Why Do You Need This New Edition?

If you're wondering why you should buy this new edition of *A Short History of the Movies*, here are six good reasons!

① **Discussion of recent films you may have seen, including** *Ashes of Time Redux, Coraline, The Curious Case Of Benjamin Button, The Dark Knight, The Diving Bell and the Butterfly, Inglourious Basterds,* and *Slumdog Millionaire.*

② **Coverage of emerging directors** like Paul Thomas Anderson, Charlie Kaufman, and Julian Schnabel is featured in this new edition, with updated discussions of established directors such as Danny Boyle, the Coen brothers, Werner Herzog, Christopher Nolan, Quentin Tarantino, Julie Taymor, Jan Troell, Gus Van Sant, and Andrzej Wajda.

③ **Fresh and updated coverage of international and independent cinema,** such as new coverage of J-horror, Zhang Yimou's Olympic ceremonies, Scorsese's documentaries, Sundance, Nigerian film, and the Mexican international production company Cha Cha Cha. "Third World Cinemas" now reflects contemporary political developments and terminology, and Bollywood is given a more objective treatment.

④ **More in-depth information on important historical developments** from the early "cinema of attractions" to today's digital 3-D. You'll also find updated discussions of independent U.S. production, transnational cinema, digital effects, HDTV, Blu-ray Discs, cell-phone cameras, and YouTube.

⑤ **The discussion of the contemporary "Return of the Myths"** has been revised to include *The Dark Knight.* Descriptions of such classic films as *The Last Laugh* and *Battleship Potemkin* have been revised based on newly restored editions.

⑥ **An expanded glossary, updated filmographies, consolidated bibliographies, and revised DVD lists** make this new edition an easier and more effective reference tool.

A Short History of the Movies

ELEVENTH EDITION

Gerald Mast
Late, of the University of Chicago

Bruce F. Kawin
University of Colorado at Boulder

Longman

Boston Columbus Indianapolis New York San Francisco Upper Saddle River
Amsterdam Cape Town Dubai London Madrid Milan Munich Paris Montreal Toronto
Delhi Mexico City São Paulo Sydney Hong Kong Seoul Singapore Taipei Tokyo

Senior Acquisitions Editor: Susan Phelps Chambers
Editorial Assistant: Erica Schweitzer
Senior Marketing Manager: Sandi McGuire
Production Manager: Stacey Kulig
Project Coordination, Text Design, and Electronic Page Makeup: GGS Higher Education Resources, a Division of
    PreMedia Global, Inc.
Cover Designer/Manager: John Callahan
Cover Image: Paramount Pictures/Photofest
Senior Manufacturing Buyer: Dennis J. Para
Printer and Binder: King Printing Co., Inc.
Cover Printer: King Printing Co., Inc.

For permission to use copyrighted material, grateful acknowledgment is made to the copyright holders on pp. 731–733, which are hereby made part of this copyright page.

Library of Congress Cataloging-in-Publication Data

Mast, Gerald, 1940–
    A short history of the movies / Gerald Mast, Bruce F. Kawin. — 11th ed.
        p. cm.
    Includes bibliographical references and index.
    ISBN 978-0-205-75557-8 (alk. paper)
    1. Motion pictures—History. I. Title.
    PN1993.5.A1M39 2010
    791.4309—dc22

                                                    2009050874

9 10—V0CR—16 15 14

Longman
is an imprint of

www.pearsonhighered.com

ISBN 13: 978-0-205-75557-8
ISBN 10:   0-205-75557-7

Contents

Preface

From its first edition, Gerald Mast's *A Short History of the Movies* helped to focus the field of film studies; it has its own role in film history. Comprehensively conceived, evocatively illustrated, and readable, drawing useful generalizations and analyzing key works in depth, it became the foundation for the modern film history course as well as an ideal book for anyone who wants to know more about movies. And as the field developed, so did the book. With each edition it grew longer and more comprehensive, responding vigorously to new movies and new conceptions of film history.

When Gerald Mast died in 1988, I took over the responsibility of revising and updating the *Short History*, beginning with the fifth edition. Like the previous editions, this 11th edition has been completely updated, scrupulously corrected, and comprehensively expanded—this time, without getting any longer. Playing the role of a respectful but aggressive editor, I have tightened and cut the text even more to make room for discussions of new or previously undiscussed films, filmmakers, and national cinemas, as well as scientific, technical, and business developments.

No vital material has been taken out; instead, a great deal has been added. Many of the discussions have been revised to make their essential points more clear, to provide more detailed examples, and to fix the mistakes. Numerous names, dates, titles, and shot descriptions have been corrected, based on such primary resources as original signatures and complete prints.

In this edition, in Chapter 17, "The Return of the Myths," much of the coverage of contemporary Hollywood filmmakers has been rewritten; the section on leading directors has been significantly revised, and there is expanded coverage of such contemporary filmmakers as Christopher Nolan, Julie Taymor, and Gus Van Sant, along with new coverage of Paul Thomas Anderson and Charlie Kaufman. Also in that chapter, the updated discussion of "mythic" films now includes *The Dark Knight*. Elsewhere there are expanded discussions of Danny Boyle, Werner Herzog, and many others, as well as discussions of directors new to this book, such as Julian Schnabel and Warwick Thornton. In Chapter 3, "Film Narrative, Commercial Expansion," there is a new section, "Complexity in Early Film," that treats the key movies and their innovations from 1893 to 1908 in chronological order without grouping them by director or country of origin, making it easier to follow the development of single-shot, multi-shot, and multi-scene films. There is more information on "the cinema of attractions," the brain's processing of sequential images, the first dream films, the Vitaphone shorts, the French "tradition of quality," the *auteur* theory, May 1968, film ratings, independent U.S. production, HDTV, Blu-ray, digital video, cellphones, YouTube, and many other topics. There are six new color photos, most of which illustrate digital effects. In Chapter 19, "Digital Cinema," the explanation of digital effects has been updated to include films as technically challenging as *The Curious Case Of Benjamin Button*, and the coverage of digital camerawork now includes such films as *Slumdog Millionaire* (a picture discussed primarily in the section of Chapter 14 that deals with England). The section on "Third World Cinemas" has been revised to reflect contemporary political developments and terminology. The discussion of Bollywood is far more objective. The glossary has been expanded, the DVD lists have been updated, the updated bibliographies have been moved to the end of the volume for greater convenience, and the filmographies have been updated to 2009. Box-office figures have been updated to 2008, and the comparison with the peak year of 1946 has been adjusted for inflation; other statistics have been updated to the last year for which figures were available, usually 2007 or 2008, while business developments and studio history have been updated to 2009. Numerous sections have been given new titles to make the information in them easier to find; for example, "From *A Hard Day's Night* to *Masterpiece Theatre*" is now "Loach, Leigh, and Others," and "Cinemas East" is now "Asia." The descriptions of many films have been corrected, often thanks to restored editions, notably *À nous la liberté, Battleship Potemkin, Cinderella, The Last Laugh* (the restored version includes another intertitle), *Memento, Persona,* and *Rough Sea at Dover.* The worldwide coverage of recent cinema is as comprehensive as the length of this book allows and includes such films as *Ashes of Time Redux, Blind Mountain, La Bohème, Encounters at the End of the World, Gomorra, The Good the Bad the Weird, Katyń, Let the Right One In, Private Century, A Prophet,* and *Vincere,* as well as such U.S. productions and co-productions as *Coraline; The Diving Bell and the Butterfly; Gran Torino; Inglourious Basterds; Synecdoche, New York;* and *Up.*

In the 21 years I have been working on the *Short History,* I have rewritten about half of it and added a great deal. But this is still Gerald Mast's book—in its solid, efficient structure; in its *auteurist* emphasis on the directors of narrative films; in its engaged and engaging tone; in its interdisciplinary approach and humanistic spirit; and in many of its analyses, arguments, and conclusions. But it has been exhaustively re-researched, corrected, expanded, and brought up to date—tasks made easier by how well the *Short History* was thought out and put together in the first place.

In his prefaces Gerald always warmly thanked those who contributed to this book through its many editions. There are those who helped him in preparing and revising the manuscripts: Joe Adamson, Richard Meran Barsam, Madeline Cook, Jeanne Eichenseer, Tag Gallagher, Steven Jack, Bruce Kawin, Antonín J. Liehm, Richard Dyer MacCann, John Matthew,

Ned McLeroy, Leonard Quart, William Reiter, Burnell Y. Sitterly, and Tom Wittenberg. There are those who helped him see films or collect stills: Mary Corliss (of the Museum of Modern Art/Film Stills Archive), Walter J. Dauler (of Audio-Brandon Films), Darrell Flugg, Bill Franz, Murray Glass (of EmGee Films), Steven Harvey, Peter Meyer (of Janus Films), Adam Reilly, Emily Sieger, and Charles Silver (of the Museum of Modern Art).

For their help in obtaining the new stills for the fifth through 11th editions, I am especially grateful to Mary Corliss and Terry Geesken (of the Museum of Modern Art/Film Stills Archive), Bruce Elder, Robert A. Harris (of Biograph Entertainment and the restorer of *Lawrence of Arabia*), the staff of the Margaret Herrick Library, Barbara Kowalczuk, Helen LaVarre (of Columbia Pictures), Rick McBride (of the Korean Cultural Center), Howie Movshovitz, Herbert Nusbaum and Joan Pierce (of MGM/UA), Martin Scorsese, Phil Solomon, the staff of the Telluride Film Festival, and William Van Wert.

The fifth through tenth editions could not have been completed without the help, advice, and support of Jack Anderson, Stan Brakhage, Ann R. Cacoullos, Ray Carney, Theresa Cecot, Bill Costanzo, Tony English, Horton and Lillian Foote, Lillian Gish, Dan Greenberg, Alan Hardy, Andrew Horton, David James, Lori Janssen, Paul Jarrico, Victor Jendras, Marian Keane, Marsha Kinder, Pablo Kjolseth, Barbara Kowalczuk, Hyung-Sook Lee, Fred Link, Susan Linville, Frank McConnell, Brock DeShane McDaniel, Bill McLeod, Charles Middleton, Howie Movshovitz, Charles Nilon, Herbert Nusbaum, Jim Palmer, David Phillips, Scott Poston, Stan Reubenstein, Donald Richie, Harold Schechter, David Shepard, Hershel and Marjorie Toomim, William Van Wert, Charles Wilcox, Donald Yannacito, and Maurice H. Zouary.

Finally, let me thank those who lent their expertise and encouragement to the immense project of researching, illustrating, and writing the 11th edition: Pablo Kjolseth, Lise Menn, and the professors who anonymously evaluated the tenth edition. All these people helped to make this book the best it has ever been.

Bruce F. Kawin

1

Introductory Assumptions

An audience first watched a motion picture flicker on a screen in 1895. Since then, the movies have developed from a simple recording device—the first films merely captured a scenic or not-so-scenic view—to a complex art and business. The important question for the first film audiences was, "Is the image discernible?" rather than, "Is the image meaningful?" From the simple beginning of cranking a camera to record a scene, filmmakers have learned that their art depends on the way the camera shapes the scene they are recording. Analogous to the novel, the completed narrative film is not just a story, but a story told in a certain way, and it is impossible to separate what is told from how it is told. Just as novelists discovered that narrative technique can be either subtly invisible—as in Flaubert or Hemingway—or intrusively self-conscious—as in Joyce or Faulkner—so too the filmmaker can construct a lucid, apparently artless story or a complex, almost chaotic maze for traveling to the story. The wonder is that while the evolution of narrative fiction can be traced back thousands of years, the movies evolved such complex techniques in little more than a century.

The history of the movies is, first of all, the history of a new art. Though it has affinities with fiction, poetry, drama, dance, painting, photography, and music, like each of these kindred arts it has a "poetics" of its own. When the early films turned from scenic views to stories, directors assumed that the poetics of the film were similar to those of the stage. Stage acting, stage movement, stage stories, stage players, and stage perspectives dominated early story films. The camera was assumed to be a passive spectator in a theatre audience, and just as the spectator has only one seat, the camera had only one position from which to shoot a scene.

Time and experimentation revealed that the camera was anchored by analogy alone, and that the analogy was false. The scene—the locale—is the basic unit of the stage because space in the theatre is so concrete. The audience sits here, the characters play there, the scenery is fixed in space behind the action. But space in the film is completely elastic; only the screen is fixed, not the action on it. Filmmakers discovered that the unit of a film is the shot, not the scene, that shots can be joined together in any number of combinations to produce whole scenes, and that scenes can be varied and juxtaposed and paralleled in any number of ways. Unity of place, a basic and practical principle of the stage, does not apply to the movie. More applicable is what the earliest film theorist, Hugo Münsterberg, adapting another stage term, called the "unity of action," a succession of images that produces the desired narrative continuity, the intended meaning, and the appropriate emotional tension of the film as a whole. By the end of the Silent Era, this principle had been superbly demonstrated.

The discovery of sound recording raised doubts about the discoveries of the preceding 30 years. Once again the analogy with the stage was pursued; once again stage actors, stage writers, stage directors, and stage techniques flooded the movies. And once again the analogy was found to be false. Just as the stage is anchored visually in space, so too is it anchored by sound. Words

1

come from the speaker's mouth; you listen to them and watch the mouth. But movies were free to show any kind of picture while the words came from the speaker's mouth. Synchronization of picture and sound also allowed for the disjunction of picture and sound. Further, the freedom of the movies from spatial confinement allowed a greater freedom in the kinds of sounds they could use: natural sounds, musical underscoring, distortion effects, private thoughts, and more. To appreciate the importance of the *integration* of picture and sound, consider a *Gone With the Wind* without Max Steiner's music or Vivien Leigh's and Clark Gable's voices, without the creaking wagons and the rustling skirts.

Just as the history of the novel is, to some extent, a catalogue of important novels, the history of film as an art centers on important films. In film history, a discussion of the significant movies is especially relevant, for the individual films are not only milestones on a historical path, but also significant artistic discoveries that almost immediately influenced other filmmakers. Although Shakespeare drew from Seneca and Brecht from Shakespeare, even more immediate was the influence of Griffith on Ford or Hitchcock on De Palma. Without years of stage tradition to draw on, film artists have drawn on the exciting discoveries of their contemporaries. The internationalism of film distribution has always guaranteed the rapid dispersal of any significant discovery.

To keep track of this dispersal of discoveries, it is necessary to know when a particular film was *released*—that is, when it was first shown to a paying public audience—for that is usually the earliest that it could have influenced audiences and other filmmakers. It is much like learning the publication date of a novel, rather than its completion date or the number of years it took to complete. For example, one could date James Joyce's *Ulysses* 1914–21, the years he wrote it, or 1921, the year he finished it; but it was first published in February 1922 and is regularly dated 1922. In this book, the date that follows a film's title is, in almost all cases, the year the film was *released in its country of origin*. If a film was released long after it was completed, both the completion and release dates are given. If it has become customary to refer to a particular film by the year in which most of it was shot (*Caligari*,

1919), but it came out the following year, both dates are given. And both dates are given if the release date is so early in the year as to be misleading; a film released on January 8, 1929, like Dziga Vertov's *The Man with a Movie Camera*, is a 1928 work as well as a 1929 release. If it matters when a foreign film opened in the United States and affected American audiences, the U.S. release date is also provided; Fellini's *La dolce vita* won a 1961 Oscar, but it came out in Italy in 1960. In any case, most films open the year they are completed and need only one date.

The title of *La dolce vita* is given in Italian, following Italian conventions for capitalization, because the film is known worldwide by its original name and was never released in English-speaking countries as *The Sweet Life*. The most reliable way to establish the actual title of a movie is to watch the movie: The original posters and most books may call Capra's picture *It's a Wonderful Life*, but the movie calls itself *It's A Wonderful Life*. Aside from cases where the Art Department has been allowed to spell the title any way it wants (*tHE tHING*), the onscreen title has an authority like that of the title page of a novel. There are, of course, exceptions. *Gone With the Wind* is, on the screen, GONE WITH THE WIND, but in this case the title of the movie had, for legal reasons, to be exactly the same as that of the novel, which, according to its publisher, has *With*, not *with*. If a film bears one title (*Corner in Wheat*) but is known by another (*A Corner in Wheat*), or if the artwork creates a title that sticks (*SE7EN*), it is best to give both the actual title and the familiar one. The use of italics for the title of a film of any length is a literary convention that has been widely adopted.

When there is a conflict over the choice or spelling of a name, professional names take precedence over birth names. Cary Grant, born Archibald Leach, is Cary Grant in film books, as Marion Michael Morrison is John Wayne; the prestudio name is a footnote. Early in the 21st century, Wong Kar-wai began spelling his name "Wong Kar Wai" in the credits of his films; that is respected as the name under which he has chosen to work. Cecil B. DeMille expressed a preference for that professional spelling of his name—which happened to be how his name was spelled at birth—but he was inconsistent about it. One reads it in the name of the company he founded, "Cecil B. DeMille Productions," and in a Silent Era article about how C. B. is DeMille, but his brother William is deMille. On the other hand, the Directors Guild calls him "De Mille," and in his own film credits the name might be "De Mille," "de Mille," "DeMille," or "deMille." Most significantly, he typed and signed "deMille" on his loyalty oath—and in the era of the blacklist, he was one of the strongest supporters of the oath, so he can be expected to have used what he considered his true name. Even if his preference for his personal name may have been "deMille," then, his repeatedly stated preference for "DeMille" as his professional name makes that the spelling used here. When there is a dispute over the spelling of a name and no conflict between birth and industry names, an original legal signature has authority, and after that a tombstone. There is no consistency in this practice, but most Western books and film distributors put the family name first for a Chinese person (as it is done in China: Zhang Yimou) but last for a Japanese person (as it is not done in Japan: Akira Kurosawa was Kurosawa Akira).

Many film historians subscribe to a basic, if far from absolute, assumption: The very best films have generally resulted from the clear vision and unifying intelligence of a single, controlling mind with primary responsibility for the whole film. Just as there is only one conductor per orchestra, they argue, there can be only one dominant creator of a movie. The "*auteur* theory," as defined by François Truffaut in France and Andrew Sarris in the United States, identifies the director (whose personal artistic signature is evident in the work) as a film's "author" or dominant creator. Whether the *auteur* improvises the whole film as it goes along or works according to a preconceived and scripted plan, a single mind shapes and guides the work of film art.

But few directors make up the stories they tell, even if they are responsible for the ways those stories are told. If an orchestra needs a conductor, it also needs a composer. What the screenwriter conceives, from the dialogue of a scene or the motivation of a character to the entire structure of a work, the director reconceives as a cinematic whole and as a creative project. It is not the writer who gets the picture made or the music written or the performances right, but without the writer there would be, in most cases,

no picture. The term *auteur* attempts to identify elements of authorship in a creative industry where there is no single, original, total author.

Although many of the best movies are dominated by an *auteur*, it is also true that any movie represents an immensely collaborative venture that may involve a hundred or more creative people. There are examples of good movies with two co-directors (Gene Kelly and Stanley Donen, Ján Kadár and Elmar Klos, Robert Rodriguez and Frank Miller). Many of the best directors have worked in frequent partnership with the same scriptwriter (Frank Capra with Robert Riskin, John Ford with Dudley Nichols), or the same cinematographer (Sergei Eisenstein with Eduard Tisse, D. W. Griffith with Billy Bitzer), or assistant director (Truffaut with Suzanne Schiffman), or composer (Alfred Hitchcock with Bernard Herrmann, Federico Fellini with Nino Rota). To study a dozen or so films by a single screenwriter would surely reveal as consistent and distinguishable a personality as a dozen or so films by a single director. Such a screenwriter might well be considered an *auteur*.

Strictly speaking, however, an *auteur* is a director who also writes the script and edits the film (for example, Japan's Takeshi Kitano or France's Agnès Varda); in practice, she or he may just work closely with the writer and the editor. But no commercial filmmaker works alone. And although any director has the authority and duty to make creative decisions that ensure the quality and coherence of the work, the *auteur* is a director whose work expresses a vision or structure that develops in the course of what may appropriately be discussed as an artistic career. Not every director is an *auteur*, and some *auteurs*—like producer Val Lewton—are guiding artists in every sense of the term but are not directors.

Even if very many movies are made outside or in opposition to the film industry, any history that intends to reveal the genesis of today's film world must acknowledge the dominant role of the industry as well as address a wealth of social and technical matters. In addition to discussing the film as art, it must deal with three related problems that have always influenced the artistic product and continue to influence it today: the cinema as business, the cinema as cultural product and commodity, and the cinema as technology.

Movies today are a multibillion-dollar business. The choice of directors, stars, and scripts is usually in the hands of businesspeople, not of artists. The company that invests more than $60 million in a picture ought to be able to ensure the safety of its investment. When push comes to shove, commercial priorities outweigh artistic ones. The name Hollywood, for some synonymous with glamour, is for others synonymous with selling out. For decades Hollywood's commercial crassness has served American novelists—from Nathanael West to Gore Vidal—as a metaphor for the vulgar emptiness of the American Dream. If the gifted young director today seems to face a distasteful dilemma—sell out or get out—directors have faced the same problem since the time of Griffith.

The awesome financial pressures of Hollywood are partly responsible for the growing number of independent films and digital videos. Young filmmakers often prefer to work alone, their sole expenses equipment and film or digital media. These filmmakers are, in a sense, returning to the earliest period of film history. Every artistic innovation since then has ironically necessitated spending more money. If lighting was a step forward in cinematic tone, it also required spending money on lighting equipment and on people who knew how to control it. Longer films required more film, more actors, more story material, and more publicity to ensure a financial return on the greater investment. It took only 25 years for the movies to progress from cheap novelty to big business.

Why do movies cost so much to make? Put the question this way: How much would you expect to pay if you employed an army of the most specialized artisans at their trade for a period of, say, three months? Making a film is such a massive and complex task it is a wonder that an artistically whole movie can be made at all. The huge sums of money required to finance a movie merely reflect the hugeness of the task of taking a movie from story idea to final print. Shooting is painfully slow. It takes time to perfect each setup: Lights must be carefully focused and toned, the shot's composition must be determined, the set must be found—or built—and dressed, background actors (extras) must be coordinated with the action of the principals, actors must have rehearsed their movements and

mastered their interpretations of lines so that a single shot fits into the dramatic fabric of the whole film, makeup must be correct, costumes must be coordinated, and so forth.

Because it takes so much time to set up a shot, producers economize by shooting all scenes together that require the same location, set, or setup, regardless of their position in the film's continuity. In other words, the film is shot "out of sequence." But even with such economies, to get two or three minutes of screen time "in the can" is a hard, well-organized day's work. A movie's production budget is calculated on the number of days it will take to shoot, and the average expense for a color film is well over $250,000 per day. Even the five-minute student film can cost thousands of dollars.

The only way to retrieve production expenses is with sales—selling tickets, renting prints, leasing television rights to networks or cable companies, selling DVDs, and licensing tie-ins from toys and computer games to novelizations.

The history of the movies as a business is inextricably linked with the history of the movies as a mass entertainment medium. To get the public to spend its money at the box office, the producer must give the public what it wants or make the public want what it gets. History indicates that the public has gotten some of both. The crassest movie maxim is the famous, "The box office is never wrong." The validity of the maxim depends on the kinds of questions you ask the box office to answer.

Film art has changed radically in the course of its history, and so have film audiences. The first movie patrons in the United States were also patrons of vaudeville houses and variety shows. When those audiences tired of the same kinds of film programs, the movies found a home with lower- and working-class patrons. Small theatres sprang up in the poor sections and commercial districts of cities; admission was a nickel or a dime. The middle class attended too, but many of the rich and educated saw movies only as an afternoon or evening of slumming. As film art and craft improved, larger and more expensive movie theatres opened in the respectable entertainment centers of the cities. Films tried to appeal to a wide range of tastes and interests, much as television does today. In this period there was little consciousness of movies as an art; they were

Fig. 1-1

Fig. 1-2

The movies as mirror of American social history.
Fig. 1-1: Social institutions responsive to human needs and challenges (Jean Arthur in the U.S. Senate of Mr. Smith Goes to Washington, *1939).*
Fig. 1-2: Three returning servicemen view the land they fought to save (from left, Dana Andrews, Fredric March, and Harold Russell in The Best Years of Our Lives, *1946).*

mass entertainment. H. L. Mencken sardonically lauded the movies as the appropriate artistic attainment of the American "booboisie." Similes linking movies with tastelessness and movie patrons with morons continually popped up in fiction and articles of the 1920s and 1930s. Sixty years later, people like Mencken were writing film criticism, a movie actor had served as president of the United States, and going to the movies had become both intellectually respectable and socially necessary.

This discussion of the evolving audiences for movies indicates the close connection between the movies as cultural artifacts and conditions in the culture as a whole. Particular cultural conditions influence, if not dictate, the particular qualities and quantities of films in any given era. For a specific movie to become a major hit at a specific time indicates, at least partially, the cultural fact that a sufficient number of people wanted, needed, demanded, or responded to just that film then. To compare *Mr. Smith Goes to Washington* of 1939, with *The Best Years of Our Lives* of 1946, with *Rebel Without a Cause* of 1955, with *The Graduate* of 1967 is to write a history of three decades of American culture. Any history of the movies must both take account of and account for these cultural shifts and conditions.

But although movies can convey an overt and explicit cultural content—a war-torn society attempting to heal its wounds in *The Best Years of Our Lives* or a working-class woman attempting to express and distinguish herself in *Flashdance* (1983)—they can also convey covert and "invisible" ideological messages. It was precisely this fear of covert ideological contamination that led to the inquiries of the House Un-American Activities Committee in the years following World War II. More recently, many contemporary film theorists, following the lead of semioticians, historians, and critics like Louis Althusser and Roland Barthes, have attempted to expose the unspoken, assumed cultural values of films—values that seem so obviously true for a culture that they are accepted as inevitable, normal, and natural rather than as ideological constructs of the culture itself. For example, happiness in an American film is so equated with a synthesis of material comfort (home, job, car, stereo) and spiritual contentment (usually a monogamous

romantic relationship) that any alternative idea of happiness, or even a critique of the idea of happiness itself, is almost unthinkable. Television is so completely structured around commercials that the very idea of buying becomes natural; it doesn't matter exactly what it is the viewer buys, just so the viewer understands that life itself consists of buying something or other and that nearly anything can be a commodity.

This ideological analysis has been especially useful to feminist critics and theorists who seek the underlying sources of sexist thinking in our cultural history. Women in films seem banished to the kitchen, the bedroom, or the pedestal. And whether they are cast in the cliché roles of virgin, whore, mother, wife, assistant, or boss, they are usually presented in terms of their relation to men. Feminist films define women as selves, not as objects. But there is a sense in which any film, not just the unfeminist *Flashdance*, turns its subject into spectacle. Following the psychoanalytic theories of Jacques Lacan, many feminist theorists explicate the ways women in movies have traditionally served as voyeuristic objects presented by male directors for the pleasurable gaze of male spectators. Although one need not accept the radical analyses of theory, there is no question that such discussions of movies have made us more self-conscious about the cultural and moral values we may have taken for granted and more wary of the ways such values are promoted.

Another radical approach to film theory suggests that our very way of looking at the world, of seeing nature, reality, and all the persons and things within it, is itself a cultural construct. The principles of Renaissance perspective—of a deep, receding space presented for the eye of the single, privileged viewer—have been ground into the lenses of cameras. Others have argued that bourgeois culture privileges a single sense— sight—over all others. The apparently innocent act of "seeing the world"—whether through our eyes or through a lens—is not at all innocent because both the seeing and the seen are cultural constructs. Hence, a final influence on the movies, important to any discussion of their history, is the dependence of film art on glass and chemicals, electricity and machines. (For more introductory topics, see the list of films and DVDs at the end of this chapter.)

Appropriately enough, our technological period has produced an art that depends on technology. The first filmmakers were not artists but tinkerers. The same spirit that produced a lightbulb and a telephone produced a movie camera and projector. The initial goal in making a movie was not to create beauty but to display a scientific curiosity. The invention of the first cameras and projectors set a trend that was to repeat itself with the introduction of every new movie invention: The invention was first exploited as a novelty in itself and only later integrated as one tool in making the whole film. The first movie camera merely exploited its ability to capture images of moving things. The first synchronized sound films exploited the audience's excitement at hearing the words that the actor's lips were mouthing. Most of the first color films were merely colorful, many of the first widescreen films merely wide.

No other art is so tied to machines. Some of the most striking artistic effects are the products of expanding film technology. For example, the awesome compositions in depth and shadow of Orson Welles's *Citizen Kane* (1941) are partially the result of the conversion to brighter arc lamps, the introduction of specially coated lenses, and the development of high-speed, fine-grain film stocks, all of which made it possible for *Kane*'s cinematographer, Gregg Toland, to "stop down" the lens (in other words, because there was now more light on the set and the film was more sensitive, he could narrow the lens's aperture) and achieve a sharper image, much richer shadows, and greater depth of field (the range within which objects are in focus; given a field that was sharp from infinity to very near the camera, Welles was free to compose shots in depth). Research has converted the camera from an erratic, hand-cranked film grinder to a smooth, precise clockwork. Research has silenced the camera's noise without using clumsy, bulky devices to baffle the clatter. Research has developed faster and sturdier film stocks, enabling greater flexibility in lighting, composition, and shooting conditions. Research has developed the computer, digital effects, and high-definition digital video. Research has improved sound recording and reproduction, developed versatile cranes and dollies, perfected a wide assortment of laboratory processes and effects, and invented special lenses and printers. Film equipment is so sophisticated that no film artist can master it all, yet despite the difficulties of money and machine—and the many achievements in the other arts—movies became the dominant art of the 20th century and remain essential to life in the 21st.

This short history will follow the road the movies have traveled to get here. To keep a history even this "short" has required several decisions. First, this history aims at revealing significant trends and turns along the road rather than detailing exhaustive lists of titles, directors, and dates. For further reading and viewing, the reader is strongly advised to consult the bibliography at the end of the book and the lists of movies and DVDs at the end of each chapter.

Second, because the history of the American film is most relevant to American readers, this short history allots more space to a discussion of American movie practices. But although American films are the dominant force in the film world, the cinema truly is an international and cross-cultural medium, and to concentrate exclusively on the United States, let alone on Hollywood, would create a misleading and impoverished record. Not every country or culture in the world is covered here, but those that have produced the most significant films are treated in as much depth as a "short history" allows.

Third, there is no room here to explain more than the most essential technical terms, equipment, standards, and procedures. The bibliography lists many introductory and advanced texts that go into all these in detail. There is also a glossary at the end of the book.

Fourth, this history concentrates heavily on the fiction film, also called the narrative film. The aesthetic principles of the nonfiction or documentary film are different enough from those of the storytelling film to require a full-length study of their own. The same is true of the animated film and of the avant-garde film. For a list of such studies, the reader is again advised to consult the bibliography. Nevertheless, the documentary *is* discussed in this book, particularly in the context of such filmmakers as Robert Flaherty, Dziga Vertov, Leni Riefenstahl, Chris Marker, and Marcel Ophuls. Animators from Émile Cohl and Walt Disney to computer-graphics artists make their appearance, and in addition to discussions of the silent avant-garde film in Europe, a significant portion of a chapter is devoted to the American avant-garde. These discussions are essential to giving a sense of the whole of film art, but they are necessarily brief and suggestive.

Finally, the reader must realize precisely what this book of history (and any book of history) really is—not a collection of all the facts that must be accepted as absolute truth but a selection of facts that have been fitted into a pattern. No matter how much it aspires to be an accurate record of change over time, a history is inevitably an interpretive narrative, a telling, a story; after all, five-sevenths of the word *history* is *story*. This story is perpetually revised and rethought: New data are selected, old data are rejected or reinterpreted, and new ways of viewing are found. Like plays, novels, and movies, histories are stories told to a particular audience at a particular time, embodying the values, hopes, ideals, and commitments of those times. Histories of movies, no less than the movies themselves, construct a view of the world and of human experience.

For Further Viewing

NOTE: The films and DVDs in these lists, found at the end of each chapter, present a range of the materials available for further research and enjoyment. The lists are suggestive but not exhaustive. Each filmography contains a representative sample of the major films of each director and period. The date after each film is the year it was released in its country of origin; within a given year, films are listed in release order if the exact release dates are known (otherwise the order is alphabetical). English, alternate, and untranslated titles are given if the films are widely known by or distributed under those titles. Most of these films are available for rental in 16mm (see the list of distributors at the end of the book), but many are also worth studying on DVD. In almost all cases, the DVDs listed here have useful supplements (not all of which are listed) and contain good, complete prints—in the case of silents, at the correct speed. Only Region 1 discs (playable in the U.S. and Canada) and region-free discs (playable anywhere) are listed.

FILMS

INTRODUCTORY MISCELLANY

SHORTS

Un Chien andalou (1929, Luis Buñuel and Salvador Dalí). Surrealism, structure.

Duck Amuck (1953, Chuck Jones). Editing, sound, reflexivity.

The Fatal Glass of Beer (1933, Clyde Bruckman), starring W. C. Fields. Language, repetition, parody, artificiality.

La Jetée (1963, rel. 1964; Chris Marker). Time, memory, stills and motion, editing.

Ménilmontant (1925, Dimitri Kirsanov). Silence without intertitles.

Meshes of the Afternoon (1943, Maya Deren). Avant-garde, structure, identity.

Mothlight (1963, Stan Brakhage). Avant-garde, filmmaking without a camera.

October: Raising of the Bridges Sequence (1928, Sergei Eisenstein). Montage, time.

Olympia: Diving Sequence (1938, Leni Riefenstahl). Editing, music.

One Week (1920, Eddie Cline and Buster Keaton). Silent comedy.

FEATURES

The Apple (1998, Samira Makhmalbaf). Realism, national cinema.

Before The Rain (1994, Milcho Manchevski). Narrative structure, national cinema.

Gabbeh (1996, Mohsen Makhmalbaf). Fantasy, realism, color, structure, national cinema.

Greed (1924, Erich von Stroheim). Realism, adaptation, mise-en-scène.

Lawrence of Arabia (1962, David Lean). Widescreen color cinematography.

The Love of Jeanne Ney (1927, G. W. Pabst). Melodrama, camerawork, editing.

The Magnificent Ambersons (1942, Orson Welles). Black-and-white cinematography.

The Man with a Movie Camera (1928, rel. 1929; Dziga Vertov). Editing, camerawork, reflexivity.

Medea (1969, Pier Paolo Pasolini). Compare von Trier/Dreyer adaptation.

Medea (1988, Lars von Trier; script by Dreyer). Authorship, adaptation.

Microcosmos (1996, Claude Nuridsany and Marie Pérennou). Extreme close-ups.

Moolaadé (2004, Ousmane Sembene). Feminism, Third World cinema.

The Passion of Joan of Arc (1928, Carl Theodor Dreyer). Faces, camerawork, editing.

Seven Samurai (1954, Akira Kurosawa). Pace, editing, national cinema.

Singin' In The Rain (1952, Stanley Donen and Gene Kelly). Early sound, studio credits, genre.

2 or 3 Things I Know About Her (1967, Jean-Luc Godard). Analyzed realism, reflexivity, language, people and objects, analysis of systems (social, economic, semiotic, cinematic), influence of Brecht, thinking with film, voice-over, auteur theory.

Weekend (1967, Jean-Luc Godard). Long takes.

DVDs

NOTE: Filmmakers, other significant figures, and restored editions are in **boldface.**

by Brakhage—an anthology. Criterion Collection. Includes 26 films, a documentary, and many interviews with **Stan Brakhage.** Excellent for detailed study of one filmmaker and his evolving thoughts on his work. Optimized for single-frame as well as full-speed viewing.

The Five Obstructions (2003, **Lars von Trier** and **Jørgen Leth**). Koch Lober. Von Trier tells Leth five different ways to remake his 1967 short, *The Perfect Human*—e.g., with no shot longer than 12 frames. Includes *The Perfect Human* and commentary by Leth.

John Cassavetes: Five Films. Criterion Collection. Includes *Faces, The Killing of a Chinese Bookie* in two versions, *Shadows* with related drama workshop footage and a **restoration** demonstration, *A Woman Under the Influence, Opening Night,* documentaries on **John Cassavetes,** interviews and commentaries, and a booklet. Excellent for detailed study of one filmmaker and his working methods.

Night and Fog (1955, **Alain Resnais**). Criterion Collection. Includes interviews with Resnais and articles by film historian Peter Cowie, music historian Russell Lack, and essayist Phillip Lopate.

Treasures from American Film Archives: 50 Preserved Films. Image Entertainment/ National Film Preservation Foundation. A great variety of silent and sound films, from home movies and cartoons to rare features and shorts, including *Blacksmithing Scene* (**Edison–Dickson–Heise**), *The Fall of the House of Usher* (**Webber** and **Watson**), *Hell's Hinges* (with **William S. Hart**), *The Lonedale Operator* (**Griffith**), *Rose Hobart* (**Joseph Cornell**), and *The Toll of the Sea* (in 2-strip Technicolor), with information on each archive and a detailed book.

2

Birth

Some film historians trace the origin of movies to cave paintings, to Balinese shadow puppets, or to Plato's mythic Cave of the Shadows in Book VII of the *Republic*. Many theorists find a valid conceptual model in Plato's mass of spectators, entranced by the flickering shadows of objects on the cave wall that are merely projections of the light behind them, diverted from the real objects they would see if they could only ascend from the shadow-show to examine them in the light itself. The nonmetaphoric history of the movies, however, begins with the steps leading to the invention of the movie camera and projector.

The 19th-century mind created machines for travel, machines for work, machines for the home, and machines for entertainment—and the lightbulb. By the end of the century, three developments had combined to create the motion picture: research into persistence of vision (wrongly thought to be the reason movies appear to move), the invention of still photography, and increasing public interest in glass-slide shows and mechanized entertainments.

Frames per Second

Movies are an optical illusion. We believe we are watching a completely continuous, fluid motion on the screen, but all we really watch are short, discontinuous bits of the motion, mere 24ths of a second of action.

To create the cinematic illusion of motion, a series of stills must be presented rapidly to the eye, which sends the information to the brain. Each picture in a movie, whether photographed

or drawn, is perceived as a clear, stable, unmoving image, as individual as a page in a flip book. But the brain does something with the information received from the eye, something that will not be fully understood until more research has been done into the neural and cognitive aspects of the perception of cinematic movement. Given certain conditions, we see the elements of one picture appear to move to their positions in the next picture. To discuss how that phenomenon has been explained, we need to understand a number of concepts and terms.

When images that present tiny changes in the photographed or drawn subject succeed each other at a rate of more than 11 or 12 per second, the viewer imagines seeing the subject move. It is, to be sure, a jerky movement. At 16 pictures per second, the apparent movement begins to seem fluid and normal, so that was the speed at which most of the first movies were photographed and projected. What we see in a movie is called *apparent movement* because no *real movement* is shown; there are only stills. Creating apparent movement from still pictures is the *cinematic illusion*.

Pictures on Film

Because each picture in a movie is an individual, rectangular image, or *frame*, on a strip of film— we'll address the digital cinema later in this book and refer until then to movies shot and printed on celluloid—the rate at which film images succeed each other is expressed in *frames per second* (*fps*) or in feet per minute (*fpm*). Most sound movies run at 24 fps, or 90 feet of 35mm film per minute. The professional, theatrical standard around the world, *35mm film*, is 35 millimeters wide (its *gauge*) and holds 16 frames per foot.

Film stock—unprocessed or *raw* film—consists of a base coated with an emulsion. The *base* is made of celluloid: originally cellulose nitrate (*nitrate film*), which was extremely flammable and deteriorated (shrank, dissolved, and worse) within a few decades, and then cellulose tri-acetate (*safety-base film*, also called *acetate film*), introduced in 1949, which burned slowly and would not deteriorate for a few hundred years. Nitrate film gave a better image but was kin to nitroglycerin. Safety-base film, which began as a cellulose acetate marketed by Eastman Kodak in 1908, was used for some 16mm and other small-gauge stocks. The improved version, cellulose tri-acetate, was adopted exclusively soon after it appeared, and since 1951 every film has been shot on safety-base stock. The exact formula has been continually improved.

One side of the base is coated with the *emulsion*, a layer of photosensitive chemicals. When film is processed, it is the emulsion that is developed. The most important chemical in a black-and-white emulsion is silver nitrate, which turns black when it is exposed to light, creating a *negative* (film that has black where the photographed subject was white, dark gray where the subject was light gray, and so on). The black-and-white values of a negative are reversed to *positive* values when it is copied onto blank film to make a projectable print. Because the printer's light shines through the negative onto raw stock that also turns black when it is exposed to light, what is white in the negative becomes black in the print. Some color emulsions—whose negatives are in the complements of the colors on the print—consist of several layers and include microscopic globules of dye. Although most professionals shoot negative film and then strike positive prints, *reversal* film, whether black and white or color, can be processed to yield a positive image.

All movie film has a line of rectangular *perforations* (informally, perfs) or *sprocket holes*, which are usually rectangular with slightly rounded corners, running just inside one or both of its edges. The holes are engaged by the teeth of *sprocket wheels* (or *sprockets*), which hold the film as the wheels advance and stop it. The base of 35mm film is perforated with sprocket holes just inside its left and right edges, one every 3/16 inch. There may also be *edge numbers* alongside one line of sprocket holes, printed every foot or so, which help identify where a particular shot is on a roll of film. There are four sprocket holes on the left side of a 35mm frame and four on the right; this standard configuration is called "8-perf 35" because there is a total of eight perforations per frame. (See Fig. 19-3 for a short strip of modern 35mm film.)

The frame itself, which appears once the film has been processed, consists of microscopic bits of silver and dye that are sometimes described as minimal picture elements (*pixels*). In most sound films, an optical soundtrack runs between the frame and one line of sprocket holes. (The film may also have several digital soundtracks printed in otherwise unused areas—even between the perforations; see Fig. 19-4.) Before the optical soundtrack was invented, a full frame was as large on a print as it was on the camera negative: approximately 1 inch wide and 3/4 inch high. In 1931, to make room for the soundtrack, the size of the frame on most 35mm prints was officially reduced to the *Academy aperture* of .868×.631 inches. All along, the proportions of a full frame have been, or been very close to, 4 units wide by 3 units high—which can be expressed, as a TV engineer would put it, as 4:3 or 4×3; with the height reduced to a constant, it is properly expressed, in film terms, as an *aspect ratio* of 1.33:1. Wider frames can be created by anamorphic squeezing and unsqueezing, as in CinemaScope, or by the equivalent of letterboxing (using an *aperture plate*—a piece of metal with a rectangular opening the dimensions of the desired frame, which can be slid into most cameras and projectors just in front of the film—to shape the exposed area so that it is less high than normal, though it is more common to letterbox the frame in a printer), as in flat widescreen. For these terms and many related ones, please see the glossary.

Speed

Sound speed is usually 24 fps, but there are exceptions: Todd-AO, for example, ran at 30 fps in the 1950s. *Silent speed* was approximately 16 fps—conveniently, 1 foot/sec—from 1895 to the late 1910s, but it often passed 20 fps in the 1920s. Many silents ran at 20.5 or 22 fps, and Edison's early films were shot at an average of between 30 and 40 fps. Because the first cameras were hand-cranked rather than run at a regular speed by a motor—and because there was no soundtrack running at a fixed rate that the film had to match—silent speed was always flexible.

Today's silent projectors run at 18 fps, which is a compromise. The problem is that if a film is shown too rapidly or too slowly—if the projector's rate differs from the camera's rate by as little as 2 or 3 fps—the movie loses its original pace and much of its impression of reality. A silent movie shown at sound speed loses its timing, its expressiveness, and even the connection one feels with its characters; what it gains is the unrealistic, comical effect of fast, silly movement. Projecting too slowly is just as bad. Fortunately, variable-speed projectors can show a film at the rate at which it was shot—and if that rate is unknown, the projector can be adjusted until natural movements look natural. The makers of the best DVDs are scrupulous about issuing silent films at their original projection speeds (which might vary within a single movie).

For the illusion of normal motion, then, the projector has to show the pictures at the same rate as the camera photographed them. The camera can shoot *slow motion* by exposing more than the normal number of frames per second; when the frames are projected at normal speed, the movement takes longer on screen than it did in the real world. For *fast motion*, the camera exposes fewer frames per second than normal.

By opening and closing a *shutter*—so called because it can shut out the light and also because window shutters open and close only to admit or block light completely—a movie camera exposes one frame at a time. Each frame is a still photograph, blurred a bit if the subject or the camera has moved. To take each picture, the camera stops the film and opens the shutter for about 1/50th of a second. To record a second of action at sound speed, it exposes and advances 24 frames during that second. The shutter on a conventional movie camera—or a very simple projector—resembles a semicircle joined halfway down its base to the end of a rod; like all movie shutters it revolves once for every frame, letting the light in when the film has stopped moving and shutting the light

out while the film is being advanced. It is called a *single-bladed shutter* because it uses a single flat piece of metal (the blade) to block the light. The one open area might be as large as 180°, but the *variable shutter* found on the best movie cameras can be set, for example, to a 140° or 120° wedge of light for a sharper exposure.

Flicker and the Continuous Signal

The shutter comes between the lens and the *film gate*, the windowed metal sandwich where film is exposed or displayed. While a camera's shutter is closed, no light reaches the film. While a projector's shutter is closed, none of the projector's light passes through the frame onto the screen. The alternation of light and dark caused by the opening and closing of the projector's shutter causes an unpleasant distraction, termed *flicker*. If it takes about 12 fps for us to perceive motion and 16 fps for the motion to begin to look smooth, it takes 48 fps or more (the human eye's CFF or *critical flicker frequency*, the point at which the stuttering light fuses) to get rid of the flicker that produced one of the cinema's early names, the flicks. *Flicker fusion* occurs when one perceives interrupted light as an uninterrupted or *continuous signal*. Below the CFF, flicker is very noticeable, and it plagued early films.

The solution to flicker, arrived at during the silent period (by Biograph in 1903), was to shoot at 16 fps and show each of the 16 frames three times, using a *three-bladed shutter* that had three blades to block the light and three open areas. That gave a flicker rate of 48/sec at a projection rate of 16 fps, with still less flicker at 18 or 20 fps. For a 24-fps sound film, which also has a normal flicker rate of 48/sec, a *two-bladed shutter*, resembling a bow tie, flashes 48 images per second, 24 of which are different. The shutter has two open areas, so every time it turns, it shows each frame twice. (A three-bladed shutter is also often used at sound speed for an even smoother effect; some shutters have five blades.) The film is advanced from one frame to another only during the last part of the shutter's revolution, so the frame remains stable no matter how many times it is displayed during its almost 1/16th or 1/24th of a second ("almost" to allow time for the film to be advanced while the shutter is closed—which can be as long as half the projection rate, but which can also be as short as the time it takes one blade of a three-bladed shutter to cross and block the light: about 1/150 of a second).

The periodic starting and stopping of the film in the gate of a camera, printer, or projector is called *intermittent movement*, and it is responsible for the sharpness of the immobilized image as well as for the shutter's alternating instants of light and black in a dark theatre. Although we see no flicker at 48 images per second, the dark periods between images are still there. There is an interrupted, off-and-on, discontinuous signal, which may be represented graphically as _ _ _ _ _ _ _ _ _ _. But our minds fill in or ignore the blanks, linking the fragments, and we perceive a continuous signal, which may be represented as ——————. Ironically, about half of the time we spend watching a movie, the screen is literally blank, devoid of any image at all.

Persistence of Vision and Other Phenomena

When darkness follows a bright image, the light receptors in the eye (whose action diminishes rapidly but does not instantly shut off) retain the image for a fraction of a second so that the retina briefly continues to send the last visual information it received to the brain.

This optical phenomenon is known as *persistence of vision* or *retinal retention*. It accounts for the way that a flashlight—or a glowing orange coal at the end of a stick—when swung around rapidly in the dark appears to produce a circle of light. In the darkness, the retina retains the individual points of light long enough to make a circle.

For many years it was assumed that persistence of vision accounted for the way we perceive apparent movement when a series of slightly different, successive images is shown to us at a certain rate. It was assumed that each image that was flashed in the dark left its imprint on the retina long enough for it to be combined with the next image. It was also assumed—before the discovery of flicker fusion—that retinally retained images were necessary to keep us from too distinctly noticing the darkness between the bright images, when the shutter is closed.

However, research begun as early as 1910 and continuing to the present has made it clear that the illusion of motion is created at a higher level of processing in the brain. Even if the retina retains an image under certain circumstances, that is not why we see movies move.

Seeing with the Brain

After the retina has delivered its information to the optic nerve, visual data are processed at a number of way stations (visual nuclei) in the brain. As the information travels, every aspect of it is interpreted by highly specialized nerve cells. It can take milliseconds, even hundreds of them, for us to become aware of what we are seeing.

One familiar, instantaneous function offers an example of how the brain constructs what we see. Because the image on the retina has been inverted by the lens of the eye and because most people have two eyes, the brain normally receives two upside-down, two-dimensional (*2-D*) images of the world at the same time. Using the distance between the eyes and the differences between the two images, the brain computes parallax and sees one three-dimensional (*3-D*) image, which it has turned right-side-up. That final image is presented by the brain as what the eyes see. Generating a 3-D mental picture of the world is a normal example of processing and interpreting visual information before what is seen by the eye can be "seen" by the brain.

Visual Masking and Retinal Retention

Images are interpreted and interrelated in the brain. Successive fragments of movement, like those shown in a series of movie frames, are misread by the brain as continuous action well after the pictures have entered the visual system. Images don't wait on the retina to be compared or combined. If they did, we would see a blurry mess of overlapping stills—not just two combined stills but many, because a retinal afterimage can last much longer than 1/20th of a second, even several seconds in the case of a very bright image. Far from accomplishing it, persistence of vision gets in the way of the cinematic illusion. Only when it has stopped processing one frame and gone on to the next can the brain notice and process any differences between the images. Late-20th-century research found that when a frame is followed by a fraction of a second of visual noise—a period of no information, like the dark interval when the shutter is closed, or a random visual signal, like a flash of TV static—the brain can stop processing the frame and can clear the mental slate. (In some experiments this process works only if white, not black, is flashed between frames.) This phenomenon, called *visual masking*, may well defeat any image-confusing effects that might be caused by persistence of vision. It is possible that visual masking works by disrupting short-term visual memory.

Although retinal retention is responsible for some images—for example, the afterimage produced by staring at a candle at night—it generally produces *unmoving* ones, like that circle made by the spun flashlight or like the apparently curved, frozen spokes of a turning wheel if it is viewed through the upright bars of a fence, a phenomenon addressed by Peter Mark Roget, the English physician best known for his thesaurus, in an 1824 paper that influenced most later discussions. (Roget's paper, "Explanation of an optical deception in the appearance of the spokes of a wheel seen through vertical apertures," responded to a query posed in 1821, probably by John Murray.)

Persistence of vision has been a persistent explanation of the cinematic illusion, and that is why it remains part of film history: because generations of scientists, camera makers, and film historians thought the explanation was accurate. It is part of the history of thinking about the cinema. Furthermore, early research into persistence of vision and the invention of devices designed to exploit it were inseparable from the invention of movie cameras and projectors. The machines based on the incorrect assumption that persistence of vision was responsible for the cinematic illusion turned out to be movie machines.

Early Observations

Under many names, persistence of vision has been known about and discussed for millennia, though it was not until the 1820s that a great deal of scientific experimentation and writing about it began in Europe. In the ancient world, Aristotle wrote about the implications of the eye's retaining an afterimage of the sun (don't try it); he thought it might be a key to the physiology of dreams, positing that many organs retain vestiges of what they have experienced or perceived and that dreams could be prompted by those fragments of sensation. Concerning persistent colors and lines, Leonardo da Vinci drew conclusions from lightning. (For the quotations and for the best history of the discovery of cinema, see Laurent Mannoni's

The Great Art of Light and Shadow.) Burning sticks were swung around and written about at least as early as 1667. No one knows who might have been the first musician to observe that a plucked string forms an oval. In Germany in 1740, Johannes Segner was the first to try to determine how long an image persists on the retina. And in 1824 Roget mentioned retinal retention in a discussion of the shutterlike slats of a fence.

A simple experiment was proposed by English astronomer and photographic chemist Sir John Herschel in 1825. He bet his friend that he could show the head and tail of a shilling at the same time. Then Sir John spun the coin, and the head and tail appeared as one image. This combining or overlapping of two distinct images was long considered an example of persistence of vision, but the rapidly recurring images were combined in the brain, not on the retina.

Told of Herschel's experiment, Dr. William Henry Fitton designed a cardboard disc with a different picture painted on each side and with strings attached to opposite edges. The strings could be twisted, then pulled, to make the card spin. When the disc turned quickly, the images on each side—in this first case, a bird and a closed, empty birdcage—were seen together as a single, unmoving image of the bird inside the cage. A version of this "scientific toy" was marketed—and long thought to have been invented—by Dr. John Ayrton Paris later in 1825. Paris called it the Thaumatrope (from the Greek "wonder turning"). Many different images were designed for the Thaumatrope; engraved drawings were printed on each side, or face, of this very popular amusement. With the invention of the Thaumatrope, the history of research into persistence of vision joins the history of entertainment. Before going on to look at the heirs of that spinning card, however, we need to consider what does generate the illusion of motion.

Separating and Integrating Frames

Although persistence of vision is not responsible for the cinematic illusion, the devices designed to exploit persistence of vision *did* produce an illusion: One did see the images move. Even if the real reasons for the perception of apparent motion were unknown, something in the persistence-of-vision experiments and toys tricked the brain correctly. They created the conditions for perceiving intermittent motion as continuous motion.

We can be sure that one of those conditions was the rapid, sequential presentation of images that were drawn or photographed to show successive parts of movements. Another condition was some kind of blank interval or imageless instant between the pictures. Yet another was the distinct space in front of the viewer, defined and occupied now by a screen but once by an eyepiece or a mirror, that allowed the images always to appear in the same place, where the viewer was already looking.

That blank interval—created by a closed shutter, by the distance between the viewing slits on a turning toy, by the flipping of a page in a flip book, by the edge of Herschel's coin, by the edges where turning mirrors are glued together, by the "field blanking" in a TV, and by other means—*separates* images so that the brain processes each one as a distinct still. (When a revolving set of mirrors directs one image after another into the eye, there is no *dark* interval, only a very briefly glimpsed, image-free line where the edges of the mirrors meet, but the illusion of motion is the same as that created by a theatrical projector.) As a separator or border, the interval between stills is read by the brain as a period of non-information—allowing the phenomenon of visual masking to work, rather than functioning as a darkness in which to watch the lingering image of a previous still. Consciously, the interval is ignored, much as the brain expects no information from the darkness that briefly descends when our eyelids blink.

Another relevant image-free area is the darkness that surrounds the picture, which can be the black rim of the screen or a whole movie theatre. Theatres—which encourage one to face the screen and see practically nothing else, which allow figures made of light to be displayed, and which keep the outside world out—were designed to be dark so that flashed images could be seen clearly and persist on the retina.

Much of the cinematic illusion depends on our seeing and processing stills as limited parts of a whole, sequential views plucked from a movement. The stills are limited by the edges of the frame, limited in time, kept separate as different images, kept together by their recurring subjects (the things that show up in every frame), and displayed in a dedicated atmosphere that encourages the viewer to concentrate while facing in a fixed direction. If there is a neural function that allows us to process frames distinctly (an essential part of which is visual masking), another neural function that misreads some stills as moving, and a neural or even preconscious function that encourages us to integrate the frames into a perceived continuity, that would be an effective combination—and one that appears to apply. Modern research suggests that many forms of processing apparent motion, including these methods, combine to turn separate, related pictures into a single imaginary vision.

The Phi Phenomenon and Beta Movement

A mental function that makes us *see light move* from one place to another when it does not move at all is a necessary element of the cinematic illusion. The first experiment concerning the brain's ability to see—or generate a mental image of—fixed lights moving was carried out in 1910. Max Wertheimer, a German psychologist, found that if two lights were flashed at a certain interval and in fixed positions a certain distance from each other, the viewer would see only one light, and it would move between the two positions; he called that the *phi phenomenon* or *phi effect*. He called it *beta movement* if the light appeared to move the whole distance from one position to another; he had other names for free movement (phi) and partial movement. If the distance or the interval was different, the viewer saw one light flash after the other. Wertheimer published his results in 1912, and Hugo Münsterberg applied them to film theory in 1916. Seeing apparent movement between positions (beta movement) is closely related to another aspect of the phi phenomenon: filling in the blanks between successive fragments of motion, imagining and perceiving what a closed shutter never allowed to be photographed. In both cases the brain generates an imaginary whole from discrete parts.

The phi phenomenon's beta movement makes certain distinct lights appear to be one moving light; in film, it might account for our thinking that we see parts of the first frame move to the positions they occupy in the second—even if, paradoxically, we can't know what those movements are until we've seen the second frame: an example of the brain's constructing experience after the fact.

Short-Range Apparent Motion

One important explanation for our seeing an illusory movement as real, posited by Joseph and Barbara Anderson in 1993, is based on research that suggests, first, that the brain processes short-range and long-range apparent motion differently and, second, that it may be unable to tell the difference between *short-range apparent motion* (whose displayed positions are spaced close together) and real motion. Therefore, because of the short distances apparently moved by figures between frames—their closely spaced positions in consecutive stills—the brain perceives the cinema's form of apparent movement as real movement. No beta movement is involved.

Another explanation concentrates on how the brain may read an interrupted signal or a set of discrete signals as a continuous signal—when it sees a flicker-free image, for example, and when it misreads short-range apparent motion as continuous motion.

Still another emphasizes that the individual photoreceptors in the retina do not perceive motion but are activated one after another by a moving light or what appears to be one. If a light is perceived by one retinal cell and then by another, the brain reads the successive lights as one moving light, as its motion-processing neurons are stimulated. The same process also may lead the brain to misread two successive stills as part of a moving image.

Whether short displacements are read as real motion or beta movement is perceived from successive stimuli, there clearly are neural functions that allow us to see certain types of apparent movement. These functions may trick the brain to ignore discontinuity.

Constructing Continuity

On the other hand, the cinéma might force the brain to *deal* with discontinuity, a discontinuity that may well be perceived. One aspect of the phi phenomenon, alluded to earlier, is that the brain fills in the action gaps between frames. That may happen preconsciously or neurally; no one knows yet. It may be a way to make sense of illusory movement or of the jumps between frames. The phi phenomenon helped Münsterberg to argue that a series of pictures requires the effects of consciousness to move, that the cinema is a psychological event in which things happen not as they do in physical reality but as they do in the mind, and that we regularly supply what is missing from a film.

The phi phenomenon implies that we perceive apparent movement in the cinema at least partly because the brain compares the successive positions of the subject and makes us see it move between those positions. That might happen because the brain decides that a photographed arm, for example, shown here in one frame and over here in the next frame, *must* have moved between the two photographed positions. The instantaneous leap from one place to another is a paradox like the quantum leap, whereby an electron is now at one distance from the atom's nucleus, now at another, without having crossed the space between those positions. The brain may deal with the leaps between frames, which contradict its experience of the world, by creating out of discontinuous parts a continuous whole—or a continuous signal—and seeing that imaginary, constructed whole rather than a series of motion fragments. (Parts and wholes are basic to Gestalt psychology, which Wertheimer helped to create. Like the systems theory of the 1970s, the continuous signal may be a more up-to-date way than Gestalt to explain how a whole can be more than the sum of its parts.) The brain has milliseconds to construct our visual reality—quite enough time to decide whether something is moving before letting us see it. The brain is certainly able to generate a mental event from partial visual data, especially if the information is gathered as regularly as that in a movie. It is already hard-wired to recognize, interpret, and organize the retinas' two flipped worlds to prepare a 3-D image to be seen only by the brain. There is so much that we only think we see.

Scientific Toys

In 1829, four years after the appearance of the Thaumatrope, the French inventor Joseph Antoine Ferdinand Plateau published his investigations on persistence of vision, and in 1832 he created his own toy to demonstrate his theoretical research. Painted on a flat, circular piece of board were individual designs in slightly varying positions. When the board was grasped by a handle, held up in front of a mirror, and then spun, the individual designs became a continuous, animated sequence. To see the designs moving

Early persistence of vision toys: the Thaumatrope, a Zoetrope wheel with paper strip, and (left rear) a primitive version of what would become a Mutoscope.

Fig. 2-1

(rather than as a blur), the viewer looked into the mirror through little slits cut into the circular board. Sales of Plateau's toy began in 1833 under various names chosen by the manufacturers. Although Plateau preferred "Phenakisticope," the name that stuck was Phenakistiscope (from the Greek "deceptive viewer"). Plateau's research was important, for in the course of it he discovered that 16 images per second was the optimal rate for producing continuous movement. In addition, the Phenakistiscope required instants of darkness, without an image (when one saw the dark or blank side of the turning card instead of the view, through a slit, of the mirror and its reflected drawings), to make the images appear to move. A successful projector would not be invented until an analogy to Plateau's slits was discovered.

A German inventor, Simon Ritter von Stampfer, developed a machine similar to Plateau's Phenakistiscope in the same year; he called it the Stroboscope (light and dark in rapid alternation, from the Greek "alternating viewer"). Based on the same principle as the Phenakistiscope and Stroboscope, many refined versions of this toy appeared throughout the

19th century. In 1834, William George Horner created a stroboscopic machine that used a circular drum rather than a flat circular board; it was first marketed in 1867. Exchangeable paper strips fit inside the circular drum. When the viewer looked through the slits in the spinning drum, which allowed instants of darkness, the pictures on the paper strips appeared in delightfully sequential motion. Horner first called his toy the Daedaleum, then the Zoötrope (or Zoetrope, from the Greek "life turning" or "wheel of life").

In 1843, English inventor T. W. Naylor adapted a magic lantern (a 17th-century glass-slide projector) to project a Phenakistiscopic disc. Apparently aware of Naylor's work, Baron Franz von Uchatius built his own Projecting Phenakistiscope in 1845 in Austria, and soon he was experimenting with multiple and sequential images. It is said that he once lined up a series of projectors side by side and focused them on the same screen. In each lantern was a glass slide with a slightly different phase of movement. By running with a torch from lantern to lantern, Uchatius threw a sequence of animated apparent movement on the screen.

Émile Reynaud

The Praxinoscope was invented by Émile Reynaud in 1877. It resembled the Zoetrope, but the drum had no slits. Instead, the viewer looked over the edge of the drum at an inner, central wheel on which mirrors were set at angles to one another. The mirrors reflected the images Reynaud had drawn on Zoetrope-like paper strips and set inside the drum, and in the instant that each mirror directly faced the viewer, it reflected that image into the eye. Between images, nothing was seen but the angled edge of a turning mirror. Reynaud soon created the Projection Praxinoscope (1880), which added the magic lantern to his mirrors, and the image-combining Praxinoscope-Théâtre (1887), in which the reflected moving image was combined with the reflection of a miniature set or a painted or printed background. These inventions finally led him to design the Théâtre Optique, a complex device, patented in 1888 and first exhibited in 1892, that showed long animated tales. Reynaud's image sequences were not limited to short repeated actions because they were painted not on turning cards or paper loops but on long transparent strips, some of them over 100 feet long and wound on a reel.

The three strips that Reynaud prepared for the Théâtre Optique between 1888 and 1892 were painted on a transparent, flexible, celluloid-like gelatin that had one perforation per frame, lasted as long as 15 minutes (the shortest was six minutes), were projected back and forth as well as straight through, and were integrated with other projected or reflected images. In the 1888 patent, Reynaud mentioned that the pictures on the long strip could be drawn, printed, or "obtained from nature by means of photography." With Reynaud, the theatrical, projected, perforated, and (even if he painted his frames) photographed cinema had been envisioned. Reynaud should also be recognized as the maker of the first animated movies. He didn't use a camera to put his paintings on film, but neither do many 21st-century digital animators.

By the end of the 19th century, hundreds of variations on these toys and shows abounded. All these heirs of the Thaumatrope were designed to exploit persistence of vision. Most were stroboscopic in the sense that they presented bright images and darkness in rapid alternation. And most of them shared several traits that were to continue as trends in later movie history. Most striking was the inventors' passion for fancy Greek and Latin names: Choreutoscope, Viviscope, Zoetrope. (There was also a Getthemoneygraph!) This passion would later dominate the first era of motion pictures—Kinetoscope, Cinématographe—and beyond it, to the age of Technicolor and CinemaScope. Also striking is the simultaneity of discoveries in different countries, primarily in France, England, Germany, and the United States. Even today, each of these four countries claims to have invented the motion picture. The validity of each claim depends on whether the motion picture was invented when it was conceived, when it was patented, when it was photographed on film, or when it was projected in public.

The early stroboscopic experiments, entertainments, and toys used drawn figures. Before the movies could become moving pictures of the natural world, the means to record the visual world had to be discovered.

Photography

Before there could be motion pictures, there had to be pictures. A moving picture was born from the union of the stroboscopic toys and the still photograph. The principle of photography dates back at least to the Renaissance and Leonardo da Vinci's drawing of a *camera obscura*. This device—literally translated as "dark room" or "dark chamber"—was a completely dark enclosure that admitted light only through a small hole. The *camera obscura* projected an inverted reproduction of the scene facing it on the wall opposite. After a lens was put in the hole to brighten and sharpen the image, all the *camera obscura* needed to become a camera was a photographic plate to replace the back wall (the portable *camera obscura* was used as an aid to sketching, with drawing paper on its "back wall" and a lid one could lift to trace the image). Inventors and scientists set out in pursuit of this plate that could fix the inverted image permanently.

As early as 1816, Joseph Nicéphore Niépce, a Frenchman, used metal plates to capture rather fuzzy images—the first photographs. He called them Heliographs, because they were drawn by the sun. (Photography, also from the Greek, means "light writing.") But it was another Frenchman, Louis Jacques Mandé Daguerre, the late Niépce's partner, who in 1839 determined the future of photography by making clear, sharp, permanent images on silvered copperplate. The very first Daguerreotype, a picture of the artist's studio, was taken in 1837, but the invention was announced and verified in 1839. The exposure time required for an image was 15 minutes, so the first sitters for Daguerreotypes had to pose motionless for 15 minutes, their heads propped up to keep them from wiggling. Before photography could become more practical, exposure time would have to be cut. There obviously could be no motion pictures, which require multiple exposures per second, until the photographic material was sensitive enough to permit such shutter speeds. (Indeed, the first still cameras used the lens cap as a shutter.) It was also in the 1830s that the English inventor William Henry Fox Talbot began his research in paper printing—the principle of the photographic negative, and with it, the reproducible photograph. Talbot's paper prints also took less time to expose than Daguerreotypes. After Daguerre's and Talbot's perfecting of the basic principles, photographic stocks became *faster* (more photosensitive), permitting a 3-minute exposure by 1841. Before 30 years had passed, the shutter had been invented, and faster photographic plates allowed exposures of a fraction of a second.

Muybridge and Marey

The first attempts at motion photography were posed stills that simulated continuous action. But a real motion picture required a continuous live action to be first analyzed into its component units and then resynthesized, rather than a simple synthesis of static, posed bits of action.

The first person to break a continuous action into discrete photographic units was an Englishman transplanted to California, Eadweard Muybridge. Muybridge was a vagabond photographer and inventor. In 1872, he was hired by the governor of California, Leland Stanford, to help win a $25,000 bet. Stanford, an avid horse breeder and racer, bet a friend that at some point in the racehorse's stride all four hooves left the ground. In 1877, after faster exposures became possible, Muybridge set up 24 cameras in a row along the racing track. He attached a string to each camera shutter and stretched the string across the track. He chalked numerals and lines on a board behind the track to measure the horse's progress. The

horse then galloped down the track, tripping the wires, and Mr. Stanford won the $25,000 that had cost him only $40,000 to win.

For the next 20 years, Muybridge perfected his multiple-camera technique. He increased the number of cameras from 12 (in the earliest experiments) to 24 and even to 40. He used faster, more sensitive plates. He added white horizontal and vertical lines on a black background to increase the impression of motion and to study human and animal movements more precisely. He shot—and published—motion sequences of horses and elephants and tigers, of nude women and wrestling men and dancing couples. He mounted his pictures on a Phenakistiscope wheel and combined the wheel with the magic lantern for public projections of his work in 1879. Unfortunately, what he mounted and projected were not his photographs but drawings made from them. He called his invention—a variation on the Projecting Phenakistiscope—the Zoöpraxiscope (from the Greek "life-constructing viewer"). Muybridge traveled to Europe, where he gave special showings of the Zoöpraxiscope to admiring scientists and photographers. Years later, in February 1888, Muybridge suggested to Edison that they combine the phonograph with the Zoöpraxiscope— or a newer apparatus on which he said he was working. Edison rejected the idea but soon began making notes for another way of integrating moving pictures and sound.

Muybridge's "series pictures," as he called them, were a major advance over a series of drawings or posed stills because they were photographs of actual movement, taken rapidly one after the other. Their limitation—aside from Muybridge's not being able to figure out a way to project the actual photographs—was the need for a separate camera to shoot each picture. Muybridge's pictures were serial photographs— not fully achieved motion-picture photography but on the verge of it—and they were of very brief actions, as short as anything in a Zoetrope loop. Continuous motion had been divided into distinct frames, but it had not yet been photographed by a single camera.

One of Muybridge's hosts in Paris in 1881 was another student of movement, physiologist Étienne-Jules Marey, who also was experimenting with serial photography. In 1882, Marey was the

Fig. 2-2
Muybridge's leaping horse.

first to shoot multiple pictures with a single camera. "Shoot" applies quite literally to Marey's experiment, for his camera looked like a shotgun. The photographic gun ("fusil") used a long barrel for its lens and a circular chamber containing a single glass photographic plate. The circular plate rotated 12 times in the chamber per second of shooting, leaving all 12 exposures arranged in a ring around the glass plate. Whereas Muybridge had gone from one camera to another, each loaded with a glass plate that had been coated with a light-sensitive emulsion, Marey moved one plate through one camera and maintained a single point of reference; Muybridge's point of view had moved horizontally, from camera to camera. Like Muybridge, Marey photographed people and

animals: runners, fencers, trotting horses, falling cats, gorgeous flying birds. But Marey's Chrono-photographs produced a much more fluid analysis of motion, the finished print resembling a surreal multiple exposure. He shot most of these sequential exposures not with the Photographic Gun of March 1882 but with a very heavy camera, shaped like a box, that produced a better image and that he patented only a few months after the gun. Marey introduced this new camera, the Photochronograph, in July 1882; it revolved a glass plate 10 times per second and exposed one picture with each revolution. In 1888, Marey redesigned the camera to use coated paper film; this new, lighter camera was called the Photochronograph until 1889, when Marey changed its name to the Chronophotographe or Chronophotographic Camera. It exposed 20 fps, though it could also run as slowly as 10 fps and—to catch the movement of flying birds—as rapidly as 40 fps. Marey called the medium Chronophotography, emphasizing its ability to photograph time (or to photograph as time progressed). Paper film could hold many more frames than a glass disc. Photography had reached the threshold of cinematography.

Because the photosensitive paper strip, wound on a spool, could be any length, Marey's 1888 camera, demonstrated to the Academy of Sciences in Paris in October, was free of the problems of the repeating loop and of the short unrepeated action. That same year, Reynaud had begun painting his extremely long strips for the Théâtre Optique and winding them on a reel. The crucial element of Reynaud's apparatus that Marey's Chronophotograph lacked was the line of perforations to help control the strip's movement. What Reynaud's perforated strip lacked was what Muybridge had brought to the project of inventing cinema: photographs.

The first paper-film movie camera was invented not by Marey in October 1888, however, but by Louis Aimé Augustin Le Prince in January 1888. Operating on unique principles, using six lenses and multiple strips of paper film, it was part of an integrated camera–projector that survives. Between January and October, Le Prince invented a single-lens camera for paper film, but it has not survived. In October 1888, the same month that Marey unveiled his own paper-film camera, Le Prince made two paper films with his single-lens camera, and they do survive on paper rolls. Le Prince also invented a three-lens projector that used perforated celluloid (March 1890)—the first celluloid-film projector. It is not known whether he made the movies for this projector by running celluloid strips through his paper-film camera or by designing a new camera—in which case he would have invented a celluloid camera before Marey did. But late in 1890, Le Prince disappeared from a train between Dijon and Paris, and nothing ever came of his work. In June 1889, English inventor William Friese-Greene patented a paper-film movie camera that took superior photographs; he also patented an integrated celluloid camera–projector in 1893, but if any movies were made with it, they haven't survived.

In Germany, Max Skladanowsky began work on his camera in 1892; his improved camera and Bioskope projector were patented in 1895.

In 1890, Marey made the first known movie camera designed to use celluloid film instead of paper film. It was his fourth camera—after the 1882 glass-disc gun, the 1882 glass-disc box, and the 1888 paper-film box—and he called it the "complete" version of the Chronophotographic Camera. He presented a movie taken with that camera, a strip of celluloid 90mm wide and about 30 frames long, to the Academy of Sciences in November 1890; the subject was that perennial favorite, a moving horse. He went on to make over 600 films. (The first Edison celluloid cameras, discussed below, were at work soon after: in November 1890, one that used a sheet of film, and in May 1891, one that used a strip.) In 1892, Marey completed his Chronophotographic Projector, which threw images from a strip of celluloid onto a screen, using electromagnetic pads to clamp and hold the film behind the lens, then release it; even with his unperforated film, Marey became the inventor most responsible for the use of intermittent movement in film cameras and projectors. By 1892, then, Marey was the first to have invented and demonstrated both a camera and a projector for celluloid movies. If Le Prince did build and use such equipment first, he did not demonstrate it as publicly as Marey did, or we would know more about his achievements.

Edison, still thinking about what he had learned from Muybridge, met Marey while attending the Paris Exposition in 1889, and from Marey—whose lab the trusting scientist invited Edison to visit—he got the idea to use a single camera loaded with celluloid that would stop in front of the lens long enough to be exposed. Edison described this idea for an invention in November 1889, 13 months after he wrote his first notes about motion pictures. (These notes were called *caveats*, notifications to the U.S. Patent Office that one was working on an invention and might later apply for a patent on it.) Because the post-cylinder cameras invented in the Edison Laboratory between 1890 and 1892 used perforated film, it is possible that Edison also saw Reynaud's work in Paris.

To produce a movie that was more than a snippet of activity, a material had to be developed that could hold thousands of images and pass through machines without tearing. Coated-paper film was an option only until celluloid—which produced sharper, richer pictures and was much stronger and more flexible—was perfected. An early version of celluloid was patented in 1872 in the United States, even though a similar product had been invented in England as early as 1855. True celluloid was invented in the United States in 1887–89.

In 1884, George Eastman began his own experiments with celluloid and with paper-roll film, the latter for use in his Kodak still camera. (Eastman perforated the still paper film, not to advance it but to mark the positions of the frames.) By 1888, photography, which had been the sole property of professionals, had become any person's hobby (Kodak's slogan was "You push the button, we do the rest"). In 1888, Eastman produced his own version of the celluloid film that had been invented and patented in 1887 by the Reverend Hannibal Goodwin. (In 1913, the courts found that Eastman had infringed on Goodwin's patents.) Its cellulose nitrate base was perfected in 1889 by an Eastman chemist named Henry M. Reichenbach, and Eastman began to produce and market celluloid film that same year. The film was transparent, thin, strong, and of the same width and quality from one batch to another, thanks to George Eastman's great skill at designing efficient, effective means of manufacturing. In 1892, the Eastman Dry Plate and Film Company (founded 1881) took the name by which it is still known, the Eastman Kodak Company.

Eastman's 1889 celluloid film became the preferred material for further experiments in motion photography. The American discovery of celluloid film shifts the history of the movies back across the Atlantic from France.

Thomas Edison

Appropriately enough, the American father of the movies is the ultimate representative of the ingenious, pragmatic American inventor–businessman: Thomas Alva Edison. In 1888, after inviting Muybridge to his lab and seeing the Zoöpraxiscope in action, the supreme tinkerer wrote his first caveat, describing "an instrument which does for the Eye what the phonograph does for the Ear, which is the recording and reproducing of things in motion, and in such a form as to be both Cheap practical and convenient." His second and third caveats concerned cylinder films, but the fourth, influenced by Marey's work and written in 1889, called for a strip of film.

It was in February 1889 that Edison assigned employees and laboratory space to the project of inventing motion pictures, but he did not personally invent them. He did, of course, invent the incandescent lamp (1879), without which most of the cinema would be impossible, and the phonograph (1877), which led to the soundtrack. Edison's original idea—in effect, a kind of music video that allowed one to see and hear a singer—was to accompany his wax phonographic cylinder with another wax cylinder on which microscopic photos were etched; one machine, invented in 1889 or 1890, did play the two cylinders in sync. Edison also ordered work on a single cylinder ringed with pictures and with grooves of sound. From the very first, he wanted to reproduce operas. But the tiny pictures looked very poor when enlarged. In addition, only their centers were in focus because they were shot on a curved surface, a cylinder coated with photosensitive chemicals.

W. K–L. Dickson and William Heise

Edison's director of the motion picture project was William Kennedy–Laurie Dickson. He was the primary inventor of the Edison cameras and viewers, and with his associate, William Heise, he made the first American films. The story of Dickson and Heise's work for Edison and the order in which the films were made have been scrupulously established by film historian Charles Musser, notably in his filmography *Edison Motion Pictures, 1890–1900.*

From early 1889 to late 1890, Dickson worked on the pinpoint-photo project with his first associate, Charles A. Brown. In October 1889, when Edison returned from the European tour during which he had met Marey, he saw the cylinder movies and agreed that they looked bad. After writing the fourth caveat, Edison told Dickson to invent a camera that used a strip of film. Dickson soon began experimenting with celluloid, but he also kept working on cylinders.

At first, Dickson bought sheets of celluloid film from inventor John Carbutt and cut them to size. (For several years, film was sliced and sometimes perforated by the purchaser.) Late in 1889, Dickson placed his first order with Eastman. He also bought 35mm film from other manufacturers—in 1893, for example, from the Blair Camera Company—but Eastman eventually became Edison's sole supplier.

Edison assigned William Heise to work with Dickson in October 1890. Dickson and Heise began wrapping sheets of coated celluloid around the cylinders instead of coating them directly, and they took bigger pictures. The first of these sheet-films survives in its entirety; called *Monkeyshines, no. 1*, it was probably shot in November 1890. *Monkeyshines, no. 1* lasts about 30 seconds and shows a man, or a set of blobs that resemble a human figure, moving its arms and legs. Entirely out of focus and almost abstract, it looks prehistoric and is—when one realizes what came from it and how much potential is already shown in it—thrilling and pure. It is the dance of precinema. *Monkeyshines, no. 2*, also about 30 seconds, offers a more recognizably human figure whose face and belt can just be made out; he waves his arms while bending from side to side and horsing around to give the camera some movement to capture—but to say what he is doing is to guess after a tenth viewing; the image is still out of focus. After one more of these camera tests (*Monkeyshines, no. 3*, which survives only in part), Dickson and Heise stopped working with cylinders but kept working with film.

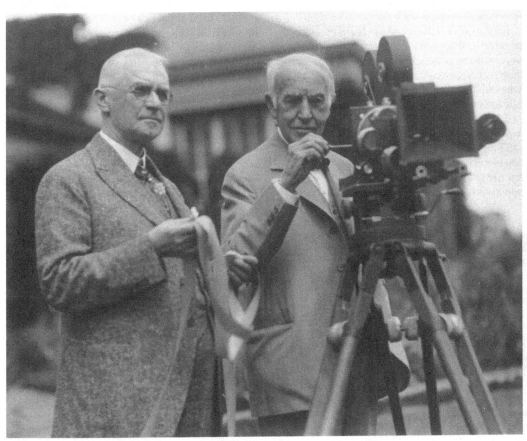

Fig. 2-3
The business of invention: George Eastman (left) and Thomas Edison, posing in 1927.

Early Cameras and Films

By May 1891, Dickson and Heise had built a camera that used perforated celluloid (a single row of perfs) that was 3/4 inch wide; the film ran horizontally through the camera. Only a fragment of the first film shot with this camera—the first American movie shot on a strip of film—survives. Called *Dickson Greeting*, it starred Dickson and was shot by Heise sometime before May 20, 1891, for it was on that date that Edison showed this film to members of the Federation of Women's Clubs when they visited his lab. Looking in the eyepiece of a boxy viewer, each woman saw a man who bowed, smiled, waved his hands to demonstrate natural motion, and gracefully took off his hat. (In what survives, he bows slightly while passing his hat from one hand to another.) When he showed that film to reporters a few days later, Edison described his plan for "a compound machine consisting of a phonograph and a kinetograph" that could reproduce an opera in one's parlor.

Edison decided the apparatus had a commercial future and applied for his first camera and viewer patents in 1891. In mid-1892, Dickson and Heise built a camera that used film that was 1 1/2 inches wide and ran it vertically. By October they had perfected the vertical-feed camera, which now used film that was 1 9/16 inches wide (a bit wider than 35mm) and had two lines of sprocket holes, with four perfs to the left and right of each frame. Film moved evenly and reliably through the October 1892 version of the huge, heavy camera (hundreds of pounds), the completed Kinetograph.

The next major improvement to an Edison camera, portability, would come in May 1896.

In April 1893, Dickson and Heise began using this camera to make 35mm films that could be shown to the public. These first pictures were shot on film made by the Blair Camera Company. The first of these—called *Blacksmithing Scene* or *Blacksmiths*—was the 16th Edison film (a count that includes the first three sheet-films); it showed a blacksmith and two assistants hammering a piece of iron, passing a bottle around while waiting for the iron to heat up, and then hammering it again. Like most of the first commercial Edison films it was 50 feet long and lasted less than half a minute. The 17th, in which one man shod a horse while another heated iron in a forge, was *Horse Shoeing*. These were the two films shown in the vertical-feed 35mm "peephole" or eyepiece viewer, the Kinetoscope, at its first public exhibition—on May 9, 1893, at the Brooklyn Institute of Arts and Sciences. The last of the known 1893 films, made in August or September, was *The Barber Shop*. Like the previous two, it was a picture of a job being done (on a set made to resemble a workplace), but it did something more: *The Barber Shop* gave the audience two things to look at, two centers of interest at once, both of which would ordinarily be in a barber shop: the man who is getting a shave and a haircut from the barber, and the waiting customers who are reading the papers (one man calls attention to a story and passes the paper to the other customer, who reads the story and laughs).

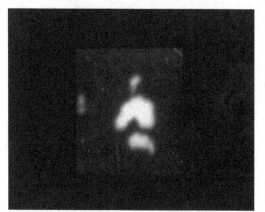

Fig. 2-4
Monkeyshines, no. 1.

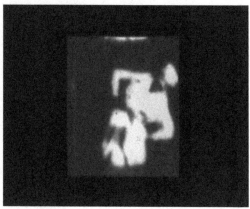

Fig. 2-5
Monkeyshines, no. 2.

Fig. 2-6
Fred Ott's Sneeze, *one of the earliest surviving, complete films.*

After *The Barber Shop* came *Fred Ott's Sneeze*, also known as *Edison Kinetoscopic Record of a Sneeze, January 7, 1894*. The 19th Edison film—and only the 6th to survive in its entirety—this 2-second picture was the first movie ever copyrighted. It was shot to appear in the pages of a magazine, *Harper's Weekly*, where it illustrated an article on Edison's work, and it was because it was to appear in a printed magazine that it was copyrighted. According to legend, one of Edison's mechanics, Fred Ott, was a comical fellow who could sneeze on cue. Dickson decided to film him, and Heise ran the camera.

After a few more experiments, in March 1894 Dickson and Heise turned entirely to films designed for commercial exhibition. They began with *Sandow* (Edison #26), which showed Eugen Sandow, "the strongest man in the world." During the next 12 months, Dickson and Heise made about 100 more of the 50-foot films. In *Annie Oakley* (1894), for example, the western star fires rapidly at fixed and moving targets. In *Billy Edwards and the Unknown* (1895), the boxers fight.

Worried about the poor quality of projected images, Edison decided on direct viewing. Rather than seeing an image projected for large groups, the customer would look through an eyepiece into a machine and view the single filmstrip inside it. Edison's decision was based on his integrity as an inventor as well as his greed. He saw the greater clarity of reproduction in the peephole machine, and he was sure he would make more money from the novelty if it were displayed to one person at a time rather than to a hall full of people. Although he was wrong about the commercial potential of projection, he made up for it a few years later by marketing an Edison projector. But another decision, made at the same time, was impossible to reverse. Perhaps because he was aware of similar work in Europe, especially Marey's patented machines, Edison decided not to spend $150 to extend his U.S. patent rights overseas. This "oversight" (if it was a mistake rather than a legitimate decision—no one knows) meant that outside the United States, the Kinetoscope could legally be cloned: broken down to discover its secret, then manufactured and sold under another name, perhaps with an improved design and perhaps with a camera to make films for it.

The Kinetoscope

When he applied for their patents in 1891, Edison called the camera the Kinetograph (from the Greek "motion writer") and the viewer the Kinetoscope ("motion viewer"). Previously he had been calling both machines the Kinetograph, to complement his phonograph. When the patents were finally granted in 1893, Edison allowed the Kinetoscope to be demonstrated in public—and soon after that was charging the public a nickel apiece.

By 1894, Edison was marketing his own machines through a firm fronted by Norman Raff and Frank Gammon. The first Kinetoscope Parlor opened in New York City on April 14, 1894; soon many more sprang up across the country. The Kinetoscope also debuted in Europe in 1894. Ancestors of the late 20th century's video arcades, the parlors offered not only phonographs, but also

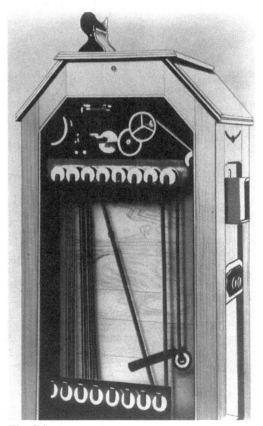

Fig. 2-7
The Kinetoscope mechanism.

Fig. 2-8

A Kinetoscope Parlor: phonographs on the left (complete with handkerchiefs for wiping the earpieces), Kinetoscopes on the right.

rows of handsomely made, nickel-in-the-slot Kinetoscopes, beckoning the customer to look at the new marvel of mechanically recorded life.

The design of the Kinetoscope strongly influenced the films Dickson and Heise shot for it. Wound around spools inside the Kinetoscope, the film's ending led continuously into its beginning, exactly as the Phenakistiscopic wheels or Zoetrope strips had done. The difference was that although the film itself had its head spliced to its tail, the *movie* could begin and end with very different images. Electronically powered, the Kinetoscope ran the loop of film only once per nickel, rather than over and over, so it was free to develop a record or narrative that moved from A to B to C...rather than from A to B to A. The space inside the Kinetoscope box limited the length of a filmstrip to 50 feet, and since Edison's cameras and viewers often ran at 40 fps, the 800 frames on the 50 feet of film might last only 20 seconds. Edison almost always said that both machines ran at 46 fps, but most of the films were shot at between 30 and 36 fps, down to the rarely used low speed of 16 fps. The continuous strip of film seemed suited to a single shot—anyway, no one had yet thought of editing—so what Dickson and Heise shot became the finished movie. The most popular filmstrips were views of famous people, like Sandow or Annie Oakley (who were the movies' first stars and human spectacles, attractive and accomplished people seen up close); animal acts; bits of dancing or clowning; and even some staged historical and news events. The most common subjects, not just of Edison films but of most films until narrative came to dominate the cinema in the early 1900s, were spectacles, events, figures, and attractions interesting to watch in themselves; film historian Tom Gunning has called this the period of "the cinema of attractions."

A Sound Film and a Studio

One of the later movies Dickson made for Edison—before resigning in April 1895 to pursue his own career—was a picture of two male employees dancing while Dickson played a violin into a funnel that gathered sound into a recording phonograph. That picture, which survives as *Dickson Experimental Sound Film* (Edison #125), was synchronized with the music the camera shows being recorded. We know that because in 1964, the long-lost recording was found: a broken wax cylinder labeled *Violin by W.K.L. Dickson with Kineto.* That 40-foot, 16-second movie, played in sync with a phonograph cylinder, was the first sound *film* (earlier experiments had synchronized a sound cylinder with a picture cylinder), and it was made sometime between

September 1894 and April 1895. The cylinder was started before the camera; about 2 minutes in, one can hear Dickson saying, "Are the rest of you ready? Go ahead." Then Heise started the camera at 40 fps, and the rest of the sound is in sync with the picture. Dickson called his apparatus the Kineto-phonograph (from the Greek "motion-sound writer"); in 1889, he claimed, he had shown an early version to Edison with a recorded greeting, but there is no surviving evidence of that. For reasons unknown, Edison decided not to pursue the Kineto-phonograph. Heise went on to shoot films for the Kinetoscope himself, notably *Annabelle Serpentine Dance* in 1895 and *May Irwin Kiss* (or *The Kiss*) in 1896; he also shot *The Execution of Mary, Queen of Scots* (1895) for Alfred Clark—the first film with two shots—and *Fatima* (1896) for James White, before leaving Edison's company and the film business in 1898.

Despite his mistake about projection, Edison certainly left his mark on the future of film. Most influential were Edison's artificial illumination and sound recording—as well as his later cut-throat behavior as a leader of the film business—and Dickson and Heise's decision to puncture the sides of movie film with sprocket holes.

The Edison–Dickson–Heise perforations quickly became the standard throughout the world and were known as the American Perforation. By the time Dickson left Edison, the experiments of Muybridge, Reynaud, Marey, and others had been integrated into a sturdy, reliable camera; motion pictures had become a viable entertainment business even without an Edison projector; and "8-perf" celluloid (that is, with four sprocket holes on the left and right sides of each frame) approximately 35mm wide had become what most people meant by movie film. (The Lumières standardized film width at 35mm and shooting speed at 16 fps, but even they were forced to adopt the American perforations in 1897 so that their films could be shown on "normal" machines. Originally they had had one circular perforation on each side of the frame.) Beyond all that, Edison and Dickson also created the movie studio.

In December 1892, at Dickson's request, Edison authorized construction of a small building that was designed for the exclusive purpose of making motion pictures. Among other things, it had to absorb the vibrations of the camera, it had to allow the subject to be adequately lit, and it had to be a dedicated space in which a single

The first movie studio: Edison's Black Maria (1893). The first studio with glass walls and roof was built by Méliès in 1897.

Fig. 2-9

task could be done well without interruption. Built on the grounds of the Edison Laboratory in West Orange, New Jersey, it was finished in February 1893. A few months later, Dickson and Heise made the first films ever shot in a studio, *Blacksmithing Scene* and *Horse Shoeing*.

Because the outside of the studio was protected with black tar paper (to exclude unwanted light), the room became known as the Black Maria, at that time slang for paddy wagon. Dickson mounted the camera on a trolley inside the Black Maria so that it could move closer or farther away, depending on the subject of the picture. The camera never changed position during the shooting. To light the action, the roof opened to catch the sunlight. The whole one-room studio—actually a shooting stage—could be rotated to catch the sun so that the scene would always be sufficiently lit.

The disadvantages of the Black Maria are obvious. The room was really a small, sunlit theatre with the camera as single spectator. There was even a specified stage area for the performer. Mobility was further curtailed by the bulky heaviness of the camera—the result of Edison's insistence on using electricity rather than a hand crank to run it, so that the machine remained perpetually indoors and inert.

To free the camera from its cage and the filmstrip from its viewing box were the next essential steps in the evolution of the movie machine. For these steps the history of film travels back across the Atlantic.

Projection

The problem of projecting motion pictures was surprisingly difficult to solve. After the principles of motion photography had been discovered and a camera developed to demonstrate the principles, one would have thought that projecting the images would come easily. In fact, early projection attempts produced blurry images, ripped film, fires, and a great deal of noise. Edison's initial decision to shelve projection was as much a realization of practical difficulties as a business error. But it was clear to other inventors that a projected motion picture was the next step. For hundreds of years audiences had delighted in projected-light shows. Even before photography, audiences had sat in darkened rooms and watched puppets' shadows or projected images on a screen.

The Magic Lantern

The invention of the magic lantern is usually attributed to Father Athanasius Kircher who, in 1646, may have made drawings of a box that could reproduce images by means of a light passing through a lens. The first working model was invented by Christiaan Huygens in 1659 or 1660. That box was similar to the 20th-century slide projector and the ancestor of all projectors.

In the 18th century, showmen trooped across Europe giving magic lantern shows, projecting glass slides with drawings, paintings, and, much later, photographs for paying customers. From the beginning, the magic lanternists sought to make their static images move. They developed lantern slides with moving parts and moving patterns. They used multiple lanterns to give the impression of depth and sequence. The most famous of these multiple-lantern shows was the Phantasmagoria (or, in French, the Fantasmagorie), in which ghosts and spirits were made to move, appear, and disappear with the aid of moving lanterns and mirrors. All the projection equipment was behind the screen, not in front of it. The showman who, overstating his role, claimed to have invented the Phantasmagoria in 1798 was Étienne-Gaspard Robert, a Frenchman who called himself Robertson. (The original inventor is unknown, but similar shows first appeared in the 1770s.) Around 1770, a "nebulous lantern" projected images of ghosts on smoke. The stroboscopic toys of the 19th century further enlarged the lanternist's repertoire.

One of the most significant of the pre-movie projection entertainments was the Photo Play. In the late 19th century, an American author and lecturer named Alexander Black combined the magic lantern slide, photography, and narration to produce a complete play with live narrator, live actors, and pictorial slides. The goal of the Photo Play was not to reproduce motion, nor to weave moving lights, but to realize the same stories and dramas that drew audiences to the live theatre. One of Black's plays lasted a full two hours and contained as many as four slides a minute, based on the same kind of melodramatic plot and suffering characters that the early movies (which were often called "photoplays") would themselves use.

By the late 19th century, several other audience entertainments combined visual images, the play of light, and the telling of a story. The Panorama, invented by English painter Robert Barker, was first exhibited in London in 1792 and remained popular for a century; it presented a huge painted mural that turned around the audience and that evolved from day to dusk to night to dawn to day again, while the action—the history of a great battle, for instance—moved across the variously illuminated surfaces of the picture. (Cinematic homages to the Panorama include the lighting changes on scenic backdrops in Chaplin's *Monsieur Verdoux*, 1947, and Hitchcock's *Rope*, 1948.) The Diorama, invented by Daguerre, debuted in Paris in 1822. Like the Panorama, it varied the light on and behind an immense painting—but the Diorama had more than one painting, and it was the audience that did the turning. Capable of presenting two different pictures—and therefore capable of scene changes—the Diorama rotated the seated audience, and the proscenium-like frame through which it looked, from a view of one large mural to the other. As we have seen, Reynaud combined a Praxinoscope with a magic lantern in 1880, and in 1892, he exhibited his Théâtre Optique, which reflected as well as projected images and whose moving pictures were painted on a celluloid-like strip that had one perforation per frame. Note that even if projection rather than reflection carried the day in the late 19th century, the chips in many 21st-century digital projectors use microscopic mirrors to reflect or block bits of light.

Even the late–19th-century live theatre was devoted to spectacular visual and mechanical effects. The conversion from oil lighting to the more controllable gas and, finally, to totally malleable electricity, coupled with the invention of elaborately mechanized scene-changing devices, led to such visual effects on stage as chases, last-minute rescues, dazzling transformations of one scene into another, and even the rapid shifts of visual setting that the movies would later codify as the cross-cut.

The Loop and Other Solutions

Such predecessors clearly indicated the potential popularity of projected movie shows. The problem was to develop a machine that could project the filmstrips. Two specific difficulties had deterred Edison: The projector needed a light source powerful enough to make the projected image clear and distinct, and the film needed to run past that light source without ripping, rattling, or burning. Flicker, Edison felt, presented no difficulty at 46 fps—very close to what was later found to be the critical flicker frequency of 48—but he never developed a projector that ran at such a high rate. The problem of flicker was not actually solved until 1903, with the invention of the three-bladed shutter, and not every projector design adopted it.

One of the first successful projections was made by a Virginia family of adventurer–inventors, the Lathams. Major Woodville Latham, former officer in the Confederate Army and former chemistry instructor, together with his two dashing sons, Gray and Otway, invented a camera and a projecting machine in 1895. The Lathams were helped significantly by their friend W. K–L. Dickson and his friend Eugène Lauste. Dickson was unhappy at Edison but had not yet left the company. In an attempt to dodge Edison's patents, Dickson and Lauste doubled the size of the film—producing a brighter, sharper image—and devised a nonintermittent way to move film through a projector. (The movement in the camera they built to go with it was intermittent.) The Lathams showed the press their projector, the Panoptikon, on April 21, 1895, and a month later they showed movies for money. By 1896, their projector was called the Eidoloscope. The most important element of the Latham projector was, as we shall see, a slack point, a curl of film called a *loop*, that Dickson and Lauste introduced into the film path (after they had put two loops in their camera, one on either side of the gate). Although the Lathams' exhibitions in New York and the urban South were very important and rewarding, the tempting life of the big cities converted the younger Lathams from scientists to playboys. The Lathams and their invention ended in the obscurity of financial disaster.

A successful projector had to do more than just enlarge the image. It had to feed and take up film on reels rather than run the film as a necessarily short, continuous circle, and it required a totally new principle of moving the film past the gate. The new principle, discovered and developed in Europe rather than the United States, was to move film intermittently through the projector: to stop each frame in front of the lamp. Thanks to Dickson and Heise's perforations, the

Kinetograph had used intermittent movement to stop the film during exposure, but the Kinetoscope had moved the film continuously—behind a rotating, slotted shutter that allowed a glimpse of each frame as the film rolled by. Intermittent movement in the projector allowed a clear, sharp image because the stationary frame used the available light more economically.

The intermittent movement of film past the shutter was, in principle, precisely the same as the slits in Plateau's Phenakistiscope; rather than a continuous succession of whirring images, each image was separated from the others into an individual piece of the whole. Although the intermittent movement of frames through the projection gate solved the problem of insufficient illumination, it could not cure the disease of ripping film without a tiny adjustment to take the tension off the jerkily speeding filmstrip. That adjustment was to create a small loop of excess film just before the gate, easing the tension from the feeding reel. Because the initial loop was first used—and patented—by the Lathams (although it was invented for them by Dickson and Lauste), it became known around the world as the *Latham loop*, a version of which all movie-film cameras and projectors still use, in most cases both before and after the gate. The loop also provided a key legal loophole that allowed Edison—once he bought the rights—to drag his competitors into court for almost a decade.

The worst problem caused by intermittent projection was the possibility of burning the highly flammable nitrate film that remained momentarily stationary in the gate. To solve this problem, the intermittent-motion projector—with its hot, bright, arc light, much fiercer than the Kinetoscope's electric bulb—required some kind of cooling system or fan to protect the film. Today, despite all the changes and improvements in movie equipment, film projectors are the same in principle as those invented in the final years of the 19th century.

The early film projectors of Le Prince (1890), Marey (1892), and Friese-Greene (1893) were mentioned above, along with their cameras. Two inventors discussed below, Charles Francis Jenkins and Thomas Armat, built in 1895 the machine that became Edison's projector (1896). Another important inventor—who worked for several years with Marey—was Georges Demenÿ,

whose Phonoscope (1891) was a Projecting Phenakistiscope—like Muybridge's except with a disc of actual photographs—and who invented a film projector in 1894 (modified for perforated film in 1896). As crucial as all these inventions were, the two most significant projectors were developed by men who began, ironically, by buying Edison machines and analyzing them. Edison's decision not to file for European patent rights allowed an Englishman, Robert William Paul, and, more significantly, two French brothers, appropriately named Lumière (French for "light"), to invent functional projectors and more versatile cameras.

The Lumière Brothers

Auguste Marie Louis Nicolas Lumière, the elder, and Louis Jean Lumière, the younger and more important of the brothers, started dabbling with Edison's Kinetoscope and Kinetograph in 1894. They also were familiar with the work of Marey. Their father, an avid photographer, had founded a factory in Lyon for manufacturing photographic plates and, later, celluloid film; when he saw the Kinetoscope, he told his sons that they could do better, that they should take the picture out of the box. Interested in the new motion photography, the brothers—who were excellent mechanics as well as budding industrialists, scientifically curious and brilliantly creative—had developed their own machine within a year. They called it the Cinématographe (from the Greek "motion recorder" or "kinetic writer," but more directly from Kinetograph, which it simply translated into French). It ran perforated 35mm film at 16 fps, and it used a unique claw mechanism to engage and advance the film. Louis always made sure his brother shared full credit, but Louis was the primary inventor of the Cinématographe—the final design came to him in a dream—and he shot the early films. Unlike Edison's bulky indoor camera, the Lumière camera was portable; it could be carried to any location. The operator turned a hand crank rather than pushed an electric button. Most significantly, the same machine that shot the pictures also printed and projected them. While the machine admitted light through its lens during filming, it projected light through its lens during projection. It printed by running raw and processed film through at once; they were in contact in the gate when light exposed

The Lumières' first film:
Workers Leaving the Lumière Factory.

Fig. 2-10

the blank film. Intermittent movement and steady alignment were guaranteed for movie photography, printing, and projection.

Early in 1895, the Lumière brothers shot their first film, *Leaving the Factory*, better known as *Workers Leaving the Lumière Factory.* Beginning in March of the same year, the Lumières projected this film and several others to private, specially invited audiences of scientists and friends throughout Europe. The first movie theatre opened to the paying public on December 28, 1895, in the basement room of the Grand Café in Paris. This date marks the generally accepted birthday of the movies, even though the first Europeans to charge admission for projected films had been Max and Emil Skladanowsky two months earlier, and the first commercial film projection in the world had been done in the United States half a year before that, by the Latham family. The choice of birthdate reflects the importance of the theatre—where the Lumière pictures continued to play for months and where money could be earned on a regular basis—but it also honors the first release to the public of what turned out to be the most comprehensive and influential solution to the problems of exposing and projecting movie film. The date the Lumières first presented their work—March 22, 1895—was as significant as

December 28, the date their theatrical exhibition defined the business.

The Lumières projected several films, among them a later version of *Workers Leaving the Lumière Factory,* a Lumière baby's meal (*Le Repas de bébé,* the first home movie), and a comical incident about a gardener getting his face doused through a boy's prank (*Le Jardinier et le petit espiègle,* the first narrative film, happily a comedy). A later film of a train rushing into a railway station (*L'Arrivée d'un train en gare de la Ciotat,* 1896)—or one called *The Sea*—provoked an extreme reaction; the audience is said to have shrieked and ducked when it saw the train or the water moving toward them. In Jean-Luc Godard's *Les Carabiniers* (1963)— Godard packs his films with history—a farm boy watches his first movie, which is also a train arriving at a station, using the same camera angle and diagonal composition as the Lumières' film. The boy ducks, trying to protect himself from a real train. Back in 1901, R. W. Paul made essentially the same joke in a film Godard may have seen, *The Countryman and the Cinematograph:* A country bumpkin stands next to a movie screen; he sees a dancing girl and imitates her, then sees a train approaching and runs from it. Finally he sees an image of himself and exclaims in surprise. It was clear from the start that audiences would have to learn how to watch movies.

The Lumière discovery of 1895—especially its elegant technical simplicity and public success—established the brothers as the most influential and important men in motion pictures in the world, eclipsing the power and prestige of Edison's Kinetograph and Kinetoscope. Within 5 years, the light of the Lumières would also begin to fade. The brothers were interested more in the scientific curiosity of their discovery than in the art or business of it, although eventually their film catalogue included more than 1,200 filmstrips for purchase. (The typical Lumière film lasted about 50 seconds.) They brought the camera out of doors, to life. The Lumières sent the first camera crews all over the globe, recording the most interesting scenes and cities of the world for the delight and instruction of a public who would never be able to travel to such places on their own. Theirs were the first films to be shown in India, Japan, and other countries, inspiring film industries and filmgoing around the world. From Russia and Sweden to Guatemala and Senegal, the Lumières were the Johnny Appleseeds of cinema; in this respect their importance far exceeds that of Edison or Marey.

The Lumière brothers adopted and established conventions and practices that have remained standard throughout the history of film. The Lumières stabilized film width at precisely 35mm, still the standard gauge today. (Dickson's had been about 39mm.) They also established the exposure rate of 16 fps, a functional silent speed until the invention of sound required a faster one for better sound reproduction. The slower exposure rate used less film—thus saving money—and allowed their machine to run more quietly and dependably, whether it was shooting, projecting, or printing—for all of which it used intermittent movement. Edison, maintaining the visual superiority of the 40-or-so fps of his Kinetoscope, scoffed that the Lumière speed would destroy the sensation of continuous movement; only a year later Edison himself adopted the Lumière speed for his projector in spite of the flicker it caused. Another Lumière contribution was the fancy name of their invention—the Cinématographe. In many countries today, the movies are the cinema, and shooting is cinematography.

R. W. Paul

Almost simultaneously with the Lumières, other Europeans were making progress on their own machines. At the Berlin Wintergarten on November 1, 1895, Max and Emil Skladanowsky offered the first commercial presentation of projected films in Europe. In the years since 1892, Max had been improving his invention, now a camera and double projector called the Bioskope or Bioscop ("life viewer," from the Greek for "life," *bios*, and "to see," *skopein*), working on completely independent principles.

In England in 1894, R. W. Paul, a maker of scientific instruments, was asked by two shady characters to build Kinetoscopes for them. Paul declined, but when he learned the surprising fact that Edison's machine had not been patented in England, he bought a Kinetoscope, took it apart to study it, and built a new one. With photographer Birt Acres, he invented a portable camera in March 1895. The Paul–Acres Camera was the first movie camera made in England. Paul and Acres soon dissolved their partnership, however, and invented competing projectors. Acres presented his projector, England's first, on January 14, 1896. Paul presented his, the more influential Theatrograph, a month later, on February 20—the very day the Lumières' films were first projected in London.

Paul's projector was the first to control intermittent movement by means of a device in the shape of a Maltese cross (a variant of which became the world standard). Converting rotary movement into intermittent movement by means of a pin that rides its curved and slotted rim, the original Maltese-cross apparatus was created for the Swiss watch, though it was adapted for the sewing machine and other devices. In cinema, it moves film through the gate: advancing it, holding it steady, then releasing it.

Paul sold cameras and projectors to others, in part so that he would have more American-perforation movies to show. His Cinematograph Camera No. 1 (built in April 1896) was the first that could be cranked in reverse, allowing the same footage to be exposed several times; thus it is of great significance that the first camera Georges Méliès used was built by R. W. Paul. (According to some sources, that camera was designed by Méliès after he studied Paul's equipment. In any case, Méliès did begin to design and market his own machines after buying some of Paul's, and he did provide Paul with movies.)

Although he left the business in 1909, R. W. Paul—an exhibitor, filmmaker, and father figure, known to his movie friends as "Daddy" Paul—was the founder of the British film industry.

The Vitascope

In the United States, a young real-estate salesman named Thomas Armat and his partner, C. Francis Jenkins—the more significant inventor of the two—developed a projector whose drive movement was intermittent. Called the Phantoscope, it was completed in August 1895 and commercially exhibited a month later. Jenkins and Armat had discovered—on their own, so they said—the equivalent of the Latham loop as well as the Lumière principle that *all* film movement should be intermittent. Soon, however, they dissolved their partnership. Early in 1896, Armat and Edison came to a business arrangement, one that Jenkins fruitlessly opposed. Edison would sell Armat's projector—the Phantoscope, with a few modifications made by Armat—as his own invention, enhancing the prestige and sales potential of the machine. Armat would silently receive a percentage of the sales. The Edison Company promptly announced the Wizard's latest invention, the projector it called the Vitascope ("life viewer"—from the Latin "life" and the Greek "to see," a linguistic mix that Armat disliked).

The Lathams projected a boxing film to a paying audience in May 1895—a world first as well as a national one, to be sure, but the machine's nonintermittent drive reduced its influence. The first commercial exhibition of an intermittent-drive projector in the United States was the premiere of the Phantoscope in September 1895, months before Armat sold the machine. But the debut that attracted the most notice was the first Edison projection for a paying audience, on April 23, 1896, at Koster & Bial's Music Hall on 34th Street and Broadway in New York City—the present site of Macy's. Edison was now popularly believed to have invented the American movie camera and projector. The "amazing Vitascope" was only one act in a vaudeville bill; movies soon became a typical part of vaudeville shows.

For the first Vitascope program, Edison converted several of his Kinetoscope strips for the projector; he also pirated a few of the R. W. Paul films from England. As with the first Lumière showings, the most exciting films were those with action that threatened to invade the space of the audience. During the showing of *Rough Sea at Dover* (1895, shot by Birt Acres and distributed by Paul), patrons in the front rows were said to have run screaming from their seats, afraid they were about to be drenched. Those cynics who were unimpressed were sure that the film had been shot in New Jersey.

The First Films

The first film audiences were amazed to see that living, moving action could be projected on an inert screen by a machine. Frank Norris's novel *McTeague* (which became the basis of Erich von Stroheim's *Greed*) records an immigrant family's first experience of the Vitascope in a vaudeville theatre, certain that the images were produced by some kind of conventional magic trick. It was an illusion all right, but not a conventional one—an illusion that allowed them to see the world as it had never been seen before.

It is easy to forget the way the world looked to our ancestors of just over a century ago—a world without automobiles, airplanes, TV, or movies. How could an American observe life in London? How could a German ever see the Pacific Ocean? How could one person in a single lifetime ever expect to view the tropics, the frigid north, the many cities of the world, and its mountains, plains, seas, and deserts? Except for the few who could afford the time and cost of laborious travel, it was impossible to experience the sights of all these places. True, there were paintings and engravings—but they were idealized impressions, and no matter how realistic, they were made by people, not by an impartial force of nature. Eventually, there were photographs—even 3-D photographed images in relief for stereopticon viewers—but none of these images moved. And, in a very real sense, life can be equated with movement—that is one meaning of "animate."

The movies were very much a part of the process that has produced what today seems a global culture: our ability to view and to travel to any place on earth. Newspapers (which rose to cultural prominence in the mid-18th century), the train (a development of the early 19th century),

Fig. 2-11
**The program for the Vitascope's debut at Koster &
Bial's Music Hall in 1896.**

the photograph (in the mid-19th century), the
automobile, airplane, telephone, radio, computer,
TV—these are the media of transportation and
communication that have shrunk the world and
practically erased the distances between its inhabitants. At the center of this communication–
transportation process are the movies. The
Lumière catalogue is the ancestor of the newsreel,
the global telecast, and the Internet.

The first films understandably exploited their
visual wonder. The films that Louis Lumière shot
for the Cinématographe and that Dickson's successors at Edison shot for the Vitascope were

similar. A movie lasted between 15 and 90
seconds. The camera was stationed in a single
spot, turned on to record the action, and turned
off when the action had finished. These films
were really "home movies"—unedited scenery,
family activity, or posed action—that depended
for their effect on the same source as today's
home movies: the wonder of seeing something
familiar and transitory reproduced in a permanent way. Nowhere is the home-movie quality of
the first films more obvious than in the Lumières'
Le Repas de bébé (*Feeding Baby*, or *Baby's Meal*,
1895), which has been duplicated uncounted
times by later generations of parents with their
own 8mm or video equipment.

A major difference between the first Edison
films and the first Lumière films is that the
Lumières have more of this home-movie quality
of merely turning the camera on to record the
events that happened to occur around it—
though many of them were more carefully
planned. The Edison films, despite their initial
lack of editing and plot, were gropings toward a
fictional, theatrical film, many of them shot
indoors. The Lumière films, with a nose for the
news, roamed around outdoors: They were freer,
less stilted, better composed, more active.

The categories of the Lumières' catalogue
indicate their conception of what the filmstrip
would provide its audience. The catalogue
breaks its films into different kinds of "views"—
visual actualities, like moving postcards—
General Views, Comic Views, Military Views,
Views of Diverse Countries. The most interesting
views are those containing the most interesting
patterns of movement: a boat struggling out to
sea against the waves, the charge of a line of
cavalry horses, the demolition of a wall.

One of the most celebrated Lumière films is
the comic jest *Le Jardinier et le petit espiègle*
(*The Gardener and the Little Scamp*, 1895),
remade in 1896 as *Arroseur et arrosé* (*The
Sprinkler Sprinkled*, or *Watering the Gardener*).
This incident—staged, but shot outdoors—
contains the seeds of what was to blossom into
one of the most important contributions of the
silent film: physical comedy. While a man waters a
garden, a boy sneaks behind him and steps on the
hose. The flow of water stops, the gardener looks
into the nozzle to see what's wrong, and the boy
steps off the hose. Water gushes into the

A "home movie": the Lumières' **Feeding Baby;** *Mr. and Mrs. Auguste Lumière with their daughter.*

Fig. 2-12

gardener's face; the boy laughs. The gardener catches the boy, drags him back into camera range (since the camera did not pan to follow the action), spanks him, and—in a hurry, because the film was running out—resumes his watering.

This little movie contains many elements of a comic art that would soon mature: The gag is completely physical; despite the improbability of the result, the causes are clear and credible; the butt of the joke is the victim of circumstances of which he is unaware; despite the victim's ignorance and innocence, the audience participates in the joke with the boy, laughing when the gardener gets drenched; the comic punishment (the spanking) is a blow to the ego more than to the body; the comic participants have obvious one-dimensional traits and roles so that complexity of character cannot interfere with the force of the jest; and the original situation is restored after the comic disruption. Above all, the comic incident is fictitious, even though the Lumières are correctly considered the fathers of the non-fiction film (the *actualité*, or direct, unbiased look at reality as well as its successor, the *documentary*, which is organized to express a conviction or make a point about the factual material it presents). It is the first movie to tell a story—the first narrative film.

For all their appearance of recording unstaged, spontaneous, real events, the Lumière films subtly incorporate the conventions of two artistic traditions that would powerfully influence the movies to follow. First, the Lumière films are very carefully composed, with symmetrical balancing of the left and right areas of the frame and interplay between the foreground and the deep space of the background (especially for those actions that move toward or away from the camera). As still photographers, the Lumières had borrowed these compositional patterns from Western representational painting—as most early photographers did. In fact, they used their movie camera almost as if it were a still camera—but the images moved.

Second, the Lumières organized their filmed events as little stories according to the most basic narrative pattern of beginning, middle, and end. This structure is easy to recognize in *Watering the Gardener*, but it is just as true of *Demolition of a Wall* (1896), which shows from start to finish the process of knocking over a wall. (Sometimes, for a startling effect, it was projected in reverse, and the wall sprang up.) The exceptions, like *Boat Leaving the Port* (1895), observe a portion of an ongoing action until the film runs out. But many of their films, as

The freedom of the outdoors and the excitement of motion: the Lumières' Boat Leaving the Port.

Fig. 2-13

brief as they are, do not begin with the event or action in progress. Instead, the camera establishes the scene before that action starts, then the event occurs, and only after the movement has terminated does the camera quit the scene. The very first Lumière film, *Leaving the Factory*, establishes this pattern. As the film begins, the large double doors of the factory are closed. They swing open for the camera, almost like the curtain rising in the theatre, and the workers pour out. Some move off frame to the right and some to the left (for compositional balance and to avoid hitting the camera), some manipulate "props" (a bicycle), and some are accompanied by a companion (a dog). In one of the very earliest examples, the movies showed their affinity for machines and animals as well as people. Only after the workers have all left the factory do the double doors begin to swing shut, concluding the film with the suggestion of the event's ending and the curtain's falling. However innocent and lifelike such a film might seem, it is not at all unstaged, unplanned, or unstructured.

It is also significant that by 1896 the Lumière company's cameramen had put the normally unmoving camera on several trains and on a gondola, creating the first moving-camera shots.

The early Edison films lack the outdoor freshness and freedom of those produced by the Lumières. Edison failed to understand and exploit the wonder and beauty of watching the world at work and at play, at rest and in motion. Typical is the staged heaviness of the first special-effects film, *The Execution of Mary, Queen of Scots* (August 1895, Edison #142), shot by Heise for the Kinetoscope and directed by Alfred Clark, one of Dickson's successors. In a total of 15 seconds, Mary is led to the block and beheaded; at the end, her head is held high for the unseen crowd (the audience).

Despite its primitive quality, several elements of this originally terrifying film are worth special attention. As in many early movies, the camera clearly thinks of itself as a spectator in the theatre. It watches from a fixed angle, a good seat. The characters move left and right in a single plane, rather than using the full depth that the movies were later to discover. Further, the film has a strong sense of entrance and exit, two more stage devices the mature film would discard. To the extent that it tells a true story, it is a kind of narrative film—made before the Lumières' gardener movie (whose fictitious story is more complicated). Beyond that, however, the film shows one clear, historically momentous realization of the potential of the film medium. After Mary (a male actor) sets her head on the block, the camera stops to allow a dummy to be substituted for

*John C. Rice and May Irwin
enact their kiss.*

Fig. 2-14

Mary and be decapitated. The ability to stop the action and start it again without any apparent break is one of the advantages that the camera enjoys over the stage. Within a very few years, a French magician, Georges Méliès, would make much of this camera advantage.

But there is more going on here than using the camera to effect a magical substitution. *The Execution of Mary, Queen of Scots* is the first film to consist of more than one shot. It was made to look like one shot and had only one scene, so it would remain for others to invent the conventional multi-shot film, where the setups change. Nevertheless, long after the camera had been stopped and restarted—important in itself as the first special-effects shot—Clark *edited the film*. He trimmed a few frames from the end of the actor footage and a few more from the start of the dummy footage, and made a splice.

A second interesting Edison film, and certainly the most famous of the early ones, is *May Irwin Kiss* (April 1896), better known as *The Kiss*. Shot originally for the Kinetoscope, this kiss, when projected on the big screen, excited the first wave of moralistic reaction to movie romance, which has remained a constant in film history. John C. Rice and May Irwin were the romantic leads in *The Widow Jones*, then a

Broadway stage success; the Edison Company got them to perform their climactic kiss in the Black Maria. When moralists and reformers saw their large, projected mouths meet, they showered the newspapers with letters and the politicians with petitions. However, *The Kiss* was also one of the biggest hits at the Vitascope shows as late as 1900, enjoyed especially for the humorous way the characters primp and prepare to kiss and then keep on kissing. Not everyone reacted to its erotic content moralistically, another constant in movie history.

Although the Lumières specialized in actualities and Edison in theatrical and staged scenes, the success of each company in its particular genre led to imitations by the other. Edison's *A Wringing Good Joke* (1899) is a descendant of the Lumières' gardener film, substituting a washtub of soapy water for the Lumières' hose.

Edison developed a portable camera in 1896 and began sending cameramen outdoors, enabling the company not only to compete in the actualities market, but also to stage their made-up scenes outside the confines of the studio. It was the ability to mix dramatic studio and location footage that eventually led to the Edison Company's 1903 masterpiece, *The Great Train*

Robbery, and beyond that to the conventional narrative film itself.

For their part, after seeing Edison's success with historical scenes, the Lumières staged some of their own, such as *The Death of Robespierre* and *The Death of Marat* (both 1897).

In addition to borrowing successful formulas—a practice that would continue throughout movie history—the two companies literally stole each other's films, made up duplicate prints (*dupes*) or reshot them without significant changes, and sold them as their own. In addition to competing with and stealing from each other, Edison and the Lumières faced competition and thievery from rivals who were springing up in England, the United States, and France. The next ten years of film history would be a period of commercial lawlessness as well as aesthetic discovery.

For Further Viewing

FILMS

THOMAS ALVA EDISON (1847–1931)
Monkeyshines, no. 1 (1890)
Blacksmithing Scene or *Blacksmiths* (1893)
Fred Ott's Sneeze (1894)
Sandow (1894)
Dickson Experimental Sound Film (ca. 1894)
Annabelle Serpentine Dance (1895)
The Execution of Mary, Queen of Scots (1895)
The John C. Rice–May Irwin Kiss or *May Irwin Kiss* or *The Kiss* (1896)
The Black Diamond Express (1896)
The Burning Stable (1896)
A Wringing Good Joke (1899)
Uncle Josh at the Moving-Picture Show (1902)

LOUIS (1864–1948) AND AUGUSTE (1862–1954) LUMIÈRE
Leaving the Factory or *Workers Leaving the Lumière Factory* (1895)
Debarking at the Congress of Photographers in Lyon or *Excursion of the French Photographic Society to Neuville* (1895)
Le Jardinier et le petit espiègle (*The Gardener and the Little Scamp*, 1895). Remade 1896 as *Arroseur et arrosé* (*The Sprinkler Sprinkled* or *Watering the Gardener*)

Le Repas de bébé (*Baby's Meal* or *Feeding Baby*, 1895)
Boat Leaving the Port (1895)
Friendly Party in the Garden of Lumière (1895)
Sack Race (1895)
The Sea (1895)
L'Arrivée d'un train en gare de la Ciotat (*Arrival of a Train at the Station*, 1896)
Demolition of a Wall (1896)
Flood at Lyon (1896)

DVDs

Edison: *The Invention of the Movies.* Kino Video and the Museum of Modern Art in association with the Library of Congress. A great, definitive collection of 140 **restored** Edison Company films (1890–1918) that starts with the *Monkeyshines* camera tests. Includes detailed scholarly notes and commentaries, interviews with film historians and archivists, and facsimiles of many drawings and documents.

Lumière & Company. Fox Lorber. Films made with the Lumière camera in 1995 by 40 directors.

The **Lumière Brothers'** *First Films.* Image Entertainment. Numerous films, 1895–97; narrated by Bertrand Tavernier. The best collection available.

Dickson *Experimental Sound Film*—with the original sound and a very useful commentary— is in *More Treasures from American Film Archives* (see Chap. 3 list).

The Movies Begin: A Treasury of Early Cinema, 1894–1913. Kino Video. An essential set of 133 films, many not available elsewhere, in archival prints with informative commentaries (unfortunately, not on a separate track) and notes. Includes *Homage to Eadweard Muybridge*, 8 **Edison–Dickson–Heise** films (*The Barber Shop, Sandow, Serpentine Dances, Feeding the Doves, The Kiss*); 27 **Lumière** films (*Leaving the Factory, The Sprinkler Sprinkled, Baby's Meal, Arrival of a Train at the Station, Demolition of a Wall, Leaving Jerusalem by Railway*); 16 **Méliès** films (*Long Distance Wireless Photography,*

A Trip to the Moon); 4 **Porter** films (*The Gay Shoe Clerk, The Great Train Robbery, The Whole Dam Family and the Dam Dog, Dream of a Rarebit Fiend*); **British** films starting with *Rough Sea at Dover*, with 5 by **Hepworth** (*How It Feels To Be Run Over, Rescued by Rover*), 7 by **Paul** (*The Countryman and the Cinematograph*), 7 by **Smith** (*Let Me Dream Again, Grandma's Reading Glass, Sick Kitten, Mary Jane's Mishap*), 5 by **Williamson** (*The Big Swallow*); also films by **Alice Guy Blaché** (*Making an American Citizen*), **Durand** (*Onésime horloger*), **Linder** (*Troubles of a Grass Widower*), **McCay** (*Winsor Mc Cay The Famous Cartoonist of the N.Y. Herald and His Moving Comics*), **Sennett** (*Bangville Police*), and **Zecca** (*The Golden Beetle*); and many other short narrative films, actualities, and documentaries.

3

Film Narrative, Commercial Expansion

The two film rulers of 1896, the Lumières and Edison, would encounter crafty and powerful competitors within the year. In France, the Lumière superiority was attacked by an artist on one side and by industrialists on the other. Georges Méliès, owner-prestidigitator of the Théâtre Robert-Houdin, saw the movies as a means of inflating his bag of magical tricks. He immediately recognized the cinematic possibilities for fantasy and illusion. In 1896, he asked the Lumières to sell him a camera and projector. When the Lumières, who insisted on licensing their own franchises to shoot and show their own kinds of actualities, refused to sell a Cinématographe, he bought a camera from R. W. Paul in London. Méliès shot his first film, *A Game of Cards*, in the spring of 1896. By 1902, Méliès was supplying the world with films, and the Lumières had almost ceased production.

Early Companies

About the same time as Méliès, two other Frenchmen, Charles Pathé and Léon Gaumont, also began building film empires.

In 1894, Charles Pathé and his three brothers formed Pathé Frères; the company started to make films in 1899. They began by imitating the familiar Lumière views and actualities. Soon they were copying ideas and techniques from Méliès and from the British—but the Pathé films had much better production values. Pathé's ultimate goal was not simply to produce the slickest entertainments, but to conquer all branches of

the French film industry. Within a few years, although it had not been able to wipe out the competition, Pathé embraced everything to do with motion pictures. It built cameras and projectors, manufactured raw film stock (after acquiring Eastman's European patent rights), produced films, and owned a chain of theatres in which to show them. This method of controlling everything from the top, from production to distribution, is called *vertical integration*, and the American film industry would grope hesitatingly toward this monolithic structure that the Pathés quickly realized.

Léon Gaumont's business perceptions were similar. In 1895, he founded a film empire whose activities ultimately ranged from manufacturing machine parts to collecting receipts at the theatre door. After seeing an early demonstration of the Cinématographe, he dedicated his photographic equipment company—eventually known simply as Gaumont—to developing a new projector, which the company began selling in 1896. It was also in 1896 that Léon Gaumont approved the suggestion of his secretary, Alice Guy, that she begin making films based on her own scripts. At 24, she became the world's first woman director as well as the first woman to head the production arm of a studio, and by 1897, Gaumont found himself at the head of the first working model of the *studio system*—in which projects are supervised by studio executives and created by writers, designers, cinematographers, directors, performers, and other artists employed by the studio, using studio equipment and facilities. Alice Guy made her first film, *The Cabbage Fairy* (*La Fée aux choux*), on 60mm stock in August and September of 1896—three months after Méliès shot his simple game of cards—and remade it on 35mm stock in 1899. By the time she left Gaumont, in 1907, Guy had produced more than 370 films, many of which she wrote and directed; among those that survive are *The Life of Christ* and *On the Barricades* (both 1906). She left for America with her husband, Herbert Blaché (an Englishman, also employed by Gaumont), where she founded her own film company, Solax (1910–13), and made films as Alice Guy Blaché (*Making an American Citizen*, 1912; *Matrimony's Speed Limit*, 1913; *A House Divided*, 1913). Back at Gaumont, Louis Feuillade—a scriptwriter who had been Guy's assistant—took over her job, selecting the scripts, directors, and performers for all Gaumont pictures; while directing 642 films of his own, he remained head of production until his death in 1925. Unlike Pathé, which did not outlast the 1930s, Gaumont is still in business today.

The English film between 1900 and 1906 was perhaps the most innovative in the world. R. W. Paul, who had been displaying the products of his Theatrograph for almost a year, began attracting other inventor–photographers to experiment with moving pictures. G. A. Smith, James Williamson—the key members of the "Brighton School"—and Cecil Hepworth made significant and rapid progress with the principles of editing and composition, realizing that the effect of a filmed story was a function of the way the individual shots were composed and stitched together. They were the first to think about the role of the camera, not just in composing shots but in defining a shot's significant elements—and, in a film like Williamson's *The Big Swallow* (1901), in which a man swallows the camera, even in the definition of space itself. Smith, discussed later in this chapter, was one of the first to define *subjective* space, with his point-of-view (POV) shots and filmed dreams. Until the emergence of D. W. Griffith, the films of these British directors were the most visually imaginative on the screen, precisely because they had discovered the importance of systematic camerawork and editing in building their stories and driving their rhythms. Among the elements of film construction discovered by the British pioneers and taken to a more expressive level by Griffith—and later by their key British heir and

biggest fan, Alfred Hitchcock—are the close-up, the cross-cut, the masked shot, the POV shot, and the pan or panoramic shot.

An American, Charles Urban, enriched the British film further in this period. Urban, who had tried unsuccessfully to peddle his Edison-imitation camera in America, journeyed to London to try his luck there. Fearing the stigma of Americanism, Urban named his London concern the Warwick Trading Company. He built it into the major distributor of early British films between 1898 and 1903, then left Warwick to found the Charles Urban Trading Company. The new company, which became the largest in the prewar British film industry, also pioneered in its production of scientific films using microcinematography and in its development of the first successful photographic (not hand-painted) color process, which Urban called Kinemacolor (1908, based largely on the discoveries of G. A. Smith).

In the United States, the two companies that would share the power with Edison—Biograph and Vitagraph—had begun making and showing films by 1897. The American Mutoscope and Biograph Company (American Biograph for short) manufactured both a peepshow machine and a projecting machine that outperformed Edison's. The primary inventive intelligence behind "Biograph" ("life writer"), as the company was to be called, was Edison's own film pioneer, W. K–L. Dickson. Having left Edison and having found the social life of the Lathams too "fast" (according to his own legal testimony), Dickson officially became the "D" of the K.M.C.D. Syndicate late in 1895. The early film companies often took their names from the initials of their owners; Dickson's initial joined Elias Koopman's, Harry Marvin's, and Herman Casler's. They had enjoyed working together before: In 1893, they had invented a miniature camera for detectives that looked like a watch.

The K.M.C.D.'s first project was the Mutoscope, their peephole machine, whose effectiveness put the Kinetoscope out of business. Like the Kinetoscope, the Mutoscope offered a series of moving photographs to the eyes of a single viewer. Unlike the Kinetoscope's celluloid frames, however, the Mutoscope pictures were large photographs mounted on individual cards. When the viewer flipped the series of cards with a hand

Fig. 3-1
The Mutoscope.

The K.M.C.D. motion-picture apparatus also bested its Edison opponent. Working with Herman Casler, Dickson invented the Mutograph—a camera that used unperforated 70mm film—in 1894 and adapted it for projection in 1895. Dickson adopted this large-format film not merely to improve photographic clarity, but also to circumvent Edison's patents on all methods of transporting perforated and small-gauge film. Dickson, in effect, invented the motion picture several times: for Edison, for the Lathams, and for Biograph. The Biograph camera's huge pictures could either be mounted on Mutoscope cards or, when combined with its intermittent-motion projector, throw the sharpest, steadiest images that had yet been seen on a screen. Beginning in 1899, however, Biograph movies were shot on standard 35mm stock. Films shot for the Mutoscope were called "mutoscopes"; those shot for life-size projection were called "biographs." In terms of their derivations, a mutoscope observes change, but a biograph writes life. Dickson's new films were also more interesting and active than Edison's: the Empire State Express (a thrilling train shot), President McKinley receiving a letter at home, the actor Joseph Jefferson performing scenes from his famous *Rip Van Winkle.*

As he had done at Edison's West Orange lab, Dickson built a special studio for shooting staged scenes. The first Biograph studio was outdoors, on the roof of the Biograph Company's offices near Broadway and 14th Street in New York City. As in the Black Maria, the stage of Dickson's roof theatre rotated to keep the sun at the best lighting angle. From this nuts-and-bolts beginning evolved the company that was to give its name to moving pictures in some parts of the world (in Danish the cinema is still called the *biograf*) and that was to launch the careers of D. W. Griffith, Mack Sennett, Mary Pickford, the Gish sisters, and many others.

Edison's second major competitor was the Vitagraph Company, which had a less spectacular career than Biograph but a longer one. Vitagraph's founder and director of production was J. Stuart Blackton, an Americanized Englishman, who began as a reporter and cartoonist for the *New York World.* Blackton first became interested in moving pictures when he visited Edison at the Black Maria; he even performed his sketching act for Edison's

crank, they were held still for an instant by a hook, allowing a good steady view of each frame and producing the same appearance of movement as a motion picture. (In principle it was similar to the flip book, which had been invented in England in 1868 by John Barnes Linnett.) The large picture cards made the Mutoscope pictures more clear, detailed, and lifelike than the Kinetoscope's. The hand crank added to the viewer's pleasure by allowing the motion to go slower, go faster, or stop. The ultimate testimony to the Mutoscope is that of all the archaic and outdated machines of the invention era, it survives today—in penny arcades and amusement parks—delighting children with some of the same moving drawings and photographs that their great-great-grandparents flicked through so long ago. The machine has also survived in "adult" book stores, engaging patrons with a type of photographic entertainment that could not have been envisioned by the Messrs. K.M.C.D.

Kinetograph. Edison leased Blackton a Vitascope franchise. Though his first films were partly distributed by Edison, Blackton soon set up his own company. Realizing the appeal of the Edison company, Blackton and his partners, William "Pop" Rock and Albert E. Smith, chose a name for their company that was as close to Edison's as the law would allow. One of Vitagraph's first films, *Burglar on the Roof* (1898), was filmed on the roof of their office building in Chelsea. For several years Manhattan rooftops doubled as film studios. Another early Vitagraph film was *Tearing Down the Spanish Flag* (1898), an attempt to capitalize on the Spanish-American War. Although the film claimed to have been shot in the heat of battle, Blackton actually staged it in the heat of Manhattan on his friendly rooftop.

While Méliès was the first to use a dissolve (in *Cinderella*, 1899), Blackton co-produced and ran the camera for the first surviving American film to include a dissolve, Edison's *The Congress of Nations* (1900).

Blackton was also a pioneer in the field of animation. He developed a camera that would expose only one frame with each turn of the crank, which made it possible to shoot one drawing after another. The first commercial film in which a drawn figure moved was Blackton's *Humorous Phases of Funny Faces* (1906). The first scientific film in which a drawing appeared to move had been made in England in 1900: R. W. Paul shot sequential drawings of magnetic lines—executed on punched cards that were mounted on pegs for the precise alignment of each frame—that had been prepared by Professor Silvanus Thompson, the designer of the experiment, and his assistant, Dennis Coales. The result, the first animated film of any kind (unless one counts the unphotographed animations of Reynaud), showed how electricity behaves when moving through an alternator. Professor Thompson first exhibited the film in 1901 as part of a lecture and explained in 1904 how he and Paul had made it; Paul first showed it to Edison in 1911.

It was also in 1911 that Blackton convinced cartoonist Winsor McCay—whose comics *Little Nemo in Slumberland* and *Dreams of the Rarebit Fiend* were the most inventive of their day, full of highly creative metamorphoses and ambitious graphics—to make animated films. Their first film, for which Blackton did the live-action sequences and McCay the animation, was *Winsor Mc Cay The Famous Cartoonist of the N.Y. Herald and His Moving Comics* (1911), familiarly known as *Little Nemo*. McCay went on to make some of the best silent American cartoons, notably the endearing *Gertie the Dinosaur* (1914).

Others all over the country were catching the movie craze, assembling machines, and capturing images. In Chicago, three men began tinkering independently: George Kleine, George K. Spoor, and "Colonel" Selig. Kleine would one day become the "K" of the Kalem (K.L.M.) Company that produced the first *Ben-Hur* in 1907. Spoor would one day become the "S" of Essanay (S&A) who, with his partner, G. M. ("Broncho Billy") Anderson—the "A"—would shoot the first series of westerns. William Selig, who liked to be called "Colonel," modeled the Selig Standard Camera and the Polyscope projector on the Lumière Cinématographe; in 1907, he sent a crew to Los Angeles to shoot parts of *The Count of Monte Cristo*, the first filming done in Hollywood. In Philadelphia, Sigmund Lubin began several tricky activities, including "duping" (illegally duplicating) films made by others to eliminate the problem of paying for them and re-enacting events like a heavyweight title bout or the Oberammergau Passion Play on his Philadelphia rooftop. Lubin even precisely re-enacted film hits like *The Great Train Robbery*. Movie projectionists trooped across the country with their filmstrips much as the magic lanternists had trooped across Europe with their slides a century earlier. One of these projectionists toured the Caribbean, drawing audiences with the unauthorized adopted name of Thomas Edison, Jr.; his real name was Edwin S. Porter.

Narrative

Despite the frenzy of movie activity in the United States, the films did not change much until 1902 or 1903. New films imitated the successes of earlier ones; like TV and film producers today, the earliest film producers copied successful formulas. The new films were longer, of course, freed from the 50-foot limit of the Kinetoscope box, but the same rushing trains, ocean and mountain views, one-joke pranks, and historical vignettes dominated the screen. Audiences began to yawn at these predictable subjects. The motion picture, formerly the highlight of a vaudeville bill, became the "chaser," the part of the program that was so dull that it chased the old audience out so that the new one could file in. By 1900, the movies were suffering the first of a series of business crises.

The rope that pulled the movies from the abyss was the development—to the point of industry dominance—of a new kind of screen entertainment. The rope-abyss image is an apt one, for the new kind of movie, the story film, was to use this and similar heart-stopping devices to weave its spell. The movies were born into the age of theatrical producer David Belasco; they have never quite outgrown that heritage. The Belasco theatre era traded on extreme emotional effects—violent tears, violent suspense, violent laughter. The two dominant theatre genres were melodrama and farce; they were to become the two dominant film genres as well. The most respected playwrights were Scribe and Sardou, Jones and Pinero, Dion Boucicault, Bronson Howard, Augustin Daly, and Belasco himself. In these plays, good and evil were as clearly distinct as black type on a white page. Though evil triumphed over good for the first 2 hours of the play, good miraculously won out in the last 15 minutes. Melodrama was a world of pathos, not of tragedy, of fears and tears and sacrifice. The era's farce was just as extroverted: A series of comic mistakes would arise, entangle, and explode until the denouement put all the pieces of the puzzle together. There was no reason a film could not tell the same kinds of stories.

The problem was to translate these dramatic stories into film terms. Many of the early narrative films merely pieced together the same kinds of static, unedited scenes that were shot for the first Kinetoscope—expanding the 50-foot strip to a whole reel. (A *reel* of film—up to 1,000 feet of 35mm—lasted about 15 minutes at silent speed.) A good example of one of these films is *Pullman Honeymoon* (1898). This Edison product (shot in the large multiset studio that replaced the Black Maria) records a series of events that might take place in one of George Pullman's sleeping cars between porters and passengers, lovers, comics, bandits, and the police. The film is strikingly inert. The movie set is a stage set: The berths line the frame at left and right; the center aisle of the

Pullman car serves as the stage-center playing area. Although the film lasts almost ten minutes, the camera never shifts its viewing angle nor its distance from any of the action. As in the earlier Edison strips, the camera is the single spectator at a staged play. The only noticeable participation of the camera in the action is that it stops after each incident and then starts again. But the slight jumps between the scenes indicate that the filmmaker tried (and failed) to make these gaps invisible, to keep the camera from participating in the event, refusing to exploit the cinema's ability to manipulate time. Further, because the film uses only one setup, the effect is ploddingly static; the passive camera never manipulates space either, never works with size and distance, never picks out any details. No action, character, or object is made to be more important than anything else. It is not that the unmoving camera or even the single-shot film cannot be expressive—the history of film is full of examples to the contrary— but that in this film the unimaginative set and action make one wish the camera would take a more active role.

French fantasist Georges Méliès was a much better film storyteller precisely because he exploited the very difference between time in nature and in the cinema that *Pullman Honeymoon* tried to cover up.

Georges Méliès

The Méliès films owe their superiority to the wild imagination and subtle debunking humor of their master. Méliès was by trade a magician; just as earlier magicians had adopted the magic lantern, Méliès adopted moving pictures. He saw that the camera's ability to stop and start again (*stop-motion photography*, an effect achieved in the camera rather than through cutting) brought to perfection the magician's two greatest arts—disappearance and conversion. Anything could be converted into anything else; anything could vanish.

One of Méliès's most enjoyable films, *The Conjurer* (1899), is nothing but one fast minute of disappearances and transformations. The magician (played by Méliès himself) vanishes, his female assistant vanishes, she turns into snow, he turns into her, and she turns into him. Pure cinema—as pure in its own way as its opposite, the realism of Lumière. For if Louis Lumière documented the world, Méliès transformed it.

If Lumière established that the camera could create a factual record of an event, Méliès proved that the camera could create an event that never happened. Lumière set the pattern for realism; Méliès opened the door to the impossible. Méliès gave the cinema the tools of fantasy, illusion, and distortion, allowing the new art to address new subject matter—notably the interior world of psychology, imagination, and dreams; the theatrical world of magic, spectacle, and set design; and the narrative world of genres and long, developing stories.

It was in 1898 that Méliès made the first or second narrative film to consist of more than one scene (the other, to be discussed shortly, was by R. W. Paul). In the first scene of *The Moon at One Meter*, also called *The Astronomer's Dream*, an astronomer falls asleep. Then the set changes, and he has a dream in which the moon comes into the room and eats him. For the final shot, when he has woken up, the set changes back to how it looked in the first shot. These set changes, bridged by simple (*straight*) cuts, are not distinct enough to make it obvious that cuts have occurred, particularly because the setup never changes. It seems likely that Méliès decided the straight cut was an unclear way to separate scenes and abandoned it in search of a new narrative device that would allow him to get from one scene to another, which he soon found in the dissolve. In 1899, Méliès made *The Dreyfus Affair*, which consisted of nine separately titled films that told a chronological story; he made the logical leap to the multi-scene film (more fully realized than in *The Moon at One Meter*) when he immediately followed *Dreyfus* with *Cinderella* (1899), a film in which the clearly different scenes are bridged by dissolves, while the camera cuts necessary for the stop-motion and multiple-exposure effects remain hidden. (Some of the camera cuts in Méliès's films were cleaned up with splices, as when the conjurer perfectly replaces his assistant in midair). It was also in 1898 that R. W. Paul made a multi-shot, two-scene film whose second shot has not survived; in *Come Along Do!*, a couple was shown outside a gallery and then, on a different set, inside it.

Having more than one shot in a film amounted not just to giving the cinema the theatre's ability to proceed from one scene to another, but even more significantly, to joining two elements that had previously been considered necessarily complete, self-sufficient visual worlds. It must have seemed as rash as putting two novels together to tell one story. On the other hand, it might have seemed as familiar as moving from one "view" to another in a magic lantern show. We may be tempted to take them for granted today, but Méliès's joined scenes—and the multi-shot films made in England between 1898 and 1903—are the beginning of *montage*, the art of editing. And the sets and costumes and props he designed, the effects he engineered—in short, the "look" he wanted each film to have—make him the first master of the cinema's other great tool, *mise-en-scène:* the art of designing and staging a scene for the camera.

Between 1896, when he founded the Star Film Company, and 1913, Méliès made at least 500 movies, of which fewer than 140 survive. He may well have been the first filmmaker ever to use superimposition (multiple exposure), hand-painting (a dab of red on the photographed dress, orange on the fire, blue on the curtain, every single frame), the dissolve, and time-lapse photography. Even allowing for the earlier *The Execution of Mary, Queen of Scots* and *The Gardener and the Little Scamp* (whose possibilities neither Clark nor Lumière pursued further), the position of Méliès as the father of the special-effects film—and every cinematic use of the fantastic—is beyond challenge, and the narrative film itself belongs on the list of his credits.

Griffith said, "I owe him everything."

In *The Magic Lantern* (1903), Méliès compared the art of the magician to that of the filmmaker. *The Magic Lantern* contains its own little history of Western visual representation and dramatic art. First, the lantern projects a static landscape (a re-creation of the painter's art); then it projects a pair of lovers in fancy costumes (a re-creation of the aristocratic theatre); finally, the lantern projects the magician himself and his clown-like servant (a comic image of the common people, of movies themselves). These reflexive films-within-the-film demonstrate at a very early date the filmmaker's conscious equation of cinema, comedy, and magic. The magic box, like a new kind of circus-clown car, is impossibly full of figures, for it can capture, store, and present any image in a world of images.

Méliès's The Magic Lantern: *The magic lantern in a toy shop projects a moving image of the clown's face while the clown himself views it—one of film's early references to its own powers.*

Fig. 3-2

Méliès's A Trip to the Moon: *A chorus line of gunners waves after loading the space ship.*

Fig. 3-3

One of Méliès's theatrical tools that served him well as a filmmaker was black velvet, which formed the background of his multiple-exposure shots, allowing only selected areas of the frame to be exposed each time the film ran through the camera. Where there was velvet, no light hit the film; if a face poked through the curtain, its image was captured on film. This was the beginning of masking and matting, on which most special-effects photography came to depend. Without the velvet, multiple exposures made the figures transparent "phantoms" or "ghosts."

Méliès was the first filmmaker to light films from the side as well as from above, thanks to the glass walls and roof of the studio he built at Montreuil (just outside Paris) in 1897. Like Dickson's Black Maria, the Montreuil studio relied on sunlight—artificial lighting truly adequate for cinematography was not introduced until 1904—but its glass walls allowed a richer, more fully modeled lighting plan and washed out the top-lit shadows characteristic of earlier studio work. In 1899, Méliès was the first to *diffuse*, or soften, light by filtering it through cotton sheets or rippled glass; not until 1902 did any other studio (Pathé) begin to use diffused lighting, and it took Edison and Biograph another 2 years to catch up.

Méliès's most famous work is the 30-scene *A Trip to the Moon* (1902), which successfully combines his fantasy and his humor into a charming film full of trick effects. Méliès parodies the intellectual doings of academics in the opening scene as a professor (played by Méliès) earnestly demonstrates his points. Méliès's parody of the intelligentsia continues in his later *The Doctor's Secret* (1909) and *The Conquest of the Pole* (1912). Delightfully whimsical in *A Trip to the Moon* are the rocket ship's landing with a splat in the eye of the man in the moon, the lines of chorus girls who wave goodbye to the moonship and lend their faces to the seven stars of the Pleiades, and the jumpy gymnastics of the moon creatures who go up in puffs of smoke when the scientists whack them with their umbrellas. In *A Trip to the Moon*, stars and planets shine above the heads of the sleeping scientists, and the explorers gesticulate with delight when they see the earth rise.

For all his cinematic inventiveness, Méliès was still very much a stage creator, shaping effects for a passive camera, delighting in the play of plaster, pulleys, and paint. The earth's rising was contrived by pulling up the earth and pulling down the rear part of the moon's crust. The ship's approaching the moon was contrived by moving the moon closer to the camera, not by moving the camera closer to the moon. He never moved the camera during a shot. Méliès clearly saw the film as parallel to a stageplay, and he referred to his technique as making "artificially arranged scenes." The structure of *A Trip to the Moon* reveals his thinking: Though the film shifts locations, each scene is presented in a single, unedited shot. Even so, *The Conjurer* reminds us that the camera could be turned off and on—and the film spliced—many times during a single Méliès "shot."

Méliès also composed the scenes as on a stage; he was conscious of limited depth, of entrances and exits. This staging is weakest in those scenes in which the performers merely line up in a row across the screen. Méliès took great pride in his scenic decor and effects, which he painted and conceived himself. In that respect alone he must be recognized as the father of art direction. (Compare the few props that set the stage in an early Edison film or the found landscapes of the Lumière films.)

Theatricality aside, however, Méliès's camera tricks relied completely on his realization of the essential difference between natural time, which is perfectly continuous, and cinematic time, which seems continuous in projection even if it was not so in filming.

Méliès had an immense influence on other directors in France and all over the world. To take only one example, Porter's *Dream of a Rarebit Fiend* (1906) is as indebted to Méliès as it is to the hallucinatory comic strip (*Dreams of the Rarebit Fiend*) by Winsor McCay.

Film theorists of a later generation—particularly Siegfried Kracauer and André Bazin—observed that Méliès and Louis Lumière established the two potential directions of the cinema in the very infancy of the art: Lumière's realism (the rendering of the world as it is) and Méliès's fantasy (the re-creation of the world—or the creation of any world—through the filmmaker's imagination). Interestingly, these theorists found Lumière's realism the more legitimate path. Many audiences, though, have preferred the Méliès path that led to *Star Wars* (George Lucas, 1977) to the Lumière path that led to Italian Neorealism. Audiences who have seen decades of later films are still capable of being delighted by Méliès's wit. His audacious sight gags and surreal surprises clearly demonstrate that a movie can result from the human acts of creation and imagination, do far more than record physical reality, and even lie.

After 1899, Méliès's peak year as a creative artist and as a businessman was 1902. His trademark, the star, was seen all over the world. That star steadily declined in the first decade of the century, if only because his painstakingly personal artisanship could not compete with the factory methods of Gaumont and Pathé. By 1914, he had lost his audience, made his last film, turned his studio into a theatre where he went back to performing magic tricks, and disappeared from the screen like a moon creature hit with an umbrella. Fourteen years later a journalist discovered him selling toys and candy at a kiosk in the Gare Montparnasse. His fame and films (some of which Méliès himself had destroyed out of bitterness; most of the rest had been requisitioned by the military during World War I and melted down for boot heels—call it disappearance and conversion) were revived. After receiving the Legion of Honor as well as a small pension from his admirers, he died in 1938.

Cohl and Others

Blackton may have been the first to move a character composed of photographed drawings, but the first genius of the animated film was Émile Cohl. Like Méliès, he was a supremely imaginative Frenchman who delighted in the irrational surprises of a world of tricks. Cohl applied the tricks that Méliès played with the natural world—and more—to animated drawings. The surreal illogic of the Cohl cartoons is much closer in spirit to the inventive transformations of characters and objects in the early Disney cartoons, in Warners' Looney Tunes, or in the trippy *Yellow Submarine* (1968) than to the realism of the later Disney cartoons. Like his American contemporary, McCay— who began making animated films a few years after Cohl, in 1911—Cohl delighted in converting one kind of drawn figure into another: a stick that becomes a man that becomes a window, an angry woman whose head rolls off and turns into a parrot, a pool cue that becomes a straw. One of the best of Cohl's transformation films is *Un Drame*

chez les fantoches (*Puppet Drama* or *A Love Affair in Toyland*, 1908), in which the constant metamorphosis of the white-on-black line drawings and figures takes farce to a whole new level—and that was only his third movie. (The first, *Fantasmagorie*, was released by Gaumont in 1908.) In *The Joyous Microbes* (1909), tiny microbic dots flow together to depict the diseases they supposedly cause. In another witty Cohl film, *The Neo-Impressionist Painter* (1910), an artist tries to sell his arty abstract canvasses, each of which consists only of a single color, to a buyer. As he describes each painting (explaining, for example, that the red canvas actually shows "a cardinal eating lobster with tomatoes by the banks of the Red Sea"), the events and qualities he discusses come alive in line drawings on the canvas of the tinted screen.

Méliès's success also influenced the films of Ferdinand Zecca. Zecca, who was director of production at Pathé, made films in all the popular genres: social commentaries, farces, and melodramas. He even remade some of the films of G. A. Smith. But Zecca also made trick films like *Whence Does He Come?* (1904), in which a man leaps out of the sea and begins putting on clothes that also leap out at him. Méliès's influence is also clear in some of Zecca's chase films. The chase was almost obligatory in the first

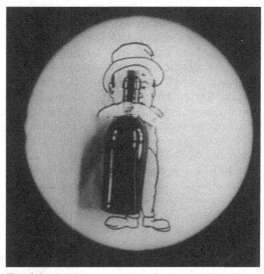

Fig. 3-4
Cohl's The Joyous Microbes: *the disease of drunkenness.*

decade of the 20th century and was perfected by the British; the excitement of people running compensated for the stasis of the camera and led the action from one shot to another. Zecca was one of the masters of the chase, but he added new excitement when he combined the chase with trick shots. In *Slippery Jim* (1905), the police chase a criminal who successfully eludes them because he has the ability to disappear, to appear in two or three places at once, to fly in the air on a bicycle, to unscrew his feet and remove the fetters, and to wriggle out of any container or bind.

One of the most influential French filmmakers in the first decade of the 20th century was more famous for his performing than for his directing of the films in which he starred. Max Linder was the first internationally famous star of motion pictures. Like the American John Bunny, who died in 1915, Linder was one of the first great film clowns. *A Skater's Debut* in 1906, in which a clumsy man meets a pair of ice skates for the first time, was also the debut of a comic character, Max, who was to become the leading figure of hundreds of comic one- and two-reel films over the next decade. By 1910, Linder's yearly salary had jumped to more than 1 million francs, and his face had become one of the most familiar in Europe. Linder, like Chaplin, Keaton, Lloyd, and Langdon who followed him, was a tiny man, and he used his smallness and his screwy wit to contrast with the bigger opponents and baffling obstacles he frequently faced. Linder's dancing moustache and dandyish mannerisms with hat and cane also set a pattern that Chaplin would follow and expand. Linder specialized in drunken routines (also a Chaplin specialty) as in *Max and the Quinquina* (1911), in which a woozy Max makes a series of comic mistakes with people and houses. He enjoyed debunking the intellectual, pretentious, and arty, as in *Max Plays at Drama* (ca. 1912), which parodies classical tragedy and romantic melodrama, primarily by means of delightful anachronisms.

Because of Max's European popularity and American anonymity, the Essanay company brought him to America in 1917 after Chaplin had left it. Both Max and Essanay soon failed. Although the films he made in America were slick and funny (especially the features *Seven Years Bad Luck*, 1921, and *The Three Must-Get-Theres*, 1922), they never recaptured the popularity of his earlier, cruder, but livelier films in Europe. Max's American adventure was unfortunate in another way: When he returned to France and made a wild haunted-house comedy with Abel Gance (*Au secours!* or *Help!*, 1923), Linder's American contracts kept it from being released.

While Pathé had Zecca and Linder, Gaumont had Cohl, Feuillade, and Jean Durand. Durand made a series of comedies that influenced the French avant-garde of the 1920s; it starred Ernest Bourbon as Onésime, a character whose bizarre logic and anarchic spirit were reflected in the aesthetics of the movies. In *Onésime horloger* (1912), when Onésime decides to speed up time so that he can collect an inheritance sooner, Durand switches to fast-motion photography, and all the events of the world rush by. In this avalanche of action, ordinary life becomes, in the words of an intertitle, "more beautiful." *Onésime horloger* announces one of the great subjects of the French cinema: the nature of time. The New Wave filmmakers of the 1960s would learn much from Durand—as well as from the dark drive and brilliance of Louis Feuillade's serials, which were also admired by the Surrealists, for these serials— *Fantômas* (1913–14), *Les Vampires* (1915–16), and *Judex* (1917)—were as uncanny as they were realistic. Charged with sexuality and menace, violence and action, they were accused of glamorizing crime. Fritz Lang's silent German films about the master criminal Dr. Mabuse were clearly inspired by Feuillade, but it was not until *film noir* arrived in the 1940s that anyone would do nearly so fine a job of portraying the world as a place full of crime, beauty, rage, and nasty surprises.

Edwin S. Porter

In most of the early French, German, and American films, one shot equaled one scene; the finished film was a series of scenes—only incidentally a series of shots. Each scene progressed chronologically, following the central character about. There were no leaps in time, no ellipses in the sequence of events. The camera was usually distant enough from the playing to include the full bodies of all the players. It remained for filmmakers from G. A. Smith in England to D. W. Griffith in America to learn to move the camera, to build scenes out of several shots, and to combine scenes and individual shots into sequences.

One of those crucial filmmakers was Edwin S. Porter. After Porter returned from the Caribbean, he paid a visit to his "father" and asked for a job. Edison hired him as a cameraman in 1900; within a year or two, Porter had become director of production for Edison's film company.

Porter was very familiar with the early British films and with *A Trip to the Moon*. From the latter he learned that a film's action could continue from one scene to the next—that a picture could tell, as he put it, "a story in continuity form"; he was sure that would "draw the customers back to the theatres." To say the least, he was right. The lure of narrative revived the industry. From Smith and Williamson he learned that a scene could consist of several shots. His work, which directly prepared the way for Griffith's, showed that actions could be made to appear continuous from one *shot* to the next, that it was unnecessary to show scenes from beginning to end, and that a movie could cover events taking place simultaneously in different locations.

Porter's two most important films were released in 1903. *Life of an American Fireman* (shot late in 1902) begins with the fireman–hero falling asleep, the subject of his reveries appearing in a superimposed white space near his head (a vignette, or "dream balloon"). This was the first time any American film had attempted to present a character's thoughts, converting part of the movie screen into a "mindscreen"; later, Griffith revealed the logic of simply *cutting* to the character's mental visions (a full-frame mindscreen).

As the fireman dreams of a mother and child, then wakes—worried about those who may be in danger from fire at the moment—there is a cut to a close-up (actually a close shot) of a fire alarm box and a hand setting off the alarm (in fact, pretending to set it off). The scene changes again to the fire station as the men tumble out of their beds—obviously in response to the alarm, which implies causal continuity from shot to shot. The cause-and-effect relationship between these shots is as important in the history of film continuity, in the very logic of film editing, as the cut to the close-up of the faraway alarm box. Before, there had been virtually no way to move a story from one shot or location to another without having the same character in both of them. Now the cut could be seen as the agency of a force exerted by one shot on another, a cinematic act that went beyond juxtaposition into the realm of asserted meaning and effective relationship. Like the British, Porter found that editing *had* a logic, one that would be explored by filmmakers from Griffith and Eisenstein to Hitchcock and Resnais. That close-up itself was not the first ever made, by the way, but it was the first one that Porter had cut into an ongoing narrative.

Having leapt out of bed, the firemen slide down the pole in one shot and reach the ground floor in the next shot. Two sets, two shots, apparently one pole, and a cut in the right place, establishing the continuity of action and location from shot to shot—and all at once Porter's audience understood the relative location of both sets, the layout not just of the two-story firehouse but of the cinematically defined landscape.

Then the firemen rush out on their horse-drawn fire engines. The exterior shots of the fire brigade charging out of the station and down the street were bits of stock footage Porter found and cut into the narrative; that was an economical move, saving the cost of shooting a new scene, but it was also a demonstration that the actors and the real firemen would be read by the audience as the same firemen. (When Lev Kuleshov expanded on this insight, he called it *creative geography* when different shots can be asserted, through editing, to be part of the same "artificial landscape.") At the site of the fire, Porter cut from the stock footage to a new shot—and achieved yet another breakthrough, for as the fire engines rush up, the camera *pans* (that is, it pivots horizontally or turns sideways) to follow the engines and reveal a burning house. It was not a simple matter of panning to cover a wide subject, like a city skyline; what it did was discover the logic for the pan, making a camera movement part of the film's dramatic strategy—because it followed a moving object and because it kept the burning house *out* of the frame until Porter chose to reveal it.

In the final sequence, the fireman rescues a mother and baby, like those of whom he dreamed, from the burning house. The entire rescue is shown twice, first from inside the house and then from outside it. Porter did not cut back and forth between the scenes; filmmakers had not yet developed cross-cutting. (The ship's landing in *A Trip to the Moon* is also shown twice, first in a view that shows the whole moon and then in a view on the moon's surface.)

It may not have been a mere economy for Porter to have used stock and new footage of entirely different fire brigades; he may have realized that he could get away with it—that the audience would integrate them into one brigade. Certainly he counted on something like that when he planned the final sequence, because the outdoor shots were clearly shot outside a real house and the indoor shots just as obviously inside a studio. Porter seems to have intuited that the cinema's narrative logic creates a unity of place where none exists in nature. As later theorists have demonstrated, we make sense of a narrative, a story, not merely on the basis of the action as presented but on the interplay between those events and our mental ability to connect them into a meaningful sequence. Porter's constructing the rescue process from two distinct views demanded that we mentally connect them into a single process—one event happening at one time—and the interior and exterior shots into views of a single building.

Porter's later film of 1903, *The Great Train Robbery*, makes even greater use of this interplay between filmed event and mental connection, and probably owes to that its terrific success as the single most popular film in America before 1912. The first series of shots in the film shows the same kind of step-by-step, one-shot–one-scene editing of the Méliès films. The outlaws enter the telegraph office and tie up the operator, board the train as it stops for water, rob the mail car and shoot the railroad man, seize the locomotive, unhook it from the rest of the train, rob all the passengers and shoot one who tries to escape, run to the locomotive and chug off, get off the locomotive, and run to their horses in the woods. Up to this point in the film any director might have made it, except for the flow and careful detail of the narrative sequences and the beauty and vitality of the outdoor shots, but the cut to the last scene of this sequence reveals a new editing idea. It is clearly an elliptical jump in time (from when the outlaws started their escape in the train to when they stopped the train and got off to find and mount their horses), and it contains a pan shot that follows the outlaws through the woods.

The next shot identifies the director's cinematic imagination more clearly. Porter *cuts back* to the opening scene, the telegraph office, and shows the discovery of the assaulted operator. Although the cut may be a backward leap in time and certainly deserts the spatial focus of the film (the outlaws and their getaway, which we understand to be an action that continues, unshown, while we watch the operator be revived), it makes perfect sense in the story's continuity. Making the mental connection, linking the film's events with our thinking about them, it *answers the question* the audience naturally asks: How will the outlaws be caught? Part of any narrative art is making the audience ask questions and

The Great Train Robbery: *composition that hides the robbers on the far left of the frame.*

Fig. 3-5

The Great Train Robbery: *the murder of a fleeing passenger, composed in depth along a diagonal.*

Fig. 3-6

delaying the answers. Almost every interesting narrative film since *The Great Train Robbery* has learned ways to make us ask ourselves what happens next, what made that happen, who did it, how will the hero get out of this one, and so on.

Porter's next shot reveals yet another ellipsis. Rather than sticking with the new focal characters (the operator and, presumably, his daughter), it jumps to a barn dance, into which the operator and the girl eventually enter to tell their tale. And then another ellipsis. The posse is tailing the outlaws in the woods. Again, the audience makes the connecting links that the director has purposely omitted. Porter was demonstrating a familiar artistic maxim in film form: The most effective way to shape a work is to omit the inessential. Although Porter may have discovered the power of ellipsis accidentally (according to legend, he was running out of film and needed to economize), the finished film demonstrates that power nonetheless.

The film's cinematic showmanship is evident in the final shot—a close shot of a bandit firing at the audience—which was intentionally unrelated to the whole film and could, according to the Edison catalogue, be shown before or after the rest of the movie. Like 3-D of later years, the shot thrilled customers with a direct assault. For the next five years, it became almost obligatory to end a film with a close shot of its major figure (*The Boy Detective* and *Her First Adventure*,

two Biograph films of 1908, are good examples)—all because of the success of the device in *The Great Train Robbery.*

For all the understandable later attention to the editing of this landmark film, several other sources of its power and popularity cannot be overlooked: its violence, its careful production design, its fluid mixing of scenes shot in the studio and on location, and its detailed demonstration of how to rob a train. Like the earliest Lumière films, *The Great Train Robbery* is a film of documentation, much as *Life of an American Fireman* is a film about a job. It is almost a little textbook called "How to Rob a Train"—first you tie up the telegraph operator so he can't send a warning, then you climb aboard the train when it stops for water, and so forth. Many of the earliest moral fears about the movies arose from their ability to teach audiences how to perform daring crimes in precise and explosive detail.

One special hand-painted copy is now widely available on film and video.

Porter's other films do not all show the same freshness in cutting or composition as *Life of an American Fireman* and *The Great Train Robbery*, even if he cut to a close-up in *The Gay Shoe Clerk* (*gay* as in playful) in 1903. His version of *Uncle Tom's Cabin*, also 1903 and the first American film to contain intertitles, is completely bound by the stage. His *Dream of a Rarebit Fiend* (1906), however, based on Winsor

McCay's series of cartoons in the *Evening Telegram* (*Dreams of the Rarebit Fiend*, 1905), is unusually inventive and memorable for its fluid use of long and close shots, its nearly film-long dream, its pan of the city, and a highly original use of superimposition and the moving camera to show how it feels to be drunk.

Perhaps the freedom of being outdoors influenced Porter's editing and shooting plan in *The Great Train Robbery*. One of the striking characteristics of American films before 1910 is that their outdoor shots look vital and fresh while the indoor shots look painted and flat. Outdoors, the accidental attractions of nature compensated for any lack of craft. Many studio films nearly reverted to the principles of the Black Maria. One reason, of course, is that the early films invested so little money and visual care in production. Nature didn't require an investment. Another reason is that the slowness of early film stock and lenses could render the world in depth only outdoors, where there was plenty of available light.

From Brighton to Biograph

While Porter was developing the tools of continuity and ellipsis in America, the "school of Brighton" was making similar and even more rapid progress in England. Porter, Zecca, and Griffith were among those who studied the early British films with care.

The group of filmmakers who clustered around the resort town of Brighton, especially George Albert Smith and James Williamson, built on the achievements of R. W. Paul, experimenting with ways to carry an action from one scene to the next, to break scenes into shots, and to use the camera and editing to define the landscape cinematically rather than theatrically. Paul had made the first multi-shot film in England, and his ideas and techniques had been imitated around the world (Edison's *Uncle Josh at the Moving-Picture Show*, 1902, was little more than a remake of Paul's *The Countryman and the Cinematograph*).

In 1900, G. A. Smith made a mindscreen film: *Let Me Dream Again*. (An earlier one was *The Moon at One Meter*, which showed the astronomer's dream. Méliès's first may have been *A Nightmare*, 1896.) In the first shot, a man romances an attractive woman; the image goes out of focus, there is a cut, and the second shot comes into focus, revealing the man in bed with his unattractive wife, whom he had begun to embrace while still asleep. The rude awakening in the second shot indicates that the first shot was a dream. Zecca remade this movie as *Dream and Reality* in 1901, joining the two shots with a dissolve—and to leap ahead of the story somewhat, Wes Craven used the technique of cutting to reality to define what came before as a dream throughout *A Nightmare on Elm Street* (1984).

The Great Train Robbery: *the freedom of the outdoors and the visual assertion of the frame's depth.*

Fig. 3-7

Haggar's Royal Electric Bioscope, an attraction at an English fair in 1902.

Fig. 3-8

Smith's first multi-shot film was *The Kiss in the Tunnel* (1899). In the first shot, the camera, mounted on the front of a train, goes into a tunnel whose darkness fills the screen; in the second shot, taken on a set, a man and a woman kiss in a private room on the train; and in the third shot, the camera and train come out of the dark tunnel into the daylight. (Many of the first three-shot films intercut the second shot into the middle of a take, which then became shots 1 and 3.)

As suggested earlier, Smith appears to have invented the POV shot, in which a shot is defined—through editing, camera position, and narrative context—as what a particular character sees. If a mindscreen shows what is seen by the mind's eye, the POV shot—also called *subjective camera*—shows what is seen by the physical eye. In his vignetted POV shots, Smith put a mask over part of the frame—an iris, for instance, so that the image became a circle surrounded by black and appeared to be seen through a telescope (*As Seen Through a Telescope*, 1900). When Pathé imitated this technique in *Peeping Tom* (1901), the mask was in the shape of a keyhole. The most important of Smith's masked-POV-shot films, *Grandma's Reading Glass* (1900), intercuts medium shots of

a boy and his grandmother—as he borrows the magnifying glass with which she has been reading the paper, and looks through it—with close-ups and extreme close-ups, shot through a circular mask, that show what he sees: the newspaper, the workings of a pocket watch, his grandmother's eye. Linking long with close views and breaking a scene into ten sharp, fascinating shots, it is a landmark in the history of editing.

Smith cut some of his other scenes into separate shots. *Sick Kitten* (1903) shows two kids taking care of their cat; shots 1 and 3 are medium views of the scene, but shot 2 cuts to a close-up of the kitten as it laps up a spoonful of medicinal oil. In *Mary Jane's Mishap*, (1903), Smith cut freely between full and close shots within a scene.

James Williamson also achieved major advances in continuity editing. *The Big Swallow* (1901) had two shots that were edited into three—but made to look like a continuous view of one scene: (1) a man walks toward the camera—from a medium view to extreme close-up—and opens his mouth until it surrounds the lens and the screen goes black; (2) the camera and the cameraman fall into the maw—a backdrop of black velvet; (3) the black screen yields an image as the mouth pulls away, and the man walks back to a medium view, chewing in triumph. All the cuts were from one completely black frame to another (similar to a technique Hitchcock would use to hide cuts in *Rope* and to the method of *The Kiss in the Tunnel*), to create the impression that shot 2 is a view from inside the mouth seen at the end of shot 1 and at the start of shot 3. Shots 1 and 3 had, of course, originally been a single take.

In another 1901 Williamson movie, *Stop Thief!*, a thief is chased out of the frame (that is, the field of view) in shot 1, runs into and out of shot 2, and runs into shot 3, where he tries to hide and is caught. Widely imitated, *Stop Thief!* set the pattern for the chase film, from *The Great Train Robbery* to Hitchcock's *The 39 Steps* (1935). That Hitchcock enjoyed Williamson's work is evident in an homage he paid in his 1955 *The Trouble with Harry* (one of the characters is so engrossed in a book that he can trip over a corpse without noticing) to *An Interesting Story*. In the seven scenes of that 1905 movie, a man finds a book so interesting that he walks, reading, from one place to another, oblivious to the people he bumps into, the objects he falls over, and even the steamroller that finally flattens him—a fate from which he is restored by trick photography.

Apart from Brighton, important work was being done elsewhere in England. Frank Mottershaw directed *Daring Daylight Burglary* in 1903, early enough in the year that it was a direct influence on *The Great Train Robbery*. Fast and violent, it follows the action from shot to shot (inspired not only by Paul but also by the way Williamson set up the chase in *Stop Thief!* and followed a longer action in continuity in *Fire!*, 1901). Unlike Porter's film, however, it told its story without ellipses; there was little left out and no doubling back, no leaping through narrative space or time. As Porter did, Walter Haggar immediately saw the potential of the violent chase film built around a crime and directed *Desperate Poaching Affray* in 1903. It was a *Daring Daylight Burglary* in which the thieves were poachers, but it was more violent, used the camera more inventively (notably in some panning shots and in the use of reverse angles), and made money for years.

Cecil Hepworth's *Rescued by Rover* (1905, with Lewis Fitzhamon behind the camera as director) is one of the most energetically edited pre-Griffith films, a decided advance over Porter

in narrative construction and rhythm. In the first expositional shot, a nurse wheeling a baby carriage insults a gypsy woman, who vows revenge. In the second shot, a carefully blocked sequence with a camera pan—a general strategy that would later be described as *plan-séquence*, the complicated blocking of a lengthy shot—the gypsy steals the baby as the nurse chats with a beau. Then Hepworth makes a huge elliptical jump. Rather than sticking with nurse, watching her discover the loss and run home to tell baby's parents, the film's third shot begins with nurse bursting into the family living room to tell her news. As she recites her tale, Rover, the family collie, listens intently; he jumps out the window in search of the stolen baby.

Then begins the most remarkable sequence in the film: a series of individual shots documenting Rover's finding baby, returning to tell his master, and leading master back to baby. The sequence, most of which is shown in Fig. 3-9, unfolds in the following shots: (1) Rover jumps out of window, (2) runs down the street toward camera, (3) turns corner, (4) swims across stream toward camera (shaking himself off after emerging from the water), (5) searches a row of shanty doors. Then there is a cut to (6) inside the shanty, where gypsy sits guzzling booze; gypsy exits, Rover enters, nuzzles baby; (7) Rover runs out door of shanty, same setup as 5; (8) swims across stream away from camera, same setup as 4; (9) runs around corner, away from camera, same setup as 3; (10) runs down street away from camera, same setup as 2; (11) jumps into house window, same setup as 1. Then, after a cut to (12) inside the house, Rover "tells" master. (13) Rover and master run down street, same setup as 2 and 10; (14) Rover and master cross stream, same setup as 4 and 8; (15) Rover leads master to door of shanty, same setup as 5 and 7; (16) master finds baby, takes it out of shanty; gypsy returns to find baby gone but is comforted by baby's clothes and her bottle of booze. In the film's final scene baby, master, mistress, and Rover are happily united in their living room; Hepworth has elliptically omitted the process of returning home, knowing that the sequence was not necessary and would weaken the emotional tension of the film. This is a crucial early instance of leaving out what the audience can figure out for itself, a basic lesson of filmmaking.

Fig. 3-9
Rescued by Rover: *the precise establishment of locations, the repetition of setups, and the consistent direction of movement within the frame produce both awareness of the process and emotional participation in the event.*

Hepworth's careful construction and editing of *Rescued by Rover* produced two effects that had not been achieved before, which communicated themselves to the audience by completely cinematic means. His systematic use of the same setups (or camera positions) to mark Rover's progress both toward and away from the baby firmly implanted in the audience's mind exactly where Rover was. Without any titles or explanations, the audience had a complete understanding of the rescue process and the spatial layout. Second, this documentation produced not only awareness, but also suspense. Because the audience knew where Rover's path was leading, it could participate in the excitement of Rover's finally reaching the end of it. Hepworth increased this excitement with the dynamic fluidity of cuts from one setup to the next. Although the locations were undoubtedly far apart, the editing created the impression that Rover ran continuously from one location to the next. Hepworth cut consistently as Rover was in motion across the frame (Eisenstein and Pabst would later develop the power of cutting on movement), impelling the viewer's eye into the next shot and producing both fluid continuity and visual energy.

Despite the slower pace of visual and narrative discovery in the American films of the period, the years from 1903 to 1908 laid the foundation on which Griffith built. To be sure, Griffith studied the British films—his first film is very similar to *Rescued by Rover,* and its editing principles would be reflected throughout his work—but he also learned from Porter. After the crucial films of 1903, Porter cleverly combined live-action comedy and graphics in *The Whole Dam Family and the Dam Dog* (1905); he used metaphoric lighting, a firelight's glow, for the final old-age scene of *The Seven Ages* (1905), predating Griffith's use of the same visual metaphor in *The Drunkard's Reformation* four years later; and he also made some of the earliest American films of social commentary, such as *The Kleptomaniac* (1905), which contrasts the one kind of law that applies to a poor and needy thief and the other kind that applies to a rich, disturbed one. Griffith would make much of such "contrasts" in *Intolerance.*

Even before Griffith (who became its leading director), the Biograph company had been producing the most interesting American films on the market. There were frantic seriocomic chases, clearly modeled on Zecca's, like *Personal* (1904), *The Lost Child* (1904), and *Tom, Tom, the Piper's Son* (1905). Within a half decade, two directors at this same studio would refine these chases into their purer but opposite types—D. W. Griffith's last-minute rescues and Mack Sennett's physical farces. Biograph also made films of ingenious thefts, like *The Great Jewel Mystery* (1905), in which the thief hides in a coffin on a train, and *The Silver Wedding* (1906), which concludes with a chase through the city sewers.

Also in this period at Biograph, G. W. ("Billy") Bitzer, the man who was to shoot all of Griffith's most inventive and important films, had begun to master the art of cinematography, notably in *Tom, Tom, the Piper's Son.* In *A Kentucky Feud* (1905), Bitzer's photography creates the appropriate visual setting for a tale of the Hatfields and McCoys. In *The Black Hand* (1906), a tale of organized crime, Bitzer juxtaposes scenes shot on sets with actual location shooting on Seventh Avenue in New York City. Biograph's *The Paymaster* (1906) may well use available light more creatively and beautifully than any other American film before 1908; especially effective are Bitzer's capturing the reflections of light on the river and his shots inside an old mill, lit entirely by oblique streams of light pouring through its window.

One question frequently debated among historians and film theorists is precisely why these early films gravitated toward narrative, toward storytelling, in the first place. Why didn't films remain depictions of real events, people, animals, and places in the world, or depictions of abstract visual qualities of light, shape, and form? Some suggest that films began to tell stories only as an act of commercial exploitation, because uneducated audiences were willing to pay for these primitive fictional shows. Others point out film's roots in documentation—that it was a small step to move from documenting real events, like the arrival of a train, to fictional ones, like the robbing of a train.

Still others suggest there was something inevitable about film's movement into storytelling, a clear outgrowth of 19th-century fiction and drama, which themselves sought the paradoxical union of two opposites—the telling of absolutely fictional and unreal stories within a visual, social, and psychological environment that seemed absolutely real and true to human experience. Movies seemed an ideal medium for combining the fictional tale with the real or realistic setting.

Whatever the theoretical, material, or spiritual reasons, between 1895 and 1908 movies changed from one-shot "views" to increasingly fluid sequences of visually effective shots that produced a continuous—if not necessarily difficult or evocative—narrative. The next evolution of narrative would require a master with a firmer and bolder sense, not so much of the individual cinematic elements but of the means to synthesize them into clearer, more credible, and more powerful narrative wholes. It would require a filmmaker not only with a strong visual sense, inherited from observing the accomplishments of Western painting, but also with a strong feeling for the plays and novels of the previous century. D. W. Griffith proved to be that artist before the end of 1909.

Complexity in Early Film

One way to understand the growing complexity of technique and narrative range in the cinema's first 15 or 16 years—as the multi-shot and the multiscene film replaced the single-shot film and as scenes began to be edited—is to set out the key films and their innovations in chronological order without dividing them up by country and director.

1893—While *Blacksmithing Scene* (Dickson and Heise at Edison) has one center of interest within the frame, in *The Barber Shop* there are two.

1894—At Edison, *Sandow* offers a relatively close view of a strongman, and *The Boxing Cats* a closer view of two fighting cats made up like boxers, while *Annie Oakley* takes an appropriately wider view of the sharpshooter and her targets. In each case the choice of camera distance enhances the subject, and the best view is selected because only one view can be photographed; each is an early example of the cinema of attractions.

1894 or 1895—Dickson makes the first film with synchronized sound.

1895—At Edison, *The Execution of Mary, Queen of Scots* is the first film to splice together two shots, even though the film appears to be a single shot. It also marks the first instantaneous substitution of a dummy for an actor. In England, *Rough Sea at Dover* directs the action at the audience. In France, the Lumières project their

first *actualités* and the first film to tell a story, *The Gardener and the Little Scamp*.

1896—In France, Méliès makes *A Nightmare*, probably the first film to include a dream. A Lumière cameraman puts the camera on a gondola for *Venice: View of the Grand Canal from a Boat*, the first known moving-camera shot.

1897—Méliès continues to explore the creative possibilities of stopping and starting the camera within what appears to be a single shot. The Lumières reflect his influence in their *Automobile Accident*, a narrative film in which the camera is stopped and started several times to allow a man and a dummy to be substituted for each other.

1898—In England, *Come Along Do!* has two scenes, each a single shot, through the second scene no longer survives. In France, *The Moon at One Meter* has three scenes; the scene transitions, which are difficult to spot, are marked by changes in the set. The Lumières market *The Life and Passion of Jesus Christ* as 13 individual, single-shot films.

1899— Méliès makes *The Dreyfus Affair* as nine individual films and shows them in one program. Méliès's next film, the 6-minute *Cinderella*, has four distinct scenes (one of which includes a hallucination that plays almost as a separate scene), bridged by dissolves. In England, Smith uses straight cuts to join the three shots of *The Kiss in the Tunnel*.

1900—In *As Seen Through a Telescope* and *Grandma's Reading Glass*, Smith invents the POV shot. *Grandma's Reading Glass* divides one scene into 10 shots, cutting between medium shots and close-ups. Hepworth's *How It Feels To Be Run Over* may be the first film to include an intertitle—actually a series of them—after a car has come close enough to run over the camera/pedestrian: "/ ?   ? / !!! / ! / Oh! / Mother / *will* / be / pleased /."

1901—Also in England, in two of the earliest reflexive films, *The Countryman and the Cinematograph* includes an image of a movie playing on a screen, and *The Big Swallow* includes the swallowing of a camera, an action seen at first through its lens. A single character is followed as he runs from one scene to another in *Stop Thief!* One fireman is followed from scene to scene in most of *Fire!*, but at one point Williamson cuts away from the firemen, directly to the interior of a burning bedroom where no fireman has yet arrived. In France, Zecca remakes

Let Me Dream Again as *Dream and Reality*, and in *History of a Crime* he inserts a moving image (a rectangle that shows a dream) into the main image, an effect borrowed from Smith. *Peeping Tom*, a Pathé film also influenced by Smith and perhaps made by Zecca, alternates shots of the main character with masked POV shots of what he sees through a series of keyholes.

1902—*A Trip to the Moon* is almost a full reel long and tells a continuous story in a great many scenes.

1903—In *Life of an American Fireman*, Porter finds new ways to link shots, including cause and effect (responding to an alarm) and having firemen slide down two views of one firepole. Porter also intercuts stock with new footage and uses a panning camera movement to keep the burning house out of the frame until he wants to reveal it. In England, *Daring Daylight Burglary* and *Desperate Poaching Affray* are crime-and-chase films that influence *The Great Train Robbery*. Smith changes the location of the camera throughout *Mary Jane's Mishap*, constructing the major scene out of full and close shots. Paul keeps important action offscreen in *A Chess Dispute*. In America, *The Great Train Robbery* cuts away from the robbers and their presumably ongoing actions to show the actions of their pursuers, leaving out the inessential and creating a relatively complex continuity that maintains two narrative lines before joining them in a final confrontation.

1904—In England, Paul adapts a popular melodrama in the multi-scene *Buy Your Own Cherries*.

1905—In England, *Rescued by Rover* uses the systematic repetition of camera setups to construct (and allow the audience to follow) a complex landscape. In America, Porter's *The Kleptomaniac* compares how the law treats the rich and the poor, showing first the rich thief, then the poor one, then a court scene in which both their fates are decided, and finally a symbol: blind Justice with the scales out of balance.

1906—In America, *Dream of a Rarebit Fiend* uses many special effects, including one in which the dreamer and his bed fly over a pan of New York City and one in which multiple exposure and the moving camera create an impression of drunkenness and indigestion. In Australia, *The Story of the Kelly Gang* is the first feature-length film (64 minutes).

1907—In France, Pathé's *The Runaway Horse* cross-cuts between the exterior and interior of an apartment building (while the delivery man is inside, his horse helps itself to a bag of oats).

1908—Pathé's *The Physician of the Castle* (also known as *A Narrow Escape*) uses a telephone to establish a link between characters, one of many way it influences Griffith's *The Lonely Villa* (1909). In England, F. Percy Smith achieves a fly-sized extreme close-up in *The Balancing Bluebottle*, later known as *The Acrobatic Fly*.

Business Wars

While moviemakers gradually discovered the elements of film construction, American movie exhibitors gradually converted commercial chaos into order. In the last 5 years of the 19th century, the American picture business enjoyed the protection of neither law nor professional ethics. Cameramen and exhibitors blatantly ignored machine patents, pirating and duplicating any instrument that could make them money. Even more vulnerable were the filmstrips themselves, which were not yet protected *as films* by copyright laws. (At first, only items on paper were covered, so the first copyrighted movies were *paper prints* of all the shots in the movie.) The French and English films were the most vulnerable; although many Méliès films were shown legitimately in the United States, his Star Film Company made no money from the prints that had been smuggled out of France and duped. Piracy had become so pervasive that film companies hung or painted their identifying logo on the sets themselves. The Edison trademark can be clearly seen on a burning wall in *Life of an American Fireman*, and the American Biograph monogram—the letters AB in a circle:

—was even pasted on the street organ of *Her First Adventure* and is easy to spot throughout *The Lonely Villa*. A war entangled all producers and exhibitors of motion pictures.

In 1899, for example, Biograph set up a huge battery of hot lights on Coney Island to record the Jeffries–Sharkey fight. The film would be the first to use electricity instead of sunlight. While the Biograph camera was grinding away in the front row, the Vitagraph camera was grinding away 20 rows back. When the Biograph boys discovered the Vitagraph camera, they sent a crew of Pinkerton detectives to seize the machine and film. The fight fans surrounding the Vitagraph camera, unaware of the causes of the attack, manfully protected their neighbors, producing more action outside the ring than in it. Eventually Vitagraph's Albert E. Smith recorded the whole fight, smuggled the film out of the arena, and developed it that night in the Vitagraph lab. The next morning Smith discovered that the pirated film had itself been pirated out of the lab by some late-night delegates of the Edison company. Ironically, although Biograph went to the trouble and expense of lighting the fight, Vitagraph and Edison (both eventually released prints of it) were the only ones to make any money on it.

In December 1897, Thomas Edison served his first legal writ, announcing his intention to eliminate all competitors in motion pictures. For the next 11 years, Edison would bring suit against any company that used a loop of film in either a projection machine or a camera, claiming he owned the rights to all loops because of the Armat patent on the Latham loop, the generic name for all loops in all film machines. Edison's private detectives roamed the country searching for shooting companies, serving any they discovered with legal writs or extralegal wreckage. Edison steadily coerced the smaller companies into accepting his terms, eventually bringing suit against the big ones like Biograph.

Then Thomas Armat, dissatisfied with Edison's taking full credit for the Vitascope, took to the courts. Edison had double-crossed Armat commercially by manufacturing his own projecting machine, the Projecting Kinetoscope, just two years after marketing Armat's. Armat, like Edison, brought suit against everyone who used his loop projector; he also sued Edison. Biograph, meanwhile, was preparing its own legal dossiers. With some careful bargaining it bought both the Armat patents and the Latham patents, arming itself with plenty of ammunition

to use against Edison. It is ironic and appropriate that these purchases put the loop back under the control of its co-inventor, Biograph's Dickson. For ten years the motion picture companies busied themselves with suits and countersuits. Some 500 legal actions were taken, more than 200 of them making their way into court.

While the company lawyers were busy at each other's legal throats, the movie companies continued making and selling an ever-increasing number of films. Originally, when movies were part of vaudeville bills or amusement arcades, the film company sold the finished picture directly to the exhibitor at between 5 and 25 cents per foot, depending on the expenses of the film, its potential popularity, whether it was hand colored, and so forth. The exhibitor then owned the film and could show it until the print wore out, then buy a new one.

But a new exhibiting development, just after the turn of the century, produced a new distributing practice. In 1902, an enterprising Los Angeles showman opened a small theatre in a store specifically for the purpose of showing motion pictures. Thomas L. Tally's Electric Theatre was the first permanent movie theatre in the United States. More and more of these store theatres sprang up until, in June 1905, a Pittsburgh store theatre opened that was a bit plusher, accompanied its showings with a piano, and charged its customers a nickel. It was the first *nickelodeon*, or "nickel theatre." Within three or four years there were more than 5,000 nickelodeons in the United States. So popular were they that in 1908 it was estimated that they drew 80 million admissions every week—at a time when the entire population of the United States was about 100 million.

The permanent movie theatre forced a fundamental change in the relationship of the movie exhibitor and the movie producer. The nickelodeon required a large number of films each week; about six films of one or one-half reel each made up a single hour-long program.

As mentioned previously, a *reel* is up to 1,000 feet of 35mm film, which has 16 frames per foot. A *full reel* is a full 1,000 feet; for decades, that was the largest roll of film a movie camera or projector could hold. At 16 fps, a full reel takes 16.67 minutes to project; at 24 fps, it takes 11.1 minutes. In practice, a reel is usually between

900 and 990 feet, and the average reel lasts about 15 minutes at silent speed, about 10 minutes at sound speed. Today, however, a "reel" is what used to be called a *double reel:* up to 2,000 feet of 35mm film, in practice between 1,500 and 2,000 feet, lasting between 15 and 22 minutes at 24 fps. When a film history book says that *Battleship Potemkin* is 5 reels long, that means that it is under 5,000 feet of 35mm film; when a projectionist today says that a feature is 5 reels long, that means that it is under 10,000 feet. To avoid confusion, this book gives lengths in feet of 35mm film (and in minutes) and uses "reel" to mean about 1,000 feet, unless otherwise specified. Division into reels does not depend purely on length but is part of the film's deep internal rhythm, coming at the end of what the editor decides is the appropriate shot to conclude a particular reel. The sound that is edited and mixed to go with a reel of film is a *reel of sound.* The ends of reels are inscribed with *changeover marks* that alert the projectionist to switch to the next reel, which in the old days was loaded on the other of a pair of projectors. (Films are still editorially constructed in reels. That is, Scene 70, to make up a figure, might be identified in a mixing session—or in a shot-by-shot description of a print—as the first 45 feet, or the first 30 seconds, of Reel 3.) *The Great Train Robbery*, which is only 720 feet long, is a one-reel picture or *one-reeler*, and so is Griffith's unusually long *After Many Years* (1908), which is 1,033 feet. For purposes of exhibition in the early Silent Era, Porter's *The Gay Shoe Clerk*, at 75 feet, was referred to as a *half-reel* picture, as was any movie under 500 feet.

To keep the customers coming, programs had to change several times a week. The theatre owner had no use for owning a film outright; after several showings, the regular patrons would not want to see it again. Between the film producer and the film exhibitor stepped a middleman who either bought the film or leased it from the producer and then rented it to the many exhibitors. The exhibitor paid less money for a larger supply of films; the producer was certain of selling films. The three-part structure of the American film industry—the producer who makes the film, the distributor who arranges for its most effective circulation, and the exhibitor who shows it in the theatre—worked out well for

all parties. That structure, with some wrinkles, survives today.

Edison tried to use this three-level structure to control the chaotic American film world. It was particularly important to work out a treaty between the two top competitors, Edison and Biograph, along with the key people and companies allied with each of them. Pressure, threats, bankruptcy, and collusion led to a combining of the nine leading film companies of 1908—Edison, Biograph, Vitagraph, Essanay, Lubin, Selig, Kalem, Méliès, and Pathé (the last two had both begun producing in America)—along with inventor Thomas Armat and distributor George Kleine (the importer of Gaumont and Urban productions). The combine, called the Motion Picture Patents Company, was incorporated on September 9, 1908, and activated on December 18, 1908; Méliès was added to the group on July 20, 1909. The members of the combine agreed to share the legal rights to their various machine and film patents (including the Latham loop, which was part of virtually every movie camera), to buttress one another's business procedures, and to keep all other parties and machine parts out of the film business permanently. The Motion Picture Patents Company could make its rules stick because it also agreed not to sell or lease to any distributor who bought a film from any other company. The exchange (distributor) that wanted to handle Patents Company films—the best pictures then on the market—could not handle any other company's films. Further, the Patents Company made an exclusive contract (on January 1, 1909) with George Eastman's factory: Eastman would sell perforated raw film stock to the Patents Company and only to the Patents Company. The Patents Company was such a big account that Eastman could not afford to sell to interlopers. After ten years of piracy and bickering, the "War of the Patents" was over. American film production was the exclusive property of nine companies. They leased their films only to those distributors who would accept their terms and pay their fees, and these "licensed" film exchanges, soon to become amalgamated as the powerful General Film Company, rented only to exhibitors who paid a weekly licensing fee ($2) and agreed to show Patents Company pictures exclusively. From first shot to final showing, law and order had come to motion pictures.

Fig. 3-10

The beckoning lure of an early nickelodeon: the Cascade Theatre in Newcastle, Pennsylvania, operated by the Warner Brothers.

Having temporarily ended the warfare within the industry, the Motion Picture Patents Company sought to silence the increasing moral clamor outside it. The staggering success of the nickelodeons, the huge numbers of Americans who had caught the "nickel madness," troubled the moral principles of both amateur advocates and professional politicians. As early as 1907, states and cities began to establish censorship boards to ensure the cleanliness of movie content and licensing boards to ensure the cleanliness and safety of movie theatres. These boards became commercially troublesome for an increasingly national industry. What if a film

were acceptable in California but not in Illinois? What if a film were acceptable in Pennsylvania as a whole but not in Philadelphia? To silence its critics and to ensure the commercial health of its product, the infant motion picture industry took the first step of the kind it would take throughout its history when faced with a moral attack that endangered its financial welfare: It established its own censorship board to control film content. The National Board of Censorship, founded in 1908 (in 1915, it changed its name to the more tolerant-sounding National Board of Review), did not put an end to state and local censorship actions, but it greatly reduced their inconsistencies by establishing standards and principles that most of them could (and did) accept.

Less fortunate for the Motion Picture Patents Company and its General Film Company was the rebellion of some distributors and exhibitors within the industry itself against this monopolistic control. It eliminated bargaining and profits from duping, and it raised prices. Within months after the peace had been signed in 1908, two distributors, William Swanson of Chicago and Carl Laemmle of New York, decided to "go independent." The two pacesetters urged other film exchanges to follow their example. The Patent War had ended; the Trust War had begun.

The independent distributor faced one problem: obtaining films to distribute that were not made by a Patents Company studio. One of the obvious solutions was for a distributor to turn producer. Carl Laemmle, film exchangeman, became Carl Laemmle, film producer, and gave birth to the organization that would eventually become Universal Pictures. William Fox, distributor and theatre owner, became William Fox, producer, and the organization that would eventually become 20th Century–Fox was born. Fox also retaliated against the Patents Company by suing them and their General Film Company as an illegal trust. The lawyers were back in the movie business—to stay.

For all Teddy Roosevelt's historical reputation as a "trust buster," it was the new Wilson administration that joined Fox's suit against the Film Trust in 1913. Governmental agencies had learned at this early date that they could attract maximum publicity in the press and interest from the public by attacking a popular and glamorous industry like the movies. By 1913, Americans had really come to care about the movies. The first U.S. fan magazine appeared in 1912.

Until 1915, movie companies fought in the courts and in the streets. Jeremiah J. Kennedy, a major executive of the Patents Company, sent gangs of gentlemen to visit unlicensed studios, shooting holes in cameras and leaving bits of wreckage about for calling cards. To escape this, some companies set up shop in faraway Hollywood. Some Patents companies set up studios there, too.

Despite the strong-arm tactics of the Trust, the Independents prospered. Adam Kessel and Charles Bauman, two former bookies, formed the New York Motion Picture Company, which eventually founded the film careers of Thomas Ince, Mack Sennett, and Charles Chaplin. When Edison had the gall to demote him in 1907, Porter left Edison to go independent, making films for his own Rex Company; it would one day be swallowed by Paramount. Most successful of all the Independents was Laemmle's Independent Motion Picture Company, known as IMP.

The Trust's barriers sprang other leaks. Unable to buy film stock from Eastman, the Independents bought stock from English, French, and other American factories. In addition, legitimate licensed film companies and film exchanges ran unlicensed, independent companies and exchanges on the side. When the smoke of this second film war had cleared, by late 1915, the Motion Picture Patents Company had been busted in court as an illegal trust (it disbanded in 1917, when the case was finally settled), and the individual companies that formed the Trust were dying or dead. The Independents propelled the movies into their next era. Three of the Independent companies (Fox, Universal, and Paramount) survive today. The last of the original Trust companies, Vitagraph, was swallowed by Warner Bros. in 1925.

The Film d'Art

An important influence made itself felt toward the end of the decade. In 1907, a French company announced the intention of creating a serious, artistic cinema—of bringing together on film the most important playwrights, directors, actors, composers, and painters of the period. The company, which called itself the Société Film d'Art, produced its first film in 1908—*The Assassination of the Duc de Guise*. Featuring actors from the Comédie Française and incidental music by Saint-Saëns, the movie was hailed as introducing the nobility and seriousness of the stage to the film. Ironically, the Film d'Art ran the movies headlong back into the theatre: theatrical staging, unedited scenes, theatrical acting. It was the first in a series of attempts to produce "canned theatre," one of the most successful of which was the American Film Theater of the mid-1970s, with its excellent filmed productions of plays like *The Iceman Cometh* and *A Delicate Balance*.

The first of these Films d'Art to be seen in the United States was *Queen Elizabeth* (1912), featuring Sarah Bernhardt and members of the Comédie Française, directed by Louis Mercanton. This bombastic film version of Elizabeth's love for Essex, whom she must eventually send to the block, reveals all the plodding staginess of the Film d'Art technique. Characters enter and exit from right and left; groups of soldiers, ladies in waiting, or courtiers stand immobile in the background; the actors, Bernhardt included, indulge in a grotesque series of facial grimaces, arm swingings, fist clenchings, and breast thumpings (once even raising dust from the costume). And yet these were among the most skillful stage actors in the world!

One clear lesson of the Film d'Art was that stage acting and film acting were incompatible. The stage, which puts small performers in a large hall, requires larger, more demonstrative movements. The artificiality of this demonstrativeness does not show in a theatre for three reasons: First, the live performance sustains the gestures with the vitality of the living performer's presence, which assimilates gesture as only one part of a whole performance. Second, the performer's voice adds another living note that makes facial expression and gesticulation also merely parts of a whole. And third, that voice carries words, which are as essential to the theatre as performance itself. The filmed play would truly flourish only with sound. In the Film d'Art of *Queen Elizabeth*, gesture and grimace were parts without a whole.

The way to improve film acting was not just to make the actors underplay but to let cinematic technique help the actors act. A camera can move in so close to an actor's face that the blinking of an eye or the flicker of a smile can become a significant and sufficient gesture. Or the field of view can cut from the actor to the subject of the actor's thoughts or attention, thereby revealing the emotion without requiring a thump on the chest. Film acting before Griffith—and before his greatest star, Lillian Gish—not only in the Film d'Art but in Méliès and Porter as well, had been so bad precisely because the camera had not yet learned to help the actors.

Although the Film d'Art had nothing to do with film art, the company had a lot to do with the direction that film art would take. *Queen Elizabeth* was a huge success. That success launched the

Fig. 3-11

Sarah Bernhardt in Queen Elizabeth: *stage composition and stage acting, with no help from the camera. As Elizabeth watches, Essex is led to his trial.*

career of its American distributor, Adolph Zukor, who decided to form an American Film d'Art called Famous Players in Famous Plays, which would eventually become Paramount Pictures. Its success also proved that highbrow pictures and, more important, *long* pictures could make money. It was to the advantage of the Motion Picture Patents Company to maintain that audiences would not sit through a single picture of more than 15 minutes, for the whole film business they had solidified was built on programs of one-reelers. The General Film Company could not distribute any film longer than two reels; it served the nickelodeons exclusively. *Queen Elizabeth*, a 44-minute three-reeler, squashed the Trust myths. Feature films were on the way.

For Further Viewing

FILMS

GEORGES MÉLIÈS (1861–1938)

A Game of Cards (1896)
The Moon at One Meter or *The Astronomer's Dream* (1898)
The Dreyfus Affair (1899)
Cinderella (1899)
The Conjurer (1899)
A Trip to the Moon (1902)
The Magic Lantern (1903)
Long Distance Wireless Photography (1908)
Hydrothérapie fantastique or *The Doctor's Secret* (1909)
The Conquest of the Pole (1912)

EDWIN S. PORTER (1869–1941)

Life of an American Fireman (1903). Completed 1902
The Gay Shoe Clerk (1903)
Uncle Tom's Cabin (1903)
The Great Train Robbery (1903)
The Kleptomaniac (1905)
The Whole Dam Family and the Dam Dog (1905)
Dream of a Rarebit Fiend (1906)

OTHER FILMS OF THE ERA

Rough Sea at Dover (1895, Birt Acres)
The Cabbage Fairy (1896, Alice Guy)
Tearing Down the Spanish Flag (1898, J. Stuart Blackton)
Come Along Do! (1898, R. W. Paul)
The Kiss in the Tunnel (1899, G. A. Smith)
Let Me Dream Again and *As Seen Through a Telescope* and *Grandma's Reading Glass* (1900, G. A. Smith)
The Big Swallow and *Stop Thief!* and *Fire!* (1901, James Williamson)
The Funeral of Queen Victoria and *The Countryman and the Cinematograph* (1901, R. W. Paul)
Dream and Reality (1901, Ferdinand Zecca)
Sick Kitten and *Mary Jane's Mishap*, (1903, G. A. Smith)
Daring Daylight Burglary (1903, Frank Mottershaw)
Desperate Poaching Affray (1903, Walter Haggar)
An Interesting Story (1905, James Williamson)
Rescued by Rover (1905, Cecil Hepworth). Directed by Lewis Fitzhamon
Tom, Tom, the Piper's Son and *A Kentucky Feud* (1905, Biograph)
Scenes of Convict Life and *Slippery Jim* (1905, Ferdinand Zecca)
On the Barricades (1906, Alice Guy)
Humorous Phases of Funny Faces (1906, J. Stuart Blackton)
The Black Hand and *The Paymaster* (1906, Biograph)
A Skater's Debut (1906, Max Linder)
The Story of the Kelly Gang (1906, Charles Tait)
Rescued from an Eagle's Nest or *The Eagle's Nest* (1908, J. Searle Dawley). Completed 1907
The Assassination of the Duc de Guise (1908, Charles Le Bargy and André Calmettes; Film d'Art)
The Balancing Bluebottle or *The Acrobatic Fly* (1908, F. Percy Smith)
Fantasmagorie and *Un Drame chez les fantoches* or *A Love Affair in Toyland* (1908, Émile Cohl)
The Music Master (1908, Biograph)
The Airship Destroyer (1909, Charles Urban)
Meeting of the Motion Picture Patents Company (1909, Biograph)
Princess Nicotine (1909, J. Stuart Blackton)
The Vampire (1910, Selig)
Little Nemo (1911, Winsor McCay and J. Stuart Blackton)
Onésime horloger (1912, Jean Durand)
Queen Elizabeth (1912, Louis Mercanton; Film d'Art)

I nomadi (*Nomadic People*, 1912, Elvira Notari)
Matrimony's Speed Limit and *A House Divided*
    (1913, Alice Guy Blaché)
Fantômas (1913–14, Louis Feuillade)
Gertie the Dinosaur (1914, Winsor McCay)

DVDs

*Georges Méliès: First Wizard of Cinema
    (1896–1913)*. Flicker Alley. Excellent prints
of most of **Méliès**'s surviving work; an essen-
tial set.
*More Treasures from American Film
    Archives, 1894–1931: 50 Films*. Image
Entertainment/National Film Preservation
Foundation. Important silent and early sound
films, most not available elsewhere, with
expert commentaries. Includes ***Dickson
Experimental Sound Film*** with the original
sound, Dickson's *Rip Van Winkle* (shot by
Bitzer), **Porter**'s *Life of an American
Fireman*, **Griffith**'s *The Country Doctor*, a
Pearl White serial episode, several early
color films, a 1910 adaptation of *The Wizard
of Oz*, a 1912 film about child labor, the original **Rin-Tin-Tin,** a film with Sioux actors, the

feature *Lady Windermere's Fan* (**Lubitsch,**
1925), *Greeting by* **George Bernard Shaw,**
two Phonofilms by **de Forest** (Eddie Cantor
in 1923, President Coolidge in 1924), field-
work footage shot in 1928 by **Zora Neale
Hurston,** many actualities and documen-
taries, a detailed book, and, of course, *Gus
Visser and His Singing Duck* (1925).
16 **Méliès** films, including *A Trip to the Moon;*
most of the early **British** films discussed in
the text, including *Rough Sea at Dover, Let Me
Dream Again, Grandma's Reading Glass,
The Big Swallow, Sick Kitten, Desperate
Poaching Affray, An Interesting Story*, and
Rescued by Rover; 4 **Porter** films, including
The Great Train Robbery and *Dream of a
Rarebit Fiend;* **McCay**'s *Little Nemo;* and
Durand's *Onésime horloger* are in *The Movies
Begin* (see Chap. 2 list).
Rescued from an Eagle's Nest (1908, **J. Searle
Dawley**) is in *Griffith Masterworks* (see
Chap. 4 list).
Les Vampires (1915–16, **Louis Feuillade**).
Image Entertainment. Complete serial, tinted.
Winsor McCay: The Master Edition. Image
Entertainment. Good prints of all 10 surviving
films.

4

Griffith

David Wark Griffith never intended to make movies. The accidental path that eventually led him to films stretched from his rural Kentucky home to selling books, picking hops in California, reporting for a Louisville newspaper, and finally writing and acting for the legitimate stage. The young Griffith had decided he was a playwright. One of his plays, *The Fool and the Girl*, even played two tepid weeks in Washington and Baltimore. Like the movies themselves, Griffith's dramatic apprenticeship was rooted in the world of Broadway producer David Belasco. It would be Griffith who would most successfully translate the Belasco effects for the screen— melodrama, suspense, pathos, purity. Griffith began with the same dramatic structures, the same sentimental characters, and the same moral assumptions of the Belasco stage, and he never deserted them, even when his audiences did.

Griffith's playwriting ultimately brought him to the movies. Like all stage actors, Griffith regarded the moving pictures as an artistic slum, but he had written an adaptation of *Tosca*, which he failed to peddle as a stageplay. He then decided to try to sell it to the pictures. In 1907, over 30 years old and out of work, he took his manuscript up to the new Edison studios in the Bronx. The film companies had deserted city rooftops for more spacious and secretive quarters in the Bronx and Brooklyn. Edwin S. Porter, by then head of production at Edison, thought Griffith's *Tosca*, with its many scenes and lengthy plot, too heady for the movies (this was five years before the Film d'Art's *Queen Elizabeth*). Instead of buying Griffith's script, Porter offered

him an acting job at $5 a day. Griffith, recently married to Linda Arvidson, needed the money and took the job. But he insisted on playing under the assumed name of Lawrence Griffith, thinking he would save his real name for the day when one of his plays opened on Broadway. Things would work out differently.

Apprenticeship

In Griffith's first role for Porter he played a lumberjack (a very thin lumberjack!) and father in *The Eagle's Nest* (1907, released 1908; also known as *Rescued from an Eagle's Nest*), produced by Porter and directed by J. Searle Dawley. When his wife informs him that their baby has been swooped away by a huge bird, Griffith climbs down a cliff to the bird's mountain lair, fights the puppet eagle to the death, and brings back the baby. This melodramatic film was not without significance for Griffith's later career. First, Porter provided Griffith's introduction to film technique. Porter was the American director before Griffith who best understood the power and logic of editing in building a story. Second, the melodramatic plot was to find its reincarnations in Griffith's movies throughout his career, from the early short films to the epics and later features. Whether Griffith acquired the taste for the last-minute rescue from the Belasco stage or the Porter screen, by the time he started to direct his own films, that taste had become his own.

After a short career with Edison, Griffith took a job at Biograph, performing the same kinds of acting chores for the head of production there,

Fig. 4-1

D. W. Griffith: a portrait of
the artist as a film director.

Wallace C. ("Old Man") McCutcheon. By 1908,
the devouring nickelodeon's demand for films
was so great that Biograph needed to step up
production to several reels per week and therefore needed another director. Griffith, whose
imagination had been noted by Biograph cameraman Arthur Marvin (brother of co-owner Harry
Marvin), was offered the job. Griffith was not
sure he wanted it. He was content with the daily
$5 wage; failure as a director might cost him the
steady income from acting. Biograph promised
him that he could go back to acting if he failed
as a director. The sincerity of the promise was
never tested. Griffith directed his first film, *The
Adventures of Dollie*, in June 1908.

Biograph: The One-Reelers

The Adventures of Dollie displays Griffith's
thorough knowledge of the successful formulas
of the past. Dollie's one-reel adventures are terribly familiar. An insulted gypsy takes vengeance
on a family by kidnapping baby Dollie and hiding
her in a water cask. As the gypsies ride away, the
cask falls off the wagon and into a stream, where
it moves steadily toward and through the vicious
rapids. Dollie eventually escapes a watery death
when her cries attract the attention of a nearby
boy who is fishing; the picture ends with the
inevitable happy family reunion. Griffith uses
two motifs that had become standard in filmed
melodrama: the spurned gypsy's revenge and the

The second shot of **The Adventures of Dollie.**

Fig. 4-2

perilous danger to an innocent child. Its clear ancestors are films like *Rescued by Rover, The Eagle's Nest,* and *Her First Adventure* (1908), Biograph's own version of the *Rover* film, made just three months before Griffith's *Dollie.* The dangerous rapids would recur in later Griffith films, most notably in *Way Down East,* made 12 years later, in which Lillian Gish floats ominously toward the falls on an ice cake.

Although Griffith's film sticks to extremely conventional narrative material, he handles those conventions with a narrative fluidity and symmetry uncommon in films of the period. Griffith establishes the agent of Dollie's rescue, the boy fisherman, in the second shot. He walks along the river bank and away from the camera at the same time that Dollie and her family walk toward the camera. This narrative linking makes the action's resolution more probable and logical. The final sequence with the floating cask also flows more continuously and rhythmically (using the consistent direction of motion across the frame and cutting on movement) than is usual for films of 1908. And the film's most interestingly planned shot is a long shot that shows a farmer cutting grain as the gypsy runs through the field with Dollie in his grasp. The shot gives the convincing feeling that these episodes of movie fiction have been plucked out of the random and continuous flow of life itself.

Another filmmaker would have left out the farmer and concentrated on the single main action, but Griffith's interest in significant contrast is already evident.

It was this paradox of film narrative—that films look so spontaneously real and natural and yet are so fictional and patterned—that Griffith would develop and master in the five years that followed. His general method would be to push each of these paradoxical qualities to its extreme—to make filmed life look as natural and random as real life and yet to make filmed stories as carefully structured and patterned as any well-constructed fictions.

Griffith, shouldering the production demand of directing several one-reel pictures every week, had been given an ideal laboratory for experimentation and development. Between 1908 and 1913, clearly Griffith's apprenticeship period, he directed more than 450 movies for Biograph; this gave him the opportunity to test a new idea immediately, see whether and how it worked, and then return to the technique the next week and develop it further. Griffith did not innovate abstractly; he could test each method day by day in front of and with the camera, rejecting what failed, refining what worked. Griffith's discoveries were empirical, not theoretical. Those discoveries embraced every component of visual, black-and-white cinematic technique.

Griffith realized that the content of the shot should determine the camera's relationship to it. The accepted shot in the film world of 1908 was what is called the *full shot* or far shot today. This shot necessarily included the full figures of all the characters in the scene, plus enough of the scenery to show the audience exactly where the characters were and how carefully the set had been painted. This standard shot enjoyed the official blessing of the Motion Picture Patents Company, whose reasoning seemed sensible: Why should the public pay the full price to see half an actor? Griffith revealed the effectiveness of showing half of an actor, a corner of a set, or even smaller areas.

In his apprentice years, Griffith developed a full series of different shooting perspectives. Beginning with the standard full shot, he moved the camera closer to the players to produce the *medium shot*—including, say, two actors from the knees up (a shot later christened the "American shot"). And then the camera moved still closer to produce the *close shot*, including only the head and shoulders of a single actor; the *close-up*, revealing only a hand or face; and the *extreme close-up*, showing perhaps just an eye. (Most of the "close-ups" in Porter's films were actually close shots.) Griffith also saw that he could move the camera in the other direction, farther away from the actors. He produced the *long shot*—a much more distant view of one or more players—which emphasized more of the scenic environment than the far shot. And then he moved the camera still farther from the players, producing the *extreme long shot* that would emphasize huge vistas and panoramas.

Griffith was not, of course, the first to use these shots. Many of the Lumière "views" were of vast panoramas. *Fred Ott's Sneeze* and the opening and/or closing of *The Great Train Robbery* both used medium to close shots, and there were true close-ups and extreme close-ups in Smith's *Grandma's Reading Glass*. But these earlier films used the nonstandard shot for some special photographic or narrative effect. Griffith made all these shots standard and combined them into sequential wholes. One could cut freely between long and medium, close and medium, close and long to produce a whole scene. Griffith broke the theatrical scene into the cinematic unit of the shot.

In a sense, his method really was another kind of analogy with the stage, but a much more subtle one than earlier film directors had perceived. Although a scene on the stage is anchored in immovable space, it really is a series of shifting "beats," of emotional pivots and silences, of thrusts and parries, of comings together and splittings apart. Despite the stasis of the setting and the audience's viewing angle, the theatrical scene is not static; it is constantly shifting, changing, and evolving. Griffith translated these stage "beats" into film terms. When the mood shifted, when the emotions changed, the camera shifted. It caught that intimate moment when a single member of a group made up his or her mind to take a significant emotional leap; it caught the smallness of a solitary soldier in the midst of a huge army on a vast battlefield. Griffith discovered that the narrative content of the scene, not the location of the scene, determined the correct placement of the camera and the correct moment to cut from one perspective or setup to another. This discovery is frequently called the "grammar and rhetoric" of film because Griffith discovered that—as with words—there was a way of combining film shots to produce clarity, power, and meaning.

Griffith discovered, at the same time, the power of two moving-camera shots: the pan and the traveling shot. Again, both of these shots had been used before. There were pans in some of Porter's films. There were traveling shots in some early Lumière views and in an American film show called *Hale's Tours* in which the audience sat in a theatre designed as a railroad car and watched films of moving scenery actually shot from a moving railroad car. But Griffith realized that these special shots were just two more potential units in creating the whole. The panoramic shot, or *pan*, with its horizontal sweeps from left to right or right to left, not only is functional for following a moving action, but also transfers its feeling of sweeping movement to the viewer. The eye is sensitive to such shifts in the field of vision, and it telegraphs this sensitivity to the brain, which translates it into a physical sensation. The *traveling shot* (also called a *track shot* or *tracking shot* because the camera's platform often rolled along, railroad style, on tracks) produces an even more magnified sensation of physical movement: the perfect tool for communicating the emotions of people riding rushing trains or walking alongside a river. Griffith's restraint in using the fast traveling shot—reserved for brief and occasional movements in the midst of a climactic chase or "race for life"—shows how thoroughly he understood its kinetic power.

Griffith also realized that just as the camera was not the servant of space, neither was the final editing of a film the servant of space or time. Most of the early films had followed a focal character slavishly from place to place, unable to leap to other places and other people regardless of the needs of the narrative. Griffith discovered that two places vastly separate in space or time could be brought together in the audience's mind. This back-and-forth editing technique, called the *cross-cut* (or parallel cut, switchback, or several other synonyms), which produced closeness out of distance, became a standard Griffith tool, fulfilling several primary functions. The cut could be a leap in space (from the victims of an attack to their potential rescuers), a leap in time (from a crisis to the earlier scene that caused it, or from modern to ancient customs), or a leap controlled by a character's mind (from the face of a sad woman to a shot of her husband lying dead on the battlefield). Such cross-cuts were attempts to interrelate and explore contrasts and parallels as well as to mirror and explore internal human sensations and thoughts in a concrete, externalized, visual form. A fourth kind of Griffith cross-cut served a more symbolic and intellectual purpose. In *A Corner in Wheat* (1909, released as *Corner in Wheat*), Griffith cross-cut between a lavish and lively banquet for the rich and a frozen portrait of the poor, waiting in line for a meager loaf of bread. The cross-cut clearly and effectively underlined the injustice of these simultaneous social conditions. When the Biograph management wondered whether audiences would be able to understand these shifts, Griffith's answer revealed both his insight and his influences: "Doesn't Dickens write that way?"

Griffith had learned, by trial and experience, what the earliest film theorist, Hugo Münsterberg, discovered by watching movies at almost the same time: Films were capable of mirroring not only physical activities, but also mental processes. Films could re-create the activities of the mind: the focusing of attention on one object or another (by means of a close-up), the recalling of memories or projecting of imaginings (by means of a flashback, flash forward, or mindscreen), the division of interest (by means of the cross-cut). Griffith had come to realize, much more firmly and consistently than Porter before him, the importance of the interplay between events presented on the screen and the spectator's mental synthesis of those events. Griffith's "discovery" was far more than a mere technique or assortment of devices; it was the way to make film narrative, storytelling with moving images, *consistently coherent and expressive.*

While Griffith's narratives learned to leap from space to space, they also began to deepen the texture of life within each of those spaces. Not content with the two-dimensional settings that dominated the interior scenes of most films of the era (so flat that many painted their furniture and props onto the backdrop), Griffith insisted on making his interior scenes appear as three dimensional as his outdoor ones. He thrust desks and tables into the shooting area, perpendicular to the walls of the set and to the frame line, rather than lining them up parallel to the walls, as they might be on the stage. He pushed pieces of furniture out at oblique angles to the set, the camera, and each other, and he shoved chairs, tables, and vases close to the camera itself, further increasing the sense of depth in the cramped quarters where the early Biograph films were shot. By 1909, Griffith's sense of the difference between theatrical and cinematic space was so clear that he could shoot a film, *The Drunkard's Reformation*, that used the device of a play-within-a-film and depended on our perceiving the contrast between shallow and deep space. By mid-1909, he was also taking his cast and crew out of New York City to shoot on location, first in upstate New York and later (1910) in California.

Griffith's innovations went beyond the camera and the editing table. Shortly before Griffith's debut in films came the debut of the electric light in the studios. Artificial lighting replaced the sun's harsh and inconstant performances. When film companies left Manhattan rooftops for the Bronx and New Jersey, they also left behind the sun and the muslin sheets that diffused its glare. But the first directors merely used the new arc lights as though they were the sun—to produce bright,

Fig. 4-3

Fig. 4-4

A Corner in Wheat: *Griffith's cross-cut from the banquet table of the rich to the bread line of the poor.*

even, untuned light with no regard to the tonal and narrative requirements of the scene. Does the scene take place indoors or out? During night or day? Should it feel harsh or gentle, cool or warm? Griffith—and G. W. ("Billy") Bitzer, the cameraman who experimented along with Griffith and taught him the ropes much as cinematographer Gregg

Toland later taught director Orson Welles—realized the importance of such questions and the ways lighting could be effective in answering them. But neither the flat, even sunlight nor all the arcs on full blast could duplicate the texture and atmosphere of indoor life, let alone create a mood or explore a character. And so—though they were not the first to do this (Porter did it in *The Seven Ages*, 1905, and Griffith had seen a similar effect while acting in Biograph's 1908 *The Music Master*)—Griffith and Bitzer lit *The Drunkard's Reformation* with a dim, flickering, low-angle light that convincingly imitated a fire's glow, giving the scene the look of real life and creating a hearth that was tonally and metaphorically related to the film's plot: the drunkard's returning from the theatre to the warmth and comfort of home and family.

Pippa Passes (also 1909, but six months and 68 movies later; it was Griffith's 159th Biograph) had much subtler and more ambitious lighting effects—including indicating the passage of time, from sunrise to night, with artificial light alone, and using light to characterize Pippa's personality as well as her room. *Pippa* was also Griffith's first attempt to tell four stories in one movie (in this case, Pippa's plus three that she passes by and affects). *Pippa Passes*, the first movie to be reviewed individually by the *New York Times*, was based on a poem by Robert Browning. Griffith often adapted classic stories, novels, plays, and even poems because he was sure that both he and the cinema could deal with great, complex material and important questions. Griffith's complete mastery of tonal lighting would culminate in 1919 with *Broken Blossoms*, which is dependent on lighting effects not only for its atmosphere and tone but also for the metaphoric contrast that underlies the film's moral system.

Griffith was as innovative with people as with machines. First, he demanded underacting: no more huge gestures and demonstrative poses. Because he had developed the expressive power of the camera and editing, he had the tools to allow a player to underact and still be understood. Second, he showed a much greater attention to selecting actors to play the roles, realizing that in a photographic medium, which depicts only visible surfaces, the actor's physical type was as crucial as acting style in the conveying of internal emotional and mental states.

Third, he developed a lexicon of gesture and movement, stylized enough to be clear and evocative, yet subtle enough to seem real and unaffected. As early as *A Corner in Wheat*, there is a basic stylistic difference in the movement and gesture of the poor and rich folks. While the poor farm people and customers at the bakery move slowly, with open, fluid hand gestures, the rich Wheat King and his cronies move briskly, with sharp, pointed, grasping hand gestures. This contrast between their styles of movement culminates in the awesome *tableau vivant* (resembling what today would be called a freeze-frame), when the movement of the poor becomes so slow that it stops altogether.

Fourth, Griffith shocked his employers with what they considered an obvious waste of time— rehearsals. The actors rehearsed the scenes before Griffith shot them. In an era when directors could scream their instructions during the shooting, Griffith's method seemed extravagant and unnecessary. It was crucial.

Finally, Griffith realized the applicability of one of the key artistic principles of the stage: A whole production requires an ensemble, not a collection of individual players. Griffith began building the Biograph stock company as a cohesive group of talented, attuned performers. His success is reflected in the number of important actors that Griffith's stock company produced, either for his own films or for the films of others. Mary Pickford, Lionel Barrymore, Lillian and Dorothy Gish, Mae Marsh, Blanche Sweet, Harry Carey, Henry B. Walthall, Robert Harron, and Donald Crisp all had worked for Griffith by 1913.

A close look at three Griffith one-reelers reveals his growing mastery of the film form. In *The Lonely Villa* (1909; onscreen title, *Lonely Villa*), his skill in cutting adds excitement to a melodrama about a mother and children who are attacked in their home by intruders. Early in the film, the fluid and rhythmic cutting adds pace to an exposition that establishes the husband's leaving home while the assailants hide outside in the bushes. The opening sequence is full of *match cuts*—shots from different angles and distances that have been assembled to give the impression of fluid, continuous movement—as the husband walks through the house and out the front door. These match cuts also establish—as systematically as the repeated locations in *Rescued by Rover*— the various domains of the house: the hallways and rooms that will play significant roles in the film's climactic sequence as the family retreats room by room from the intruders (the steady retreat into the protective depths of the home would become a consistent Griffith motif).

Fig. 4-5

Fig. 4-6

The Lonely Villa: *Griffith's
cross-cutting—the husband
gallops to the rescue . . . of the
family under attack at home.*

That climactic sequence reveals the power of Griffith's cross-cutting. As the intruders begin their assault, Griffith cuts to the husband, many miles distant and ignorant of the danger to his family. Luckily, his car breaks down and he calls home. The wife retreats to the telephone to tell her husband what's going on, and Griffith cuts to the husband as he listens to the phone and reacts; like the telephone line, the cut firmly links the two distant locations in the narrative flow despite the separation in space. Griffith then cuts back and forth between the besieged wife's trying to hold out against the attackers and the husband's getting help and rushing home to the rescue.

The Lonedale Operator (1911; onscreen title, *Lonedale Operator*) drives to its climax both more forcefully and more personally. The whole film shows a surer and more fluid technique than *The Lonely Villa*. The exposition, which establishes the relationship of the woman (Blanche Sweet) and her beau and that he is a railroad engineer and she a telegraph operator, is much clearer and more detailed than the exposition in the earlier film. The acting is much quieter, much more natural; the scene in which he courts her is credible and touching. Griffith captures the woman's spirit and her joy as she unexpectedly leaps on one of the railroad tracks and walks, tightrope-style, on the track while she talks to her beau. As soon as she and the beau separate, he to his engine and she to her office in the depot, Griffith builds toward the climax with a series of fluid match cuts showing her entering the office—door by door, as in *Villa*—and setting to work. In her office is a heavy bag full of money; two tramps see it.

Once the attack begins on her and her office, Griffith begins his relentless and rhythmic cross-cutting, which alternates among three clearly established locales: the attackers on the outside trying to get farther and farther into the depot, the operator in the inner office trying to protect herself from the assault, and the speeding train on its way to answer the distress signal that the operator intelligently wired to the next station. Griffith cuts with increasing rapidity from outside to inside to train, outside, inside, train, until the beau arrives just in time to find his sweetheart holding the culprits at bay with a "pistol" that is revealed in a close shot to be a wrench—a definitive use of the close view to show something important that cannot be seen or fully appreciated from a distance. The woman has brains as well as energy. She also has a sense of humor; she cheerfully acknowledges the comic, mock-gallant bow that the two vanquished but admiring tramps extend to her at the film's conclusion. Griffith was beginning to make his women not merely frail victims but forceful, clever, and able human beings who could take care of themselves when they had to.

Both of these films are pure stories of suspense with similar devices, although the later one has more human detail, greater realistic texture, and stronger narrative construction. *The New York Hat* (1912) dispenses with the melodramatic, suspenseful rescue altogether. With a screenplay by teenager Anita Loos (for which she received $25 and an offer to write more), featuring Mary Pickford and Lionel Barrymore, *The New York*

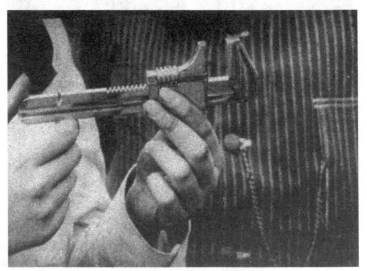

The Lonedale Operator: *the close shot reveals that the "gun" was a wrench.*

Fig. 4-7

Hat is the story of the birth of love. Young Mary (Pickford) longs to escape the drabness of her life and clothing. The young reverend of the parish (Barrymore) buys her a stylish hat from New York that she fancies. The town biddies start gossiping, linking Mary and the reverend in sin. The father cruelly tears up the hat. Finally the reverend silences their talk with a letter from Mary's dying mother asking him to look after the girl and buy her something nice with the money the mother had saved. He takes advantage of this opportunity to declare his romantic intentions; she accepts his proposal of marriage.

To establish Mary's longing for a hat, Griffith breaks down an expositional scene between Mary and her father into two different setups, alternating between a *two-shot* (a medium shot with two equally important figures) that includes both Mary and her father, and a close shot of Mary alone making wistful faces in a mirror. The two alternating setups in the scene establish the crucial emotional premise of the exposition: the gulf between Mary's little-girl relationship with her moralistic father and Mary's womanly longing to be pretty. Griffith makes the mirror a recurring thematic element in the film, for when Mary gets her hat, she returns to the mirror (and the camera to precisely the same setup) to see how charming she looks.

Fig. 4-8
The New York Hat: *the gentlemen thumb their noses at the gossipy matrons (the second from the right is Mae Marsh).*

The film is full of other sensitive touches. Mary's faces in the mirror are coy and charming; the snide, interfering town gossips are perfect comic caricatures. Griffith would draw fuller portraits of such nosy, close-minded, holier-than-thou reformers in *Intolerance* and *Way Down East.* Most personal of all in the film is the disdainful flick of the head that the church elders give, in unison, to the self-righteous gossips. Griffith is also thumbing his own nose at these morally nearsighted ladies of reform and "uplift." One must remember that in 1912 feminism was associated not only with female suffrage, but also with a moral cause that appalled Griffith: temperance. (The truth is, he drank.) The Women's Christian Temperance Union was the most powerful feminist organization in America, and its social pressure would lead to the Volstead Act and Prohibition by the end of the decade.

With a film like *The New York Hat,* Griffith had gone as far and as deeply as he could with the 15-minute picture. Those five years of one-reel films show Griffith laying the foundation not only for his technical achievements but also for the themes and motifs that would dominate his later films. He had made films about periods of American history (such as *1776 or The Hessian Renegades*, 1909), films about the contemporary social problems of poverty and of vice (such as *What Shall We Do With Our Old?*, 1910, released 1911, and *The Musketeers of Pig Alley*, 1912, the first gangster picture), films that were stylistically careful adaptations of literary classics (Shakespeare, Poe, Tennyson, Browning, Longfellow) and contemporary fiction (Frank Norris, Helen Hunt Jackson). Griffith had also begun making moral–religious allegories—Satan as the source of all human error and misery (*The Devil*, 1908); the choice between the life of sensual pleasure and the life of home and family (*The Two Paths*, 1910, released 1911) or between duty and family (*The Country Doctor*, 1909); the incompatibility of goodness and the realities of human existence (*The Way of the World*, 1910). Griffith particularly excelled at the close and affectionate study of American rural life—either the gently comic, tender study of rural customs and courtship, as in *A Country Cupid* (1911), or the compassionate view of the difficulty of rural living and survival, as in *A Corner in Wheat.* The latter

A Corner in Wheat: *an image of the natural unity of humans, animals, and field, based on Millet's painting* The Sowers. *The rest of the movie is based on Frank Norris's story "A Deal in Wheat."*

Fig. 4-9

film also provided a very early conscious reference to a specific painting—Jean-François Millet's *The Sowers*. Griffith was obviously bringing his entire 19th-century background into the movies— the paintings he had seen, the novels he had read, the plays he had performed, the Bible his mother and father had taught him.

Now that Griffith had discovered how to say things with cinema, he found he had things he wanted to say.

Two Reels and Up

Although no member of the audience yet knew Griffith's name (no Patents Company director or actor received screen credit until after 1912), they all knew that Biograph pictures were the best on the market. So did Griffith. By 1913, he wanted to break loose from the one-reel limit on his thoughts. He had earlier made two-reel films, but the General Film Company insisted on releasing them in two parts, one reel at a time. By popular demand, however, Griffith's 1911 two-reeler, *Enoch Arden*, based on the poem by Tennyson, had been shown as a single film shortly after it had been released as two; his first two-reeler, *His Trust* and *His Trust Fulfilled*, shot in 1910 and released separately in 1911, had no such luck.

Griffith's longer films used the earlier innovations to assimilate and communicate more

complex material. He wanted the images on the screen to illuminate his personal vision of good and evil. Griffith was not the cinema's first technician, nor even its first *auteur* (that would be Méliès), but he was its first moralist, poet, and master storyteller. A cliché in the criticism of Griffith is that his moral system is essentially that of the Victorian patriarchal sentimentalist. The positive values are social order, peace, intellectual freedom, loyalty, the home and family, womanhood/motherhood, children who are happy and safe, and marital fidelity. The negative values are, correspondingly, social change, war, censorship, treachery, the high life, sexual license, and the broken or abusive home. But these specific values are really consequences of Griffith's central vision rather than the vision itself.

The poles of Griffith's moral world are gentleness and violence. From gentleness come all the virtues of woman, peace, and the home. The figures of gentleness are almost always female. Griffith's young women are luminous, sweet, honest, springy, childlike, at times symbols of a delicate ideal rather than living, breathing creatures—but they can also be independent, brave, tough, and resourceful (like the Mountain Girl in *Intolerance*). Some of his women are monsters, too, and many are victims. For if Griffith saw gentleness as the ideal, he also saw

Fig. 4-10

Fig. 4-11
Griffith's framing in The Musketeers of Pig Alley. *Fig. 4-10: the tension of the oversized close-up (Elmer Booth and Harry Carey); Fig. 4-11: the social implication of money that arrives anonymously (to Elmer Booth) at the side of the frame.*

cruelty, lust, and violence as the danger. The figures of oppression and violence are almost always male, though his men can also be dedicated, honorable, valiant, and even gentle. In *Broken Blossoms*, for example, the hero is a loving, intelligent, kind, religious, artistically sensitive pacifist, and the villain is a stupid, violent lout who beats his gentle daughter to death; it is a violent, peace-loving tale of the destruction of love and tenderness—of broken blossoms.

Griffith's difficulty was integrating his vision into his melodramatic, plotty films. All too often Griffith fell back on two artificial devices that seemed superimposed on the films rather than integral to them. One of them was literally superimposed. He often thrust allegorical meanings on the films by superimposing angels and visions up in the heavens to comment on the earthly action. His allegory also extended to giving characters allegorical names—the Dear One, the Friendless One, Evil Eye. A second Griffith device was to soup up the film's meaning with purple, rhetorical titles that told the audience what moral conclusions it should draw from the actions it was about to witness. The titles constantly tell us that war's slaughter is *bitter* and *useless* (italics Griffith's), that women turn to social reform when they can no longer turn a man's fancy, that "the loom of fate weaves death." Griffith's titles (also called *intertitles* or *title cards*) were far more florid and didactic than the titles in other films of the era. Some of them even had footnotes. Griffith's last-minute rescues were so exciting partly because they required few or no titles.

Several features that Griffith shot between the one-reelers of 1912 and the epic films of 1914–16 show both his artistry in transition and his difficulties in wedding moral significance to film action. *Judith of Bethulia* (filmed 1913, released 1914) was the last picture Griffith made for Biograph. Just before *Judith*, he made one of his best two-reel Biographs, *The Battle at Elderbush Gulch* (released 1914), a western shot in California that had no difficulty in unifying action and moral significance. *Judith*, however, is a curious mixture of cinematic strengths and weaknesses. Because Griffith felt self-conscious about his biblical style and subject, his actors were much more stilted and much less carefully observed than in *The New York Hat*. Griffith's rendering of the evil of the invader, Holofernes,

is formulaic and hollow. The "orgies" in his tent, metaphoric for the man's evil mind, are represented as a series of clumsy and unevocative dances by the "Maids of the Fishes." Those Fish Maidens revealed a flaw in Griffith's vision that was to persist throughout his film career. Although Griffith knew what purity and goodness were, he either never really knew or could not honestly depict what sin and degeneracy were all about. The abstractness of the lives of sin and degeneracy that people lead in his films (a different matter from the cruelty, violence, and horror he dramatized so well) derive from the moralistic abstractions of Victorian melodrama, as in his little allegorical homily, *The Two Paths*, which signifies sin by having someone dance while holding a cocktail.

Balancing the film's artificiality and the thinness of the characters is Griffith's skill at cutting and construction. His opening expositional sequence effectively establishes the peacefulness and fertility of life in Bethulia, the importance of the well to its survival, and the thickness of the town walls for its defense. Here is Griffith's civilized ideal of peace and gentleness—an early version of John Ford's "garden in the desert." Then Griffith introduces the conqueror Holofernes and his army, the forces of violent destruction. The branches in the foreground part, revealing the awesome hordes ready to descend on peaceful Bethulia.

Griffith magnifies the horrifying intensity of the battle scenes with skillful cross-cutting from inside the walls to outside and back again. These battle scenes clearly show Griffith warming up for the huge sequences in *The Birth of a Nation*, although in *Judith* the battles feel pinched and confined by being anchored to the walls of the city. His cutting is much freer at the end of the film when the attacking hordes, without their leader, retreat in chaos. Griffith cuts from one shot in which the horses and men run furiously from screen right to screen left to the next in which men and horses stream down a hill at the top of screen left into a valley that is at the bottom of screen right. ("Screen right" is the right side of the screen as seen by the audience.) This collision of contrary movements would not only dominate the battles in *The Birth of a Nation*, but also contribute to Eisenstein's theory of the shock value of colliding images.

Four reels long, *Judith of Bethulia* was Griffith's longest film yet, but it was by no means the first feature film. The term *feature*, first used to describe any multiple-reel film, soon came to mean any film that was at least one hour long; at silent speed that meant at least four reels. The first feature film was made in Australia in 1906: *The Story of the Kelly Gang*, a four-reel movie about outlaw Ned Kelly, who wore a suit of armor, was directed by Charles Tait. The first feature made by Carl Laemmle's Universal Film Manufacturing Company (formerly IMP, later Universal) was the six-reel *Traffic in Souls* (1913), directed—without Laemmle's approval— by George Loane Tucker; a powerful film about the prostitution racket, it caused audiences literally to fight for seats. Since the nickelodeons refused to show features, being geared entirely toward the exhibition of one- and two-reelers, features were shown in legitimate theatres at higher prices (a quarter for *Traffic in Souls*, a dollar for *Quo vadis?*). Griffith was unaware of *The Story of the Kelly Gang* and the Australian features that followed it, but he certainly saw *Traffic in Souls* as well as two extraordinary spectacles imported from Italy: Enrico Guazzoni's *Quo vadis?* (1912, U.S. release 1913, eight reels) and Giovanni Pastrone's *Cabiria* (1914, 12 reels).

By late 1913, Griffith's innovativeness and the growing length and cost of his films had irked Biograph into kicking him upstairs, making him director of studio production and relieving him of the opportunity to direct movies personally. But Griffith wanted to make feature films—and the irony was, so did Biograph, which had noted the commercial success of *Queen Elizabeth;* they just didn't want to make long Griffith films.

Thoroughly angry, Griffith left Biograph for an independent company, Mutual/Reliance– Majestic (the production company was Reliance–Majestic; Mutual was the distributor), signing a contract with producer Harry Aitken that gave him the freedom to make one picture of his own each year in addition to several program pictures of the company's choosing. During that first year with Mutual, 1914, Griffith shot four features, each about five reels long: *The Battle of the Sexes; The Escape; Home, Sweet Home;* and *The Avenging Conscience.* It was a new beginning for Griffith; it was the end for Biograph, which folded in 1915. When Griffith left for

Mutual and California, he took Bitzer with him as well as nearly the entire Griffith stock company of actors. He also took out a full-page ad in the *New York Dramatic Mirror* in which he identified himself as the director of "all great Biograph successes," of which he listed 151 (out of the 455 movies he made at Biograph from 1908 to 1913, counting the two-reelers, whether released separately or together, as one film each). Griffith plainly asserted the right of the director to be called a film's creator and his personal right to be credited with "revolutionizing Motion Picture drama and founding the modern technique of the art."

The Avenging Conscience, Griffith's adaptation of Poe's "Annabel Lee" and "The Tell-Tale Heart," is intriguing and successful. In his study of the early motion pictures, the poet Vachel Lindsay used this Griffith film as a demonstration of the psychological power and intensity of the cinema. *The Avenging Conscience* concentrates intensely on the derangement and paranoid suspicions of a man (Henry B. Walthall) who believes he has murdered his guardian. The tight, methodical, nerve-racking editing of a sequence in which the killer is questioned by a relentless detective (Ralph Lewis) strongly influenced the Soviet filmmakers. Although Griffith awakens Walthall from his nightmare at the end of the film (Poe's actual murder becomes a Griffith dream), the nightmarish mood the film sustains for as long as the dream lasts is a chillingly impressive accomplishment.

The Birth of a Nation

For his own independent project for 1914, Griffith chose a novel by Thomas Dixon, *The Clansman.* The book appealed to Griffith for several reasons. It was a vast story with a strong hero, covering the final years in the graceful life of the old South before the Civil War; the turbulent, violent years of war; and the painful, political years of Reconstruction, during which the Ku Klux Klan arose to defend the rights of the whites. (The prewar and war scenes were Griffith's, not Dixon's.) In addition to this novel, Griffith also used material from Dixon's stage version of *The Clansman* and from another Dixon novel, *The Leopard's Spots,* all of which were extremely racist. Griffith, a Southerner whose father served in the Confederate Army, was attracted by Dixon's slant. Dixon, also a Southerner, saw the Reconstruction Era as a period of chaos in which the "civilized" white South, presented as the gallant underdog, struggled but survived. It was this film, with its inflammatory messages and dangerous social and political implications, that Griffith set out to make. Shooting began on the Fourth of July, 1914.

The project was vast: It took six weeks to rehearse and nine weeks to shoot, an incredible amount of time in an era when most films were cranked out in a week. It required thousands of people and animals and many huge and detailed indoor sets. Its cost, $110,000, was the most ever invested in a motion picture. At the film's official premiere in Clune's Auditorium in Los Angeles on February 8, 1915, audiences finally saw how huge Griffith's plan and project were. The 13-reel film was still called *The Clansman* at that opening. When the author of the novel finally saw the film, however, Dixon told Griffith, in his enthusiasm, that the original title was too tame. Griffith should call his film *The Birth of a Nation*. Dixon's point was that the nation was truly born only when the whites of the North and South united "in defense of their Aryan birthright." For Griffith, however, the "real nation" began when North and South united to heal the wounds of the Civil War and Reconstruction; in a 1915 interview he said that "there can exist no union without sympathy and oneness of sentiment." Though he did not acknowledge the racism that was part of that shared sentiment, he credited the KKK with beginning "the birth." Dixon's and Griffith's interpretations of the title were not all that different.

The retitled version opened in New York on March 3, 1915, still 13 reels long. But in response to social protests, Griffith deleted about nine minutes from the film (footage that has never been recovered), leaving it just over 12 reels long. The most complete surviving version lasts three hours.

The Birth of a Nation is as much a document of American social history as of film history. Though President Wilson, a former historian at Princeton, described the film as "like history written with lightning," its action openly praises the Ku Klux Klan. Wilson may well have offered the simile to help his old school chum, Dixon.

The film, which contributed significantly to the resurgence of the Klan in the 20th century, is a very difficult morsel for today's liberal or social activist to swallow. It was just as difficult for the liberals of 1915. The NAACP, the president of Harvard, social activist Jane Addams, and liberal politicians all damned the work for its bigoted, racist portrayal of the African American. The film was suppressed in some cities for fear of race riots; politicians spoke for or against it according to their dependence on the black vote. At a revival of the film some ten years after its original opening, mobs poured into Chicago to see it as well as to attend a Ku Klux Klan convention. With all the controversy over the film, it might be wise to look at Griffith's handling of the black man and woman before moving on to other aspects of the picture.

Two of the three villains—Lynch (the false reformer) and Sarah (the mistress of Congressman Stoneman)—are not pure Negroes but mulattoes. Both possess qualities that Griffith had already damned in whites—hypocrisy, selfishness, social reforming, and sexual license. That they were mulattoes may indicate that Griffith's main target was not the blacks but miscegenation—an objective of the third villain, a black soldier named Gus, when he forces his attentions on a Southern white girl. (His marriage proposal—a rape in the novel— causes Flora, the "little pet sister," to throw herself off a cliff to her death; in the novel, and reportedly in the censored footage, Gus is castrated by the KKK when they kill him.) The miscegenation theme flows through the movie like a poisonous river—in the scenes of the lecherous black legislature, in signs at the black-dominated polling place, in Lynch's attraction to Elsie (Lillian Gish) and Gus's to Flora (Mae Marsh), and in the outrages that drive the hero, Ben Cameron (Henry B. Walthall), to dream up the KKK. The mixing of bloods is one of the principal sources of "evil" in this picture. Griffith's stance against miscegenation stems from an assumption about blacks and whites that is perhaps more central to the film's offensiveness. For Griffith, whites are whites and blacks blacks; the white race is naturally superior; each race has "its own place." If Griffith's view seems outrageous—well, it is. Not every masterpiece is "politically correct," and part of dealing with *The Birth of a Nation* lies in examining, rather than explaining away, how offensive it is. Although Griffith recognized that slavery was the root of America's racial problems, his solution (proposed in part of the censored footage, an ending originally meant to balance the all-white harmony of the surviving conclusion) was to send the blacks back to Africa.

There are "good" blacks and "bad" blacks in Griffith's film. The good ones are the "faithful souls" who "know their place" and stay with their white family after the war. *Gone With the Wind*, 24 years newer fashioned than *The Birth of a Nation* and still adored by the public, makes the same distinction between good and bad blacks. Perhaps Griffith's most offensive scene is the one in which the empty state legislature suddenly (with the aid of a dissolve) springs to life, full of black lawmakers with bare feet on desks, swilling booze and eating fried chicken while they eye the white women in the gallery. But Griffith's treatment of these blacks is not an isolated expression of racial prejudice; it is a part of his lifelong distrust of the "evils" of social change and disruption. (To be consistent, of course, he should also have denounced the KKK as a disruptive social movement—but he evidently saw its actions as restorative.)

The key to *The Birth of a Nation* is that it is both strikingly complex and tightly whole. It is a film of brilliant parts carefully tied together by the driving line of the film's narrative. Its hugeness of conception, its acting, its sets, its

cinematic devices had not been equaled by any film before it and would not be surpassed by many that followed it. Yet surprisingly, for such an obviously big picture, it is also a highly personal and intimate one. Its small moments are as impressive as its big ones. Though Griffith summarizes an entire historical era in the evolution of the nation in general and the South in particular, his summary adopts an intimate, personal focus: two families, one from the North (the Stonemans), one from the South (the Camerons), who, despite the years of death and suffering, survive the Civil War and Reconstruction. The eventual marriage between the two white families becomes a symbol or emblem for Griffith's view of the united nation. Love, courage, racism, sincerity, and natural affection triumph over progressive movements and selfish reformers. The close observation of people and their most intimate feelings, the techniques of which Griffith had been developing for five years, propels the film, not its huge battle scenes, its huge dances and political meetings, or its detailed "historical facsimiles" of Ford's Theater and the Appomattox courthouse. The big scenes serve as the violent social realities with which the central characters must contend.

Even in the mammoth battle sequences Griffith never deserts his human focus. His rhythmic and energetic editing constantly alternates

Fig. 4-12

The Birth of a Nation: *Griffith's "historical facsimile" of Ford's Theater.*

between distant, extreme long shots of the battles and close concentration on the individual men who are fighting. Griffith takes the time for such touches as his cut from the living, fighting soldiers to a shot of the motionless dead ones who have found "War's peace," or his cuts from the valiant effort on the Union side to shots of a similar effort on the Confederate, including Ben Cameron's heroic charge of the Union lines, ramming the Southern flag down the barrel of a Union cannon. Griffith increases the power, the violence, the energy of these battle sequences by cutting on contrary movement across the frame, by cutting in rhythm with the action, and by cutting to different distances and angles that mirror the points of view of the different participants. But in the midst of such violence, Griffith takes time for quiet moments: the moment when the two boys, one Cameron and one Stoneman, die in each other's arms; the moment in which a mother on a hilltop views the invading army in the valley.

This shot, one of the most celebrated in the film, shows Griffith's control of the masking or irising effect, another of the techniques he and Bitzer had explored at Biograph. The *iris shot* masks a certain percentage of the frame, concentrating the viewer's attention completely on a circle of light within the blackened screen rectangle; for an example, see Figure 4-13. (The iris is a circular mask; other masks could create an image in the shape of a keyhole or show just half the screen—essential for the early matte shots, which were made in the camera—or be cut into any shape of light.) The iris, analogous to the theatre spotlight or today's zoom lens, either shrinks the audience's attention from the whole field to a single point or expands it from the single point to the whole field. G. A. Smith used an unmoving iris to frame his point-of-view close-ups in *Grandma's Reading Glass* and *As Seen Through a Telescope* (both 1900). In *The Birth of a Nation*'s most famous iris shot, Griffith begins tightly on the weeping mother's face and then irises out to reveal the awesome army below her, the cause of her sorrow. Of the many masking shots that reveal cause and effect, or event and context, in the picture, this one most brilliantly uses the iris to work with near and far views in a single but redefined visual field.

Griffith often uses animals as symbols or to define his characters and their emotional states.

In the early sequence depicting the gentle, peaceful life of the old South (analogous to the opening sequence of *Judith of Bethulia*), Doctor Cameron strokes two puppies. Significantly, one of the puppies is black and the other white; it is also significant that a kitten soon begins to play with the pups and starts a fight. The dogs become visual metaphors for Griffith's idealized prewar South, a happy mixture of different races and social classes, able to work out their own problems; the cat is the intrusive (Northern) outsider who hurts the white pup. Later in the film Griffith cross-cuts between the two lovers, Elsie and Ben, gently playing with a dove, and the savage Lynch as he mistreats a dog.

Griffith uses the main street in the town of Piedmont as a barometer of the film's emotional and social tensions. At the film's opening the street is full of people and carriages: active, sociable, friendly. As the Confederate soldiers first march off to war, the street becomes a carnival: fireworks, cheering townspeople, rhythmic columns of men. When "the little Colonel" (Ben Cameron) returns home after the war, the street is desolate, ruined, dusty. And finally, when the town is overrun with carpetbaggers and reconstructionists, gangs of blacks rove the street, which has become a very unfriendly, ungentle place. By capturing emotion in concrete images Griffith successfully renders feeling—rather than a parody of feeling, as in *Queen Elizabeth*.

Griffith never deserts the principles of his early melodramatic one-reelers as the means to keep his story moving. The suspense and excitement of Griffith's cross-cutting create the dramatic tension of many of the sequences—for example, Gus chasing the youngest Cameron sister through the woods until she jumps to her death. The most thrilling and upsetting sequence of all is the climax, in which Griffith gives us not one but two last-minute rescues. Griffith cross-cuts between two sets of victims and their common rescuers—the Ku Klux Klan—furiously galloping forth to eradicate the forces of rapine and death and social change. Not only is this rescue sequence Griffith's most complex up to this point, it is also his most sensitive to the kinetic excitement of editing rhythms and the moving camera.

But after the dust from the galloping climax has settled, Griffith makes fun of the blacks who retreat from the ballot box in fear of the Klan—

Fig. 4-13

From war's fury to "War's peace."

Fig. 4-14

and then, moving from the infuriating to the ridiculous, he celebrates the peaceful union of Elsie Stoneman and Ben Cameron with a super-imposed allegorical pageant in the heavens. Elsie and Ben see Christ replacing the military general; Christ cuts the Gordian knot, and all humanity rejoices as the City of God replaces the Kingdoms of the Earth. There are several remarkable things about this closing vision: its audacity, its irrelevance, and the passion and sincerity of Griffith's commitment to it. But exactly how is this City of God to become a reality? Certainly not by the efforts of the Ku Klux Klan alone. It is the evil in the human soul that must be exorcised. And once again Griffith reveals his nearsightedness in probing what he considers evil.

Ben Cameron (Henry B. Walthall) rams the Confederate flag down the throat of the Union cannon.

Fig. 4-15

The evil in the film is instigated by three people. They are evil (1) because they are evil or (2) because they have mixed blood. They succeed in doing evil because they entice the easily tempted Congressman Stoneman to the abolitionist cause. In the misguided Stoneman, Griffith takes another potshot at social reformers. Stoneman's temptation stems from his vanity despite his physical deformity (Griffith uses a club foot, parallel to the classic deformity of Shakespeare's Richard III, and an ill-fitting wig to define these traits) and from the "fatal weakness" of being sexually attracted to his mulatto housekeeper. According to the film's action, the chaos of the Civil War was the direct result of the nation's Stonemans, who became entangled in an evil of which they were totally ignorant or that they unwisely thought they could control. Even granting Griffith this preposterous premise, how is one to be sure the future contains no Stonemans? And how can one abolish slavery without abolition? *The Birth of a Nation*'s final vision is an innocent and mystical wish rather than the intellectual consequence of what preceded it. The film remains solid and en-

gaging as a big, complex narrative and a formal cinematic achievement, flimsy and repulsive as social theory.

Right after *The Birth of a Nation*, Griffith made *The Mother and the Law* (1915, released 1919), a tightly constructed melodrama starring Mae Marsh (the Dear One), Bobby Harron (the Boy), and Miriam Cooper (the Friendless One); it indicted reformers and big business while telling a powerful story of love, loss, and endurance. Aitken and Griffith, who had set up their own company (Epoch) to finance and distribute *The Birth of a Nation*, had by now left Mutual for the Triangle Film Corporation, whose big three were Griffith, Thomas Ince, and Mack Sennett. But the controversy over *The Birth* led to Griffith's pulling *The Mother and the Law* from Triangle's release schedule; instead, he and Aitken set up another separate company (Wark) to produce *Intolerance* (1916).

Griffith's treatment of blacks provoked public condemnation, even riots. The criticism stung Griffith deeply, since he felt he had gone to some trouble to present good and bad blacks *and* whites, as he had watered down or cut out the

Fig. 4-16

The street as emotional barometer: the total emptiness and loneliness of the "little Colonel's" return from the war.

Fig. 4-17

Ben (Walthall) and Elsie (Lillian Gish) see the City of God replacing the strife of the world—a matte shot made in the camera by masking the top left of the frame when shooting the lovers, then masking the bottom right when shooting the model of the heavenly city on the same footage.

novel's most inflammatory, racist passages. What he kept of Dixon's prose included "the opal gates of death"; what he left out sounded like this: "For a thick-lipped, flat-nosed, spindle-shanked negro, exuding his nauseating animal odour, to shout in derision over the hearths and homes of white men and women is an atrocity too monstrous for belief." The KKK had permanently disbanded in 1869, and Dixon nostalgically dedicated his 1905 "historical romance," *The Clansman*, to the memory of his "Scotch-Irish" uncle, a "Grand Titan Of The Invisible Empire"; unfortunately,

The Birth of a Nation used the medium so powerfully that Griffith's film unexpectedly but indisputably inspired the birth of the 20th-century Klan in late 1915.

Griffith began defending himself against the charges of bigotry and hatred; he angrily protested the film's suppression in several cities and wrote *The Rise and Fall of Free Speech in America*, a pamphlet that championed the "Freedom of the Screen." *Intolerance* was to be his cinematic defense, his pamphlet in film form against intellectual censorship. Fortunately for Griffith, *The Birth of a Nation* became the first authentic blockbuster in film history, earning untold millions of dollars; he would need his entire share of that money for *Intolerance*.

Intolerance

Intolerance was Griffith's longest, greatest, and most narratively complex film. It cost $1.9 million to produce—more than 15 times the cost of *The Birth of a Nation*. It was 14 reels long, though only about 12 reels survive. A formal masterpiece and an epic statement, its conception was so vast that it was to *The Birth* as *The Birth* was to *Judith of Bethulia*.

Intolerance told not one story but four. In Belshazzar's Babylon (6th century B.C.), the evil high priest conspires against the wise and just ruler, betraying the city to the Persian conqueror, Cyrus; by the end of this story, every "good" character is dead. In Judea, the close-minded Pharisees intrigue against Jesus; ultimately, the gentle savior is sent to the cross. In Reformation France (16th century A.D.), ambitious courtiers persuade the Catholic king to slaughter all the Protestant Huguenots on St. Bartholomew's Day, a massacre that includes the rape and murder of a young Protestant and the killing of her fiancé. In 20th-century America (the "Modern Story," which used to be *The Mother and the Law*), strikers are gunned down, a young man (called "The Boy") is falsely convicted of murder, and his wife loses her baby thanks to the meddling of a group of reformers; the facts eventually surface to save the Boy from the gallows. (In the release print of *Intolerance*, they get the baby back, as Griffith felt the need of a happy ending. In *The Mother and the Law*, released in 1919, the baby dies after the mother loses custody. When

Griffith edited *Intolerance* into a finished, "standard" version in 1926, he let the baby disappear into the reformers' poor care and did not resolve the issue.)

Instead of telling one story after the other, as in *Pippa Passes* or *Home, Sweet Home*, Griffith tells these stories all at once, interweaving them—and 2,500 years of history—into an intellectual and emotional argument, a demonstration that love, diversity, and the little guy have always had to struggle against the overwhelming forces of hypocrisy, intolerance, and oppression. Because the colliding, streaming, *juxtaposed fragments* of these stories implied an *idea* that went beyond the "moral" of each individual story, making the whole greater than the sum of its parts, *Intolerance* is recognized as the cinema's first great Modernist experiment in what Sergei Eisenstein would later call intellectual (or dialectical) montage. Indeed, Griffith's editing influenced the Soviets as much as his psychological lighting and control of *mise-en-scène* influenced the Germans. If *The Birth of a Nation* set the course for the American cinema, *Intolerance* did so for the Soviet cinema and *Broken Blossoms* for the German. The next American film to be organized this complexly would be *Citizen Kane* (1941); the next to be structured as a dialectical montage would be *The Godfather Part II* (1974).

The four stories are linked across time and space by the bold editing and by their consistent theme: the machinations of the selfish, the frustrated, and the inferior; the divisiveness of religious and political beliefs; the triumph of injustice over justice; the pervasiveness of violence and viciousness through the centuries. Also tying the stories together is Griffith's brilliant control of editing, which keeps all the parallels in the stories quite clear and which creates an even more spectacular climax than that of *The Birth of a Nation*. In *Intolerance*, there are three frenzied climaxes: one successful and two *failed* last-minute rescues (the Christ story is not cut for suspense). The excitement in each of the narrative lines reinforces the others, all of them driving furiously to their breathtaking conclusions. Griffith's last-minute rescues cross-cut through the centuries.

Finally, tying the four stories together, much as Pippa did, is a symbolic mother-woman, rocking a cradle, bathed in a shaft of light, representing the eternal evolution of humanity through time and

Fig. 4-18
Intolerance: *the full-scale walls of Babylon.*

fate (the three Fates sit behind her), fulfilling the purpose of the creator. The cradle, inspired by Whitman's lines, "Endlessly rocks the cradle, Uniter of Here and Hereafter," is a transitional device, an emblem of unity, and a symbol of history, out of which all the epochs and stories flow, and in which they are united. The woman is a figure of peace, of light, of fertility (sometimes flowers bloom in her cradle), of ultimate goodness that will eventually triumph. She is played by Lillian Gish, who assisted Griffith in the editing of *Intolerance.*

The film's bigness is obvious: the high walls of Babylon, the hugeness of the palace (and the immense moving camera shot that Griffith uses to span it), the battles, the care with each of the film's periods and styles. The costumes, the lighting, the acting styles, the decor, and even the intertitles are so distinct in each of the four epochs that viewers know exactly where they

are: in the squalid, drab poverty of a contemporary slum, the elegant tastefulness of the French court, or the garishness of ancient Babylon. But as with *The Birth of a Nation, Intolerance* is a big film that works because of its little, intimate moments. The film revolves around the faces of women—from the bubbling, jaunty, comically vital face of the Mountain Girl in the Babylonian Story to the luminous, tear-stained, soulful faces of Brown Eyes in the French Story and the little Dear One in the Modern Story. *Intolerance* makes it perfectly clear that social chaos takes its toll on the women. Significantly, Griffith's symbol of historical continuity is also a woman. Along with the close-ups of faces, the film is equally attentive to close-ups of hands, particularly in the Modern Story: the Dear One's wrenched hands—the rest of her body cinematically unnecessary—as the judge condemns her husband; her hand clutching one of her baby's booties after the social uplifters have carried the infant away.

The film is also rich in the same kind of metaphoric detail found in *The Birth of a Nation*. The Dear One shows her humanity and tenderness as she lovingly throws grain to her chickens; when she moves to the oppressive city, she keeps a single flower in her flat, a metaphor for all that is simple and natural and struggling to live. Yet another moving detail is the little cart pulled by two white doves in the Babylon sequence—a metaphor for the tender, fragile love between Belshazzar and his queen and for the peaceful ways of their court. After the two and the Mountain Girl have been slain, Griffith hauntingly irises out to a view of the tiny cart and doves, a touching evocation of a beauty that was but is no longer.

Griffith's technique is as effective at conveying hatred as it is at evoking tenderness. A deeply felt film, *Intolerance* makes it clear what Griffith detests: those who meddle and destroy, those who take advantage of the poor, schemers, hypocrites, and monsters of lust and power. One of Griffith's devices of caricature is the crosscut—particularly effective in the sequence in which he captures the cold inhumanity of the factory owner. Griffith cuts from the shots of the workers being mowed down by military or hired gunfire (violent, quick cutting, frenetic) to a shot of the owner of the factory sitting alone in his vast office (a long shot, perfectly still, that emphasizes the size of the office and the moral smallness and isolation of the big businessman). The contrast clearly defines the man's responsibility and his unsympathetic inhumanity.

Although Griffith's dislikes are clear, the intellectual cement uniting the four stories (and the rocking cradle) is a bit muddy. The film could as easily have been called "Injustice" or "Love's Struggle" as *Intolerance*. Griffith was interested in the word "intolerance" because he felt himself the victim of it, but in none of the four stories does intolerance seem so much the cause of evil as blind human selfishness, nastiness, and ambition (much as in *The Birth of a Nation*). It is most coherent when read as an attack on the illegitimate exercise of power by capitalists, zealots, and kings. But when the film ends with its almost obligatory optimistic vision—more superimposed angels in the heavens; the fields of the prison dissolve into fields of flowers—we once again witness an interpolated wish rather than a consequence of the film's action. Though there may be hope in the Boy's last-minute reprieve, it hardly seems enough to balance a whole film of poverty, destruction, suffering, and injustice.

The audience of 1916 found the film confusing and unpleasant. Unlike *The Birth of a Nation*, *Intolerance* aroused no social protest; it aroused little audience interest of any kind. Perhaps it was unpopular because it asked too much from its audience. Or perhaps the film was a victim of historical accident, its pacifistic statement antipathetic to a nation preparing itself to send its soldiers "Over There." Thomas Ince's pacifistic *Civilization* (1916) had made money only six months earlier. Whatever the reason, *Intolerance* was a financial disaster, costing Griffith all his profits from *The Birth of a Nation*. The failure of *Intolerance* began Griffith's financial dependence on other producers and businessmen, from which he would never recover.

1917–31

The cliché of Griffith criticism is that with *Intolerance* the director reached a peak from which the only direction was down. The final years of Griffith's career are often dismissed as years of repetition, a retreat into sentimentality, and a lack of attention to audience tastes. No matter how good some of the later pictures are, there is some truth in the truism. In the final period of his career, Griffith was less of an innovator; the cinematic advances of his youth had solidified into a stable, controlled mastery of the film form beyond which he rarely went. Some of his pictures are more striking in their parts than in their wholes: *Hearts of the World* (1918), *America* (1924). After the fiasco of *Intolerance*, Griffith also had to look to his wallet, a concern that led to uninspired program pictures to fulfill contracts: *The Idol Dancer* (1920), *One Exciting Night* (1922, dull), *Sally of the Sawdust* (1925, with W. C. Fields), *That Royle Girl* (1926, also with Fields), and more.

In 1917, Griffith went to Europe with Billy Bitzer, Robert Harron, Lillian and Dorothy Gish, and other members of his brilliant ensemble who had, under his guidance, refined the arts of cinematography and film acting to an extent unparalleled in film history. Their achievements

Fig. 4-19

Fig. 4-20

Fig. 4-21

Intolerance: *the faces of women. Fig: 4-19: the Mountain Girl (Constance Talmadge); Fig: 4-20: the little Dear One (Mae Marsh); Fig: 4-21: the poignant detail—losing consciousness, the Dear One grasps the bootie of her stolen baby.*

were comparable and related to those of Griffith, who had gone beyond all previous editing techniques in establishing absolutely that the shot, not the scene, was the basis of film construction and had learned how to break down and reconstruct actions, placing the emphasis wherever he wished: on a hand, a twitch, a prop, a mood. (Raoul Walsh, who played the role of John Wilkes Booth in *The Birth of a Nation*, had already left to direct his own films; his 1915 gangster picture, *Regeneration*, reveals Griffith's influence in every shot, but it is often sharper, more realistic, and even grotesque, anticipating the work of another Griffith pupil, Erich von Stroheim.) Their object in Europe was to film the First World War (1914–18) for Artcraft, a production company headed by Adolph Zukor, whose films were released by Famous Players–Lasky, soon to be reorganized as Paramount. Designed as a propaganda film for the British war effort and to show Americans what the suffering and valor of the war were all about, the 12-reel *Hearts of the World* deserted the labyrinth of *Intolerance* for the relatively linear narrative style Griffith was to use until the end of his career. This decidedly unpacifist film, one of whose aims was to urge America to join the war, aroused and manipulated emotion in the manner of *The Birth of a Nation*—but without causing riots (by the time the film came out, America was in the war anyway). There is no significant change in the propagandistic narrative formula when the KKK, charging to the rescue, becomes the cavalry or anyone or anything the movie has made the audience like.

Some of the Artcraft films Griffith made between 1917 and 1919, most of them six or seven reels long, were among his finest work. The best ones used a relatively small narrative canvas; their simple stories were told with rich emotion and plain humor, unpretentious lyricism and sudden suspense, all perfectly controlled. *A Romance of Happy Valley* (1918, released 1919), *True Heart Susie* (1919), and *The Greatest Question* (1919, made not for Artcraft but for his next employer, First National)—all set in something like rural Kentucky, shot by Bitzer, and starring Lillian Gish and Bobby Harron (who died in 1920)—let Griffith work with material he knew and loved. These are melodramas, often contrived, but the people in them feel real and so do

their problems (ambition, fidelity, death, the search for simplicity and happiness, the war against evil and deceit, the need to see into people's hearts). The sincerity of Griffith's engagement with these films—their settings, characters, and moral questions—is apparent and rewarding. Between *True Heart Susie* and *The Greatest Question* he made his lyrical masterpiece, *Broken Blossoms*, and his only full-length western, *Scarlet Days* (starring Richard Barthelmess). He bought *Broken Blossoms* back from Zukor and released it through United Artists, an independent distribution company that he, Charles Chaplin, Mary Pickford, and Douglas Fairbanks founded in 1919. For *Broken Blossoms*, which cost $3 to see (*The Birth* had cost $2 in its big-city runs; normal films cost well under $1) and which made a mint, Griffith designed a system of lights, concealed above and below the screen, that would wash through the image and add their colors to those that were already on the tinted and toned print— a music of light that perfectly complemented and was coordinated with the music that he co-wrote for the film. *The Birth* and *Intolerance* had also been tinted—blue for night scenes, sepia for interiors, and so on—and accompanied by an orchestra playing music co-written by Griffith, but no film before or since had those lights; the machine was reconstructed in 1980, and Lillian Gish toured the country with it, showing *Broken Blossoms* in its original form to a new generation.

In 1920, at the studio he had set up in Mamaroneck, New York, he made two awful films (*The Idol Dancer* and *The Love Flower*) and the classic melodrama *Way Down East*. He followed that with *Dream Street* (1921, a lyrical allegory with haunting, intriguing moments), *Orphans of the Storm* (1921, released 1922, a 12-reel melodrama set in the French Revolution, his last film with either of the Gish sisters), *The White Rose* (1923, a deeply moving film starring Mae Marsh), the clunker *America*, the superb *Isn't Life Wonderful* (1924, starring Carol Dempster; significantly, the last film for which he wrote the script), five more duds, and his last silent, *Lady of the Pavements* (1929), a great-looking love story starring Lupe Velez and photographed by Karl Struss, *assisted* by Bitzer.

Part of the story here is that Griffith and Bitzer found it difficult to work together after 1920; at times Bitzer worked alongside other cinematographers (notably Hendrik Sartov, who began by doing soft-focus shots for *Broken Blossoms* and co-shooting *Way Down East*), but there were many films (*Isn't Life Wonderful* among them) that Bitzer did not shoot at all. Griffith also lost some of his top players in the early 1920s—crucially Lillian Gish, who later became a producer at MGM (five films including *The Wind*, 1928) and continued to perform on stage, in films (her sound films include *The Night of the Hunter*, 1955, and *The Whales of August*, 1987), and on television; when she died in 1993, at the age of 99, an essential part of the cinema passed into history. Griffith's new leading lady, Carol Dempster, was watchable in *Dream Street* and good in *Isn't Life Wonderful*, but otherwise simply a terrible actress with bad posture, no subtlety, and a kind of hungry vanity. Unlike Gish, she could not "carry" a picture, let alone deliver a compelling close-up—but Griffith kept using her, as she was doubtless using him. Griffith's artistic and personal judgment began to falter, which is why Bitzer grew impatient with him.

As an example of bad artistic judgment and financial troubles, the following should suffice: Griffith cut into the negative of *Intolerance* in 1919, without making a copy first, so as to assemble two features, *The Mother and the Law* and *The Fall of Babylon* (with a ridiculous ending in which the unkilled Mountain Girl falls in love with the weak, untrustworthy man she avoided throughout the film, and they leave the ruins of Babylon together). Aside from how bad *The Fall of Babylon* was, and how reasonable a business decision it was to release *The Mother and the Law* on its own, the point is that the negative of *Intolerance* was all but destroyed. Two reels' worth of footage was lost, most of it forever. Griffith made this idiotic, desperate decision the same year he released four masterpieces (*A Romance of Happy Valley*, *True Heart Susie*, *Broken Blossoms*, and *The Greatest Question*) and helped to found United Artists.

Broken Blossoms and *Way Down East*

Despite Griffith's troubles, at least two of the late films rank in power and interest just behind the two great epics. In fact, *Broken Blossoms* (1919) and *Way Down East* (1920) are more entertaining and easier for today's audiences to sit through than either *The Birth* or *Intolerance*.

Fig. 4-22
***Josephine Crowell in* The Greatest Question.**

Broken Blossoms is Griffith's most polished, most finished gem, a tight triangle story of one woman between two men. Out of this triangle, rather than from Griffith's intertitles and allegorical visions, come the film's values. If the film is less weighty than the epics, it is also less pretentious. To shift terms, one could call *The Birth of a Nation* an epic, *Intolerance* a film essay or tract, and *Broken Blossoms* a lyric—an emotional poem made to be sung. Like so many Griffith films, *Broken Blossoms* is an adaptation of a work of fiction—Thomas Burke's "The Chink and the Child," from his collection *Limehouse Nights*. As with *The Clansman*, Griffith took another man's work and made it his own, as the film's metaphoric title so clearly shows (the cleaned-up subtitle, however, was "The Yellow Man And The Girl").

The film is Griffith's most explicit and poetic hymn to gentleness. It is also a film of grime and failure, terrible violence and absolute horror. Even so, an aura of tenderness and idealism suffuses the film. The gentle man in the film comes from China to bring the message of the gentle

Buddha to the vicious, violent West. Once he arrives in London's dockside slum, Limehouse, Cheng Huan (Richard Barthelmess) runs into the "sordid realities of life"—gambling, whoring, opium smoking—that constitute life in the West. He virtually gives up.

Then Griffith switches to the female figure of gentleness, Lucy (Lillian Gish). Raised by a prize fighter, Battling Burrows (Donald Crisp), Lucy is an unloved child who spends her time wandering around the Limehouse district, trying to scrape up enough tin foil to buy herself a flower. Flowers are the primary visual metaphor for gentleness in the film, as the title indicates. Lucy's gentleness, however, like Cheng Huan's, runs into sordid realities. Her reality is her father, Burrows, a brutal alcoholic who uses Lucy as both slavish servant and defenseless punching bag. One of the most poignant touches in the film is Burrows's insistence that Lucy smile for him,

regardless of her real feelings. Since she is unable to summon a genuine smile, she uses two fingers to force one. Gish improvised that gesture in a rehearsal, and Griffith decided to use it throughout the film.

Cheng Huan is attracted by Lucy's gentle purity, which he instantly perceives. They first meet, appropriately, over the purchase of a flower. She later collapses in his shop after a terrible beating by her father. Cheng Huan enthrones her in his room as a Princess of Flowers, and the two celebrate a brief but beautiful time apart from the world. Lucy even smiles without the aid of her fingers for the first time, and Cheng Huan's one weak moment of animal lust (brilliantly communicated by a painfully tight close-up) is soon conquered by his realization of the ideal perfection of his guest and their relationship.

But the world breaks in on the paradise. Burrows finds her at Cheng Huan's, trashes the

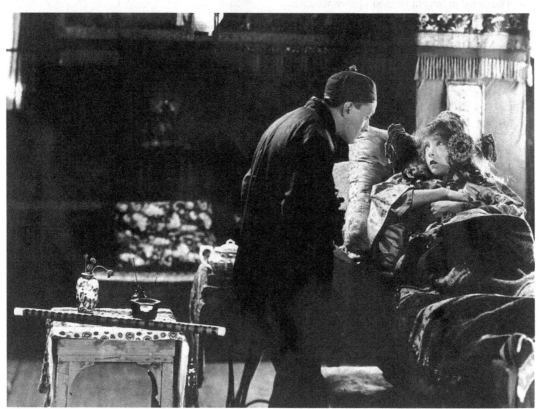

Fig. 4-23
Broken Blossoms: *Cheng Huan (Richard Barthelmess) and Lucy (Lillian Gish).*

place, drags her back to their slum room, and begins his inevitable attack. She retreats to a closet; he smashes it open with a hatchet. Gish creates one of the most accurate renditions of human frenzy in screen history as Lucy turns helplessly in a circle inside the closet—trapped, frantic, terrified. Cheng Huan, rushing to the rescue, arrives too late, and Burrows beats Lucy to death. Her final gesture is to use two fingers to raise her mouth into a smile. Cheng Huan shoots Burrows, takes Lucy's body back to his room, then stabs himself. Blossoms, despite their loveliness, cannot survive for long in a violent, unkind world. A perfectly nuanced and deeply moving drama, *Broken Blossoms* broke new narrative ground by proving that a movie could have an unhappy ending and still please an audience. And its perfect control of *mise-en-scène*, from its sets and costumes to its lighting, enhanced the control of tone and mood beyond anything Griffith or anyone else had yet achieved.

Way Down East, although more uneven than *Broken Blossoms*, is both moving and exciting. The most famous sequence in the film is the climax, the last-minute rescue of Anna Moore (Lillian Gish) who is floating toward the deadly falls. Anna Moore's unfortunate sexual error—to have "married" a rogue in a bogus ceremony and then borne him a child who died, in all of which she was honorable and innocent—has been discovered by her adopted down-east (Maine) family; she rushes out of their house into a blinding blizzard, the savagery of the wind and snow becoming visual metaphors for the chaos and misery in her own heart and the heartlessness of her oppressors. Then Griffith's cross-cutting, his most enduring tool, drives the film's climax by alternating among three separate but related locations: Anna Moore alone in the storm, prostrate on a moving ice floe; her down-east boyfriend (Richard Barthelmess), searching for her—the agent of her rescue; and the ominous falls toward which the ice is moving—the danger from which she must be saved. The river was in Vermont, and the falls were Niagara Falls; Griffith merely spliced in bits of stock footage. Here was the ultimate proof of the logic of cross-cutting: Although the actress was really nowhere near any falls (especially Niagara), the audience felt Anna's nearness because of the cuts and narrative links that bound the three locations. Soviet filmmakers would soon seize on this editing principle, naming it "creative geography."

The uneven, weaker parts of *Way Down East* are the plotty remnants of the original stage melodrama, whose rights Griffith purchased for $175,000 (far more than the entire budget of *The Birth of a Nation* and a sure indication of the film industry's rising costs). Everything in *Way Down East* related to the evildoings of the rich folks reveals the artificial, heavy, and abstract hand of Griffith trying to depict a lifestyle for which he had neither sympathy nor understanding. After all, rich people have more things to do with their money than hold fancy dress balls, act snobbish toward the pure of heart but poor of purse, and seduce innocent virgins with fake marriage vows. But the film has two compensating virtues. First, there is the face of Lillian Gish: radiant, luminous, determined, charming, alive. If the problems that the plot gives her seem contrived, the touching reactions of her eyes and mouth make sense of them. Griffith knew the power of the Gish face; he rivets our gaze on it with close-up after close-up, most of them lit to give her hair a shiny, diaphanous glow. The real action of the film takes place not in society but on her face.

The second virtue of the film is Griffith's tender, careful, comic observation of down-east life. He loves the warmth of these rural people, their pettiness, laziness, and short-sightedness as well as their sincerity, simplicity, and compassion. In down-east life Griffith saw a mirror for the gentle and fertile life of the South as well as the country life he had treated with such affectionate humor in *A Romance of Happy Valley* and *True Heart Susie*.

The Struggle

Several theories attempt to explain Griffith's creative decay in the final years of his career, years in which he struggled to find work, to move the audience as he had before, and to control his drinking. Perhaps he ran out of ideas, both technically and intellectually. Or he may not have found the right challenge. There might never have been an *Intolerance* to surpass *The Birth of a Nation* if the controversy over the first epic hadn't fired Griffith's anger and imagination.

Lillian Gish in Broken Blossoms: *the smile. The sides of her mouth pushed up by her fingers, her eyes wide with fear, Gish creates an unforgettable image of terror and submission.*

Fig. 4-24

Fig. 4-25

Griffith on location. Fig. 4-25: directing a race for life in Intolerance; *the driver, Tod Browning, later directed* Dracula *and* Freaks. *Fig. 4-26: with Billy Bitzer (left) in the snow of* Way Down East.

Fig. 4-26

Fig. 4-27

The river scenes for Way Down East *were shot in White River Junction, Vermont; Lillian Gish on location.*

He may well have been unable to do his best work in regimented studios. Indeed, *Isn't Life Wonderful* is so fine partly because it was shot outside any studio, on location in Germany during its disastrous postwar hyperinflation (where a bushel of banknotes *might* buy a loaf of bread; the exchange rate in 1923 rose to 4.2 trillion marks per dollar). Shot on the streets, with many nonprofessionals in the cast, *Isn't Life Wonderful* was the first precursor of Italian Neorealism. It was also his last independent production until *The Struggle*.

Another popular theory is that Griffith's ideas had become outmoded in the 1920s. The flapper morality of the Jazz Age rejected the sentimentality of Griffith's Victorianism. Belasco's melodrama had been supplanted by urbane, domestic comedy-dramas of sexual innuendo and visual wit. The high life of dancing while holding a cocktail, which Griffith depicted so blackly and so clumsily, was exactly what audiences vicariously wanted to experience. Griffith no longer gave the public what it wanted.

The truth probably lies somewhere among the various theories. Griffith certainly seemed to be running out of creative gas. As his pictures became more and more formulaic, he was more

and more dependent on public acceptance of his formulas—but his formulas, as formulas, were 10 to 20 years out of date. The Griffith mastery when he was working at the top of his powers could make Victorian formulas exciting; *Broken Blossoms*, *Way Down East*, and *Orphans of the Storm*, all of which were heavily Victorian and released during the Jazz Age, were huge box-office successes. When the mastery flagged, however, audiences saw the bare bones of sentimentality and took themselves to other pictures. There were also some bad films with no Victorian elements.

One thing his failure proves is that the film industry had already become a business in which "you're only as good as your last picture."

The final years of Griffith's career were scarred by his disastrous fling with the sound picture. In *Abraham Lincoln* (1930), a film that won high praise at the time, he returned to American history—but despite a moving and natural performance by Walter Huston as Lincoln, the result was narratively inert. *The Struggle* (1931) was a fervent, sentimental, sociological study of alcoholism and one man's struggle to overcome it—a struggle about which Griffith knew firsthand. The script was by John Emerson

Fig. 4-28

Fig. 4-29
***Waiting in line for food during a period of disastrous inflation. Fig. 4-28: Isn't Life Wonderful** (1924),
shot on location in Germany by Griffith, anticipated some of the techniques and values of the
Neorealists; here Carol Dempster (fourth from the left, in wide-brimmed hat) checks to see how much
the price of pork has gone up since she first got in line. **Fig. 4-29: The Joyless Street** (1925), set in
Vienna during the same economic disaster, shot on a set by G. W. Pabst. Note the differences between
street and studio realism.*

and Anita Loos, who had gotten her start with *The New York Hat*; the sound recording was of high quality. The budget was low, so the film was shot on the streets of New York and looks it: *The Struggle* has, in its best moments, a tough flavor of suffering and authenticity. It also, in typical Griffith fashion, blames alcoholism on Prohibition (1919–33), which converted a beer- and wine-drinking nation to whiskey. Audiences laughed it off the screen in a week.

The Hollywood brass was convinced that Griffith—without whom none of them would have had a job—was old fashioned, that his day was done. He spent his final 17 years barred from an art that he had practically fashioned by himself. He received an honorary Oscar in 1935, but the only job he got was as a consultant on purely visual acting for Hal Roach's *One Million B.C.* (1940), parts of which he appears to have directed. Since the cave people in that film grunt and gesture rather than speak, Roach needed someone to teach the movies how *not* to talk. Public praise for Griffith's achievements could not ease the bitterness of his rejection by the business. He died alone in Hollywood in 1948.

For Further Viewing

FILMS

D. W. GRIFFITH (1875–1948)

Griffith's Biograph films, including: *The Adventures of Dollie* and *After Many Years* (1908); *Those Awful Hats, The Drunkard's Reformation, What Drink Did, The Lonely Villa* (or *Lonely Villa*), *The Country Doctor, The Mended Lute, 1776 or The Hessian Renegades, In Old Kentucky, Pippa Passes, A Corner in Wheat* (or *Corner in Wheat*), and *The Redman's View* (1909); *The Way of the World, The Unchanging Sea, Ramona, Over Silent Paths,* and *The Sorrows of the Unfaithful* (1910); *His Trust* and *His Trust Fulfilled, The Two Paths, What Shall We Do With Our Old?, The Lonedale Operator* (or *Lonedale Operator*), *The Broken Cross, Enoch Arden,* and *A Country Cupid* (1911); *The Girl and Her Trust, An Unseen Enemy, The Painted Lady, The Musketeers of Pig*

Alley, and *The New York Hat* (1912); *The Mothering Heart* (1913); *The Battle at Elderbush Gulch,* and *Judith of Bethulia* (1914)
Home, Sweet Home (1914)
The Avenging Conscience (1914)
The Birth of a Nation (1915)
Intolerance (1916)
Hearts of the World (1918)
A Romance of Happy Valley (1919). Completed 1918
True Heart Susie (1919)
Broken Blossoms (1919)
The Fall of Babylon (1919)
The Mother and the Law (1919)
The Greatest Question (1919)
Way Down East (1920)
Orphans of the Storm (1922). Completed 1921
The White Rose (1923)
Isn't Life Wonderful (1924)
Lady of the Pavements (1929)
Abraham Lincoln (1930)
The Struggle (1931)

DVDs

Cabiria (1914, **Giovanni Pastrone**). Kino Video. One of the Italian spectacles that influenced Griffith.
The Country Doctor (1909, **D. W. Griffith**) is in *More Treasures from American Film Archives* (see Chap. 3 list).
Griffith Masterworks. Kino Video. A mixed bag. *Intolerance* looks fine but runs too slowly. *Broken Blossoms* has the wrong tints, no toning, and a new score instead of the original (for a better experience, see the Connoisseur Video VHS). However, *The Birth of a Nation, Orphans of the Storm,* and the Biographs are fine. The 23 Biographs include *The Adventures of Dollie, Those Awful Hats, A Corner in Wheat, His Trust, His Trust Fulfilled, Enoch Arden, An Unseen Enemy, The Painted Lady, The Musketeers of Pig Alley, The New York Hat,* and *The Battle at Elderbush Gulch.* Extras include *Rescued from an Eagle's Nest,* the happy ending of *The Fall of Babylon,* the song "Broken Blossoms," documents and

clips concerning the 1992 re-release of *The Birth of a Nation,* the prologue (with **Griffith** and **Walter Huston**) to the sound re-issue of *The Birth of a Nation,* footage of Griffith's funeral, a radio eulogy by **Erich von Stroheim,** short talks by **Orson Welles** and **Lillian Gish,** several documentaries, and galleries of stills.

Griffith Masterworks 2. Kino Video. Includes **Griffith**'s *The Avenging Conscience, Way Down East* (from a **restored** print), *Sally of the Sawdust, Abraham Lincoln,* and *The Struggle;* also includes Kevin Brownlow and David Gill's *D.W. Griffith: Father of Film.*

Intolerance (1916, **D. W. Griffith**). Image Entertainment. The most complete print available, based on the 1926 "standard" version but including much footage discovered in a 1917 print of the original release version.

The Lonedale Operator (1911, **D. W. Griffith**) is in *Treasures from American Film Archives* (see Chap. 1 list).

5

Mack Sennett and the Chaplin Shorts

In 1907, the year that Griffith took his ride on the "El" up to the Edison studios in the Bronx, Mack Sennett (born Mikall Sinnott in Canada) took the same ride for the same purpose. Like Griffith, Sennett then wandered from Edison to Biograph to take up a longer residence there. Like Griffith, he admired Belasco. Also like Griffith, Sennett later moved from his apprenticeship at Biograph to maturity as an independent producer and director. Sennett even worked for Griffith at Biograph, as a director, actor, and writer (he wrote the script for *The Lonely Villa*). In his years with Griffith, Sennett absorbed many lessons on cutting, shooting, and construction. Sennett would later repay his teacher both by adopting his cutting methods and by parodying Griffith's plots and last-minute rescues. Sennett always wanted to make comic films. He began directing for Biograph in 1910, and for years he tried to get them to let him make a comedy about cops. He finally got his chance with his own independent company, Keystone, in 1912.

Krazy Keystones

The marriage that Sennett effected between physical comedy and the silent film was one of those happy, inevitable unions. The purely visual film medium was perfectly suited to the purely visual comic gags that Sennett concocted. The popularity of the Lumières' first comedy, *The Gardener and the Little Scamp*, foreshadowed the future of the physical gag. Although there were comic films before Sennett—particularly the comic surprises of the trick films and the

energy of the chase films—no one before him so forcefully revealed the comic effects of motion, of human bodies and machines and inanimate objects hurtling across the screen and colliding.

It may not be coincidence that one of the most famous essays on comedy—Henri Bergson's *Le Rire* (*Laughter*, 1900)—was contemporary with the early films. Sennett—and later Chaplin, Keaton, Lloyd, and Laurel and Hardy—would unknowingly apply the Bergson theories. No theoretical aesthetic ever had the advantage of such concrete data. The Bergsonian principle that Sennett best demonstrated was that the source of the comic was the conversion of a human being into a machine. We laugh at the mechanical, inelastic motions of a man who fails to alter his responses to suit some change in the environment: the man who slips on a banana peel but continues walking as if no peel were under him until he inevitably falls. Further, we cannot laugh if we have any real fears for the man's safety; we must view him externally as a kind of imperishable object rather than as a man who can suffer pain and broken bones and lasting bruises. It is significant that, with the exception of Oliver Hardy's nosebleeds, there is virtually no blood in silent and early sound physical comedy.

This conversion of people into moving objects is at the center of Sennett's comic technique. The characters zip across the screen like mechanical toys, tossing bricks and pies and crashing into walls, furniture, and one another. Sennett furthers the impression of human machines by undercranking the camera. He saw that by recording the action at only 8 to 12 fps and then projecting it at 16 or 24 fps, the action became so speeded up that the effect became even more artificial, more frantic, and, hence, more comical. In one Sennett film, *A Clever Dummy* (1917), Ben Turpin actually plays a robot. Sennett's characters rarely experience deep emotion; they scheme rather than think, react rather than reflect; and they are individuated strictly by physical type—fat, thin, short, tall, dark, fair, male, female.

The use of people as objects makes them perfectly suited to run into trouble with the other objects and machines in their universe. Whatever terrific collisions they suffer, we know that the injury will be no more serious than a dent in a fender. Although many Sennett characters brandish guns, the audience knows that a bullet is no more lethal than a kick in the pants or a pie in the face. Their automobiles smash into each other, their boats sink, they fall down wells, they fall off roofs. Disasters that would result in death in the real world produce only a few dazed moments in the Sennett world (and in the world of the animated cartoon, where a character can be massacred in one shot and fine in the next). No damage is permanent. If we thought these characters were feeling real pain, we couldn't laugh at them. A variant of this principle is at work in the contemporary action genre, where the spectacle would be painful instead of exciting, unbearable rather than fun, if the picture urged us to care about the people who are blown up, mowed down, or in the way of a car chase.

Like a jazz musician, Sennett depended heavily on improvisation. A rough plot outline was the basis for staff meetings each week when Sennett, the cast, and the crew would get together to see what zany bits they could inject into the story line. Sennett liked to have an imaginative outside observer, whom he called his "wild card" or "joker," sit in on the staff meetings to toss out the most far-fetched and irrelevant gags he could think up. After a series of gags had been hammered together in the meeting, there was further improvisation in the course of the shooting. Sennett adhered ̶principle of construction: A gag had .d finish itself off within .id there were two kinds of gnity and the mistaken iden- .nett cared so little about whole .ual gag was the beginning and

end of his cinematic technique—many of his films are loosely structured, held together only by the pace of the movement within them. The stories seldom go anywhere; they end when the series of gags has been played out. One of the most common Sennett endings is for the clashing characters to end up dazed and exhausted or doused in a pool of water, the ocean, or a well, as in *Tillie's Punctured Romance, The Surf Girl,* and *The Masquerader.* When the characters are all wet, the action simply stops.

Sennett films usually conform to one of three structural patterns. In one of the most common, Sennett takes some conventional, almost melo-dramatic plot and then peppers it with gags. The plot merely serves as a kind of string to tie the gags together, or a clothesline on which to hang them. The second kind of Sennett structure is even less plotty and could best be described as "riffing"—taking some place or situation and then running through all the gags that might occur there. The third structure is more narrative-driven than the first two. Sennett had a great taste for parodying both the styles and the themes of famous directors and pictures. In the parody pictures, Sennett not only used individual gags but shaped the whole film in accordance with the model he was burlesquing.

Sennett's first feature—and the first American feature-length comedy—*Tillie's Punctured Romance* (1914, six reels) is a good example of the formulaic plot that strings gags together, much as a martial arts picture advances from one fight sequence to another. The completely conventional story concerns a farm girl who falls prey to the false advances of a city slicker; he wants her only for her money. She leaves the farm for the evil city, inherits money from an uncle who is presumed dead, gets mixed up with rich city folk, has troubles with her fiancé who has another girlfriend, and finally discovers his duplicity.

Tillie, the farm girl, is played by the enormous Marie Dressler in her first film role; her city-slicker boyfriend is the small and skinny Chaplin (before he adopted the tramp character exclusively). Sennett plays with the disproportion in their sizes, showing Tillie besting her beau in all sorts of contests in which Charlie winds up with a brick or a stone or a boot hitting him in the head or the seat of the pants. The "other woman" in the film is played by Mabel Normand, a coy and subtle comedienne of genius who became Sennett's creative ally. Sennett draws on the incompetent Keystone Kops for the final chase, and he throws all the main characters off the Santa Monica pier and into the Pacific Ocean to end the film. The best things in the film are the gratuitous gags, the surprises that Sennett throws in. The gratuitous becomes the essential.

Each of the Sennett "riffing" films is structured as a pure series of gags, held together only by pace and by the general locale or situation (the same could be said of an avalanche). Several of the films Chaplin made for Sennett use the riffing structure—a structure that encourages, as the name suggests, a jazz of comedy. In *The Masquerader* (1914), Sennett and Chaplin pull as many gags as they can on the premise that a disruptive actor on a movie set can wreak havoc in a studio. Chaplin plays the actor; the director boots him out; Charlie sneaks back in as a seductive woman; chaos follows until Charlie winds up soaked in a well and the riffing stops. *The Rounders* (1914) riffs on the troubles that two drunks (Chaplin and Roscoe "Fatty" Arbuckle, two obviously contrasting physical types) can get into and on the reactions of their two shrewish wives.

The Surf Girl (1916) is one of the zaniest of the riffing pictures. The two-reeler takes the beach as its starting point and then runs off every gag it can imagine in a beach setting. Sennett uses the ocean, a swimming pool, a roller coaster, a Ferris wheel, a beachfront saloon, dressing rooms for changing into bathing suits, showers, beach cabañas, an amusement park, an aviary, motorboats, whatever. The swimming pool is a crowded casserole of frantic aquatics—Sennett's undercranked camera makes the pool activities a kind of water ballet turned St. Vitus' dance. An immensely fat man rolls down a slide and into the pool; everyone in the pool (thanks to reverse motion of the camera) is vomited out of the water by the impact. A lifeguard, swinging on the rings over the pool, loses his pants; the lady who has been pushing him flies off with the pants into the pool.

This wild mêlée of gags and movement ends with a great anticlimactic joke. The cops hustle all the soaked, brawling surfers into the paddy wagon. As the wagon pulls into the station, the top part strikes the roof of the entrance and separates from the chassis. (Those incompetent cops can't even build the right-sized garage.) The surfer–felons slowly walk away from the cops, using the top part of the paddy wagon as a shell and cover for their retreat. As the dozen or so legs walk off, looking like a huge beetle, the film comes to a halt. Despite its title, there is no surf girl in the picture.

The Sennett parody films are less zany but more whole. Parodying the latest movie hit was a staple of the comic shorts. Chaplin parodied *Carmen* in 1915, the same year that two serious versions of the story were released. Both Sennett and Hal Roach parodied hits like *The Iron Horse* (*The Iron Nag*) and *The Covered Wagon* (*The Uncovered Wagon, Two Wagons Both Covered*). Some of Sennett's best parodies were of Griffith's melodramatic stories and last-minute rescues. In *Bangville Police* (1913, directed by Henry "Pathé" Lehrman) Sennett parodies such films as *The Lonely Villa* and *The Lonedale Operator* by staging the "rescue" of a woman (Mabel Normand) who has mistaken delivery men for burglars, called the cops, and barricaded herself in a room. *Barney Oldfield's Race for a Life* (1913) features a villain (Ford Sterling) who ties the young damsel (Mabel Normand) to the railroad tracks and then steals a train for the express purpose of running over her. Her boyfriend, played by Sennett, races to the rescue in an automobile. The cops pump to the rescue on a handcar. Sennett, in the best Griffith tradition, cuts among four locales: Mabel on the tracks, anxious; Ford in the train, gleefully looking forward to squashing Mabel; Mack and Barney in the auto; the cops on the handcar. Sennett draws out this rescue to an impossible length; the train, which we know is not very far from Mabel's bound body, takes forever to get to it, just long enough for Mack and the cops to get there in time.

Teddy at the Throttle (1917) parodies not only Griffith's cross-cuts but also his plots. The young man (Bobby Vernon) drops his true girlfriend for the rich society gal; the young man is being manipulated by the villain (Wallace Beery), who thinks he will make money from the society match. The society gal (large) drags the young man (small) out into an unbelievably intense storm with winds that blow the clothes off the guests at a fancy ball when the door opens, with

Fig. 5-1

The Surf Girl. *Fig. 5-1: fun in the pool; Fig. 5-2: the police wagon as beetle.*

Fig. 5-2

oceans of rain driving down, with pools of mud several feet deep. She is insistent on getting married pronto. The true girl (Gloria Swanson), who has discovered the deception, pursues them. When Gloria is tied to the railroad tracks by the villain, her dog, Teddy, carries a scribbled

message (which she miraculously managed to write while tied up) explaining her terrible plight to her boyfriend. Then comes the Griffith cutting: from Gloria tied to the tracks, to the train chugging toward her, to the agent of her rescue (the dog), who finds the boyfriend and leads him back to

Fig. 5-3

Fig. 5-4

Barney Oldfield's Race for
a Life. *Fig. 5-3: Ford Sterling
has Mabel Normand tied to
the tracks in an exaggerated
parody of melodramatic
gesture and acting; Fig. 5-4:
Mack Sennett and Mabel
Normand.*

Gloria. Gloria is saved just in time, and Teddy trees the nasty villain.

The Sennett farces set a comic standard for zaniness, non sequitur, and physical activity that has served as a model ever since—for, among others, René Clair, Richard Lester, Mel Brooks, Chuck Jones, and the Monty Python troupe. Not as technical a cinematic innovator as Griffith, Sennett still realized that the tricks the camera could play with motion were highly suited to physical comedy.

By 1915, Sennett had become a producer who no longer directed films, though he continued to supervise personally the writing and editing of every film he produced. In 1915, Sennett joined Griffith and Ince in Aitken's new venture, and Keystone became part of the Triangle Film Corporation. Sennett left Triangle in 1917—and had to leave the Keystone trademark behind him, as Triangle's property. He then founded Mack Sennett Comedies and began producing comedies for the giants like First National, Paramount, and the company from which he said he had stolen his first ideas about screen comedy, Pathé. His films became more expensive and polished, losing much of the improvisational, slaphappy quality of the Keystones that starred Chaplin, Normand, Sterling, Arbuckle, Chester Conklin, and Mack Swain. But Sennett still created hilarious 1920s films that starred the cross-eyed antihero, Ben Turpin, the antithesis of movie glamour and romance. Although Sennett produced sound shorts, the silent film was his natural medium. The particular qualities of the Sennett style become most obvious when compared with the completely different methods and emphases of his most distinguished disciple.

Charlie

In 1913, English stage comedian Charles Chaplin was touring American vaudeville stages with a music-hall act, Fred Karno's English Pantomime Troupe—also called Fred Karno's Speechless Comedians and Fred Karno's London Comedians—a troupe that included Stan Laurel. Someone—Harry Aitken, who was Griffith's and Sennett's partner; or Adam Kessel, the bookmaker-turned-owner of the Keystone Company; or Mabel Normand and Sennett—saw Chaplin's performance as a comic drunk in Karno's *A Night in an English Music Hall*. Keystone offered Chaplin a job, but Chaplin wasn't sure he wanted to work there; he shared the prejudice of many stage performers against working in films, suspecting, with his typical hard-headedness, the impermanence of a novelty that seemed more monkey business than show business. After Chaplin drove Kessel's offer up from $75 to $150 a week, including a one-year guarantee, he decided the risk was worth it. He appeared on the Sennett lot in December 1913. His first

Sennett film was *Making A Living* (1914, directed by Henry Lehrman); Chaplin hated it.

Sennett tried to use Chaplin as one more cog in his factory of human gears and puppets. Sennett capitalized on Chaplin's gymnastic abilities: his ability to fall and stagger and roll and bounce off both people and the floor. Chaplin's smallness was the perfect foil for the bigness of Arbuckle or Dressler. In *The Knockout* (1914, like all Chaplin's Keystone films), Chaplin plays a referee in a boxing match, ducking, sliding, squirming, and falling between the fighters and the ropes. This was Chaplin as pure physical comic.

But tension soon developed between Chaplin and Sennett. Sennett's rapid, pure-motion principle bothered Chaplin, who wanted to add character and individuality to his gymnastics. As early as his second and third Keystone films, *Mabel's Strange Predicament* and *Kid Auto Races at Venice* (the latter shot after *Mabel* but released before it), Chaplin began to evolve the tramp character, borrowing the idea of using a cane and hat from the earlier French comic, Max Linder, as well as an old pair of Ford Sterling's shoes (too big for Charlie's feet) and an old pair of Fatty Arbuckle's oversized pants. He also used a small derby that belonged to Arbuckle's father-in-law, Charles Avery's small jacket, and Mack Swain's false moustache (which he shortened considerably)— all found in the Keystone dressing room. Such individuation was unwanted and unneeded in Sennett's world. Sennett neither took the time nor placed the camera close enough to make such characterization count. Even so, after only one year with Sennett, the little clown with the bowler hat, baggy pants, reedy cane, and floppy shoes had become one of the most familiar figures and faces in the country. He had also, in April 1914, become a director. Chaplin directed 19 of the 35 films he acted in at Keystone; in most cases he wrote what he directed. From 1915 on, he wrote and directed—and usually edited or co-edited—every one of his films. For the record, the first Keystone he wrote and directed was *Twenty Minutes of Love*; the second was *Caught in the Rain*. In between those films, Mabel Normand directed him in *Caught in a Cabaret* (all 1914).

A brief recounting of contractual facts and figures will summarize his amazing rise to fame, fortune, power, and artistic maturity over the five years between 1913 and 1918. From $150 a week

Fig. 5-5

Fig. 5-6

Chaplin's appearance in his first Keystone releases. Fig. 5-5: as an English type with an animatedly dancing cane in Making A Living; *Fig. 5-6: in his tramp costume for* Kid Auto Races at Venice.

as a Sennett pawn in 1913–14, Chaplin signed a one-year contract with the Essanay (S&A) Company of Chicago for ten times the amount of his Keystone contract: $1,250 per week, plus a $10,000 bonus on signing—a total of $75,000 for

1915. He turned down Sennett's comparatively chintzy 500 percent raise to $750 a week (Sennett typically lost his stars when he refused to pay them their market value). In 1916, Chaplin signed a contract for almost ten times the amount of the previous year's agreement—$10,000 per week plus a $150,000 bonus, a total of $670,000 for the year—with the Mutual Corporation; it took him 18 months to fulfill this contract for 12 films. In late 1917, he signed a contract with First National for an even million dollars—at almost the same time that Mary Pickford signed her first million-dollar contract, the first time such fabulous sums entered Hollywood legend. Each of these deals brought Chaplin more money and more creative independence—to write, direct, produce, and even own the rights to his films (as he did, beginning in 1918).

Such awesome numbers indicate not only the general expansion of the movie industry (in 1914, Mack Sennett could make an entire one-reel comedy for $1,000 or less), but also the personal accomplishment of a man who became history's first truly international superstar and the first maker of movies acknowledged as a genius and primary influence by an entire generation of 20th-century artists and intellectuals.

Temperamentally, Chaplin never could see comedy as Sennett saw it. For Sennett, the comic world was a realm of silly surfaces; for Chaplin, the comic world provided the means to examine the serious world of human needs and societal structures. For Sennett, comedy was an end; for Chaplin, it was a means. Chaplin revealed another dimension of Bergson's theory of comedy in *Le Rire*—a moral force to correct the mechanical and inelastic constrictions of social norms.

Chaplin's own experience played a tremendous role in shaping his outlook. With his father and mother separated and his mother battling ill health and insanity, Chaplin spent almost two years of his Dickensian childhood in a workhouse for the poor. The boy in the workhouse quickly perceived the power of wealth and social status. The young Chaplin was an outsider, beyond the embrace of social and material comforts. The nameless screen character he created—whom we are calling Charlie (the French call him Charlot)—is also an outsider. He is a tramp, a criminal, an immigrant, a worker—someone excluded from the beautiful life. And yet Charlie yearns for that life. He longs for money, for love, for legitimacy, for social station, for etiquette, for recognition. Ironically, Charlie as outsider serves to show both the gleaming attractiveness of the beautiful life for those who don't have it and the

false emptiness of the beautiful life for those who do. Chaplin was mature enough as an artist to show ambivalence.

The critical cliché is that Chaplin slowed down Sennett's dizzy pace. He did slow it down, but he did so to put something else in. The structures of the films reveal a key shift. If Sennett's films are strings of gags, Chaplin's films are structured as three or four beads on a string. Like Sennett's, Chaplin's film structures break into clear and distinct pieces, but where Sennett's pieces are 30 to 100 seconds long, Chaplin's are three to five minutes long. He goes to the depth of a comic situation or location completely rather than flipping from gag to gag. His classic Essanay film *The Tramp* (1915), in which Chaplin first demonstrates a complete consciousness of his clown persona, breaks into four clear sections: Charlie the tramp protecting the pretty girl from other, meaner tramps; Charlie as farmhand on the girl's farm; Charlie foiling the other tramps' plot to rob the farm; and Charlie losing the girl when her wealthy boyfriend arrives. A later film he made for Mutual—*The Adventurer* (1917), whose plot resembles much of *City Lights* (1931)—also breaks into four clear sections: Charlie's escape from the police; his rescue of the drowning rich man; his attempt to join the *haut monde* at the rich man's swank party; and his second escape from the police when the rich man betrays him, coupled with his expulsion from the house by the pretty rich girl.

The shift in film structure from the gag to the scene demands that each of the sequences be more detailed, richer, fuller; each focuses attention on either the social situation or the conflict of characters and their values within it, rather than on the gags alone. The gags actually define the characters. When Charlie twirls his cane at a fancy party (in *The Count*, 1916) and then accidentally stabs the turkey, which he inadvertently swings above his head, he defines his sociable attempts to be suave and his frustrating lack of success at it. Charlie's sly and jaunty crap shooting and card shuffling when surrounded by big, mean opponents (*The Immigrant*, 1917) show he has guts as well as style. Despite the size of his opponents and the social obstacles, Charlie insists on enjoying the last laugh or the last kick in the pants. His attempts to enjoy the last boot are not only ingenious and funny; they also define his pluck. Though Charlie is comically incompetent at mastering the social graces of the *haut monde*, he consistently makes up for his lack of etiquette with his wiry toughness and his pragmatic cleverness. Chaplin's gags alone define Charlie's ironic synthesis of naïve innocence and pragmatic pluck.

Another dimension of the mature Chaplin tramp is that despite the toughness, opportunism, and dishonesty that help him survive, he has a kind and generous heart. He demonstrates this trait repeatedly by using a Griffith-like woman who evokes Charlie's milder qualities: tender and kind, instantly perceiving the redeeming characteristics in the unworldly tramp. From 1915 to 1922, Chaplin used the same actress, Edna Purviance, to portray her.

For Chaplin, the woman was not just a sentimental character—although she certainly was that; she was also a metaphor for natural human beauty uncorrupted by social definitions and unburied by material possessions. In film after film, Charlie shows his affinity with the naturally good and beautiful spirit by allying with her against those who can do him more material good. In *The Tramp* and *Police* (1916), he refuses to ally with fellow robbers and protects Edna instead. In *The Immigrant*, he retrieves Edna's stolen money and, without letting her know it, slips it back into her pocket. And yet Chaplin's sense of character and reality is such that after stuffing a wad of bills in Edna's pocket, he thinks better of it and takes a few back for himself.

Chaplin's characters also comment on the assumed values of the society that produces them. Like Sennett, Chaplin uses physical types for comic effect. Unlike Sennett, the physical type also implies moral, social, economic, political, romantic, and psychological values. Eric Campbell, the heavy, is invariably a member of the film's social in-group; he naturally hates Charlie because Charlie is not a member of that group. Eric is the giant in *Easy Street* (1917); Charlie is the runt. Eric is the waiter in *The Immigrant* who enjoys pommeling those patrons who are only a dime short of paying the bill; Charlie is the diner without any money. Eric is the lecherous rich man in *The Rink* (1916); Charlie is the poor waiter (but terrific skater!). If the social "ins" are as brutal as Eric, there is value in being "out," like Charlie.

Consistent with his social view, Chaplin's cops are very different from Sennett's incompetent and cockeyed loons. From *Easy Street* to *Modern Times* (1936), they're a rough bunch, and they often do the wrong thing. Their bullets, unlike those in Sennett comedies, look as though they might hurt somebody. In the First National three-reeler *A Dog's Life* (1918), the only crimes that the neighborhood cop finds interesting are those committed by a hungry Charlie, desperately seeking something to eat. Chaplin's films portray the police as a tramp would: men to avoid.

The short Chaplin films—like the later features—contain ironic and pointed social commentary in the action as well as in the characters. The comedies treat several controversial themes that we might think the exclusive property of today: drug addiction, poverty, hunger, crime on the streets, homosexuality, religious hypocrisy. In *The Immigrant*, Chaplin juxtaposes the Statue of Liberty with a cattle boat full of immigrants. As soon as a title announces, "The land of liberty," government officials rope all the immigrants together and start checking their identification tags. Men in uniform are inevitably damned in the Chaplin shorts, whether the uniform is a policeman's, a government official's, or a banker's. That is just one sense in which Chaplin can be seen, like Griffith, as one of the major 20th-century heirs of Charles Dickens. Griffith admired Dickens's narrative power and his controlled integration of sentiment, melodrama, and history, and he based many of his innovations, such as cross-cutting, on Dickens's techniques. But Chaplin was more like Dickens himself: in his impoverished London childhood, in his popularity, and in his brilliant use of comedy, characterization, and emotion to present the enduring qualities of the heart and the cruelty and complacency of institutions.

Aside from *The Immigrant*, *Easy Street* may be the most socially conscious of the early two-reelers. In the opening sequence, Charlie gets uplifted in the Hope Mission, singing hymns and feasting on Edna's pure face. He is so uplifted that he gives back the collection box he has stolen. The inspired Charlie goes off into the world only to find that it is a vicious place, full of hunger, poverty, thieves, drug addicts, bullies, and rapists; Easy Street is not so easy, a jungle world of animals striving to survive. As a cop in

Easy Street: *the runt and the giant (Charlie and Eric Campbell).*

Fig. 5-7

the slums (now an outcast *because of* the uniform), Charlie subdues all the foes of goodness, ironically inspired to perform his heroic deeds by a shot of dope. In the final sequence, the den of thieves has been miraculously transformed into the New Hope Mission; all the thugs, including the ominous Eric Campbell, have dressed in their Sunday suits and Sunday smiles, all of them marching meekly and politely into the mission for their own uplifting.

But social evils admit of no easy solutions; in fact, they seem to admit of no solutions. Chaplin's endings frequently imply an ironic social dimension of false happiness and solution, as in *The Vagabond* and *A Dog's Life.* In *The Bank* (1915) and *Shoulder Arms* (1918), Charlie wakes up only to discover that the happy ending literally was a dream. The other typical Chaplin ending (*The Tramp, The Adventurer*), less socially pointed but more poignant than the faked happy ones, shows Charlie losing in the end, shuffling off down the road again after failing to satisfy his longings.

Though the social and moral implications of the Chaplin shorts are striking, Chaplin never deserts the objective tool of comedy for making

his points. One of the most brilliant examples is the beginning of *The Bank.* Charlie strides into the bank, goes directly to the safe, twirls the dials of the huge safe, checking his cuff to make sure that he remembers the combination, finally opens the door of the safe, steps in, and brings out his mop and pail. Not only does Charlie demonstrate the difference between capital and labor, but he does it in a surprise that plays on our expectations. At the beginning of *The Immigrant*, people are lying about the boat, seasick. The camera cuts to Charlie, leaning over the side of the pitching ship. We expect he is sick like all his fellow passengers. Then he turns around, displaying the fish he has just caught. In *The Tramp*, he enters walking down a dusty road; a car rushes by, spraying him with dust—another contrast of rich and poor. Charlie takes out a brush, whisks himself off, buffs his fingernails, and continues on his way. The spunky tramp is a fastidious gentleman—in himself, a perfect comic contrast. As an integrator of contrasts, of the good–bad, sneaky–brave, poor–rich, lucky and out of luck in us all, Chaplin's tramp crossed worlds.

An essential element of Chaplin's comic technique—and that of every other silent

Fig. 5-8

Fig. 5-9

Easy Street: Charlie gets uplifted in the mission (Fig. 5-8), feasting on the face of Edna Purviance (Fig. 5-9).

comedian—was the ingenious use of objects. Unlike Sennett, Chaplin did not use objects simply as comic weapons (the pie in the face); the object could be either weapon or tool, could define the character using it, could be used in a surprising way, could foul Charlie up or help him out. If Chaplin's favorite structure was to exhaust a situation of some length before moving on to the next, one way to exhaust a situation was to exhaust all the objects in it. And in exhausting an object, Chaplin frequently transformed it into a completely different thing—not by stopping the camera, as Méliès had, but by manipulating the object in a witty and unexpected way. Chaplin, like Méliès, was a kind of magician, but his was a magic without camera tricks.

Chaplin's most famous short film with objects is *One A.M.* (1916). With the exception of a cab driver in the first sequence, Charlie is the only character in the film—except for a roomful of objects. In this film Charlie returns to one of his favorite incarnations, the drunk; the play with objects begins in the first section when the drunken Charlie, returning from a night on the town, gets tangled with the taxi door and then with the taxi meter. Charlie can't find the key to his front door, so he climbs in the window, stepping in a goldfish bowl as he does so. Inside the house he finds the key in his vest pocket. Back out the window he goes (foot in the goldfish bowl again) so that he can enter properly through the door.

In the second section—Charlie in the living room—Chaplin uses every piece of inanimate matter with which the set has been decorated. He feels he is being attacked by the tiger rug on the floor. He tries to walk on a circular table toward a bottle of booze and seltzer; the table spins, and Charlie walks a treadmill, unable to reach the booze. He tries to walk up the stairs only to discover himself at the bottom again.

Then, in the third section—Charlie and the bed—the game with objects culminates in a five-minute duel between the drunk and a Murphy bed. The bed flips down, flips up, reverses itself, loses its frame, bounces, rises, falls as it pleases. Charlie finally beds down in the bathtub. With the bed, Chaplin has succeeded in bringing an inanimate object to life.

The Pawn Shop (1916) is another short masterwork of comic objects. Among the shop's objects are an immense ladder that Charlie uses as a seesaw, a birdcage that he uses as a hatrack, a piece of string that he transforms into a tightrope, and a fishbowl that he mistakes for a chamber pot. But the film's culminating transformation of an object is Charlie's dismembering a clock that a needy customer (Albert Austin) has brought in to pawn. Probing the value of the

clock, Charlie's deft part-by-part dissection combines the methods of the jeweler (do its parts seem real or fake?), the doctor (is it sound? are its reflexes good?), and the shopper for meat (do the contents smell fresh?) or cloth (how many yards of material does it contain?). After the innards of the clock lie in front of him, Charlie winds its shell, and its parts begin to dance (in typical Chaplin style, he does not use Méliès's stop-action but instead uses magnets to propel the pieces without camera trickery). Then Charlie adopts the method of the gardener, spraying the jittering "bugs" with oil to exterminate them. Finally, he scrapes the clock's mauled contents into the customer's hat and hands the rubble back to him with a shake of the head: Sorry; it won't do.

Chaplin perpetually shows how things smell (either pleasant, the way he sniffs the aroma of a hot dog in the opening scene of *A Dog's Life*, or unpleasant, the way he checks the bottoms of his shoes when he steps into the tiny room packed with children in *Easy Street*), how they taste (the soapy mop and sudsy coffee in *The Bank*), how they sound (the contrast between his violin music and the brass band in the opening sequence of *The Vagabond*), and how they feel to the touch (in *City Lights*, just touching the tramp leads the formerly blind flower seller to recognize her benefactor). As film theorist Rudolf Arnheim pointed out in 1933, Chaplin's inability to manipulate any sensory data other than the visual stimulated his imaginative depiction of all the missing senses, and the fact that the view of the camera is limited allowed him to construct the fishing gag in *The Immigrant.*

As opposed to D. W. Griffith's sharp contrast of idealized goodness and idealized evil, Chaplin examined the inherent contradictions within the definitions of good and evil in bourgeois industrial society. The comic tramp was himself a walking contradiction, a figure who loathed (and feared) the falsity of the established order and who yearned toward the purity of the ideal, but also envied the comforts and rewards of the established society and realized that he had better administer a kick unto others before they kicked unto him. This tension between naïveté and instinctive, tough pragmatism in the tramp produces the moral ambivalence of the mature Chaplin films: the contrast between societal

Fig. 5-10
One A.M.: *Charlie and the tiger rug.*

definitions of paternity and more human ones in
The Kid (1921, his first feature), the ambivalent
contrasts between rich and poor in *City Lights*,
and the choice between civilization and nature in
Modern Times. In his first four years in the film
business, Chaplin created and developed the
character whom he would use to explore the
cultural landscape of civilization itself.

Most unlike discussions of Griffith, discussions
of Chaplin's contribution to the cinema focus on
what he does *on* film rather than *with* film.
Whereas Griffith combined the devices of cinema
into a coherent narrative medium, Chaplin
advanced the art by making our consciousness of
the cinematic medium disappear so completely
that we concentrate on the photographic subject
rather than the process. That does not mean (as
many have claimed) that Chaplin was "uncinematic," that he was ignorant of the means of
manipulating the cinematic language. Quite the
opposite. One indeed manipulates a language
skillfully when all consciousness of manipulation
disappears and the language serves solely to
communicate the subject matter with complete

lucidity. Chaplin's insistence on unobtrusive
composition, minimal camera movement, and
restrained, seamless editing sustained the spell of
his performance. His films were expensive to make
because he called for so many retakes. Although he
concentrated on full and medium shots, using
action and composition to direct the viewer's eye
within the frame, his close shots and close-ups
were—like the ineffably complex expression on
the tramp's face in the final shot of *City Lights*—
intimate and unforgettably moving; others—like a
close-up of a coin in the tramp's hand—made their
narrative points so clearly and so naturally that the
changes of setup went unnoticed.

Chaplin's early films demonstrated not only the
magic of a human performance on film, but also
the appeal of the performer on the minds of his
public. Millions of fans rushed to the novelty shops
that sold mechanical dolls and plaster statuettes in
the tramp's image, much as later generations of
children bought Mouseketeer and *Star Wars* paraphernalia. Chaplin was the very first national and
international craze generated by the motion-
picture industry. The craze that came next would

Fig. 5-11

The Pawn Shop: *the clock as*
patient (Fig. 5-11) and as
jewel (Fig. 5-12); Charlie
and Albert Austin.

Fig. 5-12

be Chaplin's only serious rival, Mickey Mouse. There were popular songs, like "Oh Those Charlie Chaplin Feet," some of which, like "The Moon Shines Bright on Charlie Chaplin," even crossed the Atlantic to the trenches of France. Chaplin's face, figure, and icons (bowler, cane, shoes, moustache) became more familiar to more people all over the globe than any previous face and figure in history. Chaplin hobnobbed with the most famous figures of his generation—Albert Einstein, Winston Churchill, H. G. Wells, Mahatma Gandhi. George Bernard Shaw proclaimed him the only authentic genius the cinema ever produced. Many young writers, artists, and composers of his generation grew up as his ardent fans—James Joyce, Samuel Beckett, Bertolt Brecht, Hart Crane, Fernand Léger, Pablo Picasso, Erik Satie.

If there was a single quality that most struck this generation of admirers, it was Chaplin's tremendous range, his paradoxical combinations of diametrically opposed human sentiments and reactions. Charlie was a terrific cynic and a romantic, selfish and generous, combative and cowardly, crude and delicate, vain and unselfconscious, pathetic and heroic. He was a total outsider to bourgeois middle-class propriety and its institutions, both above it in his gentlemanly disdain and below it in his destitute station. But Charlie understood the comforts and bases of those institutions as well as their constrictions. They simply weren't for the likes of him, who belonged everywhere and nowhere at all on earth.

By 1918, the time of his million-dollar contract with First National, a firm that only distributed and exhibited films, Chaplin had become a totally independent producer and the owner of his own film studio, staffed with associates like his brother (and business manager) Sydney, Rollie Totheroh (his cameraman), Henry Bergman and Chuck Reisner (his assistants), Edna Purviance (his leading lady), and Albert Austin (his deadpan character man). Many of them would never work for anyone else and would remain under contract to Chaplin even when he wasn't shooting a picture.

With First National, the later phases of his career began—with silent and sound feature films. Although the long films were among his best, Chaplin never exerted a greater cultural influence, both in America and abroad, than in those first four years between 1914 and 1918.

For Further Viewing

FILMS

Mack Sennett (1880–1960)
Comrades (1911)
Barney Oldfield's Race for a Life (1913)
Mabel's Dramatic Career (1913)
Tango Tangles (1914)
Tillie's Punctured Romance (1914)
His Bread and Butter (1916)
The Surf Girl (1916)
A Clever Dummy (1917)
Teddy at the Throttle (1917)
Mickey (1918). Completed 1916
Astray from the Steerage (1920)
The Fatal Glass of Beer (1933)

Charles Chaplin (1889–1977)
Chaplin's Keystone films, including: *Making A Living, Kid Auto Races at Venice, Mabel's Strange Predicament, Tango Tangles, His Favorite Pastime, Twenty Minutes of Love, Caught in a Cabaret, Caught in the Rain, The Knockout, Mabel's Married Life, Laughing Gas, The Property Man, The Face on the Bar Room Floor, The Masquerader, The Rounders, The New Janitor, Dough and Dynamite, His Musical Career, His Trysting Place, Getting Acquainted,* and *His Prehistoric Past* (all 1914)
Chaplin's Essanay films, including: *His New Job, A Night Out, The Tramp, Work, A Woman, The Bank,* and *A Night in the Show* (1915); *Charlie Chaplin's Burlesque on Carmen* and *Police* (1916)
Chaplin's Mutual films: *The Floorwalker, The Fireman, The Vagabond, One A.M., The Count, The Pawn Shop, Behind the Screen,* and *The Rink* (1916); *Easy Street, The Cure, The Immigrant,* and *The Adventurer* (1917)
A Dog's Life (1918)
Shoulder Arms (1918)
Sunnyside (1919)
The Kid (1921)
The Idle Class (1921)
The Pilgrim (1923)
A Woman of Paris (1923)
The Gold Rush (1925)
The Circus (1928)
City Lights (1931)
Modern Times (1936)

The Great Dictator (1940)
Monsieur Verdoux (1947)
Limelight (1952)
A King in New York (1957)
A Countess from Hong Kong (1967)

DVDs

Bangville Police (1913, **Henry Lehrman,** produced by **Mack Sennett**), a parody of Griffith featuring the Keystone Kops, is in *The Movies Begin* (see Chap. 2 list).

Charlie Chaplin *Short Comedy Classics: The Complete Restored Essanay & Mutual Collection.* Image Entertainment. **Restored.** Includes a documentary on **Eric Campbell.**

The Fatal Glass of Beer (1933, **Clyde Bruckman,** produced by **Mack Sennett**) is in ***W. C. Fields: Six Short Films*** (see Chap. 11 list).

The Gold Rush (1925 and 1942, **Charles Chaplin**). The Chaplin Collection. Warner Home Video and mk2. Excellent archival prints of both the silent and the sound versions, with many extras. Other volumes in this series offer virtually all of Chaplin's work from 1918 to 1957.

Slapstick Encyclopedia. Image Entertainment. Over 15 hours of well-selected shorts, including many by **Sennett.**

Unknown Chaplin: The Master at Work. Thames Television and A&E. With unprecedented access to **Chaplin**'s outtakes, Kevin Brownlow and David Gill produced the three brilliant documentaries on this indispensable disc. There may be no better introduction to Chaplin, to the materials of film history, or to the creative process itself. For example, one sees *The Immigrant* as it is thought out on film take by take.

6

Movie Czars
and Movie Stars

Griffith, Sennett, and Chaplin were three of the most important figures of the moving picture's second major period, 1908–19. The first, 1894–1907, was dominated by Edison (and Dickson and Porter), Lumière, and Méliès. The year 1908, when Griffith started making pictures, marks one boundary; the start of the 1920s marks the other, beginning a third period that would end with the coming of sound. The 1920s would see Keaton, Gance, Murnau, Dreyer, Eisenstein, and von Stroheim—and, of course, new work by Griffith, Chaplin, and Sennett.

After trailing the art and industries of England and France in the first years of commercial film-making, the American film asserted its dominance in the years just preceding World War I and, with the help of that war (and the films of Griffith, Sennett, and Chaplin; the star system; and the beginnings of the studio system), established a commercial supremacy that has never been challenged.

World War I came at an opportune time for the American film industry. In 1914, just as the American film imagination had begun to swell, the war came along to cripple the European film industry. The chemicals that produced raw film stock were also the essential ingredients of gunpowder. The European governments, given the choice of guns or movies, made the "obvious" decision. American films, suddenly without any competitors, ruled the screens of America and Europe during the war and just after it. When the film industries of France, Germany, Russia, and Scandinavia finally recovered, their roles in world film production were as fertile, imaginative innovators rather than as equal competitors with the big-dollar doings of Hollywood. By the time the war ended in 1918, the American film had become, as it has remained, the dominant cinema force in the world.

Wealth began pouring into the American film business with the appearance of the nickelodeons in 1905, converting that business into a powerful industry and pushing it to untangle the legal and commercial chaos of its infancy. In 1910, the war against the Trust was raging as the impish Independents valiantly kept fighting and producing pictures. Ten years later, all but one of the original Trust companies had folded, and the leaders of the opposition had themselves become more autocratic and powerful than their earlier adversaries. Carl Laemmle, William Fox, Adolph Zukor, Jesse Lasky, Marcus Loew, Samuel Goldfish, Lewis J. Selznick, and Louis B. Mayer were all lucky enough to be in the right place at the right time. They were fortunate to be running a studio or buying up theatres at the moment when everyone in America started going to the movies and when everyone abroad went to American movies because there were few others. These men, who became the first movie moguls, had outlasted their Trust competitors—the Motion Picture Patents Company—simply because they rode the crest of the new wave of film merchandising rather than trying to stop it.

The business of the Trust's distributor was to market one-hour programs of short films for the nickelodeons; the new feature films, lasting up to two hours, were for larger, more comfortable theatres devoted to and equipped for a full evening's entertainment. To produce 52 features a year (the equivalent of one film program per week) required a huge permanent staff of actors, writers, directors, and technicians; a major investment in equipment; a complex administrative office for scheduling the shooting and selling the films; and big theatres. Zukor, Goldfish, Laemmle, Fox, and some others made the investment; many of the Trust companies could not or did not, certain that the new feature craze was a passing fancy. The fancy never passed; the Trust companies did.

Although the Trust officially lost the public battle in the courts in 1917, it had already lost the war to such opponents as *Queen Elizabeth*, *Traffic in Souls*, *Cabiria*, *The Squaw Man*, *Tillie's Punctured Romance*, *The Birth of a Nation*, *The Cheat*, and *Alias Jimmy Valentine*. The public wanted feature films.

Stars over Hollywood

The years between 1910 and 1920 determined the direction the American film industry would take. By 1915, the film program consisted of a single feature film supplemented by a short or two—a one- or two-reel comedy, perhaps a serial or a cartoon. A second current practice was born at the same time—the star system. In the healthy days of the Trust, no Biograph actor ever received screen credit. Performers were known either by the names of the characters they played—"Little Mary"—or by the studio—the Biograph Girl. There even seems to have been some doubt in the minds of the earliest patrons about whether they were watching a dramatization or real life. The confusion in the mind of the country boy about fiction or reality in *Mabel's Dramatic Career* may have been quite common a few years earlier.

The First Stars

Biograph opposed giving screen credit for the same short-sighted commercial reasons that it opposed the feature film: Star actors would cost more than anonymous faces on a screen. The reasoning was correct. But the Independents reasoned that although a star would cost more, a film with a star would earn more. The Independents had the stronger argument: To

make more, it was necessary to spend more. The Independents launched their career when Carl Laemmle hired the Biograph Girl in 1910 and featured her in IMP pictures under her real name, Florence Lawrence. Laemmle and other Independents did the same with "Little Mary" Pickford, King Baggott, Arthur Johnson, and many other formerly anonymous players. The power of the star system, begun by the Independents, was such that in 1917—only a few years after its inception—two stars, Chaplin and Pickford, were vying with producers and with each other to become the highest paid performers in the business, both of them signing contracts for over $1 million. And every major producer in the industry was trying to sign them and pay them that million.

The movie star, no longer an anonymous character in a film but a human being in his or her own right, seized the imagination of the public. In 1912, just after audiences started learning their favorites' names, America's first motion picture fan magazine, *Photoplay*, appeared. It and subsequent fan magazines featured pictures, stories, and interviews that made the figure on the screen an even more intimate and personal being for each member of the audience. Producing companies needed publicity departments to sell the stars as well as the pictures to the public. In the middle of the second decade of the century, the exotic and erotic activities of the stars first became items of household gossip. One of the earliest and most impressive of the grand publicity jobs was Fox's packaging of the "lusty, seductive siren," Theda Bara, who made her debut in the gripping *A Fool There Was* (1915, directed by Frank Powell). Born in Cincinnati as Theodosia Goodman, she was transformed by Fox publicists into an Arabian beauty clad in black who survived less on oxygen and victuals than by wrecking homes and devouring men. She was a mystic semisorceress; her name, they pointed out, bore an anagrammatical relationship to death (Theda) and Arab (Bara); the blood of the Ptolemies flowed in her veins; and her astrological signs matched Cleopatra's. The character she played—a sexual vampire—was abbreviated to vamp, adding a new noun and verb to the English language. More significant than all the drivel of the Bara legend was the fact that the public loved and believed it. Movie publicists had

Fig. 6-1

Fig. 6-2

Fig. 6-3
Early archetypes. Fig. 6-1: the vamp, Theda Bara; Fig. 6-2: the rough good–bad man of the frontier, William S. Hart; Fig. 6-3: the cowboy dandy, Tom Mix.

discovered the ease of selling something the public wanted to buy. And Bara, along with a movie star of a very different type, the cowboy dandy, Tom Mix, established Fox as a major production power—their attractive presences mythified by the studio's publicity mills.

Later film theorists have speculated about the appeal, value, and utility of movie stars. For some critics, movie stars are a commodity of industrial production, another means for the film industry to package and market its products to the public. For others, movie stars are symptomatic of a superficial culture—shallow but powerful visual presences that may be uncritically accepted. Movie actors have frequently been compared unfavorably with stage actors, since film stars often seem to play one role—an onscreen persona very close to their offscreen style—over and over again. Still other critics see this unity and consistency of star personality as the most interesting and powerful accomplishment of movie stars: Movie stars do not so much play characters (as stage actors do); they *are* the characters. The movie star capitalizes on an essential paradox of movies—that they are fictional truths. A movie star is also a fictional truth, a fictional character in a fictional narrative, and yet a real human being whose face and actions have been documented by the camera and who has a powerful and familiar persona. And the character resonates with this persona; together they create the complete portrayal. As commodity, actor, and persona, the movie star had become a powerful component of American cultural experience by 1915.

The greatest stars of the silent films created their own images and types; the lesser stars merely filled the patterns that the great stars had already sketched. There were imitations of Mary Pickford's spunky, good-hearted, pranksterish little girl with the golden curls. There were sultry sirens in the Theda Bara image, many of them imported from Europe. There were gentle, soulful juveniles—Richard Barthelmess, Charles Ray. There were exotic Latin leading men—Rudolph Valentino, Ramon Novarro; perhaps even Douglas Fairbanks's conversion from zippy American go-getter to swarthy swashbuckler in the 1920s was the result of the influence of this new sexual type. There were lecherous, jaded roués, often from decadent foreign shores—Erich von Stroheim, Owen Moore, Adolphe

Menjou. There were stars from the opera, the stage, and even the swimming pool—Geraldine Farrar, Mary Garden, Alla Nazimova, Annette Kellerman. There was the basically pure woman who rose to the demands of experience (Lillian Gish); there was the stubborn, sophisticated, and often tragic lady (Gloria Swanson); there was the strong, competent, virile male (Thomas Meighan); there was the serious, tough cowboy with the sad eyes (William S. Hart); there was the fat man (John Bunny, Fatty Arbuckle), and the little man (Chaplin, Harold Lloyd, Buster Keaton), and the everyman (Lon Chaney). And as the stars flourished, so did the character actors, who specialized in playing nonromantic roles and types. Then, as now, many stars became character actors when they grew older.

California, Here We Come

As significant as the birth of the star system in this decade was the move west. As early as 1907, production companies—perhaps evading the law or the Patents Company wrecking crews—discovered southern California. According to the colorful (if not completely reliable) film historian Terry Ramsaye, during the Trust War the Independent companies took advantage of California's distance from the Trust headquarters in New York and its closeness to the Mexican border, where the company could readily flee with its negatives and machines. The trouble with this argument is that many of the Trust companies set up shop in California too. Whatever their reasons for going there, the filmmakers were soon struck by the genuine virtues of California. The vast, open plains, the dependability of the sun, the nearby mountains and deserts and ocean, all attracted the eyes of people whose art depended on the power of the visual. Griffith brought his company west in the winters of 1910, 1911, and 1912. *The Birth of a Nation* and *Intolerance* were both shot in California.

By 1915, most of the film companies had settled down to business in Los Angeles and its suburbs—known colloquially and generically as Hollywood but in fact including such diverse areas of the Los Angeles basin as Culver City, Edendale (where the first studios were located), Hollywood itself, Burbank, and North Hollywood. Real estate speculators, who suddenly discovered

Fig. 6-4

Fig. 6-5

Fig. 6-6

A gallery of stars. Fig. 6-4: "Little Mary" Pickford (note how the huge sets and furniture make her seem truly little); Fig. 6-5: the demure Lillian Gish with the slickly brilliantined Rod La Rocque; Fig. 6-6: a cool Gloria Swanson.

that miles of apparently useless land were of great use to the movie men, sold it to them by the tens of thousands of acres, at absurdly reasonable prices. Vast studios, like Thomas Ince's Inceville (1911; in 1915, he built a new lot in Culver City) and Carl Laemmle's Universal City (which opened in 1915), with rows of shooting studios, office buildings, back lots (for the outdoor sets), and even ranches completely stocked with cattle and horses and other beasts of the field, sprang up in and near Los Angeles. The founding of the movie capital was the result of three coincidental factors: weather, topography, and real estate values. Enjoying the harvests of chance, the emperors of the new film world now ruled vast, tangible empires.

The Emperors and Their Rule

The most significant accident in the history of the American film is that this first generation of influential movie producers, those gentlemen who made the concrete decisions about the artistic and moral values worthy of inclusion in films, were themselves deficient in formal education and aesthetic judgment. Most of them were either Jewish immigrants from Germany or Russia or Poland, or the sons of Jewish immigrants. Most came to the movies by accident. They sold herring or furs or gloves or secondhand clothes. They jumped from these businesses into running amusement parks and penny arcades just when Edison's Kinetoscope and Biograph's Mutoscope were bringing new life to the novelty business.

There were two reasons Jewish immigrants could thrive in this business, and they were the same reasons that Jews thrived in another contemporary entertainment business—the writing, publishing, and selling of popular music on New York's 28th Street, known colloquially as Tin Pan Alley. First, these were new businesses that had not evolved their structures of corporate control that always tend to keep newcomers out. Second, they were the kinds of risky, "illegitimate" businesses that respectable businessmen and social prejudice always allowed the Jews to run—like the lending of money in medieval and Renaissance Europe.

When movies left the peepshow box for the screen, these arcade owners converted their stores into nickelodeons. They built more and more of these theatres, which became bigger and plusher. Soon they began producing films for their theatres, what with the pressures of the Trust and its licensing fees. Such was the series of small steps by which a Goldfish (later Goldwyn) or Zukor or Mayer climbed out of the ghetto and into a multimillion-dollar throne of power over national artistic tastes. It is the same route that later generations of disadvantaged Americans have traveled; for many, the quickest and most glamorous road to the American Dream of fame and fortune is show business (sports, music, television, and movies).

It is doubtful that a first generation of producer–aesthete intellectuals would have made better movies (look at the likes of *Queen Elizabeth*), but this first generation of movie men and movie values left a legacy of sacrificing taste for dollars—or equating them—that Hollywood films have never completely shed. And they never really can. The costs of making and distributing a commercial feature demand that it appeal to many people. The curse and the glory of a popular art is that it is intended for large audiences over the entire social spectrum. Movie executives, then as now, make guesses about popular appeal. And they still are accused, regardless of their ethnic background, of running the film business as if it were the garment industry.

By 1915—even as early as 1908—there were three types of movie executives, and the differences among them reveal the structure of the American film industry as a whole. Out in Hollywood, the most famous of the movie moguls were those who controlled the actual production of films; they were the film producers and studio heads whose private lives and personal salaries made the headlines. Back in New York, on the East Coast, were the parent companies, whose executives supervised and budgeted the entire operation of the studio, marketing its products, reinvesting its revenues, and managing its assets as profitably as possible. Then, scattered throughout the country were the owners of theatres and theatre chains who needed films from the studios and returned to them the revenues that the film companies needed to make more films. The three-tiered structure of the American film industry—production, distribution (or management), and exhibition—evolved in the middle years of the century's second decade.

Major Studios

The most powerful film company of the silent era was Paramount Pictures. Paramount was the child of Adolph Zukor, the final stage in the evolution of his Famous Players in Famous Plays. Zukor, who began by distributing *Queen Elizabeth* in 1912, jumped aboard the feature-film wagon at the very beginning—one of the chief reasons for his success. Zukor's Famous Players company initiated three kinds of pictures: Class A (with stage stars and stage properties, the arty films), Class B (with established screen players), and Class C (cheap, quick features). Zukor discovered that the Class B films, the ones with Mary Pickford, were far more popular than the high-toned Class A. Zukor dropped the stagy films and concentrated on Class Bs. He soon absorbed Jesse Lasky's Feature Play Company (creating Famous Players–Lasky in 1916), Lewis J. Selznick's Picture Company, Edwin S. Porter's Rex Pictures, Pallas Pictures, and Morosco Pictures; he also absorbed a distributing exchange called Paramount Pictures, which in 1925 gave its name to the amalgamation that had been a dominant industry force since 1916. Zukor bested his competition by buying it out. The huge company then had the power and the money to hire the most popular stars and demand the highest fees from exhibitors who wanted the films of its stars.

Zukor had been working in a steady, octopodous manner, snatching up theatres as well as studios and exchanges. One of Zukor's commercial innovations was the system of block booking. The theatre owner had to agree to buy all of Zukor's products to get any of them. If he wanted Mary Pickford or William S. Hart, he had to buy all 52 weekly programs from Paramount. But even block booking, tyrannical as it was, was less efficient than owning the theatres. The studio owner not only had to produce films, but also had to guarantee that each of them would be shown. What better guarantee than to own the theatres to show them?

Another powerful studio emerged in the mid-1920s: Metro–Goldwyn–Mayer. The monolith was assembled by theatre owner Marcus Loew, who wanted to control the profit from the pictures that he showed in his national chain of theatres. In 1924, Loew bought the Metro Picture Company and merged with the Goldwyn Picture Company. Loew then put Louis B. Mayer, another theatre owner recently turned producer, in charge of production at MGM. Mayer brought with him a young assistant, Irving Thalberg, who had been at Universal, to supervise the shooting of the pictures. (In other words, Mayer was the executive in charge of the production—as opposed to the distribution—arm of the studio, and Thalberg was in charge of the actual activity of film production: planning, approving, and supervising the making of all MGM films.) From these parts, Loew assembled the most solid film factory in America. Anchored by his chain of classy and genteel theatres, Loew's MGM studio began to manufacture the kind of classy and genteel films that would perfectly mesh the ambiance of the environment to the tone of the entertainment within it. MGM took over the Goldwyn lot in Culver City to shoot its films (Goldwyn had earlier taken it over from Ince; in the 1990s it was bought by Sony); that studio then distributed its films to all of the Loew theatres. Loew, like Zukor, had succeeded in creating the kind of vertically integrated empire that Gaumont and Pathé had established 20 years earlier; he controlled all three branches of the theatrical film business: production, distribution, and exhibition.

Understandably, the theatre owner did not enjoy the strong-arm pressures of block booking or the unavailability of those popular films that had been made by the studios for their own theatres. In 1917, a group of theatre owners joined together specifically as an antidote to Zukor's commercial poison, calling themselves the First National Exhibitors Circuit. First National, managed by W. W. Hodkinson (himself elbowed out of Paramount by Zukor) and J. D. Williams, intended to diminish the power of the film production companies in filmmaking, just as the film production companies were trying to diminish the independent exhibitor's. First National contracted with individual stars (Chaplin, for example, and Harry Langdon) to make pictures for their theatres. The star gained independence and financial backing; the theatre owner gained the lucrative products of popular, established stars. The idea was so felicitous that First National was among the three great powers of the 1920s film world.

The four United Artists after the signing (from a contemporary newsreel)— from left: Fairbanks, Griffith, Pickford, and Chaplin.

Fig. 6-7

Yet another new wrinkle was the emergence of the artist as producer. If film producers could turn theatre owners and if theatre owners could turn producers, then artists could also turn producers and work for themselves. In 1919, D. W. Griffith, Charles Chaplin, Mary Pickford, and Douglas Fairbanks joined together to form the United Artists Corporation. Each would produce his or her own films (Griffith's first UA film was *Broken Blossoms*; Chaplin's was *A Woman of Paris*, 1923), which would then be distributed by the common company, United Artists. United Artists owned neither studio nor theatre; it was exclusively a distributing organization for pictures made elsewhere. However flimsy such an organization seemed compared with the giants like Paramount and First National, the company survived, eventually merging with MGM (in 1981). The idea for United Artists was years ahead of its time. Today, the major studios themselves are often merely distributors for pictures that have been made by independent producers.

Carl Laemmle went into the nickelodeon business in 1906, then into film distribution, then into film production. He formed the Independent Motion Picture Company in 1909, merged IMP with some smaller companies to create the Universal Film Company in 1912, and opened Universal City in 1915. Universal's major silent

hits ranged from *Traffic in Souls* (1913) to *The Phantom of the Opera* (1925, revised 1929).

William Fox began distributing films in 1904 and producing them in 1913; in 1915, he changed the name of his company from Box Office Attractions to the Fox Film Corporation, and in 1916, he set up a studio in Los Angeles. Fox was known for its quality productions—Fox himself received the first and only Academy Award for "artistic quality of production" for *Sunrise* (1927)—and for its early sound films and newsreels. The company merged with Darryl F. Zanuck's 20th Century Productions to become 20th Century–Fox in 1935.

The four Warner brothers—Albert, Harry, Sam, and Jack—opened their first nickelodeon in 1905, produced a feature in 1917, moved their independent operation from New York to Hollywood in 1919, and formed Warner Bros. Pictures in 1923. In 1925, they bought Vitagraph and began experimenting with sound. Warner Bros. was a minor studio until *The Jazz Singer* (1927) made it a giant; in 1928, it even took over First National.

Another major company that got a late start was founded by Harry and Jack Cohn and Joe Brandt in 1920; it took the name Columbia Pictures Corporation in 1924. What contributed to Columbia's rise was not a technology like sound but an immensely popular and gifted director: Frank Capra began working for Columbia in 1927.

Fig. 6-8

The interior of the Roxy, from the ceiling to the orchestra.

Later in the Studio Era, Columbia and Warner Bros. were very much counted among the major studios, a list that included Fox, MGM, Paramount, United Artists, Universal, and RKO. The last of these, the Radio–Keith–Orpheum Corporation, was not founded until 1928. Walt Disney Productions, a major studio today but not in the 1920s or 1930s, grew out of companies founded as early as 1922 and was incorporated in 1929.

The Hollywood film studios of the 1920s had traveled a long way from Edison's Black Maria—and even from the glass-walled studio of Méliès; now they made their own light. Vast expanses of land and a complex maze of buildings had replaced the single little tar-paper shack that pirouetted with the sun. The Hollywood studio had become an entertainment factory. One aspect of the *studio system* (see the glossary) was that it manufactured entertainment on an assembly line. Like Henry Ford's automobile plant, the Hollywood studio broke the manufacture of its product into a series of operations, and each link in the chain fulfilled its particular function. There was a specific section for writers in the studio—those who conceived the original story ideas, those who wrote the final scenarios, and even those who created the film's intertitles, a separate and highly developed art of its own. There was a specific section for costuming, one for the construction of sets, and another for the

care and maintenance of the increasingly complicated equipment, still another for the shooting of the films, and one for publicizing, marketing, and financing the finished product. The arts of the writer, the costumer, the cinematographer, the art director, the electrician, and the editor had become as significant as the contributions of the producer, director, and actor.

Movie Palaces

As the film studio evolved, so did the movie theatre. Almost simultaneous with the birth of the feature film came the huge, plush theatre to glorify the longer films and show them in comfort. The same feature phenomenon that enriched the studios enriched the theatres. The earlier nickelodeons were small and often dirty; in New York, the feature-length movies left these little stores for huge theatres on Broadway. The first of the new palaces was the Strand, constructed on Broadway in 1914, followed immediately by the Vitagraph. The new theatres could accommodate over 2,000 patrons, who trod on carpeted floors and relaxed in plush, padded chairs. The manager of the Strand Theatre, Samuel L. Rothafel (born Rothapfel), soon went on to buy, build, and conceive huge movie palaces of his own. Roxy (his nickname) opened or salvaged a string of mammoth New York houses: the Rialto, Rivoli, Capitol, Roxy,

Fig. 6-9

Fig. 6-10

Fig. 6-11

Fig. 6-12

Fig. 6-13

Grauman's Chinese Theatre. Fig. 6-9: the newly constructed theatre on Hollywood Blvd. Fig. 6-10: a few weeks before the 1927 opening, Mary Pickford and Douglas Fairbanks made their marks in the cement outside the theatre; left, Sid Grauman. It turned out that they needed two cement blocks for their names (Figs. 6-11, 6-12). Fig 6-13: in 1949, cowboy star Roy Rogers left the imprints of his gun and horse along with his hands and boots.

and the Radio City Music Hall, his finale and *chef d'oeuvre*. Roxy brought the same tone of quasi-gentility to the movie theatre that his colleagues, like Zukor and Mayer, brought to the films themselves. Roxy supplemented the film showing with symphony orchestras, corps de ballets, live variety acts, and, at Radio City, the last survivor of the Roxy era, the legendary Rockettes. Whereas vaudeville had supported the movies in their first years in America, the movies had now begun to support vaudeville.

Roxy decorated the insides of his theatres with the same kinds of flouncing that he used for the film showings. The ushers wore colorful silken uniforms that matched the carpets and walls. The walls offered ornate carvings in stone, brass, and wood; gargoyles stared from the balconies; plaster copies of Greek statues (attired in fig leaves) gazed down from trellised cupolas, bathed in a red or green floodlight.

The Roxy of the West Coast, Sid Grauman, paid as much attention to the outsides of his theatres as Roxy paid to the inside. His Chinese Theatre welcomed the patron with a complex system of pagoda roofs and Oriental carvings—and the cement footprints of the stars; his Egyptian Theatre offered patrons a waterfall and a wishing well as they walked in the door. In the 1950s, *The King and I* opened at the Chinese and *The Ten Commandments* at the Egyptian. The Roxies of the Midwest, who ran Balaban & Katz (Sam Katz and the brothers Barney and Abraham Balaban), gave the same grand treatment to the many theatres in their chain, pulling out all the stops for their glorious flagship, The Chicago. Even the smaller neighborhood theatre imitated the attractions of the movie palaces—electric stars twinkled in their stucco heavens as plaster copies of Greek gods and goddesses stared down from an Olympus decorated as a Spanish hacienda.

The Carthay Circle Theatre opened in 1926, one year before Grauman's Chinese. It too had a unique design, with its exterior patterned on a California mission, its circular auditorium (inspired by the Carthay Circle area of Los Angeles where the theatre was located), and its paintings—including one on the huge asbestos curtain—dedicated to "the pioneers of the Golden State"; the architect was Dwight Gibbs. Capable of seating 1,126 people, the Carthay was

a first-run house that opened big pictures from Walt Disney's *Snow White and the Seven Dwarfs* (1937) to Samuel Goldwyn's *Porgy and Bess* (1959). In 1928, it was converted for sound, and in 1956, it was remodeled for Todd-AO (which used a magnetic stereophonic soundtrack and an anamorphic 65mm image on 70mm film) to show Mike Todd's *Around the World in 80 Days*. The circular auditorium seemed to extend the wide, curved screen. But in 1969, it was torn down to make way for office buildings.

Even though some of them may strike us as tacky in their splendor, the movie palaces were carefully designed, luxurious fantasy worlds of their own, dedicated to the democracy of high-class entertainment. They were open to everyone, for the American movie theatre had always been a place where workers and vagabonds mingled with the middle and upper classes. They were warm in the winter, "refrigerated" in the summer. If you were a kid or out of work—particularly after 1929, as the Great Depression spread out from Wall Street to engulf the world—you could stay in that rich space all day long and dream.

Morality

The movies have waged a perpetual cold war with the forces of religion and righteousness. In 1896, the moralists denounced the improprieties of *The Kiss*. *Fatima* (1897), which depicted the bumps and grinds of a noted hoochy-coochy dancer of the day, so offended some members of certain communities that exhibitors superimposed broad white stripes across the screen to cover the areas where Fatima displayed her most lascivious wares.

Throughout the Nickelodeon Era the movies had been criticized as cultivators of iniquity; the theatres had been attacked as unsavory or unsafe. The protests of the moralistic few did not deter the entertainment-minded many from going to the nickelodeons. The parallels between the 20th-century moralistic controversy over the movies (still continuing today) and the 16th-century moralistic controversy over the Elizabethan theatre (also criticized as a breeder of licentiousness and laziness) are striking. The movie cold war escalated to a hot one in the early 1920s.

Fig. 6-14

Fig. 6-15

Fig. 6-16

Fig. 6-17

The Carthay Circle Theatre. Fig. 6-14: jammed for the 1937 premiere of Wee Willie Winkie. *Fig. 6-15: the painted asbestos curtain at the front of the circular auditorium. Fig. 6-16: the mezzanine. Fig. 6-17: one of the many snack bars.*

Fig. 6-18

Fig. 6-19

*Early film censorship: the
1897 hoochy-coochy dancer
Fatima, without and with her
censorship stripes.*

Sermons and Scandals

The content of films, reflecting the new materialism and moral relativism of the decade, became spicier and more suggestive. The sentimental films of the Griffith era had not disappeared; Griffith's own films, Mary Pickford's, Lois Weber's, and pictures like Henry King's *Tol'able David* (1921) perpetuated the tradition of innocence, purity, courage, and honor. But alongside these films were others suggesting that married couples indulge in extramarital flirtations (at the least) and that the urbane and wealthy are not inevitably evil and unhappy. The new materialistic audience (who spent as much as $2 to get into the plush movie palace before the Depression lowered prices) enjoyed films that idolized the material as well as the spiritual.

The sermonizers intensified their letter-writing and speech-making campaigns with concerted public action. Clergymen and laymen united to form panels and committees that would not exactly censor films, but that would advise parishioners and the public about which films to see and which to avoid. Behind the censorship drives of some of these organizations lay a thinly veiled anti-Semitism. The moral deficiencies of the movies were yet another stratagem of the Jewish infidels, once again poisoning the wells of a Christian nation. Against such attacks, the moral statements and strictures of the industry's own National Board of Review (its name changed from the National Board of Censorship in 1915 and its power undermined by the busting of the Trust that created it) were inadequate and powerless.

In the early 1920s, several national scandals rocked the film industry far more severely than had the letters and speeches of the zealots. Hollywood did not just sell pictures to the public; it sold the stars who sold the pictures. Scandal in the life of a star was more serious than any extra-marital wink on the screen. In 1920, Mary Pickford, "America's Sweetheart," quietly went to Nevada with her husband, Owen Moore, to get a divorce. Three weeks later "Little Mary" married her male counterpart in innocence and purity, Douglas Fairbanks. The public was not shocked by the divorce alone, since Hollywood divorces had already become old news. But this divorce, followed by the abrupt marriage of these two supposedly healthy, happy, all-American people, was something special. The Pickford–Fairbanks marriage was further complicated by the possibility that the divorce proceeding had been improperly executed ("Little Mary" eventually avoided the stain of bigamy). Though Doug and Mary had done nothing illegal, their illicit premarital romance seemed to contradict their screen purity. The tremendous public interest in this petty domestic affair clearly revealed the new social importance of the film industry and its vulnerability to attack by newspapers.

In 1921, two consecutive Fatty Arbuckle scandals fed the headlines. In July of that year newspapers ran stories about an Arbuckle party that had taken place in Massachusetts in 1917. The district attorney of a Massachusetts county had received a $100,000 gift just after the party,

and the public wondered what the district attorney had discovered that was worth such a sum to keep quiet. Then, in September 1921, Arbuckle threw a second party, this one in San Francisco's St. Francis Hotel. The next morning one of Arbuckle's guests, Virginia Rappe, was found dead in her hotel room. A week later Arbuckle gave himself up to the police, was eventually tried for involuntary manslaughter, and, after three trials (the first two ending with hung juries), was finally found not guilty. His innocence in the eyes of the law made no difference, however. He was finished.

Hollywood barred the evil Fatty from pictures. The great comedian worked in very few films, usually in small roles (for example, James Cruze's bitter 1923 satire, *Hollywood*—a film whose freeze-frames helped to popularize optical printing), although he continued to direct comic shorts under the name of Will B. Good! The moguls threw Arbuckle to the moralists, hoping to still the hissing tongues; the money men back East preferred a safe surrender to a possibly unsettling and certainly unprofitable confrontation. Some 30 years later, the film industry made an identical choice when it refused to defend the "Hollywood Ten" against the red-baiters and then instituted its blacklist.

In 1922, "handsome" Wallace Reid died suddenly, generating a posthumous scandal when the newspapers discovered he had used drugs. Early in the same year, director William Desmond Taylor was found dead in his apartment, a scandal with a vague mixture of sex, murder, and drugs. The Taylor murder hurt the careers of Mabel Normand, the gifted comedienne and early director, and Mary Miles Minter, a little-girl imitation of Mary Pickford, who were both friends of the director. The press, satisfying the hunger of its readers, turned these friendships into something salacious. There was no defense against vague rumor and veiled innuendo. Two more careers were thrown to the yapping dogs to keep them quiet.

The Hays Office

Such notoriety brought the film business to the attention of the U.S. Congress and to the edge of federal censorship—the last thing any producer wanted. The industry decided once again to clean its own house, to serve as its own censorship

Fig. 6-20

Moguls and morals—from left: Irving Thalberg, Louis B. Mayer, Will Hays, and Harry Rapf on the MGM lot.

body. Recalling the success of the baseball owners at finding a moralistic commissioner, the esteemed Judge Landis, to cleanse the "Black Sox" scandals, the film producers sought their own respected commissioner. In 1922, they found Will H. Hays, President Harding's campaign manager, Postmaster General of the United States, Presbyterian elder, and Republican.

Hays became president of the Motion Picture Producers and Distributors of America (MPPDA), an organization supported and financed by all the major film companies in America. It became known colloquially as the Hays Office, and he headed it for 23 years. In 1945, the MPPDA became the MPAA (Motion Picture Association of America), and Hays was succeeded by Eric Johnston, who headed the MPAA until 1966, when Jack Valenti became its president, a position he held until 2004.

Rather than taking concrete censorship actions, the Hays Office sought to counter bad publicity with good, to keep the press from magnifying its tales of Hollywood debauches, to regularize business procedures, and to encourage producers to submit their films voluntarily for prerelease examination. The loose, informal advising of the Hays Office in the 1920s was another in a series of successful Hollywood attempts to keep films out of the hands of government censors, a strategy that would be duplicated by the enforcement of the much stricter and more formal Hollywood Production Code of the 1930s and the MPAA Rating System (conceived by Jack Valenti) that was set up in 1968 and is still in force.

Films and Filmmakers, 1910–28

The ever-increasing problem of the American director was how to make an individualized, special film in a factory system geared toward standardization and mass production. The Griffith era of anarchy and improvisation was rapidly passing. Rather than being the artistic creator of his own films, the director was more and more expected to be the mechanic who hammered together the machine that others, the producer and writer, had earlier designed. Griffith himself noted with dismay the widening gap between producer and director, between the business of making a film and the art of making a film. Each movie, rather than being an important work in itself, became only one unit of the studio's yearly output. Though the films had gotten longer and the film business more complex, studio owners considered only the total yearly product, exactly as they did in the Patents Company days of the one-reeler. This industrialization of the film business is most relevant to the career of Thomas H. Ince, Griffith's contemporary and one of the most interesting American producers and directors of noncomic films before 1919.

Thomas Ince

Ince's films are almost the paradigmatic opposites of Griffith's. Whereas Griffith's technique aimed at developing the characters, their emotions, and the metaphoric implications of the action, Ince concentrated ruthlessly on the narrative flow. Ince was as avid a film editor as Griffith, but while Griffith cut to develop rhythm, emotion, and ideas, Ince—like Howard Hawks after him—cut to keep the story moving. Griffith's interest was in why the characters did something and what that implied symbolically; Ince's focused on what they did. Ince's symbolic antiwar epic, *Civilization* (1916), is an exception. More typical of Ince, however, is a film like *The Coward* (1915), a Civil War story that avoids all the symbolic freight of a *Birth of a Nation* to concentrate on one young man's earning his "red badge of courage." The titles of the films (the specificity of Ince's, the abstractness of Griffith's) are indicative.

The openness and movement that Griffith used for battle scenes and chases were the bases of Ince's films: the stagecoach sweeping down a mountain trail flanked by plains and sagebrush, the posse galloping across the prairies, the circling Indians, the dust and smoke and powder of the gun battle, the dust of the horses' hooves, the silhouettes of the Apaches on the mesa awaiting the moment to join the attack. One of the most common and beautiful Ince images is smoke—the swirling, enveloping movement of gunpowder or dust, shot through refractive beams of light. The producer Ince's most able director of these early westerns was Francis Ford, whose crisp, deep-focus shots established the photographic conventions of the western. Ince's productions also popularized one of the western's most enduring character types, the good–bad

man—embodied by William S. Hart. A little too tough, stubborn and ornery, sometimes even on the wrong side of the law, he could always be depended on to do the right thing in a crunch.

Contemporary with the nostalgic painting and sculpture of Frederick Remington and the pulp stories of Zane Grey, these Ince and Ford films depict a western frontier that was already disappearing under the tracks and ties of urbanization. Ince, Ford, and Hart would later pass on these legacies—the power of movement within vast western vistas and the dignity of the good–bad men who inhabit these spaces—to their successors: Ford's younger brother, John, as well as Howard Hawks, Sam Peckinpah, and many others.

As a supervisor of production, Ince could keep his finger on several projects at the same time. And as producer of his own films, he had complete control. Many current directors (Steven Spielberg, for example) have both directed and produced. Ince insisted on a detailed shooting script, which he eventually approved and stamped "Shoot as is." The Ince director then went about the business of constructing from the producer's blueprint. Ince supplemented the shooting script with a detailed production breakdown and schedule, making sure that all the people and animals and equipment went to the right place at the right time for the fewest number of hours. If Griffith was the American cinema's first real director, Ince was its first important producer, instituting the system that divided the artistic responsibility for a film between two people—or camps. Ince showed the future studio heads how to run a studio.

Ironically, Ince's career waned in the Studio Era itself. He was the hardest hit by the failure of the Triangle Film Corporation, which depended on his films and his Culver City studio. In 1915, the president of the Mutual Film Corporation, Harry Aitken, was ousted by his partner, John R. Freuler, in a power struggle. Aitken, who personally owned the Mutual contracts of Griffith, Sennett, and Ince, took the three with him to build the Triangle Film Corporation, with the three important directors as the tips of the triangle. But Griffith produced several weak program pictures, and Sennett's and Ince's drawing powers were feebler than they had been; all three left in 1917, and the company collapsed in 1919. Ince, the movie man of system and efficiency, died mysteriously (after having been shot on William Randolph Hearst's yacht—apparently by Hearst, who mistook him for someone else) in 1924, just when the era of system and efficiency had officially arrived with the Mayer–Thalberg rule at MGM, which stood on Ince's old lot.

Douglas Fairbanks

The films of Douglas Fairbanks also reveal the changing values of Hollywood. Fairbanks broke into films with Griffith at Triangle; the young actor was so athletic, so bouncy, so perpetually in motion that Griffith gave up on him and suggested he go see Mr. Sennett. Triangle eventually let Fairbanks go his own way, pairing him with writer Anita Loos, her director–husband John Emerson, and cameraman Victor Fleming. Between 1915 and 1920, the group produced a series of breezy, parodic, energetic comedies that combined the star's athleticism, energy, and sincerity with the writer's and director's wit and style. The early Fairbanks films—like the utterly outrageous *The Mystery of the Leaping Fish* (1916)—are refreshing surprises. They are parodies that make fun of a personality trait (American snobbishness, the fascination with royalty, the hunger for publicity, the ambition to achieve the impossible) or a genre of films (the western, the mystery, the melodrama). Fairbanks is the center of the parody, the magnified version of whatever the film is satirizing. But Fairbanks, because of his naïveté and enthusiasm, because of his obvious love of life and people, always succeeds in engaging our sympathies at the same time that we may be laughing at him. Loos and Emerson took advantage of the way that Fairbanks overdid everything; they made a virtue of overdoing. And Fairbanks's athleticism, his physical exhilaration, his constant movement, become a delight to watch. Fairbanks's acting technique seemed to center around such questions as: Why enter a room through a door when you can jump in through the window? Why walk up a flight of stairs when you can swing upstairs on a lighting fixture or vault through a hole in the downstairs ceiling?

One of the key contrasts in his early films is between the dull, routine, banal life Fairbanks must live in conventional society and the imaginative, free, vigorous life he wants to live.

Fairbanks was the foe of the dull and regimented; the row upon row of similar desks in the button factory of *Reaching for the Moon* (1917) was an image of everything he hated. The physical emphasis of Fairbanks's talent also led the star to value the source of the physical, the body. Fairbanks supplemented his onscreen cleanliness with magazine articles lauding the healthy life and disparaging the unhealthy lures of drink, tobacco, and gluttony.

The later Fairbanks films of the 1920s—*The Mark of Zorro* (1920, where he leads a real, not imaginary, double life as the movies' original caped crusader), *Robin Hood* (1922), *The Thief of Bagdad* (1924), and *The Black Pirate* (1926, shot in two-strip Technicolor)—make quite a contrast with the earlier, breezy ones. Fairbanks is still a great athlete; he still has his smile and energy. But he is no longer a contemporary American trying to strike a blend between his own imaginative impulses and the conventions of society. Fairbanks has been transported to faraway, romantic lands of long ago. He is free to perform exotic deeds, and although he is usually some kind of thief, he is not, paradoxically, dishonest. In addition to sparking his daring exploits, the far-off themes and places allow Fairbanks to become an explicit sex symbol, gliding through most of the films without his shirt, with limbs clearly defined by a pair of tights or slightly exposed by the scanty cloth that teasingly covers his middle.

DeMille and von Stroheim

No two directors more clearly show the problems of the filmmaker in the 1920s than Cecil B. DeMille and Erich von Stroheim (he added the "von" himself and may be referred to as Stroheim or von Stroheim). As were Griffith and Ince a few years earlier, the two are almost paradigms for the whole industry. Von Stroheim gave the public what he wanted; DeMille gave it what he thought it wanted. Von Stroheim was a ruthless realist committed to his art and his vision; DeMille was willing to throw in any faddish or striking hokum. Von Stroheim's greatest tools were close observation and detail; DeMille's were size and splash. DeMille was a big producer; von Stroheim's tragedy was that he had to depend on producers. Von Stroheim's films, despite their adult themes, were controlled by the director's

The Americano gone exotic—
Douglas Fairbanks in The
Thief of Bagdad.

Fig. 6-21

taste and intelligence; most of DeMille's films
had everything but taste and intelligence.

Both DeMille and von Stroheim served
several apprentice years before emerging as
major directors. DeMille shot his first film, *The
Squaw Man* (1914; co-directed by Oscar Apfel),
for Jesse Lasky's Feature Play Company in 1913;
it was the first feature-length western shot in
Hollywood. The Lasky company was formed by
Lasky, DeMille, and Samuel Goldfish in 1913 after
Goldfish convinced his brother-in-law, Lasky, to
go into pictures and leave vaudeville; in 1916, it
merged with Zukor's company, Famous Players
(founded 1912), to become Famous Players–
Lasky. (In 1922, Goldfish left to form a new
company with Edgar Selwyn; "Gold" + "wyn"
became Goldwyn, and Goldfish soon named
himself after the studio. With Goldfish gone,
Zukor consolidated Famous Players–Lasky and
several other companies into Paramount, for
which DeMille directed most of his films.)
DeMille began keeping track of national trends
and tastes. Von Stroheim began as a studio
adviser on European military details and an
assistant to (and player for) Griffith, then began
playing Prussian officers and other vicious

"Huns" (he was dubbed "the man you love to
hate"), and finally, in 1919, persuaded Carl
Laemmle to let him write, direct, and perform in
his own films.

The two films that most clearly reveal the
differences between the two men are DeMille's
Male and Female and von Stroheim's *Blind
Husbands*. Both were released in 1919; both
capitalized on the new audience interest in
sexual amours and the doings of the rich. Both
suggested the importance of sex in human
relationships. There the similarities stop. *Male
and Female* is a lavish, pretentious, and inconsistent examination of the class question, which
seems to suggest both that masters may marry
their servants and that masters may not marry
their servants. Although some of the film's
confusion stems from the J. M. Barrie play
DeMille was adapting, *The Admirable Crichton*
(to be adapted again by Lina Wertmüller in 1975
as *Swept Away . . .*), the most dazzling stupidi-
ties are DeMille's "additions." For example, the
film begins with an irrelevant sequence that does
not exist in the original play, a series of shots of
oceans and the Grand Canyon, followed by a
biblical quote, "God created man in his own

image." Much of DeMille's later work also uses the Bible to dignify its distinctly lay interests.

DeMille then plunges into the affairs of a contemporary British household, spending a lot of time on the elegance of Gloria Swanson's taking a bath (scented with rose water), the water temperature's being checked carefully by her maid, Gloria's striding carefully and sliding gently into the sunken tub. One of DeMille's titles asks why the bathroom shouldn't express as much elegance as anything else in life, and his even asking such a question is at the heart of what is empty about the film—although DeMille's materialistic Jazz Age audiences must surely have been delighted to see the answer. Meanwhile, DeMille contrasts the highfalutin ways of Lady Mary (Gloria), who rejects a piece of toast because it is too soft, with the simple ways of Tweeny, her maid. Simple Tweeny is in love with the butler, Crichton (Thomas Meighan). But, alas, he is not simple; he loves Lady Mary; he reads aloud poetry that Tweeny cannot understand but Lady Mary can.

Then the whole family takes a yachting trip and runs aground. Having already filmed the Creation and a chic English drawing-room comedy, DeMille can now add a kind of Swiss Family Robinson. On the island, it turns out that he who is lower class in one society is upper class in another. Crichton, the butler, becomes the natural leader of the group, and they become his servants, simply because he is competent and fit to survive, while they are all numbskulls trying to play at being posh in the wilderness. The only unaltered element is that Crichton still loves Mary (now no longer a Lady), and she discovers that she loves him. One night, fearing for her safety, Crichton follows her to the haunt of the lions where he slays a beast that is about to attack her. The male and female vow their love. And now DeMille throws in the kitchen sink.

There is an instantaneous and unmotivated cut to Babylon (the scene does not exist, of course, in Barrie's play). The motivation for the shift is the line of poetry that Crichton and Mary have read in the film (Barrie uses the line just once, but DeMille repeats it several times so we don't miss it), "If I were a king of Babylon. . . ." DeMille is not one to leave his ifs iffy. In this sequence, Crichton is indeed king, and Mary is a Christian slave. The fact that the Babylonian empire had evaporated hundreds of years before

the coming of Christ does not offend DeMille's sense of history.

This film is clearly one of the bastard progeny of *Intolerance* in its combination of different epochs in a single film. But in *Male and Female*, the diversity is pointless and pretentious, and the moralizing is hypocritical, as DeMille's often was. His racy films (like *Why Change Your Wife?*, 1920, and *Forbidden Fruit*, 1922) flirt with naughtiness and sell conventionality; his religious films—including both the 1923 and 1956 versions of *The Ten Commandments*—magnify both righteousness and lewdness.

Nevertheless, DeMille's importance is extreme. *The Squaw Man* put Hollywood on the map, and for decades DeMille remained, in many minds, the ultimate Hollywood director and producer. In *Sunset Blvd.* (1950) Billy Wilder cast him as an exemplary professional. His pictures were always big, good-looking, and entertaining, a guaranteed good time. His westerns (*The Virginian*, 1914; *The Plainsman*, 1936, released 1937) and some of his melodramas were gripping. The very best of his silents, *The Cheat* (1915, starring Sessue Hayakawa as a Japanese collector—changed to Burmese in the 1918 reissue—who brands a woman who reneges on a sexual deal), is so darkly and richly lit that it could be mistaken for a post-Expressionist *film noir*.

Von Stroheim's *Blind Husbands* is a far less complicated story than *Male and Female*. A doctor and his wife travel to the Alps; he pays her insufficient sexual attention. A German military officer named von Steuben (played by von Stroheim) does his best to seduce the young wife. The husband's blindness finally clears up; on a climactic hiking trip, the two males confront each other on the pinnacle, and the rival perishes, more a victim of the mountains and of cowardice than of the husband. The power of the film lies in von Stroheim's reduction of the quantity of incidents (quantity was DeMille's credo) to develop the quality, the feeling, the texture of the incidents he includes. Von Stroheim was such a master of *mise-en-scène* that his films remain powerful even if they were recut (actually, massacred) by lesser talents after having been taken out of his hands; we can still see what's *in the shot* and respond to that. Details develop the film's emotional dynamics: the calm husband's pipe; the wife's provocative ankles and shoes; the officer's handling of his monocle and his careful primping with brush, comb, and vaporizer of cologne to make himself sexually attractive; the soulful tune that Margaret (the wife) plays on the piano, joined by von Steuben on the violin, which shows both her loneliness and her desire. Von Stroheim's attention to detail gave him complete control of understatement.

Von Stroheim's technique owes its greatest debt to his first master, Griffith. As Griffith had, von Stroheim realized that the filmmaker's principal tools are editing (montage) and staging and design (*mise-en-scène*). Von Stroheim's care with sets, lighting, costumes, and decor is so meticulous in creating his seamy world that you can almost smell it. In *Blind Husbands*, the details of the inn courtyard, of the dining room with its posters and crockery, of the individual bedrooms, of the fog and mist on the pinnacle, all contribute to the tone of the film and the power of each scene. From *Blind Husbands* on, his films were shot or co-shot by Ben F. Reynolds, whose eye was every bit as sharp as Bitzer's.

As an editor, von Stroheim further developed Griffith's devices of the cross-cut (to show parallel events in different places at the same time) and the subjective cut (to show the mental projection of a character: what is in his or her mind's eye at a particular moment). In *Blind Husbands*, von Stroheim's cross-cutting develops both tension and irony. For example, he shows the doctor delivering a baby at the same time that von Steuben courts his wife, obviously trying to perform the act that produces babies. The most striking subjective cut in *Blind Husbands* comes just after the husband has discovered the Prussian's designs on his wife: a cut to a menacing, spot-lit head of the rival, looming out of the darkness until it fills the frame, leering grotesquely at the doctor.

André Bazin described von Stroheim's "one simple rule for direction": "Take a close look at the world, keep on doing so, and in the end it will lay bare for you all its cruelty and ugliness." Von Stroheim's films are populated with physical cripples and mental defectives (whose like the screen would not see until Tod Browning's *Freaks* and Luis Buñuel's *Land Without Bread*—both 1932 and both controversial), but even beneath the surfaces of his more elegant characters—their

polished manners, white gloves, and spray perfume—lurk animal rapacity, vicious cruelty, obsessive desire, and the brutal will to power. In von Stroheim's Naturalistic worldview, heredity, instinct, psychopathology, environment, and economics determine behavior. He observes it all with the sharp eye of a realist—but a realist to whom the resources of Expressionism are available.

The realities he strove to portray were often unpleasant. In the grimmest part of *Foolish Wives* (1921, which Universal hyped as "the first million dollar picture" and cut from just over 21 to just over 14 reels before releasing it in 1922; now about ten reels survive), a fake Russian count and con artist (von Stroheim) rapes a disabled young woman. At the end of the film, her father kills the villain and dumps his body into the sewer so it can be swept out to sea with the other garbage.

Foolish Wives made von Stroheim world famous. When Jean Renoir saw it, he decided to make movies instead of ceramics. Like *Blind Husbands* and *The Devil's Pass-Key* (1920, now lost), and even his later *The Merry Widow* (1925), *Foolish Wives* was extremely popular with audiences who appreciated its careful examination of bedroom tensions. The haughty independence of its director was less popular with the heads of studios. The greatest realist of the Silent Era, von Stroheim, in his refusal to compromise, made stunning films and lasting enemies.

Erich von Stroheim was a completist, a perfectionist, an idealist who took film and its possibilities absolutely seriously. He was forced to work with executives who maintained that they had an instinct for show business and knew better than anyone else what made a good picture—or had experience with budgets and could recognize an advisable investment. Most of them regarded von Stroheim as an egomaniac whose projects always needed to be brought under control.

Irving Thalberg, who was to become MGM's most creative production executive before his early death, hated von Stroheim and his work. When Thalberg was Carl Laemmle's assistant at Universal, he removed von Stroheim from *Merry-Go-Round* (1922) in the middle of shooting, firing him for his "inefficient" (that is, perfectionistic and uncompromising) production methods, his wasteful expenditures on "invisible" details (which were actually quite visible in the

Fig. 6-22

On location: Gibson Gowland and ZaSu Pitts in Greed.

convincing realism and texture of the film), and his insubordination (von Stroheim said they often "crossed swords"). At MGM, Thalberg would get the chance to fire von Stroheim again—and beyond that, to destroy his greatest work, in one of film history's true horror stories, the re-editing of *Greed* (1924).

Greed

Von Stroheim had long wanted to film a complete novel, and the one he chose—by Frank Norris, a writer he knew Griffith admired, for his story "A Deal in Wheat" had been the basis of *A Corner in Wheat*—was *McTeague, A Story of San Francisco* (1899). In 1922, he interested Samuel Goldwyn in backing the project and was hired by the Goldwyn Company, whose slogan was "the author and the play are the thing."

McTeague attracted von Stroheim for many reasons. It was uncompromisingly realistic, psychologically intriguing, and structured like a greased slide to Hell. Like von Stroheim, Norris was a realist (to be specific, a Naturalist in the tradition of Émile Zola) with a taste for the pathological. Many of von Stroheim's films and Norris's novels are about people who fall victim to traps they have set for themselves without knowing it, people whose very lives are traps. Further, the novel's family of German immigrants roughly

paralleled von Stroheim's own heritage (he was born in Vienna, the son of a Jewish hatter from Prussia), and the novel's familiar San Francisco and Oakland settings appealed to a man who had lived there before going to Hollywood.

Von Stroheim did not, as it is often said, set out to film *McTeague* page by page; his script includes most of the novel but changes and adds a great deal, and where the novel was strictly realistic, the film was that and more. Shot almost entirely on location in an era of studio shooting, it was also an experiment in Expressionism; it observed behavior from the outside, as tightly and scrupulously as the job has ever been done, but it also dipped into the mind and displayed its disturbing contents.

In the leading roles, he cast Gibson Gowland as McTeague, ZaSu Pitts as Trina (one of the silent screen's greatest performances), and Jean Hersholt as Marcus. In addition to Ben Reynolds, the cinematographers were William H. Daniels and Ernest B. Schoedsack. With cast and crew, von Stroheim went to San Francisco to shoot on the very streets named in the novel, and even to Death Valley (in the summer!) to obtain absolutely authentic details. Jean Hersholt had to be hospitalized after the grueling takes in Death Valley. The film took seven months to shoot and cost $470,000; then von Stroheim edited it for months.

The original version of *Greed*—previewed to two journalists, who wrote about what they saw, and one director—ran 42 reels, a mere nine hours at 20 fps. That first audience felt they had seen the greatest movie ever made or likely to be made. Von Stroheim himself shortened the film to 24 reels (just over five hours, considered the "director's version"), to be shown in two parts, with a dinner break after the wedding sequence. His friend at Metro, Rex Ingram (who had been the director in that first audience), cut the film to 18 reels and forbade von Stroheim to let anyone take another foot out of it. By this time the Maria/Zerkow and Baker/Grannis stories, to be discussed below, had been trimmed drastically but not deleted, and the film was still in two parts.

Meanwhile, as mentioned earlier, the Goldwyn Company—without Goldwyn, who had been forced out by his partners but who soon founded Samuel Goldwyn Productions entirely on his own—merged in 1924 with Metro Pictures (which was owned by Marcus Loew of Loew's Inc., the man who arranged the merger) and with Louis B. Mayer Productions, forming Metro–Goldwyn–Mayer. Mayer hired Thalberg away from Universal and put him directly in charge of production. All this made *Greed* an MGM property and put von Stroheim at Thalberg's mercy, which was not a good place to be. Fully backed up by Mayer, Thalberg turned the film over to the MGM story and editing departments; under the supervision of June Mathis, a hack cutter and title writer named Joseph W. Farnham—who had not read the book or the script—completed the hatchet job. What was left of a long, tight masterpiece was a mess; von Stroheim said the cutter had nothing on his mind but a hat.

The final version of *Greed* began with a very bad poem about gold. The lengthy prologue was cut to less than five minutes. Mathis and Farnham wrote idiotic intertitles to patch up some of the holes they had created in the story's continuity and in the characters' motivations. In addition, many scenes were shuffled out of order, and three Expressionist shots—out of all those sequences, many of which had presented the dreams and hallucinations of a crazy junkman, obsessed with discovering a huge service of solid gold, but some of which had used grotesque shadows and figures to convey the violence and madness of the waking world—were cut into the realistic footage as "symbolic" commentary on the greed of the characters. *Greed* was released at ten reels (2¼ hours with no intermission), no copies of the earlier versions were made, and except for the ten reels used in *Greed*, the negative was destroyed along with all the outtakes so that the silver might be retrieved from the celluloid.

The *Greed* that exists (the release version) must be watched as a series of parts rather than as a whole. It's all that's left. For one who hasn't read Norris's novel, the film's narrative is almost incomprehensible. The concrete process of the dissolution of the relationship between the dentist, John McTeague (Mac), and his wife, Trina Sieppe, makes no sense in the film, for in the novel Norris carefully charts it by moving the couple to shabbier and shabbier living quarters—a practice followed in von Stroheim's script (which was faithful to the novel but not afraid to add a feature-length prologue, a funeral at a wedding, or a second pet bird). Each degradation in their physical surroundings implies or contributes to their bodily, emotional, moral, and psychological degradation. But in *Greed*, although we may notice that the walls of the McTeague household change as the film progresses, we never know exactly when, why, and where the couple has moved, or how the delicate Trina became so rough and sloppy. Although in one shot we may notice that Trina's bandaged hand is missing several fingers, the film only hints that she lost them because they became infected after her husband bit them. The dissolution from happy marriage to vicious, insane combat—which is, both psychologically and economically, the meticulously observed subject of at least half of the novel (and of the screenplay)—barely exists in the film.

Another reason this sense of gradual, inevitable dissolution is lost is that the ten-reel version had to do without two other "love" relationships in the novel that undoubtedly seemed superfluous to a hack writer and cutter but that are really essential. The relationship between Trina and Mac is bounded, on the one hand, by old Grannis and Miss Baker, a couple of timid old folks who carry on a genteel, unphysical love affair, and, on the other, by Zerkow (the crazy junkman) and Maria Macapa, two obsessed, slovenly human beasts whose "love" is based on Zerkow's almost sexual pleasure in listening to the equally insane Maria's story of the golden service. Maria remains in the released film barely long enough to sell Trina the fateful lottery ticket (Trina becomes a miser after she wins the lottery); Zerkow is deleted entirely. All that remains of their love story are a few shots of skeletal, photographically distorted arms playing with distorted treasures; taken out of the Maria–Zerkow context and applied to Trina, these shots seem irrelevant and pretentious. In the novel, we understand the original love of Mac and Trina, together with their originally rational view of money, as a median between the sexual repression and parsimony of the old folks and the crazed passion of the gold lovers. Trina begins as Miss Baker's close friend, somewhat repulsed by Maria's crudeness, and gradually drifts into becoming Maria's confidante. Mac and Trina even move into the squalid hovel where Zerkow and Maria lived (which became vacant when Zerkow cut Maria's throat). Without the two poles of these other couples, *Greed* has no moral scale on which to measure the direction and degree of decay in the central couple; it is a triptych missing its outer panels.

Despite the incoherence of *Greed* as a whole, the *mise-en-scène* survives within the surviving shots. The wedding ceremony is a mixture of the comic and the somber: a parody of wedding customs that is overshadowed by the sight of a funeral cortege through an open window (a great use of deep focus and an omen of the direction the marriage will take). The scene in which Trina realizes that she is alone—with no one to protect her except the stranger who is her husband—is a rich examination of her feelings. The mad scene that climaxes her perverse confusion of money and sex, where she lies naked in bed with her gold, is daring, terrifying, and cinematically unprecedented. Mac's murder of Trina is a study in shadow—indoors, at night, as dark as any *noir*—while the showdown between Mac and Marcus in Death Valley is all pitiless light.

That same vision dominates even the fluffy trifle that Thalberg assigned von Stroheim after *Greed. The Merry Widow* (1925) was a safe property, a Viennese operetta that Thalberg was sure von Stroheim could not destroy. Von Stroheim apparently did not destroy it; the film was one of his greatest commercial successes. But von Stroheim, in adapting this operetta fairy tale, devotes a disproportionate amount of attention to the widow's first husband (before she became a widow) rather than her resulting merry widowhood. The husband is a deformed cripple (von Stroheim accentuates the deformity) with a very obvious sexual fetish: He is attracted to healthy feet—a theme that von Stroheim develops with

Fig. 6-23

The wedding scene of Greed, *composed in depth, with the funeral procession outside on the street below.*

pointed cutting. Worse, he is so excited on his wedding night that he collapses and dies on top of his bride, worn out from dragging his gnarled body up to the bed of love. Von Stroheim's handling of this unsavory relationship is not exactly operetta fare. When the widow's three suitors come to watch her perform at the theatre, all three stare at her through opera glasses. Then von Stroheim cuts to the object of their stares: the cripple watches her feet; the lecher watches her groin; the young hero watches her face. Such touches turned Franz Lehár's operetta into a salacious parody of an operetta.

Because his production methods seemed extravagant, because he seemed mean and tyrannical, unwholesome and unpleasant, Erich von Stroheim was very easy to fire, even if his films made money. *The Merry Widow* was his last film for MGM and MGM's first big hit. He went to work for Zukor and had as little success with him as with Thalberg. After two very interesting projects of 1926–29, *The Wedding March* (which starred von Stroheim, ZaSu Pitts, and Fay Wray; began as a production for Pat Powers's independent company, Celebrity Pictures; became a Paramount picture when Zukor bought Powers out; and was drastically cut before its 1928 release—although we now have the benefit of von Stroheim's 1957 recut of the first half of what was to have been a two-part film, his greatest work after *Greed*) and *Queen Kelly* (released 1932; starring and produced by Gloria Swanson, who fired him too), Erich von Stroheim directed only one other film, *Walking Down Broadway* (1932, released 1933 as *Hello, Sister!* after much tampering and reshooting by others). For the next 25 years von Stroheim continued acting in films—one of the many ways his career anticipated that of Orson Welles—most memorably as von Rauffenstein in *Grand Illusion* (1937; directed by Renoir, whose entire career and aesthetic he had decisively influenced) and as Max, the chauffeur and former movie director, in *Sunset Blvd.* The irony of this late film was not only that von Stroheim played a character whose career echoed his own (the clips Norma Desmond screens in the movie are from his own *Queen Kelly*), but also that he played the devoted servant of Gloria Swanson, who was with him at the stormy end of his Hollywood road.

Henry King

Despite his long career, Henry King may always be remembered as the director of *Tol'able David* (1921). The Soviet director and theorist V. I. Pudovkin found King's use of cutting to build a scene as instructive and effective as Griffith's. *Tol'able David* is a powerful film in which King, the student of Griffith and the employee of Ince, combines the best of both masters. King's world in *Tol'able David* is similar to Griffith's Kentucky: rural, homey, gently comic, touching, pastoral. Into the peaceful world come the violent figures from outside, three fugitives from justice, who are as vicious, as nasty, as psychotically mean as Battling Burrows—or, for that matter, as the degenerate groups in Sam Peckinpah's *Straw Dogs* (1971) and Wes Craven's *The Hills Have Eyes* (1977). Like Griffith, King defines the characters by their responses to animals: David lovingly plays with his dog, Rocket; the invaders kill Rocket out of pure meanness. And the worst thing anyone can do in a Hollywood movie is kill a dog.

King shows how to bring a story alive with significant and memorable detail by manipulating the visual, "plastic material" (Pudovkin's term). Richard Barthelmess, Griffith's own figure of gentle sincerity, plays David; his face and presence contribute greatly to the charm, warmth, and urgency of the story. King's cutting drives the emotions of the tale; the horror of the irreversible injury to David's brother, Alan, and its impact on Rose, his wife, come alive as King repeatedly cuts from the crippled, helpless Alan in bed to a shot of Rose, sitting in a rocking chair, holding their new infant, rocking relentlessly back and forth, back and forth. Brutality clashes, intentionally, with the sweeter strains of the picture. Like Ince, King actually depicted malicious violence on the screen: one of the villains digging his finger into the gunshot wound in David's shoulder, for example.

King directed Lillian Gish in two very successful silents, *The White Sister* (1923) and *Romola* (1924). His later works include *Alexander's Ragtime Band* (1938), *Twelve O'Clock High* (1949), *The Gunfighter* (1950), *Carousel* (1956), and *Tender is the Night* (1962).

Paul Robeson in the 1924 version of Micheaux's Body and Soul.

Fig. 6-24

Oscar Micheaux and the Race Movie

Oscar Micheaux, born in Metropolis, Illinois, in 1884, was one of the earliest black filmmakers. He published his first book, the autobiographical novel *The Conquest*, in 1913 at his own expense. Four years later, he nearly joined the Lincoln Motion Picture Company, formed in 1916 by black actor Noble Johnson, but the deal fell apart when they refused to allow him to direct his first picture. That was Micheaux's last brush with Hollywood, and what he did was brush it off. He became a one-man studio, based primarily in Manhattan but active in the Midwest and elsewhere. Between 1918 and 1948, Micheaux singlehandedly wrote, produced, directed, edited, and distributed more than 30 features for the Micheaux Film Corporation.

His first picture, *The Homesteader* (1918), was based on his own novel—the book that Lincoln Pictures had wanted someone else to direct. In 1919, he made *Within Our Gates* (released 1920), the first picture to present a lynching from an African-American point of view. In 1920, he showed blacks fighting back against the KKK in *The Symbol of the Unconquered*, whose title played cleverly on a line from *The Birth of a Nation*, where the burning cross is called the "symbol of an unconquered race"; the

unconquered here are brave, honest, hardworking blacks. During the 1920s, his most popular film was *Body and Soul* (1924, remade 1925), which starred the great singer Paul Robeson in the double role of a nice young man and an evil phony preacher.

As for Robeson, after starring in *The Emperor Jones* on stage and screen, he left for England, where the industry was more open to giving serious roles to blacks. There he starred in such films as *Song of Freedom* (1936), *King Solomon's Mines* (1937), and *The Proud Valley* (1940), though he also dropped back to the United States to sing "Ol' Man River" in *Show Boat* (1936), a song whose lyrics he would ironically revise in his peace concerts and leftist rallies.

Never as political as Robeson, but just as determined to make the world listen to a black voice, Micheaux set the pattern and created the market for the "race movie." Race movies were made with black casts for black audiences and played in segregated theatres (or in special after-hours showings at other theatres), and they lasted about as long as segregated theatres did, falling to the civil rights movement as much as to such all-black-cast Hollywood pictures as *Carmen Jones* (1954, directed by Otto Preminger and starring Dorothy Dandridge, the most compelling black woman on screen since Lena Horne). Although few filmmakers followed Micheaux in building their plots around mixed-blood romances, they did follow him in ditching Hollywood stereotypes of black characters and in tackling a broad range of genres, including the gangster picture (*Dark Manhattan*, 1937; directed by Harry Fraser, written and produced by George Randol, and starring Ralph Cooper), the "woman's picture" (*The Scar of Shame*, 1926, made in Philadelphia by the Colored Players Film Corporation—with a white director, Frank Perugini), and the western (*Two-Gun Man from Harlem*, 1938, directed by Richard C. Kahn).

Whether it was set in a strict religious context or in a nightclub, the battle between good and evil became a dominant theme of the race movie, without any urging from the Hays Office. From the troubling image of the duplicitous "man of God" in *Body and Soul* to the dripping holy blood that saves a soul in Spencer Williams's devout afterlife folk drama, *The Blood of Jesus* (1941), sin is a serious matter in these pictures, not something to flirt with, and choices are made at genuine moral crossroads, by real characters.

Resenting the way Hollywood portrayed blacks (whether they were cast as servants, in comic roles, or picking cotton—as they usually were—he found the actors "ugly"), Micheaux filled his films with beautiful women, decent and handsome men, and children who were as attractive and perceptive as Hollywood's white kids. Though his films did good business around the country, and great business in Latin America, Micheaux was particularly aware that his films were needed in the South, where black audiences had no other opportunity to see blacks who (like many rich blacks in the big cities of the North) lived in penthouses, had servants, and went out to the best nightclubs; only in Micheaux's films could they see African-American actors playing leading roles and, as Micheaux actress Bee Freeman put it, "really dressed up, really living, and talking like people talk." Most of his films proudly featured "An All Colored Cast"; he had a company of well-known actors recruited from Harlem and from Broadway. He also included a showgirl scene in almost every film (regardless of plot relevance,

deliberately for the black men in the Southern audience), using cabaret dancers or acts from the Cotton Club—shooting late at night, after the clubs had closed and the dancers had been picked up in a bus and taken to wherever they might be shooting. And "wherever" describes it, for Micheaux would shoot in churches, cabarets, lobbies, railroad stations—anything he could get, including farmhouses when he was shooting on the road.

Although he did not drive (and so hired a chauffeur), Micheaux was on the road much of the time, raising money, lining up bookings, and sometimes shooting on location. "A genius able to talk anyone out of their shirts," as actor Lorenzo Tucker (his "Valentino") described him, Micheaux might simply drive into a town, raise local money for shooting part or all of a movie, shoot there with locals for actors, show the film there, and add it to the collection of films he drove or shipped around the country. Often in the South, late on Saturday night in a regular movie house, a Micheaux film might be shown after the regular feature—because Micheaux would be in town with it.

But the majority of his films were made in big cities, on tight, precise budgets and with smart showmanship. He was the first African American to make a talkie: *The Exile* (1931), based on his first novel, *The Conquest*. As he had once sold that and his other novels (*The Homesteader*, *The Forged Note*) from door to door, he drove from town to town with his sound pictures, bringing the Cotton Club to Georgia and (since it went unrepresented in other pictures) Harlem to Harlem—in his own way, of course, with melodramatic plots that often turned on issues of racial identity. Many of Micheaux's films climax with the characters' finding out who they are— that is, who their parents are (*Within Our Gates*) and whether they have black or white blood. *The Exile* concerns a black man from Chicago who goes to South Dakota and falls in love with a white woman, who fortunately turns out to be partly black. *God's Step Children* (1938)—a film that combined and went beyond *Imitation of Life* and *These Three*, as its trailer pointed out— told the unhappy story of a light-skinned girl described by a schoolmate as "stuck up, and she don't want to be colored."

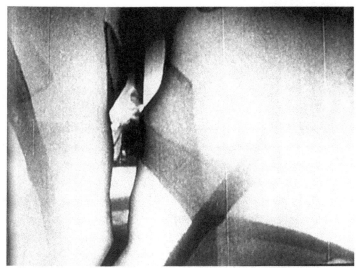

The Fall of the House of Usher: *ripping the image.*

Fig. 6-25

Micheaux's pictures looked and sounded rough. He shot no retakes. His cutting was hamhanded, and sometimes he even had problems with screen direction—as when characters in separate shots run away from each other into each other. But even when the stories were corny and the acting was awful, the films were exciting because they showed blacks living lives far more genuine than anything Hollywood had even thought of offering. A diversely talented man who, as Freeman said, "wouldn't let *anyone* tell him what to do," Micheaux got the films made, and he got them shown. He was the first black filmmaker anywhere in the world to become widely known, and not coincidentally the most persistent.

Webber and Watson

One of the challenges the narrative film has regularly set itself is that of adapting a literary work for the screen. From *Greed* to *The Maltese Falcon* (1941), the problem—and the solution—has been to discover cinematic ways of conveying the essence as well as the characters, style, plot, and point of the purely verbal original. In 1928, one of the greatest of all avant-garde teams—in effect, the American rivals of the Surrealists Luis Buñuel and Salvador Dalí in France—independently shot and released their masterpiece, *The Fall of the House of Usher,*

based on the story by Edgar Allan Poe; they were James Sibley Watson (director and cinematographer) and Melville Webber (writer and art director). This one-reel Expressionist film—a silent whose music track was added later—uses torn and multiplied images, ominous shadows, stylized figures and sets, superimposed graphics, extreme shooting angles, every special effect possible at the time, and jagged, dizzying movement to conjure a mood—entirely true to Poe—of intermingled beauty and horror. (The same year, in France, Jean Epstein directed a four-reel Impressionist version, *La Chute de la maison Usher.*) Webber and Watson's only other film was *Lot in Sodom* (1933), a biblical adaptation whose sexual content proved too strong for audiences of the day.

Weber and Women

As a producer reporting to Thalberg at MGM, but given a free hand by him, Lillian Gish took on the challenge of adapting Nathaniel Hawthorne's *The Scarlet Letter*, a project that had been opposed by every women's club in the country because its plot concerns adultery with a capital A, not to mention with a clergyman. When MGM told her "it wasn't allowed," she said, "What do you mean it's not allowed? It's an American classic, and I'm an American—why can't I make it?" When Gish contacted the women's clubs and told them she

A lobby card for Lois
Weber's The Blot (1921).
Her company's logo
(bottom left) was
Aladdin's lamp.

 A LOIS WEBER PRODUCTION   "THE BLOT"   RELEASED BY F. B. WARREN CORPORATION

Fig. 6-26

would be in charge of the project, their respect for her good taste and judgment led them to drop all opposition. To direct *The Scarlet Letter* (1926), she brought Victor Sjöström (who signed his American pictures Seastrom) to Hollywood from Sweden. The picture was a great success— as were Gish's other productions, including the 1926 *La Bohème*, adapted from the novel and play on which Puccini's opera was based. But her greatest production, and the second film Sjöström directed for her, was *The Wind* (1928), based closely on the 1925 novel by Dorothy Scarborough and shot in the Mojave Desert. In this film Gish gives one of her very finest performances—her best since *Way Down East*— as a woman driven mad by the relentless, demonic, almost sexually charged wind that drives the sand across the Texas plains and through every crack in the shack she shares with her husband. Originally ending with the same powerful scene as the novel, in which the heroine—after killing and burying the man who assaulted her— walks into the oblivion of madness and blowing sand, *The Wind* was given a happy ending (in which she and her husband stand together at the open door, powerfully facing the wind) at the

insistence of exhibitors. Even when she was not credited as producer, Gish often initiated the films in which she starred, such as *The White Sister*. She also directed a film that starred her sister, Dorothy: *Remodeling Her Husband* (1920).

Other women worked in Hollywood, and not just in front of the camera. A great many were script supervisors, screenwriters, film editors, and negative cutters. As a producer of narrative films, Mary Pickford was one of the most important figures in the industry. Margaret Winkler Mintz was the first woman to produce and distribute cartoons; in 1922, when she was 25, she founded M. J. Winkler & Co. in New York, and within a year it became the world's largest distributor of shorts. Earlier, when she had been working as Harry Warner's secretary and found that Warner Bros. had turned down Pat Sullivan's offer of a Felix the Cat series, *she* bought it. In 1923, Walt Disney asked her to distribute his first series, *Alice in Cartoonland* (which used live and animated figures in the same shots, a device that continued to interest Disney throughout his career), and she not only agreed but helped him improve it. Her husband, Charles Mintz,

Fig. 6-27

Alice Guy's **The Tigress** *played to packed houses in 1914.*

produced the Krazy Kat cartoons. (The first animated feature was made by a woman, Lotte Reiniger, in Germany in 1926.)

In the 1910s and early 1920s, at least 30 women directors were active in Hollywood, many of them—like Ida May Park and Ruth Ann Baldwin—at Universal Pictures, where Carl Laemmle was in favor of hiring women. Perhaps the greatest of them all was Lois Weber, who was born in Pennsylvania in 1882. Weber became a street evangelist and then an actress. In 1908, she began making films at Gaumont in New Jersey, under the supervision of Herbert Blaché—whose wife, Alice Guy Blaché, had been the first woman to make a film. Weber joined Universal as a contract director in 1912. Between then and the end of the Silent Era, she was the best known American woman director and the most highly paid female director in the world.

In 1917, Weber set up her own Los Angeles studio, Lois Weber Productions. Her husband, Phillips Smalley, was her "advisory director" and co-author, but she was by far the dominant creative figure. Between 1912 and 1927 she wrote, directed, and in most cases produced 45 films, many of which starred either herself or the woman she made a star, Claire Windsor. Weber was deeply concerned with social and spiritual

issues and saw the cinema as a way to spread moral messages to a vast audience. Like Griffith (*What Shall We Do With Our Old?*), she was a pioneer in what would later be called the "problem picture," and the issues addressed in her timely, insightful, compassionate, superbly crafted films remain relevant. Her works include *Hypocrites* (1914), *Where Are My Children* (1916, about abortion), and *The Blot* (1921, about underpaid professors). She lost her studio in 1923 when she and Smalley divorced. In the late 1920s, she made a few pictures for Universal and her last silent (*The Angel of Broadway*, 1927, about a Salvation Army worker) for DeMille. She directed one talkie (*White Heat*—not the one with Cagney) in 1934.

Dorothy Arzner, who was to become the best-known American woman director of the 1930s (as Ida Lupino was in the early 1950s), was born in San Francisco in 1900. She worked as a waitress in her father's Hollywood café before becoming an ambulance driver in World War I. At Paramount she went from secretary to script clerk to negative cutter to film editor. Her brilliant editing of the bullfight scenes in the Valentino hit *Blood and Sand* (1922) won her the chance to edit *The Covered Wagon*. For the next few years she was a highly respected editor and screenwriter. To keep her from leaving, Paramount made her a director in 1927. That first year, she directed what Paramount considered appropriate projects for a woman: *Fashions for Women, Ten Modern Commandments*, and *Get Your Man*. But soon she was making the films that would make her famous: *The Wild Party* (1929), *Honor Among Lovers* (1931), *Working Girls* (1931), *Merrily We Go to Hell* (1932), *Christopher Strong* (1933), *Nana* (1934), *Craig's Wife* (1936), and *Dance, Girl, Dance* (1940).

As the big studios flourished, many of the Independents folded. Pickford had been the only woman involved in the founding of a major Hollywood studio (United Artists), but some of these smaller companies had been founded by women, notably Alice Guy, Lois Weber, and Nell Shipman.

Alice Guy, now Mme. Blaché in the American press, which found the existence of a woman director newsworthy in itself—and for over 15 years, she *was* the only one in the world—founded the Solax Company in 1910. She hung signs all around her New Jersey studio that reminded the actors, "Be Natural." In the next three years she produced, supervised, and in many cases directed over 320 shorts and eight features for Solax, while Herbert Blaché handled the business affairs and directed some of the pictures. "A husband easily doubts the talent of a wife," she wrote in her autobiography. In 1913 her husband founded Blaché Pictures, which, with Guy's consent, absorbed Solax. The new company survived under various names—after 1917, without Guy—till the end of the decade, when Blaché finished it off by leaving his wife and children and debts to head for Hollywood with his leading actress. Like Weber, Guy was brought down by her husband and junior collaborator. Some of the pictures Guy directed for Solax and its successors, like *The Tigress* (1914, starring Olga Petrova), were huge hits. Guy directed her final feature in 1920; then she joined her repentant husband in California, where she was unable to find work. When she returned to France in 1922, she found no work there either—she had been forgotten. Fortunately, she was publicly acknowledged (with the Legion of Honor in 1953) before she died, at the age of 95, in 1968.

Nell Shipman worked outside Hollywood too, but not in New Jersey. She preferred wild, open country; the company of animals, her co-stars; and a small company of professionals, like her cameraman, the great Joseph B. Walker. A Canadian, she was responsible for Canada's first extant feature, *Back to God's Country* (1919, directed by David M. Hartford), starring in the film and co-producing it after having made the initial decision to adapt the novel. Revolted by the cruel ways animals were treated and the unnatural ways women were dressed and groomed—breasts strapped flat, hair in little curls—she rejected Hollywood's acting contracts and founded Nell Shipman Productions (1921–25). Her co-producer and occasional co-director was her second husband, Bert Van Tuyle.

In 1922, Shipman set up shop in a remote part of Idaho, Upper Priest Lake, where she had a complete zoo. She directed and starred in a series of shorts called *Little Dramas Of The Big Places*, about a woman who is in touch with nature and a friend to animals. In these films as in few others, nature and animals come through; deeply appreciated, they make a stronger mark. Relatively free of melodrama and of artificial violence, and as fiercely moral as the films of Weber, *Little Dramas* and *The Trail of the North Wind* (1923)—which in the course of its tense, impressively beautiful, and finally charming dog-to-the-rescue business takes a stand against animal traps—were popular, but they didn't make enough money to keep the studio going. The company left Idaho in 1924 and was bankrupt by 1925. After that, Shipman worked as a screenwriter. In 1935, she wrote the first feature about a seeing-eye dog, *Wings in the Dark*.

Entirely outside Hollywood, in France, the most important woman director of the 1920s was Germaine Dulac. Her avant-garde films—particularly *The Seashell and the Clergyman* (1927), from a Surrealist script by Antonin Artaud—broke the barriers of reason and perception along with those of gender. There were still a few years to go before the best-known woman director, in Europe or anywhere else, would be Leni Riefenstahl.

King Vidor

King Vidor effectively mixed wartime humor, antiwar propaganda, and a touching love story in *The Big Parade* (1925), the fifth or sixth top-grossing film of the decade (at the box office, it did as well as *The Jazz Singer*), then followed it with his masterpiece, *The Crowd* (1928), a brilliantly composed film full of powerful and daring camera movements, made deliberately without stars, that tells the story of an ordinary man (and his long-suffering wife) who can't stand the thought that he's not marked out for some special destiny, that he's not better than everyone else. In the extraordinary final shot, when the man and wife and their surviving child are shown having a good time in a theatre, reconciled to each other, to their little triumphs, and to being ordinary, the camera rapidly pulls back to reveal row after row of patrons, leaving the momentary hero behind in the crowd—a crowd of theatre patrons facing, in the real movie theatre, a crowd of moviegoers.

Among Vidor's many subsequent films, the one that most complements and opposes *The Crowd* is his superb adaptation of Ayn Rand's *The Fountainhead* (1949), which takes for its hero a man who *is* presented as morally and intellectually superior to most of those around him and who is last seen atop a skyscraper, well above any crowd. The hero of *The Fountainhead* is an uncompromising architect who makes his own dreams come true, and perhaps that is the key to Vidor's idealistic puzzle: that some of his characters are practical dreamers, like the heroes who bring water to their commune in *Our Daily Bread* (1934) or the architect who creates his skyscraper; and that some, whose ambitions are frustrated or self-contradictory from the start, or who *just* dream, are destroyed by their dreams, like the heroine of *Duel in the Sun* (1947), if they do not learn to find joy in what they have, like the hero of *The Crowd*. But all of them are compelling in their idealism, however misguided or on target it may be, and in the emotion and the sense of being that they pour into their obsessions. Only King Vidor, working with Barbara Stanwyck, could make the self-denying/self-fulfilling obsessive project of *Stella Dallas* (1937) so credible and involving.

Lubitsch and Others

Hollywood had begun importing many of the leading directors of Europe: Mauritz Stiller, Victor Sjøstrøm, Fritz Lang, F. W. Murnau, E. A. Dupont. But none found Hollywood so comfortable and so amicable a home as director Ernst Lubitsch, who came from Germany. Mary Pickford imported him specifically to direct a costume spectacle, *Rosita*, for her. Pickford, like her husband, sought to change her adolescent image: to grow up, cut her curls, and show she was a woman. Lubitsch, who had directed a string of costume pageants in Germany (*Gypsy Blood, Passion, Deception*) that had become popular in America for their comic "humanizing" (i.e., eroticizing) of history, was Pickford's choice. *Rosita* (1923) proved the beginning of the end of Pickford's career and the beginning of Lubitsch's. He immediately turned to polite, witty, understated drawing-room comedies: *The Marriage Circle* (1924), *Lady Windermere's Fan* (1925), *So This Is Paris* (1926).

Lubitsch's comedy derived from one essential theme: the limits and defects of human vision. Characters see either too little or too much in Lubitsch's silent comedies. They see too little because their views are blocked—by their own willful blindness, the prejudices of their society, or the simple physical fact that they can see only part of the whole picture, framed by some window or door that obscures as much as it reveals. When Mary Pickford quarreled with Lubitsch, she called him a director of doors, not of people. Lubitsch would use these doors (and windows) to reveal something about people: that human vision is always limited—by assumption, attitude, and prejudice.

If Lubitsch's people see too little, they also see too much when they make some inference about another character based on the mere sight of a physical object—the straw hats, canes, and fans that play such a large role in Lubitsch's comedies of manners—because they imply where and *with whom* a character has been. To make movies about the fallibility of human vision is a highly appropriate piece of cinematic irony and self-reference, since cinema itself depends on structuring human vision, framing visual limitations, and encouraging us to draw inferences from sights of material objects. Lubitsch's clever ability to manipulate the cinema frame and to imply so much with seemingly trivial details would soon allow him to make some of the best early American sound films.

Many other directors made interesting films in the 1920s. Some of them would be remembered primarily for one picture, as Rupert Julian is for *The Phantom of the Opera*, starring the incomparable Lon Chaney (who was directed by Tod Browning in ten films, many of them as impressive as *The Phantom*). Some would never make the transition to sound; some had only begun careers that would take clearer shape in the era ahead.

James Cruze, whose specialty was satire, made the most celebrated western epic of the decade, *The Covered Wagon* (1923). Rex Ingram, whose most famous film was *The Four Horsemen of the Apocalypse* (1921, the movie that made Rudolph Valentino a star), was a pictorial master of composition and atmosphere.

Maurice Tourneur's pictures were recognized for their artistry and consistently entertaining: the gangster picture *Alias Jimmy Valentine* (1915), the Pickford vehicle *The Poor Little Rich Girl* (1917), the beloved fantasy *The Blue Bird* (1918, designed by Ben Carré), *Treasure Island* (1920, with Lon Chaney), and *The Last of the Mohicans* (1920, co-directed with Clarence Brown). Born in France, he returned there in 1927 after a dispute with MGM over artistic control. His son, Jacques Tourneur, returned to Hollywood in 1935 and directed such genre masterpieces as *Cat People* (1942), *I Walked with a Zombie* (1943), and *Out of the Past* (1947).

Josef von Sternberg—a Viennese Jew born without a "von" and raised in New York—began his control of physical detail and cinematic atmosphere in *The Salvation Hunters* (1925), *Underworld* (1927), and *The Docks of New York* (1928). He also helped von Stroheim edit Part I of *The Wedding March*, though their version was rejected by the studio (neither of them had anything to do with the final cut of Part II, released in Europe as *The Honeymoon*). John Ford—born Sean Aloysius O'Fearna, the son of a Maine saloonkeeper—who began by taking over his brother Francis's acting troupe to shoot program westerns with Harry Carey, made his first western as epic history, *The Iron Horse*, in 1924.

Flaherty and the Silent Documentary

Many directors of the 1920s worked outside the fences of the Hollywood formulas. One of them was Robert Flaherty, the father of the documentary feature, who had been taking his camera to Hudson Bay since 1913; the eventual result was *Nanook of the North* (1922).

The first films had been nonfiction: records of actual activity, snapshots in which things moved. There were *actualités* of trains rushing by, of life in foreign lands, and of newsworthy events (on-the-spot footage of the 1906 San Francisco earthquake). There were also faked reconstructions of events, from *Tearing Down the Spanish Flag* (1898) to the *Eruption of Mount Vesuvius* (1905). From the *actualité* came the objective nonfiction film; one of the early "industrial" films, *A Visit to Peek Frean & Co.'s Biscuit Works*, made in England in 1906 and a superior example of rich indoor photography, showed the entire process of making cookies in a factory.

Beginning in 1918, Dziga Vertov made newsreels by assembling the bits of film sent to him by traveling cameramen, in which the people and activities of the new Soviet Union were recorded. In 1922, the year of *Nanook*, Vertov began shooting film and expanding his experiments both in montage and in ways to capture unstaged reality ("life unawares"); he named the new series *Kino-Pravda*, as if it were the film version of the newspaper *Pravda* ("truth"). Vertov's work led him to the genres of the "compilation film," in which a movie is created out of found footage; the "candid camera," in which people are photographed without being asked and without at first being aware of any camera, so that they have no opportunity to pose or to behave in an unnatural manner; *cinéma vérité* ("film truth"; French for *kino-pravda*), in which the camera is an acknowledged element of the scene it records; and the newsreel itself. He was also a pioneer in the feature-length avant-garde documentary, a genre that included not only his *The Man with a Movie Camera* (1928, released 1929), but also such poetic "city films" as Walter Ruttmann's *Berlin: The Symphony of a Great City* (1927).

So *Nanook* was not the first nonfiction film, even if it did set the pattern for what would later be called the documentary (the term was coined in 1926 by John Grierson—the prime mover of the British documentary film movement of the late 1920s and 1930s—in a review of Flaherty's *Moana*.) But it was the first feature-length documentary to become a huge commercial hit.

It was important to the young Flaherty not to impose a story on his materials, but to live long enough with the people whose lives he was recording, and to shoot enough film, that the material would tell its own story, that the truth would reveal itself. Once that inner story, the key to organizing the material, had become clear to him, Flaherty could edit the footage into a non-fiction narrative that would convey that truth—the essence of the subject and the point he wanted to make about it. That was the theory, and it is one that has inspired nonfiction film-makers ever since—but in practice Flaherty was a bit heavy-handed in conveying what was inevitably his interpretation of the material, the story he thought it told. Like many early ethno-graphic filmmakers, he brought back crucial records of distant cultures, but was also willing to make up a fiction that would encapsulate what he wanted to convey about the actual; he did this in several films, including *Moana* (1926) and *Louisiana Story* (1948). Edward S. Curtis had made an ethnographic film embellished by fiction in 1914—*In the Land of the War Canoes: A Drama of Kwakiutl Life*—and others would do it later. Fortunately, Flaherty did not impose a blatant fiction on Nanook's life, only an interpre-tation of what, with care and direct engagement, he found. Nevertheless, Flaherty's film has noth-ing like the objectivity of Frank Hurley's *South* (1919), the record of Ernest Shackleton's 1914–16 Antarctic expedition.

Flaherty's *Nanook* is significant for the beauty of its photography of the white, frozen plains of ice and for its care in revealing the life of the man—and the family—who lived there. Flaherty's greatest asset was Nanook's lack of inhibition before the camera. Although he was clearly conscious of being watched, suggested many of the scenes (almost every scene in the film was planned in advance), and knew he was performing, he did not quite know what a camera and movie were. Nanook was carefully directed to perform his specific business—hunting, build-ing an igloo with his family, feeding the dogs—while Flaherty's camera recorded and, inevitably, commented. From *Flaherty* on, the documentary has been defined as a nonfiction film that orga-nizes factual materials in order to make a point—as distinguished from the *actualité*, which simply records an event.

One comment, of course, was that Nanook's life was hard, a perpetual struggle for two absolute necessities, food and shelter. Flaherty's making of the film itself mirrored the hardness of Nanook's life, for Flaherty could record the severity of ice and snow only if he lived through the blizzards he was recording. Out of all that endurance came a work of art, a product of human accomplishment, like an igloo with an ice

Nanook.

Fig. 6-28

window. In Nanook's simplicity, in his skill, and in his humor, Flaherty depicted a fulfilling life.

Nanook was released by Pathé (which had, along with Revillon Frères, produced it) after Paramount and three other studios refused it. After *Nanook* proved itself at the box office, Hollywood asked Flaherty to make pictures for commercial release. For Paramount he made *Moana: A Romance of the Golden Age*—an idyllic study of life on a South Seas island. Hollywood, which expected a movie full of hula dancers, was disappointed and teamed Flaherty with other directors, W. S. Van Dyke and F. W. Murnau, for his later silents, of which the greatest was his and Murnau's exquisite, troubling *Tabu* (1931). To preserve his independence, Flaherty left for England, where a whole group of filmmakers applying his principles had begun to produce films, and where he made *Man of Aran* (1934).

In America, the success of Flaherty's first documentary stimulated his contemporaries, Merian C. Cooper and Ernest B. Schoedsack. Their silent documentaries, *Grass: A Nation's Battle for Life* (1925) and *Chang: A Drama of the Wilderness* (1927), were also close and sensitive studies of people whose existence was totally dependent on the earth, the cycles of nature, and their own skills at adapting to them. For *Chang*, shot in the jungles of Siam (now Thailand), Cooper and Schoedsack made up a story; that decision made their film not a true documentary but a narrative film shot on location. But *Grass* was the real thing. To shoot it, they and journalist Marguerite Harrison went to Persia (now Iran), where they joined a tribe of nomads on their incredibly difficult biannual journey across the Zardeh Kuh mountain range to find grass for their animals. After the 46-day

Fig. 6-29
The Bakhtiari tribe's perilous trek in search of Grass.

trek, they had 80 feet of film left to shoot an ending. With screenwriter Ruth Rose and stop-motion animator Willis O'Brien, Cooper and Schoedsack would later make the most famous and effective mixture of Hollywood fiction, documentary anthropology, and parody of documentary anthropology—*King Kong* (1933).

The Comics

One other group of 1920s films maintained an inventiveness and individuality that remain fresh today. The silent film, which had already proved itself the ideal medium for physical comedy, continued to nurture its most legitimate children. Several new comic imaginations joined the established Sennett, who still supervised films, and Chaplin, who had begun to make features: most significantly, Harold Lloyd, Buster Keaton, Harry Langdon, and Laurel and Hardy.

Laurel and Hardy and Hal Roach

Stan Laurel and Oliver Hardy perfected their material late in the silent period, then became the most popular comic team of the Sound Era. Laurel and Hardy had been put together in 1926 by Hal Roach, Sennett's major rival as a producer of comedies, who reasoned that one of his fat players and one of his thin ones might go well together. The premise was entirely Sennett-like,

and indeed Laurel and Hardy's method was a return to the solid, physical world of Sennett gags.

But Laurel and Hardy films were more tightly structured than the Sennett romps. Their films demonstrate the "snowball" principle that Bergson had developed in *Le Rire*. Like the snowball rolling down the mountain, the Laurel and Hardy film gathers greater momentum and bulk as it hurtles toward the valley. Their films demonstrate the classic structure of farce, from Plautus to Feydeau: to begin with a single problem and then multiply that problem to infinity, catastrophe. If an auto gets dented in a traffic jam at the start of the film, every car on the highway gets stripped by the end of it; if a Christmas tree branch gets caught in a door at the start of the film, the tree, the house, and the salesmen's car must be totally annihilated by the end of it. There is an insane yet perfect logic about the whole process.

As does every great silent-film comedy, a Laurel and Hardy picture depends on physical objects. But for Stan Laurel (like Chaplin, a Fred Karno alumnus) and Oliver Hardy, an object is something to throw, fall over, or destroy; most of their films are built around breaking things and getting hurt. Always trying to get away with something, get out of a jam, or get even, the "adults" of this world are overgrown, spiteful children squashing each other's mud pies. Stan

Stan Laurel (left) and Oliver Hardy.

Fig. 6-30

is the weepy, sneaky, why-blame-me kid, while Ollie is the pompous, bullying, know-it-all, incompetent kid. If the premise of the films is much thinner than Chaplin's, it is also true that they capture feelings of frustration, confusion, anger, and fear with which any child or former child can identify. Their taut, unidirectional structure ensured their success in the short film. The best loved of their sound features are *Sons of the Desert* (1933), *Our Relations* (1936), and *Way Out West* (1937, in which Stan—exploiting the potential of the sound film to play with sound/picture relationships—sings a song in three voices, two of which are impossible but in perfect sync).

When Hal Roach was a boy, he knew Mark Twain; when he died in 1992 at the age of 100, he was buried near Twain. One of the great American humorists in his own right, Roach was an actor, a writer, a director, and a producer with a genius for identifying and developing talent. He was responsible not only for developing Laurel and Hardy (who made all their films with him until 1940, after which their work became mediocre), but also for giving Harold Lloyd his start and urging him to develop his own comic persona rather than imitate Chaplin. Hal Roach Studios was the home of Will Rogers, Charley Chase, the team of Thelma Todd and ZaSu Pitts, and the Our Gang comedies. Roach put black and white children together (a first) in an integrated assault on the adult world; he created the Our Gang series in 1922 and produced it until 1938, when he sold the rights to MGM. Roach won Academy Awards for Laurel and Hardy's *The Music Box* (1932) and Our Gang's *Bored of Education* (1936). He and his son, Hal Roach, Jr., produced features—notably *Topper* (1937), *Of Mice and Men* (1939), and *One Million B.C.* (1940)—as well as a number of TV series. "The best comedy comes from children," said Roach; "Laurel and Hardy acted like children. 'Our Gang' was children acting like adults."

Harold Lloyd

Except for a brief tour at Keystone, Harold Lloyd worked with Roach from 1914 to 1923, then became his own producer. In many ways, Lloyd was a combination of Chaplin and Fairbanks. Like Chaplin, he was a little guy, slightly inept, trying to succeed. Like Fairbanks, he was

energetic, athletic, and engagingly charming, with a smile calculated to snare us as well as the heroine. Like Chaplin, he had trouble with objects and with the world while trying to achieve his desires. But unlike Chaplin—and like Fairbanks—he invariably achieved those desires.

Rather than developing character or social commentary, Lloyd generated pure comedy from the situation, from topical satire, from his own limber body, and from daring stunts. *High and Dizzy* (1920), the first of his high-rise comedies of thrills, demonstrates the variety of his comedy. The film is constructed in three loosely related episodes. In the opening sequence, Lloyd plays a doctor whose practice is so dismal that his phone is gathering cobwebs. He falls madly in love with a patient who walks in her sleep.

In the second sequence, he strolls down the hall and gets stinking drunk with another young doctor who has distilled some hooch in his medicinal laboratory. Lloyd's topical satire of doctors, admittedly rather gentle, is the same kind that he would use to portray the 1920s college generation in *The Freshman* (1925). The comic premise of two drunken doctors also allows Lloyd to demonstrate his ability and agility as pure physical comic, as the two friends dizzily weave down the street and into their hotel.

Fig. 6-31
High and Dizzy: *Harold Lloyd with a sleepwalking Mildred Davis on a scary ledge.*

Harold Lloyd rushes through New York in **Speedy.**

Fig. 6-32

Lloyd introduces his "comedy of thrills" in the film's third section. It just happens that the sleepwalking patient with whom he is in love lives in the same hotel. She starts sleepwalking out on the hotel ledge, many frightening stories above the hard pavement below. Lloyd goes out on the ledge to save her and, predictably, gets locked out there when she decides to stroll inside. Lloyd tightropes, trips, and stumbles on the ledge, playing on many emotions in us at the same time. We feel suspense because he might fall, yet we laugh because we know he won't. We wonder whether he was really on the ledge when he shot the sequence (he was—but he also used a stunt double, Harvey Perry). We laugh at his fright and perplexity; we admire his underlying competence and control. This same synthesis of cliff-hanging serial and burlesque comedy created the excitement and success of his feature *Safety Last* (1923). The greatest of his chase films, *Speedy* (1928), tore through New York rather than dangled above it.

Unlike the comedy of Chaplin and Keaton, Lloyd's remains content with emotional and psychological surfaces, never cutting very deeply, never going beyond comic sensations to confront us with ironies and paradoxes. Lloyd's films effectively distill the urges and values of American society as a whole in the 1920s—the success ethic of get up and get. Further, the Lloyd comedies reveal an extremely cunning and complex sense of comic construction, setting up a comic problem and driving it to such dizzying heights that an audience becomes helplessly hysterical in the presence of Lloyd's comic ingenuity.

Harry Langdon

Harry Langdon was Lloyd's opposite: His comic style was constructed almost exclusively of personal sensations and emotional reactions with almost no dependence on external business and physical gags. His career was also the shortest of any of the comic stars of the silents. He broke into films at Mack Sennett's studio in 1924, reached stardom with a series of features written or directed by Frank Capra in 1926 and 1927, and fell from popularity just as suddenly in 1928 when Capra went off to direct his own films and when sound invaded Hollywood.

The union of Capra and Langdon was significant for both men, for like Capra's later heroes, Langdon was a figure of innocence trapped in a mean, brutal world where angels should indeed fear to tread. Langdon was like Mr. Deeds or Mr. Smith, distilled into an essential and pure naïveté. He was like an overgrown baby. The Langdon–Capra films put this innocent hero into

The babyish Harry Langdon flirts with the vamp (Alma Bennett) in Long Pants.

Fig. 6-33

harrowing situations from which the child–man could escape only by a miracle, for only a miracle could save an infant in a lion's den.

In *Tramp, Tramp, Tramp* (1926; written by Capra but directed by Harry Edwards) Harry enters a cross-country walking race to try to win enough money to save his father's business from ruin (a clear Capra motif). Harry's opponents in this athletic contest include not only men who are bigger, tougher, and stronger, but also a cyclone that levels a town but goes away when Harry hurls a few pebbles at it. In *The Strong Man* (1926), Harry is a weightlifter's assistant who is unexpectedly forced to substitute for his boss. He manages to subdue a whole gang of bootleggers in the course of his act, ridding a small town of the mobsters who have usurped it (more Capra). Harry's girlfriend in this film is blind, a figure as pure as little Harry himself. At the end of *The Strong Man* the couple of meeklings inherit the earth. But in *Long Pants* (1927), Harry is unhappy with the purity and innocence of small-town life. He deserts the small-town gal and runs off to the "Big City" in pursuit of an exotic "Bad Woman." Harry discovers, however, that the lady of his dreams is no lady, and he scampers back to his small-town family and sweetheart, a sadder and wiser child.

Although Langdon lacked the comic range and physical gifts of the other silent clowns, his comic style revealed how restrained, how subtle, how slow, how unphysical a silent, physical comedian could be. His films were constructed so that a tiny smile, a blink of the eyes, the wave of a hand, or even, as James Agee observed, a twitch of the muscles at the back of the neck was as significant as a whole sequence of Lloyd's spectacular slips and falls.

Buster Keaton

Of the new comics, only Buster Keaton could rival Chaplin in his insight into human relationships, into the conflict between the individual and society; only Keaton could rival Chaplin in making his insight both funny and serious at the same time. The character Keaton fashioned—with his deadpan, understated reactions to the chaos that blooms around him—lacks the pathos of Chaplin's tramp, but Keaton compensates for this apparent lack of emotion with the terrific range of his resourcefulness and imagination.

A vaudevillian from childhood, Keaton was far more a classic American type than the more European working-class tramp. Born in Kansas in 1895, Keaton had a dour face and dry personality

Fig. 6-34

Fig. 6-35

The montage sequence from Sherlock Jr.: Keaton dives into the sea (Fig. 6-34) but lands in a snowy forest (Fig. 6-35).

reminiscent of Grant Wood's farmers in *American Gothic*. Beneath this "Great Stone Face," Keaton's brain conceived one outrageously inventive gag after another, many of them based on bizarre machines and gadgets. The idol of Keaton's generation was Thomas Alva Edison, the supreme inventor as tinkerer, and Keaton loved to tinker with machines (especially trains). One of those machines was the camera, and, very unlike Chaplin, Keaton loved to find new ways to

manipulate cinematic gadgetry and cinematic space. For his 1921 short *The Playhouse*, Keaton (together with his designer of special effects, Fred Gabourie) came up with a special matte box, capable of splitting the frame into as many as nine fragments. The device allowed him to play every member of a minstrel line, every member of the orchestra, or an entire audience within the same shot. He was by far the most cinematically innovative comedian in film history, but he never saw himself as a genius; he just thought he was good at gags.

On the road to the success he achieves (like growing up in *The Navigator*, 1924) or the goals he is forced to redefine (the house in *One Week*, 1920, has to be adapted to the villain's having renumbered the crates it came in, so that it is put together all wrong, but the honeymooners manage to live in it for awhile), the environment throws staggeringly huge obstacles into Buster's path: an avalanche, a locomotive, a steamboat, a spinning house, a waterfall, a cyclone, a herd of cattle. Like Chaplin, Keaton has his troubles with cops, but not just with one or two; in *Cops* (1922), Keaton runs into the entire police force. Given the size and complexity of his problems, Keaton can take no reliable action, despite his most sensible, practical efforts. The perfect metaphor for the Keaton man is in the three-reel *Daydreams* (1922) in which Keaton, to avoid the police force, takes refuge in the paddle wheel of a ferryboat. The wheel begins turning; Keaton begins walking. And walking. He behaves as sensibly as a man can on a treadmill that he cannot control, but how sensible can life on a treadmill ever be?

Keaton's *Sherlock Jr.* (1924), is one of the greatest movies about the movies. Keaton plays a projectionist in a small town (similar to the town in which Keaton was born) who falls asleep and dreams himself into the movie he is projecting. The film-within-a-film that follows permits Keaton to demonstrate spectacular physical skills. He was one of the greatest performer–athletes in film history, and his chase sequences are brilliant. As opposed to Sennett's miscellaneous chases of frantic puppets and Chaplin's chases as choreographed ballets, Keaton's chases (in *Our Hospitality*, 1923, in *Sherlock Jr.*, in *Seven Chances*, 1925, and elsewhere) are breathtaking exercises by a single racing body—running faster, leaping higher, falling more gracefully than any other body ever could, or maneuvering a vehicle at top speed through an impossible situation.

In the most celebrated sequence of *Sherlock Jr.*, Keaton is practically at rest. It is the world itself that moves, thanks to the cinema's ability to shift spaces instantaneously by means of editing. Keaton, a mortal being, has been trapped in the universe of cinema, which operates according to

spatial and temporal laws unknown to physical reality. He simply stands, sits, or jumps, occupying the identical space within the frame across the cuts, while the physical universe surrounding him switches from desert to ocean to mountain to city street. It is the ultimate comic gag created by and commenting upon the cinematic apparatus itself.

Chaplin and Keaton are the two poles of silent comics. Chaplin is sentimental; his gentle smiling women become idols to be revered. Keaton is not sentimental; he stuffs his females into bags and hauls them around like sacks of potatoes; he satirizes their finicky incompetence and praises their competence. It was especially appropriate and touching to see the two opposites, Chaplin and Keaton, united in *Limelight* (1952). Chaplin's direction of that sequence—in which they attempt to play a tune on piano and violin—shows how well he understood both Keaton and himself, for while Chaplin has trouble with his body (his leg gets shorter) and plays the romantic violin, Keaton plays the kinetic piano and has trouble with gravity (the music sheets won't stay put) and with the mechanism of the piano.

Any list of the greatest actor–directors in film history begins with Chaplin, Keaton, and Orson Welles. Keaton directed or co-directed, as well as co-wrote and co-produced, nearly all of his silent films. (His first feature, *The Saphead*, 1920, was directed by Herbert Blaché—Alice's husband.) For a while Keaton had his own studio, much as Chaplin did, and until 1928 he had complete artistic control over his pictures. But in that year he gave up his studio—and the right of artistic control—and signed a contract to make films for MGM, the first of which turned out to be the best: *The Cameraman* (1928). Without Keaton at the creative helm, the movies sank. He began playing second lead to Jimmy Durante, and eventually he was out of work and looking for bit parts. He was cast as one of the has-beens in *Sunset Blvd.* and as himself in *Beach Blanket Bingo* (1965), but the most memorable of his late appearances, aside from *Limelight*, came in two 1965 shorts (both shot in 1964): *The Railrodder*, in which he rides the rails across Canada, creating a functioning environment for himself in a handcar, and *Film* (directed by Alan Schneider and written by Samuel

The Gold Rush: *Charlie's forks dance the "Oceana Roll."*

Fig. 6-36

Beckett), in which he plays the double role of a man (Object, who wants no one to look at him) pursued by his own faculty of perception (Eye, whose view is the camera's).

The Gold Rush and *The General*

No two films more clearly reveal the contrasting strengths and interests of the two clowns than *The Gold Rush* (Chaplin, 1925) and *The General* (Keaton and Clyde Bruckman, 1926, released 1927). Like Chaplin's short comedies, *The Gold Rush* is an episodic series of highly developed, individual situations. *The Gold Rush* uses one of Chaplin's favorite figures, the circle, to structure the sequence of episodes: Prologue (arriving in Alaska), the Cabin, the Dance Hall, the Cabin, Epilogue (leaving Alaska for home).

The individual sequences of *The Gold Rush* are rich both in Chaplin's comic ingenuity and in his ability to render pathos. Several of the comic sequences have become justifiably famous. In the cabin, a hungry Charlie cooks his shoe, carves it, and then eats it like a gourmet, twirling the shoelaces around his fork like spaghetti, sucking the nails like bones, offering his disgruntled partner (who has been chewing the upper half of the shoe as if it were just a shoe) a bent

nail as a wishbone. This is the Chaplin who treats one object (a shoe) as if it were another kind of object (a feast), the same minute observation he used in dissecting the clock in *The Pawn Shop*; it is also the definitive example of the tramp as a gentleman—that is, of comic contrast. And unlike the Sennett world where bullets can't kill, the funny business here has permanent consequences: Characters really die in *The Gold Rush*, and once his boot has been boiled, Charlie spends the rest of the picture with his foot wrapped in rags.

But the comic business is matched by the pathos that Charlie can generate, often growing out of the comic business itself. Charlie's saddest moment is when Georgia (played by Georgia Hale), the woman he loves, stands him up on New Year's Eve. When Charlie realizes that it is midnight and she is not coming, he opens his door and listens to the happy townspeople singing "Auld Lang Syne." The film cuts back and forth between Charlie, the outsider, standing silently and alone in a doorway, and the throng of revelers in the dance hall, clasping hands in a circle and singing together. But this pathetic moment would have been impossible without the previous comic one in which Charlie falls asleep and dreams he is

Fig. 6-37
The General: *Johnny Gray (Buster Keaton) goes about his business while his train carries him behind the enemy's lines.*

entertaining Georgia and her girlfriends with his "Oceana Roll." Charlie's joy, his naïve sincerity, his charm, his gentleness, all show on his face as he gracefully makes the two rolls kick, step, and twirl over the table on the ends of two forks. The happiness of the comic dream sequence sets up the pathos of the painful reality.

The Gold Rush consistently indicts what the pursuit of gold, power, and even food does to the human animal; as in *Greed*, it makes people into inhuman animals. Charlie has come to the most materialistic of places—a place where life is hard, dangerous, brutal, uncomfortable, and unkind. The quest for gold creates a Black Larsen who casually murders lawmen and purposely fails to help his starving fellows. It creates a Jack, Georgia's handsome boyfriend, who treats people like furniture. Just as Charlie's genuine passion reveals the emptiness of Jack's protestations of love, Chaplin's film technique makes an

unsympathetic bully out of the conventional Hollywood leading man.

The rush toward gold perverts both love and friendship. Georgia herself, though Charlie perceives her inner beauty, has become hardened and callous from her strictly cash relationships with people in the dance hall. And Charlie's partner, Big Jim McKay (Mack Swain), is one of those fair-weather friends whose feelings are the functions of expediency. When Big Jim gets hungry, he tries to eat Charlie; although Jim's seeing his buddy as a big chicken is comic, the implied cannibalism is not. Later, Big Jim needs Charlie to direct him to his claim; once again Charlie becomes a friend because he is needed. In the end, Big Jim shares the claim with Charlie, as he promised, and the two millionaires head for home on a steamship—the same one Georgia has taken. Charlie dresses in his tramp outfit for a news photographer, and Georgia, thinking he is

Fig. 6-38
The pragmatist turns obstacles into tools.

a stowaway, offers to pay for his passage—an *un*materialistic gesture that shows her moral growth and leads properly to her and Charlie's romantic union.

While *The Gold Rush* combines a thematic unity with the episodic structure that exhausts individual situations, the thematic coherence of *The General* is itself the product of the film's tight narrative unity. *The General* is the first, probably the greatest comic epic in film form. Like every comic epic, *The General* is the story of a journey, of the road (albeit a railroad). As in every comic epic (think of the *Odyssey*), the protagonist suffers a series of hardships and dangerous adventures before achieving his or her goal, which may include a marriage or a return to the stability of the home. As in every comic epic (think of *Don Quixote*), there is a comic insufficiency in the protagonist and a disparity between his powers and the task he sets out to accomplish—but Buster triumphs despite his insufficiencies. Everything in the Chaplin film, every gag, every

piece of business, every thematic contrast, is subordinate to the delineation of the tramp's character. Everything in *The General*—every gag, every piece of business—is subordinate to the film's driving narrative, its story of Johnny Gray's race to save his three loves: his sweetheart, his country, and, most important of all, his locomotive (whose name is "The General").

The great question posed by *The General* is how to perform heroic action in a crazy universe, where the easy and the impossible are reversed, as are the heroic and the mundane. Buster tries to go about his business; he is an understated hero. At one point, Johnny/Buster is so busy chopping wood to feed his engine that he fails to notice that the train is racing past row after row of blue uniforms marching in the opposite direction; he has inadvertently crossed behind the enemy's lines. Johnny Gray simply wants to run his train; unfortunately, Union spies have stolen the train and want to use it to destroy the Confederate railroad (a real incident in the

Civil War). In the course of trying to save "The General," chasing it with another train, Johnny rescues his sweetheart and accidentally wins a terrific victory for the South.

That heroism occurs as a series of frantic yet graceful accidents in *The General* is at the center of its moral thrust. It is a lucky accident and a triumph of geometry, the core of Keaton's visual comedy, that a cannon, aimed squarely at Johnny, does not go off until the train rounds a curve, discharging its huge ball at the enemy instead. It is another accident, also a matter of trajectory and line (much as the chases in *Sherlock Jr.* play with vacuum and volume), that Johnny's train comes to a rail switch just in time to detour the pursuing train. How less heroic, how less pretentious can a person be than the pragmatic and unassuming Buster?

The denigration, or redefinition, of the heroic is as constant an element in *The General,* as the denigration of gold (the redefinition of wealth) is in *The Gold Rush*. The plot is triggered by Johnny Gray's rejection by the Confederate Army. He fears he has been found wanting, but the Confederacy vitally needs him at home, running his locomotive. Nevertheless, his girlfriend and her family ostracize Johnny as an unheroic coward, a shirker, and the rest of the film demonstrates what heroism really is and what it is worth. Hardheadedness and improvisation, not ego and gallantry, win the day.

What distinguishes *The General* is the clarity of its journey, laid out on a maze of rails but aiming and arriving at fulfillment. Johnny Gray's sweetheart (played by Marion Mack), a typical figure of sentiment and romance (her name is Annabelle Lee!), is an incompetent twit—until she learns the ropes. In the course of the film, Johnny becomes an actual officer and Miss Lee grows up.

The ultimate proof of the power of *The Gold Rush* and *The General* is that they need not be referred to as great silent films; they are merely great films. For both, silence was not a limitation but a virtue. It is inconceivable that they could have been any better with talk; by removing our complete concentration on the visual, they could only have been worse. With such control of physical business, thematic consistency, narrative structure, camera placement, and functional editing, neither *The Gold Rush* nor *The General* requires speech to speak.

Hollywood and the Jazz Age

American movies of 1915–27 are important collectively as a social barometer, indicating the evolving spirit, values, and attitudes of American society during that period. But the cinema was only one of the arts that grew to maturity at this time. There were startling innovations in American fiction (with the first major novels of Ernest Hemingway, John Dos Passos, William Faulkner, F. Scott Fitzgerald, and Sinclair Lewis), in American drama (whether the tragedies of Eugene O'Neill or the fast-paced social comedies of George S. Kaufman and Marc Connelly, of Ben Hecht and Charles MacArthur), in American poetry (with Ezra Pound, T. S. Eliot, Gertrude Stein, Wallace Stevens, and the flourishing little magazines, like Harriet Monroe's *Poetry*), in American theatre music (with Jerome Kern, George and Ira Gershwin, Richard Rodgers and Lorenz Hart), and in American painting, journalism, and dance (when Grant Wood, Ben Shahn, H. L. Mencken, Martha Graham, Katherine Dunham, and Virgil Thomson first appeared on the scene).

Modernism

It was a period of creative excitement and invention—the profuse flowering of an artistic tradition over the full spectrum of arts and letters. Later critics would find a name—Modernism—for this international explosion of artistic activity that rebelled against the forms and norms of a previous generation. And somewhere in the middle of it were the movies. They may not have been as consistently committed to experimental innovation as some of the other arts, but all the artists went to the movies, and so did everyone who read their novels, saw their plays, discussed their poems, and hummed their tunes. James Joyce and Sergei Eisenstein knew of each other's work, Eisenstein found the seeds of montage in Dickens (although they were also evident in Whitman's 1855 *Leaves of Grass* and earlier work by others), and Beckett studied the films of Eisenstein and Pudovkin. The great montage experiments of the 1920s were not confined to the cinema but included such poems as Eliot's "The Waste Land" (1922) and Pound's *The Cantos* (which began appearing in 1919) as well as such novels as Joyce's *Ulysses* (1922) and Faulkner's *The Sound and the Fury* (1929). Fragmentation

Fig. 6-39
Before the feature, some theatres offered a live stage prologue.

and synthesis, essential concerns of Modernism from Cubist painting to 12-tone music, had been recognized as the essence of montage since *Intolerance*, but the cinematic apparatus itself had long posed exciting phenomenological questions about the continuous and intermittent recording of reality. Both the montage novelist John Dos Passos and the definer of the "continuous present," Gertrude Stein, readily admitted that they were doing what the cinema was doing.

Jazz, Booze, and "It"

The postwar years of the late 1910s and 1920s saw many important changes in American life. It is all too easy to mystify history by selecting a single image to stand for a whole period, but there is something inevitable about the image of a flapper, a "jazz baby," in a short beaded dress and bobbed hair, wearing a jeweled headband, holding a glass of champagne, dancing the Charleston.

More than anything else, the Jazz Age seems a period of contradictions. Conservative Republican presidents (Harding, Coolidge, and Hoover) explicitly pledged to return the nation to "normalcy" in the 1920s, one of the least conservative and least "normal" decades of the century. The sale and purchase of liquor may have been against the law, but more Americans drank more booze than they ever had before. Lubitsch's and DeMille's comedies about the rich elite, who lived either in Europe or on Long Island, were as popular as Lloyd's comedies about the most normal mid-American, middle-class aspirations. There were Chaplin's comedies that despised the pursuit of merely material goods, while American society seemed hell bent on acquiring as many of those goods as possible—especially the new automobiles, refrigerators, and radios. Those domestic machines and gadgets by which modern life is often defined first entered middle-class American lives in the 1920s.

The word *jazz* entered mainstream American language at the same time. It didn't mean anything very precisely; for those who hated it, jazz

Fig. 6-40
Jazz Age partying of the Veddy Veddy Rich in MGM's **This Modern Age** *(1931)—with Joan Crawford, Neil Hamilton, and champagne poolside (Figs. 6-40, 6-41); Fig. 6-42: Clara Bow, the "It" Girl.*

meant musical noise that was loud and vulgar, too disorganized to be an art. For those who loved it, jazz was rhythm and riffs, the music you danced to and made love to, music that could go anywhere, whether by black composers and musicians like Fats Waller, Bessie Smith, Ethel Waters, and Duke Ellington or white composers and musicians like George Gershwin, Paul Whiteman, Bix Beiderbeck, and Helen Kane. Jazz meant about the same thing that rock did a half-century later—the exuberant, liberating music to which young Americans danced. It was also a word that sold movie tickets; a 1927 poster read, "William Fox presents *Cupid and the Clock*: A Jazz Version of the O. Henry story."

At the center of these changes and contradictions was the new American woman—or, rather, women. The many new types of women on movie screens indicated the conflicting varieties of experience in modern American life. At one extreme there was Mary Pickford, "America's Sweetheart," who personified the woman as child—sweet, innocent, virgin (for sure), but perky, bright, and charming too. At the other

extreme there were several alternatives to Pickford. One was the woman of adventure and daring, personified by Pearl White, the Queen of American serials, beginning with *The Perils of Pauline* in 1914. White represented the woman less as suffering victim than as active challenger of villainy. Another alternative was the more dignified, controlled woman of grace and manners, represented by such stars as Gloria Swanson and Pauline Frederick—women who personified the era's notions of a true Lady.

The rebellious alternative to Pickford's adolescent spunk was Clara Bow, the "It" Girl, and It, like jazz, was another of the important if vague words that indicated the values of the decade. It was coined and popularized by British author Elinor Glyn in a series of books from *Three Weeks* (1907) to *It* (1927)—sexually scandalous bourgeois novels for women readers. It was a vague euphemism for sex (hence the deliberate irony of Cole Porter's 1928 song hit, "Let's Do It") and implied a wide range of suggestions: sex appeal, sexual drive, the sex act itself, or a more general attitude toward that sexual activity. The girl, like Clara Bow, who had It exuded sexual energy and appeared as if she might welcome a sexual invitation (even if she coyly never accepted It). One could have It, want It, show It, or think about It, but not *do* It.

American It was somewhat different from European It. While American-born stars with It (Clara Bow, Joan Crawford, Mae McAvoy) were bouncy flappers with get-up-and-go, European-born stars with It were deep, intriguing Circes (Greta Garbo, Pola Negri) with lie-back-and-wait. Louise Brooks was the rare American It girl who flowered in German soil (*Pandora's Box* and *Diary of a Lost Girl*, both directed by G. W. Pabst and released in 1929). Brooks and Garbo (who did her best work in such MGM films as *Flesh and the Devil*, 1926, and *Queen Christina*, 1933) were more than international stars: They were essential mysteries, icons of the cinema, whose intimate relationship with the camera promised but withheld absolute knowledge. The camera studied Garbo—her face, her moods, the mask of her thoughts—as it had no one else, and always came away with a rich set of questions, energized by the enigmatic power of her being, which felt as simple and complex, as familiar and strange as one's own.

Fig. 6-41

Fig. 6-42

Fig. 6-44

Fig. 6-43
European It. Figs. 6-43, 6-44, Greta Garbo.

In the 1920s, these European It goddesses distilled and incarnated the experience of that generation of American males who marched off to France singing "Over There," met the mademoiselles about whom they sang "Hinky Dinky Parley Voo," and returned to America singing "How Ya Gonna Keep 'Em Down on the Farm, After They've Seen Paree?"

When Hollywood reflected on its own cultural history, with the writing of those explicit moral instructions that became the Production Code of 1930, it confessed that its films of the 1920s were more lascivious and suggestive than they ought to have been. The writers of the Code then blamed that permissiveness on the mores of the period itself, whose "roaring" hedonism and "wonderful nonsense" came tumbling down with the Wall Street crash of October 1929 (which led to a worldwide depression that lasted until the munitions buildup for World War II created jobs). This recantation of Jazz Age values indicated not only the differences in American social attitudes just one decade later, but also the changes in an industry seeking not to lose the patronage of its most dependable middle-class customers.

The powerful images of female stars are among the most enduring and revealing traces of this era's films. There were exceptional male figures—the virtuoso comics (Chaplin, Keaton, Laurel and Hardy), the masculine counterparts of European exotica (Valentino, Ramon Novarro, Rod La Rocque), the jazzy Jolson, the intense John Barrymore, the dashing American It boys (Fairbanks, John Gilbert), and the unclassifiable Lon Chaney. But relatively few male faces from the 1920s have survived in our cultural memory. Of course, many of the films themselves have been lost, so little did anyone think of preserving them. The faces of the era's women suggest a portrait of American life as a whole. As Norma Desmond (played by Gloria Swanson) put it in *Sunset Blvd.*: "We had faces then." For most of us, those faces are the Jazz Age.

For Further Viewing

FILMS

LON CHANEY (1883–1930)
The Miracle Man (1919)
The Penalty (1921)
The Hunchback of Notre Dame (1923)
HE Who Gets Slapped (1924)
The Phantom of the Opera (1925, revised 1929)
The Unholy Three (1925)
The Blackbird (1926)
The Unknown (1927)
West of Zanzibar (1928)
The Unholy Three (1930)

MERIAN C. COOPER (1893–1973) AND ERNEST B. SCHOEDSACK (1893–1979)
Grass (1925)
Chang (1927)
The Four Feathers (1929)
The Most Dangerous Game (1932)
King Kong (1933)
This Is Cinerama (1952). Co-producers, Mike Todd and others

CECIL B. DEMILLE (1881–1959)
The Squaw Man (1914). Co-director, Oscar Apfel
The Virginian (1914)
The Cheat (1915)
Don't Change Your Husband (1919)
Male and Female (1919)
Why Change Your Wife? (1920)
The Affairs of Anatole (1921)
Forbidden Fruit (1922)
The Ten Commandments (1923)
The King of Kings (1927)
Madame Satan (1930)
The Sign of the Cross (1932)
Cleopatra (1934)
The Plainsman (1937). Completed 1936
Union Pacific (1939)
North West Mounted Police (1940)
The Greatest Show on Earth (1952)
The Ten Commandments (1956)

DOUGLAS FAIRBANKS (1883–1939)
His Picture in the Papers (1916)
Flirting With Fate (1916)
The Mystery of the Leaping Fish (1916)
The Americano (1916)

Reaching for the Moon (1917)
The Mark of Zorro (1920)
The Mollycoddle (1920)
The Three Musketeers (1921)
Robin Hood (1922)
The Thief of Bagdad (1924)
The Black Pirate (1926)
The Iron Mask (1929)

ROBERT FLAHERTY (1884–1951)
Nanook of the North (1922)
Moana: A Romance of the Golden Age (1926)
Tabu (1931). Co-director, F. W. Murnau
Man of Aran (1934)
The Land (1942)
Louisiana Story (1948)

THOMAS H. INCE (1882–1924)
The Taking of Luke McVane (1915). With W. S. Hart
Keno Bates, Liar (1915). With W. S. Hart
The Coward (1915). With Charles Ray
Civilization (1916)

BUSTER KEATON (1895–1966)
Shorts, including: *One Week, Convict 13, The Scarecrow,* and *Neighbors* (1920); *The Haunted House, The Goat, The Playhouse, The Boat,* and *The Paleface* (1921); *Cops, My Wife's Relations, The Blacksmith, The Frozen North, Daydreams,* and *The Electric House* (1922); and *The Balloonatic* (1923)
The Saphead (1920)
The Three Ages (1923)
Our Hospitality (1923)
Sherlock Jr. (1924)
The Navigator (1924)
Seven Chances (1925)
Go West (1925)
Battling Butler (1926)
The General (1927). Completed 1926; co-director, Clyde Bruckman
College (1927)
Steamboat Bill, Jr. (1928)
The Cameraman (1928)

HARRY LANGDON (1884–1944)
Shorts, including: *Picking Peaches, Smile Please, The Luck of the Foolish, All Night Long,* and *Feet of Mud* (1924); *Remember*

When?, *Boobs in the Woods*, and *Lucky Stars*
(1925); and *Saturday Afternoon* (1926)
Tramp, Tramp, Tramp (1926)
The Strong Man (1926)
Long Pants (1927)

STAN LAUREL (1890–1965) AND OLIVER HARDY (1892–1957)

Shorts, including: *Finishing Touch* and *The Call of the Cuckoo* (1927); *Leave 'Em Laughing* and *Two Tars* (1928); *Liberty, Big Business, Double Whoopee, Perfect Day, Wrong Again,* and *Bacon Grabbers* (1929); *Brats* and *Another Fine Mess* (1930); *Beau Hunks* (1931); *County Hospital* and *The Music Box* (1932); and *Thicker Than Water* (1935)
Pardon Us (1931)
Sons of the Desert (1933)
Our Relations (1936)
Way Out West (1937)
Block-Heads (1938)

HAROLD LLOYD (1893–1971)

Shorts, including: *Lonesome Luke* (1915); *The Cinema Director* (1916); *Birds of a Feather* (1917); *The Non-Stop Kid* and *Nothing But Trouble* (1918); *The Chef, Don't Shove, Just Neighbors, Chop Suey & Co.,* and *Going, Going, Gone* (1919)
High and Dizzy (1920)
Never Weaken (1921)
Dr. Jack (1922)
Safety Last (1923)
Hot Water (1924)
The Freshman (1925)
Speedy (1928)
The Milky Way (1936)
The Sin of Harold Diddlebock (1947). Recut version, *Mad Wednesday*, released 1950

OSCAR MICHEAUX (1884–1951)

The Homesteader (1918). First New York showing, 1920
Within Our Gates (1920). Completed 1919
The Symbol of the Unconquered (1920)
Birthright (1924)
Body and Soul (1925). First version, 1924
Spider's Web (1926)
Wages of Sin (1928)
The Exile (1931)
Ten Minutes to Live (1932)

Harlem After Midnight (1934)
Lem Hawkins' Confession (1935)
Murder in Harlem (1935)
God's Step Children (1938)
The Notorious Elinor Lee (1940)
The Betrayal (1948)

KING VIDOR (1894–1982)

The Big Parade (1925)
The Crowd (1928)
Hallelujah (1929)
Street Scene (1931)
Our Daily Bread (1934)
Stella Dallas (1937)
Duel in the Sun (1947)
The Fountainhead (1949)

ERICH VON STROHEIM (1885–1957)

Blind Husbands (1919)
Foolish Wives (1922). Completed 1921
Greed (1924)
The Merry Widow (1925)
The Wedding March (1928)
Queen Kelly (1932). Shot 1928–29

LOIS WEBER (1882–1939)

Suspense (1913)
Hypocrites (1914)
Where Are My Children (1916)
The Hand That Rocks the Cradle (1917). Original title: *Is a Woman a Person?*
Too Wise Wives (1921)
The Blot (1921)
The Angel of Broadway (1927)

REPRESENTATIVE FILMS

Vitagraph Comedies: *Stenographer Wanted* (1912), *Goodness Gracious, or, Movies As They Shouldn't Be* (1914), *Professional Patient* (1917)
Broncho Billy's Capture (1913, Gilbert M. Anderson)
Traffic in Souls (1913, George Loane Tucker)
The Perils of Pauline (1914 serial, Louis J. Gasnier). With Pearl White
The Tigress (1914, Alice Guy Blaché)
Alias Jimmy Valentine (1915, Maurice Tourneur)
A Fool There Was (1915, Frank Powell). With Theda Bara
Regeneration (1915, Raoul Walsh)
Young Romance (1915, William C. deMille; directed by George H. Melford)

The Toll Gate (1920, Lambert Hillyer). With W. S. Hart

The Four Horsemen of the Apocalypse (1921, Rex Ingram). With Rudolph Valentino

Tol'able David (1921, Henry King). With Richard Barthelmess

Blood and Sand (1922, Fred Niblo). With Rudolf Valentino

Salomé (1922, rel. 1923, Charles Bryant). With Alla Nazimova

The Covered Wagon and *Hollywood* (1923, James Cruze)

The Hunchback of Notre Dame (1923, Wallace Worsley). With Lon Chaney

The White Sister (1923, Henry King). With Lillian Gish

The Big Parade (1925, King Vidor)

Tumbleweeds (1925, King Baggot). With W. S. Hart

The Unholy Three (1925, Tod Browning). With Lon Chaney; sound version, 1930, directed by Jack Conway

Ben-Hur (1926, Fred Niblo)

The Scar of Shame (1926, Frank Perugini)

The Scarlet Letter (1926, Victor Sjøstrøm). With Lillian Gish

Son of the Sheik (1926, George Fitzmaurice). With Rudolf Valentino

Sparrows (1926, William Beaudine). With Mary Pickford

What Price Glory (1926, Raoul Walsh)

The Cat and the Canary (1927, Paul Leni)

It or *"it"* (1927, Clarence Badger). With Clara Bow

Wings (1927, William Wellman)

The Crowd (1928, King Vidor)

The Fall of the House of Usher (1928, James Sibley Watson and Melville Webber)

Lonesome (1928, Paul Fejos)

The Wind (1928, Victor Sjøstrøm). With Lillian Gish

DVDS

The Art of Buster Keaton. Kino Video. The only **Buster Keaton** set to consider. Includes 11 features and 19 shorts—every film he made from *One Week* (1920) to *Steamboat Bill, Jr.* (1928)—and over three hours of rare footage, including home movies. The best prints of *The General, The Navigator, Our Hospitality,* etc.

The Best Arbuckle Keaton Collection. Image Entertainment. **Roscoe "Fatty" Arbuckle** and **Buster Keaton** in their 12 surviving shorts, from *The Butcher Boy* (1917, Keaton's first appearance on film) to *The Garage* (1919, rel. 1920; their last collaboration, Keaton's favorite).

The Black Pirate (1926, Albert Parker). Kino International. Starring **Douglas Fairbanks. Restored;** two-strip color.

Blind Husbands (1919, **Erich von Stroheim**) and *The Great Gabbo* (1929, **James Cruze,** starring Stroheim). Kino International. An excellent tinted print of *Blind Husbands* (from the Museum of Modern Art) with many extras, including a radio play and excerpts from the pressbook. *Gabbo* was **restored** by the Library of Congress.

The Blot (1921, **Lois Weber**). Image Entertainment/Milestone. **Restored.**

Cecil B. DeMille's Manslaughter and The Cheat. Kino International. The print of *The Cheat* (1915, **DeMille**) is superb but is the 1918 re-issue.

The Charley Chase Collection. Kino International. **Charley Chase** in six Hal Roach shorts.

The Douglas Fairbanks Collection. Image Entertainment. **Fairbanks** in *The Mark of Zorro, The Three Musketeers, Robin Hood, The Thief of Bagdad, Don Q Son of Zorro,* and *The Black Pirate,* with extras. (A better version of *The Black Pirate* is listed separately.)

The Fall of the House of Usher (**Webber** and **Watson**) is in *Treasures from American Film Archives* (see Chap. 1 list).

Foolish Wives (1922, **Erich von Stroheim**) and *The Man You Loved To Hate* (a 1979 documentary on Stroheim). Kino Video. This excellent print of *Foolish Wives* was carefully **restored** by the American Film Institute to 143 minutes and has the original score. Commentary by biographer Richard Koszarski, censorship information, a note by Stroheim, and more.

Grass (1925, **Merian C. Cooper** and **Ernest B. Schoedsack**). Image Entertainment. Includes an audio interview with Cooper.

The Harold Lloyd Collection. Kino International. **Harold Lloyd** in *Grandma's Boy* and seven shorts.

Harry Langdon . . . the forgotten clown. Image Entertainment. **Harry Langdon** in *Tramp,*

Tramp, Tramp; The Strong Man; and *Long Pants.*

Laurel & Hardy. Lions Gate/Fox. **Laurel** and **Hardy** in the feature *Sons of the Desert* and the shorts *Another Fine Mess, Busy Bodies, County Hospital,* and *The Music Box.*

The Lon Chaney Collection. Warner Home Video. Contains *The Ace of Hearts; The Unknown* (the crucial film in this group, directed by **Tod Browning**); *Laugh, Clown, Laugh;* commentary by **Lon Chaney** biographer Michael Blake; stills from *London After Midnight* (offered as a reconstruction); and a documentary.

The Lost Films of Stan Laurel and Oliver Hardy: The Complete Collection. Image Entertainment. The best available prints; each volume about two hours of **Laurel** and **Hardy,** separate or together. Volume One includes *Big Business.* Volume Three includes *Liberty.* Volume Eight includes *Two Tars* and *From Soup to Nuts.*

Male and Female (1919, **Cecil B. DeMille**). Image Entertainment. Also in a DeMille set.

The Man Who Laughs (1928, **Paul Leni**). Kino Video/Universal. Excellent **restoration** with the original Movietone soundtrack, home movies, many stills, an excerpt from the Italian release version, an informative essay by **Conrad Veidt** biographer John Soister, a documentary, etc.

Nanook of the North (1922, **Robert Flaherty**). Criterion Collection. Director's cut at 21.5 fps.

The Origins of Film: 1900–1926. Image Entertainment. The Library of Congress Video Collection. Includes *Alias Jimmy Valentine, Within Our Gates, Too Wise Wives, The Scar of Shame,* other features, and many shorts.

The Phantom of the Opera: The Ultimate Edition (1925 and 1929, **Rupert Julian** and others). Image Entertainment. Starring **Lon Chaney.** With a new score by Carl Davis and the original Vitaphone soundtrack, color sequences, stills including deleted scenes, trailers, and both versions of the film.

Salomé (1922, rel. 1923, **Charles Bryant**), starring **Alla Nazimova,** and *Lot in Sodom* (1933, **Melville Webber** and **James Sibley Watson**). Image Entertainment. *Lot in Sodom* has the original music by Alec Wilder.

The Seashell and the Clergyman (**Germaine Dulac**) is in *Avant-Garde: Experimental Cinema of the 1920s and '30s* (see Chap. 10 list).

Arbuckle, Chaplin, Keaton, Langdon, Lloyd, Sennett, and others are in *Slapstick Encyclopedia* (see Chap. 5 list).

The Stan Laurel Collection. Kino International. **Stan Laurel** in 17 shorts.

Tabu (1931, **Robert Flaherty** and **F. W. Murnau**). Image Entertainment. Commentary by film scholar Janet Bergstrom.

Without Lying Down: Frances Marion and the Power of Women in Hollywood (2001, Bridget Terry). Image Entertainment. Informative documentary. DVD includes a 1917 film written by **Frances Marion:** *A Little Princess,* starring **Mary Pickford** and **ZaSu Pitts.**

7

The German Golden Age

In the final year of World War I, the German government wondered whether preferring bullets to pictures had been a tactical error. Whatever the results of the battles at the front, the German nation and German character were losing terribly on the screens of the world. In a number of very popular films made in America during and after the war, the enemy was portrayed as a villainous, vicious Hun; the evil, sinister, outwardly polished and inwardly corrupt Erich von Stroheim was the perfect stereotype of this newest movie bad guy. There was no screen antidote to this single stereotypic portrait, so the German government decided to produce one.

In November 1917, the government set up a private company that soon began to buy and merge many studios into a single, large filmmaking unit, Universum-Film AG, known subsequently to the world as Ufa. Ufa's job was to make movies that would boost the German spirit at home and sell the German character and position abroad. The war ended before Ufa could accomplish either goal—but the immense movie company was still in business after the armistice had been signed. In 1920, Ufa moved into a huge new studio at Neubabelsberg, near Berlin, and it was there that the great era of German films was born.

Expressionism, Realism, and the Studio Film

The German Golden Age of film was a very short one, from the shooting of *The Cabinet of Dr. Caligari* in 1919 to Hitler's absorption of the German film industry in 1933. The great burst of artistic activity that followed the fall of the Kaiser and the founding of the Weimar Republic, the new spirit of intellectual and creative freedom in Germany, made itself felt in all the arts, but especially in the cinema.

If Griffith's two great accomplishments were his realization of the power of atmosphere, decor, and texture within a shot and the power of editing to join shots, it was the genius of the German film to refine and develop the former; the Soviet film developed the latter. The German film, in an era of silence, made the aura, the mood, the tone of the shot's visual qualities speak—so well that the best German films of the era contain the barest minimum of intertitles, or none at all. As the Soviet films emphasized montage and politics, the German films emphasized *mise-en-scène* and psychology. In general, the Soviets shot on location and rarely moved the camera, while the Germans shot in studios and moved the camera freely. If Griffith's *Intolerance* was the decisive influence on Soviet filmmaking in the 1920s, many German films of the 1920s can be seen as an extension of *Broken Blossoms*— which looked realistic but was shot in a studio; conveyed its psychological insights through lighting, gesture, and costume and set design; and told the intense, tragic story of a small number of characters.

In addition to liberating the camera, the Germans realized that it could function as a window into the mind. The camera, rather than taking the stance of an impartial observer, could itself mirror the perceptions, thoughts, and feelings of a character experiencing an event. To use an analogy with the novel, the German filmmaker realized that the camera, like the pen, could narrate a story in the first person as well as the third. Griffith used an occasional flight into subjectivity—his cutaways to reveal a character's thoughts, even the long dream in *The Avenging Conscience*—but Griffith's subjective moments were always in brackets. He used specific conventions to inform the audience that it was entering the personal experience of a character. Subjectivity in the German film is rarely set off in brackets; instead, the boundary between subjective and objective perceptions becomes indefinite: The world might look crazy because someone sees it that way or because it *is* that way, burdened with wordless meaning. To this idea—that the look or style of the visible, external universe can take its shape, color, and texture from the artist's intuition of its essential inner being or from internal human sensations—critics assigned a single term: Expressionism. The principle dominated the early 20th-century painting and drama of Germany as well as the often theatrical, always moving, graphic art of German cinema.

The harsh, bold graphics and revelatory distortions of German Expressionist drawing and painting inspired an attempt, in *The Cabinet of Dr. Caligari*, to film a completely Expressionist universe—one so unnatural that it had to be created in a studio. If an Expressionist painter might distort the look of an object to express its nature, to reveal the energy of an inner essence bursting to reveal itself—in effect, to show the skin of the nightmare or the scream of a lake—the Expressionist filmmaker had to design and construct an artificial landscape that was graphic in inspiration and boldly disturbing, on and beneath the surface.

But having made one world from scratch, the German filmmakers realized that they could create *any* kind of artificial world, including a realistic one. Whereas the Soviets' "artificial landscape" (or "creative geography") was assembled by cutting together shots taken in different locations, the Germans built and lit their artificial landscapes in studios, determining and controlling their every detail, often in the service not of Expressionism but of realism. The controlled, artificial realism of the studio film—as practiced,

for example, by Wyler or Hitchcock—was firmly established at Ufa.

The dependence of the German film on the evocations of its *mise-en-scène* led to its becoming completely a studio product. The only way to make sure that the lighting, the decor, the architectural shapes, the relationships of blacks, whites, and grays were perfect was to film in a completely controlled environment. Even some outdoor scenes were shot inside the four walls and ceiling of a studio. The vastness, the freedom of the outdoors that had become one of the sources of power of both the American and the Swedish film, was rejected by most of the Germans. (Among the exceptions were the makers of "mountain films," in which climbers rose to the physical and spiritual challenges of the elements.) The totally studio-produced films emphasized the importance of the designer, whose job was to conceive and decorate everything from one-room sets to enormous indoor cities (often "built" or realized with the aid of special effects). These designers—later called art directors or in some cases production designers—came to films from painting, theatre, and architecture, having absorbed the styles of many of the new artistic movements of postwar Europe: Expressionism, Cubism, Constructivism, and other forms of abstraction and analysis. The German film could never have exerted its influence without its talented painter–architect designers, the most notable of whom were Hermann Warm, Walter Röhrig, Walter Reimann, Robert Herlth, Albin Grau, and Ernö Metzner.

The emphasis on the studio production and the consolidation of talent in a single company produced a studio system very different from Hollywood's. Unlike the competing factories of Hollywood, the German studio was far more a combination of artists working with each other rather than trying to outguess each other. Although there were competitors with Ufa in the 1920s (Decla-Bioscop, for example), many of them worked so closely with the major producer that merger was inevitable. Ufa's great producer, Erich Pommer, was a man of artistic judgment and business acumen who stimulated mediocre directors to do their best work (E. A. Dupont's *Variety*, 1925, for example). Instead of building a star system, the German studio developed a repertory company, emphasizing the play and not the player, the character and not the personality. The German film actor needed variety and range, not a single trait to be milked over and over again. Among the best of the German repertory actors were Emil Jannings, Werner Krauss, Conrad Veidt, Fritz Körtner, Lil Dagover, Brigitte Helm, Asta Nielsen, Lya de Putti, and Pola Negri.

Many of these actors had been trained by the greatest German stage director of the period, Max Reinhardt, who had conceived a style of theatre that depended as much on decor as on the actor and playwright. Among the directors who studied with Reinhardt were F. W. Murnau (later his assistant) and Lotte Reiniger, whose animated films, inspired by the German shadow-play and by the Greek and Balinese shadow puppets, featured detailed paper figures in silhouette. In 1926, Reiniger made the world's first full-length animated feature, *The Adventures of Prince Achmed.*

Reinhardt was influential on the German cinema of the Weimar Republic not only for his actors, pupils, and Expressionist visual conceptions, but also for the style and genre he pioneered in his theatre, the *Kammerspiele*, a "chamber theatre" for small audiences, with small casts, intimately psychological portraits, and dim lighting (with spotlights to isolate part of the stage or action and with extensive use of *chiaroscuro*). Some of the greatest German films of the 1920s would be intimate "chamber dramas," a genre called the *Kammerspielfilm.*

Weimar cinema went through three major stages: (1) Expressionism, the best examples of which are *Caligari* and Karl-Heinz Martin's *Von Morgens bis Mitternacht* (*From Morning to Midnight*, 1920); (2) the *Kammerspielfilm*, which had few or no intertitles in order to intensify and deepen what the actors, lighting, and set design conveyed, and which featured psychological studies of a few characters in ordinary middle- and lower-class environments; examples include Lupu Pick's *Sylvester* (1923) and Murnau's *The Last Laugh* (1924); and (3) *die neue Sachlichkeit*, or the "New Objectivity," whose often fatalistic and grimy lower-class realism found a home in the studio (Pabst's *The Joyless Street*, 1925) and in the streets (Metzner's *Überfall* [usually called *Accident*, the film's title would more accurately be translated *Police Report: Surprise Assault*], 1929). These stages

were inspired by and related to movements in the arts; although German Expressionism had passed its prime by the time *Caligari* was made, *die neue Sachlichkeit* was contemporary with the artistic movement of the same name, which produced the bitterly sarcastic drawings of George Grosz. The most important abstract films—films of pure form—were made by Swedish-born Viking Eggeling (*Diagonalsymphonien* or *Symphonie diagonale*, 1924) and painter Hans Richter (*Rhythmus 21*, 1921), who had joined the international Dada movement and who worked together in Germany until Eggeling's early death.

Many key figures worked in more than one of these movements. Murnau directed both *The Last Laugh* and the Expressionist *Nosferatu* (1922). Producer Erich Pommer closely managed films as diverse as *Caligari, The Last Laugh, Variety, Metropolis* (1926, released 1927), and *The Blue Angel* (1930)—and later, in the United States, even Dorothy Arzner's *Dance, Girl, Dance.* Carl Mayer co-wrote *Caligari* and was the sole author of a great number of the most important films of the period, including *Sylvester* and *The Last Laugh;* he also conceived the genre of the "Street film" and dominated both it and the *Kammerspielfilm*, writing rhythmically charged scripts that suppressed intertitles and included precise lighting and camera directions. And in the hands of the great cinematographers Karl Freund (*The Last Laugh, Variety*) and Fritz Arno Wagner (*Nosferatu* and *M*, 1931), the moving camera, the unconventional angle, the subjective image, and expressive low-key lighting showed the world what the camera could really do.

The German films of this great era fell generally into two types: either fantastic and mystical or realistic and psychological. One was steeped in the traditional German Romanticism of love and death; the other revealed the new German intellectual currents of Freud and Weber. In the films of fantasy and horror, the action revolves around the occult, the mysterious, the metaphysical. These are films of fantastic monsters in human dress, of what lives beyond the grave, of dream kingdoms of the past and future. The architect–painters could turn these eerie, abstract, intangible regions into concrete, visual domains. In the psychological film, the action revolves around the thoughts and feelings of the characters, their needs, their lusts, their jobs, their frustrations. Unlike the fantasy films, which usually are set in some romantic time and place, the psychological films are set in the urban present. The architect–painters could turn the tawdry, dirty, depressing rooms and streets into complex, detailed, realistic studio slums.

Fantasy

Caligari

The film that signaled the start of the new era, *The Cabinet of Dr. Caligari* (released in February 1920), is a tale of fantasy and horror with a psychological twist. It was produced by Erich Pommer for Decla-Bioscop before that company was absorbed by Ufa. The camerawork is primitive, and the direction is uneven, but the mood of this definitively antirealist film is unshakably disturbing.

Its central plot is a story of horror, murder, and almost mystical power. An enigmatic and menacing yet oddly seductive hypnotist, who calls himself Dr. Caligari (Werner Krauss), opens a stall at a fair in the town of Holstenwall; his act demonstrates his mastery over a sleepwalker he has apparently hypnotized, Cesare (Conrad Veidt). A rash of murders breaks out in the town. The police have no clues. The film's narrator–protagonist, Francis (or Franz, played by Friedrich Feher), suspects Caligari, shadows him, and eventually discovers that he forces his slave, Cesare, to murder the victims while the hypnotist substitutes a life-sized dummy resembling Cesare in the coffin-like box (the cabinet) to fool the police. Francis continues to follow the master who, it turns out, is also the director of the state insane asylum. The keeper of the insane is himself insane, a monster who has discovered the medieval formula of Caligari for controlling men's minds and who has set out to "become Caligari." Francis exposes the monster; the monster goes mad. The orderlies stuff Caligari into a strait-jacket and lock him in a cell. This is as far as the central plot of *Caligari* goes. It is also as far as its writers, Carl Mayer and Hans Janowitz, wanted it to go.

But *Caligari* goes further. The entire central plot is bracketed by a frame, conceived by Fritz Lang. The film begins with Francis informing a listener (and us) that he has a dreadful story to tell. To set a horrific, supernatural tale within a frame is, of course, a traditional literary device (as in Mary Shelley's *Frankenstein* or Henry James's *The Turn of the Screw*), the means to anchor a fantastic story in reality (as well as isolate it, fence it in) and thereby increase our credulity. The setting of this opening, framing sequence seems like a park—there are trees, vines, a wall, benches. But it is too bare, too cold; the woman (Lil Dagover) who walks past seems somnambulistic, ethereal. Only at the end of the film do we discover that the opening and closing framing sequences are set not in a park but on the grounds of an asylum, that Francis himself is a patient, that many of the characters in his tale (like the gentle Cesare—who had died in the inner narrative but is now quite alive) are also patients, and that the so-called Caligari is the director of the asylum. And it is not Caligari who winds up in a cell in a strait-jacket but Francis. The surprise at the end of the film is our discovery that the tale we assumed to be true is a paranoid's fantasy.

Our discovery of the disease in the narrator's brain suddenly illuminates the principle of the film's unnatural decor. Throughout the film the Expressionist world of the horror tale has been striking: the grotesque painted shadows on streets and stairs; the irregular, nonperpendicular chimneys, doors, and windows; the exaggerated heights of the furniture; the boldly painted makeup. This grotesque world is not simply a decorative stunt; it is, thanks to Lang's psychological "twist," the way Francis sees the world. That was how Lang, the original director assigned to the project, saw it; how Robert Wiene did direct it; and why the writers objected to the changes. Rather than exposing an insane world (that could tyrannically send an innocent—or soldier—like Cesare to kill against his will), their story now implied that the world is fine, Francis is mad, and Caligari knows best.

The striking effect of the film's Expressionist design (by Warm, Röhrig, and Reimann) is not just the look but the unnatural feel of it. Walls, floors, and ceilings bear a structurally impossible relationship to one another; buildings so constructed could never stand. Most unnatural of all, the world of *Caligari* is a world without sunlight: Shadows of light and dark, shafts where the sun would normally cast its shadow, have been

Fig. 7-1

The Cabinet of Dr. Caligari: *a madman's vision of the world—impossibly shaped windows, exaggeratedly high furniture, and geometric shadows.*

painted on the sets. Hermann Warm, the principal designer, belonged to a group that believed "films should be drawings brought to life," and *Caligari* lives up to that demand; it is an inhabited graphic world, an Expressionist visual conception that moves.

Caligari is interesting not just for how it looks but for the ambiguities generated by the tension between its inner and framing narratives. The central story is no simple tale told by an idiot. If the kindly doctor is really not the demented Caligari, why does it feel so creepy when he says, at the very end, that he now knows "how to cure" Francis? And why does the asylum look no more natural in the closing framing sequence (supposedly an objective point of view) than it did in Francis's narration?

Perhaps the film's ambiguities and internal contradictions stem from the conflict between the writers, who conceived one kind of story, and the director, who accepted another. Whatever the underlying reason, the ambiguities and ambivalences of *Caligari* enrich it.

Although it started the Expressionist film movement, decisively influenced the horror film (which had flourished in Germany since 1913), and set the pattern for a film with an "unreliable narrator"—one of the key devices of modern fiction—*Caligari* has been attacked since it

came out. Theorists André Bazin, Erwin Panofsky, and Siegfried Kracauer are unanimous in believing that the film is a cinematic mistake, that it "prestylizes reality," that it violates the inherent photographic realism of the medium, that it substitutes a world of painted artifice for the rich resources of nature. Despite these later arguments, the film had an immense influence not only in Germany, but also in France, where "Caligarism," though detested by some, inspired many of the early avant-garde experiments in abstract cinema, in film as "painting in motion" rather than as realistic narrative. If it was the first feature-length "art film" and the first feature that *had* to be shot in a studio, *The Cabinet of Dr. Caligari* has also been capable of scaring and fascinating audiences for scores of years.

Destiny and *Metropolis*

Of the mystical children of *Caligari*, Fritz Lang's *Destiny* (*Der müde Tod*, 1921) is among the most interesting. Lang, in collaboration with his author–wife, Thea von Harbou, who wrote most of his German films, is more famous for a series of psychological studies of the activities of gamblers, murderers, master criminals, and spies (*The Spiders*; *Dr. Mabuse, the Gambler*; *Spies*; *M*). But he also made several metaphysical–fantasy films. In *Destiny*, based on a dream Lang

Fig. 7-2

Fig. 7-3

Caligari's *faces of paint.* Fig. 7-2: Dr. Caligari (Werner Krauss); Fig. 7-3: Cesare (Conrad Veidt).

had as a child, a young woman (Lil Dagover) and her lover enter a new town; on the road they encounter a shadowy, spectral stranger. The stranger has bought a piece of land near the town's cemetery and has enclosed it with an immense stone wall that lacks a door or any other physical means of entering. The lover disappears; when the woman discovers that he is a prisoner beyond the wall, she starts to drink a

Fig. 7-4

Destiny: *the Cave of the Candles (Lil Dagover and Bernhard Götzke).*

poisonous drug. Lang cuts to the wall where she sees the transparent images of souls entering the region beyond the wall. The way in is metaphysical, not physical.

The wall surrounds the kingdom of death; the mysterious stranger is Death himself, a weary Death (the meaning of the title's "*müde Tod*"), superintending the candles of human life that inevitably flicker out. The woman pleads for the life of her lover; Death tiredly offers her a chance to save him, pointing out three candles whose lights have begun to flicker. The woman claims that love can conquer death, and she sets off to save at least one of the three lights.

Each of these "lights" is a story in a far-off land: a Middle Eastern Moslem city, Renaissance Venice, and a magical China. In all three the woman and her lover are reincarnated as two young lovers whose monarchs have declared war on their love. In all three reincarnations, the young man dies. After her failure, Death gives her one more chance; she can return to life and redeem her lover if she can offer another life in trade. She soon runs into a burning hospital to save an infant trapped there. Death meets her inside and asks her for the child. She considers and then refuses; she will not kill the infant to save her lover. Instead, the woman herself dies in the fire; her soul and her lover's are reunited as their transparent images climb a hill and stand against the sky. Love, in dying, has conquered death.

The power of the film lies in its combination of the pictorial sense of the director and the magnificent visual creations of the designers (Warm, Röhrig, Herlth). The huge, gray wall of Death dwarfs the black-clad figures who stand in front of it; its horizontal and vertical lines run off the frame at top, right, and left—a powerful visual metaphor for the infiniteness and inaccessibility of fate. Equally memorable is the care taken in creating each of the fantastic kingdoms for the stories of the three lights.

A later Lang film, *Metropolis* (1926, released 1927), was the most important science fiction film since *A Trip to the Moon*. The film depicts a socially engineered world of the future where the rich and intelligent live on the earth's surface with their airplanes and trams and skyscrapers, and the workers—who make the society go— live beneath the surface in a drab, utilitarian "city," below which are dark, labyrinthine caverns. The hero (Freder, played by Gustav Fröhlich), a young rebel, rejects the sheltered lifestyle of the rich—his father, who dresses and behaves like a modern executive, runs Metropolis—and goes to live and struggle with the workers of the underworld. There he meets the spirit of the workers—Maria (played by Brigitte Helm), a proletarian version of the Virgin Mary and Christ all in one—who urges peaceful change and nonviolent progress. Maria is a Christian Democrat–Humanist (literally Christian since she delivers her political sermons in a candlelit cave full of crosses) who formulates the film's political argument: The heart must mediate between head and hands.

The young hero's father, the Master of Metropolis, will have none of this. He hires the evil scientist–magician, Rotwang (played by Rudolf Klein-Rogge: the direct ancestor of Dr. Strangelove, even to the black glove), to manufacture a sexy, vicious robot (Brigitte Helm) who looks exactly like Maria and who will incite the workers to riot; the father's troops can then use the riot to enslave the workers. The workers riot, flood their underground city, and almost destroy the whole society, until the kidnapped Maria escapes and the hero kills Rotwang. The Master learns his lesson, and his enlightened son, who has lived in both worlds, is designated the society's official "heart" to mediate between head (administration—his dad) and hands

(labor—he shakes hands with the foreman of the workers).

The film demonstrates the dangers of the purely architectural–pictorial premise of many of the German studio films. Shot by Karl Freund and Günther Rittau, *Metropolis* is a series of stunning images, sequences, and effects, held together by a silly and oppressive fable. Many of its images were composed in vast geometrical patterns: row upon row of black-clad workers in boxy elevators; the geometrical machines and the patterns of workers who serve them.

Part of the emptiness of the film lies in the way it reduces people to patterns—to units of geometrical architecture. What is most Fascistic about *Metropolis* is its portrayal of the general lot of human beings as a mass of plodding slaves or wild rioters—in either case, indistinguishable ciphers. Unable to take care of themselves, swayed just as easily by the robot as they are by Maria, the workers are utterly dependent on the beneficence of the ruler above.

The implications of *Metropolis* did not pass unnoticed in its time. It was one of Hitler's favorite films; another was Lang's *Die Nibelungen* (1924), which contained the story of Siegfried, with whom Hitler identified. (No one knows what Hitler thought about Lang's 1922 *Dr. Mabuse, the Gambler*, in which a mesmerizing, power-mad criminal exercises his irresistible will to control the people and world around him, until he is destroyed by his own demons.) After Hitler had seized control of the government, he invited Lang to make films for the Nazis. That Lang sometimes diminished people into puppets, crowds into patterns, and political problems into romantic abstractions exactly suited Hitler's purposes. Lang, however, fled the country.

Much as *Caligari* influenced the horror film in Germany and abroad, *Metropolis* foreshadowed many developments in the science fiction film (as did Lang's *Woman in the Moon*, 1928 [released 1929], which introduced the countdown), particularly in its vision of the futuristic upper city, in its use of telescreens for spying and communication (seen in Universal's Flash Gordon serials as well as in Chaplin's *Modern Times*), and in the design of Rotwang's laboratory, where scientific apparatus, Expressionistic magic, and pure light bring the robot to life. The film's most influential special-effects shots were

Fig. 7-5

Fig. 7-6

Metropolis: *human beings reduced to dispirited masses of architecture.*

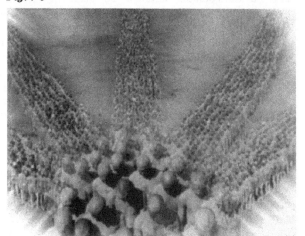

Fig. 7-7

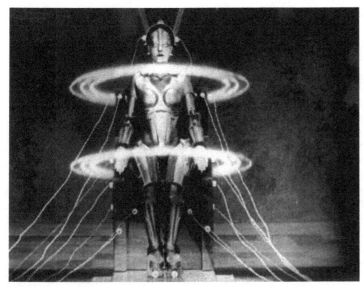

Fig. 7-8

Science as magic: bringing the robot to life in Metropolis.

achieved through the "Schüfftan process," which was invented by Eugen Schüfftan specifically for *Metropolis*. The Schüfftan process allowed actors and miniature or model sets to be photographed together. Between the actors, who might be on a full-scale but partial set, and the camera, a mirror was placed at a 45° angle; the model set, which was off to the side, was reflected in the mirror. One or more holes were made in this reflected image by scraping the silver off the back of the mirror, and through those areas of clear glass the actors could be seen and photographed; the partial set behind them would match and line up with the miniature, creating the impression of a complete full-scale set with actors in it. In Figure 7-5, for example, the buildings in the background are a miniature set, and the actors and gong are full size. Although the Schüfftan process was superseded by the traveling mattes, front and rear projection, and sophisticated optical printing perfected in *King Kong* and other films of the 1930s, it was revived in the 1990s by Introvision, which used an improved version of it to create the effects for such films as *The Fugitive* (1993) because it allowed work to be done in the camera, with faster and cheaper results than could be achieved in a lab.

Originally 153 minutes, *Metropolis* was soon re-edited—not by Lang—for release in Germany

and America. Both the Ufa and the American versions shortened the film to just under two hours and rewrote many of the intertitles; they changed and reinterpreted the story (in different ways) while removing numerous subplots and motivations. It was not until 2001 that *Metropolis* was successfully restored. The restored version, while not quite complete (124 minutes; some of the deleted material, about 20 minutes, was discovered in Argentina in 2008), is much more coherent, thanks in part to the discovery of the original text of the intertitles, which allowed the surviving footage—which was digitally restored, then transferred back to film—to be put in its proper order. Unfortunately, the head, heart, and hands business is still there.

Nosferatu and Others

Of the other films of fantasy and the supernatural, Paul Leni's *Waxworks* (1924) included an Expressionist dream sequence that centered on Jack the Ripper. Co-director Paul Wegener's *The Golem* (1920, but previously made in 1914)—the story of a magician–rabbi who brings a clay statue to life to protect the Jews in the ghetto—is significant for the twisted architecture of its settings (designed by Hans Poelzig); the fiery, demonic special effects in the scene when Rabbi Loew brings the man of clay to life; and its great influence on the

Frankenstein series, including the monster's attraction to an innocent playing child. Galeen's version of *The Student of Prague* (1926, previously made by Stellan Rye and Paul Wegener in 1913) is the mythical story of the *Doppelgänger*, or double, a genre dating back at least to Poe's "William Wilson" and Dostoyevsky's *The Double;* in *The Student of Prague*, a man sells his reflection only to effect a divorce between his internal and external selves—and to leave on the loose a bad guy who looks just like him. Arthur Robison's *Warning Shadows* (1923, designed by Albin Grau and shot by Fritz Arno Wagner) is interesting for its complex and consistent use of shadows: as an element of the film's action; as the profession of one of the main characters, who, like a filmmaker, entertains audiences with shadow-plays; as a means of creating a mysterious mood and

mystical atmosphere; and as one of the film's key metaphoric motifs.

The most noteworthy and effective of the purely horrific descendants of *Caligari* was F. W. Murnau's *Nosferatu, a Symphony of Horror* (1922), an unauthorized adaptation—with a script by Henrik Galeen—of Bram Stoker's *Dracula. Nosferatu,* Murnau's first major success, was distinguished in the aura of horror and gloom with which it surrounded the vampire's activities. Unlike later incarnations of Dracula— Bela Lugosi, Christopher Lee, and many others— Murnau's vampire (Max Schreck) was no sexy, suave, intriguing gentleman. Murnau's vampire was hideous—a shriveled, ashen man with rat teeth, not long canines. He is pestilential, and his visits are mistaken for a rat-borne plague. *Nosferatu* creates a feeling of mystical

Fig. 7-9
Nosferatu: *The vampire (Max Schreck).*

parasitism, of the way that death perpetually feeds off the living. Also memorable are the shots that evoke the deadly emanations of the vampire: the rats in the streets; the phantom ship sailing by itself; the use of negative film and single-frame exposure to depict the gulf between the natural world and the supernatural world of the vampire's castle; the bare, stony walls of the castle itself. Murnau had Fritz Arno Wagner shoot these sequences outdoors, in nature; rather than "prestylize" reality as *Caligari* had, Murnau and Wagner and art director Albin Grau found ways to make reality creepy—in many respects, the most crucial and impressive of *Nosferatu*'s achievements.

Significantly, the underlying theme of *Nosferatu* is similar to *Destiny*'s: the conflict of love and death. The film's heroine consciously seduces the deadly menace, who is attracted to her beauty. Sacrificing her life, she keeps him out of his coffin until after the sun rises, and he dissolves into the morning air. Love is the strongest power in the mystical German film.

Psychology

The Last Laugh

F. W. Murnau's *The Last Laugh* (*Der letzte Mann*, 1924) is the most influential of the films that concentrated on psychology and realism rather than fantasy and the unnatural. Although it contains an Expressionist dream sequence, for the most part the film is a good example of the *Kammerspiel* movement. *The Last Laugh* teamed the greatest of Ufa's talents: director, Murnau; producer, Pommer; writer, Carl Mayer; cinematographer, Karl Freund; designers, Röhrig and Herlth; and central figure, Emil Jannings. The plot is as simple as the plots of the mystical–fantasy films were complex; its emotions are as personal and as carefully motivated as the concepts of the metaphysical films were abstract.

A porter–doorman at a posh hotel (Jannings) bases his self-respect on his belief in the importance of his job, which is symbolized by his passionate devotion to his ornate uniform. The almost military uniform (he salutes when he wears it) both defines his existence and impresses his status-conscious, less fortunate neighbors. Because he is old and beginning to slow down, the doorman is stripped of this uniform and given a new one: the plain linen jacket of the lavatory attendant. The film then details the impact of this loss of dignity on his emotions—his ego collapses—and on his family and acquaintances, who reject and taunt him. Rather than leaving the old man stooped in abject despair, the film "takes pity on him" (apparently at Erich Pommer's insistence) and gives him a happy ending: a sudden inheritance of money that turns him into a kindly but gluttonous gobbler of caviar. The effect of this deliberately contrived ending will be discussed in a moment. Worthy of the fullest and most immediate attention in the film is the rendering of the steady deterioration of the old man's soul once he has lost the uniform that covers his body.

One of the film's great virtues is the performance of Jannings, his clear yet subtle portrayal of the two states of the unnamed doorman's mind. Wearing his uniform, Jannings walks quickly and erect; his gestures are smart and precise; his whole body exudes pride and self-esteem, as well as smugness and vanity. Without the gaudy coat he ages 25 years—his body stoops; his gestures are vague and languid; he becomes a hunched, shuffling, broken man.

The director and cameraman give Jannings a new and useful ally—the camera itself. Freund's camera tracks and swings and tilts at key moments in the film. The key principle is not just that the camera moves for the sake of visual variety, but that it has been freed from its stationary tripod in order to illuminate narrative and psychological content. The camera becomes, in effect, the other major character with whom Jannings plays his scenes, and they work so well together that verbal explanations (titles) become almost unnecessary. *The Last Laugh* has no intertitles for dialogue, but it does have two narrative intertitles—one to introduce the unrealistic ending—and several shots of objects that we read: a newspaper article about the legacy, a wedding cake. (One surprise in the restored version is that it opens with an intertitle: "One day you are preeminent, respected by all—a minister, a general, maybe even a prince. But, what will you be tomorrow?")

The power of the moving camera—which, more than anything else, made *The Last Laugh* internationally famous—strikes the viewer in the

Fig. 7-10   Fig. 7-11

The Last Laugh: *the old man (Emil Jannings) in the treasured, prestigious uniform of a hotel doorman (Fig. 7-10) and in the humble uniform of a hotel lavatory attendant (Fig. 7-11).*

very opening of the film. In the first shot, the camera (strapped to the cameraman, who was on a bicycle) rides down the elevator of the Hotel Atlantic; after a cut, it tracks through the bustling lobby, as if it were a guest who had walked out of the elevator, and over to the constantly revolving door, where it stops to look through the door at the rainy night and the doorman, with his big umbrella, ushering patrons to and from cabs. In the next shots, the camera joins the old man in the rain. This fast, busy sequence imparts excitement with its movement, but also establishes every crucial expository detail the film's action requires: the size and importance of the hotel, the old man's conscientious devotion to his job, the difficulty and triumph of his managing a heavy trunk in the rain (which leads him to take a rest, which leads the manager to decide he's too old for the job, which precipitates the catastrophe and motivates the rest of the story), and the indifference of that symbol of the inhuman, continuous efficiency of business, the revolving door.

When the old man receives his notice of demotion from the manager, the subjective camera (a POV shot) shows us the letter and then blurs; the doorman can no longer read the piece of

paper. When he gets drunk at his daughter's wedding party, the room whirls; the spinning camera mirrors his spinning head and makes the audience a bit dizzy. In his drunken reverie (an Expressionistic dream sequence in which he demonstrates his power by tossing and catching a trunk while guests and bosses marvel and clap), the world becomes distorted. In this elaborate mindscreen, the hotel's revolving door, now immensely tall, casts bizarre shadows, and the faces of the musicians (who wake him) have been squeezed, stretched, and curved like faces in the mirrors of a funhouse. Murnau even translates sound into subjective visual effects by blurring the shots of the musician's trumpet, implying that the doorman can hear it only as a blur. Whereas the distortion and superimposition in a film like *Destiny* reveal the supernatural and the immaterial, those same techniques in *The Last Laugh* reveal natural sensations and unsupernatural dreams; the effect of a technique is defined by the narrative context of the whole film.

In spite of its oddly "Hollywood" ending, *The Last Laugh* differed markedly from the Hollywood films of the 1920s, both in its

Fig. 7-12

Subjective vision in **The Last Laugh:** *the hungover porter's view of a woman (Emilie Kurz) bringing his morning coffee (Fig. 7-12); the distorted face of a neighbor (Fig. 7-13).*

Fig. 7-13

emphasis on psychology rather than action and in its depiction of a world of moral grays rather than blacks and whites. On one hand, the film condemns the callous social process that values the man's function rather than the man himself. On the other hand, our particular hotel doorman is portrayed as foppish, vain, class-conscious, and image-conscious. For a man to define his essence by a uniform and by what others think of him is false and foolish.

But the other members of the doorman's own lower-middle-class world are themselves callous and petty, unsympathetic and inhumane, and prone to define a man by his uniform. They gossip at top volume. They are as vicious as the hotel manager is indifferent. They snigger behind his back when the former doorman walks down the street and into his apartment. Even his own family rejects him. And to some extent the old man deserves this, for his earlier attitude toward them, as he smugly paraded down the street in his uniform like a peacock, was as class-conscious as their present one. Although he gave candy to the children, he did it as a benevolent celebrity. He was his neighbors' connection to the military and economic ruling classes, and they honored him only until he fell, when they could take their revenge on him (now that he had become ordinary, one of them, or even lower) and on the oppressive social system he once incarnated. As social analysis—precisely focused on the uniforms of doorman and lavatory attendant and on the individual who wears them both, before he ends up in the "uniform" of a rich gentleman— this is a far more insightful reading of the class structure than anything in *Metropolis*.

The one odd note in the film is the old man's sudden good luck. In a way like *Caligari*, whose revised ending was also approved by Pommer, *The Last Laugh* has an ending that doesn't "fit," dividing the film against itself in an act of self-contradiction. Before our eyes, a tragedy switches to a comedy. It even uses an American character to motivate the happy ending, which is a parody of a Hollywood happy ending, seen from a Brechtian distance.

Wrenching us out of the story and announcing that the rest of the film is chimera, Carl Mayer's title card reads: "Here, in the place of his disgrace, the old man wastes away miserably for the rest of his life. And the story would end here. However—the author has decided to look after this person long after he has been abandoned by all the others, by giving him an epilogue, wherein things turn out—unfortunately—as they seldom do in real life." Whereas the film had not previously required a single title to clarify the thoughts or feelings of its characters, it suddenly uses one to show that the writer is sticking something on with narrative paste. Then, after shots of people laughing in the hotel as they read the paper, an insert shot of the article allows us to read with them that an American millionaire had left his fortune to the man who would be by his side when he died, and that the rich man had died in the washroom of the Atlantic Hotel. The German title of the film, *Der letzte Mann*, translates as *The Last Man*—the last who, says the Bible, shall be first; the "last man" of the will; and the old man when he is at his lowest.

The artificiality of the film's conclusion is so obvious, the solution so facile, that our minds immediately sniff parody—or commercialism. However, our hearts are also gladdened by the man's good fortune, particularly because he shares it with the only person who showed compassion for his suffering—the night watchman. In a way, he's still giving out candy, but with a difference, for now he has discovered the compassion for his fellows—notably the current lavatory attendant and, at the end of the film, a beggar—that he once lacked. He has no compassion, however, for those who turned their backs on him. He makes the hotel manager eat crow, and his own family is noticeably absent in his moment of good fortune. The ending satisfies our sense of

poetic justice. We just don't know whether—or, more precisely, *how*—to believe it.

Pabst and *die neue Sachlichkeit*

If one kind of German realist film was the close examination of a single psyche (usually a man's), the other examined the whole political or social milieu. Some of these movies, later known as "Street films," consistently use "street" in their titles: Karl Grune's *The Street* (1923), Bruno Rahn's *Tragedy of the Street* (1927). They use the unifying locale of the street as a means of tying together diverse kinds and classes of people—often to force a sheltered or repressed middle-class man to confront the seamy dangers of the real world. The street becomes a microcosm of society as a whole. And it's rough out there.

Among the most interesting of the Street films is *The Joyless Street* (1925), the first important film of the Austrian G. W. Pabst. Pabst's street runs through postwar Vienna, a city of striking contrasts: of feast and starvation, of family traditions and whoring. On Pabst's street the poor wait in line in front of a butcher's shop, hoping that the brutal man (Werner Krauss, who played Dr. Caligari) will give them a shred of meat. In the same building as the butcher's shop is Mrs. Greifer's nightclub, a frivolous, orgiastic late-night gathering spot for the rich, which also serves as a brothel. The film examines several lives on that street of contrasts where the women must choose between the poverty of standing in the slow line for the butcher's meat or the fast line to riches at Mrs. Greifer's—where the butcher is a steady customer. Two women take opposite paths. One (Asta Nielsen) sells her body and eventually commits murder; the other (Greta Garbo) holds out as long as she can and is rescued at the last minute. *The Joyless Street* was so realistic and controversial that it was banned in England and recut for distribution in many countries, including Italy, France, and even Austria.

Pabst typically combines a social theme with melodramatic action. The unity of this film lies in Pabst's consistent condemnation of the society that allows such poverty and opulence to exist at the same time, that gives no choice to the poor except starvation or capitulation to the perverted values of the rich. But while we are thinking about these social and moral issues, we are also rooting for Garbo; we are still in the world of melodrama, where goodness confronts evil and emotions are extreme.

Pabst was a psychological realist, sometimes a great one. In 1926, he made a film designed to explore and explain Freudian psychoanalysis, *Secrets of a Soul*; the film, which had the cooperation and blessing of two of Freud's assistants, arranged the life of a patient (Werner Krauss) into a puzzle of Expressionist dream sequences, memories, therapy sessions, and conventional action scenes, then solved the puzzle. Here and in general, Pabst's forays into Expressionism were visually creative but lacked the tortured drivenness of Expressionist art, the need one sees in the paintings of Van Gogh or Munch to get the vision *out*, to express its truth and its energy with raw, bold brilliance; nor did they show Murnau's gift for transforming the natural world into a new kind of nightmare (*Nosferatu*).

Pabst belonged to the third major movement in German film (after the Expressionist and *Kammerspielfilm* movements), the "New Objectivity" (*die neue Sachlichkeit*); this "new realism," which included but went beyond the Street films, took a close look at the surfaces and circumstances of reality without "prestylizing" it or pouring on the symbolism. So although he dabbled in Expressionism, Pabst was better at looking at people from the outside. From that vantage point, his psychological insight was flawless. Although some of his villains are as hissable as the butcher in *The Joyless Street* or the con artist in *The Love of Jeanne Ney* (1927), and some of his heroes are as true-hearted as Jeanne Ney and her Bolshevik lover, there are also characters who are scrutinized profoundly and yet remain impossible to label or sum up, like Lulu (Louise Brooks) in *Pandora's Box* (1929). Both in the terms of melodrama and in those of social and moral consciousness, everything in a Pabst film is examined for its value, to see what values it possesses or reflects. And the answers are not always simple.

In keeping with his psychological objectivity, in his greatest films Pabst strives for a realistic *mise-en-scène*—whether in the studio-made worlds of Ufa (*The Joyless Street*, like *The Last Laugh*, was shot entirely in the studio) or on the actual streets of Paris (*Jeanne Ney* combines location and studio footage). He defines characters through their possessions and surroundings as well as their behavior, using *mise-en-scène* in a way that is both relentless and subtle, telling but not overstated. *The Love of Jeanne Ney* opens not with an establishing long shot but with a close-up of the worn-out shoes on the villain's feet (with one foot nervously twitching), which goes exactly against narrative convention, puts extreme emphasis on a realistic detail, and does establish a great deal about this cheap character (the despicable con artist Khalibiev, played by Fritz Rasp). As the shot continues, the camera moves down his legs—he's lying on a shabby couch in cheap pants—and over to survey what is on the table alongside him: a mess of papers, a crudely drawn pornographic sketch, a lamp, some half-smoked cigarettes. After the camera has held on the table-top for a few seconds, a dirty hand with manicured nails reaches into the frame and fumbles for one of the butts; the camera pans right, following the hand, to reveal at last the face that we are not surprised to find weak and unpleasant, as the man puts the cigarette in a holder decorated with an amorous couple, lights it and finds it bitter, tosses it away, and sulks with the cigarette holder slack in his teeth. (*Jeanne Ney* was shot by Fritz Arno Wagner and Robert Lach.) A few shots later, the holder goes up when he looks at a sexy picture and down when he looks at a bill. That is a cinematic psychological realism that is daring, insightful, material, and precise.

But what Pabst is most known for is the fluidity of his camerawork and editing. He might well be thought of as the director who perfected classical film continuity. His camera tracks so readily, pauses or turns so appropriately, that we accept it as an element of the film's world and as the transparent vehicle of our attention. But if he wants us to notice the camera, we *do*—as in the shot in *Jeanne Ney* when an old woman screams and the camera moves in so close and so fast that the cracks in her tongue almost fill the screen. His lighting can appear natural but can just as easily plunge us into a world of shadows, madness, and evil (as in the murder of Jeanne's greedy uncle). His editing is so rapid and smooth that we can watch sequences in *Jeanne Ney* that contain more than ten shots per minute (like the one in which Khalibiev meets Jeanne and her father) and hardly be conscious of a cut. At its

Fig. 7-14
The realistic* mise-en-scène *of Pabst's* The Love of Jeanne Ney; *Fritz Rasp as the seedy villain.

most extreme, this is called "invisible editing," the exact opposite of the Soviet practice of calling attention to montage. But Pabst did not hide every cut; his skillful combination of cross-cutting and the moving camera often produces vividly effective cuts that are meant to be noticed. Between *The Joyless Street* and *The Love of Jeanne Ney*, Pabst saw Eisenstein's *Battleship Potemkin* and Pudovkin's *Mother* (which were great hits in Germany, as *The Last Laugh* was in Russia), and that is why *Jeanne Ney* is so much more intricately edited than any previous German film, why it was based on a novel in which the heroine's true love is a Bolshevik, and why it implies socialist solutions that had not been available to the characters of *The Joyless Street.*

The smoothness of Pabst's cuts depends on the absolute coordination and integration of

camerawork and editing, which themselves work in concert with the movements of the actors and even the movements of the audience's eyes. Pabst discovered that one could charge a scene with invisible energy by cutting in the middle of a character's motion. The moving hand or leg, the rising body, the opening door all hide the camera's shift in distance and angle while propelling the eye into the next shot. Pabst also cut on *eye* movement—as when we watch one thing or person move from the left side of the screen to the center, and then something totally different move at the same pace from the center to screen right, and the trajectory of our eye movement is neither changed nor interrupted, so that it feels as if we're watching one motion even if the moving subject changes. Having mastered this, Pabst could direct a movie so that cuts were hidden or revealed at will.

The End of an Era

The key question about the death of the German film is whether it ended with a bang or a whimper—with Hitler's tyranny over the individual artist and the state's tightening control of Ufa, with the gradual decay that had been afflicting the German film mind even before Hitler came to power, or with its export to Hollywood. There is evidence that the claustrophobia of the studio production, the dependence on architecture and paint, which had liberated the visual imagination in 1919, began to inhibit it by 1926. The weakest parts of *Metropolis* employed decoration for the sake of pure decorativeness. It was time to take to the streets—the real ones.

Beyond the Studio

In 1927, the great writer of studio films, Carl Mayer, and the great photographer of studio films, Karl Freund, broke out of the studio completely to shoot a candid documentary of Berlin life. Directed, edited, and co-written (with Freund; Mayer, who disliked the director's purely pictorial approach, left the picture and was credited with having had the idea for *Berlin*) by the abstract artist and architect Walter Ruttmann, *Berlin: The Symphony of a Great City* (1927) was the antithesis of the traditional German film. It used no story; it was merely a chronological progression of some 18 hours in the city's life,

from the arrival of an early morning train to the late-night activities of the Berliners. The film had no protagonist but the city itself, a place where people sit in cafés in the sun and where a woman commits suicide by jumping off a bridge. The whole genre of the "city symphony"—a form of avant-garde documentary that includes Dziga Vertov's *The Man with a Movie Camera*—was named after Mayer's idea and Ruttmann and Freund's film. The earliest examples of the genre, however, include Alberto Cavalcanti's *Rien que les heures* (1926) and Mikhail Kaufman's *Moscow* (1927; Kaufman was Vertov's brother).

The power of *Berlin* lies in its candid photography and its rhythmic cutting. To guarantee the authenticity of revealing the city at work and play, Freund hid the camera in a truck. Though the shooting of the film was haphazard, Ruttmann's editing of it was not. His two controlled editing principles were form and rhythm (this was, after all, two years after *Battleship Potemkin*, and Ruttmann had also read Vertov's theoretical manifestos). As he cut from shot to shot, constructing the film, Ruttmann capitalized on either parallels or contrasts in form (circles, verticals, heavy masses). To combine whole sections of shots he used principles of music composition, endowing the sequence with a rhythm and tone appropriate to its content (an idea Vertov published in 1922). The opening

Berlin: The Symphony of a Great City—*the geometry and visual music of everyday life.*

Fig. 7-15

movement of this "symphony," the train approaching the sleeping city, is *allegro moderato*—alive with expectation but a bit cautious, sleepy, hesitant. The next sequence, of the city's waking, is a *largo*—slow, peaceful. As the city wakes and goes to work, the tempo changes to *allegro vivace*—vibrant, active. There is an *andante* at the lunch hour when work stops, another *allegro* when it begins again, and another *andante* in the quiet, gear-changing hours of the evening between work and play. The film ends with a *presto finale*, a fast, frenzied sequence of neon lights, night life, dancing, movies. With its use of pure visual form, musical rhythms, and real life, *Berlin* is clearly an attempt to exceed the limits of studio production.

Exodus to Hollywood

If the limitations of the studio film had begun to cramp the German imagination, it was also possible that the exodus of so much film talent to Hollywood had not left enough imaginations in Germany to get cramped. Murnau had gone to Hollywood to work for William Fox. After making his formal masterpiece—the lyrical study of a married couple's antagonism and reunion, *Sunrise: A Song of Two Humans* (1927, written by Carl Mayer, starring George O'Brien and Janet Gaynor, and photographed by Charles Rosher and Karl Struss), which won the first Oscar for Cinematography as well as a special Oscar for "Artistic Quality of Production" and was one of the pictures that won Gaynor the first Oscar for Best Actress—Murnau directed the now-lost circus drama *Four Devils* (1929) and the beautiful and moving *City Girl* (1929, released 1930), worked with Flaherty on *Tabu*, then died in California in 1931, the victim of an automobile crash. Lubitsch had left Ufa for Hollywood in 1922, never to return. Schüfftan went to France, where he worked on such films as Marcel Carné's *Port of Shadows* (1938) and Georges Franju's *Eyes Without a Face* (1960); in the United States, where he changed his name to Eugene Shuftan, he won an Academy Award for Robert Rossen's *The Hustler* (1961). Mayer went

Fig. 7-16
German filmmakers and film practice come to Hollywood: **Sunrise** *(1927); George O'Brien and Janet Gaynor get on the tram that will take them out of the big city that was built, German-studio style, on the Fox lot.*

Fig. 7-17
German filmmakers and film practice come to Hollywood: **The Mummy** *(1932), directed by Karl Freund at Universal; Boris Karloff, as the reanimated Imhotep, takes the Scroll of Thoth from an unbeliever in a scene strongly influenced by German Expressionist horror.*

to Hollywood with Murnau but settled in England, where he adapted plays for the screen and worked with Paul Rotha on documentaries. Between 1927 and 1933, actors such as Marlene Dietrich and Peter Lorre; the Reinhardt-trained directors William Dieterle, Otto Preminger, and Edgar G. Ulmer; other important directors, including Paul Leni, Robert Siodmak, Billy Wilder, and Fred Zinnemann; as well as Reinhardt, Brecht, Freund, and Lang all headed for Hollywood.

Even those filmmakers who never went to Hollywood could not avoid its influence. As the German film industry had more and more financial difficulties, it was more and more underwritten by Hollywood production dollars—particularly from Paramount and MGM in an agreement known as "Parufamet." With dollars came directives, especially since Paramount and Metro were interested in destroying the fortunes of their most powerful European competitor.

The export of German talent to Hollywood would powerfully stimulate the American film for

the next three decades. Many of the best directors of American films between 1933 and 1960 had either worked in the German industry or been trained there: Alfred Hitchcock, Max Ophüls, Douglas Sirk, Michael Curtiz, and others already mentioned. The great American horror films of the 1930s and 1940s at Universal (the dark tales of Frankenstein, Dracula, the Mummy, and the Wolf Man) descended either directly or indirectly from the German horror films. Karl Freund shot *Dracula* (1931) for Tod Browning and *Murders in the Rue Morgue* (1932) for Robert Florey, both at Universal, before directing his own horror classics, *The Mummy* (1932, Universal) and *Mad Love* (1935, MGM). One of the cinematographers on *Mad Love*, Gregg Toland, was decisively influenced by Freund—an influence that is clear in the film Toland shot six years later, *Citizen Kane*. Freund's contributions to the American industry would extend to the three-camera shooting technique that he developed for Desi Arnaz at Desilu for the *I Love Lucy* and *Our Miss Brooks* television series in the 1950s.

Moody Expressionist lighting and claustrophobic decor dominate American crime films of the 1940s and 1950s, the *films noirs;* despite the name given them by postwar French film critics, the disturbing themes and moods of these films came directly from the German cinema. Like Lang's *M* (1931), these are paranoid nightmares in which there is little difference between the aims and methods of cops and crooks. It is difficult to imagine the history of American cinema without this infusion of both visual imagery and thematic commentary from Weimar Germany.

Using Sound

It is also possible that Hitler's political victory in 1933 killed a thriving film culture with terrible suddenness. The early German sound films were as good as anyone's, or better. *The Blue Angel* (1930), despite its American director (von Sternberg), was a completely German film. Its heritage is evident in its careful studio-controlled atmospheres (the smoky chaos of the nightclub hung with nets) and even in its close examination of a Jannings character (Professor Immanuel Rath's steady degeneration into a humiliated clown). The film was as careful with sound as with pictures: the singing of Lola Lola (Marlene Dietrich), the crowing of the humiliated professor, the contrast between the noisy chaos in Rath's classroom before he enters and the deadly silence when he does.

Lang's use of sound was equally astute. In *M*, his first talkie, a mother's calls—for the daughter she does not know has been abducted and murdered—are heard offscreen while the camera reveals the empty spaces where no living being stirs. The murderer (played by Peter Lorre, whose first American film was Freund's *Mad Love*) is identified by the Grieg tune he repeatedly whistles, and Lang effectively depicts the moment when a blind man, who is totally dependent on sound, recognizes the murderer. The principal cinematographer on *M* was Fritz Arno Wagner, who shot *Nosferatu* and co-shot both *Destiny* and *The Love of Jeanne Ney.*

M is also a significant example of Lang's interest in the trial as a dramatic opportunity for a society to investigate itself, or for a movie to investigate a society. In *M* the child-murderer is tried by criminals, and the insanity defense is explored. In Lang's first American film, *Fury*

Fig. 7-18

Fig. 7-19

Fig. 7-20
Sound and image in **M.** *As her mother calls for "Elsie," Lang shows her absence.*

(1936), the apparent burning alive of an innocent man (Spencer Tracy) is explored in an equally complex trial in which movies (newsreel close-ups) provide crucial evidence against the members of the often architecturally arranged lynch mob, and the victim's showing up alive in court proves a triumph for conscience without dismissing the moral culpability of the violent mob. Lang continued to examine the nature of justice, and the complementary nature of revenge, in such American films as *Rancho Notorious* (1951, released 1952, starring Marlene Dietrich), *The Big Heat* (1953, a crucial *noir*), and *Beyond a Reasonable Doubt* (1956).

As for the man who played Cesare, the somnambulist conscripted by Dr. Caligari, Conrad Veidt left Nazi Germany for America, where—with a vengeance—he played the Nazi villain in Michael Curtiz's *Casablanca* (1942). Werner Krauss—Caligari—stayed and was honored as an Actor of the State.

Leni Riefenstahl

Rather than dying slowly, the German age may well have been transformed abruptly from one of gold into one of iron. As of 1933 the Nazis were in, Jewish filmmakers were out, and there was a new agenda. The German sense of architecture and composition, the rhythms of cutting and movement, found a new use in the masterful propaganda films of Leni Riefenstahl. The heroic architectural configurations of her documentary on the 1934 Nazi Party Convention at Nuremberg, *Triumph of the Will* (1935), are descendants of *Metropolis*; the stirring integration of musical motifs, the control of camera angle, the incorporation of mythic elements all aim at presenting the Führer as a combination of Pagan god of strength and charismatic savior.

An athlete, dancer, and actress, Riefenstahl appeared in mountain films—notably *The White Hell of Piz Palü* (1929), directed by Arnold Fanck and G. W. Pabst—before directing her own beautiful, mystical, and powerful mountain film, *The Blue Light* (1932). She liked Hitler and thought he could lead Germany out of its economic troubles, but after the war she maintained that she had known nothing about the genocidal campaigns and had never joined the Nazi Party. In the autobiography she published at age 90, she insisted that even the Nazi convention she documented in *Triumph of the Will* was merely an artistic opportunity. She also said she went out of her way to arrange private rather than government funding for *Olympia* (1938), one of the reasons that Hitler's minister of propaganda, Joseph Goebbels—as she put it—hated her guts. When she made *Tiefland* (shot 1945, edited 1954), she borrowed gypsies from a concentration camp to act as extras. After the war she devoted herself primarily to still photography—working first with African tribes and then underwater—and to defending her reputation, which rests not only on the films whose propaganda content and

Spencer Tracy (right) in Fury.

Fig. 7-21

Fig. 7-22　　　　　　　　　　　　**Fig. 7-23**

The triumph of Metropolis: *Human beings become architecture again in Leni Riefenstahl's 1935 Nazi celebration film,* Triumph of the Will.

function she attempted to deny, but also on the most physical and metaphysical of all documentaries, *Olympia*. In that grand, two-part masterpiece, a record of the 1936 Berlin Olympic Games—which she edited for 18 months and which ranks her among the greatest of all filmmakers—the techniques used to consecrate and glorify the body, the athlete, a physicality so pure that it becomes transcendent, build on the achievements in purely rhythmic editing of Ruttmann (who assisted her) and Pabst but take them to an entirely new level of power, notably in the diving sequence that climaxes the film.

Obeying the dictates of Goebbels, the German industry turned out musicals, comedies, period pieces, and melodramas that were calculated to entertain—with none of that annoying, depressing, psychological rot, let alone the decadence of Expressionism—and to convince the public that it was a sensitive, well-meaning bunch whose values and valuables needed to be defended against a host of deceitful enemies. Some of these enemies, particularly Jews, were portrayed as subhuman, whereas the Aryan characters had real feelings and suffered real losses (the propagandistic method of *The Birth of a Nation*). Other films simply took the dominant ideology for granted and set out to deliver romantic comedy or melodrama (the as-if-apolitical method of bourgeois cinema in general). In 1939–40, when the campaign against the Jews had intensified, several features

(notably Veit Harlan's *Jew Süss*, 1940) and documentaries (Fritz Hippler's *The Eternal Jew*, 1940) were devoted to portraying Jews as worthy only of expulsion or extermination; in contrast to the majority of Nazi films, which may have contained a few scenes or subplots directed against the Jews and other designated "enemies," such as the British and the Bolsheviks, these were full-length efforts in support of the Final Solution.

Architecturally grandiose, glossily lit, and intensely serious when they were not viciously comic, such stirring, manipulative melodramas as *Jew Süss* and *Hitler Youth Quex* (1933, directed by Hans Steinhoff) were about as subtle as the Nazis. If the German cinema began with horror films, it ended with films that were horrors.

For Further Viewing

FILMS

FRITZ LANG (1890–1976)
The Spiders (1919)
Destiny (Der müde Tod, 1921)
Dr. Mabuse, the Gambler (two parts, 1922)
Die Nibelungen (two parts, 1924)
Metropolis (1927). Completed 1926
M (1931)
The Testament of Dr. Mabuse (1933)
Fury (1936)

F. W. MURNAU (1888–1931)
Der Januskopf (1920)
Schloss Vogelöd (1921)
Nosferatu, a Symphony of Horror (1922)
The Last Laugh or *The Last Man* (*Der letzte Mann*, 1924)
Tartuffe (1926). Completed 1925
Faust (1926)
Sunrise: A Song of Two Humans (1927)
City Girl (1930). Completed 1929
Tabu (1931). Co-director, Robert Flaherty

G. W. PABST (1885–1967)
The Joyless Street (1925)
Secrets of a Soul (1926)
The Love of Jeanne Ney (1927)
Pandora's Box (1929)
Diary of a Lost Girl (1929)

LENI RIEFENSTAHL (1902–2003)
The Blue Light (1932)
Triumph of the Will (1935)
Olympia (two parts, 1938)

REPRESENTATIVE GERMAN FILMS
The Student of Prague (1913, Stellan Rye and Paul Wegener)
The Golem (1914, Paul Wegener and Henrik Galeen)
Homunculus (1916, Otto Rippert)
The Cabinet of Dr. Caligari (1920, Robert Wiene). Shot 1919
The Golem: How He Came into the World (1920, Paul Wegener and Carl Boese). Script by Paul Wegener and Henrik Galeen
Hintertreppe (*Backstairs*, 1921, Paul Leni and Leopold Jessner)
Rhythmus 21 or *Rhythm 21* (1921, Hans Richter)
Warning Shadows (1922, Arthur Robison)
The Street (1923, Karl Grune)
The Hands of Orlac (1924, Robert Wiene)
Symphonie diagonale or *Diagonalsymphonien* (1924, Viking Eggeling)
Waxworks (1924, Paul Leni)
Variety (1925, E. A. Dupont)
The Student of Prague (1926, Henrik Galeen)
Berlin: The Symphony of a Great City (1927, Walter Ruttmann)
Überfall (*Accident* or *Police Report: Surprise Assault*, 1929, Ernö Metzner)

Mädchen in Uniform (1931, Leontine Sagan)
Kuhle Wampe (1932, Slatan Dudow and Bertolt Brecht)
Hitlerjunge Quex (1933, Hans Steinhoff)

DVDs

Rhythmus 21, *Symphonie diagonale*, and *Überfall* are in *Avant-Garde: Experimental Cinema of the 1920s and '30s* (see Chap. 10 list).
Berlin: The Symphony of a Great City (1927, **Walter Ruttmann**). Image Entertainment. Includes Ruttmann short, *Opus II*.
The Blue Angel (1930, **Josef von Sternberg**). Kino Video. Includes both versions of the film—the German original, **restored,** and the "English" version—plus **Marlene Dietrich**'s screen test, and more.
The Cabinet of Dr. Caligari (1920, **Robert Wiene**). Kino International. **Restored** authorized edition. Despite some print damage near the beginning, a terrific archival restoration. The intertitles match the original in style and wording (there's a sequence in German for comparison) and divide the film into its original six acts; tinted and with the Decla logo.
Destiny (1921, **Fritz Lang**). Image Entertainment. Tinted.
Diary of a Lost Girl (1929, **G. W. Pabst**). Kino Video. **Restored** and uncensored.
Dr. Mabuse, the Gambler (1922, **Fritz Lang**). Kino Video. **Restored;** 30 minutes longer than other prints. Includes a German documentary, *The Story Behind Dr. Mabuse.*
The Last Laugh (1924, **F. W. Murnau**). Kino International. **Restored.**
The Love of Jeanne Ney (1927, **G. W. Pabst**). Kino Video. An Ufa print.
M (1931, **Fritz Lang**). Criterion Collection. **Digitally restored.** Includes interviews with Lang, a **Chabrol** film inspired by *M*, production sketches, and more.
Metropolis (1927, **Fritz Lang**). Kino International. Excellent **digital restoration** with full restoration information and demonstrations, documentaries, commentary, script and novel excerpts, etc. Edited correctly into a more coherent story.

The Mummy is in *The Mummy: The Legacy Collection* (see Chap. 11 list).

Nosferatu: A Symphony of Horror (1922, **F. W. Murnau**). Kino Video. **Restored** authorized edition. This version has well-designed and well-translated intertitles, includes the original act breaks, is more convincingly edited than earlier restoration attempts, and was mastered from an archivally restored negative with the original tints. At the correct projection speed and with some previously missing shots, it runs 12 minutes longer than most versions; it also shows more of the frame.

Pandora's Box (1929, **G. W. Pabst**). Criterion Collection. **Restored.** Includes two documentaries on Brooks, a book of essays, and an interview with Pabst's son.

Triumph of the Will (1935, **Leni Riefenstahl**). Synapse. Includes a Riefenstahl short, *Tag der Freiheit,* and commentary by historian Anthony R. Santro.

8

Soviet Montage

The Soviet film was born with the Russian Revolution. Before 1917 the Russian film industry was a colony of Europe—of Pathé or Lumière or Scandinavia's Nordisk; no film was shot in Russia by a Russian company until 1908. However distinguished the features of Evgenii Bauer (*A Child of the Big City*, 1914; *Daydreams*, 1915) and the stop-motion animations of Ladislas Starewicz (*Revenge of a Kinetograph Cameraman*, 1912), the majority of czarist films followed the narrative patterns set by other industries, and very few of them were exported. Costume films, horror films, and melodramas—the typical formulas of Europe and America—were the staples of the pre-1917 Russian film diet. The revolution changed all that.

There were three Russian Revolutions. The first, in 1905, was a workers' uprising that lasted months and ran the gamut from brutally suppressed protests to general strikes; the revolt even had support within the military, as the mutiny on the battleship *Potemkin* indicated. The czar responded by promising a constitution and an elected legislature (the Duma). The second revolution, in February (on the old Russian calendar; March elsewhere) 1917, overthrew the czar; a Provisional Government, led in part by the Mensheviks, took power. The Mensheviks were socialists and liberal social democrats who were willing to work with the bourgeois capitalists and who eventually supported Russia's continuing to fight in World War I, unlike the radical Bolsheviks who believed in a proletarian revolution directed by a party of committed revolutionaries and who

opposed participation in the war. The liberal Provisional Government, headed at that time by socialist Alexander Kerensky, was overthrown in the Bolshevik revolution of October (again on the old calendar) 1917, whose most significant leaders were Leon Trotsky and Vladimir I. Lenin. After Lenin's death in 1924, there was a power struggle that ended with Joseph Stalin in charge (1927) and Trotsky—who later was murdered—in exile (1929).

Marxist political and economic philosophy, which had evolved in the age of machines, adopted the machine art as its own. Lenin considered the cinema the most influential of all the arts. Movies not only entertained but, in the process, molded and reinforced values. The film was a great teacher; with portable power supplies it could be shown to huge groups of people in every remote corner of the new Soviet Union. While the flickering images held their audiences captive, the events on the screen emphasized the virtues of the new government and encouraged the people to develop those traits that would best further it. Whereas the American film began as an amusing novelty, the Soviet film was created explicitly as teacher, not as clown. In 1919, after a chaotic year in which the Soviets had let the film industry go its own commercial way, the Russian industry passed under government control.

"The foundation of film art is editing," wrote Pudovkin in the preface to one edition of his book on film technique. Whereas the German innovators concentrated on the look, the feel, the psychological and pictorial values of the individual shot, the Soviet innovators concentrated on the effects of joining the shots together. Like so many of the earlier innovations in film technique, the Soviet discoveries were the products of experience and experimentation; they did not grow out of abstract theorizing. But as early as 1919, the Soviets began developing a bold new literature of film theory; many of the writings of Vertov, Eisenstein, and Pudovkin proved as influential as their films and grew out of the experiments undertaken in those films—as well as the Russians' legendary fondness for debate.

The Kuleshov Workshop

Two significant accidents determined the paths Soviet experimentation would take. The first was the shortage of raw (unexposed) film stock. As in the rest of Europe, film stock was scarce in Russia during and just after the war years. The Russian film famine was even more severe, for the still-fighting Red and White armies erected blockades against each other to keep supplies from getting through. Lacking quantities of stock, the Soviet filmmakers had to make the most of what they had.

The raw stock that was available consisted mostly of the tail ends of reels left in the czarist studios and labs; it was not the material with which to develop an aesthetic of the long take. Shots had to be planned carefully and were necessarily brief; the art grew out of joining these rigorously composed fragments into wholes. And with so little stock available, regardless of the length of the individual celluloid strips, it was more important to use film for newsreels rather than features. (In 1922, Lenin established that a set—in practice, variable—ratio of documentaries and narrative films should be made each year; it was called "the Lenin proportion.") One of the first major newsreels, *Kinó-Nedelia* (*Cinema Weekly*), was supervised by Lev Kuleshov and employed the services of a young editor who called himself Dziga Vertov. The editing of these newsreels—and the full-length compilation films that began to appear in 1919—was exceptionally brisk and dynamic, largely because the cameramen had to shoot on mere scraps of film.

The scarcity of film stock also created the Kuleshov workshop (1919–25). Lev Kuleshov, who taught a workshop class at the newly established Moscow Film School, led his students in a series of editing experiments. Pudovkin was to become the most famous of those students (Vertov was not in the workshop), but even those filmmakers who did not study with Kuleshov (for example, Eisenstein) could not escape his influence. Lacking the raw stock to shoot films of their own, the Kuleshov workshop experimented in drafting scenarios, in editing and re-editing the pieces of film they already had on hand, and in re-editing sequences of feature films imported from the West.

The second of the influential accidents directly affected the Kuleshov group. In 1919, a print of Griffith's *Intolerance* successfully wriggled through the anti-Soviet blockade. *Intolerance*, which Lenin greatly admired, became a Kuleshov primer. His students examined its boldness in cutting—cuts to drive the narrative, to integrate tremendously diverse and disjointed material, to imply concepts and draw conclusions, to intensify emotion with its rhythms, to mirror thoughts and sensations. The Kuleshov workshop screened *Intolerance* incessantly, even reediting its sequences to examine the resulting effects on the film's power and to discover the reasons for Griffith's particular choices. With such a thorough mastery of the principles of Griffith's cutting (and of the 1922 Abel Gance film, *La Roue*, as important for its rapid cutting and its use of real locations as *Intolerance* was for its dialectical "drama of comparisons"), the Soviet directors would extend those principles to their limits—when they got the money and the film.

Until then they experimented. Each of the experiments furthered their control of the effects of editing and their conviction that editing was the basis of film art. In the "Mozhukhin Experiment," conducted in or before 1923, Kuleshov used some old footage of a prerevolutionary actor, Ivan Mozhukhin. Kuleshov cut the shot of Mozhukhin's face into three pieces. He juxtaposed one of the strips with a shot of a plate of hot soup; he juxtaposed the second with a shot of a child (in some accounts, an old woman) in a coffin; he juxtaposed the third with a shot of a little girl playing with a toy bear. When viewers, who had not been let in on the nature of the experiment, saw the finished sequence, they praised Mozhukhin's acting: his hunger when confronted with a bowl of soup, his sorrow for "his dead child" or "his dead mother" (their interpretation), his joy when watching "his daughter" playing. Mozhukhin's neutral expression was identical in all three pieces of film. The juxtaposed material (face + soup = hunger) evoked the concept or emotion in the audience, which then projected it into the actor. Editing alone had created the scenes, their emotional content and meaning, and even a brilliantly understated performance!

In another Kuleshov experiment the audience sees a series of five shots: (1) a man walks from right to left; (2) a woman walks from left to right; (3) they meet and shake hands, the man points; (4) we see a white building; (5) the two walk up a flight of steps. The audience connects the five pieces into a single sequence: A man and woman meet; they go off toward a building that he sees. In reality, the two individual shots of the man and woman walking were made in two different parts of the city; the building he points to is the White House, snipped out of an American film; the steps they ascend belong to a church in yet a third section of the city. Kuleshov's experiment revealed that the impression of geographical unity in a film was unrelated to geographical unity in space. Kuleshov called the result the "artificial landscape," or "creative geography." It was the same method Griffith used when he spliced Niagara Falls into the climax of *Way Down East*. A third Kuleshov experiment might,

by analogy, be called "creative anatomy." Kuleshov created the impression of a single actress by splicing together the face of one woman, the torso of another, the hands of another, the legs of yet another.

The Kuleshov student learned that editing served three primary purposes in building a film. First, a cut could serve a *narrative* function. For example, a man walks toward the camera; something to his right catches his attention and he turns his head. The audience's natural question is: What does he see? The editor then cuts to an old tramp who pulls a pistol on the man. The audience's next question is: How will the man react to this attack? The editor cuts back to the man to show his fear or his courage. And so forth. The narrative cut allows the director–editor to analyze an action into its most interesting psychological elements and then to resynthesize these elements of the event into a powerful sequential action. Another kind of narrative cut is the flashback or flash forward—a cut to a past or future event. One can also cut to reveal what a character is thinking. A woman stares dreamily into space; the editor cuts to her husband in a faraway prison, then cuts back to the woman's face. Yet a third kind of narrative cut is the cross-cut. While the tramp attacks the man with a pistol, the police charge to the rescue. All this had been learned from Griffith.

But the Soviet film students realized that a cut could do more than narrate: It could generate an *intellectual* response. One kind of intellectual

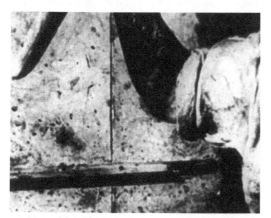

Fig. 8-1   *Fig. 8-2*

From the final montage sequence of Strike: *the butcher's hand thrusts downward to kill the animal, the people's hands thrust upward in an appeal for mercy.*

cut was the metaphorical or associational cut. From a group of workers running from soldiers, the director could cut to the slaughter of a bull in a stockyard (as Eisenstein did in *Strike*). The image of the dying animal comments on the killing of the workers; two shots at the end of the sequence (the bleeding bull, then the dead workers) also generate a metaphor of "slaughter." The director can cross-cut between a procession of demonstrators and a river thawing in the spring, a mass of cracking and flowing ice (as Pudovkin did in *Mother*). The naturalness, the inevitability of the progress of the ice comments on the force of the workers and metaphorically treats revolution as a thaw, a breakup of the old order. A second intellectual effect could be produced by the contrast cut. The filmmaker cuts from the dinner table of a poor man, who eats only a few pieces of bread, to the table of a rich man laden with meats, candles, and wine. The contrast comments on the injustice of the fact that two such tables can exist at the same time. Such cuts can also be traced back to Griffith, who executed precisely this intellectual contrast between the table of the rich and the bread line of the poor in *A Corner in Wheat*. The parallel cut produces a third kind of intellectual response. From the condemned man sentenced to die at five o'clock, the filmmaker cuts to a thief who murders a victim at precisely five o'clock. The parallel acts of violence at the same time reinforce each other. Significantly, the intellectual cut—metaphoric, contrast, or parallel—also has an emotional dimension. The cut not only comments on the injustice of the rich man's dinner, but also makes us hate the rich man for his gluttony and pity the poor man for his need.

The third kind of cut that the Kuleshov students discovered is a purely *emotional* one: The very method of joining the strips of celluloid together, rather than their content, produces an almost subliminal kinetic response in an audience that the director—working with or as the editor—can unobtrusively control. First, the director can cut a sequence rhythmically. He or she can use shorter and shorter pieces of film, increasing the tempo and tension of the action—or else can cut a sequence with long pieces of film, producing a feeling of slowness or ease. By splicing together a series of strips of equal length the director can produce the feeling of a regular,

measured beat. The tonal cut is the director's second method of manipulating an audience's emotions without its conscious awareness of manipulation. He or she can cut a sequence with steadily darker pictures, producing the impression of oncoming night and growing despair, or with steadily lighter pictures, producing the impression of dawn and rising hope. A third kind of emotional editing is the form cut, cutting on a similarity or difference in the form of the object in the frame. The director can cut from a spinning roulette wheel to a turning wagon wheel, from a jabbing pencil to a thrusting sword. A fourth kind of kinetic editing is the directional cut, in which the director uses the direction of movement across the frame either to keep the action flowing or to produce a dynamic collision. The director can cut from a group of workers streaming from right to left, to a group of foot soldiers streaming from right to left, to a group of Cossacks on horseback streaming from right to left—or can cut from a group of workers streaming from right to left to a group of Cossacks streaming from left to right. Whereas the first series of directional cuts would produce the feeling of speed, continuousness, and flow (and show a chase), the second would produce the sensation of two huge masses smashing into each other. Significantly, a cut that is intended to have an intellectual effect—from pencil to sword—may also serve as a form cut, as part of a tonal sequence, as part of the film's rhythm, and as a shift in the film's narrative structure. A single cut can function on all three levels—narrative, intellectual, emotional—at once. In fact, the Soviet directors discovered that most cuts *must* function on all three levels at once.

To this set of discoveries they gave the name "montage." In French, *montage* simply means editing; for the Soviet directors and theorists, the word signified dynamic editing and the ways it could control a film's structure, meaning, and effect. Fragmentation (breaking the world or the text into little bits) and synthesis (bringing the parts together into a whole) were the key elements of montage. By 1924, the Kuleshov students had acquired the stock, the equipment, and the budgets to turn their lessons into films. They went out to develop their personal notions of montage.

Sergei M. Eisenstein

Eisenstein was the greatest master of montage. Eisenstein's sense of cutting transformed his didactic lessons on the virtues of brotherhood and Marxism into dynamic, moving works of art— even for the non-Marxist. The Eisenstein silents break all the rules of "good" narrative construction. They lack central protagonists, and they move from action to commentary to analysis at Eisenstein's whim. Although they lack a conventional plot, they lack neither compelling action nor a unified structure.

The Eisenstein film holds together by means of its theme rather than its story: the experience of the workers who learn what it means to strike and to take collective action against a wicked state, the ability of a single revolutionary action on a battleship to unite a whole people, the replacement of a false revolutionary government by a true one, the superiority of the new agricultural and social methods to the old ones. The theme gets its flesh from Eisenstein's depiction of the people who embody it. Although the central character is the mass, the people as a whole, Eisenstein never forgets that the mass is made up of individuals.

Eisenstein's geometric compositions, as careful and as visually attractive as they are, are never static. The individual shots are full of dynamic movement. And Eisenstein's montage increases the sense of movement and tension as the individual shots collide, crash, explode into each other.

Eisenstein defined his principle of montage as one of collision, of conflict, of contrast. He does not simply build shots with particular meanings into a whole, but sees each shot, even each frame, as a unit with a dynamic visual charge of a particular kind. His goal is to bring the dynamic charge of one shot into conflict with the visual charge of the next. For example, the shots can conflict directionally—a ship sailing from right to left, followed by a wave breaking from left to right. The shots can conflict in rhythm—a group of people running chaotically, followed by a group of soldiers marching steadily, inexorably. The shots can conflict in bulk—from a mass of workers to a single worker's face. The shots can conflict in number—from one dead sailor to a crowd of mourners. The shots can conflict in camera angle—from an extreme downward view

(a high-angle shot) of a large crowd to a noble upward (low-angle) shot of a member of the crowd. The shots can conflict in the intensity of light— from a dark, dim shot to a blazing, bright one. The shots can conflict in time—from the end of an action to its middle. And so forth. Eisenstein's great films are the products of his combining many and diverse gifts—his visual sense of composition, his feeling for rhythm and tempo, his ability to understand and manipulate emotion, and his perceptive intellect, which could create meaning by joining two or more apparently unrelated images.

Eisenstein devoted special attention to the editing together of shots that were, at first glance, entirely different from each other, though when juxtaposed they might reveal that they could be related thematically. This method, which he called intellectual or *dialectical montage*, set the terms, the shots, in opposition; out of their conflict would develop a synthesis of the two shots, an idea or concept that would be impossible to shoot on its own. It is notoriously difficult to photograph an idea, while it is easy to set out an idea in words. The first shot operates as the thesis, or first term; in opposition to it appears the antithesis, the second term; and out of their conflict arises the synthesis, a third term that would be, as Eisenstein put it, "graphically undepictable." This kind of editing is called dialectical because it operates in much the same manner as the dialectics of Georg W. F. Hegel, which influenced the dialectical materialism of Marx. (If Hegel felt there was an idealistic spirit manifesting itself through history, Marx felt the primary force was materialism.) In history, Hegel argued, a first term or condition, the thesis, gives rise to its polar opposite, the antithesis, and out of their conflict arises a synthesis of the two, which becomes the new thesis, and the process repeats. For example, the thesis of the French monarchy was opposed by the French Revolution, which at its most chaotic and frenzied was a Reign of Terror; the synthesis was Napoleon, an emperor who arose from the ranks of the Revolution. For Eisenstein, a shot of a bull and a shot of dead workers could create the metaphoric statement that the workers had been "slaughtered," or shots of two religious figures— one with a rounded form and the other ringed with spikes or rays—could "explode" religion.

Eisenstein formally studied engineering and architecture. During the Civil War of 1918–20, he organized an impromptu theatre troupe in the Red Army. Attracted to the theatre, he started directing plays in Moscow after the war, where he was heavily influenced by the innovative, anti-Naturalist director Vsevolod E. Meyerhold. A committed formalist and Constructivist, Meyerhold later became one of the first to oppose Socialist Realism. In one of Eisenstein's stage productions, Ostrovsky's *Enough Simplicity in Every Wise Man* (1923), he included his first short film, *Glumov's Film Diary*, within the context of the play. He staged his last play, *Gas Masks* (1924), in the Moscow Gas Works. Eisenstein could go no further with stage reality; the leap into films was inevitable. Many of the actors he had worked with in the Proletkult Theatre followed him. His first feature film, *Strike* (1924, released 1925, made when he was 27), revealed the bold, broad strokes of a new master. From its opening montage sequence—of whirring machines, spinning gears, factory whistles; of traveling shots along the length of the factory complex; of dynamic, dizzying movement—the film proclaimed that a brilliant cinematic imagination was at work.

Strike contains many of the traits that make an Eisenstein film distinctly his own. There is the director's control and alternation of moods: from the peaceful, idyllic sequences of the striking workers at rest and play to the violent, vicious slaughter of the workers in their tenements. There is the satirical treatment of the rich and the informers for the rich: The company finks are depicted as sneaky animals; the rich factory owners sip cocktails while the workers starve and die. There is the director's sense of visual composition: the geometrical patterns and shapes of the factory and of the workers' tenements where the Cossacks attack. There is Eisenstein's construction of a metaphor out of two images, to comment on the action: the shot of the dying bull juxtaposed with the shot of the dead workers. And uniting the film is the Eisenstein vision: that the capitalistic, czarist system is fundamentally inhumane, an obstacle not only to physical survival, but also to human fellowship, family, and brotherhood. *Strike* was co-shot by cinematographer Eduard Tisse, who would shoot or co-shoot all of Eisenstein's major films through the first

part of *Ivan the Terrible* (1944). Indeed, Eisenstein and Tisse are regarded as one of the greatest director–cinematographer teams in film history, along with Griffith and Bitzer, and Chaplin and Totheroh. Another figure who began working with Eisenstein on *Strike* and would continue throughout his career was assistant director Grigori Alexandrov.

Battleship Potemkin

Battleship Potemkin (1925) was Eisenstein's next film. Originally titled *1905*, the work was intended to depict the general workers' revolt in Russia of that year. Instead, Eisenstein pared down his conception to linking two events in that revolt—the rebellion on the battleship *Potemkin* and the attack on Odessa citizens by the czar's troops and Cossacks—to serve as a microcosm for the 1905 revolution, whose 20th anniversary both *Battleship Potemkin* and Pudovkin's *Mother* (1926) were commissioned to celebrate, just as Eisenstein's *October* (1928) and Pudovkin's *The End of St. Petersburg* (1927) commemorated the tenth anniversary of the more successful 1917 Bolshevik revolution. The five-reel film's five parts, deliberately mirroring the five-act structure of classical drama, form a taut structural whole: from the unity the sailors build on the ship, to the unity between ship and shore, to the unity of the entire fleet.

In the first part, entitled "People and Worms," Eisenstein builds the dramatic reasons for the sailors' discontent. Their food is infested; the czarist doctor looks at the meat closely through his spectacles and declares it wholesome, although his glasses magnify the presence of the worms. The sailors are beaten, insulted, and treated unfairly by the officers. Eisenstein brilliantly shows a sailor's pain by simply photographing the twitching muscles of his back as he sobs. Aware of the uprising going on across Russia, a sailor named Vakulinchuk urges the others to demonstrate their solidarity with the workers.

In the film's second part, "Drama on the Deck," the men have had enough. They refuse to agree that their food is edible; when the captain orders all dissenters to be shot, the sailors rebel. By the end of this violent sequence, the ship belongs to the workers. Significantly, it is a moment of nonviolence that begins the transfer of power.

Fig. 8-3

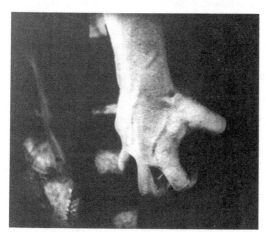

Fig. 8-4

Fig. 8-5

Battleship Potemkin: *from the mass to individual detail, from geometry to people.*

The sailors who are to be shot are covered with a tarp. The soldiers appear hesitant to fire; then Vakulinchuk asks them to think whom they are shooting. The soldiers lower their rifles, expressing solidarity with their "brothers"; then the fight begins. Vakulinchuk is shot to death by an officer, and the sailors take his body to lie in state on the shore, bearing the sign "For a spoonful of soup."

The film's third part, "The Dead Man Calls Out," is a requiem, a pause between the violent capture of the ship and the violence to follow on the Odessa Steps. The workers of Odessa file past Vakulinchuk's body, touched and united in spirit by the sailor's sacrifice. They too have been radicalized, for which they will soon be punished. Their growing anger and solidarity are dynamically portrayed. At the end of this part, a red flag is raised over the *Potemkin*. (It looks like a white flag, which can be confusing—as if they were surrendering—but it was white so that it could be vividly hand-colored.)

The fourth part, "The Odessa Staircase," better known as "The Odessa Steps," begins gaily enough. The workers of Odessa race out to the *Potemkin* in their boats, carrying food and joy to their fellow workers on the ship. There is a union of ship and shore, of sailors and citizens. Other Odessans watch and wave from an outdoor staircase. Suddenly, czarist troops march down the steps, shooting everyone in their path. The citizens scurry for protection. At the bottom of the huge staircase, mounted Cossacks join the attack. Firing and slashing without mercy, the soldiers slaughter young and old, men and women, children and mothers. The *Potemkin* retaliates by firing at the generals' headquarters in the Odessa theatre. A statue of a sleeping lion, perhaps in front of the theatre, wakes up and rises in alarm. Tisse shot three stone lions to create the effect.

The fifth part of the film, "Rendezvous with the Squadron," is another emotional contrast. From the violence and chaos of the previous section, the mood becomes subdued, tense, expectant. The single battleship races toward the fleet; the ship prepares for battle. Eisenstein builds the suspense with shots of whirring gears, pumping pistons, rising guns. Will the fleet fire? The fleet does not. The "brothers" on all the ships cheer one another. The *Potemkin* has united them all.

Eisenstein's uniquely powerful editing brings the film to life. At the end of the first part, Eisenstein wants to emphasize that the men have had it, that the last straw has been laid on the camel's back. A sailor washing the dishes sees a plate inscribed, "Give us this day our daily bread." The biblical platitude infuriates him since they have no decent daily bread. He smashes the plate (see Fig. 8-6). To emphasize this act of smashing, Eisenstein divides this physical action, which takes only a few seconds, into 11 different shots, some as brief as four frames (1/4 second): (1) a close shot of the man's face reflecting his decision to smash the plate; (2) a medium shot as he pulls his arm back with the plate in his right hand; (3) a medium shot as he swings the plate over his left shoulder; (4) a medium close shot of the farthest reach of his swing, the plate behind his left shoulder; (5) a medium shot of his swinging the plate violently downward; (6) a close shot of his arm extended high above his *right* shoulder as he begins to hurtle the plate downward; (7) a close-up of his face; (8) a medium shot of his swinging the plate down from above his right shoulder; (9) a medium shot of the table as the plate smashes against it, scattering the silverware; (10) a medium close shot of his rising shoulder, the smashing completed; (11) a medium shot of the orderlies standing around the table where the plate has been smashed, a lengthy shot that ends with a fade-out. Dividing an action into such a process analyzes the event *and* makes it more violent, more purposeful, more dynamic—particularly in the impossible movement created by the jump cut from (5) to (6)—and more memorable as a pivotal point in the film. The edited version of the action (six seconds without the fade-out) takes longer than the physical act itself if one could perform it.

Having expressed their solidarity with the mutineers, the people of Odessa become targets. The most dazzling editorial sequence in all of *Battleship Potemkin* is the massacre of the citizens of Odessa on that city's great outdoor staircase: the second half of the "Odessa Steps" section. Eisenstein constructs this horrifying, brutal sequence from many different kinds of shots: far shots from the bottom of the steps showing the citizens running chaotically; traveling shots along the side of the steps that flee with

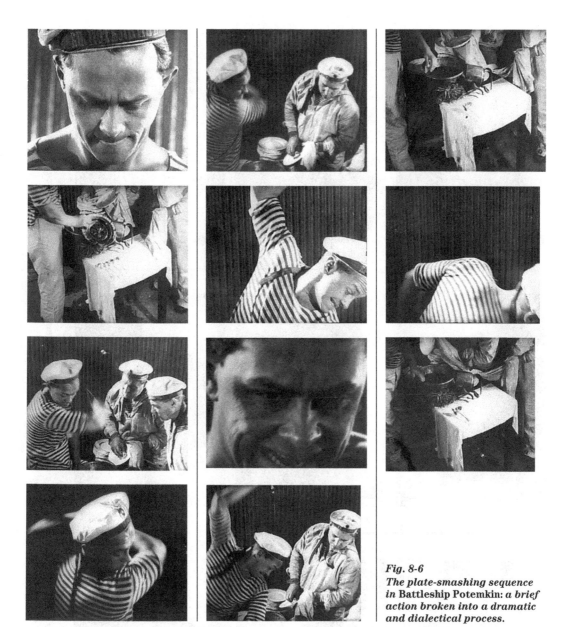

Fig. 8-6
The plate-smashing sequence in Battleship Potemkin: *a brief action broken into a dramatic and dialectical process.*

the workers; shots from the top of the steps showing the relentless, metric pace of the marching soldiers, sometimes with only their boots, their bayonets, and their awesome shadows in the frame; close-ups of faces in shock, pain, horror, fear, confusion, anger. Eisenstein intercuts all these different shots, alternating them according to different principles of his montage of collisions, each of them sustained on the screen for

the rhythmically correct number of seconds (or fractions of seconds). And as in the plate-smashing scene, the film time for the sequence on the Odessa Steps is longer than the actual time it would take a group of people to run down a flight of steps. Subjective time, the way it felt to be there, replaces natural time.

But *Battleship Potemkin* is more than montage. For a film with a mass protagonist, the

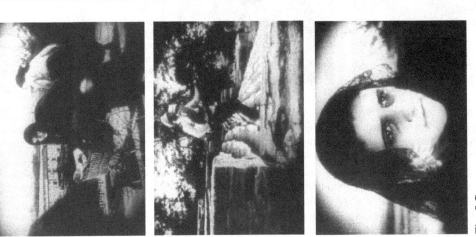

Fig. 8-7
Nine shots from the "Odessa Steps" sequence. Note the graphic conflicts between long and close shots, symmetrical and asymmetrical compositions, a human face and the inexorable march of an armed machine.

faces of individuals are strikingly memorable. Out of the geometric organization of sailors' hammocks emerge the faces of the young sailor who gets beaten and Vakulinchuk, the sailor who leads his comrades in revolt. The sharp-featured, beady-eyed faces of the sneaky ship's doctor, the cunning ship's mate with the moustache of a melodrama villain, and the egomaniacal captain convey Eisenstein's condemnation of the vicious ruling class. The most maniacal face of all is that of the incongruous if not completely symbolic priest, his hair streaming in close-ups framed with light and smoke, his huge iron cross more a symbol of authority and a dangerous weapon (it sticks in the ship's deck like a hatchet) than a symbol of love and sacrifice. But the most memorable faces are those in the most active and violent sequence of all—the Odessa Steps. Eisenstein creates the horror of the slaughter not just with mass murder, chaotic movement, fast cutting, and conflicting compositions, but also with the individual reactions and sensations of the victims: the elderly lady with the pince-nez, the mother with her shot and trampled son, the student near the mirror, the dark-clad mother with the baby carriage. As the soldiers attack, Eisenstein follows the fortunes and reactions of each of these individuals, using their emotional responses to evoke ours.

So much of the viewer's experience of *Battleship Potemkin* proceeds not from the eyes to the brain (the film's ideological statements) but from the eyes to the nerves. Like music, one *feels* the film as rhythm, mood, tone, and texture in addition to perceiving its concrete images. Eisenstein's "music" can be generally described as tensely violent, as a nervous, surging, discordant dissonance—qualities that parallel those of the modern music then being composed by his countrymen and contemporaries, Dimitri Shostakovich and Sergei Prokofiev. Both composers later wrote music for the Soviet sound film, and the effective collaboration of Eisenstein and Prokofiev on *Alexander Nevsky* (1938) and *Ivan the Terrible* revealed how kindred were the spirits of these two "musicians."

October

Eisenstein's next film, properly titled *October* (1928, co-directed by Grigori Alexandrov), was released in a shortened and oversimplified version in the United States and England as *Ten Days that Shook the World* (its title chosen to exploit the interest in John Reed's book). In his theoretical writings, Eisenstein continually refers to the experiments with montage in *October*, the most sustained and intense attempt at defining the language of cinema since Griffith and until Godard. *October*, a loose historical survey of the months between the February Revolution of 1917 and the Bolshevik Revolution of October, is more intellectual, more satirical, and more specifically political than *Battleship Potemkin*. It is also, unfortunately, less unified dramatically, less consistent thematically, and less effective emotionally. Unlike *Battleship Potemkin*, its parts are far more striking than its whole. One reason it feels lacking is that it was censored: Stalin insisted, when the film was nearly finished, that Trotsky be virtually removed from the story of the October Revolution.

October's montage makes its points and drives its rhythms. During the scenes of rebellion, Eisenstein uses extremely quick cuts (shots two frames long!) that smash the viewer with an impression of violence. The alternation of these two-frame pieces, the one of a machine gun, the other of the gunner's face (or a different angle on the gun), creates the kinetic impression of gunfire although no gun is actually firing. Eisenstein uses an opposite editing principle to emphasize that St. Petersburg has been cut in half, extending, slowing down, and intensifying the sequence of the raising of the bridges (set in July 1917), just as he expressively extends the plate-smashing scene and the Odessa Steps sequence in *Battleship Potemkin*. Two halves of a drawbridge pull apart and slowly rise. On one of the halves lies the body of a woman whose hair crosses the gap between the halves. Her hair flows and falls repeatedly as Eisenstein makes the bridge rise over and over. On another half (perhaps of another drawbridge) lies the body of a white horse, still attached to a wagon full of revolutionary banners. The horse falls into the gap; the wagon remains on the bridge; the horse remains suspended in midair as the bridge continues to rise. After an agonizing wait, the white body falls into the river. Immediately after, Eisenstein cuts to a shot of Bolshevik leaflets and banners, also falling into the river. The white pamphlets of the true revolution (*Pravda*) have been cast away, like the dead white horse. The Provisional Government, the result of the February Revolution, is portrayed as a triumph for the bourgeoisie and a failure for the real revolutionists.

Eisenstein's consistent method in this film is to use inanimate objects to comment, often sarcastically, on the activities of the living. Although he used the method rarely in *Battleship Potemkin, October* is full of "stone lions" that come to life.

A series of objects comments on the values of Kerensky, leader of the Provisional Government. As Kerensky poses, Eisenstein cuts to a statuette of Napoleon. Eisenstein further debunks Kerensky's imperial ambitions by showing all the possessions in his quarters, formerly occupied by the czar and his family—gleaming china plates, goblets of cut glass, an army of toy soldiers, the king he plays with from a chess set—or by showing him repeatedly ascending the same staircase every time he gets promoted. Most damning of Kerensky is the series of shots that shows him hiding under pillows from the horns blasting their warning of the advance of counterrevolutionary General Kornilov; he and Kerensky battle it out symbolically as "Two Napoleons," and one of the little statues gets broken.

Eisenstein uses other objects satirically. To burlesque the glories of war, he shows a collection of gaudy medals; to burlesque the emptiness of religion (a consistent Eisenstein theme, since the church supported the czar as well as the Provisional Government), he shows a rapid series of icons: crosses, statues of Buddha, wooden figures of gods. None of this religious satire exists in the overseas release version, *Ten Days that Shook the World*—nor do most of the montage sequences. To burlesque the futility of the government officials, Eisenstein plays geometric games with the empty coffee glasses on their conference table. The parodic yet urgent tone of *October*, and the rigor of its montage experiments, hold together its sprawling, essayistic, semihistorical structure.

Eisenstein's next film, his last silent, was *Old and New* (1929). Often called *The General Line* and also directed with the assistance of Alexandrov, *Old and New* demonstrates the difficulties and the virtues for the peasant of discarding the old ways of farming and thinking, of

Fig. 8-8

Fig. 8-9

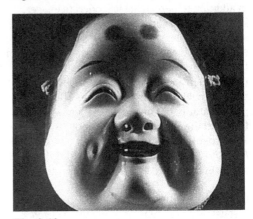

Fig. 8-10
October: *Eisenstein "explodes" religion with a satiric montage of revered cultural objects.*

adopting the new collective ways and the new machines, notably a cream separator and a tractor. The film represents some departures for Eisenstein. In the manner of Pudovkin, he uses natural rather than inanimate imagery—fields, soil, animals, and crops—and he also uses a central figure—a peasant woman who supports collective farming—rather than the masses to embody the film's social progress.

But Eisenstein was beginning to run into trouble with the Soviet line and leaders. Stalin was dissatisfied with the ending of *Old and New*, finding it untrue to the spirit of the new nation and the people. Eisenstein—a half-Jewish, bisexual iconoclast, a devoted artist, an avid reader of everything from T. S. Eliot and Proust to Joyce and Kafka, from Dickens to Japanese poetry—began to feel the pinch of tightening state control. He did not complete another feature for nearly ten years.

Sound and Color

Both political problems and aesthetic challenges frustrated and motivated Eisenstein during this hiatus. Sound had suddenly overtaken the world's industries, and in 1929, Eisenstein, Alexandrov, and Tisse were sent abroad to study foreign studio methods and sound techniques. Eisenstein lectured all over Europe and met, among others, George Grosz and Luigi Pirandello in 1929 and Abel Gance, James Joyce, and Jean Cocteau in 1930. In France, in 1930, he made his first sound film, the 16-minute *Romance sentimentale;* it was commissioned by Mira Giry, a Russian émigrée, and used both natural and domestic imagery—and even scratching on the film—to interpret and accompany the old Russian ballad she sang, a woman's powerful lament for lost Russia and lost love. When Giry insisted on an uplifting ending, Eisenstein took his name off the project, and the film was finished by Tisse and Alexandrov (and credited, at Eisenstein's insistence, to Alexandrov). With the money they made from this film, the trio was able to continue on to Hollywood.

Eisenstein spent most of the rest of 1930 in America, where he met Chaplin, Disney, and Theodore Dreiser. For several months he was under contract at Paramount, trying to get them to accept any of the projects he had developed (notably Dreiser's *An American Tragedy* and a

biopic called *Sutter's Gold*). Paramount decided otherwise. In 1931, Eisenstein, Tisse, and Alexandrov were in Mexico, filming an epic of the Mexican people, *¡Qué viva México!*, financed by Upton Sinclair. Eisenstein fought with Sinclair, and the film was canceled. Eisenstein never got the chance to edit the finished footage, much of which he never saw. A bowdlerized version of the film, assembled by Sol Lesser, was released in 1933 as *Thunder Over Mexico*. Marie Seton put together a better version, *Time in the Sun*, in 1939, and Alexandrov released his own cut of the footage, as he believed Eisenstein would have edited it, in 1979. The dullness of the latter version revealed how much of an assistant director Alexandrov truly was; he was never a genuine co-director.

Returning to the Soviet Union, Eisenstein submitted several projects that were rejected by the state film committee. Eisenstein was accused of formalism—to Stalin, a pedestrian realist, the great sin of Soviet art—of paying too much attention to the formal beauty and structure of the work and not enough to its narrative content and political clarity. His methods were wasteful and time-consuming. His perfectionism was demanding and inconsiderate of budgets and schedules. He seemed to be a director without a country, too political for 1930s Hollywood, too aesthetic for 1930s Moscow, and too intellectual for both of them. *Bezhin Meadow*, the project he cared the most about during the 1930s and had begun to shoot in 1935, was canceled by official order in 1937. Finally, in 1938, he made his first sound feature, *Alexander Nevsky*.

Eisenstein's theory of the sound film—expressed in a 1928 "Statement" co-signed but probably not co-written by Pudovkin and Alexandrov—was that the "talkie" was a fundamental error in the use of the medium. There was no artistic purpose in showing an actor's lips move while the audience hears the words pour out. "Satisfying simple curiosity," he wrote, "increases the inertia of each shot as a montage element." For Eisenstein, sound was to be used asynchronously and contrapuntally: to become one more element of a film's montage. The visuals and sound should play *against* one another, not plod in unison. Although Eisenstein's theory of the sound film was contrary to the practice of his contemporaries—except for Vertov, who wrote that sounds could be edited as easily as pictures, "in harmony or not" with the visuals—years of experience with the sound film have since proved the solidity of his theory.

Eisenstein, whose use of images had always been musical, was especially interested in the precise synchronization of visual images with musical passages and motifs. One of the best demonstrations of his musical theory is in "The Battle on the Ice" sequence in *Alexander Nevsky*, as the invading Teutonic hordes (symbolic of the Nazi threat) encounter the valiant Russians who have gathered to defend themselves. Aided by the power and complexity of Prokofiev's score, Eisenstein turns "The Battle on the Ice" into a cinematic symphony. The successive tones and rhythms of the music—slowly expectant, playfully fast, steadily victorious—play both with and against the content of Eisenstein's images of battle and the rhythms and shapes that control the editing of the images.

Eisenstein's only other completed works before his death in 1948 were two of the three intended parts of *Ivan the Terrible* (Part I released 1944, Part II [1946] released 1958, Part III [1946]

unfinished). In Part II, he experimented with Expressionist color in two sequences. As with sound, Eisenstein believed that color should not be exploited for its novelty, its colorfulness, but that color should play a functional role in controlling the film's tone and effects. Again, the years would prove his sensitivity to one potential of a cinematic device. The interrelation of color, cutting, movement, and music in *Cabaret* (1972), for example, can be related to Eisenstein's theories of using sound, color, music, and montage in film. The color experiments of Antonioni (*Red Desert*, 1964) and the use of Expressionist color in parts of Kobayashi's *Kwaidan* (1964, released 1965) and Kurosawa's *Dodes'ka-den* (1970) are directly indebted to the color sequences in *Ivan the Terrible, Part II*. But the most striking fact of Eisenstein's career is that he completed four full-length pictures in his first five years and three in his next 20 years. Eisenstein became a teacher and theoretician; he taught at the State Film School; he wrote lengthily and convincingly on the powers and effects of montage, although Stalin suppressed the publication of many of Eisenstein's books. But his greatest achievements in filmmaking had been accomplished before the end of the Silent Era. Indeed, his sound films display a self-consciousness in the handling of montage that was somewhat deadening to the vitality and exuberance of the method he applied instinctively in his youth; they also have central protagonists (Nevsky and Ivan) and relatively conventional narrative structures.

To some extent his career mirrors the artistic vitality of the Soviet film as a whole. The Russian film made the transition into the Sound Era with great difficulty, partly because the Soviet cinematic method was so visual, partly because the great Soviet directors became politically suspect, and partly because the Soviet industry had difficulty acquiring reliable machines to shoot and project sound pictures.

Vsevolod I. Pudovkin

Pudovkin and Eisenstein were friendly opponents. Whereas Eisenstein's theory of montage was one of *collision*, Pudovkin's was one of *linkage*. For Pudovkin, the shots of the film combine to build the whole work rather than conflict with one another in dynamic suspension.

Fig. 8-11
Ivan the Terrible, Part I: *A master of editing,*
Eisenstein was also a master of composition.

Pudovkin, a trained scientist, sometimes considered film viewers to be a bit like the dogs in the experiments of his contemporary, Pavlov: The proper cinematic stimulus could elicit the desired intellectual, physical, or emotional response. Eisenstein, however, following the theories of Hegel, Marx, and Engels, believed that the method of argument itself must be rigorously dialectical: Shot A collides with shot B to create concept (or metaphor) C. Eisenstein's goal was to convert cinematic practice into a means of dialectical reasoning. If his primary method was dialectical montage, Pudovkin's was *constructive editing*, also called *linkage editing*. In the terms of later semiotic theory, Pudovkin's film theory and visual compositions tended to emphasize the signifieds and referents of film images—*what* the images were images of, *what* they meant. Eisenstein's film theory and visual compositions tended to emphasize the complex play of signifiers themselves—*how* the images and their elements evoked concepts, *how* they meant.

Whereas the tone and pace of an Eisenstein film are generally nervous and tense, exciting and jostling, the tone and pace of a Pudovkin film are more intimate and measured. He reserves the shocking, violent montage effects for sequences of fighting and rebellion—or exuberance. Whereas Eisenstein's usual human focus is the mass, Pudovkin's is the individual, a single person's revolutionary decision rather than the revolutionary action of a whole group. Whereas Eisenstein's montage is rich in intellectual commentary, Pudovkin's montage assembles the scene or sequence out of *relatively* complementary shots to construct the action and advance its metaphoric and emotional complexity.

Pudovkin, unlike Eisenstein, depended heavily on the performances of individual players; like Griffith, Pudovkin realized that the context of the scene, the nearly immobile face of an actor in close-up, a flickering in the eyes, could communicate more than overstated gestures. An actor who wrote the first important book on the theory of film acting, Pudovkin took Kuleshov's experiment with Mozhukhin's face seriously—far more seriously than Kuleshov himself took it (as the overacting in Kuleshov's 1926 film, *By the Law*, shows). Pudovkin believed that the "plastic material"—visually expressive objects and images—could communicate emotions and ideas

more effectively than any other cinematic tool. The writer or director must, he wrote, "know how to find and to use plastic (visually expressive) material: that is to say, he must know how to discover and how to select, from the limitless mass of material provided by life and its observation, those forms and movements that shall most clearly and vividly express in images the *whole content* of his idea." The fact that he followed this principle throughout his career gives his work a deeply rewarding degree of richness, power, and precision. Pudovkin also made far greater use than Eisenstein of natural imagery: trees, rivers, mud, the wind.

After studying physics and chemistry, Pudovkin decided to work in films, originally intending to act rather than direct. His admiration for *Intolerance* strongly influenced his decision to direct. (As a theorist, he illustrated many of his points with examples from *Intolerance, Way Down East*, and Henry King's *Tol'able David*.) In 1920, Pudovkin began his studies at the State Film School, entering Kuleshov's workshop two years later. His scientific training ably suited him for his first major project, *Mechanics of the Brain* (1926), a cinematic investigation of Pavlovian research on conditioned reflexes in animals and children. He took time off from the Pavlov picture to shoot his first fiction film, *Chess Fever* (1925), an ingenious and charming short comedy that paid homage to his teacher, Kuleshov.

Unlike the American comedies, *Chess Fever* is a comedy of editing. Pudovkin surprises us with gags that are solely the results of montage. During the filming of *Chess Fever*, an international chess tournament actually took place in Moscow. Pudovkin sent his camera crew—masquerading as newsreel photographers—to film the tournament and the champion players. Pudovkin then spliced the "newsreel" footage into the comedy, making the film's action seem to revolve around the tournament. For example, a girl is so upset by her boyfriend's fanatic devotion to chess that she throws one of his chess pieces away. Pudovkin then cuts to a shot of the chess champion, Capablanca, standing and holding a chess piece. It looks as if he caught the piece that the girl just threw. Purely an editing trick! Pudovkin took Kuleshov's notion of "creative geography" and produced "creative continuity."

Mother

Pudovkin's unique style emerged in his later fiction films. In *Mother* (1926), he reveals his ability to combine sensitive treatment of a human story, montage, and natural images that comment on the action and reinforce the film's values. Produced, like *Battleship Potemkin*, for the 20th anniversary of the ill-fated 1905 revolution, *Mother* is a loose adaptation of Gorky's novel about a woman (Vera Baranovskaya) who learns that radical action is the only protection against a wicked state. In 1905, her abusive, drunken husband (who isn't in the novel) is lured into helping a group of strikebreakers; he is shot and killed in a scuffle. The mother then betrays her own son, Pavel (Nikolai Batalov), revealing to the police, whose promises she naïvely trusts, that the youth was in collusion with the strikers. At Pavel's trial—Pudovkin's version of the Boy's trial for murder in *Intolerance*—she sees the corruption of justice. The judges are more interested in dozing or in breeding race horses than in administering justice; the unsympathetic gallery has come to the trial for a good sadistic show. The unjust social process turns the old woman into a radical. She helps her son escape from prison, and together they march in the forefront of a workers' demonstration. Although both she and Pavel die, cut down by the bullets of the Cossacks and the hooves of their horses, the story of her education serves as a model for all the workers of Russia and a metaphor for the results of their education that would eventually surface in 1917.

Pudovkin's handling of actors and shaping of scenes are exceptional. His principle of acting—that the film's context, its decor, its business, its use of objects work with the actor to create a performance—is demonstrated throughout *Mother*. A most effective example is the scene of mourning in which the mother sits by the corpse of her husband. Pudovkin alternates among several setups: a far shot of the mother sitting beside the bier, the walls gray and bare behind her; a close shot of water dripping in a bucket; a close shot of the mother's face, motionless. The mother's face needs no motion. The bareness of the room, the steadily dripping water, and the husband's corpse create all the emotion the scene needs. Her still, quiet face—expressive plastic material, as much as the pan—mirrors all the sorrow that has been built around her.

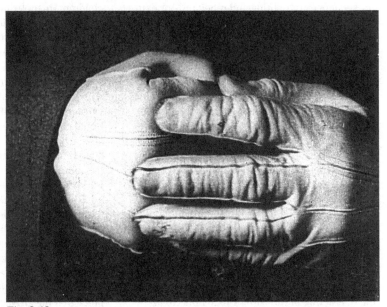

Fig. 8-12
Mother: *Pudovkin's use of the "plastic material." Defining a bureaucratic policeman by his gloved hands.*

The camera angle Pudovkin uses to shoot a scene is always significant. The far shot of the mourning mother beside the corpse is a downward shot from a high camera position (a *high-angle shot*). Pudovkin discovered that the downward angle emphasizes the characters' smallness, their feeling of being alone, their insignificance. Conversely, the extreme upward angle (a *low-angle shot*) can magnify the self-importance of characters, their smugness and petty self-esteem—or can make them appear more formidable, like the guard outside the courthouse. A slight upward angle produces not satire or intimidation but ennoblement, making the character grand without delusions of grandeur. Pudovkin's final shots of the mother marching at the head of the demonstration are low-angle shots. Pudovkin mirrors the state of the mother's mind and the progress of her education with his choice of camera positions. He often shoots her from above before her conversion; he shoots her from below to ennoble her after it.

Pudovkin relies primarily on the narrative cut, breaking down, analyzing, and constructing scenes in a manner that builds on Griffith's. Like

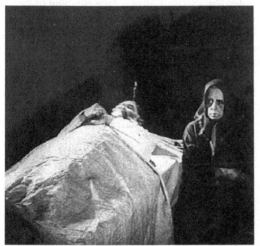

Fig. 8-13

Fig. 8-14

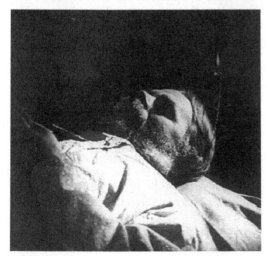

Fig. 8-15
Mother: *the scene of mourning—built with four shots.*

Fig. 8-16

Griffith, he works for fluidity in building a scene, constructing it out of shots that work together; the montage is evident and strong but not disruptive. Most reminiscent of Griffith is the subjective flashback (or mindscreen) in which the mother remembers her son's hiding the guns. Such fluid, narrative cutting was infrequent in Eisenstein. But like Eisenstein, Pudovkin could also use bold montage effects. To reveal the joy in Pavel's heart when he discovers that his comrades will soon free him from prison, Pudovkin splices together a series of images to evoke the sensation of joy. The director's sensitivity to the actor's needs told him that merely to show a smile on Pavel's face would be phony and punchless. Instead, Pudovkin cuts from Pavel's face to a rapid series of beautiful natural images: water flowing in conflicting directions, a happy child lifted high in the air, a brook upside down. Pudovkin uses a similar method to reveal the other prisoners' thoughts of home: He uses shots of fields, of horses, of plowing, of hands feeling the soil. Like Eisenstein's cuts, the shots are related thematically, not narratively; unlike Eisenstein's, the images are natural rather than artificial, warm rather than satirical. Pudovkin's famous ice shots, the parallel montage with which the film's climax begins, also echo Eisenstein's metaphorical cuts as well as Griffith's cross-cutting. Pudovkin cuts repeatedly from the shots of marching workers, steadily growing in mass, rhythm, and purpose, to shots of ice flowing and crashing on the river, steadily growing in momentum, rhythm, and direction. Although the image of the ice cakes echoes *Way Down East* as well as *Uncle Tom's Cabin*, here the thawing ice means something quite different: the energy of revolutionary upheaval as spring begins to melt a world frozen by tyranny.

Like Eisenstein, Pudovkin knew how to analyze a quick action into its component movements to add emphasis, shock, and drama to the event. For example, in the climactic demonstration sequence, Pudovkin emphasizes the brutality of the slaughter by breaking the moment of the soldiers' initial attack into 13 shots: (1) a gloved hand of the commanding officer is raised, close-up; (2) the soldiers raise their rifles, full shot; (3) the workers see the rifles and start to scurry, far shot; (4) the mother and Pavel embrace, medium close; (5) the commanding

officer's gloved hand drops, close-up; (6) the rifles fire, full shot; (7) a fallen worker's body crashes in a pool of muddy water, close shot, very quick; (8) another worker plunges face first into the water, close, very quick; (9) another body falling, close on midsection, quick; (10) the red flag starts to fall, silhouetted against the sky, close; (11) the falling flag and its bearer reflected in the water as they both fall into the mud, close; (12) the mother continues to hold Pavel, who has been shot to death, medium close; (13) Pavel falls, full shot. Out of the sudden loss and violence of this moment the mother learns her last political lesson; courageously, she picks up the fallen flag and walks toward the charging troops (an excellent series of cuts with contrasting directions and rhythms). When a sunlit cloud is seen through the red flag she holds, the film's images of nature and of politics are unified. Though the soldiers kill her, she dies a rebel, the metaphorical mother of the nation that is born with her death.

Later Works

Like *Mother*, *The End of St. Petersburg* (1927) is a story of political education, of a character who betrays the revolutionists early in the film only to join them before the end of it. A young peasant from the country must leave for the city to survive; there is neither enough land nor enough food on the farm to support him. Pudovkin draws a visual contrast between city and country with the opening shots of animals, fields, rivers, and trees, and the later shots of factories and buildings and statues. The youth feels dwarfed in the city of St. Petersburg, with its huge statues, high buildings, and vast public squares.

The youth, ignorant of political realities, becomes a strikebreaker and betrays the leaders of the strike, one of whom is his own cousin. It takes the rest of the movie for him to redeem himself.

The second half of the film brings a sharp structural shift. Pudovkin temporarily abandons the narrative focus on the youth to treat the political events of 1914–17 that "ended" St. Petersburg by converting it to Leningrad: World War I, the February Revolution, the Provisional Government, and the October Revolution. Although *The End of St. Petersburg* was intended to commemorate the tenth anniversary of the final, Bolshevik Revolution, it goes beyond

Fig. 8-17
The beginning of the slaughter in Mother.

Fig. 8-18

Fig. 8-19

Fig. 8-20

Fig. 8-21

The End of St. Petersburg: *the deflation of war—soldiers without heads, flying flags, a fancy orator, as men die in the smoke and carnage on the battlefield.*

that to become an epic of the people and the land, embracing all the country in its tale of farm and factory, class and change. Although the film's second half lacks narrative unity (the thin unifying thread is the youth's development into a Bolshevik soldier), it contains some powerful thematic contrasts that Pudovkin draws with his control of montage.

The film makes a relentless visual contrast between the idealistic glories and the realities of war. When war is declared, Pudovkin shows the military leaders only from the neck down—their uniforms, their medals, their gold braid, their boots. Not their heads. They obviously have no heads. As the parade of soldiers marches off to war, Pudovkin cuts the sequence rhythmically to

look and feel like a gaudy carnival. From the rhythmic shots of celebration, Pudovkin cuts to a quiet shot of the sky; a shell explodes, splattering the earth in the foreground. The glory of war has been replaced by the reality. Later he cuts back and forth between the violent war at the front and violent men haggling at the stock exchange, in a sequence clearly inspired by *A Corner in Wheat*. While men die in the military war, others get rich in the financial war.

Like Eisenstein, Pudovkin believed that the value of the sound film would be its asynchronous, tonal use of sound rather than a synchronized dialogue and picture. In discussing the way he would have used sound in *Mother*, Pudovkin said he would have evoked the sorrow of the mourning scene not with the synchronized sound of the mother's weeping but with the steady, hollow sound of water dripping into a bucket. Like Eisenstein, Pudovkin had difficulty putting his theories into practice. *The Story of a Simple Case* (1932), planned and apparently shot as a sound picture, was released silent. His next picture, *Deserter* (1933), is his most respected sound film: the story of a young German worker who, like the protagonists of Pudovkin's silent films, receives an education in radicalism.

Pudovkin's major films were shot by Anatoli Golovnya and written by Nathan Zarkhi. One reason *Deserter* is the last masterpiece is that Zarkhi died in a car accident in 1935. Pudovkin continued to direct and act in films until his death in 1953. Like Eisenstein, he was castigated for his formalism and spent much of his later life teaching and writing.

Other Major Figures

Alexander Dovzhenko

Alexander Dovzhenko was the third of the great Soviet directors. Though he shared both the political philosophy of Marx and the montage methods of Kuleshov with Eisenstein and Pudovkin, Dovzhenko's style was completely original. Unlike Eisenstein and Pudovkin, Dovzhenko came from the provinces, not the capital, from Ukraine, not Moscow or St. Petersburg. As early as his first major work, *Zvenigora* (1928), Dovzhenko's films are saturated in Ukrainian life and customs as well as in the folk-legend spirit and poetry of the country. (The next major Ukranian director to appear would be Sergei Paradjanov in the 1960s.) Dovzhenko's films desert realism and linear construction even more completely than Eisenstein's and use nature even more richly than Pudovkin's. His is a world where horses talk, where paintings of heroes in picture frames roll their eyes at the bastardization of their principles, where animals sniff the revolutionary spirit in the air. The Dovzhenko film is structured not as narrative but as lyric, a visual poetry that develops a theme and allows immense elliptical jumps in time, space, and continuity.

Arsenal (1928, released 1929) is the first of his mature film poems. Its subject is, roughly, the birth and growth of the revolutionary spirit in Ukraine. Whereas Pudovkin might develop such

a theme by showing a single Ukrainian's radicalization, Dovzhenko seems to spread all the events of the revolutionary years before him and then to select those images and vignettes that appeal to him. The film darts from place to place, from social class to social class, from political meeting to war to church procession to factory to a train chugging through the snow.

Dovzhenko uses a central figure—a soldier who deserts the czar to serve the revolution—as a loose peg on which to hang the film's action. Scenes with the soldier flow through *Arsenal's* many vignettes. In the final sequence, the White army captures the soldier and shoots him. The Ukrainian soldier does not die; the bullets do not strike him. He stands there defiantly. Although the forces of tyranny can capture a single arsenal, although they can shoot a single rebel, they cannot murder the spirit of rebellion and freedom in the hearts of the people. The Ukrainian becomes an image of that spirit. His presence throughout the film has been as metaphor, not as traditional protagonist. Dovzhenko's films are not narratives of events but metaphors for the feeling and the significance of the events.

Dovzhenko's striking compositions in light and space reveal the eye of the painter he once was. Though his montage sequences are vivid and powerful, even more effective are the relatively long takes in which he allows a great image all the time it needs. And his painter's eye sees the power and tension of shooting with the tilted camera, on an angle to rather than parallel with the world he is filming.

But Dovzhenko's compositions are as impressive for their content as for their look. In *Arsenal*, Dovzhenko cuts to a frozen hand sticking out of the dirt, to a frozen smile on the face of a corpse, to the frenzied laughter of a German officer who has been gassed.

Dovzhenko's films are composed of metaphors within metaphors, of isolated vignettes, of scenes and characters manifesting themselves without preparation or introduction, playing themselves out on the screen and then disappearing, often never returning to the film at all. The film's general theme and the unity of the director–poet's imagination keep the apparently random scenes together. Dovzhenko's greatest silent film poem, *Earth* (1930), is another series of images and vignettes, this one revolving around the earth, the

Fig. 8-22

Fig. 8-23

Fig. 8-24

Fig. 8-25

Arsenal: *the horrors of war. A hand . . . a frozen smile . . . a mad laugh . . . death in silhouette.*

harvests, the relationships of people, machines, and the cycles of life. His sound films, *Ivan* (1932), *Aerogard* (1935), and *Shchors* (1939), also were daring, episodic, and imagistic. Not surprisingly, Dovzhenko ran into stiff Soviet criticism; he was the most elliptical director of them all. How could his films be socially useful if the audiences could not follow them? Dovzhenko made only two films in his last 15 years and died in 1956, another great innovative mind stifled by the state's ever-narrowing definitions of artistic utility.

Dziga Vertov

Dziga Vertov, one of the Soviet Union's pioneers in combining documentary footage with political commitment, experimental cinema with

ideological statement, suffered similar artistic strangulation as Stalinism took hold—partly because he was a Jew, partly because his aesthetic was formalist, and partly because he didn't praise Stalin enough in the last film he was allowed to make, *Three Songs About Lenin* (1934). His brother, cameraman Boris Kaufman, left Russia to shoot all the films of Jean Vigo in France before going to Hollywood, where he shot such pictures as *On the Waterfront* (1954) and *The Pawnbroker* (1965). His other brother, cameraman Mikhail Kaufman, stayed to direct documentaries; he also shot Vertov's *The Man with a Movie Camera* (1928, released 1929), one of the most distinctive and adventurous films of any era.

Dziga Vertov's intense energy was evident not only in his documentaries and manifestos, but also in the name he chose for himself, which translates roughly as "fidgety spinning top" (*Dziga* is Ukrainian for "spinning top" or "restless person"; *Vertov* is derived from the Russian verb "to rotate" or "to fidget"); he was born in Poland as Denis Kaufman. As mentioned in Chapter 6, Vertov began by compiling footage into weekly newsreels in 1918–19, went on to edit full-length compilation films and shoot some of his own footage in 1920–22 (he called the camera his "Kino Eye"), then invented a documentary form that went beyond the reportage of the newsreel into creative journalism: a series of shorts that were called newsreels but each focused on specific topics and themes. That series, which ran from 1922 to 1925, was *Kinó-Pravda* ("film truth"; the French term, in homage to Vertov, is *cinéma vérité*), and its powerful emotional and didactic effects were created by the ways Vertov and his wife, editor Elizaveta Svilova, assembled the absolutely unstaged footage that was sent in from all over Russia. Beginning in 1919, he also published manifestos that were as brilliant and playful as they were radical; no film theorist is more fun to read. He attacked not only the narrative feature, but also the ordinary ways of looking at things, explored the cinema's relation to radio and television, and argued that montage—of pictures as well as sounds—was an art not of the sequence but of a film's concept from start to finish.

In many of his films, Vertov brings to life the ordinary, laborious tasks of building a nation (laying an airstrip, planting crops, finishing a tram line) by examining the progress of the task from many stirring and awesome angles, endowing the ordinary with wonder and exploring, as would many later Soviet films, the vitality of machines and the powerful potential of the union of people and machines. One of the reasons for Vertov's dynamic editing was that he had to work with mere scraps of film stock. But by 1924, when film became more available, Vertov was able to shoot more, and he sent his brother Mikhail into the streets to capture "life unawares"—candid footage, inventively shot and edited into such full-length documentaries as *Kinó-Eye* (1924) and *The Man with a Movie Camera*. It should also be noted that full reels of film stock were needed to make and export prints of the new Soviet films.

Like Ruttmann's *Berlin*—which was influenced by Vertov's writings and popularized his ideas, since little of Vertov's work was seen outside the Soviet Union—and Mikhail Kaufman's *Moscow* (1927), *The Man with a Movie Camera* is organized as an examination of life in a major city—its work and play from morning to night. Unlike Ruttmann, however, Vertov depicts the ways that the cinema itself has become an intrinsic part of modern life and a marvelous aid to seeing and understanding that life. Early in the film, we see an empty movie theatre. When the patrons arrive, the seats fold down by themselves

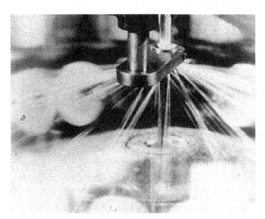

Fig. 8-26
Two consecutive frames from **The Man with a Movie Camera.**

to greet them. Thus the film begins itself. The film they see is the film we see—for *The Man with a Movie Camera* is a film-within-a-film about filmmaking. Vertov compares the lens of the movie camera and its operations to the human eye and its operations—declaring the cinema an extension of human vision. He demonstrates the processes of editing (in the most brilliant of the film's reflexive sequences, the movie "stops" while the editor decides which shot to use next) and the relationship of still frames to moving shots. He also draws parallels between the processes of cinema and other societal occupations that depend on machines that spin, wheel, or cycle repeatedly—the pumping of pistons, the winding of threads.

Like everyone else in the society, the man with the movie camera has a job to do. His special work is to record and reveal the work of everyone else. And like everyone else in the society, the man with the movie camera likes to play. Vertov allows the playful camera to dazzle us with accelerated motion, split screens, superimpositions, stop-motion animation—demystifying the cinema even as it gives the audience the visual treats it came to the theatre to enjoy. Grounded in daily life as much as in the theory and practice of cinema, this brilliantly reflexive documentary renders cinema and life inseparable.

Despite this inspired synthesis of radical form and radical ideology, Vertov made few films after 1930, the most important of which were *Enthusiasm* (1931), which had a loud, complex, contrapuntal soundtrack, exploding with the energy of sound/picture montage, and *Three Songs About Lenin*, which combined documentary footage with lyrical passages in honor of the founding father. He died in 1954 after 20 years of reduced influence and enforced idleness.

Socialist Realism

Before the Stalinist clampdown, a number of other filmmakers did important work. The greatest comic director of the silent Soviet cinema was Boris Barnet, best known for *Girl with the Hatbox* (1927) and the extraordinarily inventive *House on Trubnaya Square* (1928).

Esther Shub used montage effects to bring old newsreel footage to life, providing a striking, imaginative, and officially sanctioned view of

what it was like to live in *The Russia of Nikolai II and Lev Tolstoy* (1928) and other eras.

Some of the less inventive figures enjoyed longer careers. Abram Room—who was trained by Meyerhold and Kuleshov, and whose great silent film, *Bed and Sofa* (1927), combined a sensitive study of a love triangle with the social problems of abortion and inadequate housing—made merely competent films in the Sound Era. Room's realistic human focus and conventional plotting were more consistent with the new official aesthetic of "Socialist Realism" than were the methods of the more adventurous silent masters.

Stalin's pet aesthetic, Socialist Realism, sometimes called Stalinist Realism, demanded that art serve the interests of the state—not by stimulating and challenging people but by entertaining them with obvious, inspiring tales that had to be clear to anyone. To concentrate on the form of a work was to be arty and confusing, and to deviate from the Stalinist line was to fail to communicate plain reality. By the mid-1930s, this was the only permissible way to make a film.

In the early years of sound, the more realistic and less elliptical directors triumphed. Behind the struggle between realism and abstraction in the cinema lay a more general battle that was being waged between two conflicting forces in all the Soviet arts: the struggle between Socialist Realism and Constructivist abstraction for control of the "true path" of the People's Revolutionary Art.

The central arena for the struggle was the theatre, where the principles of Stanislavski's Moscow Art Theatre (detailed, realistic characters; lucid stories of human interaction in a clear social setting) triumphed over those of Vsevolod Meyerhold's brand of Constructivism (more abstract and symbolic settings; epic stories of vast social forces and movements). The official canonization of the Stanislavski method (despite the Moscow Art Theatre's czarist and elitist origins) led to the vilification and ostracizing of Meyerhold. Bertolt Brecht, who first fled Hitler's Germany for the Soviet Union, found a very cool reception there in 1933, for Brecht and Meyerhold held similar theories of the stage. This conflict of values in the theatre necessarily spilled over into the cinema, where several film directors (Eisenstein, for example) had been extremely influenced by Meyerhold.

Nikolai Ekk, whose *Road to Life* (1931) was the first commercially successful Soviet sound film, found the assumptions of Socialist Realism quite congenial. His film is a close, warm study of human feelings and exertion as well as a social lesson on how the "wild boys" of Russia—the homeless juvenile delinquents roaming the streets—found a purpose in life through collective labor. The Vasiliev Brothers' *Chapayev* (1934) became the model for the study of revolutionary heroes, the intimate portrayal of a military leader whose great strengths are his energy, passion, humor, and love for the people, and who overcomes his great weaknesses—excessive individuality, a stubborn refusal to study the new ways—to unite his heroic band of guerrillas with the spirit of the entire Red Army.

Yakov Protazanov was another of the successful realist directors of the first decade of sound, one of the few film directors of the czarist era to return to Soviet Russia. Grigori Kozintsev and Leonid Trauberg founded the actor-oriented "FEX" group (Society for Eccentric Actors) in the silent period in answer to the montage-oriented Kuleshov group; they continued to make films into the 1960s. Mark Donskoy made the careful, literate biographical trilogy of Maxim Gorky's growth from youth to maturity (*Childhood of Gorky*, 1938; *In the World*, 1939; *My Universities*, 1940).

But for almost 25 years the imagination and creativity of the Soviet film were tightly reined by a government policy and aesthetic that forced artists into prescribed channels of expression. The battles within the Soviet arts of the late 1920s mirrored the larger battle in Soviet politics, as Joseph Stalin seized control of the Central Soviet Communist Party in 1927 (Lenin had died in 1924) and forced Leon Trotsky—a key theorist and organizer of the Bolshevik Revolution, equal in importance to Lenin, and Stalin's most serious political and ideological rival—into exile in 1929.

For the critical years from 1929 to 1937—the transitional years between silence and sound—Stalin replaced Lenin's sympathetic commissar for information, Anatoly Lunacharsky, who encouraged artistic innovation, with a flunky, Boris Shumyatsky, a business-minded bureaucrat who viewed his job as bringing the eccentric, "formalistic" artists in line. Shumyatsky's "bringing the artists in line" was as responsible for the silence of Eisenstein in those key years as the triumph of Socialist Realism. Stalin dismissed Shumyatsky in 1937 for failing to produce enough films and enough significant films; the Soviet filmmakers then enjoyed a few years of freedom. But the war against Germany in 1941 (ending a nonaggression pact that had lasted two years) imposed restrictions again; certain kinds of films were needed to boost morale. After the war, Stalin clamped down on the directors and the people yet again. Only with his death in 1953 did the Soviet film begin to regain prestige on the international screen.

For Further Viewing

FILMS

ALEXANDER DOVZHENKO (1894–1956)
Zvenigora (1928)
Arsenal (1929). Completed 1928
Earth (1930)
Aerogard (1935)
Shchors (1939). Asst. director, Yulia Solntseva

SERGEI M. EISENSTEIN (1898–1948)
Strike (1925). Completed 1924
Battleship Potemkin (1925)
October (1928). Co-director, Grigori Alexandrov
Old and New or *The General Line* (1929). Co-director, Grigori Alexandrov
Romance sentimentale (1930). Finished by and credited to Grigori Alexandrov
¡Qué viva México! (1930–32). Unfinished. Co-director, Grigori Alexandrov. Portions of the footage assembled and released as *Thunder Over Mexico* (1933, Sol Lesser), *Time in the Sun* (1939, Marie Seton), and *¡Que Viva Mexico!* (1979, Grigori Alexandrov)
Alexander Nevsky (1938). Co-director, Dmitri Vasiliev
Ivan the Terrible (1944). *Part II*, 1946, released 1958; *Part III*, unfinished, shot 1946

VSEVOLOD I. PUDOVKIN (1893–1953)
Chess Fever (1925)
Mechanics of the Brain (1926)
Mother (1926)
The End of St. Petersburg (1927)
The Heir to Genghis Khan or *Storm Over Asia* (1928)
Deserter (1933)

Dziga Vertov (1896–1954)

Kinó-Pravda (1922–25)
Kinó-Eye (1924)
The Man with a Movie Camera or *Man with Movie Camera* (1929). Completed 1928
Enthusiasm (1931)
Three Songs About Lenin (1934)

Pre-Soviet and Soviet Miscellany

Revenge of a Kinetograph Cameraman or *The Cameraman's Revenge* (1912, Ladislas Starewicz)
A Child of the Big City (1914, Evgenii Bauer)
Daydreams (1915, Evgenii Bauer)
Father Sergius (1918, Yakov Protazanov)
Shackled by Film (1918, Nikandr Turkin). Script by Vladimir Mayakovsky
Extraordinary Adventures of Mr. West in the Land of the Bolsheviks (1924, Lev Kuleshov)
By the Law (1926, Lev Kuleshov)
The Cloak (1926, Grigori Kozintsev and Leonid Trauberg)
Bed and Sofa (1927, Abram Room)
Girl with the Hatbox (1927, Boris Barnet)
Moscow (1927, Mikhail Kaufman)
House on Trubnaya Square (1928, Boris Barnet)
The Russia of Nikolai II and Lev Tolstoy (1928, Esther Shub)
Road to Life (1931, Nikolai Ekk)
Chapayev (1934, Sergei and Georgy Vasiliev)
Lieutenant Kije (1934, Alexander Feinzimmer). Score by Sergei Prokofiev

DVDs

Battleship Potemkin (1925, **Sergei Eisenstein**). Kino International. **Restored.** Includes two discs, one with Russian intertitles and one with newly translated English intertitles; the 1926 music; and a documentary on the film and the restoration.

The Cameraman's Revenge & Other Fantastic Tales (1912 and later, **Ladislas Starewicz**). Image Entertainment. Contains *Revenge of a Kinetograph Cameraman, The Insects' Christmas, The Frogs Who Wanted a King, Voice of the Nightingale, The Mascot,* and *Winter Carousel.*

Eisenstein: The Sound Years. Criterion Collection. **Restored** prints of *Alexander Nevsky* and *Ivan the Terrible, Parts I and II,* a reconstruction of *Bezhin Meadow,* an audio essay by film historian David Bordwell, deleted scenes from *Ivan,* drawings and production stills, a **restoration** demonstration, as well as multimedia essays on **Eisenstein**'s collaboration with **Prokofiev,** Eisenstein's visual vocabulary, etc.

Kinó-Eye and Three Songs About Lenin (1924 and 1934, **Dziga Vertov**). Image Entertainment. The last reel of *Kinó-Eye* has been reconstructed from outtakes; this feature version was rarely shown outside the Soviet Union. *Three Songs* is a sound film.

The Man with a Movie Camera (1928, rel. 1929, **Dziga Vertov**). Image Entertainment. Commentary by film historian Yuri Tsivian. Music by the Alloy Orchestra.

Mother (1926, **V. I. Pudovkin**). Image Entertainment. The only available DVD but not a great print; be sure to turn off the 1968 music-and-effects soundtrack (the sound transfer is so poor that you can hear the projector). There are similar problems with other DVDs not listed here: relatively poor print quality for **Dovzhenko**'s films, 40 minutes missing from the only DVD of *October,* etc.

¡Qué viva México! (1930–32, **Sergei Eisenstein**). Kino Video. Alexandrov's attempt to restore Eisenstein's unfinished film. Also includes *Romance sentimentale* and representative documents concerning production and release.

9

Sound

According to legend, sound unexpectedly descended on the film industry from the skies, like an ancient god out of a machine, when *The Jazz Singer* opened on Broadway on October 6, 1927. Although the success of *The Jazz Singer* overthrew the film industry of 1927 with incredible speed, preparation for the entrance of sound had been building for over 30 years. The idea for the sound film was born with the film itself. W. K–L. Dickson claimed to have produced a rough synchronization of word and picture in 1889, and he did use the Kineto-phonograph to synchronize music and picture in 1894 or 1895 for the first surviving sound film.

Throughout the first 20 years of film history, inventors worked to wed sight and sound. In France, between 1896 and 1900, Auguste Baron, Henri Joly, and Georges Demenÿ patented various processes for synchronizing moving pictures with sounds recorded on a disc. Between 1900 and 1910, Léon Gaumont demonstrated synchronized-sound pictures, both at the World Exposition of 1900 and in his own Paris theatres. The first attempts to record sound on film, rather than on cylinders or discs, were made in France in 1904 by Eugène Lauste—the same man who worked with Dickson on the Latham camera and projector and was the co-inventor of the loop. In 1910, the German pioneer Oskar Messter produced a film with synchronized sound, *The Green Forest.* And in America, the Edison Company produced a 15-minute, vaguely synchronized musical version of *Mother Goose Tales* (shot in one continuous take) in 1912. Edison's six-minute *Nursery Favorites* came out

in 1913, projected from what he called the Kinetophone. Like the pioneers of an earlier film era, the first sound pioneers decorated their inventions with Greco–Latin names that almost required a special apparatus to pronounce, such as the Graphonocone. Aside from these early picture–sound novelties, live sounds were extremely common in the nickelodeons of 1905–12. Not only was there the piano, the organ, or a trio of musicians, but live actors sometimes stood behind or beside the screen to speak the lines accompanying the pictures—or a narrator (called the *benshi* in Japan, where this practice flourished throughout the Silent Era) might comment on the action as well as deliver the dialogue. It seemed inevitable that movies would make their own noise.

Processes

The first practical, dependable synthesis of picture and sound came just after World War I. Two primary problems confronted the inventor of a sound-film process. The first was synchronization. How were the film and the sound to be kept permanently and constantly "in sync"? (*Sync* is short for synchronization.) The problem with using one machine was that the picture had to stop and start for every frame but the sound had to roll evenly, like a tape. The problem with two machines was that they *were* two machines. The method of coupling a projected film with a recorded disc was risky; it was terribly easy for the two to slip "out of sync." The film could break; the stylus could skip. *Singin' In*

The Rain (1952), a marvelous parody of the transitional era from silent to sound films, revealed the unintentionally comic results when the cavalier's voice issued from the damsel's moving lips.

Although the first commercially successful American sound-film process, the Vitaphone, synchronized a record player with the film projector, a more stable method had been developed as early as 1919: the optical soundtrack. Three German inventors had discovered the means of recording the soundtrack directly on the film itself (*optical sound*) and crucially smoothing, with a simple flywheel, the movement of film through a sound projector; they were Josef Engl, Joseph Massole, and Hans Vogt. Using the principle of the oscilloscope, the Germans used a photocell to convert the sound into light beams, recorded the beams on one side of the strip of film, and then built a reader on the projector that could retranslate the light beams into sound. This German discovery, known as the Tri-Ergon Process, later became the ruling sound-film patent of Europe. Successfully demonstrated in 1922, the Tri-Ergon Process was very similar to the optical-sound process on which the American inventor Lee de Forest had begun working in 1913 and which he perfected in 1920: the Phonofilm.

An earlier de Forest invention solved the second problem of the sound film—amplification. The sound not only had to be synchronized, it had to be audible. A film had to make enough noise to reach all the patrons who filled the movie palaces. The earliest phonographs and radios, lacking the means of amplification, could entertain only one listener, who wore a listening tube. In 1906, de Forest invented the audion tube, the little vacuum tube that, among other things, magnified the signals it received. The key element of any electronic amplifier, whether it is used to pick up weak signals (from microphones or even satellites) or to modify sounds and drive them into a loudspeaker, de Forest's tube gave birth to many children—the radio, public address system, long-distance telephone, television, stereo components—in short, modern electronics and mass communications. It also gave birth to the sound film. Whatever the system of synchronization, the audion tube magnified the sound so that an entire audience could hear it. De Forest patented an early version of the audion tube in

1906 and the perfected version in January 1907. It used three electrodes: a cathode to produce electrons, a plate to attract them, and—the crucial innovation—a grid to control them, so that a signal could be reduced or increased without distortion. The tube's amplifying power was increased in 1913 by Edwin Howard Armstrong.

It was in 1913 that de Forest experimented with the photographing of sound; his first subject was an acrobatic barking dog. The phonograph, he said, was "a triumph over a bad principle" because it relied on a needle that could scratch the record; his solution—similar to that employed in today's compact disc—was to use light, not a metal shaft, to write and read the sound. From 1919 to 1921, he invented and improved the Phonofilm, whose optical soundtrack ran between the picture area and one row of sprockets (the row on the other side of the film directly adjoined the picture; the Germans had run the soundtrack between one row of sprocket holes and the outer edge of the film). He began shooting sound films in 1921, making hundreds of shorts between then and 1927. He demonstrated the Phonofilm in 1922 and premiered it in New York theatres on April 28, 1923. Among his first subjects were the singer and comedian Eddie Cantor (1923), pianist Oscar Levant (1922), and monologist Monroe Silver (1922); his first narrative film was *Love's Old Sweet Song* (1924). In 1924, he invented the sound newsreel; his first subject was President Calvin Coolidge.

The optical soundtrack in use today is a direct outgrowth of de Forest's Phonofilm—as the Academy of Motion Picture Arts and Sciences acknowledged when it awarded him a special Oscar in 1959. But de Forest made little money, and for decades received little credit, for bringing sound to the motion picture. And the optical-sound processes demonstrated in 1922 in Europe (the Tri-Ergon Process) and America (the Phonofilm) were not the first to succeed commercially.

A competing process that recorded the soundtrack on 78 RPM records (*sound on disc*), with each record large enough to hold ten minutes of sound so that there could be one disc for each reel of film, had good sound quality and was used on the right movie: *The Jazz Singer*. Both sound-on-film and sound-on-disc processes, as well as all subsequent sound filming, required that the speed with which film was exposed and projected be standardized, so that the sound could be played back at the speed at which *it* had been recorded and remain in sync with the picture. By the mid-1920s, film speed had drifted upward to between 18 and 22 fps, and of course it still varied from one movie to another. The faster sound is recorded and played back, the better it sounds. So the faster speed of 24 fps was established as an industry standard, the normal duration of a reel became ten minutes, and film length began to be given in minutes rather than feet or meters.

The sound-on-disc process—a "double system" that relied on two interlocked machines, the projector and the turntable, as opposed to the "single system" of sound-on-film projection—was developed by Bell Telephone's research lab, Western Electric. In 1925 they began trying to market the invention, which they named the Vitaphone.

Western Electric offered the Vitaphone to the biggest producer in Hollywood, Adolph Zukor. Paramount did not want it. Neither did any other major company. Their reasons for rejecting sound were obvious: It was an untried and expensive innovation that could only disrupt a business that had become increasingly stable and profitable. Sound recording was ticklish and expensive; it would slow down production schedules. Sound equipment was expensive to buy, especially for the exhibitors whose houses would have to be converted, at up to $20,000 per theatre, before any sound film could be shown. Nor did the competing sound-film processes make the decision easier. On which should the wise theatre owner place a commercial bet? The confusion was like that surrounding the competing color television processes of the early 1960s, the competing home-video cassette and disc formats of the late 1970s, or the competing computer platforms of the 1980s. The wise theatre owner did nothing.

Rejected by the most powerful producers, Western Electric offered Vitaphone in 1926 to Warner Bros., a family of four producing brothers whose small company had recently embarked on a costly program of major expansion. Having bought the remains of the Vitagraph Company (the last of the original Trust Companies) in 1925 and made it their distribution chain, the Warners wished to expand their small network of theatres, to achieve full vertical integration, and to take on

the big boys—Loew, Zukor, First National—who controlled enough theatre and distribution chains to choke the market for Warners' films. The Warner brothers bought the Vitaphone. Within three years they had swallowed First National and digested most of the theatres in that chain.

The Warner sound films started cautiously enough. On August 6, 1926, the Warners presented a program of short sound films; the first was an address by Will Hays praising the possibilities of the sound film, followed by the New York Philharmonic Orchestra and by leading artists of the opera, the concert, and the music hall. The Vitaphone shorts were similar to de Forest's Phonofilms. But on the same program, the Warners presented a feature film, *Don Juan* (directed, like *The Jazz Singer*, by Alan Crosland), with a synchronized musical score. A canned orchestra had replaced the live one in the pit. This put many musicians out of work, but it allowed filmmakers to decide *exactly* what music would accompany their images, a significant advance in artistic control. For over a year Warner Bros. presented a series of similar film programs: highly entertaining musical or comedy shorts that have long been underrated (see the collection on the DVD of *The Jazz Singer*) and a feature with synchronized score. The Warners were wary of films that talked, or that just talked. Sam Warner was reported to have said, "If it can talk, it can sing."

Like the Warners, another lesser producer, William Fox, was a film businessman who gazed enviously at the Zukors and Loews on the

Fig. 9-1
Will Hays welcomes moviegoers to aural wonders in the first Vitaphone program of 1926.

heights; like Carl Laemmle, the independent producer who founded Universal, he had fought Edison in the courts and won. Fox decided to use sound the same way as the Warners did. Early in 1927 Fox began presenting mechanically scored films, the greatest of which was Murnau's *Sunrise* (planned and shot as a silent), whose music and sound effects were post-synchronized. The effects on these soundtracks were recorded in a studio rather than created on the spot with musical instruments, an advance in realism. Like the Warners, Fox presented a series of short novelty films—performances by famous variety artists and conversations with famous people. In addition, Fox started his own sound newsreel, the Fox Movietone News. Unlike Vitaphone, the Fox system, called Movietone, was a sound-on-film process, exactly like the Phonofilm. Through Theodore Case, Fox bought the rights to a modified version of de Forest's system; Fox also purchased the American rights to the Tri-Ergon patents.

Fox exploited the novelty of coupling the sound of the human voice with the picture of moving lips. In the Movietone short referred to as *Shaw Talks for Movietone News* (1928) and as *Greeting by George Bernard Shaw, 1928*, the audience is amused by seeing the image of the crusty playwright, hearing his voice, enjoying his garrulous, improvised pleasantries, and recognizing the mechanical reproduction of other natural sounds like birds chirping and gravel crackling on the garden path. The five-minute film uses only two setups: a brief far shot as Shaw walks down the path, then a medium shot of Shaw's head and torso that lasts for the rest of the film (over four minutes without a cut). Perhaps the only reason the film splurged with the second setup was that the honk of an automobile horn (clearly audible on the soundtrack) "spoiled" the first take a minute after the camera started rolling. The moving pictures had become a simple recording device once again. The camera stopped speaking as the movies learned to talk.

By the late 1920s, then, there were a number of competing film-sound systems: sound on disc and two kinds of sound on film: variable-density optical and variable-area optical. *Vitaphone* was the sound-on-disc process developed by Western Electric and used by Warner Bros. from 1926 to 1931. (Some of today's digital systems put the soundtrack on a CD; that too is sound on disc.) *Movietone*, used by Fox; de Forest's *Phonofilm*; and a new optical sound system developed by

Shaw Talks for Movietone News: *the playwright scowls his "Mussolini look."*

Fig. 9-2

Western Electric and used by MGM, Paramount, United Artists, Universal, and even Warners, which issued films with disc and optical tracks from 1928 to 1931, were virtually identical sound-on-film processes. Their optical soundtracks were "variable density," becoming darker (more "dense") or lighter as the sound varied. The last major system, the *Photophone*, was perfected in 1927 by RCA and used by RKO as well as in much of Europe. It had a "variable area" optical sound-track, which had a transparent area, resembling a transparent line surrounded by black, whose amplitude increased and decreased as the sound changed, producing the squiggly soundtrack familiar today. The variable density track, which looked more like a gray stripe than like a rubber band gone nuts, is obsolete today, but the variable area track is common, and the Stereo

Variable Area (SVA) track is the basis of Dolby Stereo, which when it was used in *Star Wars* (1977) was an optical format with two variable area tracks and four channels.

The Jazz Singer was neither the first sound film nor the first film to synchronize picture with speech and song. It was, however, the first full-length feature to use synchronized sound as a means of telling a story. Most of the film was shot silent, with intertitles and a post-synchronized score. In this respect Warners' *Jazz Singer* went no further than their *Don Juan*. But at least five sequences used synchronized speech.

In one, the jazz singer (Al Jolson) returns to his Orthodox Jewish home to visit his parents. His mother (Eugenie Besserer) enjoys seeing him and listening to his "jazzy" singing of "Blue Skies." His father (Warner Oland), a cantor,

Fig. 9-3
The Jazz Singer: *Jolson sings "Blue Skies" for his mother (Eugenie Besserer) and a frozen camera.*

orders an end to all profane jazz in his house. The father's command to stop the music is the cue for the film to revert to silence—then the old orchestral music and the intertitles start. That brilliant strategy made the sound film modern and the silent film old-fashioned.

In another of the lip-synchronized (*lip sync*) sequences, Jolson sings his "Mammy" number, in blackface, to an audience in a theatre. The number is exactly like the vaudeville shorts recorded earlier on the Phonofilm, the Vitaphone, and the Movietone—with two differences. First, Jolson performed for two specific people who were watching him: his sweetheart (backstage) and his beloved mother (in the audience). Second, his song played a role in the thematic action of the film: The cantor's son had synthesized the sacred and profane functions of music—and the contradictory demands of showbiz and the family—by becoming an entertainer who sang from the heart to a responsive, involved audience that could almost be thought of as a congregation.

The divided nature of *The Jazz Singer*—part silent, part talkie—revealed both the disadvantages and the advantages of the new medium. Whereas the silent sections of the film used rather flowing camera work and terse narrative cutting, the synchronized sections were visually inert. For Jolson's third song, "Blue Skies," the camera was restricted to two setups: a medium shot of Jolson at the piano, and a close shot of Besserer responding (intercut sparingly). Most visually inert of all is the dialogue shot: a rambling, improvised series of Jewish jokes between choruses of the song—a full shot of Jolson and mama, one long take. When the film starts making synchronized noises, the camera stops doing everything but exposing film.

On the other hand, this moment of informal patter at the piano is the most exciting and vital part of the entire movie. In the silent sequences Jolson is a poor mime, with hammy, overstated gestures and expressions. But when Jolson acquires a voice, the warmth, the excitement, the vibrations of it, the way its rambling spontaneity lays bare the imagination of the mind that is making up the sounds, convert the overgesturing hands and the overactive eyes into a performance that seems effortlessly natural. Another element that is more natural in the sound film is the use of more words than would be included in an intertitle; this makes real dialogue possible. "Wait a minute," Jolson tells an applauding audience in his first song-and-dialogue scene, "You ain't heard nothin' yet! Wait a minute, I tell ya, you ain't heard nothin'. You want to hear 'Toot Toot Tootsie'? All right, hold on . . ." The addition of a Vitaphone voice revealed the particular qualities of Al Jolson that made him a star. To reveal the whole complex of identity and experience expressed by the human voice, the sound film had to be invented. A sound mix has three parts: dialogue, music, and effects. The silent film already had music and some effects; now the music could be synchronized and the full sounds of nature could be brought to the microphone— but it was dialogue (and other sounds people make, like the anguished crowing of the professor in *The Blue Angel*, which had to be heard and was enacted because it could be heard) that was the crucial addition. Not only the eyes are a window on the soul.

Problems

The Jazz Singer was a huge hit; it put new zip in a film business that had begun to sag in 1927. Warner Bros.' next Jolson vehicle, *The Singing Fool* (1928), was the top-grossing film of the 1920s and the top-grossing sound film until Disney's *Snow White and the Seven Dwarfs* (1937). The movie czars who resisted sound because it would disrupt their stable business now had to convert to sound to stay in business. Although studio executives predicted that sound and silent films would continue to co-exist, the admission dollars of the public punctured the theory. Americans no longer wanted to see silent films. Silent films had taught them to see; the new invention of radio had taught them to hear, and its programs were free, like broadcast TV today. They would not leave their homes and spend their money if they could not both see and hear at the same time. By 1929, the silent film was virtually dead in America. Even the hell-bent-for-action serials went talkie. Hollywood produced a few silent versions of sound films for foreign theatres and for rural American houses that were not yet equipped for sound. (A few countries made silent films until the mid-1930s.) In 1926, a few silent films used synchronized music and sound effects as a commercial

A weekly lobby card for one of the first "all-talking" serials: **The Lone Defender** *(1930), from Mascot Pictures.*

Fig. 9-4

novelty; in 1929 and 1930, a few synchronized sound pictures were released silent as a commercial necessity. Only Chaplin resisted sound for aesthetic reasons, releasing *City Lights* with synchronized music but no dialogue—a silent that did tremendous business in 1931.

The new sound film caused filmmakers and film critics three primary problems: artistic, technical, and commercial. The camera, which had spent the previous 32 years learning to take an active part in filmed fiction, suddenly became motionless and inexpressive, unless the scene was shot silent and then post-synchronized. Cuts were rare. Although the silent film had declared its independence from the stage, the early sound film became the vassal of the theatre once again—and rushed to hire its actors for their voices. The moving picture stopped moving and stopped using pictures. Critics and theorists sang a requiem for the film art and said amen.

Typical of the aesthetic blunders of the earliest sound films was the very first "all-talking" film, *Lights of New York* (Warner Bros., 1928, directed by Bryan Foy). The camera stood still to record scenes of seemingly endless and very bad dialogue. The film was cut sparingly. The camera rarely panned more than two feet. Space was no longer charged with beauty or meaning. The decor no longer served any tonal, metaphoric, or

narrative function; it was merely something to talk in. And the talking bodies huddled together so they could all be heard by the single microphone. In a scene in a barbershop, a character stops talking when he walks across the room. He could not speak unless he was parked under the mike. In a later scene, two thugs talk to their mobster boss in his office; the crooks sit on the edge of the sofa leaning toward the boss; the boss sits in his desk chair leaning toward his boys. All three actors strain to make sure that their voices can be heard by the mike, obviously buried in a canister on a table that has no function in the scene except to hide the microphone.

Worse, the film not only strains to record the dialogue, but the dialogue, once recorded, is not worth hearing. The film's speech is crammed with mixed metaphors ("You think you can take any chicken you want and throw me back in the deck?"), with clichés ("You needed me to stick by you through all the tough times")—with the blatantly obvious and unnecessary. Especially ludicrous are the actors' attempts to render gangster slang with the most precise, theatrical diction ("Take him—for—a—ride"). Compared with the fluidity of a silent gangster film like Josef von Sternberg's *Underworld* (1927), *Lights of New York* was an abominable regression.

Many of the aesthetic shortcomings of the first sound films were less the result of theoretical problems than of the practical and technical problems of mastering the new machines. The stasis, the inertia, of the early sound films resulted partly from the difficulty of silencing the whirring camera and partly from the difficulty of recording with a single, fixed microphone. To baffle the camera's clatter, the machine and its operator were imprisoned in a soundproof, windowed booth. The camera could neither tilt nor travel. The most it could manage was a slight pan. Scenes soon were shot from several booths at once; footage from the secondary setups could be cut into the synchronized footage from the primary camera, as long as the new footage was exactly the length of the footage it replaced. That helped. But in the years before sound mixing and the boom microphone, a single mike had to be buried in a pivotal, stationary spot on the set; the easiest scenes to shoot were those in which an actor spoke into a telephone. Of necessity, the microphone nailed the action to a tiny circle. The comic attempts to hide the mike in *Singin' In The Rain*—in a bush, in the star's bosom—are exaggerated but accurate.

Yet another problem of the new sound equipment was its cost. Studios invested huge sums in the new machines and new soundproof buildings (sound stages) in which to use them. The theatre owner also faced enormous expenses, forced to buy new sound projectors, new speakers, and new wiring to link the two. Both studios and theatres borrowed from the banks to convert to sound. The movies, big business though they were, became subsidiaries of the banks. The two major sound processes in 1930, Western Electric's and RCA's, came from companies that were subdivisions of the Morgan and Rockefeller holdings. Studios borrowed from these very banks to buy the equipment that bank money had developed. The interrelationship of movies and high finance has continued ever since. By acquiring this large debt, the movie industry became dependent on Wall Street brokerage houses and banks to underwrite the costs of production.

The new invention caused commercial problems with people as well as with paper. Studios suddenly discovered that popular stars and directors of the silent films were liabilities in the era of speech. The incoming tide of foreign talent—the Negris and Janningses and Stillers—reversed and started flowing back to native shores. The actor or director with faulty English had no place in the Hollywood world of dialogue film. Lubitsch and Garbo stayed, but most returned home. (The next influx came in response to the rise of Hitler; by the time Peter Lorre arrived, colorful foreign voices were welcome.) American-born stars also had troubles with dialogue; their voices had to harmonize—as Keaton's, for example, did not—with the visual images they had projected in the Silent Era. The beautiful actress with a nasal rasp and the handsome Latin with a squeaky twang might as well have been unable to speak at all. Diction coaches opened offices in the studios to polish the pronunciation of those voices that did not irreparably offend the microphone. (Stage actors with great unique voices, like John Barrymore or Groucho and Chico Marx, were left alone.) Along with the diction coaches came dialogue writers, many of them novelists or playwrights, whom the studios also needed. Old stars and old jobs died; new ones were born.

Writer Ben Hecht had come to Hollywood in 1925, when his friend Herman Mankiewicz—who later wrote *Citizen Kane*—sent him a telegram that read in part, "Millions are to be grabbed out here and your only competition is idiots. Don't let this get around." By 1930, the news had gotten around.

Eisenstein predicted that the sound film would try to solve its problems by taking the path of least resistance: by drifting into dialogue films and merely exploiting the audience's interest in seeing and hearing a person or event at the same time. Hollywood did just that, grandly advertising its films as "all-talking" and even as "100% all-talking, all-singing, and all-dancing." Gunshots, ringing telephones, and banging doors were everywhere. Musical numbers became obligatory—and soon the previously impossible genre of the film musical was born. Hollywood imported Broadway directors, players, and plays. At least the talk in a play had already been tested, and its actors (for example, Bela Lugosi in the stage version of *Dracula*) had demonstrated their ability to speak it. Moving pictures were in danger of becoming hand-servants of the theatre once again, oblivious to the years of development that had created a unique narrative art.

Solutions

While film aesthetes sang the blues, a few creative film artists worked to turn talkies into moving pictures with sound, certain that the movies could absorb sound rather than the other way round. Hollywood began to solve some of the technical problems. Although the noisy camera had to be encased, it could be released from its glass-windowed prison for those shots that did not require synchronized dialogue. In *Hallelujah* (1929), King Vidor let the camera roam silently over the fields, through a forest, aboard a train, and then dubbed in the singing of spirituals. Music in *Hallelujah*, its rhythms precisely synchronized with the visual action and emotional "beats," carried much of the film's meaning and effect. In *The Love Parade* (1929), Lubitsch shot ladies sitting in Parisian windows or soldiers marching gallantly in formation with a silent, tracking camera and then dubbed in the song that Maurice Chevalier or Jeanette MacDonald sang. In *All Quiet on the Western Front* (1930), Lewis Milestone shot battle scenes with silent, sweeping tracking shots of the lines of attacking armies and post-synchronized the sounds of machine guns and grenades during the editing. Luis Buñuel and Salvador Dalí's Surrealist feature, *L'Age d'or* (1930), had its entire sound-track added after the picture was shot; in a way that would have pleased Eisenstein, the "wrong" sound was often synchronized with the picture, putting the sound and image tracks in a montage relationship so that they could conflict with each other or work in counterpoint. But that was, to say the least, not a Hollywood movie.

Soon even the dialogue scenes gained mobility with the invention of the camera blimp, a device that slipped over the camera to muffle its noise without banishing it to a soundproof booth; one blimp was invented by Lee de Forest. By 1929, Victor Fleming (in *The Virginian*) could shoot dialogue sequences outdoors, including tracking shots in which men on horseback spoke to passengers on a moving train. And by 1930, Lubitsch (in *Monte Carlo*) could shoot a long tracking shot on a gravel path in which camera movement, dialogue, and editing worked together with complete fluidity.

Hollywood solved the microphone problem, too. Rouben Mamoulian, one of the theatre directors imported from New York, suggested

Fig. 9-5

Fig. 9-6

Fig. 9-7
Applause: *Mamoulian adds visual energy to the early talkies with silhouettes and striking camera angles (Fig. 9-5), effects shots like the split screen that shows Helen Morgan serenading her lover's picture while he caresses the chorus girl down the hall (Fig. 9-6), and location shots to which sound could be added later (Fig. 9-7).*

using two microphones to shoot a single scene, balancing and regulating the relative volumes of the two with a sound mixer. In Mamoulian's *Applause* (1929), two characters could speak to each other from opposite ends of the room without trotting together to speak into the same flowerpot. Mamoulian added zip to his film by recording indoor scenes with a moving camera, tracking toward and away from the speakers. He shot other scenes on location, taking advantage of actual New York sights like the Brooklyn Bridge, the Chrysler Building, and the subway, dubbing in the dialogue later.

An even more flexible method of capturing the voice was the invention in 1929 of the boom, a rod or mechanical arm that kept the microphone hovering above the speaker's head, just out of the camera's frame. Whenever the actor moved, the microphone could silently follow. Although the invention has been credited to sound technician Eddie Mannix (at MGM), to director Dorothy Arzner, and to actor–director Lionel Barrymore, the idea for the boom was probably born when someone improvised by tying the mike to a long stick. If the boom became a boon for fluidly mobile sound-film recording, it became the bane of lighting design. How could scenes be lit without throwing its long tell-tale shadow across the walls of the set?

Just as technicians began to conquer the mechanical problems of sound filming, directors began to discover the means of using sound artistically in a primarily visual medium. Even a deadly talkie like *Lights of New York* contained a few imaginative combinations of sound and picture: The sequence in which the gangsters shoot a cop is staged in enlarged shadows on a wall coupled with the sounds of a shout, a policeman's whistle, a shot, and the motor of the getaway car. René Clair was impressed with some of the effects of MGM's first all-talking, all-singing picture, *Broadway Melody* (1929): While Bessie Love watches her lover leave, the director (Harry Beaumont) keeps the camera riveted on her tearful face, dramatizing the departure with sound alone—the door slams, the lover's car drives off.

Several of Ernst Lubitsch's juxtapositions of sound and picture reveal the comic ingenuity that would soon develop a mature sound-film masterpiece like *Trouble in Paradise* (1932).

In *The Love Parade* (1929), as Chevalier starts to tell the queen's chamberlain a sexual anecdote (how Madame Curie cured him of a cold but gave him a French accent), Lubitsch cuts to a camera position outside the window. The rest of the scene is silent; we cannot hear the joke at all. We don't need to. The slyness of the silence, Lubitsch's joke, is funnier than the joke itself. Similarly, as Chevalier and the queen dine tête-à-tête in her boudoir, Lubitsch shows us the queen's ladies-in-waiting, ministers, and servants narrating what they can see from outside her window. Sound allowed Lubitsch to develop one of his favorite comic devices: A scene inside a room can be much more interesting and fun if the camera stays outside the room.

In *Monte Carlo* (1930), a Jeanette MacDonald musical, Lubitsch's most famous device was to set the song "Beyond the Blue Horizon" as a duet between the soprano and a speeding train. As MacDonald sings the song, the sounds of the train (chugging wheels, tooting whistle, puffing smoke) become her percussion accompaniment, underscored by the equally percussive rhythms of the editing. This was an innovative and ingenious combination of picture, sound, and cutting—a synthesis of Soviet montage and American musical comedy.

The most innovative early sound films, however, were the animated cartoons of Walt Disney. Disney began as a commercial artist and cartoonist in Kansas City; he made his film debut with animated ads and satiric, short cartoons—*Fred Newman's Laugh-O-Grams*. He migrated to Hollywood in 1923 and produced a series of short films that integrated cartoons and a living girl (each cartoon in the series was "An ALICE Comedy"; hence, the *Alice Comedies*); Disney would again mix people and drawings in *Song of the South* (1946) and *Mary Poppins* (1964), and his studio would continue the tradition after his death with *Who Framed Roger Rabbit* (1988). By the end of the Silent Era, he and his animator, Ub Iwerks, had mastered the methods and art of animation. The *Alice* films were rich in the mature Disney imagination, particularly in his credible transposition of physical reality into almost surreal impossibility. For example, as a mouse (Mickey's progenitor) serenades his mousette (Minnie's) in *Alice Plays Cupid* (1925), a barrage of notes flies out of his guitar and streams into her face as she stands on her balcony. The mouse then uses these notes as a ladder, climbing them up to her chamber; that accomplished, he gathers them together with his tail, transposing the ladder of notes into a bouquet of flowers.

But it was sound that turned Disney into one of the most influential producers in the film industry. Adding sound to a cartoon was considered commercially insane and an artistic mistake—until Disney pulled it off. He also pioneered the Technicolor cartoon (*Flowers and Trees*, 1932) and the American animated feature (in 1937, *Snow White* was billed as the first full-length animation, in ignorance of Reiniger's work in Germany). Disney's cartoons, which were not compelled to photograph the real world, escaped the tyrannies of sound recording that enslaved the directors of theatrical features. Disney's drawn worlds were shot and edited with all the fluidity of the silents, as if by a real camera moving through an artificial landscape to a perfectly synchronized soundtrack; because the animation camera shot no live action and required no soundproof booth or blimp or microphone, the Disney films moved like movies. The cartoon—which is free from all natural laws, from all human and spatial realities—also granted its creator complete freedom in playing with sound. Just as the pictures could depict impossibilities—animals that act like people, physical stresses that a living organism could never endure—the soundtrack could be equally free and fanciful. Handmade pictures could combine in fantastic ways with made-up sounds. Or the animated film could develop a counterpoint between its fanciful, unreal sights and the concrete reality of familiar sounds. The Disney sound cartoon united three of the great traditions of silent filmmaking and carried them into the Sound Era: the wacky, speedy physical comedy of Mack Sennett; the fantasy world of Méliès, in which what cannot happen happens; and the genius of Chaplin, Winsor McCay, and especially Émile Cohl for transforming one kind of object into a totally different one.

Iwerks and Disney's first sound film, *Steamboat Willie* (1928, the first Mickey Mouse cartoon to be released), used optical sound and shows complete mastery of the counterpoint of picture and sound. The most imaginative sequence is the "Turkey in the Straw" number.

A goat has eaten a guitar and the sheet music for the tune "Turkey in the Straw." Mickey Mouse (voice by Disney) twists and starts to crank the goat's tail; the notes pour out of the animal's mouth; the music on the soundtrack accompanies the visual notes. Then Mickey (or "Willie") uses whatever he can find as an accompanying percussive instrument. He rattles on a garbage pail and a series of different-sized pots; he scratches a washboard; he swings a cat around by its tail to produce syncopated wails; he squeezes a duck's throat to produce rhythmic quacks; he pulls the tails of nursing piglets to produce a scale of squeaks; he bangs on a cow's teeth to produce the tones of a xylophone. (The subtle sadism of Disney's work is already evident here.) Whereas silent montage created meaning by juxtaposing dissimilar images, Disney perceived the similarity of apparently dissimilar sounds and images. An Eisenstein simile that the workers (visual) are like a bull (visual) contrasts with Disney's that a cow's teeth (visual) are like a xylophone (sound).

The Skeleton Dance (1929), the first of the Silly Symphonies, is an even more skillful weaving of motion, music, and rhythm. Its opening sequence—an atmospheric painting of the mood of midnight and goblins—combines the eerie, tense whine of violins with percussive effects produced by an owl hooting, bats' wings flapping, wind whistling, and cats screeching. Then the skeletons creep out of their graves. The surprising activities of the bones are carefully coordinated with the beats of the music. Disney is sensitive not only to the possibilities of the kinds of sound that a visual image might generate, but also to the punch of coordinating animated movement with the rhythmic effects of the score. This sensitivity to musical tones and rhythms (which, when the sound and picture beats are *too* tightly coordinated, is still pejoratively known as "Mickey Mousing") became the outstanding feature of every Silly Symphony, eventually culminating in the cinematic tone-poem *Fantasia* (1940). Though his studio's greatest achievements were the animated features *Snow White and the Seven Dwarfs* and *Pinocchio* (1940), Disney's synthesis of image, music, and rhythm had begun with his first sound cartoons. The means of turning sound into a resource for film rather than a liability were being found.

Fig. 9-8

Disney's clever wedding of sound and image. Two xylophones: a cow's teeth in **Steamboat Willie** *(Fig. 9-8), a human skeleton in* **The Skeleton Dance** *(Fig. 9-9).* © *Disney Enterprises, Inc.*

Fig. 9-9

For Further Viewing

FILMS

WALT DISNEY (1901–66)
Alice Comedies Series (1923–27)
Steamboat Willie (1928)
Plane Crazy (1928)
The Skeleton Dance (1929)
Flowers and Trees (1932)
Mickey's Pal Pluto (1933)
The Three Little Pigs (1933)
Thru the Mirror (1936)
Moving Day (1936)
The Old Mill (1937)
Snow White and the Seven Dwarfs (1937)
Pinocchio (1940)
Fantasia (1940)
Dumbo (1941)
Bambi (1942)
Song of the South (1946)
Seal Island (1948)
The Adventures of Ichabod and Mr. Toad (1949)
Cinderella (1950)
Treasure Island (1950)
Alice in Wonderland (1951)
The Living Desert (1953)
Peter Pan (1953)
20000 Leagues Under the Sea (1954)
Lady and the Tramp (1955)
Sleeping Beauty (1959)
Mary Poppins (1964)

ERNST LUBITSCH (1892–1947)
Gypsy Blood or *Carmen* (1918)
Passion or *Madame Du Barry* (1919)
Rosita (1923)
The Marriage Circle (1924)
Lady Windermere's Fan (1925)
The Love Parade (1929)
Monte Carlo (1930)
Trouble in Paradise (1932)
Design for Living (1933)
The Merry Widow (1934)
Ninotchka (1939)
The Shop Around the Corner (1940)
To Be or Not To Be (1942)
Cluny Brown (1946)

ROUBEN MAMOULIAN (1898–1987)
Applause (1929)
City Streets (1931)

Dr. Jekyll and Mr. Hyde (1932). Completed 1931
Queen Christina (1933)
Becky Sharp (1935)
The Mark of Zorro (1940)
Blood and Sand (1941)
Silk Stockings (1957)

ILLUSTRATIVE TRANSITIONAL FILMS
Love's Old Sweet Song (1924, Lee de Forest)
Don Juan (1926, Alan Crosland)
The Jazz Singer (1927, Alan Crosland)
Sunrise: A Song of Two Humans (1927, F. W. Murnau)
Greeting by George Bernard Shaw, 1928 or *Shaw Talks for Movietone News* (1928, Fox)
Lights of New York (1928, Bryan Foy)
The Sex Life Of The Polyp (1928, Fox)
The Singing Fool (1928, Lloyd Bacon)
Broadway Melody (1929, Harry Beaumont)
The Virginian (1929, Victor Fleming)
The Younger Generation (1929, Frank Capra)
L'Age d'or (1930, Luis Buñuel and Salvador Dalí)
All Quiet on the Western Front (1930, Lewis Milestone)
King of Jazz (1930, John Murray Anderson)
Whoopee! (1930, Thornton Freeland)
Minnie the Moocher (1932, Max and Dave Fleischer). With Betty Boop and Cab Calloway
Scarface (1932, Howard Hawks). Uncensored version completed 1930
Vampyr (1932, Carl Theodor Dreyer)
Duck Soup (1933, Leo McCarey)
Modern Times (1936, Charles Chaplin)

DVDs

L'Age d'or (1930, **Luis Buñuel** and **Salvador Dalí**). Kino Video. **Restored.**
Betty Boop Cartoons. Platinum Disc Corp. Betty in *Minnie the Moocher* and 22 other black-and-white cartoons by **Dave and Max Fleischer.**
The Cocoanuts (1929, Joseph Santley and Robert Florey), starring the Four **Marx Brothers,** is in *The Marx Brothers Silver Screen Collection* (see Chap. 11 list).
Greeting by **George Bernard Shaw** and two Phonofilms by **Lee de Forest** are in *More Treasures from American Film Archives* (see Chap. 3 list).

The Jazz Singer (1927, **Alan Crosland**). Warner Home Video. **Restored.** Includes 3 1/2 hours of Vitaphone musical and comedy shorts, plus documentaries and Jolson shorts.

Modern Times (1936, **Chaplin**). The Chaplin Collection. Warner Home Video and mk2.

Pinocchio (1940, **Disney**). Disney Studios/ Platinum Edition. **Digitally restored.** Other Disney features have been released in this series and others.

Snow White and the Seven Dwarfs (1937, **Disney**). Disney Studios/Platinum Edition. Includes many documentaries, storyboard-to-film comparisons, live-action test footage, **restoration** information, and other extras.

Walt Disney *Treasures: Mickey Mouse in Black and White*. Walt Disney Home Video. Includes *Steamboat Willie, Plane Crazy, Mickey's Service Station*, and 31 other black-and-white Mickey Mouse cartoons.

Walt Disney *Treasures: Mickey Mouse in Living Color*. Walt Disney Home Video. Includes *The Band Concert, Thru the Mirror, Moving Day*, and 25 other color Mickey Mouse cartoons.

Walt Disney *Treasures: Silly Symphonies*. Walt Disney Home Video. Includes *The Skeleton Dance, The Three Little Pigs* (censored), *The Old Mill*, and 38 other cartoons.

10

France between the Wars

The French film in the first decade of sound may have been the most stimulating of its generation: a subtle blend of effective, often poetic dialogue; evocative visual imagery; perceptive social analysis; complex fictional structures; rich philosophical implications; wit and charm. The maturity of the French film in the 1930s was partially the result of the growth of the French film in the 1920s. The final ten years of silent films laid the foundations for the great sound structures that would follow in the next ten. Abel Gance, René Clair, Jean Renoir, Jacques Feyder, Julien Duvivier, and Jean Epstein all conquered purely visual expression before they began combining picture and sound.

Surrealism and Other Movements

Paris of the 1920s was the avant-garde capital of the world in art, literature, music, and drama. It was the city of Picasso and Dalí, of Stravinsky, Milhaud, Poulenc, and Satie, of Proust and Cocteau, and the home away from home of Joyce and the American expatriate writers. Modernism— the urge to experiment, to create new forms, to challenge the established artistic norms in music, painting, sculpture, poetry, fiction, and drama— also dominated the new machine art of the motion picture, which had, after all, begun with Marey, Lumière, Guy, and Méliès as much as with Muybridge, Edison, and Dickson, and which depended on the French invention of photography. Paris was the city of many movements: Surrealism, Cubism, Dadaism. Painters exulted in manipulating pure shapes and colors—often

"ugly" ones, difficult and stimulating, as dissonant as much of 20th-century music. The painting did not need to reproduce external reality— photography could handle that—or honor Renaissance codes of perspective; it could mirror life's moods, tones, hidden structures, and dreams, or depart from "reality" altogether. Time and consciousness were investigated to the point of reinvention, notably by Gertrude Stein, Marcel Proust, and James Joyce. If the world was irrational, art could mirror that irrationality or dispense with the whole job of mirroring and description. All bets were off: Practically anything could be done in a new, modern way. In fact, given the fragmentation of the postwar world—whose ideal aesthetic was montage—the history and resources of art had to be *made* new to become viable and useful.

It was the age when a premiere—like that of Igor Stravinsky's *The Rite of Spring*—could spark a riot or start a movement. Colonies of artists would gather at parties or salons to show each other works they had sculpted, painted, or written—works devoted to form and sensation as well as to unconventional logic and new ways of creating meaning. At these parties some of the artists would show little movies, created on the same formal principles, to their gathered friends. They discovered that of all the arts, the moving picture was capable of the most bizarre tricks with form and time: a series of purely visual images, of shapes, of lights, of double exposures, of dissolves; a series of worlds out of focus, moving too fast or too slow, making their own chronology with cuts that defied ordinary sequence and development.

Ironically, the great experimental leap forward of the French film in the 1920s was also a step into the past, analogous to Ezra Pound's lifelong effort "to gather from the air a live tradition." In 1919, at the dawn of this avant-garde decade, Louis Delluc and Ricciotto Canudo, two zealous film buffs, founded the first of many subsequent French societies for the presentation and preservation of great films of the past. Delluc and Canudo canonized the movies as the Seventh Art and urged attention to the directors of an earlier era: to Méliès, Zecca, Cohl, Linder, Durand, Feuillade. They ignored the theatrical, stagey, Comédie-Françaiseish, Film d'Arty pictures of the decade of the war. This first generation of *cinéastes* urged a return to the wild fantasies of Méliès, to the motion-filled chases of Zecca and Sennett, to the tricks with camera speed and motion of Jean Durand's *Onésime horloger* (1912), in which a special clock makes the world speed up so that Onésime can collect his inheritance "sooner." Like the French *cinéastes* of the 1960s—Godard, Truffaut, Malle—those of the 1920s used film history not only to pack movies with historical echoes and allusions, but also to embellish earlier film ideas with the filmmakers' own distinct and personal extensions of them. The Parisian avant-garde filmmaker of the 1920s used one hand to rip up accepted film conventions and assumptions and the other to pull the traditions of the film past into the movies of the present.

The experimental French films of the 1920s were of three approximate types: (1) films of pure visual form; (2) Surrealistic fantasies in which tricks with time, juxtaposition, transition, and form create a symbolic–dreamlike–irrational universe; (3) Naturalistic studies of passion and sensation in which symbols and surreal touches help to render elusive human feelings. The three types were far from distinct. A movie could begin as an essay in pure form and then change into a surreal dream–fantasy (René Clair's *Entr'acte*, 1924). Sometimes the film would begin as a surreal journey and change into a study of form (Man Ray's *Mysteries of the Chateau Dé*, 1929). Or the film could begin as an impressionistic study of emotions and relationships only to end as a dream (Jean Renoir's *The Little Match Girl*, 1928). Dadaism, Surrealism, and Poetic Naturalism—sometimes called Poetic Realism, especially when it brought out the beauty of the unglamorized

world—flowed into one another to create new compounds in the movies. Germaine Dulac, known primarily as an Impressionist in 1923 (*The Smiling Madame Beudet*), turned to Surrealism for *The Seashell and the Clergyman* (written by Antonin Artaud, inventor of the "theatre of cruelty") in 1927. In 1924, Dulac wrote, "What is more mobile than our psychological life with its reactions, its manifold impressions, its sudden movements, its dreams, its memories? The cinema is marvellously *equipped* to express these manifestations of our thinking." Jean Cocteau's *The Blood of a Poet* (1930) is a personal film poem, not part of any movement.

The films of Man Ray, a photographer and painter born in America, are the purest examples of movie Dada—of a collage of visual shapes and

Fig. 10-1

Fig. 10-2
Man Ray's Return to Reason: *exposing the celluloid to nails (Fig. 10-1) and thumbtacks (Fig. 10-2) directly, without a camera.*

234   A SHORT HISTORY OF THE MOVIES

patterns with no meaning other than the chaos of forms themselves. Ray's films began quite literally as collages: In *Return to Reason* (1923)—an ironic title, since the film rejects reason—he randomly scattered springs, nails, tacks, salt and pepper, and other items over strips of film and then exposed the littered film to light, leaving shadows of the objects imprinted on the celluloid. Ray gradually abandoned such random methods for more controlled essays in form, such as *Emak-Bakia* (1927), in which visual similarities and differences of form control Ray's choice of images. Fernand Léger's Cubist *Ballet mécanique* (1924) and Marcel Duchamp's comic jest of spinning spirals, puns, rhymes, and invented words, *Anémic cinéma* (1926), also begin with the premise of using a succession of images related in form, shape, and rhythm.

The most famous of the Surrealist films is the Salvador Dalí–Luis Buñuel fantasy, *Un Chien andalou* (1929). Like the title (*An Andalusian Dog*), the film is a series of non sequiturs, scenes that only seem to be related logically; its "logic" is that of a dream. The film teasingly suggests thematic and narrative unities amid rampant discontinuity; whatever rules it has, it makes up. Its action consistently arises from the sexual desires, tensions, and confrontations surrounding one woman. Much as in their 1930 sound film, *L'Age d'or*, Buñuel and Dalí seem to contrast sexual desire and social convention. (They worked together as writers on both films, but Buñuel did most of the directing, and on *L'Age d'or* he may even have done all of it.) *Un Chien andalou* is a series of daring vignettes juxtaposed irrationally, as in the leaps of a dream, to amuse, shake up,

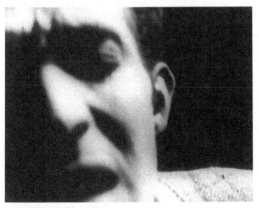

Fig. 10-3

Fig. 10-4

Fig. 10-5

Fig. 10-6

The dream-space of Un Chien andalou. *Four consecutive shots: the man falls, indoors (Fig. 10-3), to slither against the torso of an outdoor nude (Figs. 10-4, 10-5), who evaporates (Fig. 10-6).*

and even attack the viewer. From the opening sequence in which Buñuel slits an eyeball with a razor in gruesome close-up (the film's continuity suggests the eye belongs to the woman, but if you look closely—rather than away, as your organ of vision is assaulted—you can see animal hair around it) to the final one in which a man and woman are inexplicably buried in the wasteland/sand of a rocky beach, the film's goal is to excite, to shock, to surprise, to make us "see" differently rather than to preach or explain. The French writer Lautréamont defined Surrealism as the fortuitous meeting of a type-writer and an umbrella on an operating table. *Un Chien andalou* is one of cinema's most powerful demonstrations of Surrealist juxtaposition.

On the other hand, Jean Epstein's *The Fall of the House of Usher* (1928) uses gentler dream effects to create the atmosphere for his relatively lucid Poe plot. Epstein uses the tools of cinematic Impressionism—slow-motion effects; out-of-focus lenses; multiple exposure; contrasts of light and shadow; distortion; cavernous, dreamworld sets—as a means of turning the House of Usher into a house of visual music. The films of Germaine Dulac and of Marcel L'Herbier (*The Late Mathias Pascal*, 1926) use, among other devices, slow motion, distortion, and soft focus subjectively to illuminate almost inaccessible mental and emotional states.

Even the Naturalistic psychological studies of human interaction try to probe beneath familiar surfaces to reveal irrational, chaotic passions, often using the devices of the Surrealists to illuminate this subjective world. Alberto Calvalcanti's *Rien que les heures* (1926), on the surface a documentary study of 24 hours of Paris life, relies on avant-garde juxtapositions and special effects to paint the city's moody picture, including freeze-frames, double exposures, split-screen effects, matte shots, and obtrusive wipes. Louis Delluc's *Fièvre* (1921), a tense story of desire and death in a seamy waterfront saloon, weaves images of gliding ships and a symbolic rose into its tapestry of Naturalistic human conflict in the café. A less Naturalistic example of Poetic Realism, Jean Vigo's *L'Atalante*, is discussed later in this chapter.

Dimitri Kirsanov's *Ménilmontant* (1925), a half-hour narrative film without any intertitles, uses quick cutting, unique images that visualize thought and feeling, and the sordid atmosphere of Paris slums to tell its story of two sisters from

Fig. 10-7
Nadia Sibirskaïa in Ménilmontant.

the country whose parents are killed by an ax murderer in the opening montage; later, as adults in the city, they are sexually betrayed by the same man. Even with its Naturalistic elements, it is committed to showing the beauty in reality. In the original release version, the sisters are reconciled, raise the younger sister's baby together, and restore a sense of home violated at the film's merciless, brutal start. The version most often seen today, which Kirsanov donated to the Museum of Modern Art, ends shortly after the murder of the false-hearted lover with a return to the banal, repetitive world of work; the continuity in this later version is harder to follow, either because it is missing scenes or because Kirsanov recut it to make it less rounded and reassuring. As rapid and violent as *Ménilmontant* often is—in either version—it slows down to present the monotony of ordinary life; its control of the pace of scenes and the passage of time is complete. *Ménilmontant* is as insightful, stirring, and beautiful as the French cinema gets, and a good introduction in itself to the art of silent film.

Gance and Dreyer

Abel Gance was French; Carl Dreyer, who made films all over Europe, was Danish. They were among the greatest filmmakers of any country or period, and they suffered rejection, unemployment, and incomprehension throughout their careers. The more they awakened the cinema to a new day, the more the film business hit the snooze button.

Abel Gance

The most important commercial director of the decade, whose Promethean ambitions led many a bureaucrat to feast on his liver and whose vast energy pushed his films beyond the limits of commerce and convention, Abel Gance applied an experimental, almost avant-garde concern with visual forms, tricks, and devices to the narrative feature. This should not be surprising, since his 1915 short, *The Folly of Dr. Tube,* used distorting mirrors to convey distorted perception and may well have been the first "experimental" film. His *J'accuse* (*I Accuse*, 1919) and *La Roue* (*The Wheel*, 1922) explored war and tragedy, respectively, in the context of intimate, passionate, grand melodramas. *J'accuse*, which took its title from Émile Zola's 1898 article in defense of Alfred Dreyfus, let the ghosts of the soldiers

Fig. 10-8

Speaking with their bodies, soldiers of the First World War spell out "J'accuse," the title of Gance's 1919 film and an accusation against the masters of war.

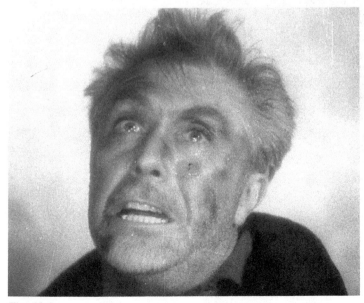

Fig. 10-9

The hero of Gance's 1937 J'accuse (played by Victor Francen) calls up the spirits of the soldiers of all nations, hoping to stop another war.

of World War I ("the war to end all wars") return. Shot in 1918 with soldiers on temporary leave from the front, who expected—in most cases, correctly—to be killed within the month, so that they knew they were playing their own ghosts and trusted Gance to carry their message into a future they would not see but urgently demanded to affect, *J'accuse* was the greatest antiwar film yet made. In 1937, Gance remade the film, hoping to stop the Second World War by re-evoking the horrors and lessons of the First. Another masterpiece, the second *J'accuse* did not halt the coming conflict but remains a gesture of immense belief in the power of the cinema.

Of *La Roue*, a roughly seven-hour movie (shown on three successive nights at first, then cut for wider exhibition) that was released in the pivotal year that *Ulysses* and "The Waste Land"

were published (1922), Jean Cocteau observed that "There is the cinema before and after *La Roue* as there is painting before and after Picasso." A tragic story of the wheel of fate (a crushing wheel that doubles as a rack), told with the romantic energy of a Victor Hugo and the melodramatic impact of a Euripides, this compelling and realistic picture (shot on location in a trainyard near Nice and on Mont Blanc) brought its first audience to a standing ovation—no matter how long it was, they refused to leave until the final reel had been shown again—and decisively influenced the Soviets. Its rapid cutting—some of its shots only one frame long—came to be called "Russian cutting" once *La Roue* had, like Gance, been forgotten. Gance resembled Griffith in many ways, not the least of which is that neither could find work in the conservative

Fig. 10-10
La Roue: *Séverin-Mars as Sisif, the tragic "Man of the Wheel."*

Studio Era, though each had, through his vision of what the cinema could be, brought the art to the peak of its powers. When they met in 1921 (immediately after the editing of *La Roue*), Gance and Griffith congratulated each other for having independently discovered the possibilities of the close-up, the dolly shot, and rhythmic editing. Each made films that were inseparably melodramatic and political, and each put much of himself into his typical romantic hero: for Griffith, the caring man who finds himself in right action, and for Gance, the inventor–genius who wants to change the world.

Although Griffith was virtually unemployed from *The Struggle* to his death, and Gance was kept from making films for periods as long as 12 years, Gance did make one great silent after *La Roue* (*Napoleon seen by Abel Gance*, 1927) and at least two important sound films in addition to the 1937 *J'accuse*. His abridged version of *Napoleon* (*Napoleon seen and heard by Abel Gance*, 1935) introduced stereophonic sound—which he had patented in 1929—and *Un Grand amour de Beethoven* (*A Great Love of Beethoven*, 1936) used sound and silence to convey what it meant for a composer to go deaf; in *Beethoven*, of necessity, images became music.

Like *The Birth of a Nation*, the 1927 *Napoleon* (which originally ran nine hours—42 reels at 20 fps, polished by Gance to 29 reels—about 6 1/2 hours—and premiered at 17 reels in a special short version) used individuals to explore the history of an entire nation in a period of political instability and crisis. Unlike Griffith's concentration on a group of ordinary citizens, Gance's is on Napoleon, the idealized leader, the mythic man of destiny who pulls a divided nation out of the ideological chaos of the French Revolution. Some critics have found *Napoleon* either naïvely worshipful of a heroic leader or implicitly fascist. But one must note the stern warning delivered near the end of the film by ghosts of the leaders of the Reign of Terror (a key to Gance's plans), that Napoleon will fall if he betrays the original goals of the Revolution. Because of a lack of funding, Gance was prevented from showing Napoleon's tragic development and fall in subsequent films (*Napoleon* closes with the Italian campaign, well before the general became the emperor). The energy of *Napoleon* is, like that of *La Roue*, the energy of an idealized cinema: a grand, vaulting belief in what unhindered genius can accomplish. The hero of *Napoleon* is Gance.

Among the many breakthroughs of *Napoleon* was its use of multiple imagery, for which Gance's general term was polyvision. Polyvision referred to superimposition (as many as 16 images laid on top of one another), the split screen (as many as nine distinct images in a frame), and the multiple screen (the triptych—used three times in *Napoleon*, although two of them have been lost—whereby three cameras and projectors and screens could create a single wide-screen image with an aspect ratio of almost 4:1, or three separate, side-by-side images that reinforced, reversed, or played against each other in counterpoint). With polyvision and rapid cutting, Gance became the master of montage in France. The triptych, which was later reinvented as Cinerama, was an invention whose inventor was conveniently forgotten. The final reel of *Napoleon* was also shot in 3-D and again in color, though Gance disliked the results and decided to release the surviving triptych instead.

Most of Gance's films were lost or ruined over time, but restoration efforts are under way. In 15 years of work, stitching together fragments of abridged and mutilated versions, British film historian Kevin Brownlow restored *Napoleon* to more than six hours; in 1975, he was joined in the effort by Robert A. Harris, who produced the final restored version, which was premiered at the 1979 Telluride Film Festival in Colorado with Gance in attendance. In 1980, Francis Ford Coppola lent his clout—and his father's music—to the project, and Harris and Coppola premiered a four-hour, sound-speed version of *Napoleon*, tinted and toned according to the original instructions, in 1981 at Radio City Music Hall in New York. (The six-hour version, with music by Carl Davis, continues to play at 20 fps at festivals and archives in Europe.) Seeing a revival of *Napoleon*, projected from a sparkling 35mm print in a huge movie palace, supported by a live symphony orchestra and giant Wurlitzer organ, reveals not merely the grandeur of this single film but the potential magic and beauty of any properly presented "silent" epic.

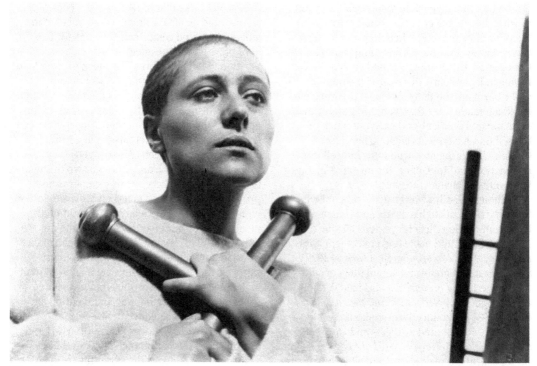

Fig. 10-11

Fig. 10-12

Fig. 10-13

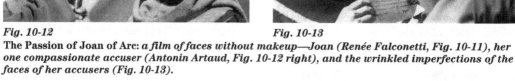

The Passion of Joan of Arc: *a film of faces without makeup—Joan (Renée Falconetti, Fig. 10-11), her one compassionate accuser (Antonin Artaud, Fig. 10-12 right), and the wrinkled imperfections of the faces of her accusers (Fig. 10-13).*

The Passion of Joan of Arc

For many, the culminating film of the 1920s in France was Carl Theodor Dreyer's *The Passion of Joan of Arc* (1928; shot 1927). Despite its Danish director and German art director

(Hermann Warm, the principal designer of *The Cabinet of Dr. Caligari*), the film's aesthetics and effects are also consistent with the French. Narratively, the film condenses Joan's long trial and eventual execution into a single day, but the trial feels both endless and, in the transcendental sense, timeless. For emotional continuity, it was shot in sequence.

The details of Joan's trial are precise and intense; the enormity of her suffering, her sorrow, her spiritual fire are clear. The film examines Joan the immense emotional being rather than Joan the militant, or even Joan the religious iconoclast. The sainthood of Dreyer's Joan (played by Renée Falconetti) can be seen on her face and exists within her; it is in her faith and her intense ability to feel and suffer and glow. Dreyer's Joan contrasts strikingly with Shaw's, although the film uses some of the same dialogue as Shaw's *Saint Joan* (because both Shaw and Dreyer consulted the same historical documents, in which there was renewed public interest and to which there was greater public access after the Church canonized Joan in 1920). In Shaw's play, Joan's comments are witty, intelligent, and shrewd; Dreyer's Joan, with her glowing face and visionary eyes, keeps her answers short and operates primarily on a level beyond verbal expression. Dreyer's film presents and transcends the tale of the trial and death of Joan in the same way that Bach's *The Passion According to St. Matthew* relates, dramatizes, and goes beyond Matthew's account of the martyrdom of Christ.

To create a feature film of almost musical sensations and ritual power, Dreyer fills the frame with faces and seeks out each one's essence. Rudolf Maté's camera travels ceaselessly over the faces of the judges and Joan—or holds on one. The bare white walls of the set make the richly textured human features and make-up–free skin leap out at the viewer. Warm's decor gives the film the flavor of medieval starkness *and* the texture of modern design and abstract painting with its sharp, clean lines.

If the interiors are a kind of *Kammerspielfilm*, the exteriors—where onlookers and soldiers wait, a gravedigger shovels up a skull, contortionists perform, and Joan's execution leads to a riot—are like an action movie from Hell, realistic and disturbing and (like the entire film) stylized not on the surface but somehow from within. Dreyer's stark eye and his compassion are at work throughout the film, even at its most violent.

For many critics, *The Passion of Joan of Arc* was the ultimate silent film, the ultimate example of the power of purely visual expression. In fact,

it was planned as a talkie but shot silent because of the lack of equipment; that turned out to be a good thing. In its silence, *Joan* is one of the most expressive pictures ever made. In comparison with its pictorial rigor, its artistic wholeness, its intellectual and emotional maturity, most pictures—particularly the silly, static talking pictures that were already playing at competing theatres—were ludicrous.

But even *Joan* contained its own limitations. Printed intertitles—the necessary evil of the silent film—became uncomfortably intrusive here. Just as there is something anomalous in this Joan's uttering any words at all, there is something anomalous in interrupting the rush of compelling and brilliantly composed images and the passionate conflict of faces to flash words on the screen. The intertitles disrupt the rhythm and the pictorial unity of *The Passion of Joan of Arc* just as obviously as sound disrupted the pictorial imagination of early talkies. To sustain an unbroken flow of visual images, the film needed sound rather than printed words to perform vital narrative functions. *Joan of Arc* needed a nondisruptive means of showing us what those compelling faces were saying.

Dreyer went on to make four of the greatest and most demanding of all sound films, in which people still didn't talk very much, and which continued his examination of the conflict between the earthly, mortal, and material, and the mystical, spiritual, and eternal: *Vampyr* (1932), *Day of Wrath* (1943), *Ordet* (1954, released 1955), and *Gertrud* (1964).

René Clair

René Clair mastered the purely visual cinema, the painting-in-motion of the 1920s, before he began to address both eye and ear in the 1930s. Clair began as cinematic trickster, a choreographer of irrational film ballets; later he used his tricks to turn the realistic and rational world into a place of fantasy and song. Clair looked back admiringly at the zany, frenetic worlds of Sennett, Zecca, and Durand, and that looking backward allowed his own kind of zany frenzy to move forward. Despite Clair's historical influences, despite his maturing as an artist, despite the new adjustments that the talking machines forced him to make, a René Clair movie—silent or sound—is unmistakably his own. The clearest Clair traits are his delight in physical movement and his comic fancy, which converts two things that are obviously different into things that are surprisingly the same: a funeral becomes a wedding party; a prison is a factory, and a factory is a prison. Clair's dissolving of differences into similarities is designed as much for imaginative fun as for social commentary. Clair's best silent films, *Entr'acte* (1924) and *The Italian Straw Hat* (1927), and his best sound films, *Le Million* (1931) and *À nous la liberté* (1931), are those in which his flights of visual fancy drop the most explosive intellectual bombs on his two favorite targets—social convention and money.

Clair's first two silents contained the seeds of everything that would grow afterward. *Paris qui dort* (*The Crazy Ray* or *Paris Asleep*, 1923) is a fantasy, the story of a scientist whose ray has put the populace of the world to sleep, paralyzed (in effect, by the cinema) in the midst of their activities. Only a handful of Parisians avoid the professor's sleep ray: those who were above the beams of his machine on the top of the Eiffel Tower or in an airplane. Many of the effects were achieved on an optical printer.

Clair's second film, *Entr'acte*, less satirical, less logical, and far more daring than his first, was made specifically as the intermission piece, the *entr'acte*, for a performance of the Ballets Suedois in Paris. The film is pure romp, the whimsical, choreographic Clair who does not stop at satirizing the social order but brings down order itself. The film begins with a series of Dadaist non sequiturs: two men playing checkers on a high building, two others hunting birds on skyscrapers, a ball dancing on jets of water, a ballerina (shot from underneath) whose billowing skirt spreads and shuts like the petals of a flower. Then the two checker players see the Place de la Concorde materialize on their checkerboard; the dancing ball dangles inexplicably in midair, defying gravity, after the water jets have been turned off; the ballerina turns out to be a bearded man.

In the second half of the film, society gathers for a funeral. But the mourners dress in white and they throw rice at the hearse. When the hearse starts running away by itself, the mourners rush after it. Clair uses fast motion, slow motion, traveling shots, freeze frames, and interpolated cuts of racing cars and roller coasters to energize the chase. Eventually the coffin falls off the hearse, and the corpse rises from the box and blithely makes everyone disappear. A man leaps through the screen that dares to say "The End."

Clair's silent feature *The Italian Straw Hat*, set in 1895, takes its visual style from the era of the pre-Griffith French "primitives," from the decor of the Zecca and Linder films. A young bridegroom's horse eats a young lady's straw hat as the groom drives to meet his bride. Since the young lady lost her hat while enjoying an extramarital afternoon with a beau, she must replace the rare hat to allay her husband's suspicions. The young groom, who looks suspiciously like Max Linder, must juggle his wedding party with his comically frantic attempts to replace the hat.

In his first sound film, *Sous les toits de Paris* (*Under the Roofs of Paris*, 1930), Clair—always the choreographer—discovered the effectiveness of using music as a leitmotif and as a means of creating the film's fantasylike breezy spirit. Music became the perfect unrealistic accompaniment for the balletic Clair fantasy world.

Le Million is an even more interesting mixture of movement, sound, and music. It revolves about two favorite Clair motifs—money and the chase. A poor artist discovers that he has won a million francs in the lottery; unfortunately, the lottery ticket is in the pocket of a coat that has been stolen by a fleeing thief. The film becomes a furious chase after the jacket. When the artist finally finds his coat at the Opera, he grabs it, only to find that the tenor insists on using the old coat as part of his pauper's costume. The artist, the tenor, and the police engage in a mock-heroic struggle for the jacket. Clair adds crowd noises, officials' whistles, and cheering to the soundtrack while the men play keepaway in the Opera's corridor. The coat has become a football, the struggle a game.

Clair's next film, *À nous la liberté* (*Liberty For Us*), was to be his last masterpiece. Clair again combines his comic and musical inventiveness with thematic wholeness and seriousness. Two convicts try to break out of prison, though only one of them gets away. The successful escapee steals some money, works his way up in the record business, and builds a huge factory to manufacture phonographs; the other, his friend in prison, becomes a worker in that factory. The tycoon eventually discovers that the life of a "respectable" factory owner, with its rules, its social obligations, its emotional infidelities, its devotion to money and machines, is no different from the life of a prisoner. Neither plutocrat nor prisoner is truly free. The film ends as the capitalist and the worker turn their backs on the factory to head off down the road, two tramps, finally free of restraint and convention.

Uniting the film is its consistent examination of the term *liberty*. For Clair, society and freedom are incompatible. Everyone attached to the factory—Clair's microcosm for society—is a prisoner of his or her role in the system: owner, member of the board, worker, foreman, secretary. The film's brilliance lies in the translation of this Marxist–humanist cliché into imaginative images. The two central characters, one tall and fat, the other short and skinny, are spirits from the world of silent comedy, reminiscent of Fatty and Charlie, of Laurel and Hardy. Their ultimate choice of vocation—tramp—also echoes the asocial yet human choice that Charlie so often makes. If Clair's tramps seem indebted to Charlot, Chaplin later collected the debt by borrowing one of *À nous la liberté*'s assembly-line scenes for *Modern Times* (1936). Clair's little prisoner sits in his place on the monotonous assembly line. As the unfinished machines roll down the conveyor belt, he fails to put his particular screw into the destined hole. He scampers down the line following the machine, trying to remedy his error. The assembly line quickly becomes a chaotic heap of unfinished machines and brawling workers. Clair's assembly-line chaos is a perfect way of showing inhuman enslavement to the machines that humans have built.

Clair's consistent technique for illuminating the lack of liberty is to set up visual parallels. The film opens with shots of men in prison, manufacturing little toy horses as they sit in rows on the prison's assembly line; they eat their meals as they sit in rows in the prison's dining room. Later, Clair shows the factory workers sitting in the same rows as the men in prison, eating in almost the same formations as the men in the prison mess hall. Factory and prison are visually identical. Prison uniforms have become factory uniforms; prison guards have become factory foremen.

Clair's choice of a phonograph factory is itself a part of the film's metaphorical wholeness: The factory turns music into a mechanical artifact and a commodity. Even music lacks liberty in this society. Reflexive as ever, Clair implies that the sound film will have to become a place where sound and music are free to play.

The film hits its visual and thematic climax in the wild scene in which the social elite gather to honor the great factory owner who has created this phonographic empire and is about to automate it. The ceremony begins with perfect formality: the guests wearing top hats and tails, the orators sitting stiffly on the rostrum, the workers standing in formation listening to the boring, droning speeches. Suddenly a wind sweeps through the factory courtyard. It blows the top hats all over the courtyard; it scatters the factory's profits—paper money—all over the ground. The liberating wind turns the factory into a swarming mass of chaotic free activity. In the most Sennett-like manner, the dignitaries abandon their dignity to chase their hats and the blowing bills all over the courtyard in frenzied, choreographed patterns.

After this climax, a peaceful coda shows the effect of this whistling wind of freedom. The factory's workers are shown at play, then singing while fishing and dancing; the now totally automated factory produces phonographs by itself. In Clair's idyll, the people are free to be human, leaving the machines to make the machines. They have been freed from the assembly line, and the two old friends have become tramps who are happily on the road and staying out of jail.

After two less important films in France, Clair made his first English-language film, *The Ghost Goes West* (1935), a fantasy about a social-climbing American who buys a Scottish castle and transports it, block by block, complete with ghost, back to Florida. During the war years, Clair stayed in Hollywood where he made more fantasies (notably *I Married a Witch*, 1942, and his personal favorite, *It Happened Tomorrow*, 1944) and the ingenious mystery *And Then There Were None* (1945). When Clair returned to France after the war, his wit was gentler, the whimsy thicker, the decor lusher. Later Clair films never matched the combination of exuberance, style, cinematic control, structural parallel, and thematic consistency of *Le Million* and *À nous la liberté*.

Fig. 10-14

À nous la liberté: *Clair's visual parallels—the prison as assembly line (Fig. 10-14), the assembly line as prison (Fig. 10-15).*

Fig. 10-15

Jean Renoir

Like René Clair, Jean Renoir—son of the Impressionist painter Pierre Auguste Renoir—started making films in the 1920s and reached the peak of his powers in the 1930s. Like Clair, Renoir was a social satirist. But there the similarities stop. Renoir's satire was bitter and melancholy, whereas Clair's was ebullient and whimsical. Clair's satire condemned institutions

and praised the human spirit; Renoir's satire declared hollow institutions to be the inevitable products of flawed, erroneous humans. If Clair let his films go crazy once in a while, Renoir kept his tightly structured even when they lightened up. Like Clair, Renoir saw that the claims of nature and civilization were antithetical; unlike Clair, Renoir never resolved the dilemma by simplistically espousing one of the two alternatives because Renoir realized both the attractiveness of nature that seems so innocent and the need for civilization that seems so complicated.

Renoir emphasizes the inseparable connection of civilization and nature with a favorite setup, shooting from indoors through windows and doorways that frame the outdoors with their architectural presence. His visual signature, composition in depth, allows the *mise-en-scène* to make its own statements; foreground and background figures, civilization and nature, upper and lower classes, winners and losers—all are included in Renoir's complex comedies of manners. If Clair's roots were in ballet and in song, Renoir's were in painting and ceramics, in the sensitivity to light and shadow, form and texture.

The Renoir silents are darker, slower, more brooding than Clair's. In his fifth movie, *The Little Match Girl* (1928), Renoir adapts Andersen's fairy tale of the little match seller who dreams of toyland and perishes in the snow. The film is suffused with the heavy atmosphere of death. The opening sections, Renoir's depiction of reality in the cold, snowy city, paint the world with exaggerated harshness, with extreme blacks and whites—glaring lamps, black silhouettes, grotesque shadows—so that the real world becomes surreal; the visual contrasts of dark and light are that intense.

In the second sequence, the girl's dream, Renoir is free to play with multiple exposures, irrational sequences of images, blurred focus. Even in the toy-shop window the atmosphere is dark. The shapes of this toy world are jagged and sharp; the lighting is tonal and moody. The toys threaten her—soldiers in formation, an aggressive ball, the ominous jack-in-the-box who becomes the pursuing figure of death.

In the final section of the film, the girl and her soldier–protector flee from their black pursuer. Their flight through the clouds becomes a horrifying, nightmare chase that ends with the girl's dream death in an Impressionistic cemetery. The petals of flowers descend onto her dying body; then the petals of the dream dissolve into the snowflakes of reality. The little match girl lies frozen, buried under a mound of snow. Only a few scattered boxes of matches reveal that she once existed.

Although later Renoir films became less fantastic, the effects of tonal lighting, the overhanging mood of death, the complexity of his irony, and the sadness underlying the superficial gaiety were all constants. But Renoir's world was, even so, not utterly bitter and dark. It was characterized just as much by its vast, humanistic acceptance of life, an acceptance based on a rich understanding of the world, whose ironies, contradictions, satisfactions, and failures he observed with what can only be called wisdom. His best films are among the great contributions to world culture, and their profundity deepens with every viewing.

Throughout the 1930s Renoir's films threw a cold, hard light on the crumbling social and political structures of Europe. An effete aristocracy was gradually sinking under the weight of its own artificial conventions, and the new rising classes were barrenly following in the steps of their former masters. The 1930s, in France as well as in America, had become the age of the scenarist, and Renoir's screenplays (which he wrote in collaboration with other writers) novelistically emphasized parallel structures, parallel characters, parallel details. The attention to visual and intellectual parallels gave the Renoir film the rich complexity of the novel. But the literary structures of the films were enhanced by Renoir's sensitivity to the visual: Shots of nature, of faces, of social groupings in deep space visually generate the film's meaning and control its tone. *La Chienne* (1931), a comedy of betrayal and survival that in Fritz Lang's hands became the fatalistic *Scarlet Street* (1945); *Boudu Saved from Drowning* (1932), an exuberantly comic clash between a tramp, a rough man of nature, and the stifling conventions of polite, bourgeois society; *Toni* (1935), a sensitively tragic clash between the passions of love and restrictive societal codes—and a crucial precursor of Neorealism; *The Crime of Monsieur Lange* (1936), a comedy about a publishing house that becomes a successful co-op, almost a communist utopia, after the boss leaves; *La Marseillaise* (1938), a historical study of the French Revolution, made for the French Popular Front, which reveals its leftist sympathies by its focus on the common foot soldiers; and an adaptation of Gorky's *The Lower Depths* (1936), which attracted Renoir with its bitter microcosmic study of society—all show the director warming up for his greatest films at the end of the decade.

Grand Illusion

Grand Illusion (1937) is also a microcosmic study. Its superficial action is the story of two French soldiers who eventually escape from a German prisoner-of-war camp during World War I—and one who does not. Its real action is metaphor: the death of the old ruling class of the European aristocracy and the growth of the new ruling classes of the workers and bourgeoisie. The prisoner-of-war camp is a microcosm of European society. The prison contains French and Russian and English, professors and actors and mechanics and bankers, Christians and Jews, nobility and capital and labor.

At the top of the social hierarchy are the German commander, Rauffenstein (played by Erich von Stroheim, the director whose films most influenced Renoir's), and the French captain, Boeldieu (played by Pierre Fresnay). Though the two men fight on opposite sides, they are ideologically identical: They both use a monocle; they both wear white gloves; they both share the same prejudices and snobberies, the same educated tastes in wine, food, and horses. They are united by class more than they are divided by country. The supreme irony of the film is that the German commander must kill this man to whom he feels most closely allied because the rules of the war game demand that the commanding officer of the prison shoot men trying to escape, just as they demand that the prisoner (gentleman or not) attempt to escape. The two men are inflexibly, tragically responsible to their codes, their rules, and their duties. United as members of the cultured international elite, divided as prisoner and warden, they both transcend boundaries and acknowledge them in a paradox of roles whose only constant is honor. They are part of a dying breed that, like the old Europe, would not survive the war.

The two tougher, hardier prisoners do escape, while Boeldieu, attired in his white gloves, smartly covers for them and gives up his life in gentlemanly sacrifice. Maréchal (played by Jean Gabin), a mechanic, and Rosenthal (played by Marcel Dalio), a Rothschildean Jew whose family owns banks, land, and several chateaux, escape together from the German prison. The animosities, the tensions, the prejudices of the two men surface as the going gets rough, but the two finally make it to Switzerland—and they make it

together. Overcoming their own set of social boundaries, they are the new Europe.

Grand Illusion opens on a gramophone horn: The machine plays "Frou-Frou," a popular French song; we are in the French camp. A few minutes later, the camera captures a second gramophone horn; the machine plays a Strauss waltz; we are in the German camp. The songs have changed; the camps are the same. Most indicative of the film's control of tone is the drag-show sequence in which the prisoners entertain each other by putting on a show, a French revue that includes a number performed by British prisoners dressed and made up as cancan girls. Just before the show, the French prisoners receive word that the German army has captured the French town of Douaumont. Despite their sadness, the show must go on—to show their *esprit*. In the middle of the drag show, the French receive word that the Allies have recaptured Douaumont. Maréchal makes the announcement; the cancan boys stop dancing and remove their wigs. Led by one of the British dancers, everyone sings the "Marseillaise." Renoir's shots of these rouged, lipsticked men singing the patriotic anthem are simultaneously stirring and tawdry, transcendent and transvestite.

Music is used to create leitmotifs. The trifle "Frou-Frou" recurs several times. When the captured French prisoners first hear a German military band, united by the rhythmic tramping of marching feet and the soaring descant of piping fifes, Boeldieu remarks, "I hate fifes." Another unifying musical motif is "Il était un petit navire," which we hear played for the first time by Boeldieu on a little toy fife as a ruse to help Maréchal and Rosenthal escape; the tune diverts Rauffenstein's attention but leads to the death of the man who hated fifes. Later, on the icy road, when the crippled Rosenthal and the impatient Maréchal quarrel and threaten to separate, Rosenthal starts singing "Il était un petit navire" in defiance and anger. As Maréchal stalks away from his lame comrade, he starts to sing the same song. The song ultimately brings Maréchal back to his slower comrade; he will not desert him again.

Consistent visual imagery is another source of the film's unity. Renoir's camera contrasts things that are hard, cold, and dead with things that are soft, warm, and vital. The final

Fig. 10-16

Fig. 10-17

Grand Illusion. *Fig. 10-16: the coldness of stone and metal; Rauffenstein (von Stroheim), Boeldieu (Pierre Fresnay), and Maréchal (Jean Gabin) in the German fortress. Fig. 10-17: Maréchal finds warmth on the little farm; a farm instead of a prison, straw instead of stone, loose clothing instead of uniforms, farming tools instead of rifles.*

sequences take place during the winter; the consistent pictures of snow and frozen ground throw their cold, damp shadow over the entire film. The two escaped prisoners must struggle across an immense meadow of snow to reach safety in Switzerland. But the Swiss border is invisible. It is impossible to distinguish different nations beneath a common blanket of snow. Only the German officer's announcement that the two have made it—to freedom, in one of Renoir's characteristically open endings—informs us where the snow of Germany ends and the snow of Switzerland begins. That one can make such

nationalistic distinctions is one of the film's grand illusions—as a breeder of war, perhaps the most destructive and coldly heartless.

Equally cold is the bare, stony castle that keeps the prisoners captive. And unforgettable is the piece of iron that replaces Rauffenstein's chin; it supports his face since his real chin has been shot away. The rigid, inflexible Rauffenstein himself is literally held together by metal—in the chin, the back, the knee—the embodiment of the film's contrast of the vital and the dead. The one soft thing in the prison castle is Rauffenstein's little geranium (a prop—and an insight into the man's character—contributed by the film's art director, Eugène Lourié), which he carefully nurtures. When Boeldieu dies, Rauffenstein lops off the single blossom; he knows that his world is dead. Emphatically warm and vital are the woman and child, Elsa and Lotte, that Maréchal and Rosenthal encounter on their flight. Elsa's warmth touches Maréchal, and he vows to return to her after the war is over. But he tells her in French, a language she cannot understand.

It is, of course, another sign of Renoir's brilliance that he has built this dialogue film around the ironies of language (the soundtrack is crowded with French, German, and English; the most educated, upper-class characters speak them all with equal facility), languages that separate people or bind them together as effectively as national boundaries. Indeed, language differences are national differences. So in this film that is full of disastrous political illusions, it is difficult to determine which is the "grand" one. That war is noble? That old social and political ideals remain viable? That national boundaries exist? That national boundaries do not exist?

Grand Illusion shows how, with the Great War, the aristocracy of Europe committed elegant suicide. To turn life into a cold, murderous game with a series of artificial rules is ultimately to turn life into death. But how can a class that has lived according to certain codes and manners for centuries suddenly change to fit the new bourgeois and proletarian times? Rauffenstein and Boeldieu are admirable for their taste, their elegance, their integrity, and their honor. Is it their fault that they have been condemned by history to live in a century that barely understands those virtues? As Renoir would put the problem in his last film of the decade, "Everyone has his reasons."

The Rules of the Game

These ironies and paradoxes become the central issues of that last 1930s film, perhaps Renoir's greatest, *The Rules of the Game* (*La Règle du jeu;* shot, released, censored, and banned in 1939; restored in 1956). The film uses sex rather than war to provoke a crisis of values in a dying society—two mutually dependent societies, in fact: the society of wealthy masters and the society of genteel servants. Both masters and servants value good form over sincerity and the

open expression of emotion; both are equally aware of class distinctions. The rabbit hunt is one of the key sequences that shows how death is the price—paid by nature, innocence, and the innocent—for the masters' dying way of life. But as in *Grand Illusion*, the dancers in this dance of death try to balance the demands of social form with the demands of human spontaneity. Like the aristocrats of *Grand Illusion*, they find that the conflicting demands are ultimately, and unfortunately, mutually exclusive and unbalanceable.

Renoir's complex structural parallels play several love stories against each other. In the main plot, a romantic aviator, André Jurieux, petulantly confesses his love for a stylish, upper-class married lady, Christine de la Chesnaye. Although the rules of the game do not prohibit adultery, they do condemn such frank, impulsive, sincere expressions of it. In a subplot, the lady's maid begins her own adulterous dabbling with a new servant, Marceau: a poacher, an outsider (like André), not a genteel (if excitable) servant like her own husband, Schumacher. Other subplots concern Christine's husband's attempts to break off a boring love affair and André's best friend's discovery that he, Octave (played by Renoir), loves Christine. The love plots cross paths, as in a dance with changing partners or a wildly complicated bedroom farce. The maid's jealous husband, who also has problems observing the rules of the game, mistakenly shoots the aviator, thinking that André is really Octave, that Octave has become his wife's new lover (he has not), and that the woman wearing his wife's coat is his wife (it is Christine). The romantic aviator dies, and the game of lies goes on, but both represent codes that are dying out. The Marquis de la Chesnaye, Christine's husband (played by Marcel Dalio), formally announces to his guests that André has met with a "regrettable accident"; the group admires and accepts the baron's lie as a gentlemanly display of good form.

Renoir's sense of style and imagery again sustain the film. Its most memorable visual sequence is the rabbit hunt, a metaphor for the society's murderous conventionality and insensitivity. The wealthy masters go off to shoot rabbits; this hunt, like the lives of the rich, has its etiquette, its rules, its gentility. It is a civilized form of killing. The servants also serve as accomplices in the murder, for their job is to beat the

Fig. 10-18
The Rules of the Game: *the perfect orderliness of conventionalized murder—the aristocrats at the hunt.*

trees and bushes, driving the pheasants and rabbits out of cover and into the open where they can be gunned down. Servants and masters are partners in this murderous game. Renoir fills the screen for five minutes with an agonized ballet of helpless, dying animals: They run across the screen accompanied by the bushy scamper of their little feet on the soundtrack; we hear a shotgun, and the furry animal stops, flips, spins, and stretches out to die. The sickening, horrifying beauty of this dance of death is at the heart of the film's meaning and tone. The whole film is a dance of death. Skeletons dance on stage at the marquis' evening party, and men shoot real bullets at one another in the audience. When André, in some ways as natural, impulsive, innocent, and naïve as an animal, is killed with a shotgun, the victim of another murderous, elegant game, he rolls over and dies "like a rabbit."

One of the film's key visual metaphors is the marquis' collection of mechanical toys—ornate clockwork birds and music boxes. The marquis

collects people the way he collects toys, and he prefers winding up intricate predictable machines to manipulating unpredictable people. But even the machines break down—chaotically but momentarily, like the supposedly inviolable rules of correct behavior.

And yet Renoir's method is not so naïve as to condemn artifice and praise the simplicities of spontaneity. For one thing, the Marquis de la Chesnaye—Renoir's representative of polite civilization—is a compassionate, considerate man who is trying not to hurt anyone, whereas the aviator—Renoir's representative of spontaneity—is a selfish, blundering fool. Although the music boxes are indeed mechanical, they also represent a degree of orderly and delicate perfection. De la Chesnaye's problem is that he would like to achieve an impossible ideal: a world in which the demands of love (which can be notoriously disruptive) and order are harmonious rather than mutually exclusive—or at least are pursued with restraint and good manners, with "class." As he

Fig. 10-19
The marquis (Marcel Dalio, left) with one of his mechanical pets and Octave, the sponger (played by Renoir).

tells his gamekeeper, he wants no fences around his property, and he also wants no rabbits.

It is not de la Chesnaye's fault that the perfect grace of the 18th century (the century that produced his chateau, his lifestyle, many of his toys, and the Mozart on the soundtrack), a world in which the demands of spontaneity and convention may seem to have been properly balanced, no longer existed in the 20th century with its airplanes, motor cars, radios, and *nouveau riche*, and its Nazis massing on the borders of France. As in *Grand Illusion*, the source of ruin in *The Rules of the Game* is complex: It is rooted partly in the human personality, partly in the demands of social convention, partly in nature itself, and partly in history, which has posed dilemmas greater than the powers of people to solve.

Renoir's comedies of manners are dark and very ironic. If *Grand Illusion* is a tragedy with a comic ending, *The Rules of the Game* is a comedy full of failure and death. Even such comedies of survival as *Boudu* and *La Chienne* have an almost Chaplinesque sense of loss, along with a delight in reversed expectations.

During the World War II, Renoir, like Clair, made excellent films in the United States: *Swamp Water* (1941), *This Land Is Mine* (1943), *The Southerner* (1945), *Diary of a*

Chambermaid (1946). After the war, he, like Clair, returned to France. But he took a while to get there. In India, where he inspired Satyajit Ray, Renoir made his first color film, *The River* (1951). By way of Italy and another movie, he was back in the Paris studios by 1954 for *French Cancan*, which starred Jean Gabin. His eye, his sense of style, his perception of social structures and human relationships were still keen. For many of the New Wave filmmakers, especially Truffaut, Renoir would serve as a living bridge to the past and its cinematic traditions.

Vigo and Others

Not all French filmmakers were as successful as Renoir at combining literary values with the visual powers of moving pictures. As in America, the early sound years in France produced a curious and inert hybrid, the filmed play. "Canned theatre" became one obvious but clumsy way to solve the dialogue problem in French as well as American films. The success of the French playwright, Marcel Pagnol, as a producer and director of dialogue films (*Marius*, 1931; *Fanny*, 1932; *César*, 1936) was symptomatic. But in translating his own plays and novels for the camera, Pagnol showed more cinematic sense than did many theatre-inspired French or Hollywood directors. He often preferred shooting outdoors to shooting on the sound stage, a very untheatrical choice. He also had the vision to ask cinematically minded directors to work for him, like Jean Renoir (*Toni*).

Jean Vigo

The young iconoclast Jean Vigo, however, was totally unfettered by the theatrical and literary biases of the early 1930s. Vigo made only four films—two shorts, one picture of medium length, one feature—before his death in 1934 at the age of 29. That Vigo should be free of theatrical and even cinematic conventions was appropriate, for freedom was his primary theme. His characters struggle to create temporary pockets of freedom in the midst of the society that confines them.

His first short, *À propos de Nice* (1930), was an avant-garde documentary, more sexually playful and creatively outrageous than the city symphonies that influenced it. His other short, *Taris Swimming* (1932), experimented with underwater photography and prepared the visual means for one of the greatest sequences in *L'Atalante* (in which a heartbroken husband dives into the water in search of the image of his lost wife). He followed these with the 44-minute *Zéro de conduite* (*Zero for Conduct*, 1933)—which was as daring and original as the poetry of Arthur Rimbaud (Vigo has been called "the cinema's Rimbaud")—and the beautiful, tender, unsentimental, compelling, lyrical, gross, wild, rough, deeply moving *L'Atalante* (1934), which opened the day he died.

Zéro de conduite contrasts the energetic freedom of boyhood with the prison-like school that the children must attend. The boys eventually rebel against the institution, staging a demonstration on alumni day in front of all the wooden guests. They lower the flag of France and raise the skull and crossbones. They stand against the sky as the film ends. The freedom of Vigo's surprising images reveals the spirit of this film about freedom, which strongly influenced both Truffaut's *The 400 Blows* (1959) and Lindsay Anderson's *If. . .* (1969).

Vigo's primary visual choice is to subvert realistic, three-dimensional space and replace it with an imaginative, metaphoric sense of space that takes its spatial coordinates from the emotions and sensations of his characters. In the opening sequence, two boys, in a moment of youthful communion, transform the cramped space of a train compartment into an imaginative realm of play and joy, almost a mental universe. There are surprising shots from varied angles and perspectives in the tiny train compartment, brilliantly photographed by Boris Kaufman, the émigré brother of Dziga Vertov. Kaufman's ability to shoot improvisationally in real locations—which he learned with his brothers and of which Vigo made excellent use—would contribute significantly to the 1950s American film. The spatial magic of the opening sequence is matched by that of the final shot, as four young rebels, apparently climbing to the peak of a tiled roof, seem to ascend into the sky itself, since Vigo has deliberately stripped the shot of all familiar spatial coordinates.

Surprisingly beautiful is the slow-motion pillow fight in the bare, sterile dormitory. This scene—another radical transformation of space, here achieved by transforming time, and obviously influenced by the pillow fight in Gance's *Napoleon*—is a metaphor for the whole film: In the midst of the confining, regularized room the children leap and bound, swing pillows, spill feathers in slow motion, the feathers falling about their bodies and laughing faces like snow. In a completely different tone—the film has handfuls, changes tone every few minutes—Vigo presents the teacher–jailers as comic grotesques. They sneak around corners; they steal the kids' candy. Most grotesque of all is the school's principal—a dwarf with a scary streak. The only good teacher has an irreverent sense of humor and mimics Chaplin. This wild, iconoclastic film was itself given a zero for bad behavior: It was banned by the French government in 1933 because it ridiculed authority. The film was not shown in France until after the war in 1946, when all forms of repression became understandably unpopular.

If *Zéro de conduite* was the young director's anarchistic, sarcastic swipe at authority and the system, his next film and only full-length feature, *L'Atalante*, was a mature, romantic look at two young adults as they discover what is important. Recently married and deeply in love, they discover each other's flaws, then drift apart and

Fig. 10-20

Fig. 10-21

Fig. 10-22
Zéro de conduite: *the subversion of three-dimensional space: two boys puffing cigars in the train car (Fig. 10-20), the slow-motion procession after the feathers fly (Fig. 10-21), the final ascent toward the sky (Fig. 10-22).*

separate, and then find each other again, now knowing how empty their lives are without each other. It is a movie in which unsentimentalized reality and romantic dreams are equally vivid. Tying the film together is the river barge, L'Atalante, where the newlyweds must live. The man (Jean, played by Jean Dasté) owns the barge, and running the boat is his life. Juliette (the bride, played by Dita Parlo) longs for life on the shore. The barge becomes the rival that drives the couple apart. Although Juliette does not know it, the open space of the shore, which seems so attractive, is really more confining, less free than the apparently cramped space on the barge. As in Zéro de conduite, Vigo set himself the problem of translating emotion into spatial coordinates. Jean surrenders to love by diving underwater in search of love's image, where the world has no form or limit—a triumph of romantic space. Juliette learns that the cramped, cluttered, but at times unforgettably lyrical space on the barge is spiritually and emotionally richer than the deep space on shore, where excitement and "fun" turn out to be loveless, painful, costly, and unfulfilling. The barge, adrift on the river, gliding on the water, in the sunlight, through the fog, becomes, like the community established by the boys in Zéro de conduite, an ideal community— man, wife, old crew member, young apprentice—because it is not contaminated by contact with "official" society at all.

Whatever romantic heights the film reaches, Vigo's approach remains unglamorous and tight. By turns ecstatic at the beauty that shines through reality and cluttered with reality's debris, L'Atalante is one of the greatest achievements of Poetic Realism, even if its ending is unusually positive; most Poetic Realist films have fatalistic or melancholy endings.

Vigo's understated sincerity in rendering emotions is evident in images that imply much more than they say: the lonely Juliette sitting huddled up alone in the fog; the man and woman in separate beds. Vigo's sense of the grotesque adds a symbolic air to the shamelessly gross old sailor (played by Renoir's Boudu, Michel Simon), who has made the water his home, and the clownish peddler who evokes Juliette's longings for the life on shore. Because the two young people really love each other, and because Vigo has rendered that love so intimately and sincerely, we feel

Fig. 10-23
Jean Dasté (Jean) and Dita Parlo (Juliette) in L'Atalante.

complete relief when, after their painful separation, they wordlessly return to each other and life on L'Atalante. The barge casts off and continues its journey up river.

Carné and Prévert

The films of Jacques Feyder and Marcel Carné took their literary qualities from the novel rather than the stage. In this age of the screenwriter, both directors enlisted talented writers. Charles Spaak (who also wrote *Grand Illusion* for Renoir) wrote for Feyder the scripts of *Le Grand jeu* (1934), *Pension Mimosas* (1935), and *Carnival in Flanders* (1935). Even more fruitful was the collaboration of Carné and the novelist–poet Jacques Prévert. Prévert, whose poetic obsessions with fatalism and death dominated both romantic melodramas (like *Le Jour se lève* or *Daybreak*, 1939) and light comedies (*Drôle de drame* or *Bizarre Bizarre*, 1937),

wrote Carné a series of scripts in which admirable men die (for no reason other than that men die), in which people are dragged against their wills into complicated webs of human interactions from which there is no escape, in which people lose what they want and achieve what they do not want, in which symbolic figures of death weave pointedly through the realistic action, in which images of fog and gloom and chaos are pervasive.

Like Renoir, Clair, and Vigo, Carné and Prévert explore what is clearly the key theme of the 1930s, freedom. But for Carné and Prévert the limit to human freedom is human life itself: its fallibility, its mortality, its futility, its existence in an indifferent universe. Prévert's existential void is the precursor of Camus's or Beckett's, but charged with a romantic sense of doom. The seriocomic irony of Renoir contrasts with the vivid despair of Carné.

In *Port of Shadows* (*Quai des brumes,* 1938)—whose romantic fatalism and moody power make it, like *Le Jour se lève*, both an example of Poetic Realism and a recognizable precursor of the American *film noir*—a young soldier, past unknown (we know only that he is a deserter), is steadily dragged into a net of murderers, thieves, and outcasts, all because of the woman he loves, who loves him in return. Like the small dog that follows the soldier everywhere, the soldier (played by Jean Gabin) is instinctively, irrationally attached to Nelly (Michèle Morgan). He abandons his own attempts to escape, protects Nelly instead, and is gunned down at the end. The film is dominated by images of shadows and fog.

The richest of the Carné–Prévert films is *The Children of Paradise* (shot under the Nazi occupation in 1943–44, released 1945). Like the reader of Hugo, Tolstoy, or Dickens, the viewer of *Les Enfants du paradis* lives through a novelistically complicated series of interlocking events with many interesting figures over a long period of time. There are six central characters: two actors, two women (the possessive Nathalie and the unpossessable Garance), an aristocrat, and a murderous thief. All have difficulty deciding what they really want; each achieves material success only to discover that it is meaningless.

Central to the film is the contrast between the two actors: One, Frédérick Lemaître (Pierre Brasseur), is the man of words; the other, Baptiste Deburau (Jean-Louis Barrault), is the mime. Although both Frédérick and Baptiste are historical figures—two famous French actors of the 19th century—the film treats them as metaphorical opposites rather than as biographical subjects. Frédérick is the man of surfaces, of words, of fine talk and phrases; he becomes a success in cheap, hack dramas that he saves with his own imaginative theatrics. Baptiste is the man of deep feeling and the real artist, moonstruck and vulnerable; he transforms his emotions into theatre. Although Frédérick is the matinee idol of Paris, Baptiste is the delight of artists and the common people.

Between the two actors stands a woman named Garance (played by Arletty). She casually becomes Frédérick's mistress, although Baptiste is the shy man who really loves her. Garance thinks love is simple, but Baptiste thinks it's terribly complicated. When she casually offers him her body, he, seeing her as a pure spirit of beauty, declines the offer—a decision for which he never forgives himself. Only years later, after she has found wealth and glamor as the mistress of a fastidious count (Louis Salou), does she realize the power of Baptiste's passion, the power that makes him a great mime. But when she returns, Garance sees that Baptiste is saddled with a possessive wife he does not love (Nathalie, played by Maria Casarès, who later starred in Cocteau's *Orpheus*) and a child.

The last major character is Lacenaire (Marcel Herrand). He is not a man of the theatre but a thief with a taste for murder, a man who lives his life as though it were the theatre. And Carné and Prévert use the theatre as the film's central metaphor. Both the first and second parts of the film open on a theatre curtain, which rises to reveal the movie world of *Les Enfants*. Both parts of the three-hour film end with the curtain's coming down. Carné and Prévert sustain the theatre metaphor by paralleling the dramatic, fictional roles of the actors on stage with their actual longings and choices off the stage. In one pantomime created by Baptiste, the character played by Frédérick—Harlequin—is, like Frédérick, bouncy, playful, spirited, charming. Baptiste's dramatic role as Pierrot is like Baptiste himself: sad, moonstruck, tender, idealistic. Pierrot loses the beautiful moon lady (played by Garance) to Harlequin; Baptiste loses Garance to Frédérick. The theatre is life, and life is the theatre.

The "Paradise" of the title is not a heavenly, metaphysical one but an earthly one: It is the slang name for the second balcony (in English theatre, "the gods"), the highest, cheapest seats in the theatre, the seats where sit the masses, those who love the theatre and mix intimately in all its passions. The chaotic, energetic masses (the "gods" who watch, who are to be pleased, and without whom the entertainers would not exist) in "Paradise" parallel the masses just outside the theatre on the teeming, vital, packed Boulevard du Temple, the "Street of Crime."

At the end of the film, Baptiste loses Garance once more, perhaps never to see her again. He follows her through the "Street of Crime," vainly calling her name. But Garance, on her way to meet a man she does not know is dead, cannot hear him; the masses of humanity—carnivalesque

Fig. 10-24

Fig. 10-25
Les Enfants du paradis: *the theatre as life and life as the theatre. Fig. 10-24: the seething activity in "the gods." Fig. 10-25: Frédérick (Pierre Brasseur, left) as Harlequin, Garance (Arletty) as the Moon Lady, and Baptiste (Jean-Louis Barrault) as Pierrot, acting out a version of their offstage love triangle in a pantomime scripted by Baptiste.*

revelers on the theatre of the street—slow Baptiste's pursuit, keeping him from reaching his love. Surrounded by all this activity, so alive and yet so senseless, Baptiste is swallowed by the crowd, and the curtain falls.

For the first 15 years after the war, many French films would look backward to the literary-scenario films of the prewar era, a cycle whose major wartime expression was *Les Enfants du paradis* itself. The postwar studios' "Tradition of Quality" would produce such slick and literate films as Jean Delannoy's *La Symphonie pastorale* (1946) and Claude Autant-Lara's *The Red and the Black* (1954). Not until 1959—when the New Wave (*la nouvelle vague*), which had been building since the mid-1950s, crested and broke on the shores of the film world it was to transform—would the French cinema strike off in a new direction.

For Further Viewing

FILMS

MARCEL CARNÉ (1906–96)
Drôle de drame (*Bizarre Bizarre*, 1937)
Quai des brumes (*Port of Shadows*, 1938)
Le Jour se lève (*Daybreak*, 1939)
Les Visiteurs du soir (1942)
The Children of Paradise (1945). Shot 1943–44

RENÉ CLAIR (1898–1981)
Paris qui dort (*The Crazy Ray*, 1923)
Entr'acte (1924)
The Italian Straw Hat (1927)
Sous les toits de Paris (1930)
Le Million (1931)
À nous la liberté (1931)
The Ghost Goes West (1935)
I Married a Witch (1942)
It Happened Tomorrow (1944)
And Then There Were None (1945)

GERMAINE DULAC (1882–1942)
The Smiling Madame Beudet (1923)
The Seashell and the Clergyman (1927)

JULIEN DUVIVIER (1896–1967)
Poil de carotte (1932)
Pépé-le-Moko (1937)
Panique (1946)

ABEL GANCE (1889–1981)
La Folie du Docteur Tube (1915)
J'accuse (*I Accuse*, 1919)
La Roue (*The Wheel*, 1922)
Au secours! (*Help!*, 1923). With Max Linder
Napoléon vu par Abel Gance (*Napoleon*, 1927)
La Fin du monde (*The End of the World*, 1931)
Napoléon Bonaparte vu et entendu par Abel Gance (1935)
Un Grand amour de Beethoven (1936)
J'accuse (1937)
Bonaparte and the Revolution (1971)

MARCEL PAGNOL (1895–1974)
Marius (1931, Alexander Korda)
Fanny (1932, Marc Allégret)
César (1936)

MAN RAY (1890–1976)
Return to Reason (1923)
Emak-Bakia (1927)
L'Etoile de mer (1928)
Les Mystères du Château du Dé (1929)

JEAN RENOIR (1894–1979)
The Little Match Girl (1928)
La Chienne (1931)
Boudu Saved from Drowning (1932)
Toni (1935)
The Crime of Monsieur Lange (1936)
The Lower Depths (1936)
A Day in the Country (1936). Unfinished; first shown, 1946
Grand Illusion (1937)
La Bête humaine (1938)
La Marseillaise (1938)
The Rules of the Game (1939)
This Land Is Mine (1943)
The Southerner (1945)
The River (1951)
The Golden Coach (1952)
French Cancan (1954)

JEAN VIGO (1905–34)
À propos de Nice (1930)
Taris Swimming (1932)
Zéro de conduite (1933)
L'Atalante (1934)

Fièvre (1921, Louis Delluc)

Ballet mécanique (1924, Fernand Léger)

Ménilmontant (1925, Dimitri Kirsanov)

Anémic cinéma (1926, Marcel Duchamp)

Rien que les heures (1926, Alberto Cavalcanti)

The Passion of Joan of Arc (1928, Carl Theodor Dreyer). Shot 1927

The Fall of the House of Usher (1928, Jean Epstein)

Un Chien andalou (1929, Luis Buñuel and Salvador Dalí)

The Blood of a Poet (1930, Jean Cocteau)

Carnival in Flanders (1935, Jacques Feyder)

DVDs

À nous la liberté (1931, **René Clair**). Criterion Collection. Includes deleted scenes, *Entr'acte*, and a BBC interview with Clair.

L'Age d'or (1930, **Luis Buñuel** and **Salvador Dalí**). Kino Video. **Restored.**

L'Atalante (1934, **Jean Vigo**). New Yorker Video. **Restored** version.

Avant-Garde: Experimental Cinema of the 1920s and '30s. Kino Video. Short films from the Raymond Rohauer Collection. Includes **Man Ray**'s *Return to Reason* and *Emak-Bakia*, **Léger**'s *Ballet mécanique*, **Kirsanov**'s *Ménilmontant*, **Duchamp**'s *Anémic cinéma*, and **Dulac**'s *The Seashell and the Clergyman*, as well as **Richter**'s *Rhythmus 21* and *Ghosts Before Breakfast*, **Eggeling**'s *Symphonie diagonale*, **Metzner**'s *Überfall*, and many others.

The Blood of a Poet is in *The Orphic Trilogy* (see Chap. 13 list).

Un Chien Andalou (1929, **Luis Buñuel** and **Salvador Dalí**). Transflux Films. Includes two interviews with Buñuel's son that cover Buñuel's life, personality, working methods, relations with Dalí, etc.

The Children of Paradise (1945, **Marcel Carné**). Criterion Collection. Includes a digital **restoration** demonstration and **Prévert**'s original treatment.

Grand Illusion (1937, **Jean Renoir**). Criterion Collection. Digital transfer from the recently discovered camera negative, with a commentary by film historian Peter Cowie, a trailer with Renoir, Renoir and **Stroheim** on the radio, and a **restoration** demonstration.

The Passion of Joan of Arc (1928, **Carl Theodor Dreyer**). Criterion Collection. **Restored** from newly found original materials.

La Roue (1922, **Abel Gance**). Flicker Alley. **Restored** to 4 hours 21 minutes.

The Rules of the Game (1939, **Jean Renoir**). Criterion Collection. **Digitally restored** image and sound, an introduction by Renoir, side-by-side comparisons of both endings of the film, unique information on the release version, Jean Gaborit and Jacques Durand on their restoration and re-release of the film, an excerpt from a TV program on Renoir by **Rivette,** other documentaries and interviews, essays by **Truffaut** and others, and a commentary by film scholar Alexander Sesonske.

Under the Roofs of Paris (1930, **René Clair**). Criterion Collection. Includes *Paris qui dort.*

11

The American Studio
Years: 1930–45

In the 1930s, Americans went to the movies; in the 2000s, they went to a movie. The difference is not merely semantic. In 1938, there were some 80 million movie admissions every week, a figure representing 65 percent of the population of the United States. In 1994, there were some 25 million movie admissions every week, less than 10 percent of the population of the United States. Over 500 feature films were produced by the major studios in the United States in 1937, but fewer than 100 in 1983. In the relatively active year 1987, the major studios released 135 features and the independents another 380. In 2008, the majors released 148 pictures, the independents 462. The film industry of the 1930s thrived on a felicitous circle of economic dependence on attendance, exhibition, and production. The huge number of movie admissions necessitated a huge number of theatres, which necessitated a huge number of films to be shown in the theatres, which necessitated large, busy studios that could produce enough films to keep the theatres filled. Only after World War II did the circle of dependence reverse itself and turn vicious.

The need for enormous quantities of films guaranteed the survival of the studio system, which was geared for production in quantity. The huge studios of the 1920s converted to sound by adding new departments to their already complex organizations; specialization and division of labor, two pillars of the silent-film factories, became even more essential to the sound-film factory. New departments of music, of sound mixing and dubbing, of sound technicians and machinery joined the older, established

departments on the lot. The writing department became even more specialized; some writers roughed out general treatments, others converted and expanded the treatments into screenplays, and still others polished the dialogue.

The film property traveled through the studio, from department to department, from story idea to finished script, until it finally landed in the hands of its director, sometimes just before shooting began. After 15 to 30 shooting days (for a typical "program picture"), the director relinquished the negative to the cutting department, which edited the picture and sound into final form, as instructed by the film's producer. Only the most important directors of the most special films enjoyed the opportunity to shape the script before shooting and to cut the footage afterward. From the cutting department the film went to distribution offices, and from there to the waiting chains of theatres that the company itself owned. The film product rolled down the assembly line from the original idea to final showing, all stages controlled by the studio factory. The film industry had evolved its structure for the next 16 rich years, from 1930 to 1946.

The years of wealth were not without their moments of worry. At first, the Wall Street crash of 1929 had little effect on the film business. Although America was officially broke, Americans kept scraping up dimes, quarters, and dollars to see movies. The economic sag first hit the movie industry in 1933; admissions declined, theatres closed, production dropped. But prudent studio economy measures and a new moralistic path of righteousness helped to nurse the movie business back to health.

Film Cycles and Cinematic Conventions

The Studio Era was dominated not only by big filmmaking companies, but also by a number of assumptions about how movies should be produced, who should star in which kinds of films, and the need to acknowledge the ordinary conventions of society.

The Production Code

In 1930, Martin Quigley and Daniel Lord drafted the Hollywood Production Code, another in a series of the motion picture industry's official statements on the proper moral content of films. But the Code might never have been enforced if the Catholic Legion of Decency had not threatened an economic boycott in 1933, the same year that movie revenues first began to feel the effects of the Depression. In July 1934, Joseph I. Breen went to work for the Hays Office (see Chapter 6) as the head of its new Production Code Administration (PCA), an agency that would award the industry's seal of approval only to those films that observed the Code's moral restrictions. Any producer or distributor who released a film without the industry's seal would be fined $25,000. Because every major producer and distributor was a member of the Motion Picture Producers and Distributors of America (MPPDA, later the MPAA), they all subscribed to the PCA's rulings and, as of 1934, submitted all their scripts to the Hays Office for approval before shooting.

The Code declared that movies were to avoid brutality (by gangsters and especially by the police), they were to avoid depicting any kind of sexual promiscuity (unwedded, extramarital, or "unnatural"), and they were to avoid making any illegal or immoral life seem either possible or pleasant (goodbye to the gangsters who lived well until the law gunned them down). The Production Code viewed marriage as more a sacred institution than a sexual one; even the sophisticated Nick and Nora Charles of *The Thin Man* (1934) slept separately in twin beds—which became known as "Hollywood beds." Even more restrictive were the new Code's specific prohibitions against certain words. Not only were "sex," "God," "hell," and "damn" forbidden, but so were

such flavorful and healthy Americanisms as "guts," "nuts," and "louse," which were considered deficient in gentility and "tone." Ironically, the Code, which Hollywood adopted for business reasons in 1934, perished 34 years later for the same reasons. The very words and deeds that crimped sales in the 1930s spurred them in the 1960s.

Some historians see the Code as the era's institutional means for eliminating political dissent and narrowing discussion of the important social issues. The large banks, whose investment capital allowed the movie industry to function, could dictate the conservative content of films through the Code, constricting political change and cultural consciousness. Within the film industry at the time, the Code was a particularly useful instrument for studios to keep writers in their place. A producer could always settle a dispute with a writer by claiming that the Code said "No."

But its administrators claimed that the purpose of the Code was not to keep films from being made, but to allow them to be made—without damaging the commercial health of the film, the studio that made it, and the industry as a whole. Americans inside and outside the film industry knew that adultery, crime, and injustice were not only a part of life but the elementary materials of playacting and storytelling from their beginnings. It's hardly a joke to say that the Greek tragedies would have been sent back for rewrite. The Code was a unique historical document that attempted to formulate, concretely and precisely, the publicly admissible mores of an entire culture—the kinds of deeds suitable for public depiction and, especially, the kinds of words (now that movies could talk) suitable for public utterance.

In advising producers and writers—particularly about adaptations of prestigious plays and novels—the PCA trimmed as little of the original material as possible but as much as was necessary to conform to the moral sensibilities of an American majority—as envisaged and articulated by the Code.

In addition to soothing its audiences' moral sensitivities, Hollywood pulled itself out of the Depression by offering a bargain. Double features—two pictures for the price of one—became standard in all but the poshest of first-run theatres. Hollywood added a third attraction to the two movies (plus trailers, cartoons, shorts, and a newsreel): Audiences could play exciting games between the films—Keno, Bingo, Screeno—that sent the winner home with cash or a set of dishes. The studios survived the financial crisis of 1933, and profits shot up in 1935; they survived the crisis of 1938, and profits shot up in 1939. The boom years of the war eliminated all money crises for several more years. World War II lasted from 1939 (1941 in America) to 1945. The film industry enjoyed its biggest business year in 1946.

Despite the blockbuster years of the late 1970s and 1980s, the film industry's profits have never been proportionately higher than those of 1946, when over 78 million Americans went to the movies. In 1989, for example, domestic grosses topped $5 billion for the first time, but the dollar wasn't what it used to be (what cost nine cents in 1946 cost a dollar in 1989), the films cost much more to make and to advertise, independent distributors took their cut off the top, and a much smaller percentage of the population was buying tickets.

The studio system produced an obvious tension between film art and film business. Art cannot be mass produced; creativity does not flourish in departments and on schedules. The unexceptional program picture was the resulting rule, the fresh and original film the vital exception.

Despite this tension between commerce and creativity, there are surprising parallels between the Hollywood film of 1930 to 1945 and the richest era of English dramas, 1576 to 1642. Like the Renaissance dramas, the studio films were popular with vast audiences of diverse social, economic, and educational backgrounds. The Elizabethan and Jacobean plays and players were products of repertory theatre companies with permanent staffs of writers, actors, managers, costumers, and designers; the films were products of repertory film studios with similar permanent staffs. Like the theatre company, the film studio spread the acting parts among its regular stable of actors, each of whom played a specific kind of role over and over again—old man, comic, juvenile, leading man or lady, dancer, singer, child. Just as Shakespeare's Will Kemp and Richard Burbage bounced from comic or tragic part to comic or tragic part, Spencer Tracy and Clark Gable bounced for MGM. And like the

films of the Studio Era, the Elizabethan and Jacobean plays were drenched in the theatrical customs, clichés, and conventions of their age: the tragic scenes of Senecan gore, the bawdy use of the comic Vice, the pastoral convention of a magical forest. And just as a Shakespeare, a Marlowe, or a Jonson could turn a convention into a trait of personal style, so too a Lubitsch, an Astaire, or a Ford could make a studio convention completely his own.

There are two ways of looking at the artistic products of a repertory system for the manufacture of popular dramatic entertainment. The critic can look at the greatest products of the system—its Shakespeares and Jonsons—or at its most typical and conventional products. Any fair assessment of the studio system must do both.

Cycles

The studio system controlled both the subjects of film narrative and the styles in which they were shot. Formulas for story construction, characterization, casting, decor, music, and photography dominated Hollywood's films. A key principle in the selection of story material was—and remains—simply that an idea that had worked before would probably work again. Films were not seen as special, individual conceptions but tended to bunch together as types, in cycles.

The new sound equipment introduced audiences to the hard-bitten street slang of mobsters; Hollywood produced a cycle of pictures that made the tough talk of gangsters as familiar as polite conversation around the family dinner table. The first gangster cycle condemned and glorified the brutality of the underworld: *Little Caesar, Scarface, The Public Enemy*. Later gangster cycles, purified by the antiviolence, anti-illegality sections of the Breen Code, merely put the tough-talking guys on the right side of the law—that is, on the other side of the badge: *The Public Enemy*'s James Cagney in *"G" Men*. A cycle of films about prison, the "big house," spun off from the mobster films; the big house also had its slang, its underworld morality, its tough guys behind bars and behind the warden's desk: *The Big House, San Quentin, The Criminal Code*. Yet another close relative of the mobster cycle was the journalism cycle. The newspaper reporters often seemed like gangsters who had accidentally ended up behind a typewriter rather than a tommy

Fig. 11-1   Fig. 11-2

The assault of gangsters on American life. Fig. 11-1: Paul Muni as the hero/villain of the 1932
Scarface; Fig. 11-2: George Raft as his coin-flipping friend.

gun; they talked and acted as rough as the crooks their assignments forced them to cover: *The Front Page*, *Big News*, *The Power of the Press*. It is no accident that Ben Hecht, the greatest screenwriter of rapid-fire, flavorful tough talk as well as a major comic playwright, wrote gangster pictures (including *Underworld*, for which he won the first Oscar for best original story), prison pictures, and newspaper pictures. And Hecht had scores of imitators.

A succession of musical cycles accompanied the cops-and-robbers cycles. Just as synchronized sound brought the pungent, brittle crackle of thug talk to American audiences, synchronization also brought the possibility of complex rhythmic and musical effects. Singing and dancing could be synchronized to the exact beat; picture and sound could be wed in their own kind of audio-visual montage. The first talking pictures were inevitably singing pictures. De Forest's earliest Phonofilms and the Warners' earliest Vitaphone shorts used singers and vaudeville entertainers. *The Jazz Singer* was more a singie than a talkie; even *Lights of New York*—the first of the gangster talkies—used several long musical numbers in Hawk Miller's nightclub. Musical sequences were almost obligatory in early talkies, just as most 1940s films included at least one song—whether integral and relevant, as in

Casablanca, or unnecessary, as in *The Big Sleep*. Among the first "100 percent" talkies released by every major studio in 1929 was a musical— MGM's *Broadway Melody*, Fox's *Sunny Side Up*, and *Paramount on Parade*.

The first musicals were either filmed versions of Broadway shows or suave, continental musical–comic pictures à la Lubitsch. The second cycle of musicals was a series of "backstage" stories—the struggling young composer, the young hopeful in the chorus (who is catapulted to stardom when the leading lady falls ill), the down-and-out director who needs one last hit— epitomized at Warner Bros. by *42nd Street* and other films with musical numbers directed by Busby Berkeley.

The Berkeley musicals were contradictory mixtures of bland, formulaic dramatic sections (which Berkeley did not usually direct) and visually dazzling musical sections. Berkeley's accomplishment was not merely that space itself became a "dancer" in these numbers but that his radical shifts of camera position stripped the frame of any clear geographical or theatrical referents. His numbers may begin or end on a stage, but most could never be performed on one; they happen in cinematic space and are addressed to the camera, which may be on the ceiling. Berkeley's numbers invite us into a visual labyrinth; the viewer's eye absorbs a kind of visual "music," scored solely by abstract contrasts of black and white, circle and line, camera angles and editing rhythms.

A cycle of smoother, more integrated comedies-of-romance-with-music starred Fred Astaire and Ginger Rogers at RKO. For Astaire and Rogers, dancing was not merely a generic inevitability of backstage musicals but a means of human interaction and connection. The characters embodied by Astaire and Rogers discovered one another's feelings through the dances they performed together, discovered that, no matter what social obstacles confronted them, they belonged together because they danced so perfectly together. Their dancing celebrated not just rhythm, motion, grace, and style, but also the way that physical activity can become a spiritual expression and spatial extension of inner feelings and harmonies.

America's greatest composers for the musical theatre wrote original songs and scores for Hollywood films: the Gershwins (*Shall We Dance?* and *A Damsel in Distress* for Astaire at RKO in 1937); Jerome Kern (*Swing Time*, 1936, and *You Were Never Lovelier*, 1943, also for Astaire); Irving Berlin (*Top Hat*, 1935, *Follow the Fleet*, 1936, and *Carefree*, 1938, for Astaire; *Alexander's Ragtime Band*, 1938, for Fox); Rodgers and Hart (*Love Me Tonight*, 1932, for Maurice Chevalier and Jeanette MacDonald at Paramount); Cole Porter (*Born to Dance*, 1936, and *Broadway Melody of 1940* for MGM's Eleanor Powell).

There were the ornately costumed operettas at MGM with Nelson Eddy, Jeanette MacDonald, and Allan Jones—musicals that brought the stage hits of a previous generation to life for a new one in cinema. There were musicals for children (Shirley Temple and Bobby Breen), musicals for fresh, young ingenues (Deanna Durbin and Gloria Jean), musicals on ice (Sonja Henie), and musicals under water (Esther Williams).

Any successful Hollywood film spawned many imitations, just as one successful television show begets half a dozen progeny on all the major networks. Like television, the Hollywood of the 1930s faced the weekly pressure of entertaining a huge percentage of the national population; as in television, fear of a dollar disaster was a constant spur to produce safe mediocrities.

The parallels with TV programming are even more obvious with those successful films that spawned not only imitations but sequels. The film series was the ancestor of the TV series: the Andy Hardy pictures, the Maisie series, the Charlie Chan films, Mr. Moto, Philo Vance, Henry Aldrich, and—the closest possible parallel with network TV—the series of films springing from MGM's *Young Doctor Kildare*. Yet another studio formula was to patch together a film with what seemed like all the stars they had under contract: Paramount's *Big Broadcasts* (of 1932, 1936, 1937, and 1938), MGM's *Broadway Melodies* (of 1936, 1938, and 1940). The studios made the same films over and over again, with similar titles or different ones. And they put their stars into roles they felt would suit them—the star system was a key element of the studio system—so that audiences could enjoy their favorite actors doing what was expected of them. Even today, the right star in the right genre is the key to big profits.

Studios and Style

Formulas for style were as binding as formulas for plotting. Hollywood films of the decade, with surprisingly few exceptions, looked strikingly alike. Many directors' impulses toward personal style were suppressed before shooting began by the studio's general policies of lighting, design, cinematography, and cutting.

The key characteristic of film style in the Studio Era was that sound films were talking films. The talk was better now that writers of screen dialogue knew how to write screen dialogue. The scenes of talk were smoother now that the speakers could move from place to place and both camera and microphone could follow them. The careful decor added insightful nuances and contrapuntal resonances to the scenes of talk. But talk still propelled the talkies.

The reign of talk produced further stylistic consequences. The camera's position and angle illuminated the speaker and the other characters' reactions to the speech rather than obscuring them in the hope of illuminating something else. Extreme high and low angles, extreme close shots, extreme far shots, tilts, and whirls were uncommon in even the most visually imaginative films. Cutting was as functional as the shooting. Quick cutting distracted the audience from the speaker's words. Rapid montage was reserved

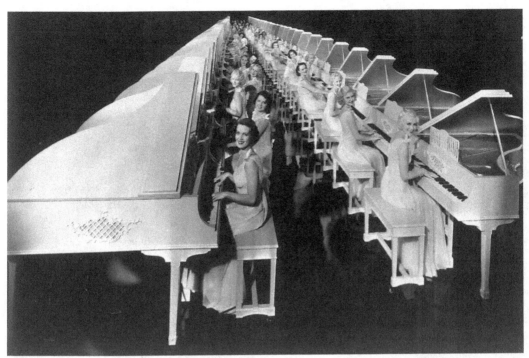

Fig. 11-3
The monochrome musical. Busby Berkeley's kaleidoscopic white pianos on a black floor (**Gold Diggers of 1935**).

for occasional and obvious showcase effects: the passage of time, a summary of a character's activities. Scenes were lit first for the stars, then for the dramatic atmosphere. Designers and cameramen used light to make the pretty people even prettier, shaping their heads with light to make those box-office faces stand out from the backgrounds. Yet for all their apparent standardness, the movies never demonstrated a higher degree of craftsmanship and artisanship—neither in America nor elsewhere—than in these 15 years of Hollywood studio style.

Despite their common assumptions and conventions, each of the studios displayed a unique personality in applying them. The two giants— MGM and Paramount—were the most distinctive and the most different from one another. MGM was the studio with almost dictatorial central control—exerted by Louis B. Mayer and Irving Thalberg. Paramount, under B. P. Schulberg, was a much looser organization, granting more freedom to individual producers, directors, and writers. MGM was a studio of stars: Greta Garbo,

Jean Harlow, Joan Crawford, Norma Shearer, Katharine Hepburn, Mickey Rooney, Clark Gable, James Stewart, Lionel Barrymore, Spencer Tracy. Paramount was a studio of writers and directors: Ernst Lubitsch, Josef von Sternberg, Cecil B. DeMille, Leo McCarey, Preston Sturges, Billy Wilder. In the early 1930s, Paramount was the iconoclast's haven: the home of Mae West, W. C. Fields, and the Marx Brothers. The studio permitted the sensual excesses of von Sternberg and the sexual sniggers of Lubitsch. Unless it was making a horror film like *Mad Love*, MGM flattened all excesses into a shiny, respectable, beautifully lit wholesomeness. When the Marx Brothers left Paramount for MGM, they lost much of their lunacy and spark. Ironically, in the 1930s the MGM policy seemed the wiser of the two, for Louis B. Mayer's devotion to family entertainment made MGM the most respected and successful film factory in Hollywood—a studio that could release *The Wizard of Oz* and *Gone With the Wind* in the same year (1939)—while B. P. Schulberg's chaotic individuality ran Paramount into severe financial difficulties, resulting in the

Fig. 11-4
RKO's I Walked with a Zombie, *produced by Val Lewton and directed by Jacques Tourneur.*

studio's loss of many of its stars (Jeanette MacDonald accompanied the Marx Brothers to MGM) and Schulberg's loss of his job.

Warner Bros., which invested less money in production values (sets, costumes, crowds), was more dependent on good talk, and the dialogue in the early Warners pictures was as sharp, as fast, and as good as anyone's. The studio specialized in gangster films, biographies, and musicals, directed by William Wellman, Mervyn LeRoy, William Dieterle, Michael Curtiz, Lloyd Bacon, and Busby Berkeley, and starring such sharp talkers as James Cagney, Edward G. Robinson, Paul Muni, Humphrey Bogart, Bette Davis, Dick Powell, Ruby Keeler, Joan Blondell, and Ida Lupino (who became a director in the late 1940s). Warner Bros. was also the studio most committed to the depiction of contemporary social problems—whether in its musicals (the "Forgotten Man" and "Shanghai Lil" numbers of Berkeley musicals), its gangster pictures (like *Little Caesar* and *The Public Enemy*), its problem pictures (like *I Am a Fugitive From a Chain Gang*), its socially conscious "biopics," as *Variety* called them (the biographies of Zola, Pasteur, and Curie), or its "woman's pictures"— the choices and conflicts of women in contemporary American society (often embodied by Bette Davis). Warners was also the most pro-Roosevelt of the studios: the most supportive of his New Deal and, like FDR, openly critical of the Nazi menace abroad. And Warners had the best cartoons, thanks to the vocal talents of Mel Blanc; the musical direction of Carl Stalling; the scripts

Fig. 11-5
RKO's The Curse of the Cat People: *another Lewton masterpiece, this one directed by Robert Wise and Gunther Von Fritsch.*

Universal's Frankenstein, *directed by James Whale, was influenced more by German Expressionism than by Mary Shelley's novel; sets by Charles D. Hall.*

Fig. 11-6

by Michael Maltese, Tedd Pierce, and Warren Foster; the directors Tex Avery, Bob Clampett, Friz Freleng, Chuck Jones, Robert McKimson, and Frank Tashlin; the producers who started the Looney Tunes (1930) and Merrie Melodies (1931) series, Hugh Harman and Rudy Ising (as in "harmonizing"); and the personalities of some of Warners' top stars, from Bugs Bunny to Daffy Duck. In contrast, the Disney cartoons were bourgeois, reverent, and tame. On the level of sheer visual inventiveness, Warners' only competitors were the independent Max and Dave Fleischer, who first brought Ko-Ko out of an inkwell, then created the Betty Boop, Popeye, and Superman cartoons.

Twentieth Century–Fox excelled in historical and adventure films directed by John Ford, Henry King, and Henry Hathaway with Tyrone Power and Henry Fonda, in show business musicals with Don Ameche and Alice Faye (and, later, with Betty Grable and Dan Dailey), and in the folksy comedies of Will Rogers and Shirley Temple. If Warners was committed to general social problems, Fox was committed to the problems of American family life. Even Fox musicals confront a woman (the Fox stars of musicals were always women—from Janet Gaynor to Marilyn Monroe) with the difficult choice between career and family.

RKO, the least financially stable of the major studios, was most memorable for the smooth musicals of Fred Astaire and Ginger Rogers, the suave comedies with Cary Grant, the literate horror B pictures produced by Val Lewton, and the occasional film by Howard Hawks (*Bringing Up Baby*), Orson Welles (*Citizen Kane, The Magnificent Ambersons*), and John Ford (*The Informer*)—not to mention *King Kong*.

Universal excelled in the horror films— *Frankenstein, Dracula,* and *The Wolf Man*— directed by James Whale, Tod Browning, George Waggner, and others; in the later comedies of W. C. Fields; and in the saccharine singing pictures of Deanna Durbin and Gloria Jean.

Columbia was the creation of a single producer, Harry Cohn, who hitched his "minor" studio to director Frank Capra in 1927 and rode to respectability on the coattails of Capra's many successes (especially *It Happened One Night* in 1934). Although Cohn was the Hollywood mogul whom more actors and writers hated more

deeply than any other, he respected directors (like Capra, Howard Hawks, and George Cukor) and left them alone to do some of their finest work.

The most aesthetically and commercially successful of the independent production companies were Samuel Goldwyn, Inc., Selznick International Pictures, and Walt Disney Productions; at some point, each distributed its films through United Artists, which remained the independents' releasing company of choice but also had begun to produce films on its own.

The two "Poverty Row" studios, Republic and Monogram, specialized in cheap westerns, cheap hoodlum pictures, and—like Universal—serials. A later generation of French *cinéastes* canonized the B-picture offerings of these cheapie–quickie studios as superior to many of the glossier offerings of the major studios.

The studios forced their directors to be eclectic. A director jumped from jungle adventure to backstage musical to historical pageant to contemporary comedy. The director's sole qualification for handling so many styles and settings was the ability to get any job done well.

Typical of the competent impersonality of the Studio Era are the careers of Warner Bros.' Mervyn LeRoy and MGM's W. S. Van Dyke. LeRoy, within a four-year period, directed *Little Caesar*, the tough story of a mobster's rise and fall; *I Am a Fugitive From a Chain Gang*, a true story of brutality in a southern prison; and the "dramatic" sections of the backstage musical *Gold Diggers of 1933*. In those same four years, 1930–33, LeRoy directed 20 other films, including journalism pictures, homespun comedies, and show-business musicals. LeRoy's later work was just as eclectic, from the patriotic adventure, *The FBI Story*, to the musical, *Gypsy*. Woody Van Dyke's films are equally diverse; he directed adventure (*Trader Horn; Tarzan, the Ape Man*), mystery–comedy (the *Thin Man* series), costume pageant (*Marie Antoinette*), disaster movie/historical romance with music (*San Francisco*), operetta (*Rose Marie, Sweethearts*), as well as contributions to MGM series pictures (*Andy Hardy Gets Spring Fever, Dr. Kildare's Victory*).

The Studio Era produced several of these "smorgasbord" directors who could be depended on to cook up a palatable, powerful product

Fig. 11-7

Clark Gable and Vivien Leigh in Gone With the Wind.

Fig. 11-8

Along with Swing High, Swing Low *(1937), this Depression-era theatre offered a chance at a $500 prize on "Bank Nite."*

regardless of its particular ingredients: Michael Curtiz (*Mystery of the Wax Museum, The Walking Dead, The Charge of the Light Brigade, The Adventures of Robin Hood* [co-director, William Keighley], *Dodge City, The Private Lives of Elizabeth and Essex, Yankee Doodle Dandy, Casablanca, Mildred Pierce, Life with Father,* and more), William Dieterle (*The Firebird, The Story of Louis Pasteur, The Life of Emile Zola, Juarez, The Hunchback of Notre Dame, Love Letters, Portrait of Jennie*), Lewis Milestone (*All Quiet on the Western Front, The Front Page, Rain, Anything Goes, Of Mice and Men*), Victor Fleming (*Red Dust, Treasure Island, The Wizard of Oz, Gone With the Wind, A Guy Named Joe*). Although most of *Gone With the Wind* was directed by Fleming, the film's *auteur* was producer David O. Selznick, who planned and supervised the project from the time he bought the rights to the novel to the time he released the movie through MGM; it was also Selznick who hired the picture's first director, George Cukor, and replaced him with Fleming at the insistence of the male lead, Clark Gable. Other directors who shot important sequences were Sam Wood and King Vidor. Nevertheless, it is remarkable that Fleming had a major hand in directing two of the best-loved movies ever produced by Hollywood, *Gone With the Wind* and the entirely

different *The Wizard of Oz,* in the same year, by taking the jobs assigned to him by the kings of the studio system.

In addition to asking their directors to select from the smorgasbord, the studios found that some directors did a better job with a single dish. Some directed comedies primarily: Gregory LaCava (*She Married Her Boss, My Man Godfrey*), Sam Wood (*A Day at the Races; A Night at the Opera; Goodbye, Mr. Chips*), Leo McCarey (*Duck Soup, Ruggles of Red Gap, Going My Way*), Edward Sutherland (*Mississippi, Poppy*). Other directors specialized in adventure, horror, or mystery: Tod Browning (*The Unholy Three, Dracula, Freaks*), William Wellman (*The Public Enemy, The Ox-Bow Incident, The Story of G.I. Joe, The High and the Mighty*), James Whale (*Frankenstein, The Old Dark House, The Invisible Man, Bride of Frankenstein*), Henry Hathaway (*Come On Marines, The Lives of a Bengal Lancer*). Clarence Brown, who worked well with actors and dialogue, specialized in adapting stageplays—not to mention Faulkner's novel *Intruder in the Dust*—into films; Mark Sandrich and Roy Del Ruth directed musicals primarily.

If the most conventional studio films displayed any personality, it often reflected the general moral assumptions and values of the

Fig. 11-9
Along with **Music for Millions** *(1944), the Capitol Theatre in Manhattan offered a stage show with Tommy Dorsey; it was World War II, and war bonds were sold "day and night."*

era as a whole. Almost all the films took the view that the sincere, the sensitive, the human would inevitably triumph over the hypocritical, the callous, the oppressive. From the screwball comedies to the horror films, wit and resourcefulness saved the day. American audiences, escaping from the realities of the Depression outside the movie theatre, withdrew inside to see grit triumph over suffering and kindness triumph over financial, political, and moral chicanery. If the optimism of Hollywood films provided the audiences with the tranquilizer they needed, it also strengthened the audience's belief that eventually good people would make bad times better.

The American film offered not only escape but also subtle propaganda. While many Americans lacked the money to buy warm clothing, American movie characters wore fashionable gowns and well-tailored suits. While many Americans lacked the money to pay the rent, American movie characters lived in elegant apartments filled with expensive furniture. The tasteful richness of the studio films, supported by the inexorable workings of poetic justice in their plots, answered a very deep need in a people working hard to achieve the kind of comfort, plenty, and fairness that it saw in the films every week. Just as the cynical materialism of the 1920s succeeded the innocence and honor of the Griffith era, the optimism and wholesomeness of the 1930s succeeded the values of the Jazz Age.

Women in the Studio Era

Ginger Rogers said it, and when she danced with Fred Astaire she demonstrated it: "A woman can do anything a man can do, but she can do it backwards and in high heels."

In the Studio Era, there were many crucial women in front of the camera, but there were not very many women behind the camera. There was Katharine Hepburn, for example, who as a strong role model got women to wear pants, and there was Shirley Temple, who was the most popular star in the United States from 1934 to 1938. (In 1937, royalties from Shirley Temple dolls and other merchandise earned the nine-year-old almost $4 million a year, on top of her $307,000 salary; her nearest competition was Clark Gable,

who made $272,000 that same year.) But there was only one director: Dorothy Arzner.

The unions and guilds were virtually closed to women during the 1930s and 1940s. Of course the studios would have collapsed without their typists, and the editors would have been lost if the "script girls"—later called Script Supervisors—had not kept track of all the changes of dialogue on the set, take by take; these jobs were given almost exclusively to women. But most of the big jobs were reserved for men. Many women were employed as assistant film editors because of their relatively small fingers, but there were very few women editors. Marjorie Fowler, who became an editor in the silent period and was still at work in the 1970s, was the first film editor to use a diagonal splicer for sound editing. Cutting diagonally across the tape spread the splice along as it crossed the tape head or sound reader, instead of making the cut hit the head all at once; it made the difference between an inaudible cut and a pop.

Of the women who were talent scouts and agents, one of the most powerful and distinguished was Kay Brown. Her first job was to read for RKO in search of literary properties that would make good movies. She found Edna Ferber's novel *Cimarron*, which won the Oscar for Best Picture of 1931. She represented such writers as Isak Dinesen, Lillian Hellman, and Arthur Miller and such actors as Montgomery Clift, John Gielgud, Alec Guinness, Rex Harrison, and Fredric March. For producer David O. Selznick she found the books *Rebecca* and *Gone With the Wind*, which also won Best Picture Oscars, and such overseas talent as Ingrid Bergman, Vivien Leigh, and Alfred Hitchcock.

Some women exercised significant influence over the film industry as uncredited advisors to their husbands. Walt Disney ran all his ideas past his wife, Lillian, and she was recognized within the studio as having played an integral part in its growth. The most famous example is this: When Walt told her that he had thought of a new character, Mortimer Mouse, Lillian made it clear that she preferred the name Mickey.

Frances Marion, the first woman to win the Oscar for Best Screenplay (*The Big House*, 1930), began writing for the pictures in 1916; before that, she had worked for Lois Weber as a production assistant. In the 1930s, she wrote

Katharine Hepburn reads a script.

Fig. 11-10

primarily for MGM. For decades she was Hollywood's highest-paid screenwriter. Her scripts include *Rebecca of Sunnybrook Farm* (for Pickford), *The Scarlet Letter* and *The Wind* (for Gish), *The Son of the Sheik* (for Valentino), *Love* and *Anna Christie* and *Camille* (for Garbo), *Min and Bill*, *Dinner at Eight*, and *Stella Dallas*. She also directed Pickford in *The Love Light* (1921) and directed numerous films starring Marion Davies. Another writer, Joan Harrison, who co-wrote *Rebecca* for Hitchcock, became a producer in 1944 with *Phantom Lady*; she was one of the very few female producers in the Studio Era. Later, Harrison was the associate producer for TV's *Alfred Hitchcock Presents*.

One of the first black women to make a memorable appearance onscreen in the mainstream cinema (as opposed to the race movies) was Etta Moten Barnett, who sang a chorus of "Remember the Forgotten Man" in *Gold Diggers of 1933*. Lena Horne, who made her own debut in 1938 (*The Duke is Tops*), called her a role model. (Horne became a star in two 1943 films, *Cabin in the Sky* and *Stormy Weather*.) The first black to

win an Oscar was Hattie McDaniel, for her work as Best Supporting Actress in *Gone With the Wind*; the night of the awards ceremony, held in 1940, she was also, according to *Variety*, the first black ever to sit at an Academy banquet.

Mae Questel was the voice of Betty Boop (after the very first cartoons) and Olive Oyl; she was offscreen and unknown to the public but one of the best-loved performers of the period. Hedy Lamarr was a famous actress, widely recognized onscreen, but one of her most interesting achievements was unknown for many years; in fact, it was classified. In 1942 Lamarr and composer George Antheil patented a frequency-hopping radio encryption technique; later it was called spread-spectrum technology. They donated it to the Navy as an antijamming device for torpedoes that were controlled by radio signals, but the military did not manage to employ it during the war. Now spread-spectrum technology is found in cellular phones, military radios, and wireless Internet connections.

Dorothy Arzner, who began as an editor (see Chapter 6), used her editing skills to great effect

Fig. 11-11

A poster for The Love Light, *featuring the star and the writer–director.*

in Paramount's first talkie, *The Wild Party* (1929), breaking up the rock-still dialogue takes with shots in which the camera moved or was not fixed on the characters' talking faces; the result was a film directed as if it were not crippled by the demands of sound recording. While shooting *The Wild Party*, she decided the microphone could be dangled over the actors from a fishing pole and follow them; her "fishpole" mike may have been the first boom microphone. She worked at Paramount, Columbia, RKO, and MGM, and for most of her career she was the only woman director in Hollywood. Her slick, professional pictures all made money. She chose scripts with strong and interesting female leads, women whose desires and ambitions determined the story and who were portrayed by some of the top actresses of the period. She showed a complete control of emotion—for example, she turned the audience's sympathies toward the unlikable heroine of *Craig's Wife* (1936) with a single, subtle close-up at the end of the picture. When the heroine of *Dance, Girl, Dance* (1940)

is told by Mr. Right at the happy ending to "Go ahead and laugh, Judy O'Brien," it is a safe bet that many members of the audience laugh through tears, responding to the emotional undercurrents of the whole picture as they are gathered together and focused in that line. A minute earlier, Judy wanted to laugh when she realized how simply things could have turned out if only she had known who he was at first—but what that means is how much comic business would have been unnecessary, how many comic misunderstandings and bad decisions would have been avoided: in short, how much of life could have been missed. It is a great insight into comedy.

Arzner caught the nuances of life as well as its big gestures, as can be seen in Crawford's brazen attitude in *The Bride Wore Red* (1937) or Hepburn's noble suicide—and her breaking an altitude record—at the climax of *Christopher Strong* (1933). Her women know themselves or, like Clara Bow in *The Wild Party*, are capable of learning the truth about themselves. Her heroines are always fully realized human beings, even

Fig. 11-12
Dorothy Arzner looks through the camera.

if the period's story formulas may make them seem less so. Arzner found in the "woman's picture" a way to address the universal ambition to do honorably and well, even if many others do not understand why one considers it right to behave as one does. There is, after all, always the hope that someone else will understand one's view of the world. Such a person, Arzner would argue, would be a genuine friend and perhaps a mate.

Arzner always worked to express what she called "a woman's point of view." In a 1932 interview she said, "There should be more of us directing. Try as any man may, he will never be able to get the woman's viewpoint in directing certain stories."

The Comics

Some of the most distinctive American films of the 1930s, like those of the previous two decades, were comedies. It was the great period of screwball comedy. Sophisticated romantic comedies flourished along with low-budget

spoofs. There were also films that took a dark look at some of the roughest and most disappointing aspects of life, using comedy to set the world as right as it could be.

Late Chaplin

Chaplin survived the transition to sound by making no apparent transition at all. His first two sound films, *City Lights* and *Modern Times*, used a synchronized score and clever sound effects but little synchronized speech (none at all in *City Lights*). Chaplin was certain that Charlie, the little tramp, was a man of mime, a character not made for a world of words.

In *City Lights* (1931), Charlie's pantomime takes him into the society of the rich, where he makes friends with a suicidal millionaire who is friendly and generous when drunk, cold and callous when sober—and forgetful of whatever had happened while he was drunk. Charlie's intermittent closeness to the world of the rich, as the millionaire remembers or forgets him, allows him to help a poor blind girl (Virginia Cherrill) who,

Fig. 11-13

Fig. 11-14

Modern Times: *a televised Boss spies on Charlie in the washroom, then feeds him by machine.*

Fig. 11-15

Fig. 11-16

Fig. 11-17

Fig. 11-18

Chaplin's women. With the ideally beautiful statue (Fig. 11-15) and flowerseller (Virginia Cherrill, Fig. 11-16) in City Lights; *with the unbeautiful realities of his "wives" (Margaret Hoffman, Fig. 11-17; Martha Raye, Fig. 11-18) as the bigamist in* Monsieur Verdoux.

significant in the Chaplin symbolism, sells flowers to keep herself alive. Charlie scrapes up enough money to pay for the young woman's operation; she recovers her eyesight, opens a flower shop, and eventually discovers her benefactor, recognizing him by touch. The audience is not told whether they have a romantic future. An agonizingly poignant close-up of Charlie's face ends the film. The final shot of *City Lights* is so memorable because it is so open; it stops at the climax and refuses to provide a resolution.

In *Modern Times* (1936), Chaplin asks whether the tramp is capable of achieving marriage, for marriages require homes, and homes require payments, and payments require jobs. And this is the Depression. So in *Modern Times*, the little tramp, as always, is at the mercy of the social order, especially of the immense industrial machinery of an increasingly technological society. At the end of *Modern Times*, the tramp and his "wife" (Paulette Goddard, soon to become Chaplin's actual wife) walk away from the camera and from society, literally heading for the hills, for their kind of marriage cannot survive in such a society.

Modern Times would be Chaplin's last stand against the modern dialogue times and the last pure incarnation of the Everyman Tramp. Consistent with the metaphors of enslaving machinery in *Modern Times*, Chaplin depicts the synchronized soundtrack as another enslaving machine—a television with which the factory boss monitors his workers' most private activities or a phonograph that subordinates human movement to a recorded verbal message. Chaplin lets us hear the record and the boss's voice as it blasts from the monitor's speaker, but when people talk normally to each other, we read their words. In the climactic restaurant sequence of the film, Charlie finally makes synchronized sounds, but with a sly difference: not talking sense but singing nonsense. Otherwise—except for a chorus of singing waiters—only the machines talk. The silent intertitle, and Chaplin's performance and music, convey a more human language; the talking picture is a talking machine.

In his next picture, the talkie *The Great Dictator* (1940), Chaplin played two roles: a Jewish barber, closely akin to his underdog tramp, and the villainous top-dog Führer, whom Chaplin—with his short, toothbrush moustache—resembled. The comic action of the film pleads eloquently and ironically for the rights of individual human expression against the stifling, murderous power of the tyrant. Unfortunately, Chaplin discovered that the dialogue film could plead with speeches as well as with comic action. The didacticism of the film's final speech, a fervent but overlong and sentimental appeal for world peace, is a dramatic letdown.

The same overt moralizing clouds Chaplin's last two masterpieces, *Monsieur Verdoux* and *Limelight. Monsieur Verdoux* (1947) begins with a brilliant seriocomic premise (suggested to Chaplin by Orson Welles): A delightful, witty, urbane gentleman marries a series of rich women specifically to bump them off, using their legacies to support his crippled wife and child on an idyllic country estate. The film necessarily questions the relationship of the means of an action to its end, whether murder is justifiable if its ultimate purpose is virtuous. The film develops its theme with a series of acidly hilarious vignettes in which Verdoux goes about his murderous business in the most fastidious, matter-of-fact way. Most hilarious of all are his frustrating attempts to dispose of the coarse, clumsy, big-mouth wife played in perfect counterpoint to Chaplin's diminutive suaveness by Martha Raye.

But as in *The Great Dictator*, Chaplin deserts comic objectivity at the end of *Monsieur Verdoux* to spell out the film's implications in a bald and unnecessary speech: Society commits the same crimes and accepts the same assumptions as Monsieur Verdoux, except on a much larger scale.

Comic insight and uncomfortable sentimentality pull *Limelight* (1952) in two directions. The flashback scenes that re-create the music-hall routines of the old vaudevillian, Calvero (Chaplin), are funny and touching, the former music-hall clown's ultimate tribute to the world that fostered his mime and art. The scenes in the present—of the clown's love for a ballerina (played by Claire Bloom) whom he saves from suicide and despair—suffer from overstatement. Even so, *Limelight* is profoundly moving, and the climactic routine with Keaton is a revelation.

It was only in his last two pictures that Chaplin really faltered. *A King in New York* (1957), which takes on everything from McCarthyism to the wide screen, is interesting but rarely engaging, and *A Countess from Hong Kong* (1967) has a severe, classic style that interferes with the film's painful attempts to be funny.

Chaplin maintained his power and individuality in the Studio Era because he needed to make no concessions to Hollywood's commercial structure. Chaplin produced and owned his own pictures, ran his own studio, and released through United Artists; the popularity of his films earned him the profits to make more pictures just as he wanted to make them. At the opposite extreme, the career of Buster Keaton, who in the Sound Era was "just an actor," no longer in charge of his films, turned into a disaster.

Chaplin's cinematic technique was never dependent on montage or intrusive camerawork. The antagonism of Cold War America ended his American career in 1952. Only after 20 years did Chaplin return briefly to America from Switzerland, where he died in 1977.

Disney's World

Walt Disney, like Chaplin, made the transition into the Studio Era by maintaining his commercial and, consequently, artistic independence. Disney, whose fantasies of drawing and music, movement and rhythm had evolved in the first years of sound, found one further ally in the 1930s—color. Whereas the realistic, live-action studio films were trying to tame the effects of color, to blur its garishness, to make its hues mirror nature, Disney's animated fantasies could use color as one more controlled, artificial element. The counterpoint of picture and music in the Disney cartoon acquired a third contrapuntal line. Shifts in color could accompany the shifting tones of the music and action. Expressive color, like rhythm and music, became a kinetic element. The same advantage that Disney enjoyed over realistic films in the free use of sound also gave him the freedom to manipulate color—surrealistically, as in the "pink elephants" sequence of *Dumbo* (1941), or realistically, as in most of *Bambi* (1942). Disney brought Technicolor to his Silly Symphonies, to his animal characters (Mickey, Donald, and Pluto), and eventually to his first feature, *Snow White and the Seven Dwarfs* (1937), one of the biggest hits of the decade and of all time.

The Disney fantasies of color and motion were perfectly suited to the audience's craving for happiness, wholesomeness, and optimism in films—even if they often terrified children. His "Who's Afraid of the Big, Bad Wolf?" from *The Three Little Pigs* (1933) became not only a popular song but also a metaphor for the whole country's cheerful defiance of the big, bad "wolf at the door," the Depression. The film itself was a socially acceptable Protestant-ethic lecture: to build with bricks, not straw. (Less acceptable anti-Semitic elements have been deleted from most prints still in circulation.) But Disney's happy cleanliness began taking its toll on his visual imagination. Disney gradually deserted the short for the feature, the fantasy–abstract film of color, music, and movement for the sentimental story film that attempted to blend fantasy and realism. Even in 1937, critics noticed a tension in *Snow White* between the fantastic rendering of the witch and the dwarfs and the clumsy, sticky attempts at realism in rendering Snow White and her prince. After the climactic *Fantasia* (1940), his films took fewer chances. Everything became too controlled and perfect—an aesthetic he extended in the 1950s to Disneyland.

Lubitsch and Sound

Ernst Lubitsch, whose camera had learned to comment on a character or situation by shooting an apparently insignificant detail that was loaded with implications, discovered that sound, as well as pictures, could make such touches. In his first sound films, the continental musicals, he mastered the new machines and learned to make the sound film as fluid and effortless as the silent one. But his greatest sound films were dialogue pictures, slick comedies of manners, translated by his cinematic imagination (often from the stage) into his unique film terms: *Design for Living* (1933), *Angel* (1937), *Ninotchka* (1939, with Garbo), *To Be or Not To Be* (1942, with Jack Benny and Carole Lombard), and, especially, *Trouble in Paradise* (1932). *Trouble in Paradise* is such a subtle, deceptively artless film that its bold, imaginative mixture of picture and sound seems completely consistent with the shiny conventionalities of Studio Era films.

Trouble in Paradise is the story of an urbane, elegant crook whose charm and social graces allow him to work his way into the hotels and hearts of the very rich where he performs his

Trouble in Paradise: *elegant veneers. The two thieves (Miriam Hopkins and Herbert Marshall, right) use an elegant supper as an occasion for fleecing one another.*

Fig. 11-19

Fig. 11-20

Fig. 11-21

Lubitsch's sexual wit in **Trouble in Paradise**—*from a reflection of the embracing lovers in the mirror (Fig. 11-20) to the shadows of their bodies on the bed (Fig. 11-21).*

high-stakes thievery. Eventually the master crook, Gaston Monescu (Herbert Marshall), finds himself caught between his love for two women, Mariette Colet (Kay Francis), the rich perfume heiress he is swindling, and Lily (Miriam Hopkins), his clever accomplice. Because he is a thief, because he is merely a pretender to propriety in the gleaming world of the rich and proper, because his past has determined his future, Monescu eventually leaves Mariette for Lily.

Lubitsch brings his droll carnival of thieves to life with his dry, witty control of picture, sound effects, and speech. The film opens on a shot of a garbage pail. A man picks up the pail and tosses its contents into his "truck." Except that "truck" turns out to be a gondola, for this is a garbage man in Venice, city of romance. As the garbage gondola journeys on its route, Lubitsch shoots the gleaming water of the canals and the picturesque *palazzi* surrounding them; the garbage gondolier sings plaintively, "O sole mio." The romantic song continues when the garbage gondola is offscreen. Not only has Lubitsch used the contrast of sound and image to deflate picture-postcard romance, one of the film's themes, but he also has underscored, metaphorically, the film's action, which reveals the "garbage" beneath the pretty surfaces in the lives of the film's "beautiful people."

Lubitsch handles Monescu's sexual relationships with the two women with the greatest wryness and subtlety. In the first sequence, Lily and Monescu fall in love by discovering each other's crooked cleverness. The two dine in Monescu's elegant hotel suite. Like the opening's garbage gondola, the scene plays the elegant surfaces off against the corruption beneath: The two are not Baron and Countess enjoying a slyly seductive supper but two crooks trying to fleece each other. As the two trade polished banalities, they steal each other's watches, wallets, jewelry. After they discover and sort out each other's goods, Monescu bends over to kiss Lily as she sits on a sofa. Lubitsch dissolves to an empty sofa. Then he cuts to a male arm, its white sleeve implying a discarded dinner jacket, hanging a "Do Not Disturb" sign on the door of his hotel room. Later, Lubitsch implies the direction of Madame Colet's and Monescu's intentions by throwing the shadows of their embracing bodies on the coverlet of her bed. The implications of such juxtapositions are obvious, clearly a sign of the screen's pre-Breen sexual suggestiveness.

Add to Lubitsch's subtle images and clever music his satiric handling of the minor characters (Edward Everett Horton, Charles Ruggles, C. Aubrey Smith), and Samson Raphaelson's sparkling dialogue, which consistently pins a new tail on an old cliché: "A bird in the hand is worth two in jail"; "If you behave like a gentleman, I'll break your neck"; "I love you as a crook, but don't become one of those useless, good-for-nothing gigolos"; "a member of the *nouveau* poor." The combined ingredients make *Trouble in Paradise* one of the most polished comedies of manners in the history of film.

Frank Capra

Frank Capra also turned to comedies of manners in 1934. But instead of the suave manners of Lubitsch's shiny Europe, Capra, born in Sicily, focused on the ingenuous, homespun manners of

the most American America—and, in an insightful part-talkie, *The Younger Generation* (1929), on the conflicts that assimilation raises in a family of immigrants. Although Capra's career in films stems from silent comedy (recall his work with Harry Langdon) when he was a gag man and staff director at both the Sennett and the Hal Roach studios, Capra became an important director in the era of the talkies after he signed with Columbia Pictures, where producer Harry Cohn guaranteed him creative freedom. At Columbia, he met Robert Riskin, who was to write most of his important scripts. The Capra–Riskin film was generally a witty contemporary morality play that pitted a good man—usually a "little guy" who is naïve, sincere, folksy, unaffected, unintellectual, apolitical—against evil social forces: money, politics, affectation, social status, human insensitivity. The "little guy" emerges from the struggle not only victorious but also wiser about the ways of the world—but so does a good, intellectual, political man like the hero of Capra's *Lost Horizon* (1937).

It Happened One Night (1934), the first movie to "sweep" the Oscars—winning Academy Awards for best picture, director, actor, actress, and adapted screenplay—examines the clash of a snooping newspaper reporter (Clark Gable) and a rich society woman (Claudette Colbert) fleeing her wealthy father to marry a worthless boyfriend. The two travel cross-country by bus, discovering the hazards as well as the charms of rural, uncitified America—motels, bad roads, hitchhiking, and people. Among the people they discover are themselves and one another—what makes them alike and makes them like others despite the gulf between their material and intellectual backgrounds.

In *Mr. Deeds Goes to Town* (1936), a man from the country (Gary Cooper) inherits a pile of money and comes to the city to discover how to spend it. The city folk belittle the country ways of the hero "hick," and leading the laughter is the snobbish reporter (Jean Arthur) with whom Deeds has fallen in love. Deeds eventually converts the woman, discovers that he must use his money to help the poor and starving, and vanquishes the rich who try to prove him insane so they can control his fortune. A whole family of happy, poor eccentrics struggles comically against the forces of money, sophistication, and

It's A Wonderful Life: *"Little guy" George Bailey (James Stewart, right) refuses to abandon his values and sell out to the heartless big capitalist, Potter (Lionel Barrymore, seated).*

Fig. 11-22

industrialization in *You Can't Take It With You* (1938). In *Mr. Smith Goes to Washington* (1939), Mr. Deeds has changed to Mr. Smith, Gary Cooper has changed to James Stewart, and his problem has changed from money to politics. The woman is still Jean Arthur. Although Capra's vision may seem corny and populistic, the consistency of Capra's material, the solid scripts, the sharp cinematography, the unforced acting in his films and their crisp comic timing make them sincere, intelligent statements of the era's optimism and humanism—as well as batty celebrations of comic anarchy. It is hard to find a movie more hilarious than *Arsenic and Old Lace* (1941, released 1944), which has no significant social content and is one of the greatest examples of comic rhythm—and the intelligent adaptation of a play—in the sound film.

But there is a dark side to the Capra films as well. *The Bitter Tea of General Yen* (1932) never turns sweet. Mr. Deeds must endure the courtroom malice of his accusers for an agonizingly long time, until the judge finally pronounces him the sanest man who ever entered his courtroom. Mr. Smith suffers another ordeal, a Senate filibuster that pushes his physical endurance to the limit, until his enemy finally capitulates to the strength of his honest courage. In *Meet John Doe* (1941) Capra demonstrates that the folksy

slogans of an ordinary John Doe (Gary Cooper again) are uncomfortably close to the fascistic slogans of a corrupt politician (played by Edward Arnold, Capra's favorite representative of plutocratic oppression). In *It's A Wonderful Life* (1946, released 1947), made one year after World War II and widespread knowledge of the Nazi death camps, George Bailey (James Stewart, who co-produced the film) has become so frustrated by his drab middle-American existence that only a heavenly miracle can rescue him from suicide and restore his faith in his own accomplishments. The legions of God and the Devil struggle mightily in these allegorical Capra comedies, and it takes a terrifyingly long time for justice, truth, and salvation to triumph.

Preston Sturges

Preston Sturges wrote and directed witty moral comedies on American subjects, but he was an ironist and satirist who stood many of the era's wholesome and optimistic conventions on their ear. He was also the first major writer–director of the Sound Era—and in Hollywood, the first writer allowed to direct his own scripts. *The Great McGinty* (1940), the first film Sturges directed after a distinguished career as a screenwriter (he wrote *The Power and the Glory*, 1933, and *Easy Living*, 1937), ridicules American democratic

Sullivan's Travels: *Aided by his valet (Eric Blore, left), millionaire director John L. Sullivan (Joel McCrea) tries on his hobo outfit.*

Fig. 11-23

politics and the naïve notion that the voter really controls the government. *Christmas in July* (1940) satirizes the American dream of getting rich quick without hard work. *The Lady Eve* (1941) is a burlesque of American sexual–romantic conventions, particularly the puritanical insistence on virginity and innocence. It may well be his funniest work, rivals *Sullivan's Travels* as his best, and gives Henry Fonda and Barbara Stanwyck their greatest comic roles. *Sullivan's Travels* (1941) is the story of a Hollywood director (Joel McCrea) who is weary of making entertaining fluff and aspires to make films laden with Serious Moral and Social Significance; he decides that in order to make such films, he must learn firsthand what it feels like to be poor. In the course of his travels, the director discovers true love (Veronica Lake) as well as the value of "merely" making people laugh.

During the war years, Sturges courageously extended his satire to American perceptions of the war, our confused sexual standards in wartime (*The Miracle of Morgan's Creek*, 1943, released 1944, and which D. W. Griffith found hilarious), and our superficial definitions of heroism and patriotism (*Hail the Conquering Hero*, 1944). His last major work was a blisteringly funny romantic comedy, *Unfaithfully Yours*

(1948); it starred Rex Harrison as a jealous conductor and Linda Darnell as his wife. Sturges could get away with his audacious iconoclasm because of the unmatched verbal richness of his scripts, the spirited wit of his acting ensemble, and the ingenuity of his physical slapstick comedy.

George Cukor

George Cukor was another comic ironist, but of a very different sort. Like Lubitsch, Cukor also made comedies of sexual manners; but unlike Lubitsch, these were the manners of monogamous America. And as in Sturges's films, these were American manners filtered through the lens of Hollywood convention.

Cukor was known best as a "woman's director." After he was removed as director of *Gone With the Wind*, Vivien Leigh and Olivia de Havilland insisted that he continue to coach them, which he did in his home. (He also coached Judy Garland early in the making of *The Wizard of Oz*.) At RKO and especially MGM, he specialized in adaptations of novels (*Little Women*, 1933; *David Copperfield*, 1935) and Broadway plays (*A Bill of Divorcement*, 1932; *Dinner at Eight*, 1933; *Holiday*, 1938; *The Women*, 1939; *The Philadelphia Story*, 1940).

Fig. 11-24
The Four Marx Brothers in Duck Soup. *From left, Chico, Zeppo, Groucho, and Harpo.*

He also teamed with writers Ruth Gordon and Garson Kanin on a series of Spencer Tracy–Katharine Hepburn vehicles at MGM (*Adam's Rib*, 1949) and Judy Holliday vehicles at Columbia (*Born Yesterday*, 1950). From Hepburn to Harlow to Garbo (*Camille*, 1936, released 1937) to Holliday to Judy Garland (*A Star Is Born*, 1954) to another Hepburn (Audrey in *My Fair Lady*, 1964), Cukor elicited superb performances from female stars.

The reason was Cukor's consciousness that the sharp distinctions between male and female sexual identity were not as simple as they seemed in American movies. Cukor was the one major director of Hollywood's Studio Era who was gay—or, at least, was willing to admit it in the 1970s, when it was safe to come out. He disguised his alternative sexual taste behind heterosexual comic arguments that challenged the prevailing assumptions of male domination.

For example: why shouldn't the male lawyer, Adam (Tracy), and the female lawyer, his wife Amanda (Hepburn, defending Judy Holliday), adopt fundamentally different strategies of law in *Adam's Rib*, since these laws have been written by men for men?

Cukor's films never answer such questions; instead, the director presents his carefully balanced and amusingly paradoxical evidence. He is very much an outside observer looking in, refusing to take a side in the battle of the sexes. He presents his own oblique self-portrait in *Adam's Rib*—Kip Lurie, a successful composer for Broadway shows, a sort of Cole Porter or Noël Coward who lives across the hall from Adam and Amanda. Like Cukor, Kip is clearly gay—as clear as Hollywood could make such matters in 1949—an outsider to the marriage of Adam and Amanda (just as, offscreen, Cukor was a friendly outsider to the relationship of Tracy and Hepburn).

In *Adam's Rib*, there is a difference between male and female, Adam and Amanda, Tracy and Hepburn, and yet there is no difference. *"Vive la différence,"* Adam concludes, yet no one can say precisely what that difference happens to be.

Cukor's cinematic style presents these ironies and paradoxes with a balanced detachment that creates a dialectic between characters and incidents in the plot as well as within the frame itself. In Cukor's carefully balanced frames, conflicting decor and symmetrical composition often indicate the moral and social paradoxes of the film. Though less idiosyncratic than the social comedies of his contemporaries, Cukor's films have worn wonderfully well, for social and sexual consciousness have finally caught up with his subtle ironies.

The Marx Brothers

As with the silent comedies, many of the sound comedies wore the personalities of their comics rather than their directors. Because Langdon and Keaton and numerous other clowns who were schooled in the silent tradition never successfully combined talk and movement, Hollywood imported clowns from Broadway who had already effected the combination. The Marx Brothers even shot their first films in New York. In 1929, they re-created their current stage hit, *The Cocoanuts*, for the screen. The Marx Brothers combined the great traditions of American physical comedy with a verbal humor that perfectly suited their physical types. The plots of the Marx Brothers' films were irrelevant, providing occasions for gags and irreverent parodies of the conventional behavior in the self-important worlds into which the zany comics dropped.

The Marx Brothers made some of the funniest movies in history. People are still arguing about whether *Duck Soup* (1933) and the Paramount films are better than *A Night at the Opera* (1935) and the MGM films. Starting with the eldest, the

Fig. 11-25
Groucho in **Duck Soup.**

five brothers were Chico (Leonard), Harpo (Adolph, called Arthur), Groucho (Julius Henry), Gummo (Milton), and Zeppo (Herbert). In vaudeville, Gummo was part of the team; on Broadway and in the first films, he was replaced by Zeppo. When Zeppo left after *Duck Soup*, the Four Marx Brothers became three: Groucho, Chico, and Harpo. In a number of the best pictures, Margaret Dumont played a conventional woman trying to manage the chaos but also attracted to it. Almost all of their movies featured musical sequences in which Chico plays the piano or Harpo plays the harp; they were part of the act as much as Groucho's cigar and painted mustache—or the verbal and visual puns.

The Marx Brothers pictures were brilliantly written and directed at a screwball pace that could slow down to watch in wonder as an almost infinite joke became more funny the more it went on. They were masters of timing, both visual and verbal, and they were planted in the silent and the sound comedy by Harpo's miming

and Groucho and Chico's dialogue. In themselves they were figures as fundamental as Chaplin's tramp. The films abound with physical comedy and mad visuals: the football sequence in *Horse Feathers* (1932), the mirror scene in *Duck Soup*, the stateroom packed with human sardines or the split-second timing of the bed-shifting sequence in *A Night at the Opera*. And for brilliant verbal doubletalk there is the "Why-a-duck?" sequence in *The Cocoanuts*, in which Groucho tries to sell Chico a piece of island property with a viaduct; the "Party of the First Part" sequence in *A Night at the Opera*, in which Groucho and Chico tear apart a contract (literally) clause by sanity clause; and the "Tootsie Frootsie Ice Cream" sequence of *A Day at the Races* (1937), in which Chico sells Groucho a coded manual for betting the ponies, and then another manual to decode the first manual, and then yet another to decode that one. Like their puns, their gags built and built until audiences were weak with laughter. From Harpo's horn

Mae West: *The caricature of female sensuality poses beside a caricature of her own sensuality in a 1932 publicity photo.*

Fig. 11-26

to Groucho's walk, the Marx Brothers films revealed the key elements of sound comedy—comic physical types suited to their comic personalities, to the physical-comedy situations, and to the verbal wit. Comic talkies had to move as well as talk.

Mae West

And sometimes the talk was dirty. Mae West, another Broadway import, had her own comic personality, a parody of the amoral, sensual female hedonist who frankly enjoyed nice clothes, nice food, and a nice tumble in the hay. She physically suited that personality. No petite, lithe, virginal ingénue was Mae, but a buxom, hefty broad. Her rolling eyes, her gyrating hips, her falling, throaty voice consciously tried to unmask an opponent or undress a friend. And her comic lines fit the eyes, the voice, and the body: "Beulah, peel me a grape"; "Are you packin' a rod or are you just glad to see me?" Even her croaking "Oh" said much more than oh. Like the Marx Brothers' plots, Mae West's film stories, which she wrote herself, were slender lines on which to hang her own personal business: her gyrations, her comments, her songs. The films' action inevitably ran Mae up against the forces of respectability and legality.

Ironically, only one of her films, *She Done Him Wrong* (1933), is, because of its pre-Code date, fully a Mae West film. Most suggestive (and most characteristic of Mae's style) in the film are her songs. One of them is her set of dirty lyrics to the familiar tune "Frankie and Johnny"; after all, Frankie didn't shoot Johnny just because she saw him with another woman in a public bar. The second song was often referred to as "THAT song"; its noneuphemistic title was "I Like a Guy What Takes His Time." When she was casting the picture and saw beginner Cary Grant, she said, "If he can talk, I'll take him."

The effect of the Production Code was obvious in her next film, which was forced to change its title from *It Ain't No Sin* (with its obvious implications) to *I'm No Angel* (1933). Despite the financial success of *She Done Him Wrong*, Mae West's film career was cut up and cut short by the Breen sanctions against overt sexuality and the glamorous portrayal of vice. (Still, she worked in as many suggestive lines as she could, and of censorship she said, "I believe in it. I made a fortune out of it.") In her later films—*Goin' to Town* (1935), *Klondike Annie* (1936), and even *My Little Chickadee* (1940) with W. C. Fields—Mae West becomes a clean-scrubbed caricature of her

W. C. Fields caught in the trap of respectable American life in **The Bank Dick.**

Fig. 11-27

own sexuality, which was, in its original frankness, a caricature of sexuality in the first place.

W. C. Fields

W. C. Fields was another great comedian of the sound stage. Like Mae West and the Marx Brothers, Fields's comedy stemmed from himself rather than from the stories in which he found himself. Like Mae West and the Marx Brothers, Fields combined a comic personality, a comic physical type, and a style of verbal wit that fitted both his mind and his body. Fields also came to films from the stage, but the former vaudevillian, famous today for his gravelly, whiskey voice, began his film career in silent comedies directed by Edward Sutherland, Gregory LaCava, and D. W. Griffith. Although it is impossible to imagine Fields without his voice, an occasional sequence from one of the sound films reveals his powers as pure physical clown: his clumsy attempts to play croquet in *Poppy* (1936), the battle with bent pool cues in *Six of a Kind* (1934), his deft juggling in *The Old-Fashioned Way* (1934), and the car crashes in *If I Had A Million* (1932). Physically funny too is the Fields body—the booze-bloated nose, the beer belly—which he tries to dignify with the spiffiest, most fastidiously selected period costumes.

Fields is the great spinner of words—of melodious euphemisms, euphonious malapropisms, florid rhetoric. Some of his greatest comic routines—as in *The Fatal Glass of Beer* (1933)—push repetition to the limit. At once obnoxious and charming, his affectation of polite speech is like all his other pretensions to politeness—pure sham. Beneath the fancy waistcoats and purple prose beats the heart of a dirty old man who drinks, smokes, swears, and gambles, who hates women (especially sweet old ones), children (especially cute little ones), animals, sobriety, and all respectable social institutions (especially marriage, work, honest business dealings, and the law). In *Never Give a Sucker an Even Break* (1941), he tells the audience that the soda-shop scene he is in was supposed to have been set in a bar, but the censors changed it. (Other great reflexive films of that year were *Sullivan's Travels* and Ole Olsen and Chic Johnson's *Hellzapoppin'*, which was directed by H. C. Potter.) In films like *Tillie and Gus* (1933), *It's a Gift* (1934), and *The Bank Dick* (1940), Fields—like the Marx Brothers and Mae West—was the foe of everything sentimental and nice. In an era of glamorized

The Blue Angel: *the chaotic clutter of the nightclub; Marlene Dietrich on stage.*

Fig. 11-28

sentimentality and niceness, their essential vulgarity and comic crudeness were especially refreshing. They provided the era's comic snore to puncture the Hays Office's American Dream.

Masters of Mood and Action

A number of noncomic directors made individualistic films that were powerful exceptions to the studio rule. The most significant of these *auteurs* were Josef von Sternberg, John Ford, Howard Hawks, Alfred Hitchcock, and Orson Welles.

Josef von Sternberg

By turns brooding and extravagant, the *mise-en-scène* of von Sternberg's films was obsessive and intricate; at times it was more impressive than the movies themselves. Visually, the von Sternberg films were gleaming gems, rich in atmospheric detail, shimmering pools of light and contrasting shadow, the excitement of a perpetually moving, prowling camera, the luminous face of Marlene Dietrich—in shadow, in blazing light, veiled, feathered, powdered, hazed. But beneath von Sternberg's gleaming surfaces—the exotic locales, the symbolic details, the smoke, the shafts of light, the audacious sexual innuendoes that could have gotten past the censors only because they didn't understand visual symbols—his films reveal certain problems of plotting and characterization. (This cannot be said of his early, relatively understated, dramatically

powerful works *Underworld* [1927], *The Last Command* [1928], and *The Docks of New York* [1928], all of which are tightly constructed.)

The Blue Angel (1930), von Sternberg's second sound film, was shot in Germany for Ufa. In the early sound years, Hollywood discovered a new problem: the language barrier. The silent cinema—a genuinely international language—simply substituted new titles in new languages as a film leaped from country to country. But with sound, before film distributors discovered dubbing and subtitling, it was common to shoot the same film in different languages and sometimes with different casts. Von Sternberg, born in Vienna without the "von" and raised in America, went to Germany to take part in this cinematic internationalism and direct, in German and English versions, Ufa's first talkie.

The Blue Angel is a Circe story. A bewitching woman, the nightclub singer Lola Lola (Marlene Dietrich) steadily turns a compulsively orderly schoolteacher (Emil Jannings) into a beast; he even crows like a cock to show his transformation. It is also the tale of a siren (or, in German terms, a Lorelei) whose singing lures men to their doom. If the film is among von Sternberg's best, that is because it is based on a strong novel, Heinrich Mann's *Professor Unrat*, and because the director renders every step in Professor Rath's demise with the greatest intimacy and clarity. Atmosphere and visual images in the film

The Blue Angel: *the antiseptic order and clarity of Emil Jannings's classroom, invaded by the influence of Lola Lola.*

Fig. 11-29

Fig. 11-30
Von Sternberg putting his Blonde Venus through hoops: Dietrich as a sleazy whore...

Fig. 11-31
...and as an international star.

are the means to depict the two conflicting characters and lifestyles. Professor Rath's classroom is clean, bright, with desks arranged in geometric regularity; the Blue Angel club where Lola sings is smoky, hazy, chaotic, dim, and hung with entangling nets.

Like the great films of Jannings's past, *The Last Laugh* and *Variety*, *The Blue Angel* refuses to draw simplistically sentimental or romantic conclusions. Professor Rath's ascetic life is sterile, schematic, so crammed with routine that it lacks the breath of life; like his caged bird (whose singing contrasts with that of the unconfinable Lola Lola), he is dead. Lola's sensual life is selfish and amoral; she is committed to love, not to loving someone—as her famous song, "Falling in Love Again," so clearly indicates. The film's business is not moral comment but the tragic story of what happens to a man from one life who tastes a drop of another. The wine that at first makes Rath drunk eventually poisons him. His final metamorphosis is into the kind of pathetic clown that he saw in Lola's dressing room when he first met her, a figure who foreshadows Rath's fate. Rejected and humiliated, the shattered professor creeps back to his old classroom to die. The only simple moral comment in the film is against the professor's students, who pervert his name to *Unrat* ("garbage") and who fail to see that, as both strict disciplinarian and broken clown, Rath is a human being who deserves understanding. When Lola does betray him—and the troupe's return to the Blue Angel exposes him to the jeers of his former students, bringing the wreck full circle—the students are as heartless and vicious as the fallen doorman's neighbors in *The Last Laugh*.

The von Sternberg–Dietrich American films are as dazzling visually as *The Blue Angel* (in fact, even more so), and like it they are suffused with a pervasive sexual energy. Their rich surfaces point to the sexual and psychological intensity beneath the surface. But with the exception of *The Shanghai Gesture* (1941, made without Dietrich), von Sternberg's later films are weak in story value. *The Blue Angel* stood up to the atmospheric pressure; most of the others collapsed, leaving films that were strings of rich, obsessive scenes. The best scene in *Morocco* (1930), the first of von Sternberg's Dietrich films made in America, shows Marlene's first

appearance in the Moroccan nightclub. She is dressed as a man in tails; she sings, Eve-like, about selling apples, which she offers as she sings. A lesbian in the audience is obviously attracted to the male-clad performer. Marlene, knowing the woman's intentions, toys with her while singing and then matter-of-factly walks up to her and kisses her on the mouth. It is a stunning moment of sexual power.

The later von Sternberg–Dietrich films became progressively more bizarre, as if the director were (like von Stroheim) daring the race of Puritans to stop him and, at the same time, were (like Lubitsch) laughing at the sexual childishness of the Puritans for believing these Circean parables. *Blonde Venus* (1932)—which contains enough plot for four films—features Marlene as loving wife, tempted adulteress, devoted mother, cheap whore in a border town, and international sensation of the music hall. Despite the film's wandering plot, it is redeemed by its moments of intensity and audacity: the sensuous opening scene as Dietrich swims in a shimmering stream (and as Herbert Marshall, impersonating a Boy Scout—at the age of 42!—voyeuristically watches her); the dusty, smoky chiaroscuro of the cheap dive in the Tex–Mex border town; the astonishing visual contrasts of the "Hot Voodoo" number, in which the Blonde Venus, complete with platinum fright wig, pokes her head out of a gorilla costume; Dietrich in white top hat and tails, the masculine guise that attracts the adoration of her male admirers. More than anything else, von Sternberg seems to wonder how many grotesque and outlandish hoops he can make his Blonde Venus jump through without his audience's catching on to the sardonic and satirically contemptuous game.

The coming of the Code and the Hays Office in no way inhibited the director's sexual fantasies but seemed to spur them to new heights. *The Scarlet Empress* (1934), his most sumptuous exercise in *mise-en-scène*, begins with the dreams of the sweet blonde seven-year-old Sophie who later becomes Catherine the Great of Russia. The child's nighttime visions are sadomasochistic fantasies, including the screams of tortured men on the rack and, in what may be the most de Sade–like image ever presented in a "respectable" Studio Era film, the hanging of a male body inside a huge bell, so that his swinging legs and heels can bang against the bell and send its peals out over the town and countryside. This image of swinging torture dissolves into a shot of Sophie herself, moving in pseudosexual rhythm on her childhood swing.

Von Sternberg broke away from Dietrich to direct films without her after the ultimate study of Circean hypnosis, *The Devil Is a Woman*, in 1935. His later work includes the unfinished *I, Claudius* (1937), with Charles Laughton, Emlyn Williams, and Merle Oberon, and *The Saga of Anatahan* (1953), a film he directed for the Japanese film industry and in which he returned to the theme and image of the *femme fatale*. But von Sternberg's period of greatest influence—on both cinematic and cultural fashions—ended when he and Dietrich separated. In von Sternberg's hands, Dietrich became a modern goddess of Sexual Mystery—a celluloid icon of Circe, Aphrodite, Leda, Helen, and Galatea, all wrapped into a single key-lit face. And seven movies.

John Ford

John Ford continued the traditions of D. W. Griffith. Ford was an Irish Catholic born in Maine. He made westerns. Like Griffith's, Ford's values are traditional and sentimental: father, mother, home, and family; law, decency, democracy. Like Griffith—and Frank Capra—Ford was a populist. He praised the little people and

damned those who twisted the system to grab money and power. More like Griffith than Capra, Ford emphasized visual images rather than talk and counterpointed violent dramatic action with rich comedy and wringing pathos. In his westerns, Ford used the settling of the frontier as his basic myth and central metaphor for the emerging American spirit—the bringing of civilization and fruitfulness to the savage wilderness. But Ford's films were neither naïve nor simple in their mythic vision. The "savage" could be very accomplished, evil could be awesomely powerful, and the forces of civilization could be stupid, rigid, and cruel.

The Ford films are as visually striking as von Sternberg's, but more direct and uncluttered. Unlike von Sternberg's Germanically moving camera, Ford's camera composes in space, in width and depth. Dominating Ford's films are the vast vistas of the plains, mountains, and sky, and the shots-in-depth of a group of faces or figures, tensely composed. But Ford never substituted picture taking for picture making. Although the films became complex allegories of good and evil—the lighting, the settings, the weather, the characterizations all supporting the symbolic structure—Ford never forgot the studio prescription that a film must tell a good story.

Ford's directorial career began in 1917 with a series of inexpensive program westerns starring the good badman, Harry Carey. He did not

The Informer: *Ford's feeling for people is reflected in the strength and uniqueness of their faces.*

Fig. 11-32

achieve wide recognition, however, until 1935 with *The Informer* (written by Ford's frequent collaborator, Dudley Nichols), which brought him the first of his many Academy Awards. *The Informer* is a story of the Irish Revolution, with which Ford, the son of an Irish immigrant, was in sympathy. Ford would return frequently to Irish, Catholic, or Irish-American themes—as in *Mary of Scotland* (1936), *The Plough and the Stars* (1936), *The Quiet Man* (1952), and *The Last Hurrah* (1958). In *The Informer*, Gypo (played by Victor McLaglen), a former member of the Irish Republican Army, betrays his closest friend and former comrade to the hated British. The film traces the consequences of his succumbing to this weakness and eventually paying, both physically and mentally, for his betrayal. The film's power lies in Ford's achievement in making Gypo's tortured mind manifest, in showing the man's hurts, hopes, fears, and conflicts.

Like many of Ford's prestigious projects of the late 1930s and early 1940s, *The Informer* was an adaptation of a respected literary work, a novel by Liam O'Flaherty. So were his adaptations of Eugene O'Neill's one-act plays about men at sea, *The Long Voyage Home* (1940), of John Steinbeck's *The Grapes of Wrath* (also 1940), and of Richard Llewellyn's *How Green Was My Valley* (1941). These adaptations were less impressive for their faithfulness to the original source material than for Ford's fondness for his characters and his feeling for the visual surroundings in which they worked, loved, and died. With their awesome contrasts of dark and light, photographed in deep focus (twice by Gregg Toland), these three films convert light and space into both tactile and moral qualities. Indoors, there is the warmth, peace, light, and comfort of family life; outdoors, the dark uncertainty of the world—in the depths of a Welsh mine, in the dark at sea, in the night of a California desert. Whether indoors or out, Ford invests his faith in "the people"—working people, poor people, religious people, family people—never in commercial institutions like banks, mining companies, or government camps.

Ford poured his feelings for America—its history, its destiny, and its people—into his westerns, the kinds of films in which he and brother Francis began. Francis played a small but pivotal role in almost every John Ford film, like the hard-drinking but fair-minded frontiersman in the coonskin cap who serves as a choric member of the jury in *Young Mr. Lincoln* (1939). For John Ford, the coonskin-cap spirit of the frontier suggests the true spirit of American aspiration and civilization, the link between a Lincoln, a Harry Carey, a Francis Ford, and a John Wayne. Two of Ford's major westerns—*Stagecoach* (1939) and *My Darling Clementine* (1946)—are allegorical studies of American history in the years just before and just after World War II.

The coach itself of *Stagecoach* becomes Ford's metaphor for "civilized" society. Like the trains in *The Iron Horse* (1924) and *The Man Who Shot Liberty Valance* (1962), the stagecoach is a manufactured vehicle the makers and occupants of which set out to tame the vast western wastes—in one of Ford's recurring metaphors, to plant a garden in the desert. Although Ford's films examine what civilization does *to* people as well as *for* people (particularly in *The Searchers*, 1956; *Liberty Valance*; and *Cheyenne Autumn*, 1964), in *Stagecoach* the key dramatic conflict is between the microcosm inside the coach and the "savagery" of the land and the Apaches outside it.

Inside Ford's stagecoach is a whole society of white people, of different social classes and mental habits: banker, sheriff, outlaw, salesman, doctor, prim wife, dance-hall "singer," gambler, stage driver. Ford and Dudley Nichols carefully distinguish between the human traits of each: the gambler's chivalry and polish, the outlaw's sense of fairness, the delicate lady's shedding of her prejudices, and so on. Beneath their superficial tensions and differences, all these people (with one exception) eventually reveal an underlying warmth, kindness, and camaraderie that make them equally decent human beings: The sheriff lets the good-hearted outlaw get away with Dallas, the singer (a euphemism for prostitute); Dallas, despite her toughness, gently helps the doctor deliver a baby; the outlaw—the Ringo Kid, played by John Wayne—loves Dallas despite the societally defined shadiness of her past.

The single unredeemed character in the film is Gatewood, the rich banker, who has stolen $50,000 from his own bank and is now running away with it. Despite his violation of the law, Gatewood is the most outspoken on the immorality of the doctor, singer, and outlaw and the most dogmatic in pontificating on the government's duty to protect his own

Fig. 11-33

Stagecoach: *Bringing white civilization to the wilderness.* *Fig. 11-33: Ford's stagecoach slices through the barren beauty of Monument Valley.* *Fig. 11-34: Inside a rustic shack, a microcosm of European–American society breaks bread.*

Fig. 11-34

self-important person. Ford's preference for the good-hearted, simple people over the evil-hearted rich is like Griffith's. And the prim, proper, moralistic, uplifting society of old hens, who viciously toss Doc and Dallas out of town at the beginning of the film, seems to have leaped directly out of *The New York Hat, Intolerance,* or *Way Down East.* Despite the exciting staging and cutting of the climactic battle with the Apaches, *Stagecoach* is primarily about character and values.

So is *My Darling Clementine*, although the enemy has shifted from Native American "savages" to savage members of the white race, and the battleground has shifted from the desert to a town. On its surface *My Darling Clementine* is an installment in the legend of Wyatt Earp. He and his brothers no longer enforce the law but live the private life of ranchers, out on the plains. The riot and disrule of a frontier town bring him back to "civilization" and its law.

Earp, played by Henry Fonda, Ford's embodiment of American backwoods, self-educated social consciousness (Lincoln and Tom Joad), restores peace to the town. It builds a church and holds a dance, two of Ford's favorite emblems of communality, along with a gathering at a funeral, having a friendly fight, and sharing a meal.

Despite its western surfaces, the film's allegorical suggestions link it closely to the recent war in Europe and the Pacific. Ford soldiered with his camera in the Pacific, often at the front, where he made documentary films for the Navy (*The Battle of Midway*, 1942; *December 7th*, 1943, co-directed by Toland). "What kind of a town is this?" Wyatt asks when he cannot even get a shave and haircut in peace—two marks of a civilized man. Ford might just as well be asking, "What kind of a world is this?"

The nighttime sneak attack of the vicious Clanton family on the youngest and unarmed Earp brother parallels the attack of the Japanese

Fig. 11-35

Fig. 11-36

More civilization in the wilderness: the dance at the dedication of My Darling Clementine's *church (Fig. 11-35); the architectural expanse of the saloon and its hanging lamps (Fig. 11-36).*

on Pearl Harbor or the Nazi invasion of Poland. Wyatt parallels the American fighting forces—peacekeeper in a former time (World War I), now withdrawn and isolated from the battle, steadily drawn into it when it engulfs him. Between the Earps and the Clantons stands Doc Holliday, a man of science (he is a doctor) and culture (he can quote Shakespeare), a former citizen of Boston (the most Eastern and European of American cities, and a favorite center of decadent mischief for Ford). Doc has fallen into the Slough of Despond—into decadence and drink. He no longer practices medicine but makes his living at cards; he has deserted the faithful woman back home, Clementine, for the dancehall slut, Chihuahua; he is also dying of tuberculosis. Holliday seems the emblem of a sick and degenerate Europe, unable to defend itself, dependent on America—as Doc is dependent on Wyatt—to restore it to moral health.

Even the town's saloon is a mythic edifice: Row upon row of hanging lanterns stretch into the deep space of the frame, illuminating the perfectly planed and proportioned building, which is less a frontier drinking place than a monument to civilization. The question of the film (and of many Ford westerns) is how civilization can be protected, how it can survive.

Ford's usual answer is that civilization requires a vigilant gunfighter to keep the peace. Many Ford films define two conflicting principles of "Law." On the one hand, the Law is a book—a series of abstract rules, principles, and statutes that can be understood and practiced by all rational and responsible persons in a society. On the other hand, there are certain gifted persons in a society, like the biblical prophets, who carry the Law within them because they write or correctly interpret the books. They are the Law because they embody the idea of Law. Sometimes, like Fonda in *Fort Apache* or Raymond Massey in *The Hurricane* (1937), they are inflexibly bound to the rules and must choose between bending the Law (which often involves situational ethics, compromise, and forgiveness) and destructive rigidity. Given the Fall of Man (Ford's religious background shows clearly in his view of history), many people are not rational and responsible—whether they are Nazis or Clantons. Civilized society cannot exist without its soldiers, within whom the Law is as strong as villainy in the

wicked and whose ability and determination match those of the wicked.

My Darling Clementine expresses grave doubts whether a civilization can survive without the violent man of honor, the vigilant gunfighter and peacekeeper who carries the Law within him. Ford's westerns for the next 15 years (from the cavalry films—*Fort Apache*, 1948; *She Wore A Yellow Ribbon*, 1949; and *Wagon Master*, 1950—through *The Searchers* to *The Man Who Shot Liberty Valance*) would continue the exploration of this mythic theme.

Howard Hawks

If John Ford was the sound film's Griffith, Howard Hawks was its Ince. Compared with Ford's, Hawks's films are more brutal and less sentimental, more active and less mythic. Like Ince's, Hawks's movies are more striking in their driving narratives than in their examinations of psychology or emotional interaction. The psychological insight in a Hawks film functionally serves the narrative line. If Ince used his "soul fights" to move his narratives, Hawks showed that character motivates and is best judged by what one does. For all their verbal energy, his are films of action. This is as true of his crazy comedies as it is of his dramas, the two categories into which his work can be divided.

Howard Hawks is the most deceptively artless of the great Hollywood directors. His visual style is free of the tricky idiosyncrasies of a von Sternberg or a Lubitsch; his narrative style avoids the political and moral allegories of a Ford or a Capra. Direct and unsentimental, Hawks films merely seem to be well paced, well told, functionally shot genre pictures—gangster films, war films, westerns, screwball comedies, and the like. But the ultimate testimony to Hawks's powers and abilities may well be that he created at least one film that might serve as the very best representative example of almost every genre: the best gangster film (*Scarface*, 1930, released 1932), prison picture (*The Criminal Code*, 1931), racing picture (*The Crowd Roars*, 1932), western (*Red River*, 1948), backstage comedy (*Twentieth Century*, 1934), newspaper picture (*His Girl Friday*, 1940), whodunit (*The Big Sleep*, 1945, revised and released 1946), and screwball comedy (*Bringing Up Baby*, 1938). When a director succeeds so deeply and so broadly with these genre films, it is necessary to look more closely at the unique spirit and talent that created them.

That these films are at least arguably the very best examples of their genres is perhaps the result of two facts. First, Howard Hawks was not really a studio director, a staff member employed by a single studio (like Curtiz at Warners or Fleming at MGM). He was an independent producer for much of his career, and his films were released by various studios (Warner Bros., RKO, and Columbia among them). He was not *assigned* genre pictures; he made the films he wanted to make in the way he wanted to make them. Second, Hawks was one of the greatest storytellers—perhaps the greatest—of the entire Studio Era. He revised or co-authored every script he shot, and his ability to shape the scenes he wanted to shoot and eliminate those he did not was so extraordinary that he was frequently called in to help other directors solve narrative problems with whole films or single scenes.

The aesthetic of omission, of implying what is not explicitly and overtly stated, is an essential feature of Hawks's narrative mastery. Beneath the generic surfaces of his narratives lie complex tensions between the characters' verbal façades and their unverbalized feelings. In both the comedies and the adventure films, Hawks characters tend not to talk about their feelings overtly—first, because words can be hollowly

manipulated; second, because Hawks characters attempt to protect themselves, either with silence or with torrents of chatter, not wanting to make the costly emotional mistake of investing their trust in someone unworthy of it. Most of the great Hawks films are stories of the evolution of trust, of growing faith in another human being, and the goal of the entire narrative is to reveal to the central pair (either two men or a man and a woman) that they have good reason to invest their faith in one another. Most Hawks films are like tennis games between mind and feeling (in contrast to many other Hollywood directors, like Ford, Capra, or von Sternberg, for whom the central interest is exposing the naked heart). The intellect controls the character's surface, the genuine feelings lie beneath, and the resolution of the Hawks narrative almost always brings the characters to a synthesis of the perceptions of the brain and the affections of the heart.

On the surface, *Twentieth Century* is a battle of wills, a study of two egomaniacal theatre people (played by Carole Lombard and John Barrymore) who fight to the egoistic death. Beneath the battle there is love (for they would not fight if they did not love), respect for each other's abilities, each other's strength, each other's egos. In the same way, although Hildy (Rosalind Russell) in *His Girl Friday* thinks she wants a sweet, normal married life with an insurance salesman (Ralph Bellamy), the fact is that

Fig. 11-37   *Fig. 11-38*
Going screwball in Bringing Up Baby. *Fig. 11-37: Katharine Hepburn nets Cary Grant; Fig. 11-38: singing "I Can't Give You Anything But Love" to a leopard on a rooftop in Connecticut.*

she belongs with Walter Burns (Cary Grant) because, beneath their arguments and banter and battles, they complete each other. They are both newspaper "men." (In the source, the play *The Front Page*, Hildy was male.) Hildy's life can be full only if she *does* what she does well, not if she tries to feel what she feels she ought to feel. And in the same way, the scientist, David (Grant), in *Bringing Up Baby* can free himself from his emotional and psychological cage only by experiencing the spontaneity and unpredictability of a Susan (Katharine Hepburn) rather than by working joylessly with his more proper fiancée, Miss Swallow. Although the plot of *Bringing Up Baby* seems to be a loony chase after dinosaur bones and escaped leopards, it really is an adventure in emotional education in which David learns how to be a complete person. The journalistic adventures of *His Girl Friday* and the theatrical adventures of *Twentieth Century* teach their characters the same lesson. From the comedies to the action films, Hawks tells stories of what people have to do (love, fight, work . . .) and have to be good enough to do.

Hawks's alterations of Raymond Chandler's *The Big Sleep* clearly reveal both his psychological interests and his thematic commitments. With the aid of screenwriters William Faulkner, Leigh Brackett, and Jules Furthman, Hawks builds the surface of the film as a maze of murders and bewilderingly proliferating names designed to lead the central pair, Marlowe (Humphrey Bogart) and Vivian (Lauren Bacall), to the knowledge that they can trust each other, if only because they work well together. It would be both foolish and dangerous for Marlowe to trust her if she is not really "wonderful" (as he ironically describes her); many of the film's murdered men go to their "big sleeps" because they trust the wrong women. The twists of Hawks's narrative allow Vivian (a less romantic character in the Chandler novel) to demonstrate her loyalty and sincerity not by telling Marlowe about them but by proving them.

Despite its apparently different cowboy surface, *Red River* is also about suspicion and trust. The prologue (which does not exist in the Borden Chase story on which Hawks's film is based) carefully establishes every narrative detail the film will require for its conclusion. Thomas Dunson (John Wayne) builds an immense cattle spread from the mating of his bull with the calf of a young boy, Matthew Garth (Montgomery Clift). After the Civil War, it becomes necessary to drive the now huge herd a thousand miles to market, from Texas to Kansas City. During the drive, Dunson's inflexibility—his refusal to change his mind or alter a decision, his strict sense of vengeful justice—threatens the success of the entire venture. Matthew usurps Dunson's authority and proves more flexible and more popular with the men he leads. The younger, "softer" man succeeds by altering the ultimate destination, bringing the herd to the new railroad line in Abilene and establishing the Chisholm Trail.

Instead of stealing the herd, Matt sells it for a good price and holds the money in trust for Dunson. His honorable, courageous, and professionally appropriate behavior answers the essential question Hawks asks of all his characters: "Are you *good enough*?"—good enough at who

Fig. 11-39
The climactic gun battle that doesn't take place in Red River: the unswerving determination of Dunson (John Wayne) overcome by the quiet, loving strength of Matthew Garth (Montgomery Clift), producing—with the help of the tough woman (Joanne Dru, offscreen in Frame 7) who shoots at them and tells them they love each other—the final reunion of "father" and "son." (continued on next page)

you are and what you do to be trusted. Dunson too is finally satisfied with Matt and promotes him to full co-owner of the herd, saying he's "earned it." A family and an economy are established in *Red River*, which truly is an epic—not just because it includes an arduous journey and a significant battle, but because it is the tale of the founding of a tribe and dramatizes the myth of fertility and achievement, love and work, that Hawks saw at the center of American culture and as the key to a fulfilled, fun, strong, sexy, successful life.

If Capra's allegories were addressed to Democrats, *Red River* expressed a businesslike optimism that appealed to Republicans. (Both Ford and Hawks were right-wingers.) The film was directly inspired by *Mutiny on the Bounty*, with Matthew in the role of Mr. Christian and Dunson as the rigid captain. Dunson can create an empire, but Matthew can keep it together; Dunson can fall in love (in the prologue) and lose the woman by refusing to change his plans about when they should get together—a rigidity that gets her killed—but Matt can marry. Thanks to the film's elegant, tight structure of repetition, the woman Matt finds (Joanne Dru) is the image of the one Dunson lost. And because this is a Hawks film, the woman is—like most of his female leads—tough, smart, experienced, sexy, witty, and able to take care of herself.

The climax of the film, a showdown between the two leaders, reveals the ultimate Hawks synthesis of love and trust demonstrated by action. Although some find the ending of *Red River* an optimistic, arbitrary avoiding of the gunfight toward which westerns invariably build, this opinion reflects a lack of understanding of both Hawks in general and the particular narrative he has carefully built. Dunson has come gunning for Matthew because he views the boy's taking the herd from him as a disloyal act, a usurpation, a denial of their love and work together that built the immense herd in the first place. Matthew, on the other hand, has taken the herd from Dunson as an extension of his love and loyalty, knowing that only his leadership can bring their invested labors to fruition. Matthew knows (from that very prologue added by Hawks) that Dunson will not shoot a man who does not intend to shoot him; he also knows (again established in the prologue) that Dunson reads a man's eyes to

determine if and when he intends to shoot. As Dunson strides toward Matthew, the younger man's eyes (carefully scrutinized by the camera) reveal that he will never shoot. One does not shoot the people one loves. Dunson must observe that love in action, and Matt accordingly demonstrates in action (as every major Hawks character must do) exactly what he feels beneath the surface. The film ends with an affirmation of love, friendship, fraternity, paternity, and marriage, as almost every Hawks film does.

As opposed to Ford, who saw American history as the movement of pioneers, prophets, and soldiers, followed by the spread of their civilized institutions—the law, the cavalry, the church, the dance, the home—Hawks saw American history as the assertion of individual wills. It is as Protestant an ethic of individualism and professionalism as Ford's is a Catholic view of fallible mortals within earthly institutions that invoke, interpret, and administer an ideal. While Ford's films test the responsiveness of those groups and institutions, Hawks's films test the firmness and responsiveness of human wills, both their resoluteness and their recognition of limits and limitations—the point at which they require the complementarity of another.

Unlike the decor and lighting of Ford's frontier saloon in *My Darling Clementine*, the typical Hawks setting suggests the fragility of human existence and institutions—a small circle of men (and a woman or two) huddled together under the light from a single oil or electric lantern in a ramshackle cabin barely able to withstand the assault of wind and rain. The more cynical Hawks would take one look at his good friend John Ford's monumental saloon in Monument Valley, then playfully ask, "Where the hell did they get all that wood?"

Alfred Hitchcock

Alfred Hitchcock was not a product of the American studio system at all, but a combination of the German studio style and the British studio industry. But the British film industry has maintained a symbiotic relationship with Hollywood since the end of World War I (Hitchcock's first film job was with a British branch of Paramount), made even more dependent by the common language after the conversion to sound. Hitchcock's affinity with the American system is clear in the popularity of his British films in America and in his smooth, effortless emigration from London to Hollywood in 1939.

Hitchcock served part of his apprenticeship as an art director at Ufa. Murnau gave him tips on staging and lighting. The German influence would persist throughout Hitchcock's career—in the murky shadows and studio-controlled Expressionist lighting of his black-and-white films, in the equally controlled universe of his color films, in the paranoia that consumes his characters and spreads to the audience, in the claustrophobic decor that confines his figures, in the inexorable and implacable sense of fate from which his characters cannot escape. Perhaps more British is Hitchcock's dry irony, which allows him to chortle at this doom and gloom that he finds as funny as it is alarming.

Although Hitchcock directed his first film in 1925 (*The Pleasure Garden*), he did not become a major figure until sound allowed him to complement his visuals with talk. Hitchcock's—and perhaps England's—first sound film, *Blackmail* (1929), already reveals much of the Hitchcock world in miniature. There is odd sexuality (a painter invites a woman to his flat so he can rape her while she wears a special costume), a murder (the woman defends herself with a handy knife), paranoid psychology (she fears both the forces of law and the blackmailer pursuing her, seeing and hearing their menace in every ordinary conversation), a climactic chase in an ironic public place (the British Museum), and a moral twist at the end (the woman gets away with the murder, although the painter's clown picture still laughs at her). But the first three Hitchcock films to make a major impact in America were *The Man Who Knew Too Much* (1934), *The 39 Steps* (1935), and *The Lady Vanishes* (1938), all of them rich in subtle psychology, ironic humor, and gripping suspense.

The 39 Steps is a prototype Hitchcock film of his British period. The plot is a mad chase from London to Scotland and back again. The chase throws the crime-tracking runners into the most wildly diverse and incongruous settings: a Scottish farmhouse, a plush manor, a vaudeville theatre. The action is a mad attempt to solve the film's great riddle (the narrative pretext that appears to motivate and integrate the film's intriguing incidents—a whatsit that, in the deep regions of character and irony where the film really oper-

ates, doesn't matter—which Hitchcock called the "MacGuffin"), the meaning of the "39 steps." The solution to that riddle is buried inside the head of the vaudeville performer, Mr. Memory, who, when publicly confronted with the question in front of an audience, is torn by his commitment to his art (he prides himself in knowing all) and his commitment to his fellow conspirators.

As in so many of his films, Hitchcock delights in showing the most horrible crimes taking place in the most public places: amusement parks, concert halls, trains. And like so many Hitchcock films, *The 39 Steps* is a completely apolitical story of political intrigue. Except for the wartime films (*Foreign Correspondent*, 1940; *Saboteur*, 1942; *Lifeboat*, 1944; and *Notorious*, 1946), which are explicitly

Fig. 11-40

Fig. 11-41
Subjectivity in Hitchcock's first sound film, Blackmail: *The fleeing woman sees an electrified cocktail shaker become the knife with which she murdered her assailant.*

anti-Nazi, and *North by Northwest* (1959), which is an anti-Communist film from the Cold War, the two political sides in Hitchcock films are us and them. He refuses to cloud a good story with ideology. For the same reason, Hitchcock films frequently take place in the world of the rich; they are divorced from such social–realist problems as poverty and hunger. The Hitchcock actors are smooth, slick males like Cary Grant, Ray Milland, and James Stewart and cold, sleek ladies (usually blonde with strong features) like Grace Kelly, Vera Miles, and Eva Marie Saint. *The 39 Steps* uses the slick Robert Donat and the cool Madeleine Carroll.

The Hitchcock films are a unique blend of story, style, mood, and a deceptively complex

Fig. 11-42

Fig. 11-43
Subjectivity in Strangers On A Train. *Fig. 11-42: the "normal" American, Farley Granger (right), drawn into the shadows of Robert Walker's psychotic aberration; Fig. 11-43: the maniac as a tiny black blot on the white marble monuments of American values.*

technique. Hitchcock mixes the macabre and the funny, mystery and whimsy, suspense and sardonic laughter. While the gripping story drives relentlessly forward, Hitchcock takes time out to focus on a subtle physical detail or ironic element. The plots revolve about the wildest improbabilities: vast international conspiracies; little old ladies who are really spies; psychotic killers who impersonate their dead mothers; chases that culminate on carousels, in concert halls, in a bell tower, on the Statue of Liberty, or on Mount Rushmore. Beneath almost every Hitchcock film is the structure of the chase, the accelerating rush toward a climactic solution. But Hitchcock personalizes the improbable chase by making each of the racers surprisingly familiar and vulnerable, fallibly credible. The most intricate tales hang on the most trivial details—a rare brand of herb tea, a cigarette lighter, an inquisitive cocker spaniel. Frenzied suspense and wry understatement are the ultimate Hitchcock ingredients; bizarre psychological states beneath the most banal surfaces, the essential Hitchcock theme.

Hitchcock's two greatest technical tools are his command of editing and his control of what Pudovkin called the "plastic material." Hitchcock's films are rich in tiny yet revealing plastic details, from facial tics to physical objects, from the body in clothes to embodied dreams. *Strangers On A Train* (1951) is as much about a cigarette lighter and a pair of glasses as it is about two men, one "normal" and one "crazy."

Hitchcock's awareness of the power of concrete detail is such that when the detail is not exactly right in its natural state, he fixes it up to emphasize it. In *Suspicion* (1941), to hypnotize us with a glass of milk that Joan Fontaine thinks is poisoned, Hitchcock puts a tiny light inside the glass to make the milk truly glow in the darkness. In *Spellbound* (1945), he makes a revolver dominate the foreground by photographing an immense, six-times-larger-than-life model. (He also cuts to pure red when the gun shoots the character/camera; the rest of the film is in black and white.) The power of these objects in Hitchcock films reveals the origins of his style in art direction and the dependence of his technique on "storyboarding" his shots. After tight scripting, Hitchcock planned a film by having pictures drawn of exactly the way he wanted every image to look, then set up each shot to duplicate the drawing.

In an era of functional narrative cutting, Hitchcock's editing alone tightened the screws of suspense. As Sylvia Sidney slices roast beef at the dinner table in *Sabotage* (1936), Hitchcock's cutting shows her passion building until she drives the knife into her villainous husband. The same quick editing creates the suspense of the final fight in *Saboteur* as the Nazi spy slips off the Statue of Liberty to his death, the frenzy of the spinning carousel at the end of *Strangers On A Train*, and the brutality of Janet Leigh's death in *Psycho* (1960) as Hitchcock cuts from shots of the victim's face, to shots of the slashing knife, to shots of the bloodstreaked water swirling down the drain of the shower.

Hitchcock films provide perfect examples of how to cut picture and sound together. In *The 39 Steps*, the charwoman walks into a room where she sees the shadow of a corpse; her eyes widen and her mouth begins to erupt into a scream. Hitchcock immediately cuts to the shriek of a train whistle and a shot of the train racing toward Scotland. The screaming train replaces the human scream and startles us with its unnatural shrillness.

When he moved from England to America in 1939 at the invitation of producer David O. Selznick (who at the time was making *Gone With the Wind* and arranging its release with MGM), Hitchcock's first Hollywood project was an adaptation of Daphne du Maurier's *Rebecca* (1940), which was set in England. A gothic romance that was atmospheric and suspenseful, it won the Academy Award for Best Picture. The greatest films of his early Hollywood period include *Rebecca* and *Shadow of a Doubt* (1943), but the best of them all may be *Notorious* (1946). It starred Cary Grant, Ingrid Bergman, and Claude Rains in a spy story that was really about character, about finding out and believing in what another person is made of. The most elegantly shot and tensely paced of his 1940s thrillers, it was also a superior romance; the thrills of romance and danger were often linked in Hitchcock's films, and *Notorious* is one of the great examples of the control of pace and tone such a combination requires.

Working in Hollywood, as he did for the rest of his career, Hitchcock began to make pictures

Fig. 11-44

Fig. 11-45

Fig. 11-46
The 39 Steps: *the sound-and-picture montage, from the cleaning woman's discovery to the train's scream.*

that could be as disturbing as they were witty and entertaining—films such as *Shadow of a Doubt* and *Rope* (1948) and, ultimately, *Vertigo* (1958). He turned the dry drollery of his English wit to observations of the American scene that had a corrosive subtlety beyond anything he had shown in England. One of his favorite subjects became the superficial placidity of American life, whose clean, bright surfaces disguised the most shocking moral, political, psychological, and sexual aberrations: the wealthy members of an American cultural elite who happen to be Nazis (*Saboteur*); the small-town Americana wholesomeness that protects a psychopathic killer (*Shadow of a Doubt*). For Hitchcock, the most striking, funny, and terrifying quality of American life was its confidence in its sheer ordinariness. Beneath the surface, ordinary people and normal life were always "bent" for Hitchcock. This conviction would make him one of the most insightful and irreverent directors of the 1950s, when American culture retreated behind a façade of cheerful normality.

Orson Welles

Unlike Hitchcock, Chaplin, Hawks, or Ford, whose reputations rest on a great number of impressive films, critical respect for Orson Welles rests primarily on one film, *Citizen Kane* (1941), widely considered the greatest sound film ever made. *Kane*'s greatness can be discussed on several different levels: its technical innovation, structural complexity, complicated handling of narrative point of view, controversy as a biography of a famous American, philosophical search for meaningful values, sociological study of the "American Dream," acting, literacy, individuality. Orson Welles, the young sensation of both the stage and radio, had been invited to bring his Mercury Theatre group to Hollywood in 1939 to make virtually any film he chose. Welles was 24 when he signed with RKO. The film, *Citizen Kane*, was both his first and the last he would ever be so free to make. Like an earlier *enfant terrible* of Hollywood, Erich von Stroheim, Welles insisted on participating in every production detail: acting, directing, writing, editing, sound, design. And like von Stroheim, Welles soon saw the Hollywood lords giving his negatives to other hands for slicing and later found the gates of the lords' studios locked against him.

From its opening sequence, *Citizen Kane* is no ordinary film. It begins in quiet and darkness: a wire fence with a "No Trespassing" sign; a series of tracking shots and dissolves past a weird menagerie that brings us closer to the creepy mansion, Xanadu, and eventually into the room of a dying man (Kane, played by Welles); his

Expressionistic death, with the echoing, rasping sound of the word "Rosebud" on his lips; the glass ball dropping silently through snowy space before shattering; the distorted view of the nurse, seen through the curved glass of the fallen globe as she enters the room to attend to the dead man. As if this beginning were not elliptical enough, Welles shatters the dark mood of death with the blaring music and glaring images of a newsreel documentary. From moody Expressionism, the film jumps to a brilliant parody of *The March of Time:* the musical fanfare, the booming "voice-of-God" narration, the overly descriptive printed titles, the purple prose, the diagrams and maps, the lifeless newsreel photography, the tendency to reduce motion pictures to stills that merely illustrate a verbal commentary. The newsreel ends as abruptly as it began and is followed by a scene in the projection room in which the reporters discuss the newsreel's defects as a biography of Kane, a scene played entirely in shadow, drenched in smoke, backlit by shafts of light from the projection booth. The scene is as garishly shadowed as the preceding news footage was flat and thin. Three sequences, three completely different film styles.

The film's technical brilliance continues throughout. Even today it seems striking in its extreme low-angle shots (how conscious were we that Hollywood sets before *Citizen Kane* had ceilings?), its consistently extreme contrasts of dark and light, its vast shots in depth revealing interaction between foreground and background. Welles was lucky to have the cinematic eye of Gregg Toland behind his camera and the designer's eye of Perry Ferguson in front of it. Toland, who did most of his work at Samuel Goldwyn Productions but was hired out for occasional other projects—to RKO for *Kane*, for example, or to MGM for *Mad Love* (1935)—had challenged the limits of early sound filming in *Bulldog Drummond* (1929) and had learned Expressionist cinematography while working under director Karl Freund on *Mad Love*. Toland had perfected his craft while working with director William Wyler at Goldwyn on such pictures as *These Three* (1936), *Dead End* (1937), *Wuthering Heights* (1939), and especially *The Little Foxes* (released a few months after *Kane* in 1941), whose climactic scene he shot in deep focus; his last great work with Wyler was

Plate 1

Plate 2

Plate 3

Coloring of black-and-white silent films. Plate 1: Edison's Annabelle Dances; *swirls of motion and hand-painted color. Plate 2: Méliès's* Paris to Monte Carlo; *the hand-painted automobile is always red. Plate 3: Porter's* The Great Train Robbery; *the dude dances to a volley of hand-painted golden gunfire. Plate 4: Griffith's* Intolerance; *worshipping the fiery red Ishtar in a tinted and toned frame. Plate 5:* Intolerance; *in this blue-toned frame, masked to create a wide-screen image, the invading hordes rush toward Babylon.*

Plate 4

Plate 5

Plate 6

The colors of reality. Plate 6: a race through the slums in Slumdog
Millionaire; *scenes like this one were shot with a 2K digital camera.*
Plate 7: *the colors of nature, restored and then slightly enhanced, in* Ashes
of Time Redux.

Plate 7

Plate 8

Digital effects. Plate 8: In this scene from The Curious Case Of
Benjamin Button, *Brad Pitt's computer-generated head (based
partly on a motion-capture performance by Pitt) was digitally
attached to the body of another actor, who went through the scene in
costume for the production camera. Plate 9: a digital composite
from* Star Wars: Episode III—Revenge of the Sith.

Plate 9

Plate 10

Outdoor and indoor cinematography. Plate 10: The White Balloon, *shot by Farzad Jowdat; set design by the director, Jafar Panahi. "It looks like they are dancing when they move their fins," a girl (Aïda Mohammadkhani) tells her mother (Fereshteh Sadr Orfani), begging for money to buy a special goldfish; less than two hours of afternoon light remain before the New Year begins in Tehran. Plate 11:* McCabe & Mrs. Miller, *shot by Vilmos Zsigmond. McCabe (Warren Beatty) tracks his enemies in the wet and icy outdoors. Plate 12:* The Godfather, *shot by Gordon Willis. Don Vito Corleone (Marlon Brando) conducts business inside, in the dark, rich light of his office.*

Plate 12

Plate 11

Plate 13
Colors inspired by a graphic novel: Watchmen.

Plate 14
Subtle politics: Do The Right Thing; *Da Mayor (Ossie Davis) offers flowers to Mother Sister (Ruby Dee). Whereas Hollywood used to maintain that black actors could not be photographed well, using that as one excuse to keep them out of leading roles, this frame with its painted building offers one of many color compositions designed to show that black is beautiful; note the use of starch-white and rose-red, here and in Plate 12, to organize the color schemes.*

Plate 15

Plate 16

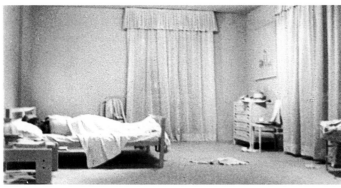

Plate 17

The color system of Red Desert. *Giulia (Monica Vitti) in the drab, imprisoning environment of contemporary reality (Plate 15); Giulia and Corrado (Richard Harris) in the sexual atmosphere of the red-walled shack (Plate 16); rocks like flesh in the brilliant sunshine (Plate 17); the hotel room gone pink after sexual consummation (Plate 18).*

Plate 18

Plate 19

Bold colors in the darkness. Plate 19: Batman (Christian Bale) descends to the streets of Gotham in an IMAX shot from The Dark Knight. Plate 20: David Lynch's Blue Velvet; Dennis Hopper as the murderous pervert, sucking an unidentified gas and striking Isabella Rossellini for looking at him, while light and color create a seductive, intimate mood.

Plate 20

Plate 21

Wide-screen cinematography: Lawrence of Arabia. *Plate 21: an extreme long shot. Plate 22: a close shot; Peter O'Toole as T. E. Lawrence. Directed by David Lean,* Lawrence *was shot in Technicolor on 65mm stock by Frederick A. Young; Plates 21-25, were made directly from an original 70mm print (the extra 5mm allowed room for the soundtrack).*

Plate 22

Plate 23

Camera movement and composition for the wide screen: the attack on Aqaba. Plates 23 and 24 are from the beginning and end of a single sequence. In Plate 23, the heroes begin their charge toward screen right, filling the huge screen with movement. Plate 24 is the end of a shot in which the camera pans right and then briefly tracks right to follow the invaders (seen in extreme long shot) as they ride into and through the city, all the way to the gun. The gun makes attack from the sea—that is, from screen right—impossible; this brilliant view of the gun and coast is composed both laterally and in depth—as well as in relation to the rightward camera movement.

Plate 24

Plate 25

Depth of field and the wide screen. While the preceding frames from
Lawrence of Arabia (notably Plate 24) have a broad depth of field,
the depth of field in Plate 25 is shallow: The statue in the central
background, though only a few feet behind O'Toole and the match, is
out of focus. The meticulously composed image from 2001: A Space
Odyssey (Plate 26) is in focus from foreground to background,
drawing our attention to the set and props as well as to the
astronaut (Keir Dullea).

Plate 26

Plate 27

Plate 29

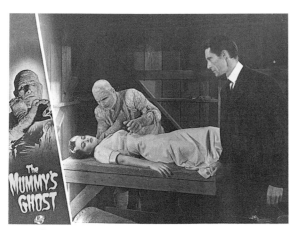

Plate 28

Plate 30

*A selection of colored lobby cards, all of them for black-and-white movies;
original size, 11×14 inches. Plate 27: Robin Hood (1922), a production
still subtly hand-painted to suggest the mood of the scene. Plate 28: The
Mummy's Ghost (1944), featuring a crucial scene from the movie, as most
lobby cards did, and based on a production still rather than a frame
enlargement, as most of them were, but with an almost Expressionist
color scheme that enhances the horror. Plate 29, Gun Crazy (1949,
released 1950), and Plate 30, Kiss of Death (1947): two cards in the same
genre, one capturing the bloody red of noir, the glandular excitement of
violence, sex, and action, and one going for the black—the world of
shadows in which the film noir sets its moral battles.*

Plate 31

François Truffaut in The Green Room. *As the sharp left side of the frame shows, the distortion is caused by uneven glass; in this way a realistic setup motivates a painterly effect, a portrait of the artist.*

Plate 32

Plate 33

Disney color animation. Fig. C-32: Three Little Pigs. *The Big Bad Wolf huffs and puffs until he turns purple in the face. Fig. C-33:* Fantasia. *The sorcerer's apprentice, afloat in the darkness on a flood of his own making, searches desperately in the sorcerer's book for a solution.*

Plate 34

Plate 35

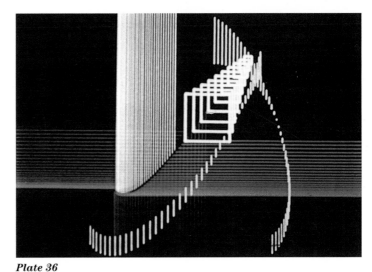

Plate 36

Abstract color animation.
Plate 34: Oskar
Fischinger's Allegretto.
Plate 35: Jordan
Belson's Allures.
Plate 36: John Whitney's
computerized Matrix.
Plate 37: Norman McLaren's
Begone Dull Care—*painted,*
scratched, and drawn
directly on celluloid.

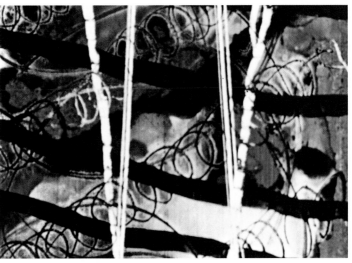

Plate 37

Plate 38

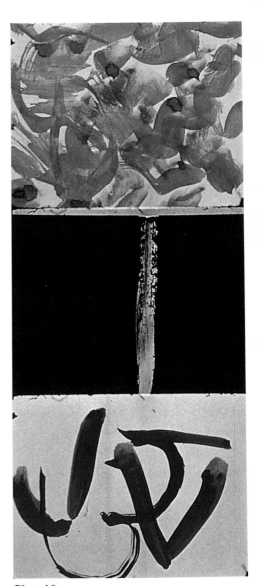

Plate 40

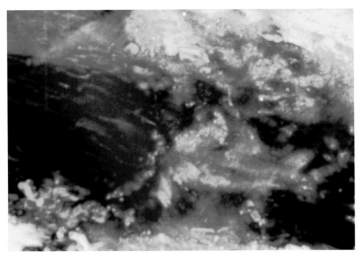

Plate 39

Plate 41

Plate 44

Plate 42

Plate 43

Experimental color films.
Plate 38: a real fern in Stan Brakhage's
Mothlight. *Plate 39: a frame from Mary Beth*
Reed's **Moon Streams,** *created on an optical*
printer. Plate 40: three consecutive frames from
Robert Breer's **Blazes.** *Plate 41: Kenneth Anger's*
Scorpio Rising—*the biker's sensuous dream*
image. Plates 42, 43: compositions in green and
in red from Im Kwon-Taek's sung and enacted
narrative, Chunhyang. *Plate 44: using color,*
light, and focal length to alter the same space
in Michael Snow's Wavelength.

Plate 45

Painting and film. Plate 45: Stan Brakhage's existence is song, *painted directly on IMAX film. Plate 46: the energy of painting, captured in this frame from* Life Lessons, *Martin Scorsese's contribution to* New York Stories.

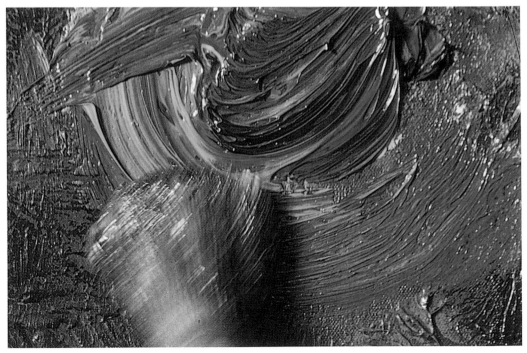

Plate 46

The Best Years of Our Lives (1946). Toland had further expanded his stylistic range through his rich, dark work for Howard Hawks (*The Road to Glory*, 1936) and John Ford (*The Grapes of Wrath* and *The Long Voyage Home*, both 1940). For his work on *Citizen Kane*, Welles awarded Toland a credit equal to his own for directing; as much as Welles pushed Toland to devise even newer ways of shooting, Toland taught cinematography—and what he had learned about filmmaking from Freund, Wyler, Hawks, and Ford—to Welles.

If Welles was learning the arts of camerawork and editing while directing *Kane*, he was also rapidly becoming their master. His genius for the cinema is evident in the editing, and again he learned from the person he was supervising— Robert Wise, who edited *Kane* before he became a director himself, and who was pushed by Welles into creating a pace and complexity never before attained in the sound film.

Although it is full of quick cutting and has a narrative structure that functions as a montage, the visual style of *Citizen Kane* is primarily a triumph of camerawork and *mise-en-scène*. Welles often shoots long takes, composed in depth, and moves the actors and the camera from one composition to another within the same shot, instead of cutting from setup to setup.

Welles's control of sound is as careful as his manipulation of image. The years in radio made

him aware of sound's dramatic power, an advantage he enjoyed over those directors who graduated to sound from the silents. The overloud narration of the news digest, the echoing emptiness of Thatcher's mausoleum–library, the contrast between the amplified and unamplified human voice at Kane's political rally, the flat tones of the ungifted opera singer, the echoing voices in the immense rooms of Xanadu, all are examples of an ear trained in the power of the microphone and the loudspeaker to create aural space. The sound field in this movie has as much depth as the deep-focus visual field.

Citizen Kane, one of the most complexly structured pieces of film narrative in cinema history, resembles nothing so much as William Faulkner's *Absalom, Absalom! Citizen Kane* is, like the Faulkner novel, an immense jigsaw puzzle (like the puzzles Susan assembles in Kane's castle). Welles and screenwriter Herman J. Mankiewicz (whose favorite novel, F. Scott Fitzgerald's *The Great Gatsby*, had a more direct influence) lead the audience through a seemingly chaotic collection of events and personal fragments until all the pieces of the puzzle are fitted together—the last piece being the identity of "Rosebud." Although both Welles and Faulkner seem to wander confusingly over an immense expanse of time and space, both artists carefully follow a well-charted if intricate map to the ultimate revelation. Although Welles and

Fig. 11-47

Citizen Kane: *dominated and distorted by the fallen glass ball, the Expressionistic and richly symbolic image of Kane's death.*

Fig. 11-48

The deliberate overexposure
of the peeping news camera,
trying to catch a glimpse of
Kane (Fig. 11-48), and the
shafts and shadows of the
projection sequence, lit
almost totally from behind
(Fig. 11-49).

Fig. 11-49

Mankiewicz may not have been directly influenced by Faulkner (though Toland knew Faulkner and had worked with him on *The Road to Glory*), Welles had gone to RKO with the original intention of adapting Joseph Conrad's *Heart of Darkness* (rejected by the studio because Welles planned to use subjective camera throughout), whose complex story-within-a-story, imagery, theme, questing narrator (Marlow), and

central character (Kurtz) bear obvious affinities to *Kane* and strongly influenced both *Absalom, Absalom!* and *The Great Gatsby*.

The cinematic structure of *Citizen Kane*'s first sequence is a microcosm of the whole film. Just as Welles's camera begins outside the fence of Charles Foster Kane's house and then steadily moves closer until it comes to rest on the man himself (the camera is itself curious and goes

Fig. 11-50
The shot in depth. Jed Leland (Joseph Cotten, left) and Bernstein (Everett Sloane) speak in the foreground while Charlie Kane (Orson Welles) dances with chorus girls in the background.

Fig. 11-51
Welles's "dissolve-montage." As Leland tells his story in the foreground, the events dissolve into the frame in the background—a technique borrowed from the stage.

through all barriers), so the whole film begins on the outside of Kane and steadily moves inward, seeking the man's core. The first section (of six) that sets out to convey a vision or interpretation of Kane, the news digest, is the most externalized report of all, a sweeping summary of the facts and dates of Kane's public life—and the details of his private life that were made public—with no attempt at understanding his character. The newsreel is useful not only because it gives us a documentary report, but also because it gives us a series of road signs—concrete incidents, images, and dates—to which Welles will return later; it provides a chronological skeleton for an unchronological film. In the projection-room scene that follows, the reporter who made the newsreel, Thompson (William Alland), is sent out to find the meaning of "Rosebud."

The second section is narrated by Thatcher (George Coulouris), the banker who first brought young Charles to the city. Or rather it is narrated by Thatcher's memoirs, which Thompson reads, since the man is now dead. Thatcher's section primarily covers Kane's boyhood and youth, from the time he left his parents in Colorado to the time he took over the newspaper in New York, though it goes all the way to the Depression, when Kane's empire foundered. Because Thatcher never cared for Kane and because, as a banker, he concentrates on Kane's

financial history, his report remains very much on the outside of Kane. It is, however, part of the narrative game of *Citizen Kane* that many of the events narrated by "Thatcher" (and the others) could not possibly have been perceived in the way we witness them (the closeness of mother and boy captured in the close shot of their faces; the boy's sled lying alone in the snow, as the howl of a train whistle on the soundtrack reveals that Thatcher and the boy have already departed and Bernard Herrmann's music sounds the haunting "Rosebud" theme). Despite the human narrative voices in the film, the primary narrator is the camera, which sees more clearly and crosses more barriers than any mortal observer.

In the next four sections, Thompson interviews the four surviving people who knew Kane best, and what they tell him appears onscreen, just as Thompson's memoirs had: as flashbacks mediated by the narrators' attitudes (so that they are mindscreens) and further scrutinized and interpreted by the relentlessly curious and insightful camera.

The third section, narrated by Bernstein (Everett Sloane), Kane's business associate, begins to turn inward. Bernstein begins more or less where Thatcher left off—from the founding of the newspaper through the marriage with the first Mrs. Kane (Ruth Warrick). But because Bernstein idolized Kane and never deserted him, the section concentrates on the young, energetic,

Fig. 11-52

The erosion of time: the
youthful Leland, Kane, and
Bernstein (Cotten, Welles,
Sloane) and the aged
Thatcher, Kane, and
Bernstein (George Coulouris,
Welles, Sloane). In his youth,
Kane signs a "Declaration
of Principles" (Fig. 11-52);
broken by both age and the
Depression, he signs away
his holdings (Fig. 11-53).

Fig. 11-53

iconoclastic "Charlie" Kane, the man with spirit
and vision.

The fourth section, Jed Leland's, begins the
depth sounding. Jed (Joseph Cotten) is Kane's
former best friend, now his cynical enemy. Kane
fired Jed when Jed refused to desert his principles to suit his boss; Jed's very presence
reminded Kane of the principles he had left
behind. Jed's section picks up where Bernstein's

leaves off—from the marriage with the first Mrs.
Kane to the Chicago opera debut of Susan
Alexander, who has become the second Mrs.
Kane. Bernstein's section takes Kane to the peak
of his happiness and success; Jed's shows the be-
ginning of Kane's bitter descent.

The fifth inner narrative, Susan Alexander's,
continues the descent. Now a singer in sleazy
cafés, Susan (Dorothy Comingore) begins her

Fig. 11-54

Fig. 11-55

The final views of Kane. Fig. 11-54: as a tiny dark figure, dwarfed by exotic arches. Fig. 11-55: as a mystery—holding the glass ball and walking between mirrors, his reflection multiplied to infinity.

tale with her operatic career under Kane (which was, as she says, all his idea) and continues it through their horrifying life in the huge castle, Xanadu, that Kane supposedly had built for her; she ends with the time she finally walked out on him (which was *her* idea). Kane, attractively youthful and rebellious in the film's early sections, is now seen as a broken, loveless, ugly old tyrant.

The sixth section and the epilogue focus, like the prologue, on Xanadu, the house, as well as on Kane, the man. The final inner narrator is Kane's butler, Raymond (Paul Stewart), his final human contact. Raymond tells how Kane trashed her room after Susan left—but said "Rosebud" when he picked up the glass ball, then walked down the hall between two mirrors (producing an infinite image of Kane that is as important an emblem of the quest to understand Kane—and human character itself—as the jigsaw puzzle, because a puzzle can be put together if one finds all the pieces, but an endless succession of images is paradoxical and unresolvable). Raymond also says he heard Kane say "Rosebud" when he died—though he is not shown in the death scene. The reporter, who has remained faceless throughout the film (as a sort of audience surrogate—like the camera, a vehicle of our curiosity), gives up, and the film goes into its epilogue.

Realizing that he never will find Rosebud, the "missing piece" of the puzzle—and that even if he found it, it wouldn't explain Kane completely—Thompson resigns the search. As the

news crew leaves Xanadu, Raymond orders some workmen to throw into a furnace the least valuable of the items that Kane had collected during his lifetime. One of the pieces of junk is Kane's childhood sled; we see that its name is "Rosebud." The wood goes up in flames; the object becomes a column of smoke, ascending into the night sky as Herrmann's "Power" and "Rosebud" leitmotifs are finally resolved. The camera pulls and dissolves steadily away from the mansion until it stands once more outside the fence with the "No Trespassing" sign. Having trespassed to discover as much as could be known about any human being, the camera now leaves Kane his privacy.

Rosebud is an object of Kane's youth, an object that he did not buy, something he loved—and lost, given to him by parents he loved and lost. He kept Rosebud (from his mother's estate) because, like his mother's old wood stove, it had great sentimental value. He was also sentimentally attached to Susan's glass ball, a paperweight whose snow scene deliberately recalls the snowy images of Thatcher's visit to young Charles in Colorado. Young Kane was ripped away from his snowy childhood, his family, and life with Rosebud, by the discovery of the Colorado lode, a gold mine whose deed was left to Kane's mother (Agnes Moorehead) in exchange for rent at her boarding house. And so Rosebud, in Kane's mind anyway, represented the opposite of everything his life had become, youth rather than corrupt maturity, genuine human emotion (with his mother particularly) rather than cash substitutes.

Significantly, no human observer discovers the meaning of "Rosebud." The camera alone discovers the answer to the film's opening riddle, completing its trespassing and the work's artistic pattern. That pattern is, arguably, the only Elizabethan tragedy—in spirit and shape—that Hollywood ever produced out of American materials.

Like the hero of Marlovian tragedy, a Dr. Faustus or Tamburlaine, Kane is an immense human being with immense power. Like Marlowe's Faustus or Shakespeare's Macbeth (a favorite Welles role), Kane is an overreacher, a man who dares the cosmos by seeking to accomplish more than a mortal can. The very virtues of such a figure—his energy, will, ambition—lead directly to his tragic flaw, as virtues do in classical tragedy. Finally, as in the classical and the Elizabethan tragedy, there is something inevitable about Kane's fate; elements inherent in the man's character and in the human condition itself conspire to produce the tragic result.

While many in later generations felt that it showed what a film could really be, *Citizen Kane* was both shocking and confusing to its audiences in 1941. Instead of Hollywood's flat gloss, the film was sombre and grotesque. The action sprawled over more than 60 years, requiring its performers to make tremendous transitions in acting and appearance. There were no last-minute changes of heart, no romantic reconciliations. *Citizen Kane* followed its tragic premises to their logical, gloomy end. Even more

Fig. 11-56
The Magnificent Ambersons: *Agnes Moorehead and Tim Holt on the grand staircase.*

The Lady from Shanghai:
Orson Welles and Rita Hayworth prove that love has many angles.

Fig. 11-57

disturbing for Hollywood was the enmity the film produced in the press, particularly in the Hearst chain. William Randolph Hearst saw obvious and infuriating parallels between himself and Charles Foster Kane; between Susan Alexander and his own artistic protégée, Marion Davies; and between Kane's Florida castle, Xanadu, and his own California castle, San Simeon, where screenwriter Mankiewicz had been a regular guest. The pressures of the Hearst press—refusing advertisements for the film, pressuring theatres that showed it with threats not to print any future ads or notices—and the film's unspectacular showing at the box office led RKO to deny Welles total artistic control over his next project, an adaptation of Booth Tarkington's *The Magnificent Ambersons*. From then on, his life and career became a struggle to make films and have them released intact—which they virtually never were.

The Magnificent Ambersons (1942) might have been as great as *Kane* if Welles had not left the country—after he and Robert Wise, who also edited *Ambersons*, had assembled a rough cut— to shoot the ill-fated documentary *It's All True* (uncompleted; a 1993 documentary on the making of *It's All True* includes much of the footage). With the help of the cutting instructions Welles cabled from South America, Wise presented RKO with a lengthy masterpiece that flopped with

preview audiences. Some new scenes were shot and old ones rearranged, disastrously wrapping up the film's last hour in a few rushed minutes. Like *Greed*, the complete *Ambersons* has proved impossible to restore, but what remains is extraordinary.

Its story of a vain, selfish brat (Tim Holt as George Amberson Minafer) who finally gets his "come-uppance" and sees the world more clearly once he has been brought down a peg allowed Welles to tell the larger, more nostalgic story of the old ways—incarnated in the rich, graceful, high-society Amberson family—that perished with the coming of the automobile. It was a movie designed for the moving camera (manned by Stanley Cortez, whom Welles taught much of what Gregg Toland had taught him); the great staircase in the Amberson mansion was built to facilitate the phenomenally varied use of a crane. As in *Kane*, scene elements moved fluidly from one to the other through changes of camera angle and composition, not with the previously obligatory cuts. Figures moved in and out of shadow, as if into their own ominous or unknown depths, as the camera kept pace with the action or stopped for an intense slow look. The superb cast included Dolores Costello, Joseph Cotten, and— in the performance of a lifetime—Agnes Moorehead.

Even without a Hearst seeking its destruction, the abridged version of *The Magnificent Ambersons* opened to dismal business. RKO relieved Welles of his duties on his next film, *Journey Into Fear* (1942), in the middle of production.

Later Welles films—*The Stranger* (1946), *The Lady from Shanghai* (1946, released 1948), *Macbeth* (1948), *Othello* (1952), *Mr. Arkadin* (1955), *Touch of Evil* (1958, restored 1998), *The Trial* (1962), and *Chimes at Midnight* (1966, also known as *Falstaff*)—are, like *Citizen Kane*, obsessed with the themes of the corrupting influence of power and money, with treachery and desire, with guesswork in a labyrinth, with egotism and gamesmanship, with the dark side of greatness and the limits of ambition and friendship. These later films also reveal Welles's unmistakable visual style, regardless of their budgets or their cinematographers: baroque, backlit contrasts of dark and light; claustrophobic interiors whose ceilings squash their occupants; a seemingly infinite depth of field, often surveyed from a very low angle; and magnificently planned, complexly choreographed tracking shots.

The opening shot of *Touch of Evil*—the last true *film noir*—which begins with the close-up setting of a time-bomb, travels high above and then through the streets of Tijuana as it follows the bomb-laden car and the walking heroes on their complexly intersecting paths, and concludes, over three minutes later, with medium-shot reactions to the explosion, is one of the greatest and most complicated crane shots in cinema history. But the studio ran the opening credits over it and re-edited the rest of the film. Welles's editing remained as inventive as his camerawork. The climactic shootout in *The Lady from Shanghai*, as Everett Sloane and Rita Hayworth shoot repeatedly at each other's reflections in a house of mirrors, is one of the most memorable metaphors of cinematic death, translated into the shattering crash of glass and the annihilation of images.

Until his death in 1985, Welles was forced to contend with inadequate budgets and production schedules. He acted to make money to make films. Like Griffith and Gance and von Stroheim before him, he was a great artist rejected by the industry. Like Kane, he left many things unfinished. But even when the script, the budget, the

producers, or the studios let him down, a Welles film never looked or sounded like anything other than a Welles film.

For Further Viewing

FILMS

DOROTHY ARZNER (1900–79)
The Wild Party (1929)
Honor Among Lovers (1931)
Working Girls (1931)
Merrily We Go to Hell (1932)
Christopher Strong (1933)
Nana (1934)
Craig's Wife (1936)
The Bride Wore Red (1937)
Dance, Girl, Dance (1940)
First Comes Courage (1943)

TOD BROWNING (1882–1962)
The Unholy Three (1925)
The Unknown (1927)
London After Midnight (1927)
Dracula (1931)
Freaks (1932)

FRANK CAPRA (1897–1991)
The Younger Generation (1929)
Platinum Blonde (1931)
The Bitter Tea of General Yen (1932)
It Happened One Night (1934)
Mr. Deeds Goes to Town (1936)
Lost Horizon (1937)
You Can't Take It With You (1938)
Mr. Smith Goes to Washington (1939)
Meet John Doe (1941)
Why We Fight Series (1942–45)
Arsenic and Old Lace (1944).
    Completed 1941
It's A Wonderful Life (1947).
    Completed 1946
State of the Union (1948)
Hemo the Magnificent (1957)

GEORGE CUKOR (1899–1983)
A Bill of Divorcement (1932)
Dinner at Eight (1933)
David Copperfield (1935)
Sylvia Scarlett (1935)
Camille (1937). Completed 1936

Holiday (1938)
The Women (1939)
The Philadelphia Story (1940)
A Woman's Face (1941)
Keeper of the Flame (1942)
Gaslight (1944)
Adam's Rib (1949)
Born Yesterday (1950)
Pat and Mike (1952)
A Star Is Born (1954)
My Fair Lady (1964)
Rich and Famous (1981)

MICHAEL CURTIZ (1888–1962)
Doctor X (1932)
Mystery of the Wax Museum (1933)
The Kennel Murder Case (1933)
Black Fury (1935)
Captain Blood (1935)
The Charge of the Light Brigade (1936)
The Walking Dead (1936)
The Adventures of Robin Hood (1938).
  Co-director, William Keighley
Angels With Dirty Faces (1938)
The Sea Hawk (1940)
Casablanca (1942)
Yankee Doodle Dandy (1942)
Mildred Pierce (1945)
Life with Father (1947)

WILLIAM DIETERLE (1893–1972)
A Midsummer Night's Dream (1935). Co-
  director, Max Reinhardt
The Story of Louis Pasteur (1936)
The Life of Emile Zola (1937)
The Hunchback of Notre Dame (1939)
Juarez (1939)
Love Letters (1945)
Portrait of Jennie (1948)

W. C. FIELDS (1879–1946)
Shorts: *The Barber Shop, The Fatal Glass of
  Beer,* and *The Pharmacist* (all 1933)
Million Dollar Legs (1932)
Tillie and Gus (1933)
It's a Gift (1934)
The Bank Dick (1940)
My Little Chickadee (1940)
Never Give a Sucker an Even Break
  (1941)

VICTOR FLEMING (1883–1949)
Lord Jim (1925)
The Virginian (1929)
Red Dust (1932)
Treasure Island (1934)
Captains Courageous (1937)
The Wizard of Oz (1939)
Gone With the Wind (1939)
Dr. Jekyll and Mr. Hyde (1941)
A Guy Named Joe (1943)

JOHN FORD (1895–1973)
The Iron Horse (1924)
The Lost Patrol (1934)
The Informer (1935)
Mary of Scotland (1936)
The Prisoner of Shark Island (1936)
The Plough and the Stars (1937). Completed 1936
The Hurricane (1937)
Stagecoach (1939)
Young Mr. Lincoln (1939)
The Grapes of Wrath (1940)
The Long Voyage Home (1940)
How Green Was My Valley (1941)
My Darling Clementine (1946)
The Fugitive (1947)
Fort Apache (1948)
She Wore A Yellow Ribbon (1949)
Rio Grande (1950)
Wagon Master (1950)
The Quiet Man (1952)
The Searchers (1956)
The Man Who Shot Liberty Valance (1962)
Donovan's Reef (1963)
Cheyenne Autumn (1964)

GRETA GARBO (1905–90)
The Story of Gösta Berling (1924)
The Joyless Street (1925)
Flesh and the Devil (1926)
Mata Hari (1931)
Grand Hotel (1932)
Queen Christina (1933)
Anna Karenina (1935)
Camille (1937)
Ninotchka (1939)

HOWARD HAWKS (1896–1977)
Fig Leaves (1926)
The Dawn Patrol (1930)

The Criminal Code (1931)
Scarface (1932). Uncensored version
    completed 1930
The Crowd Roars (1932)
Today We Live (1933)
Twentieth Century (1934)
Ceiling Zero (1935)
The Road to Glory (1936)
Bringing Up Baby (1938)
"—only Angels have wings" or *Only Angels
    Have Wings* (1939)
His Girl Friday (1940)
Ball of Fire (1941)
Air Force (1943)
To Have and Have Not (1944)
The Big Sleep (1946). Shot 1944, revised 1945–46
Red River (1948)
I Was a Male War Bride (1949)
Monkey Business (1952)
Gentlemen Prefer Blondes (1953)
Rio Bravo (1959)
Hatari! (1962)
El Dorado (1967)
Rio Lobo (1970)

ALFRED HITCHCOCK (1899–1980)

The Lodger (1926)
Blackmail (1929)
Murder! (1930)
The Man Who Knew Too Much (1934)
The 39 Steps (1935)
Sabotage (1936)
Young and Innocent (1937)
The Lady Vanishes (1938)
Rebecca (1940)
Foreign Correspondent (1940)
Suspicion (1941)
Shadow of a Doubt (1943)
Lifeboat (1944)
Spellbound (1945)
Notorious (1946)
Rope (1948)
Under Capricorn (1949)
Strangers On A Train (1951)
Dial M for Murder (1954). 3-D, but released flat
Rear Window (1954)
To Catch a Thief (1955)
The Trouble With Harry (1955)
The Man Who Knew Too Much (1956)
The Wrong Man (1956)
Vertigo (1958)

North by Northwest (1959)
Psycho (1960)
The Birds (1963)
Marnie (1964)
Frenzy (1972)
Family Plot (1976)
TV series: *Alfred Hitchcock Presents* (1955–62),
    The Alfred Hitchcock Hour (1962–65)

FRITZ LANG (1890–1976)

Fury (1936)
You Only Live Once (1937)
Hangmen Also Die! (1943)
Scarlet Street (1945)
Rancho Notorious (1952). Completed 1951
Clash by Night (1952)
The Big Heat (1953)
Beyond a Reasonable Doubt (1956)

VAL LEWTON (1904–51)

Cat People (1942, Jacques Tourneur)
I Walked with a Zombie (1943, Jacques
    Tourneur)
The Leopard Man (1943, Jacques Tourneur)
The Seventh Victim (1943, Mark Robson)
The Ghost Ship (1943, Mark Robson)
The Curse of the Cat People (1944, Robert Wise
    and Gunther Von Fritsch)
The Body Snatcher (1945, Robert Wise)
Isle Of The Dead (1945, Mark Robson)
Bedlam (1946, Mark Robson)

THE MARX BROTHERS (CHICO, 1886–1961; HARPO, 1888–1964; GROUCHO, 1890–1977; ZEPPO, 1901–79)

The Cocoanuts (1929, Joseph Santley and Robert
    Florey)
Animal Crackers (1930, Victor Heerman)
Monkey Business (1931, Norman Z. McLeod)
Horse Feathers (1932, Norman Z. McLeod)
Duck Soup (1933, Leo McCarey)
A Night at the Opera (1935, Sam Wood)
A Day at the Races (1937, Sam Wood)

LEO MCCAREY (1898–1969)

Duck Soup (1933)
Ruggles of Red Gap (1935)
The Awful Truth (1937)
Make Way For Tomorrow (1937)
Love Affair (1939)
Going My Way (1944)

My Son John (1952)
An Affair to Remember (1957)

LEWIS MILESTONE (1895–1980)
All Quiet on the Western Front (1930)
The Front Page (1931)
Rain (1932)
Anything Goes (1936)
Of Mice and Men (1939)
A Walk in the Sun (1945)
The Strange Love of Martha Ivers (1946)
Pork Chop Hill (1959)

PRESTON STURGES (1898–1959)
The Great McGinty (1940)
The Lady Eve (1941)
Sullivan's Travels (1941)
The Palm Beach Story (1942)
The Miracle of Morgan's Creek (1944).
    Completed 1943
Hail the Conquering Hero (1944)
The Sin of Harold Diddlebock (1947).
    Recut version, *Mad Wednesday*,
    released 1950
Unfaithfully Yours (1948)

JOSEF VON STERNBERG (1894–1969)
The Salvation Hunters (1925)
Underworld (1927)
The Last Command (1928)
The Docks of New York (1928)
The Blue Angel (1930)
Morocco (1930)
An American Tragedy (1931)
Blonde Venus (1932)
Shanghai Express (1932)
The Scarlet Empress (1934)
The Devil Is a Woman (1935)
The Shanghai Gesture (1941)
Anatahan or *The Saga of Anatahan* (1953)

RAOUL WALSH (1887–1981)
Regeneration (1915)
What Price Glory (1926)
The Big Trail (1930). Wide screen
The Roaring Twenties (1939)
They Drive by Night (1940)
High Sierra (1941). Completed 1940
They Died With Their Boots On (1941)
White Heat (1949)

ORSON WELLES (1915–85)
Citizen Kane (1941)
The Magnificent Ambersons (1942)
It's All True (1942). Unfinished
Journey Into Fear (1942)
The Stranger (1946)
The Lady from Shanghai (1948). Completed
    1946
Macbeth (1948)
Othello (1952)
Mr. Arkadin or *Confidential Report* (1955)
Touch of Evil (1958). Reconstructed 1998
The Trial (1962)
Chimes at Midnight or *Falstaff* (1966)
The Immortal Story (1968)
The Other Side of the Wind (1970–76).
    Unfinished

WILLIAM A. WELLMAN (1896–1975)
Wings (1927)
The Public Enemy (1931)
Night Nurse (1931)
Wild Boys of the Road (1933)
A Star Is Born (1937)
Nothing Sacred (1937)
The Ox-Bow Incident (1943)
Ernie Pyle's Story of G.I. Joe or *The Story of
    G.I. Joe* (1945)
Battleground (1949)
The High and the Mighty (1954)

MAE WEST (1892–1980)
She Done Him Wrong (1933)
I'm No Angel (1933)
Belle of the Nineties (1934)
Klondike Annie (1936)
My Little Chickadee (1940)

JAMES WHALE (1889–1957)
Journey's End (1930)
Frankenstein (1931)
The Old Dark House (1932)
The Invisible Man (1933)
Bride of Frankenstein (1935)
Show Boat (1936)
The Man in the Iron Mask (1939)

WILLIAM WYLER (1902–81)
Dodsworth (1936)
These Three (1936)
Dead End (1937)

Jezebel (1938)
Wuthering Heights (1939)
The Letter (1940)
The Little Foxes (1941)
Mrs. Miniver (1942)
The Memphis Belle (1944)
The Best Years of Our Lives (1946)
Roman Holiday (1953)
The Big Country (1958)
Ben-Hur (1959)
The Collector (1965)

THE WARNER BROS. BUSBY BERKELEY (1895–1976) CYCLE
42nd Street (1933, Lloyd Bacon/Busby Berkeley)
Gold Diggers of 1933 (1933, Mervyn LeRoy/
   Busby Berkeley)
Footlight Parade (1933, Lloyd Bacon/
   Busby Berkeley)
Dames (1934, Ray Enright/Busby Berkeley)
Gold Diggers of 1935 (1935, Busby Berkeley)
In Caliente (1935, Busby Berkeley)

THE RKO FRED ASTAIRE (1899–1987) / GINGER ROGERS (1911–95) CYCLE
Flying Down to Rio (1933, Thornton Freeland)
The Gay Divorcée (1934, Mark Sandrich)
Roberta (1935, William A. Seiter)
Top Hat (1935, Mark Sandrich)
Swing Time (1936, George Stevens)
Shall We Dance? (1937, Mark Sandrich)
The Story of Vernon and Irene Castle (1939,
   H. C. Potter)

STUDIO ERA MISCELLANY
Little Caesar (1930, Mervyn LeRoy)
Grand Hotel (1932, Edmund Goulding)
I Am a Fugitive From a Chain Gang (1932,
   Mervyn LeRoy)
If I Had A Million (1932, James Cruze, H. Bruce
   Humberstone, Stephen Roberts, William A.
   Seiter, Ernst Lubitsch, Norman Taurog, and
   Norman Z. McLeod)
The Mummy (1932, Karl Freund)
Island of Lost Souls (1933, Erle C. Kenton).
   Completed 1932
Baby Face (1933, Alfred E. Green)
King Kong (1933, Merian C. Cooper and Ernest
   B. Schoedsack)

The Black Cat (1934, Edgar G. Ulmer)
Imitation of Life (1934, John M. Stahl)
Manhattan Melodrama and *The Thin Man*
   (1934, W. S. Van Dyke)
Tarzan and His Mate (1934, Cedric Gibbons)
"G" Men (1935, William Keighley)
Mad Love (1935, Karl Freund)
Mutiny on the Bounty (1935, Frank Lloyd)
Flash Gordon (1936 serial, Frederick Stephani)
My Man Godfrey (1936, Gregory LaCava)
The Petrified Forest (1936, Archie Mayo)
Dark Manhattan (1937, Harry Fraser)
Easy Living (1937, Mitchell Leisen)
The Good Earth (1937, Sidney Franklin)
Destry Rides Again (1939, George Marshall)
Gunga Din (1939, George Stevens)
Midnight (1939, Mitchell Leisen)
The Biscuit Eater (1940, Stuart Heisler)
Dark Victory (1940, Edmund Goulding)
Kitty Foyle (1940, Sam Wood)
Now, Voyager (1940, Irving Rapper)
Hellzapoppin' (1941, H. C. Potter)
Kings Row (1941, Sam Wood)
The Wolf Man (1941, George Waggner)
The Pride of the Yankees (1942, Sam Wood)
This Gun For Hire (1942, Frank Tuttle)
Double Indemnity (1944, Billy Wilder)
The Fighting Seabees (1944, Edward Ludwig)
Since You Went Away (1944, John Cromwell)
Brewster's Millions (1945, Allan Dwan)
Detour (1945, Edgar G. Ulmer)
The House on 92nd Street (1945, Henry
   Hathaway)
Murder, My Sweet (1945, Edward Dmytryk)

DVDs

The Big Sleep (1946, **Howard Hawks**). Warner
   Studios. Includes the 1944 pre-release version
   and the 1946 release version, with a documen-
   tary on their differences.
The Blue Angel is listed in Chap. 7.
Bringing Up Baby (1938, **Howard Hawks**).
   Warner Home Video. Two-Disc Special
   Edition. Includes documentaries on Hawks
   and Grant, plus a cartoon and a short from
   1938. Commentary by Peter Bogdanovich.
Citizen Kane (1941, **Orson Welles**). Warner
   Home Video. Includes commentaries by critic
   Roger Ebert and Welles expert Peter

Bogdanovich, premiere newsreel, studio correspondence, storyboards, and a documentary.

The Complete Mr. Arkadin (1955, **Orson Welles**). Criterion Collection. Includes three cuts of the film: *Confidential Report*, the "Corinth" version of *Mr. Arkadin*, and a "comprehensive" version that attempts to reconstruct Welles's planned film out of all the existing footage. Also includes outtakes, relevant radio, alternate scenes, a documentary on the comprehensive version, and the printed novel.

Dr. Jekyll and Mr. Hyde (1932, **Rouben Mamoulian,** starring Fredric March). Warner Home Video. Also includes the 1941 version, directed by **Victor Fleming** and starring Spencer Tracy.

Fort Apache (1948, **John Ford**). Turner Home Entertainment. **Digitally restored.**

42nd Street (1933, **Lloyd Bacon**). Warner Home Video. Includes three shorts and information on **Busby Berkeley.**

Freaks (1932, **Tod Browning**). Warner Home Video. Includes a documentary, a commentary by horror scholar David J. Skal, the reissue prologue, and three alternate endings.

Gone With the Wind (1939, **Victor Fleming**). Warner Home Video. Four-Disc Collector's Edition. The best **digital restoration** of this film yet, with hours of documentaries, newsreels, restoration information, and more.

The Lady Eve (1941, **Preston Sturges**). Criterion Collection. Commentary by film historian Marian Keane, introduction by Peter Bogdanovich, and the 1942 radio adaptation.

The Man Who Shot Liberty Valance (1962, **John Ford**). Paramount Home Video. Centennial Collection. Includes a documentary and archival recordings.

The **Marx Brothers** *Collection.* Warner Home Video. Includes *A Night at the Opera, A Day at the Races, Room Service, At the Circus, Go West, The Big Store*, and *A Night in Casablanca*, with documentaries, shorts including **Robert Benchley** in *How to Sleep*, cartoons, and more.

The **Marx Brothers** *Silver Screen Collection.* Universal. Includes *The Cocoanuts, Animal Crackers, Monkey Business, Horse Feathers, Duck Soup*, and some extras.

The Mummy: The Legacy Collection (1932–44). Universal. Includes *The Mummy* (1932, **Karl Freund**) with commentary by film historian Paul Jensen, a documentary by horror scholar David J. Skal, and the Kharis sequels: *The Mummy's Hand, Tomb, Ghost*, and *Curse* (1940–44); the only extras for the sequels are their trailers. Other Legacy sets for *Dracula, Frankenstein*, and *The Wolf Man* include the originals and all their pre-Abbott-and-Costello sequels (though some sequels show up in surprising sets), with good extras and silly ones. Unfortunately, some of the films in these sets are not as sharp as the others (they were compressed at different **bit rates;** see Chap. 18). The *Dracula* set includes the U.S. and Spanish versions of *Dracula*.

Notorious (1946, **Alfred Hitchcock**). Criterion Collection. Commentaries by film historians Rudy Behlmer and Marian Keane.

Rear Window (1954, **Alfred Hitchcock**). Universal. Collector's Edition. **Restored,** with a documentary on the production and restoration. The screenplay is in the DVD-ROM section.

Rebecca (1940, **Alfred Hitchcock**). Criterion Collection. **Digitally restored.** Includes commentary by Leonard J. Leff, screen tests, production correspondence, the preview questionnaire, several radio versions, and more.

Red River (1948, **Howard Hawks**). MGM/UA Home Video. This is the longer of the two versions, the "book version"—preferred by Hawks, though not the release version—in which the narration comes from a written history of early Texas. (The shorter version is narrated voice-over by Walter Brennan.)

The Scarlet Empress (1932, **Josef von Sternberg**). Criterion Collection. Includes a BBC documentary and essays by filmmaker **Jack Smith** and film critic Robin Wood.

The Searchers (1956, **John Ford**). Warner Home Video. Two-Disc Anniversary Edition. **Digitally restored.** Commentary by Peter Bogdanovich. Includes several short documentaries on the film, director, cast, location, etc.

Stagecoach (1939, **John Ford**). Warner Home Video. Two-Disc Special Edition. Includes documentaries on Ford and Wayne and on the film; also includes a radio adaptation.

Sullivan's Travels (1941, **Preston Sturges**). Criterion Collection. Includes four commentaries, interviews, a documentary, and Sturges singing a song and reciting a poem.

The 39 Steps (1935, **Alfred Hitchcock**). Criterion Collection. **Digitally restored,** with a documentary on Hitchcock's British period, the 1937 Lux Radio Theatre version, production design sketches, and a commentary by film historian Marian Keane.

Touch of Evil (1958, **Orson Welles**). Universal. The 1998 **restored** version, with Welles's memo regarding the editing of the picture.

Tracy & Hepburn: *The Signature Collection.* Warner Home Video. Includes *Adam's Rib* (1949, **George Cukor**), *Pat and Mike* (1952, **Cukor**), *Woman of the Year* (1942, **George Stevens**), and *The Spencer Tracy Legacy*.

Trouble in Paradise (1932, **Ernst Lubitsch**). Criterion Collection. Includes a Lubitsch 1917 short, *The Merry Jail*; a commentary by Lubitsch biographer Scott Eyman; and a 1940 radio show with Lubitsch, Jack Benny, Claudette Colbert, and Basil Rathbone.

The Val Lewton Horror Collection. Warner Home Video. Contains all nine of the horror films **Val Lewton** produced for RKO as well as a documentary on Lewton.

Vertigo (1958, **Alfred Hitchcock**). Universal. Collector's Edition. **Restored,** with commentary by the restorers, Robert A. Harris and James C. Katz. Includes a documentary on the production and restoration**.**

Warner Bros. Pictures Gangsters Collection. Warner Home Video. Contains *Little Caesar* (1930, **Mervyn LeRoy**), *The Public Enemy* (1931, **William A. Wellman**), *The Petrified Forest* (1936, **Archie Mayo**), *Angels With Dirty Faces* (1938, **Michael Curtiz**), *The Roaring Twenties* (1939, **Raoul Walsh**), and *White Heat* (1949, **Walsh**). Each feature is accompanied by a cartoon, a newsreel excerpt, a trailer, and a short from the same year as the film; these extras, introduced by Leonard Maltin, partially recreate a night at the movies. The set also includes some radio versions.

W. C. Fields: *Six Short Films* (1915 and 1930–33). Criterion Collection. Good prints—from original materials, some **restored**—of *Pool Sharks* (silent), *The Barber Shop, The Fatal Glass of Beer, The Pharmacist, The Golf Specialist,* and *The Dentist.*

The Wizard of Oz (1939, **Victor Fleming**). Warner Home Video. Three-Disc Collector's Edition. **Digitally restored,** with a documentary on the restoration. Includes deleted scenes, outtakes, hours of unedited musical recordings, radio programs, many documentaries, five previous Oz films, printed stills and facsimiles, and much more.

Young Mr. Lincoln (1939, **John Ford**). Criterion Collection. **Digitally restored.** Includes the radio version, audio interviews with Ford and **Henry Fonda,** and a BBC documentary on Ford's early career.

12

Hollywood in Transition: 1946–65

In 1946, the American film business grossed $1.7 billion domestically, the peak box-office year in the 50-year history of the American film industry. Twelve years later, in 1958, domestic box-office receipts fell below a billion dollars; by 1962, domestic receipts had fallen to $900 million, slightly more than half the 1946 gross. And inflated ticket prices hid an even more devastating statistic: By 1953, weekly attendance at film theatres had fallen to about 25 percent of the 1948 figure. While box-office income steadily fell, production costs—unionized labor, new equipment, costly materials—steadily rose along with the nation's soaring, inflated economy. The two vectors of rising costs and falling revenues seemed to point directly toward the cemetery for both Hollywood and the commercial American film.

Yet in 1968, American box offices collected $1.3 billion (domestic box-office receipts having risen every year since 1963). In 1974, American theatres grossed almost $2 billion, and in 1983, over $3 billion. In 1989, domestic box-office grosses exceeded $5 billion for the first time (by then, "domestic" included American and Canadian theatres). In 2000, they reached a new high of $7.7 billion, and in 2004, they reached $9.2 billion, representing 1.52 billion tickets (at an average cost of just over $6) to movies that each cost, on the average, $63.8 million to produce. (In 1960, *Psycho* was produced for under $1 million, and only the makers of *Spartacus* could figure out how to spend more than $11 million.) In 2008, average ticket prices were over $7, admissions had held steady at about

1.4 billion for several years, and the box office took in $9.6 billion. Adjusted for inflation (what cost $1 in 1946 cost $10.91 in 2008), this was still not as high as the 1946 box-office gross, which was $18.55 billion in 2008 dollars.

Even if films are still attended by a much smaller percentage of Americans than went to the movies in 1946, the figures indicate that the American film industry emerged from a difficult transitional period and solidified itself commercially by redefining its product and its audience. Between 1948 and 1963, however, lay 15 years of groping.

Enemies Within: Freedom of Association and Free Entertainment

Even before World War II, the two forces that would crush the old Hollywood had begun their assault. First, U.S. courts had begun to rule that the film industry's methods of distributing motion pictures represented an illegal restraint of open trade. Block booking was unfair to the individual competitive exhibitors, requiring them to book many pictures they did not want in order to get the few they did. Over the course of the 1920s and 1930s, the general tendency of American judicial and legislative pressure was to reduce the number of films the independent exhibitor could be forced to buy as a block. The studio-owned chains of theatres gave even greater monopolistic control of the market to the "majors," the five biggest Hollywood production companies—MGM,

Paramount, Warner Bros., 20th Century–Fox, and RKO—who could use their commercial and artistic power to control the industry's profits and practices. The industry knew that the day would come when the line that tied theatre to studio would have to be cut. The war postponed that day.

Second, by the mid-1930s a new electronic toy that combined picture and sound—television—had been demonstrated by its scientist creators. At first Hollywood laughed at the visually inferior upstart whose programs—like those of its parent, radio—were both live and free; by the late 1940s, Hollywood had begun to fight. National television broadcasting began in the United States in 1948, and in 1949, there were only a million television receivers in America. By 1952, there were 10 million. By the end of the decade, there were 50 million, and Hollywood had surrendered.

World War II helped postpone the domestic battle because fighting America needed movies to take its mind off the war. Both soldiers overseas and their families at home needed to escape to the movies. America also needed films for education: to train the soldiers to do their jobs, to teach them "why we fight," to give both information and encouragement to the folks at home. Hollywood sent many of its best directors—Frank Capra, William Wyler, George Stevens, John Huston, John Ford—to make documentaries for the government and the armed forces. Hollywood also sent 16mm prints of its newest releases for distribution—without charge—to the fighting men at thousands of "Beachhead Bijoux."

While Hollywood did its part, its profits conveniently rose. The government added special war taxes to theatre tickets and sold bonds in the lobby; Americans who went to the movies not only enjoyed themselves, but also contributed to the war effort (see Fig. 11-9). Many Hollywood writers, directors, and producers took new pride in the educational and documentary projects. Frank Capra's *Why We Fight* series (1942–45), Ford's *The Battle of Midway* (1942), Ford and Toland's *December 7th* (1943), Wyler's *The Memphis Belle* (1944), Huston's *The Battle of San Pietro* (1945) and *Let There Be Light* (1946, released 1981), and Disney's *Victory Through Air Power* (1943) were among the most powerful wartime documentaries.

Even fictional feature films of wartime battles—Delmer Daves's *Destination Tokyo* (1943), Tay Garnett's *Bataan* (1943), Howard Hawks's *Air Force* (1943), Lewis Milestone's *A Walk in the Sun* (1945), William Wellman's *The Story of G.I. Joe* (1945)—borrowed the visual styles of documentary authenticity. It was almost obligatory in these war films that an American fighting platoon was composed of one Italian from Hackensack, one WASP mainliner from Philadelphia, one Jew from Brooklyn, one farmboy from Kansas, one Irish Catholic from Boston, one Pole from Chicago—a mythical cross section of America, pulling together to win the "big one." Not until Wellman's *Battleground* and Mark Robson's *Home of the Brave* (both 1949) did a black soldier join that cross section.

Henry Hathaway made a series of postwar films that looked and sounded like documentaries. Some of them re-created true stories, and all of them were shot outside the studio, on the locations where the actual events occurred (or, in the case of a realistic fiction, would be likely to occur). Of the true stories, *The House on 92nd Street* (1945) and *Call Northside 777* (1948) stand out. The greatest of his melodramas are *Kiss of Death* (1947), a *film noir*, and the rich, dark *Niagara* (1953), which has many of the elements of *noir*. Hathaway's nonstudio style was launched before that of Italian Neorealism.

The government's Office of War Information established a Bureau of Motion Picture Affairs, while Hollywood responded with its War Activities Committee. After the war, the relationship between the industry and the government would not be so cozy.

The Supreme Court's 1948 decision in *U.S. v. Paramount Pictures, Inc.* was the ultimate in a lengthy series of court rulings that the studios must sell ("divest" themselves of) their theatres. The guaranteed outlet for the studio's product—good, bad, or mediocre—was closed. Divestiture changed the film economy: Each film would have to be good enough to sell itself.

Meanwhile, more and more Americans bought television sets. Special events like the 1948 Rose Bowl game and parade and the 1948 political conventions, or regular events, like Milton Berle, "Uncle Miltie," on the *Texaco Star Theater* every Tuesday night at eight, kept Americans looking at the box. The film industry denied the box its products. Until 1956 (1954 for RKO), no Hollywood film could be shown on television, and no working film star could appear on a television program. So Americans stayed home to watch British and public-domain movies, their favorite radio stars made visible, and the new stars that television itself developed.

The Hollywood Ten and the Blacklist

These specific legal and commercial woes were accompanied by a general shift of American mood in the years following the war that also contributed to the ills of a troubled industry. The Cold War years of suspicion—dislike of foreign entanglements in general and the increasing fear of the "Red Menace" in particular—also produced a distrust of certain institutions within the United States. Because the film industry was so active in the war effort against the Nazis, because so many Hollywood producers and screenwriters were Jewish, because so many Jewish intellectuals seemed sympathetic to liberal political positions, and because the most extreme right-wing American opinion saw the entire war as a sacrifice of American lives to save the Jews in Europe and help the Soviets defend the Eastern front, it was not surprising that these rivers of reaction coalesced into an attack on the motion-picture industry as a whole. Whereas for

four decades American suspicion had concentrated on Hollywood's sexual and moral excesses, in the decade following the war distrust shifted to Hollywood's political and social positions: to the subversive, pro-Communist propaganda allegedly woven—mainly by the writers—into Hollywood's entertainment films.

The first set of hearings of the House Committee on Un-American Activities, called by its detractors the House Un-American Activities Committee (or HUAC), in the fall of 1947, investigating Communist infiltration of the motion-picture industry, produced the highly publicized national scandal of the "Hollywood Ten." Asked "Are you now or have you ever been" a Communist, the Ten—screenwriters Alvah Bessie, Lester Cole, Ring Lardner, Jr., John Howard Lawson, Albert Maltz, Samuel Ornitz, and Dalton Trumbo; director Edward Dmytryk; writer–producer Adrian Scott; and director–producer Herbert J. Biberman—accused the Committee of violating the Bill of Rights by its existence. When the Ten were cited for contempt of Congress, the motion-picture industry reacted fearfully by instituting a blacklist—no known or suspected Communist or Communist sympathizer would be permitted to work in any capacity on a Hollywood film. Convicted, their appeals denied, the Ten began to serve one-year sentences in 1950. (When he got out, director

The Hollywood Ten: a 1950 demonstration.

Fig. 12-1

Dmytryk named names—that is, gave the Committee the names of possible subversives—and went back to work.)

The second set of congressional hearings (1951–52) gave witnesses two choices. If they admitted a previous membership in the Communist Party, they were obligated to name everyone else with whom they had been associated at that time or suffer a contempt of Congress sentence as had the Hollywood Ten. The other choice was to avoid answering any questions whatever on the basis of the Constitution's Fifth Amendment guarantee against self-incrimination. Although "taking the Fifth" kept the witness out of prison (whereas invoking the First Amendment, which protects freedom of speech, of the press, of religion, and of association, did not), it also kept the witness out of work—thanks to the industry's blacklist.

A number of the blacklisted writers found work under pseudonyms. Many left Hollywood, and some left the country. So did such directors as Jules Dassin and Joseph Losey. (While living in Mexico, Hugo Butler wrote for Buñuel.) In 1953, an independent film called *Salt of the Earth* was shot in New Mexico by three blacklistees: writer Michael Wilson, director Herbert Biberman, and producer Paul Jarrico. Wilson's script, the true story of a mining strike that lasted more than a year, was critiqued by and rewritten to the satisfaction of the hundreds of people who had participated in the strike, many of whom played themselves in the movie. The primarily Mexican-American cast was led by professional Rosaura Revueltas (who was deported to Mexico during the shooting and effectively blacklisted thereafter) and nonprofessional Juan Chacon; they play a couple who discover the dignity of resisting economic and racist oppression as equals. *Salt of the Earth* rigorously and dramatically analyzes a problem common to many political movements: that as the boss or tyrant treats the worker, so the male revolutionary often treats the female revolutionary. In this film the miners learn to stop treating their wives as underlings, and the newly unified community wins its battles. Completed despite concerted attacks, *Salt of the Earth* had practically no distribution in America, though it won awards and acclaim in both Western and Eastern Europe as well as the People's Republic of China. It was to become a

Fig. 12-2
Salt of the Earth: *beyond sexism, beyond racism, and way beyond Hollywood.*

cult film on American campuses during the 1960s and 1970s and is widely regarded now as a classic.

The result of the congressional hearings—and the controversial blacklist, the damaging publicity in the press, the threats of boycott against Hollywood films by the American Legion, the lists of suspected Communists or Communist sympathizers in publications such as *Red Channels*—was an even greater weakening of the industry's crumbling commercial and social strength.

The biggest, richest studios were hit the hardest. Two former assets suddenly became liabilities: property and people. In 1949, MGM declared wage cutbacks and immense layoffs. The giant studio's rows of sound stages and acres of outdoor sets became increasingly empty; the huge film factories now owned vast expanses of expensive and barren land. Even more costly than land were the contracts with people—technicians, featured players, and stars—that required the studio to pay their salaries although it had no pictures for them to make. MGM allowed the contracts of its greatest stars, formerly the studio's richest commercial resource, to lapse. Every big studio extricated itself from the tangle of its obligations with financially disastrous slowness. By the late 1950s, the star system and the studio system were as good as dead. A minor studio like Columbia, with very few stars under contract, a small lot, and no theatres, stayed healthier in those years of thinner profits. Columbia also showed foresight by being the first film studio to establish a television-producing division, Screen Gems, in 1951, when television was still an infant. The big movie houses suffered with the big studios. On a weeknight, only a few hundred patrons scattered themselves about a house built for thousands. One by one the ornate palaces came down, to be replaced by supermarkets, shopping centers, and apartment buildings.

3-D, CinemaScope, Color, and the Tube

Television was not the sole cause of the film industry's commercial decay. The American demographic shift from the cities to the suburbs began just after the war. Movie theatres had always been concentrated in the city centers, and the multiplex cinemas of suburban shopping malls were two decades away. There were also many new ways to spend leisure time and the leisure dollar. Professional and collegiate sports events, stimulated by television exposure, drew increasingly larger audiences. The DC-6 and DC-7 airliners and, by 1960, DC-8 and 707 jets made long-distance travel more accessible and affordable. The RPM 33 1/3 long-playing microgroove phonograph record appeared in 1949, as did the 45 RPM single; first high-fidelity ("hi-fi"), then stereo music systems became household necessities within the next decade. A booming music industry ate into former movie dollars as voraciously as television did.

Fig. 12-3
Hollywood executives watch 3-D dailies in 1952.

By 1952, Hollywood knew that television could not be throttled. If films and TV were to co-exist, the movies would have to give the public what TV did not. The most obvious difference between movies and TV was the size of the screen. Television's visual thinking was necessarily in inches, whereas movies could compose in feet and yards. Films also enjoyed the advantage of over 50 years of technological research in color, properties of lenses, and special laboratory effects; the younger television art had not yet developed color, and videotape was in its infancy. Hollywood's two primary weapons against television were to be size and technical gimmickry.

One of the industry's first sallies was 3-D, a three-dimensional, stereoscopic effect produced by shooting the action with two lenses simultaneously at a specified distance apart. Two interlocked projectors then threw the two perspectives on a single screen simultaneously; the audience used cardboard or plastic glasses (with red and blue lenses for black-and-white films, polarized clear lenses for color films) to read the two overlapping, flat images as a single three-dimensional one. The idea was not new; even in the 19th century, a viewer could see a three-dimensional still photograph by looking at two related photos through a stereopticon; all that is necessary is to show the image taken by the right camera only to the right eye, and the left image only to the left eye. Kodak had been marketing "stereo" still cameras since 1901, and Edwin S. Porter and William E. Waddell had presented the first 3-D movie (non-narrative scenes of New York and New Jersey) in 1915. Abel Gance had shot a 3-D roll for *Napoléon* in 1927, but decided not to use it.

Despite the familiarity of the stereoscopic principle, to see it in a full-length, active feature film was a great novelty. The first 3-D feature was Harry K. Fairall's *The Power of Love* (U.S., 1922); Russia released its first 3-D film, *Day Off in Moscow*, in 1940. Hollywood rushed into 3-D production in 1952 with Arch Oboler's *Bwana Devil*, which was followed by pictures like *House of Wax, It Came From Outer Space, Fort Ti, Kiss Me Kate,* and *I, the Jury* (all 1953); *Creature from the Black Lagoon, The French Line,* and *Gog* (all 1954); and finally, *Revenge of the Creature* (1955). Audiences eagerly left their TV sets to experience the gimmick that attacked

them with knives, arrows, avalanches, stampedes, vats of chemicals, Ann Miller's tap shoes, and Jane Russell's bust; the thrill of 3-D was that the formerly confined, flat picture convincingly threatened to leap, fly, or flow out of its frame at the audience.

Some blame the death of 3-D on the headache-inducing glasses that it required, but the more obvious cause of death was that any pure novelty becomes boring when it is no longer novel. 3-D, as used in the 1950s, was pure novelty; the thrill of being run over by a train is visually identical to that of being run over by a herd of cattle. Further, because 3-D required the theatre owner to make costly additions and renovations (in order to perform changeovers, mere startup costs included four projectors—two for each reel), the exhibitors declared a war of neglect against the process and hastened its demise. Business for 3-D films fell off so quickly that Hitchcock, who had shot *Dial M for Murder* (1954) in the new process—taking full advantage of the opportunity to compose in depth—released it in the conventional two dimensions. Among the later attempts to revive two-projector 3-D have been a few "sexploitation" films (in 1970, *The Stewardesses*) and Paul Morrissey's *Flesh for Frankenstein* (released as *Andy Warhol's Frankenstein*, 1974). In the 1980s, a single-projector 3-D system, with half the normal resolution but simplified installation, gave audiences everything from *Friday the 13th Part III* (Steve Miner, 1982) to the 3-D release of *Dial M for Murder* (1983). The superior optical system of digital 3-D, which appeared during the first decade of the 21st century, reduced the complaints about the glasses and headaches and allowed many versatile new effects, as in Henry Selick's stop-motion animated *Coraline* (2009), which made its alternate world deeper than its real one, or Pixar's first 3-D picture, *Up* (2009), which displayed many uses for the process beyond that of hurtling images at the audience, creating a world with the texture and deep fullness that the best 3-D can offer.

A second movie novelty also promised thrills. Cinerama, unlike 3-D, brought the audience into the picture, not the picture into the audience. Cinerama originally used three interlocked cameras and four interlocked projectors (one for stereophonic sound). The final prints were

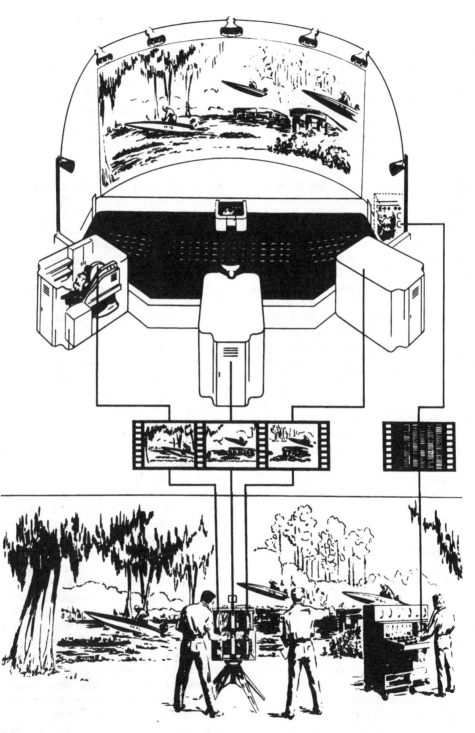

Fig. 12-4
A contemporary diagram of Cinerama: the widest of screens broken into three frames with six-track stereo sound. The six-perf frames were taller than they appear here.

projected not on top of one another (superimposed, as in 3-D), but side by side—with barely visible vertical lines where the images met. The result was an immense wraparound image that was really three images. The wide, high, deeply curved screen and the relative positions of the three cameras worked on the eye's peripheral vision to make the mind believe that the body was actually in motion. The difference between a ride in an automobile and a conventionally filmed ride is that in an automobile the world also moves past on the sides, not just straight ahead. Cinerama's huge triple screen duplicated this impression of peripheral movement.

Like 3-D, the idea was not new. As early as the Paris World's Exposition of 1900, the energetic inventor–cinematographers had begun displaying wraparound and multi-screen film processes. (Multi-screen experiments have long been popular at world's fairs—for example, the New York fair of 1963–64 and Expo '67 in Montreal.) In 1927, Abel Gance had incorporated triple-screen effects, both panoramic and triptych, into his *Napoléon*. In 1938, Fred Waller, Cinerama's inventor, began research on the process. But when *This Is Cinerama* opened in 1952, audiences choked—quite literally—with a film novelty that sent them racing down a roller coaster track and soaring over the Rocky Mountains. A six-track (in later Cinerama films, seven-track) stereophonic sound system accompanied the thrilling pictures; sounds could travel from left to right across the screen or jump from behind the screen to behind the audience's heads. Co-produced by Merian C. Cooper, Lowell Thomas, Louis B. Mayer, Robert L. Bendick, and the great showman Michael Todd, and partly directed by Ernest B. Schoedsack (Cooper and Schoedsack made both documentaries like *Grass* and spectacular fictions like *King Kong*), *This Is Cinerama* had one foot in show business and the other in documentary.

Cinerama remained commercially viable longer than 3-D because it was more carefully marketed. Because of the complex projection machinery, only a few theatres in major cities were equipped for the process. Seeing Cinerama became a special, exciting event; the film was sold as a "roadshow" attraction with reserved seats, noncontinuous performances, and high prices. Customers returned to Cinerama because they could see a Cinerama film so infrequently. (The second, *Cinerama Holiday*, came out three years after *This Is Cinerama*.) After the travelogues, Cinerama was used for narrative films: *The Wonderful World of the Brothers Grimm* (1962), *It's a Mad Mad Mad Mad World* (1963), *How the West Was Won* (1963). In 1968, Stanley Kubrick's *2001: A Space Odyssey* subordinated a modified Cinerama (shot with a single camera but projected on a Cinerama screen) to the film's sociological and metaphysical journey, letting the big screen and sound work for the story rather than letting the story work for the effects, as some of the Cinerama narrative films had done.

A third innovation of the early 1950s also took advantage of the size of the movie screen. The new format, CinemaScope, was the most durable and functional of them all, requiring no extra projectors, special film, or special glasses. It did, however, require theatre owners to invest in "scope" or anamorphic projection lenses; wide, curved screens; and, in most cases, stereophonic sound systems. The action was recorded by a conventional movie camera on conventional 35mm film. A special anamorphic lens squeezed the image horizontally to fit the width of the standard film. When projected with a corresponding anamorphic lens on the projector, the distortions disappeared and a huge, wide image stretched across the curved screen. (It was curved not only to emulate Cinerama, but also to keep the entire image in focus by having the left, center, and right of the screen equidistant from the projector.) Once again, the "novelty" was not new. As early as 1928, a French scientist named Henri Chrétien had experimented with an anamorphic lens for the motion-picture camera; in 1952, the executives of 20th Century–Fox visited Professor Chrétien, then retired to a Riviera villa, and bought the rights to his anamorphic process. The first CinemaScope feature, Henry Koster's *The Robe* (1953), whose size itself was spectacular, convinced both Fox and the industry that the process was viable. The screen had been made wide with a minimum of trouble and expense. A parade of screen-widening "scopes" and "visions" followed Fox's CinemaScope, some of them using an anamorphic lens, one non-anamorphic process (VistaVision) printing the image sideways on the celluloid strip to achieve width without loss of resolution, and some of them achieving screen width by widening the film to 55mm, 65mm, or 70mm, notably Todd-AO, MGM Camera 65, CinemaScope 55, Super Panavision 70, and Ultra Panavision 70 (some of these also used anamorphic lenses to widen the wide-film image). The first 70mm film of the 1950s was *Oklahoma!* (1955), directed by Fred Zinnemann and shot in Todd-AO.

Ultimately it was size and grandeur that triumphed, not depth perception or motion effects. As early as 1930, Eisenstein advocated a flexible screen size, a principle he called the "dynamic square." He reasoned that the conventional screen, with its four-to-three ratio of width to height (an aspect ratio of 4:3, or 1.33:1), was too inflexible. The screen should be capable of becoming very wide for certain sequences, narrow and long for others, a perfect square for balanced compositions. But Eisenstein's principles were much closer to Griffith's use of masking or irising than to the wide screen's inflexible commitment to width. George Stevens complained that CinemaScope was better for shooting a python than a person. How could a horizontal picture frame, with a 5:2 ratio of width to height, enclose a vertical subject?

Despite these complaints, which echoed those about synchronized sound in the late 1920s, some directors came to terms with the new frame format right away. In the wide-screen musical *It's Always Fair Weather* (1955), directors Gene Kelly and Stanley Donen could make a little in-group joke. When Dan Dailey retires to a telephone booth, a sign informs us that a call to California costs only **$2.50** for **1** minute, with the numbers in boldface. That ratio of 2.5 to 1 was roughly the CinemaScope format of this very film, made in California. (The actual aspect ratio of this and other early CinemaScope films was 2.55 to 1. CinemaScope later changed to 2.35:1. The current 35mm anamorphic format, Panavision, began at 2.35:1 but changed in the early 1970s to 2.4:1.)

The film also demonstrates that the familiar American object most like a CinemaScope frame is a dollar bill (2.33:1). The plot of *It's Always Fair Weather* rips a dollar bill into three pieces, one for each of three GIs, to remind them of their reunion ten years later. In the same way, Kelly and Donen repeatedly rip the CinemaScope frame into three compositional pieces, one for each of the buddies. The movie industry hoped it would rake in plenty of dollar bills from this frame that resembled a dollar bill.

Like sound in the early years, the new technological invention was a mixed blessing, adding some new film possibilities and destroying many of the old compositional virtues. What many critics of the wide screen did not perceive at the time was that just as deep focus permitted contrapuntal relationships between near and far within the frame (as in *Citizen Kane*), the wide screen permitted contrapuntal relationships among left, center, and right.

George Cukor's *A Star Is Born* (1954), a great remake of William Wellman's great 1937 melodrama, provides powerful proof of this potential. Two sequences demonstrate not only Cukor's mastery of the format, but also his awareness of its history and value. In one scene, Oliver Niles (Charles Bickford), the head of the studio, fires the aging matinee idol, Norman Maine (James Mason). Maine's popularity has been slipping, and the studio itself has been slumping. The cause? Television. During this conversation, the men stand between two flickering black-and-white images on the far left and right edges of the frame. To the far left is a TV set; Niles has been watching the fights on TV (even a studio head cannot stay away from a TV screen). To the far right of the frame is a motion picture, projected in the next room for Maine's party guests. The discussion between Maine and Niles takes place precisely between a video image and a film image—a visual translation of the historical crossroads where all the studio heads and studio stars found themselves in 1954.

Cukor uses television again in the film's Academy Awards ceremony. While Cukor shoots Vicky Lester's (Judy Garland) triumph with the CinemaScope lens in medium long shot, a TV monitor in the upper right-hand corner of the frame displays the moment in typical TV close-ups. The shot is simultaneously a long shot and a close-up, a wide-screen color image and a small-screen black-and-white TV image, a revelation of CinemaScope's visual power and television's cultural power, capable of bringing this moment, "live," into people's homes in close-ups.

The wide CinemaScope frame enabled Cukor to shoot whole scenes—even Garland's entire rendition of "The Man That Got Away"—in a

Fig. 12-5

Fig. 12-6
Composition for the wide screen in A Star Is Born. *Fig. 12-5: Judy Garland surrounded by jazz musicians for "The Man That Got Away"; primary interest at center. Fig. 12-6: Garland, with Jack Carson, surrounded by the photographic faces of stardom; primary interest at the sides, in a CinemaScope approach to the two-shot.*

continuous, complexly choreographed shot without a cut. (Of course, Welles and Toland had done that with the standard frame in *Citizen Kane.*) In the work of Cukor, Donen, Ophüls, Preminger, and others, the 1950s saw an explosion of interest in the uses of the wide screen, an interest that remained evident in the 1960s and 1970s works of such directors as Lean, Kurosawa, Leone, Peckinpah, and Godard. By the mid-1960s, the wide-screen revolution was as

complete as the sound revolution of the late 1920s, and the wide screen, like sound, would become the basis of a new generation's film aesthetics.

The battle with television was partially responsible for another technical revolution in the 1950s—the almost total conversion to color. From the earliest days of moving pictures, inventors and filmmakers sought to combine color with recorded movement. Some of the early

Méliès films were hand-painted frame by frame. Many silent films were bathed in color tints, adding a cast of pale blue for night sequences, sepia for interiors and yellow for sunlight, a red tint for certain effects, a green tint for others. Such coloring effects were obviously tonal, like the accompanying music, rather than an intrinsic part of the film's photographic conception. As early as 1908, Charles Urban patented a superb color photographic process, Kinemacolor, that was inspired by the work of G. A. Smith. But opposition from the Motion Picture Patents Company kept Kinemacolor off American screens.

In 1917, the Technicolor Corporation was founded in the United States. Supported by all the major studios, Technicolor enjoyed monopolistic control over all color experimentation and shooting in the country. Douglas Fairbanks's *The Black Pirate* (1926) and the musicals *Rio Rita* (1929) and *Whoopee!* (1930) used the early Technicolor process, which added a garish grandeur to the costumes and scenery. In the 1920s, Technicolor was, like Urban's Kinemacolor, a two-color process: two strips of film exposed by a single lens equipped with a beam-splitter prism, one strip recording the blue–green colors of the spectrum, the other sensitive to the red–orange colors; the strips were bonded together in the final processing. But by 1933 Technicolor had perfected a more accurate three-color process: three strips of black-and-white film, one exposed through a filter to red, the second to blue, the third to green, originally requiring a bulky three-prism camera—with a single lens—for the three rolls of film, copies of which were used to transfer red, blue, and green dyes to a print. The first two-strip Technicolor feature had been *The Toll of the Sea* (1922); the one that used color most creatively was *Doctor X* (1932). The first film made in the three-strip process was Disney's cartoon *Flowers and Trees* (1932). RKO's *La Cucaracha* (1934) was the first three-strip Technicolor live-action short, and Rouben Mamoulian's *Becky Sharp* (1935) the first three-strip Technicolor feature. Hollywood could have converted to color at almost the same time it converted to sound. But expenses and priorities dictated that most talkies use black-and-white film, which was itself becoming faster, subtler, more responsive to minimal light, easier to use under any conditions. Color was reserved

for cartoons or for lavish spectacles that could afford the slowness and expense of color shooting (for example, Michael Curtiz and William Keighley's *The Adventures of Robin Hood*, 1938; Victor Fleming's *Gone With the Wind* and *The Wizard of Oz*, both 1939).

Before World War II, color was both a monopoly and a sacred mystery. Color negatives were processed and printed behind closed doors; special Technicolor consultants and cameramen were almost as important on the set of a color film as the director and producer. Natalie Kalmus, the ex-wife of Herbert Kalmus, who invented the process, became Technicolor's artistic director and constructed an official aesthetic code for the use of color (she preferred mutedly harmonious color effects to discordantly jarring ones), a code as binding on a film's color values as was the Hays Code on its moral values. Until 1949, every film that used Technicolor was required to hire Mrs. Kalmus as "Technicolor Consultant."

World War II, which demanded that the film industry keep up production while tightening its belt, generally excluded the luxury of color filming—unless the film had propaganda value and was likely to improve morale. England put up the money for Laurence Olivier's *Henry V* (1944), whose splendid and complex use of color intensified the film's propagandistic appeal. Most wartime American color films also had propaganda value—Vincente Minnelli's *Meet Me in St. Louis* (1944), which depicted the homespun life and traditions that the boys were fighting to save; DeMille's *The Story of Dr. Wassel* (1944), a hymn to an American war hero.

After the war, Hollywood needed color to fight television, which—at least until the late 1950s—could offer audiences only black and white. Technicolor, formerly without competitors, had kept costs up and production down. Hollywood began encouraging a new, competing single-strip process, Eastmancolor. The new process was one of the spoils of war, a pirated copy of the German Agfacolor monopack. The monopack color film bonded three color-sensitive emulsions onto a single roll of filmstock. A color film could be shot with an ordinary movie camera. Color emulsions became progressively faster, more sensitive, more flexible. A series of new processes—DeLuxe, Metrocolor, Warnercolor—were all variations of Eastmancolor, which was less expensive and of lower quality than monopack Technicolor (introduced in 1942). What these monopack color processes gained over three-strip Technicolor in cheapness and flexibility they sacrificed in intensity and brilliance. (Technicolor's clean dyes were picked up and transferred directly onto the print by three strips or matrixes struck from the camera's three strips, but the Eastman dyes were *in* the stock and had to go through chemical processing in the lab.) So unstable and impermanent were their color dyes that Eastmancolor prints of the 1950s have already faded badly. Not until the development of the CRI (color reversal internegative) printing process of the 1970s—and Martin Scorsese's successful campaign of the 1980s for an Eastman stock that would hold its color values for at least 50 years—would monopack prints approach the clarity, brilliance, and permanence of three-strip Technicolor.

During the 1950s, black and white gradually became the exception and color, even for serious dramas, little comedies, short subjects, and low-budget westerns, became the rule. As the technology of color cinematography became more flexible, film artists learned, as they did with sound, that a new technique was not only a gimmick, but also a way to fulfill essential dramatic, aesthetic, and thematic functions.

Sound quality improved drastically after World War II, thanks to the introduction of magnetic tape (another of the spoils of war, invented in Nazi Germany), a superior recording technology. Until 1949, optical film was used to record all soundtracks. From the 1950s to the end of the 20th century (when magnetic soundtracks became obsolete), a release print might have a magnetic or an optical soundtrack. Magnetic tape and magnetic film (called "mag stock") are still used for virtually all analog sound recording, editing, and mixing. Even digital tape and a computer's hard disk record data magnetically.

Hollywood finally capitulated to TV by deciding to work with it rather than against it. (Radio had not posed such a threat because it couldn't show pictures.) If TV would not die, then it could be fed old movies and would need to film installments of series. Columbia Pictures, Walt Disney (*Disneyland*), Warner Bros., 20th Century–Fox, MGM, and Universal all began making 30- and 60-minute weekly shows—as well as commercials—for TV, while several new companies bought old film studios expressly to make television films: Revue bought the old Republic studio and Desilu the RKO studio. Hollywood also lifted its ban against films and film stars appearing on TV. In 1954, RKO began to show its own movies on its own stations; as in a theatre, the "Million Dollar Movie" (conceived by Thomas F. O'Neil, the TV executive who bought RKO to pull this off) repeated the week's picture several times a day. It was in 1956 that the other Hollywood studios first sold their films to TV, the sole provision being that the film had to have been produced before 1948. Since 1956, however, Hollywood has sold more and more recent films to the networks or cable stations; many of last year's movies appear on this year's television. In a sense, TV has replaced the old fourth- and fifth-run neighborhood movie houses, most of which had disappeared by 1965—much as the rentable video has nearly wiped out the revival house (a theatre that shows films that are out of release).

It was the theatre owners who were hit hardest by a medium that could deliver entertainment directly to the home. Theatres countered by offering sights and sounds that televisions could not deliver. They still do. The brilliance and immensity of the image and, the fullness of sound in the movie theatre remain basic reasons to go there, even though 21st-century home video has been narrowing the gap between the experiences offered by the movie theatre and by TV.

By 1956, the war with TV was over, and although the armistice had clearly defined the movies' future relationship with its living-room audiences, the future with its audiences in theatres was still uncertain.

Films in the Transitional Era

With the collapse of the studio structure, the dictatorial head of production, and the quantitative demands of a large yearly output, producing films became similar to producing stage plays. Like the theatre producer, the new film producer concentrated on shaping and selling a single project at a time rather than a whole year's output of more than a dozen films. Like United Artists, David Selznick, and Samuel Goldwyn of earlier years, Hollywood feature-film production, even within the studios, had "gone independent." The more independent producer selected the property, the stars, and the director; raised the money; and supervised the selling of the finished film. Perhaps the production company rented space on a studio lot; perhaps it used the studio's distribution offices to help sell the film. But the producer, not the studio, made the picture. With no lot, no long-term contracts with stars, no staffs of writers and technicians, the producer assembled a production company for a particular film, disbanded it when the film was finished, and assembled another for the next film.

Although independent production freed film-makers from dictatorial studio heads, the new system had its own tyrannies. Veteran directors like Howard Hawks complained that they spent more time making deals than making movies. Now the director–producer handled all the petty problems—dickering to raise the money, compromising with bankers to get it—that a studio previously managed for him. And the large pool of expert studio craftsmen and technicians began to dry up—with fewer films to make and (since many were no longer full-time studio employees but were hired for one film at a time) no way to know when or whether they would make them.

The individual producers, forced to make each film pay for itself, searched for stable, pre-dictable production values. One of the axioms they discovered was that the most dependable films were either very expensive or very cheap. A very expensive film could make back its invest-ment with huge publicity campaigns and high ticket prices at roadshow engagements. The the-ory translated itself into practice with big films like *Oklahoma!*, *The Ten Commandments*, *The Bridge on the River Kwai*, *Ben-Hur*, and *Spartacus*. Even unpretentious directors of fast-paced action pictures like Howard Hawks and Nicholas Ray joined the parade of Colossal Spectacles (*Land of the Pharaohs*, 1955, and *King of Kings*, 1961, respectively). The biblical–historical epics disappeared after *Cleopatra* (1963) cost and lost more than any film ever had before.

But the 1950s were also the years of *I Was a Teenage Werewolf*, *Hercules*, *Not of This Earth*, *Joy Ride*, and *Riot in Juvenile Prison*. American–International Pictures, the only new producing company to be founded in a decade of studio col-lapse, built itself entirely on low-budget films with topical teenage themes—horror, science fic-tion, rock and roll, juvenile delinquency, and beach parties—that could be shot in less than two weeks for under $250,000. Joseph E. Levine built a commercial empire on Steve Reeves and a cast of Italians, films that were produced for under $150,000 in Italy and then dubbed into English. Roger Corman, the master of cheap monsters and outrageous scripts, enlarged his empire by teaming Vincent Price with Edgar Allan Poe. The inexpensive film could make back its investment in two weeks of saturation book-ing at neighborhood theatres and, most of all, drive-ins, a 1930s innovation that joined the 1950s war to pull people out of their living rooms. In an era of unstable business values the movies had become a lure for daring speculators, just as they had been before 1917.

For major productions, major producers became dependent on popular novels, musicals, and plays, properties that had excited the public in other forms and might excite it again. Lacking large, permanent staffs of screenwriters with original ideas, both studio and independent producers bought established, already written properties that simply required an artful, profes-sional translation into film form: *The Caine Mutiny*, *Exodus*, *A Streetcar Named Desire*, and so forth. It was easier for a producer to raise money for a film that was considered "presold," and it was easier to sell one of these familiar properties back to the public after the film had been finished.

Because both fiction and the stage have tradi-tionally remained freer of sexual and moral re-strictions than films, it was inevitable that fresh breezes would blow from the original works into the screen adaptations of them. Because televi-sion applied even stricter moral regulations to its programs than the Production Code did to films, producers could lure audiences to the movie the-atre with promises of franker, racier, "more adult" entertainment. Films adapted from novels like *Peyton Place*, *From Here to Eternity*, *Compulsion*, *Advise and Consent*, *Lolita*, and *Butterfield 8* could not possibly avoid references to adultery, fornication, or homosexuality, topics perfectly suited to Hollywood's audience war with television.

Freedom of Speech, Preminger, and the End of the Blacklist

A landmark Supreme Court ruling, the so-called *Miracle* case of 1952 (formally, *Burstyn v. Wilson*), declared that movies were part of the nation's "press," entitled to Constitutional guarantees of freedom of speech. A 1915 Supreme Court ruling *(Mutual Film Corp v. Ohio Industrial Commission)* had decided exactly the opposite—that movies were a novelty and amusement, conducted solely for profit, not "speech" at all. That ruling stood until a foreign "art film," *Ways of Love*, opened in New York in 1950. It was composed of three unrelated segments (one of which was Jean Renoir's *A Day in the Country*, made in 1936), the most important of which was Roberto Rossellini's *The Miracle* (1948), starring Anna Magnani. *The Miracle* had originally appeared with another short Rossellini film starring Magnani: *The Human Voice*, based on Cocteau's play *La Voix humaine*.

The story of a simple-minded peasant woman, seduced by a stranger, who believes she has been impregnated by St. Joseph, *The Miracle* was condemned as sacrilegious by the archdiocese of New York and seized by New York's commissioner of police. After repeated losses in lower courts, Joseph Burstyn, the film's American distributor, took the case to the Supreme Court, which ruled that the term "sacrilegious" had no clear meaning and that films could no more be suppressed than any other forum for public debate. In addition to its liberating effect on film exhibition, this ruling undermined the legitimacy of the Production Code, even if the PCA was not a government office. That it took a foreign "art film" to effect this important change in American law foreshadowed many other changes that "art films" would effect within the decade. Produced outside America and shown in little theatres whose owners were not members of the Motion Picture Association, these "art films" were never subject to the industry's Code.

The war against the Code began officially in 1953 with Otto Preminger's decision to release *The Moon Is Blue* without the Code's seal of approval. Preminger's was the first major American movie since the first Code seal of approval was awarded in 1934 to be released without one; that turned out to have immense publicity value. The war declared by Preminger would end in 1968

with the elimination of the 1930 Production Code (already modified in 1966) and the adoption of the more flexible system of rating the "maturity" of a film's content. During the years between 1953 and 1968, the strict moral principles of the Code repeatedly slid and bent, for in the search to find a lure that television lacked, the film industry seized on sexual relationships and social criticism.

The resulting sexual–social films of the transitional years were very different from the "liberated" films of the 1970s. The sharp producer of the 1950s had merely found a clever way of injecting sexual tidbits and social questions into the old 1934 formulas for morality, motivation, and plotting. Otto Preminger and Stanley Kramer were particularly good at turning "explosive," "controversial" material into films that could offend almost no one.

Preminger, a Lubitsch protégé, had begun with ironic, unpretentious genre films at 20th Century–Fox (from *Laura* in 1944 to *River of No Return* in 1954) only to move toward more monumental, controversial, and socially conscious literary adaptations in the era of independent production. His *cause célèbre*, *The Moon Is Blue*, merely added a few "naughty" words (for example, *virgin* and *mistress*), leering eyebrows, and bedroom situations to a conventional comedy of manners. But his camerawork and his mastery of the crane and (beginning with *River of No Return*) of the wide screen never were conventional. Two of Preminger's steadily gripping adaptations, *The Man With the Golden Arm* (1955) and *Anatomy of a Murder* (1959), use quiet, understated acting and evocatively moody jazz scores (by Elmer Bernstein and Duke Ellington, respectively) to make the stories of drug addiction and rape more absorbing.

Preminger was instrumental in vanquishing the blacklist, as he had challenged the Code; he hired Dalton Trumbo, one of the Hollywood Ten, to write the script for *Exodus* (1960) under his own name. At approximately the same time, Kirk Douglas hired Trumbo to write *Spartacus* (1960), and the nearly simultaneous release of those two major spectacles broke the power of the blacklist.

Although there is some disagreement about who hired Trumbo first, Preminger was months ahead of Douglas in announcing that Trumbo was working for him and would receive screen credit. Eventually, Trumbo's credits on those films he had written during the blacklist period were acknowledged; they included *Gun Crazy* (1949, released 1950), *Roman Holiday* (1953), and *The Brave One* (1956), and the latter two had won Oscars for their writing. It took years for some of the blacklisted writers to find work. Ring Lardner, Jr., finally returned with *The Cincinnati Kid* (1965, written for Peckinpah) and triumphed with *MASH* (1970). Only after his death did Michael Wilson—whose only credit after winning an Oscar for *A Place in the Sun* (1951) had been *Salt of the Earth*—receive credit for his work on *Friendly Persuasion* (1956), *The Bridge on the River Kwai* (1957), and *Lawrence of Arabia* (1962).

Message Pictures: Kazan and Others

Stanley Kramer became the era's sentimental liberal. In *The Defiant Ones* (1958), he examined race relations by showing a black man (Sidney Poitier) and a white man (Tony Curtis) escaping from a southern prison. Chained together, they are forced to come to terms with each other. Although the terms, the problems, and their solutions are predictable from the moment the men flee, Kramer's loud and clear plea for racial tolerance would dominate his career from *Home of the Brave*, which he produced in 1949, to *Guess Who's Coming to Dinner*, which he directed in 1967. In *On the Beach* (1959), the last of the human race is about to perish from atomic fallout; Kramer's film depicts the sentimental consequences of universal death, but none of its

Fig. 12-7

Fig. 12-8

Fig. 12-9

Fig. 12-10

Two films shot by Boris Kaufman. Kazan's **On the Waterfront:** *the realism of "Method" acting; Marlon Brando with Eva Marie Saint (Fig. 12-7), and Rod Steiger (Fig. 12-8). Lumet's* **The Pawnbroker:** *Steiger trapped in the cage of his pawnshop (Fig. 12-9) and in the cage of New York's modern architecture (Fig. 12-10, with Geraldine Fitzgerald).*

political or social causes, because in the face of nuclear annihilation, none of the reasons matters.

The impetus for these socially committed films is clear enough—Kramer and others wanted to do something meaningful, important, relevant. But some of their films lend unintentional support to one of Samuel Goldwyn's classic pronouncements: "If you want to send a message, go to Western Union." The tension between social consciousness and Hollywood cliché is uncomfortably strong in some message pictures.

Elia Kazan, originally a Cold War liberal in the era of Hollywood blacklisting, had the problem of making social-problem films that would neither offend an audience nor cost him his job. He solved the problem in his public life by cooperating with the HUAC; he solved the problem in his films by turning social statements into "human" statements—*A Streetcar Named Desire* (1951), *Viva Zapata!* (1952), *On the Waterfront* (1954), *East of Eden* (1955), *A Face in the Crowd* (1957), *Splendor in the Grass* (1961)—all of which sustain their social issues with dynamic performances by Marlon Brando (the prototypic Kazan actor), Vivien Leigh, James Dean, Jo Van Fleet, Rod Steiger, Andy Griffith, Warren Beatty, Natalie Wood, Pat Hingle, and others. In these films Kazan brought to the screen the earthy, introspective "Method" acting style of the Group Theatre (founded in New York in 1931 by Lee Strasberg, Harold Clurman, and Cheryl Crawford) and of the Actors Studio (founded in New York in 1947 by Crawford, Robert Lewis, and Kazan; Strasberg was the key teacher and artistic director). Because of their intelligent writing, rich composition, and powerful acting, Kazan's literary adaptations of the 1950s—especially the CinemaScope masterpiece *East of Eden*—look better than his social-problem films of the 1940s (*Gentleman's Agreement*, 1947; *Pinky*, 1949).

Several other American filmmakers of the era also used New York styles to escape the studio clichés of Hollywood—in particular, the use of real New York locations and established New York actors (*Marty*, 1955; *12 Angry Men*, 1957; *A View from the Bridge*, 1962; *The Pawnbroker*, 1965). Many of these "New York films" owed their texture and impact not only to their director (usually Sidney Lumet, the most perceptive

and unsentimental of the "message picture" directors, whose *The Hill*, 1965, and *Prince of the City*, 1981, are among the most powerful and complex examples of the genre), but also to their informal origins in television styles and to the apparent spontaneity of location shooting and lighting. The improvisational "look" of these New York films can often be attributed to Boris Kaufman, the cinematographer who shot many of them and who had demonstrated the same spontaneity in his collaboration with Jean Vigo two decades earlier.

In 1950, New York was not only the center of American theatre—as it had been for a century—but the center of American television production as well, with a large pool of talented actors, writers, and directors. Many of them would move from television to New Yorky "little" movies and then on to Hollywood itself. In the era before videotape, color, and its own move to Hollywood, television was very much a medium for writers and actors, not designers, and for intimate direction. Television directors were more like theatre directors, interpreters of the dialogue rather than manipulators of montage.

Many important screenwriters of this generation came from television: Paddy Chayefsky (*Marty*; *The Bachelor Party*, 1957; *The Goddess*, 1958; *Middle of the Night*, 1959), Reginald Rose (*12 Angry Men*), Abby Mann (*Judgment at Nuremberg*, 1961), Rod Serling (*Patterns*, 1956; *Requiem for a Heavyweight*, 1962; *Seven Days in May*, 1964). A generation of new directors also came from television: Sidney Lumet, Daniel Mann (*Come Back, Little Sheba*, 1952; *The Rose Tattoo*, 1955), Delbert Mann (*Marty*; *Separate Tables*, 1958; *Middle of the Night*), Arthur Penn (*The Left-Handed Gun*, 1958; *The Miracle Worker*, 1962; *Bonnie and Clyde*, 1967), Sam Peckinpah (*Ride the High Country*, 1962; *The Wild Bunch*, 1969), Irvin Kershner (*A Fine Madness*, 1966; *The Empire Strikes Back*, 1980), John Frankenheimer (*The Manchurian Candidate*, 1962; *Seven Days in May*; *Seconds*, 1966). Although many of these directors would later adopt Hollywood's familiar genres, most of them were initially committed to detailed social and psychological portraits of people who are either very typical (like Ernest Borgnine in *Marty*) or atypical (like Kim Stanley in *The Goddess*).

Adaptations and Values:
John Huston and Others

A moralist with a taste for irony and for great literature, John Huston also faced the tension between cinematic style and significant statement. Some of his films, like *The Maltese Falcon* (1941, the first film he both wrote and directed) and *The Asphalt Jungle* (1950), match style and statement so unobtrusively that the results have classical status; others, like *Moulin Rouge* (1953), foreground their experiments at the expense of stylistic balance but remain of interest; and still others, like *Freud* (1962) and *Reflections in a Golden Eye* (1967), experiment in a manner that comes to seem pretentious. Most of his works are literary adaptations, and again it can be said that some, like *The Maltese Falcon* and *The Treasure of the Sierra Madre* (1948), brilliantly convey the essence of their originals through a careful adaptation of literature and film to each other's demands and a perfect balance of tone and substance; some, like *The Night of the Iguana* (1964), *Fat City* (1972), *Wise Blood* (1979), and *Under the Volcano* (1984), strong films in their own right, share enough of the tone, power, and intent of the original works to be considered valid, intriguing adaptations; and some, like *Moby Dick* (1956) and *The Bible* (1966), fail to rise to the challenges posed by the original material.

While Kazan's films, with their credibly earthy acting, revealed his background in the theatre, Huston's revealed his background as a screenwriter with their taut and subtle scripts in which individual human weaknesses usually destroy the best-laid plans. (He did not, however, write the scripts for all of his films.) In Huston's films, the characters who survive are usually those who accept the limits of their humanity and navigate a moral crisis (the detective in *The Maltese Falcon*) or are flexible and resourceful enough to modify their projects (*The African Queen*, 1951). Those who fall—or fail, but remain of consuming interest—often are obsessed, inflexible overreachers possessed by their projects (*The Man Who Would Be King*, 1975; *Wise Blood*) or people who are too good at their jobs, or trapped in them, to give them up (*The Asphalt Jungle*; *Prizzi's Honor*, 1985). Of the three men who set out to mine gold in *The Treasure of the Sierra Madre*, it is the one driven mad by gold—who abandons his humanity and forgets that of others,

who is utterly consumed by the project, and who talks the most about ideals—who is destroyed, while the other two are able to accept the loss of the gold and do not lose sight of larger values. The "black bird" or its equivalent is the quest object in most Huston films: the dangerous, problematic, and possibly worthless icon of desire, riches, and power. The best of Huston's moral tales are both idealistic and ironic; behind them one senses the shrewd, wry cackle of a student of the aspirations and failures of human nature.

Joseph L. Mankiewicz, whose brother Herman wrote *Citizen Kane*, adapted theatrical works as diverse as the tragedy *Julius Caesar* (1953), the musical *Guys and Dolls* (1955), the melodrama *Suddenly, Last Summer* (1959), and the mystery *Sleuth* (1972). He also adapted novels to make thrillers like *5 Fingers* (1952) and family moral dramas like *House of Strangers* (1949). His skills as a writer and a director of sharp, ironic dialogue made his witty comedies of manners into grenades of manners and gave field days to great actors. One of the themes he returned to most often was the danger of celebrity, notably in *Julius Caesar*; in *Cleopatra* (1963), which gave him a second chance at Caesar, played this time by Rex Harrison (as well as a shot at the too-famous lovers Antony and Cleopatra, played by the too-famous lovers Richard Burton and Elizabeth Taylor); and in his masterpiece, *All About Eve* (1950), a tale of the theatre at its most brilliant and cruel, where celebrity draws evil as well as attention, bringing out the worst in the worst people even as it lets a major actress (Bette Davis as Margo Channing) appropriately adopt, for as long as she chooses, the language, power, and magnitude of a star.

One of the greatest films of the 1950s was a study of values, a literary adaptation, and a compelling story realized in purely cinematic terms: *The Night of the Hunter* (1955). Scripted by James Agee from the novel by Davis Grubb, it was the only movie ever directed by actor Charles Laughton. (Agee was a major writer and film critic who had also written the script for *The African Queen*.) This hauntingly photographed, lyrically evocative film tells of two children, on the run from a killer (Robert Mitchum), who find sanctuary in the home of a tough, practical woman (Lillian Gish). In place of money and horror, the film finds value in the enduring power

Fig. 12-11

Fig. 12-12
Humphrey Bogart (left) and Elisha Cook, Jr., in The Maltese Falcon *(Fig. 12-11)*. **The**
Treasure of the Sierra Madre: *from left, Tim Holt, Humphrey Bogart, and the director's*
father, Walter Huston (Fig. 12-12).

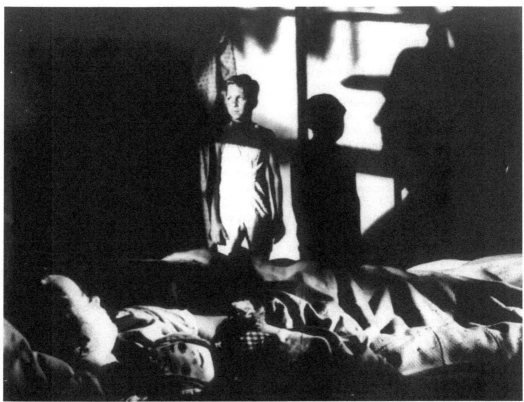

Fig. 12-13
The children and the shadow of their pursuer: an Expressionistic moment from **The Night of the Hunter.**

of love, and it does so without the least trace of sentimentality.

Film Noir and Other Genres

Although it was not apparent at the time, the most enduring Hollywood movies of the period wore the disguises of familiar genres. The two basic metaphors for American life—the open frontier and the dense modern city—had been the movie means for examining the promise and exposing the failures of American society since well before John Ford. The western provided the generic terms for mythifying American history, its aspirations in building a nation from a wasteland, the actions that hindered or furthered it. The gangster film established the generic terms for diagnosing the corruption and diseases of the present. It depicted America after the Fall, after the virgin wilderness had been cleared and densely packed with people and steel buildings.

The western remained one of the most exciting and entertaining genres of the Transitional Era: George Stevens's *Shane* (1953), Fred Zinnemann's *High Noon* (1952), Nicholas Ray's *Johnny Guitar* (1954), as well as several by Budd Boetticher, Anthony Mann, and Samuel Fuller. But in the Transitional Era the conventions of this long-lived genre began to stretch in several different directions. Some western films—most notably Anthony Mann's (*Winchester '73*, 1950; *Bend of the River*, 1952; *The Man from Laramie*, 1955) and Budd Boetticher's (*Decision at Sundown*, 1957; *The Tall T*, 1957; *Ride Lonesome*, 1959)—maintained the conventional attitudes of the genre toward violence and killing. Violence was a legitimate means of establishing law and civilization or a legitimate assertion of one's self and self-respect against elemental enemies. Like Ford's *Stagecoach* and Hawks's *Red River*, they were attempts to examine the essential human and social qualities that produced the American nation and its ideals in the first place.

But other westerns of the 1950s began bending the conventions of the genre to other ends. On the one hand, a filmmaker could use the mythic background of the Old West to attack contemporary American values (disguise was an especially useful ploy in an era of blacklisting). *High Noon*, in its attack on the timidity of the respectable majority and in its contempt for the think-alike, act-alike mentality, is clearly about the American social climate of 1952 and mixes contemporary moralizing with the western's setting and action. On the other hand, a filmmaker could take the violence of westerns as symptomatic of deranged behavior and imply that the forging of this "ideal" American nation was ruthless and corrupt from its very beginning: hence the nearly psychotic gunman in *Shane* and the rich man he works for.

The mystery and gangster films began turning very dark, concentrating on the inevitability of crime in urban America, on criminals who are not simply selfish and tough (like Little Caesar) but crazy (like the giggling maniac played by Richard Widmark in Henry Hathaway's *Kiss of Death*, 1947), on policemen who are as diseased as their quarry, on lovers and partners who betray each other, and on visual images that are consistently shadowy, dark, and sharp. French critics coined the name for this genre—the *film noir*—a term derived from the black (*noir*) covers of crime novels in the French *Série noire*, many of which were translations of American novels by Dashiell Hammett, James M. Cain, Raymond Chandler, David Goodis, and Jim Thompson. But for all they owe to American crime fiction, both the style and the spirit of these *films noirs* were unmistakably German, from their fatalism to their looming shadows. Some were even directed by Germans and Austrians (Wilder, Preminger, Ulmer, and Siodmak among them).

Fig. 12-14
Reflection of death: Tom Neal and Ann Savage in Edgar G. Ulmer's film noir, Detour (1945).

Edward Dmytryk's *Crossfire* (1947) is a dark mixture of murder, anti-Semitism, and homosexuality; almost everyone who worked on this film was targeted by the HUAC. Robert Rossen's *Body and Soul* (1947) and Abraham Polonsky's *Force of Evil* (1948) both use John Garfield as a child of the slums facing the decision between an unprofitable honesty and lucrative dishonor. Garfield was a prototypic *film noir* hero (another was Robert Mitchum) and the "bad girl"—Gloria Grahame, Jean Hagen, Shelley Winters, the early Marilyn Monroe—a prototypically used and abused woman. Another prototypical *noir* figure is the *femme fatale:* the seductive woman who is deadly treacherous (for example, the women played by Barbara Stanwyck in Billy Wilder's *Double Indemnity*, 1944, and Jane Greer in Jacques Tourneur's *Out of the Past*, 1947).

The titles of Dassin's *Night and the City* (1950), Joe Lewis's *Gun Crazy*, and Huston's *The Asphalt Jungle* themselves evoke the *noir* world.

The first *films noirs* appeared in the early 1940s, and the form was fully defined by the time—and the example—of *Double Indemnity.* The film that marked the end of the *noir* cycle was Welles's *Touch of Evil* (1958). (Attempts to revive *noir* as a genre include *Chinatown*, 1974; *Body Heat*, 1981; and *Blood Simple*, 1983.)

The *noir* world is a dark place, psychologically and morally as well as cinematographically. James Cagney stars in Raoul Walsh's *White Heat* (1949), in which the old-style breezy Cagney gangster has become psychotic. Jules Dassin depicts the brutality of prison life (*Brute Force*, 1947), of urban life (*The Naked City*, 1948), and of the San Francisco vegetable market (*Thieves' Highway*, 1949). In Fritz Lang's *The Big Heat* (1953), women become pawns (and the victims of gruesome crimes) in the war between cops and criminals. The only *noir* made by a woman was *The Hitch-Hiker* (1953); its director and co-writer, the established actress Ida Lupino, was virtually the only female

Fig. 12-15
Out of the Past: *shadows in a world of traps and betrayals—the* **femme fatale** *(Jane Greer) left, the* **hero** *(Robert Mitchum) in a trenchcoat, and the* **blackmailer** *(Steve Brodie) speaking from the darkness; before the film ends, all three will die.*

director working in Hollywood in the late 1940s and 1950s. She also directed *Not Wanted* (1949) and *The Bigamist* (1953).

An outgrowth of the *film noir* was a new genre that also showed marked affinities with the western. The "rebellious youth" films of the 1950s—particularly Laslo Benedek's *The Wild One* (1953) and Nicholas Ray's *Rebel Without a Cause* (1955)—were also a violent reaction against a decaying and diseased society. But whereas the gangster chose violence as a weapon against the brutal hardness of city life, the youths rebelled against the sterility, monotony, and conformity of normal adult life. "What are you rebelling against?" someone asks the smirking Johnny (Marlon Brando) on his motorcycle in *The Wild One*. "What'ya got?" he answers. The highway death of the young James Dean not only robbed Hollywood of a rich acting talent and translated an actor into a legend, it also seemed a symbol of the ultimate rebellion against what'ya got.

While a western looked at the past and a mystery or thriller at the present, science fiction looked at the future. Inspired by both the new fear of atomic annihilation and the hope of interplanetary travel, science fiction films brought atomic mutants and extraterrestrial visitors to Earth or sent Earthlings to the Moon, Mars, and the stars. In *The Thing From Another World* (1951), directed by Christian Nyby and produced by Howard Hawks, atomic science and outer space combine to produce a death-defying vegetable monster. But in *Forbidden Planet* (1956, directed by Fred M. Wilcox)—the first feature to have an electronic music score (composed by Bebe Barron)—Earthlings take their monster with them into space:—a Freudian menace, emanating from the id of the scientist himself. Martians attack Earth in *The War of the Worlds* (1953), directed by Byron Haskin and produced by the great special-effects designer, George Pal. But in Robert Wise's *The Day the Earth Stood Still* (1951), a sage interplanetary visitor brings reason, sense, and peace to an Earth intent on destroying itself and everything else in the galaxy.

Interplanetary travel took humans into space in Kurt Neumann's *Rocketship X–M*, George Pal's *Destination Moon* (both 1950), and Joseph

Fig. 12-16   *Fig. 12-17*
Icons of 1950s rebellion. Fig. 12-16: Marlon Brando in The Wild One; *Fig. 12-17: James Dean in* Rebel Without a Cause.

Fig. 12-18

Fig. 12-19

They came from outer space:
The Thing *(Fig. 12-18)*
and **The War of the Worlds**
(Fig. 12-19).

Newman's *This Island Earth* (1955) while Earth was overrun by atom-strengthened ants in *Them!* (1954), consumed by interstellar slime in *The Blob* (1958), and stomped by atom-wakened dinosaurs in many films from Japan (*Godzilla King of the Monsters!*, 1954, U.S. version 1956; *Rodan*, 1956, U.S. version 1958; both originally directed by Ishiro Honda)—which had suffered the reality of atomic devastation. (*Gojira*, the original *Godzilla*, makes the atomic issue more

central; it is also more moving and tells its story without the excessive voice-over of the American version.) During the Red Scare, some science fiction films cast high-tech enemy agents as another kind of threat; the best of these is the 3-D *Gog* (1954, directed by Herbert L. Strock), and the one that has to be seen to be believed is *Red Planet Mars* (1952, directed by Harry Horner).

One of the most socially and politically re-vealing of the science fiction/horror films was

Don Siegel's *Invasion of the Body Snatchers* (1956, from the novel by Jack Finney), in which vegetable pods from outer space replace the Earth's inhabitants, resembling the Earthlings in every way but one: They have no feelings. These pods seem (but were not meant as) a possible allusion to Communism: the way some Americans, who appear "normal," are really selfless agents of an evil foreign power—the Red Menace of the Cold War 1950s. But the pods also strongly suggest an indictment of American conformity, a uniform society that appears human but lacks the essential human qualities of emotion, moral judgment, and independent action. Either way, the point is that all the pods think alike. Don Siegel later said Hollywood was full of pods. While American horror films of a previous generation (like *Frankenstein*) doubted the ability of science to transcend the limits of mortality and the mysteries of experience ("There are some things man is not meant to know..."), science fiction films of the 1950s surveyed a universe with no limits whatever on our knowledge or on our potential for creation or destruction—an attitude most memorably expressed in *The Day the Earth Stood Still, Forbidden Planet, Gog, This Island Earth*, and Jack Arnold's 3-D *It Came From Outer Space* (1953).

The newest comic performers were Danny Kaye at Goldwyn and Bud Abbott and Lou Costello at Universal. Abbott and Costello seemed to be built on the old physical premises of teams like Laurel and Hardy—one fat (Costello), one thin (Abbott); one clumsy, one suave. But despite their physical humor, Abbott and Costello were primarily verbal comics (their most famous routines, like "Who's on First?," originated on radio); the only other way to use them in a film was to plunge the bungling, cowardly Lou into scary situations. And so Abbott and Costello went into jungles or the Army or met all the monsters under contract to Universal in an attempt to squeeze laughs from spine-tingling contrasts of humor and horror (*Bud Abbott and Lou Costello Meet Frankenstein*, 1948). The Danny Kaye films also juxtaposed comedy and danger, surrounding Kaye with rings of murderers, kidnappers, spies, and thieves who gave him his trademark comic jitters and stutters, which complemented his tongue-twisters (*The Court Jester*, 1956).

Succeeding Abbott and Costello in 1950 were Dean Martin and Jerry Lewis at Paramount, another team combining a zany clown and a slick "straight" man. Lewis and Martin contrasted both physically and mentally: the one brash, noisy, nasal, infantile; the other oily, loose, controlled. But their wacky personalities were frequently drowned in predictable, overplotted situation comedies.

The same overplotting plagued the films that Jerry Lewis made alone after 1956. Although some French intellectual critics rate Lewis alongside Chaplin and Keaton, few Americans can sit through a Jerry Lewis film. Lewis's problem seems to be a conflict between character and plot, a zany conception forced to march through a completely formulaic story. Unlike most of the great film clowns, Lewis's funniness stems more from technique than from a vision of experience.

After Frank Capra made his dark comedy of postwar doubt, *It's A Wonderful Life*, the lightweight comedies that followed were dull. Even Preston Sturges, cramped by a production contract with Howard Hughes, made less successful comedies after the war, but had great moments: *The Sin of Harold Diddlebock* (1947), starring Harold Lloyd—badly recut by Hughes and released as *Mad Wednesday* in 1950—and the wicked *Unfaithfully Yours* (1948).

Among the best postwar comedies of manners were Billy Wilder's, who with his co-author, I. A. L. Diamond or Charles Brackett, preserved the tradition of comic collaboration between director and scenarist. Born in Vienna and trained as a screenwriter in Berlin, he left Germany when Hitler came to power in 1933. Wilder's comedy juxtaposed verbal wit with a sinister, morally disturbing environment: the corruption of a postwar Berlin in rubble (*A Foreign Affair*, 1948), the dark estate of a deranged has-been of the silent screen (*Sunset Blvd.*, 1950), a concentration camp (*Stalag 17*, 1953), the gangster underworld (*Some Like It Hot*, 1959), the corruption of Madison Avenue (*The Apartment*, 1960), and the Cold War in the now rebuilt and industrialized Berlin (*One, Two, Three*, 1961). His *Double Indemnity* (1944) was a highly influential *film noir. The Lost Weekend* (1945) was a grueling study of alcoholism. The comedies of manners ran the gamut from the hilarious *Some Like It Hot*, which dramatizes the problems two men can encounter when passing as women, to the moral darkness of *The Apartment* and the brooding tragedy of *Sunset Blvd.*, a film as dark as his great and not at all comic *Double Indemnity*.

The Freed Musicals

Musicals in the postwar years were also undergoing a transition, one that produced Hollywood's greatest musical films. Before the war, Hollywood musicals were breezy concoctions that focused mostly on the doings of show folk; works as free of the stage as *The Wizard of Oz* were the exception. Musical numbers wove through a scanty plot about love among entertainers as Ruby Keeler, Dick Powell, Fred Astaire, Ginger Rogers, Eleanor Powell, or Rita Hayworth sang and danced in the show business world of theatres and nightclubs. The 1930s musicals had few pretensions to psychological realism or complex (as opposed to complicated) human relationships; the plots were trifles to hold the numbers together. By the mid-1950s, however, filmed musicals, following the pattern of Broadway shows (which, of course, they were often adapting), became more realistic and psychological. World War II and street gangs had become subjects for Broadway musicals like *South Pacific* and *West Side Story*. The fluff of Rodgers and Hart had been replaced by the romantic seriousness of Rodgers and Hammerstein.

The "integrated" musical, as the Rodgers–Hammerstein type and its successors came to be known, tried to imagine under what conditions a human being might sing in reality—"feel a song coming on" or, in some cases, "think" a song. Although it was difficult enough to convince a Broadway audience that a group of juvenile delinquents would sing to one another before cutting one another's throats, the task was even more difficult for films. The stage, at least, enjoys the unreality of cardboard and plaster and paint and spotlight. The stage musical could draw on the conventions of two other theatrical forms—opera and the dance—as its stylized means of translating song and dance into a representation of reality. But how to make a film audience believe that a woman would sing a song standing on a real tugboat in the middle of New York harbor?

The director of early musical films did not have such problems. Musical films were obviously unreal, unserious spoofs that never tried to be credible. Busby Berkeley could twirl his camera, his dancers, their pianos, fiddles, and fountains in grandiose and grotesquely imaginative patterns precisely because his musical numbers owed no allegiance to either spatial logic or social reality.

Musical films just after the war, while they did become lavish, ornate, Technicolor spectaculars (as so many films did), maintained their stylized unreality. The MGM musicals produced by Arthur Freed in particular combined surrealistically imaginative musical numbers, pleasant scores, an exciting use of color, and funny, spoofing plots that often still revolved around showfolk.

Of the directors of musicals for Freed's unit, Vincente Minnelli was the most conscious of the traditions of painting and modern art. His musicals (*Meet Me in St. Louis*, 1944; *The Pirate*, 1948; *An American in Paris*, 1951; *The Band Wagon*, 1953) are masterful in their attention to color and light, to details of costume and decor, and to their layering of perspectival space for the lens. Charles Walters was most sympathetic to individual performers, especially to the manic moods of Judy Garland (*Easter Parade*, 1948; *Summer Stock*, 1950). Stanley Donen (with or without Kelly) was most committed to defining visual space itself as an emanation and external projection of musical energy, movement, and feeling (*On the Town*, 1949; *Singin' In The Rain*, 1952; *Seven Brides for Seven Brothers*, 1954; *It's Always Fair Weather*, 1955).

The best of the Freed musicals were those with musical numbers conceived and choreographed by Gene Kelly, particularly *An American in Paris* and *Singin' In The Rain*. In the former, Kelly's ballet, combining George Gershwin's tone poem with French Impressionist painting, received the most critical attention. Although the lengthy ballet borders on the pretentious and fits very loosely into the film's plot, the dream–ballet by itself is a brilliant demonstration of the powers of a nearly abstract cinema. Its integration of music, color, dance, decor, costumes, editing, and camera movement is as sensually and formally "pure" cinema as any that has ever been attempted.

Singin' In The Rain, co-directed by Donen and Kelly, boasts perhaps the funniest screenplay of any musical film, the best of Betty Comden and Adolph Green's many Hollywood spoofs. Every

The exuberance of song and dance: Gene Kelly Singin' In The Rain.

Fig. 12-20

musical number in *Singin' In The Rain* combines music and fun, pleasant movement and wry spoof—from the staging of the title song in which Kelly tap dances in rain puddles to the surrealistic ballet, "Broadway Melody," in which Kelly romanticizes a young entertainer's rise to the top.

In addition to its parodic historical representation of Hollywood's conversion to synchronized sound, the technology that made musicals possible, *Singin' In The Rain* contains its own reflexive history of MGM musicals, from their 1929 beginning to the 1952 present. The film's score, with music by Nacio Herb Brown and lyrics by Arthur Freed (the film's producer), is a virtual compilation of hit tunes from MGM musicals.

By the mid-1950s, MGM had begun deserting original musical ideas, assigning Minnelli to adapt stage shows like *Brigadoon* and *Kismet*.

The original screen musical died with the original musical screenplay. It also died with the studio system that produced a certain number of musicals each year and employed a stable of musical talent expressly for that purpose. The road for independent production was being cleared.

The next great musicals would come out in 20 years—notably those directed and choreographed by Bob Fosse (*Cabaret*, 1972; *All That Jazz*, 1979), who had danced in 3-D in *Kiss Me Kate*; those that truly re-imagined stage musicals for the cinema (Luis Valdez's *Zoot Suit*, 1981); and those that experimented with the form and idea of the musical (Herbert Ross's *Pennies From Heaven*, 1981, based on Dennis Potter's 1978 British teleplay, which was the primary experimental work). But in the 1990s, after the deaths of Jerome Robbins, Betty Walberg, Bob Fosse, and Dennis Potter, it was often said that there was no one left who knew *how* to do a musical, who had the feel for it and the skill.

Things were changing, and not only for the musical. By the turn of the 1960s, there were signs that a powerful new sense of cinema was on the way—not just from the New Wave films arriving from Europe, but from such brave American pictures as John Cassavetes's *Shadows* (1959), Alfred Hitchcock's *Psycho* (1960), Robert Rossen's *The Hustler* (1961), David Miller's *Lonely Are the Brave* (1962), John Frankenheimer's *The Manchurian Candidate* (1962), and Frank and Eleanor Perry's *David and Lisa* (1963).

Surfaces and Subversion

To understand those American films of the 1950s that seem most interesting decades later requires a careful look at the differences between the clear values on their narrative surfaces and the more complicated social and psychological questions beneath. As a representative sample, or an intriguing set of films worth a closer look, consider *Pickup on South Street*, *Rear Window*, *Rebel Without a Cause*, *The Searchers*, and *Imitation of Life*.

Unlike the American message films and European art films of the period, these Hollywood films wear thick disguises, masquerading as ordinary westerns or thrillers or weepies—the derogatory term for "women's pictures," itself a derogatory enough term. To wear a thick disguise was an understandable strategy in an era of blacklisting, when it was safer to make films with no apparent "message" at all. But these genre films, like those of the previous era, felt comfortable raising the important questions within the boundaries of familiar genres. Although few critics took even the best of these genre films seriously in the 1950s, most of the movies made money—accomplishment enough in that decade—and many of them have proved more durable than the critics who casually dismissed them.

Samuel Fuller
Beginning in 1949, Samuel Fuller directed, wrote, and often produced a series of inexpensive genre films that fell somewhere between A and B pictures in their budgets, styles, stars, and

shooting schedules: westerns (*I Shot Jesse James*, 1949; *Run of the Arrow*, 1957), gangster films (*Pickup on South Street*, 1953; *Underworld U.S.A.*, 1961), and disturbing melodramas (*Shock Corridor*, 1963; *The Naked Kiss*, 1964). Fuller's war films about the war in Korea (*The Steel Helmet* and *Fixed Bayonets*, both 1951) are shockingly violent and honest. For the subject of his last war film, *The Big Red One* (1980), he turned to World War II. In 1982, he made a controversial film about racism, *White Dog*, that was barely released. Some of his pictures, including *Shock Corridor* and *The Naked Kiss*, were restored and re-released before he died, still full of energy and tough charm, in 1997. Sometimes instead of yelling "action," he fired his .45 in the air.

On its surface, *Pickup on South Street* is a simple enough story about a petty thief, Skip McCoy (Richard Widmark), who picks the purse of a woman (Jean Peters) passing atomic secrets to the Russians. The thief finds himself surrounded by powerful enemies: The police want to send him back to prison, the FBI wants the secret documents and the spy ring, the woman wants the documents to appease her boyfriend, the boyfriend and his Communist allies want the documents at any human cost. The thief has only himself to depend on; a real model of individualism and free enterprise, he plays the parties off against one another until he lands on his feet.

Fuller brought this curious mixture of political espionage and petty crime to life by scrambling its moral system, shifting audience allegiances to characters that most Americans (and the Production Code) found loathsome. The studio was as surprised as Fuller when *Pickup on South Street* won at the Venice Film Festival.

The thief's urge to steal is uncontrollably sexual, as the opening sequence in a crowded subway car makes powerfully clear. He sidles up to his attractive victim and eyes her closely, hiding his hand behind a newspaper as he slides it toward her body. Then, without her realizing it, he bumps against her, enters her purse, removes its contents, and withdraws. But if the thief is a kind of rapist, and certainly no ordinary hero, his victim is a kind of prostitute. She does the bidding of her boyfriend (Richard Kiley) because he offers her nice clothes and a nice apartment, and she uses her body as bait to retrieve the stolen

Fig. 12-21

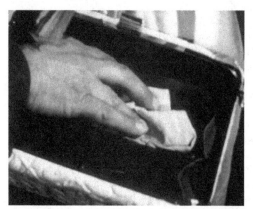
Fig. 12-22

Fig. 12-23
Three consecutive shots from the opening sequence of Pickup on South Street: *The victim (Jean Peters) waits alluringly, (Fig. 12-21) a hand fingers her purse (Fig. 12-22), and the thief (Richard Widmark) gazes intently (Fig. 12-23).*

documents from the thief. The film's title suggests its deliberate mixing of the criminal and the sexual: A cop "picks up" a crook, a stranger "picks up" a lover, a prostitute "picks up" a trick.

While Fuller's "Commies," as his films always call them, look like plutocrats, his thieves are the ironic embodiment and protectors of capitalism: They are all in the business of selling, and most of them are poor. One of the film's quirkiest creatures is "Lightning Louie," a fat informant who picks up and pockets his bribery fees with the same chopsticks he uses to shovel Chinese food into his face. Even the thief's close friend, "Moe" (Thelma Ritter), sells him out several times—for her business is selling information to anyone who pays her price. Nothing personal, she tells him, just business. And the one time "Moe" refuses to sell him out, she dies for her loyalty.

The one moral precept for these thieves—one Fuller shared—is that it's better to be a patriotic crook than a rotten Commie. Betrayal is the worst sin here, of a country or a friend, and the best solutions are direct ones. By the end of the film the good guys have won, but the dirt remains. Fuller's supposedly simple story spins a complicated web of sexuality, thievery, politics, law, government, business, loyalty, and love.

Late Hitchcock

While the opening scene of *Pickup on South Street* implicates the movie viewer's voyeurism, most of Alfred Hitchcock's work from *Rope* (1948) to *Psycho* makes voyeurism a major theme. Hitchcock's films of this period seem convinced that normal American life is shockingly abnormal. Like *Pickup on South Street*, *Rope* begins with an odd sexual climax—but the camera must wait outside a penthouse apartment, its curtains drawn, not permitted a view of the brutal homosexual murder, modeled on the sensational Leopold–Loeb murder case, in the dark. Only after the murder can the camera and the light be invited inside, to permit the audience's identification with the two handsomely murderous boys, who in the course of the picture are given enough "rope" to hang themselves (to complement that theme, the camera pursues its own long-take trajectory and rarely reveals any cuts, as if it were visually following one line). The Code prohibited the depiction of explicit sexual and "unnatural" acts; still, Hitchcock implied a great deal. In a similar way, *Strangers On A Train* (1951) balances the audience's antipathies between a maniacal homosexual murderer, Bruno (Robert Walker), and a bland model of straight American normality, the tennis pro, Guy (Farley Granger).

In this decade committed to the "straight" and normal, Hitchcock's sly examinations of sexual aberration beneath the placid surfaces of 1950s American life were deliciously subversive. He enjoyed exposing the dark sexual undersides of familiar movie stars—James Stewart and Cary Grant in particular—so familiar and safe as sexual beings: the calm rationality of Stewart, astonished that he has a libido; the graceful suavity of Grant, always verging on the hysterical and scatterbrained. Near the conclusion of *Vertigo* (1958), James Stewart grasps the female fantasy of his own construction, embodied by Kim Novak, in his arms. Hitchcock's sleazy hotel room begins spinning slowly, its walls, bathed in aqueous blue-green light, briefly replaced by Stewart's memory of that location where he last encountered this woman before her apparent death. While the embracing couple stands at the center of this vertiginous circling (both they and the complex, rear-projected set turn), the erotic highpoint of 1950s cinema, Stewart pulls away slightly from Novak to glance over his shoulder, as if to ask, "Where the hell am I?" These great American stars didn't quite know where they were in Hitchcock films; like the audience, they were often kept off-balance.

Rear Window (1954), based on a story by Cornell Woolrich, puts all these disturbing themes together in a masterful comic thriller. A professional photographer, L. B. Jeffries (Stewart), confined to his apartment with a broken leg, has just one amusement during the hot summer days: gazing at the activity in the courtyard surrounding his apartment window. As he watches the activities of his neighbors through their windows, he notices something wrong in one of the apartments: A woman mysteriously disappears. After a lengthy period of puzzling, spying, and piecing the evidence together, Jeffries exposes the missing woman's husband, Thorwald (Raymond Burr), as her murderer. Until the murderer comes after him, Jeffries's experience with the life outside his window is virtually identical to the spectator's experience at the cinema: looking through a rectangle at the world, sometimes with the feeling that one is spying. Jeffries extends his vision with parallels to the movie camera—a pair of binoculars and his still camera's telephoto lens.

Jeffries is more turned on by the activity outside his window than by the visits of his flesh-and-blood girlfriend, Lisa (Grace Kelly). Hitchcock fills the frame with other frames, drawing a parallel between Jeffries's vicarious experience and the moviegoer's. Through the courtyard's many

The vertiginous kiss in Vertigo: *James Stewart almost remembers the last place he saw Kim Novak.*

Fig. 12-24

window frames, Jeffries catches glimpses of other human beings, whom he converts into characters: "Miss Lonelyhearts" and so on. The courtyard full of window frames—suggesting long shots and close-ups, even CinemaScope, paralleling the varied formats of frames through film history—is really full of framed movie shots. This set of movies could be compared to a television with a choice of channels.

The spectator gets into trouble when experience violates his voyeuristic privacy. When Thorwald discovers Jeffries's prying gaze (and, in person, Lisa's snooping), he steps out of the movie frame of his own apartment and into the auditorium of Jeffries's apartment. Unable to fight or run, Jeffries temporarily blinds Thorwald with flashbulbs, defending himself with characteristically photographic resources—but Thorwald throws him out the window. In a literal visualization of that classic movie metaphor, the "cliffhanger," Jeffries clings to the ledge—but over a metaphorical abyss that is more Hitchcock than Pearl White. If Hitchcock heroes often hang from such "cliffs" as the Statue of Liberty (*Saboteur*), the edge of a roof (*Vertigo*), or Mount Rushmore (*North by Northwest*, 1959), those who fall (as in *Vertigo*'s major dream sequence) lose their grip on more than a ledge, plummeting into the mystery of personal annihilation and secrets that are melodramatic and subconscious. Jeffries hangs just long enough for the police to capture Thorwald; then he falls, breaks his other leg, and finally is shown—in a richly ironic ending—as a comic figure whom Lisa can marry and domesticate, but whose legs, now both in casts, imply castration and passivity rather than the romantic resolution the film appears to present. Both the "last-minute rescue" and the closing view of the "couple" have something failed, askew, and unsettling about them.

Hitchcock followed *Rear Window* with some of his greatest movies, disturbing even when they were comic and profoundly witty even in terror and despair. They include *Vertigo*, which many consider his masterpiece and which was certainly his best film since *Notorious* (1946). In black and white he made *The Wrong Man* (1956), a realistic tragedy, and *Psycho*, a rich and bold nightmare; like *Vertigo*, each went to the heart of his concerns with the nature of identity and guilt. The slick color comedies, whose surfaces are charged with hidden danger and emotion, and whose brilliant camerawork (by Robert Burks, who shot every 1950s Hitchcock film as well as *The Birds* and *Marnie*), symbolic and expressive colors, and absolutely controlled *mise-en-scène* are characteristic of his work in the 1950s, include *To Catch a Thief* (1955), *The Trouble With Harry* (1955), and *North by Northwest*. Bernard Herrmann, the composer of *Citizen Kane*, wrote his greatest score for *Vertigo* and his most experimental score (nothing but strings) for *Psycho*. Hitchcock's lifelong interest in Freudian psychology (about which one can never tell whether he is serious or has his tongue wedged in his cheek), seen in such earlier works as *Spellbound*, is a complex and ironic factor in *Vertigo*, *North by Northwest*, and *Psycho*—which were made in that order—as well as in the last of his great movies: *The Birds* (1963), in which he continued his demonstration that the apparently innocent and unnoticed can turn deadly; *Marnie* (1964), the "sex mystery," as he described it in the trailer, in which he took a deep look at the psychological links between sex and crime; and *Frenzy* (1972), which he returned to London to shoot and in which he showed more shocking and troubling (and unglamorized rather than elegantly stylized) violence than anyone had yet seen in a mainstream movie.

Nicholas Ray

A loner and a rebel, Nicholas Ray began making films in 1948. Like Fuller, Ray became a director on the fringes of the Hollywood establishment with films that he often wrote himself. Although he began in the theatre and came to Hollywood as Elia Kazan's assistant, Ray would feel more comfortable with Hollywood genres than with theatrical ones: westerns (*Johnny Guitar*), war films (*Flying Leathernecks*, 1951), the combination of *film noir* and wild youth (*They Live By Night*, 1948, released 1949; *Knock on Any Door*, 1949; *Born to Be Bad*, 1950). But like *Johnny Guitar* (a wildly stylized film with a showdown between two women), his pictures often leave their genres behind. *The Lusty Men* (1952) is a rodeo picture and more. Ray's disturbing movie about the film industry, *In A Lonely Place* (1950), features Humphrey Bogart as a Hollywood screenwriter who is unjustly suspected of murder but who *is* emotionally destructive.

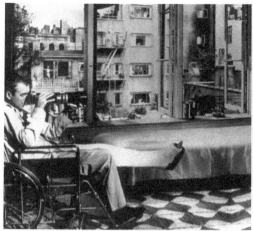

Fig. 12-25

Fig. 12-26

Fig. 12-27

Fig. 12-28

Fig. 12-29

Rear Window: *window frames as movie frames. The spectator–voyeur (James Stewart, Fig. 12-25), observes the framed stories of the newlyweds (Fig. 12-26), "Miss Lonelyhearts" (Fig. 12-27), "Miss Torso" (Fig. 12-28), and the murderer, Thorwald (Raymond Burr, Fig. 12-29).*

Fig. 12-30
Alfred Hitchcock on the set of The Birds.

Rebel Without a Cause (1955), which gave birth to the James Dean legend (Dean starred in only two other films: Kazan's *East of Eden*, earlier in 1955, and George Stevens's *Giant*, 1956), is one of Ray's most personal works. The rebellion in the film's title is the only detail Ray borrowed from Robert Lindner's bestselling 1944 case study of a young psychopathic criminal. The title is a smokescreen for the film's real issue—the attempt of three outsiders, strangers alike to the materialistic values of their weak but rigid parents and the desperately insecure values of their teenage contemporaries, to form an alternative community of genuine human sympathy.

Jim Stark (Dean) begins the film as a hopeless drunk because he sees no value in a future represented by the enslavement of his father (Jim Backus—the voice of Mr. Magoo) to material possessions and a nagging wife. "Jimbo's" father is a man of no commitments or aspirations, except to keep the peace amongst the sterile bric-a-brac of his bourgeois home. Judy (Natalie Wood) also has problems with a father who spurns her confusedly provocative need for affection, sending her off in search of thrills and easy sensual power over boys her own age. Plato (Sal Mineo), the rich kid who never sees his

divorced parents (as Ray's son rarely saw him), is the most vulnerable and intellectual of the three, the most socially unskilled, and implicitly homosexual. Plato recognizes the fragility of human experience in a cold and awesome universe—suggested by the hypnotic planetarium show, a spectacle of sound and light analogous to movies. Plato, like Judy, searches for love and finds it in the same source—Jim.

Ray chronicles Jim's discovery of what it means to be a man and a responsible human being. The seeming alternative he sees to his father's emasculation is the world of his violent contemporaries, with their knife fights and chicken runs, car races that may be to the death. Jim, Judy, and Plato try to be good—and they are—but always seem to end up being called bad. Only love can unscramble their hearts, can give an uncontradictory message, can let them find themselves beyond the empty and unfulfilling hypocrisy of imposed social roles.

The trio withdraws—from both worlds of adult bourgeoisie and adolescent *machismo*—to found a perfect community. A deserted mansion in the Hollywood Hills, Falcon's Lair, serves as home to this affectionate alternative family, in which Plato is the child. The outside world,

A new and more perfect union in Rebel Without a Cause: *from left, Sal Mineo, James Dean, and Natalie Wood at Falcon's Lair.*

Fig. 12-31

however, invades this fragile oasis—both adolescents seeking revenge and the police trying to clean up the mess by making more mess. With the death of Plato, the sacrificial victim, Jim and Judy come even closer, and their parents appear to be ready to listen to them.

Rebel Without a Cause had great power for young audiences in the 1950s, urging them to abandon conformity and to seek values that made personal sense. At the same time, it urged parents to face up to their own problems. Ray described Dean's red jacket, in contrast with his black Mercury, as a danger sign, a personality about to explode. Ray consistently identified with oddballs and loners who saw themselves as different from everyone else.

Late Ford
Ethan Edwards of John Ford's *The Searchers* (1956) is another oddball and loner, different from everyone else. In *The Searchers*, Ford continued his mythic investigation of American history. Like Ford's postwar *My Darling Clementine*, the cavalry trilogy of 1948–50 (*Fort Apache, She Wore A Yellow Ribbon, Rio Grande*), and the 1962 *The Man Who Shot Liberty Valance*, *The Searchers* exposes the conflict of irresolvable historical forces: the clash between inflexible civilized institutions designed to patrol the peace and individual qualities of human will

required to fight for peace; between the struggle to establish and protect a civilization and the values of civilization that make it worth establishing and protecting. Both Ford and Wayne show the violence under the tightly controlled surface of a culture or a face.

The searchers are Ethan Edwards (John Wayne), whose obsessiveness dominates the film, and Martin Pawley (Jeffrey Hunter), who is part Cherokee. Ethan's brother, Aaron, and Aaron's wife, Martha, whom Ethan may himself once have loved, are brutally slaughtered in a Comanche attack soon after the film begins. The Comanches carry off two daughters, Debbie and Lucy. Though Lucy is raped and murdered, Debbie remains among the Comanches. Ethan's search for Debbie, which consumes him for five years, is an act of determination and revenge: to murder the man responsible for the death of his kin (the Indian warrior Scar, played by Henry Brandon) and to rescue Debbie from the Comanches before she has suffered sexual contamination—or to murder her if he is too late (since, for Ethan, to be a white squaw is worse than death for a Christian woman). In this context, Martin's project is not only to find Debbie, but also to protect her from Ethan.

Ethan refuses to surrender the search, just as he has never surrendered any cause—he still honors his oath to the Confederacy. Ethan and Martin pursue the search for years, living nomadically, like the Comanches they pursue. Martin, however, strongly feels the pull back toward home: His sweetheart, Laurie Jorgensen (Vera Miles), will not wait forever.

The film's dominant contrast is between those who settle and those who search. Ethan feels uncomfortable indoors, within the comforts of a home, covered by a ceiling. Ford's beautiful and parallel shots, which begin and conclude the film, looking outdoors into the glaring sunlight through the dark arch of a doorway, are visual metaphors for the contrasting regions—of indoors and outdoors, civilization and wilderness, garden and desert, settling and searching. In Ford's metaphor, these two regions are contiguous; the warm familial peace indoors cannot be secure without taming the threat from the outdoors. There can be no settlers without searchers—and perhaps, in Ford's view, no peace without war. In *The Quiet Man* (1952) a willingness to be violent is presented as psychologically healthy, and in *Liberty Valance* it is the key to popularity as well as to establishing the rule of law.

Ethan remains connected to but apart from the world of settlers; he is not just more comfortable outside, but an outsider. And he has a ruthless, crazy streak that gives the film its edge and a rigidity that appears to be headed straight for tragedy.

In the film's climax, Ethan chases the fleeing Debbie (Natalie Wood). Martin runs after them, terrified that Ethan intends to kill her, but Ethan sweeps her into his arms, up on his horse, and simply says, "Let's go home, Debbie." Like the film's opening and closing shots, this action completes a circle, for Ethan had lifted Debbie in much the same way when she was a little girl. This act of loving acceptance makes the civilized family possible and brings Ethan's obsessive quest for revenge to an unexpected but appropriate solution. Like the by-the-rules, code-driven official (Raymond Massey) in Ford's *The Hurricane* (1937), but unlike the rigid officer (Henry Fonda) in *Fort Apache*, Ethan rises above his own inflexibility. From *The Informer* to *The Quiet Man*, Ford tells stories of moral education whose heroes learn the meaning of honor, courage, love, and law (and, often, how and when to fight). *The Searchers* is typical in the way its lesson comes clear only at the end, with no sense of the formulaic or pat: Up to the last moment, the audience cannot predict whether or not Ethan will tragically set his rigid code above the demands of love.

Douglas Sirk

In contrast to Ford's complex, energetic, and mutually enriching opposition of the settler's hearth and garden and the loner's wide open spaces, Douglas Sirk shrinks the world into a modern, bourgeois interior that has been arranged and ordered to death. Born in Denmark, Sirk moved to Germany, where he began making films in the 1930s. A leftist, he left Germany in 1937 and arrived in America in 1939 to direct anti-Nazi war films (*Hitler's Madman*, 1943), *films noirs* (*Sleep My Love*, 1948), and domestic comedies (*No Room for the Groom*, 1952). Sirk's major work began in 1954 after his move to Universal, where he became a director of glossy melodramas (adult soap operas, at the time called weepies or women's pictures) under producer Ross Hunter.

The Sirk melodramas are odd mixtures of contradictory qualities. On the one hand, they seem slick depictions of the most tawdry values of materialistic, middle-class life. On the other hand, they seem brutally funny comments on this very tawdriness, on the values of bourgeois life that the characters automatically accept and on the values of movies and movie audiences that accept them just as automatically. To see a Sirk film, like *Imitation of Life*, in a 1959 movie theatre was a fractured experience: half the audience sobbing hysterically into wet handkerchiefs, the other half laughing hysterically in sheer disbelief. These same contradictory reactions have divided audiences of Sirk films ever since.

The reason is that Sirk films are powerful bourgeois melodramas and, at the same time, powerful comments on the assumptions of bourgeois melodrama. In *All That Heaven Allows* (1955, U.S. release 1956), an attractive, middle-aged widow (Jane Wyman) falls for a younger man (Rock Hudson), her own gardener, depicted as Thoreau's "man of nature." Her friends find the man unsuitable—not rich enough, not old enough, not a member of her own social class. The single attraction they see in him is physical—what they can see. She sees him as spiritually different. But if he is such a "natural spirit," why does nature play such a tame visual role in the film—embodied by one symbolic deer behind a plate-glass window in a sound-stage forest? Why is almost every scene of nature in the supposedly Thoreauvian *All That Heaven Allows* so obviously an indoor imitation of the outdoors? Is it a mere studio convention, or is Sirk debunking the convention—along with the contrast between nature and artifice on which the film depends? This question is always at the center of a Sirk film. We are never quite sure who is kidding whom.

Sirk shoots his bourgeois world filtered through reminders of Hollywood's presence. Doorways, partitioning screens, window panes, mirrors, reflective surfaces (even the glass screens of television sets) dominate Sirk frames, calling attention to the fact that we look not at life but at a frame. Unnatural prismatic lighting effects in Sirk's color films raise questions about the source and purpose of this oddly colored light. Is the *mise-en-scène* merely decorative, an exercise in cold good taste, or is Sirk "deconstructing" the very images he constructs (pointing out their internal contradictions)? Is he using Brechtian distancing devices to separate the audience from the illusion of the work? Or is he, without irony—and with or without contempt—simply giving the audience what it wants: the slickly artificial and maudlin? Does the Sirk film proclaim that everything about it is manufactured— from the way it looks, to the characters who inhabit it, to their value and moral systems—or is it merely proud of itself as an artificial product?

Imitation of Life (1959) is the ultimate Sirk film—both his last and his most powerful at posing these questions. It is a story about race relations, one of the few serious social subjects that films could explore in the 1950s without fear of right-wing protests and boycotts. An unemployed white actress, Lora (Lana Turner), meets a black woman, Annie (Juanita Moore), early in the film while their daughters play together on a crowded beach. The actress rises to success, aided by the financial support and household service of Annie, who has moved in with her. Lora's daughter, Susie (Sandra Dee), enjoys a typical upper-middle-class adolescence (boarding school and college), while the black daughter, Sarah Jane (Susan Kohner), who looks white, suffers the pain of social exclusion. She tries to escape her black heritage, seeking sexual affairs with white boys, working as a showgirl in a white nightclub—but returns in the end for her mother's funeral to suffer agonies of grief.

In remaking this Fanny Hurst novel (originally directed by John M. Stahl for Universal in 1934, starring Claudette Colbert and Louise Beavers), Sirk and Hunter made a crucial change. While in the original (novel and film), Lora makes a public success of Annie's private recipe for pancake flour (a clear allusion to Aunt Jemima), the black woman in the 1959 film has no direct relation to the white woman's

Fig. 12-32   *Fig. 12-33*

Imitation of Life: *Whether in a dressing room (Fig. 12-32) or a kitchen (Fig. 12-33), Annie (Juanita Moore) finds it "natural" to become the maid of her friend and equal, Lora (Lana Turner).*

vocational success. The world of pancake mix has been abandoned for the glittering world of Broadway stardom. What happens to the black woman in this new world? Quite simply, she becomes Lora's maid.

There is no indication in the film of why this black woman—the social and financial equal of the white woman at its beginning—should automatically accept her "place" as the white woman's servant. Lora wears an endless number (actually 34) of shapely, bright-colored, high-fashion outfits and a great deal of jewelry. But Annie wears drab, nondescript clothes with plain collars and little jewelry. However many of these outfits she wears, they all look the same and always suggest the domestic. Neither Annie nor Lora sees anything odd in this visual inequality (as if it were "natural" for a black woman to become or resemble the servant of a white woman). The question is, does Sirk? Is this a plea for interracial respect and personal authenticity, or a sentimental exaltation of the problems of racism and role playing? Although the white woman and the black woman inhabit the same house, the same film, and the same frame, they don't inhabit the same universe. Class and race have nothing and everything to do with their friendship. Who's kidding whom here?

Does *Imitation of Life* reveal what makes its characters' lives false and empty, or is it itself a deliberately fake world within which the characters deal only with the artificial crises of romantic melodrama, making even civil rights a sentimental issue? Even if its plot of Lora's stardom and love life, and Annie's daughter's rebellion, is the disguise, and friendship and understanding—and suffering—between women is the film's official subject, the ways it is actually about—or an example of—the contradictions of its culture and period can be found in plain sight: for example, in the differences between Lana Turner's and Juanita Moore's wardrobes. If Sirk's melodramas are about surfaces, that does not make them superficial.

Whatever adjectives one might seek to describe these films by Fuller, Hitchcock, Ray, Ford, and Sirk, escapist wouldn't be one of them. The moral, economic, social, psychological, and sexual ambiguities of such films suggest an America that was itself as genuinely confused as it was superficially assured about its purpose and direction.

Finding the Audience

Despite the gimmicks, despite the wide screen, despite the sexual innuendos, despite the industry's claim that movies were better than ever, movie income and movie admissions continued to fall throughout the 1950s. In an effort to give the public what television could not, Hollywood had to discover who its public was. It could not assume, as studio moguls Mayer and Cohn did in the 1930s, that its public was all of the people all of the time.

The signs that would eventually point the way had begun to appear just after the war. A series of foreign films—with De Sica's *The Bicycle Thief* (1948) the first highly publicized import—proved that a particular kind of film, inexpensively produced, more obviously sociological and less idealized than the Hollywood film, could attract interested audiences to small theatres while slick Hollywood films played to empty houses in large ones. More and more little neighborhood theatres that could no longer do business as fourth-run houses for Hollywood films found a second life as "art houses" by replacing the popcorn machine with an espresso maker and showing foreign pictures like *Rashomon* (1950), *Seven Samurai* (1954), *La strada* (1954), *Diabolique* (1955), and *The Seventh Seal* (1956) as soon as they were released in the United States. In 1959, for example, the art houses' competition wasn't all *Ben-Hur*, *Some Like It Hot*, and *North by Northwest.* Two of the dumbest American films ever made (Martin Ritt's *The Sound and the Fury* and Edward D. Wood, Jr.'s *Plan 9 From Outer Space*) were released in 1959—but so were such foreign films as Marcel Camus's *Black Orpheus*, François Truffaut's *The 400 Blows*, Jack Clayton's *Room at the Top*, and Louis Malle's *The Lovers.* The better films were better received, and many patrons went back to see them again and talked about them seriously with their friends.

A foreign film was certainly unlike anything that the networks could or would present on television: introspective, with dialogue requiring the audience to read subtitles, sensitive to intellectual and political questions, treating sexual matters frankly, with refreshing insights into other cultures, other values, and other ways of seeing. And these foreign imports had never been required to submit themselves to the moral approval of the Hays Office Code. There had been a call for "art houses" and an "art movement" in the 1930s, which had been answered in a few major cities by a few theatres. But the small art house of under 500 seats, with its elite fare, ran contrary to the old financial tides of the 1940s, when the movie palaces of several thousand seats filled up every night. With television, however, the commercial tides had turned.

Hollywood discovered that movies had indeed become an elite as well as a popular art. Just as the legitimate theatre had been the art for *some* in the 1930s when movies were the art for *everyone*, so movies had become the art for some when television became the art for all. Movies had been the casual everyday form of entertainment before World War II, but TV supplied that kind of entertainment after it. Movies, then, had to be aimed at the minority audience that wanted the kind of show that television could not or would not provide; *Psycho* found that audience in 1960, as did *Dr. Strangelove* in 1964, *Bonnie and Clyde* in 1967, *Faces* in 1968, and *Medium Cool* in 1969. The elitism of the movie audience by 1970 becomes clear when comparing the average cost of a ticket in 1946 and 1970. Although films grossed almost the same amount of money in both years, in 1946 the average movie seat cost about 40¢; in 1970, the average seat cost $2. (Inflation played a minor role here; what cost 40¢ in 1946 cost 80¢ in 1970.) By 1980, the average cost had risen to $3.50, and in 1990, it was normal to pay $5.50 (top big-city prices rose to $4 in 1978 and to $7 in 1989; in 2006, they reached $12, which was three times above the rate of inflation since 1946). Movies were no longer the "nickel" entertainment, the easiest to get for the least cost, that they had been since the turn of the century. But the programs on TV, like those on radio, were free.

To keep any share of the entertainment market at all, the motion-picture industry needed to reflect about who still went to movies and why. Families were one answer; movies still provided an outing for the whole family. But the combined cost of four, five, or six tickets meant that the outing would be rare and special—perfect for those family-oriented "specials," like the biblical blockbusters of the 1950s or the musical blockbusters of the 1960s.

The professional college-educated elite, who still lived in the cities or frequently visited them, was another answer. A strongly committed moviegoing generation of upwardly mobile Americans had discovered the cultural importance of movies—both American and foreign, both classic and new—during their college days.

Finally, there were the young, aged about 14 and upwards, for whom movies were an essential part of the socialization process. These young people used movies to get out of the house, away from the society of their parents (increasingly symbolized by that TV set), into a society of their own contemporaries.

It was easy for the movie industry to attract members of these two groups—the cultural elite and the adolescent—away from the TV set. Hollywood aimed its films at their values, their interests, their styles, using their themes, their music, their moral codes. If movies were directed at the young, educated, and urban, television, like many films in the 1930s, was aimed at rural and suburban families—at the kind of audience who went to the movies in the 1930s and 1940s; in fact, much of its audience in the 1950s was composed of those very people. Television formulas—family comedies, mysteries, westerns, hospital dramas, courtroom dramas—were the old movie formulas (with a strong dash of radio, evident not only in the soaps and the news, but also in variety shows, situation comedies, dramatic series, and the many programs that began on radio, like *Dragnet* and *The Jack Benny Show*). TV formulas did not change because the audience did not change. Films and film audiences had changed.

The movies learned to coexist with television, as we have seen. They made TV movies and licensed their films to be shown on TV. They recruited directors, writers, and actors with TV experience. (Ultimately, in the mid-1980s, Fox launched its own network.) They scrapped their movie palaces and replaced them with 500-seat theatres that were easier to fill despite their high ticket prices. They chopped big theatres into two or three or even multiplex theatres on the same property, a much more economical use of land and space. Most of the few great movie palaces that still survive—the Empire in London, the Chinese in Los Angeles—are multiple cinemas now. In 1973, both the MGM and the 20th Century–Fox back lots were sold to make room for real apartment houses, office buildings, stores, restaurants, and streets.

Television, which threatened to swallow the film studios, also subsidized them. The old studios survived the years of drift and struggle—if they survived at all—thanks to the steady income from TV filming.

Because of pressures and problems ranging from the blacklist to the "box," in the 1950s there was terrific uncertainty about what might be said, how it might be said, and to whom it might be said—an uncertainty that increased with every passing year until the film business bottomed out in the early 1960s. The best films of the postwar decades preserved the old studio styles, structures, and genres, even as the studios were crumbling—or took wild creative chances in spite of those conventions. Hollywood stumbled through the maze of conflicting production values and social controversies, eventually emerging in a Renaissance that was strongly influenced by foreign films and by the most adventurous films of the 1950s and early 1960s in America.

For Further Viewing

FILMS

JACK ARNOLD (1912–92)
It Came From Outer Space (1953). 3-D
Creature from the Black Lagoon (1954). 3-D
Tarantula (1955)
The Incredible Shrinking Man (1957)
The Mouse That Roared (1959)

ROGER CORMAN (1926–   )
Not of This Earth (1957)
A Bucket of Blood (1959)
The Little Shop of Horrors (1960)
The Pit and the Pendulum (1961)
The Raven (1963)
X or X—The Man with the X-Ray Eyes (1963)
The Masque of the Red Death (1964)
Gas-s-s-s (1970)

JULES DASSIN (1911–2008)
Brute Force (1947)
The Naked City (1948)
Night and the City (1950)
Rififi or Du Rififi chez les hommes (1955)
Never on Sunday (1960)

10:30 PM Summer (1966)
A Dream of Passion (1978)

STANLEY DONEN (1924–   )
On the Town (1949). Co-director, Gene Kelly
Royal Wedding (1951)
Singin' In The Rain (1952). Co-director, Gene Kelly
It's Always Fair Weather (1955). Co-director, Gene Kelly
The Pajama Game (1957)
Bedazzled (1967)
Two for the Road (1967)

SAMUEL FULLER (1911–97)
Fixed Bayonets (1951)
The Steel Helmet (1951)
Pickup on South Street (1953)
House of Bamboo (1955)
Run of the Arrow (1957)
Underworld U.S.A. (1961)
Shock Corridor (1963)
The Naked Kiss (1964)
Dead Pigeon on Beethoven Street (1972)
The Big Red One (1980)
White Dog (1982)

HENRY HATHAWAY (1898–1985)
The Lives of a Bengal Lancer (1935)
Trail of the Lonesome Pine (1936)
The House on 92nd Street (1945)
The Dark Corner (1946)
Kiss of Death (1947)
Call Northside 777 (1948)
Niagara (1953)
True Grit (1969)

JOHN HUSTON (1906–87)
The Maltese Falcon (1941)
Let There Be Light (1946). Released 1981
Key Largo (1948)
The Treasure of the Sierra Madre (1948)
The Asphalt Jungle (1950)
The African Queen (1951)
The Night of the Iguana (1964)
Fat City (1972)
The Man Who Would Be King (1975)
Wise Blood (1979)
Under the Volcano (1984)
Prizzi's Honor (1985)
The Dead (1987)

Elia Kazan (1909–2003)
A Tree Grows in Brooklyn (1945)
Boomerang (1947)
Gentleman's Agreement (1947)
Pinky (1949)
A Streetcar Named Desire (1951)
On the Waterfront (1954)
East of Eden (1955)
A Face in the Crowd (1957)
Splendor in the Grass (1961)
America, America (1963)

Henry King (1888–1982)
Tol'able David (1921)
The White Sister (1923)
Alexander's Ragtime Band (1938)
The Black Swan (1942)
The Song of Bernadette (1943)
Twelve O'Clock High (1949)
The Gunfighter (1950)
King of the Khyber Rifles (1953)
Carousel (1956)
Tender is the Night (1962)

Stanley Kramer (1913–2001)
The Defiant Ones (1958)
On the Beach (1959)
Inherit the Wind (1960)
Judgment at Nuremberg (1961)
It's a Mad Mad Mad Mad World (1963)
Ship of Fools (1965)
Guess Who's Coming to Dinner (1967)

Jerry Lewis (1926–   )
The Bellboy (1960)
The Nutty Professor (1963)
The Patsy (1964)

Joseph Losey (1909–84)
The Boy With Green Hair (1948)
The Prowler (1951)
The Damned or *These Are the Damned* (1962)
The Servant (1963)
King & Country (1964)
Accident (1967)
The Romantic Englishwoman (1975)

Sidney Lumet (1924–   )
12 Angry Men (1957)
Long Day's Journey Into Night (1962)
A View From the Bridge (1962)

Fail-Safe (1964)
The Hill (1965)
The Pawnbroker (1965)
The Deadly Affair (1967)
Bye Bye Braverman (1968)
Serpico (1973)
Dog Day Afternoon (1975)
Network (1976)
Prince of the City (1981)
The Verdict (1982)
Before the Devil Knows You're Dead (2007)

Joseph L. Mankiewicz (1909–93)
All About Eve (1950)
Julius Caesar (1953)
The Barefoot Contessa (1954)
Guys and Dolls (1955)
Suddenly, Last Summer (1959)
Cleopatra (1963)
Sleuth (1972)

Anthony Mann (1906–67)
T-Men (1947)
Raw Deal (1948)
Winchester '73 (1950)
Bend of the River (1953)
The Far Country (1955)
The Man from Laramie (1955)
El Cid (1961)

Vincente Minnelli (1903–86)
Cabin in the Sky (1943)
Meet Me in St. Louis (1944)
The Clock (1945)
The Pirate (1948)
An American in Paris (1951)
The Band Wagon (1953)
Tea and Sympathy (1956)
Gigi (1958)
Some Came Running (1959)
Bells Are Ringing (1960)
Two Weeks in Another Town (1962)

Otto Preminger (1906–86)
Laura (1944)
The Moon Is Blue (1953)
Carmen Jones (1954)
River of No Return (1954)
The Man With the Golden Arm (1955)
Anatomy of a Murder (1959)
Porgy and Bess (1959)

Exodus (1960)
Advise and Consent (1962)
Bunny Lake is Missing (1965)

NICHOLAS RAY (1911–79)
They Live By Night (1949). Completed 1948
Knock on Any Door (1949)
In A Lonely Place (1950)
The Lusty Men (1952)
Johnny Guitar (1954)
Rebel Without a Cause (1955)
55 Days at Peking (1963)
Lightning Over Water or *Nick's Film* (1980).
    Co-director, Wim Wenders

ROBERT ROSSEN (1908–66)
Body and Soul (1947)
All the King's Men (1949)
The Hustler (1961)

DON SIEGEL (1912–91)
Star in the Night and *Hitler Lives* (1945 shorts)
The Verdict (1946)
Private Hell 36 (1954)
Riot in Cell Block 11 (1954)
Invasion of the Body Snatchers (1956)
Baby Face Nelson (1957)
Flaming Star (1960)
The Killers (1964). Made for TV
Madigan (1968)
The Beguiled (1971)
Dirty Harry (1971)
The Shootist (1976)
Telefon (1977)
Escape from Alcatraz (1979)

DOUGLAS SIRK (1900–87)
Magnificent Obsession (1954)
All That Heaven Allows (1955)
Written on the Wind (1956)
The Tarnished Angels (1957)
Imitation of Life (1959)

GEORGE STEVENS (1904–75)
Alice Adams (1935)
Swing Time (1936)
Gunga Din (1939)
Penny Serenade (1941)
The Talk of the Town (1942)
Woman of the Year (1942)

A Place in the Sun (1951)
Shane (1953). Completed 1951
Giant (1956)

BILLY WILDER (1906–2002)
The Major and the Minor (1942)
Double Indemnity (1944)
The Lost Weekend (1945)
Sunset Blvd. (1950)
The Big Carnival or *Ace in the Hole* (1951)
Stalag 17 (1953)
The Seven Year Itch (1955)
Some Like It Hot (1959)
The Apartment (1960)
One, Two, Three (1961)
The Fortune Cookie (1966)
The Private Life of Sherlock Holmes (1970)

ROBERT WISE (1914–2005)
The Curse of the Cat People (1944). Co-director,
    Gunther Von Fritsch
The Body Snatcher (1945)
The Set-Up (1949)
The Day the Earth Stood Still (1951)
Somebody Up There Likes Me (1956)
I Want to Live! (1958)
Odds Against Tomorrow (1959)
West Side Story (1961). Co-director, Jerome
    Robbins
The Haunting (1963)
The Sound of Music (1965)
The Sand Pebbles (1966)

FRED ZINNEMANN (1907–97)
The Men (1950)
High Noon (1952)
From Here to Eternity (1953)
Oklahoma! (1955)
A Man for All Seasons (1966)
The Day of the Jackal (1973)
Five Days One Summer (1983)

TRANSITIONAL ERA MISCELLANY
The Killers (1946, Robert Siodmak)
Crossfire (1947, Edward Dmytryk)
Out of the Past (1947, Jacques Tourneur)
Easter Parade (1948, Charles Walters)
Force of Evil (1948, Abraham Polonsky)
Home of the Brave (1949, Mark Robson)

Intruder in the Dust (1949, Clarence Brown)

Gun Crazy (1950, Joseph H. Lewis). Completed 1949

Destination Moon (1950, Irving Pichel)

Ways of Love (1950). Includes Pagnol's *Jofroi* (1934), Renoir's *A Day in the Country* (1936), and Rossellini's *The Miracle* (1948)

The Thing or *The Thing From Another World* (1951, Christian Nyby)

My Son John (1952, Leo McCarey)

Red Planet Mars (1952, Harry Horner)

The 5,000 Fingers of Dr. T. (1953, Roy Rowland)

The Hitch-Hiker and *The Bigamist* (1953, Ida Lupino)

House of Wax (1953, André de Toth). 3-D

Invaders From Mars (1953, William Cameron Menzies)

Kiss Me Kate (1953, George Sidney). 3-D

Lili (1953, Charles Waters)

Little Fugitive (1953, Morris Engel, Ruth Orkin, and Ray Ashley)

The Robe (1953, Henry Koster)

Salt of the Earth (1953, Herbert Biberman)

The War of the Worlds (1953, Byron Haskin)

The Wild One (1953, Laslo Benedek)

Bad Day at Black Rock (1954, John Sturges)

The Bridges at Toko-Ri (1954, Mark Robson)

The Caine Mutiny (1954, Edward Dmytryk)

Gog (1954, Herbert L. Strock). 3-D

Them! (1954, Gordon Douglas)

Blackboard Jungle (1955, Richard Brooks)

Kiss Me Deadly (1955, Robert Aldrich)

Marty (1955, Delbert Mann)

The Night of the Hunter (1955, Charles Laughton)

This Island Earth (1955, Joseph Newman)

The Court Jester (1956, Norman Panama)

Earth vs. the Flying Saucers (1956, Fred F. Sears)

Forbidden Planet (1956, Fred M. Wilcox)

Picnic (1956, Joshua Logan)

I Was a Teenage Werewolf (1957, Gene Fowler)

Sweet Smell of Success (1957, Alexander Mackendrick)

The Blob (1958, Irvin S. Yeaworth, Jr.)

The Fly (1958, Kurt Neumann)

Elmer Gantry (1960, Richard Brooks)

The Magnificent Seven (1960, John Sturges)

The Savage Eye (1960, Ben Maddow, Sidney Meyers, and Joseph Strick)

The Connection (1961, Shirley Clarke)

Lonely Are the Brave (1962, David Miller)

What Ever Happened to Baby Jane? (1962, Robert Aldrich)

David and Lisa (1963, Frank Perry)

Dr. Strangelove Or: How I Learned To Stop Worrying And Love The Bomb (1964, Stanley Kubrick)

Nothing But a Man (1964, Michael Roemer). Co-director, Robert M. Young

Point of Order (1964, Emile de Antonio)

The World of Henry Orient (1964, George Roy Hill)

The Spy Who Came In from the Cold (1965, Martin Ritt)

A Thousand Clowns (1965, Fred Coe)

DVDs

All That Heaven Allows (1955, **Douglas Sirk**). Criterion Collection. Includes BBC documentary with Sirk interview; **Fassbinder** essay, "Imitation of Life: The Films of Douglas Sirk"; and notes by film theorist Laura Mulvey.

Blacklist data, interviews, and shorts are included with *Spartacus* (see Chap. 15 list). Also see *Salt of the Earth*, below.

The Day the Earth Stood Still (1951, **Robert Wise**). 20th Century Fox Home Video. Includes a 1951 Movietone newsreel, a commentary by Wise and Nicolas Meyer, a documentary, **restoration** comparisons, and the shooting script.

Dirk Bogarde Collection. Anchor Bay. Dirk Bogarde stars in *The Mind Benders* (1963, Basil Dearden), *The Servant* (1963, **Joseph Losey**), and *Accident* (1967, **Losey**).

Film Noir Classic Collection. Warner Home Video. Contains *Murder, My Sweet* (1945, **Edward Dmytryk**), *Out of the Past* (1947, **Jacques Tourneur**), *The Set-Up* (1949, **Robert Wise**), *Gun Crazy* (1949, rel. 1950, **Joseph H. Lewis**), and *The Asphalt Jungle* (1950, **John Huston**), with commentaries.

Film Noir Killer Classics. Questar. Includes *Detour* (1945, **Edgar G. Ulmer**), *Scarlet Street* (1945, **Fritz Lang**), *The Stranger* (1946, **Orson Welles**), *Too Late for Tears* as *Killer Bait* (1949, **Byron Haskin**), *D.O.A.* (1950,

Rudolf Maté), 38 *film noir* **trailers,** posters, documentaries on *noir* and *femmes fatales,* and more.

From Here to Eternity (1953, **Fred Zinnemann**). Columbia TriStar. Includes documentaries, biographies, and commentaries.

The Hitch-Hiker (1953, **Ida Lupino**). Kino Video. **Restored** from the Library of Congress print.

Invasion of the Body Snatchers (1956, **Don Siegel**). Republic Studios. Letterboxed (with the pan-and-scan for comparison), and with an interview with actor Kevin McCarthy.

The Manchurian Candidate (1962, **John Frankenheimer**). MGM Home Entertainment. Special Edition. Includes commentary by Frankenheimer, interviews, and shorts.

On the Waterfront (1954, **Elia Kazan**). Columbia TriStar. Includes an interview with Kazan; short biographies of **Budd Schulberg, Marlon Brando,** etc.; a documentary; and commentaries.

Pickup on South Street (1953, **Samuel Fuller**). Criterion Collection. Interviews with Fuller, a poster filmography, trailers for eight Fuller films, and a booklet with excerpts from his autobiography.

Rififi (1955, **Jules Dassin**). Criterion Collection. The best *noir* ever made in France, famous for its long, silent robbery sequence. Includes an interview with Dassin.

The Robe (1953, **Henry Koster**). 20th Century Fox. Special Edition. **Digitally restored,** with a making-of documentary.

Salt of the Earth (1953, **Herbert Biberman**). Geneon/Pioneer. Includes the documentary *The Hollywood Ten* and much information on the blacklist and on the making of the picture.

Singin' In The Rain (1952, **Stanley Donen** and **Gene Kelly**). Warner Home Video. Special edition, with a digital transfer from **restored** elements, a documentary on Freed musicals, other shorts and clips, and commentary by the screenwriters and cast.

Sunset Blvd. (1950, **Billy Wilder**). Paramount Home Video. Special Collector's Edition. **Restored,** with commentary by Wilder scholar Ed Sikov, documentaries, script pages for the original morgue prologue, and a map.

The Treasure of the Sierra Madre (1948, **John Huston**). Warner Home Video. New transfer from **restored** picture and sound elements.

West Side Story (1961, **Jerome Robbins** and **Robert Wise**). MGM Home Entertainment. Special Edition Collector's Set. Includes a scrapbook with the complete working film script, memos, and reviews.

13

Neorealism, the New Wave, and What Followed

The French and Italian postwar cinemas revolutionized the values and aesthetics of the motion picture itself. The changes in content and style that began in Italy and culminated in France affected and influenced the entire world's cinema as much as Griffith, Murnau, or Eisenstein did in the Silent Era.

Italian Neorealism and the French New Wave were the two most important movements of the Sound Era. They forced filmmakers to re-think everything from the social value of movies to the realism of photography and from the politics of form to the metaphysics of cinematic time and space. They made the world care and think. They used film to investigate its own language. They used film to interrogate the world. They inspired and excited viewers with entirely new kinds of movies. As they rose to the defining challenges of political crisis and aesthetic opportunity, they urged the world to follow them into the next cinematic era.

After World War II, European directors did exactly what they did after World War I. They climbed out from under years of wartime rubble and disrupted production, somehow scraped together enough money and film stock, and began making films that showed extraordinary sincerity, insight, and artistic control. While American films groped for a new identity, many of the films that struck audiences and critics as the best came from Europe. The European films seemed best not because they revealed portions of naked bodies, not because they were obscure, and not because Americans had become cultural snobs—as so many American film executives claimed.

The films seemed best because they raised the same questions in cinematic form that had been raised in the best novels, plays, poems, and philosophical essays of the 20th century. And the adult Americans who had become the new movie audience, those who found it easy to leave their TV sets, were precisely those who were reading the books.

It was not that American films were mindless but that the best films from Europe were so explicitly serious, more aggressively existential, Modernist, and adult than the familiar genres and attitudes of Hollywood. In the tradition of Mann, Proust, Pirandello, and Sartre (and, by the way, of Renoir, Eisenstein, Murnau, and Pabst), the new European film searched for meaningful, life-giving values in a world in which absolute values had crumbled. The social and psychological problems of these European films could not be solved by Hollywood's two most frequent forms of closure—the killing of a bad guy or the marriage of John and Jane. Many European films began with a marriage rather than ended with one.

The great films of postwar Europe, despite the individuality of the particular directors, shared several traits that contrasted with the typical American film. First, very few of them were adaptations of familiar books and plays. Most were original conceptions, carefully shaped by the director and screenwriter working in unison.

Second, those postwar European films that reached American viewers continued the prewar tradition of structuring themselves around a theme or a psychological problem more than around a story. The films of Roberto Rossellini,

Vittorio De Sica, Federico Fellini, Ingmar Bergman, Alain Resnais, Jean-Luc Godard, and Michelangelo Antonioni were not so much linear narratives as they were experiments in cinematic narration, often concerned with political and philosophical issues, as well as investigations of human conduct in the face of emotional, economic, and conceptual crises.

Third, the focus on form and theme brought these films back into the mainstream of 20th-century thought and literature. The philosophical and psychological questions in these films, and to some degree the ways they were handled, from Bergman to the New Wave, were related to those in Kafka, Pound, Joyce, Proust, Mann, Woolf, Faulkner, Camus, Ionesco, and others.

Fourth, the films looked different from each other and from the product of Hollywood or any big studio. European directors discovered different ways to define film style, realizing that certain kinds of thematic inquiries or psychological states required a totally different handling of the *mise-en-scène*, camera, and soundtrack.

The postwar European cinema—especially the New Wave—brought the movies back into the mainstream of Modernism (to which they had not been widely considered central since the 1920s, when the works of Keaton and Vertov, for example, were as Modernist as anything by Stein or Joyce), the key 20th-century movement that produced nonrepresentational painting, atonal music, absurd drama, and the stream-of-consciousness novel, and whose tenets included the self-conscious questioning of all social and moral values, the duty to "make it new," the study of perception, the determination to work creatively with fragmentation (from Cubism to montage), and the self-conscious manipulation of the conventions of the art itself. If the first major Modernist film was *Intolerance* and the best known for decades was *Battleship Potemkin*, the audiences of the 1950s and 1960s recognized the breakthroughs made by filmmakers from Rossellini to Resnais, and an invigorated social and intellectual discussion found the movies crucial both to art and to political analysis. The years after 1945 were a great period in film history, one in which wave after wave of European directors and writers had something to say and knew how to say it.

Italian Neorealism

Not since 1914 had Italy been an important international film power. Early Italian sound films traveled between the two poles of pro-Mussolini propaganda and of escapist comedies, historical spectacles, and musical romances, so-called "White Telephone" pictures (because of the inevitable white telephone in the fancily decorated apartments that served as sets for these films). Mussolini extended considerable aid to the film industry, founding both a huge film studio (Cinecittà) and a film school (Centro Sperimentale). Although opposite the Soviets in ideology, Mussolini believed just as firmly in the persuasive power of cinema to shape a people. Like the Germans and Japanese, Mussolini banned the importing of American films—an isolation that protected the Italian populace from American contamination and the Italian film industry from American competition, allowing its consolidation into a native cinema that was commercially vigorous if artistically dead. The occasional work of great artistic merit that dared to concentrate on important social, political, and philosophical matters—such as Goffredo Alessandrini's *We the Living* (1942; U.S. release 1988), based on the novel by Ayn Rand—was confiscated by the Fascist authorities or—like Visconti's *Ossessione*—recut after a brief release. If society, art, sex, politics, and independent thought were problematic, economics was untouchable: Any portrayal of unemployment was absolutely forbidden.

After the overthrow of Mussolini and the expulsion of the Nazis from the country and of the Fascists from power, the Italian filmmakers, highly experienced in film production, used the new freedom to combine their skill in making pictures with the subjects about which they wanted to make pictures.

Roberto Rossellini

Even as the Nazis were evacuating Rome, Roberto Rossellini began to work on *Open City* (*Roma, città aperta*, 1945). An "open city" is one that is immune from attack because it has been declared demilitarized, as Rome was. Rossellini made the film under the most difficult conditions, closely resembling the early production problems of the Soviets: Raw film stock was scarce, money for constructing sets was even scarcer, actors were difficult to find, slickness and polish were

Fig. 13-1   *Fig. 13-2*

Open City: *From the death of a single valiant priest (Fig. 13-1, Aldo Fabrizi), the boys walk back to the city, arm in arm.*

impossible without the controlled lighting of studio filming. Rossellini turned defects into virtues. He willingly sacrificed polish for authenticity, sets for real locations, fiction for life. Rossellini often preferred laborers and peasants to actors (a parallel with Eisenstein and Pudovkin). He and cinematographer Ubaldo Arata carried their camera all over and fleetingly shot the real city on the run.

Open City (written by Sergio Amidei, Rossellini, and Fellini, who also collaborated on *Paisan*) contrasts the humane, committed, unified struggle of the Italian people for freedom—the unity of priests, workers, intellectuals, adults, children—with the brutality of the Nazi invaders, who used the most loathsome methods (torture, bribery, addiction) to enslave the weakest Italians or to force them to betray their fellows. The two styles of the film—the natural, open, realistic, crisply lit texture of the scenes with the Resistance figures and the cramped, artificial, shadowy texture of the scenes with the Nazis—support the film's thematic contrast.

At the end of the film a single member of the Resistance, a committed priest (Don Pietro, played by Aldo Fabrizi), is executed by the Nazi oppressors for his service to the people. This priest is a notable political exception (the Italian clergy generally supported Mussolini's Fascist government), and his alliance with the Resistance is also an alliance with the Communists who led it. As the partisan priest dies, Rossellini's camera captures the activities of the children of Rome and a far shot of the city itself, for from the death of this one man

will come a solidarity that was to be the hope of the new Rome. *Open City* became the unofficial cornerstone of a new movement in Italian cinema—Neorealism, a "new realism" characterized by the use of nonprofessional actors and realistic dialogue, an emphasis on the everyday struggles of common people and the unvarnished look of nonstudio reality, and the determination to present the characters in relation to their real social environments and political and economic conditions.

Rossellini's next film, *Paisan* (1946), further defined his commitments. A collection of separate vignettes, each of the film's six sequences moves progressively north with the Allied invasion and Nazi retreat. Despite its documentary structure, mirroring the movement of the campaign, Rossellini concentrates on the human texture within each of the vignettes—some lighter and some more brutal, some dominated by the imagery of battle-scarred cities and some by the apparent placidity of the countryside. As is usual for Rossellini, he neither makes simple judgments nor takes simple positions; he is neither for nor against the insensitivities of the invading liberators and neither for nor against the Italians, themselves terribly divided by the struggle. Rossellini's camera, managed by Otello Martelli, records the luminous countryside in which the struggle takes place, seemingly unaffected by the brutal battle within it. The counterpoint between human action and the landscape that contains it would remain Rossellini's dominant visual technique and personal theme.

Rossellini completed this "War Trilogy" with *Germany Year Zero* (1947), in which he examined the rubble, hunger, and unemployment of postwar Berlin. Edmund (played by Edmund Meschke), a resourceful 12-year-old, is the sole support of his family, struggling to survive in the bombed-out city where civilization is as ruined as the buildings. By the end of the film, the boy has killed himself by jumping off a gutted building, an emblem of the world that looks as if it could never be reconstructed and whose children are at a dead end. This bleak and scrupulously realistic tale, shot on location in Berlin in 1947, is related in an objective tone, but it reveals in the opening voice-over its compassionate hope that German children will "relearn to love life."

Rossellini then tracked inward from cross-sectional surveys of an entire society to close studies of personal moralities and internal sensations—featuring Ingrid Bergman, the great star who defied Hollywood propriety and world opinion by abandoning her husband to remain with Rossellini in Italy. (Their daughter, Isabella Rossellini, became a famous actress in her own right, particularly with the 1986 release of David Lynch's *Blue Velvet*.) In *Stromboli* (1949), scripted by Amidei, Bergman plays a war refugee from Northern Europe, desperately seeking a new life with an Italian husband on a tiny island off the Italian coast. The isolation of the primitive island and its brutal people, the craggy rock of the treeless volcanic soil, the gleaming white houses baking in the brilliant and brutal sun all metaphorically imply the woman's loneliness,

frustration, and isolation. Rossellini's landscape reflects her internal state, a stranger in a strange land, tied to a small-minded, old-fashioned man, as unresponsive to her needs as the soil on which she walks. At the end, she both transcends her situation and comes to terms with it largely by confronting the landscape.

Viaggio in Italia (*Voyage to Italy*, 1953), one of Rossellini's greatest works, began his move away from Neorealism. A British couple (Ingrid Bergman and George Sanders) travels to Naples to settle the property and business affairs of a deceased relative. Rossellini depicts their emotional distance from each other by their emotional distance from the countryside and its customs. Their clothing is wrong for the weather; their habits are insensitive to native custom. But simply by walking around and observing—Rossellini's awesome visual recording of the statues in a museum, of the ruins of Pompeii, of the bubbling volcanic lava of Vesuvius—the woman especially begins to feel the fertile energy of that vital setting called "Italy."

Sightseeing becomes a powerful moral and emotional force. By seeing these sights, the man and woman begin to internalize their visual resonances, giving them at least some hope of continuing together in the future. For Rossellini to convert sightseeing into a poetic force is to redefine the landscape—as Antonioni would do later—as the companion of consciousness. Landscape and architecture are important elements of his 1960s and 1970s films, which analyze historical and philosophical structures with rigor and brilliance and whose camerawork is tight and understated; most of them, including *The Rise to Power of Louis XIV* (1966), were made for TV. Rossellini's ability to render the moral, emotional, architectural, philosophical, and poetic power of sights and systems would make him a major influence on a new generation of directors in both Italy and France.

De Sica and Zavattini

Cesare Zavattini, who wrote virtually all of Vittorio De Sica's Neorealist films, defined the principles of the movement: to show things as they are, not as they seem, nor as the bourgeoisie would prefer them to appear; to write fictions about the human side of representative social, political, and economic conditions; to shoot on

Fig. 13-3
The power of sightseeing in Viaggio in Italia.

Fig. 13-4
The Bicycle Thief: *Father (Lamberto Maggiorani) and son (Enzo Staiola) search for the irreplaceable bicycle.*

location wherever possible; to use untrained actors in the majority of roles; to capture and reflect reality with little or no compromise; to depict common people rather than overdressed heroes and fantasy role models; to reveal the everyday rather than the exceptional; and to show a person's relationship to the real social environment rather than to his or her romantic dreams. As can be seen from the last of these tenets, the movement was as opposed to Expressionism as it was to Hollywood. The Neorealist film developed the influence of the social environment on basic human needs: the need for food, shelter, work, love, family, sex, honor. In the tradition of Marxist thought (yet another parallel with the classic Soviet films), the Neorealist films repeatedly show that unjust and perverted social structures threaten to pervert or destroy essential human values.

Vittorio De Sica became the most popular Italian Neorealist with American audiences, probably because his melodramas effectively combined the political, the sentimental, and the traditional story—as opposed to the detached ironies, paradoxical observations, conceptual framing, and elliptical narratives of Rossellini. De Sica, a popular stage and film actor in the 1930s and, at first, a director of escapist fluff films, directed the Neorealist *Shoeshine* in 1946 (script by Zavattini), a brutally poignant study of the destruction of a pair of Roman boys by both the gangsters and the police who are using them. *Shoeshine* was preceded by *The Children Are Watching Us* (shot in 1942 but not released until 1944), a transitional film, co-written by Zavattini, in which suicide—a taboo subject—and other realistic elements were presented; it has an uncompromising ending in which a boy rejects his mother for having a love affair that led to his father's death. With this film, De Sica left fluff and tales of adolescent romance behind, and he began to work with Zavattini exclusively (though other writers contributed to some of the scripts). *The Bicycle Thief* (1948, Zavattini's most important script) is a study of degradation and pain. Its literal title, *Bicycle Thieves* (*Ladri di biciclette*), is more appropriate than the accepted American translation because there are two thieves in the film: the man who steals the protagonist's bike and the protagonist himself (Antonio, played by Lamberto Maggiorani), who eventually becomes a bicycle thief out of necessity.

From the film's opening shots De Sica and Zavattini begin their relentless development of the kind of social environment that turns men into bicycle thieves: There are many men without work; there are very few jobs; the men have wives and children to support; the man with a bicycle is one of the lucky working few. To get his bicycle out of the pawn shop (for a job pasting up posters all over the city—for *Gilda*, a glamorous American *noir*), Antonio's wife takes her wedding sheets to pawn in exchange for the bike. The poignancy of her sacrifice is underscored by De Sica's long shot of piles of pawned bridal sheets—others have been forced to make the same sacrifice. De Sica's camera emphasizes the quantities of people and things that are embraced by this story rather than implying that this is a tale of the exceptional few. The film is filled with panning or tracking shots of rows and rows of men, of houses, of bicycles.

The film's powerfully simple narrative premise is Antonio's desperate need to find his stolen bicycle. Without the bicycle he has no job; without a job his family starves. The man and his young son, Bruno (Enzo Staiola), roam the streets, catching an occasional glimpse of the bike or the figure who stole it. Throughout the film the boy's relationship with his father serves as barometer of the effects of the agonizing search on the man's soul. Father and son drift further apart; the man even strikes the boy. When Antonio finally corners the thief, the thief's mother and neighbors protect him, and neither the police nor the local Mafia are any help, since Antonio has no evidence.

Realizing the impossibility of ever getting his own bicycle back, Antonio is tempted by the sight of the many unattended bikes around him. In desperation, he steals a bicycle himself, is swiftly caught, and then is beaten and abused by the angry citizens. Bruno sees his father's ultimate degradation. When the father tries to hurry away from the boy in shame, Bruno catches up with him and slips his hand inside his father's. Despite the terrible social humiliation, the humanity and affection of father and son have been restored. Then they disappear into a crowd of people who, the film implies, are struggling with analogous problems; this tragedy, made from such unglamorous materials, is one among thousands.

De Sica claimed that an American producer offered him millions to make *Bicycle Thieves* with Cary Grant as Antonio. De Sica rejected both the money and the star. Instead, he cast a metal worker, a nonactor, as the desperate father. De Sica's preference reveals many of the principles of Neorealism: authenticity rather than pretense, earthiness rather than sparkle, the common man rather than the idol. Instead of Hollywood's bright sets and stylish clothes, these films showed primitive kitchens, squalid living rooms, peeling walls, torn clothing, streets that almost stank of urine and garbage (no telephones here, much less white ones!). Instead of the Hollywood love goddess, the Neorealist heroine incarnate was Anna Magnani: coarse, fiery, indefatigable, sexual, strong, sweaty. Zavattini claimed that the Neorealist film was as attached to the present as sweat was to skin.

It is worth noting that *The Bicycle Thief* and *Open City* were edited by the same man. One of the most versatile editors in film history, Eraldo Da Roma edited the major films of Rossellini, De Sica, and Antonioni.

The essential theme of the Neorealist film was the conflict between the contemporary common person and the immense social, economic, and political forces that determined his or her existence: first the war, after it the means of making a living and the struggle to keep a home and family together. In the late 1940s, many Italian directors developed their own variations on this essential theme: Alessandro Blasetti's *Un giorno nella vita* (1946); Luigi Zampa's *Vivere in pace* (1946), *L'onorevole Angelina* (1947), and *Anni difficili* (1948, script by Amidei); Alberto Lattuada's *The Crime of Giovanni Episcopo* (1947) and *Senza pietà* (1948); Giuseppe de

Santis's *Caccia tragica* (1947) and *Bitter Rice* (1949). In many of these films, despite the social squalor and economic misery surrounding them, the central figures succeed in asserting their humanity. The films are about misery without surrendering to misery.

But by 1950 Neorealism had either run or begun to change its course. The new stability of postwar Europe, the new prosperity of the Italian film industry, or the new Andreotti Law (which simultaneously supported film production but denied export permits to any film that depicted Italian society unfavorably) shifted the Italian film's focus away from the sociological struggle with squalor. The films became increasingly psychological and less sociological. Although critics tried to elucidate the continuity of the movement by coining terms like "Poetic Neorealism" or "Historical Neorealism," such terms were not quite compatible with the original Neorealist premise. The Italian film for the international market, while still valuing the realist actor and the realist milieu, had begun to use more polished scripts, more carefully constructed sets, more conventional fictional structures and themes, and professional actors. Even the original Neorealist directors wandered away from earlier styles and themes.

De Sica and Zavattini made a utopian folk fantasy, *Miracle in Milan* (1950), a joyous combination of political and Christian myth, and *Umberto D.* (1952), a wrenching film of typical De Sica pathos, far more interested in Umberto's personal feelings than in the social problem of old-age benefits. De Sica, however, probably strayed least from the original Neorealist principles, as his later *The Roof* (1956) and *Two Women* (1960) show. Sophia Loren won an Academy Award for her ability to play an unglamorous, Anna-Magnaniesque woman in *Two Women*, valiantly fighting the classic problems of Neorealism: the war, hunger, and the assault on her family.

Fig. 13-5
The Sicilian fishing boats of La terra trema.

In *The Garden of the Finzi-Continis* (1971), De Sica and Zavattini again depicted the struggle against the viciousness of social systems and the brutalities of war; even so, this late film—with its nostalgic look back at the world of the rich and its lush color pictorialism—seemed antithetical to the style and spirit of the earlier, earthier De Sica. But in their final collaboration, *A Brief Vacation* (1973, De Sica's last film), they told the story of a working-class woman who, to be cured of tuberculosis, takes the only vacation of her life in *The Magic Mountain*–like retreats of the rich. Here the glossy look of the sanitarium—and the concerns of the rich—contrast effectively with the dim, brutal, unchanged world to which she must return.

Luchino Visconti

The potential direction of Italian realism was predicted by a much earlier film: Luchino Visconti's *Ossessione* (*Obsession*, 1942, released 1943). Visconti's film, an unauthorized adaptation of James M. Cain's novel of sexual sordidness and murder, *The Postman Always Rings Twice*, uses squalid settings and realistic rather than romantic human types as background for its personal, psychological action. Social realism becomes the film's milieu, its soil, rather than its subject. Visconti's films consistently depart from the Zavattini definitions, using the social reality to define the personal problems of the characters rather than as the focus of the films themselves. For this reason, Visconti felt equally comfortable in the social reality of contemporary lower-class life: *Ossessione*, *La terra trema* (*The Earth Trembles*, 1948), *Rocco and His Brothers* (1960), shot in black and white—or historical sumptuousness: *Senso* (1954), *The Leopard* (1963), *Death in Venice* (1971), shot in color.

Of the three major Neorealist directors, Visconti had the most elegant visual sensibility, an almost sensuously formal approach to camera movement and composition. An aristocrat and Marxist, Visconti made the most uncompromisingly authentic of Neorealist pictures (*La terra trema*, shot in a dialect most Italians could not understand) and the most artificial of grand romantic meditations (*Senso*, *Death in Venice*); the contradictions of his tastes and concerns were reconciled in the operatic approach he took to all his subjects. The long takes—three or four

minutes each in *La terra trema*—that pan and track from one brilliant composition to another; the fixation on the characters' environments and tools (whether they were real, as in *La terra trema*, or carefully chosen props and stylized sets); the vision that was at once tragic, romantic, skeptical, hard-edged, and ecstatic; and the integrated revelation of character, morality, and *mise-en-scène* are consistent throughout his work. An excess of desire and a commitment to analysis characterized not only Visconti's films, but also those of the next generation of Italian masters, from Fellini to Pasolini.

Romantics and Antiromantics

Federico Fellini

Although Federico Fellini's apprenticeship was to Rossellini and Amidei on the screenplays for *Open City*, *Paisan*, and *The Miracle*, Fellini's own films reveal the flamboyant romantic. He preferred the places of mystery, magic, and make-believe—the circus, the variety theatre, the nightclub, the opera house—to the slums of reality. His characters search for happiness, for love, for meaning, not for social security. If Anna Magnani or Ingrid Bergman is the soul of Rossellini's Neorealism, Giulietta Masina is the soul of Fellini, his wife offscreen—she survived him by only a few months—and the central figure of many of his films, including *La strada* (*The Road*, 1954) and *Nights of Cabiria* (1956), two of his greatest. Giulietta Masina, with the glowing eyes, the smirking mouth, the deep dimples, wildly joyful, wildly sad, is to Anna Magnani as a sunbeam is to a lion. In both *La strada* and *Cabiria* Masina plays a pure spirit of love, a being of the heart.

In the earlier film, Masina is Gelsomina, the clownish fool, apprenticed to the strong man, Zampanò (Anthony Quinn), who uses her as servant, performer, cook, and concubine—human chattel. Despite her rough treatment from the boorish animal–man, Gelsomina comes to love him. But he—afraid of human commitment, of emotional strings—betrays her, leaving her alone to die in the snow. He kills her in the same careless and callous way that he killed that other clownish soul, the acrobat (Richard Basehart) who had felt the rays of Gelsomina's hypnotic passion. Only after Gelsomina is dead, when the strong man hears the haunting, sweet–sad song that she once played on her trumpet, does the strong man learn how weak and alone he is.

As Cabiria, Giulietta Masina plays once again the spirit of love trampled by the realities of human selfishness. Cabiria is the pure-hearted whore, forced to sell her love since no one wants it for nothing. The film opens with a boyfriend's stealing her purse and throwing her in the river. Later, a more serious lover does much the same. Cabiria's final disillusionment is the ultimate magnification of the opening scene, the comedy of the opening scene turned tragic. But Cabiria does not die. In the ironic and metaphorical ending, the weeping Cabiria encounters a group of festive, singing youngsters as she walks on the road back to town (and, metaphorically, to life). They sing as she sobs; they do not notice her tears; their singing does not stop her tears, but she continues walking with them, participating vicariously in their song. The laughter and tears of Cabiria's life, of Everyman's life, have been brilliantly juxtaposed.

Fellini's greatest international success was *La dolce vita* (*The Sweet Life*, 1960, U.S. release 1961). In this wide-screen epic of the superficiality of modern life, with its unforgettable score by Nino Rota (who wrote the music for Fellini's major films as well as for *The Godfather*) and stellar performance by Marcello Mastroianni, Fellini deserted Neorealism forever; in fact, there had been little of it in his work since *I vitelloni* (1953). Even his first picture, *Variety Lights* (1950, co-directed with Alberto Lattuada), is in love with clowns and the stage from the start. From *La dolce vita* on, Fellini would be best known for fast-paced movies that were at once carnivalesque and introspective.

The contrast between sensuality and spirituality dominates *La dolce vita* from its first sequence, in which a helicopter pilot, towing a statue of Christ, looks down and waves at three women in bikinis, sunning themselves on a Roman roof. The film's themes are already clear: Christ has been petrified; he is a tool of the modern world (the helicopter); people have lost faith without finding an adequate substitute. Showing the effects of this moral superficiality, Fellini continues for three hours, contrasting

Fig. 13-6
La strada: *Zampanò (Anthony Quinn) and Gelsomina (Giulietta Masina).*

sensual things—nightclubs, orgiastic parties—with the corruption of spiritual things—an intellectual commits suicide, children pretend to see a miraculous vision. But excess is part of his point, even this numbing excess of schematic examples. There is too much of everything in this film—everything but what the characters really need: some fulfilling kind of peace and self-knowledge. The hedonistic, narcissistic, highly publicized "sweet life" is an existential vacuum.

Fellini continued to examine the duality between sensuality and spirituality throughout his career. *Fellini Satyricon* (1969) synthesized the sensual and the spiritual by pushing the purity of sensual expression to its limit, so that this elevation of the sensual became an apotheosis of spirit as well (*Casanova*, 1976, attempted the same synthesis). *Satyricon* is a hypnotic journey through a Surrealistic narrative world that, like Fellini's other circuses (his primary image for the world of art), is an endless and self-sufficient procession of masks and thrills and dangers, a place full of cages, a place to be free.

What characterizes and energizes Fellini's work is a romantic rebelliousness and an ambivalent reaction to the grotesque. A consistent Fellini target is the Roman Catholic Church. For Fellini, the Church is a hypocritical and empty show that bilks its public by playing on its insecurities and fears. The Church is the archsensualist masquerading as a spiritualist, hiding its confusion behind a mask of dogma and ritual. In *Nights of Cabiria*, a society of human unfortunates takes a desperate outing to a religious festival, where they are greeted by canned prayers on loudspeakers and greedy vendors hawking sacred candles and secular candies. In *8½* (1963), the Church offers the main character not spiritual guidance but a ritualistic structure of nostalgia and guilt. *Fellini Roma* (1972) includes a monstrously funny clerical fashion show.

Whereas Fellini treats organized religion with grotesque bitterness and comical contempt, he treats the glamorous world of the rich with a stylish grotesqueness that reveals both its emptiness and its fascination. The patrons of the health spa in *8½*, the orgiasts in *Fellini Satyricon*, and the first-class passengers in *And the Ship Sails On* (1983) are all examples of the grotesque—in costume, make up, gestures, features, shapes, sizes—that Fellini finds hauntingly attractive.

Juliet of the Spirits (1965), his first color film, uses bright colors to make the wealthy sensualists even more beautiful–ugly. (The previous year, Antonioni put color to subtler uses in *Red Desert*.)

Fellini's greatest film, his most impressive synthesis of dramatic power, personal vision, and cinematic control, may well be *8½*. (Before this, Fellini had directed six features and three "half films"—two episodes in compilation films and one co-directed feature; *8½* is named only as Fellini's 8½th movie.) Perhaps the quintessential postwar Modernist feature, the subject of *8½* is simply itself. It is not merely about filmmaking (like Truffaut's *Day for Night*); it is about the making of a film very much like this one: a film the director finds impossible to make. The protagonist of *8½* (Guido, played by Marcello Mastroianni) is a director himself. Because of his nervousness and tension, he is relaxing, preparing for his next film, at a fashionable health spa. Preparing for the project, the director is flooded with images out of his film and memories out of his life. He puts his living relationships into fictional structures; he draws his fictional ideas from his personal experiences of the past and present (just as Fellini does with more tenderness and less agony a decade later in *Amarcord*, 1973). The director's emotional problem in the film is wondering whether he is successful at either life or art. His memories and fantasies not only intrude on the action but become it; the filmmaker's mindscreens and his moviemaking project unfold together, in a brilliantly integrated construct of stress and desire, analysis and nostalgia.

At the end, Guido attends a gala party for his film. Unable to resolve his personal conflicts or to finish the film, he imagines crawling under a table and shooting himself. The party becomes a gigantic circus comprising all the characters of his memories and his film. Fellini's camera swirls in an excited circle as the parade of Guido's creatures dances about a circus ring, that familiar Fellini setting. Guido stares at the dancing creatures; he then steps into their circle and joins the dance. His life is what it is; his art is what it is. There is nothing for him to do but live it and create it. The artist's tension has been resolved in acts of acceptance and reflexivity; he cannot be separated from the dancing ring of his

Fig. 13-7

8½: *the artist (Marcello Mastroianni) among his memories and fantasies.*

thoughts, his loves, his creations, his memories—and his original, innocent love of art. The film that could not be made has been abandoned, but *8½* has been completed. Whatever Guido's (and Fellini's) deficiencies as a human being, he is a maker of films. That is his act in the big circus.

Michelangelo Antonioni

Like Fellini's, Michelangelo Antonioni's roots were in Neorealism. While Rossellini and De Sica were making their documentary-style features, Antonioni was making documentary shorts about the lives of street cleaners and farmers. But Antonioni soon deserted the documentary for the highly polished and understated drama of perceptions, emotions, epiphanies, moods—eventually to return to documentary filmmaking for the 1972 *Chung Kuo Cina*, shot in the People's Republic of China. Antonioni, who died in 2007, was as much an Abstract Expressionist painter as a documentary photographer. His series of 184 paintings, "Montagne Encantate" (Enchanted Mountain), reveals some of his visual values. These are colorful representations of living rocks, vaguely sensuous landscapes dominated by clashes of color and contrasts of

forms. Such enigmatic shapes, charged with ambiguous significance, would dominate Antonioni's films as well, their evocative landscapes closer to Rossellini's disciplined psychological imagery (and, in France, Robert Bresson's pure, severe, unsentimental, understated intensity) than to Fellini's flamboyance or Zavattini's Neorealism. While Neorealism used the external social environment to define a human being, Antonioni found a way to present landscape and character as an integrated mystery—a subtle Expressionism in the service of psychological, sociological, and philosophical insight.

After making seven short documentaries (1943–50) and directing his first features, including *Cronaca di un amore* (*Chronicle of a Love*, 1950) and *I vinti* (*The Vanquished*, 1952), and doing even better work on *Le amiche* (*The Girlfriends*, 1955) and *Il grido* (*The Cry*, 1957), Antonioni achieved complete mastery over his method with *L'avventura* (*The Adventure*, 1960), the first film of a trilogy that includes *La notte* (*The Night*, 1960) and *L'eclisse* (*Eclipse*, 1962). In declaring a new Italian cinema, this trilogy was at least as significant as *La dolce vita* and *8½*, partly because the two filmmakers were so stylistically assured and such opposites. If Fellini's films are

The white wall in L'avventura.

Fig. 13-8

fast, flamboyant, grotesque, and richly emotional, Antonioni's are slow, spare, unwilling to draw pointed conclusions, and often about characters who are unable to feel deeply—or to be sure what it is they feel.

Antonioni's method concentrates as much on the scenic environment as on the people in it. The environment reflects the people, and not just socially. The emotional resonances of the environment convey the internal states of the people within it. Antonioni's favorite photographic subjects include both nature—for example, the sea and rocks in *L'avventura*—and the slick, hard-surfaced materials of modern architecture: glass, aluminum, terrazzo. The angular furniture, the stony objects, and the glossy floor of the apartment at the beginning of *L'eclisse* brilliantly evoke the coldness, the emptiness, the deadness in an alienated relationship as Vittoria (Monica Vitti) breaks off with her lover. *La notte* begins with a similar feeling of cold alienation, created by the shiny windows and slick, bare corridors of the hospital where an author and his wife (Marcello Mastroianni and Jeanne Moreau) visit a dying friend. The beginning of *Blowup* (1966, based on a story by Julio Cortázar and shot in London) surrounds a group of carnivalesque merry-makers with wet, shiny terrazzo courtyards and aluminum-and-glass apartment buildings. The beginnings of Antonioni films

consistently use the environment to define both the film's social milieu and its emotional climate. The ending of *Eclipse* may be unique in film history: It presents the location where the main characters have *not* shown up and spends in a study of the sounds and details of the meeting-place the screen time they would have spent together.

Other Antonioni environments come to mind, many of them reminiscent of his paintings: the rocky barren island where the barren holidaymakers search for Anna in *L'avventura;* the steel flag-poles with the ropes hollowly clanging against them in *L'eclisse;* the gray-brown ugliness of the factory belching smoke in the color masterpiece *Il deserto rosso* (*Red Desert*, 1964); the compelling desert of *Zabriskie Point* (1970, shot in Death Valley). Perhaps Antonioni's favorite object for emotional definition is the white wall: Sandro's flat in *L'avventura*, the hospital corridors in *La notte*, the hotel corridor in *Red Desert*, the photographer's studio in *Blowup*. The Antonioni character's feeling of affinity with the hard white wall is emphasized by a piece of business that recurs through many of the films: The character stands against the wall and then circles the room, back and palms pressing against the plaster.

A cliché of Antonioni criticism is that all his characters live lives that are boring and empty, meaningless and sterile, and that his films are accordingly boring, sterile, and abstract. But *La notte* has a deep emotional power that sneaks up on you, and *Blowup* does not deny meaning but complicates our view of its nature. Ironically, most of Antonioni's characters manage to survive (Jack Nicholson in *The Passenger*, 1975, is an exception). Most of the central Antonioni figures find some value that helps them live. And what they learn most often is how to live with ambiguity. Like the characters, the films struggle to communicate things that are almost impossible to put into words or express in actions and images. With great effort, Antonioni's movies communicate emotional and moral states that can never be entirely clear or resolved.

Antonioni de-emphasizes words for two reasons. First, words are not a very effective tool for communicating states of feeling. Vague, imprecise feelings of loneliness, uneasiness, and angst do not lend themselves to the terse summary required of movie dialogue. Second, there is much more to human interaction than communicating. "Our drama," he once said, "is noncommunication." *Red Desert* contains Antonioni's ultimate metaphor for the irrelevance of words when the heroine addresses her lengthiest and most explicit revelation of her innermost feelings to a Turkish sailor who cannot understand a word of the Italian she is speaking. His 1995 *Beyond the Clouds* (based on several of his short stories, with linking scenes directed by Wim Wenders), another film about love and silence, touching and not touching, waiting without meeting, and insight and misunderstanding, opens with two people who in any other movie could be an ideal romantic couple. Instead they *almost* get together, and the space between them becomes the romantic subject.

L'avventura may be Antonioni's most completely realized film. It is at once rewarding and frustrating, stunning and boring, uplifting and depressing. When a group of friends go on an adventure to an uninhabited island, Anna (Lea Massari) disappears; her lover, Sandro (Gabriele Ferzetti), and her best friend, Claudia (Monica Vitti), try to find her. Sandro and Claudia eventually become lovers—and never do find Anna. Despite the impression that the plot wanders, it travels steadily toward its final, ambiguous moment of reconciliation and compassion in which Claudia can feel sympathy for the weakness of Sandro and in which Sandro can feel the terrible pathos of his need to betray Claudia.

But if Sandro's education is to discover the human weakness that makes betrayal so inevitable (and education is the subject of most Antonioni films), Claudia's education is to discover that betrayal is a fact of human life. "Human" and "fallible" are unfortunately synonymous; any meaningful human relationship may have to start from that definition. *L'avventura* is a journey and adventure that bring Sandro and

Fig. 13-9

Clutching at love: Monica Vitti and Gabriele Ferzetti in L'avventura.

Claudia to that potential starting point, but their relationship may be over. The ending of the film is both open and final; *L'avventura* leaves many questions unanswered—What happened to Anna? What will happen to Sandro and Claudia?—and is complete. It offers figures in a landscape that is often more interesting than they are, and it has no interest in genre or formula. For all its emotional complexity, it is beyond the characters that *L'avventura*, like other Antonioni films, finds a coherence that can be expressed only by the camera.

If *L'avventura* is the fullest and most sensitive statement of Antonioni's vision, *Red Desert*, his first color film, is the most revealing of his technique. Its revolutionary, self-conscious use of color inspired Fellini, Resnais, Godard, and others to work in color, though few were so bold as to re-paint real landscapes to get the hues they desired, as Antonioni did in *Red Desert* and *Blowup*. After *Ivan the Terrible, Part II* (1946), *Red Desert* is the next crucial step in the history of Expressionistic color filmmaking; the next major advance would come with Kurosawa's *Dodes'ka-den* (1970).

Color in the film is not Fellini's flamboyant, saturated show but Antonioni's subtle use of the environment to mirror the character's internal states and, ultimately, to communicate the film's subject. *Red Desert* often uses a long lens that blurs the background into a mass of indistinguishable colors; that effect mirrors the way Giulia (the protagonist, played by Monica Vitti) sees color: frightening, aggressive, uncontrollable, indistinguishable, out of focus. She is so uncomfortable with colors—in fact oppressed, threatened, overwhelmed, and even erased by them—that she cannot pick one to cover the walls of her shop. Giulia's discomfort with colors is a metaphor for her discomfort with the reality that surrounds her—all of its sights, sounds, smells, uncertainties. In a later sequence in the engineer's hotel room, the walls change color from their original hard gray to warm pink. The walls are now pink because Giulia feels them pink, with her body next to a warm, strong man. He, ironically, cares neither how she feels nor how she feels the walls.

Though Antonioni's method disparages words, he does not forget sounds. Sound is a crucial element in *Red Desert* and in all Antonioni films (even his deliberate silences reveal a knowledge of the power of sound). In *Red Desert* sound and color operate similarly. Giulia sees her everyday life as a grayish, poisonous, choking existence, punctuated by the frightening, grotesque colors of the factory pipes (hence the gray–brownishness of the shots of the factory, the mud, the fog, and the striking blues and oranges of the pipelines). Accompanying the shots of the oppressive factory are the incessant thumping, beating, chugging noises of the factory machines on the soundtrack.

Nevertheless, the ending of *Red Desert* is relatively positive. Just as she did in the opening sequence, Giulia walks by the factory, which is still belching its poisonous smoke. Her young son asks whether the smoke will kill the little birds that might fly through it. Giulia answers that the birds have long since learned not to fly through the smoke.

Pasolini and Bertolucci

The two most interesting and influential Italian *auteurs* to emerge in the mid-1960s were Pier Paolo Pasolini and Bernardo Bertolucci. Like most of the earlier Neorealists, both were Marxists who sought to combine a passion for politics with a passion for cinema. But if Bertolucci was a romantic, Pasolini was profoundly antiromantic. If a bird were to fly through the smoke of a factory chimney in a Pasolini film, it would find itself not just choking but being eaten alive by the owner of the factory.

Pasolini began his career as a street bum and a poet. All his life, he wrote poetry and interrogated systems. He was expelled from the Italian Communist Party in 1949 because of his homosexuality. "Rational and irrational to the utmost," as he said of himself in a poem, he began making films in the Neorealist mode—the protagonist of *Accattone* (*Beggar*, 1961) is a poor, brash young man in a Roman slum, trying to earn enough money to survive—but soon was questioning and exploding its conventions. Abandoning Neorealism but not the poor and not the question of power, Pasolini made elliptical, satiric, and often brutal films about moral and political degradation and the poetry of rebellion.

Bertolucci's first major success, *Before the Revolution* (1964), set the pattern for his more famous films to follow—a study of the interrelationship between political structures and sexual or emotional fulfillment. While Pasolini's films are more abstract, more complexly structured, and more ferociously aggressive moral–political investigations, enlivened and propelled by dazzling bursts of unforgettable imagery, Bertolucci's conform to a more familiar narrative pattern, which combines political events in a particular society with richly rendered characters, emotionally expressive color settings, and carefully structured strings of narrative action, sinuous but linear (like the rich movements of his camera). Bertolucci might be thought of as combining the leftist social conscience of a Zavattini with the more intimately psychological and sexual perceptions of a Visconti or Antonioni. Pasolini was more the Eisenstein or Vertov of Italian political cinema (like the two Soviet masters, Pasolini wrote rich and complex theoretical essays on film "language" as a form of visual–intellectual poetry) while Bertolucci was more its Pudovkin.

In Pasolini's *Teorema* (*Theorem*, 1968), its very title informing us that it is a logical demonstration, a beautiful young man—a kind of angel—succeeds in blasting apart the apparently solid foundations of a bourgeois family by making every member of it fall in love with him—the maid, daughter, artist son (whose notions of truth

and beauty are so devastated by the confrontation that his "action painting" becomes a process of urinating on canvas), mother, and high-finance businessman father. At the end of the film, the businessman has been so overwhelmed by his passion, his commitment to a forbidden, anti-bourgeois love, that he wanders about the town's railroad station, seeking to pick up hustlers. The final image of the film shows him wandering in a wasteland, naked, the rocks and sand of the hilly desert seething with volcanic steam. The grand bourgeois has been stripped of all the moral, social, and political apparatus by which he lived his life—no clothes, no sense of direction, no civilization, no concrete location, no purpose, a total moral and social leper. The theorem that underlies this stripping process is, quite simply, that sexual passion knows no moral or social boundaries and that those who least know this truth are the most easily overwhelmed by the discovery of the flimsy assumptions on which their lives are based. His next film, *Porcile* (*Pigsty*, also called *Pigpen*, 1969), was about cannibalism, bestiality, and capitalism.

Salò (1975) was Pasolini's last film before he was murdered in a sexual incident that might well have occurred in one of his films. Based on the Marquis de Sade's *The 120 Days of Sodom*

Salò: *sexual slavery as a metaphor for moral and political bondage.*

Fig. 13-10

(which also inspired the ending of Buñuel and Dalí's *L'Age d'or*) and named for the northern lake town that was Mussolini's last capital (as the Fascist government withdrew steadily toward the Austrian border), *Salò* is an even more extreme, aggressive, and repellent allegorical theorem than *Teorema*. In this piece of cinema cruelty (in Antonin Artaud's sense of the term), the audience is subjected to a horrifying vision of political totalitarianism disguised as sadomasochistic sexuality. In 1943, four pillars of Italian Fascistic society—a duke, a priest, a judge, and a banker—gather a specially selected group of beautiful boys and girls in a mansion and then proceed to make them perform every imaginable sexual atrocity for their own pleasure. The young people are permitted to indulge in any sexual wish, so long as it is not a natural or tender one. Pasolini fills the screen with orgies of sexual torture and oppression—buggery, voyeurism, casual murder, pornographic songs and stories (a vital part of the dirty old men's pleasure), mutilation, branding, scalping, the consumption of human feces. And yet this cruel, obscene, ironic film is uncompromisingly ethical. Presenting Fascism in all its horror and absolutely rejecting it, the film refuses to express a conventional, holier-than-thou preference for the "normal"; instead it problematizes the normal.

His other films, all of which rejected studio values, varied greatly in structure and tone, alternating among the shattering allegorical mode of *Salò* (*Porcile*); a neo-Neorealism with speed, humor, and bite (*The Gospel According to St. Matthew*, 1964; *Hawks and Sparrows*, 1966); and fabulous, intricate experiments in narration that were inspired by great literary sources and that set stories within stories as well as story against story (*Medea*, 1969; *The Decameron*, 1971; *The Canterbury Tales*, 1972; and *The Arabian Nights*, 1974).

The political films of Bernardo Bertolucci are more sensuous, more meticulous in their stylish attention to visual detail, and less schematic in their abstract arguments. As a result, they are also much more popular. In *Before the Revolution, The Conformist* (1970, based on a novel by Alberto Moravia), and *Last Tango in Paris* (1972), Bertolucci examines the

Fig. 13-11
Stefania Sandrelli and Dominique Sanda dance in The Conformist.

interrelationship between political issues and sexual drives not, as Pasolini does, by revealing the radical anarchic power of sexual passion but, instead, by showing that political and sexual commitments weave together in complex and mysterious ways. The rich, bored dilettantes are no more committed to Marxist ideology than they are to their own lusts and seductions in *Before the Revolution*. They play around with both and succeed in fulfilling neither. In *The Conformist*, the central figure's ideological emptiness is intimately connected with his lack of sexual identity, his need to assert his masculinity while evading his unacknowledged homosexuality. An unprincipled conformist, he is a Fascist only until the Fascists are defeated. He can betray ideals, his friends, his professor, his lover, his wife, because he is a zero—both ideologically and sexually. *Last Tango in Paris* was not one of Pasolini's abstract sexual theorems but an intimate and detailed portrait of human carnality, dominated by the pervasive lust and persuasive confusion of the lost American portrayed by Marlon Brando, in one of his greatest screen roles.

1900 (1976) is an epic history of Italy in the 20th century. Here Bertolucci shifts his personal focus from lust to friendship—a study of the limits on and the possibilities for friendship of two men, born on the same day on the same estate in 1900 but in the opposite classes of landowner (Robert De Niro) and peasant (Gérard Depardieu). Bertolucci examines the closeness of the two boys (their comradely discoveries of nature, sex, and death together; the genuine emotional ties that bind them) and the barriers to that friendship (their different financial, educational, and moral backgrounds; their different romantic decisions; their different attitudes toward the phenomena of the century—two wars; the rise and fall of Fascism; the labor, union, and workers' movements—and toward private property itself). Ultimately, Bertolucci's synthesis (and, in contrast to Pasolini, there is a synthesis, not an insistently irreversible analysis) does not erase the fact that the two men are and are not close, can and cannot be friends, can and cannot overcome the facts of social history that both bind and separate them. Their inseparable opposition determines the synthesis: the century.

Politics and sexual politics continued to concern Bertolucci in a series of extravagant international co-productions: *The Last Emperor* (1987), *The Sheltering Sky* (1990), *Little Buddha* (1993). *The Last Emperor*, like *1900*, is an epic with real political intelligence and carefully observed human drama. *The Sheltering Sky* is his most

sensually complex work since *Last Tango*, and it opens the return to romance in his later films, *Stealing Beauty* (1996) and the more political *Besieged* (1998) and *The Dreamers* (2003). *Little Buddha*, on the other hand, yielding to the weakest tendencies in his work, is romantic and sumptuous and almost fatuously empty—the kind of happy, extravagant film that would give nightmares to a Pasolini.

Germi, Leone, and Others

Pietro Germi was Italy's greatest film satirist of the postwar period. Germi made several Neorealist films just after the war, the most interesting of which was *In the Name of the Law* (1948), a contrast between social hypocrisies and the underlying moral realities in a Mafia-dominated Sicily. This contrast of the appearance and the reality, the external show and the internal emotion, later became Germi's dominant theme in his great satirical comedies, *Divorce—Italian Style* (1961, U.S. release 1962), *Seduced and Abandoned* (1963), and *The Birds, the Bees, and the Italians* (1966; literal title, *Ladies and Gentlemen*). In the first of these films, murder seems a practical social tool, there being no easier legal way to break a stifling marriage contract. In *Seduced and Abandoned*, a Sicilian family insists on maintaining its honor to the death. And death is precisely the result of their obsession with honor, despite all the hilarious machinations to get the deflowered daughter engaged, disengaged, and eventually married.

Landowner (Robert De Niro) and worker (Gérard Depardieu) in Bertolucci's 1900.

Fig. 13-12

The code of honor becomes a rigid absurdity that the characters uphold with the most frenzied seriousness. And in *The Birds, the Bees, and the Italians* Germi presents a world that is farcical, cruel, and grotesque—the Fellini world gone bourgeois, with warts.

The paths of Neorealism took several other directions. Mario Monicelli's *The Organizer* (1963, U.S. release 1964) applied Neorealist principles to a historical study, the fight for fair wages and working conditions by a group of early-20th-century strikers. Vittorio De Seta, a documentary filmmaker, combined documentary and fiction for his first feature, *Bandits of Orgosolo* (1961). After his debut film, the ferociously iconoclastic *Fists in the Pocket* (1965), Marco Bellocchio satirically examined the clumsy attempts of the bored rich to carve a meaning out of their lives by dabbling in romance and Marxist politics in *China Is Near* (1967). And Lina Wertmüller, who served her apprenticeship with Fellini, sought to combine broad satire with sharp political analysis. Her major films (*The Seduction of Mimi*, 1972; *Love and Anarchy*, 1973; *Swept Away . . .*, 1974; *Seven Beauties*, 1976) reveal both a Marxist analysis of contemporary social problems and an exuberant comic sensitivity to the dilemmas of sexuality, power, morality, and survival. In *The Battle of Algiers* (1966), Gillo Pontecorvo combined a Neorealistic tale of political resistance with a visual style that suggested newsreel actuality—to "document" the Algerian struggle for freedom from the French.

Most Neorealistic of the second-generation postwar directors was Ermanno Olmi. In *Il posto* (*The Job*, also called *The Sound of Trumpets*, 1961), Olmi studies an adolescent boy's absorption into the machinery of bureaucratic industrialized society. The boy leaves home, takes a civil service examination, gets a job as messenger, and finally earns a clerk's desk in the bureaucratic office. The film ends with a terrific sound effect, not the glorious sound of trumpets but the cranking of a mimeograph machine. The boy has been "duplicated," cranked through the industrial process to emerge as one more identical sheet of paper on which his future for the next 50 years has been printed.

Olmi's masterpiece, *The Tree of Wooden Clogs* (1978), set in Northern Italy around 1900, relates economic conditions and "minor" subjects to the crucial concerns of real life as relentlessly as any of its Neorealist predecessors. A rigorously shot

Fig. 13-13
The Battle of Algiers: *political fiction as newsreel reportage.*

color study of a year in the lives of three peasant families, it focuses on the story of a man who cuts down a small tree to make a new pair of clogs for his son (who has a 6-kilometer walk to school and has broken one clog); for this act, the family is evicted.

A third generation of Italian masters emerged in the 1970s—Ettore Scola, Paolo and Vittorio Taviani, and Francesco Rosi—all of them fully conscious of their Neorealist roots; indeed, Rosi had been making films for decades before attracting wider international attention. Scola is the subtle ironist and comic stylist of the group (*We All Loved Each Other So Much*, 1974; *A Special Day*, 1977; *La Nuit de Varennes*, 1982). Like many of his contemporaries, Scola is dedicated to exploring the processes of history: political history, like the French Revolution (in *La Nuit de Varennes*, scripted by Sergio Amidei, whose scripts were so important to Rossellini), or cinema history, like Scola's explicit homage to De Sica and the succeeding quarter century of Italian film styles (*We All Loved Each Other So Much*).

The Taviani brothers closely examine Italian social structures within periods of historical crisis. *Padre Padrone* (1977) is a careful dissection of Italy's paternalistic familial structures, collapsing beneath the attack of modern literacy. *The Night of the Shooting Stars* (1982) pays explicit homage to Rossellini and *Paisan* in the same way that Scola's *We All Loved Each Other So Much* pays homage to De Sica and *The Bicycle Thief*. The Taviani films might also be described as explorations of language: the language of cinema in *Good Morning, Babylon* (1987, about working on *Intolerance*), literacy itself in *Padre Padrone*, and storytelling in *KAOS* (*Chaos*, 1984—a group of stories by Pirandello, followed by one about him).

The films of Francesco Rosi (*Salvatore Giuliano*, 1962; *The Mattei Affair*, 1972; *Christ Stopped at Eboli*, 1979; *Three Brothers*, 1981) are also attracted to periods of historical crisis. As a political tragedy, *Salvatore Giuliano* has been compared to *Julius Caesar* and *Citizen Kane*. At the center of a conspiracy that may involve the police, the government, and the Mafia, Giuliano is on camera only after he is dead. Out of chronological order, the film presents the past of this powerful bandit—and the events that followed his death—but the events are shown as the consequences of his decisions; we do not see him,

as in the conventional Robin Hood or war movie, making the decisions. Only once, climactically, do we hear him off-camera and catch a glimpse of his hand. The film is very concerned with the unknown reasons for one of his ruthless decisions: to fire on a group of demonstrating workers. The sharp, deep cinematography of Gianni Di Venanzo, at once stark and rich, enforces the sharp, unimpeachable realism of Rosi's style and the pointedness of his political approach, which exposes the conspiracies that defined an era of Sicilian history.

For 50 years the Italian film has started with the surface of reality as its initial premise. But the Italian filmmaker has been free to manipulate the realistic surfaces of rich or poor, of past or present, and to probe beneath those surfaces with sociological commentary, psychological insight, sexual allegory, farcical comedy, philosophical ennui, bizarre romance. The postwar Italian film has been so rich and diverse not only because of the rich and contradictory challenges of Neorealism and Modernism, but also because, ironically, the Italian film industry was supported first by American dollars and later by the Italian government to stimulate even more production.

The Hollywood dollar stimulated not only postwar Italian "art films," but several cycles of genre films as well. In the 1950s, a series of quasi-mythological "spectacle" films starring the American muscleman, Steve Reeves, could be shot for under $150,000 in Italy and then dubbed into English for mass release in American theatres (*Hercules*, 1959). In the 1960s, a series of Italian "spaghetti westerns," the best of which (*A Fistful of Dollars*, 1964, closely based on Kurosawa's 1961 *Yojimbo;* and *For a Few Dollars More*, 1965) starred Clint Eastwood and were directed by Sergio Leone, not only made money but attracted a cult of admirers. Leone's success with the cheap violent western—and the wide screen—was so great that he was given the chance to shoot a major high-budget western, *Once Upon a Time in the West* (1968), which may be the slowest paced, most naturalistically detailed, and most visually intense collection of western clichés ever assembled—but with a difference (Henry Fonda smiles as he shoots a child . . .). The West is demystified, shown in all its grossness, while Leone weaves a new myth. A film of sudden, intense close-ups and boldly composed long shots, enthusiastically filling the wide screen and magnificently scored by Ennio Morricone (who had composed the music for all of Leone's films—becoming well known for *The Good, the Bad and the Ugly*, 1966—and who would go on to score *1900* and, in America, *Days of Heaven*, 1978), *Once Upon a Time in the West* shares much with the Eastwood "man with no name" westerns but explores history, mythology, and a wider range of tones.

As romantic as Leone, for whom he once worked, and as committed to the genre film, Dario Argento became a master of horror. Surrealistic, lushly colored, full of bold camera movements and naggingly serial music (usually by Goblin), unsettling, suspenseful, moody, shocking, and gory, Argento's cult hits have much in common with Antonioni's sense of mystery and Bertolucci's operatic visions of conspiracy and perverse evil; they also reflect the influence of the Italian horror films of Mario Bava (*Black Sunday* or *The Mask of the Demon*, 1960; *Blood and Black Lace*, 1964; *A Bay of Blood* or *Twitch of the Death Nerve*, 1971). His first movie, *The Bird with the Crystal Plumage* (1970), was made in the *giallo* genre—Italy's version of *film noir*, inspired by a series of mystery novels with yellow (*giallo*) covers, comparable to France's *Série noire*, with an emphasis on slashers and a respect for American pulp fiction from the 1920s to the 1950s. After several more *giallo* thrillers, Argento pushed his camera and his imagination to new extremes and made his most disturbing, beautiful, and uniquely terrifying pictures, *Deep Red* (1975) and *Suspiria* (1977).

The reflexivity of the Italian film did not end with *8½* and *We All Loved Each Other So Much*. Giuseppe Tornatore's movie about watching and projecting movies, *Cinema Paradiso* (1989), touched audiences around the world, and Maurizio Nichetti's *The Icicle Thief* (1989) may be the funniest picture ever made about the problems of showing a film on television—in this case a Neorealist film, interrupted by commercials, that is being watched by a contemporary Italian family whose problems are comically analogous to those in the old movie.

Confirming the continuing importance of the theme of the family in society, Marco Bellocchio's *My Mother's Smile* (2002) tackled religious hypocrisy and opportunism, telling the story of an atheist who finds that his mother is a candidate for sainthood. The family wants the social prestige as well as the spiritual "life insurance" of this canonization, and the hero finds a way not to join their efforts. He also finds that he shares his mother's mocking, ironic, detached, and secretly destructive smile—which is not the smile of a saint. Bellocchio continued to critique Italian institutions in *Vincere* (2009), a biography of Mussolini's mistress and a dark study of Mussolini's rise to power.

The crime film made a comeback with Matteo Garrone's *Gomorra* (2008), a fact-based, multifaceted examination of a big crime organization in Naples and the many people whose lives it affects or ends. This film is as tight and violent and as forcefully intercut as it is expansive.

France—Postwar Classicism

The postwar Italian film sprang from the reality that the filmmaker sought to capture with camera and film; the postwar French film sprang from the filmmaker's stylistic concern with the way a camera can capture reality. That the postwar French cinema should be committed to style and form is not surprising; the prewar French cinema was just as committed to formal experiment, from the innovative silents of Gance, Dulac, Ray, Kirsanov, Duchamp, Epstein, and others to the stylistic powerhouses of Clair, Vigo, and Renoir. To approach consciousness and reality through the manipulation of style and form has been an aesthetic premise of the French creative mind from Racine to Proust to Ionesco. The postwar French cinema is very much in the same tradition.

Cocteau and Others

The most important surviving directors of the 1930s—Clair, Renoir, Carné, and Cocteau—continued to make films after World War II. René Clair combined fantasy, song, and social satire once again in films that were frothy mixtures of physical movement, stylized decor, and music—among them *Le Silence est d'or* (*Silence is Golden*, 1947, starring Maurice Chevalier; U.S. title, *Man About Town*), a nostalgic tribute to the Zecca–Méliès years of the French film; *Beauty and the Devil* (1949), an ironic treatment of the Faust legend; and *Beauties of the Night* (1952), the romantic reveries of a daydreaming musician.

While Clair returned to France to make films that were softer, sweeter, and weaker than his earlier work, Renoir made at least three films that are arguably as great as his masterpieces of the 1930s. The three films—*The River* (his first in color; shot 1949–50, released 1951), *The Golden Coach* (1952, shot in Italy), and *French Cancan* (1954, shot in France)—are a kind of trilogy. All three use color as a metaphoric and thematic element in their investigations. All three are set in periods or places far from postwar France: India's Bengal region (*The River*), South America of the 1700s (*The Golden Coach*), and Montmartre of the 1890s (*French Cancan*). Their primary duality is the familiar Renoir conflict between art and nature, but in these late films the conflict becomes a communion as the very artfulness of the films themselves—their visual beauty as well as their structural complexity—reveals how one can indeed make life into art and thereby synthesize the opposites of art and nature.

The River, shot in India by a French director with a French and Bengali crew, featuring a cast of both Indians and Westerners, masterfully addresses this interplay of cultures and values. Using the vibrant colors of the Indian landscape and drawing on Indian mythology, religion, philosophy, and music, *The River* (based on the book by Rumer Godden, who co-wrote the script

with Renoir) shows a group of "crippled" Westerners—crippled physically or spiritually by the war, by political chaos, and by personal disappointment—healing their minds and feelings by seeking to achieve a harmony with the eternal cycles of nature: birth, life, and death.

Marcel Carné, deprived of Jacques Prévert's scripts, never regained the power of *Le Jour se lève* and *Les Enfants du paradis*, although he made almost a dozen films. In 1994, a poll of French filmmaking professionals found that they considered *Les Enfants du paradis* the greatest film made in any country during the past 50 years—but at the same time, no one in the industry was willing to finance a new Carné film, *Mouche*, which had run out of money after shooting had begun. He was still trying to raise the money when he died in 1996. The last film he completed was a documentary, *La Bible* (1977).

Jean Cocteau, whose only prewar film was the 1930 *The Blood of a Poet* (an experimental, personal attempt to "picture the poet's inner self"), made several films in strikingly different though equally formalistic film styles: the claustrophobic realism of *Les Parents terribles* (1948); the poetic symbolism of *Orphée* (*Orpheus*, 1950), a Surrealistic study of the artist's ambivalent relationship with love and death as well as a rich realization of some of the ways that poetry and

Cocteau's union of opposites in Beauty and the Beast— *loveliness (Josette Day as Beauty) and ugliness (Jean Marais as the Beast), human and animal, nature and artifice, animate and inanimate (note the candelabra's arm).*

Fig. 13-14

film can work together; and *Beauty and the Beast* (1946), a perfectly realized fairy tale that mixed Cocteau's surreal romanticism and evocative symbolism quite effectively in the story of Belle's growing love for the ugly yet loving beast. The impression of these stylistically eclectic Cocteau films is that they are the works of a cinematic amateur (in the original sense of the word). The artist, having given birth to his personal and symbolic world on the stage, on the page, and on canvas, also decided to people the screen with his personal fantasies, images, motifs, and symbols. Cocteau felt that only the work of art was capable of effecting a synthesis of the conflicting demands of art and nature, of form and freedom. In the films, Cocteau's commitment to art is even more fervent than Renoir's. As befits his elevation of art, Cocteau's films are generally more fanciful, more symbolic, more claustrophobically stylized, more otherworldly than those of Renoir, who, even in his late period, holds the demands of art and social reality in balance.

Max Ophüls

Of the new directors of French cinema in the 15 years following the war, the three greatest were Max Ophüls, Robert Bresson, and Jacques Tati. All three of them had made films in the Clair–Carné–Renoir tradition; all three had, in fact, made films before 1945. Whereas the end of the war signaled a shift in an entirely new direction for the Italian film, the end of the war in France extended an earlier one. The break with French tradition came in 1959, and, as we shall see, it was not a complete break at all.

Max Ophüls made films in Italy, Holland, and the United States after fleeing his German homeland and Hitler in 1933 (he was Jewish). Ophüls's reputation today rests primarily on the last films he made in America (*Letter From An Unknown Woman*, 1948; *Caught* and *The Reckless Moment*, both 1949) and the four he directed and co-wrote in France before his death: *La Ronde* (1950), *Le Plaisir* (1952), *Madame de . . .* (*The Earrings of Madame de . . .*, 1953), and *Lola Montès* (1955, shot in Paris and Munich); all the French films were shot by Christian Matras and are noted for their fluid, highly charged camerawork. *Lola Montès* features a wide-screen camera whose movements are so graceful and comment with such authority on the action that they have been considered the best of the 1950s, the great experimental period of anamorphic camerawork (Ray, Kazan, Preminger, and many others). Ophüls was clearly an international rather than a French director. And yet he found a place in French

Max Ophüls's urbane narrator–chorus (Anton Walbrook) with the whore (Simone Signoret) and the metaphoric carousel of La Ronde.

Fig. 13-15

studios at a particularly apt time for his talents—a time when French film values favored the literate, almost theatrical script and the ornate, carefully styled studio production (the "tradition of quality"). Ophüls's greatest artistic resemblance is to two other internationalized Europeans, the German Ernst Lubitsch and the Austrian Erich von Stroheim, whose contrasting qualities he seems to synthesize. Ophüls's films combine Lubitsch's light, mocking, sexually wise touch with von Stroheim's perception of human desire and social corruption.

The last Ophüls films all revolve around sexual intrigue in conflict with social regulations. The Ophüls characters continue to carry on their intrigues while either hypocritically ignoring the social tensions (as in *La Ronde* and *Madame de . . .*) or openly defying social convention (as Lola does). In developing a consistent theme, Ophüls also prefers consistent stylistic conventions. Each film's plot is less a single driving narrative than a string of vignettes, held together by the setting (the Vienna of *La Ronde*, the circus tent of *Lola Montès*), by an object (the earrings of *Madame de . . .*, which are passed from person to person in a fatal circle), or by a concept (in *Le Plaisir*, which retells three stories by Guy de Maupassant, how pleasure is found easily but happiness is elusive). By deemphasizing story, Ophüls illuminates key structural balances, comparisons and contrasts of similar actions in different circumstances or different actions in similar ones. Such balancing—itself both intellectually distant and passionately involved—takes the viewer directly to the center of Ophüls's moral statement on love, feelings, and social custom. And Ophüls's deliberate choice of an artificial, theatrical setting (the soundstage in *La Ronde*, the circus in *Lola Montès*) provides a nonrealistically appropriate setting for Ophüls's comedies of sociosexual manners and also raises intentional questions about the shams of real human activity and the realness of acting and impersonation. Lola Montès, for example, is put on display to act the role of herself.

La Ronde is one of the finest translations of a stage work (Arthur Schnitzler's *Reigen*) into film. The film is both theatrical and cinematic. The setting in *La Ronde* is both an undisguised soundstage and the city of Vienna around 1900. The camera wanders about the soundstage at will between the two poles of obvious stage set and realistic bedroom, between a metaphorical carousel, symbolic of the film's everturning dance of sexual relationships (a conjugal merry-go-round in which A loves B who loves C who loves A), and a real boudoir. Ophüls keeps the camera perpetually on the move; his German heritage is especially clear in his use of the moving camera and emphasis on *mise-en-scène*. The gliding photography adds not only visual energy but also continuity between the vignettes. And Ophüls's wandering camera has an ally: The director has invented a narrator, a character who does not exist in the original play, who speaks directly for the filmmaker to the audience. The urbane, perceptive, witty narrator (Anton Walbrook) wanders, as the camera wanders, as he speaks for Ophüls. Director, camera, and narrator are one.

The single view they present is of sexual desire and the lies people tell to others and to themselves to obtain the objects of their desire. Schnitzler's play is a series of ten wryly comic seductions, all of which, except the last, denote the sexual climax with a line of asterisks in the text. The play's unique structure gives its author several interesting perspectives, which Ophüls pointedly borrows. Because the scenes do not depict sexual activity but show only the events leading up to and away from the activity, the obvious focus of each scene is on the emotional reactions before (usually sexual excitement, clichéd lies, mental fencing) and after (usually disillusionment, callousness, and guilt) the asterisks.

La Ronde poses a moral tension between natural human responses and unnatural social restrictions. The result is that the only time the characters cannot lie to each other is when they are lying with each other, during the unshown "asterisks" of each scene.

The same antithesis between authentic experience and convention propels *Lola Montès*, but Lola (Martine Carol) resolves the contradiction by remaining unflinchingly true to her feelings, regardless of the risk, regardless of the consequences. The story of Lola is the fictional biography of a real person, a notorious courtesan of the 19th century, who took a series of brilliant lovers—a famous composer (Liszt) and a ruling Bavarian prince (Ludwig) among them. But Lola falls on evil fortune; she becomes a circus performer, forced to parade her life's story before a crass and ogling audience, selling gossip and

Fig. 13-16
Lola Montès: *composition for the wide screen—contrapuntal verticals (Martine Carol and Anton Walbrook).*

letting her hand be kissed for a dollar. Lola has, on the surface, fallen from great lover to romantic exhibit; once free, she is now controlled. The new man in her life is the slimy ringmaster (Peter Ustinov) who revels in Lola's past, his present mastery over her, and the money he makes from her life. Lola's conquerors are circumstance and time, as her sick and aging body requires more whisky to keep it going.

Despite the change in her fortunes, Lola is still Lola. Even her deliberate public display of her past is an unconventional act of defiance. If people want to look at her, let them.

But *Lola Montès* is more than an examination of a romantic lifestyle. It is one of the most dazzling of visual shows—in both color and CinemaScope. Each of the sequences has its own unique color and tone: the warm browns, oranges, and ambers of the rustic affair with the composer; the cold whites, silvers, and pale blues of the affair with the prince; the dazzling reds and golds of the circus, glowing in the blackness of the tent. The film's composition is as dynamic as its color.

Ophüls was one of those early directors to compose not *in* the wide screen but *for* the wide screen. The big shots—in the circus tent, in the palace—truly fill the frame. Ophüls's constantly moving camera, panoramic staging, and careful decor decrease the impression of the screen's great width by adding fullness and balance to the frame. Ophüls often splits the wide screen with contrapuntal verticals, breaking the horizontal expanse with lamps, chandeliers, ropes, drapes, pillars. His favorite camera maneuver in the film is the circular track that moves round and round the action, keeping the figures contrapuntally balanced around an invisible pole in the center of the wide frame. The circular motion is not only active and interesting pictorially; it is the perfect cinematic parallel for the film's metaphorical circus tent, which becomes a microcosm for all earthly places and all human experience. Ophüls's turning camera, his metaphorical setting, and the very structure of *Lola Montès* turn all human experience into a vivid circus and all spectators in the movie theatre into spectators in the circus tent.

Lola Montès was Max Ophüls's final film before his death in 1957. His son, Marcel Ophuls, became a major documentary filmmaker of the next generation (*The Sorrow and the Pity: Chronicle of a City under the Occupation,* 1969; *The Memory of Justice,* 1976). These personal, political films, with their pointed montages and revelatory long takes, were quite different from his father's elegantly formal romances.

Robert Bresson

Robert Bresson, though equally careful with narrative structure, details of decor, and pictorial composition, was a completely different kind of filmmaker. Subdued rather than flamboyant, quiet rather than gaudy, introspective rather than extrovertedly spectacular, Bresson's films are as far apart from Ophüls's as Brittany is from Vienna. Bresson made only 15 films in 40 years, from *Les Anges du péché* (1943) to *L'Argent* (1983); the most important are *Les Dames du Bois de Boulogne* (1945), *Diary of a Country Priest* (1950), *A Man Escaped* (1956), *Pickpocket* (1959), *Au hasard Balthazar* (1966),

Mouchette (1967), *Une Femme douce* (1969, his first in color), and *Lancelot du lac* (1974). He died in 1999 at the age of 98. His slowness and care as a craftsman seem to mirror the quietness, the slow pace, the austere rigor, the internalized probing of his films. Like Antonioni, Ozu, and Dreyer, Bresson was a purist and a perfectionist. Whereas the Ophüls films are intricate visual shows, the Bresson films feel more like ascetic, introspective novels. Like the novelist, Bresson could tell his story through an omniscient third person (*Les Dames du Bois de Boulogne*) or a confessional first person (*Diary of a Country Priest*). Most of his stories seem to be trying to find ways to tell themselves. Like the films of Dreyer and Antonioni, Bresson's are often about expressive silence. And some of his characters are caged into silence, while others choose it as a discipline.

Bresson's primary theme is the battle of spiritual innocence with the corruption of the world. This is particularly clear in his film about the Christ-like humility and suffering of a virtually silent donkey, *Au hasard Balthazar*

Fig. 13-17
Diary of a Country Priest.

(*Watch out, Balthazar*). Bresson, a devout Roman Catholic, sought spiritual meaning and salvation in a world that had lost touch with them. In *Diary of a Country Priest*, a young, innocent curé faces the worldly evils about him: A cynical, nihilistic doctor commits suicide; a wealthy count substitutes money and influence for morality and faith; the faith of the count's wife wavers at the loss of her son; the count's neurotic daughter viciously implicates the priest in the countess's death; the peasants of the countryside remain indifferent and hostile. As a priest, the man fails. He succeeds only in bringing a moment of faith and peace to the countess. The other members of his parish remain tied to their selfish cares and material concerns. But as a man, the priest succeeds completely. He dies of cancer, unshaken in his faith to the end, certain that "all is grace." His spirit wins the battle with his body. Bresson's cinematic technique—unself-conscious, unspectacular, rigorously dispassionate, effortlessly transparent—never diverts our attention from the man's internal struggle and the thematic basis of that struggle, spiritual maturity and endurance.

Tati, Clouzot, and Others

Jacques Tati was the great comic of the French film, probably the greatest film mime and visual comic since Chaplin and Keaton. Like Bresson, Tati worked slowly, controlling every detail of the film himself from script to cutting; like Bresson, Tati refused to compromise with either technicians or producers. As a result, though Tati's first film appearance was as early as 1932, he made only six feature films: *Jour de fête* (1949), *Mr. Hulot's Holiday* (1953), *My Uncle* (1958, his first in color), *Playtime* (1967, in 70mm), *Traffic* (1970), and *Parade* (1973). Like Chaplin and Keaton, Tati came to films from the music hall. Before taking to the stage, Tati took to sport—tennis, boxing, soccer. Tati's comedy— for example, his famous tennis pantomime— often combined the athletic field and the music hall. But Tati was sensitive not only to the comic possibilities of his body but also to the visually comic possibilities of film.

Tati plays essentially the same character in each picture: a charming fool whose incompetence is preferable to the inhuman competence of the life around him. Tati's Mr. Hulot merely goes about his business, totally unaware that the world around him has gone mad and that his naïve attention to his own business turns its orderly madness into comic chaos. Tati's Hulot neither looks nor moves like anyone else in the universe. He leans forward at an oblique angle—battered hat atop his head, pipe thrusting from his mouth, umbrella dangling at his side, trouser cuffs hanging two inches above his shoes—an odd human construction of impossible angles, off-center and off-kilter. His bouncy walk implies an elastic spring, ready to launch him off the earth.

In his first feature film, *Jour de fête* (a feast-day or holiday), Tati plays a clumsy rural postman who discovers the apparent efficiency and speed of the American postal system. Tati's zany attempts to convert himself into a speedy efficient machine produce great visual gags as well as chaos in the little town. As always with Tati, that which seems efficient and modern is ultimately inefficient and wasteful.

For *Mr. Hulot's Holiday*, Tati created Monsieur Hulot, an apparently conventional, pipe-smoking, easygoing, middle-class gentleman who comes to spend a conventional week at a completely conventional middle-class resort. Hulot, like Chaplin and Keaton, runs afoul of objects. His troubles with bathers on the beach, with his sputtering little car, even with the twang of the hotel's dining-room door, reduce the conventional, routinized tourist resort to unconventional hysteria. Tati's comic attack exposes the resort—supposedly a place devoted to leisure and fun—as the domain of the dull and monotonous. M. Hulot is the spontaneous, disruptive force who enlivens the dead place of play by bombarding it with uncanny objects, sounds, and movements.

My Uncle (*Mon oncle*) features Monsieur Hulot again—this time as the old-fashioned uncle of a family of upper-middle-class suburbanites. Hulot's simple, unaffected ways contrast with the complicated machinery of his relatives' lives: their fancy gadgets that open the garage doors and kitchen cabinets (inconsistently); their bizarrely shaped furniture that is designed for everything but comfort and function; their gravel-lined, flagstone-paved "garden" that is suitable for everything but growing things and enjoying the sun. In this struggle of humanity

Fig. 13-18
The first entrance of M. Hulot (Jacques Tati, right) in **Mr. Hulot's Holiday.**

versus the artifact, the gadgets win the battle (they always do in physical comedy), but M. Hulot wins the satirical war.

Playtime brings a group of American tourists to Paris. Hulot, more a passive observer than the central figure of this film, accompanies the group on their tour of a modern industrial exposition and a fancy nightclub that has just been glued together for fashionable Parisians and American tourists. Tati ridicules the slick surfaces of modern life with hilarious visual gags: The tiles of the dance floor have been pasted down so recently that they stick to the dancers' high-stepping shoes; a plate-glass door has been cleaned so well—to the point of invisibility—that the customers cannot tell whether the doorman actually opens the door or merely mimes it. Tati also uses sound brilliantly. Although *Playtime* has so little dialogue that it requires no subtitles, Tati develops sound gags like a plastic-and-foam-rubber sofa that makes grotesque breathing and sucking noises when Hulot sits on it and a miraculous modern door that makes absolutely no noise even when slammed with the most violent force.

Like *Mr. Hulot's Holiday*, the underlying theme of *Playtime* is the creative use of leisure and the genuine fun that can result from active perception rather than the passive acceptance of planned and canned routines. *Playtime* is very much about itself, about our having fun by watching a film closely and finding its comic inventions for ourselves rather than being fed them by a prepackaging film director. Shot in 70mm, its geometric

modern city planned and constructed by Tati himself (humorously called "Tativille," its cost drove him into bankruptcy, from which he never recovered), *Playtime* invites us to explore its vast spaces without a dictatorial guide; in a film virtually without close-ups, our eye must pick out visual and comic significance for itself. In their blend of social satire, wry charm, imaginative physical gags, and the creative use of the visual and aural devices of the cinema itself, the films of Jacques Tati have not been surpassed by those of any other postwar film comic, French or otherwise.

Two other major French directors of the years just following the war were Henri-Georges Clouzot and René Clément. Clouzot was, like Hitchcock, an assured director of extremely suspenseful melodramas. Both *The Wages of Fear* (1953) and *Les Diaboliques* (*Diabolique*, 1955) mix chills, horror, sexual intrigue, and taut suspense. *Diabolique* is the more celebrated of the two, a story of sexual intrigue and shocking cruelty. But *The Wages of Fear* is a purer representative of the Clouzot method: an agonizingly tense, long journey of two trucks transporting nitroglycerin through the jungles of South America. Audiences that screamed at *Diabolique* sat frozen with tension through *Wages*.

Clément's most important film is *Forbidden Games* (1952), a wartime story of two children who are both affected and infected by the murderous world of their elders. A young girl's parents and puppy are machine-gunned by a strafing German airplane. The girl, horrified by the death of her parents, fixes her fascination on the dead puppy, refusing to believe it is dead; she tries to keep it and play with it. She is adopted by a family of Pyrenees farmers who, through their young son, teach her that dead things must be buried. The girl buries the puppy. She becomes so fascinated with burying things that she and the boy go about the countryside killing things so they can bury them. It is how they deal with death, gaining some measure of control over it. They are severely punished for their activity, which ironically merely mimics that of their elders.

Jean-Pierre Melville, who started his own small production company in 1946, shot his tough, methodical films on the streets of Paris, on available locations (real apartments and cafés, for example), and occasionally in a small studio. If the New Wave filmmakers learned from the Neorealists the advantages of shooting in the streets and on location, working with a small budget and without big studio support, they learned from Melville how to make such films in Paris. He directed and co-wrote, with Cocteau, an adaptation of Cocteau's novel *Les Enfants terribles* (1950). An unsentimental writer and director, Melville often follows a central character through a process that is difficult and isolating: the last job planned by a lifelong gambler (*Bob le flambeur*, 1955), the activities of the French Resistance supervised by an efficient and dedicated organizer (*Army of Shadows*, 1969), the killings carried out by a cool, solitary hit man (*Le Samouraï*, 1967). Most of his films, from the rough-edged *Bob le flambeur* to the cold, elegant *Le Samouraï*, were shot by Henri Decaë, whose low-budget, street-smart look contributed so much to *The 400 Blows*, for Truffaut borrowed not only Melville's independent methods but also his cameraman.

1959 and After

In the years following the war a new generation of the French became addicted to the movies. Many of these *cinéastes* first became film critics rather than filmmakers, simply because in France, as in America, the studio establishment had solidified enough to keep new minds and small budgets out. These cinephiles did not like the film establishment's ornately staged, heavily plotted, unspontaneous films. In *Cahiers du cinéma*, the journal founded by film critic and theorist André Bazin, the young critics François Truffaut, Jean-Luc Godard, and Claude Chabrol ripped apart the films of Clément, the screenwriters Jean Aurenche and Pierre Bost (*La Symphonie pastorale*, 1946), and others of what they considered the same literary, talky, tasteful, studio-crafted, theatrical type (the "tradition of quality"). Following Bazin's example, they emphasized the work of directors, and the *auteur* theory—which identified directors as the authors of their films and found ways to analyze their recurring themes and structures—was born at *Cahiers*. It was Roberto Rossellini, one of the idols of these critics, who urged them to stop writing about films and start making them.

These *Cahiers* critics retreated a generation, to the 1930s of Clair, Renoir, and Vigo, where they found the zest and spontaneity of what they considered the authentic French tradition. Just as the French directors of the 1920s leaped backward to the primitive exuberance of Cohl, Zecca, and Méliès, the French directors of the 1960s leaped backward to the films of the 1920s and 1930s. Just as the French films of the 1920s combined echoes of the past with bizarre innovations for the future, the films of Truffaut and Godard were to be full of echoes of Vigo, Bogart, Hitchcock, Feuillade, Hawks, Welles, and more, combined with ingeniously elliptical techniques. The year 1959 was the year that the critics, heeding Rossellini's advice, became filmmakers—the year of Truffaut's *The 400 Blows*.

The New Wave

The New Wave ("*la nouvelle vague*") was a term coined in France to describe the sudden appearance, on many fronts, of brilliant films by new directors. Although there were several directors (such as Louis Malle) affiliated with neither camp, the New Wave consisted primarily of two parts: the *Cahiers* group of critics-turned-directors (Claude Chabrol, Jean-Luc Godard, Jacques Rivette, Eric Rohmer, and François Truffaut) and the "Left Bank" group of Chris Marker, Alain Resnais, and Agnès Varda, who had gone directly into filmmaking. The Left Bank group has often been characterized as having taken literature, philosophy, politics, and the possibilities of documentary more seriously than the *Cahiers* group. They were also the more professionally experienced filmmakers, and Varda's *La Pointe-Courte* (shot and privately premiered in 1954, released in 1956, and edited by Resnais) has been called by some the first New Wave film; it is certainly the crucial precursor, as *Ossessione* prepared the way for Neorealism.

Although influenced by the Neorealists, the avant-garde, American pulp, and any cinematic, literary, political, or philosophical text that fired their imaginations, the New Wave filmmakers set out to make films that were their own reference points. Each film took a new approach to its subject, as if no one had ever made a film about young love or political commitment, a film with intellectual conversations, a film about time or war or language. Every subject stimulated an original style. The camera might swing freely through the streets or refuse to move; it might track elegantly through any type of location to indicate the movement of a character's—or the film's—consciousness. The image might show a character's thoughts or the film's abstract argument or a day spent playing hooky. Time could proceed chronologically or in an original manner that problematized time itself. Politics could be dramatized as a fable, tackled as a governmental or social problem, or made the subject of conversations that reflected political conditions and philosophies in themselves. Any subject was ripe for filmmaking. The nonstudio look of most of the films and their use of real locations gave an air of realism to the New Wave films, and their intellectual rigor, reflexivity, and free-spirited openness to varieties of form made the films seem the first to have brought film into the major discussions of the day. The movies seemed determined to be brilliant, to find the rules and

expand the boundaries of filmmaking. It was a time for great films, ambitious films, new films—films that took as their starting point the power and nature of the cinema.

In France as well as abroad, the perceived crest of the New Wave was *The 400 Blows*, which was completed and released in France in 1959 and—something almost unprecedented—released in America that same year. America saw *The 400 Blows, The Lovers, Look Back in Anger*, and *Room at the Top* in 1959; *Hiroshima mon amour* and *Shoot the Piano Player* in 1960; *Breathless, La dolce vita*, and *L'avventura* in 1961; and *Jules and Jim* and *Last Year at Marienbad* in 1962—and perceived itself in the midst of something new and exciting: A wave of films was breaking on its shores, a wave of films from England, Italy, and especially France.

Fig. 13-19
The 400 Blows: *Antoine Doinel (Jean-Pierre Léaud) in the classroom. Both the feeling and the candid style of Vigo's* Zéro de conduite.

François Truffaut

The young François Truffaut, like the young Vigo and the young Renoir, built his early films on the central artistic idea of freedom, both in human relationships and in film technique. Truffaut's early protagonists are rebels, loners, or misfits who feel stifled by the conventional social definitions. Antoine Doinel (Jean-Pierre Léaud), the 13-year-old protagonist of *The 400 Blows* (*Les Quatre cents coups*—its title a reference to the expression "*faire les 400 coups*": to raise hell or make mischief), must endure a prisonlike school and a school-like prison, sentenced to both by hypocritical, unsympathetic, unperceptive adults. Charlie Kohler (Charles Aznavour) of Truffaut's *Shoot the Piano Player* (1960) has deliberately cut himself free of the ropes of fame and fortune as a concert pianist, preferring his job in a small smoky bar, where he thinks he can remain—uncommitted, unburdened, unknown. Catherine (Jeanne Moreau) of *Jules and Jim* (1961, released 1962) feels so uncomfortable

Fig. 13-20
***Antoine at the sea: the final scene of* The 400 Blows.**

with all definitions—wife, mistress, mother, friend, woman—that she commits suicide. Truffaut's early cinematic style was as anxious to break free as his characters were. The early films are dazzlingly elliptical, omitting huge transitional sections of time and emotional development. These narrative leaps—and a camera that moved unpredictably but always effectively, as if possessed by a vision of cinema and its renewed possibilities—gave the Truffaut films an intensity, a spontaneity, a freshness that other films lacked.

Truffaut delighted in mixing cinematic styles. Breezy, startling, and deeply moving, *The 400 Blows* (shot by Henri Decaë) ranges from sentimental traveling shots of Antoine's tear-stained face, underscored by Jean Constantin's lush music, to scenes shot on the streets with the unpretentious intensity of the Neorealists—but shot in scope—to candid comic scenes in the schoolroom, echoing Vigo's work with school-children; from a *cinéma vérité* interview between Antoine and a social worker (actually, Léaud's screen test, with Truffaut offscreen asking the questions; the social worker's voice was dubbed in later) to long, subjective traveling shots as Antoine escapes the reform school and races toward the sea. The film then ends with what was, at the time, an unprecedented surprise: a freeze-frame of the boy's face (presumably implying the ambiguity of his future). *Shoot the Piano Player* contains a most audacious interruption. A character swears that he is telling the truth. "May my mother drop dead if I'm lying," he says. Truffaut then cuts to a shot of an old lady by a stove who suddenly clutches her heart and collapses to the floor. In *Jules and Jim* (shot by Raoul Coutard), Truffaut undercranks the camera for Sennettesque effects; he uses a subjective traveling shot as the three characters race across a bridge; he uses newsreel footage of World War I that is distorted by his anamorphic lens; he uses a brief freeze-frame to capture a moment of Catherine's beauty. The trick and the surprise were intrinsic to Truffaut's method.

Charlie Kohler finds it impossible to divorce himself from commitment and emotion in *Shoot the Piano Player* (based on a novel by David Goodis, *Down There*). Charlie, as a flashback reveals, was once the famous concert pianist Edouard Saroyan. After his wife's suicide, for which Saroyan's absorption in himself and his

Fig. 13-21

Fig. 13-22

Jules and Jim. *Fig. 13-21: supremely sunny moments;*
Fig. 13-22: Jeanne Moreau.

career is largely responsible, the pianist changes
his identity, becoming Charlie Kohler, honky-
tonk pianist, determined to avoid any further
human involvement, conflict, love. He sits at his
piano, grimly banging out his honky-tonk tunes.
But life catches up with Charlie, forcing him to
respond. The film paradoxically maintains that it
is the nature of love to be lost but that to protect
oneself from the pain of loss by not loving is not
to live at all.

Jules and Jim (based on the novel by Henri-
Pierre Roché) is another cinematically fresh
study of the relationship of love and life.
Catherine refuses to live any longer than she can
love, feel, respond freely, act impulsively. She is a
creature of whim, of impulse, of change. She can
dress up like a Jackie-Cooganesque kid; she can
dive into the Seine to shake up her complacent
companions. Her face and smile match those of
the statue of the love goddess that Jules and Jim
first encounter in a friend's slide show, then track
down. But the pure spirit of love has difficulties
surviving in the real world of geographical
boundaries, marriage laws, child-bearing, and
war. Though Catherine enjoys supremely sunny
moments with Jim (Henri Serre), with Jules
(Oskar Werner), and with her daughter, the
moments lose their sunlight when they become

months and years. She cannot remain happy with
anyone for very long. And so she cuts the rope
that binds her both to life and to Jules and Jim by
driving her car off a pier, taking Jim with her,
while Jules can only watch.

The Truffaut filmography splits into two
unequal halves—a group of early films in black
and white (which earned him his initial respect
and reputation) and two decades of films in color.
The two recurrent themes of Truffaut's later films
are education and art, both of which grow out of
his earliest work. After several transitional pieces
in a variety of styles—the realistic love triangle of
The Soft Skin (1964), a repressive, antiliterate
world of the future in *Fahrenheit 451* (1966, in
color, based on the novel by Ray Bradbury), and a
Hitchcock dissertation in *The Bride Wore Black*
(1968, also in color, based on the novel by Cornell
Woolrich, and made after Truffaut published his
book-length interview with Hitchcock)—the
more commercial, less experimental half of
Truffaut's career begins with the return to
Antoine Doinel in *Stolen Kisses* (1968).

Antoine Doinel is Truffaut's alter ego; his
adventures on film parallel Truffaut's own
personal experiences as a child and young man;
the maturing of the actor who plays Doinel, Jean-
Pierre Léaud, parallels the maturing of the film

director behind the camera who discovered the young boy and nurtured his early career. Léaud is Truffaut's spiritual son, much as Truffaut claimed André Bazin as his own spiritual father.

In *Stolen Kisses*, young Doinel blunders at both love and work, clumsily groping toward self-fulfillment in both. In *Bed and Board* (1970), Antoine is married, with a child of his own as well as a mistress; he is still a half-committed blunderer, the consistent trait of his adult life. And in *Love on the Run* (1979), Antoine gets divorced, but his novel has finally been published—a novel that is really an autobiographical exploration of his own experiences with women, transmuted into art.

The Wild Child (1969, released 1970), Truffaut's only black-and-white film after *The Soft Skin*, is also devoted to education. A late-18th-century scientist (played by Truffaut) succeeds in taming a wild boy—a child (played by Jean-Pierre Cargol) who had spent his entire early life in the forest—and introduces him to the luxuries of civilization: speech, clothes, shelter, discipline, and love—which make him unfit for life in the wild.

The central Truffaut theme had evolved into one that was quite close to Renoir's: the relationship of art to nature. *The Wild Child* looks more ambivalently at the claims of nature than *The 400 Blows* or *Jules and Jim;* though civilization constricts, it also humanizes. As in the films of Renoir, socialization is a tragic necessity here. But the educated lose as well as gain, and teaching in this film is as horrific and tyrannical as it was in *The 400 Blows* (particularly the scene in which the scientist locks the boy in a closet to teach him the meaning of injustice), while nature has never looked so beautiful in a Truffaut film. The camera, managed by cinematographer Nestor Almendros, consciously evokes the visual values of that earlier, more primitive cinematic era of Feuillade, Gance, and Griffith: the use of irising, pure silence, and black and white, whose silvery monochrome looks more like the older orthochromatic film than the newer panchromatic stock, as well as the decision to shoot in the old aspect ratio of 1.33:1 (most of his films were shot in European widescreen [1.66:1, flat] or in scope [2.35:1, anamorphic])—all reveal the director's turning to the cinematic past for his study of nature and the historical past.

Fig. 13-23
Day for Night: *life as art as life as art. An adult Jean-Pierre Léaud (with Valentina Cortese) as a love-sick actor, playing a love-sick character, in a Truffaut movie, featuring Truffaut in the role of a film director.*

The tension between art and nature also propels *Day for Night* (1973), whose subject is the process of filmmaking. As in *The Wild Child*, the film develops the conflict and resultant synthesis of art and nature, for the commercial filmmaking process is one of converting the arranged and the artificial into the seemingly natural. A movie produces candle effects with electric lights, rain and fire with valves and hoses, snow with suds of foam. The term that gives the film its title, *day-for-night* (in French, *la nuit américaine*— "American Night"), is itself an artifice that transforms nature, the term that Hollywood coined in the era when the movies produced the effect of nighttime by shooting during the day with a filter or with the lens opening reduced. Art and nature approach a synthesis in the twist—reminiscent of late Renoir—that the dedication to art becomes natural for people who define themselves as being artists.

In *Small Change* (1976), Truffaut returned to the classroom experience but made it much brighter and more positive than it was in *The 400 Blows* or *The Wild Child. Small Change* is a colorful, sunny film in which the teachers are nice and a kid who falls out of a high building lands unharmed. A much more complex and coldly affecting treatment of the problems of life, *The Green Room* (1978), stars Truffaut as a figure taken from two Henry James stories ("The Altar of the Dead" and "The Beast in the Jungle"), a highly educated man who is obsessed with art and death virtually to the point of missing out on life.

Truffaut was never a committed political filmmaker. Like Renoir, he was too much the sympathetic but detached observer and ironist who saw the validity of competing ideological positions. And like Ophüls, he was too much the romantic and formalist in his quest for emotional satisfaction and artistic perfection. Truffaut faced his evasions directly in *The Last Metro* (1980), his most political film. The director of a Parisian acting ensemble during the Nazi Occupation (Catherine Deneuve) insists on continuing business as usual, performing the escapist plays the public and the authorities expect of her, refusing to take a stand against the anti-Semitic regulations that devastate her own acting company. Although her detachment angers the new leading man of the troupe, he discovers that her apolitical stance is a ruse to protect her own husband, the company's former director and leading man, who is hunted by the Occupation authorities and hiding in the basement of the theatre.

Here Truffaut made two points about his own apolitical films—in response to the activism of his colleague and contemporary, Jean-Luc Godard, who took quite the opposite path. First, the genuine political effects of art are frequently unknowable on the surface; second, the business of artists is to make art. The artist who rejects his *métier* for explicit political and rhetorical

programs might produce bad art. In one of his last films before his death in 1984, Truffaut reaffirmed his belief in the value of making personal movies.

Jean-Luc Godard

Jean-Luc Godard took the idea for his first feature film, *Breathless* (*À bout de souffle*, shot in 1959 and released early in 1960), from Truffaut. Michel Poiccard, the gangster–lover–hero of the film, is very much a Truffaut figure, a synthesis of Charlie, Catherine, and Antoine Doinel. Except for the fact that the cinema was both directors' ultimate subject, *Breathless* was as close as Godard's films ever came to Truffaut's. Whereas Truffaut's films are consistent in both theme and technique, the Godard films are consistent in their inconsistency, their eclecticism, their mixing of many different kinds of ideas and cinematic principles.

Godard, paradoxically, supports several contradictory ideas and filmic methods at the same time. He finds human experience irrational and inexplicable: the sudden, almost arbitrary deaths at the end of *Vivre sa vie* (*My Life to Live*, 1962), *Contempt* (1963), and *Masculine Feminine* (1966), and the chance murder of the policeman in *Breathless*. But we do not cry over these deaths, from which we are distanced by the director's unsentimental treatment. Godard embraces Brechtian devices and politics, and

Breathless: *Jean-Paul Belmondo playing Michel Poiccard playing Humphrey Bogart.*

Fig. 13-24

one of Brecht's premises was that both art and human problems must be viewed as strictly rational and hence solvable. The parable of turning a man into a soldier in *Les Carabiniers* (*The Riflemen*, 1963) echoes that parable in Brecht's *A Man's a Man* (written in 1924); the numbered scenes of *Vivre sa vie*, *A Married Woman* (1964), and *Masculine Feminine* and the references to B. B. in *La Chinoise* (1967) are unmistakable. On one hand, Godard is fond of allegorical, metaphorical parables: *Les Carabiniers*, *Alphaville* (1965, starring Eddie Constantine), *Weekend* (1967). On the other, he is fond of citing concrete facts and figures: the prostitution figures in *Vivre sa vie*, the Maoist students' speeches in *La Chinoise*, the truck drivers' debate in *Weekend*, the discussions of image making in *Le Gai savoir* (1968, released 1969) and of radical politics in *One Plus One* (1968; also known as *Sympathy for the Devil*).

Like Truffaut's, Godard's film career breaks into two parts—the works preceding and following 1968. But Godard's films never evolve toward Truffaut's synthesis of life and art; instead, Godard's films progressively reflect a fear that the familiar solutions of art are precisely antithetical to the necessary solutions for life, particularly political life. Bourgeois films cannot solve bourgeois problems, let alone Marxist and Maoist ones; such films cannot even ask the right questions. One cannot think with these films. The old forms provide their own oversimplified answers.

And so Godard's films become not more whole and dramatic but more fragmented and questioning, in search of "new forms for new contents," as the director (Yves Montand) says in Godard and Jean-Pierre Gorin's *Tout va bien* (1972). Rather than resolving his contradictions, Godard's evolving work seeks to explore and analyze them. To the extent that he characteristically presents a dialectic rather than its resolution and that he thinks so deeply about the cinema as a language, Godard may well be considered the filmmaker who picked up where Eisenstein left off.

Breathless remains the strongest narrative of the Godard films. Godard examines the life of Michel Poiccard (Jean-Paul Belmondo), alias Laszlo Kovacs (the same name as the American cinematographer who began by filming B pictures for American International and who later shot *Easy Rider*). Poiccard is indeed a petty crook in the B-picture tradition, a casual car thief who kills a policeman virtually by chance, gets emotionally entangled with his girlfriend (Jean Seberg), whom he wants to run away with him, and is eventually gunned down by the police after the woman tips them off. The remarkable thing about the film is not just its simple story and the choppy, exciting, refreshing way it is told, but its Bogartesque character: brazen, charming, free, refusing to warp emotions into words or conduct into laws. Remarkable also are the emotional moments of the film: the startlingly real interaction between Michel and

Breathless: *Michel (Belmondo) and Patricia (Jean Seberg) in the bedroom.*

Fig. 13-25

Patricia in her room and bed, or the moving but tough ending as the dying Michel bids a funny–sad farewell to the woman who betrayed him because she was afraid to love him.

To like Godard for *Breathless* is perhaps to wish he were another Truffaut. But even in *Breathless* the unique Godard devices—the logical assault against logic, the sudden and abrupt event, the Brechtian detachment of the viewer from the illusion of the film—control the work. As Michel drives the stolen car, his monologue on life and the countryside is addressed directly to us, an artifice that Godard emphasizes with his jump cutting, which destroys—or excitingly charges—the visual continuity of time and space. As Michel walks on the Champs Elysées, an automobile strikes and kills a pedestrian. Godard's jump cutting and Raoul Coutard's hand-held camera give the event the convincing feeling of accident, chance, the unexpected. Michel takes a casual look at the dead pedestrian, shrugs, and keeps walking. This is pure Godard, not Truffaut.

The primary strength of Godard's early films is his ability to catch flashing, elusive moments of passion, joy, or pain with the most surprising and unconventional narrative techniques. *Vivre sa vie* is a cold and moving, compelling and detached study of a woman (Nana, played by Godard's first wife, Anna Karina), who drifts into prostitution (a consistent Godard metaphor for the relationships of people under capitalism) and is shot to death when one pimp tries to sell her to another (in an understated, realistic scene of almost arbitrary violence—as far from a big "Hollywood ending" as possible). Nana goes about the business of being a prostitute in the most matter-of-fact way while Godard's soundtrack gives us, in counterpoint, a dry recitation of facts and figures on prostitution. Nana weeping at a screening of Dreyer's *Joan of Arc* (the film itself moves her, she recognizes her own suffering on the screen, and Godard compares her face with Joan's) and her lengthy discussion of the meaning of life with an old philosopher in a café also contribute to the roundness of her portrait.

Les Carabiniers and *Weekend* get their energy from the power of Godard's fable rather than the engaging nature of his characters. *Les Carabiniers*, based on an idea by Rossellini, is a wryly comic Brechtian parable of two country bumpkins—ironically named Michelangelo and

Ulysses, a synthesis of classical, Renaissance, and modern civilization—who leave the farm to go to war. The recruiting officer promises them the world; instead, the yokels merely bring back picture postcards of the world, which they insist are deeds to the things they signify. Throughout the film, the reality of still and motion photography is interrogated by the director and a matter of some confusion to the characters. When they write to the women at home (Venus and Cleopatra), they make no separation between the pleasant places they visit and the people they butcher. This naïvely bitter, Brechtian device points directly to the moral of this black comedy: Those who butcher get butchered in return.

Weekend, another film about butchery, begins realistically enough; Godard takes realistic man's animal-like possessiveness toward the automobile as the film's starting point. As the central couple—who are not all that civilized in the first place—travel on a highway to a weekend with their in-laws, Godard transports them from the land of the living to parable land. Using an agonizingly long traffic jam on the highway—shot in two long takes cut together as one—Godard leads us gradually from reality into metaphor: from traffic jam to a land of wrecked automobiles and mutilated crash victims; soon the couple find themselves in a land of open human hostility and warfare, and finally in a land of cannibalistic outsiders slaughtering pigs and people with equal appetite. There the husband who was willing to murder for money ends up in a stew enjoyed by his wife. In *Weekend*, cannibalism becomes the ultimate metaphor for modern society.

But on his way to this ultimate reduction, Godard cannot restrain himself from adding capricious touches. The secret code employed by the cannibalistic bands is based entirely on film titles and characters—Potemkin, Gösta Berling, Arizona Jules. The last is one of the inmost of in-group jokes, a combination of Arizona Jim (the pulp hero in Renoir's *The Crime of Monsieur Lange*) and *Jules and Jim*. Godard is often wry when serious and serious when wry.

If Godard's overall career reveals a consistent pattern, it is that he began by using bizarre devices of cinematic perception as a means to tell rather conventional narratives—the means to bring his characters to life—and he became progressively

Vivre sa vie: sudden, meaningless death during a business transaction (Anna Karina as Nana).

Fig. 13-26

more concerned with a critique of cinematic perception as an end in itself. The one subject Godard's films consistently explore is the cultural process of making and receiving images—on film, television, radio news, printed advertisements, billboards, book jackets, and video. The first shot in Godard's first feature captures Jean-Paul Belmondo's gazing upon a sexy pin-up in a tabloid newspaper. While this shot in *Breathless* served to define the interests, the cultural level, and the sexual commitments of the character, successive Godard films became increasingly interested in precisely what people were seeing and reading in those magazines and other media of cultural dissemination rather than in who these people were—or, rather, Godard became convinced that people unwillingly and unconsciously become the products of those very drawings and advertisements.

Three of Godard's pre-1968 films are most clearly committed to a study of image making. *Contempt* is a film explicitly about the making of film images (with Fritz Lang in the role of a director and Brigitte Bardot as a sex-object star). *A Married Woman* is an analysis of the commodification of women, marriage, "beauty," and "romance" in modern society. *2 or 3 Things I Know About Her* (1967), which some consider his greatest film, is a return to the milieu of prostitution

of *Vivre sa vie* but with the emphasis on the milieu (cafés, cars, city streets, architecture) and the cultural, political, and economic system of which prostitution is an integral part and for which it is a valid symbol. *2 or 3 Things* is also about the problem of knowing, defining, and filming anything—a major investigation of the phenomenology and epistemology of the filmed world. The director questions the objects and people at which he looks, as well as the look itself, and the film becomes a self-conscious, self-aware exploration of the nature and limits of cinematic expression. As his films moved toward 1968, Godard became increasingly convinced that one cannot make movies—or any other kind of artwork—without first understanding how one is making them and why.

The upheavals and demonstrations of May 1968, when leftist students took to the streets of Paris and workers went on strike, intensified Godard's political commitment, leading him to organize a political cell (he and co-founder Jean-Pierre Gorin called it the Dziga Vertov film collective, after the Soviet innovator of *Kinó-Pravda*) for making films, in opposition to the Apollonian, bourgeois model of the individual artist–creator. The character played by Yves Montand in *Tout va bien* is, like Godard, a film director who explains that he could no longer continue making auteurist films after the events of 1968. But Montand's choice becomes a cynical one; he decides to shoot the most vapid and exploitative television commercials exclusively. Unlike this character, Godard decided to become the analyst rather than the manipulator of modern cultural packaging. In that same film, Jane Fonda plays Montand's wife (they met on the barricades in 1968), a news correspondent who now feels she "corresponds to nothing." They get caught in a strike whose leaders have a flair for guerrilla theatre; re-think their politics, work, and marriage; and begin to think of themselves in historic terms. *Tout va bien* constructs itself as it goes and comments on the choices it makes. As long as there is a growing level of consciousness in art, sex, work, and politics, "tout va bien"—everything's going well.

In addition to the events of 1968, another important influence on Godard's work must have been the revolutionary political films from embattled Third World countries (like the mammoth *Hour of the Furnaces* from Argentina), which were first shown frequently in Europe the same year as the Paris riots. The political discussions in Godard's films, beginning with *La Chinoise* (especially the colonialism debate in *Weekend* and black radical rhetoric in *One Plus One*), seem to have been inspired by similar discussions in Third World films—much as his earlier films were influenced by and offered their own take on American B pictures, back when he considered Hawks the most precise analyst of the laws of cinema. But while these Third World films advocate stirring political actions and passionately address a unified working-class audience, Godard's discussions are abstracted, antidramatic analyses of semiotic and political theory; like much post-1968 film theory, they are likely to make more sense to the highly educated than to the proletariat. This fact makes it important to educate the audience about politics and about representation, a consistent project of Godard's post-1968 work. Many of those films were made in collaboration, co-directed either with Jean-Pierre Gorin—in 1969, *Pravda* and *Vent d'est* (*Wind from the East*); in 1970, the PLO-inspired *Till Victory;* in 1972, *Letter to Jane* and its companion piece, *Tout va bien*—or with Anne-Marie Miéville: in 1975, *Numéro deux* (or *Breathless Number Two*, not a sequel but a

Fig. 13-27
France/Tour/Détour/Deux/Enfants: *Godard and Miéville put "truth" ("vérité") on TV. Photo by Erika Sudeuburg.*

film made for the same cost as *Breathless*) and *Ici et ailleurs* (*Here and Elsewhere*, a meditation on *Till Victory* and the view from here of the politically and geographically elsewhere); in 1976, *Comment ça va? (How's It Going?)*, a reflexive conversation about and from a work in progress.

The investigation of language is an aspect of every Godard film, but it reaches its philosophical peak in *2 or 3 Things I Know About Her* and its political apex in *Wind from the East*. Beginning in 1968, Godard also made films for TV about language (*Le Gai savoir*, released 1969); with Anne-Marie Miéville, he made two important series for TV, the 1976 *Communication* (*Six fois deux/Sur et sous la communication* [*Six Times Two*—the series was in six parts and had two directors—*On and Under Communication*, where *sur* means "over" as well as "about"]) and the 1978 *France/Tour/Détour/Deux/Enfants*. Godard's controversial *Hail Mary* (1985) opened with a short film by Miéville—which many preferred to the Godard feature; that same year they made *Soft and Hard (A Soft Conversation on Hard Subjects)*. In the 1980s, Godard made a number of richly theatrical films that investigated art, religion, and genres (*Passion*, 1982; *First Name: Carmen*, 1983; *Hail Mary; Detective*, 1985). His wry, enigmatic, meditative, questioning voice was fully engaged in a film advertised as the sequel to *Alphaville*, again starring Eddie Constantine, *Germany Nine Zero* (1991); its subtitle—*Solitudes: A State and Variations*—indicated his growing interest in the musical structuring of observations and arguments, an interest carried further in his study of the politics of variations and repetition, *For Ever Mozart* (1996). In *Notre musique* (*Our Music*, 2004), a meditation on violence on film and in the world, Godard argued that the cinema is built on the "shot and counter-shot" of the imaginary and the real: "Imaginary: certainty. Reality: uncertainty. The principle of cinema: go toward the light and shine it on our night. Our music." In *Éloge de l'amour* (*In Praise of Love*, 2001), he shot in color and in black and white, on 35mm film and on digital video, an essay on love, global economics, memory and history, the quality of contemporary cinema, old age, literature, and many other subjects—a view of the world from a critic who never stops looking.

Extending the investigation of self, divination, and spirit begun in *Passion* and *Hail Mary*, and facilitating the leap from *Germany Nine Zero* to *For Ever Mozart*, *Hélas pour moi* (*Alas for Me*, or *Woe Is Me*, 1992, released 1993) is a meditation on mortality and disappointment. If Wittgenstein was the philosopher most important to *2 or 3 Things*, *Hélas pour moi* extrapolates the work of Jacques Derrida—seeking the traces of a god in a legend and in the ordinary contemporary world, while knowing that the traces can lead to no final knowledge and that there can be no absolute universal center or foundation of knowledge. Nevertheless, Godard meditates from a kind of center (which he

calls *ici-bas*, "down here" or "here as over there," a pun on *là-bas*) in which he finds that things are "absent—but nowhere else." As in *2 or 3 Things*, Godard is still investigating objects, analyzing images and sounds, and trying to construct a basis for the cinema; he is also still doing a lot of quoting. Even if, as he admits, parts of the world and his subject refuse to be told, Godard's mature understanding of distance allows him to continue to probe the nature of engagement.

Alain Resnais

Although Alain Resnais has been consistently linked with both Truffaut and Godard, he is a completely different kind of filmmaker. Ten years older than Truffaut and Godard, Resnais began his career in films not as *cinéaste* and critic but as film editor and documentary filmmaker. His most important early films were documentaries that studied the works of artists (Van Gogh, Gauguin, Picasso's *Guernica*) or examined the horrors of the Nazi concentration camps (*Night and Fog*, 1955, in which monochrome footage of the camps when they were in use is intercut with color footage of the camps in the mid-1950s, a harrowing film about the importance and the limitations of memory). But as with Truffaut, 1959 was the year of Resnais's first feature, *Hiroshima mon amour*, and critics considered his work part of the same "wave" despite the differences in his films.

Emmanuelle Riva and Eiji Okada in Hiroshima mon amour.

Fig. 13-28

Resnais begins with a far more literary premise than Truffaut or Godard. His films are neither improvised nor spontaneous. Like Bresson and Renoir, Resnais begins with detailed, literate, highly polished scripts. Although Resnais does not usually adapt novels into films, he often asks novelists to write his original scripts: Marguerite Duras, Alain Robbe-Grillet, Jean Cayrol. (In his later films, he did adapt plays.) Resnais respects literateness, complex construction, and poetic speech. His films are thoughtful, astonishing, tightly controlled, and at times operatic. Because one of the key Resnais themes is the effect of time, the interrelation of past, present, and future, of memory and event, his narratives are frequently elliptical, cutting in time and space even more freely than Truffaut's or Godard's.

In *Hiroshima mon amour* (1959), written by Marguerite Duras, a French woman and a Japanese man try to build something more between them than a single night in bed. She is an actress who has come to Hiroshima to make a peace film; he is an architect trying to build the ruined city up from its ashes. But they are separated by more than cultural distance. Between them is the past. For him, there is Hiroshima, the burned-out home of his youth; for her, Nevers, the little French town where she loved a German soldier in the occupation army whom the villagers murdered when the Nazis evacuated. Both have burned-out pasts.

To show the intrusion of these pasts into the present, Resnais cuts shots of Nevers and the Hiroshima carnage into the shots of the present. At the film's opening, the two embracing lovers' arms seem to be covered with radioactive dust. As they make love, Resnais's camera tracks through the Hiroshima war museum, showing the burnt buildings and mutilated bodies. When the woman (Emmanuelle Riva) glances at the twitching hand of her sleeping lover (Eiji Okada), Resnais cuts to a short, sudden flash of her experience in Nevers: the moment she held her German lover and saw his hand twitch as he died. The result of this assault of the past on the present is an emotional gulf between them that can never be bridged.

Last Year at Marienbad (1961) is a film that is richly formal and narratively challenging. Resnais captures the ornate details of an

Fig. 13-29

Fig. 13-30

Fig. 13-31
Framing and space in Last Year at Marienbad. *Fig. 13-29: X, the suitor (Giorgio Albertazzi), watches a couple we see framed in a mirror; Fig. 13-30: a board game against a painted checkerboard; Fig. 13-31: the woman, A (Delphine Seyrig), poses in front of a formal garden that might be either real or trompe l'oeil.*

elegant and elaborate chateau: its mirrors and chandeliers, its carved walls and ceilings, its formal gardens. His editing adds to the visual excitement, jumping about the castle so freely that he erases—or renews—time and space completely. Alain Robbe-Grillet, who wrote *Marienbad*, said that "elsewhere" and "formerly" are impossible in the continuously renewed present tense of cinema, so that whether a given shot or sequence presents objective or subjective material (fantasies, dreams, memories), the events of *Marienbad* happen not in two years at two chateau-resorts, nor in a week at one resort, but in the hour and a half it takes to project the film. Resnais (whose early features were edited by Henri Colpi and Jasmine Chasney) treats virtually any straight cut as a leap in time, not only as a shift from one physical or mental space to another; this is most clear in his science fiction film about love and memory, *Je t'aime, je t'aime* (1968), but it begins in *Night and Fog* and catalyzes all the features. In *Marienbad*, every event is ambiguous. A man (X, played by Giorgio Albertazzi) meets a woman (A, played by Delphine Seyrig) at what may or may not be an elegant resort near the town of Marienbad; he may or may not have met her there or at a different resort one year before. He relentlessly implores her to leave the resort with him, to leave the man (M, played by Sacha Pitoeff) who may or may not be her husband. At the end of the film, she may or may not remember having met him (X may have convinced her of a lie), but she does appear to leave with him.

Resnais followed *Marienbad* with *Muriel or The Time of a Return* (1963), his first feature in color. Written by Jean Cayrol, the Auschwitz survivor who had written *Night and Fog*, *Muriel* sticks to the present (rather than allowing direct views of the past, as *Night and Fog* and *Hiroshima* do, or refusing to define the present while scrambling the objective and subjective past and present, as *Marienbad* does) as its characters attempt to deal with the past. Even as the characters remember and talk about the past, and figures from the past show up (some with lies and some with the hidden truth), forcing all of them to deal with old political atrocities and romantic betrayals, *Muriel* shows how they and the city in which the action is set (Boulogne—like Hiroshima, reconstructed after World War II) are part of a system. That systemic approach directly influenced Godard in *2 or 3 Things I Know About Her* and helped to make *Muriel*

the most formally satisfying and emotionally powerful of Resnais's films, the perfect climax to his four-film investigation (beginning with *Night and Fog*) of the difficulty and necessity of remembering, of coming to terms with the lessons of horror and love. As cold and intellectual as some people find Resnais's formally perfect films, they are deeply romantic and intensely political in addition to being philosophically profound. Like Godard and Chris Marker, Resnais is someone who thinks with film.

After returning to black and white to make a relatively accessible story of love and contemporary politics in the context of the Spanish Civil War, lost long ago, *La Guerre est finie* (*The War is Over*, 1966), Resnais concentrated on formal color style pieces: some of them as elegantly structured as operas, some as rigorous as investigations. *Je t'aime, je t'aime* used science fiction to experiment with the tenses of film narrative—but for Resnais, the true time machine is cinema itself. While some Resnais color films—notably *Muriel* and the controversial *Stavisky . . .* (1974)—maintain a political focus, *Providence* (1977, his first film in English) uses his athletic, subjective editing to examine the narrative process, studying a novelist's consciousness, and wandering from his life to his dreams to the novel he is writing. In *Mon oncle d'Amérique* (1980), an almost clinical study of stress, Resnais likens the edited pieces of film to the tiles of a mosaic, gathered into a unity by the codes of cinematic narration and the audience's perception of formal connection.

Because of what many perceive as a growing lack of interest in serious, complex films, Resnais's films of the 1980s—*La Vie est un roman* (1983), *L'Amour à mort* (1984), *Mélo* (1986), and *I Want to Go Home* (1989, written by Jules Feiffer)—were released in France but had little or no exposure abroad. But he hit the perfect tone and method in 1993 with *Smoking and No Smoking*, two complementary films based on six plays (from a sequence of eight two-part plays written by Alan Ayckbourn), presenting 12 possible conclusions; the permutations vary further depending on which of the films one sees first, and neither film is inherently "first." All of the female characters are played by Sabine Azéma, all of the males by Pierre Arditi. The two had starred in *La Vie est un roman* (*Life is a Novel*),

L'Amour à mort (Love until Death), and Mélo, but even for such versatile performers, this was a stretch. The audience enjoys and plays along with their impersonations—and the game that keeps no more than two of the nine characters, necessarily a man and a woman, onscreen at a time—even as it cares about the characters and the branching, alternative consequences of their decisions (to have an affair or not, go to school or not, say this instead of that). "Or else," the film announces as it doubles back on itself to show how an event might have gone differently and then follows that different plot development to its conclusion. Theatrical, reflexive, witty, and, like all his pictures, *tight*, this double film is as systematic as anything Resnais has ever done, but it is also compulsively engaging and finally very funny and moving. Like the disciplined but wacky actors, the contradictory sequences are graceful, clean, controlled, and formally perfect without pointing it out—a marked difference from the self-consciousness of *Marienbad;* everything is artificial and rings true. Widely exhibited, except in the United States, *Smoking/No Smoking*—and the prize-winning work that followed, *On connaît la chanson (Same Old Song,* 1997), inspired by the teleplays of Dennis Potter, especially *Pennies From Heaven* and *The Singing Detective,* in which characters break not into song but into recorded popular songs—reminded audiences of the existence of one of the world's greatest filmmakers. His mysterious and romantic *Wild Grass* (2009) was more widely exhibited.

Chabrol, Rohmer, and Rivette

Many important directors—though not of the stature of Godard, Truffaut, and Resnais—also contributed to the reputation of the French film in the 1960s. Claude Chabrol was the first of the *Cahiers* critics to make a feature film (*Le Beau Serge,* 1958). In films such as *Les Cousins* (1959), *A double tour* (*Leda,* 1959, also called *Web of Passion*), *Les Bonnes femmes* (1960), *Landru* (1962), *Les Biches* (1968), *Que la bête meure* (*The Beast Must Die,* 1969), *Le Boucher* (1970), *La Rupture* (1971), *Wedding in Blood* (1973), and *Violette* (1978), Chabrol reveals—rather like Hitchcock, whom he often emulates—a superb contrapuntal tension between the sexual passions of his characters and the carefully detailed

social environment. Chabrol, who often adapts *noir* fiction, specializes in romantic case studies that often culminate in a grotesque murder.

Eric Rohmer began making his "Six Moral Tales" in 1962 (the first was a short, the second less than an hour long) and found a worldwide audience with the fourth one, *My Night at Maud's* (1969), a tale of love and religion and serious conversation. The mental battle over desire was joined again, almost as memorably, in the last two films in the series, *Claire's Knee* (1970) and *Chloe in the Afternoon* (1972). In 1976, he turned his austere eye to literature, adapting Heinrich von Kleist's *The Marquise of O . . .,* and in 1978, he retold Chrétien de Troyes's 12th-century version of the legend of the grail-seeking Parsifal (also called Parzival or Perceval) according to the conventions and in the imagery of medieval art (*Perceval*). He then began another cycle, "Comedies and Proverbs," which includes *The Aviator's Wife* (1981), *Le Beau mariage* (*The Perfect Marriage,* 1982), *Pauline at the Beach* (1983), and *Full Moon in Paris* (1984). His characters continued to pursue desire and achieve epiphanies in his later films, particularly *Le Rayon vert* (*The Green Ray,* or *Summer,* 1986) and *A Tale of Winter* (1992); the latter is part of another series, "Tales of Four Seasons," begun in 1989 with *A Tale of Springtime* and completed with *Autumn Tale* in 1998. In 1987, he made *Four Adventures of Reinette and Mirabelle,* an exuberant and unpredictable film in which he sought "to return to my roots and to the tone of the first short films that we shot, Rivette, Truffaut, Godard, and myself."

Of the five *Cahiers* critics-turned-filmmakers, Jacques Rivette has had the least commercial success, but his long, labyrinthine explorations of the nature of film and the paradoxes of narration are central to the New Wave's spirited reinvention of the cinema. His first feature—begun at the same time as Chabrol's *Le Beau Serge* but so intricate and ambitious that it was not finished and released until 1961—was *Paris nous appartient* (*Paris Belongs to Us*); produced by Truffaut, it's the picture the family goes to see in *The 400 Blows.* Using both narrative and antinarrative methods, Rivette dramatized and analyzed narration itself in *L'Amour fou* (1968), *Out 1* (1971, nearly 13 hours), *Out 1: Spectre* (1974, a different film made from the footage of *Out 1*), and especially the mysterious, intricate, and playful *Céline and Julie Go Boating* (1974).

Varda, Marker, and the Documentary

The "Left Bank" group of Chris Marker, Alain Resnais, and Agnès Varda worked in the documentary as well as the feature film, and they often worked together. Marker and Resnais co-wrote and co-directed *Les Statues meurent aussi* (1953)—and both concentrated in their later works on the problems of time, politics, and the nature of truth; both also learned much about stasis and editing from comic books, and both turned at some point to science fiction in search of the freedom to explore their ideas about memory and time. In 1954, Resnais edited Varda's *La Pointe-Courte*, which as previously mentioned was either the first of the New Wave features or the film that most decisively anticipated the movement. But Varda was also connected with a New Wave filmmaker who belonged to neither the Left Bank nor the *Cahiers* group: her husband, Jacques Demy.

Demy might be considered the Busby Berkeley of the movement. His first great film was *Lola* (1961), which intertwined several love stories and was both enchanting and moving. In *The Umbrellas of Cherbourg* (1964), which introduced Catherine Deneuve to the screen, Demy took the tritest of melodramatic plots (boy loves girl; he goes into the army; she marries a rich suitor; he returns; their love can never be again), decorated it with the richest frosting he could find, and made audiences weep. The film is 100 percent all-singing; even the most banal ideas—needing a penicillin shot, asking for a liter of gas—get the benefit of Michel Legrand's lush score in what may be the first opera written for the cinema. The color scheme of *The Umbrellas of Cherbourg* was fabulously creative, and it had the good luck to come out the same year as *Red Desert*, when self-conscious color was newly being scrutinized and valued. His later films include *Les Demoiselles de Rochefort* (1966) and *Donkey Skin* (1970); he died in 1990.

Agnès Varda is a totally different kind of filmmaker: probing, thoughtful, intellectually sensitive to the problems of the artist and the difficulty of living fully. Her first film, *La Pointe-Courte*, was inspired by William Faulkner's

The Wild Palms, a novel written in what Eisenstein would have called parallel montage (two short, systematically opposite novels about the nature of love and freedom, presented in alternating chapters), two of whose characters leave the city to nurture their love in the woods. That image of hard-won romantic freedom, paradoxical loss, and sense of place dominates *La Pointe-Courte* and shows up, somewhat more simplistically, in other New Wave films—notably Godard's *Pierrot le fou* (1965)—as an image of romantic escape. Eventually Godard adapted the *structure* of *The Wild Palms:* two films—*Made in U.S.A* (1966) and *2 or 3 Things I Know About Her*—both shot in the summer of 1966 and meant to be shown in alternating reels (but never shown that way, since *Made in U.S.A* was banned before *2 or 3 Things* was released). Godard acknowledged both Varda and Faulkner by having Patricia read *The Wild Palms* in *Breathless*. A cinematic generation later, Wim Wenders acknowledged Godard with the same novel in *Kings of the Road* (1976).

The film that made Varda famous was *Cléo from 5 to 7* (1961), which follows a woman (Corinne Marchand) in virtually real time while she confronts the possibility that she has cancer. *Le Bonheur* (*Happiness*, 1965), shot in deliberately beautiful color, tells the moral tale of a happily married man who has a happy extramarital affair and decides to share his happiness with his wife, who takes the news rather badly. *Daguerréotypes* (1975), one of Varda's many documentaries, presents the people who live on her street, which is named after Daguerre. (All her documentaries are personal as well as objective; the most moving is *Jacquot de Nantes*, 1991, a film about Demy.) *One Sings, the Other Doesn't* (1977) returns to fiction to examine, in feminist terms, a long friendship between two women. *Documenteur: An Emotion Picture* (1981), whose title is a pun—documentary filmmaker and liar—exemplifies the wit of her hard, incisive look at the world. *Sans toit ni loi* (literally, *Without Roof nor Law*, 1985; U.S. title, *Vagabond*) investigates the rewards and costs of a free life, re-creating the final weeks in the life of a young drifter (Sandrine Bonnaire); the film is appropriately dedicated to the French writer Nathalie Sarraute, author of *Tropisms* and master of the neutral observation of the behavior of

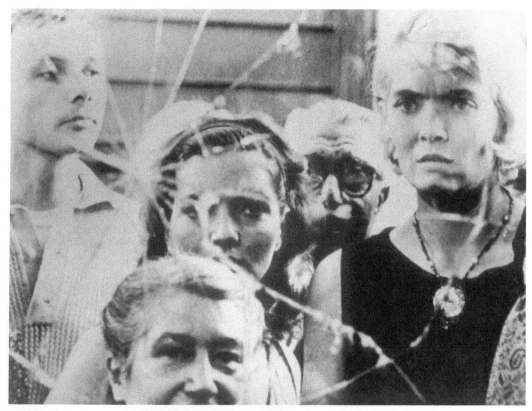

Fig. 13-32
Cléo from 5 to 7: *a look at life and death (Corinne Marchand, right).*

organisms. The personal and careful way she studies what she gathers is clear in the title of her documentary *The Gleaners and I* (2000). She filmed her lyrical and unconventional memoir, *The Beaches of Agnès*, in 2008. A true *auteur*, Varda writes, directs, and edits or co-edits her films, which are characterized by her great eye for strong compositions and colors and by the complex, painful problems with which she forces her characters to deal.

Chris Marker, who was born Christian François Bouche-Villeneuve, established himself as an author and world-traveled journalist before co-directing his first documentaries with Resnais in the early 1950s. His own documentaries have enlarged the possibilities of the art; he has worked in the neglected genres of the letter (*Letter from Siberia*, 1957), the essay (*Cuba sí!*, 1961), and the meditation (*Sans soleil*, 1983). Some of his narrative films are as much fiction as

nonfiction (one would be hard pressed to call *The Koumiko Mystery*, 1965, a pure fiction); what drives them is narration itself. Even his science fiction short, *La Jetée* (1963, released 1964)—perhaps the best film ever made on the subject of time travel—is told in words, voice-over, as much as it is shown, and it is shown almost entirely in a paradoxically cinematic succession of stills (frozen moments in the museum of the main character's memory, like the fragments of time caught and held as individual still frames of movie film—and like the "stills" in a comic book). In the early 1960s Marker experimented with *cinéma vérité* (*Le Joli mai*, 1962, released 1963). In the mid-1960s he organized the SLON film cooperative (the Society for the Launching of New Works), through which he produced several highly political compilation films—the most important of which was *Far from Vietnam* (1967), for which Resnais,

Chris Marker's Sans soleil: *a travelogue through the culture of images in an attempt to define the self, the other, and actual others.*

Fig. 13-33

A frozen moment from La Jetée.

Fig. 13-34

Godard, and others made short films about what it meant to be far from the combat (making movies in safety) but inevitably, philosophically, politically involved in it—and released such controversial films as the long, powerful documentary *The Battle of Chile* (directed by Patricio Guzmán; Parts I and II, 1973–77).

Marker's film essays often take the form of travel journals, narrated voice-over, in which the alien observer looks at and tries to make sense of what interests him: faces, videos, cats— fragments of the mystery of life, with which he is gravely and wittily engaged; the most representative and moving of these is *Sans soleil*. A powerful essay that is not a travel film but a revisiting of the history of Communism and Soviet cinema in the form of "missives" to a Soviet filmmaker, *The Last Bolshevik* (1993) continues his investigation of memory and reality, and a 1994 short, *Prime Time in the Camps*, takes a guerrilla-video approach to the war in Bosnia. One of the greatest films ever made about one filmmaker by another is his study of Tarkovsky's directing, *One Day in the Life of Andrei Arsenevich* (1999).

Since 1998, he has done a great deal of his work on computer media.

In 1960, ethnographic filmmaker Jean Rouch, in collaboration with sociologist Edgar Morin, made *Chronique d'un été (Paris 1960)* (*Chronicle of a Summer,* released 1961), the first and most influential film in the French documentary movement that was another contribution of the New Wave, *cinéma vérité.* Here and in Marker's more personal *Le Joli mai,* people on the street are interviewed about their lives and feelings, provoked by the filmmakers (who, with their equipment, are not always hidden from view) to reveal their true selves, virtually to confess to the camera. In *cinéma vérité*—made possible by the invention of portable 16mm sync-sound equipment—the primary drama is the interaction of the unrehearsed subject, warts and all, with the camera, whose presence is always acknowledged. In *direct cinema,* which developed in England, America, and Canada in the 1960s, the camera is less obtrusive.

Marcel Ophuls created his own form of the investigative documentary, characterized by a cagey, well-informed style of interviewing that lasts so long and proceeds so congenially that the interviewee, given enough rope and footage to hang himself or herself, reveals events and attitudes that he or she may have kept secret for years and may not even be conscious of revealing to Ophuls and the patient camera. Ophuls expresses his own attitudes in three ways: by pouncing on the interviewee at a critical moment, pointing out contradictions and lies; by intercutting the interviews; and by cutting to archival footage from the period under investigation. Sometimes playful, sometimes sarcastic, and sometimes devastating, Ophuls's montage intrusions are the release valve for the tensions accumulated during his long, patient interviews. In *The Sorrow and the Pity* (1969) he exposed the ways many of the French felt all right about collaborating with the Nazis during the Occupation. In *The Memory of Justice* (1976), the most powerful and demanding of his works, he compared the war crimes, and the military trials and investigations that followed, in World War II, the Algerian War, and the Vietnam War—finding, for example, that the French lawyers were harder on the Nazis than they were on the French officers who committed atrocities in Algeria. *A Sense of Loss* (1972) addressed the situation in Northern Ireland, and *Hôtel Terminus: The Life and Times of Klaus Barbie* (1988) detailed not only the hunt for the "butcher of Lyon" but also the covert military and government activity that allowed Barbie to escape justice for so long. *November Days* (1992) looked at the last days of East Germany, and *The Troubles We've Seen: A History of Journalism in Wartime* (1994) concentrated on Sarajevo.

Inspired by Ophuls's work, Claude Lanzmann made *Shoah* (1985), a 9 1/2-hour documentary about the Holocaust. Lanzmann's extremely long interviews stick rigorously to the present; there is no archival footage, only an intense look at what remains. As Lanzmann noted, his approach was precisely the opposite of that adopted by Spielberg in his 1993 *Schindler's List,* which took what Lanzmann considered the easier route of historical re-creation.

Fig. 13-35

*Shoah: **Simon Srebnik, a survivor of the Holocaust, meets with the Polish gentiles who remember him from 40 years ago and listens— outside the town church where Jews were rounded up—to their reminiscences and unexamined prejudices.***

Lacombe Lucien: *Lucien (Pierre Blaise), a French peasant who becomes a German agent during the Occupation, practices his slingshot in front of a portrait of Marshal Pétain, the head of the Vichy government.*

Fig. 13-36

Malle and Others

Louis Malle was one of the most eclectic of the New Wave directors. After studying political science and then filmmaking, he virtually co-directed Jacques-Yves Cousteau's underwater documentary *The Silent World* (1956), which won an Academy Award; then he assisted Bresson on *A Man Escaped*. His first feature, *Elevator to the Gallows* or *Frantic* (1957, released 1958), was a thriller with a score by Miles Davis, starring Jeanne Moreau, and shot by Henri Decaë (who was soon to shoot *The 400 Blows* and *Le Beau Serge*; Decaë was the vital cinematographer for the *Cahiers* group before the advent of Raoul Coutard, who worked primarily with Godard, and Nestor Almendros, who worked primarily with Rohmer and Truffaut). In later years he would make a multi-part documentary on India as well as two of the best movies ever to attempt to sort out the moral complexities of living in France under the Nazi occupation: *Lacombe Lucien* (1974) and *Au revoir les enfants* (1987). His first contribution to the New Wave was *The Lovers* (1958), a graceful and erotic tale of the manners and world of the rich, culminating in the woman's throwing over both industrialist husband and polo-playing lover to leave with the young student with whom she spends the night. *Zazie dans le Métro* (1960) is a delightfully breezy, illogical, spirited film that uses cinematic tricks to re-create the literary and linguistic gags of Raymond Queneau's novel. The film is one of surprise and freedom, the director's hymn to the spontaneous and unfettered. *Murmur of the Heart* (1971) seems a synthesis of these earlier styles with its child's-eye view of the restraints of adult life and a wealthy, attractive mother's attempts to manage both her family and her love life. Malle would later desert his French environment for the American scene—*Pretty Baby* (1978), *Atlantic City* (1980, a Canadian–French co-production), *My Dinner with Andre* (1981), *Damage* (1992)—a prime example of the internationalization of film production since the late 1970s. The last film he completed before his death in 1995 was *Vanya on 42nd Street* (1994).

France itself has long had an internationalized industry, dating back to the American arm of Star Films established by Gaston Méliès, Georges's brother, at the turn of the 20th century (Gaston was the first to hire John Ford—as an actor in his westerns). The Spaniards Dalí and Buñuel made their Surrealist films in France in 1929–30, and during the blacklist such American directors as Jules Dassin (*Rififi*, 1955) found a home in the French industry. Since the 1960s, many important films have been made in France by directors born, and sometimes trained, in other countries. Among these are the Swiss directors Claude Goretta (*The Lacemaker*, 1977) and Alain Tanner (*The Salamander*, 1971; *The Middle of the World*, 1974; *Jonah Who Will be 25 in the Year 2000*, 1976). Tanner, who applies a Marxist analysis to the lives of middle-class citizens, examines the tangles of love, work, and politics as his characters attempt to form a more responsive human community. The Greek director Costa-Gavras—who was born Constantinos (familiarly, "Costas") Gavras—made a series of violent and probing political films (*Z*, 1969; *The Confession*, 1970; *State of Siege*, 1972, released 1973) that combined radical analysis with the radical styles of the New Wave; like *Breathless* and *Jules and Jim*, *Z* was shot by Raoul Coutard. Some of Costa-Gavras's American films, particularly *Missing* (1982), maintained an active political focus and continued his investigation into the differences between true and false accounts of events.

In the 1990s and early 2000s, the astute reader of credits would find that many films from the emerging industries of Algeria (Merzak Allouache's *Bab El-Oued City*, 1994; Rachid Bouchareb's *Dust of Life*, 1994), Romania (Lucian Pintilie's *An Unforgettable Summer*, 1994), Tunisia (Moufida Tlatli's *Silences of the Palace*, 1994), and Vietnam (Hung Tran Anh's *The Scent of Green Papaya*, 1992) were French co-productions; some of them, like *The Scent of Green Papaya*, were even made in France, on French sets, by international directors. The most significant French films of the early 1990s were made by the Polish director Krzysztof Kieślowski: *The Double Life of Veronique* (1991) and *Three Colors* (1993–94, comprising the features *Blue*, *White*, and *Red*); his intensely moody, intuitive dramas trace the paradoxes of relationship in a way that raises huge, deep questions rather than settles them. One of the most visually inventive films of the early 2000s was a U.S.–French co-production with American producers and an American director, Julian Schnabel; *The Diving Bell and the Butterfly* (2007; literally, *The Diving Suit and the Butterfly*)—based on the memoir by Jean-Dominique Bauby, the editor of the fashion magazine *Elle*, who suffered a stroke that left him with "locked-in syndrome," where his mind worked normally but he was almost completely paralyzed, having the use of only one eye and its lids—adopts the POV of that one eye for much of its running time, experimenting with camera movement and exposure (almost in the manner of Stan Brakhage) as the eye rolls to get a grasp of the room, refocuses, seizes on faces. Bauby learns to blink when the letter he wants is recited to him from a usage-frequency alphabet, painstakingly composes sentences, and lives just long enough to write a book about his experience. It is an inspiring and deeply original film.

Still, native French talent continued to prosper both in the last years of the New Wave and after its demise in the early 1970s. Truffaut's assistant, Bertrand Blier, studied male sexuality in *Going Places* (1974) and *Get Out Your Handkerchiefs* (1977). Roger Vadim's *and God . . . created woman* (1956) made an international sex symbol out of Brigitte Bardot and prepared the way for the theatrical exhibition of New Wave films by demonstrating that sexually frank films could be nonpornographic and bring in big audiences. (Bardot, who later became an animal-rights activist, said in the 1990s, "I gave my youth to men and my wisdom to animals.") Jean Eustache made one of the more interesting experiments in cinematic form and sexist commentary before his suicide (*The Mother and the Whore*, 1973; considered by many the last film of the New Wave). Claude Miller made one of the few French feature films to explore repressed homosexual feelings (*The Better Way*, 1975). And Alain Robbe-Grillet made films that, like *Marienbad*, extended the principles of the "new novel" to the cinema (*The Man Who Lies*, 1968; *La Belle captive*, 1982).

Four women directors joined the post–New Wave generation of French filmmakers—two of whom worked within the French film industry, and two of whom worked very much outside it. Diane Kurys (*Peppermint Soda*, 1977; *Entre nous*, 1983; *C'est la vie*, 1990) and Nelly Kaplan (*A Very Curious Girl*, 1969; *Néa*, 1976; *Charles and Lucie*, 1979) moved from apprenticeships with Gance, Resnais, and Truffaut to direct their own relatively commercial, industry-backed films, frequently concentrating on young women or maturing adolescents at turning points in their lives. The novelist Marguerite Duras went from writing scripts for Resnais (*Hiroshima mon amour*) to writing and directing films, often based on her own novels and plays (*La Musica*, 1966; *Destroy, She Said*, 1969;

Nathalie Granger, 1973; *The Woman of the Ganges*, 1974; *India Song*, 1975; *Days in the Trees*, 1976; *Le Camion*, 1977). She died in 1996 at the age of 81. Like her novels, Duras's films experiment with both narrative form and psychological representation—often in the interplay between minimal visual imagery and densely rich soundtracks. The Belgian Chantal Akerman is influenced by experimental filmmakers on both sides of the Atlantic—Godard, Michael Snow, Stan Brakhage. In her first ten years as a filmmaker, she directed 17 movies. Her films (especially *Jeanne Dielman/23, Quai du Commerce/1080 Bruxelles*, 1975, and *Meetings with Anna*, 1978) reduce plot and dialogue, emphasizing the duration of uninterrupted temporality and the resonance of spaces. Like Varda, these directors have given France the claim to the longest of woman-centered cinematic narrative traditions, one that goes back to Alice Guy, Germaine Dulac, and Marie Epstein. Duras's films, which carry out avant-garde experiments with narrating voices and minimal plotting, are like those of her predecessors in that they are outside the mainstream of commercial narrative filmmaking, while those of Kurys are not. The works of Kaplan and Akerman are, in their own distinct ways, radical in form and feminist in politics.

In the 1990s and early 2000s, France remained a major presence on world screens, thanks not only to the new films of Akerman, Chabrol,

Godard, Resnais, Rohmer, Varda, and other established artists, but also to the compelling and fully realized works of many newcomers. *Microcosmos: The People of the Grass* (1996, a French–Swiss–Italian co-production) showed a day in a meadow—created by Claude Nuridsany and Marie Pérennou out of years of extreme close-ups—as it might be experienced at ground level, primarily by insects. Gaspar Noé, who was born in Argentina and signs his films "Noe," took psychological and social horror to new extremes with a short (*Carne*, 1991) and a feature (*Seul contre tous* or *I Stand Alone*, 1998) about a horsemeat butcher whose life is destroyed by his violence, his sweeping hatred, and his love for his daughter. *Seul contre tous* actually stops to flash a warning for 30 seconds so that the audience can leave before the most violent and perverse scene, which may be a Postmodern joke but which is also, for some people, good advice. Noé's next feature, *Irreversible* (2002), starts with the butcher but soon abandons him to tell the story of an extraordinarily vicious rape and a misguided revenge, neither of which can be undone. In a structure similar to that of *Betrayal* (directed by David Jones and written by Harold Pinter in the U.K., 1983), *Irreversible* presents the story in reverse order, from the last event to the first, creating a uniquely painful experience as it moves back through horror to a stability that brings the wildly careening camera to a stop,

Fig. 13-37
Amélie (Audrey Tautou) watches a movie.

closing the film with a peaceful, symmetrical image of doomed fertility and hope. At the beginning, the camera tries to swing around and get behind the credits, as if it could reverse the image and the course of the action—which is irreversible at the start because everything has already happened. Noé's subject matter is violent and upsetting, and the damage his characters suffer is permanent. His pictures are relentless, realistic, and moral. By following characters who make one catastrophic decision after another and advance ever further into personal hells of hatred, desire, and ruin, they confront social problems, psychological labyrinths, and the responsibilities that go with making a choice.

Alain Berliner's *Ma vie en rose* (*My Life in Pink*, 1997, a Belgian–French–British co-production) is a sex comedy about a boy who wants to be a girl; the title is a play on a song made famous by Edith Piaf, "La Vie en rose," and the film asserts the power of imagination to transform the look and even some of the reality of oneself and the world. In *Irma Vep* (1996), a movie that could be timed not in frames per second but in film references per minute, Olivier Assayas portrays the last gasp of the New Wave—the attempt of an obsessed director, played by Jean-Pierre Léaud, and a real martial arts star, Maggie Cheung, to create something perfectly new and old, a shot-for-shot remake of Feuillade's silent serial *Les Vampires*—as a nervous breakdown. In *The Dreamlife of Angels* (1998), Érick Zonca offers an unforced, realistic look at what it is like, in the cities of northern France, for two young women to find and lose— or live always on the fringe of—a job, a place to live, and someone to care about. Chilean filmmaker Raul Ruiz made the best film yet adapted from Marcel Proust's overwhelming novel, *A la recherche du temps perdu* (*In Search of Lost Time*); in his long, rich adaptation of the novel's final volume, *Time Regained* (1999), Ruiz found his own impressionistic terms—gliding across subjectivity through moments and rooms—for Proust's narrator's discovery of the range of one's being in time. Catherine Breillat took an unexcited look at desire in *Romance* (1999) and *The Fat Girl* (2001). Vincent Paronnaud and Marjane Satrapi made the animated *Persepolis* in 2007; it was based on Satrapi's autobiographical graphic novel and showed what it was like for a girl to grow up during the Islamic Revolution in Iran. The team of Jean-Pierre Jeunet (*metteur-en-scène*) and Marc Caro (artistic director—that is, production designer) crammed the screen with vibrant, deeply colored images in complex compositions; their fast cutting, poetic writing, surreal comedy, and exhilarating special effects (by far the best computer work in France at the time) made their wild, dark fables, *Delicatessen* (1991) and *The City of Lost Children* (1995), as entertaining as they were demanding. (Jeunet and Caro were in some ways the French complement of England's Michael Powell and Emeric Pressburger, the most inventive team of the 1940s.) On his own, Jeunet directed the squirmy *Alien Resurrection* (1997— the fourth in the series) in America, then returned to France to make the most positive film he could dream up, the popular and endearing *Amélie* (2001). In the excellent prison drama *A Prophet* (2009), Jacques Audiard tells the story of how a young man learns how to survive and succeed in prison and as a criminal in the outside world. Its contemporary gangs, both those on the rise and those in decline, are sharply observed; the dialogue is as pointed and tight as the violence; and the long movie goes by as if it were short.

Currently the elder statesman of the post–New Wave directors, Bertrand Tavernier is the most conscious of uniting the traditions of past and present cinema. Although a committed leftist, Tavernier, like Renoir of the 1930s, gives ordinary citizens their dignity in their attempts to understand the political, social, and military structures that contain them, for "everyone has his reasons." Although the middle-class father (*The Clockmaker*, 1974) cannot understand his son's acts of political radicalism, he comes to understand that his son must have a reason for them. *Coup de torchon* (1981), based loosely on Jim Thompson's novel *Pop. 1280*, satirizes the political commitments of both right and left, while *Deathwatch* (1979) imbeds its critique of cinema's exploiting the images of women within the framework of science fiction. His greatest commercial success of the 1980s was *Round Midnight* (1986), an evocative realization of the jazz scene in 1950s Paris; it experimented with jazz rhythms in its own structure and starred Dexter Gordon as an expatriate master of the tenor sax. Most reminiscent of Jean Renoir is *A Sunday in the Country* (1984)—from its title, which evokes Renoir's 1936 film, *A Day in the Country*, to its central character, an aging Impressionist painter and a contemporary of Auguste Renoir, the film director's father. Set early in the 20th century, at the time that photography and the cinema had come to supplant or supplement painting as the culture's dominant mode of pictorial representation, the film shows how the elderly painter comes to realize that the process of making images is not simply an act of craft or beauty but a reflection and a shaper of moral commitment. But the most impressive of all his films may be *L.627* (1992), a realistic look at the problems of drug use, the legal system, and police work in the world Tavernier faced every day.

Among the New Wave characteristics these later films share are their careful rendering of the textures of sensations and experiences, their antistudio look, their interest in political analysis (including the politics of gender), and their elliptical narrative structures that emphasize thematic development rather than a linear, chronological presentation of events.

For Further Viewing

FILMS

ITALY

MICHELANGELO ANTONIONI (1912–2007)
N.U. or *Netezza urbana* (*Trash Collectors*, 1948)
Cronaca di un amore (*Story of a Love Affair*, 1950)
I vinti (*The Vanquished*, 1952)
Le amiche (*The Girlfriends*, 1955)
Il grido (*The Cry*, 1957)
L'avventura (*The Adventure*, 1960)
La notte (*The Night*, 1960)
L'eclisse (*Eclipse*, 1962)
Il deserto rosso (*Red Desert*, 1964)
Blowup or *Blow-Up* (1966)
Zabriskie Point (1970)
Chung Kuo Cina or *China* (1972)
The Passenger (1975)
Beyond the Clouds (1995). Co-director, Wim Wenders

BERNARDO BERTOLUCCI (1940–   )
Before the Revolution (1964)
The Spider's Strategem (1970)
The Conformist (1970)
Last Tango in Paris (1972)
1900 (1976)
The Last Emperor (1987)
The Sheltering Sky (1990)

VITTORIO DE SICA (1902–74)
The Children Are Watching Us (1944). Completed 1942
Shoeshine (1946)
Bicycle Thieves or *The Bicycle Thief* (1948)
Miracle in Milan (1950)
Umberto D. (1952)
Two Women (1960)
A Brief Vacation (1973)

FEDERICO FELLINI (1920–93)
Variety Lights (1950). Co-director, Alberto Lattuada
I vitelloni (*The Calves* or *The Young and the Passionate*, 1953)
La strada (*The Street* or *The Road*, 1954)
Nights of Cabiria (1956)
La dolce vita (*The Sweet Life*, 1960)
8½ (1963)
Juliet of the Spirits (1965)
Fellini Satyricon or *Satyricon* (1969)
The Clowns (1971)
Amarcord (1973)
Casanova (1976)
Orchestra Rehearsal (1979)
Intervista (1988)

SERGIO LEONE (1921–89)
For a Fistful of Dollars or *A Fistful of Dollars* or *Fistful of Dollars* (1964)
For a Few Dollars More (1965)
The Good, the Bad and the Ugly (1966)
Once Upon a Time in the West (1968)
Once Upon a Time in America (1984)

PIER PAOLO PASOLINI (1922–75)
Accattone (*Beggar*, 1961)
The Gospel According to St. Matthew (1964)
Hawks and Sparrows (1966)
Teorema (*Theorem*, 1968)
Porcile (*Pigpen* or *Pigsty*, 1969)
Medea (1969)

The Decameron (1971)
The Canterbury Tales (1972)
The Arabian Nights (1974)
Salò or The 120 Days of Sodom (1975)

ROBERTO ROSSELLINI (1906–77)
Rome, Open City or Open City (1945)
Paisan (1946)
Germany Year Zero (1947)
The Miracle and *The Human Voice* (1948)
Stromboli (1949)
Europa '51 (1951)
Viaggio in Italia (*Voyage to Italy or Strangers*, 1953)
India (1958)
General Della Rovere (1959)
The Rise to Power of Louis XIV or The Taking of Power by Louis XIV (1966)
Socrates (1970)
The Messiah (1975)

ETTORE SCOLA (1931–   )
We All Loved Each Other So Much (1974)
A Special Day (1977)
La Nuit de Varennes (1982)

LUCHINO VISCONTI (1906–76)
Ossessione (*Obsession*, 1943). Completed 1942
La terra trema (*The Earth Trembles*, 1948)
Senso (1954)
Rocco and His Brothers (1960)
The Leopard (1963)
The Damned or *Götterdämmerung* (1969)
Death in Venice (1971)
The Innocent (1976)

ITALIAN MISCELLANY
Bell' Antonio (1960, Mauro Bolognini)
Bandits of Orgosolo (1961, Vittorio De Seta)
Divorce—Italian Style (1961, Pietro Germi)
Il posto (*The Job* or *The Sound of Trumpets*, 1961, Ermanno Olmi)
Salvatore Giuliano (1962, Francesco Rosi)
Il sorpasso (*The Easy Life*, 1962, Dino Risi)
The Organizer (1963, Mario Monicelli)
Seduced and Abandoned (1963, Pietro Germi)
Sei donne per l'assassino (*Blood and Black Lace*, 1964, Mario Bava)
Fists in the Pocket (1965, Marco Bellocchio)
The Battle of Algiers (1966, Gillo Pontecorvo)
The Seduction of Mimi (1972, Lina Wertmüller)

Swept Away . . . or *Swept away by an unusual destiny in the blue sea of August* (1974, Lina Wertmüller)
Deep Red (1975, Dario Argento)
Seven Beauties (1976, Lina Wertmüller)
Padre Padrone (1977, Paolo and Vittorio Taviani)
Suspiria (1977, Dario Argento)
The Tree of Wooden Clogs (1978, Ermanno Olmi)
The Beyond (1981, Lucio Fulci)
The Night of the Shooting Stars (1982, Paolo and Vittorio Taviani)
KAOS (*Chaos*, 1984, Paolo and Vittorio Taviani)
Cinema Paradiso (1989, Giuseppe Tornatore)
The Icicle Thief (1989, Maurizio Nichetti)
Elective Affinities (1996, Paolo and Vittorio Taviani)
Life is Beautiful (1998, Roberto Benigni)
The Son's Room (2001, Nanni Moretti)
The Best of Youth (2002, Marco Tullio Giordana)
My Mother's Smile (2002, Marco Bellocchio)
Gomorra or *Gomorrah* (2008, Matteo Garrone)
Vincere (2009, Marco Bellocchio)

FRANCE

ROBERT BRESSON (1901–99)
Les Anges du péché (*Angels of Sin*, 1943)
Les Dames du Bois de Boulogne (1945)
Diary of a Country Priest (1950)
Un Condamné à mort s'est échappé (*A Man Escaped*, 1956)
Pickpocket (1959)
The Trial of Joan of Arc (1962)
Au hasard Balthazar (1966)
Mouchette (1967)
Une Femme douce (1969)
Lancelot du Lac or *The Grail* (1974)
The Devil, Probably (1977)
L'Argent (1983)

CLAUDE CHABROL (1930–   )
Le Beau Serge (1958)
The Cousins (1959)
A double tour or *Leda* or *Web of Passion* (1959)
Les Biches (1968)
The Beast Must Die or *This Man Must Die* (1969)
Le Boucher (1970)
La Rupture (1971)
Wedding in Blood (1973)
Violette Nozière or *Violette* (1978)

Une Affaire de femmes or *Story of Women* (1988)

La Cérémonie or *A Judgment in Stone* (1995)

Bellamy (2009)

JEAN COCTEAU (1889–1963)

The Blood of a Poet (1930)

Beauty and the Beast (1946). Asst. director, René Clément

Les Parents terribles (1948)

Orpheus (1950)

The Testament of Orpheus (1959)

JEAN-LUC GODARD (1930–   )

À bout de souffle (*Breathless*, 1960). Shot 1959

Le Petit soldat (1963). Completed 1960; banned until 1963

Vivre sa vie or *My Life to Live* (1962)

Les Carabiniers (*The Riflemen*, 1963)

Contempt (1963)

Bande à part (*Band of Outsiders*, 1964)

A Married Woman (1964)

Alphaville, A Strange Adventure of Lemmy Caution (1965)

Pierrot le fou (1965)

Masculine Feminine (1966)

Made in U.S.A (1966)

2 or 3 Things I Know About Her (1967)

La Chinoise (1967)

Weekend (1967)

One Plus One or *Sympathy for the Devil* (1968)

Le Gai savoir (1969). Completed 1968

Wind from the East (1969). Co-director, Jean-Pierre Gorin

Tout va bien (1972). Co-director, Gorin

Numéro deux (1975). Co-director, Anne-Marie Miéville

Ici et ailleurs (*Here and Elsewhere*, 1975). Co-director, Miéville

Comment ça va? (1976). Co-director, Miéville

Communication (six parts, 1976). Co-director, Miéville

France/Tour/Détour/Deux/Enfants (1978). Co-director, Miéville

Sauve qui peut/La vie or *Every Man for Himself* (1980)

Passion (1982)

Hail Mary (1985)

Germany Nine Zero (1991)

Hélas pour moi (*Woe Is Me*, 1993). Completed 1992

JLG/JLG: Self-Portrait in December (1994)

For Ever Mozart (1996)

Histoire(s) du cinéma (four two-section parts, 1998–99)

Éloge de l'amour or *In Praise of Love* (2001)

Notre musique (*Our Music*, 2004)

LOUIS MALLE (1932–95)

Ascenseur pour l'échafaud (*Elevator to the Gallows* or *Frantic*, 1958). Completed 1957

The Lovers (1958)

Zazie dans le Métro (1960)

Phantom India (1970)

Murmur of the Heart (1971)

Lacombe Lucien (1974)

Atlantic City (1980)

My Dinner with Andre (1981)

Au revoir les enfants (1987)

Damage (1992)

Vanya on 42nd Street (1994)

CHRIS MARKER (1921–   )

Letter from Siberia (1957)

Cuba sí! (1961)

Le Joli mai (1963). Completed 1962

La Jetée (1964). Completed 1963

The Koumiko Mystery (1965)

Far from Vietnam (1967)

Le Fond de l'air est rouge (1977)

Sans soleil (1983)

The Last Bolshevik (1993)

One Day in the Life of Andrei Arsenevich (1999)

MARCEL OPHULS (1927–   )

The Sorrow and the Pity: Chronicle of a City under the Occupation (1969)

A Sense of Loss (1972)

The Memory of Justice (1976)

Hôtel Terminus: The Life and Times of Klaus Barbie (1988)

The Troubles We've Seen: A History of Journalism in Wartime (1994)

MAX OPHÜLS (1902–57)

Letter From An Unknown Woman (1948)

Caught (1949)

The Reckless Moment (1949)

La Ronde (1950)

Le Plaisir (1952)

Madame de . . . or *The Earrings of Madame
de . . .* (1953)
Lola Montès (1955)

ALAIN RESNAIS (1922–   )
Night and Fog (1955)
Hiroshima mon amour (1959)
Last Year at Marienbad (1961)
Muriel or The Time of a Return (1963)
La Guerre est finie (1966)
Je t'aime, je t'aime (1968)
Stavisky . . . (1974)
Providence (1977)
Mon oncle d'Amérique (1980)
Life is a Novel (1983)
L'Amour à mort (1984)
Mélo (1986)
I Want to Go Home (1989)
Smoking and *No Smoking* (1993)
Same Old Song (1997)
Hearts or *Private Fears in Public Places*
   (2006)
Wild Grass (2009)

JACQUES RIVETTE (1928–   )
Paris nous appartient (*Paris Belongs to Us*,
   1961). Shot 1957–59
L'Amour fou (1968)
Out 1 (1971)
Out 1: Spectre (1974)
Céline and Julie Go Boating (1974)
La Belle noiseuse (1991)
Up Down Fragile (1995)
Va savoir or *Who Knows?* (2001). Completed 2000
Don't Touch the Axe (2007)

ERIC ROHMER (1920–   )
La Boulangère de Monceau (1962)
My Night at Maud's (1969)
Claire's Knee (1970)
Chloe in the Afternoon or *Love in the
   Afternoon* (1972)
The Marquise of O · · · (1976)
Perceval le Gallois or *Perceval* (1978)
Le Rayon vert or *Summer* (1986)
A Tale of Springtime (1990)
A Tale of Winter (1992)
A Summer's Tale (1996)
Autumn Tale (1998)
The Lady and the Duke (2001)
The Loves of Astrée and Céladon (2007)

JACQUES TATI (1908–82)
Jour de fête (1949)
Mr. Hulot's Holiday (1953)
Mon oncle (1958)
Play Time or *Playtime* (1967)
Traffic (1970)
Parade (1973)

BERTRAND TAVERNIER (1941–   )
The Clockmaker (1974)
Deathwatch (1979)
Coup de torchon (1981)
A Sunday in the Country (1984)
Round Midnight (1986)
Life and Nothing But (1989)
Daddy Nostalgia (1990)
L.627 (1992)
It All Starts Today (1999)
In the Electric Mist (2009)

FRANÇOIS TRUFFAUT (1932–84)
Les Mistons (1957)
The Four Hundred Blows or *The 400 Blows* (1959)
Shoot the Piano Player (1960)
Jules and Jim (1962). Completed 1961
The Soft Skin (1964)
Fahrenheit 451 (1966)
The Bride Wore Black (1968)
Stolen Kisses (1968)
Bed and Board (1970)
The WildChild (1970)
Two English Girls (1971). Revised 1984
Day for Night (1973)
The Story of Adèle H. (1975)
Small Change (1976)
The Man Who Loved Women (1977)
The Green Room (1978)
The Last Metro (1980)
The Woman Next Door (1981)
Vivement dimanche! or *Confidentially Yours*
   (1983)

AGNÈS VARDA (1928–   )
La Pointe-Courte (1956). Completed 1954
Cléo from 5 to 7 (1961)
Le Bonheur (1965)
Les Créatures (1966)
Lions Love (1969)
Daguerréotypes (1975)
One Sings, the Other Doesn't (1977)
Murs murs (1981)
Documenteur: An Emotion Picture (1981)

Sans toit ni loi or *Vagabond* (1985)
Jacquot de Nantes (1991)
The Gleaners and I (2000)
The Gleaners and I: Two Years After (2002)
The Beaches of Agnès (2008)

FRENCH MISCELLANY
La Symphonie pastorale (1946, Jean Delannoy)
Les Enfants terribles (1950, Jean-Pierre
  Melville)
Forbidden Games (1952, René Clément)
The Wages of Fear (1953, Henri-Georges Clouzot)
Bob le flambeur (1955, Jean-Pierre Melville)
Les Diaboliques or *Diabolique* (1955, Henri-
  Georges Clouzot)
Du Rififi chez les hommes or *Rififi* (1955, Jules
  Dassin)
and God . . . created woman (1956, Roger Vadim)
The Red Balloon (1956, Albert Lamorisse)
Black Orpheus (1959, Marcel Camus)
Eyes without a Face (1960, Georges Franju)
Le Trou (1960, Jacques Becker)
Chronique d'un été (Paris 1960) (1961, Jean
  Rouch). Co-director, Edgar Morin
Sundays and Cybèle (1962, Serge Bourguignon)
Life Upside Down (1963, Alain Jessua)
The Umbrellas of Cherbourg (1964, Jacques
  Demy)
King of Hearts (1966, Philippe de Broca)
The Two of Us (1966, Claude Berri)
Jeu de massacre (1967, Alain Jessua)
Le Samouraï (1967, Jean-Pierre Melville)
L'Enfance nue or *Me* (1968, Maurice Pialat)
The Man Who Lies (1968, Alain Robbe-Grillet)
A Very Curious Girl (1969, Nelly Kaplan)
Z (1969, Costa-Gavras)
The Valley or *The Valley Obscured by Clouds*
  (1972, Barbet Schroeder)
State of Siege (1973, Costa-Gavras). Completed
  1972
The Mother and the Whore (1973, Jean Eustache)
India Song (1975, Marguerite Duras)
*Jeanne Dielman/23, Quai du Commerce/1080
  Bruxelles* (1975, Chantal Akerman)
Idi Amin Dada (1976, Barbet Schroeder)
Jonah Who Will Be 25 in the Year 2000 (1976,
  Alain Tanner)
Lumière (1976, Jeanne Moreau)
Meetings with Anna (1978, Chantal Akerman)
Série noire (1979, Alain Corneau)
Diva (1982, Jean-Jacques Beineix)

Shoah (1985, Claude Lanzmann)
Jean de Florette and *Manon of the Spring*
  (1986, Claude Berri)
Delicatessen (1991, Jean-Pierre Jeunet and
  Marc Caro)
Three Colors (three parts, 1993–94, Krzysztof
  Kieśowski). *See* Poland
The City of Lost Children (1995, Jean-Pierre
  Jeunet and Marc Caro)
Irma Vep (1996, Olivier Assayas)
Microcosmos (1996, Claude Nuridsany and Marie
  Pérennou)
Ma vie en rose (1997, Alain Berliner)
The Dreamlife of Angels (1998, Érick Zonca)
Seul contre tous or *I Stand Alone* (1998, Gaspar
  Noé)
Time Regained (1999, Raul Ruiz)
Amélie or *The Fabulous Destiny of Amélie
  Poulain* (2001, Jean-Pierre Jeunet)
Irreversible (2002, Gaspar Noé)
Belleville Rendez-vous or *The Triplets of
  Belleville* (2003, Sylvain Chomet)
Tell No One (2006, Guillaume Canet)
The Diving Bell and the Butterfly (2007, Julian
  Schnabel; U.S./France)
Persepolis (2007, Vincent Paronnaud and
  Marjane Satrapi)
The Class (2008, Laurent Cantet)
A Prophet (2009, Jacques Audiard)

DVDs

ITALY

L'avventura (1960, **Michelangelo Antonioni**).
  Criterion Collection. Includes Antonioni's
  statements on the film after its premiere,
  selected Antonioni writings read by Jack
  Nicholson, a documentary, and more.
The Battle of Algiers (1966, **Gillo Pontecorvo**).
  Criterion Collection. Includes an informative
  booklet and many documentaries (one narrated by postcolonial theorist Edward Said)
  on Pontecorvo, the making of the film,
  Algerian history, terrorism, etc. One documentary shows French soldiers recalling the
  torture and execution of rebels.
Bicycle Thieves (1948, **Vittorio De Sica**).
  Criterion Collection. **Digitally restored**
  and newly translated; with documentaries

on Zavattini, Neorealism, and working with De Sica (which includes a 2005 interview with Enzo Staiola) and with a booklet of essays.

Blow-Up (1966, **Michelangelo Antonioni**). Warner Home Video. Commentary by film historian Peter Brunette.

Deep Red (1975, **Dario Argento**). Anchor Bay. This director's cut (126 min.) improves on the uncut release version (120 min.); includes a documentary and filmographies.

L'eclisse (1962, **Michelangelo Antonioni**). Criterion Collection. Includes a documentary on Antonioni as well as essays, a commentary, and a short about *Eclipse*.

8½ (1963, **Federico Fellini**). Criterion Collection. Includes Fellini's documentary *Fellini: A Director's Notebook*, a booklet with essays by Fellini and others, a documentary on composer **Nino Rota,** and many interviews.

The Leopard (1963, **Luchino Visconti**). Criterion Collection. **Restored;** includes both versions (the European original and the American release cut—with **Burt Lancaster**'s voice in the latter instead of the previous dubbed one), a commentary by film historian Peter Cowie, a documentary, interviews, and newsreels.

Medea (1969, **Pier Paolo Pasolini;** starring **Maria Callas**). Vanguard Cinema. Compare with the von Trier–Dreyer version (see Chap. 14 list).

My Mother's Smile (2002, **Marco Bellocchio**). New Yorker Films. Includes an interview with the director.

1900 (1976, **Bernardo Bertolucci**). Paramount Home Video. Collector's Edition. The uncut, two-part, original version—both dubbed and subtitled.

La notte (1960, **Michelangelo Antonioni**). Fox Lorber. Will have to do until a restored print becomes available.

Open City (1947, **Roberto Rossellini**). Image Entertainment. The same company offers *Paisan* and *Germany Year Zero*.

Pier Paolo Pasolini Collection: Volume 2 (1961–66, **Pier Paolo Pasolini**). Water Bearer Films. Contains Pasolini Foundation prints of *Accattone, The Gospel According to St. Matthew*, and *Hawks and Sparrows;*

includes a documentary on Pasolini. Volume 1 includes *Porcile*.

Il posto (1961, **Ermanno Olmi**). Criterion Collection. Includes an interview with Olmi; an Olmi short, *La cotta;* a **restoration** demonstration; and a deleted scene.

Salò or the 120 Days of Sodom (1975, **Pier Paolo Pasolini**). Criterion Collection. **Digitally restored.** Includes several documentaries and a booklet of essays.

Salvatore Giuliano (1962, **Francesco Rosi**). Criterion Collection. An essential set, with a **restored** print, an exemplary commentary by film historian Peter Cowie, part of a 1950 newsreel about Giuliano's death, a documentary about Rosi, an interview with Rosi about realism, written tributes by Coppola and Fellini, and more.

Umberto D. (1952, **Vittorio De Sica**). Criterion Collection. Includes a documentary on De Sica and writings about the film by De Sica, novelist and theorist Umberto Eco, and others.

I vitelloni (1953, **Federico Fellini**). Criterion Collection. **Restored.**

FRANCE

The Adventures of Antoine Doinel (1957–79, **François Truffaut**). Criterion Collection. Includes all the Doinel films—*The 400 Blows, Antoine and Colette* (from *Love at Twenty*), *Bed and Board, Stolen Kisses*, and *Love on the Run*—and the early short *Les Mistons*, along with **Jean-Pierre Léaud**'s screen test and many documentaries, TV-show excerpts, commentaries, and interviews.

Au hasard Balthazar (1966, **Robert Bresson**). Criterion Collection. **Digitally restored;** includes an insightful interview with film historian Donald Richie and a 1966 French TV program about Bresson and the film.

Band of Outsiders (1964, **Jean-Luc Godard**). Criterion Collection. Includes interviews with Godard, cinematographer **Raoul Coutard,** and star **Anna Karina,** and a silent comedy by **Agnès Varda.**

Beauty and the Beast (1946, **Jean Cocteau**). Criterion Collection. **Restored;** includes Philip Glass's opera and the original fable.

Bob le flambeur (1955, **Jean-Pierre Melville**). Criterion Collection. Includes a radio interview with Melville.

Les Carabiniers (1963, **Jean-Luc Godard**). Fox Lorber.

Cléo from 5 to 7 (1961, **Agnès Varda**). Criterion Collection. Varda **restored** the opening color sequence and supervised the digital transfer.

Contempt (1963, **Jean-Luc Godard**). Criterion Collection. Includes a conversation between Godard and **Fritz Lang,** with many other extras.

Diary of a Country Priest (1950, **Robert Bresson**). Criterion Collection. **Digitally restored,** with a commentary by film historian Peter Cowie.

Eyes without a Face (1960, **Georges Franju**). Criterion Collection. **Digitally restored;** includes Franju's short documentary, *Blood of the Beasts*, and an interview with Franju about the fantastic and horror.

The Gleaners and I (2000, **Agnès Varda**). Zeitgeist Films. Includes the sequel, *Two Years After* (or *The Gleaners and I: Two Years Later*), and Varda's production notes.

Hiroshima mon amour (1959, **Alain Resnais**). Criterion Collection. Includes excerpts from writer **Marguerite Duras**'s script notes, interviews with Resnais and star **Emmanuelle Riva,** commentary by film historian Peter Cowie, and more.

Jeanne Dielman, 23, Quai du Commerce, 1080 Bruxelles (1975, **Chantal Akerman**). Criterion Collection. **Digitally restored.** Includes documentaries, interviews, and Akerman's first film.

La Jetée and *Sans soleil* (1963 and 1983, **Chris Marker**). Criterion Collection.

Jules and Jim (1962, **François Truffaut**). Criterion Collection. **Digitally restored;** includes interviews with Truffaut, cinematographer **Raoul Coutard,** and others; commentaries by star **Jeanne Moreau,** Truffaut collaborator **Suzanne Schiffman,** co-writer **Jean Gruault,** editor **Claudine Bouché,** and others; a discussion between

film scholars Dudley Andrew and Robert Stam; TV-show excerpts; and more.

Last Year at Marienbad (1961, **Alain Resnais**). Criterion Collection. **Digitally restored.** Includes a new interview with Resnais, two documentaries on *Marienbad*, and the shorts *Toute la mémoire du monde* and *Le Chant du styrène*.

Mon oncle (1958, **Jacques Tati**). Criterion Collection. **Restored,** with a 1947 Tati short.

Night and Fog (see Chap. 1 list).

The Orphic Trilogy (**Jean Cocteau**). Criterion Collection. Includes *The Blood of a Poet, Orpheus*, and *The Testament of Orpheus*; a documentary on Cocteau; a collection of Cocteau's writings on the trilogy; a filmography; and a Cocteau short, *Villa Santo Sospir*.

Playtime (1967, **Jacques Tati**). Criterion Collection. **Restored.** Includes a making-of documentary, a BBC program on Tati, a 1967 short written by and starring Tati, and more.

Rififi (see Chap. 12 list).

Le Samouraï (1967, **Jean-Pierre Melville**). Criterion Collection. **Digitally restored.** Includes archival interviews with Melville and new ones with Melville experts.

Shoot the Piano Player (1960, **François Truffaut**). Criterion Collection. **Digitally restored;** digital transfer supervised by Raoul Coutard. Includes scholarly commentaries as well as interviews with Coutard, Suzanne Schiffman, and others.

Six Moral Tales (1962–72, **Eric Rohmer**). Criterion Collection. Includes all six films, the original stories, five Rohmer shorts, a Rohmer TV program on Pascal, essays, and interviews.

Tout va bien (1972, **Jean-Luc Godard** and **Jean-Pierre Gorin**). Criterion Collection. Includes their film *Letter to Jane* and several interviews with both directors.

2 or 3 Things I Know About Her (1967, **Jean-Luc Godard**). Criterion Collection. **Digitally restored** and newly translated.

The Wages of Fear (1953, **Henri-Georges Clouzot**). Criterion Collection. **Digitally restored;** includes an analysis of how the film was censored for U.S. release, numerous interviews, and a documentary on Clouzot.

14

National Cinemas 1: 1945–

The flourishing of the French and Italian cinemas was not an isolated postwar occurrence. Forces similar to those of the New Wave affected cinemas of many other countries. First, the postwar period encouraged personality and individuality in the cinema—new things to say and new ways to say them—because the old formulas and stylistic assumptions were breaking down. Second, the audience, the technology, and the world were all changing. Times of instability and change tend to encourage originality rather than formula. Third, the American film industry was in trouble commercially. Prizes at international film festivals (a new sign of the times) brought not only honor to previously unknown film artists and industries, but also, and perhaps more important, bookings. American films were no longer powerful or attractive enough to keep foreign films off the screen, either abroad or in America.

Finally, feature film production has been either directly or indirectly supported by government policies in almost every country except the United States. Foreign governments have established quotas to limit the importation or exhibition of American films, have levied exorbitant taxes on profits from showing American films or limited the currency that American companies could export, and have invested directly in film production or indirectly through state-supported television systems. While the American film industry has always had to sink or swim on its own, in the lean postwar years of shrinking feature-film production, the American government let the Hollywood

industry sink, while other governments kept their industries afloat.

In the mid-1970s, the wheel came full circle. By adopting the styles and assumptions of the foreign film movements, the American cinema not only became strong enough again to keep most foreign competition off American screens—clearly a loss for the audience—but began winning the prizes at the international film festivals as well.

Sweden and Denmark

The name of Ingmar Bergman is as synonymous with the new cinematic directions of the second half of the 20th century as those of Fellini, Antonioni, Resnais, or Godard. Like them, Bergman is the product of a rich national film tradition. The Swedish film industry, though never producing a great number of films, enjoys a long history. Bergman, an actor, playwright, and stage director, learned his film craft from Alf Sjøberg, Sweden's most important director in the first two decades of sound production. And Sjøberg learned his craft in the Silent Era of Victor Sjøstrøm and Mauritz Stiller. Bergman also learned much from the films of Denmark's Carl Theodor Dreyer.

Stiller and Sjøstrøm combined the visual and poetic power of the northern landscapes with stories of realistic passions and mystical influences—much as Bergman would do 40 years later. The three consistent traits of the Swedish silents were: first, their use of natural imagery to evoke and convey human passions, as in Sjøstrøm's use of the sea in *A Man There Was* (1916, released 1917) and of the mountains and fjords in *The Outlaw and His Wife* (1918) and Stiller's use of the lake of ice in *Sir Arne's Treasure* (1919) and of the snow and mountains in *The Story of Gösta Berling* (1924, starring Garbo); second, their satirical and critical condemnation of social hypocrisies and injustices, as in Sjøstrøm's *The Outlaw and His Wife* and Stiller's *Erotikon* (1920); third, also Dreyer's great theme, the influence of cosmic, metaphysical forces in human affairs. The eerie, ghostly carriage that comes for the tramp who dies at precisely midnight on New Year's Eve in Sjøstrøm's *The Phantom Chariot* (1920, released 1921) is the ancestor of the hearse that comes for Isak Borg in Bergman's *Wild Strawberries;* Sjøstrøm's figure of death is an ancestor of Death in Bergman's *The Seventh Seal.* The metaphorical unity in the Swedish film tradition is striking, for Victor Sjøstrøm—Sweden's first film master—played the role of the old doctor in Bergman's *Wild Strawberries.*

One break in that continuity occurred in the 1960s, when Swedish films found an international market for their frank and realistic uses of partial or even complete nudity; Vilgot Sjöman's *I am Curious (Yellow)* (1967) went so far as to simulate intercourse. Bergman treated passionate sexual love intensely in films as diverse as *Summer with Monika* (1953) and *The Silence* (1963), and in using partial nudity he was not being prurient but acting in accordance with the liberal standards of the industry, which allowed him to be realistic.

Much as the Swedish cinema looks back to Sjøstrøm, the Danish cinema takes continuing inspiration from Dreyer, every one of whose films was a fresh experiment—in T. S. Eliot's words, another "raid on the inarticulate." As in his French *The Passion of Joan of Arc* (1928) and his German *Vampyr* (1932), a central theme in the works Dreyer made when he returned to Denmark is the intersection between the mortal and the immortal. In *Vampyr,* humans are touched by the supernatural—a vampire—and the realm of shadows, reversals, and dreams into which evil turns the world is transcendental and terrifying. In *Day of Wrath* (1943), it is hard to be sure whether what may be supernatural

intrusions come from Satan, God, or the characters' immersion in religion and its sexual politics; the film is plotted and shot in such a way that the main character might or might not be a witch. No modern view completely dispels the belief the filmed world has in witchcraft. The divine intervenes directly in *Ordet* (*The Word*, 1954, released 1955). Dreyer's last planned film was a life of Jesus; his last completed film was *Gertrud* (1964), which is purely about the mortal world and the importance of believing in love, and which, like *Ordet,* was based on a play. Gertrud believes in love as unreservedly as Joan believes in God. When Gertrud leaves an unfulfilling marriage to begin a new life, her courage and self-knowledge, the deeply understood pain of the whole situation, and her eventual destiny go beyond a work that may appear to be similar, Ibsen's play *A Doll's House.* In all these films, Dreyer's subtle work with actors and bold, insightful camerawork—from his absolute mastery of lighting to the camera movements that almost seem conscious—remained at the height of the art; the few movies for which he was able to obtain funding secured his place as one of the most interesting minds on film.

Three decades after Dreyer's death, the Danish director best known to international audiences was the audacious Lars von Trier (born Lars Trier), who delighted in making up rules—like those in the Dogme95 manifesto, discussed below, most of which he wrote—and breaking them to arrive at new forms of expression: using theatrical and realistic sets—and black and white and color—in the same scene, as in *Zentropa* (the U.S. title; it was released in 1991 as *Europa*); turning the rigid expectations of religious and sexual convention against themselves, as in *Breaking the Waves* (1996); handing the narration over to characters who would not ordinarily have access to the action or be able to explain it, as in the movies made from his TV series *The Kingdom* (1994, 1997); or having a dream end with the death of the dreamer and of the audience that has been hypnotically addressed, in the second person, as the main character (*Zentropa*). If an oppressive concept of Europe has persisted since the end of World War II, a "dream of Europa" from which it is impossible to awake as long as one follows the rules, then rebellion and madness are only partial solutions unless they arise from an intuitive, visionary conviction, the kind that Dreyer—whose characters may be possessed by visions and paradoxes (*Ordet*) or by bad ideas (*Day of Wrath*)—would have understood. In fact, von Trier's first and in many ways most powerful movie, *Medea* (1988), was made from an old script co-written by Dreyer; the film has a stark simplicity that complements and advances the tragedy, and it plays no games.

Where von Trier differs from Dreyer is in the range of his style, which can be flamboyant and full of effects or ruggedly low-budget and anti-artistic, and in the quality of his vision: He parodies vision instead of being possessed by the real thing. Even so, his parodies of crazy visionaries are terrific—for example, the possessed bureaucrats who use the regulations, which they break, as a screen for their madness and who want their crazy institutions to endure (*The Kingdom*). If, like the characters in his 1998 film *The Idiots*, one nurtures one's "inner idiot," the results may well include the orgiastic, the stupid, and the brutal, in any order and in no conventional hierarchy. In the worlds of Lars von Trier, you never know what will save you (*Breaking the Waves*) or that nothing will (*Zentropa*).

In 1995, von Trier convinced directors Thomas Vinterberg, Søren Kragh-Jacobsen, and Kristian Levring to take a "Vow of Chastity" and agree to film according to a strict set of rules; they took the vow and formed the movement, Dogme (or "dogma") 95, written Dogme95. They vowed not to shoot in black and white (too "artistic") or use filters, not to make genre films or include murders and similar "superficial action," not to credit the director, not to use superimposed titles or other effects, not to use any lights unless it was necessary to mount a single one on the camera, to hand-hold the camera and go where the actors and the action were (as opposed to the studio practice of putting the actors where the heavy camera was), to record the sound and action at the same time (no post-synchronization of dialogue or music), to shoot on 35mm film in the Academy ratio of 1.33:1, and above all not to build sets or bring props but to shoot on location and use the props and buildings found there. One of the central goals—for the bravely improvising actors as well as the other filmmakers, who ideally worked as an artistic collective—was, as von Trier put it,

"to force the truth out of the characters and settings." Most of them shot their movies with camcorders in spite of the rules. The first of the Dogme95 films were released in 1998: Vinterberg's *The Celebration* and, shortly after it, *The Idiots*. Kragh-Jacobsen's *Mifune* (1999) was the first of the Dogme95 films to be shot on film and the first to be a comedy. The fourth Dogme film was Levring's *The King is Alive* (2000). *The Celebration* is the roughest and deepest, wringing surprising truths out of its actors and recording not like a TV camera but like an eye untrained by the movies or journalism and ready to pick up everything as it happens with full energy. In its iconoclastic and conservative mix *The Celebration* is entirely Danish, but it also resembles the tense, intimate, character-wrenching realism of Cassavetes—who was, by the way, a lifelong admirer of Dreyer.

Ingmar Bergman

From the late 1950s through the 1970s, no single filmmaker was as respected, worldwide, as Ingmar Bergman. His complex films were dense and disturbing, both emotionally and philosophically. Audiences began to follow his films as links in an argument about the nature of life. Some theatres showed his pictures in 24-hour marathons. Every new film was an advance on what had become Bergman's central concerns: our often painful relations with each other and with a silent or perhaps absent God. Audiences came to know Bergman's mind and to await his next film. He may have been the first writer—director to demonstrate that movies could be central to intellectual and cultural life, that they could be profound, essential, necessary. Further, many audiences learned first through Bergman that there were certain statements and kinds of drama that could be reached only with film. Those who found it urgent to discuss "the new Bergman" with their friends evolved into those who were discussing the latest New Wave picture or trying to figure out *Blowup*; they became the core of a new filmgoing generation that looked to the art theatres and revival houses rather than to the first-run Hollywood theatres for stimulating, important movies. They were ready to accept the *auteur* theory because Bergman had shown them how a single person could express his preoccupations through the collaborative art of cinema.

Bergman directed his first film, *Crisis*, in 1945. For ten years Bergman and his first cinematographer, Gunnar Fischer, felt their way together within the film form, discovering how to synthesize the theatre (Bergman's first love) with the visual image, building a stock company of actors sensitive to each other and to the director: Max von Sydow, Gunnar Björnstrand, Eva Dahlbeck, Ingrid Thulin, Harriet Andersson, Bibi Andersson, Gunnel Lindblom. Later regulars would include Liv Ullmann and Erland Josephson. *Smiles of a Summer Night* (1955) was probably Bergman's first fully mature work, although critics in retrospect now point to signs of the Bergman mastery in *Thirst* (1949), *Monika* (*Summer with Monika*, 1952), and especially *The Naked Night* (*The Clown's Evening*, 1953; also known as *Sawdust and Tinsel*).

But it was *The Seventh Seal* (1956, released 1957) that first conquered audiences throughout the world, and soon Bergman had released two more films, *Wild Strawberries* (1957) and *The Magician* (*The Face*, 1958), to cement his reputation.

The Seventh Seal is the story of a medieval knight who returns home from the crusades only to encounter Death waiting for him on a desolate, rocky beach. The knight (Antonius Blok,

Fig. 14-1
The Seventh Seal: *Death as confessor. The equation of black, death, darkness, restraints, and the Church; from left, Bengt Ekerot and Max von Sydow.*

Fig. 14-2
The Seventh Seal: *Mary (Bibi Andersson) and Joseph (Nils Poppe), two actors in the sunlight.*

played by Max von Sydow) challenges Death (Bengt Ekerot) to a game of chess, knowing the inevitable result but playing for time. He wants the time for one reason: to discover the value of living. Everywhere around him he sees death: from the crusades, from the plague, from flagellation and superstition.

At the end of the film, the knight loses the chess game, and Death overtakes him and his party. But as the knight himself says, the delay has been most significant, for he has found some good people and learned, partly through them, to value life and hope, and he has helped a young family escape Death. This innocent, happy family of father (named Joseph), mother (named Mary),

and infant becomes the film's trinity of life. At the end of the film, they stand in the sunlight as Joseph watches Death lead the knight and his party across a hilltop in shadow.

The film's central contrast is the opposition of the ways of life and the forces of death. The Church—organized, dogmatic religion—becomes emblematic of superstition and death. In fact, the knight mistakes the figure of Death for a priest when he makes confession. Bergman surrounds the minions of death with darkness, shadows, and the religious smoke of the censer or the stake.

Opposed to the film's dark moments are its moments of life, clarity, and light. Many scenes between Joseph (Nils Poppe) and Mary (Bibi

Andersson)—the two strolling players—are brilliantly bathed in light. Actors and the theatre would remain a perpetual source of joy for Bergman, as he demonstrates in *Fanny and Alexander* (1982). The scene in which the knight partakes of their happiness, when the group sits in the sunshine to eat wild strawberries, is natural, peaceful, and bright. The real religion, the real humanity in the film stems from the sincere, unselfish feelings of the characters for one another—husband for wife; parent for child; the cynical squire (Gunnar Björnstrand) for his master, the knight, and for the tormented farm girl. In the course of the film, the knight discovers the value of those feelings and feels them himself.

In Bergman's allegory we all play chess with Death. The only question about the game is how long it will last, not who will win. To play it well, for the highest stakes, is the best we can do.

Wild Strawberries puts the same theme in modern dress. The film begins with a vision of death, the old man's dream in which he sees a hearse roll down a desolate street, in which he sees himself inside the hearse's coffin (Bergman's homage to Dreyer's *Vampyr*), in which the vision of himself in the coffin grabs hold of the dreamer and tries to pull him into it, in which he sees that time has stopped, that the clocks have no hands. Bergman increases the dream's impression of bleakness and desolation by overexposing the whole vision. Then the old doctor wakes up. Since he perceives the closeness of death, he is haunted by questions about the value of the life he has lived. Ironically, this doctor, Isak Borg (played by Sjøstrøm), aged 78, is about to be honored by society for the value of his life's work; a university is to award him an honorary degree. Despite the university's assessment of his life's worth, the doctor is not so certain about it. The rest of the film shows him groping for an answer, through his memories and through the events of the day (as well as a final dream). Like *The Seventh Seal*, the film is structured as a journey. As Borg travels along the road toward the university, three kinds of encounters influence his thought: with his present relationships (son, housekeeper, daughter-in-law, mother), with people on the road (three young, robust hikers and a bickering, middle-aged married couple), and with the visions of his past that keep crowding into his brain.

When Borg examines his present relationships, he sees nothing but empty sterility. Borg's great legacy to his son has been to transfer his nihilism, his contempt for life. So successfully has Borg passed on this dowry that the son and daughter-in-law are in danger of separating. The son hates life so bitterly that he refuses to bring children into it.

The two groups that Borg encounters on the road are diametric opposites. The young hikers are shining, vital, energetic; they devour life with a callous yet honest robustness (Ibsen called it the Viking Spirit), unfettered by social convention, disillusionment, and failure. The middle-aged couple are tied to one another by habit, by argument, and by the need to share futility. Both encounters trigger Borg's visions. The pair with blasted lives evokes Borg's bitterest dream, in which he attends a hell-like school (the scene echoes the school scene in Strindberg's *A Dream Play*, a work that influenced Bergman throughout his career) and fails an examination administered by the husband. Uncompassionate and guilty, he must learn to ask forgiveness.

But the hikers, particularly the young woman (Bibi Andersson), stimulate Borg to dream of his childhood, his summers at the family summer house, where he felt both disappointment in romance and the happiness of youth. Bergman shoots these scenes with a clarity and a whiteness that echo the scenes between Mary and Joseph in *The Seventh Seal*. Summer and sunshine—not overexposure, which he saves for nightmares—are consistent metaphors for moments of happiness in *Smiles of a Summer Night, Monika, Summer Interlude* (1950, released 1951), and even the violent *The Virgin Spring* (1959, released 1960, where the metaphor is used ironically, turned against itself to intensify a sunlit horror).

Like the knight of *The Seventh Seal*, Isak Borg translates his vision into action, primarily by offering to ease his pressure on his son and, in effect, reconciling son and daughter-in-law to each other. Borg has taken a journey toward life and finally helped his son do the same. Borg contentedly falls asleep, no longer haunted by clocks without hands.

The films that Bergman designated as his trilogy—*Through a Glass Darkly* (1961), *Winter Light* (*The Communicants*, 1962), and *The Silence* (1963)—all seek meaningful, sometimes spiritual values in a world in which God can be scary or absent and there are many barriers to communication. *Cries and Whispers* (1972) shows how the awareness of an impending death defines the values of living. And *Persona* (1965, released 1966) combines the self-conscious cinematic tricks of *The Magician* with a psychoanalytic and metaphysical study of a person who, like Isak Borg, views the experience of living as a bleak and terrible lie.

But despite the similarities of these to the earlier films, the Bergman cinematic style had altered radically, becoming more subtle and complex. Bergman's stylistic shift was partly the result of his switching to a more experimental cinematographer, Sven Nykvist, who replaced Gunnar Fischer in the 1960s. The late Bergman films are increasingly concerned with psychology—the fears, anguish, and even mental diseases of individuals—and painful relationships. The characters are caught in institutions through which they can fulfill or destroy themselves but which they can never fully understand: the Church, the theatre, marriage.

Persona is Bergman's masterpiece, his most complex and reflexive film, and his truest display of technical virtuosity. On its surface, the film is the story of a cure, a psychological case study of Elisabeth Vogler (Liv Ullmann), an actress who went blank onstage during a performance of *Electra* and has refused to speak since. Her refusal to communicate is symptomatic of her feeling that human existence is merely a collection of lies. For Elisabeth, to speak is to lie. (The problem is, to be silent is not necessarily to be honest and good.) She is treated in a mental hospital by a young, energetic, and dedicated nurse, Alma (Bibi Andersson), and the cure then takes both of them out of the hospital to the seaside home of the hospital's head psychiatrist. At that seaside retreat, where the nurse does all the talking, the two women share moments of intimacy and hatred. The end of this process is the actress's apparent return to communication, to her life on the stage and with her family, and Nurse Alma's return to her job, shaken by the experience but continuing on her way.

What complicates the case study is Bergman's elliptical and nonlinear way of telling this story, which gives rise to several motifs that extend far beyond a simple examination of a neurotic artist. Bergman presents *Persona* not as a record of events but (1) as a film and (2) as a kind of mental movie screen on which the "events" appear

(an advanced construct of the mindscreen). Film itself plays a role in the movie. *Persona* begins with the illumination of an arc-light projector, with the spooling of a reel of film on the projector, with the familiar projection leader that counts down the numbers before a film begins, and with several miscellaneous clips and shots interspersed (a slapstick comedy, a blood sacrifice, an animated cartoon). It ends with a loop of film slipping out of the projection gate, with sprocket holes, with the white glare of a blank screen and the extinguishing of the projection arc with which the film began. Between these two self-referential frames the film repeatedly refers to itself—at one point, having the film appear to stop, rip, and burn in the projection gate. This picture, which starts and defines and ends itself, was crucial in the development of the self-conscious film in the mid-1960s, a development also seen in the work of Godard, notably in *2 or 3 Things I Know About Her*, shot the year *Persona* was released.

Bergman calls attention to the film as a film because he wants to emphasize that what follows is a fiction, an illusion—a sequence of light and shadow on a flat screen. The audience has entered the world of art and chimera—of magic and theatre, not of nature and reality. But Bergman's film then gives this clear dichotomy another twist, for is the world of nature—or personal identity itself—any more solid, any more real than the one of artistic illusion? That is the question that propels the rest of the film after its projectionist prologue. For example, at one point in the film Alma believes she hears Elisabeth Vogler speak to her—and we hear her, too. But Elisabeth denies speaking, and we begin to wonder whether Alma imagined it. At another point in the film, Alma believes she hears a noise and discovers Elisabeth's husband, who mistakes the nurse for his own wife and begins making love to Alma as Elisabeth watches. He cannot possibly be there and would not make that mistake; he could be the product of Alma's imagination, an anxiety dream about how similar she and Elisabeth are. And yet there he stands, concretely before us and before the nurse and his wife. Is the concrete world any more tangible, any more "real" than the intangible world of dreams and the imagination? And does the distinction make any sense in a movie?

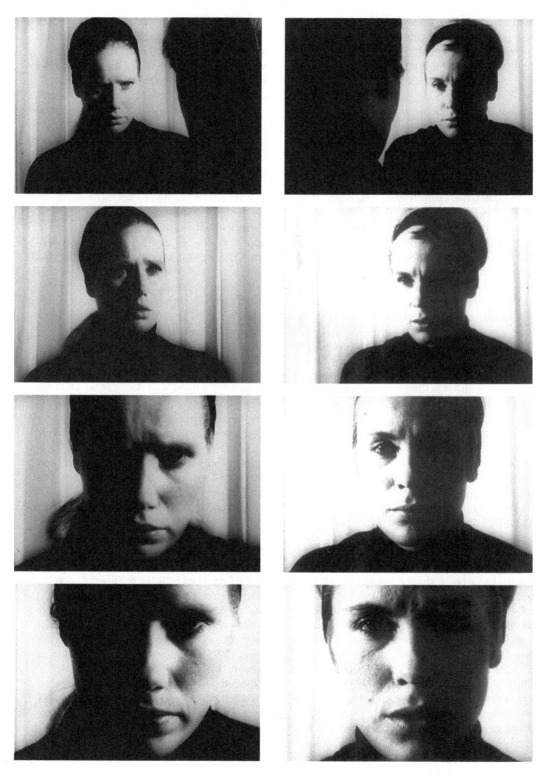

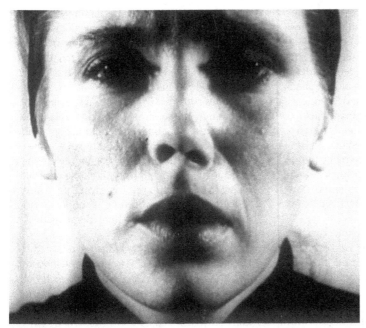

Fig. 14-3

Persona. *Merging two personae into one: the joining of Elisabeth Vogler (Liv Ullmann, left column) and Sister Alma (Bibi Andersson, right column). As the two women face each other across a table, the scene is side lit, from Alma's right and Elisabeth's left, leaving complementary halves of each character's face in darkness; at the end of the last shot, with the illuminated side of Alma's face on the left side of the screen, the dark half is filled in with the lit side of Elisabeth's face.*

This phenomenological collapse of the familiar distinction between illusion and reality leads Bergman to collapse another familiar kind of distinction. Nothing is usually so unique and consistent, in art or in the psychoanalyst's definitions, as individual human personality. Bergman has titled his film *Persona*, a term that can refer to the mask assumed by a narrator or an author, or worn by an actor in a play (as in *dramatis personae*), to a role played in a drama or in real life, and to an individual's personality. The film apparently presents us with two antithetical *personae*—talkative nurse and silent patient. Each has her own part to play and even her own "costume" (patient's gown, nurse's uniform) at the start. And each is an entity wearing the mask of personality—masks that Bergman shows can be exchanged. In addition, the mask can be compared to a frame: the mask of imagery, or the filter, placed in front of the projector's white light.

Then Bergman collapses these opposites—nurse and patient—into one. For the nurse does all the talking; she ironically is the one actually undergoing the psychoanalytic treatment while Elisabeth plays the psychiatrist and merely listens. The film is Alma's psychodrama as much as Elisabeth's. It is Alma who confesses her doubts

and insecurities; it is Alma who is driven to acts of violence, inconsistency, jealousy, frenzy, and paranoia by Elisabeth's manipulative behavior and aloof silence, a silence that makes Elisabeth comparable to the silent God of the trilogy that preceded *Persona*. The film was partly inspired by Strindberg's play *The Stronger*, a power struggle between one woman who speaks and one who does not.

Bergman's film constantly emphasizes that the two women are one and the one is two. The two women look strikingly alike. Often they dress alike, and in several scenes they are shot so that parts of each woman form a composite body. Crucially, there is the lengthy scene at the kitchen table that Bergman shows in its entirety twice. First, he shoots Alma's tale (ironically, Alma speaks aloud Elisabeth's silent thoughts about her child) from Alma's point of view, camera riveted on Elisabeth—who is wearing a black sweater and black headband—moving the camera steadily toward Elisabeth's face with a series of dissolves (four shots, each closer than the last). Then Bergman shoots the scene over again from Elisabeth's point of view, camera riveted on Alma (a conventional film would shoot the scene twice but cut back and forth between the two points of view in the final editing, showing the scene once)—who is wearing an identical "costume" of black sweater and black headband—the camera again moving steadily closer to the subject's face with another series of identical dissolves (at exactly the same points of the speech as in Elisabeth's previous sequence). Identical and reversed, the faces begin to mirror each other. Finally, Bergman literally blends the two faces into one (thesis–antithesis–synthesis), using half of each woman's face to make the composite portrait. The two opposite *personae* become literally, tangibly one—a concrete illusion that Bergman has produced by means of the filmmaker's art.

Persona was followed by the grim, powerful, nightmarish trilogy of *Hour of the Wolf* (1966, released 1968), *Shame* (1967, released 1968), and *The Passion of Anna* (1969), all of which starred Liv Ullmann and Max von Sydow. After several more emotionally painful works—notably *Cries and Whispers* and *Scenes from a Marriage* (1974, condensed from the 1972 TV version)—Bergman returned to the sustaining vision of theatricality. Most of his later films reaffirm his faith in illusion, in the imagination, in art, and in magic. The three-part structure of *Fanny and Alexander*, fashioned from a longer version made for Swedish TV, seems Bergman's own spiritual autobiography. It begins happily, surrounded by family, in the theatre—the place where Bergman began, the place of joyous illusion, of smiles and light. It then plunges into a middle section of dark despair, dominated by Calvinist severity and mortification—which parallels Bergman's despairing black-and-white films of the 1960s. But it escapes once again into the light, back to the celebration of magic and theatre—and the performance of Strindberg's *A Dream Play*.

After *Fanny and Alexander*, Bergman officially retired from filmmaking, then promptly made *After the Rehearsal* (1984, for TV but soon shown in theatres) and a short, personal film about his mother (in the form of a look through the family scrapbook). In the 1990s, he went back to directing plays, notably *A Doll's House* and *The Winter's Tale*, and writing scripts for others to direct (*The Best Intentions*, by Bille August, and *Sunday's Children*, by his son Daniel Bergman, both 1992; *Faithless*, by Liv Ullmann, 2000). He apparently considered a TV movie something

other than a film, because he continued to maintain that he had retired from filmmaking in spite of *After the Rehearsal* and *In the Presence of a Clown*, a picture he wrote and directed for TV in 1997. In 2003, he wrote and directed the film he announced was his very last: *Saraband*. A sequel to *Scenes from a Marriage*, again starring Liv Ullmann as Marianne and Erland Josephson as Johan, it was shot on high-definition digital video and promptly shown on TV. Bergman was unhappy with the attempts to transfer the picture to film and held up the theatrical release until 2004, when a satisfactory print was struck. Like most of his earlier works, *Saraband* is emotionally grueling and ultimately enlightening. Bergman died in 2007.

Although Bergman was the unquestioned directorial star of the postwar Swedish industry, several later lights appeared: the lush, pictorial, fatalistic romanticizing of Bo Widerberg's *Elvira Madigan* (1967); the close, affectionate observation of Swedish immigrants in Jan Troell's two-part epic, *The Emigrants* (1971) and *The New Land* (1972); and the disciplined realism of Sven Nykvist's *The Ox* (1991). Troell made a distinguished comeback in 2008 with *Maria Larsson's Everlasting Moment*, better known as *Everlasting Moments*, in which he told the true story of a woman whose life is changed by her learning to take photographs. That same year, Sweden had another international hit in Tomas Alfredson's *Let the Right One In*, the violent and emotionally engaging tale of the friendship between a young boy and a vampire who appears to be a young girl. It was also in 2008 that the Norwegian cinema came to world attention with Bent Hamer's *O'Horten*, a warm comedy about a man who searches for a fulfilling life after he retires.

England

With certain notable exceptions, the British film took a long time to recover something like the experimental uniqueness of the era of Hepworth, Smith, and Williamson. The common language made England—the center of filmmaking activity in the British Isles—such a Hollywood colony that in 1927 the British government passed quota laws to protect the native cinema. A British theatre owner was obliged to show a certain quota of British-made films. These quotas produced a flood of cheapies—called "quota quickies"—that served as second features (sometimes screened at 10 A.M.) for the American films that everyone came to see.

If a British film did score an international success in the 1930s—such as Alexander Korda's *The Private Life of Henry VIII* (1933) or Hitchcock's *The 39 Steps*—its director or star almost immediately departed for Hollywood. Charles Laughton, Cary Grant (born Archibald Leach in Bristol), Laurence Olivier, John Gielgud, Ralph Richardson, Jack Hawkins, Stan Laurel, Charles Chaplin, Claude Rains, Basil Rathbone, Deborah Kerr, Boris Karloff, and Leslie Howard were as much a part of the Hollywood of the past as Richard Burton, James Mason, David Niven, Sean Connery, Albert Finney, Dirk Bogarde, Maggie Smith, Julie Andrews, Anthony Hopkins, Julie Christie, Peter Sellers, Glenda Jackson, Alec Guinness, Richard Attenborough, Michael Caine, Peter O'Toole, Ben Kingsley, Peter Cushing, Daniel Day-Lewis, John Cleese, Kate Winslet, Judi Dench, and Emma Thompson have been of the "Hollywood" of the recent past.

Postwar Masters

David Lean's first great film was the restrained, deeply moving romantic drama *Brief Encounter* (1945); he followed it with two of the most highly regarded of all Dickens adaptations, *Great Expectations* (1946) and *Oliver Twist* (1948). He first revealed his eye for the sumptuous in *Summertime* (1955), then began directing a series of spectacles, literate and long and flexibly paced, that were overwhelmingly pictorial, organized around complex characters, and designed to explore moral questions under pressure. The first and best of these were *The Bridge on the River Kwai* (1957) and *Lawrence of Arabia* (1962, shot by Frederick A. Young); they were followed by *Doctor Zhivago* (1965), *Ryan's Daughter* (1970), and *A Passage to India* (1984). At the time of his death in 1991, Lean was working on an adaptation of Joseph Conrad's *Nostromo*.

Carol Reed made his mark with economical, precisely observed films as diverse as *The Stars Look Down* (1939) and *Outcast of the Islands* (1951). He did his best work in two tightly constructed, haunting thrillers: *Odd Man Out* (1947) and *The Third Man* (1949). When he worked in America, he directed the compelling circus

melodrama *Trapeze* (1956), a highlight of Burt Lancaster's career.

For the 15 years after World War II, British film seemed synonymous with four kinds of movies, all carefully crafted. London was—and still is—the world capital of a style of English theatre and literature that has evolved over many centuries. These literate, well-spoken films displayed taste, style, grace, and intelligence.

First, there were the polished, fluently acted adaptations of literary classics: Lean's films of Dickens, Anthony Asquith's adaptations of Rattigan (*The Winslow Boy*, 1948; *The Browning Version*, 1951) and Wilde (*The Importance of Being Earnest*, 1952), and Olivier's later adaptations of Shakespeare (*Hamlet*, 1948; *Richard III*, 1955). Olivier's *Henry V* (1944) had created much of the momentum for this genre: More than an effective wartime propaganda film, it showed how cinematically original a literary adaptation could be.

Second, there were the tightly edited, intelligently written contemporary dramas, many of which adopted the terms of familiar genres. Some of these concerned themselves with wartime military assignments or postwar political cabals, but the majority were romances (*Brief Encounter*), thrillers (*Odd Man Out*), mysteries (Sidney Gilliat's *Green For Danger*, 1946), and horror films (*Dead of Night*, 1945, directed by Alberto Cavalcanti, Charles Crichton, Basil Dearden, and Robert Hamer).

Third, there were the biting, richly dry and satiric "little" comedies made at the Ealing Studios by Robert Hamer (*Kind Hearts and Coronets*, 1949; *Father Brown*, 1954), Alexander Mackendrick (*Tight Little Island*, 1949; *The Man in the White Suit*, 1951; *The Ladykillers*, 1955), Charles Crichton (*The Lavender Hill Mob*, 1951), and Anthony Kimmins (*The Captain's Paradise*, 1953). Many of these masterpieces of comic construction, irony, and understatement—including some not made at Ealing, such as Ronald Neame's *The Horse's Mouth* (1958)—featured the protean performances of Alec Guinness, who could transform himself into any kind of comic character—fuddy-duddy scientist, bohemian painter, old lady.

And fourth, there were the elegant Technicolor spectacles produced by the Archers, an independent company formed by Michael Powell, who directed the films, and Emeric Pressburger, who wrote them; their collaboration

Fig. 14-4
Olivier's **Henry V:** *France as an English Renaissance audience might have imagined it while watching Shakespeare's play, thanks to an art direction based on the art of the period.*

was attested to by the credit they always used, "Written Produced and Directed by Michael Powell and Emeric Pressburger." Before joining Pressburger, Powell made numerous low-budget pictures. His first, which deserves to be better known, was most unlike the fantasies and psychological dramas for which he became famous, a harsh and realistic tale shot on location on a rugged island north of Scotland: *The Edge of the World* (1936, released 1937). The Archers were best known for their intense use of color, their spectacular fantasies, and their social and psychological boldness. Their key works include *The Life and Death of Colonel Blimp* (1943, an epic satire), *A Matter of Life and Death* (1946, a fantasy released in the U.S. as *Stairway to Heaven*), *Black Narcissus* (1947), and *The Red Shoes* (1948). *Black Narcissus*, which is convincingly

set in India, high in the Himalayas, was shot (by Jack Cardiff) entirely at Pinewood Studios, London; the intent, in Powell's words, was to create "a perfect color work of art." As realistic as the world of *Black Narcissus* looks and sounds, its artificiality is complete, and its contrast of cultures, expectations, moods, and personalities develops as a contrast and metamorphosis of colors as well as of music and sound effects. The story concerns a group of Anglo-Catholic nuns, led by Sister Clodagh (Deborah Kerr), who attempt to set up a school and dispensary in an old palace on a mountain shelf above a remote Indian village. The longer they stay, the more their former, organized ways of doing and thinking about things come to seem irrelevant. Each of the nuns is disturbed by the place, some more than others. One sister, assigned to work in the garden, finds herself listening to the endless wind, looking through the clear air at the great mountains, thinking too much, spacing out, and—caught up in an almost metaphysical simplicity—planting flowers instead of potatoes; another sister, assailed by the forces of desire and madness, turns murderous. This sensuous, rigorous film was banned in many countries. And *The Red Shoes* was no fairy-tale backstage musical, but another beautiful, disciplined, adult film made with absolute artistic control. Like the ballet danced within it—"The Red Shoes," based on Hans Christian Andersen's story—*The Red Shoes* tells of a woman (Moira Shearer) who puts on the red shoes, cannot take them off, and dances to her death. She is torn between two men, the impresario who offers her the great career she wants and deserves and the young composer who wants her to quit dancing and love him. Neither of these men will give her a break, and the conflict they represent is, in any case, between the lover and artist in herself; the choice proves impossible, and she is destroyed—in a moment that intricately represents the triumph of artifice. Powell and Pressburger collaborated from 1938 to 1957; Powell went on to direct the savage, brilliant *Peeping Tom* (1960, written by Leo Marks), to advise Coppola on the creation of artificial worlds (during the development of electronic cinema and of *One from the heart*, 1982), and to script an adaptation of Ursula K. Le Guin's *The Wizard of Earthsea* before his death in 1990. *Peeping Tom*, released earlier in the same year as Hitchcock's *Psycho*, is, like *Psycho*, a forerunner of the slasher film, a disciplined masterpiece, and an ironic mixture of voyeurism and murder—reflexively linked by the making of images literally taken from life.

The general traits of all four of these British categories were a subtle understatement, expert acting, detailed decor, and a firm control of taut narrative construction.

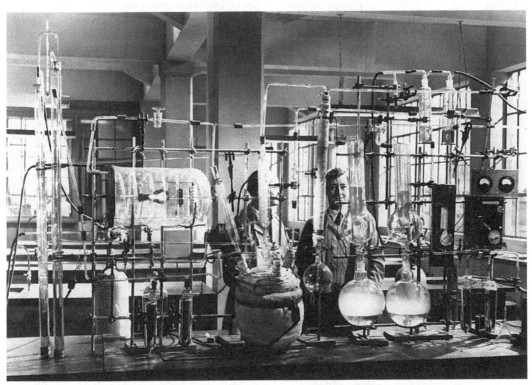

Fig. 14-5
The Man in the White Suit: *the realistic texture of the British documentary tradition flavoring the comedy of Alec Guinness, surrounded by the tubes and wires of his scientific apparatus.*

Among the most distinctive and significant work in the British film between the era of Charles Urban and 1959 was the documentary film movement of the 1930s and 1940s. Sponsored by the government and directed by filmmakers like John Grierson, Paul Rotha, Basil Wright, Harry Watt, Edgar Anstey, and Humphrey Jennings, the British documentaries developed the craft of capturing the surfaces of reality to illuminate the essences beneath them. The realist texture that seemed to distinguish British fictional films from Hollywood's was especially obvious in the purely realist documentary films. To some extent, the new British film of 1959—which found a ready international market as part of the generalized new wave of European cinema—began with a similar premise. This new British film was the product of several influences: of the British documentary tradition; of the new class-conscious British novels and plays by authors like John Osborne, John Braine, Arnold Wesker, Shelagh Delaney, Alan Sillitoe, and Alun Owen; of the Italian Neorealist films; and of the new spirit of free cinema that was emerging in France at the same time. The result of these many influences was a series of films that were radically different from the polished, elegant films of Asquith and the Archers.

Another New Wave

The new British films, like the Italian Neorealist ones, emphasized the poverty of the worker, the squalor of working-class life, the difficulty of keeping a home and keeping one's self-respect at the same time, the social assumptions that sentence a person with no education and a working-class dialect to a lifetime of bare survival. British directors turned their cameras on the oppressive smoke of factories, the dull and drizzly weather at their stifling seaside resorts, the dingy and smoky feel of the pubs, the faded austerity of the rooms people can afford to rent. In the midst of this intentionally barren and gray world, the directors focus on a common man reacting to his surroundings—bitter, brutal, angry, tough. These heroes of the films, traditionally labeled "angry young men" (a term first applied to the writers and antiheroes of the plays on which many of these films were based), react in one of two ways to the working-class prisons of their lives: They try to grab some of the swag of the upper-class life for themselves, or, failing that, they

get nasty, yell at women, and break things. Angry young men aside, Tony Richardson's *A Taste of Honey* (1961) and Bryan Forbes's *The L-Shaped Room* (1962) were among the best of the new films whose central characters were female.

Jack Clayton's *Room at the Top* (1959) was the first of the working-class British films to earn an international reputation and to make money. Clayton came to films not as a young rebel but as a tireless perfectionist who had worked his way up in the British film industry. Joe Lampton (Laurence Harvey), an ambitious young man with a provincial accent and a provincial education, takes a job at Brown's factory in a northern industrial city. Joe quickly learns the economic facts of life. He believes the old line that there is always "room at the top." He becomes enamored of a posh residential area of the city known as the "top," a hill that dominates the town. Most attractive of all the houses on the "top" is that of Mr. Brown (Donald Wolfit), the owner of the factory and commercial lord of the industrial town. On billboards, outside railway windows, reflected in the puddles on the street, hanging on one of his smokestacks, is the name of Brown, an ever-present reminder of the temptation of money and power, the temptation to which Joe yields, damning himself.

Joe sets his sights on Susan (Heather Sears), Brown's daughter, a pretty but emotionally shallow young woman who responds to affection with the same intensity as to a brisk set of tennis. Then Joe meets Alice (Simone Signoret), an older, warmer woman who reveals to him what two people are capable of feeling for each other. Just when Joe has decided that the relationship with Susan is valueless, she becomes pregnant, and her father compels Joe to marry her. When Joe tells Alice that he is going to marry Susan, she kills herself in a car accident. And so Joe marries Susan. He gets what he wanted—makes it to the top—but no longer wants it.

That Clayton's commitment was more to his craft than to any class-conscious subject matter became clearer in his subsequent films—*The Innocents* (1961), *The Pumpkin Eater* (1964, script by Harold Pinter), *Our Mother's House* (1967), and *The Great Gatsby* (1974). *The Innocents* is the best adaptation yet of Henry James's *The Turn of the Screw. The Pumpkin Eater*, the story of a troubled middle-class marriage, reflects the influence of

Fig. 14-6

Fig. 14-7

Black Narcissus: *two worlds. Fig. 14-6: Sister Clodagh (Deborah Kerr) tries to find comfort in the well-organized Christian world of her office, where everything fits within the frame assigned to it. Fig. 14-7: Having renounced her vows, Sister Ruth (Kathleen Byron) runs through the rich darkness of the old palace, losing her scarf on a Hindu wall sculpture. Production designed by Alfred Junge.*

Fig. 14-8
Peeping Tom: *Carl Boehm as the photographer who, spied on and abused as a child, has become obsessed with recording the ultimate private moment—the confrontation with one's own fear at the point of death. In the background, Anna Massey as his observant friend.*

Resnais in its time-defiant editing and complex narrative structure. *The Great Gatsby*, however, is merely well photographed. *Our Mother's House*, *Something Wicked This Way Comes* (1983 and, like *Gatsby*, made in the U. S.), and *The Lonely Passion of Judith Hearne* (1987) all reveal Clayton's masterful control of tone.

In 1959, Tony Richardson directed the film version of John Osborne's *Look Back in Anger*, three years after he had directed the sharp, tongue-lashing stageplay at London's Royal Court Theatre. Within three years Richardson had directed three similar films: two adaptations of realist, class-conscious plays (*The Entertainer*, 1960, starring Laurence Olivier, from the play by John Osborne; *A Taste of Honey*, starring Rita Tushingham, from the play by Shelagh Delaney) and an adaptation of Alan Sillitoe's antiestablishment, class-conscious novel *The Loneliness of the Long Distance Runner* (1962, starring Tom Courtenay; at one point the film was called *Rebel*

With a Cause). These four early Richardson films depend heavily on the literateness of the original works. All are brilliantly acted, both in the major roles and in the character parts. Richardson's experience as a stage director no doubt aided his actors, but actors like Richard Burton, Claire Bloom, Mary Ure, Laurence Olivier, Brenda DeBanzie, Rita Tushingham, Murray Melvin, and Tom Courtenay made his task somewhat easier. *The Loneliness of the Long Distance Runner* is the most adventurous of the films cinematically; the freeness of the novel and the influence of the French New Wave helped Richardson escape the traditions of the stage. It remains the best example of the social realism of the period.

Later Richardson films—*Tom Jones* (1963), *The Loved One* (1965), *The Charge of the Light Brigade* (1968), *A Delicate Balance* (1973)—leave the grime of working-class England and the bitterness of social-outcast laborers far behind. Like *The Charge of the Light Brigade*, the best of them are ironic comedies. His final film, made in America, was *Blue Sky* (released 1994); he died in 1991.

Richardson's collaboration with playwright John Osborne indicates that English fashions in its cinema are inseparable from fashions in its theatre. As British playwrights moved away from working-class characters and themes, so did British cinema. A parallel movement can be seen in the collaboration of playwright Harold Pinter and the blacklisted American director Joseph Losey, who emigrated to England. Losey turned a number of Pinter screenplays into elegantly acted, coolly mysterious, and psychologically insightful films—*The Servant* (1963), *Accident* (1967), *The Go-Between* (1971)—that had nothing to do with angry young men, let alone with Joe McCarthy's America. *The Servant* concerned the nature of power, a struggle between a weak master (James Fox) and a strong servant (Dirk Bogarde) that was taken from a novel by Robin Maugham but was similar to the relationships in many of Pinter's plays. Elegant and decadent, yet efficiently directed, *The Servant* gave Losey's career a new start and launched Pinter as an innovative screenwriter (on *The Pumpkin Eater*, for example, he was responsible for the montage structure that made the picture so distinctive; his brilliant script of Proust's *A la recherche du temps perdu* remains unproduced). Pinter once

Fig. 14-9

Fig. 14-10

Two angry young men surrounded by the shabby respectability of their working-class lives.
Fig. 14-9: Laurence Harvey in Room at the Top, with Simone Signoret (left) and Hermione Baddely.
Fig. 14-10: Richard Burton and Mary Ure in Look Back in Anger.

said that Losey taught him how to write screen-plays by cutting out the pauses.

None of the social-realist films was shot in color. Color was as antithetical to the smoke and fog of working-class Britain as it was to the poverty of postwar Italy. Karel Reisz's *Saturday Night and Sunday Morning* (1960) and Sidney J. Furie's *The Leather Boys* (1963)—and even Reisz's *Morgan, a Suitable Case for Treatment* (1966), which is a comedy—mix stories of rebellious young have-nots with a carefully realistic depiction of the social milieu that condemns them to the prison of their economic class. Other British films of the same era, with widely different themes and characters, share the same texture and smell of Naturalism—from the factory tensions of Guy Green's *The Angry Silence* (1960) to the realistically brutal rugby games in Lindsay Anderson's *This Sporting Life* (1963) and the fashionable social world of John Schlesinger's *Darling* (1965).

Loach, Leigh, and Others

One obvious exception to this school of social realism is the work of Richard Lester, an American expatriate who united the Beatles with the cinematic ellipticality of Truffaut and Resnais. The results—*A Hard Day's Night* (1964) and *Help!* (1965)—were buoyant romps through the fields of illogic. Lester, who began by making

television commercials, invests his imaginative energy in terrific bits. Lester does best when the parts propel a whole that is conceived as an elliptical string of bits—from the Beatles films and *How I Won the War* (1967) to *The Three Musketeers* (1974) and *The Four Musketeers* (1975). Lester's greatest film after *A Hard Day's Night* is the psychological drama *Petulia* (1968).

From the Renaissance stage to the music hall, the British have enjoyed a witty and often outrageous comedic tradition. In the 1950s, some of the best working talent was on the radio, as it was on television in the 1970s, and the stars of these shows often went on to significant film careers. The BBC's *The Goon Show*, one of the most bizarre and hilarious programs in the history of radio, starred Spike Milligan, Harry Secombe, and Peter Sellers. Lester's first comedy, *The Running, Jumping and Standing Still Film* (1960), was a short that starred the Goons; its sheer craziness and comic energy led straight to *A Hard Day's Night*. Peter Sellers, whose voice was as protean as Lon Chaney's face, became one of England's great screen comedians, starring in films as diverse as *The Mouse That Roared* (1959), *I'm All Right Jack* (1959), *The Wrong Arm of the Law* (1962), *Lolita* (1962), *The Pink Panther* (1964) and its sequels, *Dr. Strangelove* (1964), *The World of Henry Orient* (1964), and *Being There* (1979).

Fig. 14-11
**The Servant: *Dirk Bogarde and James Fox
(right) as the manservant and master who
exchange roles in Losey and Pinter's brilliant
study of decadence and power.***

Just over a decade after the Goons, the BBC's
silliest and most creative comedians were the
Pythons: Graham Chapman, John Cleese, Terry
Gilliam, Eric Idle, Terry Jones, and Michael Palin.
They broke into film in 1972 with *And Now For
Something Completely Different* (directed by Ian
McNaughton), an anthology of routines from
their TV show, *Monty Python's Flying Circus*.
Their first original feature, *Monty Python and
The Holy Grail* (1974)—which made cinematic,
literary, and historical jokes with equal skill in an
outrageous sendup of the Arthurian legend—was
directed by Terry Jones and Terry Gilliam (an
American and the troupe's animator); the ones
after that were directed by Jones alone and
include *Monty Python's Life of Brian* (1979), the
tale of a fellow whose life runs parallel to that of
Jesus, and *Monty Python's The Meaning of Life*
(1983), a guide for the perplexed. Cleese, Idle,
and Palin went on to establish themselves
independently as actors and writers in such films
as Richard Loncraine's *The Missionary* (1982)
and Charles Crichton's *A Fish Called Wanda*

(1988), and Gilliam became a controversial director with his grotesque dystopia, *Brazil* (1985).
The Pythons ceased to exist as a troupe after the
death of Graham Chapman in 1989.

Economically and internationally, England's
biggest hit was the James Bond series, based on
the spy novels of Ian Fleming and starring Sean
Connery (succeeded by Roger Moore and
others). Released through United Artists and
becoming one of that company's chief assets, the
Bond films have, since the 1960s, offered sophisticated adventure, witty dialogue, state-of-the-art
gadgetry, spectacular sets, elaborate action
sequences, and generous helpings of sex and
death. Produced by Albert R. Broccoli and Harry
Saltzman, the series began with *Dr. No* (1962,
directed by Terence Young), won over the critics
with *From Russia With Love* (1963, Terence
Young), and consolidated its position at the
center of the new spectacle—displacing all those
Hollywood ancient-world extravaganzas—with
Goldfinger (1964, Guy Hamilton). If the first
Bond films were strongly influenced by the
elegance, action, and long-distance chases of the
witty spy thriller *North by Northwest*, they added
high tech to the mix and became, in their turn,
the prototype for the contemporary action
movie.

Hammer Films also attracted loyal audiences worldwide with its boldly colored, bloody
horror films, beginning with Terence Fisher's
The Curse of Frankenstein (1957), which
starred Peter Cushing and Christopher Lee—
two actors who soon became as important to
the studio as its head writer, Jimmy Sangster.
But Britain still turned out a number of restrained, relentless, black-and-white chillers—
such as Jacques Tourneur's *Night of the Demon*,
1957—that were as effective as the gruesome
color pictures.

Not every British filmmaker moved to
America as Hitchcock did; there was a lot of
traffic both ways. Many who rushed to see that
very English import, *The Servant*, did not realize
Joseph Losey was American, let alone the director of *The Prowler* (a 1951 *noir*) and the controversial antiwar film *The Boy With Green Hair*
(1948), whose release Howard Hughes had tried
to stop. Between *The Entertainer* and *A Taste of
Honey*, Tony Richardson made *Sanctuary* in the
United States. Karel Reisz opted for the

Technicolor internationalism of *Isadora* (1968) and the literary games of *The French Lieutenant's Woman* (1981, script by Pinter from the novel by John Fowles). Lindsay Anderson's surface realism continued in *If . . .* (1969), augmented by the new Hollywood conventions of youthful romanticism and Technicolor pictorialism and by his own Pirandellian games with reality and illusion (games that turned Brechtian in his next major feature, *O Lucky Man!*, 1973, and that had been abandoned by the time he directed his final film, the American *The Whales of August*, 1987). John Schlesinger was almost as comfortable with the American social fringes in *Midnight Cowboy* (1969) as he was with the British ones in *Darling*. In spite of all this crossover, there will always be an England, and no one would mistake a British heist comedy like *The Lavender Hill Mob* for an American heist comedy like *Take the Money and Run* (1969, Woody Allen).

Since the beginning, when the Brighton group led the world in narrative complexity and momentum—anticipating a cinema that would range from *Peeping Tom* to *Dr. No*, respectively—and certainly throughout the Sound Era, the British cinema has excelled in comedy, mystery, drama, literary adaptation, social realism, fantasy, and documentary. Through every period of its history, even when it was reduced to quota quickies, the British produced memorable pictures in all these areas. But from a longer perspective—taking the comedies and mysteries as constants—the thesis and antithesis of British cinema, the extremes where the action is, are social realism and triumphant artifice. If the 1940s offered audiences a choice between the artificial worlds of Powell and Pressburger and the realistic dramas of Carol Reed, and if the social realism of the 1960s was balanced by Hammer's elegant period horror films, it is no surprise that the British cinema after 1970 was divided between the social realists, led by Ken Loach and Mike Leigh, and the fantasists, led by Peter Greenaway. England has

Fig. 14-12
King Arthur (Graham Chapman, central foreground) and his knights receive their mission from God in Monty Python and The Holy Grail.

always produced great writers, and some of them, including Graham Greene and Harold Pinter, have worked in film; in this period one of the greatest was Dennis Potter, who wrote for TV (*Pennies From Heaven*, 1978; *The Singing Detective*, 1986) and the movies (*Dreamchild*, 1985). Literary adaptation was dominated by Merchant Ivory Productions (the team of producer Ismail Merchant and director James Ivory, whose adaptations include *A Room with a View*, 1986; *Howards End*, 1992; and *The Remains of the Day*, 1993). The spectacle has been in eclipse since the death of David Lean, and the documentary waits for another Peter Watkins, but the comedies and the underclass dramas have kept coming. The biggest box-office hit in Britain to date was 1997's working-class sex comedy, *The Full Monty* (Peter Cattaneo), and the hit of the year before was *Trainspotting* (Danny Boyle), a brazen, unvarnished look at a group of aimless Edinburgh junkies.

Some of the directors who established themselves in the 1970s continued to do important work for decades. Ken Loach, a compassionate realist whose work is free of embellishment or overstatement, keeps his camera on a developing scene, no matter how painful, or on a character's truthful expression, no matter how unpleasant, until his look—his decision to keep shooting and not edit out—becomes in itself a moral statement, a commitment to the abused and the excluded, the confused and the graceless, the silenced and the rebellious who are all utterly valuable and who may be surrounded by cruel and stupid people. They are surrounded by powerful, destructive people in their own families (*Family Life*, 1971, also called *Wednesday's Child*, the first insightful film about schizophrenogenic families), in the courts and the welfare system (*Ladybird Ladybird*, 1994, based on the true story of a woman whose children were repeatedly taken from her by the social services, one of them virtually in the delivery room), and on the battlefield (*Land and Freedom*, 1995, the only narrative film about the Spanish Civil War that can stand up to the documentaries). Loach's matter-of-fact, grueling, and at times horribly funny pictures are crucial works in the history of realist cinema, from the first, *Poor Cow* (1967), through the essential *Family Life* and the slices of raw life like *Raining Stones* (1993) to the war film in which he put two brothers through the Irish

rebellion of the early 1920s, *The Wind That Shakes the Barley* (2006), a film whose characters have realistic political discussions and whose violence is unglamorized—but also a film that, however realistic, has the romantic force of which memorable political ballads are made.

In marked contrast to a grim master like Loach, Ken Russell is the most audacious and gaudy British stylist, a director with a brilliant sense of decor and a gift for big cinematic flourishes. Russell, whose training came in filming biographies for TV, continued to direct for TV while he made movies (one of his best studies of music and the psychology of a composer, made in black and white for TV, is *Song of Summer*, 1968; the cinematic equivalents and complements he finds for music charge the biography—of Frederick Delius, from the point of view of his assistant—with a respect for art, in which he finds horror and ecstasy as well as discipline and accomplishment). He directed his first highly acclaimed film in 1969, *Women in Love*. The physicality of the D. H. Lawrence characters and the effectiveness of the novel's symbolism helped anchor Russell's visual flights of fancy in solid fictional ground. His film of *The Boy Friend* (1971) flirted with innocence and cynicism while it turned the musical on which it was based into the onstage portion of a reflexive backstage musical. Russell's "psychological" studies of Tchaikovsky (*The Music Lovers*, 1970) and medieval religious fanaticism (*The Devils*, 1971) were stylistically astounding—especially *The Devils*. There was more style than substance—too much more—in the later *Altered States* (1980) and *Gothic* (1986).

John Schlesinger was a completely different kind of stylist, more restrained. For Schlesinger, "abnormal," "aberrant" people live lives that make perfect sense from their point of view, and the Schlesinger films develop precisely this subjective point of view. The young man's erratic and erotic fantasies in *Billy Liar* (1963), the bizarre sexual and career values of the world of high fashion in *Darling*, the complex desires and problems of those who live *Far from the Madding Crowd* (1967, based on Thomas Hardy's novel and, like *Darling*, scripted by Frederic Raphael and starring Julie Christie), the down-and-out lives of hustlers and bums in *Midnight Cowboy* (one of the first American films to be rated X), and the bisexual triangles in *Sunday Bloody Sunday* (1971) are not examples of human freaks but examples of people trying to satisfy the most common human needs: security and love.

Lindsay Anderson remained the British director most devoted to rebellion against a stagnant and repressive bourgeois society and mentality. Anderson's rebellion was embodied by his violent central characters, who usually want to attack the elements in society that oppress and restrict them: Richard Harris in *This Sporting Life* and Malcolm McDowell in *If . . .* and *O Lucky Man!* Anderson's rebellion determined his cinematic style: violent attacks on the continuity of space, time, and action. Whereas structure, character, and dialogue are Schlesinger's strengths (the dramatic values) and spatial composition is Russell's (the pictorial values), Anderson's primary strength is his battle with continuity at the editing table. Anderson was the British director

Fig. 14-13

In Ken Loach's Ladybird Ladybird, *Crissy Rock stars in the true story of a woman's struggle against the social-service system and the courts to keep her children and live as she sees fit.*

Fig. 14-14

Gorging on desire: Peter Greenaway's The Cook The Thief His Wife & Her Lover. *In contrast to the psychological, social, and political realism and the flat, unstylized look of Loach, Greenaway probes artificial worlds structured by the rules of games, especially games of power, numbers, sex, and art.*

most obviously influenced by the French, from Vigo to Godard, and the most closely linked to the British documentary movement. Like many of the French New Wave directors, Anderson was a film critic (and the influential editor of a film journal, *Sequence*) who turned filmmaker.

Nicolas Roeg was a cinematographer (he did second-unit work on *Lawrence of Arabia*, then shot *The Masque of the Red Death*, 1964, for Roger Corman, *Fahrenheit 451* for Truffaut, *Far from the Madding Crowd* for Schlesinger, and *Petulia* for Lester) who moved to directing. His dominant interests are sexual ambiguity, scientific paradox, the power of the otherworldly, and the mystical influence of cultural myth— sometimes featuring rock stars (Mick Jagger in *Performance*, 1970, which Roeg co-directed with Donald Cammell; David Bowie in *The Man Who Fell to Earth*, 1976). His superb horror film, *Don't Look Now* (1973), intercuts subjective and objective visions as rapidly and complexly as it intercuts the past, present, and future; the daring, originality, and narrative significance of montage in his films puts Roeg in the tradition of Eisenstein and Resnais. He is also, as *Don't Look Now* plainly reveals, a master of *mise-en-scène*. His Australian production, *Walkabout* (1971), proved enormously influential, suggesting themes and images that the new Australian feature-film industry would explore later in the 1970s, particularly in films such as Peter Weir's *The Last Wave* (1977). From *Performance*, *Walkabout*, and *Don't Look Now* to *Bad Timing* (1980) and *Track 29* (1988, written by Dennis Potter), his films have proved mysterious and fascinating, laying out labyrinths that circle back on themselves in a trap of revelation. Yet he is also capable of turning out a polished, linear narrative whose very simplicity is formal, such as the Jim Henson film he directed in 1990, *The Witches*.

Peter Watkins, who began as an editor for the BBC, became the most distinguished British documentarist of the period. His BBC production, *The War Game* (1965), was so powerful an indictment of atomic competition and British vulnerability to its terrifying consequences that it was banned from British television and has never been shown on the BBC. Watkins's biographical re-creation of the life of painter *Edvard Munch* (1974) is its formal opposite—one of the most tactile cinematic examinations of a painter's creative activity, scratching and scraping his obsessive images onto the canvas. His politically radical fiction films—which often deal, much as *The War Game* does, with the urgency of finding, circulating, and preserving an image of the truth, despite government censorship— include *Privilege* (1967) and *Punishment Park* (1971).

The most labyrinthine and intellectual of the British directors is Peter Greenaway; his *The Draughtsman's Contract* (1982) elicited as many attempts at summary or symbolic explanation as *Blowup* had. Greenaway has pursued the trails of desire and formal signification through films that are constructed as elegant, dangerous puzzles. Not surprisingly, he lists *Last Year at Marienbad* as one of his favorite films; in the 1980s and 1990s, his films were shot by Sacha Vierny, who had been Resnais's cinematographer. Greenaway organizes all of his films by taxonomy (systematic classification), using numbers (*1–100*, 1978; *Drowning by Numbers*, 1987), alphabets (*H is for House*, 1973; *A Walk Through H*, 1978; *26 Bathrooms*, 1985), alphanumeric puns (*A Zed & Two Noughts* [*ZOO*], 1985), menus (*The Cook The Thief His Wife & Her Lover*, 1989), postcards (*5 Postcards from Capital Cities*, 1967; *The Belly of an Architect*, 1987), autopsies (*Death in the Seine*, 1988), books (*Prospero's Books*, 1991; *The Pillow Book*, 1996), and other systems of linear and nonlinear narrative.

Provoked by the sexually and politically conservative regime of Prime Minister Margaret Thatcher, Stephen Frears made films that took homosexuals for their central characters (*Prick Up Your Ears*, 1987); unsentimentally portrayed the nihilistic, anarchistic spirit that swept England's new generation of rebels (*Bloody Kids*, 1983); and examined racial and economic conflicts in an England grappling with everything from new sexual attitudes to old colonial attitudes, illuminated now by fluorescents and now by the fires of a street riot (*My Beautiful Laundrette*, 1985, and *Sammy and Rosie Get Laid*, 1987, both from scripts by Hanif Kureishi). Frears also displayed a talent for the cruel tale of the manipulative, sexually charged war for power (*Dangerous Liaisons*, 1988; *The Grifters*, 1990). After making several films in America, of which *The Grifters* was the most influential, he returned to England to make such noteworthy films as *The Snapper* (1993) and *The Queen* (2006).

Mike Leigh makes slice-of-life comedies and dramas about ordinary but extraordinary people, some of whom are endearing oddballs (*High Hopes*, 1988; *Life Is Sweet*, 1991; *Happy-Go-Lucky*, 2008), while at least one is the terminal "angry young man" whose ideas are as bleak and violent as his behavior (*Naked*, 1993). His detailed period film, *Topsy-Turvy* (1999), both a character study and a meticulous analysis of the genesis and production of *The Mikado*, offers an unglamorous but affirmative portrayal of the backstage world of Gilbert and Sullivan. His skill at social realism and his mastery of tone are evident in that film and in *Vera Drake* (2004), the story of a working-class abortionist. One of his most popular films was *Secrets & Lies* (1996), a comic family melodrama full of sexual, racial,

and emotional surprises. Leigh's actors inhabit their roles and improvise the story and dialogue together; then Leigh writes the script, which is filmed without further improvisation. This helps to give the movies their characteristic balance of structural control and apparently spontaneous realism; it is similar to the practice of John Cassavetes.

If Leigh is the most significant of the newer realists, the fantasist to complement him may be horror writer Clive Barker; his first film, *Hellraiser* (1987), takes huge artistic chances, both visually and conceptually. Kenneth Branagh, born in Northern Ireland, is best known for his cinematically and dramatically energetic adaptations of Shakespeare's *Henry V* (1989) and *Much Ado About Nothing* (1993); his adaptation of *Hamlet* (1996), however, was bombastic and superficial. Other directors who did their first

Fig. 14-15
Walkabout: *the aborigine (David Gulpilil), silhouetted by the Australian sun.*

important work in the 1980s but became famous in the 1990s include Mike Hodges, whose *Croupier* (1998) was a crisp, literate thriller, and Terence Davies, whose *Distant Voices, Still Lives* (1988) was a profound, upsetting, and darkly beautiful study of family life and whose adaptation of Edith Wharton's *The House of Mirth* (2000) was maturely considered and precisely shot, a worthy complement to Scorsese's adaptation of Wharton's *The Age of Innocence* (1993).

Danny Boyle made his first movies in Scotland: *Shallow Grave* (1994), a black comedy about death, money, and betrayal, and *Trainspotting*, his 1996 hit about a group of drug addicts. Like these two, the best of his films are vivid, fast, witty, and emotionally engaging, and they often take a surprisingly upbeat tone in spite of their sometimes upsetting subject matter, the result of a commitment to the energy of life. Travel became a theme not only of the director's career—his greatest success, *Slumdog Millionaire* (2008), was shot in India—but also of many of his films: the journey to find a refuge from the zombies in the horror film *28 Days Later* (2002), the flight to the sun in the science fiction film *Sunshine* (2007). Working in India with co-director Loveleen Tandan, Boyle staged and shot much of *Slumdog Millionaire* on location, using many nonprofessionals and capturing the crowded streets and much of the tight interior action with a digital movie camera (it was a 2K camera; see Chapters 18 and 19); the equipment had the advantage of being lightweight and easy to conceal. About 40 percent of the finished picture was shot on film. Energetically and complexly edited, *Slumdog* tells the story of a young man whose life—shown throughout the film in sets of flashbacks—has prepared him to answer correctly the questions on a TV quiz show. The picture is about destiny, which brings the young man a fortune in spite of many hardships and, more importantly, brings him together at last with the woman he has loved since they were children. Grueling and violent, funny and romantic, and grounded at once in the social and economic realities of India and in the fantastic way things can be mixed up and still work out in Bollywood (the film ends with a dance that gives it a Bollywood touch), *Slumdog Millionaire* became an international hit, and in America this low-budget, tonally complicated, original movie earned the Oscar for Best Picture, an honor won in the past by such British films as *Lawrence of Arabia* and *Gandhi* (Richard Attenborough, 1982).

Central and Eastern Europe

The Czech Golden Age

No cinema better demonstrates the interrelationship of film art and political freedom than the cinema of Czechoslovakia, a country that may have been invaded, occupied, and liberated more times in the 20th century than any other. In January 1993, it became two countries: the Czech Republic and Slovakia; though the Czech Republic now has the more active industry, both parts of the former Czechoslovakia contributed to its Golden Age. The Czech Golden Age of cinema (or "Czech film miracle" or "Czech New Wave" as it has also been called) was an extremely short one—roughly, 1961 to 1969—during which time over a dozen Czech films won major awards at the important international film festivals as well as the Academy Awards for Best Foreign Language Film of 1965 (*The Shop on Main Street*) and 1967 (*Closely Watched Trains*, Czech release 1966). The years of Czechoslovakian film mastery coincided with the only years between the Munich Agreement of 1938 and the fall of the Berlin Wall in 1989 that the Czech people and Czech artists had enjoyed a measure of intellectual and creative freedom. Before this brief eruption, the Czech cinema was one of promising beginnings cut short by political repression and artistic censorship—and as we shall see, the censors were still active even in the Golden Age.

In the late silent and early sound periods, the Czech cinema had begun to develop an integrity and individuality (as in the films of Gustav Machatý, Otakar Vávra, Karel Lamač, and Martin Frič) that was destroyed by the Nazi occupation of 1939. After the war the Czech cinema made another new beginning. Led by a group of young filmmakers who had organized their intentions in the final year of the Nazi occupation, the cinema was the first of the industries that was nationalized after the liberation. But this promise was cut short by the Soviet occupation and Stalinization of 1948, and there followed over a decade of repressive rule: the purges, the hardening of the Iron Curtain, the cultural isolation of the Cold War. The fears and repressive climate of the McCarthy years in the United States were marked and mirrored by parallel and much more severe activities on the other side of the Iron Curtain (as can be seen in Jaromil Jireš's 1969 Czech film, *Joke*). Signs of a political thaw began to appear in 1961, and the Czech Golden Age of cinema—which began with Věra Chytilová's *Ceiling* (1962) and Štefan Uher's *Sunshine in a Net* (1962)—sprang up through the cracks until the Soviet tanks rolled into Prague in August 1968.

During the decades of occupation and repression, two significant institutions were founded that would later contribute to the greatness of the Czech film. Just as the Fascists founded a film school and built an efficient studio in Mussolini's Italy that would later be put to use by significant artists, the noted Czech film school, the F.A.M.U., was founded in 1947, and the Barrandov Studios were built into one of the best-equipped production facilities in Europe during the Nazi occupation. (Both were in Prague.) The great Czech films and filmmakers would come from this film school (five intensive years of training at state expense) and film studio as soon as the filmmakers were free to combine their artistic imaginations with their technical capabilities.

The Czech masterpieces were of four general types, including two that had undergone a transformation in the previous years of Soviet repression. First, there was the tale centered on resistance to the Nazi occupation, a safe subject in the Stalinist era, since opinion of the Nazis was quite unanimous. But under the Soviets, the Czech resistance film mirrored the values of Socialist Realism, primarily by presenting a positive, heroic, almost superhuman figure as the embodiment of political resistance—like Shchors and Chapayev in those Stalinist Soviet sound films. In the mature Czech films of the 1960s, however, the central figures of resistance are frequently weak, lazy, and comic—nonheroic, ordinary, all-too-human figures who eventually choose or are forced to take a political stand. Such a study of the comic antihero confronted by the demands of war is a tradition in Czech literature, perhaps most memorable in Karel Hašek's novel *The Good Soldier Schweik*.

Such are the "heroes" of Jiří Weiss's *The Coward* (1961), the study of a cowardly rural schoolteacher who eventually decides to sacrifice himself rather than to select ten of his fellow townspeople to be slaughtered by the Nazis; of Ján Kadár and Elmar Klos's *Death Is Called Engelchen* (1963), about a wounded Czech partisan who wonders whether his sacrifice has been worth the struggle; of Otakar Vávra's *Golden Rennet* (1965), a study of intellectual cowardice; of Zbyněk Brynych's *The Fifth Horseman Is Fear* (1964), the story of the tenants of an apartment house in Nazi-occupied Prague, particularly an old Jewish doctor who must choose between protecting himself and helping a fugitive who has dedicated himself to helping the doctor's people; as well as of both *The Shop on Main Street* and *Closely Watched Trains*.

A second genre, the historical costume drama, popular during the years of suppression, was less popular in the 1960s but still produced films of significance. As in Hitler's Germany and Mussolini's Italy, a film could avoid delicate political issues by avoiding contemporary life altogether. In the 1960s this escapist tendency continued, but of special note are František Vláčil's *Marketa Lazarová* (1967), a mammoth and carefully detailed historical spectacle set in 13th-century Bohemia, and Jiří Weiss's *The Golden Fern* (1963), a beautiful adaptation of a Czech fairy tale.

The third of the Czech genres of the 1960s— the film of contemporary life—had a very different analogue in the era of Soviet suppression. Under the Soviets, Czech cinema eulogized the noble worker, sang the praises of the collective society, depicted the beauty of the factory, and dedicated itself to the proposition that with hard work and cooperation Life Would Be Beautiful. The mature Czech films of the 1960s doubted the values of collectivization, suggested that work did not equal happiness, refused to glamorize the everyday, and implied that the essential human problems were personal rather than societal.

These films of contemporary life tend in two opposite directions. Many of them set their studies of human personality against a clear social and political background. Věra Chytilová, among the most important and accomplished women directors of postwar Europe, made careful studies of feminist problems (*Ceiling; Something Different*, 1963; *The Fruit of Paradise*, 1969; *The Apple Game*, 1975, released 1978; *Trap, Trap, Little Trap*, 1998). Her most entertaining film is a bold, visually inventive satire, *Daisies* (1966), the zany story of two young women who decide to "go bad." A picture with creative energy to burn, *Daisies* can cut from a shot of green apples to a shot taken through an apple-green filter; it can make its characters squeak like dry wood when they move. Jan Němec's *Report on the Party and the Guests* (1966), a satire on conformity, was banned for over a year, even in the liberalized Czechoslovakia. *Daisies* was banned at the same time. Jaromil Jireš's *Joke* is explicitly anti-Stalinist and anti-Soviet, the story of a man who seeks revenge for his earlier imprisonment in the 1950s era of the purges. Evald Schorm's *Courage for Everyday* (1964) and Jiří Weiss's *Ninety in the Shade* (1964, a British co-production) both use suicide as a means of exposing the alienation and sterility of living in such a highly regulated and at times brutally absurd society.

The other tendency of the contemporary films is to concentrate more on character than on politics, to study the human comedy. These "experiential" films—studies of experience—represent one of the truly unique and most influential accomplishments of the Czech cinema: personal, subtle, touching, probing. Many have simple plots; much as in Chekhov's plays, almost nothing happens. But in the course of this nothing the audience discovers how it feels to be these people, how they feel life, and how they feel about life. The purest expressions of these "experiential" films are the sympathetic satires by Miloš Forman (*Black Peter*, 1963; *Loves of a Blonde*, 1965; *The Firemen's Ball*, 1967) and the delicate, perfectly constructed comedy *Intimate Lighting* (1965), by Ivan Passer, who began as Forman's scenarist and later made movies in America (*Cutter's Way*, 1981), as Forman did. Regardless of their settings, the primary focus of the great Czech films of the 1960s is the texture of human experience.

The fourth genre was the surreal or futuristic allegory. Jan Schmidt was the master of this genre, and his short film *Josef Kilian* (1963), co-directed by Pavel Juráček, has been compared to the work of another Czech master, Franz Kafka. Josef K's world becomes a frightening, infinite nightmare, and the experiential quality that Schmidt and Juráček develop is that of wandering in a labyrinth of terrifying dreams. Schmidt's riveting, post-apocalyptic *The End of August at the Hotel Ozone* (1966, released 1968), scripted by Juráček, is a brutal odyssey of survivors of an atomic holocaust, all of them women, roaming about the countryside on horseback, killing.

The Czech cinematic style reveals the pervasiveness and influence of both the French and Italian movements and might be described as a perfect synthesis of Italian Neorealism—particularly its emphasis on the problems of ordinary people and its rejection of the "studio look"—and the compositional and editing spontaneity of the French New Wave—its elliptical cutting, its jumbling of film time, its *cinéma vérité* authenticity. No surer sign of French influence exists than the half dozen major Czech films—Forman's *Black Peter* and Passer's *Intimate Lighting* among them—that end with a Truffaut freeze frame.

Although the Czech filmmakers usually preferred to shoot in real locations, the dominant imagery of this cinema is not nature but the human face. By keeping the camera much closer to the faces of the actors, who were often non-professionals, the Czech films achieved a feeling of naturalness, imperfection, spontaneity, and authenticity.

Another trait of these films is their intermingling of humor and seriousness, producing films that were quite remarkable in their range of emotions, from hilarity to pathos to sudden horror. And this range of effects was also one of the ideas and subjects of the films, for the Czech films implied that life was a mixture of lightness and seriousness, of living through a time fraught with danger. A most difficult existence still remains rich in smiles and jokes, though death waits (and not even unexpectedly) around the next corner. In their seriocomic blend the Czechs distilled the tragic modern history of their tyrannized nation into a positive vision of life that saw humor in even the darkest moments and that (with a few exceptions) refused to surrender its faith in exertion, commitment, and integrity.

Jiří Menzel's *Closely Watched Trains* (1966) is a good example of this Czech spirit. The film's story (scripted by Bohumil Hrabal, from his short story) is of a comical young man, Miloš Hrma, who has taken a job as an apprentice at a train station during the Nazi occupation—primarily to avoid any serious or difficult labor. Despite its wartime setting, the film is a sex comedy, concentrating on the failures and fears of the inexperienced boy. At the film's climax, the boy performs the mission of blowing up a Nazi ammunition train (just as successfully as he made love, the night before, with the woman who brought him the explosives) and is suddenly machine-gunned by a Nazi guard. The clumsy boy has become a man, both sexually and politically, but in gaining his manhood he has lost his life. In this strange variation on the familiar *Bildungsroman*, the long comic apprenticeship produces a period of maturity that is strikingly brief.

The Shop on Main Street (1965), produced and directed by Ján Kadár and Elmar Klos, also mixes the comic and the serious, although not so exuberantly or contrapuntally as *Closely Watched Trains*. According to Kadár, in his collaboration with Klos he took responsibility for the shooting and the handling of the actors while Klos served as producer and supervised the

cutting. If so, *The Shop on Main Street* owes its greatest debt to Kadár's work with actors, and the earlier *Death Is Called Engelchen*, with its brilliant leaps backward and forward in time and space, was more dependent on the editing of Klos.

Of the pure comedies, Miloš Forman was the master. An affectionate satirist who pokes fun at human folly, he also realizes that folly is what makes people human. Two of Forman's Czech films (*Black Peter*, *Loves of a Blonde*) and two of his American films (*Taking Off*, 1971; *Hair*, 1979) are youth films that deal with self-discovery and the generation gap. His other major films, *The Firemen's Ball* and *One Flew Over the Cuckoo's Nest* (1975), as well as the later *Ragtime* (1981), *Amadeus* (1984), *The People Vs. Larry Flynt* (1996), and *Man on the Moon* (1999), keep in touch with the bad-boy spirit of *Black Peter* while they examine the follies of adulthood.

One further contribution of the Czech cinema that cannot be overlooked is its accomplishments in cel animation and in puppet cinema, most notably the work of Jiří Trnka (*The Devil*

Closely Watched Trains: *the human texture of Czech realism. Miloš (Václav Neckár) whispers his secret to the pro-Nazi train inspector (Vlastimil Brodsky).*

Fig. 14-16

on Springs, 1946; *The Czech Year*, 1947; *The Emperor's Nightingale*, 1948; *The Hand*, 1966), Karel Zeman (*Christmas Dream*, 1945; *The Invention of Destruction*, 1957; *On a Comet*, 1970), and Jan Švankmajer (*Dimensions of Dialogue*, 1982; *Conspirators of Pleasure*, 1996). Švankmajer's influence, which remains worldwide in the 21st century, is most keenly evident and richly acknowledged in the animated films of two Americans who have done most of their work in the United Kingdom—the Quay Brothers (Stephen and Timothy), whose creepy, atmospheric, unforgettable shorts and features have taken stop-motion and drawn animation (sometimes including live action) as well as set design to new levels of expression (*Street of Crocodiles*, 1986; *In Absentia*, 2000; *The Piano Tuner of EarthQuakes*, 2005).

So far, the most arresting Czech film of the 21st century is an extraordinary collection of home movies that makes its intimate and vivid way through the 20th century, Jan Šikl's *Private Century* (2007). In eight 52-minute parts (first shown on TV), it presents and analyzes a family and the changing world around it.

Poland

The other cinemas of Eastern and Central Europe endured the same Stalinist and anti-Stalinist twists and turns as the Czech cinema, producing similar periods of fertility and barrenness.

The most fertile period of the Polish cinema preceded the Czech era by almost a decade (1955–64), produced primarily by the founding of another major film school (the Łódź Film School in 1948) and the splitting of the Polish industry into individual artistic production units in 1955. (One of the greatest films made before these changes was *The Last Stop*, 1947, which Wanda Jakubowska shot in Auschwitz—where she herself had been a prisoner.) These smaller production units granted the Polish directors a new freedom and allowed the exercise of more individuality; the two most talented directors, Andrzej Wajda (of the KADR unit) and Roman Polanski (of the KAMERA unit), took advantage of this new opportunity.

As in Czechoslovakia, the Nazi occupation and the resistance to it were favored subjects of the Polish cinema, and no one made more powerful films on the Occupation era than

Andrzej Wajda, whose first feature, *Generation* (1955), became the first work of the new "Polish school." As opposed to the seriocomic, intimate style of the Czech war films, Wajda's style is more active, more violent, more baroque, and less internalized. The greatest early Wajda films (*Kanal*, 1957; *Ashes and Diamonds*, 1958) consistently use arresting, grotesque visual imagery (for example, the claustrophobic Warsaw sewers in *Kanal*), often dwelling on shots of rubble, ashes, and garbage, but these images can turn suddenly beautiful and unforgettably disturbing, as do the sheets hung out to dry in *Ashes and Diamonds*, which become a deadly labyrinth even as they wave neutrally in the breeze. *Ashes and Diamonds* is a spectacularly visual film, with vivid lighting effects (its extreme backlighting and low-angle camerawork influenced by *Citizen Kane*) and with the compelling performance of one of the most interesting and least-known stars in the history of cinema, Zbigniew Cybulski—in many ways the Polish James Dean.

Wajda's filmmaking career is itself a miniature of the political history of Poland over the decades. With the constriction of Polish freedoms in the mid-1960s (and the early death of Cybulski, Wajda's friend and leading actor), Wajda's work became more introspective (particularly the devastating film he made in response to Cybulski's death, *Everything for Sale*, 1969) and more ambiguous in its treatment of politics. But with the return of Polish dissent in the 1970s, spearheaded by Lech Walesa's Solidarity organization of workers and intellectuals, Wajda's films again became openly political. He identified strongly with Solidarity in *Man of Marble* (1977, also influenced by *Kane*) and *Man of Iron* (1980).

Wajda's *Danton* (1982) feels the weight of Solidarity's defeat beneath the Polish capitulation to Soviet policy in December 1981. A French–Polish co-production shot in France (many of Wajda's films had to be shot outside Poland), ostensibly detailing the ideological battle between Danton and Robespierre during the French Revolution, the film uses the familiar strategy of paralleling historical conflicts to contemporary events. When Danton dies beneath the blade of Robespierre's guillotine, the drops of his blood suggest the color and design of the Solidarity insignia. Wajda implies that although

Walesa's Solidarity movement may be as dead as Danton, the ideas for which both stand are alive. In the late 1980s, when Walesa proved victorious, Wajda was free to mix politics and melodrama without reaching for big symbolic effects. In 2007 Wajda directed *Katyń*, the story of the Soviets' slaughtering thousands of Poles in a forest in 1940. In a way, it was the story of his own father's death and his mother's struggle to find out what happened to him, and it returned to the realism and urgency of such early "Polish school" films as *Kanal*.

Roman Polanski's career represents another kind of historical metaphor, centered on horror; though he has attempted to flee from it and deny its power, along with that of the state, horror and trouble have found him in one country after another. From *Repulsion* to *Rosemary's Baby*, his characters don't escape, and as in *Chinatown*, the state is too corrupt to do any good. Even in his early Polish films, Polanski's primary theme is not the rubble of war but the ominousness of the universe itself. Polanski's black-and-white films use a simple situation and very few characters (two men carry a wardrobe out of the sea in *Two Men and a Wardrobe*, 1958; three people sail a boat in *Knife in the Water*, 1962). But Polanski charges the universe with a menacing spirit that turns the simplest events into terrifying combats of great magnitude. In *Repulsion* (1965, made in England) the most commonplace settings and items become tactile enemies, magnified by the growing madness of the withdrawn protagonist (Catherine Deneuve).

Polanski was born in France, but the family soon returned to Poland. Polanski's parents were taken to a concentration camp when he was eight (the mother died there). He was on his own for the next four years, first in the ghetto and then in the countryside, where he found, on the one hand, families that would put him up for awhile, and on the other hand, German soldiers who shot at him for fun. The visions he developed as an adult—of cosmic malevolence, mortal power games, and psychological ambiguity—were incompatible with any Socialist theory of justice. Polanski could resolve his nihilistic conflict with a repressive state only by escaping to a more indulgent West to make films in England, France, and the United States: *Repulsion; Cul-de-Sac*, 1966, a devastating black comedy;

The Fearless Vampire Killers or: Pardon Me, But Your Teeth Are In My Neck, 1967, a parody; *Rosemary's Baby*, 1968, a straightforward, glossy horror film and his first American picture; *Macbeth*, 1971, a version of Shakespeare's play that is short on poetry and—perhaps because it was the first film he made after his pregnant wife, Sharon Tate, was murdered by the Manson "family"—long on violence; *Chinatown*, 1974, a classic mystery and a latter-day *noir; The Tenant*, 1976, a horror film comparable to *Repulsion; Tess*, 1979, from the novel by Thomas Hardy; *Bitter Moon*, 1992, a tale of sexual revenge; *Death and the Maiden*, 1994, a tale of political revenge; and *The Pianist* (2002), a tale of survival. He left the United States in 1978 after a sex scandal and since then has worked in Europe.

Jerzy Skolimowski was, like Polanski, a younger-generation filmmaker who fled Poland. After serving as scriptwriter for both Wajda (*Innocent Sorcerers*, 1960) and Polanski (*Knife in the Water*), he wrote and directed *Identification Marks: None* (1964), *Walkover* (1965), and *Barrier* (1966) in Poland. After his anti-Stalinist *Hands Up!* (1967) was banned, he made *Le Départ* (1967) in Belgium, *Deep End* (1970) in Germany, and *The Shout* (1978) and *Moonlighting* (1982) in England. Skolimowski has made incisive political films (*Hands Up!*, *Moonlighting*) as well as intricate apolitical films (*The Shout*).

An intellectually demanding director whose films explore moral and philosophical dilemmas, Krzysztof Zanussi is, after Wajda, the most important Polish filmmaker still working in the country (though he was forced out of Poland after the fall of Solidarity and worked in Germany for much of the 1980s). His characters—often scientists (Zanussi's degree was in physics)—struggle with ideas and intuitions within networks of social and moral codes; his major works include *The Death of a Provincial* (1966), *The Structure of Crystals* (1969), *Camouflage* (1977), *The Constant Factor* (1980), *Contract* (1980), *The Year of the Quiet Sun* (1984), and *Life As a Fatal Sexually Transmitted Disease* (2000).

For various reasons, by choice or compulsion, the three most important new Polish filmmakers of the 1980s and 1990s did not work in Poland. For directing *Interrogation* (1982)—the relentless, compelling story of a woman (Krystyna

Ashes and Diamonds: *the death of a political assassin (Zbigniew Cybulski).*

Fig. 14-17

Krystyna Janda as the citizen detained for years in Ryszard Bugajski's Interrogation.

Fig. 14-18

Janda) who is imprisoned and questioned for years and develops a complex relationship with her Stalinist inquisitor—Ryszard Bugajski found his film immediately banned, not to be shown until 1990, and himself a political exile. Working in Canada, he made such important films as *Clearcuts* (1991). Agnieszka Holland studied under Forman, was jailed in 1968 after the Prague Spring, collaborated on several films with Wajda (for example, she co-wrote *Danton* and *A Love in Germany*), acted in *Interrogation,* had some of her own films—notably *A Woman Alone* (1981)— banned, made a pro-Solidarity film in 1988 (*To Kill a Priest*), and then became internationally famous with *Europa Europa* (1991), a French–German

co-production that told the true story of a Jewish youth who survived the war by pretending to be an Aryan Nazi. Her next films were made in France (*Olivier Olivier*, 1992) and America (*The Secret Garden*, 1993).

Krzysztof Kieślowski also made important films in Poland before finally settling in France: *Camera Buff* (1979) and the ten-part *Dekalog* (*The Decalogue*, 1988, for TV), each of whose probing and ironic, roughly hour-long tales was based on one of the Ten Commandments; two of them were expanded into features: *A Short Film About Killing* and *A Short Film About Love* (both 1988). Working in France and Poland, Kieślowski and his regular co-writer, Krzysztof

Piesiewicz, went on to make *The Double Life of Veronique* (1991), an intuitive study of two women, living in different countries, who are virtually identical. They climaxed their exploration of the almost inexpressible connections between people with the Swiss–French–Polish trilogy *Three Colors*, whose parts—*Blue* (1993), *White* (1993, released 1994), and *Red* (1994)—are named after the colors of the French flag and ironically investigate liberty, equality, and fraternity. But what liberty means to the woman in *Three Colors: Blue* is solitary grief after her husband and child die in a car accident—an unwelcome freedom at best, even if she uses it to find herself and heal. Equality in *White* is a matter of getting even, a consummation of shared deprivation, and fraternity in *Red* is a matter of eavesdropping, coincidence, and hidden connections. Color-coded to the core and insightfully interrelated, these three films marked Kieślowski as the long-sought heir of Antonioni and Bergman—but at the premiere of *Red*, he announced his retirement, and he died in 1996.

Hungary

The early Hungarian cinema is probably most notable for the talents it exported to the rest of the world after their Hungarian apprenticeships: Béla Lugosi; Hollywood directors Michael Curtiz, André de Toth, and Paul Fejos; the noted British producer and director, Alexander Korda; and the international film theorists, László Moholy-Nagy and Béla Balázs. The best-known international representative of the new Hungarian cinema of the 1960s and 1970s was Miklós Jancsó (*Cantata*, 1962; *The Red and the White*, 1967; *The Confrontation*, 1968). Jancsó's films combine Hungarian folk tales and history with extremely lengthy and carefully planned tracking shots that choreograph cinema space as complexly as those of Orson Welles; his use of the wide screen, especially in *The Red and the White*, is among the most impressive in the history of the art.

István Szabó, originally a member of Balázs's experimental workshop, makes psychologically detailed portraits of citizens who must make difficult choices between the personal and the political. The actor of *Mephisto* (1981, starring Klaus Maria Brandauer) refuses to take a stand against the Nazi oppressors because he's "only an actor." He becomes the slave of his satanic role, both onstage and off. *Colonel Redl* (1985) explores what it means to care only about power. In 1999, Szabó made *Sunshine*, which follows three generations of a family that is under pressure to renounce its Jewish identity.

Béla Tarr makes long, slow films. *Damnation* (1988), for instance, consists almost entirely of carefully composed, slow-paced, long takes in sharp black and white; the film tells the story of a failed romance and a kind of spiritual espionage in a muddy town where there is little to do but watch the rain. In a 2001 interview, he said that his films are not about telling stories—which he keeps as banal as possible—but about getting closer to people. By understanding everyday life, he hopes, the films may achieve an understanding of human nature: "why we are as we are, how we commit our sins, how we betray one another, and what interests lead us." He said it about *Werckmeister Harmonies* (2000), but it applies to all of his films to date—including the eight-hour *Satantango* (or *Satan's Tango*, 1994)—whose shots spend a long time with characters, concentrating on their present-tense being in time and space until part of their nature is revealed. Tarr leaves in what most directors since Griffith have taken out: the parts of scenes in which not much happens, the long transitions between actions, shots with little or no movement (in *Satantango*, for example, characters may walk half a mile directly away from the camera in long shot, a very long take in which almost nothing changes on the screen, or they may remain almost still and look at the camera for minutes after a scene appears to be done). Often the camera observes the weather, spending time with it as the characters must; the weather, the landscape, and time itself are given the screen time they need to become fully declared presences in Tarr's films.

Nimród Antal made a devastating black comedy about fantasy and murder in the subway, *Kontroll* (2003). He then went to Hollywood to make a tight and atmospheric horror film, *Vacancy* (2007).

Of Hungary's women directors, two have achieved international recognition: Ildikó Enyedi with her first feature, *My 20th Century* (1988), a playful, moving exploration of the nature of light (as starlight, electric light, movies) and communication (wireless telegraphy, homing pigeons) as two sisters lose and find each other while the young century also tries to find its way through a maze of sexual, political, and technological changes; and Márta Mészáros with a career of films about the everyday lives of working women and the attempt to live truthfully in the midst of social and political hypocrisy (*Adoption*, 1975; *Diary for My Children*, 1982; *Fetus*, 1993).

The Balkan States

Of all the countries known collectively as the Balkan States, Greece and the former Yugoslavia have had the greatest impact on world cinema.

When it was still called Yugoslavia, the country built its international cinematic reputation with the productions of the Zagreb studio, which since 1957 had been the most innovative and influential source of animated films in the world. Yugoslavia's best known director of feature films, particularly in the late 1960s and 1970s, was the irreverent satirist Dušan Makavejev, whose movies resist narrative continuity and test taboos (*WR—Mysteries of the Organism*, 1971; *Sweet Movie*, 1974); he also made satiric montages that are primarily political (*Innocence Unprotected*, 1968) and sociopolitical tragicomedies full of unpredictable twists (*Love Affair, or The Tragedy of a Switchboard Operator*, 1967; *Montenegro, or Pigs and Pearls*, 1981; *Gorilla Bathes at Noon*, 1993).

In 1991 and 1992, the former Yugoslavia split into separate countries: Bosnia–Herzegovina, Croatia, Tfyrom (The Former Yugoslav Republic of Macedonia), Slovenia, and the Federal Republic of Yugoslavia (which included Serbia and Montenegro, which separated from each other in 2006; finally, in 2008, Kosovo split off from Serbia). Ethnically driven civil wars broke out in 1992, and in the context of the new map it became significant that Emir Kusturica was a Bosnian Muslim, Makavejev a Serbian. The three major production centers, now in different countries—Belgrade in Serbia, Zagreb in Croatia, and Ljubljana in Slovenia—became more stylistically and politically independent of each other. In Bosnia–Herzegovina during the 1990s, most of the filming was done by news cameras. Kusturica, who had won audiences around the world with two occasionally surreal coming-of-age films—*When Father Was Away on Business*

(1985) and *Time of the Gypsies* (1989)—shot *Arizona Dream* (1993) in the United States. Like the most important Romanian film of the period (*An Unforgettable Summer*, 1994, the first film Lucian Pintilie had been allowed to make in 30 years) and the first film made in Tfyrom (Milcho Manchevski's brilliant, circularly structured *Before The Rain*, 1994), *Arizona Dream* was a French co-production. Foreign money also helped Kusturica make his next pictures in Prague and Belgrade (*Underground*, 1995) and on the Danube (*Black Cat, White Cat*, 1998). The best features to come out of the wars were the buddy film *Pretty Village, Pretty Flame* (1996), by Srdjan Dragojević, and *The Powder Keg* (1998), also known as *Cabaret Balkan*, by Goran Paskaljević, a film in which any vignette can turn comical or violent.

Greek cinema came to international attention in the early 1960s, thanks primarily to *Never on Sunday* (1960) and three films by the Cyprus-born Michael Cacoyannis: *Stella* (1955), which introduced Melina Mercouri in the role of a woman who loves deeply but defies marriage—a significant break with Greek social and artistic conventions; *Electra* (1961), which starred Irene Papas and remains the greatest cinematic adaptation of a Greek tragedy; and *Zorba the Greek* (1964), which was a popular hit based on a novel by Nikos Kazantzakis. Like *Electra*, the strongest of Cacoyannis's later films—*The Trojan Women* (1971) and *Iphigenia* (1977)—are Greek tragedies set not on the stage but in the rough natural world. Particularly in *Electra* and the archetypically feminist *Iphigenia*, our engagement with the characters—which successfully evokes the Aristotelian responses of pity and horror, or empathy and dread—is enhanced by their appearing to be real people (not common or ordinary, but credible) in unstylized environments. Cacoyannis creates a convincing picture of the ancient world in which the tragedies unfolded, an approach exactly opposite to the spectacular approach of the Hollywood "epic."

Never on Sunday, a comedy about a prostitute (Melina Mercouri) with a mind of her own, was a worldwide hit; its director, Mercouri's husband, was the blacklisted American Jules Dassin. Dassin's other major Greek film was *A Dream of Passion* (1978), his response to *Persona*, in which an actress portraying Medea

(Mercouri) meets a woman who really has murdered her children (Ellen Burstyn). If some directors, like Dassin, came to Greece in the 1950s and 1960s, others left—notably Costa-Gavras, who went to France, where he learned the trade and eventually made his gripping film about political assassination, Fascism, and the struggle for truth in Greece, *Z* (1969).

After the military junta of 1967 was overthrown in 1974, conditions improved to the point that Mercouri, who had been declared an enemy of the state and exiled for her opposition to the ruling colonels, was elected to Parliament and eventually became Greece's Minister of Culture; she died in 1994, a popular hero.

With help from the government-backed Greek Film Centre and other production and funding agencies—and the moral support, since the late 1990s, of an annual film festival in Thessaloniki—many independents made their first films, which ranged from the original and artistic (Antoinetta Angelidi's *The Hours: A Square Film*, 1995) to the human-interest contemporary (Constantine Giannaris's *From the Edge of the City*, 1998).

The most stylistically rigorous of the Greek directors is Theodoros Angelopoulos, whose long takes (often in long shot, but also in full and medium shot) follow and meditate upon their subjects with the patience of a Godard and the transcendental intensity of a Tarkovsky. Episodic, ambiguous, and slow-paced, his films present the "other Greece"—not the one of stunning beaches and crowded cities, the *Never on Sunday* Greece, but the rhythmically different land of peasants, refugees, nomads, and soldiers, a place where continuity (emphasized in the long takes and following shots) is the essential structure of life and perception, while the definitions according to which people attempt to organize their lives prove elusive and sometimes destructive. His works include the trilogy *Days of '36* (1972), *The Traveling Players* (1975), and *The Hunters* (1977), as well as *Alexander the Great* (1980), *Voyage to Cythera* (1983), *The Beekeeper* (1986), *Landscape in the Mist* (1988), *The Suspended Step of the Stork* (1991), *Ulysses' Gaze* (1995), *An Eternity and a Day* (1998), and *Trilogy: The Weeping Meadow* (2004), the last of which begins the story of a woman whose tragic life is an image of 20th-century history (carried

forward in *The Dust of Time*, 2008). History is vividly dramatized in his most important and challenging film, *The Traveling Players*, which tells the story of a troupe that travels through Greece between the years 1939 and 1952—years of war, of partisans, of Fascists, of political betrayal—performing the pastoral drama, *Golpho the Shepherdess*. The leader of the troupe and his family live out a modernized version of Aeschylus's trilogy of Greek tragedies, the *Oresteia* (the murder—in this case the betrayal and execution—of the father, the son's revenge on the mother and her lover, the son's flight); the son is even named Orestes. It is as if the lives of the players were positioned between two determining texts: the *Oresteia*, which no one ever mentions, and *Golpho*, which never changes. The story is told out of chronological order in a manner that is architecturally masterful and compelling. During the time covered by the action, the players often return to the same cities; that makes it possible for Angelopoulos to show them

Fig. 14-19
Iphigenia: *Greek tragedy in a realistic setting; Clytemnestra (Irene Papas) and her daughter Iphigenia (Tatiana Papamoskou), the elder sister of Electra and Orestes, who is about to be sacrificed by her father, King Agamemnon, so that the Trojan War can be successful.*

in the same places at different times, and for the film to start with the troupe in a certain city in 1952 and to end with them in the same city in 1939. So unusual is the treatment of time in this picture that in one shot several men walk down the street at dawn on New Year's, 1946, to a political rally taking place in 1952. So elegant is the camerawork that one shot shows the father's ascending a staircase (one of two that reach the same level), going into the bedroom where his wife is waiting, telling her he's enlisted, hitting her when she laughs at him, then going out of the bedroom and down the other staircase, where he says goodbye to his daughter and leaves; then the camera pans back to the first staircase to watch the lover come upstairs and go into the bedroom. *The Traveling Players* unites the mythical past and the political recent past into a radical picture that crosses and recrosses Greece in space and time.

The Suspended Step of the Stork is a profound meditation on the nature of borders—between people, countries, epochs, states of apprehension—epitomized in the transcendental monologues of an alienated politician (played by Mastroianni) and in two shots in which first a border guard and then, near the end of the film, a TV journalist (who has been trying to track down the vanished politician) stand in midstride—like a stork with one leg raised—at the Greek–Albanian border, realizing that to complete that step would be to enter the undefinable realm of "elsewhere." The primary setting is a town filled with international dropouts and refugees who have mythologized the "elsewhere" they hope to find if they are ever given papers and allowed to cross the border—which never will happen, so that their condition is one of permanent liminality. The formal highlight of the film is a wedding sequence that is shot without close-ups because of the scale and tone of the event—and because the bride and groom cannot see each other close up, for they are on opposite sides of the wide river that has artificially become a political boundary dividing the region in which they grew up as childhood sweethearts into parts of separate countries.

These Central and Eastern European films suggest that no matter how the map of Europe might be drawn, moral, psychological, and stylistic concerns transcend political borders even as they respond to political conditions.

Asia

Japan

The Japanese cinema first conquered the West when Akira Kurosawa's *Rashomon* (1950) won the Golden Lion at the Venice Film Festival of 1951. In the wake of *Rashomon* followed a series of imaginative and impressive films from Japan, directed by Kurosawa and by other masters of a cinema that had previously been unknown to most Western audiences: Kenji Mizoguchi, Yasujiro Ozu, Teinosuke Kinugasa, Kon Ichikawa, Hiroshi Inagaki, Masaki Kobayashi, Tadashi Imai, Mikio Naruse. The decade of the 1950s proved to be Japan's richest cinematic era—both commercially and artistically—as a result of many of the same forces that stimulated the new Western film industries in the same period: the receptivity to new forms of film expression, the new market for non-American films, and the new period of political and intellectual freedom. As in many European nations, the Japanese cinema emerged from over a decade of political constraints caused by World War II and its aftermath of normalization. The awards given to *Rashomon* restored the esteem of a defeated generation, the warriors who had lost the war. What surprised Western audiences was not simply the maturity of Japanese films in this decade but the richness and depth of the Japanese film tradition: Mizoguchi and Kinugasa had been directing since the 1920s, and the 1930s had been a great period.

The Japanese cinema developed under conditions that kept it approximately ten years behind the cinemas of the West, a lag that worked in its favor in the 1950s, for the Japanese film industry felt the crippling effects of television almost a decade later than the industries of America and Europe. So too the early period—in which Japanese narrative and philosophical traditions developed along native lines into a unique cinematic syntax—lasted a decade longer in Japan, at least into the mid-1920s. Although there were commercial and technological reasons for this delay—a lag in organizing the industry, problems with machines and film—the primary reasons were aesthetic. First, women did not appear in Japanese films until the mid-1920s, women's roles being played by female impersonators called *oyama* (Kinugasa began his career as an *oyama*). This sacrifice of naturalness and authenticity tended to keep the Japanese cinema tied to its theatrical roots (where men also played the female roles, as they did on the Elizabethan stage) and kept it from asserting the kind of naturalness and spontaneity that gradually evolved in the films of the West between 1905 and 1915.

Second, the Japanese cinema used a narrator to explain the film to the audience. Called the *benshi*, this narrator's presence eliminated the need for printed titles and partly accounts for the way the Japanese cinema developed its own cinematic grammar and rhetoric, which had nothing to do with the Griffith tradition. Although narrators occasionally accompanied film screenings in American nickelodeons, they disappeared with the nickelodeons. In Japan, where the commentary of a narrator was a convention of Kabuki theatre, some films became so dependent on a human speaker that the cinema itself did not need to "speak" in its own unique and powerful terms. (On the other hand, the absence of intertitles let the best of the Japanese filmmakers achieve a scroll-like flow of carefully chosen images.) All the early Western masters of the cinema—Griffith, Eisenstein, Murnau, and others—were specifically those who discovered ways to make a purely visual "language" communicative. A highlight of the Japanese silent cinema is Kinugasa's tale of devotion and insanity, *A Page of Madness* (*Crazy Page* or *A Page Out of Order*, 1926), as elliptical in its construction as anything by the French Surrealists, as daring in its editing as Kirsanov's or Eisenstein's montage, and with no intertitles, more stream-of-consciousness sequences than *Napoléon*, and a more cinematic grasp of Expressionism than *Caligari* (which had not yet been shown in Japan). Many people who see it feel a *benshi* would have helped. Still, the film is coherent, and there is no doubt that it speaks the language of cinema. Kinugasa's *Crossroads* (1928) was the only Japanese film before *Rashomon* to be shown widely in the West, and his *Gate of Hell* (1953) was one of the biggest hits to follow *Rashomon*, along with Kurosawa's own *Seven Samurai* (1954) and, of course, Ishiro Honda's *Gojira* (1954; U.S. version, *Godzilla King of the Monsters!*, co-directed by Terry Morse, 1956).

Third, lacking an active tradition of popular, bourgeois prose fiction (even though the first post-Roman novel was written in Japan in the early 11th century: *The Tale of Genji*, by Lady Murasaki Shikibu), Japan's cinema descended from the rich theatrical traditions of Noh, Kabuki, and Bunraku, as well as the highly developed arts of painting, poetry, and design. While Western cinematic conventions evolved as combinations of and compromises between enacted and written storytelling, the indigenous Japanese cinema evolved from the stylizations of its theatrical and visual arts. Not only did the *oyama* and *benshi* come to Japanese cinema from the theatre but, according to Japanese film critic Tadao Sato, so did a key distinction between two types of leading men. One was the *tateyaku*—strong, powerful, virile (to be embodied by Sessue Hayakawa and Toshiro Mifune—parallel to America's Clark Gable and John Wayne); the other was the slighter, sweeter, milder figure, the *nimaime*—literally, the "second lead" of Kabuki (parallel to such American stars as Richard Barthelmess and Montgomery Clift). Many Japanese film stories derive from expectations about these two opposite types of actors.

The confining Japanese cinematic traditions died slowly and unwillingly. The *oyama* disrupted film production in 1922 by calling a strike when they saw they were to be replaced by women. The *benshi*, who had made themselves into one of the primary attractions of the Japanese cinema (often an audience attended a film merely to enjoy the commentary of a clever and popular *benshi*), fought extinction even more vigorously. In 1932, the *benshi* and the theatre musicians called a strike against the entire film industry. Some *benshi* turned off the soundtracks of the early talkies so they could do their act. On at least one occasion the *benshi* union hired thugs to assault an official of one of the studios that was converting to sound.

When sound finally came to the Japanese cinema, it came almost a decade later than to the film industries of the West. (For that matter, the first unhidden kiss scene was shot in 1946.) Although the first successful sound film was shot in Japan as early as 1931—*The Neighbor's Wife and Mine*, directed by Heinosuke Gosho—in 1932 only 45 of some 400 Japanese films used synchronized sound. Ozu did not shoot his first sound film until 1936, and silent production did not die completely until 1937.

The coming of sound to Japan was quickly followed by the coming of war, and the Japanese government demanded that the film industry support the war effort with films reflecting national militaristic policies. An equally repressive policy restricted the Japanese film industry after the war when the American Occupation Forces created a cultural "reorientation" committee, which banned certain subjects (for example, all Japanese period dramas because they were feudalistic and militaristic) and demanded others (for example, the values of peaceful living and democratic institutions).

On the other hand, the Japanese film industry had developed a number of practices and traditions that would work for rather than against it when a period of commercial, technical, and political equality would enable it to compete on the world's screens. The Japanese film industry, like the American one, was composed of several competing commercial companies, with their own writers, directors, actors, and technicians working under contract, which were in the business of conceiving, making, and selling films. The four Japanese studios that became most familiar to Western audiences were Nikkatsu (the oldest, founded in 1912—Ichikawa's studio); Shochiku (founded in 1920 and for three decades the commercial leader—Ozu's studio); Toho (founded in the 1930s by the amalgamation of several smaller companies—Kurosawa's primary studio; exploiter of Japanese monster pictures, like *Godzilla*; developer of Japan's own wide-screen, anamorphic process, Tohoscope); and Daiei (founded during the war—producer of *Rashomon*, *Gate of Hell*, and Mizoguchi's later films).

The Japanese studio system avoided many of the evils of the American system, but it produced others. A primary advantage was that the system was built around the director rather than the producer or star. The Japanese "producer" is comparable to the production manager in Hollywood who manages production details but makes no creative decisions. The Japanese director is a more powerful audience attraction than a film's star. The Japanese director is the paternalistic head of his own production "family." The disadvantages of such a system—more comfortable and less competitive than Hollywood's—are, first, that talented directors must serve long apprenticeships to work up the ladder (in the

case of a mentorship under a great senior director, this may be an advantage). Japan does not import instant talents from outside its studio system—no Rouben Mamoulians or Bob Fosses who come from the theatre; no Jean-Luc Godards or Lindsay Andersons who come from film journals. A second disadvantage is that the paternalistic system keeps women from rising to positions of authority.

Japanese films tend to bunch themselves in clear-cut genres and cycles. The basic division is between the *jidai-geki*, a period or costume film set in Japan's past (in most cases, in the feudal period before the emperor returned to power in the 1868 Meiji Restoration), and the *gendai-geki*, a film of modern life. But within these two basic genres there are many subgenres. The *jidai-geki* can be further subdivided into the particular period of Japanese history it depicts (for example, the Tokugawa era, 1615–1868). As the terms are used in the Japanese industry, however, the *jidai-geki* treats only the Tokugawa period, the *Meiji-mono* treats the period from the Meiji Restoration to 1912, and there is no specific term for films set before the Tokugawa era (such as *Rashomon*, which is set in the Heian period, no later than the 12th century). The *gendai-geki* has such subgenres as the *shomin-geki* (the drama or comedy of middle-class and lower-middle-class life), the "mother picture" (a mother's relationship to her children), the "wife picture" (the difficulties of marriage for women), the "nonsense picture" (farcical comedies), the *yakuza* or gangster picture, and the "youth picture" (the wild doings of youth). In 1998 *Ringu* (*Ring*) instituted a new modern-life genre, "J-horror," which was more violent than the conventional ghost story.

Two consistent structural traits do seem to dominate the best Japanese films, and both are descendants of the Japanese theatrical traditions of the Kabuki and the Noh. The first trait is an economical concentration on the central theme; the second is a concern for symmetry, for parallels and contrasts that find a balance. But no single consistent stylistic trait dominates the Japanese cinema. Those three directors who, at least from a Western perspective, appear to be Japan's greatest film artists—Akira Kurosawa, Kenji Mizoguchi, and Yasujiro Ozu—have three completely different visual senses and are unique, individual stylists.

Akira Kurosawa is the Japanese director most popular in the West—perhaps because he was so obviously influenced by films of the West (he once listed Gance's *La Roue* and the works of Hawks, Stevens, Capra, Ford, and Wyler as major influences—and Antonioni and Mizoguchi as favorites rather than influences). He is one of the only filmmakers to have made effective movies in both the *jidai-* and *gendai-geki*. Kurosawa's samurai films are closely related to American westerns (and have been remade as westerns), and he was clearly influenced by Western cinematic styles, especially the use of the subjective traveling camera, the wide screen, rapid cutting, the Expressionist color experiments of Eisenstein's *Ivan the Terrible, Part II*, and deep-focus cinematography. He is most Japanese in his long takes and subtle but powerful control of mood.

Rashomon clearly demonstrates Kurosawa's thematic concerns and stylistic maturity (he had been directing films since 1943). The film is famous as the essential cinematic demonstration of the relativity and subjectivity of truth—and that it is, though it is also about lies. But it is also notable for Kurosawa's stylistic control and for what he says people should do, given the problematic nature of truth and the imperfection of human beings.

Rashomon presents several levels of narration—most significantly, two frames and four inner tales. One of the frames is primary: In the narrative present, two men tell a third about a trial they have witnessed. The trial itself is an inner frame within which the three primary characters relate their versions of what happened (the fourth tale is told later). Each of the inner tales reflects the attitude, personality, and self-justifications of the witness, and each presents a version of what happened that cannot be reconciled with the others. The one known fact is that a man lies dead in the forest; but what emerges as worse, the real moral problem, is that the inquest has been filled with immoral lies. Since people need to assign a cause, to see a reason for a catastrophic fact, the film becomes a search for answers and reasons: how he died, why they lied, and whether people are any good.

The film's primary frame introduces this search as two men, a Woodcutter and a Priest (representatives of the secular and sacred orders), feel compelled to tell their story to a stranger. Kurosawa sets this frame during a furious rainstorm, from which the only refuge is a pitiful shelter of architectural ruins. Kurosawa uses the ruins and the storm as concrete external images of the social instability of the era: a period of lawlessness, bandits, plagues, famine, civil war, and, like the Rashomon Gate itself (and the old values it represents), collapse and loss. What is intriguing about the Woodcutter's introduction is that he tells the Listener that this incident is especially terrible, worse even than the social chaos of the present. The Listener, whose curiosity is aroused—he serves as the viewer's surrogate in this respect—agrees to listen to the tale while waiting out the storm.

The first three versions of the incident (given after a policeman has explained how he caught the bandit and the Woodcutter has—we find out later—lied about how he found the man already dead) are those of the three principal participants. Each testimony is completely different in motivation, tone, and style. The first version is that of the boastful, impulsive bandit, Tajomaru (Toshiro Mifune). Tajomaru's version emphasizes the physical sensations of the confrontation—the heat of the day, the glare of the sun, the sting of the gnats that he repeatedly swats—that Kurosawa depicts subjectively, from Tajomaru's point of view. Kurosawa's primary subjective device in the sequence, however, is the violent, furious pace of the camera's incessant movement, translating Tajomaru's energy into visual terms and expressing how he sees himself: aggressive, restless, dominant.

According to Tajomaru, his rape of the woman was a romantic conquest. The bandit then bests the husband in fair, valiant combat ("He fought marvelously"), killing him with a sword. Kurosawa's camera catches the flashy swordsmanship as Tajomaru perceives it—or, more to the point, describes it: with violent movement of the skillful participants.

The woman (Machiko Kyo) tells a version that is completely different in tone, emphasis, and action. According to the way she sees both herself and the event, she is a "poor helpless woman." Although her version begins after the sexual act, her obvious implication is that she had no choice but to submit to the rape. The bandit plays a small role in her relatively subdued version of the incident, and the few glimpses she provides are of a whooping savage, a grotesque caricature of the bandit's masculinity in his own version. She presents herself as a selfless, proper wife whose real concern is her husband, the only one whose reaction to the rape matters. And his reaction is a cold, pitiless, piercing stare. She retrieves her knife, still stuck in the trunk of a tree (a point of agreement with Tajomaru's version), and advances on him with the knife. Then she faints. Upon awaking she finds the knife (a different murder weapon than in Tajomaru's story) in her husband's chest.

The ghost of the husband tells the third version of the story—through a female medium who has summoned his spirit from the other world. As the dead man's voice issues from the medium's lips, sounding like a phonograph record played at too slow a speed in an underground cavern, her veils float and flap violently in the wind that has suddenly entered the courtyard, clashing with its previous stillness. The wind is, or is like, a blast from the supernatural.

In contrast to the writhing agony of the medium is the still, dark tone of the husband's version of the incident. For the husband (Masayuki Mori), the woman proves herself unworthy, as dishonorable as the bandit. According to the husband, he does not die by the sword in combat (Tajomaru's version) nor as the result of a "trance" that impels his shamed, rejected wife toward him with the knife (as in hers) but as the result of his own decision—to kill himself with the knife to redeem his honor and end his pain. Each of the narrators claims to have killed the man and to have acted according to his or her best nature.

But the Woodcutter (Takashi Shimura), who discovered the body and who, we now find out, actually witnessed the entire incident, sees all three versions as lies—even the dead man's. If this is true, one cannot depend even on supernatural beings for the truth. The Woodcutter then tells his version of the incident, the "objective account" of an outside observer. In the Woodcutter's account, all three characters are weaker than in their own. The bandit blubberingly offers to marry the woman he defiled; the husband is a jittery coward; the wife is selfish (she does care about herself), and she dares the two men to fight over her. Because both men are so cowardly in this version, they have a good deal of trouble working up a fight. They both shake with fright, their hands and swords

trembling. Eventually the fight blunders to its climax as the husband loses his weapon and is killed—by the bandit, with a sword.

Several questions arise, however, from this "objective" report. Are the participants lying—as the Woodcutter believes—or are they telling part of the truth as they perceived it (called by some psychologists "the *Rashomon* effect")? Clearly, some lying is going on: The husband cannot have killed himself with a knife if the bandit killed him with a sword. On the other hand, the bandit and woman surely experienced the rape differently. With regard to many of the plot's contradictions, one is left asking where the characters are distorting their stories to make themselves look good and where they are simply telling what they "know" to be true.

Rashomon's final sequence, which returns us to the ruins of the Rashomon Gate, provides Kurosawa's resolution of all this despair and ambiguity through human action. As the Woodcutter's story ends, the three men hear the cries of an infant, abandoned to the storm and the ruins by its parents. The Listener's reaction is to steal the baby's clothes and blanket: "We can't live unless we act selfishly these days." The Woodcutter protests, but the Listener accuses him of not being so perfect himself and correctly guesses that the Woodcutter stole the valuable knife. Because the Woodcutter left that out of his supposedly objective report (and also out of his earlier report of finding the body), he too is a liar as well as a thief, and he is in no position to play holier than thou. But the audience may finally be in a position to guess what happened. The Listener leaves with the baby's clothes. The Woodcutter reaches for the baby, but the Priest interferes—assuming now that this second thief wants to steal what little protection the infant still has. When the Woodcutter explains that he wants to adopt the child, that he already has six children and another won't make much difference, the Priest becomes ashamed of himself for having judged the man too harshly. Thus every major character has proved fallible and done something wrong. The Priest hands over the baby and finds that the Woodcutter's generous act has restored his faith. People can admit their failures and be unselfish, and the world can make sense. The rain stops, and the Woodcutter leaves with his new child. The sun shines.

Fig. 14-20

Fig. 14-21
Rashomon. *Fig. 14-20: husband (Masayuki Mori), bandit (Toshiro Mifune), and swords;*
Fig. 14-21: husband, wife (Machiko Kyo), and knife.

Many of Kurosawa's films are battles with despair, and like the majority of Japanese films (even those with "happy endings"), they end on a sad or emotionally mixed note. *Seven Samurai* (1954) ends with a shot of the graves of the heroes who fell in battle, rather than a shot of the survivors. If *Rashomon* gives us an unusually happy ending, it is only after showing us that the search for truth must lead to ambiguity; that people can be cowardly, vain, and immoral; that ideals, codes of honor, and roles may not be lived up to; and that nostalgia for goodness and honor is a sad emotion, since for every moral success one finds many more moral failures and brutal acts. These points are made with equal conviction in Kurosawa films from *Ikiru* (*To Live*, 1952) to *Ran* (*Chaos*, 1985).

Kurosawa's two most interesting samurai films—*Seven Samurai* and *Yojimbo* (*Bodyguard*, 1961)—work the theme of existential action into two opposite situations, both borrowed from the western. *Seven Samurai* is a variation on the farmers-against-the-ranchers western, except in Kurosawa's film they are the farmers against the bandits. *Yojimbo* is the story of the paid gun (sword) for hire who rides (walks) into a small town that is split between two warring but equally crooked rival factions and succeeds in cleaning up both sides. *Seven Samurai* develops the theme of assertion and action through cooperation; *Yojimbo* develops the theme of self-assertion and individual integrity. Kurosawa paid his debt to the American western when both *Seven Samurai* and *Yojimbo* were made into westerns (John Sturges's *The Magnificent Seven*, 1960, and Sergio Leone's *Fistful of Dollars*, 1964, respectively). His *jidai-geki* also had a significant effect on another genre: George Lucas's *Star Wars* (1977) owes as much to Kurosawa's *The Hidden Fortress* (1958) as it does to *The Wizard of Oz*, and the editing and pace of both *Star Wars* and *The Empire Strikes Back* (1980) were strongly influenced by the fast wipes and stirring editing of *Seven Samurai*.

Kurosawa's most important *gendai-geki* is *Ikiru*, a story of the assertion of dignity through significant action. *Ikiru*'s hero is a petty bureaucrat (played by Takashi Shimura) who has wasted most of his life and who discovers that he is dying of cancer. He finally decides to dedicate his last days to accomplishing one important thing—which is discussed at his wake in the film's second part. *Ikiru* is as sensitive as the samurai pictures are active and violent.

As Lucas recalled the incident on the DVD of *The Hidden Fortress*, Kurosawa once told an interviewer that all his films attempted to answer the question, "Why can't people be happier, and why can't they be happier together?"

Kurosawa continued to make great films until his death in 1998. *Dodes'ka-den* (1970) is an Expressionist color study of the lives and dreams of the homeless. *Dersu Uzala* (1975), a Japanese–Soviet co-production, contrasts the values of a hunter who dwells in the forests, living close to the land and its creatures, with the aimlessness of modern, indoor city dwellers who have lost their contact with nature and even with the power of dreams. And *Kagemusha* (1980) is a return in color to the feudal world of *Seven Samurai* and *Yojimbo*, more critically dissecting the political inequities, class distinctions, and illusions of identity that supported feudal society. The stylized dream sequences of *Kagemusha* and *Dodes'ka-den*, painted by Kurosawa himself, are spectacular displays of color.

Five years after *Kagemusha* came *Ran*, Kurosawa's adaptation of *King Lear*. In this version, Lear has three sons rather than daughters, and several of Shakespeare's characters are condensed and combined. *Akira Kurosawa's Dreams* (1990), a series of sequences that re-create dreams the director felt were the most significant ones in his life, ends with a plea for ecological awareness; his last great film, *Rhapsody in August* (1991), set in Nagasaki in 1990, takes up the memory of nuclear war. At 83, he made *Not Yet* (*Madadayo*, 1993), about a professor who leaves academia, maintains a lifelong relationship with his former students, and repeatedly asserts that he is "not yet" ready to die.

Kenji Mizoguchi was a director of an earlier generation whose career came to its artistic culmination as Kurosawa's began to expand. Compared with Kurosawa, Mizoguchi employs a more consistent visual style, a more consistent theme and setting, and a much narrower range of emotion and tone. Mizoguchi specializes in period dramas, and his milieu is not simply the past but the past as seen in folk legends, plays, and paintings. Mizoguchi develops the distant mildness and stateliness of the past as well as some of its harsher realities. His primary attraction to the past is its apparent synthesis of art and nature—a synthesis that is fundamental to the motion picture. Many of Mizoguchi's central figures are artists: the actress Taki no Shiraito in the 1933 silent film of the same name; the troupe of Kabuki players in *The Story of the Last Chrysanthemum* (1939); the artist Utamaro in *Utamaro and His Five Women* (1946); the potter in *Ugetsu* (1953). For Mizoguchi, the business of the artist is the conversion of life into the perfection and precision of art, and the business of the cinema is both the conversion of life into art and the reverse conversion of art (a folk tale, for example) into the "living" vitality of cinema. Blending the domains of art and nature, *Ugetsu* begins with paintings of nature and dissolves into shots of nature.

In his photographic style Mizoguchi mirrors this art-as-nature-as-art synthesis, which is typical of Japanese aesthetics. Where Kurosawa often uses a traveling camera and deep focus, Mizoguchi uses a generally fixed camera (when it travels, it does so slowly and gracefully) and softer focus. Mizoguchi's shots of Japanese settings—fields, mountains, lakes (often shot by cinematographer Kazuo Miyagawa, who also shot *Rashomon*)—are much softer and flatter than Kurosawa's shots of nature, deliberately turning these natural settings into evocations of Japanese prints and paintings. Mizoguchi tends to use back- and side-lighting for these outdoor shots, not only softening them and reducing the depth of field but also giving them a hazy, limpid glow. Even in the moments of human agitation (for example, the sister's suicide in *Sansho the Bailiff*, 1954), nature remains soft, still, and quiet. Like Akerman, Antonioni, Bergman, and Cukor, Mizoguchi is a great director of women, and many of his movies are centered around the lives, perceptions, and ordeals of women (*Sisters of the Gion*, 1936; *Women of the Night*, 1948, which so realistically revealed the lives of prostitutes that it affected legislation; *The Life of Oharu*, 1952; *Sansho the Bailiff*).

In his structure, Mizoguchi is also more classical than Kurosawa; Mizoguchi's major films are perfect examples of the Japanese sense of symmetry. Whereas Kurosawa's symmetry (in *Yojimbo* and *Throne of Blood*—but not in *High*

and Low) is sometimes blurred by the violence and energy of his action, Mizoguchi's stately pace emphasizes his structural purity (and symmetry is another of the ways that art resembles nature). Mizoguchi's primary structural device is the separation of the leading characters, each of them traveling different paths—quite literally, since the journey is essential to many Mizoguchi films. *Taki no Shiraito* traces the separate paths of the actress and the young law student until fate draws the paths together; *Utamaro* follows the artist's "journey" as well as that of each of the women; *Sansho* is a series of separations and eventual reunions with both the living and the dead. The symmetry of *Sansho* is so perfect that there are two fathers in the film (Sansho and Zushio's father), two sons (Taro and Zushio), two separations (the mother from Zushio and Anju; Zushio from Anju), two children (Zushio and Anju), two reunions with the living (Zushio with Taro and Zushio with his mother), and two reunions with the dead at their shrines (Zushio at his father's tomb and at the lake where Anju drowned).

Ugetsu is a perfect Mizoguchi film in structure, theme, visual style, and tone (and it ought to be, since he edited and co-wrote the movie as well as directed it and thought about it for years before making it). There are four central characters—a potter and his wife, the potter's brother and his wife—each of whom travels a separate path and comes to a different end. The men, pursuing the false goals of money, fame, and lust, both discover the worthlessness of these goals, primarily because the wives—in many respects, the main characters—follow paths that lead to their undoing (one is murdered by soldiers, the other becomes a prostitute). Mizoguchi brings the film to life by the elegance of this symmetry and the magnificence of his visual technique, which dissolves nature into the mystical and concretizes the mystical into nature.

As the characters travel by boat on a misty lake to bring their goods to market (the potter is driven by his desire for riches), a thick fog converts the natural lake into an apparently supernatural netherworld. Out of this fog, the characters see a boat floating toward them, a mystical and eerie boat, seemingly floating on the fog itself. Inside the boat lies a figure who looks like a ghost. No, he says, he is not a ghost but a man who has been beaten and robbed by

Ugetsu. *Mizoguchi's elegantly balanced composition as the potter enjoys a picnic with a ghost.*

Fig. 14-22

pirates. He warns the characters against going farther—especially because of the danger to the women. But the potter presses onward.

Soon the potter falls under the spell of Lady Wakasa (Machiko Kyo), who tempts him by flattering his artistry and satisfying his sensuality. But Mizoguchi keeps his comment on the action clear by cross-cutting between the other characters on their "paths." While the potter enjoys Lady Wakasa, his wife is murdered by a group of soldiers on the road, his brother cheats his way into fulfilling his dreams of becoming a samurai, and his brother's wife is raped on the road by bandits.

The potter awakes one morning to discover that Lady Wakasa has been dead for years and that her house is—and long has been—a pile of ruins (Mizoguchi has this "morning after" discovery shot in a much harsher and brighter light than is usual for him). The potter, penniless and broken, returns home to join his wife. Although his wife greets him, he discovers the next morning from his neighbors that she has been killed and that he has spent the night with yet another ghost (a second "morning after" discovery—and a clear example of symmetry). He decides to devote his life to honoring his wife's grave (just as the son honors the graves of his sister and father in *Sansho*), and the spirit of his wife returns to him again—this time as a voice. She tells him

that her spirit will remain perpetually beside him and their son (a beneficent supernatural presence, in contrast to Lady Wakasa—a reversed parallel, or mirror image, that is another kind of symmetry) and that he should return to his pottery. Both the potter and the brother renounce their false ambitions and return to the normal cycles of their lives. (The warrior brother's renunciation was insisted upon by the studio; Mizoguchi considered it out of character.)

Far more than Kurosawa, Mizoguchi—whose moral system is relatively conventional—values the traditional Japanese virtues (not always observed in real life) of patience, honor, self-control, humility, and resignation. But his moral judgments are no less insightful than those of Kurosawa.

Yasujiro Ozu, Mizoguchi's contemporary, is the master of the *shomin-geki*—films about ordinary, modern-day people, often but not always comedies. Ozu's primary subjects are the surfaces, forms, rituals, and processes of middle-class and lower-middle-class life. His films are dominated by scenes of conversing and eating, both at home and in restaurants; scenes at the office; scenes of men drinking together in bars. They are films about the central social processes—work, marriage, family life, friendship—and life and death.

As a stylist Ozu challenges most of the West's cinema theory. He abjures the visual conventions of Western cinema—traveling shots, montage, movement within the shot, dissolves, fades, even the boundary of the 180° line, whose crossing within a Hollywood scene is thought to confuse the viewer. The titles of many of Ozu's films are so similar that they are hard to keep straight (*Late Spring*, 1949; *Early Spring*, 1956; *Late Autumn*, 1960—a color remake of *Late Spring*; *End of Summer*, 1961; *An Autumn Afternoon*, 1962). In truth, their subjects are similar— parents and children; whether, when, and whom to marry—and the actors recur from one film to another (as in the work of Griffith or Bergman). His films are visually spare, use many long takes, and have a similar tone: an understated pathos and comedy that play against one another in delicate counterpoint. And their endings are more likely to be wistful and complexly balanced than simply "happy"; virtually all of them share an attitude or tone the Japanese call *mono no aware:* a wistful acceptance of the evanescence of all things. But for all that they share, the films are unique, and the differences between them construct a multifaceted view of life.

There is a great deal of talk in Ozu's films, but there are also moments of contemplation and silence. Sometimes the camera will hold for as long as ten seconds on a room the characters have left; on the other hand, many of his shots are only five to seven seconds long. If these talky family melodramas and comedies are "soaps"— as some Ozu-bashers have suggested—they are the kind of soaps made by Dreyer (*Day of Wrath*, *Gertrud*) and Antonioni (*La notte*, *Eclipse*); Ozu's style is as spare, rigorous, and subtly flexible as Bresson's. Ozu's editing is functional, and the camera rarely moves—but when it does move, the shot is momentous. The camera is very often put at a low eye level—quite logically, as if it were the view of someone sitting on the floor in a Japanese house—but even if it has been invited, so to speak, to sit at the family table, it remains neutral, an impersonal but not unkind observer (see Fig. 14-23).

Ozu's masterpiece, *Tokyo Story* (1953), is a film about ordinary life that must be called extraordinary. It tells of an elderly couple—Shukichi, the father, played by Chishu Ryu, and Tomi, the mother, played by Chieko Higashiyama—who take their first trip to the big city to visit their children. Shortly after their arrival in Tokyo, it becomes clear that the son and daughter are far more interested in their own problems than in devoting respectful, loving attention to their parents. (In this film, as in the novels of Henry James, the amenities reveal and conceal matters of the greatest seriousness; watching it, one flinches at a disrespectful line or tone.) Only

Fig. 14-23

Tokyo Story: *Noriko (center) extends her hospitality to her parents-in-law; from left, Chishu Ryu, Setsuko Hara, and Chieko Higashiyama. Note the position of the camera.*

Noriko (Setsuko Hara), the widow of their second son, is genuinely glad to see them, spends time talking with them, and sincerely extends them the proper hospitality. In the loud, fast world of the town, Noriko is a rarity; much of the film concerns the differences between old and modern ways as well as between small town and big city living *and* between generations, and all these themes become especially clear, both intellectually and emotionally, in the scenes with Noriko and her parents-in-law.

The son and daughter send their parents to a resort—obviously to get rid of them, but supposedly because the old couple will enjoy themselves more there. The mother's strength, which has been failing, takes a turn for the worse, and shortly after they reach home, she dies. Now it is the children's and in-laws' turn to travel from Tokyo to the small town (a good example of symmetry in Ozu's work); they pay their respects, but leave soon enough. Noriko stays longer, to comfort the father and keep him company, but he tells her that she needs to get on with her life and that he is content to be alone. His acceptance of life and the solitude to which it has brought him—*mono no aware*—is profound and moving.

After Kurosawa, Mizoguchi, and Ozu, Kon Ichikawa is among the most interesting directors of that generation. Ichikawa savagely and openly criticized political, social, and personal corruption as he examined the depravity of the human animal. Ichikawa's first noted film, *The Burmese Harp* (1956), is one of his milder studies: the examination of a soldier in Burma (now Myanmar) in the final days of World War II who first disguises himself as a priest in order to survive and then becomes a true convert to the priestly values. *Fires on the Plain* (1959), which has been called the most powerful antiwar film ever made in Japan, concentrates on the last days of the war. He died in 2008.

Mikio Naruse, a contemporary of Ozu, also begins within the *shomin-geki* world. As opposed to Ichikawa's brutal dissection of perversities, Naruse's pessimistic bourgeois dramas (*Floating Clouds*, 1955; *As a Wife, As a Woman*, 1961; *Yearning*, 1963) observe postwar white-collar workers trapped by modern life—stifling marriages, boring jobs, and inadequate salaries—for whom adultery and theft promise escape but lead to ruin. Like Mizoguchi, Naruse takes

women seriously and portrays their situation under patriarchy with moving conviction (*When a Woman Ascends the Stairs, Flowing Night, Autumn is Beginning*, and *Mother, Wife, Daughter*—all 1960).

Kinugasa's *Gate of Hell* (1953) and Hiroshi Inagaki's *Samurai* (1954) were among Japan's first color films and are magnificent in their application of splendid color photography to the *jidai-geki*. Inagaki went on to make a color, wide-screen version of the Legend of the Loyal 47 Ronin (a favorite subject of the Japanese drama for hundreds of years), the 1962 *Chushingura*.

Masaki Kobayashi's first great work was the 9 1/2-hour trilogy *Human Condition* (1958–61), a wide-screen epic, in black and white, about the treatment Manchuria received at the hands of the Japanese and the efforts of the powerfully beset Japanese hero, an idealist around whose prewar and wartime experience the trilogy is organized, to escape a prison camp (he drowns an oppressive guard in a vat of excrement) and walk home. The best of his later films are *Harakiri* (1962)—which resembles the work of Alain Resnais and Peter Watkins with its story, told through flashbacks, of an atrocity and a revenge that are both covered up—and *Kwaidan* (1965), a wide-screen, Expressionist color anthology of beautiful and scary ghost stories adapted from the writings of Lafcadio Hearn. In 1983, he made a documentary, *The Tokyo Trial*, about the tribunal on war crimes committed by Japan during World War II, a film that was unpopular at home.

The Japanese film industry, like the industries of the West, underwent severe commercial changes in the decade following 1950. The Japanese discovered that many of their cheaper productions—monster pictures (*Godzilla, Rodan*), invasions from outer space (*The Mysterians*)—could make money abroad. And so Japan was continually invaded by prehistoric monsters or visitors from space who stomped or incinerated models of Japan's cities before they were repulsed by some new weapon or by each other. As the Japanese bought (and manufactured) more and more TV sets, Japanese film attendance dropped. The Japanese film industry had learned from the earlier experience of the West, however, that this was one monster that could not be repulsed. Japanese studios began production for TV from the start—and even began operating TV stations. Then the Japanese invented the VCR and changed video history.

Of the generation of directors influenced by the New Wave, Nagisa Oshima, who mixes radical film techniques, radical politics, and a radical sexuality, may have worked in the most styles and tones. Like the films of Godard, *The Man Who Left His Will on Film* (1970) is both a deconstruction of cinema and an essay on the context of film images. *Death by Hanging* (1968) is a Brechtian attack on easy definitions of social crime and personal identity in bourgeois society. *Cruel Stories of Youth* (1960) links big business and crime. *Boy* (1968) is the dispassionate story of a boy whose parents have trained him to get hit by cars so that they can extort money from the drivers. *In the Realm of the Senses* (1976), a Japanese–French co-production, is pornographic and obsessive.

Shohei Imamura seemed to be a descendant of both Ozu, for whom he worked, and Godard, whom he admired. Called the "cultural anthropologist" of modern Japanese cinema, Imamura's films (*The Pornographers*, 1966; *A Man Vanishes*, 1967; *Vengeance Is Mine*, 1979; *The Ballad of Narayama*, 1983; *Black Rain*, 1989; *The Eel*, 1997; *Dr. Akagi*, 1998), often mix fictional and documentary styles, dissecting characters and societies that either resist or suffer modernization. He died in 2006.

Two of the most experimental and culturally probing films of the 1980s were Katsuhiro Otomo's *Akira* (1988) and Shinya Tsukamoto's *Tetsuo* (1989). A metaphysical epic about bikers and orphans with superhuman powers, set in "Neo-Tokyo" three decades after World War III, *Akira* was an *anime*, or feature-length animated film, adapted by Otomo from his own multivolume graphic novel, that made spectacular use of computer animation, the wide screen, and more than 200 colors. *Tetsuo* (or *Tetsuo: The Iron Man*), a black-and-white film whose camerawork and editing can be described as frenzied, was made with the Kaijyu Theatre; the 1992 sequel, *Tetsuo II: Body Hammer*, was shot in color. *Tetsuo* explored the growing overlap and confusion between people and objects, notably by having a man slowly push a long piece of metal into his leg.

The 1990s and early 2000s saw the generation that followed Oshima begin to take shape. For some, like Hirokazu Kore-eda, that meant finding a way to build on the work of Mizoguchi, Ozu, and Naruse; for Takashi Miike, it meant testing or breaking the rules of logic, taste, and respect; for Takeshi Kitano, who performs in his movies and others' under the name Beat Takeshi and who is particularly good at turning from quiet to violent, it meant finding a way to work in the art film and the genre film at once, violating expectations while subtly or brutally controlling the mood of a scene (*Boiling Point*, 1990; *Hani-bi* or *Fireworks*, 1997; *Zatoichi*, 2003); and for the animators, it meant giving Japan an epic cinema charged with conservationist messages while deepening their treatment of character and perfecting their skills (*Princess Mononoke*, 1997, and *Spirited Away*, 2001, both directed by Hayao Miyazaki). In *Dead or Alive* (1999) Miike built a *yakuza* picture to a cosmic showdown, and in *Audition* (1999) he turned what looked like a romantic comedy into a horror picture that is unforgettable in both its whispering softness and its gruesome violence. Kitano's *Hana-bi* is a powerfully controlled mix of tones: quietly intimate, ruthlessly bloody, resigned, resourceful, vengeful, and calm—the tale of an ex-cop who wants to take his dying wife on a trip, all the people he kills or avenges first, and how fireworks mostly fizzle when you expect them but explode (into action sequences, trouble, murder) when you do not.

Miike's and Kitano's films are examples of the wildest work being done in spite of the strict definitions of genre—and examples of the many artfully violent pictures made in Japan. But the genre film is by no means dead. Japanese horror made a comeback with *Ringu* or *Ring* (1998, directed by Hideo Nakata) and its sequels, in which the threat is both supernatural and technological, a media horror from the afterlife. On the less violent side, the current master of the artfully observed psychological film appears to be Kore-eda, whose interest in memory led him to make *After Life* (1998), a sad, funny, reflexive, and touching film about having to choose one moment, and only that moment, to remember from your whole life, and *Maborosi* (1995), a beautiful, slow, and quiet film about a woman who tries to understand why her husband killed himself—why he succumbed to the lure of the eternal and unknown, compared by one of the characters to a *maborosi*, a strange enticing light out at sea. He followed those with a realistic human-interest picture, *Nobody Knows* (2004), based on the true story of a woman who abandoned her children in the big city. However differently Kore-eda, Miike, Miyazaki, and Kitano approach the questions of filmmaking and of human nature, they are all major stylists in a cinema with an exceptionally rich stylistic history.

India

The West discovered the Indian cinema much as it did the Japanese. Satyajit Ray's *Pather Panchali* (*Song of the Little Road*, 1955) won a prize at the 1956 Cannes Film Festival, and his next film, *Aparajito* (*The Unvanquished*, 1956) won the Golden Lion Award at Venice the following year. *Apur Sansar* (*The World of Apu*, 1959) completed the trilogy.

The Indian film industry was prolific: India produced some 300 feature films in 1958, second only to Japan in the quantity of feature production. In the 1970s, India became the world leader in the number of feature films produced each year. In the 1980s and 1990s, India remained the world's top producer, releasing an average of two films a day (one fifth of all the features made worldwide)—and even more in the early 2000s; it produced over 1,000 features in 2005, a year in which the U.S. produced about 600 and Japan about 350. It should be noted that some of the most formulaic, mass-market Indian films are exported to more than 100 nations—primarily in the Third World—where they have long proved extremely popular.

Several considerations have influenced the popular turn taken by the dominant Indian cinema and the complex challenges it faces. First, India is a vast nation of over a billion people, and movies remain the only form of popular entertainment accessible to the masses, although the video industry is very much on the rise. The pressure on the studios to provide film after entertaining film for a huge, largely uneducated audience has led to a devotion to formula and convention. The dominant narrative formula calls for a lengthy love story, many problems standing in the way of the lovers' happiness (he might be from the wrong caste, she might be

kidnapped by gangsters . . .), endless musical numbers, a happy ending in which all problems are resolved, and three hours of footage.

Second, and even more difficult for the film industry, India is a nation without a common language. There are hundreds of Indian languages, 20 of them spoken by more than 10 million people, and seven of those spoken by over 40 million people. The most common include Hindi, Urdu, Bengali, Telegu, Marathi, and Tamil. This language barrier caused little difficulty in the Silent Era. The Indian silent film industry, effectively established in 1913 by the magical, mythological films of Dadasaheb Phalke and developed by pioneers such as Dhiren Ganguly, Debaki Bose, and Chandulal Shah, may have been more artistically advanced than the silent Japanese cinema. But the coming of sound, which liberated the Japanese cinema from the *benshi*, imprisoned the Indian cinema in the Tower of Babel.

Most films for the all-India market are now made in Hindi in the commercial film capital, once called Bombay. Adopting in the mid-1990s a term coined by a non-Indian journalist, Bombay's commercial cinema has taken the name Bollywood. (The term has stuck despite the fact that Bombay has been Mumbai since 1995.) In Madras and elsewhere, many films—some more mainstream than others—are made in regional languages for regional and, in some cases, international distribution. The art film, or alternative cinema (also called "Parallel Cinema" in the 1970s), has flourished in Mumbai and Calcutta and runs parallel to the commercial film establishment, never touching it. This "Indian New Wave" or "New Cinema" finds little distribution in India and acknowledges the inspiring example of Ray (most of whose films were shot in Bengali and adopted a lyrical realist aesthetic). In the early 2000s, two of the best-known art filmmakers were Shyam Benegal and Buddhadeb Dasgupta.

Third, the Indian cinema has been subject to ruthless government intervention and censorship. Under the British, themes of independence were forbidden; under the government of free India, "decadent" Western influences were forbidden. Kissing scenes first appeared in the 1970s. In addition to limiting its artistic freedom, the Indian government taxes the film industry heavily; its huge audiences provide handsome revenues, even with the low ticket prices. Further, the government has levied severe import quotas that restrict the supply of raw film stock. Even more ironic, an Indian print that has been shown abroad is subject to duty as an "imported" film upon returning home. If the government restricted the movement of commercial films, it encouraged alternative production by financing personal films. Satyajit Ray's first films—as well as those of Mrinal Sen, Shyam Benegal, and Aparna Sen—were supported by the Indian government.

Fourth, the Indian film industry itself has employed corrupt profiteering practices. Independent producers who want to make a quick killing, rather than established film companies, have been the rule. In the 1930s, however, India's studios were more solid organizations; the most famous of them, Bombay Talkies, was a cooperative familial studio—modeled on Germany's Ufa, where Bombay Talkies' married owners, Himansu Rai and Devika Rani, had worked. But the independent speculator, who usually did not have enough money to complete a film once it was started and therefore needed to beg, borrow, deal, and swindle more as the shooting went along, came to dominate the industry in the 1940s.

The speculator could get that money only because, fifth, the Indian film industry has been totally dominated by the star system since the familial studios collapsed in the 1940s. And it has been a star system with a vengeance, making the power of the Hollywood luminaries look puny. Because only a producer with a major star could get the money to finish a film, stars became so popular and enjoyed such power—even political clout—that they commanded immense salaries (at least half of it paid under the table in untaxable "black money") and might work on as many as two dozen films at once, dropping in periodically on each of the production units as the star's schedule and inclinations permitted. Music was the supporting "star" of an Indian film (the music director has one of the highest-paid positions in the Bollywood industry); for decades, of the hundreds of films shot each year in India, there was *not one* without singing and dancing. The Indian film became so conventional that its foremost historians (Barnouw and Krishnaswamy) described the formula succinctly as "a star, six songs, and

three dances." These formulaic Hindi films are called *masala* films; "masala" means a mixture of spices, and the sense of the term is that these films consist of a number of appetizing ingredients in combinations that vary only slightly from film to film—as if one were adding a little more garlic to a successful recipe or substituting turmeric (pirates) for fenugreek (gangsters).

To such assumptions and conventions Satyajit Ray remained a stranger. His father was a friend of Rabindranath Tagore, the greatest Indian poet of the 20th century. Well read in Indian literature and philosophy, Ray studied painting after receiving a degree in economics. But Ray was also a *cinéaste*; with Chidananda Das Gupta, Ray was co-founder of the first film society in India, the Calcutta Film Society, in 1947. So one might see Ray as uniting the traditions of Indian literature, painting, and music with those of Western cinema. The meeting of Western and Indian values is one of his recurring subjects. The influence of European films is unmistakable in Ray's films, particularly Italian Neorealism and the French cinema of the 1930s—though when he was a young man, he preferred Hollywood movies. Ray was particularly influenced by observing Jean Renoir make *The River* in Calcutta in 1949–50, when he spoke frequently with the classical French director. Although Ray, who died in 1992, was a Bengali, his outlook was always international.

In the Indian cinematic tradition, the two dominant genres are "socials" and "mythologicals." The mythologicals, as the name suggests, use the cinema to bring to life the traditional tales and settings of Indian folklore, ancient literature, and myth. The socials, or contemporary melodramas, address social problems but use them primarily as plot complications. There are also "devotionals," which feature religious figures, and "historicals," which are set in the past, unlike the socials. Ray avoided the majority of Indian film traditions, from the sentimentality of the socials to the conventions of the studio system—in other words, not just how films were conceived but how they were produced. *Pather Panchali*, which he was inspired to begin after seeing *Bicycle Thieves* in London, had no star (in the manner of the Soviets and Italians, Ray even used some nonprofessional actors) and no songs and dances (although there was an instrumental

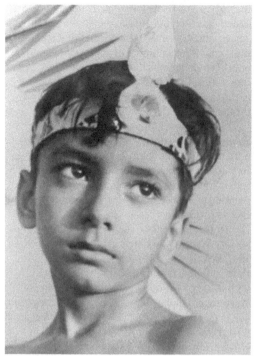

Fig. 14-24
Pather Panchal: *the worlds of youth and age. The young Apu (Subir Banerji).*

score by Ravi Shankar). Furthermore, it was shot on location (Indian films were exclusively studio films, even for outdoor scenes, a choice that aided their flight from reality and linked them with the stylized conventions of Indian theatre). Ray's film wanted to have as much to do with reality as possible.

Ray's Apu trilogy (*Pather Panchali*, *Aparajito*, and *Apur Sansar*, commonly referred to as *The World of Apu*), adapted from two mammoth novels by Bibhutibhusan Banerjee (*Pather Panchali*, which covers the first film, and *Aparajito*, which covers the last two), employs a complex, careful structure that is apparent in the unity of the individual films as well as in the overall conception of the trilogy. The subject of the trilogy is the growth of a young Indian boy (Apu) from his peasant, rural youth to a mature and educated adulthood in the city—an Indian *Bildungsroman*. The three films devote themselves to childhood, adolescence, and adulthood, respectively. In all three films, deaths play a pivotal role in the boy's growth and development:

the deaths of the old aunt and his sister in *Pather Panchali*, the deaths of his father and mother in *Aparajito*, the death of his wife (the hardest one for him to accept) in *The World of Apu*. In counterpoint to these deaths, all three films end identically: Apu is on the road ("Pather Panchali" means "Song of the Little Road"), moving from the country to the city, implying the continuity of life and growth.

At the end of *Pather Panchali*, the remaining family members leave their village to try to live better in the city (Benares). At the end of *Aparajito*, Apu pulls himself together after the death of his mother and takes the path back to the city (Calcutta) and the university. At the end of *The World of Apu*, Apu is back on the road, returning to Calcutta again, his son on his back. A sign of the precision of Ray's structural conception is that at the end of this final installment Apu's young son is almost exactly the same age as the child Apu in the first one, now on his way to the city with a newly returned father. The song of the road has come full circle.

Perhaps Ray's essential theme may be found in his ultimate commitment to life, to human exertion, and to the cycles of nature of which man is a small and uncomprehending part. Ray's films acutely show that life is often painful, that people can be petty, that sorrow is inescapable and death inevitable, and that nature is an ever-present mystery.

Ray's other films are equally interesting in their careful views of Indian life and are often quite as effective. In *The Music Room* (1958) Ray examines the collapse of the old India—its traditions and its art—and the rise of the new bourgeoisie. *Devi* (*The Goddess*, 1960) is also a clash of old and new, a study of the old religious prejudices and fanaticism that can destroy happiness. *Mahanagar* (*The Big City*, 1963) examines family life in the new Calcutta, particularly the new status of women. *Three Daughters* (1961, released abroad in a shortened version, *Two Daughters*) and *Charulata* (*The Lonely Wife*, 1964) are both based on stories by Tagore; the latter is as much about the late-19th-century impact of British ideas on Bengali intellectuals as it is an insightful exploration of a woman's growing desire to define herself. *Kanchanjungha* (1962), his first color film, tells of the problems of the members of a wealthy family on vacation in

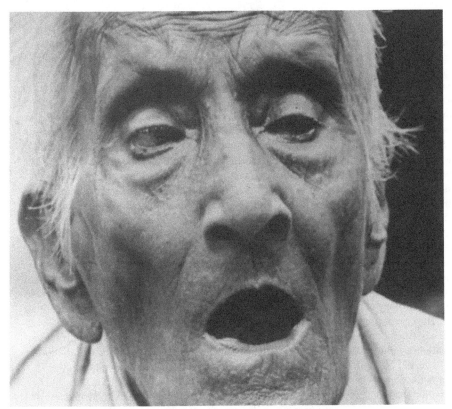

Fig. 14-25
Pather Panchali: *the worlds of youth and age. The old aunt (Chunibala Devi).*

Darjeeling and how they and other characters rebel against the aristocratic, authoritarian father—and, implicitly, the patriarchy he represents. *The Chess Players* (1977), Ray's first film in Urdu rather than Bengali, is the chilling–amusing story of two men who concentrate so much on the chess games they play with each other that they do not notice—or pretend to be above—how the political world is playing games with them. Though it may have been as elegant as a Mozart opera, *Days and Nights in the Forest* (1970) was also a devastating, ironic analysis of the increasingly evident failures of post-Independence India. *Distant Thunder* (1973) depicted a terrible famine, but on an intimate rather than a massive scale. In the darkest and most political of his films, referred to as the "Calcutta trilogy"—*The Adversary* (1970), *Company Limited* (1971), and *The Middleman*

(1975, whose title, *Jana Aranya*, literally means *The Jungle of Human Beings*)—Ray targeted cultural and spiritual corruption. While a major theme of the Apu trilogy is the importance of learning to read and write, which enlarges Apu's concept of the world as well as his opportunities in it, the Calcutta trilogy shows how education is one of the many values under assault in the modern urban world, the values people have grown up with but choose to betray. The Calcutta trilogy presents crises of choice in a corrupt system; some characters make the ethical choices that define their humanity, while most trade their integrity for money and petty power.

But Ray's are not the only nonmainstream films made in India. One of his most significant contemporaries, in many ways his opposite (loud sound effects, jarring editing, a ruthless vision of the interconnected evils of the world), was

Ritwik Ghatak, whose best-known film is *Meghe Dhaka Tara* (*The Cloud-Capped Star*, 1960); he followed that with *Komal Gandhar* (*E Flat*, 1961), *Subarnarekha* (1962), and *Jukti Takko ar Gappo* (*Reason, Debate, and a Tale*, 1974), then drank himself to death. Ray's other great contemporary, Mrinal Sen, is a Marxist whose denunciations of the exploitation of the poor (*Akaler Sandhaney/In Search of Famine*, 1980) and of women (*Ek Din Pratidin/And Quiet Rolls the Day*, 1979) and whose attacks on middle-class hypocrisy (*Khandhar/The Ruins*, 1983) have found an international audience. Sen was influenced by Godard (*Calcutta '71*, 1972) and is an influence on the many new *auteurs* who have found the political content of his works inspiring.

Adoor Gopalakrishnan's films draw on the history and culture of his native Kerala in south India. Kerala's transition from feudalism to modernity serves as a backdrop to his complex meditations on the psychology of power, the nature of oppression, the corruption of patriarchy, and the coexistence of the modern and the feudal in post-Independence democratic India. *Elippathayam* (*The Rat Trap*, 1981), his key film, vividly captures the descent into paranoia of a man trapped within his feudal universe. In *Mukhamukham* (*Face to Face*, 1984), a study in failed idealism, a Communist leader gives up on revolution and decides to go to sleep instead. Gopalakrishnan's later films—*Anantaram* (*Monologue*, 1987), *Mathilukal* (*The Walls*, 1989), *Vidheyan* (*The Servile*, 1993), and *Kathapurushan* (*Man of the Story*, 1995)—display a new concern with interiority and reflexivity, foregrounding time, memory, consciousness, and the nature of storytelling.

Although few Indian art films other than those of Ray have been widely seen outside India (while the Bollywood socials have a huge international audience), many Western films have been shot there. India was both the visual setting and primary metaphor of Renoir's *The River* and Lean's *A Passage to India*. Roberto Rossellini (*India*, 1958) and Louis Malle (*Phantom India*, 1969) made careful documentary studies of Indian life and culture, both commissioned by European television. And Danny Boyle went there for *Slumdog Millionaire*. An American director, James Ivory, and his Indian partner, producer Ismail Merchant, began their career with Calcutta films (*Shakespeare Wallah*, 1965; *Bombay Talkie*, 1970), heavily influenced by the films of Satyajit Ray, only to switch loyalties to the novels of Henry James (*The Europeans*, 1979) and E. M. Forster (*A Room with a View*); most of their later films were British or American productions.

The New Cinema began in the late 1960s. As mentioned before, this parallel or alternative cinema is completely distinct from the artificial worlds of the Hindi romances and violent adventures—whose colors and camerawork are flashy, whose sets range from the studio-realistic to the theatrical and fantastic, and whose heroes may spring up from vicious beatings as free from permanent damage as the heroes of cartoons. The New Cinema examines social problems (often from a Marxist perspective), prefers to shoot on location, seeks to create a Neorealism for the expression of Indian reality, rejects formulaic narrative structures, uses the camera subtly and effectively, occasionally uses Brechtian and reflexive devices, and promotes the concept and creative authority of the *auteur*. None of these notions has any place in the mainstream Bollywood industry.

The New Cinema began with Mrinal Sen's *Bhuvan Shome* (*Mr. Shome*, 1969), an irreverent comedy that had been financed by a loan from the government's Film Finance Corporation (FFC). When *Bhuvan Shome* proved to be a critical and popular success, the FFC made more money available for quality, low-budget films, much as the French government helped to finance the New Wave. The key *auteurs* fall into two groups, those in Mumbai and those in the south of India. In Mumbai are Shyam Benegal (*Ankur/The Seedling*, 1974), Mani Kaul (*Uski Roti/Daily Bread*, 1969), Ketan Mehta (*Mirch Masala/Spices*, 1986), Govind Nihalani (*Aakrosh/Cry of the Wounded*, 1980), and Kumar Shahani (*Maya Darpan/Mirror of Illusion*, 1972). In the south are Malayali G. Aravindan (*Chidambaram*, 1985), Adoor Gopalakrishnan (see above), Girish Karnad (*Kaadu/The Forest*, 1973), Girish Kasaravalli (*Ghatashraddha/The Ritual*, 1977), and Pattabhi Rama Reddy (*Samskara*, 1970). To this list must be added a group of gifted filmmakers from Bengal: Buddhadeb Dasgupta (*Tahader Katha/Their Story*, 1992), Utpalendu Chakravarty (*Moyna*

Salaam Bombay! *After working hard at a wedding, Krishna (Shafiq Syed, second from left), Manju (Hansa Vithal, right), and their friends are paid practically nothing but allowed to eat their fill.*

Fig. 14-26

Tadanta/Post Mortem, 1981), Gautam Ghosh (*Patang/Kite*, 1993), and Rituparno Ghosh (*Dahan/Crossfire*, 1997).

The New Cinema has brought new opportunities for women directors. Aparna Sen was already a famous actress when she directed *36 Chowringhee Lane* (1981), the carefully detailed story of an Anglo-Indian schoolteacher who must come to terms with loneliness and old age. Mira Nair's first feature, *Salaam Bombay!* (1988), which is "Dedicated to the children on the streets of Bombay" and whose profits funded shelters for homeless children, is the story of a nice, honest boy (Krishna, played by Shafiq Syed) who tries, while making a living on the street at menial jobs, to save enough money to go home to his family and village. Like the homeless kids in *The 400 Blows* and *Shoeshine*, Krishna and his friends endure rough times until they are taken under the care of the social services, which make things worse. Nair's later films include *Mississippi Masala* (1992), the controversially sexy *Kama Sutra: A Tale of Love* (1996), and *Monsoon Wedding* (2001). Gurinder Chadha, who was born in Kenya and raised in London but now has her base of operations in Los Angeles, often focuses on the experience of Indians living outside the country; her most successful films to date are *Bend It Like Beckham* (2002, a soccer comedy set in London) and *Bride & Prejudice*

(2004, an attempt to give Jane Austen the Bollywood treatment). Deepa Mehta, who was born in India but has set up shop in Canada, wrote and directed a politically and socially controversial trilogy—*Fire* (1996), *Earth* (1998), and *Water* (2005)—that made her a political target; she was even forced to shoot *Water* in Sri Lanka after the Indian sets were sabotaged and she was threatened. *Fire* raised the subject of lesbian love. *Earth* addressed the partition of India and Pakistan, an important subject that had been ignored by the mainstream cinema. And *Water* dealt with the customs regarding widowhood, particularly as they affect an eight-year-old girl.

China

The People's Republic of China, founded in 1949, has for the most part encouraged film production. Between 1949 and the beginning of the Cultural Revolution (1966–76), the state abolished commercial filmmaking and then nationalized and completely subsidized the industry, ten major studios were built, and the number of theatres increased from 646 to 20,363. As in the Soviet Union, the films' essential task was to communicate the ideals of the Revolution to a huge and far-flung population; not surprisingly, many of the best Chinese films have been works of art as well as of propaganda. Zheng Junli's *Lin Zexu* (1959), for example, told a patriotic war story *and*

New and old ways and values meet in Yellow Earth.

Fig. 14-27

attempted to find visual equivalents for the subtle tropes of Chinese poetry. During the Cultural Revolution, censorship was at its most formidable, many filmmakers were sent away from the cities and studios to learn from the peasants, and very few pictures were made. By 1978, however, the "rehabilitated" filmmakers were back at work, determined to make artistic movies, and they encountered no government opposition. In the early 1980s, the studios were given the responsibility of planning their own budgets, working with only partial government financing, and raising the rest of their production money at the box office. In 1983, billions of movie tickets were sold. In 1984, Wu Tianming's *Life* portrayed both peasants and intellectuals as good characters. Things were opening up.

The first major work of "the Fifth Generation"—a group of younger directors who were the fifth set to graduate from the Beijing Film Academy—appeared late in 1984: Chen Kaige's *Yellow Earth*, a magnificently photographed, complexly constructed drama about a soldier who goes to a remote feudal village to learn folk songs that he can adapt for use by the army; the effect he and the villagers have on one another; and a young woman who must choose between going through with an arranged

marriage (the old ways of the peasants, which—as most Chinese films emphasize—tend to oppress women) and leaving the village and her world to join the army, for which she would very much like to write inspiring songs. As so many Chinese films do, *Yellow Earth* dramatizes the confrontation of new and old ways, presenting the military representative of the Socialist revolution (the film is set in 1937) as the bringer of new information and attitudes ("Men can sew," says the amazed heroine of *Yellow Earth* when the soldier takes up needle and thread), but its deep sense of character goes well beyond the simple, allegorical role assignment (you be Capital, you be Labor) typical of propaganda. Its color cinematography was the work of Zhang Yimou.

The Fifth Generation's evolution from an artistically sophisticated social realism to an outright art cinema that denounced tyranny and outraged the censors can be seen in the differences between *Yellow Earth* and Chen's 1993 international hit, *Farewell to My Concubine* (released, after full-length premieres at film festivals, in a shortened version called *Farewell, My Concubine*). Rather than concentrating on what the Revolution has to offer the peasants, the later film emphasizes how much is lost when the old ways—especially the traditions of Chinese art—are destroyed by

Farewell to My Concubine:
*Leslie Cheung (left), Zhang
Fengyi (center), and Gong Li
(lower right).*

Fig. 14-28

military and political groups who are sure of the
new way things ought to be done. The rich artistic
tradition of the Beijing Opera is set against over
50 years (1924–77) of political upheaval, culminating in the Cultural Revolution's complete purge of
the "Old Society." From childhood, two males have
been trained to perform the roles of the King of
Chu and his Concubine Yu in the opera *Farewell to
My Concubine;* when the king is defeated, his
faithful concubine kills herself with his sword.
Shitou, who takes the stage name Duan Xiaolou
(Zhang Fengyi), plays the king—though he turns
out, unlike the brave and steadfast king, to be willing in real life to "go with the times" and survive all
the shifts of political fashion, even if it means betraying his wife (Juxian, played by Gong Li). Douzi,
whose stage name is Cheng Dieyi (Leslie Cheung),
so strongly identifies with the female role of
Concubine Yu that he falls in love with Xiaolou and
wants them to be as close in life as they are on the
stage; this creates problems not only when Xiaolou
marries Juxian, a prostitute, but more significantly
when the Communists reject the beauty and the
rigorous practice to which he has dedicated his
life. He is as faithful to his art as the concubine is
to her king, and eventually he manages to die in
the work as he has lived in it.

After *Farewell to My Concubine* shared the
top prize at Cannes (with Jane Campion's *The
Piano*), it played for one day in Beijing before
being banned for its treatment of homosexuality
(particularly in scenes in which Dieyi is sexually
abused by powerful patrons of the arts, but also

in the ambiguous treatment of Dieyi's concept of
his own sexuality). Within two months, the ban
was lifted—no reason given. But another masterful film that showed the destructive effect of
Maoism, this time on an urban family—Tian
Zhuangzhuang's *The Blue Kite* (1993)—was
banned permanently; not only that, Tian (who
had made one of the most beautiful and starkly
moving, practically nonverbal films of the new
Chinese cinema, the 1985 *Horse Thief*) first was
not allowed to edit the film and then was forbidden to make films in China. By that time, ticket
sales were down to 10.6 billion, the studios had
been entirely cut off from government support
(forcing them into numerous productions
bankrolled by Taiwan and Hong Kong), and the
new Chinese films had been recognized—
everywhere but in China—as the most consistently excellent works of the late 1980s and the
1990s. Chen Kaige, Tian Zhuangzhuang, Wu
Tianming, and especially Zhang Yimou had taken
their place beside the world's great directors.

Wu Tianming, who headed the Xi'an studio for
most of the 1980s and helped to make it the center of Fifth Generation filmmaking, directed *Old
Well* in 1987, a film that not only told the story of a
Party member with a better idea for a well and a
village woman who cuts her ties to the dowry system, but also made extraordinary use of the only
true Technicolor lab in the world, which happened to be in China. (In the West, Technicolor
laboratories had processed only Eastmancolor
stock or its equivalent since the mid-1970s; until

2000, when Coppola's *Apocalypse Now Redux* went through the lab, the last American film shot in Technicolor and imbibition printed was Coppola's *The Godfather Part II*, 1974.) The colors in *Old Well* and in Zhang Yimou's *Red Sorghum* (1988) are intense beyond words.

Red Sorghum has an additional level of intensity, however: outright exuberance. Although like virtually all Chinese films it keeps sexual activity offscreen, *Red Sorghum* is full of raw sexual energy, which it celebrates along with life, love, the earth, action, resistance. Although the movie is, like most Chinese art, subtly and carefully structured, it pulls no punches: Its violent scenes are absolutely violent, its scenes of collective action are irresistibly inspiring, its humorous scenes are outrageous, its tender moments and fine characters ring true, and its wild beauty is stunning and uncompromised. In the summer of 1988, when Chinese politics were at their most liberal, young people expressed their idealism, energy, determination, and revolutionary optimism by humming and singing the songs from *Red Sorghum*. But in the summer of 1989, when a pro-democracy demonstration, held primarily by students in Beijing's Tiananmen Square, was brutally put down by the government, China entered another oppressive phase. "Stupid Old People Should Resign Quickly," read one banner hung in Tiananmen Square; they didn't. The Xi'an studio was virtually shut down. Wu Tianming left the country. And Zhang Yimou's next film, *Ju Dou* (1990, co-directed with Yang Fengliang), which is both more politically critical and more sexually frank than *Red Sorghum*, became another hit at the festivals but was not allowed to be shown in China.

Ju Dou tells a story indebted to the plot and feverish sexuality of *The Postman Always Rings Twice*, with the difference that the lovers have to deal not with an insurance investigator but with a vicious kid who behaves like a little Red Guard before his time (the film is set in the 1920s); it was bankrolled in Japan, where Gong Li, who played the heroine, was a big box-office draw. In Zhang's next film, *Raise the Red Lantern* (1991), she played one of several wives who compete for their husband's sexual attention and the power that gives them; set well before the Revolution, the film dramatized how women were oppressed not only by polygamy and by limited options in life, but also by each other.

This rigorously composed and richly photographed film had none of the earthiness of the earlier films but was every bit as moving. It was followed by *The Story of Qiu Ju* (1993), which had a low-tech look (it was shot in Super-16mm and included nonprofessional actors) that suited its subject: the heroic but unglamorous struggle of a peasant woman (Gong Li) to enlist the aid of the contemporary justice system to force the village leader to apologize and make restitution for kicking her husband in the genitals. Zhang was gratified that "a film that talks about the everyday life of simple people in today's China," as he described it, could be appreciated in the West; when it won the Golden Lion for best picture at the Venice Film Festival, he dedicated the award to China's peasants. When his next film, *To Live* (1994), which took a dim view of what the Chinese have had to endure in order to survive recent Chinese history, competed at Cannes—entered by its Taiwanese producer despite the fact that it had not been approved by the Chinese censors—Zhang did not attend, hoping that that gesture, and a public "self-criticism," would calm down the authorities. But his next film

Fig. 14-29
Red Sorghum: *Gong Li (right, as Nine) carries food for the resistance fighters through a field of sorghum.*

(*Shanghai Triad*, 1995) was held up, and he was forbidden to work on foreign co-productions for at least two years—and ordered to stay away from those pernicious film festivals.

In 1999, Zhang made two films about teachers, both produced in China: *Not One Less*, about a girl put in the role of teacher and told not to allow any truancy, and *The Road Home* (released 2000). The latter tells the story of a young woman transfixed by love for the village teacher and their romance as it is remembered by their son 40 years later. The father has died, and the old mother wants his body carried back on "the road home" to the village so that his soul will know the way back; this is a "superstitious" custom not practiced since the Cultural Revolution. She also wants her son to teach for just one day, so that her husband's desire that he be a teacher will be satisfied. When all has been done according to her wishes, she sees a vision of herself as a young woman in love, running down the road to her home—reminiscent of the drive down "the road home" her son took from the city for the funeral—as we have seen her running to the schoolhouse to listen to the teacher lead his students in a recitation that includes the line, "Know the present, know the past," or waiting on the road in the winter for the teacher's return from an interrogation in the city. While the present is shown in a bluish monochrome, the scenes of the past are in color—not the Technicolor of *Raise the Red Lantern* but the found colors of nature, food, a red jacket. As it urges China to keep in touch with its past—a pre-Revolutionary custom and the indelible face of Zhang Ziyi as the mother when she was young—*The Road Home* offers an integrated vision of how life can be complete.

Chen Kaige's *The Emperor and the Assassin* (1998, released 1999) told the story of the king of Qin, who after 550 years of civil war wanted to unify the seven warring kingdoms into one China and, in 221 B.C., succeeded. His problem is that he is in love with a woman (Gong Li) who believes that he will conquer without bloodshed and who, with the aid of an assassin whose role is ironic and paradoxical, turns against him when he fails to keep his promises. In a way it is like a movie about an Ivan the Terrible in love with a Katharine Hepburn. Produced in China with money from France and Japan, it told the human cost of empire building. When Zhang Yimou told

much the same story in the martial-arts drama *Hero* (2002), the politics and the characters' motivations were more conservative, perhaps reflecting the increased power of the censors. The heroic assassin decides to spare the king and to let himself be killed so that the empire—a unified China, "our land"—can be realized and bring peace. In *Hero* and the martial-arts film that followed it, *House of Flying Daggers* (2004), his painterly eye and sharp ear first took advantage of the computer. Zhang's next picture, the contemporary story of a father's attempt to become part of his dying son's life, *Riding Alone for Thousands of Miles* (2005), was shot on location and mostly with amateurs; throughout his career he has alternated between big studio productions and smaller-scale stories of what he has called the real relationships of common people. He returned to the studio to shoot a sumptuous period piece, the court melodrama *Curse of the Golden Flower* (2006). In 2008, he was chosen as artistic director of the opening and closing ceremonies for the Beijing Olympic Games, an integration of computers, dancers, and film that was both spectacular and state of the art; the four-hour opening in particular gave him a great opportunity as a choreographer of movement and light. His being chosen indicated that he was no longer controversial.

A number of filmmakers who call themselves the Sixth Generation have, since the mid-1990s, produced a new realistic cinema, most of it shot on 16mm or video. (They call themselves the Sixth Generation because they are the new filmmakers after the Fifth, not because they were the next graduating class at the academy; they are not a cohesive, defined group with a common background.) Zhang is a great painter, they argue, and there's nothing wrong with that, but he and Chen are now the older generation, and their films do not show the real China. Often using mini-DV cameras and acknowledging the influence of Agnès Varda, they make both documentaries and features on what modern urban life is really like. The Sixth Generation has taken its small cameras to the streets, even at times concealing them. They favor long takes. They work without permits and often without lights. They shoot only on location—often in apartments—and have nothing to do with the studios. Most of their unpolished films concern the daily lives of artistic and social outsiders. Because they work as cinematic outsiders—without shooting permits, state financing, censorship, or authorized distribution—the Sixth Generation has not been able to exhibit its films in China except underground—in bars, for instance, or in special secret showings. *Beijing Bastards* (1993, directed by Zhang Yuan), the first Sixth-Generation film, tells the mundane story of a rock'n'roll band and their friends. *Frozen* (1996, directed by Wang Xiaoshuai) is about a performance artist whose project involves freezing himself to death. *Beijing Suburb* (2002, directed by Hu Ze) is about artists who live in a suburb of Beijing; those without regular IDs or Temporary Residence Permits are subject to harassment and arrest. Performance artists, painters, poets, and others are shown at work and in relationships. Two scenes in *Beijing Suburb* actually depict sexual intercourse; in two other scenes, people talk about what is wrong with Chinese culture. Many other scenes show people talking about the nature, marketing, and exhibition of art, especially performance art and painting. There is, in fact, a performance-art quality to the entire project. *Beijing Suburb* has little narrative momentum, but the stories are true, and the artists play themselves.

In 2007, Li Yang's *Blind Mountain*, an involving narrative film that did not belong to any particular school, was released abroad but not in China (it did play in Hong Kong); it deals forthrightly with the effect of Chinese population directives, which have left a generation of young men without enough young women to marry, by telling the story of a woman who is kidnapped to become a wife and does everything in her power to escape, finally taking matters into her own hands when the authorities prove inadequate. One hopes that China will again prove ready for the works of its most adventurous filmmakers.

Taiwan

After the founding of the People's Republic of China in 1949, the former Chinese government and many of the commercial filmmakers—particularly those who had worked in the Shanghai industry—set up shop on the island of Taiwan. The industry that developed in Taiwan was formulaic and commercial, emphasizing martial arts films and melodramas. An art cinema appeared in the 1980s; its two most important directors were Edward Yang (*That Day, On the Beach*, 1983) and Hou Hsiao-hsien (*City of Sadness*, 1989), whose films examined what it meant to live in a country that was continually changing hands, where cultural backgrounds and languages were diverse but not shared, and where urban life was a maze of contradictions that could be intimate or general, exhausting or perilous. In the late 1990s, Chinese reviewers were debating Hou's apparent turn away from the "nostalgia" of his earlier films—the intellectually rich, perfectly composed long takes that explored moments of crisis and transition in childhood, the family, and the history of Taiwan (*A Summer at Grandpa's*, 1984; *A Time to Live and a Time to Die*, 1985; *City of Sadness;* and the first film he shot with synchronized sound, *Puppet Master*, 1993)—in favor of a rougher but still long-take look at contemporary Taiwan (*Goodbye South, Goodbye*, 1996); he followed that with a deliberately beautiful, formally composed, long-take look at life in the Shanghai brothels of the late 19th century, *Flowers of Shanghai* (1998). In 2003, Hou directed—in Japanese and at the invitation of the Japanese—*Café Lumière*, an homage to Ozu in honor of the centenary of his birth; "we shot similar themes but with different methods of shooting," Hou said in an interview; "that's how we honor him." Meanwhile, Yang's fans were trying to unravel *A Confucian Confusion* (1994) and studying how he managed to cover 40 or more characters in the mere four hours of his urban epic of disaffected youth, *A Brighter Summer Day* (1991). In 1999, Yang was writing a new script, and every day when he sat down at the typewriter, he got himself up to speed by saying "A one and a two..."—and the closest Chinese translation to that was *Yi Yi* (2000), which can mean "one one" or "two," or, roughly, "a one and a one." Like many of his earlier films, *Yi Yi* has a large number of characters who are eventually interrelated by a tight, converging plot. While it is hard at the start of some of his movies to figure out who all these people are and how they relate, by the end one knows them like family members and can find satisfaction in their confrontations and share their revelations. At that point his movies do not seem so long. One character in *Yi Yi* is a little boy who uses his still camera to shoot the backs of people's heads, to show them what they don't know and what they haven't seen (and to help them see the other side of the truth, not just the side in front); one needs a camera like that boy's or like Yang's to venture into the complexity of others' points of view and into unsuspected or forgotten regions of one's own experience. Yang died in 2007.

If the dominant theme of the new Taiwan cinema has been the ways people adjust to cultural conflict and change, the films of Ang Lee (*The Wedding Banquet*, 1993; *Eat Drink Man Woman*, 1994; *Sense and Sensibility*, 1995; *The Ice Storm*, 1997; *Crouching Tiger, Hidden Dragon*, 2000; *Brokeback Mountain*, 2005; *Taking Woodstock*, 2009) might be considered an extension of the movement, even if most of them are accessible comedies of manners co-produced and sometimes shot in the United States. *The Wedding Banquet* presents the "two men and a girl" triangle with a difference: the lovers are the two men, and the cross-cultural and cross-generational hurdles leaped in the course of winning the Taiwanese man's parents' approval of the household he sets up with his American lover and pregnant Chinese wife are both universal and culturally specific. (Lee returned to the theme of homosexual love, but in a tragic mode, in *Brokeback Mountain*.) *Eat Drink Man Woman* also uses food and family gatherings to define and catalyze emotional and cultural conflicts, but it is far more sophisticated in structure and ambitious in concept (the dialectical terms of human life, including gender and experience, as the *yin* and *yang* of the foods that come together as a meal, like the conflicting but complementary elements that make up a family); like a Jane Austen novel, it finds in its focus on a chef and his daughters an intimate, concentrated way to organize within a work of art practically everything that matters about living. The aptness of the comparison with Jane Austen was confirmed in his next picture, *Sense and Sensibility*, a U.S.–U.K. co-production based on a masterful screenplay by Emma Thompson—by far the most faithful and spirited of Austen adaptations, a 1995 film immersed in the look and rules of the dawn of the 19th century.

Feeling that he would not be a real filmmaker until he had made a martial arts movie like those he had grown up on, and also that there was more to do with the character dynamics explored in *Sense and Sensibility*, Lee made what he told Michelle Yeoh (with Chow Yun-fat and Zhang Ziyi, one of the three leads) was "*Sense and Sensibility* with martial arts." As choreographed by Yuen Wo-Ping and shot by Peter Pau, the result, *Crouching Tiger, Hidden Dragon*, goes where the martial arts film has gone and beyond. Nothing in this picture is entirely new, but its wirework and camerawork and fast, graceful action (the chase across the walls and roofs, the fight in the waving trees) are integrated with more beauty, rigor, and complexity than the genre usually affords; the reach into the depths of character and decisive action is more profound; and the open ending gives the image and the story an awe-inspiring reach.

In the 1990s, as previously mentioned, money from Taiwan and Hong Kong fueled much of the film production on mainland China. For some of these capitalist producers, China became a low-rent backlot whose spectacular range of landscape could not be duplicated in the choked streets of Hong Kong or on the island of Taiwan. The first entirely Taiwanese film to be shot entirely in China was Huang Jianxin's *The Wooden Man's Bride* (1994), an action-packed tale of forbidden romance. But many things were changing by then: Trade borders opened even as political borders hardened (Tibet) or were redefined (Hong Kong became part of China again in 1997, with a limited degree of self-regulation and the promise of economic continuity).

International co-production also stimulated the cinemas of Southeast Asia. One example was the new Vietnam, officially at peace with China, France, and the United States. When Tran Anh Hung, who was living in Paris, made *The Scent of Green Papaya* (1992), he shot it in a Paris studio, re-creating the Saigon of the 1950s with an appropriately slick and artificial style. When he shot *Cyclo* (*Xich Lo*, 1995) in Vietnam, he used an equally appropriate style, just as meticulous but vivid and rough, to capture the very different Ho Chi Minh City of the 1990s, with its bureaucracy, inflation, unemployment, and crime. Tran was still using European financing when he shot *Vertical Ray of the Sun* (or *At the Height of Summer*, 2000) in Vietnam. His films called attention to the work of earlier Vietnamese filmmakers, especially Dang Nhat Minh (*When the Tenth Month Comes*, 1984; *The Girl on the River*, 1987; *Hanoi—Winter 1946*, 1997).

Hong Kong

Although it has produced such distinguished artists as Wong Kar Wai, the most single-mindedly commercial and artificial cinema in the world is that of Hong Kong. Whether they are gritty and gory or sentimental and magical, whether they are gangster stories or fairy tales or martial arts spectaculars, the majority of the films defy the limits of space and time and endurance and even gravity in a realm of impossible wonders where dreams turn real, wounds never kill unless they bear a thematic charge, "perpetual-motion editing" keeps sorcerers and combatants pinwheeling and sweeping through the air for minutes on end, spells work, honor matters, style and skill are one, and every action and skill is an expression of good or evil.

Loyalty—to a friend, a teacher, a ritual, a code—is a recurring theme in these films, and it is tested by deception and contamination at every turn. Romantic, even chivalric, and directed entirely toward exciting and entertaining the audience, these films adapt the conventions of Cantonese opera to the cinema (one source of the colorful costumes and aerial choreography) and create a fantastic and action-oriented universe in which ideals are as real as corruption.

These values are central to the martial arts films, examples of which range from Chang Cheh's *One-Armed Swordsman* (1967) to Lo Wei's *The Chinese Connection* (1972, starring Bruce Lee, who consistently portrayed a figure of honor and power and who was also a superb fight choreographer) and Liu Chia-Liang's *Drunken Master II* (1994, starring Jackie Chan). These values are just as evident in the supernatural extravaganzas such as Ching Siu-tung's *A Chinese Ghost Story* (1987, produced by Tsui Hark), in the police/gangster thrillers such as John Woo's *Hard-Boiled* (1992), and in the buddy films (which are also known as the Masochistic Flaming Brother genre) such as John Woo's *A Better Tomorrow* (1986) and *The Killer* (1989).

Another important genre is the urban comedy–drama. Wong Kar Wai (who used to spell his name Wong Kar-wai) makes romantic movies that are cinematically daring and combine a complex of emotional states into rich, rewarding structures. Almost everything in his films seems connected to everything else: The two halves of *Chungking Express* (1994) systematically parallel and contradict each other, and *Fallen Angels* (1995) refers to both halves. Two neighbors do not become lovers in *In the Mood*

for Love (2000); one of them lives in Room 2046. In *2046* (2004) that number becomes the basis of a maze of nostalgia and desire. As much as his characters struggle with time in their relationships, trying to come into emotional sync with each other, time becomes a complex element in the image itself. The signature shot in his early films, made famous in *Chungking Express* and so widely imitated that Wong no longer uses it, mixed slow and fast motion in the same image. The divisions in his scripts—like those between the two parts of *Chungking Express*—separate and join characters who are trying to find someone, maybe their counterpart in Wong's romantic labyrinth, the person who is just on the other side of the present.

In 2008, Wong restored and then recut *Ashes of Time* (1994), one of his most beautiful and lyrically constructed works, as *Ashes of Time Redux*, making it a bit easier to follow and slightly enhancing its extraordinary colors. Like many of his other films, it is a study of solitude and connection; its plot is organized by the turning of the year and by the sayings and prophecies appropriate to each season.

Unlike Japanese films, Hong Kong films delight in mixing genres. *The Killer*, for instance, is a buddy film about a hit man and a policeman—and a blinded singer from the "doomed songstress" pictures. Some use genre to break new ground, like Woo's *Bullet in the Head* (1990), a buddy–war movie about three friends whose civilian experiences in Vietnam test their loyalty and values—a film influenced by *The Deer Hunter* and *Apocalypse Now* but offering a uniquely Asian point of view on the war as well as a formulaic vision of friendship. But genre and formula have always been at the heart of Hong Kong cinema—and have continued to be, even after the British left in 1997 and the former Crown Colony came under Chinese control—providing structures within which the creative imagination can run wild.

Korea

Largely isolated for 500 years, the "Hermit Kingdom" of Korea was traumatically wrenched into modernity at the end of the 19th century as Japanese, Russian, and Chinese territorial ambitions began to be played out across the peninsula. Annexed by the Japanese in 1910, it

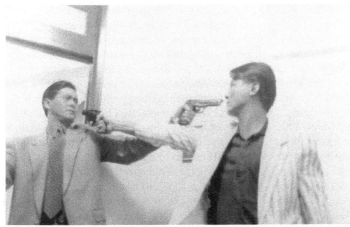

The "unusual killer" (Chow Yun-fat, left) and "unusual cop" (Danny Lee), who both believe in honor and justice and keeping promises—and whose guns almost never run out of bullets—in John Woo's The Killer, *whose original title, literally translated, is* A Pair of Blood-Splattering Heroes.

Fig. 14-30

remained occupied until the liberation in 1945, but the Korean War (1950–53) brought division and new occupation, leaving the North in the Soviet sphere and the South dependent on the West—a most brutal experience of the Cold War that persists to the present. All the films produced under the Japanese occupation were lost during the wars of the mid-century, and about the films made in the North we know little more than that they have adhered to Kim Il-Sung's policies of self-reliance and the aesthetic of Socialist Realism. But since the 1990s, the South Korean cinema has been twice revitalized, first with the internationally recognized New Korean Cinema, parallel in many ways to the contemporary art cinemas of China and Taiwan, and then again more recently with the *hanryu* or "Korean Wave" of films and TV dramas that have become enormously popular across East Asia.

The South Korean cinema had its heyday in the 1960s, producing as many as 200 films a year, most of them genre pictures for domestic consumption. With the increasing popularity of TV in the 1970s, a decline set in, and the country was flooded with foreign imports. But opposition to the military dictatorship and the subsequent political liberalization that culminated in democratic presidential elections in 1992 led to a renewal of the cinema. Its core was a group of directors debuting in the mid-1980s, including Chung Ji-Young, Bae Yong-Kyun, Jang Sun-Woo, Park Kwang-Su, and Park Jong-Won. They used innovative narrative structures and camera styles to approach Korea's

troubled history with a directness that had previously been censored. Park Kwang-Su has best sustained the impetus of this group with *To the Starry Island* (1994), about wartime social conflicts on one of Korea's remote islands, and *A Single Spark* (1996), about a young man whose suicide ignited the labor movement in Korea.

In the early years of the 21st century, South Korea developed a popular genre cinema, the "Korean Wave." The breakthrough came with *Shiri* (or *Swiri*, 1999, directed by Kang Je-Gyu), an action film centering on the tragic love story of a secret agent from North Korea and her opposite number in the South. Often referred to as the first Korean blockbuster, *Shiri* prompted a series of further big productions, the first of which was *Joint Security Area* (2000, directed by Park Chan-Wook), a mystery thriller portraying the friendship among soldiers of the two Koreas at the Demilitarized Zone. Its commercial success led the industry to increase production budgets for genre films. Action and gangster films like *Friend* (2001, directed by Kwak Kyung-Taek) were commercially the most viable, but a variation on the genre, the action comedy, was also very successful, notably in *My Wife is a Gangster* (2001, directed by Cho Jin-Gyu). Although that film had a female hero, most Korean action films are still male-centered, such as the next record-breaking action films, *Silmido* (2003, directed by Kang Woo-Suk), based on the true story of a group of soldiers trained as assassins to be sent secretly to North Korea, and *Tae Guk Gi: The Brotherhood of War* (2004, directed by Kang Je-Gyu), which portrays the love of brothers who are conscripted during the Korean War. Although not as successful as the action films, the romantic comedy *My Sassy Girl* (2001, directed by Kwak Jae-Yong) was enthusiastically received in both the Korean and Asian markets and precipitated a series of imitations. And beginning with *Whispering Corridors* (1998, directed by Park Ki-Hyung), Korean horror films became extremely popular; the genre grew to include such bizarre tales of cruelty as Park Chan-Wook's *Sympathy for Mr. Vengeance* (2002) and *Oldboy* (2003). In 2005, the top-grossing film was *The King and the Clown* (Lee Jun-Ik), a period piece portraying homosexuality in 16th-century Korea; the next box-office smash was a monster movie, *The Host* (2006, directed by Bong Joon-Ho). *The Good the Bad the Weird* (Kim Jee-Woon), a tremendously energetic homage to the westerns of Sergio Leone, was released in 2008, a triumph both of the genre film and of the Postmodern revisiting of genres. These developments demonstrate the diversified range of genres that reconstructed Korean cinema—but the chief figure who brought Korean cinema to the world's attention in the first place was Im Kwon-Taek, who had been making films since the 1960s.

Born in 1936, Im began as a set builder, eventually became an assistant to an action-film director, and debuted with his own first film in 1962. He made almost 70 features in the next 15 years, most of which were routine genre productions. By his own testimony, he first discovered his personal style in *Genealogy* in 1978, a film about the worst excesses of the Japanese occupation just before World War II. Since then his work has followed two main currents. One current has continued the genre films' box-office orientation, culminating in the enormously successful *The General's Son* (1990), a martial-arts epic, again set in the period of the Japanese invasion, that spawned two sequels. Generally the financial success of works like these has subsidized the other current, a series of works meditating on the ordeals of modern Korean history, often using an abused woman character as a figure for Korea and attempting to translate into film the qualities of traditional Korean culture. These include *Mandala* (1981), *Gilsottum* (1985), *Ticket* (1986), *Surrogate Mother* (1986), *Sop'yonje* (1993), *Festival* (1996), and *Chunhyang* (2000).

Set in the period after the Korean War, *Sop'yonje* is about *p'ansori*, a traditional form of folk opera practiced since the 19th century by itinerant musicians, in which a soloist, accompanied by a barrel drummer, sings a long musical story—a highly disciplined and emotionally rich performance that can last for hours and that depends on a practiced yet flexible bond between the singer and the drummer who guides and follows him or her. As a narrative, *Sop'yonje* is both remembered by and told to Dongho (Kim Kyu-Chul) who, orphaned as a child, was taken as an apprentice by a *p'ansori* singer called Yubong

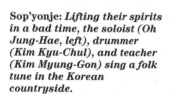

Sop'yonje: *Lifting their spirits in a bad time, the soloist (Oh Jung-Hae, left), drummer (Kim Kyu-Chul), and teacher (Kim Myung-Gon) sing a folk tune in the Korean countryside.*

Fig. 14-31

(Kim Myung-Gon), who had already similarly adopted a daughter, Songhwa (Oh Jung-Hae). Yubong is uncompromising as a teacher, and eventually Dongho flees his harsh treatment and the misery of life on the road in an impoverished Korea where traditional culture is rapidly being eroded by foreign pop music. But in doing so, he leaves Songhwa to Yubong, who goes so far as to give her a poison that blinds her, forcing her to concentrate her whole being in her voice. But he cannot force her to become an artist, to survive and use her pain the way he wants. She does the job herself, singing alone in the wild, in a sequence whose integration of art and nature is awesome.

If Yubong makes an obsession out of his egotism, Songhwa makes art out of her accepted fate and survived grief, not masochistically but with the grounded autonomy of an artist who brings into resonant unity—exactly as the film does—not only her own character and experience but Korean tradition and nature itself. Pivoted on Dongho's reunion with Songhwa after their father's death—a scene in which she sings and he drums to the height of the art, fusing and transcending their suffering into an intensely painful and beautiful expression, after which they separate without putting into words that they have recognized each other—the film is a seamlessly integrated mosaic of flashbacks, distinguished by the melancholy beauty of both Songhwa's *p'ansori* singing and the Korean countryside. (*Chunhyang* takes an entirely different approach: The narrative frame is a *p'ansori* concert, sung by one man with a male drummer on a bare, elegant stage, with cuts to the dramatized action. Despite the engaging 13th-century tale and its rich, moving enactment, our minds, ears, and eyes are never far from the singer–narrator and the astounding color—so various and subtle, natural and arranged, that it addresses a question posed by avant-garde film poet Stan Brakhage in *Metaphors on Vision*: "How many colors are there in a field of grass to the crawling baby unaware of 'Green'?") *Sop'yonje* was a major cultural event in South Korea, occasioning a storm of media attention, breaking all previous box-office records, and sparking a national revival of interest in traditional arts. In the West, *Sop'yonje* did for South Korea what *Rashomon* had done, so long ago, for Japan.

For Further Viewing

FILMS

SWEDEN AND DENMARK

INGMAR BERGMAN (1918–2007)
Thirst (1949)
Summer with Monika or *Monika* (1953)
The Naked Night or *Sawdust and Tinsel* or *The Clown's Evening* (1953)
Smiles of a Summer Night (1955)
The Seventh Seal (1957). Completed 1956
Wild Strawberries (1957)
The Magician or *The Face* (1958)
The Virgin Spring (1960). Completed 1959
Through a Glass Darkly (1961)
Winter Light or *The Communicants* (1962)
The Silence (1963)
Persona (1966). Completed 1965
Hour of the Wolf (1968). Completed 1966
Shame (1968). Completed 1967
The Passion of Anna (1969)
Cries and Whispers (1972)
Scenes from a Marriage (1974). TV version 1972
The Magic Flute (1974)
Fanny and Alexander (1982)
After the Rehearsal (1984)
Saraband (2004). Completed 2003

CARL THEODOR DREYER (1889–1968)
Leaves from Satan's Book (1919)
Michael (1924)
The Passion of Joan of Arc (1928). Shot 1927
Vampyr (1932)
Day of Wrath (1943)
Ordet (1955). Completed 1954
Gertrud (1964)

SWEDISH AND DANISH MISCELLANY
The Black Masks (1912, Mauritz Stiller)
Ingeborg Holm (1913, Victor Sjøstrøm)
A Man There Was (1917, Victor Sjøstrøm). Completed 1916
Thomas Graal's Best Film (1917, Mauritz Stiller)
The Outlaw and His Wife (1918, Victor Sjøstrøm)
Sir Arne's Treasure (1919, Mauritz Stiller)
Erotikon (1920, Mauritz Stiller)
The Phantom Chariot (1921, Victor Sjøstrøm). Completed 1920

Häxan or *Witchcraft Through the Ages*
   (1922, Benjamin Christensen)
The Saga of Gösta Berling (1924, Mauritz Stiller)
Torment (1944, Alf Sjöberg)
Miss Julie (1951, Alf Sjöberg)
Raven's End (1963, Bo Widerberg)
Dear John (1966, Lars Magnus Lindgren)
Elvira Madigan (1967, Bo Widerberg)
I am Curious (Yellow) (1967, Vilgot Sjöman)
The Emigrants (1971, Jan Troell)
The New Land (1972, Jan Troell)
My Life as a Dog (1985, Lasse Hallström)
Babette's Feast (1987, Gabriel Axel)
Medea (1988, Lars von Trier). Script by Dreyer
Pelle the Conqueror (1988, Bille August)
Europa or *Zentropa* (1991, Lars von Trier)
The Ox (1991, Sven Nykvist)
The Kingdom (1994, Lars von Trier). From TV
   series; *Kingdom II*, 1997
The Celebration (1998, Thomas Vinterberg)
The Idiots (1998, Lars von Trier)
Mifune (1999, Søren Kragh-Jacobsen)
Faithless (2000, Liv Ullmann)
The King is Alive (2000, Kristian Levring)
Dogville (2003, Lars von Trier)
The Five Obstructions (2003, Lars von Trier
   and Jørgen Leth)
Let the Right One In (2008, Tomas Alfredson)
Maria Larsson's Everlasting Moment or
   Everlasting Moments (2008, Jan Troell)

ENGLAND

LINDSAY ANDERSON (1923–94)
This Sporting Life (1963)
If. . . (1969)
O Lucky Man! (1973)
The Whales of August (1987)

DANNY BOYLE (1965–   )
Shallow Grave (1994)
Trainspotting (1996)
A Life Less Ordinary (1997)
28 Days Later or *28 Days Later. . .* (2002)
Millions (2004)
Sunshine (2007)
Slumdog Millionaire (2008). Co-director in
   India, Loveleen Tandan

JACK CLAYTON (1921–95)
Room at the Top (1959)
The Innocents (1961)

The Pumpkin Eater (1964)
Our Mother's House (1967)
Something Wicked This Way Comes (1983)
The Lonely Passion of Judith Hearne (1987)

DAVID LEAN (1908–91)
Blithe Spirit (1945)
Brief Encounter (1945)
Great Expectations (1946)
Oliver Twist (1948)
The Bridge on the River Kwai (1957)
Lawrence of Arabia (1962)
Doctor Zhivago (1965)
A Passage to India (1984)

MIKE LEIGH (1943–   )
High Hopes (1988)
Life is Sweet (1991)
Naked (1993)
Secrets & Lies (1996)
Topsy-Turvy (1999)
Vera Drake (2004)
Happy-Go-Lucky (2008)

RICHARD LESTER (1932–   )
*The Running, Jumping and Standing Still
   Film* (1960)
A Hard Day's Night (1964)
Help! (1965)
How I Won the War (1967)
Petulia (1968)
The Three Musketeers (1974)
The Four Musketeers (1975)
Robin and Marian (1976)

KEN LOACH (1936–   )
Poor Cow (1967)
Family Life or *Wednesday's Child* (1971)
Hidden Agenda (1990)
Raining Stones (1993)
Ladybird Ladybird (1994)
Land and Freedom (1995)
My Name is Joe (1998)
Bread & Roses (2000)
The Wind That Shakes the Barley (2006)

LAURENCE OLIVIER (1907–89)
Henry V (1944)
Hamlet (1948)
Richard III (1955)
Three Sisters (1970). Co-director, John Sichel

MICHAEL POWELL (1905–90)

The Edge of the World (1937). Completed 1936
The Thief of Bagdad (1940). Co-directors,
Ludwig Berger and Tim Whelan
The Life and Death of Colonel Blimp (1943).
Co-creator, **EMERIC PRESSBURGER (1902–88)**
A Canterbury Tale (1944). Co-creator,
Pressburger
I Know Where I'm Going! (1945). Co-creator,
Pressburger
A Matter of Life and Death or *Stairway to
Heaven* (1946). Co-creator, Pressburger
Black Narcissus (1947). Co-creator,
Pressburger
The Red Shoes (1948). Co-creator, Pressburger
Peeping Tom (1960)

CAROL REED (1906–76)

The Stars Look Down (1939)
Kipps (1941)
Odd Man Out (1947)
The Fallen Idol (1948)
The Third Man (1949)
Outcast of the Islands (1951)
Trapeze (1956)
Our Man in Havana (1960)
Oliver! (1968)

KAREL REISZ (1926–2002)

Momma Don't Allow (1955). Co-director, Tony
Richardson
Saturday Night and Sunday Morning (1960)
Morgan, a Suitable Case for Treatment or
Morgan! (1966)
The Loves of Isadora (1968). Condensed as
Isadora
Who'll Stop the Rain (1978)
The French Lieutenant's Woman (1981)
Sweet Dreams (1985)

TONY RICHARDSON (1928–91)

Momma Don't Allow (1955). Co-director, Karel
Reisz
Look Back in Anger (1959)
The Entertainer (1960)
Sanctuary (1961)
A Taste of Honey (1961)
The Loneliness of the Long Distance Runner
(1962)
Tom Jones (1963)
The Loved One (1965)

The Charge of the Light Brigade (1968)
Ned Kelly (1970)
A Delicate Balance (1973)
Joseph Andrews (1977)
Blue Sky (1994). Completed 1991

NICOLAS ROEG (1928–   )

Performance (1970). Co-director, Donald
Cammell
Walkabout (1971)
Don't Look Now (1973)
The Man Who Fell to Earth (1976)
Insignificance (1985)
Track 29 (1988)
The Witches (1990)

KEN RUSSELL (1927–   )

Song of Summer (1968). Made for TV
Women in Love (1969)
The Music Lovers (1970)
The Boy Friend (1971)
The Devils (1971)
Tommy (1974)

JOHN SCHLESINGER (1926–2003)

Billy Liar (1963)
Darling (1965)
Far from the Madding Crowd (1967)
Midnight Cowboy (1969)
Sunday Bloody Sunday or *Sunday, Bloody
Sunday* (1971)
The Day of the Locust (1975)
Marathon Man (1976)
The Tale of Sweeney Todd (1998). Made for TV

THE EALING COMEDIES

Kind Hearts and Coronets (1949, Robert Hamer)
Tight Little Island or *Whisky Galore!* (1949,
Alexander Mackendrick)
The Lavender Hill Mob (1951, Charles Crichton)
The Man in the White Suit (1951, Alexander
Mackendrick)
The Captain's Paradise (1953, Anthony Kimmins)
The Ladykillers (1955, Alexander Mackendrick)

UNITED KINGDOM MISCELLANY

A Cottage on Dartmoor (1929, Anthony Asquith)
Dead of Night (1945, Alberto Cavalcanti,
Charles Crichton, Basil Dearden, and
Robert Hamer)
Green For Danger (1946, Sidney Gilliat)

Scrooge or *A Christmas Carol* (1951, Brian Desmond-Hurst)

The Importance of Being Earnest (1952, Anthony Asquith)

The Holly and the Ivy (1953, George More O'Ferrall)

An Inspector Calls (1954, Guy Hamilton)

Romeo and Juliet (1954, Renato Castellani)

Night of the Demon or *Curse of the Demon* (1957, Jacques Tourneur)

Dracula or *Horror of Dracula* (1958, Terence Fisher)

The Horse's Mouth (1958, Ronald Neame)

I'm All Right Jack (1959, John Boulting). Producer, Roy Boulting

The Angry Silence (1960, Guy Green)

Sons and Lovers (1960, Jack Cardiff)

Tunes of Glory (1960, Ronald Neame)

Billy Budd (1962, Peter Ustinov)

Dr. No (1962, Terence Young)

The L-Shaped Room (1962, Bryan Forbes)

From Russia With Love (1963, Terence Young)

Lord of the Flies (1963, Peter Brook)

Séance on a Wet Afternoon (1964, Bryan Forbes)

Zulu (1964, Cy Endfield)

The War Game (1965, Peter Watkins)

Marat/Sade or *The Persecution and Assassination of Jean-Paul Marat as Performed by the Inmates of the Asylum of Charenton Under the Direction of the Marquis de Sade* (1966, Peter Brook)

Privilege (1967, Peter Watkins)

The Prime of Miss Jean Brodie (1969, Ronald Neame)

Punishment Park (1971, Peter Watkins)

The Ruling Class (1972, Peter Medak)

Edvard Munch (1974, Peter Watkins)

Monty Python and The Holy Grail (1974, Terry Jones and Terry Gilliam)

The Rocky Horror Picture Show (1975, Jim Sharman)

The Long Good Friday (1980, John Mackenzie)

Excalibur (1981, John Boorman)

The Draughtsman's Contract (1982, Peter Greenaway)

Pink Floyd—The Wall (1982, Alan Parker)

Betrayal (1983, David Jones)

Bloody Kids (1983, Stephen Frears)

Local Hero (1983, Bill Forsyth)

The Killing Fields (1984, Roland Joffe)

Dreamchild (1985, Gavin Millar)

My Beautiful Laundrette (1985, Stephen Frears)

28 Up (1985, Michael Apted)

Drowning By Numbers (1987, Peter Greenaway)

Hellraiser (1987, Clive Barker)

Distant Voices, Still Lives (1988, Terence Davies)

A Fish Called Wanda (1988, Charles Crichton)

The Cook The Thief His Wife & Her Lover (1989, Peter Greenaway)

Henry V (1989, Kenneth Branagh)

Prospero's Books (1991, Peter Greenaway)

Hedd Wyn (1992, Paul Turner)

Howards End (1992, James Ivory)

Orlando (1992, Sally Potter)

The House of Mirth (2000, Terence Davies)

Iris (2001, Richard Eyre)

Shaun of the Dead (2004, Edgar Wright)

Wallace & Gromit: The Curse of the Were-Rabbit (2005, Nick Park and Steve Box)

The Last Station (2009, Michael Hoffman; U.K./Germany/Russia)

CENTRAL AND EASTERN EUROPE

THEODOROS ANGELOPOULOS (1935–)

Days of '36 (1972)

The Traveling Players or *The Travelling Players* (1975)

Voyage to Cythera (1983)

Landscape in the Mist (1988)

The Suspended Step of the Stork (1991)

Ulysses' Gaze (1995)

Eternity and a Day or *An Eternity and a Day* (1998)

Trilogy: The Weeping Meadow (2004)

The Dust of Time (2008)

MILOŠ FORMAN (1932–)

Black Peter (1963)

Loves of a Blonde (1965)

The Firemen's Ball (1967)

Taking Off (1971)

One Flew Over the Cuckoo's Nest (1975)

Hair (1979)

Amadeus (1984)

The People Vs. Larry Flynt (1996)

JÁN KADÁR (1918–79) AND ELMAR KLOS (1910–93)

Death is Called Engelchen (1963)

The Shop on Main Street (1965)

Adrift (1971)

MIKLÓS JANCSÓ (1921–　　)
Cantata (1962)
My Way Home (1964)
The Round-Up (1965)
The Red and the White (1967)
Silence and Cry (1968)
The Confrontation (1969)
Red Psalm (1972)

KRZYSZTOF KIEŚLOWSKI (1941–96)
Camera Buff (1979)
Blind Chance (1987). Completed 1982
Dekalog or *The Decalogue* (ten parts, 1988).
  Made for TV
A Short Film About Killing (1988)
The Double Life of Veronique (1991)
Three Colors: Blue (1993)
Three Colors: White (1994). Completed 1993
Three Colors: Red (1994)

DUŠAN MAKAVEJEV (1932–　　)
Man Is Not a Bird (1965)
*Love Affair, or The Tragedy of a Switchboard
  Operator* (1967)
WR—Mysteries of the Organism (1971)
Sweet Movie (1974)
Montenegro or Pigs and Pearls (1981)

ROMAN POLANSKI (1933–　　)
Two Men and a Wardrobe (1958)
The Fat and the Lean (1961)
Knife in the Water (1962)
Repulsion (1965)
Cul-de-Sac (1966)
Rosemary's Baby (1968)
Macbeth (1971)
Chinatown (1974)
The Tenant (1976)
Tess (1979)
Bitter Moon (1992)
The Pianist (2002)

JERZY SKOLIMOWSKI (1938–　　)
Identification Marks: None (1964)
Walkover (1965)
Barrier (1966)
Le Départ (1967)
Hands Up! (1967)
Deep End (1970)
The Shout (1978)
Moonlighting (1982)

ANDRZEJ WAJDA (1926–　　)
A Generation or *Generation* (1955)
Kanal (1957)
Ashes and Diamonds (1958)
Everything for Sale (1969)
Landscape After the Battle (1970)
Man of Marble (1977)
Man of Iron (1980)
Danton (1982)
A Love in Germany (1984)
Katyń (2007)

**MISCELLANY: FORMER CZECHOSLOVAKIA, POLAND,
  HUNGARY, FORMER YUGOSLAVIA, GREECE**
The Last Stop (1947, Wanda Jakubowksa;
  Poland)
Man on the Track (1955, Andrzej Munk;
  Poland)
Stella (1955, Michael Cacoyannis; Greece)
Professor Hannibal (1956, Zoltán Fábri; Hungary)
The Invention of Destruction (1957, Karel
  Zeman; former Czechoslovakia)
Dom (*House*, 1958, Walerian Borowczyk;
  Poland)
Ceiling (1961, Vera Chytilová; former
  Czechoslovakia)
Electra (1961, Michael Cacoyannis; Greece)
Sunshine in a Net (1962, Štefan Uher; former
  Czechoslovakia)
Josef Kilian (1963, Jan Schmidt and Pavel
  Juráček; former Czechoslovakia)
The Passenger (1963, Andrzej Munk; Poland).
  Unfinished at his death in 1961
The Fifth Horseman Is Fear (1964, Zbyněk
  Brynych; former Czechoslovakia)
Les Jeux des anges (1964, Walerian Borowczyk;
  Poland)
Ninety in the Shade (1964, Jiří Weiss; former
  Czechoslovakia)
Intimate Lighting (1965, Ivan Passer; former
  Czechoslovakia)
Closely Watched Trains (1966, Jiří Menzel; for-
  mer Czechoslovakia)
Daisies (1966, Vera Chytilová; former
  Czechoslovakia)
Report on the Party and the Guests (1966, Jan
  Němec; former Czechoslovakia)
I Even Met Happy Gypsies (1967, Aleksandr
  Petrović; former Yugoslavia)
Marketa Lazarová (1967, František Vláčil; for-
  mer Czechoslovakia)

The End of August at the Hotel Ozone (1968, Jan Schmidt; former Czechoslovakia). Completed 1966

The Paul Street Boys (1968, Zoltán Fábri; Hungary)

Joke (1969, Jaromil Jireš; former Czechoslovakia)

The Structure of Crystals (1969, Krzysztof Zanussi; Poland)

Camouflage (1977, Krzysztof Zanussi; Poland)

Iphigenia (1977, Michael Cacoyannis; Greece)

Women (1977, Márta Mészáros; Hungary)

Angi Vera (1978, Pál Gábor; Hungary)

The Constant Factor and *Contract* (1980, Krzysztof Zanussi; Poland)

Fever (1980, Agnieszka Holland; Poland)

Mephisto (1981, István Szabó; Hungary)

Diary for My Children (1982, Márta Mészáros; Hungary)

Contest or *Orientation Course* (1983, Dan Piţa; Romania)

When Father Was Away on Business (1985, Emir Kusturica; former Yugoslavia)

My 20th Century (1988, Ildikó Enyedi; Hungary)

Time of the Gypsies (1989, Emir Kusturica; former Yugoslavia)

Interrogation (1990, Ryszard Bugajski; Poland). Completed 1982

Europa Europa (1991, Agnieszka Holland; Poland)

Tito and I (1992, Goran Markovic; former Yugoslavia)

Fetus (1993, Márta Mészáros; Hungary)

Before The Rain (1994, Milcho Manchevski; former Yugoslavia)

Satantango or *Satan's Tango* (1994, Béla Tarr; Hungary)

An Unforgettable Summer (1994, Lucian Pintilie; Romania)

Underground (1995, Emir Kusturica; former Yugoslavia)

Conspirators of Pleasure (1996, Jan Švankmajer; former Czechoslovakia)

Pretty Village, Pretty Flame (1996, Srdjan Dragojević; former Yugoslavia)

Cabaret Balkan or *The Powder Keg* (1998, Goran Paskaljević; former Yugoslavia)

Life As a Fatal Sexually Transmitted Disease (2000, Krzysztof Zanussi; Poland)

Werckmeister Harmonies (2000, Béla Tarr; Hungary)

L'Après-midi d'un tortionnaire (2001, Lucian Pintilie; Romania)

Kontroll or *Control* (2003, Nimród Antal; Hungary)

4 Months, 3 Weeks and 2 Days (2007, Cristian Mungiu; Romania)

Private Century (eight parts, 2007, Jan Šikl; former Czechoslovakia). Made for TV

Dogtooth (2009, Yorgos Lanthimos; Greece)

JAPAN, INDIA, CHINA, TAIWAN, HONG KONG, KOREA, AND VIETNAM

CHEN KAIGE (1952–   )

Yellow Earth (1984)

Big Parade (1985)

King of the Children (1987)

Life on a String (1991)

Farewell to My Concubine (1993). Shorter version, *Farewell, My Concubine*

The Emperor and the Assassin (1999). Completed 1998

Together (2002)

HOU HSIAO-HSIEN (1947–   )

A Summer at Grandpa's (1984)

A Time to Live and a Time to Die (1985)

Daughter of the Nile (1987)

Dust in the Wind (1987)

City of Sadness or *A City of Sadness* (1989)

Puppet Master or *The Puppetmaster* (1993)

Goodbye South, Goodbye (1996)

Flowers of Shanghai (1998)

Coffee Time or *Café Lumière* (2003)

Three Times (2005)

KON ICHIKAWA (1915–2008)

The Burmese Harp (1956)

Fires on the Plain (1959)

Odd Obsession or *The Key* (1959)

An Actor's Revenge (1963)

Tokyo Olympiad (1965)

The Makioka Sisters (1983)

IM KWON-TAEK (1936–   )

Genealogy (1978)

Mandala (1981)

Surrogate Mother (1986)

Ticket (1986)

Adada (1988)

The General's Son (1990)

Sop'yonje (1993)

Festival (1996)

Chunhyang (2000)
Chihwaseon or *Painted Fire* (2002)
Lower Class Life (2004)

AKIRA KUROSAWA (1910–98)
Drunken Angel (1948)
Stray Dog (1949)
Rashomon (1950)
Ikiru (*To Live*, 1952)
Seven Samurai (1954)
The Lower Depths (1957)
Throne of Blood (1957)
The Hidden Fortress (1958)
Yojimbo (1961)
High and Low (1963)
Red Beard (1965)
Dodes'ka-den (1970)
Dersu Uzala (1975)
Kagemusha or *Kagemusha, The Shadow Warrior* (1980)
Ran (*Chaos*, 1985)
Rhapsody in August (1991)
Madadayo (*Not Yet*, 1993)

ANG LEE (1954–   )
Pushing Hands (1992)
The Wedding Banquet (1993)
Eat Drink Man Woman (1994)
Sense and Sensibility (1995)
The Ice Storm (1997)
Crouching Tiger, Hidden Dragon (2000)
Brokeback Mountain (2005)
Lust, Caution (2007)

KENJI MIZOGUCHI (1898–1956)
Osaka Elegy (1936)
The Story of the Last Chrysanthemum (1939)
The 47 Ronin (two parts, 1941)
Utamaro and His Five Women (1946)
Women of the Night (1948)
The Life of Oharu (1952)
Ugetsu or *Ugetsu Monogatari* (1953)
Chikamatsu Monogatari (*A Story from Chikamatsu*, 1954)
Sansho the Bailiff (1954)
Street of Shame (1956)

MIKIO NARUSE (1905–69)
Street Without End (1934)
Mother (1952)
Floating Clouds (1955)

Autumn is Beginning (1960)
Flowing Night (1960)
Mother, Wife, Daughter (1960)
When a Woman Ascends the Stairs (1960)
As a Wife, As a Woman (1961)
Yearning (1963)

NAGISA OSHIMA (1932–   )
Cruel Story of Youth (1960)
Boy (1968)
Death by Hanging (1968)
Diary of a Shinjuku Thief (1969)
The Man Who Left His Will on Film (1970)
The Ceremony (1971)
In the Realm of the Senses (1976)
Merry Christmas, Mr. Lawrence (1983)
Gohatto (*Forbidden*, 2000)

YASUJIRO OZU (1903–63)
I Was Born, But . . . (1932)
Woman of Tokyo (1933)
A Story of Floating Weeds (1934)
The Brothers and Sisters of the Toda Family (1941)
There Was a Father (1942)
Late Spring (1949)
Early Summer (1951)
The Flavor of Green Tea over Rice (1952)
Tokyo Story (1953)
Early Spring (1956)
Floating Weeds (1959)
Ohayo (*Good Morning*, 1959)
Late Autumn (1960)
End of Summer (1961)
An Autumn Afternoon (1962)

SATYAJIT RAY (1921–92)
Pather Panchali (*Song of the Little Road*, 1955)
Aparajito (*The Unvanquished*, 1956)
The Music Room (*Jalsaghar*, 1958)
The World of Apu (*Apur Sansar*, 1959)
Devi (*The Goddess*, 1960)
Three Daughters (1961)
Kanchanjungha (1962)
Mahanagar (*The Big City*, 1963)
Charulata (*The Lonely Wife*, 1964)
Days and Nights in the Forest (*Aranyer Din Ratri*, 1970)
Distant Thunder (*Ashani Sanket*, 1973)
The Middleman (*Jana Aranya*, literally *The Jungle of Human Beings*, 1975)

The Chess Players (*Shatranj Ki Khilari*, 1977)
Ganashatru (*The Enemy of the People*, 1989)
Shakha Proshakha (*Branches of the Tree*, 1990)

WONG KAR WAI OR WONG KAR-WAI (1958–   )
The True Story of Ah Fei or *Days of Being Wild* (1990)
Ashes of Time (1994)
Chungking Express (1994)
Fallen Angels (1995)
Happy Together (1997)
In the Mood for Love (2000)
2046 (2004)
Ashes of Time Redux (2008)

ZHANG YIMOU (1950–   )
Red Sorghum (1988)
Ju Dou (1990). Co-director, Yang Fengliang
Raise the Red Lantern (1991)
The Story of Qiu Ju (1992)
To Live (1994)
Not One Less (1999)
The Road Home (2000). Completed 1999
Hero (2002)
House of Flying Daggers (2004)
Riding Alone for Thousands of Miles (2005)

ASIAN MISCELLANY
A Page of Madness or *Crazy Page* or *A Page out of Order* (1926, Teinosuke Kinugasa; Japan)
Gate of Hell (1953, Teinosuke Kinugasa; Japan)
Two Acres of Land (1953, Bimal Roy; India)
Godzilla (*Gojira*, 1954, Ishiro Honda; Japan). U.S. version, *Godzilla King of the Monsters!*, with new material by Terry Morse, 1956.
Rodan (1956, Ishiro Honda; Japan)
Mother India (1957, Mehboob Khan; India)
Human Condition (three parts, 1958–61, Masaki Kobayashi; Japan)
Chushingura (1962, Hiroshi Inagaki; Japan)
Harakiri (1962, Masaki Kobayashi; Japan)
Onibaba (1964, Kaneto Shindo; Japan)
Woman in the Dunes (1964, Hiroshi Teshigahara; Japan)
Kwaidan (1965, Masaki Kobayashi; Japan)
Shakespeare Wallah or *Shakespeare–Wallah* (1965, James Ivory; U.S./India)
The Pornographers (1966, Shohei Imamura; Japan)

One-Armed Swordsman (1967, Chang Cheh; Hong Kong)
Bhuvan Shome (1969, Mrinal Sen; India)
Double Suicide (1969, Masahiro Shinoda; Japan)
Uski Roti (*Daily Bread*, 1969, Mani Kaul; India)
Eros + Massacre (1970, Yoshishige Yoshida; Japan)
A History of Postwar Japan As Told by a Bar Hostess (1970, Shohei Imamura; Japan)
Fist of Fury or *The Chinese Connection* (1972, Lo Wei; Hong Kong)
Insiang (1976, Lino Brocka; Philippines)
The Rat Trap or *Rattrap* (1981, Adoor Gopalakrishnan; India)
The Ballad of Narayama (1983, Shohei Imamura; Japan)
The Ruins (1983, Mrinal Sen; India)
That Day, On the Beach (1983, Edward Yang; Taiwan)
Life (1984, Wu Tianming; China)
Horse Thief (1985, Tian Zhuangzhuang; China)
Peking Opera Blues (1986, Tsui Hark; Hong Kong)
A Chinese Ghost Story (1987, Ching Siu-tung; Hong Kong)
Old Well (1987, Wu Tianming; China)
Akira (1988, Katsuhiro Otomo; Japan)
Salaam Bombay! (1988, Mira Nair; India)
The Killer (1989, John Woo; Hong Kong)
Tetsuo (1989, Shinya Tsukamoto; Japan)
Boiling Point (1990, Takeshi Kitano; Japan)
Autumn Moon (1992, Clara Law; China)
Hard-Boiled (1992, John Woo; Hong Kong)
The Blue Kite (1993, Tian Zhuangzhuang; China)
The Bride with White Hair (1993, Ronny Yu; Hong Kong)
Drunken Fist II or *Drunken Master II* (1994, Liu Chia-Liang *a.k.a.* Lau Ka Leung; Hong Kong). Released in U.S. as *The Legend of Drunken Master* (2000)
Cyclo (*Xich Lo*, 1995, Tran Anh Hung; Vietnam)
Maborosi (1995, Hirokazu Kore-eda; Japan)
A Single Spark (1996, Park Kwang-Su; South Korea)
The Eel (1997, Shohei Imamura; Japan)
Hana-bi or *Fireworks* (1997, Takeshi Kitano; Japan)

Princess Mononoke (1997, Hayao Miyazaki; Japan)

After Life (1998, Hirokazu Kore-eda; Japan)

Ringu or *Ring* (1998, Hideo Nakata; Japan)

Audition and *Dead or Alive* (1999, Takashi Miike; Japan)

Yi Yi or *A One and a Two . . .* (2000, Edward Yang; Taiwan)

Spirited Away (2001, Hayao Miyazaki; Japan)

Zubeidaa (2001, Shyam Benegal; India)

Sympathy for Mr. Vengeance (2002, Park Chan-Wook; South Korea)

Old Boy or *Oldboy* (2003, Park Chan-Wook; South Korea)

Nobody Knows (2004, Hirokazu Kore-eda; Japan)

Water (2005, Deepa Mehta; Canada/India)

Blind Mountain (2007, Li Yang; China)

The Good the Bad the Weird or *The Good, the Bad, and the Weird* (2008, Kim Jee-Woon; South Korea)

Window (2009, Buddhadeb Dasgupta; India)

DVDs

SWEDEN AND DENMARK

The Celebration (1998, **Thomas Vinterberg**). Focus Features/Umvd. Marked "Dogme #1" on the cover.

Dreyer Box Set (1943–64, **Carl Theodor Dreyer**). Criterion Collection. Contains *Day of Wrath*, *Ordet*, and *Gertrud*; interviews with Dreyer and others; a biographical essay by Dreyer scholar Edvin Kau; and a documentary by Torben Skjødt Jensen, *Carl Th. Dreyer—My Métier*, with outtakes.

A Film Trilogy by Ingmar Bergman (1961–63, **Ingmar Bergman**). Criterion Collection. Contains *Through a Glass Darkly*, *Winter Light*, and *The Silence*, with discussions and essays by Bergman scholar Peter Cowie and others.

The Five Obstructions (see Chap. 1 list).

Häxan (1922, **Benjamin Christensen**). Criterion Collection. Contains the 1922 version **restored** by the Swedish Film Institute, running at 20 fps, with the original music and some outtakes; a gallery of "diabolical" images

and other sources Christensen consulted; a commentary by Danish-film expert Casper Tybjerg; and the 1968 recut version, *Witchcraft Through the Ages*, narrated by novelist William S. Burroughs.

The Ingmar Bergman Special Edition DVD Collection (1966–77, **Ingmar Bergman**). MGM Home Entertainment. Contains the uncensored, original Swedish versions—in their correct aspect ratios, with readable subtitles—of *Persona* (whose opening includes an erection, in case one needs a warning), *Hour of the Wolf*, *Shame*, and *The Passion of Anna*, as well as, for some reason, *The Serpent's Egg*. Also includes several interviews with Bergman; new, important interviews with stars **Bibi Andersson, Erland Josephson,** and **Liv Ullmann;** the original Swedish trailers; interpretive shorts and commentaries; and documentaries on Bergman, his island, and cinematographer **Sven Nykvist.**

Light Keeps Me Company (2000, **Carl-Gustaf Nykvist**). First Run Features. A documentary on **Sven Nykvist**'s life, thoughts, and methods. Includes interviews with **Bergman** and others.

Medea (1988, **Lars von Trier**; script by **Dreyer**). Facets Video. Compare with the Pasolini–Callas version (see Chap. 13 list) and von Trier's later films.

The Passion of Joan of Arc (see Chap. 10 list).

The Seventh Seal (1957, **Ingmar Bergman**). Criterion Collection. **Restored** from the camera negative; includes a **restoration demonstration,** an illustrated filmography, and a commentary by Bergman scholar Peter Cowie.

Vampyr (1932, **Carl Dreyer**). Criterion Collection. **Restored** German version. Includes the screenplay, a documentary on Dreyer's career, a 1958 radio program with Dreyer, and many other extras.

Wild Strawberries (1957, **Ingmar Bergman**). Criterion Collection. With a commentary by Peter Cowie and a documentary by Jörn Donner, *Ingmar Bergman on Life and Work*.

ENGLAND

*The **Alec Guinness** Collection.* Anchor Bay. Contains *Kind Hearts and Coronets*, *The Lavender Hill Mob*, *The Man in the White*

Suit, The Captain's Paradise, and *The Ladykillers.*

Billy Liar (1963, **John Schlesinger**). Criterion Collection. Includes commentary by Schlesinger and actors **Tom Courtenay** and **Julie Christie.**

Black Narcissus (1947, **Michael Powell** and **Emeric Pressburger**). Criterion Collection. The excellent commentary track is a conversation between Powell and **Martin Scorsese.**

The Edge of the World (1937, shot 1936; **Michael Powell**). Image Entertainment. Includes Powell's 1978 follow-up documentary, *Return to the Edge of the World*; a Powell short, *An Airman's Letter to His Mother*; the original press kit, in the DVD-ROM section; and commentaries by **Thelma Schoonmaker Powell,** film historian Ian Christie, and others.

A Hard Day's Night (1964, **Richard Lester**). Miramax Entertainment. Includes many interviews and, in the DVD-ROM section, the first draft of the script.

Henry V (1944, **Laurence Olivier**). Criterion Collection. Remastered from Technicolor elements, with information on the kings of England and a commentary by film historian Bruce Eder.

The Horse's Mouth (1958, **Ronald Neame**). Criterion Collection. Includes a **D. A. Pennebaker** short, *Daybreak Express,* and an interview with Neame.

Lawrence of Arabia (1962, **David Lean**). Columbia TriStar. Superbit Collection. **Restored.** Mastered at a higher **bit rate** than most DVDs, leaving no room for extras but giving a better image and single-frame capability. The only DVD that approaches the correct colors and the sharp, rich look of **Robert A. Harris**'s 70mm restoration (the basis of most DVD editions), this is the best available substitute for Criterion's out-of-print laserdisc.

Peeping Tom (1960, **Michael Powell**). Criterion Collection. Includes commentary by theorist Laura Mulvey and a documentary on screenwriter **Leo Marks.**

Richard III (1955, **Laurence Olivier**). Criterion Collection. **Restored;** includes a 1966 interview with Olivier.

The Ruling Class (1972, **Peter Medak**). Criterion Collection. The original, uncut version, with a commentary by Medak, star **Peter O'Toole,** and writer **Peter Barnes.**

The Servant and *Accident* are in the *Dirk Bogarde Collection* (see Chap. 12 list).

Slumdog Millionaire (2008, Danny Boyle). 20th Century Fox Home Entertainment. Includes a making-of documentary and deleted scenes.

The Third Man (1949, **Carol Reed**). Criterion Collection. **Digitally restored;** includes an episode from **Orson Welles**'s radio series, *The Lives of Harry Lime;* the Lux Radio Theatre adaptation of *The Third Man;* a reading of part of **Graham Greene**'s treatment; and **Joseph Cotten**'s alternate voice-over opening for the U.S. version.

The 39 Steps (see Chap. 11 list).

CENTRAL AND EASTERN EUROPE

Black Peter (1963, **Miloš Forman**). Facets Video.

Daisies (1966, **Věra Chytilová**). Facets Video. Includes letter about the banning of the film.

The Decalogue (1988, **Krzysztof Kieślowski**). Facets Video. Includes interviews with Kieślowski and writer **Krzysztof Piesiewicz,** a visit to the set, and more.

Everything for Sale (1969, **Andrzej Wajda**). Vanguard Cinema.

The Firemen's Ball (1967, **Miloš Forman**). Criterion Collection. Includes an interview with Forman and a look at the **digital transfer** process.

Knife in the Water (1957–62, **Roman Polanski**). Criterion Collection. Includes *Two Men and a Wardrobe, The Fat and the Lean,* and six other Polanski shorts; the feature, with new subtitles by Polanski; and an interview with Polanski and co-writer **Jerzy Skolimowski.**

Mephisto (1981, **István Szabó**). Anchor Bay. Includes a documentary featuring Szabó and actor **Klaus Maria Brandauer.**

The Red and the White (1967, **Miklós Jancsó**). Facets Video.

Satantango (1994, **Béla Tarr**). Facets Video. The director's cut, seven hours long, made for this video.

Stella (1955, **Michael Cacoyannis**). Fox Lorber. Includes filmographies.

Three Colors Trilogy (1993–94, **Krzysztof Kieślowski**). Buena Vista Home Video. Contains *Blue, White,* and *Red*.

Three War Films (1955–58, **Andrzej Wajda**). Criterion Collection. Contains *A Generation, Kanal,* and *Ashes and Diamonds* (the "War Trilogy"). Includes many interviews with and about Wajda, his film-school short, and more.

Ulysses' Gaze (1995, **Theo Angelopoulos**). Fox Lorber. *The Traveling Players* is available only on VHS (Facets Video).

JAPAN, INDIA, CHINA, TAIWAN, HONG KONG, KOREA, AND VIETNAM

Ashes of Time Redux (2008, **Wong Kar Wai**). Sony Pictures. *Ashes of Time* (1994), **restored** and recut.

Audition (1999, **Takashi Miike**). Chimera Entertainment. The unrated director's cut (avoid the poorly labeled R version), plus an interview with Miike and a partial commentary by him.

Beijing 2008 Complete Opening Ceremony (2008). NBC Universal. U.S. network coverage of **Zhang Yimou**'s opening ceremony for the Olympic Games.

Café Lumière (2003, **Hou Hsiao-hsien**). Wellspring. Includes an interview with Hou on Ozu and a French TV documentary, which also includes many interviews, on the transnational context of the film, its planning, and its production.

Chungking Express (1944, **Wong Kar Wai**). Criterion Collection. **Digitally restored** and newly translated.

Chunhyang (2000, **Im Kwon-Taek**). New Yorker Films.

Chushingura (1962, **Hiroshi Inagaki**). Image Entertainment. Compare with *The 47 Ronin*.

Crouching Tiger, Hidden Dragon (2000, **Ang Lee**). Columbia TriStar. Includes a commentary by Lee and writer–producer **James Schamus,** an interview with star **Michelle Yeoh**, and a making-of documentary.

Cyclo (1995, **Tran Anh Hung**). New Yorker Films.

The Emperor and the Assassin (1999, **Chen Kaige**). Columbia TriStar. Commentary by Chen. *Yellow Earth* is not on DVD, and *Farewell to My Concubine* is available only in the shortened version (Miramax).

Fireworks (1997, **Takeshi Kitano**). New Yorker Films. Includes a making-of documentary.

The 47 Ronin (1941, **Kenji Mizoguchi**). Image Entertainment. Contains both parts. Compare with *Chushingura*.

Harakiri (1962, **Masaki Kobayashi**). Criterion Collection. **Digitally restored.** Includes part of an interview with Kobayashi, an introduction by Donald Richie, and more.

Hero (2002, **Zhang Yimou**). Buena Vista Home Video. Includes storyboards, a short about the film, and a conversation between **Quentin Tarantino** and star **Jet Li.**

The Hidden Fortress (1958, **Akira Kurosawa**). Criterion Collection. **Digitally restored;** includes an interview with **George Lucas.**

Ikiru (1952, **Akira Kurosawa**). Criterion Collection. **Digitally restored;** commentary by film scholar Stephen Prince; includes documentaries on the film and on Kurosawa, one featuring several interviews with him.

In the Mood for Love (2000, **Wong Kar Wai**). Criterion Collection. Includes interviews with Wong, deleted scenes with his commentary, a making-of documentary, a short by Wong (*Hua Yang de Nian Hua*), biographies, a press conference, and the electronic press kit.

Pather Panchali (1955, **Satyajit Ray**). Columbia TriStar. The same company also offers *Aparajito* and *The World of Apu*.

The Pornographers (1966, **Shohei Imamura**). Criterion Collection.

Rashomon (1950, **Akira Kurosawa**). Criterion Collection. **Digitally restored.** Includes the original short stories, "In a Grove" and "Rashomon"; newly translated subtitles; and a commentary by the film historian who knew Kurosawa best, Donald Richie.

The Road Home (2000, **Zhang Yimou**). Columbia TriStar.

Seven Samurai (1954, **Akira Kurosawa**). Criterion Collection. Three-disc set. A **digitally remastered** edition of the

restored version, supplemented by several long documentaries and a booklet of essays.

A Story of Floating Weeds/Floating Weeds (1934 and 1959, **Yasujiro Ozu**). Criterion Collection. **Digitally restored,** with new subtitles; contains the silent and sound versions of the film. *A Story of Floating Weeds* has an exemplary commentary by Ozu scholar Donald Richie; *Floating Weeds* has an excellent commentary by film critic Roger Ebert.

Tokyo Story (1953, **Yasujiro Ozu**). Criterion Collection. **Digitally restored,** with new subtitles, a commentary by film scholar David Desser, a documentary on Ozu (*I Lived, But...*), and a short in which directors such as **Hou Hsiao-hsien** and **Wim Wenders** talk about him.

15

Hollywood Renaissance: 1964–76

It is not entirely certain when the old American movie reawakened as the new American cinema: *Bonnie and Clyde* (1967)? *Seconds* (1966)? *The Crazy-Quilt* (1966)? *The Pawnbroker* (1965)? *Dr. Strangelove* (1964)? *David and Lisa,* (1963)? *Lonely Are the Brave* (1962)? *To Kill a Mockingbird* (1962)? *The Hustler* (1961)? *Psycho* (1960)? Hollywood arose for its fifth era, its renaissance, gradually, just as it had slipped into its transitional fourth phase—quite unlike its sudden leaps into the second era of the feature film and the third era of synchronized sound.

All ten of these films (of which only *Bonnie and Clyde* is in color) contain seeds of the period's values: the offbeat antihero protagonists, the explicit treatment of sexual conflicts and psychological problems, the mixing of the comic and the serious, and the self-conscious use of cinematic effects (slow motion, quick cutting, stylized memory and dream sequences, and so forth).

Most of the films give evidence of the two clichés that critics used to describe films of the era: sex and violence. But films have always used sex, whether it was the sexiness of Griffith's Friendless One, of Valentino's Sheik, of Dietrich's veiled face in a key light, or of bare breasts and buttocks in a Paris apartment (*Last Tango in Paris*). And films have always been violent—whether it was violent death on a Civil War battlefield in *The Birth of a Nation*, the violent death of a hoodlum on the cathedral steps in *Little Caesar*, or the violent deaths on the highway in *Easy Rider* (1969, directed by Dennis Hopper). The question is not whether a movie includes sex and violence but how it uses them.

The graphic sex and violence of this "new" Hollywood cast a cynical look back on the genre films of the old Hollywood, suggesting that their assured and optimistic conclusions simplified the unresolved divisions in American life.

This new cinema in America evolved for several reasons. The first was a negative cause: The old, regular movie patrons now stayed home to watch television. The industry had to find new regular customers, not those who would go to the occasional movie that seemed special enough but those who would go every week—who still liked movies and considered them important to their social and leisure experience, and who appreciated the adult dialogue and treatment TV was forbidden to offer.

Second, the new cinema of Europe eventually converted American producers. The innovations of Godard, Truffaut, Fellini, and Antonioni, along with those of Kurosawa and Bergman, had already conquered the rising generation of young filmmakers and audiences at the art houses. Even more convincing, Truffaut and Fellini could make money. The years 1959–61 were as important as any to the future American film: the years of *Breathless, The 400 Blows, L'avventura, La dolce vita, Through a Glass Darkly,* and *Hiroshima mon amour.*

Third, though Hollywood repeatedly scoffed at the Underground Cinema, the underground crawled up to enjoy the last laugh. Not only did underground filmmakers succeed financially—for example, Andy Warhol, Robert Downey, and Brian De Palma—but the underground films conditioned a whole generation of young filmgoers

Fig. 15-1
Love, thrills, and bullets. Michael J. Pollard, Faye Dunaway, and Warren Beatty (right)
in **Bonnie and Clyde.**

(precisely those who became the steady customers for Hollywood films) to understand and accept innovations in cinematic form, visual stimulation, and elliptical construction.

Fourth, the film industry pushed its discovery of the elitism of the new film audience to its limits. Rather than attempting to make all the films for all the people, producers and exhibitors realized they must appeal to very special tastes. They made a few family pictures to serve that special need. They capitalized on the racial makeup of urban audiences by making "blaxploitation" cops-and-robbers films (Gordon Parks's *Shaft*, 1971, and its descendants). They made "sexploitation" films for that special audience—not "stag" shorts but full-length movies: *The Devil in Miss Jones* (1973), *Deep Throat* (1972), and *Boys in the Sand* (1971) were three of the most commercially successful pornographic features. (For a horrifying account of the making of *Deep Throat*, read Linda Lovelace's autobiography,

Ordeal.) There were even special cult films shown at midnight for late-night "film freaks" in the cities. Among the most popular of these cult films were Andy Warhol's *Sleep* (1963), Russ Meyer's *Faster, Pussycat! Kill! Kill!* (1966), Alexandro Jodorowsky's *El Topo* (1969), John Waters's *Pink Flamingos* (1971), Hal Ashby's *Harold and Maude* (1971), Jim Sharman's *The Rocky Horror Picture Show* (1975), and David Lynch's *Eraserhead* (1977). There were also old films that attracted cults (*Casablanca*) and cult films that never became "midnight movies."

In the same way, the American industry aimed its "art films" (those directed by Arthur Penn, Mike Nichols, and others) at the minority audience that liked such films. These films, however, found a wide audience and were precisely those that served as America's best examples of film art and the key representatives of its fifth era.

Finally, the values of these new American "art films" reflected the sexual and social values of American film audiences in the period. The American college student, the core of this audience, had discovered politics, drugs, and premarital sex, and protested against the covert and overt policies of the government as well as the racism, materialism, and hypocrisy of American society. The vision of reality on the screen did not entirely shape its audience; as in the 1930s, the screen still reflected the values of those who sat in front of it. Those values had changed.

Arthur Penn's *Bonnie and Clyde* was perhaps the first full statement of the new cinema's values; it was so popular that many of its daring innovations became conventions in the years that followed. In most cases, the protagonists of the films were social misfits, deviates, or outlaws; the villains were the legal, respectable defenders of society. The old bad guys became the good guys; the old good guys, the bad guys. The surprising element in *Bonnie and Clyde* (and *Easy Rider, Cool Hand Luke, The Wild Bunch, Butch Cassidy and the Sundance Kid, Thieves Like Us*, etc.) was not simply that the protagonists were criminals, for films had depicted their Little Caesars and Bonnie Parkers for decades. The surprise was that these new murderers were also charming, exciting, compassionate, and funny—and that the violence was much more graphic. The pursuers with badges were the cruel ones; even the pursuers without badges—as in *The Graduate* (1967, directed by Mike Nichols) and *Easy Rider*—had no sense of humor, of fair play, of love. The new obligatory ending was unhappy (*Joe*, 1970) or open (*Billy Jack*, 1971) rather than happily resolved (a rare exception among counterculture movies was Alan Myerson's *Steelyard Blues*, 1973).

The crucial thing about the new antihero heroes was not that they died violently, but that how they lived and what they stood for were validated. Even if evil regularly triumphed over goodness, rationality, and freedom, the American film was still essentially romantic and Manichean, just as it was in the 1920s and 1930s. There were still film characters who lived beautiful lives and others who lived vile ones; it was clear who the good guys were, even if they would have been called bad guys in the 1950s and even if they lost.

Rather than effacing the film's artfulness, as a Ford or Hawks intentionally did, the new directors threw in as many cinematic tricks as possible, which both intensified the film's moods and reminded the audience that it was watching a film. Slow motion, grainy filmstock, jump cutting, splitting the wide screen, self-conscious camerawork, mixtures of black and white and color were all standard tricks of the new trade. There was an emotional power in the visual assaults of the medium itself. And the flashes both forward and backward in time as well as into and out of a character's mental experience broke down the definitions and distinctions of time and space, of now and then, of reality and fantasy, of "proper" linear continuity.

The new films played as trickily with sound as they did with images. Gone was the old principle of studio scoring—to underscore a scene with music that increases the action's emotional impact without making the viewer aware of the music's existence. In the new films, there was little of this kind of background music. If there was to be music, it had to be either clearly motivated (playing on a radio or record player nearby) or deliberately artificial (a song on the soundtrack that existed specifically to be noticed and played either in harmony with or in counterpoint to the sequence's visuals). Coppola's *Apocalypse Now* (1979) starts with The Doors' "The End." In Haskell Wexler's *Medium Cool* (1969), the patriotic speeches and songs inside the Democratic Convention hall accompany the sounds of the riots in Grant Park. The soundtrack of Altman's *Thieves Like Us* (1974) is a compendium of 1930s radio broadcasts that sometimes comment ironically on the action (for example, an installment of *Gang Busters* during a bank robbery). Some films distorted sound purposely (for example, Coppola's *The Conversation*, 1974, whose subject is sound recording). Most of the new films used rock music heavily (the scores of Martin Scorsese's *Mean Streets* and George Lucas's *American Graffiti*, both 1973, were anthologies of highly relevant rock hits), for rock was the other artistic and social passion of the young audiences who supported the movies. Scorsese's soundtracks continued to feature period hits, rock and otherwise, to evoke and comment on the emotional and social worlds of his characters, notably in *GoodFellas* (1990).

Fewer films were shot on soundstages; directors preferred the authenticity of shooting on location. Whereas the old Hollywood style was devoted to eliminating the imperfections of reality—uneven lighting, unwanted noise—the new films required accident and imperfection for their visual style and human credibility. The lighting styles of Bergman's Sven Nykvist and of the New Wave cinematographers (Raoul Coutard, Nestor Almendros), who bounced light off the ceilings of rooms and caught it as it poured through windows, influenced a new generation of American cinematographers—Haskell Wexler, Gordon Willis, Vilmos Zsigmond, Robert Surtees, Lucien Ballard, Laszlo Kovacs, John Alonzo. Inside the old studios, the only light that poured through a window flowed from an electric pitcher.

The new American films were gladly influenced by French films, Italian films, Czech films, British films, underground and avant-garde films, and even rediscovered films (an old Hawks movie in Bogdanovich's *Targets*, 1968). Many of the new American films, like the new European films, depicted how actions *felt*, not just actions, so that character became more important than plot; they also tackled big issues, much as the Europeans did (whereas the 1980s and 1990s would be decades in which big issues were generally avoided).

However Europeanized the fifth American era had become, it still maintained its old inclination toward rigid genres and marketable cycles. Producers still felt safer with a formula that had succeeded before, and so a series of films about compassionate thieves followed *Bonnie and Clyde*, a series of ironic romantic comedies followed *The Graduate*, the chase scene in *Bullitt* was topped by the chase in *The French Connection*, and so forth. Despite their new experiential and stylistic commitments, the new films were descendants of the old genres: the western, the gangster, the *policier*, the screwball comedy, and the rest. The basic generic division in the new films was between city films and country films. Beyond these lay the road films (*Easy Rider*), the wilderness of horror (George Romero's *Night of the Living Dead*, 1968), and the world of fantasy (*Willy Wonka & the Chocolate Factory*, 1971, directed by Mel Stuart).

Many of the city films developed a thematic opposition between the unnaturalness and brutality of the city and the freedom and openness outside the city. (*Midnight Cowboy* is the story of a country mouse, played by Jon Voight, and a city mouse, played by Dustin Hoffman.) While the *noir* city films shove law and crime, promise and corruption up against one another in tempting proximity, the city films of the "new" Hollywood suggest a seething human hell, augmented by location shooting and gory "effects" makeup. The cities breed paranoid fantasies, whether the sounds of San Francisco (*The Conversation*) or the sights of New York viewed through a windshield—smoke, steam, and brimstone rising from the entrails of the city (Martin Scorsese's *Taxi Driver*, 1976). In the black comedy *Little Murders* (1971, written by Jules Feiffer and directed by Alan Arkin), New York is a city of snipers. And cities are where big business and the corrupt government plan—and get away with—their awesome conspiracies (Alan J. Pakula's *The Parallax View*, 1974). There were also paranoid glimpses of cities of the future (George Lucas's *THX-1138*, 1971; Richard Fleischer's *Soylent Green*, 1973).

Close cousins to the city films, thematically as well as geographically, were the suburb films—such as *The Graduate*, Paul Mazursky's *Bob & Carol & Ted & Alice* (1969), and Romero's *Dawn of the Dead* (1978, released 1979). If, compared with the densely packed older cities, these suburb–cities were clean, bright, and new, they were also rootless and soulless. They lacked a center—either geographical or moral.

The new "experiential" western—for example, Sam Peckinpah's *The Wild Bunch* (1969), George Roy Hill's *Butch Cassidy and the Sundance Kid* (1969), and Robert Altman's *McCabe & Mrs. Miller* (1971)—was more violent, sensual, and antiestablishment than earlier westerns. For the new films, the vast plains and deserts were (like the highways in road movies) the last outposts of the free spirit of America. Both *The Wild Bunch* and *Butch Cassidy* were set in an era when the Old West was crumbling, when the city's values were swallowing the country's. Like the hero of *Lonely Are the Brave*, the heroes of both films prefer to remain anachronisms rather than surrender to "decency" and the machine. The slow-motion sequences in these new westerns heightened and lyricized the moment of death.

The new gangster film mirrored the same basic generic division between past and present, city and country, rural criminals and urban

Fig. 15-2
Pike (William Holden) gets shot in Sam Peckinpah's masterpiece, The Wild Bunch.

criminals. The country-crime genre was essentially a subgenre of the new western. Whereas the protagonists of the western depended on their horses, the central figures of *Bonnie and Clyde*, *Thieves Like Us*, and Terrence Malick's *Badlands* (1973) used the automobile as their means of slicing through the country. In *Easy Rider* they used motorcycles; the open road was romantic and free, but sullied, and corruption and bigotry won in that movie's unexpected, violent ending.

If the upsetting death sequence was obligatory in the western and country-crime films, as well as many urban dramas, the assaultive chase was obligatory in the city-crime films. The essential technical tool of the city film was editing—rather than composition as in the country films—and a familiar subjective device was the violent rushing of the traveling or hand-held camera. Cops in the city-crime films (Peter Yates's *Bullitt*, 1968; William Friedkin's *The French Connection*, 1971; Don Siegel's *Dirty*

Harry, 1971) usually faced two sources of tension: within themselves (are they just doing their job or are they neurotically driven to violence and sadism?) and within their own departments (the pressures of politicians, bureaucrats, and incompetents). The *film noir* of the Transitional Era (for example, Lang's *The Big Heat*, 1953) was a truly transitional link between the detective films of the Studio Era in which the cop fought crime and of the new era in which a cop fought himself and cops fought each other (Lumet's *Serpico*, 1973, and *Prince of the City*, 1981). The new focus of the gangster city films was less on the push to the top and the inevitable fall (*Little Caesar* or *Scarface*) and more on the problems of living legitimately once the top had been reached (the conflict between the old life of crime and the new respectability in *The Godfather Part II*).

The most obvious link with the old Hollywood was the one "new" genre of the 1970s—what might be called the genre genre. These Postmodern films parodied the plots, conventions, and stars of Hollywood Past, usually by compiling a reflexive catalogue of Studio Era clichés—the Neil Simon–Robert Moore comedies (*Murder by Death*, 1976), Stanley Donen's *Movie Movie* (1978), some of the early Woody Allen films (*What's Up, Tiger Lily?*, 1966; *Take the Money and Run*, 1969; *Play It Again, Sam*, 1972, written by Allen but directed by Herbert Ross, as Allen's *What's New Pussycat*, 1965, had been directed by Clive Donner), and, of course, almost everything by Mel Brooks, the writer–director of *The Producers*, 1968; *Blazing Saddles*, 1974; *Young Frankenstein*, 1974; *Silent Movie*, 1976; and *High Anxiety*, 1977—and the producer of *The Elephant Man* (1980, directed by David Lynch).

If a single American film of the 1970s put all these themes together, it was *Chinatown* (1974). Like many of the most perceptive film dissections of American society—from Chaplin's to Lang's to Hitchcock's—*Chinatown* was not directed by an American. Roman Polanski— whose view of life, American or otherwise, stretched from the concentration camp where his mother died to Bel Air and the brutal Manson murder of Sharon Tate, Polanski's wife—directed the film from a masterful script by Robert Towne. The film explored American political and sexual corruption in a supposedly saner, cleaner social era of "wholesome values"—the 1930s of Frank Capra and the New Deal. While the 1930s films generally reaffirmed the myths of American purpose and destiny (after serious setbacks and struggle), *Chinatown* exposed the myths themselves as naïve falsehoods.

On its surface, *Chinatown* is a detective movie set in California—like the studios themselves and like the Dashiell Hammett and Raymond Chandler novels that the studios made into movies like John Huston's *The Maltese Falcon* and Howard Hawks's *The Big Sleep*. Huston himself appears in *Chinatown* as its master villain. Instead of traveling with Jake Gittes (Jack Nicholson) toward a successfully solved case, the film conducts him—much as *film noir* would—on a tortuous journey through a bewildering maze of murders and sordid sexual encounters to arrive at the core of moral corruption within American life itself. Polanski weds the country's "Watergate mood"—the suspicion

of invisible strands of corruption binding everyone in high places—to a Technicolor, Panavision world of beautiful images (shot by John Alonzo), which intensify the terrifying ugliness beneath an apparently beautiful surface. The American Dream is shown as a nightmare of power, lust, and money. In its paranoia, its many specific references to American film history and genres, its depiction of a modern city perverting the essential natural resource (water) of the Edenic garden, and its explicit sexual corruption (from mere adultery to layers of incest), *Chinatown* captures the mood of an entire era.

The period that began with the assassination of one president ended with the disgrace of another. The national mood of anger, doubt, and distrust understandably differed from the optimism, commitment, or vigilance of prewar, wartime, and postwar America. Not every American shared that mood, but the most vocal Americans against the war and in favor of civil rights—who marched on Washington in immense numbers and disrupted college campuses—were the ones who went to the movies. The American film business—much leaner than it had been a decade earlier—could afford to play a central role in this national debate.

Not coincidentally, the old Hollywood Production Code, which had always been a hypocritical compromise between the facts of life and the pressures of public opinion, came to an end as this era began. After several years of hedging, of making exceptions for prestige films like *Lolita* (1962), Lewis Gilbert's *Alfie* (1966), or *Who's Afraid of Virginia Woolf?* (1966), in 1968 the Motion Picture Association of America (MPAA, formerly the MPPDA), headed from 1966 to 2004 by Jack Valenti, finally replaced the PCA (Production Code Administration) with the CARA (Classification and Rating Administration). The new board— which, as a service to parents, *rated* the "level of maturity" a film assumed of its audience rather than prohibited certain kinds of material altogether—instituted four categories: originally, G (for all audiences), M (suggested for mature audiences—which became GP, then PG), R (restricted to audiences of 17 years and older, except when accompanied by a parent or guardian), and X (restricted to audiences of 18 and over). PG-13, a warning stronger than PG (parental guidance suggested) but weaker than R, was added in 1984; it identified films considered too violent or upsetting for children under 13 and "strongly cautioned" parents. In 1990, the NC-17 (no one under 17) rating replaced the X. In CARA's first 20 years, half of the nearly 9,000 features rated received an R, one third a PG.

While the new MPAA ratings system unleashed more explicit sexual talk and activity and a more open critical attack on society's norms than had ever been seen in American movies before, there was still plenty of uncertainty, bargaining, and hypocrisy. Who was to say what a 17-year-old did or should know? CARA repeatedly revised the guidelines and the age limits. There was considerable bargaining between film producers and CARA over what a film might cut to receive a more commercially "desirable" rating—just as there had always been bargaining between producers and the PCA over what a film could show or say.

In 1968 and 1969, many respected commercial films with sex and violence and antiestablishment messages received an X rating (*Midnight Cowboy, Medium Cool*). Originally conceived to describe films with serious adult content, the X quickly became a euphemism for "porn"—films that were never rated at all. Shot by producers and exhibited in theatres that never belonged to the MPAA, these films rated themselves as X to attract customers. By 1971, the debasement of the X had so shaken CARA's standards that a film like Altman's *McCabe & Mrs. Miller*, rated R, contains words, shots, and actions that could never have received an R rating in 1968; the same could be said of Friedkin's *The Exorcist*, which received its R in 1973. To distinguish rated films with adult content from unrated films brimming with prurient sex (or uncompromised violence, as in the case of *Dawn of the Dead*, which Romero had refused to re-edit for an R and had released unrated in 1979), the MPAA instituted the NC-17, hoping that certain films could be rated "adults only" without falling prey to the many ordinances that prohibited X-rated films from advertising in local papers or playing in local theatres. But many organizations simply boycotted NC-17 films. Another 1990 change in the ratings system was that CARA was required to give the reasons (sex, violence, language) a picture had been rated R. The industry's new rating system changed the shape of public debate about personal morality and public exhibition but certainly did not end the discussion.

Although the $10 million blockbusters with G ratings could make a lot of money (Robert Wise's *The Sound of Music*, 1965, starring Julie Andrews), they could also lose a lot of money (Robert Wise's *Star!*, 1968, starring Julie Andrews). The iconoclastic, risk-taking films, which cost near to or less than the 1970 industry average of $3 million, made consistent, if modest, profits. If smashing the idols of American myth and exposing the ideals of American genres made money, then movie executives could only assent to the evidence of their balance sheets.

American *Auteurs*

Like the film industries of Europe and Japan, the American cinema became more a directors' cinema, granting proven directors a higher measure of control over the scripting, production, and editing decisions, allowing them more freedom in selecting their projects, and giving them more credit for their contributions than the studios once did in the era of the moguls. A film was frequently labeled *by* or *of* its director (an attribution that the Writers Guild of America, West vigorously opposed for decades), whose name often appeared above or before the film's title. The American director became one of the film's stars, and it is significant that many 1970s directors were allowed to make films without any major star at all (*The Last Picture Show, Thieves Like Us, Days of Heaven*), an unheard-of practice for major studio films.

When François Truffaut in France and Andrew Sarris in America developed the "*auteur* theory" (or *auteur* policy), they did so as a means of distinguishing directorial individuality in the Studio Era, since individuality was often buried beneath the decisions of producers and the scripts of the Story Department. The new American *auteurs* were film authors in the full sense of a Griffith, Gance, Dreyer, Ford, Hitchcock, Godard, Fellini, Bergman, or Kurosawa—the ones who control the responsibility for the entire project so that their own personal visions and visual styles get recorded on film.

John Cassavetes

John Cassavetes got his start in television, but as an actor. Like Orson Welles, he acted in features (*Rosemary's Baby*, *The Dirty Dozen*, *The Fury*) primarily to pay for the films he directed, the most significant of which are *Shadows* (1959, improvised version shown 1958), *Faces* (1968), *Husbands* (1970), *Minnie and Moskowitz* (1971), *A Woman Under the Influence* (1973, released 1974), *The Killing of a Chinese Bookie* (1976, recut 1978), *Opening Night* (1978), and *Love Streams* (1984). His films reveal a unique fusion—of narrative cinema, candidly documentary shooting styles, confessional explorations of character, and an unswerving commitment to filmmaking as personal statement—that remained fresh, experimental, honest, and intense throughout his career (he died in 1989). As a director, he was an actor working with actors, trying to get them to reveal the essential being and unstylized behavior of their characters; as a writer, he strove to present the ways people really talk and behave, charting a fine line between the too tightly organized and the pointlessly rambling; as a complete filmmaker, he sought an invisible style that would not be arty, pretty, or in the way. His wife, Gena Rowlands, and his friends Seymour Cassel, Peter Falk, and Ben Gazzara gave their finest performances in his films, probing their own, their characters', and Cassavetes's vital energies and personal mysteries in an atmosphere that was kept utterly free of artificiality, phoniness, and formulaic solutions.

As an independent who freelanced on the fringes of the studio system, Cassavetes wrote, produced, directed, distributed, and sometimes acted in his films, all of which conceptualize experience in terms of the interactions of a tightly knit cluster of individuals. One acts out one's destiny in front of an audience in Cassavetes's work, whether that be a paying audience and a metaphoric family (*The Killing of a Chinese Bookie*), a literal family (*A Woman Under the Influence*), or people linked by a dynamic system of intimate relationships (*Faces*). However deeply personal its sources, experience is public and social. Cassavetes's characters function within a force field of social "influences" that can never be escaped or avoided. The only course of survival is to master these ever-shifting, often fiercely predatory forces; the

alternatives are misery and destruction. As his characters maneuver for position, power, and self-knowledge within volatile networks of mutual responsibility, Cassavetes reveals just how complex living can be. The intricacy of Cassavetes's depiction of his characters' negotiations with each other—along with the deliberately unpolished quality of the shooting and editing—give his scenes the appearance of having been improvised, but all these hesitations, ellipses, and obliquities of expression were actually scripted and rehearsed in advance.

Although the relentless pressures and the fierce conflicts in his work gave Cassavetes the reputation of being a pessimist, he repeatedly denied the accusation that his films were negative or despairing. He argued that he was as idealistic as Capra (who, with Dreyer, was among his favorite filmmakers), that he was celebrating his characters' heroic capacities of creative response to the dangers and problems they confront.

That heroic creative response is one Cassavetes shared with his characters. A Hollywood outsider fighting the studios, distribution systems, and publicity machinery for his vision of the feature film not as a commercial product but as a personal expression, this fiercely independent, embattled filmmaker was not discouraged but challenged and energized by the forces that sought to destroy or dismiss his uniquely demanding, historically significant work.

Woody Allen

Woody Allen is the American comic *auteur* who is most conscious of the older American comic-film tradition that he inherits. His glasses create a "glasses character" who resembles Harold Lloyd, his physical clumsiness and unattractiveness parallel Harry Langdon's, and his dryly quiet, offbeat comic ironies suggest the flavor of Buster Keaton and the wit of Groucho Marx. But more than anyone else, Allen resembles Chaplin as an observer and chronicler of the social scene. Although his characters wear different names (Fielding Mellish in *Bananas*, 1971; Miles Monroe in *Sleeper*, 1973; Boris Grushenko in *Love and Death*, 1975; Alvy Singer in *Annie Hall*, 1977), a device that parallels Keaton's different names and costumes, Woody Allen's comic persona is a

Fig. 15-3
Gena Rowlands and John Marley in Faces.

single, familiar, established being, like Charlie
(the British tramp), who wanders across the landscape of modern urban life, contrasting that persona with the less observant, less sensitive—and
probably married and employed—characters who
surround him. One might call Woody Allen's entire *oeuvre* "Modern Times," and if the problem
for Allen's city dwellers has shifted from the
external one of finding a job and founding a home
to the internal one of feeling secure enough to
survive between appointments with the analyst,
that shift is symptomatic of almost seven decades
of change in American life. Like Charlie, Woody
(the Jewish *schlemiel*) is out of tune and out of
step with the society that threatens and excludes
him but that he wants to join and comically reflects.

Allen's cinematic technique in his earliest films
was, like that of Mack Sennett, truly flip—in two
senses of the term. First, it was casual and flip-
pant, taking nothing as sacred (racial and religious

stereotypes, political philosophies, politicians,
intellectuals, revolutions, conformity, cultural
crazes, sexuality, psychology), especially the making of the movie itself. He was also flip in that he
leapt from gag to gag, often wearing out the audience (and his ideas) before the end of the film.
But Allen's three late-1970s films (*Annie Hall*;
Interiors, 1978; *Manhattan*, 1979) show far more
care and consciousness of cinematic style and
"art"—possibly because all three were shot by
Gordon Willis (cinematographer of the *Godfather*
films), the most distinguished cinematographer
with whom Allen had yet collaborated.

But it is with *Love and Death* that Allen's
movies became increasingly reflexive, committed to exploring the condition of comic movies
more than his own fixed comic persona—a commitment taken to its greatest richness in *Annie
Hall*, his most reflexive movie. *Love and Death*
alluded to Soviet cinema—from Eisenstein's
images to Prokofiev's film scores—as often as

Fig. 15-4
New American archetypes: the arty Gentile kook and the neurotic Jewish schlepp (Diane Keaton and Woody Allen in **Annie Hall***).*

to 19th-century Russian fiction; it reimagined Russian history in the terms of Russian art, as well as in the personal terms of Allen's comedic mythology. *Stardust Memories* (1980), like Fellini's *8½*, which it deliberately echoes, shows the way a popular artist can be trapped by his own success and the expectations of fans and critics. *A Midsummer Night's Sex Comedy* (1982) combines Shakespeare's *A Midsummer Night's Dream* and Bergman's *Smiles of a Summer Night*, linked by midsummer sexuality, the confusions of lust-blinded lovers, and the magic of cinema itself—as symbolized by the inventor Allen's "spiritball," capable of projecting images from air and light. Thanks to Gordon Willis's hard work, inserting Woody's image into old film clips and making new footage look old, *Zelig* (1983) is virtually an entire movie in the style of *Citizen Kane*'s newsreel—an ironic examination of the way American hype converts anonymous nonentities into media superstars. *Broadway Danny Rose* (1984), one of the best in this cluster of pictures, accomplishes the unlikely task of dumping a Jewish *schlemiel* into a gangster film with a deli-*vérité* frame.

The Purple Rose of Cairo (1985) contrasts the realities of Depression America with the escapist joy of Depression Hollywood's films, symbolized by Allen's contrast of realist color cinematography with dreamlike black and white. Like *Broadway Danny Rose*, some of his best later films are nostalgic and engaging looks at show business (*Radio Days*, 1987; *Bullets Over Broadway*, 1994) or formal experiments (*Everyone Says I Love You*, 1996, a Postmodern musical with actors who can't sing but do anyway: "the musical" with one element systematically altered), but the major theme of his work since *Annie Hall* has continued to be the nature of contemporary intimate relationships (*Manhattan; Hannah and Her Sisters*, 1986; *Crimes and Misdemeanors*, 1989; *Husbands and Wives*, 1992; *Mighty Aphrodite*, 1995; *Match Point*, 2005; *Vicky Cristina Barcelona*, 2008), with an emphasis on the problems of authenticity and fallibility. Many of his comedies of manners are little romantic tragedies that follow the forms or rules of comedy.

Hannah and Her Sisters—its title lifted from Thomas Mann's *Joseph and His Brothers*—starred Allen, Mia Farrow, Barbara Hershey, Max von Sydow, and others in an intricately plotted examination of love and marriage, guilt and personal growth. But Allen's most complex and troubling film since *Manhattan* was *Crimes and Misdemeanors*. Although *Manhattan* ends by urging Woody to learn to have a little faith in people, *Hannah* and *Crimes* make it clear that few people, including one's most intimate friends and lovers, deserve the honor.

The question raised in *Crimes* is whether God sees the evil that goes on in the world and does anything about it. The villains are a superficial media star (Alan Alda) who leads a charmed life and gets everything and everybody he wants, and an eye doctor (Martin Landau) who gets away with adultery and murder. Contrasted with them both is Woody, who would like to be as famous as Alda and who has an adulterous affair—but the woman (Farrow) ends up with Alda, and Woody's desires and failings become the misdemeanors that we compare with Landau's crimes. Landau suffers from the guilt he entirely deserves; he unburdens himself to a rabbi (Sam Waterston—who is going blind but sees ethical problems clearly, in contrast to the confused eye doctor) and worries for months—until he simply stops worrying. It appears that the good and evil in the world are neither rewarded nor punished appropriately. But at the very end, with Landau, Farrow, and Alda enjoying their lives and Woody trying to make sense of his own, Allen the writer–director gives us a powerful image: the now blind rabbi dancing at a family wedding. With that image of ethical continuity, of acceptance, and of personal strength, Allen arrived at last at a profundity that would have pleased Chaplin.

Robert Altman

Robert Altman made 15 feature films in the 1970s alone.

Altman's work comes in two narrative sizes. The first is a small, close study of people who lead bizarre lives or are possessed by their dreams—the boy who wants to become a bird and fly in *Brewster McCloud* (1970), the hiply updated Philip Marlowe in *The Long Goodbye* (1973), the thieves who want to rob enough banks to settle down to respectable lives in *Thieves Like Us*, the possessed gambler–friends of *California Split* (1974), Nixon in a room (*Secret Honor*, 1984).

The second Altman narrative structure requires a much larger canvas. It is a broad study of a particular American institution, built from a great number of interwoven characters, adding up to a cross-sectional view of American life. *MASH* (1970), Altman's first major success, used the sexy, funny, gory activities of a group of American medics in Korea to examine (at the height of the Vietnam crisis) American attitudes toward war, particularly wars against soldiers of other races in distant parts of the world; the script was by Ring Lardner, Jr., one of the Hollywood Ten. *MASH* led to a hit TV series, *M*A*S*H*, and to more advanced experiments in complex film soundtracks. *Nashville* (1975), probably Altman's most solid and respected film, used the American country-and-western recording industry—and all the people it touched or who wanted to be touched by it—to investigate American political, sexual, and economic structures, as well as the American dreams of fame and success. *Buffalo Bill and the Indians, or Sitting Bull's History Lesson* (1976), one of Altman's more pretentious films (the worst is *Quintet*, 1979), used the Wild

West show to examine the rape of the American continent and the debasement of the pioneer spirit. And *A Wedding* (1978) used a suburban upper-middle-class wedding ceremony to examine the relationship of love and lucre in contemporary life.

One of Altman's consistent strengths is the compelling spontaneous authenticity of the moments of human interaction. Altman works improvisationally with his actors, and the scenes they build together (between Donald Sutherland and Elliott Gould in *MASH*, Julie Christie and Warren Beatty in *McCabe & Mrs. Miller*, Gould and Sterling Hayden in *The Long Goodbye*, Keith Carradine and Shelley Duvall in *Thieves Like Us*, Gould and George Segal in *California Split*, Barbara Harris or Lily Tomlin and everybody else in *Nashville*) are encounters with acting that feels like life. That remains true throughout his career; the acting and the rhythm of events are assured and authentic all the way to *A Prairie Home Companion* (2006), the last film he released before his death in 2006.

The second Altman strength is his perceptive scrutiny of American social institutions, which he explores with haunting and startlingly memorable images. *Brewster McCloud* is dominated by images of the bare, sterile Astrodome. Fleeting but repetitive images are woven like recurring musical motifs through the impressionistically constructed narratives of *Images* (1972) and *Three Women* (1977). The brilliance of Altman's

Fig. 15-5
McCabe & Mrs. Miller: *no idealized civilization in this wilderness. The dirty frontier town of Presbyterian Church, blanketed by perpetual snow, rain, and mud—its church spire barely visible in the background.*

perceptive, evocative imagery frequently overcomes the dreamlike meanderings of his weaker narratives. But there certainly are Altman films whose meandering cannot be redeemed (*Health*, 1979) and whose ideas are superficial (*Prêt-à-Porter*, 1994, also called *Ready to Wear*).

Consistent with the spirit of the era, Altman's work attacked the myths of American life as articulated in the genres of American movies. *McCabe & Mrs. Miller* does to the western what *The Long Goodbye* does to the detective film: explodes its assumptions and picks up only a few of the pieces. In this ragged frontier town, ironically named Presbyterian Church, there is no mythic showdown between good and evil in the glaring light of high noon. The "good guy," McCabe, is a drunken profiteer from gambling and prostitution who shoots his assailants in the back. The sun almost never shines in this muddy town; the rain or snow almost never stops. The "bad guys" are not desperadoes but methodical killers hired by the mining company that first tries to buy McCabe out but finds it easier to kill him. The "dance-hall girls" are not euphemisms but whores, plain and simple, and their madam, Mrs. Miller, reveals no heart of gold when trouble comes but retreats into her opium haze.

Despite the town's name, its church, that great icon of civilization in John Ford westerns, is only half-built (the film's pre-release title was *The Presbyterian Church Wager*). Its major purpose in the film is to catch fire and distract the town's citizens from the real battle between McCabe and the hired killers—just as western movies, Altman perhaps implies, distracted American citizens from political realities with mythic façades.

After the mid-1970s and the passing of that era's attack on movie myth, Altman found it increasingly difficult to finance projects and please audiences. In the 1980s, he turned to theatre (where he had never previously worked), staging productions and then filming them cheaply, sometimes using television equipment and techniques (*Come Back to the Five and Dime, Jimmy Dean, Jimmy Dean*, 1982; *Streamers*, 1983; *Secret Honor*). His most ambitious and disturbing films of this period—*Jimmy Dean, Fool for Love* (1985, written for the screen by playwright Sam Shepard), and *Vincent & Theo* (1990, the story of the brothers Van Gogh)—attracted

critics and audiences but still failed to convince producers that Altman could be trusted to turn out a commercially viable project. During this period Altman lost several assignments when he told studio heads that he intended to make an Altman film rather than, for example, an MGM film. But in 1992 he made a genuine comeback with *The Player*, a relentless satire of the Hollywood food chain. His next picture was *Short Cuts* (1993), a long ensemble piece set in Los Angeles. His later works ranged, as usual, from the awful (*Prêt-à-Porter*) to the artful (*Gosford Park*, 2001) to the brilliantly comic and insightful (*A Prairie Home Companion*).

Francis Ford Coppola

If Robert Altman was a foe of movie myth and the industry during the 1970s, Francis Ford Coppola was central to the American film industry in this period. Coppola is less a film director than an all-around man of the movies. He began as an assistant to Roger Corman—where he learned to cut, dub, write, and direct films. He has written scripts for other directors (notably the Oscar-winning *Patton*, 1970, for Franklin Schaffner, co-written by Edmund H. North), and he has become a producer or co-producer of others' films—whether for a slightly younger generation of American directors (George Lucas, Carroll Ballard), an established generation of non-American directors (Kurosawa, Wim Wenders), or the forgotten masterpiece of a silent director (Abel Gance's *Napoléon*). He founded his own independent company, American Zoetrope. More than anything else, Coppola is committed to the cinema—to its past and its future, its genres and its possibilities. He might be thought of as a combination of D. W. Griffith and Thomas Ince.

Coppola's films tend to be either big commercial epics (*Finian's Rainbow*, 1968; *The Godfather*, 1972; *The Godfather Part II*, 1974; *Apocalypse Now*, begun in 1976 and finally released in 1979; *The Cotton Club*, 1984; *The Godfather Part III*, 1990) or smaller, more offbeat style pieces (*You're a Big Boy Now*, 1966; *The Rain People*, 1969; *The Conversation*, 1974; *One from the heart*, 1982—spelled like an Italian film title, one way Coppola announced that this film did come from his heart; *The Outsiders*, 1983; *Rumble Fish*, 1983; *Gardens of Stone*, 1987; *Youth Without Youth*, 2007; *Tetro*, 2009).

The Conversation, with its clever use of sound as both the central subject and the dominant stylistic device of the film, with its furtive *cinéma vérité* sequences shot in Union Square that are an exact visual equivalent of the sound-recording process, with its effective settings (the modern, barren, absolutely impersonal office building; the matter-of-fact detail of the commercial exposition displaying the newest products for snooping and bugging), is the most profound and disturbing of his "smaller" films as well as the most highly respected. Like the *Godfather* films that came just before and after it—the greatest of his "big" movies—*The Conversation* is morally intense and intellectually solid. One might see the film's theme as the clash between a person's craft and conscience, the pure devotion to artisanship as opposed to the moral responsibilities of engaging in any business that affects the lives of other people.

The first two parts of *The Godfather*, adapted from Mario Puzo's bestselling novel, constitute a monumental American epic about the conflict between doing business and living according to meaningful values—a conflict built into the very familial and economic structure of American society. *The Godfather* opens with a wedding—a family celebration of fertility, union, and the future—and it ends just after the bride (Talia Shire) has become a widow. Vito Corleone (Marlon Brando) spends his time not outdoors, in the bright and open sunlight, but in his dark cave-like office, where he does business with his wedding guests. The negotiations indoors represent the dark underside of the brightly visible activity outdoors; for Coppola, every American business has this dark underside. As an Italian American, Coppola is terribly conscious of the suspicion that all Italian and Sicilian immigrant families are branches of the illegitimate Mafia tree. Instead, Coppola argues that no American and no American business, of whatever ethnic extraction, can escape the conflict between business dealings and personal values. The Mafia is not a disease within American life; it is a symptom of American life itself.

The Godfather Part II extends the examination historically into both past and future—an epic chronicle of achievement and degradation, the dissolution of the American Dream that brought immigrants to the United States in the

Fig. 15-6
The Godfather: *the public dance, outdoors, in the sunlight. Family ceremony in contrast to the dark interior of family business (Marlon Brando, Talia Shire, and guests).*

first place. The temporal leaps in Coppola's narrative—late-19th-century Sicily, the arrival of immigrants at Ellis Island, life in New York's Little Italy in the 1910s and 1920s, Batista's corrupt Cuba of the 1950s, Las Vegas of the 1960s—produce a political conversation between the simple hopes of the past and the complex corruption of the present, as the stories of Vito's and Michael's careers are cross-cut. Like the Ricos and Tony Camontes of Hollywood Past, Michael Corleone (Al Pacino) accumulates wealth and power at the expense of losing everyone close to him—associates, friends, wife, children, brother. Unlike those earlier gangsters, Michael himself does not lose his life but remains—a lonely, tragic, coldly powerful head of a corporation of crime.

The Godfather Part II, widely considered the best sequel ever made, is so different in style and structure that it and *The Godfather* form a genuine historical dialectic. Although no Marxist,

Coppola's dialectical method within and between the two films suggests a historical analysis of the assumptions of Old and New World capitalism and is a vivid way to dramatize the rise and fall of the family and all it stands for. *The Godfather Part II* is the most ambitiously constructed parallel montage since *Intolerance*. It may also reveal the depth of character and the tragic paradoxes of power more effectively—and formally—than any film since *Citizen Kane*.

Paramount was determined from the start that *The Godfather Part III* would have a linear narrative, as *The Godfather* did, rather than pursue the bold cross-cutting of *The Godfather Part II*. Even though both films had won the Oscar for Best Picture (an unprecedented achievement), the studio felt that *Part II* was confusing. What Coppola and Puzo (who co-wrote all three scripts) wanted *Part III* to do was give Michael an opportunity to redeem himself spiritually, to suffer as he had made others suffer. In *Part III*,

then, Michael completes his project of shifting all the family's business interests to legitimate activities—but everywhere he turns, even the Vatican, he encounters corruption and more enemies. After confessing his sins to an insightful cardinal, Michael asks God for an opportunity to atone for killing his brother (Fredo, at the end of *Part II*—the most important of his sins, since it was against the family), and he gets it: Michael loses his daughter, who is shot to death right in front of him. His silent scream as he holds her body is the beginning of his penance. While not a complete betrayal of the first two parts, *The Godfather Part III* is nowhere near them in power and range.

Coppola's Vietnam epic, *Apocalypse Now*, has a stunning surround soundtrack, many unforgettable sequences, and a muddled ending. Coppola's foe is again the system itself, the military mentality that produces a Kurtz (Brando), insane with power; a Willard (Martin Sheen),

Fig. 15-7
Apocalypse Now: *the grotesque juxtaposition of surfboards and napalm.*

who must search for Kurtz by becoming Kurtz; and a Kilgore (Robert Duvall), who can make little distinction between the fun of surfboarding and the fun of napalming. Coppola's metaphoric journey upriver—adapted from Joseph Conrad's *Heart of Darkness*—is dominated by powerful images: Playboy bunnies entertaining the troops (deliberately reminiscent of those Bob Hope GI shows), the psychedelic nighttime carnival in which Willard wanders through an eerie wasteland of stoned soldiers, the collection of severed human heads that decorates Kurtz's camp, and many more. In 2000, Coppola and Walter Murch, the great sound designer and editor, recut and expanded the film into *Apocalypse Now Redux* (released 2001), adding scenes and experimenting with a rhythm that tried to make the long journey and the climactic encounter with Kurtz work even better. Still, many believe that the very first version of *Apocalypse Now*, the one shown without titles at Cannes and in a few big-city previews, was the most emotionally and cinematically powerful of all; it ended without an attack sequence.

Coppola's musicals (*Finian's Rainbow, One from the heart, The Cotton Club*) are stylistic exercises that explore the central paradoxes of the musical as a genre—the relation of convention to credibility, stylization to reality, number to story, and entertainment to social commentary. In these films, Coppola sacrifices his characters and their actions for intrusive style: references to a trunkful of other movies in *Finian's Rainbow;* breakthrough experiments in electronic cinema (see Chapter 18), but with more decor than drive, in *One from the heart;* another trunkful of references in *The Cotton Club*. Unfortunately, these musicals have at times (despite that title) very little heart—the ultimate element that gives a musical its artistic sense. *Bram Stoker's Dracula* (1992—and not a faithful adaptation of the novel, despite its title) has an analogous problem: It is a horror film that is not scary—drenched in romantic imagery, overwhelmed by style and getting nowhere, and sunk by a ridiculous ending. But when Coppola's romantic energy and grand imagination are focused by a compelling subject, as they were in his four great films of the 1970s—*The Godfather, The Conversation, The Godfather Part II,* and *Apocalypse Now*—his mastery of style is beyond challenge.

Martin Scorsese

Martin Scorsese brings a tense urban sensibility and a vision of spiritually charged moral conflict to the Italian-American film. An admirer of filmmakers as different as Cassavetes and Powell, Scorsese puts his characters through explosive scenes that have the flavor of improvisation and chaos but are profoundly determined. Scorsese seems to succeed most with carefully textured psychological portraits of people who are entangled in their detailed social environments—New York's Little Italy (*Mean Streets*, 1973), a diner in the American Southwest (*Alice Doesn't Live Here Anymore*, 1974), New York street life (*Taxi Driver*, 1976; *Bringing Out the Dead*, 1999), late-19th-century high society (*The Age of Innocence*, 1993), mid-19th-century slums (*Gangs of New York*, 2002), 1920s and 1930s Hollywood (*The Aviator*, 2004). *Raging Bull* (1980) was an interpretive biography of boxer Jake La Motta, but it went much deeper. Combining Italian Neorealism and the visual style of 1950s New York films (set in that period, shot primarily in black and white), *Raging Bull* related the violence of boxing to sexual violence in general, as well as to the limits of theater and the beginnings of religion.

As fast and violent as Scorsese's films often are, they are also intensely meditative; many also have thoughtful voice-over narrators. He moves the camera with more zest and authority than any American now making movies. He is scrupulously attentive to technical quality and wildly excited about the work of classic directors like Michael Powell—or Lean, Rossellini, Welles, Bresson, Hawks, Hitchcock, Cassavetes—because this is one director who knows film history and loves watching movies as well as making them. The visceral editing (often by Thelma Schoonmaker), the evocative music (not only the carefully selected popular hits, but also the original scores: Bernard Herrmann composed the music for *Taxi Driver* shortly before his death), the state-of-the-art soundtracks, and beyond all that the ironies and depths of Scorsese's films have vaulted him to the first rank of American directors. As a professional and as an artist, he is the most highly respected director of his generation.

"I'm God's lonely man," says Travis Bickle (Robert De Niro), the psychopathic taxi driver who wants to cleanse the world of sin—and many of Scorsese's central characters are isolated (often within the limits of an obsession, whether it be an idea, a desire, or a view of the world) and do think about God. At the beginning of *Mean Streets*, Charlie (Harvey Keitel) observes, voice-over, "You don't make up for your sins in church. You do it in the streets; you do it at home." Charlie would like to do penance for his sins on his own, in his own terms, with actions rather than prayers. For a character like Jake La Motta (De Niro) in *Raging Bull*, punishing himself and impulsively, blindly seeking redemption might mean screaming at and fighting with everyone he loves or getting punched to a pulp in the ring and destroyed through all his mistakes. In *The Color of Money* (1986, the sequel to *The Hustler*), Fast Eddie Felson (Paul Newman) has to face himself, find himself, and in fact redeem himself not before a conventional altar, but on the spiritual and profane battleground of a pool table.

Most of Scorsese's pictures are as complexly unsettling as *Raging Bull*, where we watch a man stupidly wreck his life, or *Taxi Driver*, where we share the meditations and worldview of an oddly innocent but genuinely crazy and violent man as he prepares a private apocalypse—and both La Motta and Bickle are characters we cannot shake, scary mysteries whose solution is emotional.

The King of Comedy (1983) transfers the obsessiveness of *Taxi Driver* to the world of entertainment (*Raging Bull* was already there; at one point Scorsese cuts from the line "That's entertainment!" to a loud, bloody smash to the face): Rupert Pupkin (De Niro), whose single-minded desire to appear on a talk show leads him to kidnap its host (Jerry Lewis), becomes a celebrity with his own show when he gets out of prison—if one takes the ending literally. *After Hours* (1985) is a black comedy about a night in Manhattan, a night full of promise during which everything goes wrong; the movie doesn't let up.

Fig. 15-8
Mean Streets: *Charlie (Harvey Keitel) in church, crossing himself before the lighted candles and thinking of "the pain of Hell," the burning heat "from a lighted match increased a million times. Infinite."*

GoodFellas (1990), the true story of a boy (Ray Liotta) who grew up to join the "wiseguys"—the friendly brotherhood of criminals who ran his neighborhood—and thought it was great until some of the crazy murderousness of his buddies (Joe Pesci, Robert De Niro) got out of hand, is Scorsese's return to the world of *Mean Streets*, this time with the matured skills of a world-class filmmaker. Highly charged, fast paced, full of sudden violence, and very funny, its tones and rhythms masterfully varied and controlled, *GoodFellas* presents the work and home life of its gangsters in a realistic, understated manner (unlike the romanticized *Godfather*)—at 100 miles an hour and changing direction without warning. *GoodFellas*, *The Age of Innocence* (faithfully adapted from the novel by Edith Wharton), and *The Departed* (2006, a cops-and-gangsters picture—based on a 2002 film from Hong Kong: Wai Keung Lau and Siu Fai Mak's *Infernal Affairs*—that reaches almost Jacobean levels of darkness and betrayal) reveal the absolute stylistic control and the emotional range of the films of his maturity.

The great question in the majority of Scorsese's films is whether this is a world in which one can attain salvation; it is assumed that one cannot be saved by the church. When Scorsese turned at last to his long-delayed adaptation of Nikos Kazantzakis's *The Last Temptation of Christ* (1988; it took ten years to find a studio that would not be intimidated by Fundamentalist protests), he showed that even Jesus might have had trouble finding salvation, that even he might have felt that his destiny was bound up with the entanglements of this world—and that when Jesus accepted his true destiny, which was to be martyred rather than live out the life of an ordinary man (the last temptation), he entered a state of radical

Fig. 15-9
Raging Bull: *Jake La Motta (Robert De Niro), at home, fighting with his first wife (Lori Anne Flax).*

isolation, chose suffering, and expressed his spiritual conviction in an active, physical language of pain and blood, along with a few intense words. In all these respects Jesus is a prototypical Scorsese character, one whose suffering and confusion Scorsese has learned to understand. Although *The Last Temptation* was deeply devoted to celebrating the Christian sacrifice, albeit in Kazantzakis's and Scorsese's terms, it became the most controversial film of the late 1980s; around the world, screens were slashed and theatres were picketed, mostly by people who had not seen the movie.

Scorsese has also produced films directed by others (starting with *The Grifters*, with which he was involved from 1986 to 1990) and has directed documentaries. Both he and Thelma Schoonmaker were editors on and the assistant directors of Michael Wadleigh's *Woodstock: 3 Days of Peace & Music* (1970). While his excellent concert documentaries—*The Last Waltz* (1978), with The Band, and *Shine a Light* (2008), with the Rolling Stones—are better known, Scorsese has also made such revealing, stylish, intelligent, and well-researched documentaries as *Italianamerican* (1974), *A Personal Journey with Martin Scorsese Through American Movies* (1995, co-directed by Michael Henry Wilson), *My Voyage to Italy* (1999), and *No Direction Home: Bob Dylan* (2005). In the 1980s, as a direct result of Scorsese's efforts, Eastman Kodak began to manufacture camera and printing stocks that would hold their colors far longer than any previous Eastman film; these extremely high-quality filmstocks soon were used throughout the American film industry.

Malick, De Palma, and Others

Terrence Malick, who has been influenced by Murnau as much as by George Stevens and who once taught philosophy, is the film poet of this generation. Until he made a comeback in 1998 with a meditative war film, *The Thin Red Line*, Malick had directed only two features: *Badlands* and, five years later, *Days of Heaven* (1978). Both these films manipulate several complexly contrapuntal lines; both juxtapose violent narrative events with a spectacularly lush and rhythmically languid series of stunning visual images; both use ironic, immature voice-over narrators (Sissy Spacek in *Badlands*, Linda Manz in *Days*

of Heaven) who understand, to varying degrees, the events they are involved in and whose unpolished voices contrast tonally with the rigorous, magnificent shots. The radiant, almost transcendent look of *Days of Heaven* (shot primarily by Nestor Almendros), supported by the superb music of Ennio Morricone and a Dolby Stereo mix that could unforgettably put one in the middle of a firefight or a windswept field of wheat, had a luminous beauty, a richness of texture, and a subtle palette that aspired to see into the heart of the physical world and to imply, on film, the full range of its essential being. Both films are parables of good and evil, but *Badlands* is flatter—and for that, funnier and more frightening; its love anthem is the strange rock song "Love Is Strange," and its narrator thinks in clichés (which, as we compare what she says with what we see, generate narrative complexity). The narrator of *Days of Heaven*, however, is a reliable commentator whose remarks are on target and have their own poetry and wit, without being the least bit arty.

The multiple voice-over narrators of Malick's later films, however, do not introduce narrative tension or complexity; they simply make the films—*The Thin Red Line* and *The New World* (2005, his version of the Pocahontas story)—more psychological, as we hear so much of what the characters are thinking. If there is irony in his later work, it is stimulated not by the conflict between words and images but by the conflict between the living landscape and the destructive actions that take place on it. What the later movies have in common with the earlier ones is a determination to honor the beauty of nature; it was appropriate, then, that *The New World* was shot without any artificial lighting.

Paul Schrader, like Coppola and Scorsese, came to filmmaking from film school. His scripts for Scorsese (*Taxi Driver*), Brian De Palma (*Obsession*), Sidney Pollack (*The Yakuza*), and others led to directing his own scripts. Raised in a strict Calvinist home and not permitted to see a movie until he was 18 (a background reflected in his *Hardcore*, 1979), Schrader explores the repressions and guilt of characters with enormous sexual appetites and inflexible moral codes, characters who are fanatically attracted to ritual and seek redemption through discipline and violence or find it through grace. His first

Fig. 15-10
Linda Manz as the narrator of Days of Heaven. *Photo by Edie Baskin.*

feature, *Blue Collar* (1978), took a sharp and intensely political look at labor unions and at the "divide and conquer" strategy that frustrates class awareness in America. The later films have been more redemptive and philosophical than political, and extremely self-conscious in their rich use of *mise-en-scène*; the finest of these are *American Gigolo* (1980) and *Mishima* (1985). Most of his work, from his book on transcendental style in film to pictures as recent as *Touch* (1996, released 1997), *Affliction* (1997, released 1998), and *Adam Resurrected* (2008), is concerned with the expression of spirit in a fallen world. Schrader's films are not strictly about religion—although *Touch* plays with the possibility of a Christian solution—but about the ways people blunder toward redemption in their own terms, often through radical acts of self-redefinition (*Taxi Driver, Mishima*) and a violent rage too hard to tell from love (*Affliction*).

Paul Mazursky specialized in psychological—sociological case histories, usually of city dwellers, but he added offbeat comic ironies to his solidly and charmingly acted portraits (*Bob & Carol & Ted & Alice*, 1969; *Harry and Tonto*, 1974; *Next Stop, Greenwich Village*, 1976; *An Unmarried Woman*, 1978; *Enemies, A Love Story*, 1989).

Hal Ashby, who died in 1988, made a string of solidly scripted, subtly acted, wryly comic films (*The Landlord*, 1970; *Harold and Maude*, 1971; *The Last Detail*, 1973; *Shampoo*, 1975; *Bound for Glory*, 1976; *Coming Home*, 1978; *Being There*, 1979), often about romantics in conflict with conventional American values. With their engaging characters and zealous satiric tone, whether they were as outrageous as the cult hit *Harold and Maude* or as understated as *Being There*, Ashby's films were among the most creative and widely admired of the period.

Through the mid-1970s, the most respected and accomplished African-American director was Gordon Parks. After 20 years as a photographer for *Life*, he made *The Learning Tree* (1969), which he produced, directed, and adapted from his own autobiographical novel; he also wrote the music. *The Learning Tree*, which was among the first group of 25 films selected in 1989 by the Library of Congress for its Hall of Fame, the National Film Registry, is a realistic, humanistic, visually rich, and often tender coming-of-age drama set in Kansas in the 1920s. Parks's biggest commercial success was *Shaft* (1971), a witty and violent film that inspired, as previously mentioned, a commercial wave of "blaxploitation" pictures. After *The Learning Tree*, his most tonally complete and culturally powerful work, though it found only a limited audience, was his biography of the great blues composer and singer, *Leadbelly* (1976). When he died in 2006, *Variety* remembered Parks as "Hollywood's first major black director."

Parks's contemporary, Melvin Van Peebles, had a festival hit in *The Story of a Three-Day Pass* (*La Permission*, 1967, made in France) and a box-office smash in the sexually frank and politically revolutionary *Sweet Sweetback's Baad Asssss Song* (1971). His son, Mario Van Peebles, made one of the most vivid and stylish of the inner-city crime dramas, *New Jack City*, in 1991.

Brian De Palma began with offbeat projects (*Greetings*, 1968; the film version of an environmental theatre work, *Dionysus in '69*, and *Hi, Mom!*, both 1970). He graduated to reflexive parodies (*Phantom of the Paradise*, 1974), wonderful horror films (*Carrie*, 1976, whose "zinger" open ending has been imitated in half the horror films made since; *The Fury*, 1978), gangster pictures (*Scarface*, 1983; *The Untouchables*, 1987), and ingenious thrillers combining Hitchcock psychoses with Roger Corman atrocities (*Sisters*, 1973; *Obsession*, 1976; *Dressed to Kill*, 1980; *Raising Cain*, 1992). His best slow-motion sequence, the one you can't look away from, is in the middle of *The Fury*. His best reflexive intrusion and the first of his major statements on voyeurism and moviemaking is at the end of *Greetings*. His *Carrie* may be the best adaptation of a Stephen King novel. But he went into a big-movie slump. After a string of vacuous big-budget pictures including *Mission: Impossible* (1996), De Palma regained some of his audience with the opening of *Snake Eyes* (1998), a 20-minute sequence shot as remarkable for its sound editing as for its intricate camerawork.

In De Palma's *Mission to Mars* (2000) two historically significant shots define the surround sound field precisely. The first shot, just over half a minute long, rotates a fixed sound source (a video monitor) around to the right of the theatre, not in a square but in a circle, as the camera pans to the left across a cylindrical meeting area in a space ship. At the start of this shot, the camera swings past the monitor, whose sound comes from the front center, and it pans 180° until a character speaks on camera, his voice heard from the front, while the monitor is heard from directly behind. Then there is a reverse-angle cut to the monitor that also reverses the sound field so that the monitor is heard from the front. These were not the first shots to define the sound field's left/right/surround orientation in terms of the left/right orientations of what was seen on screen, but they were the most exact and deliberate, the most like a map. The earliest stereo and surround fields maintained a consistent orientation regardless of where the camera was pointed. In a scene set in a garage, for instance, the left front side's sound would always come from the left front speaker, and the right front from the right, whether the camera showed the front of the garage or the rear; this kept the garage a consistent sound environment in the theatre, even if for the second shot in that example the left/right/front/rear relations of the sound should have been reversed. The surround sound field developed relatively conservatively, took longer than the visual to evolve to a shot-specific, changing field—a sound field whose changes (in this example, bouncing the front and rear of the garage across the theatre to match a shot/reverse-shot conversation) were at first expected to confuse the audience.

Doubling and disguise are running themes in his work, whether the linked figures are twins, look-alikes, or parts of a multiple personality. His films do not question reality so much as question our knowledge of it. How we know anything about ourselves or each other or the network of danger within which we may be forced to act is the natural subject of the thriller, at which De Palma excels, and an invitation to explore some of the ways of knowing that for him have the greatest cinematic resonance: identification, psychoanalysis, and voyeurism. In many cases he reflexively frames his subject with extensive citations of earlier films (*The Phantom of the Opera* in *Phantom of the Paradise*, *Vertigo* in *Obsession* and *Dressed to Kill*, *Peeping Tom* in *Raising Cain*, and *Psycho* in practically everything). De Palma makes the sexual repressions of his characters and the psychological aggressions of movie voyeurism increasingly explicit. *Dressed to Kill* is, in part, an attack on movie voyeurism as pornography, a theme De Palma takes further in *Blow Out* (1981) and *Body Double* (1984). In *Redacted* (2007), he uses video cameras, computers, cell phones, and the other media with which the U.S. soldiers were covering their lives, dramatizing an atrocity that took place during the war in Iraq and reflecting on the nature of information and self-knowledge.

Peter Bogdanovich was strongly influenced by the *auteur* theory and its application to the old Hollywood movie. Like many of the French New Wave directors, Bogdanovich began as a film critic, his favorite subjects being Hawks, Ford, and Welles. His interviews with Ford and Welles are invaluable. Bogdanovich's first film, *Targets* (1968), in many ways his cleverest, is a film buff's film, taking its style from the Roger Corman low-budget terror factory (Corman produced the film), complete with Boris Karloff as its star. For *The Last Picture Show* (1971) and *Paper Moon* (1973) Bogdanovich re-created the dry, dusty look of America's rural past—of the 1950s and 1930s, respectively. He also used the textures of American films of those decades, in particular his radical decision to use black and white. Some of his later films have succumbed to Hollywood formulas (*Mask*, 1985), while the best have avoided or undermined them (*Saint Jack*, 1979).

William Friedkin was the tightest and most impersonal technician of the new directors. Among the problems he has posed himself are translating talky stage plays into cinema (*The Birthday Party*, 1968; *The Boys in the Band*, 1970); capturing the texture and flavor of the old burlesque houses, customers, and performers (*The Night They Raided Minsky's*, 1968); translating the violence of urban police life into kinetic imagery (*The French Connection*, 1971); bringing a demon to the screen with convincing effectiveness (*The Exorcist*, 1973); and capturing the atmosphere of New York's sadomasochistic homosexual underworld (*Cruising*, 1980). Friedkin described his own intention in all his films as that of producing powerful but crude emotional effects—terror, tension, suspense. With the exception of *To Live and Die in L.A.* (1985), however, most of Friedkin's later films have struck audiences as more crudely leaden than crudely exciting.

One of the period's great satirists, Mike Nichols (*Who's Afraid of Virginia Woolf?*; *The Graduate*; *Catch-22*, 1970; *Carnal Knowledge*, 1971), a very successful director of comedies on the stage, made his most important film in 1967 when *The Graduate*—released a few months after *Bonnie and Clyde*—seemed to summarize the attitude of the younger generation toward the hypocritical world of bourgeois adulthood. With *The Day of the Dolphin* (1973), his films turned surprisingly weak, lacking the cinematic verve of *The Graduate* and the tight writing of *Carnal Knowledge* (script by Jules Feiffer). In the 1980s, Nichols spent most of his time back in the theatre but made two commercially successful films, *Silkwood* (1983) and *Working Girl* (1988). As a satirist and an insightful observer of human behavior, he was back in form with *Wolf* (1994), a look at werewolves in the publishing business, and *Wit* (2001, made for cable TV), adapted from a play in which a literature professor faces cancer. He also directed, from scripts by Elaine May, *The Birdcage* (1996)—the funny and one hopes final remake of *La Cage aux folles* (1978)—and *Primary Colors* (1998), one of the few films critical of American politics to come out of Hollywood in a decade; its complement was the fact-based political satire *Charlie Wilson's War* (2007). Elaine May, his partner in the 1950s nightclub-and-LP comedy team Nichols and May, has directed several films, the most biting and funny of which are *A New Leaf* (1971) and *The Heartbreak Kid* (1972). Her major independent film, *Mikey and Nicky* (shot 1973, released 1976, re-edited and re-released in the 1980s), was strongly influenced by the work of John Cassavetes and starred Cassavetes and Peter Falk. On the other hand, she also made *Ishtar* (1987). With the exception of Mel Brooks's *The Producers*, the most biting satire of the late 1960s was Robert Downey's *Putney Swope* (1969), a hilarious and racially daring tale of an ad agency taken over by blacks, complete with commercials and ironic stereotypes.

Arthur Penn was a director of the old school (*The Miracle Worker*, 1962) who came to the movies from television dramas and became one of the central figures of the new school. His dominant interest is the creation of folk legends out of outsiders, rebels, and misfits (*The Left-Handed Gun*, 1958; *Mickey One*, 1965; *Bonnie* and Clyde; *Alice's Restaurant*, 1969; *Little Big Man*, 1970), a concern that, like *The Graduate*, made its greatest impact on younger audiences in the anti-myth late 1960s and early 1970s. Of his later films, the most interesting and underrated is *Night Moves* (1975). The least appreciated of his great films is *Alice's Restaurant*.

Sidney Lumet began as an off-Broadway director, then became a highly efficient TV director. His first movie was typical of his best work: a well-acted, tightly written, deeply considered "problem picture," *12 Angry Men* (1957, written for TV and film by Reginald Rose). Since then, Lumet has divided his energies among idealistic problem pictures (*Fail-Safe*, 1964; *The Hill*, 1965; *Serpico*, 1973; *Prince of the City*, 1981; *The Verdict*, 1982), literate adaptations of plays (*A View from the Bridge*, 1961; *Long Day's Journey Into Night*, 1962) and novels (*The Pawnbroker*, 1965; *The Deadly Affair*, 1967), big stylish pictures and artificially tense melodramas (*The Wiz*, 1978; *Guilty As Sin*, 1993), and New York–based black comedies (*Bye Bye Braverman*, 1968; *Dog Day Afternoon*, 1975; *Network*, 1976). Lumet's sensitivity to actors and to the rhythms of the city have made him America's longest-lived descendant of the 1950s Neorealist tradition and its urgent commitment to ethical responsibility. *The Hill* is one of the most politically and morally radical films of the 1960s. Beneath the social conflicts of Lumet's films lies the conviction that love and reason will eventually prevail in human affairs, that law and justice will eventually be served—or not. He continued to investigate family conflicts and the nature of justice, and to get great performances from great actors, in many films, including *Before the Devil Knows You're Dead* (2007), a family melodrama in which all plans unravel and a murder offers the only resolution.

Martin Ritt, who acted with the Group Theatre in the 1930s, directed hundreds of TV shows and dramas before he was blacklisted. He spent the early 1950s at the Actors Studio, teaching Paul Newman, Joanne Woodward, Rod Steiger, and others how to act. His first feature film, *Edge of the City* (1957)—a realistic look at race relations and corrupt union practices in and around the docks of New York, starring Sidney Poitier and John Cassavetes—indicated Ritt's great skill with actors and the controversial,

nonconformist direction the best of his films would take: *Paris Blues* (1961), *Hud* (1963), *The Spy Who Came In from the Cold* (1965), *Sounder* (1972), *The Front* (1976, about the blacklist), and *Norma Rae* (1979). He died in 1990.

Other blacklisted directors who went on to do major work, but outside the country, include Cy Endfield (*Zulu*, 1964), Jules Dassin, and Joseph Losey. Dassin, who had made conventional studio films (*The Canterville Ghost*, 1944) and important *noirs* (*The Naked City*, 1948), left to work in England (*Night and the City*, 1950, another key *noir*), France (*Rififi*, 1955, the definitive caper movie and his greatest work, famous for its long, silent burglary sequence), and Greece (*Never on Sunday*, 1960; *A Dream of Passion*, 1978). Losey, who had made politically controversial, symbolic dramas (*The Boy With Green Hair*, 1948) and *noirs* (*M* and *The Prowler*, both 1951), worked in France (*Mr. Klein*, 1976) but was best known for his work in England (*King & Country*, 1964; *The Romantic Englishwoman*, 1975; and three films written by Harold Pinter: *The Servant*, 1963; *Accident*, 1967; and *The Go-Between*, 1971).

Like Lumet, Penn, and Ritt, John Frankenheimer directed for TV before making movies; his first feature, *The Young Stranger* (1957), was a remake of a TV drama he had directed. His best picture, *The Manchurian Candidate* (1962, from the novel by Richard Condon), was withdrawn from distribution after the assassination of President Kennedy because it includes a number of political assassinations, one virtually at the presidential level. For similar reasons, Bogdanovich's *Targets* was withdrawn after the murder of Robert Kennedy, never again to be shown theatrically—but *The Manchurian Candidate* had better luck and was re-released in 1987; the industry was surprised that audiences would be so interested in an old black-and-white movie that took politics seriously and played games with perception (near the beginning, it cuts between what is seen by characters who have been hypnotized and by those who have not), especially when the revival houses were closing and old movies had been relegated to the world of video. The best of his later works is *Seconds* (1966), a cautionary tale about the desire to recapture one's youth. Others that merit a look include *Seven Days in May* (1964),

Fig. 15-11
The Manchurian Candidate: *The brainwashed Raymond (Laurence Harvey) enjoys a little game of solitaire and goes into a trance as his mother (Angela Lansbury) watches.*

The Train (1964), *The Iceman Cometh* (1973), and *Black Sunday* (1977).

Sam Peckinpah also came to films from television, where he was primarily a writer. Without question, he made the greatest westerns of the 1960s. Peckinpah's three best films study the old men (Randolph Scott and Joel McCrea) who personify the last gasp of the Old West (*Ride the High Country*, 1962), the necessity of defining one's relation to violence (*Straw Dogs*, 1971), and the bonds one makes in a crummy world (*The Wild Bunch*, 1969).

Most of Peckinpah's films were recut by the studios before release—even *The Wild Bunch* lost ten crucial minutes. Charlton Heston once stood outside the cutting room with a rifle so that Peckinpah could edit *Major Dundee* (1965) without interference—but the film was simply recut after Peckinpah delivered it. MGM executive James Aubrey told Peckinpah to cut an hour from *Pat Garrett and Billy the Kid* (1973)—in

three weeks!—when he had no intention of using that cut; while Peckinpah slaved away, managing to remove 40 minutes without changing the picture's structure, Aubrey had the editing department prepare the shortened, straightened-out, ruined release version. Among Peckinpah's lesser works, the films that best managed to survive such mutilation include *The Ballad of Cable Hogue* (1970, in which the Old West figure is run over by the first car he has ever seen), *The Getaway* (1972, from the novel by Jim Thompson, which has a much nastier ending; however, Thompson's hellish conclusion was not cut from the film, as one might by now imagine—it isn't in the script and was never shot), *Bring Me The Head of Alfredo Garcia* (1974), and his only war film, *Cross of Iron* (1977). The final film of this artist who was, in his own way, an embattled last survivor of the Old West—and whose work amounted to much more than rapid cutting and bloody, slow-motion death sequences—was *The Osterman Weekend* (1983); to see it was not only to feel that it could have been better but to know that it *had* been better.

Whether they are set in the wide open spaces or modern cities, most of the films of Clint Eastwood are westerns. Like the classic westerns, they define moral stature through the assertion of individual will and the exercise of personal style, and as they pit civilians and outlaws against each other, they examine the values of civilization (and, in many of his films, the value of religion). From the 1960s "spaghetti westerns" directed by Sergio Leone (*Fistful of Dollars; For a Few Dollars More; The Good, the Bad and the Ugly*) through the "Dirty Harry" city-crime films of the 1970s and 1980s directed by Don Siegel (*Dirty Harry*, 1971), Ted Post (*Magnum Force*, 1973), and Eastwood himself (*Sudden Impact*, 1983), the films in which Eastwood acts depict a society ungovernable by laws, lawmakers, procedures, and bureaucrats. Only a vigilante enforcer like Harry Callahan, tight with anger, can bring criminals to a primitive justice, for he is as mean and "dirty" (if neat in appearance and methodical in strategy—the name means that he gets stuck with all the dirty jobs) as the creeps he blows away.

Aside from his screen personae of the almost uncontrollably violent Harry Callahan, embattled with the rules and the rulemakers, and Leone's terse "Man with no name," Eastwood is an accomplished director of action films (*The Enforcer*, 1976), westerns (*High Plains Drifter*, 1973), and thrillers (*Play Misty for Me*, 1971) who also has a serious interest in jazz—evident not only in his biography of Charlie Parker, *Bird* (1988), but also in his having persuaded Warner Bros. to co-finance Tavernier's *Round Midnight*. Like *Unforgiven* (1992) and *A Perfect World* (1993), most of his pictures show that the world is imperfect and corrupt (*Absolute Power* and *Midnight in the Garden of Good and Evil*, both 1997); his heroes *and* villains seek what order they can. They know when things feel right (*The Bridges of Madison County*, 1995); feel just (*Sudden Impact*); or feel sick, cruel, crazy, and wrong (*Misty*). But sometimes, beyond any question of how they feel, his protagonists *are* wrong; a film of Eastwood's maturity, *Mystic River* (2003), investigates the actions, social forces, and assumptions that distort the world into a place where violence appears the only way to set things right. When a gun is fired in *Mystic River*, the action is tragic rather than fulfilling.

Eastwood's late films are sharp, polished, tight, and classically restrained, even when they deal with violence (boxing in *Million Dollar Baby*, 2004; war in *Flags of Our Fathers* and *Letters From Iwo Jima*, both 2006; and cleaning up a violent neighborhood in *Gran Torino*, 2008). *Flags* shows the Battle of Iwo Jima from the American perspective (though it cuts away from the island to follow the story of three soldiers who were photographed raising the flag), and *Letters* shows the same battle from the Japanese perspective. Visually Eastwood's most arresting work, these complementary war pictures have had varying amounts of color removed from the image, giving an almost monochrome sensibility to both the big and the intimate scenes, a bleak and understated toughness; this palette paradoxically enhances the films' realism while offering the filmmakers total control over the erasure and eruption of color. *Gran Torino*, a visually simpler film that features one of Eastwood's best performances, picks up the theme of the man who feels the need to make the world right, which had been important in his work since his portrayal of Dirty Harry and his interrogation of heroism in *Unforgiven*, and works out an unusual solution for the contemporary vigilante.

Eastwood's status as a total filmmaker had been confirmed when he had picked up two Oscars—one as producer and one as director—for the film voted Best Picture of 1992, *Unforgiven*, a western that showed the unglamorous reality behind the myth of the gunfighter—and then, without contradicting itself, reaffirmed the power of that myth. Eastwood plays Bill Munny, a once-famous outlaw reformed by his late wife and scraping along as a farmer with two kids. Hardly able—at first—to shoot or ride, he agrees to kill some bad guys to get enough money to give his kids a fresh start; as he tells Ned, his old partner (Morgan Freeman), who joins him—and a youth (Jaimz Woolvett) who will learn how final and horrible it is to shoot a person—he is not going back to his old ways just because he is taking this job. But eventually the old imperatives take hold—revenge, justice, fair play, violence—and when Ned is murdered, Munny comes fully into his power, and that of his legend, as he avenges his black friend. Terrifying a corrupt town into at least the beginnings of a sense of justice, and blasting sexism and racism, Munny rides off, back to his family, and makes that fresh start. Because of his essential strength of character and his refusal to romanticize murder, he has performed a dirty job without becoming corrupt and has inhabited a mythic space without losing his bearings or his credibility.

As Eastwood acknowledged in his dedication of *Unforgiven* "to Sergio and Don," he learned the trade by watching Sergio Leone and Don Siegel. Siegel was a great action director with a tough sense of humor; his major works include *Riot in Cell Block 11* (1954), *Invasion of the Body Snatchers* (1956), *Baby Face Nelson* (1957), *The Killers* (1964, not broadcast because it was too violent, but the first movie made for TV), *Madigan* (1968), *The Beguiled* (1971), *Dirty Harry*, *Charley Varrick* (1973), *The Shootist* (1976), and *Escape from Alcatraz* (1979).

A new generation of horror directors appeared during this period, though some (in America, John Carpenter and Wes Craven; in Canada, David Cronenberg; in Italy, Dario Argento) were not widely known until after 1976. While studio pictures from *Rosemary's Baby* and *The Exorcist* to *Jaws* (1975, directed by Steven Spielberg) and *Carrie* kept the genre alive in the mainstream, independently produced films

Fig. 15-12
Kept back by fire, but not for long: the flesh-eating zombies of George Romero's **Night of the Living Dead.**

catered to the drive-in crowd with explicit gore (Herschell Gordon Lewis's *Blood Feast*, 1963, was the first gore film), sadistic sex and violence (Wes Craven's *The Last House on the Left*, 1972), and troubling fantasy (Herk Harvey's *Carnival of Souls*, 1962).

The most important American horror film since *Psycho* was George A. Romero's *Night of the Living Dead* (1968), a gory, low-budget, black-and-white, tightly organized shocker that remains as frightening and revolting as it is thought-provoking. *Night of the Living Dead* takes a hard look at the world that is in danger of being taken over by flesh-eating zombies, and few of the living measure up; most are selfish, violent, stupid. The strongest, smartest, most resourceful character is played by a black man (Duane Jones—one of the very first black actors to be cast in a leading role *regardless* of the fact that he was black, rather than because of it), and though he survives the night, he is shot and burned the next morning by a redneck posse—shown in grainy stills and brief shots that resemble 1960s news coverage of racist incidents in the South. The Vietnam War and the civil rights movement made their presence felt in this film, though it did not set out to be a political or racial allegory and simply happened to express—as horror often does—the tension of the time with unprecedented force.

The sequels, however, took on social issues deliberately—for as an officially despised genre, the low-budget horror film was (and still is) free to take outrageous creative chances and adopt controversial attitudes toward the issues of the day—or of eternity. Daring and iconoclastic, *Dawn of the Dead* (1978, released 1979) did not just satirize consumerism (the heroes are isolated in a besieged shopping mall this time, not in a besieged farmhouse) but presented the imminent death of the whole racist, sexist, materialistic world—and the media too. In *Day of the Dead* (1985), which is set in an underground government storage facility (another museum of human culture, like the mall in *Dawn*), military solutions fail and scientific ones are compromised. In *Land of the Dead* (2005), the audience begins to feel some sympathy for the zombies as they march like an army of the homeless, the new have-nots, on a socially and economically corrupted city. *Diary of the Dead* (2007, released 2008), produced at the same time as the similar *Redacted*, uses the point of view of contemporary media as some of the victims use digital cameras and computers to shoot and edit a video that tells the truth about the zombie plague, which starts anew in this picture (it is not a sequel to *Land of the Dead*). (The device of using hand-held video to record a horror in which the camera operator is involved also was employed in *Cloverfield* [2008, directed by Matt Reeves] and the Spanish *[Rec]* [2007, directed by Jaume Balagueró and Paco Plaza].) The *Dead* films put a new, ravenous face on the end of the world; in this horrific context they make it clear what is, or was, worth saving about humanity. The best of Romero's other horror films is *Martin* (1978), a disturbing, formally experimental tale about a young man who is not your average vampire.

The Texas Chain Saw Massacre (1974) was another independent first feature made far from Hollywood (in Texas; *Night of the Living Dead* came from Pittsburgh) that put its director, Tobe Hooper, in the permanent annals of the genre. A deranged family melodrama that lives up to its title, *The Texas Chain Saw Massacre* is painfully violent, grossly repulsive, and full of ghoulish art (like *Psycho*, it was inspired by the case of Ed Gein, the Wisconsin ghoul), for one of its principal subjects is the art of horror. Hooper's most reflexive horror film, *The Funhouse* (1981), and his most commercially successful film, *Poltergeist* (1982, produced by Spielberg), have higher production values but continue to investigate, as *Texas Chain Saw* did, the nature of the "normal" and "abnormal," particularly in terms of the family. Larry Cohen's *It's Alive* (1974) takes another approach to the institution of the family: a monstrous killer baby, destroyed by killer police and representatives of a killer society. Cohen's tongue-in-cheek monster movie, *Q* (1982), prepared the way for his sharpest satire, *The Stuff* (1985), in which the monster is a truly organic health food.

Stanley Kubrick

Discussions of science fiction in this period inevitably come around to one film: Stanley Kubrick's *2001: A Space Odyssey* (1968), released one year before the first moon landing but still offering a completely realized vision of outer space—which is not surprising, since Kubrick was always such a meticulous and demanding artist. In the early 1960s, Kubrick detached himself from the constraints of American studios to produce films in England, where he died in 1999. A perfectionist who decided on every detail of the film himself, from scripting to editing—with the advantage of being his own producer—Kubrick worked very slowly. His reputation rests on only ten films: *The Killing* (1956), *Paths of Glory* (1957), *Lolita* (1962), *Dr. Strangelove Or: How I Learned To Stop Worrying And Love The Bomb* (1964), *2001*, *A Clockwork Orange* (1971), *Barry Lyndon* (1975), *The Shining* (1980), *Full Metal Jacket* (1987), and *Eyes Wide Shut* (1999). Kubrick's early films, *Fear and Desire* (1953) and *Killer's Kiss* (1955), are melodramatic apprentice work, and on *Spartacus* (1960) Kubrick was not the primary director, having been brought in halfway through production by Kirk Douglas.

From the *noir* world of *The Killing* to the military world of *Full Metal Jacket*, the essential Kubrick theme is man's love affair with death. Kubrick seems to be a social critic in that his films consistently rip apart the hypocrisies of polite society: the military society of World War I France (*Paths of Glory*), the pseudointellectual society of suburbia (*Lolita*), the political society of the White House and Pentagon (*Dr. Strangelove*), the sterilized banality of a society of the future (*2001* and *A Clockwork Orange*), the elegant hypocrisies of Europe's 18th-century aristocracy (*Barry Lyndon*). As with Renoir, Kubrick's social evils are human evils; the problem is with human

nature. Without a society, men slaughter each other individually, as they do in "The Dawn of Man" sequence in *2001* after the first ape/man discovers the use of a weapon. With society, men slaughter each other *en masse* under the pretext of patriotism, military justice, potency, or national defense.

Kubrick's great cinematic gift is not just his ability to develop this bitterly ironic theme but his gift for finding the right ironic tone—part horror, part humor, a cold mixture of burlesque and Grand Guignol—for developing it. Kubrick does not always appear to care about his characters; sometimes it is as if he puts them in boldly

Fig. 15-13

Fig. 15-14
Full Metal Jacket: *Kubrick's relentless parody of the Vietnam War takes the recruits from the point where they are taught by the machine to be part of the machine (Fig. 15-13) to their survival or death in combat (Fig. 15-14, one of the few images to acknowledge the high number of black casualties in the war).*

decorated freezers, to calculate their behavior and cackle at their struggles. But there is compassion, even vulnerability, in his long look at the married couple in *Eyes Wide Shut;* there is sorrow in *Full Metal Jacket,* rage in *Paths of Glory,* awe in *2001.* There is a tone of sympathy in *Barry Lyndon* that modifies the cold irony—but the merciless, cynical, sardonic, ironic tone is relentless in *Lolita, A Clockwork Orange, The Shining,* much of *2001,* all of *Dr. Strangelove,* at the end of *Full Metal Jacket,* and wherever else it pleased Kubrick to weave it into his work, from the cold vantage point of his masterfully controlled compositions.

Dr. Strangelove is the fullest and the least ponderous expression of the Kubrick theme and tone. The film begins with an audacious visual joke: Two jet planes, one refueling the other in mid-air, appear to be copulating. Kubrick emphasizes the gag by underscoring the planes' passion with a lush romantic version of the popular tune,

Fig. 15-15

Fig. 15-16

Dr. Strangelove: *Farcical madmen decide the fate of the world. Dr. Strangelove (Peter Sellers, Fig. 15-15) and General Buck Turgidson (George C. Scott, right, Fig. 15-16) in the War Room.*

"Try a Little Tenderness." As it turns out, the whole film synthesizes copulation and death. The American general Buck Turgidson (George C. Scott) acts the same in the bedroom as he does in the War Room. The crazed army commander, Jack Ripper (Sterling Hayden), develops his whole theory about the Commies attacking his "precious bodily fluids" with fluoridated water based on how depleted he felt after making love. The American pilots in the atomic bomber work feverishly to drop their bomb on the Rooskies although the plane has been critically damaged. When they finally succeed in dropping it, the plane's commander (Slim Pickens) rides the bomb down to his destruction, whooping like a cowboy on a bronco, the bomb looking like an enormous surrogate phallus.

The ultimate symbol of man's romance with machines and death is the wheelchair-bound Dr. Strangelove himself, the "converted" Nazi atomic scientist (Wernher von Braun, a former Nazi, headed America's space and weaponry research) who still delights in the means of mass murder and who cannot keep his black Rotwang glove from rising into a "Sieg heil." (Strangelove was one of three roles played by Peter Sellers in this film; the others were Lionel Mandrake and President Merkin Muffley. All three names include sexual puns.) The film ends as it began, with a romantic orgy performed by death-dealing machines. The bombs explode in silent beauty, while Vera Lynn sings her romantic tune of the 1940s, "We'll Meet Again"—the audience and the Bomb, that is; "some sunny day," we have a hot date.

2001: A Space Odyssey really is two films, one mystical, one cynical, which Kubrick holds in balance. On the one hand, Kubrick's astronauts travel toward the meaning of life itself, apparently known by the extraterrestrials who have planted metal slabs on Earth, beneath the surface of the moon, and near Jupiter at the "dawn of time," in order to influence human progress—and reward it at the correct stage, for to find the moon's monolith, human technology would have to have developed to the point of landing people on the moon. Thus the mysterious silent slabs are both beacons and goads, and the central theme of the film is evolution. The first slab provokes the discovery of the first tool, a discovery that culminates in the invention of rocket ships and computers. Kubrick's brilliant cut from the soaring bone to the floating space shuttle visually establishes the connection between these tools. The second slab provokes the Jupiter Mission, which takes human beings to their next stage of evolution, "beyond the infinite." After some form of maturation in a strange room, climaxed by the appearance of another monolith, a cosmic force sends the reborn astronaut back to Earth in a different kind of space capsule—a womblike bubble. Another stage of evolution begins with this starchild. This metaphysical theme necessarily remains elusive; the monoliths and the force behind them are never explained—which leaves the feeling of metaphysical mystery intact.

On the other hand, the film's social commentary is quite clear, a satirical study of a race that can improve its machines but not its instincts. The first tool becomes a weapon. When humans travel to the moon, they take their capitalistic establishments with them—Pan Am, Howard Johnson's, Bell Telephone. The scientist–diplomat also takes his tribal, nationalistic prejudices and loyalties, not being free to discuss scientific problems with his colleagues from other countries. When human beings build supermachines—the computer, HAL—they build them with human weaknesses. HAL is a superbrain; he also kills because he has been programmed to distrust his associates. The Jupiter Mission becomes a battle between man (Keir Dullea) and tool (HAL): which one is more evolved, more deserving of reaching the outermost monolith and learning its secrets. Produced without computers, *2001* remains one of the most impressive and intelligent "big" films ever made. Its influence on George Lucas, among others, was definitive. Always intriguing, often breathtaking, it still looks absolutely fresh and contemporary—even after decades of progress in space operas, special effects, and computers.

Kubrick's final project, *AI*—the story of a robot boy who wants to be loved like a real human child and who does not age while those around him die and ages pass—was ironically kept from production by the limitations Kubrick perceived in contemporary computer effects technology. Though he worked on *AI* for many years, drew storyboards for it, and often consulted by transatlantic phone with his friend Steven Spielberg, he could not solve the problem of a convincing special-effects robot—necessary because Kubrick shot so slowly and methodically that a real boy would age during the years of production. Before his death, Kubrick turned the project over to Spielberg, who solved the problem by using a live actor and making the film in under a year. Spielberg's *A.I. Artificial Intelligence* (as it was advertised; the onscreen title is *Artificial Intelligence AI*), as much an homage to Kubrick as an original vision of love in a mechanized, frozen future, was released in 2001.

The Independent American Cinema

The Independent American Cinema has been called by many names: the American Underground, the American Avant-Garde, the New American Cinema, and the Experimental American Cinema among them. By whatever name, an alternative cinema tradition has existed in the United States since the 1920s with a series of assumptions that differ markedly from those of the commercial American cinema. This cinema is highly personal and individual (often one person literally makes the entire film); like poetry, it has virtually no commercial aspirations; and it is necessarily revolutionary in structure, or visual technique, or intellectual attitude, or all three. These personal, experimental films first attracted wide attention in the late 1950s. Nevertheless, the American avant-garde, independent, poetic cinema was not only a 1950s or even a 1960s movement. Rather, a tradition of avant-garde filmmaking that had grown along with, and been influenced by, the avant-garde cinema of Europe since the 1920s, and that had its own major films and figures and movements all along, went through a particularly creative phase just when public interest in film as an art was at its height.

There are three conflicting critical attitudes about the Independent American Cinema. For some, it represents the narcissistic visual scribblings of the lunatic fringe whose work is ultimately irrelevant to the development of serious film art (that is, commercial, narrative, feature-length "art films"). In support of this position, it is probably true that a vast majority of American filmgoers has never even heard of the most respected Independent filmmakers. A second position finds the Independent American

Cinema a fertile testing ground for techniques and devices that are later absorbed and practiced by the mainstream of filmmaking (that is, commercial, feature-length narrative films). In support of this position one can point to the influence of the French avant-garde on the later features of Clair, Epstein, Cocteau, and Buñuel (all of whom came out of the avant-garde), as well as the fact that many of the stylistic devices and moral attitudes of the commercial films of the 1960s and 1970s (their sensuality, the use of slow motion, multiple exposure, accelerated motion, rock music, *musique concrète*, computer graphics, shock cutting, split screen) were first seen in Independent films. Many of the experiments undertaken by New Wave directors were inspired by those they had seen in 1958 (at the Brussels World's Fair and, a week later, in Paris) at screenings of films by Kenneth Anger, Jordan Belson, Stan Brakhage, Robert Breer, Jim Davis, Maya Deren, Ian Hugo, and others. More recently, the credits of *SE7EN* (1995) reflected the influence of Brakhage. Yet a third position finds the Independent American Cinema the only significant and serious works of film art in America. In support of this position, they observe that these are the only films free of commercial pressures, totally dependent on the vision of a single artist, and totally aligned with the parallel movements in modern painting, music, and poetry. The business of these independent films is perception: the way the devices of an art can aid, extend, and complicate one's ability to perceive inner and outer realities. That goal might be taken as the ultimate intention of all the Modernist arts.

Early History

Rather than engaging in this controversy of values, it would be useful simply to trace the history of this movement, to define its principles and principal types, and to mention the accomplishments of its most distinctive filmmakers. The tendency of the earliest avant-garde American films (in the 1920s and 1930s) was to avoid the Hollywood assumptions by making films of pure visual form, films that were, in effect, moving paintings, virtually abstract, whose content was that of form in motion. Although Robert Florey and Slavko Vorkapich's *The Life and Death of 9413—A Hollywood Extra* (1928, shot by Gregg

H_2O: *the abstract play of moving light and water.*

Fig. 15-17

Toland) protests against the facelessness and inhumanity of the modern industrial system (using the movie business as its industry), it is really a series of Expressionist models and paintings made to move, combining the visual settings of the German Expressionists (especially *Caligari*) with the camera trickery of the French Surrealists. Another avant-garde film that tells a story but is primarily a triumph of pure Expressionism is James Sibley Watson and Melville Webber's *The Fall of the House of Usher* (1928). Ralph Steiner's H_2O (1929), which is composed exclusively of images of light reflecting on water, begins with beautiful and recognizable images (say, raindrops splashing in a rippling stream) and steadily becomes more abstract, so that the shots of light and shimmering water cease to look like anything except waving abstractions (a sort of moving Klee or Pollock painting). Among the few early exceptions to this purely formal rule were Joseph Berne's sensitive *Dawn to Dawn* (1934) and Webber and Watson's sexually symbolic *Lot in Sodom* (1933).

The best early films of pure form, movement, rhythm, and (later) music were made not in America, however, but in Europe. In the Silent Era, Hans Richter and Viking Eggeling excelled in rhythmically moving forms that also manipulated the restrictions of black and white. For example, Richter's *Rhythmus 21* (1921) features a variety of kinds of rhythmic movement: Rectangular shapes move about the screen, they change their sizes and shapes (expanding and contracting into lines, squares, trapezoids, and so forth), and they change their shades (shifting from white on black to black on white to gray on black, etc.). Fernand Léger's *Ballet mécanique* (1924) was another film that strongly influenced the Americans. In the 1930s, Len Lye (whose *A Colour Box*, 1935, was animated without the use of a camera) in England and Oskar Fischinger in Germany developed the film of pure form and movement to its height by using color and by accompanying the dizzily changing forms with appropriate music. In effect, these films became dances of color and shape. Other European filmmakers of the 1920s and 1930s—along with the Americans Man Ray (who worked in Europe) and Webber and Watson—whose influence on later Independent film poets was strong include Buñuel and Dalí, Alberto Cavalcanti, René Clair, Jean Cocteau, Marcel Duchamp, Dimitri Kirsanov, and Walter Ruttmann.

The most important American Independent filmmaker of the 1940s was Maya Deren (born

Fig. 15-18
Maya Deren with her 16mm camera.

Fig. 15-19
Maya Deren meets herself in **Meshes of the Afternoon.**

Eleanora Derenkowsky in Kiev), who combined her interests in dance, in voodoo, and in subjective, phenomenological psychology in a series of surreal perceptual films. *Meshes of the Afternoon* (1943, soundtrack added 1959), *At Land* (1944), and *Ritual in Transfigured Time* (1946) defy the continuity of space and time, erase the line between dream and reality, and turn the entire vision of the film into the streaming consciousness of the filmmaker. In *Meshes* and *At Land*, she is the central performer—both the mind behind the film and the body within it. *Meshes of the Afternoon* uses a series of repeating dreamlike motifs—a shadow walking down a garden path, a flower, a key, a knife, a mirror, attempts to mount a flight of stairs—that prefigure the use of similarly repeating motifs in *Last Year at Marienbad* almost two decades later. The motifs weave together musically and subconsciously rather than rationally, tangling the viewer in a systematic labyrinth of unresolvable resonances. As such, the film serves as a clear bridge between the Surrealism of *Un Chien andalou* and the dream-realities of *Marienbad, Persona,* and *8½.* Her very brief *A Study in Choreography for Camera: Pas de Deux* (1945), which, like most of her films, is silent, combines Deren's two dominant interests— the movement through space of dance and the

movement of space through editing—to reveal how editing may create the impression of continuous motion through discontinuous space.

Film Poets

Greatly influenced by Maya Deren and Marie Menken, the American avant-garde began building itself into a movement in the mid-1950s— aided by the expanding availability of 8mm and 16mm equipment—with the recognition of the work of a great many major filmmakers. Joseph Cornell and Harry Smith, who preceded Deren, made their first films in 1939. Mary Ellen Bute began work a decade before that. Marie Menken started as the cinematographer of *Geography of the Body* (1943), directed by her husband, Willard Maas, whom she photographed with his male lover. She soon began her own career with sweeping hand-held images of sculptor Noguchi's works, followed by a series of gently critical visions of her husband's homosexual life, metaphorically using everything from microscopic sperm to the huge Versailles. Her epic "city film" *Go! Go! Go!* (1964) was imitated by filmmakers as diverse as Godfrey Reggio (*Koyaanisqatsi,* 1983) and Jonas Mekas. Her work throughout a variety of subjects—the Alhambra, *Moonplay* (mid-1960s; part of a lifelong *Notebook* of films), an *Arabesque for Kenneth Anger* (1961), Greek Orthodox and

Christmas *Lights* (1965)—is characterized by a perfected hand-held camera in the service of an incisive lyricism.

American Independents who began to make films in the 1940s, and of course continued to work for decades, include Kenneth Anger, James Broughton, Rudy Burckhardt, Douglas Crockwell, Maya Deren, Dwinell Grant, Alexander Hammid, Curtis Harrington, Hy Hirsch, Willard Maas, Gregory Markopoulos, Marie Menken, Sidney Peterson, Frank Stauffacher, James Whitney, and John Whitney. European film poets starting at the same time included Georges Franju and Humphrey Jennings.

The 1950s saw the first films of Jordan Belson, Stan Brakhage, Robert Breer, Shirley Clarke, Bruce Conner, James Davis, Robert Gardner, Ian Hugo, Ken Jacobs, Larry Jordan, Helen Levitt, Christopher MacLaine, Ron Rice, and Stan VanDerBeek. In Europe novelist Jean Genet was making films, as were Jean Isidore Isou, Kurt Kren, and Peter Kubelka; in Canada there was Jack Chambers.

In the 1960s, they were joined by Bruce Baillie, Robert Beavers, Les Blank, Nathaniel Dorsky, Ed Emshwiller, Hollis Frampton, Ernie Gehr, James Herbert, Will Hindle, George Kuchar, Mike Kuchar, George Landow, Saul Levine, Adolfas Mekas, Jonas Mekas, Richard Meyers, Gunvor Nelson, Robert Nelson, Andrew Noren, Pat O'Neill, Peter Rose, Carolee Schneemann, John Luther Schofill, Paul Sharits, Jack Smith, Chick Strand, Michael Wallin, and Andy Warhol. Takahiko Iimura was working in Japan; Dr. Noel Brinckmann, Werner Nekes, and Dore O were in Europe; and Keewatnin Dewdney, David Rimmer, Michael Snow, and Joyce Wieland were in Canada.

Americans who did their first work in the 1970s include Dan Barnett, Sandra Davis, Gary Doberman, Curt McDowell, Su Friedrich, Robert E. Fulton, Amy Greenfield, Barbara Hammer, Peter Hutton, Marjorie Keller, Annie Charlotte Robertson, M. M. Serra, Phil Solomon, Willie Varele, and Fred Warden; in Canada were Bruce Elder, Ellie Epp, and Vincent Grenier.

Some of the new American film poets of the 1980s were Carolin Avery, Alan Berliner, Emily Breer, Mary Filippo, Nina Fornoroff, Peter Hurwitz, Jim Otis, Luther Price, Bill Stametz, Stacy Steers, Mark Street, and Leslie Thornton. Europeans following their own avant-garde

impulses while influencing independent filmmakers around the world included Martin Arnold and Matthias Müller. New Canadian artists included Amy Bodman, Rick Hancox, Mike Hoolboom, Henry Jesionka, Richard Kerr, and Chris Wellsby.

Of those who began their film work in the 1990s, the following are exemplary: in America, Carl Fuerman, Joel Haertling, Nisi Jacobs, Mary Beth Reed, Jennifer Todd Reeves, Erin Sax, Robert Schaller, Eric Waldemar, Timoleon Wilkins, and John Writer; in Europe, Jürgen Reble and Sistiaga; and in Canada, Susan Oxtoby and Garina Torossian. To enlarge on only one of these examples, Mary Beth Reed achieved the abstract images and startling colors of *Moon Streams* (2000) through hand-painting and sometimes hand-processing film, working with the result on an optical printer, then combining that with other images—sometimes the same image in negative, sometimes another hand-painted shot or a photographed shot—in bi-pack and running them through a contact printer.

Since the 1950s, the Independent Cinema has tended to gravitate toward four vague but recognizable "genres": the formal, the social–satirical, the sexual, and the reflexive. As with the avant-garde French films of the 1920s, these categories are neither rigid nor mutually exclusive. A film devoted primarily to the visual effects of imaginatively dancing forms can imply a social and a reflexive dimension (Robert Breer's *Jamestown Baloos*, 1957; *Horse Over Teakettle*, 1962; and *Fist Fight*, 1964). A sexual film often satirizes the assumed social values of normality (Kenneth Anger's *Scorpio Rising*, 1963). And many of the films devoted to a reflexive meditation on the nature of film devote themselves to the manipulation of visual forms.

The film of pure form, one of the oldest experimental styles of cinema, persisted in the American Underground, much of it influenced by the earlier work of Fischinger, Léger, and Lye. Among the outstanding formal dances are the computer films of John Whitney, who, like Fischinger, combined his ceaselessly changing color-forms with synchronized music (*Catalog*, 1961; *Permutations*, 1968; *Matrix*, 1971). Whitney's films differ from Fischinger's in being more precise and mathematical in their symmetrical visual forms (not surprising, since those forms were being spun to symmetrical perfection

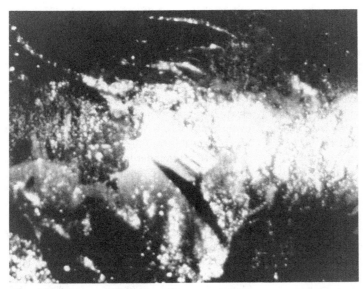

Fig. 15-20

Mary Beth Reed works in the tradition of the film of pure form; this frame is from **Moon Streams.**

by a computer). The best known work of his brother, James Whitney, is *Lapis* (1966).

Other films in the formal tradition include those of Jordan Belson (*Mandala*, 1953; *Allures*, 1961; *Re-Entry*, 1964; *Phenomena*, 1965; *Samadhi*, 1967), who uses his colorfully amorphous evolving forms as mandalas, indescribable objects of spiritual reflection and contemplation. Belson's meditational colors and forms flowed into the commercial mainstream with the astronaut's shimmering visions in Philip Kaufman's *The Right Stuff* (1983). Many of the animated films of Robert Breer are sorts of spatial dancing: *66* (1966) is a sequence of evolving forms and colors. Scott Bartlett's stroboscopic *OffOn* (1967) succeeds in turning more concrete referents (the eye, a bird, a head) into pulsing forms in ceaseless motion, accompanied by *musique concrète*. Indeed, this form of Modernist music—often a rhythmic assemblage of various abstract noises such as buzzing, scratching, grinding, whining, and found sounds—is one of the primary accompaniments of many avant-garde films, though it is also true that many are silent.

Bruce Conner is the funniest and most reflexive of the social satirists; he is essentially an editor, and his best films (*A Movie*, 1958; *Cosmic Ray*, 1961; *Report*, 1963–67; *Marilyn × Five*, 1965) cleverly splice together existing stock footage to make their satirical point. Conner's point is that people

are murderous, destructive, and ultimately suicidal, conducting an assault against their fellows and against nature itself that will eventually kill everyone. Conner supports his view in *A Movie* with found footage of violence and destruction exclusively: tanks in battle; collisions of racing automobiles; the burning of a zeppelin; the collapse of a bridge; the detonation of the atomic bomb. Conner's movie implies that the business of the movies is to chronicle and eroticize catastrophe.

Equally satirical is Stan VanDerBeek's *Breathdeath* (1963), which combines his interest in collage and cartooning with his own apocalyptic vision of a society warring, breathing, and boring itself to death. Tom DeWitt's *Atmosfear* (1967) is a satirical view of "pollution": of the air, of the landscapes (with ugly factories and smokestacks and architecture), of the cities (with repressive and restrictive signs), and, ultimately, of the mind. In this same satirical tradition are the films of James Broughton (*Mother's Day*, 1948; *Loony Tom the Happy Lover*, 1951; *The Pleasure Garden*, 1953; *The Bed*, 1968) and Robert Nelson (*Confessions of a Black Mother Succuba*, 1965; *Oh Dem Watermelons*, 1965; *The Great Blondino*, 1967; *Bleu Shut*, 1970).

Yet another kind of satirical "underground" film burlesques the business of aboveground movie making (also an implication of the Bruce Conner films), for society's art mirrors society's values.

The comical, usually camp films in this tradition are those of the Kuchar brothers (*Sins of the Fleshapoids*, 1965, by Mike, and *Hold Me While I'm Naked*, 1966, by George) and some of the early films of Andy Warhol (*Harlot*, 1965; *The Chelsea Girls*, 1966), though Warhol was also an important Minimalist (*Sleep*, 1963). Paul Morrissey directed the majority of the later "Warhol" features (*Flesh*, 1969; *Trash*, 1970; *Andy Warhol's Frankenstein*, 1974, in 3-D), which Warhol produced.

As can be seen from the Warhol films, the satires are close cousins to the sexually oriented films, whose studies of "abnormal" sexuality often comment satirically on society's concepts of normality. The master in the field was Kenneth Anger, the son of a famous Hollywood agent of its Golden Age. The young Anger translated his Hollywood experiences into a scandalous book about Hollywood sexual practices, *Hollywood Babylon*, which includes such gossipy morsels as the "real" murder weapon in the Virginia Rappe murder case; the "real" reasons for the deaths of Thomas Ince, William Desmond Taylor, and Paul Bern (Jean Harlow's husband); and the various genital sizes of the Hollywood matinee idols. Anger's outrageousness also dominates his films, beginning with *Fireworks* (1947), which he made when he was only 15 years old. The film is clearly his own adolescent and masochistic fantasy, the symbolic dream journey of a lonely, horny boy (played by Anger himself) who is picked up, beaten, and raped to satiety by sailors, climaxing (literally and figuratively) with the image of a penis metamorphosizing into a Roman candle.

Fetishism and sadomasochism dominate Anger's most important film, *Scorpio Rising*, an examination of the practices, perversions, and paraphernalia of the motorcycle "man": his attachment to costume and symbol (chains, boots, belts, leather, Levi's, jacket), his idolization of Marlon Brando (in *The Wild One*) and James Dean (another motorcycle freak), his hatred of society's lifeless symbols of goodness (personified by recurring shots of a kitschy Christ in film clips from DeMille's *King of Kings*), and his adoration of cruelty (personified by film clips and stills of Hitler). The motorcycle freak's worship of the macho external is, Anger implies, a literal cover-up of his homosexual essence, and Anger uses the soundtrack to comment contrapuntally (and comically) on

this gap between self and projected self-image. Popular rock-and-roll tunes of the era (a clear precursor of *Easy Rider*) dominate the soundtrack, and at one point, as the cyclist adoringly dons his macho Levi's, the song goes, "She Wore Blue Velvet." Anger's film served as the basis for several of the country's crucial obscenity test cases, first seized and then judged not obscene by the State of New York in 1965. This film alone was responsible for the demise of that censorship board, a reminder that "underground" films, because of their artistic seriousness, have played a major role in American social history as test cases for definitions of pornography.

One of the famous sexual films that has not yet been thus exonerated is Jack Smith's *Flaming Creatures* (1963), an outrageous, funny, and violent attack on sexual definitions, propriety, and normality. Smith's friend, Ken Jacobs, has made films in the sexual–social–satirical tradition (*The Death of P'town*, 1961; *Blonde Cobra*, 1963), though he is better known for his Structuralist, reflexive films (*Little Stabs at Happiness*, 1963; *Soft Rain*, 1968; *Tom, Tom, the Piper's Son*, 1971). Some of Warhol's early works—in particular, *Blow Job* (1964), a 30-minute reaction shot of the face of a man apparently receiving one—are not only attacks on normal and accepted sexual practices but also Warhol's attack on the normal definition of a movie.

The fourth kind of Independent film, the cinematically self-conscious, reflexive one, also attacks the commonly accepted assumptions of what a movie is or ought to be. As the term *reflexive* (or the redundant but widely used *self-reflexive*) implies, these films are meditations on themselves—as works of film art. As meditations, these films consciously test the possible definitions of cinema and its processes, revealing the different purposes to which cinema can be put. The underlying commitment of these films is to the act and art of perception itself, to "seeing" (in both senses of sight and insight)—the ways that cinema records the world and the things we can discover about both the world and the cinema as a result.

Stan Brakhage was the most lyrical, poetic, and romantic of the reflexive filmmakers. Brakhage combined the Romantic's investigation of nature, innocence, and experience with the Modernist's meditation on the processes and

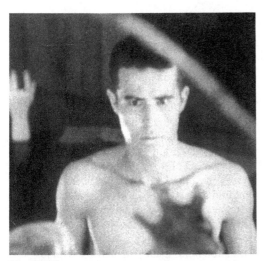

Fig. 15-21
Kenneth Anger seeks to complete himself
in Fireworks.

materials of his art. For Brakhage, the love of film intensifies the love of life and nature, and his films simultaneously celebrate both the world and the remaking of the world with cinema. Brakhage treated celluloid itself as a living, organic substance—growing mold on it (which he called "a little garden"), baking film in the oven, cutting individual frames of film into pieces and reassembling them as celluloid collages, scratching and painting directly onto the celluloid, assembling an entire film (*Mothlight*, 1963) by scattering bits of leaves, flowers, seeds, and moths' wings on pieces of Mylar splicing tape and then printing the results (a completely unphotographed film—and a link with Man Ray's scatterings of the 1920s, except that Man Ray never used organic materials). Brakhage combined these nonphotographic film methods with photographic and montage manipulations like the extreme use of superimposition (up to four images printed in the same frame), radical varying of the focus and exposure settings within individual shots, and elliptical yoking of images that demand mythic and allegorical interpretation as well as a quick eye.

Brakhage's early films tended to be sexual mood pieces in black and white, partly influenced by Kenneth Anger's tortured dream-fantasies (*Reflections on Black*, 1955; *Flesh of Morning*, 1956). But he converted to color and to the autobiographical recording of his own family and life in

1959 with *Window Water Baby Moving*, in which the filmmaker lovingly observed and captured the birth of his own first child. One of Brakhage's most important works is *Dog Star Man* (1961–64), a 79-minute silent work (allowing exclusive concentration on the dense visual imagery) in four parts plus a prelude. This mythic film combines an adoration of nature (mountains, forests, snow, moon, mists, clouds, sun) with the tortuous journey of a man (Brakhage himself) and his dog up a mountainside to create Brakhage's cosmological view of man's relation to the universe, shaped by his ability to translate his visions into works of art. Perhaps the most stunning of his later achievements is *The Dante Quartet* (1982–87), a series of four hand-painted films that takes the viewer from Hell to Paradise: *Hell Itself*, *Hell Spit Flexion* (on 35mm stock), *Purgation* (on 70mm stock), and *existence is song* (on IMAX stock, each frame a nearly 3-inch by 4-inch layered painting, up to ⅛-inch thick). These short, silent, hypnagogic films are fast, gripping, visionary. The title of one of Brakhage's major works, *The Text of Light* (1974), a lengthy abstract study of the prismatic play of light beams in a glass ashtray, might serve as the key to all his texts of light.

After nearly dying of cancer and going through chemotherapy in the mid-1990s, Brakhage said that he wished "to leave something like a snail's trail in the moonlight." He abandoned the paints and dyes it had turned out his body was unable to tolerate, but he did not give up on the "hand-tooled film." Although he made some films with a camera (*Commingled Containers*, 1997, a tight, macrophotographic look at underwater air-bubble formation, contrasted with the surface of the rushing stream), most of his energy went into a primarily handmade film begun in 1996 and called ". . ." (or, for convenience, *Ellipsis*). This long film is divided into reels, not parts, that can be shown in any order; some are in black and white, some are in color, some have sound, some are collaborations. In this "effort to avoid language," Brakhage scratched film leaders of various colors (and some photographed footage), then printed them—superimposed, in negative, and so forth—to create a further variety of color. Unlike Len Lye and others who scratched animation, in ". . ." Brakhage was scratching "moving visual thinking." Right up to his death in 2003, his efforts and artistic passions remained romantic and analytic, documentary and fantastic, phenomenological and synaptic, pursuing, as Gertrude Stein did, a simultaneous perception and expression of the exact, changing nature of being.

Although strongly influenced by Brakhage and by Ken Jacobs, both for their uniquely personal visions of reality and for their foregrounding of the means of vision even to the point of silence, Phil Solomon's work is original. He made all of his early films on an optical printer, one multi-layered frame at a time, in a meditation whose time is measured by the vertical line of sprocket holes, not by the circle of hours. They include *What's Out Tonight Is Lost* (1983), *The Secret Garden* (1988), *The Exquisite Hour* (1989, revised 1994), and *Remains To Be Seen* (1989, revised 1994). In *Clepsydra* (1992), whose name means "water clock," time drips in minutes or drenches the frame like a waterfall, a layer of the image through which we glimpse the dreamlike, secret action: more layers of image, undoing and reinforcing each other in clashing silence as the memory of childhood abuse and the resistance to memory tangle and unfold as if under a sleep of water. A crackling fog of light charges many of his films, and a will to control time; Solomon is as likely to probe his own memory as to manipulate old, found footage in his search for the living past.

Bruce Baillie combines Brakhage's romantic consciousness of nature with the social analyst's perception of the corruption of modern life. *Mass for the Dakota Sioux* (1964) and *Quixote* (1964–65) examine the ways in which the pioneer spirit of America—as symbolized by its original inhabitants—has been corrupted by the building of cities, the buying and selling of food, the digging and erecting of edifices by machines. *To Parsifal* (1963) contrasts the natural imagery of woods and water with the modern machines of fishing boat and railroad train. *Castro Street* (1966) explores the relationships among consciousness, film, and the environment—in this case a train yard and an oil depot. Just as Brakhage recorded his own life in a cinema diary, *Scenes from Under Childhood* (1967–70), Baillie constructed his own autobiographical cinema diary, *Quick Billy* (1967–71). Perhaps the most dedicated of the film diarists is Jonas Mekas, who seeks subjective and objective authenticity with the concentration of a jazz musician on the

moment, recording his life and the course of his art: *Diaries, Notes and Sketches (Walden)* (1968); *Lost Lost Lost* (1976).

The films of Hollis Frampton are more logical exercises than romantic quests. *Zorns Lemma* (1970), a complex, three-part, hour-long film, may be Frampton's most important—and most difficult—work. In its first section, about four minutes long, the viewer sees a completely black, blank screen during the reading of an alphabetical lesson out of the *Bay State Primer*, one of those early moralistic texts for teaching Puritan children their ABCs. The second section, about 43 minutes long, is also alphabetical—a silent series of images of New York signs, each one beginning with a different letter of the alphabet. Frampton holds each sign on the screen for exactly one second (24 frames), and he reduces the English alphabet to the Roman one of 24 letters (combining i and j, u and w)—so that the number of letters and the number of frames are identical. Frampton then goes through the entire alphabet 108 times—but as he does so, he systematically substitutes a visual image for each letter of the alphabet (a fire replaces x, a shot of waves replaces y, a shot of woods replaces another letter, beans filling up a jar replaces another). The second section concludes when, on its 108th cycle, all 24 letters have been converted to 24 visual images, producing, in effect, an entirely new alphabet of purely visual cinema imagery.

The first section of the film uses sounds without images—dominated by blackness; the second, images without sounds—dominated by colors; its third part combines word and image—dominated by whiteness—in a single, apparently unbroken 12-minute shot (whereas the second part used editing extensively—2,592 images of one second each). A man, woman, and dog cross a snowy white field as a group of female voices recites a visionary text according to a strict, one-second, 24-frame, metronomic beat. The point of Frampton's mathematical and alphabetical games is to reveal how insidiously our vision and knowledge are constricted by our methods of seeing and knowing. To create a new alphabet of images is to see the world and the means of recording it differently.

Perhaps the most celebrated and controversial of the reflexive films came from Canada

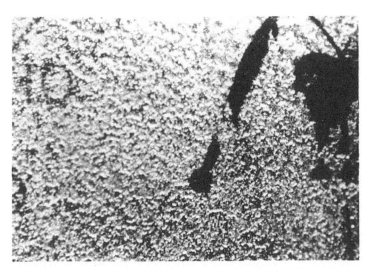

Clepsydra: *Phil Solomon's frame-by-frame meditation on time and memory, light and water, and the fight for clarity under a torrent of interference and emotion.*

Fig. 15-22

rather than America: Michael Snow's *Wavelength* (1967)—the film credited with establishing the Structuralist film movement—which is, on its surface, nothing more than an agonizingly slow 45-minute zoom shot through a single loft, beginning with a full shot of the entire room and the street outside, ending as an extreme close-up of a portion of a photograph on the far wall of the room. In the course of this inexorable forward zoom, human figures wander into the space of the frame—two men who move a bookcase, two women who listen to the radio, a man who breaks into the loft and collapses on the floor, a young woman who uses the telephone—but all of these humans leave the frame (or the frame leaves them—as it does the man on the floor, when it zooms past his body), never to return. These people, and whatever pattern of narrative causality has brought them to this particular space, are never developed, investigated, or explicated. The usual center of human interest for the usual movie is not at all central to this film.

The central concern of *Wavelength* is the space—indeed, space itself. As in *Zorns Lemma*, the structural logic of the film is rigidly formal and precisely deductive. It begins with a three-dimensional space that might be defined as 12 feet high, 22 feet wide (the usual width of a brownstone), and, say, 100 feet deep (the length of the room plus the signs visible outside its windows across the street). The film ends with a

two-dimensional space less than 8 inches high and less than 10 inches wide (part of an 8 × 10 photograph). It begins with the zoom lens at its most wide-angle setting (the shortest focal length) and ends at the most telephoto setting (the longest focal length). It also begins as a moving picture in color and ends—at the end of its focal and temporal "length"—as a still photograph in black and white (of a wave). The zoom lens flattens the visual field the most when it is at its telephoto setting, and it is at that setting when it shows the two-dimensional photograph. The film's structural logic is this implacable narrowing of space and flattening of depth as the focal length steadily increases and the frame, or the field of view, appears to move the length of the room.

A film like *Wavelength* once again raises the question about the significance of the Independent American and Canadian Cinema. On the one hand, the critic can respond to *Wavelength* with a "So what?" Space that lacks human significance is empty and boring. On the other hand, the critic can respond to *Wavelength* as one of the most perfect expressions of the cinematic condition (that movies necessarily frame spaces) as well as one of the most perfect means of educating us about the human condition—that cinema can provoke viewers to perceive the mystery, the expressiveness, and the variety of the shapes around them, not only in the frame but in the world.

For Further Viewing

FILMS

WOODY ALLEN (1935–   )
What's Up, Tiger Lily? (1966)
Take the Money and Run (1969)
Bananas (1971)
Sleeper (1973)
Love and Death (1975)
Annie Hall (1977)
Interiors (1978)
Manhattan (1979)
Stardust Memories (1980)
Zelig (1983)
Broadway Danny Rose (1984)
The Purple Rose of Cairo (1985)
Hannah and Her Sisters (1986)
Crimes and Misdemeanors (1989)
Mighty Aphrodite (1995)
Match Point (2005)
Vicky Cristina Barcelona (2008)

ROBERT ALTMAN (1925–2006)
The James Dean Story (1957). Co-director,
    George W. George.
MASH or *M*A*S*H* (1970)
Brewster McCloud (1970)
McCabe & Mrs. Miller (1971)
Images (1972)
The Long Goodbye (1973)
Thieves Like Us (1974)
California Split (1974)
Nashville (1975)
*Buffalo Bill and the Indians, or Sitting Bull's
    History Lesson* (1976)
Three Women (1977)
*Come Back to the Five and Dime, Jimmy Dean,
    Jimmy Dean* (1982)
Secret Honor (1984)
Fool for Love (1985)
Vincent & Theo (1990)
The Player (1992)
Short Cuts (1993)
Gosford Park (2001)
A Prairie Home Companion (2006)

HAL ASHBY (1929–88)
Harold and Maude (1971)
The Last Detail (1973)
Shampoo (1975)

Bound for Glory (1976)
Coming Home (1978)
Being There (1979)

PETER BOGDANOVICH (1939–   )
Targets (1968)
The Last Picture Show (1971)
Paper Moon (1973)
Saint Jack (1979)
Noises Off (1992)
The Cat's Meow (2001)

MEL BROOKS (1926–   )
The Producers (1968)
The Twelve Chairs (1970)
Blazing Saddles (1974)
Young Frankenstein (1974)
Silent Movie (1976)
High Anxiety (1977)
Spaceballs (1987)

JOHN CASSAVETES (1929–89)
Shadows (1959). Earlier version shown 1958
Faces (1968)
Husbands (1970)
Minnie and Moskowitz (1971)
A Woman Under the Influence (1974).
    Completed 1973
The Killing of a Chinese Bookie (1976). Recut
    1978
Opening Night (1978)
Love Streams (1984)

FRANCIS FORD COPPOLA (1939–   )
Dementia 13 (1963)
You're a Big Boy Now (1966)
The Rain People (1969)
The Godfather (1972)
The Conversation (1974)
The Godfather Part II (1974)
Apocalypse Now (1979)
One from the heart or *One From The Heart* (1982)
Rumble Fish (1983)
The Godfather Part III (1990)
Bram Stoker's Dracula (1992)
Apocalypse Now Redux (2001). Completed 2000
Tetro (2009)

BRIAN DE PALMA (1940–   )
Greetings (1968)
Hi, Mom! (1970)

Sisters (1973). Completed 1972
Obsession (1976)
Carrie (1976)
The Fury (1978)
Dressed to Kill (1980)
Blow Out (1981)
Scarface (1983)
Body Double (1984)
Mission to Mars (2000)
Redacted (2007)

CLINT EASTWOOD (1930–   )
Play Misty For Me (1971)
High Plains Drifter (1973)
Sudden Impact (1983)
Bird (1988)
Unforgiven (1992)
A Perfect World (1993)
Mystic River (2003)
Million Dollar Baby (2004)
Flags of Our Fathers and *Letters From
    Iwo Jima* (2006)
Gran Torino (2008)

JOHN FRANKENHEIMER (1930–2002)
The Young Stranger (1957)
The Manchurian Candidate (1962)
The Train (1964)
Seconds (1966)
The Iceman Cometh (1973)
Black Sunday (1977)

STANLEY KUBRICK (1928–99)
Fear and Desire (1953)
Killer's Kiss (1955)
The Killing (1956)
Paths of Glory (1957)
Spartacus (1960). Begun by Anthony Mann
Lolita (1962)
*Dr. Strangelove Or: How I Learned To Stop
    Worrying And Love The Bomb* (1964)
2001: A Space Odyssey (1968)
A Clockwork Orange (1971)
Barry Lyndon (1975)
The Shining (1980)
Full Metal Jacket (1987)
Eyes Wide Shut (1999)

TERRENCE MALICK (1943–   )
Badlands (1973)
Days of Heaven (1978)

The Thin Red Line (1998)
The New World (2005)

ROBERT MULLIGAN (1925–2008)
Fear Strikes Out (1957)
To Kill a Mockingbird (1962)
The Other (1972)
Same Time, Next Year (1978)

MIKE NICHOLS (1931–   )
Who's Afraid of Virginia Woolf? (1966)
The Graduate (1967)
Catch-22 (1970)
Carnal Knowledge (1971)
The Fortune (1975)
Primary Colors (1998)
Wit (2001). Made for TV
Angels in America (2003). Made for TV
Charlie Wilson's War (2007)

ALAN J. PAKULA (1928–98)
Klute (1971)
The Parallax View (1974)
All the President's Men (1976)
Sophie's Choice (1982)
The Pelican Brief (1993)

SAM PECKINPAH (1925–84)
Ride the High Country (1962)
Major Dundee (1965)
The Wild Bunch (1969)
The Ballad of Cable Hogue (1970)
Straw Dogs (1971)
The Getaway (1972)
Pat Garrett and Billy the Kid (1973)
Cross of Iron (1977)
The Osterman Weekend (1983)

ARTHUR PENN (1922–   )
The Left-Handed Gun (1958)
The Miracle Worker (1962)
Mickey One (1965)
Bonnie and Clyde (1967)
Alice's Restaurant (1969)
Little Big Man (1970)
Night Moves (1975)
Inside (1996). Made for TV

GEORGE A. ROMERO (1940–   )
Night of the Living Dead (1968)
Martin (1978). Shot 1976

Dawn of the Dead (1979). Completed 1978
Day of the Dead (1985)
Land of the Dead (2005)
Diary of the Dead (2008). Completed 2007

PAUL SCHRADER (1946–   )
Blue Collar (1978)
Hardcore (1979)
American Gigolo (1980)
Mishima (1985)
Affliction (1998). Completed 1997

MARTIN SCORSESE (1942–   )
Who's That Knocking At My Door (1969)
Boxcar Bertha (1972)
Mean Streets (1973)
Taxi Driver (1976)
The Last Waltz (1978)
Raging Bull (1980)
The King of Comedy (1983)
After Hours (1985)
The Last Temptation of Christ (1988)
GoodFellas (1990)
The Age of Innocence (1993)
Gangs of New York (2002)
The Departed (2006)
Shine a Light (2008)

HOLLYWOOD RENAISSANCE MISCELLANY
The Crazy-Quilt (1966, John Korty)
Faster, Pussycat! Kill! Kill! (1966, Russ Meyer)
Lord Love a Duck (1966, George Axelrod)
Cool Hand Luke (1967, Stuart Rosenberg)
The Dirty Dozen (1967, Robert Aldrich)
In Cold Blood (1967, Richard Brooks)
Point Blank (1967, John Boorman)
Bullitt (1968, Peter Yates)
Planet of the Apes (1968, Franklin J. Schaffner)
Pretty Poison (1968, Noel Black)
Salesman (1968, Albert Maysles, David Maysles, and Charlotte Zwerin)
Bob & Carol & Ted & Alice (1969, Paul Mazursky)
Butch Cassidy and the Sundance Kid (1969, George Roy Hill)
Easy Rider (1969, Dennis Hopper)
The Learning Tree (1969, Gordon Parks)
Medium Cool (1969, Haskell Wexler)
Midnight Cowboy (1969, John Schlesinger)
Putney Swope (1969, Robert Downey)
Beneath the Planet of the Apes (1970, Ted Post)

Five Easy Pieces (1970, Bob Rafelson)
Joe (1970, John G. Avildsen)
Patton (1970, Franklin J. Schaffner)
Woodstock: 3 Days of Peace & Music (1970, Michael Wadleigh)
Billy Jack (1971, Tom Laughlin)
Dirty Harry (1971, Don Siegel)
The French Connection (1971, William Friedkin)
The Last Movie (1971, Dennis Hopper)
Little Murders (1971, Alan Arkin)
The Panic in Needle Park (1971, Jerry Schatzberg)
Shaft (1971, Gordon Parks)
Sweet Sweetback's Baad Asssss Song (1971, Melvin Van Peebles)
Willy Wonka & the Chocolate Factory (1971, Mel Stuart)
Deliverance (1972, John Boorman)
The Heartbreak Kid (1972, Elaine May)
Sounder (1972, Martin Ritt)
Tomorrow (1972, Joseph Anthony)
The Exorcist (1973, William Friedkin)
The Sting (1973, George Roy Hill)
The Way We Were (1973, Sydney Pollack)
Death Wish (1974, Michael Winner)
The Texas Chain Saw Massacre (1974, Tobe Hooper)
Hester Street (1975, Joan Micklin Silver)
Not a Pretty Picture (1975, Martha Coolidge)
Smile (1975, Michael Ritchie)
The Front (1976, Martin Ritt)
Leadbelly (1976, Gordon Parks)
Mikey and Nicky (1976, Elaine May). Shot 1973
The Omen (1976, Richard Donner)
Rocky (1976, John G. Avildsen)

AMERICAN INDEPENDENT CINEMA
Manhatta (1921, Paul Strand and Charles Sheeler)
The Fall of the House of Usher (1928, James Sibley Watson and Melville Webber)
The Life and Death of 9413—A Hollywood Extra (1928, Robert Florey). Co-creators, Slavko Vorkapich and Gregg Toland
H_2O (1929, Ralph Steiner)
Lot in Sodom (1933, James Sibley Watson and Melville Webber)
A Colour Box (1935, Len Lye; England)
Composition in Blue (1935, Oskar Fischinger; Germany)
Allegretto (1936, Oskar Fischinger; Germany)

Meshes of the Afternoon (1943, Maya Deren). Soundtrack added 1959

At Land (1944, Maya Deren)

A Study in Choreography for Camera: Pas de Deux (1945, Maya Deren)

Dreams that Money Can Buy (1944–46, Hans Richter; Germany)

The Potted Psalm (1946, Sidney Peterson and James Broughton)

Ritual in Transfigured Time (1946, Maya Deren)

Fireworks (1947, Kenneth Anger)

Motion-Painting I (1947, Oskar Fischinger)

Mother's Day (1948, James Broughton)

The Petrified Dog (1948, Sidney Peterson)

Begone Dull Care (1949, Norman McLaren; Canada)

The Lead Shoes (1949, Sidney Peterson)

Loony Tom the Happy Lover (1951, James Broughton)

Bells of Atlantis (1952, Ian Hugo)

Colour Cry (1952, Len Lye; England)

Analogies #1 (1953, James Davis)

Mandala (1953, Jordan Belson)

The Wonder Ring (1955, Stan Brakhage)

Flesh of Morning (1956, Stan Brakhage)

NY, NY (1957, Francis Thompson)

Anticipation of the Night (1958, Stan Brakhage)

A Movie (1958, Bruce Conner)

Pull My Daisy (1959, Robert Frank and Alfred Leslie)

Wedlock House: An Intercourse and *Window Water Baby Moving* (1959, Stan Brakhage)

The Flower Thief (1960, Ron Rice)

Allures (1961, Jordan Belson)

Blazes (1961, Robert Breer)

Catalog (1961, John Whitney)

Cosmic Ray (1961, Bruce Conner)

Guns of the Trees (1961, Jonas Mekas)

Horse Over Teakettle (1962, Robert Breer)

Blonde Cobra (1963, Ken Jacobs)

Breathdeath. A Trageede in Masks (1963, Stan VanDerBeek)

Flaming Creatures (1963, Jack Smith)

Little Stabs at Happiness (1963, Ken Jacobs)

Mothlight (1963, Stan Brakhage)

Scorpio Rising (1963, Kenneth Anger)

Sleep (1963, Andy Warhol)

To Parsifal (1963, Bruce Baillie)

Dog Star Man (1961–64, Stan Brakhage)

Blow Job (1964, Andy Warhol)

Fist Fight (1964, Robert Breer)

Mass for the Dakota Sioux (1963–64, Bruce Baillie)

Re-Entry (1964, Jordan Belson)

The Art of Vision (1961–65, Stan Brakhage)

Quixote (1964–65, Bruce Baillie)

Oh Dem Watermelons (1965, Robert Nelson)

Phenomena (1965, Jordan Belson)

Sins of the Fleshapoids (1965, Mike Kuchar)

Castro Street (1966, Bruce Baillie)

The Chelsea Girls (1966, Andy Warhol)

Film in which there appear sprocket holes, edge lettering, dirt particles, etc. (1966, George Landow)

Hold Me While I'm Naked (1966, George Kuchar)

Inauguration of the Pleasure Dome (1966, Kenneth Anger)

Lapis (1966, James Whitney)

Relativity (1966, Ed Emshwiller)

66 (1966, Robert Breer)

Report (1963–67, Bruce Conner)

Fuses (1964–67, Carolee Schneemann)

David Holzman's Diary (1967, Jim McBride)

OffOn (1967, Scott Bartlett)

Pas de deux (1967, Norman McLaren; Canada)

Portrait of Jason (1967, Shirley Clarke)

Samadhi (1967, Jordan Belson)

Wavelength (1967, Michael Snow; Canada)

Chinese Firedrill (1968, Will Hindle)

Diaries, Notes and Sketches (Walden) (1968, Jonas Mekas)

Maidstone (1968, Norman Mailer)

Permutations (1968, John Whitney)

⟵⟶ (1969, Michael Snow; Canada)

Invocation of My Demon Brother (1969, Kenneth Anger)

Scenes from Under Childhood (1967–70, Stan Brakhage)

Multiple Maniacs (1970, John Waters)

Zorns Lemma (1970, Hollis Frampton)

Matrix (1971, John Whitney)

La Région Centrale (1971, Michael Snow; Canada)

Reminiscenses of a Journey to Lithuania (1971, Jonas Mekas)

Tom, Tom, the Piper's Son (1971, Ken Jacobs)

Film about a woman who . . . (1974, Yvonne Rainer)

The Text of Light (1974, Stan Brakhage)

Kristina Talking Pictures (1976, Yvonne Rainer)

Four Journeys Into Mystic Time (1978, Shirley Clarke)

Re-born (1979, Ian Hugo)

Two Figures (1980, James Herbert)

What's Out Tonight Is Lost (1983, Phil Solomon)

The Man Who Envied Women (1985, Yvonne Rainer)

The Dante Quartet (1982–87, Stan Brakhage)

Marilyn's Window (1988, Stan Brakhage)

The Lost Domain (1990, Peter Herwitz)

Opening the Nineteenth Century: 1896 (1990, Ken Jacobs)

Clepsydra (1992, Phil Solomon)

The Book of All the Dead (1975–95, Bruce Elder; Canada)

". . . " or Ellipsis (1998, Stan Brakhage)

Moon Streams (2000, Mary Beth Reed)

Occam's Thread (2000, Stan Brakhage)

Persian Series 1–18 (1999–2000, Stan Brakhage)

The Jesus Trilogy and *Coda* (2001, Stan Brakhage)

Razzle Dazzle: The Lost World (2008, Ken Jacobs)

DVDs

Apocalypse Now: The Complete Dossier (1979 and 2001, **Francis Ford Coppola**). Paramount Home Video. Includes the original film (it appears close to the Cannes version) and *Apocalypse Now Redux*, with commentary by Coppola.

by Brakhage—an anthology (see Chap. 1 list).

Chinatown (1974, **Roman Polanski**). Paramount Home Video. Widescreen Collection. Includes interviews with Polanski, writer **Robert Towne,** and producer **Robert Evans**.

Dawn of the Dead Ultimate Edition (1978–79, **George A. Romero** and **Dario Argento**). Anchor Bay. Includes all three versions: the release cut (127 min., Romero's favorite), the European cut re-edited by Dario Argento (118 min.), and the extended edition premiered at Cannes (139 min., preferred by many), along with several documentaries (including *Document of the Dead*), commentaries by all concerned, an original commercial for the Monroeville Mall, many shorts, and more.

Dr. Strangelove Or: How I Learned To Stop Worrying And Love The Bomb (1964, **Stanley Kubrick**). Columbia TriStar. 40th Anniversary Special Edition. Includes documentaries on Kubrick and Sellers, interviews with Robert McNamara and others, an essay by film critic Roger Ebert, and a split-screen interview with stars **Peter Sellers** and **George C. Scott.**

Easy Rider (1969, **Dennis Hopper**). Columbia TriStar. Includes commentary by Hopper and a documentary featuring interviews with star **Peter Fonda,** Hopper, and others.

The Fall of the House of Usher and *OffOn* are in *Treasures from American Film Archives* (see Chap. 1 list).

The Films of Kenneth Anger, Vol. 1 (1947–54, **Kenneth Anger**). Fantoma. **Restored.** Includes *Fireworks* and *Inauguration of the Pleasure Dome*. Vol. 2 includes *Scorpio Rising*.

The Godfather: The Coppola Restoration (1972–90, **Francis Ford Coppola**). Paramount Home Video.

The Godfather and *The Godfather Part II* have been **restored;** *The Godfather Part III* has been remastered. Contains many making-of and other documentaries.

H_2O, The Life and Death of 9413, Lot in Sodom, and *Manhatta* are in *Avant-Garde: Experimental Cinema of the 1920s and '30s* (see Chap. 10 list).

John Cassavetes: *Five Films* (see Chap. 1 list).

Martin Scorsese Collection (1969–90, **Martin Scorsese**). Warner Home Video. Contains *Who's That Knocking At My Door, Mean Streets* (Special Edition), *Alice Doesn't Live Here Anymore, After Hours,* and *GoodFellas* (two-disc Special Edition), all with commentary by Scorsese.

Maya Deren: Experimental Films (1943–59, **Maya Deren**). Mystic Fire Video. Contains *Meshes of the Afternoon, At Land, A Study in Choreography for Camera, Ritual in Transfigured Time, Meditation on Violence,* and *The Very Eye of Night.*

Medium Cool (1969, **Haskell Wexler**). Paramount Home Video. Commentary by Wexler and others.

Nashville (1975, **Robert Altman**). Paramount Home Video. Commentary by Altman.

A Prairie Home Companion (2006, **Robert Altman**). New Line. Commentary by Altman and actor **Kevin Kline.**

Salesman (1968, **Albert Maysles, David Maysles,** and **Charlotte Zwerin**). Criterion Collection. **Digitally restored.** Includes an interview with Albert and David Maysles, commentary by Albert Maysles and Zwerin, filmographies, and the original trailer.

Spartacus (1960, **Stanley Kubrick**). Criterion Collection. The only DVD offering **Robert A. Harris**'s complete **restored** edition. Includes deleted scenes; interviews with stars **Peter Ustinov** and **Jean Simmons;** the first **blacklist** documentary, *The Hollywood Ten,* and further information on the blacklist; storyboards by **Saul Bass;** a **restoration demonstration;** writer **Dalton Trumbo**'s scene-by-scene analysis; and a commentary by novelist **Howard Fast,** star–producer **Kirk Douglas,** Peter Ustinov, Robert Harris, Saul Bass, and others.

Straw Dogs (1971, **Sam Peckinpah**). Criterion Collection. Includes a documentary on Peckinpah.

Targets (1968, **Peter Bogdanovich**). Paramount Home Video. Commentary by Bogdanovich.

To Kill a Mockingbird (1962, **Robert Mulligan**). Universal. Commentary by Mulligan and producer **Alan J. Pakula.**

Unseen Cinema: Early American Avant-Garde Film 1894–1941. Image Entertainment. Over 150 films, most of them long unseen outside of archives, with the familiar films' benefiting from being put in context with the others; includes many scholarly notes.

The Wild Bunch: The Original Director's Cut (1969, **Sam Peckinpah**). Warner Studios. Contains the 145-minute cut (longer than the release version) and a documentary.

Young Frankenstein (1974, **Mel Brooks**). Twentieth Century Fox. Special Edition. Commentary by Brooks.

16

National Cinemas 2: 1968–

As in the first two decades after World War II, new national cinemas have attracted international attention since the political upheavals of the late 1960s, promoted by the international film festivals, supported by their governments or national television systems, and welcomed by audiences and critics. The most exciting new movements were those in Germany, Australia, Russia, Iran, and that collection of developing nations problematically called the Third World, although the increasing internationalism of film production was as striking as any single national movement.

Das neue Kino

For 35 years, from 1932 to 1967, Germany produced very few films of international significance. Among the scattered postwar German films to be exported were Rolf Thiele's *Rosemary* (1959), a Neorealistic study of the life and death of a Berlin prostitute; Kurt Hoffmann's *Aren't We Wonderful?* (1958), a biting political comedy; and Swiss-born Bernhard Wicki's *The Bridge* (1959), the story of a group of German school-children who were killed while defending a worthless bridge in the last days of World War II. Volker Schlöndorff's *Young Törless* (1966), which parallels sadomasochistic torture in a boy's school with the moral and psychological conditions for Nazism in Hitler's Germany, was either the last of these occasional German films to achieve international recognition or the first representative of the new and genuine German film movement.

In 1960, the German film industry produced some 70 feature films, almost exclusively for local consumption in their simple themes and conventional styles. The Oberhausen Manifesto, formulated by 26 German screenwriters and directors at the Oberhausen Film Festival of 1962, called for a "new German cinema," free from the stifling habits and conventions of the German film industry. Through its leaders, especially Alexander Kluge (*Yesterday Girl*, 1966; *Strongman Ferdinand*, 1975), the group successfully pressured the West German legislature to set up a film board and allocate subsidies for film production in 1967. The new German cinema flowed from these subsidies.

In the late 1960s and early 1970s appeared the first feature films of three young German filmmakers—Werner Herzog (*Signs of Life*, 1968), Rainer Werner Fassbinder (*Love Is Colder Than Death*, 1969), and Wim Wenders (*Summer in the City*, 1970; *The Goalie's Anxiety at the Penalty Kick*, 1971). All three were born within a few years of one another (Herzog in 1942, Wenders in 1945, Fassbinder in 1946); each was about 24 when his first feature appeared; each was supported by government subsidy, either directly through the Film Subsidies Board or indirectly through subsidized television production. These three directors, who steadily achieved international recognition, formed the nucleus of one of the most interesting and productive new national film movements since the French New Wave.

Although American and European critics and festivals had realized as early as 1972 that something important was happening in West Germany—particularly after watching *The Goalie's Anxiety*, Herzog's *Aguirre, the Wrath of God* (1972), and Fassbinder's *The Bitter Tears of Petra von Kant* (1972)—American audiences did not take to the New Cinema (*das neue Kino*) as rapidly as they had to the films of the New Wave. The new German films were not more difficult to understand than previous European films, but they were difficult in a different way—colder, harder edged, more ironic, and less charming than the films of Fellini or Truffaut.

The surprising commercial success of Fassbinder's *The Marriage of Maria Braun* (1979) accompanied international financing for English-language productions by Fassbinder (*Despair*, 1977), Wenders (*The American Friend*, 1977; *Paris, Texas*, 1984) and Herzog (*Fitzcarraldo*, 1982). The major American publicity campaigns for these films, Wenders's collaboration with Coppola and playwright Sam Shepard, and the posthumous interest in Fassbinder's last films—from the epic *Berlin Alexanderplatz* (1980, 15½ hours, made for TV) to *Querelle* (1982)—indicated that these filmmakers had attracted the critical attention and the audiences they deserved in the United States.

That the New German Cinema initially made little impact in America was ironic, for one of its traits was a conscious debt to the American cinema. Wenders's *Kings of the Road* (1976) is both a western (two buddies riding in open spaces) and a road movie like *Easy Rider* (they ride in a truck rather than on horseback, accompanied by American rock music). His *American Friend* is a *film noir* that evokes many American movies: Hitchcock's *Strangers On A Train* (one stranger proposes the murder of another stranger; the film is based on *Ripley's Game*, a novel by Patricia Highsmith, the author of *Strangers On A Train*), Bette Davis's *Dark Victory* (a man is going blind as a result of a mysterious terminal disease), *The French Connection* (an international Mafia-style conspiracy, shot all over the globe), American westerns (the American wears a cowboy hat and describes himself as "a cowboy in Hamburg"—and that cowboy is played by American actor Dennis Hopper, the director of *Easy Rider*). There are also appearances by two of Wenders's favorite American directors, Samuel

Fuller and Nicholas Ray (who directed Hopper in *Rebel Without a Cause* and who collaborated with Wenders on *Lightning Over Water*, 1980, the record of Ray's endgame with cancer). Wenders also acted as backup co-director for Antonioni on *Beyond the Clouds*.

Fassbinder's films are packed with conscious homages to Douglas Sirk and Max Ophüls. His *Ali: Fear Eats the Soul* (1973) is a revisionist remake of Sirk's *All That Heaven Allows*. Fassbinder's repetitive use of glass reflections on windows, mirrors, and tabletops deliberately recalls Sirk's complex use of windows and mirrors; the graceful, lengthy tracking shots in many of Fassbinder's films recall the camera style of Max Ophüls. One of the more interesting lines of movie genealogy can be traced with the appearance of Eddie Constantine in *Beware of a Holy Whore* (1970), who came to Fassbinder via Godard's *Alphaville*, and who came to Godard via a series of low-budget French crime films based on American Monogram mysteries. Fassbinder also acknowledges Godard as a way station between American movies and the New German Cinema by using Anna Karina, Godard's first wife and lead actress, as the French mistress in *Chinese Roulette* (1976). Although Werner Herzog's conscious debt to American culture and American movies may be smaller than Wenders's or Fassbinder's, *Stroszek* (1977) contains an endearing satire of the plastic surfaces of American life (mobile homes, fast-food restaurants, Formica) as well as of American bank-robbing westerns. Herzog's homages are more likely to be paid to Murnau.

If one characteristic of the New German films is their debt to foreign movies, another is their debt to a native German film tradition—the Expressionist masterpieces of the 1920s. The Fassbinder films often evoke the stylized, statuesque, highly patterned visual world of Fritz Lang. The opening shots of *Fox and His Friends* (1974) at a circus sideshow clearly link Fox, who performs as the "talking head," with Cesare of *The Cabinet of Dr. Caligari*.

Herzog's works recall the spiritual, mystical aspects of such films as *Caligari*, *Destiny*, *Warning Shadows*, and *Nosferatu*—the last one quite literally, since Herzog modeled his *Nosferatu* (1979) on Murnau's. The slow rhythms of the Herzog films, their lengthy shots of frozen figures and hypnotically entrancing landscapes, evoke the dreamlike mysteries and rhythms of the Expressionist world—as well as the emotional and symbolic intensity, the deep pull to nature, and the visionary ambitions of 19th-century German Romanticism. Many of Herzog's central figures are possessed by manias and demons that drag them inexorably into the realms of their desires and their imaginations—as well as to the ends of the earth. The most Expressionist of Herzog's experiments was *Heart of Glass* (1976), in which he hypnotized almost the entire cast during shooting, to achieve the impression that the world of the film had been plunged into a deep trance.

Although Wenders is the most apparently realist of the three directors (in the sense that Fassbinder is theatrical and Herzog is visionary), his work can be compared with such German classics as the more realistic works of Murnau and Pabst—in particular Wenders's unsentimental look at characters in undistorted environments (as in Pabst's *Pandora's Box*) and his contrast of cramped, indoor architectural spaces with open, freer outdoor spaces (as in Murnau's *Sunrise* or Pabst's *Jeanne Ney* and *Kameradschaft*). Nevertheless, of the three directors only Fassbinder could present a world as *grossly* realistic as the opening of *The Love of Jeanne Ney*.

Rainer Werner Fassbinder

Rainer Werner Fassbinder was the most prolific of the new German directors until his death from a drug overdose in 1982. Directing some 40 feature films in a dozen years, in addition to producing television programs and radio plays, as well as writing and staging theatrical productions in the same period, he worked—and ate and drugged—himself to death.

Fassbinder's work is consciously Brechtian; even the title of one of his films, *Mother Küster's Trip to Heaven* (1975), is a deliberate echo of Brecht's *Mother Courage*. The Fassbinder narratives, like those of Brecht, develop a detached irony that prods the audience to examine the political, psychological, or moral implications of the tale rather than to become intimately attached to the feelings and fortunes of its central characters. Fassbinder's parables, however melodramatic (and in that sense un-Brechtian) they

may become, tend toward the allegorical and take the form of complex and explicit elaborations of a simple moral–political lesson: that personal catastrophe gives one great economic power in contemporary society (*Mother Küster*), that even social outcasts like homosexuals are more loyal to their economic class than to their sexual comrades (*Fox and His Friends*), that the myth of the bourgeois artist—tyrannically reducing everyone in life to slaves for the sake of Art—is also the myth of Fascism (*Satan's Brew*, 1976), that the political and economic recovery of postwar Germany was achieved by acts of moral prostitution (*Maria Braun*).

Fassbinder's roots, like Ingmar Bergman's, were in the theatre, and his films never deserted the theatre's elegant, economical stylization. Like Bergman and D. W. Griffith, Fassbinder preferred the theatrical method of working with an acting ensemble rather than with individual types and stars, and over the 1970s the faces of the Fassbinder players became almost as familiar as the Griffith or Bergman stock companies—Irm Hermann, Margit Carstensen, Hanna Schygulla, Brigitte Mira, Kurt Raab, Volker Spengler, Marquard Böhm, Harry Baer. Despite the speed of his production and shooting, Fassbinder's style and control evolved slowly and steadily. His frenetic productivity of 11 films in 1969–70 slowed greatly to permit greater investment of his time, care, and control. The stylistic experiments of these early films, which tended in any number of contradictory directions—the mannered *film noir* of *The American Soldier* (1970), the maniacal mixture of movie making and sexual tyranny in the chaotic *Beware of a Holy Whore*, and the undramatic, almost *cinéma vérité* study of dull, drab middle-class life of *Why Does Herr R. Run Amok?* (1969)—fused into a consistent Fassbinder look, style, and tone.

There are three primary Fassbinder visual and social settings: the stifling, tawdry world of the working and middle class—their apartments, bars, and shops (*The Merchant of the Four Seasons*, 1971; *Mother Küster*; *Ali*); the hard, shiny world of the rich and famous (*Petra von Kant*; *Chinese Roulette*; *Satan's Brew*); and the detached elegance of the world of the near or distant past (*Effi Briest*, 1974; *Despair*). The visual characteristic that links these three social realms is their unrelenting hardness and coldness, their lack of comfort or human charm. Both private homes and places of public habitation become uninhabitable in the Fassbinder world; they are mausoleums or, like Fox's apartment, museums. Whether cutely cluttered or chicly bare, Fassbinder films are almost exclusively indoor films, claustrophobically enclosed by the rooms his characters are forced to inhabit (another clear parallel to the tradition of German Expressionism and to the Sirk and Ophüls films, which depicted similarly claustrophobic worlds).

The central theme of Fassbinder's work is power—social power, economic power, psychological power, erotic power, often translated into specific scenes of sadomasochistic dominance and subservience. The characters in Fassbinder films exercise terrible power over others, just as the filmmaker exercises a terrible power over the audience. *Satan's Brew* begins and ends with a quotation from Antonin Artaud, and the union of Artaud and Brecht, the theatre of cruelty with the theatre of ideas, mental punishment with political discussion, is as important to Fassbinder as it was to Pasolini and Polanski. Appropriately enough, one of Fassbinder's final works was an adaptation of Jean Genet's *Querelle de Brest*, for Genet, like Fassbinder, evolved a radical politics based on sadomasochistic, homosexual alternations of dominance and subservience. Many central Fassbinder figures are completely mistaken in the power they think they possess—the sexual power of Effi Briest and Fox is much lighter than the social and economic power that engulfs them, and the mercantile power of the merchant of the four seasons is equally illusory and inadequate. As in the plays of Jean Genet, the characters in Fassbinder films love to dominate and to be dominated, and many of the films chronicle the economic, social, political, and romantic revolutions of this sadomasochistic circle.

Ali: Fear Eats the Soul (in German, ungrammatically, as Ali would say it, *Fear Devour the Soul*) is one of Fassbinder's most popular and accessible works, the love story of a middle-aged widow and a young, black Moroccan who meet, marry, and confront societal rejection and isolation. The film is clearly based on Sirk's *All That Heaven Allows*, but the differences between the Sirk film and the Fassbinder film show a degree of psychological perceptivity and artistic courage in the German work that the American one either did

Fig. 16-1
Effi Briest: *Effi (Hanna Schygulla) engulfed by the curtains, carvings, mirrors, and paintings of her world.*

not or could not achieve. Sirk's middle-aged widow, Carrie, is an upper-class, graceful, and attractive woman (played by Jane Wyman); Fassbinder's widow, Emmi, is an old, wrinkled, frumpy, working-class cleaning lady (played by Brigitte Mira, who plays most of Fassbinder's matrons). Sirk's young sexual male, Ron, was impersonated by Rock Hudson, who played a gardener (which put him in a lower social class from those whose trees he pruned, but also gave him a "natural" dignity—a quality that the film emphasized by frequently mentioning Thoreau's *Walden*). Although Sirk's film made it clear (or as clear as a 1955 Hollywood film could) that the gardener was an attractive sexual object, his embodiment by the picture-perfect Hudson converted the sexual male into a pretty mannequin. Fassbinder's Ali (El Hedi Ben Salem), on the other hand, is a total social outcast and a target of extreme social pressure (a black, unlettered stranger in a strange land) but a very powerful, graceful male presence, seething with energy and sexuality—and an anxiety that eats him alive. Whereas the central narrative question in Sirk was, "Can she marry this man?"—a marriage opposed by all her friends, family, and social set—Fassbinder goes beyond to a more ironic problem: Can they stay married?

Fox and His Friends, despite its homosexual milieu, is a similarly ironic parable of the conflict between personal erotic relationships and the surrounding economic and moral landscape. Fox, a working-class boy–man (played by Fassbinder) who survives by working in carnivals and as a hustler, wins a great sum in the lottery. The money gives him an entry into the world of "finer things," and he manages to acquire a very pretty new lover, a "smart set" of new friends, a fancy apartment stocked with paintings and antique furniture, an expensive sports car, and other cultural benefits, such as pretentious meals in French restaurants. He lends immense amounts of money to Eugen, his lover, and he carelessly signs legal contracts that will defraud him of both his money and his property.

Fassbinder carefully details the conspiracy to fleece Fox, particularly showing that everyone with whom he does business is, like Fox himself, a homosexual—the antique dealer, the clothes salesman, the lawyer, and Eugen. All of these supposedly unconventional men are perfectly acceptable in the proper bourgeois world because they accept all the bourgeois assumptions about money and property. Their economic loyalties are much stronger (and more socially significant) than their sexual ones. Fox, who has blindly, romantically, sincerely, willingly done everything for the love of Eugen, ends completely stripped of everything—no lover, no friends, no car, no apartment, no money, and no life. In an ironic final image, Fox lies dead of an overdose on the cold, white, shiny tiles and stones of a public building—appropriately enough, one of the new underground shopping emporia—while two teenage boys rob the corpse of its remaining cash and the denim jacket that has been Fox's trademark, accompanied by the bitterly cold gaiety of carnival music. Fassbinder's death as Fox grimly foreshadows his own, seven years later.

Werner Herzog

Werner Herzog makes both documentaries and fictional feature films, but the differences between them are not nearly so great as such terms imply. Even Herzog's documentaries are far less concerned with the objective recording of events, processes, or conditions than with the subjective and symbolic aspects of undergoing a particular event, process, or condition. *Fata Morgana* (1970) is a transcendental documentary shot in the Sahara and as concerned with creation myths as it is with looking at the desert through new eyes. *Land of Silence and Darkness* (1971)

Ali: Fear Eats the Soul: *Emmi (Brigitte Mira) and Ali (El Hedi Ben Salem) as Fassbinder's radically odd couple.*

Fig. 16-2

attempts to re-create the sensation of experiencing the world as a blind and deaf person (quite a task for film, whose two tools are images and sounds). *The Great Ecstasy of the Sculptor Steiner* (1974) attempts to transfer the ski jumper's sensation of flying from the film's subject to its audience. *La Soufrière* (1976), a documentary about an anticipated volcanic catastrophe on the island of Guadaloupe that does not take place, is more interested in communicating the mysterious emptiness of the evacuated city of Basse Terre than in chronicling a seismic event. *La Bohème* (2009), a four-minute short, consists simply of shots in which a series of African couples face the camera while a love duet from the opera plays on the soundtrack. It is a film in which cultures clash but the universality of love is affirmed. In *Little Dieter Needs to Fly* (1997), Herzog makes it very clear—by taking him back to the jungles and prison camp from which he had escaped during the Vietnam War—exactly why Dieter, now a claustrophobic whose house is stocked with food, *needs* to fly, free in his plane in the unbounded space of the air. *Grizzly Man* (2005) follows an engaging, obsessed man to his death. In *Encounters at the End of the World* (2007, wide release 2008) Herzog went to Antarctica to meet people whose dreams, work, and sense of adventure had led them to the ultimate south. Herzog was lured to shoot this high-definition video when he saw footage shot under the Antarctic ice by Henry Kaiser, some of which he includes in his beautiful and meditative documentary. Even if his words, whether voice-over or in dialogue, are richly significant, Herzog depends finally on the poetic evocations of his visual imagery, distinguished by its intense silence, its haunting colors, its hypnotic slowness, its stare through the surface of light.

Among Herzog's favorite images are natural settings that are mysterious and untamed. He once said that he searches this planet for extraterrestrial landscapes. The arid rocky island of Cos in *Signs of Life* and the lushly dense Amazonian jungle of *Aguirre, the Wrath of God* and *Fitzcarraldo* are some of the environments to which Herzog's German characters have been transported. Herzog's soundtracks are as careful as his visual imagery; he gives particular attention to music and to the musical scoring of both speech and noises—the repetitive use of intense silences; the calls of birds; the use, in film after film, of music by South American Indians; the intense adagio that opens *The Mystery of Kaspar Hauser* (whose German title translates, *Everyone for Himself and God Against All* 1974); the clash of languages and of musical styles (glockenspiel and rock) in *Stroszek*, or the chant of the auctioneer in the same film, a chant that is both a rapid stream of language and a complex musical passage. He has also directed some American films, the best of which may be his black comedy *The Bad Lieutenant: Port of Call: New Orleans* (2009), which in spite of its title is only partly a remake of Abel Ferrara's *Bad Lieutenant* (1992).

At the center of most Herzog narratives is a character who follows his single-minded determination to an ironic and irreversible end. The Herzog characters are driven by destinies or inner compulsions that can be neither softened nor averted. Aguirre (played by Klaus Kinski, whom Herzog once called the only true demon of the cinema and about whom he made a documentary, *My Best Fiend*, in 1999), the Spanish conquistador, is driven to seek the mythical city of El Dorado in the depths of the South American jungle. He tyrannically and unswervingly pushes his steadily dwindling band of Europeans into the heart of the unknown continent, refusing to alter his determination despite the poisoned darts, the devastating heat and diseases, the dense forest, and the angry uncharted waters. Aguirre ignores the arguments of men and the evidence of nature. The result is complete catastrophe: the death of everyone on the raft that Aguirre—the stranded imperialist, the demon of European power, the self-proclaimed wrath of God, a Hitler before his time—has forged to tame the continent. The final shot of the film is both an inspired cinematic device and an unforgettable visual metaphor for Aguirre's mind and world. As the leader stands firmly atop his raft, littered with the bodies of his followers and the frenetic scrambling of hundreds of monkeys, Herzog's camera (now in a helicopter) circles the raft, ringing the man and his kingdom of monkeys off from the rest of the world, revealing that Aguirre's physical and mental universes are a circumscribed world of one—and that one a figure of pure will who set his will against nature, now helpless but unwilling to capitulate, locked in the

Aguirre, the Wrath of God:
*Aguirre (Klaus Kinski)
demonically enclosed in his
universe of one.*

Fig. 16-3

world of his obsession and continuing to deny the power of any force outside himself: first the jungle, then the king, and now death.

Other Herzog figures attempt to mold the physical world according to the shapes of their imagination. Like Aguirre, the residents of a small town in *Heart of Glass* become obsessed with a mythical quest that leads to death and destruction—not the search for El Dorado but the attempt to rediscover a secret formula for making the ruby-red glass for which the town is famous. Like Aguirre, the innocent child–man Kaspar Hauser (played by Bruno S., who had been institutionalized as a schizophrenic before Herzog starred him in *Kaspar Hauser* and *Stroszek*) sees the universe with a singleness of personal vision that clashes with the assumptions of all those citizens who try to teach him to see it differently by teaching him to speak. Like Truffaut's *The Wild Child*, *Kaspar Hauser* shows what it means to live with and without language, but it goes further, adding the problem of language's inability to describe what lies outside the realm of words and of well-ordered perceptions. Fitzgerald (Kinski again), of *Fitzcarraldo*, is determined to haul his ship up and over the top of a

mountain—a feat that had to be duplicated by Herzog and his crew—contrary to gravity and common sense, so that he can bring the voice of Enrico Caruso to the jungle and raise money for an opera house. The journey of that ship—all to create an edifice for art, the opera house Fitzgerald envisions—seems an emblem for Herzog's art and for Herzog himself: fixing one's sights on an impossible task and refusing to look away from it until the film is finished and the limits of experience have been challenged and extended once again.

Wim Wenders

Wim Wenders has made films that are austere and rigorous (*The Goalie's Anxiety at the Penalty Kick*), films that are long and loose (*Kings of the Road*), and films that address the terms of American films (*The American Friend*). Many of them are about American movies and the pervasive force of American culture in the former West Germany. Characters in Wenders films drink Jack Daniel's whiskey, listen to American rock, discuss American novels, drive American cars, delight in American names, and attempt to re-create the lifestyles and values of characters in American films. The goalie in *The Goalie's Anxiety* attends a showing of Howard Hawks's *Red Line 7000* (1965), and a newspaper in *Alice in the Cities* (1974) announces the death of John Ford. If Wenders's films glorify—and investigate and critique—American culture and American movies, they also pay homage to cinema itself. French directors Jean Eustache and Gerard Blain play roles in *The American Friend*, as do American directors Ray and Fuller. The two buddies of *Kings of the Road*, in explicating a passage from Faulkner's *The Wild Palms*, also pay their respects to Godard's *Breathless*, in which Patricia and Michel discuss a passage from the same novel. Such internationalism (an American author and a French *auteur* in one scene of a German movie) is typical of Wenders's films, many of which show Germans and Americans trying to figure each other out.

The vocation of one of the two major characters in *Kings of the Road* is to service motion picture projectors, maintaining the machines that allow the cinema to exist. The crimes against life in *Kings of the Road* are crimes against cinema—projectionists who do not care whether the image is properly framed or focused or whether their equipment is clean and well oiled. The two men in the truck, like the cowboys on their mounts, belong everywhere and nowhere—perhaps like Wenders, whose films have been said to manifest "a worldwide homesickness" and whose independent production company is called Road Movies. But it is also true of Wenders that he can find himself at home anywhere in the world, anywhere his camera takes him—to Cuba and Amsterdam, for example, for his music documentary *Buena Vista Social Club* (1999).

Given Wenders's affection for the styles, themes, and images of American film, it was no surprise that he began to make films in America: *Hammett* (1982), produced by Coppola (and employing the advanced technology developed for *One from the heart*), a fictionalized biography of Dashiell Hammett, and *Paris, Texas* (1984), written by Sam Shepard. In this return to *Alice in the Cities* and *Kings of the Road*, the two wandering "buddies" are father and son, searching (in a conscious homage to Ford's *Searchers*) the Hollywood Hills and Texas plains for a missing woman (the wife and mother, played by Nastassia Kinski, Klaus's daughter); when they

find her—since this is a western, a form that both Shepard and Wenders continually explore—the husband heads for the hills.

Wings of Desire (1987; literally, *The Heavens over Berlin*), a French–German co-production, was written by Wenders and novelist Peter Handke (author of *The Goalie's Anxiety*). It tells of two angels (Bruno Ganz and Otto Sander), assigned to Berlin since prehistoric times, who move through the city in 1987, eavesdropping on people's thoughts and wondering what it would be like to be human, to live in time rather than eternity. Since the angels can remember everything that ever happened on a particular street, Wenders can show that street in the present, then during the Third Reich, then in the present again or after an Allied bombing, summarizing all that Berlin has been, has done, and has endured. The movie takes the long view of history and of the fates of individuals, but it also moves in close to show all the concerns and uncertainties of the present and of individuals—and so does the camera, which may look at Berlin from above or at people straight on (or may reflexively imitate the camera movements from a shot in Murnau's *Sunrise*; this is, after all, a Wenders film). What the angels see is in black and white, while mortal experience is in color; angels hear the thoughts of others (sometimes the soundtrack is a chaos of minds), while people hear only themselves. The ultimate questions this movie raises about life are posed by Rainer Maria Rilke, one of whose poems is quoted repeatedly, and by the everyday/cosmic attitude the movie adopts with such calm, authority, and love. It turns out that some angels may become mortal; Peter Falk plays one of these "former angels," and the film is dedicated to three more: Ozu, Truffaut, and Tarkovsky. *Wings of Desire* is certainly the *It's A Wonderful Life* of the 1980s, but it is also a movie that feels on the verge of some great historic change. A film about the present and for the future, it ends on a note of setting out on the adventure of life, its story to be continued. When Germany was reunified in October 1990, after 45 years of division, that seemed to fit perfectly into the film's worldview—and rather than become dated, *Wings of Desire* became even more relevant and inspiring.

After making another long road movie, *Until the End of the World* (1991), Wenders returned to

Fig. 16-4
Alice in the Cities: *Rüdiger Vogler, Wenders's alter ego in the early black-and-white features, surveys the bleak American landscape with his Polaroid.*

Berlin to tell the story of the other angel (Otto Sander) in *Far Away, So Close!* (1993), the companion film to *Wings of Desire* (Wenders insisted it was not a sequel). Six years later, Wenders and the angel find Berlin an increasingly hostile place whose citizens are disoriented and disunited, but the film suggests they may be healed—perhaps if they discover compassion and learn to use their eyes (especially in the loving look) not only to take and to take in, but also to give. As a female angel puts it, "They've forgotten that light enters the heart through the eye and then shines back out through the eye from the heart."

Von Trotta and Others

The new German cinema has not been confined to its three major voices. Alexander Kluge has already been mentioned. Volker Schlöndorff excels in stylish literary adaptations—of Heinrich von Kleist (*Michael Kohlhaas*, 1969), Heinrich Böll (*The Lost Honor of Katharina Blum*, 1975), Günter Grass (*The Tin Drum*, 1979), and Margaret Atwood (*The Handmaid's Tale*, 1990).

He also excels at the political melodrama, bringing out the irony and the commitment in a story like that of Katharina Blum or the heroine of *The Legends of Rita* (2000). His then wife, Margarethe von Trotta, wrote Schlöndorff's scripts, co-directed *Katharina Blum*, and writes and directs films that are often confrontationally and controversially feminist (*Sisters, or The Balance of Happiness*, 1979; *Marianne and Juliane*, 1981; *Sheer Madness* or *Friends and Husbands*, 1982; *Rosa Luxemburg*, 1985; *Three Sisters*, 1988; *Vision*, 2009). Though all of the 26 filmmakers who signed the Oberhausen Manifesto were men, many women directors became active in Germany, notably Helma Sanders-Brahms (*Germany Pale Mother*, 1979), Ulrike Ottinger (*Freak Orlando*, 1981), Doris Dörrie (*Inside the Whale*, 1984; *Men . . .*, 1986; *Enlightenment Guaranteed*, 1999), and Monika Treut (*Didn't Do It for Love*, 1998).

The husband–wife team of Jean-Marie Straub and Danièle Huillet, for years the most radical filmmakers at work in Germany, were influenced

Fig. 16-5
Franka Potente in **Run Lola Run.**

by Bresson as well as by Brecht and Godard. They were committed to deconstructing both the ordinary processes of film narrative and the usual strategies of film imagery. Straub/Huillet, as they are usually referred to, together wrote, produced, and directed their films, which include *Not Reconciled* (1965), *Chronicle of Anna Magdalena Bach* (1967), *History Lessons* (1972), *Moses and Aaron* (1974), *Class Relations* (1983), and *The Death of Empedocles* (1987). Huillet died in 2006.

Films from the "Berlin Underground" include Frank Ripploh's *Taxi zum Klo* (1981), an amusingly frank account of Germany's gay subculture. At the opposite extreme, Hans-Jürgen Syberberg makes operatic films on an epic scale. While his *Parsifal* (1982), a staging of Wagner's opera, recalls the German traditions of Romanticism and Expressionism (and puts a Nazi parade inside Wagner's head, which is used as a set), *Our Hitler* (1977) more directly confronts those traditions and German history in search of the roots of Nazism.

One of the most popular German films of the early 21st century was Florian Henckel von Donnersmarck's *The Lives of Others* (2006), a story about political surveillance in East Berlin in the early 1980s and the effect it has on the listener as well as the targets. Herzog called it the best German film he'd seen in ages.

Tom Tykwer sets up limits for his characters to transcend. In *Run Lola Run* (literally, *Lola Runs*, 1998), the main character (Franka Potente as Lola) has 20 minutes to get a lot of money and take it to her boyfriend; she begins running at 11:40. By noon, things have worked out as badly as possible. She says "Stop" and it's 11:40 again. The second 20 minutes work out badly in a different way, but the third time everything is fine. Lola has a power that is like magic; she can pull time back so that events take a different path. *Heaven* (2002) was shot from a script by Krzysztof Kieślowski and Krzysztof Piesiewicz, part of an unproduced trilogy called *Heaven, Hell and Purgatory*. It resembles *Dekalog* and *Three Colors* as a close study of a paradoxical and ironic situation. In Italy, an English woman plants a bomb in the office of a bad guy, but the janitor unknowingly takes out the bomb with the trash, and when the bomb goes off, it kills the janitor and a man with two young daughters. When she confesses, a policeman who acts as an interpreter falls in love with her. He helps her escape; in fact, he goes with her. At the end, surrounded, they get in a helicopter and fly straight up until they disappear into the blue sky, which no helicopter can do; figuratively, they go to heaven. In *Perfume: The Story of a Murderer* (2006), based on the novel by Patrick Süskind, Tykwer set himself the problem of conveying that a character has no personal odor at all but does have a strong and cultivated sense of smell; the world of the film is rich with odors the cinema is equipped only to suggest.

Michael Haneke was born in Germany but raised in Austria, and he established himself as an Austrian filmmaker, working both in German and (via Austrian–French co-productions) in French. His tone is cold, distanced, and clear. The stories he tells tend to be cruel and violent, but in most cases he keeps the violence off-screen. A great many of his shots are long takes, sometimes separated by blackouts that turn the films into collections of fragments. What links the fragments is usually not stated. Haneke leaves out crucial story information so that the viewer will ask questions about what she or he is shown. If all the information were given, the story might be banal—or the ambition to tell everything about a situation might appear too outmoded, too like a 19th-century novel. (He does, however, tell a complete, long story in *The White Ribbon*, 2009.) *The Seventh Continent* (1989) tells everything about a suicide except the reason the parents decide to kill themselves and their child. *Funny Games* (1997, remade in English in 2008), the story of two extremely polite home invaders who torture and kill a family, offers a few possible motives for the villains' actions but confirms none of them. *Funny Games* also asks the audience how it feels about what it is seeing and raises the possibility that the audience is complicit in the sadistic events. (Haneke has said that most of his films are about culpability; the best example of this may be *Benny's Video*, 1992, in which a bourgeois couple covers up a thrill murder committed by their son.) In

71 Fragments of a Chronology of Chance (1994) and *Code inconnu* (*Code Unknown: Incomplete Tales of Several Journeys*, 2000), the viewer struggles to discover how the various scenes are related. *The Time of the Wolf* (2003) is a breakdown-of-civilization story in which the reasons for the breakdown are never specified. And in *Caché* (*Hidden*, 2005) it is never said who is making and sending the videos that remind the main character of a shameful and destructive incident in his childhood. For all that he leaves out, however, Haneke makes fascinating films that pose questions in much the same direct, unexplained way that life so often does.

Third World Cinemas

"Third World" is a dated term, once referring to nations that were not allied with the First World of the United States and its allies or the Second World of the Soviets, but it has stuck to many of the films and many of the discussions of them, so as a film term it has some currency. An alternative term, "Third Cinema," has been proposed to distinguish politically oppositional films from the First Cinema of Hollywood and the Second Cinema of *auteurs*. (It should be noted, however, that a developing country will not necessarily produce works of Third Cinema.) "Third World cinema" does not so much describe a national tradition as provide a heading for many politically and economically related but geographically scattered national cinemas: those films from the underdeveloped emerging nations of Africa, Asia, Latin America, and elsewhere that explicitly examine the political, social, and cultural issues of those nations. Although Brazil is one of those countries that has produced Third World films, the popular romantic–erotic fantasy *Dona Flor and Her Two Husbands* (1976, directed by Bruno Barretto), with its escape from social realities, would not be considered one of them. Nor would the Kung Fus from Hong Kong. On the other hand, some European films (*The Battle of Algiers*, *State of Siege*) and some American black or Latino films (like Melvin Van Peebles's *Sweet Sweetback's Baad Asssss Song*, 1971, and Anna Thomas and Gregory Nava's *El Norte*, 1983) have been considered spiritual products of the Third World even though the films were produced or directed by Americans or Europeans; they may well be called Third Cinema, as *Dona Flor* may not. Michel Khleifi's *Wedding in Galilee* (1987), officially an Israeli production, was made primarily with money from Belgium and France, has a distinctly Palestinian point of view, and is usually discussed as a Third World Palestinian picture (much like the films Khleifi did produce in Palestine, again with European money but without the participation of Israel), with a flavor of having been made under the nose of the enemy and a running theme of having to get Israeli approval for everything. (Israeli cinema itself took a surprisingly radical turn in *Waltz with Bashir* [2008, directed by Ari Folman], an animated film—except for a documentary sequence at the end—that investigates an atrocity and the many ways of thinking about it.) *Yol* (1982), a realistic, socially critical Turkish film directed by Şerif Gören and written by Yilmaz Güney—who wrote the script while in jail and had to smuggle it out—is certainly a Third World film. To keep an already muddy metaphor from becoming any more murky, it would make sense to define a Third World film by both its national origin and its cultural content.

These developing, often postcolonial countries produce films either to educate their own citizens about the cultural history and contemporary conditions of the nation or to present that nation's problems and positions to the citizens of the rest of the world—sometimes both. To make feature films up to the technical standards of the international market costs a lot of money, particularly for countries with limited economic resources. Those Third World films that have been widely screened outside local markets must pass a strict test of social utility—serving a country's national and international interests—or they must be artistically striking enough to do well at film festivals and find distribution, which brings prestige to the country and support for its film industry, pictures like Colombia's *Rodrigo D. No Future* (1989, released 1990), Victor Gaviria's violent, depressing, tough, Neorealist look at a group of doomed young men in Medellín (its title a play on De Sica's *Umberto D.*), or Cuba's *Who the Hell is Juliette?* (1997), Carlos Marcovich's wonderfully jerky collaboration with a young woman to define herself and the world around her on film—"if anyone's still in the audience," she says to us through his camera.

Whether or not they are films of revolt, almost all of them are films of national and cultural self-definition. Their clearest historical analogy is to the Soviet silent classics of the 1920s. Like the new Soviet Union, many of these nations are emerging from decades or even centuries of cultural exploitation—economic domination by foreign interests, political domination by autocratic governments that concentrated power in the hands of the few for the benefit of the few and kept the bulk of the population largely illiterate and very poor. As in the new Soviet Union, films could be used to educate an audience unable to read and ignorant or dubious of the goals and methods of a new government. As in the Soviet Union, films could be projected in remote regions of these often topographically tortuous countries with the aid of portable power supplies. One Cuban documentary, Octavio Cortázar's *For the First Time* (1967), describes the wondrous introduction of motion pictures—Chaplin's among them—to a village of Cuban peasants. As in the Soviet Union, films could combine their political lessons with moving stories of human action, often mingling native symbols and folk elements with their didactic tales of social values.

No clearer parallels with the early Soviet movement can be found than in several specific devices of these Third World films. The ending of the Cuban film *The Last Supper* (1976), directed by Tomás Gutiérrez Alea, reflects the influence of Pudovkin: A montage of metaphoric cross-cuts links the uprising of an oppressed people with the inevitable and irreversible processes of nature. The ending of Miguel Littin's Chilean film *The Promised Land* (1973; never released in Chile), like Pudovkin's *Mother*, shows a failed revolution of the past passing on its spirit to the future and, like Dovzhenko's *Arsenal*, develops the mystically unkillable power of the people. The Argentinian *The Hour of the Furnaces: Notes and Testimonies on Neo-Colonialism, Violence and Liberation* (1968), directed by Fernando Solanas and Octavio Getino—which calls for that revolutionary "Third Cinema" energized by Neorealism and the documentary, politically engaged and collaboratively produced—includes such specific Eisenstein echoes as the use of stone statues in a Buenos Aires cemetery as a metaphor for cultural deadness (paralleling Eisenstein's similar use of statues in *Battleship Potemkin* and *October*) and the metaphoric killing of beasts in a slaughterhouse (parallel to the montage symbolism of *Strike*—except that the Argentine film's soundtrack ironically juxtaposes its slaughter with the jaunty counterpoint of the merry Swingle Singers). Finally, like the Soviet cinema, the cinema of the Third World includes many works that are mere propaganda (telling the audience what to think) and many that present ideas for the audience to think about (comparable to a Brechtian theatre of ideas). Third World cinema is both an international phenomenon and a set of national cinemas, bursting with important movements (*Cinema Nôvo* in Brazil) and exciting director/theorists (Solanas and Getino in Argentina, Glauber Rocha in Brazil) and essential films (Rocha's *Antonio das Mortes*, 1969) whose international influence has been enormous.

Emerging Cinemas, Emerging Concerns
The methods and goals of film production in these developing countries can be divided into three very broad categories. First, one country, Cuba, with a well-developed, sophisticated, and nationalized film industry, can rival the industries of all but a few countries of the world in the quality of its output. Like Lenin, Fidel Castro declared the cinema the most important and socially useful of the arts; as a result, the Cuban government, like the Soviet Union, founded and funded a national film school and film production company (ICAIC—Instituto Cubano del Arte e Industria Cinematograficos). Although ICAIC produces mainly documentaries, it also makes several narrative feature films each year, for the Cubans discovered, as did the Soviets, that the populace preferred Hollywood-style stories to didactic documentaries.

During the brief periods of the progressive Torres regime in Bolivia and the Allende regime in Chile, the cinemas of these two South American nations began to move toward a Cuban-style nationalized industry. But the right-wing *coups d'état* that ended both leftist regimes also ended their developing cinemas and forced many leading artists into exile. Conversely, expanding political freedoms in 1980s Brazil stimulated Brazilian film production.

Second, several developing countries have made a small number of feature films for both national consumption and international distribution (for example, Senegal, Egypt, Ethiopia). Because the population of many of these countries is small, these films seek international distribution to expand their impact and justify their cost. (Nigeria, with a larger population and with a democratic government since 1999, built a larger industry based on video production and achieved wide distribution on DVD and over the Internet. Called Nollywood, the Nigerian industry produces over 1,000 feature-length videos per year, and their content is not at all political.) Because the governments of some of these countries are still politically repressive, the political content of these films, if there is any, is often guarded and metaphoric—more ironic, less radical, less explicitly Marxist, less dominated by revolutionary rhetoric than the films of Cuba or those of the third group.

The third group of films comprises those from countries with such repressive governments that the films become underground acts of rebellion and sedition in themselves. Because these films are so dangerous to make, they could never be shown in the countries that produced them without a revolutionary change in their governments; two outstanding examples are *The Hour of the Furnaces* and Parts I and II of *The Battle of Chile* (1973–77, directed by Patricio Guzmán and edited in Cuba, a Chilean–Cuban co-production released in France). These films have been produced almost exclusively for international distribution, to rally international opinion against the ruling regimes.

Despite these differences in the methods of their production and distribution, Third World films share several general themes. The first is an attack on the dominating cultural presence of the more affluent nations of Europe and America—the British presence in *The Night of Counting the Years* (Egypt, 1969), a film by Shadi Abdes-Salam; the French presence in the films of Ousmane Sembene (Senegal); the American presence in South American films. These movies often reveal the power of colonial and postcolonial influences in their conflict between imported products or customs and strictly native ones—the bottles of Evian water, Coca-Cola, and J&B Scotch in Sembene's *Xala*

Fig. 16-6

Fig. 16-7

Clashes of cultures. Black
African song and a sleeping
white aristocrat in The Last
Supper *(Fig. 16-6); traditional*
African dress with
Westernized gifts at the
wedding in Xala *(Fig. 16-7).*

(*The Curse*, Senegal, 1974) or the conflict of both Christianity and Islam with African religious rituals in his *Ceddo* (Senegal, 1978); the magazine advertisements for American consumer products in *The Hour of the Furnaces;* the juxtaposition of the ritual magic of black African slaves with the rituals of Christian Easter in Tomás Gutiérrez Alea's *The Last Supper;* the presence of the American "Progress Corps" in Jorge Sanjiné's *Blood of the Condor* (Bolivia, 1969).

A second major theme is the crushing, unimaginable poverty of vast segments of the peasant population—whether of the Andes Indians of *Blood of the Condor*, the feudal farmers of Haile Gerima's *Harvest: 3000 Years* (Ethiopia, 1975), the migrant workers of Miguel Littin's *The Jackal of Nahueltoro* (Chile, 1969) and *The Promised Land* (1973), the impoverished family in the barren drought-burned plains of Brazil's Northeast in Nelson Pereira dos Santos's *Vidas secas* (*Barren Lives;* Brazil,

1963), or the impoverished street children in the Rio de Janeiro slums of Hector Babenco's *Pixote* (Brazil, 1981).

A third theme, like the title of Eisenstein's 1929 film, might be called "Old and New," the contrast of the old backward ways of farming, living, thinking with newer, more progressive ones—the conflicts of national and tribal laws in *The Night of Counting the Years*, of ancient and modern customs in *Xala;* the examinations of the new systems of education and the new social role of women in the Cuban documentaries *The New School* (1973) and *With the Cuban Women* (1975), and of the general patterns of historical evolution in the Cuban fictional classic, *Lucía* (1968). Some of these films celebrate the old ways, the founding rituals and unique look of their land and culture—as Souleymane Cissé treats Africa in *Brightness* (or *Yeelen*, Mali, 1987). Others say that it is about time for a change in customs: A powerful example is Ousmane Sembene's *Moolaadé* (2004), a study of female circumcision that is revolutionary, compelling, and easy to understand; the last point is important because Sembene went from writing novels to making movies so that he could reach more people in more direct, clear terms.

A final theme that unites many of these films is the implication that these scattered countries, continents, and peoples are indeed united by common cultural problems and goals whether they are problems of political exploitation or of economics and whether the goal is global communication or national self-definition.

Instructive Dramas

Like Humberto Solás's *Lucía*, many of these films from developing and postcolonial nations have been recognized as classics from world-class directors. *Lucía* is a film in the tradition that stretches from Griffith's *The Birth of a Nation* to Bertolucci's *1900*: the political epic that juxtaposes personal dramas with immense historical events and sociopolitical processes. Solás divides his epic into three periods—1895, 1932, and 196 . . .—each of them reflecting a particular political struggle of the Cuban people (first, the War of Independence from Spain; next, the first Cuban political revolution against the dictator Machado; finally, the continuing worker's revolution under Castro). Uniting the

film is a woman named Lucía—or rather, three different women with the same name. In each of the film's eras, there is a conflict between Lucía's romantic love and the political events that surround and threaten that love.

The 1895 Lucía surrenders to her sexual passion for Rafael, although such a passion is forbidden in the proper, highly Europeanized upper-class world of 1895 Cuba. Her Rafael, an undercover Spanish agent, seduces Lucía as a means of capturing an arsenal held by the Cuban guerrilla army. The result is that Lucía becomes the unknowing cause of her country's defeat, of her brother's death, and of her own horrifying rape. The 1932 Lucía is a member of the *haute bourgeoisie* who falls in love with and marries Aldo, a young radical student. She supports his political struggle by, in effect, joining the working class (she goes to work in a factory) and participating in the street demonstrations of the Cuban women. After the success of the insurrection against Machado, Aldo discovers that their revolution has become corrupt (this was, after all, an insurrection of the bourgeoisie—and Batista would be its end product). Aldo continues his fight against the new status quo, machine-gunning the mayor of Havana on the steps of the city hall (this assassination is a piece of Cuban history), himself dying in the struggle. Lucía remains alone with her personal and political futures shattered.

The 196 . . . Lucía is a member of the working class who has recently married the very energetic and attractive Tomás. Unfortunately, Tomás, in addition to his masculine charm, is also enslaved by the old masculine ways of thinking; he converts his new wife into his domestic prisoner, refusing to allow her to work in the fields, to be seen in public, or to learn to read and write, all because of his sexual jealousy and macho possessiveness. Lucía rebels and deserts him, but the two live very unhappily apart. (This section sets itself the propagandistic problem of supporting marriage while opposing the enslavement of the wife.) In the film's final shot, after their reunion, Lucía continues to insist on her right to be free and Tomás on his right to possess her. The film ends on this unresolved argument— implying that the battle has not been won and that the struggle of Cuban women still continues. The open-ended, ongoing, present nature of this social and political change is emphasized by the ambiguous date of the 1960s (196 . . .) sequence.

The Brazilian Nelson Pereira dos Santos's *Vidas secas* is in a very different style and single key—a hard, close, unflinching look at the desperate poverty of a single family of "Nordestinos," the rural peasants of Brazil's Northeast, in 1940. This family—husband, wife, two boys, and faithful dog—roams the barren, burned plains in search of a farm or ranch where they can earn their keep. Fabiano, the hard-working husband, runs into trouble with a petty government policeman, but rather than take the path of rebellion (he gets the opportunity both to join a band of guerrillas and to murder this toad in uniform), he remains the hard-working docile slave with an incompletely evolved political consciousness.

One of the film's remarkably effective devices is its brilliantly cinematic use of available light for both indoor and outdoor sequences. The scorching, blazing power of the sun, the cause of the land's dryness, is also the film's central metaphor and the source of its absolutely authentic depiction of people living in the midst of their genuine surroundings, either outdoors when exposed to its pitiless glare or indoors when trying to escape into the temporary shade of rooms and houses. Although the film pretends to be set in the past (many radical films, like *Antonio das Mortes*, must masquerade as apolitical and unconnected to the present), it nevertheless successfully implies that the journey of such people continues, unsolved and unresolved, into the present.

A later dos Santos film, *How Tasty Was My Little Frenchman* (1972), is a political tale of a very different type. A period film photographed in lush color, it depicts the experiences of a 17th-century Portuguese mercenary captured by a Brazilian tribe. They sentence him to death because they believe him to be French, the tribe's enemy. They fail to understand that he is Portuguese—also an enemy of the French—and that he came to South America to fight the French. Portuguese look just like Frenchmen to them, and the different European languages sound indistinguishable to their ears—an ironic comment on the way Europeans of that period believed all "savages" looked and talked alike.

Their law demands that he live for a year with the tribe, in material comfort and wedded bliss, after which they will ceremonially kill him and eat him. The "Frenchman" spends his time both trying to escape from the tribe and luxuriating in the simple beauty of its natural life. He cannot believe that they will actually murder him after a year of such community and companionship. But they do—with his sensuously loving wife leading the ceremony. (As the title says, he was *her* tasty little Frenchman.) The film implies that, whether French or Portuguese, the white European is an exploitative colonizer who deserves to experience both the integrity of indigenous custom and the severity of its justice.

Documentaries

The Third World political documentaries, like Solanas and Getino's *The Hour of the Furnaces*, have a very different kind of artistic power and political purpose. *The Hour of the Furnaces* is a three-part, 260-minute analysis of the political, economic, and cultural landscape of Argentina, past and present. Part 1 examines Argentinean political–cultural life in the present (1968) and the roots of that life in the past—the dependence on foreign investments and capital, the domination by foreign culture and customs, the concentration of wealth in the hands of the few, the political alienation of the working class, and the extreme impoverishment of the native Indian population. Part 2 examines Perónism, which the film calls the only genuine working-class political movement in Argentinean history—first, the decade of Perón rule, 1945–55, then the decade of underground Perónist sentiment and activity following the coup that overthrew the Perón regime. Part 3 is a call to arms, urging armed revolution and resistance as the only way to establish a just and equitable government in Argentina. The film's three parts exhibit the three-part argument of Marxist dialectic: thesis, antithesis, and synthesis.

The Hour of the Furnaces is interesting on a number of levels and for a number of reasons. First, the film shakes its audiences—regardless of their political convictions—with the sense of witnessing and participating in a series of historically important and humanly shattering events. The film presents the country's social chaos and cultural antagonisms so sharply, so clearly, and so comprehensively that audiences from more stable, less divided cultures in happier times can only marvel at a spectacle with the intensity of

Vidas secas: *the homeless*
family of "Nordestinos."

Fig. 16-8

historical fiction but the authenticity of historical fact. Second, the film adopts the stance of Marxist (rather than Fascist) rhetoric—asking the audience to think about the issues it has presented, to discuss them (indeed there are sections where the film abruptly breaks off and asks the audience to have a discussion), to formulate questions and to argue about them. This request for conscious and active participation seems antithetical to the Fascist propaganda strategy, also common to bourgeois cinema, of hypnotizing viewers by manipulating ideologically loaded plots (where only the right people get the happy endings or the audience's sympathy) and symbols that strike beneath the viewer's threshold of conscious awareness.

But these differences may be only superficial. Plenty of propaganda remains in the film; much is also left unsaid. For example, *The Hour of the Furnaces* treats the Roman Catholic Church very gingerly (a clear departure from Marxist theory and from Eisenstein's satiric practice), occasionally linking a bishop visually with the forces of governmental repression but never accusing the Church as a whole of any role in subjugating the people. Given the close attachment of the South American working classes to the Church, the film would rather not raise this sensitive issue at all. On the other hand, the soundtrack is a stream of verbal rhetoric that repeats its accusations like a

litany. We hear the accusations that the government of Argentina is an oligarchy, that the oligarchy is supported and controlled by the American CIA, that Argentinean intellectuals and universities are mere servants of decadent European tastes and culture (the film purposely develops an antagonism between workers and intellectuals), but we see little or no precisely documented evidence. The film assumes that merely to flash images on the screen of classic European paintings or of modern magazine ads is in itself an indictment of America, Europe, and Western civilization as a whole.

A great documentary that makes its case with precision and force is Guzmán's two-part, 191-minute *The Battle of Chile* (released in 1977; a third part was added in 1979), which chronicles the six months of social agitation that led to the military *coup d'état* against the constitutionally elected left-wing government of Allende in 1973.

Unlike the Marcel Ophuls documentaries, these chronicles tend to be ideologically one-sided. Ophuls is painfully aware of the complexities and ironies in the commitment to any single political position. These enriching ironies and complexities are luxuries that only pluralistic democratic nations can usually afford. Two Third World directors, Tomás Gutiérrez Alea of Cuba, who received his cinema education at Italy's Centro Sperimentale, and Ousmane Sembene of

Senegal, a novelist who began writing in France and studied filmmaking in Moscow, reveal many of the same broader ironies and complexities of a more international outlook.

Gutiérrez Alea and Sembene

Tomás Gutiérrez Alea's first major work to be seen in the United States, *Memories of Underdevelopment* (1968), is an ironic portrait of a member of the bourgeoisie (Sergio Corrieri) who, unlike many other members of his class, remains in Cuba after the fall of Batista. This highly influential film carefully and comically reveals the man's difficulty in finding a place for himself in the new society. His sexual tastes (rather graphically recorded), his cultural tastes (in books, paintings, music) simply do not belong in the new Cuba, and the film simultaneously condemns the man's spiritual emptiness and ironically sympathizes with his isolation. But an even more careful and elegant Gutiérrez Alea film is *The Last Supper* (1977), a costume drama in color. *The Last Supper* is, like the first section of *Lucía*, set in the Cuba of the late 18th century—on a sugar cane plantation owned by the aristocracy and worked by black African slaves. As the film's

title indicates, the story takes place during Easter week, and the entire work is built on a religious, allegorical foundation. The landowner of the plantation suffers a seizure of aristocratic *Weltschmerz*—he knows not why he is living nor what the value of life may be. In order to regain his faith, he decides to perform an ideal act of Christian penance and charity; he selects 12 of his own slaves, washes their feet, and invites them to sit at his table as his disciples. The meal they eat together is intended to mirror the ideals of Christian charity and equality—master with slave, all equals in the eye of God.

The lengthy supper sequence becomes a rare moment of emotional togetherness and ideological separation. As the diners consume more and more wine, they feel closer to one another. (Like Brecht's *Herr Puntila* and Chaplin's *City Lights*, the film uses alcohol as the great eradicator of class barriers.) The one slave who refuses to be seduced by the master's kindness is Sebastian (whose Christian name evokes martyrdom as well as militance and transformation). Only when the host falls asleep does Sebastian tell his own mythic story, a pagan version of the "Fall of Man," which presents humankind as a mixture of

Fig. 16-9
The Hour of the Furnaces: *testament to political oppression and social violence.*

human and beast—the head of a pig surmounts the heart of a human. The master will indeed reveal that, despite his kindly sentiments, a pig's head rules this human's heart. The pig's head is economic interest—a metaphor for vicious capitalism—that draws a sharp distinction between business and religious sentiment; in other words, the master has no trouble believing in both slavery and Christianity.

The next day is Easter Sunday, and the slaves — according to the master and the sympathetic plantation priest (another deliberate attempt to attack not the spirit of Christianity but its bastardization)—are to spend the holy day at rest and worship. But the brutal foreman of the plantation can think of nothing but productivity. This foreman represents the hard economic reality beneath the spiritual and philosophical façade of the master, the man who does the ruling class's dirty work. He demands that the slaves get to work. A violent rebellion of slaves results—led by those very 12 disciples who sat at the master's table and believed in his commitment to the sanctity of the next day. In the struggle, the slaves deliberately kill the vicious foreman (a man who had earlier cut off Sebastian's ear as punishment), accidentally kill his wife, and set fire to the

plantation. The master's pigheaded answer is the equally violent subduing of the rebellion by armed force and the deliberate murder of the 12 slaves who, the night before, sat with him at table—as an example of the price of revolution.

But Sebastian manages to escape, using the magic dust he brought with him from Africa, the spirit of his homeland, to convert himself into a tree, a rock, a river, a bird. With Sebastian's escape—Gutiérrez Alea cross-cuts between the running Sebastian and images of a tree, a rock, a river, a bird—we understand that his rebellious spirit is, like that of St. Sebastian (who reportedly had to be killed several times), an unkillable human force that will be reborn in later generations of followers. The black African spirit of Sebastian becomes the film's metaphor for the spirit of the Cuban working-class people—many of them descendants of these African slaves— that would arise and rebel against the shams of Christian social justice in 1959.

Gutiérrez Alea's next major film (he died in 1996), co-directed with Juan Carlos Tabío, was *Strawberry and Chocolate*, a film about different tastes in sex, politics, and ice cream. Completed in 1992, it was shown at a Cuban festival in 1993 and immediately banned; the producer was

Memories of Under-development: the bourgeois intellectual surrounded by books, physical embodiments of his attitudes and values; the book in his hands is Lolita.

Fig. 16-10

forced to leave the country. The film attacks the homophobia of the Castro regime and outlines many of the failures of the revolution by allowing a character who is both intellectual and gay (Diego, played by Jorge Perugorría) to express his view of the world to a party-line heterosexual (David, played by Vladimir Cruz) who comes to care about him and to understand—even to share—some of his perspective. This consciousness-raising film, in which a radical becomes aware of a new radical agenda (a new sexual politics and an openness to world culture and new ideas), attempts to advance the essence of social and political revolution while opposing the limited vision of the dominant regime. In other words, it is a Third World film that appears counterrevolutionary only to a government that sees the revolution as a fixed and established entity, rigid in its political and cultural agendas and social attitudes.

Ousmane Sembene, the most important director in sub-Saharan Africa, had been adapting his own stories and novels into films since 1966, when he made *Black Girl*, a study of an African woman who feels stifled, deceived, and corrupted when brought to the South of France to work as a cleaning lady. Born in Senegal, he became a dockworker and union activist in France in the 1950s before turning to writing and—thanks to a scholarship to the Moscow film school in 1962—to filmmaking. He died in 2007. One of Sembene's most complex films is his adaptation of his novel *Xala*, an ironic study of the difficulty of exercising power well after having seized it. The prologue is a comic allegory of political change—the native-dressed black Africans enter a marble-halled, mausoleum-like, European-style building, the Chamber of Commerce, and jauntily evict its white occupants and their symbols—busts of European figures, army boots, institutional paintings—spouting rhetoric about "Africa for the Africans." But in the very next shot, the African deputies sit in the Chamber's conference room, dressed in European tuxedos and tailcoats; in succeeding shots, a white commander, one of those previously expelled from the Chamber, directs a perfect line of metronomically marching black policemen; two other formerly expelled white deputies present attaché cases stuffed with greenbacks to each of the current deputies, who sit in perfect symmetrical lines around the conference table. (Sembene deliberately uses the unnaturally straight line and the overperfection of sharp, rectangular compositions as satiric devices.) The prologue's point is clear: A group of Africans throw the rascals out of the Chamber of Commerce and become the rascals themselves; they are not true revolutionaries, charting a new and indigenously African course, but examples of mere neocolonialism.

The rest of *Xala* tells the story of one of those bureaucratic deputies, a respected businessman, whose business, significantly, is importing food. This minister has decided to indulge his sexual appetite by taking a third wife. (Sembene ironically reveals that the sexist Africans have preserved those vestiges of African culture that suit their pleasure under the guise of perpetuating "Africanness.") The wedding party is a curious mixture of African customs (the groom need not even attend the church service) and Western ones (the guests drink cocktails and Coca-Cola; gifts include African ones, like gold jewelry, and a Western one, a red-ribboned automobile; a band plays a terrible but funny pastiche of pop-rock music). This marriage begins the minister's downfall—he sinks steadily into debt, beggary, and social disgrace.

Unfortunately, the minister is mysteriously incapable of sexual arousal with this new young bride he took for sexual purposes. The minister believes that someone has put a curse—a *xala*—on his virility. So he seeks a variety of native magical cures (again Sembene shows that these Westernized Africans become very Africa-conscious when it suits their needs), but his impotence is incurable. At the end of the film, the minister has fallen lower than the outcast poverty of a group of beggars and cripples that has wandered symbolically through the film—beggars who have been swindled out of the food they need to survive by the minister's own economic machinations. The man's true *xala* is that he is a stranger to his own people—not white and not black, not traditional and not modern, not African and not Western. Like all of the hypocritical swindlers and thieves in the outwardly respectable Chamber of Commerce, he is a not.

One of *Xala's* consistent motifs is to draw a contrast between men and women in this society—a sure sign, for Sembene, that the new

Fig. 16-11
Xala: *Africans in the Chamber of Commerce with Westernized clothing and identical, geometrically arranged attaché cases.*

culture is as stagnant, as immature, as unresponsive to the genuine needs of the African people as the one it replaced. The men in the film all speak French, while the women all speak the native language, Wolof. The men dress in black-and-white Western clothing, while the women dress in colorful native garb. This contrast of neutrality and color plays a consistent symbolic function in this color film. The single colorful object in the conference room of the Chamber of Commerce is the table around which they sit (which is, in effect, their altar); it is green, like dollars. The minister's sexual problem becomes a metaphor for the general sexist and material corruption of the "new" African male, the continent's true *xala*. In *Xala's* ironic contrasts of black and white, old and new, male and female, Africa and Europe, developing world and developed world, political justice and political repression, self-definition and imitation, power and impotence, economic freedom and economic dependence, the film brilliantly, maturely, comically, perceptively summarizes the essential issues of the political cinema of the developing world as a whole.

Other English-Language Cinemas

If the British film industry once was a Hollywood colony, ruled by the common language, the English-language film industries of former British colonies—from Australia to Canada (which also has a French-language industry)—have faced even greater difficulty. While England

possessed the resources to develop projects that Hollywood could not do at all or as well, the industries of the former colonies struggled to find the economic means and cultural distinctiveness to flourish as alternatives to both London and Hollywood.

Australia

Australia's film-production problem paralleled that of any developing, postcolonial nation—with important differences. Founded by the British as a penal colony in 1788 (which it remained until 1840), not federated as a commonwealth until 1901, Australia has a population most of which descends directly from Britain. While an emerging country of Africa or Latin America could draw upon its own native culture, customs, and language that had been usurped by colonizers, the dominant customs and language of Australia came from the colonizers, from England, and it was this culture that would produce most of its films.

Given its direct British descent, Australian culture is not without its parallels to America's. As opposed to the verdant unity of the English countryside, Australia remains a largely untamed frontier continent with awesome topographical contrasts—plains, seas, mountains, deserts, forests. Like modern America, it has both vast modern cities and vast open spaces. Also like America, it has an indigenous culture that the European white settlers pushed back and pushed aside but could neither ignore nor assimilate. The clash of European immigrants and Australian Aborigines paralleled that between white pioneers and Native Americans. While some Australian films (notably Peter Weir's *The Last Wave*, 1977) set Australian whites in the context of Aboriginal culture, as colonizers who need to learn from or at least stop oppressing the natives, the majority (like Weir's *Gallipoli*, 1981) celebrate white Australian culture in itself and bitterly resent the ways Australians are treated by *their* imperialist oppressors, the stuck-up and sometimes cruel British. The Australian films of the 1970s defined their identity by combining local themes with models from both London and Hollywood: British traditions of literary elegance and polished acting (many Australian actors and directors have trained at the London dramatic academies and have apprenticed in British repertory companies) with the vitality of American images and Hollywood genres.

Before there could be films, there had to be funds. Shot in Australia, Nicolas Roeg's British film, *Walkabout* (1971), was among the first to demonstrate the power of Australian themes and visual imagery (the contrast of white and Aboriginal children's worldviews in the frontier Australian Outback). If the British could make such films (or a Canadian—Ted Kotcheff's harrowing *Outback*, also 1971), why couldn't Australian directors make them as well? As in so many film production centers outside America, the stimulus came from governmental subsidies for feature films with "local content," consistent with international standards of technical expertise and stylistic polish, through the Australian Film Development Commission, established in 1970 (which became the Australian Film Finance Corporation, or FFC). Produced with just such support, one of the first Australian films to be shown at international festivals was John Power's *The Picture Show Man* (1977).

Although many Australian films try to sort out modern Australian life (for example, Gillian Armstrong's comic rock-musical, *Star Struck*, 1983, or Stephan Elliott's *The Adventures of Priscilla, Queen of the Desert*, 1994), some impressive Australian films look back at the nation's history—particularly the two decades between the Boer War in South Africa and World War I, the very period of Australian confederation. Australian troops had fought for the British in both wars, with great loss of life and little Australian gain, and Australians had been forced to fight British economic wars against colonial insurgents very much like themselves. Bruce Beresford's *'Breaker' Morant* (1980) and Peter Weir's *Gallipoli* are two powerful depictions of the Australian soldier as hero and cannon fodder, under the yoke of sneering British superiors.

If the British and New Zealanders have often characterized the Australians as rough and uncouth, Beresford's *The Adventures of Barry McKenzie* (1972, sequel 1974), a film in extremely bad taste, only confirmed their suspicions. Beresford's breakthrough film was *Don's Party* (1976), and he captured the international market with *'Breaker' Morant*, a film that picks up the debate in John Ford's cavalry films between the laws of peace and the necessities of

Fig. 16-12
Edward Woodward in 'Breaker' Morant.

war. Morant's platoon had been specially trained to fight the Boer guerrillas by using the enemy's informal and improvisational tactics rather than the rules of British military protocol. But when Morant's Australian platoon performs one of the actions for which it was expressly created, the British disown it for political and diplomatic reasons, court martial Morant and his fellow officers as criminals, and execute two of them on a beautiful morning.

The films Beresford later directed in America include several distinguished "small" films (that is, independent productions in which studios had no interest until they won Academy Awards, characterized by low budgets, excellent scripts, and superb acting) and a few big studio mistakes (he directed *King David* for Paramount in 1985). The best of the "small" films is *Tender Mercies* (1983), which won its author, Horton Foote, his second Oscar (the first had been for adapting Harper Lee's novel *To Kill a Mockingbird*, directed by Robert Mulligan in 1962). That

Beresford works best when he has a good script is clear from *'Breaker' Morant, Tender Mercies,* and *Driving Miss Daisy* (1989). With Beresford's move to Hollywood, the filming of "rough" Australian types was left to Paul Hogan and Peter Faiman, whose *Crocodile Dundee* (1986) was an international hit—and eventually to Greg McLean, whose *Wolf Creek* (2004) features a serial killer as rough and merciless as the Outback he inhabits.

Gillian Armstrong's *My Brilliant Career* (1979), set in the same period as *'Breaker' Morant* and within the same visual environment, is a *Bildungsroman*—the coming of age of Australia's first major woman novelist (Miles Franklin, played by Judy Davis). The film examines both the social disadvantages of women in colonial Australia and the cultural prejudices against Australian thought and art within the entire British Empire. The woman's lowly status in her patriarchal culture mirrors the country's lowly status in the Empire. Her growing maturity and confidence suggest the growth and confidence of Australia in the same period—and of creative, powerful women in any period. From *Star Struck* to her most popular American film, *Little Women* (1994), Armstrong's movies have continued to explore the ways her female characters learn to define and express themselves.

Both Peter Weir and Fred Schepisi contrasted Australia's Europeanized culture with that of its Aboriginal natives. Schepisi's *The Chant of Jimmy Blacksmith* (1978) is a study of a brutally disturbing incident in Australian history. Jimmy Blacksmith is a native Australian who gives up his values, his customs, even his name to serve the whites. When he discovers that he has been betrayed, that he has gained neither the promised material wealth nor social equality, he goes berserk and murders as many white settlers as he can find. He is of course sentenced and executed by white courts of law. Schepisi's film is both a political plea for the rights of Australia's exploited Aborigines as well as a warning about inevitable retribution—a persistent fear of British colonialism. Rebellion and punishment also play major roles in his intense study of sexual repression in a 1950s parochial school, *The Devil's Playground* (1976). Schepisi later made a number of fine films in America, including *Plenty* (1985, starring Meryl Streep), *A Cry in the Dark*

(1988, again with Streep; a U.S.–Australian co-production based on an Australian infanticide case), *The Russia House* (1990, a spy thriller much of which was shot in Moscow and Leningrad with the full participation of the Soviets—the first post–Cold War film), and *Six Degrees of Separation* (1993).

Peter Weir's *The Last Wave* also envisions Aboriginal retribution—not as overt violence but as a quietly subversive power, more psychic and metaphysical than conventionally political. In contrast to the modern man of law (Richard Chamberlain), Weir's Aborigines are in touch with the "dreamtime" and with supernatural influences capable of summoning a wave that will drown the puny white civilization. More than any other Australian director, Weir suggests the doubt beneath the surfaces of Australian culture—that "modern," "rational," "civilized" white European society is a mere shadow and delusion in the mystical eyes of Australia's original inhabitants—the ones who were there *ab origine,* "from the beginning." One of the most elegant films of the late-1970s horror renaissance, *The Last Wave* is in the same league as Roeg's *Don't Look Now.* Weir's previous film, *Picnic at Hanging Rock* (1975), is a very elegant mystery— the inexplicable disappearance of three girls and a teacher from a proper boarding school during an outing, leaving no physical traces behind. Set in the same period as *'Breaker' Morant, Picnic at Hanging Rock* contrasts the rational, orderly appearances of repressive white European society (the school itself) with the operations of an inexplicable universe—just as *The Last Wave,* his best film, does in modern dress.

Gallipoli and *The Year of Living Dangerously* (1982) were the last films Weir made in Australia. His American films have been well received (*Witness,* 1985; *Dead Poets Society,* 1989; *Master and Commander,* 2003), except when they depart markedly from Hollywood formulas (*The Mosquito Coast,* 1986). The best of them—*The Mosquito Coast, Fearless* (1993), and *The Truman Show* (1998)—push some of the same boundaries and have some of the unsettling and rich imagery, the compelling rhythms, and the mysterious overtones of his great Australian films.

George Miller's Mad Max films—*Mad Max* (1979), *The Road Warrior* (*Mad Max 2,* 1981), and *Mad Max Beyond Thunderdome* (1985, co-directed by George Ogilvie)—are futuristic fantasies that combine several genres and traditions while creating an original myth; together they constitute an epic. The central character, Max (American-born Mel Gibson, who emigrated to Australia with his parents), is an "enforcer" like Dirty Harry, a searcher and a loner like Ethan Edwards, a wanderer of the wasteland like an Arthurian knight, a founder like Aeneas, a fighter like Achilles, and a wily survivor like Odysseus. He makes his own rules and establishes his own loyalties (the reason he helps the good guys in *The Road Warrior* is that the bad guys killed his "horse"—his V8—and his dog). The setting is the Australian Outback after a war that has destroyed the old world, which depended on fossil fuels and collapsed without them. Now gasoline is the most precious commodity, and most of the characters spend their time killing each other—for fun, and to steal gas from the losers' disabled vehicles. A burned-out ex-cop whose wife and son were run down by murderous bikers, Max is incapable of settling down but makes vital contributions to the pockets of civilization that are humanity's only alternative to an age of barbarism. *The Road Warrior* tells how Max helps a besieged group—occupying a refinery that resembles a fort in a western but also echoes the tiny, walled city of Troy— escape to found "the great northern tribe" (much as the Trojans were said to have founded Rome), and *Thunderdome* ends with a foundation story that is also a creation myth. The Mad Max films draw, then, on the genres of the biker film, the action–adventure spectacle, and the road movie as well as the older, related traditions of the medieval romance and the ancient epic—but more than anything else, they are westerns: from *Thunderdome*'s wide-open town to *The Road Warrior*'s climactic chase, which converts Ford's stagecoach into a speeding truck and his Indians on ponies into brutal crazies driving wild cars. The Mad Max films are clear examples of the vital Australian blending of classic genres and images with uniquely modern and Australian issues: What would happen to an immense, isolated continent like Australia after an atomic war, when the world was already plagued by oil embargoes? In addition to the Mad Max films, George Miller is responsible for another series,

the Babe films, whose hero is a gallant and unusually talented pig; he produced *Babe* in Australia and the United States in 1995, and in 1998, he directed its sequel, the American production *Babe: Pig In The City.*

Among Australian directors who did their first significant work in the 1980s and 1990s, Baz Luhrmann (*Strictly Ballroom*, 1992; *Moulin Rouge!*, 2001; *Australia*, 2008) is the most flamboyant stylist; Ray Lawrence (*Lantana*, 2001), the most intense choreographer of complex characters; and Rob Sitch (*The Castle*, 1997), the most congenial and outrageous comedian. Paul Cox, who was born in the Netherlands but made his mark as an Australian filmmaker (*Man of Flowers*, 1983; *A Woman's Tale*, 1991; and especially *Innocence*, 2000), extended the range of his probing, distinguished, emotionally rich work with the Dutch production *Molokai: The Story of 'Father Damien'* (1999), a tale of leprosy and heroism shot with no frills. In the early 2000s, one of the most interesting new directors was Warwick Thornton, whose *Samson & Delilah* (2009) was the realistic, understated, unconventional love story of two young Aborigines who spend some time in town. Continuing the trend of those who, like Weir, direct their most original and daring works in Australia only to make what are for the most part less interesting films in America, Phillip Noyce left after the brilliantly realistic drama *Newsfront* (1978) and the fiercely tense *Dead Calm* (1989) to make such American pictures as *Clear and Present Danger* (1994) and *The Bone Collector* (1999). He returned to Australia to make *The Quiet American* (2001, released 2002) and *Rabbit-Proof Fence* (2002), which are among his finest works. But not everyone leaves. One filmmaker who has bucked the trend and stayed to work in Australia is Rolf de Heer. Born in Holland and raised in Australia, de Heer became known for such domestic dramas as *The Quiet Room* (1996) and *Alexandra's Project* (2003) before making a breakthrough picture with a cast of Aborigines, *Ten Canoes* (2006). Narrated and performed in an Aboriginal language spoken today by 200 people, and told in an Aboriginal style, *Ten Canoes* is set before the coming of the whites; it is a tale of the ancestors, a profound and entertaining tragicomedy of conflict and kinship that completely immerses one in its world. The Aborigines improvised much of

Fig. 16-13
Richard Chamberlain in **The Last Wave:** *discovering his own fate—and face—while probing an Aboriginal mystery.*

the dialogue, though de Heer wrote the script; as he told a *Time* interviewer, "They're telling the story, largely, and I'm the mechanism by which they can."

New Zealand

New Zealand was settled by the Maori, a people of Polynesian origin, in the 10th century and by Europeans in the 17th and 18th centuries. The Maori called the country Aotearoa—and still do. A British colony since 1840, it became self-governing in 1907 and has been an independent member of the Commonwealth since 1947. While the Maori continued to control their own lands, white New Zealanders nurtured their Britishness along with their independence. The film industry, given a boost by the founding of the New Zealand Film Commission in 1978, is independent and original as well as linked with the industries of Great Britain, America, and Australia.

For some time, the most important filmmakers from New Zealand were *from* New Zealand and did their major work in England or the United States—notably Len Lye, whose *A Colour Box* (1935) made the first great use of painting directly on celluloid and is considered a British film. Beginning in the late 1970s, however, Roger Donaldson drew attention to New Zealand filmmaking with his *Sleeping Dogs* (1977) and *Smash Palace* (1981). Like Lee Tamahori's *Once Were Warriors* (1994), whose main characters are Maoris living in the big city, *Smash Palace* is a violent family melodrama about the conflict between the way things are and the way heroes and antiheroes think they ought to be; there is a tendency in both films to revert to the old codes in the face of the wreck of everything important.

The black comedies and outrageous horror films of Peter Jackson (beginning with *Bad Taste* in 1987) became cult favorites and prepared audiences for his horrific family melodrama, *Heavenly Creatures* (1994), the true story of two infatuated, murderous girls. After the premature death of his longtime producer, Jim Booth, in 1994, Jackson went on to make an authoritatively phony documentary about early film history,

Forgotten Silver (1996, co-directed with Costa Botes), and his first big-budget horror film, The Frighteners (1996), in which he revealed a gift for managing large teams and a command of slick special effects, rich visuals, solid performances, and relatively good taste, all of which he put to use in his next major project, the three-part/three-year adaptation of J. R. R. Tolkien's trilogy, The Lord of the Rings. Its first part, The Fellowship of the Ring, was released in 2001 to critical acclaim and increased book sales. The second part, The Two Towers (2002), and the final part, The Return of the King (2003), were equally impressive. With each film, Jackson and his New Zealand effects teams broke new ground. Although produced with American money, the trilogy was made in New Zealand. Joining The Wizard of Oz and King Kong, The Lord of the Rings proved to be one of the cinema's great works of fantasy and adventure, even if its vision was darker and it had fewer songs and poems than the original novels. Appropriately, Jackson's next project was a U.S.-financed remake of King Kong (2005). In 2009, he helped to produce Neill Blomkamp's District 9, a science fiction film set in South Africa.

After Jackson, the most authoritative stylist of the 1990s, who also started with horror films that were hard to take, was Scott Reynolds; his The Ugly (1996) and Heaven (1998) worked multiple levels of vision, dream, and reality together with unusual skill and emotional power.

The hero of Niki Caro's Whale Rider (2003), a modern version of an ancient story, is Paikea, a young Maori whose brother, who was supposed to become the next leader, died at birth. Although the boys are educated in their culture and rituals, Paikea (Keisha Castle-Hughes), as a female, is barred from the teaching sessions. At the climax, she rides a whale, recreating the journey of her ancestor, celebrated in myth, who rode a whale to bring his people to Aotearoa, and she is accepted as the new leader. A feminist film as well as a mythic one, Whale Rider brought another powerful woman director to world attention; Caro joined Jane Campion as one of New Zealand's vital artists.

Jane Campion was born in New Zealand and made her first films in Australia: the shorts Peel (1982), A Girl's Own Story (1984), and Passionless Moments (1984); the TV film Two

Friends (1986); and her first theatrical feature, Sweetie (1989). She returned to New Zealand to make An Angel at My Table (1990, originally for TV) and to shoot the Australian–French–New Zealand co-production that made her famous, The Piano (1992, released 1993). Beautifully photographed, The Piano had a polished style that was carried forward in The Portrait of a Lady (1996), from the novel by Henry James, and Bright Star (2009), a look at the last years of poet John Keats's life and his romance with Fanny Brawne—a rare example of successful communication in Campion's work. Most of Campion's films are about women whose means of expressing themselves are met with rejection and incomprehension—sometimes because the people around them refuse to let go of power long enough to listen, sometimes because their gestures and decisions are paradoxical and unexplained.

Sweetie is about a dysfunctional family dominated by a spoiled, obnoxious daughter who, the audience finally realizes, was probably sexually abused by her father and has been expressing, in her own way, all the tension and chaos the family denies. Her language is to explode. An Angel at My Table, based on the autobiographies of Janet Frame, who became one of New Zealand's most famous authors, tells how Frame's shy ways, coupled with a nervous breakdown, were misdiagnosed as schizophrenia and led to her being incarcerated for eight years of shock treatment. She was saved from brain surgery only when the stories she had been writing were published and the authorities around her realized that she had a rich and sane inner life. If the withdrawn person she presented to the world seemed hard to know, isolated in some private space, her language—written words—got through the barrier. The woman in The Piano, who can speak but until the end of the story does not (a decision she has held to since childhood), has her language too: music. Her inner life and essential being come forward when she plays the piano. In what is both a feminist fable and a kind of D. H. Lawrence fantasy, she resists her controlling husband—who believes that since she is his property, she can have none of her own, and gets rid of the piano—and falls in love with a man who uses the piano as a way to get to her heart and her body. Using what she calls the voice of

Fig. 16-14
Maori boys are taught the history and rituals of their culture in **Whale Rider.**

Fig. 16-15
Harvey Keitel and Holly Hunter in **The Piano:** *love in another language.*

her mind, this silent woman speaks to the audience voice-over, and eventually the characters learn to listen to her too; when she finally abandons her isolation, however, she also has to let go of the piano—though it remains a vital emblem in her memory, an image of nonverbal power buried deep in the self.

Canada

Australia and New Zealand struggled with or adapted to the cultural imperatives of British domination before developing original cinemas, but they enjoyed the cultural oddity of isolation as Western societies in the oceans south of Southeast Asia. Even more severe have been the cultural handicaps on a Canadian cinema, not only a former British colony, but also a former French colony, a nation of two cultures and two languages, just across the border from the country with the West's most powerful film industry. The earliest Canadian feature was *Evangeline* (1913), directed by E. P. Sullivan; the earliest that survives is *Back to God's Country* (1919), directed by David M. Hartford and starring the woman who masterminded the project, Nell Shipman (see Chapter 6).

For decades, Canadian cinema was synonymous with the National Film Board of Canada, founded by the British documentarist John Grierson in 1939. Government-supported and famous for the experimental films of Norman McLaren (*Fiddle-de-dee*, 1947; *Begone Dull Care*,

1949; *Neighbours*, 1952; *Blinkity Blank*, 1955; *Pas de deux*, 1967), the Film Board was committed almost exclusively to short films—documentary or animated, in English or in French. Canadian feature-film production, though it dates from 1913, and though the National Film Board did produce a few features—few, but superb, like Don Owen's *Nobody Waved Goodbye* (1964)—was a relatively minor activity. Instead, Canada's international prestige rested on its animated films and documentaries, as well as on the avant-garde films of Michael Snow (*Wavelength*, 1967), Bruce Elder (*The Book of All the Dead*, 1975–95), and others. Many feature-oriented Canadian directors (Norman Jewison, Arthur Hiller) and actors (Donald Sutherland, Christopher Plummer) left to work south of the border, as Mack Sennett had.

The changes in Canadian feature-film production began in 1978, stimulated (as usual) by government policy—seed money for film investment through the Canadian Film Development

Corporation (established in 1967) and new, attractive tax laws for film companies to shelter profits. While postwar European governments used tax laws to combat American films, the Canadian government used tax laws to lure film projects, many of which seemed thoroughly American. Louis Malle's *Atlantic City* (1980) was officially a Canadian film, despite its French director, American setting, and clear relationship to American genres like the *film noir*. Other Canadian productions included apparently Italian films, like Ettore Scola's *A Special Day* (1978), and French films, like Claude Lelouch's *Us Two* (1979).

Finding Canadian subjects for Canadian films has been an ongoing project. Although *Nobody Waved Goodbye* and Paul Almond's *Act of the Heart* (1970) attracted international attention, Ted Kotcheff's *The Apprenticeship of Duddy Kravitz* (1974), based on the bestselling Canadian novel by Mordecai Richler and supported by the Canadian Film Development Corporation, was the first thoroughly Canadian feature film to make a great deal of money outside Canada. Canadian themes have since been seen in Richard Benner's affectionate tribute to Canadian transvestite performer Craig Russell (*Outrageous!*, 1977), Ralph L. Thomas's tracing the paths of Canadian youth to the brainwashing camps of the "Moonies" (*Ticket to Heaven*, 1981), and Phillip Borsos's exploring the legends of Canada's own Wild West and exotic outlaws (*The Grey Fox*, 1983). *The Fast Runner* (2001), shot on video in the Arctic by a group of Inuit film-makers led by Zacharias Kunuk, was based on an ancient Inuit legend.

One of the first French–Canadian directors to reach an international audience, with his small-scale *Mon oncle Antoine* (1971) and grand-scale *Kamouraska* (1974), Claude Jutra first made animated films and "direct cinema" documentaries (helping to found Canada's own vastly influential *cinéma vérité* movement) at the National Film Board. In the late 1980s, the most popular French–Canadian films were those of Denys Arcand: *The Decline of the American Empire* (1986), a witty, sexy comedy of manners, and *Jesus of Montreal* (1989), a reflexive satire about the production of a Passion Play; he also had great success with the sequel to *Decline*, *The Barbarian Invasions* (2003), in which the

characters deal with a death. In the late 1990s, Montreal's bravest director was Denis Villeneuve, whose *August 32nd on Earth* (1998) broke the rules of continuity editing and narrative connection to explore the paradoxical ways people nearly connect, rather like an episode of *The Twilight Zone* based on Buñuel and Dalí's *L'Age d'or*.

Of the newer English-language directors who established their reputations with Canadian features and continued to pursue the themes of their early works in the films they made in the United States and elsewhere, the best known are Ted Kotcheff and David Cronenberg. Kotcheff left Canadian TV to make films in England (*Life at the Top*, 1965, the sequel to *Room at the Top*) and Australia (*Outback*, 1971—a richly atmospheric and disturbingly violent film, certainly his best, that was released in the same violent year as *Straw Dogs* and *A Clockwork Orange*) before returning to Canada to make *Duddy Kravitz*. His most successful American film, *First Blood* (1982), inaugurated the Rambo series but was more thoughtful and intense than its sequels. The heroes of all these films are at war with the world around them, either because they have been forced to fight groups they would rather ignore (*Outback*, *First Blood*) or because they have chosen to "conquer" groups they want to join (*Life at the Top*, *Duddy Kravitz*); in all these battles, whether physical or verbal, moral values and self-definition are at stake—and not every hero survives, or wants what he wins.

The horror films of David Cronenberg are even more tightly interrelated, taking for their essential subject the nature of evolution, both of "the flesh" and of consciousness. The changing body is a cancerous horror in some of his films, a pubescent paradox in others, and it is often accompanied by a scary but fascinating change in mental ability and sexual behavior. There is no thematic break between his major Canadian films (*Shivers*, 1975, released in the United States, with cuts, as *They Came From Within*; *Rabid*, 1977; *The Brood*, 1979; *Scanners*, 1980, released 1981, his first international hit), his Canadian/U.S. co-productions (*Videodrome*, 1982, released 1983; *Dead Ringers*, 1988), his American pictures (*The Dead Zone*, 1983; *The Fly*, 1986; *M. Butterfly*, 1993), and his Canada-based international co-productions that have included France, the United Kingdom, and sometimes Japan (*Naked*

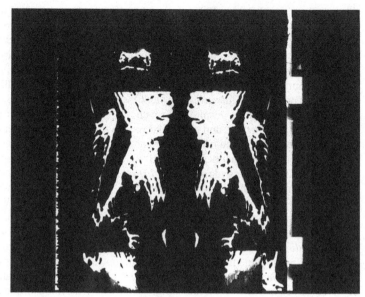

"From **The System of Dante's Hell,** *the first region of* **The Book of All the Dead.** *One who lives with the knowledge of death—of the deaths of love, desire, and creative power—abides from moment to moment with the horrible question, 'Am I acceptable to the Creator?' and so must constantly reaffirm his poetic capacities. Out of this urgence has emerged a long, and densely allusive text, that like Pound's* **Cantos,** *after which it is fashioned, seeks to fashion a paradiso terrestre."—Bruce Elder*

Fig. 16-16

Lunch, 1991; *Crash,* 1996; *eXistenZ,* 1999). They all fit and advance together on a dramatic definition of the nature and psychology of flesh, the metaphoric and sometimes gory route he takes into the study of people in bodies. (Nevertheless, *Eastern Promises,* released in 2007, confirmed that he had turned away from the horror film and the theme of flesh, a move that began with *A History of Violence* in 2005.)

In *The Brood,* the story of a woman whose angry thoughts cause her to give birth to little monsters who kill her enemies—so that they are the children of her anger, "the shape of rage"—the horror is characteristically mental and physical. The protagonist in *Spider* (2002) suffers mental anguish, and the audience shares his painful, contradictory visions and memories; he also is uncomfortable in his body and wears extra layers of clothing to separate himself from the outside world and keep track of who he is. *Spider* offers a view of mental illness, seen both subjectively and objectively, that is inseparable from how the character inhabits the physical world. The hero of *Videodrome* (Max) attains a new level of consciousness partly as the result of a brain tumor induced by a video signal, and the hero of *The Dead Zone* (one of the best Stephen King adaptations and the first Cronenberg film not based on a Cronenberg story) gains telepathic abilities, from

brain injuries, that allow him to save the world. In *Shivers,* sluglike glandular parasites infect the bodies and drastically affect the minds and behavior (compulsive erotic violence) of everyone living in a fancy bourgeois housing complex; rather than evolve, they devolve. But *Videodrome*'s Max evolves morally and metaphysically—and suffers vivid hallucinations—as his body evolves into the "new flesh," the incarnated Word of video philosopher Brian O'Blivion (inspired by Canadian media theorist Marshall McLuhan). Experimental flesh grafts turn skin-flick star Marilyn Chambers into the carrier of a plague in *Rabid.* The "mad scientist" in *The Brood* is a psychiatrist, as the one in *Rabid* is a plastic surgeon. *Scanners* concerns a generation of telepaths whose projected thoughts have physical effects, created through *in utero* chemistry by a scientist who wants to accelerate human evolution—unlike the mad scientist in *Shivers* who invents squirmy monsters to pull humanity back to a primitive level of development. In the original version of *The Fly* (1958, directed by Kurt Neumann), the scientist ends up with the fly's head and arm immediately, as soon as the teleportation experiment goes wrong; in Cronenberg's version, the emphasis is on the scientist's slow evolution into a man–fly and on the way he learns to enjoy, as his body changes,

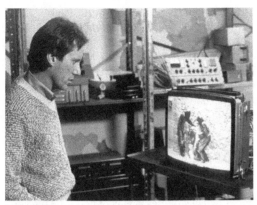

Fig. 16-17
Videodrome: *Max (James Woods), a cable TV programmer, gets his first look at a sadistic Videodrome program.*

the way a fly thinks. The characters in *Crash* attempt to merge flesh and metal, lust and death, through the power of sheer erotic will. And the end of *Scanners* shows two brothers in one body (one's mind and voice in the other's body), while *Dead Ringers* examines the problem of twin brothers with disturbingly separate minds in disturbingly similar bodies, who come together to die.

Ivan Reitman, the producer of *Shivers* and *Rabid*, was born in the former Czechoslovakia and raised in Toronto. His full-length student film, *Columbus of Sex* (1970, based on the anonymous Victorian autobiography *My Secret Life*), was the first Canadian feature to be charged with obscenity. After producing *National Lampoon's Animal House* (1978, directed by John Landis) in the United States, he moved to Hollywood, where he directed movies that were silly (*Stripes*, 1981; *Twins*, 1988), smart (*Dave*, 1993), and no-holds-barred entertaining (*Ghostbusters*, 1984).

Of course, not every Canadian director has commuted or emigrated to Hollywood. Atom Egoyan, born to Armenian parents in Egypt in 1960, remained in Toronto even after *Exotica* (1994) and *The Sweet Hereafter* (1997) made him famous. One of his most personal films, *Ararat* (2002), told the little-known story of the mass murder of Armenians in 1915, the Armenian genocide still denied by those who carried it out. Like many of his other films, it is about bearing

witness with a camera. Egoyan's characters are always looking at each other, sometimes in person but usually through some kind of mediator: the phone, a video camera, a TV set, a surveillance camera, a movie, a computer. They peek into others' lives, usually maintaining an excited, voyeuristic distance but sometimes involving themselves with the people they have met through the camera, whom they sometimes cannot even see without a camera (in *Family Viewing*, 1987, one character becomes introspective only when looking at herself on closed-circuit video). As a phone can be used for phone sex, video can become an erotic interface (*Family Viewing*; *Speaking Parts*, 1989; *The Adjuster*, 1991); *Speaking Parts* combines the metaphors in a sexy scene with a teleconferencing apparatus, and *Family Viewing* shows a couple acting out phone sex in front of their video camera. Video can also become, like film, a window to the past: the mausoleum stone in *Speaking Parts* on which the mourner imagines a video of a memory, or the home videos the grandmother watches in *Family Viewing*. The title of the latter is a massive pun, encompassing a family's private viewing of a deceased relative, a family that spends its time together watching TV, a family whose members watch each other on video, entertainment suitable for the whole family, and a look at a family made out of the survivors of families we have watched fall apart. Some of Egoyan's characters depend on films and tapes to maintain their real or imagined relationships with the dead. In *Felicia's Journey* (1999) a man whose late mother hosted a cooking show from her own kitchen keeps the kitchen just as she had it and watches her old shows on a TV set in that kitchen, following her instructions exactly in an effort at last to win—or at least be worthy of—her approval.

Many of Egoyan's characters have lost their ability to make an unmediated erotic connection; many are estranged from themselves and from where they live. His films are filled with Canadian Armenians who feel displaced from their homeland, victims of fire who have been displaced from their homes (*The Adjuster*), people who live and work in hotels. In *Speaking Parts* there is a writer who has been kicked off her own project—a script based on her own life, from which she now has been removed.

In *The Adjuster* a man pretends to be a director who needs, as a set (but actually as the site for an apocalyptic sex game whose fetishes are cameras and the identities of others), the furnished home of an insurance adjuster; by offering enough money he convinces and displaces the adjuster, who moves with his family into the motel where he has been arranging temporary housing for his clients. Soon after the adjuster has become a member of this city of transients, he loses his family and house.

Transience is one of Egoyan's central themes: the ephemeral nature of commitments, relationships, places to live, and life. Capturing life with a video camera is a transient (erasable) way to stay partly in touch with all that one has lost or will lose. Nevertheless, the woman in *Family Viewing* (Arsinée Khanjian) who is given a tape of her mother's funeral, who was deprived of the ritual of the family viewing—strictly defined—and the chance to bury her mother in person, tosses the tape away, to the incomprehension of the youth who thought that she would be as comforted by watching the tape as by having been there; in other words, Egoyan knows the difference between media and life, but some of his characters don't. Beyond video, another way to spy on life and create a record of it is to investigate: not to tape people but to question them, getting a thrill of connection from probing their wounds while doing all one can to restore their losses (*The Adjuster, The Sweet Hereafter*). The latter film—adapted from the novel by Russell Banks and the first of his pictures for which Egoyan did not write an original story—makes it especially clear that the ambulance-chasing lawyer is trying to get a life by getting other people's lives, that some secrets will always be kept private, and that some losses cannot be restored. When the Academy nominated Egoyan for an Oscar as best director for *The Sweet Hereafter*, it was, for once, not trying to lure a Canadian to Hollywood but honoring a major artist of the Canadian cinema.

Ireland and Elsewhere
The United Kingdom comprises Wales, Scotland, and Northern Ireland as well as England; the Republic of Ireland is a separate country. This survey of alternative English-language cinemas is happily obliged to call attention to the small but developing industries of Wales (Paul Turner's *Hedd Wyn*, 1992), Scotland (Bill Forsyth's *Gregory's Girl*, 1981) and Ireland (Jim Sheridan's *My Left Foot*, 1989), as well as independent productions such as Jamie Uys's *The Gods Must Be Crazy* (1981), from Botswana, and international co-productions such as *Hotel Rwanda* (2004, directed by Terry George), partly from South Africa.

Hedd Wyn (pronounced "Heth Win") was not only the first Welsh feature, but also one of the best films ever made about poetry, the story of a prize, a chair, and a war. It was shot in Welsh and bore English subtitles, a way of honoring the language and its poets. Many of the legends and poetic traditions that England adopted as its own were of Welsh origin, and *Hedd Wyn* reminds us of the depth and complexity of a culture, people, and region that England has sometimes denigrated. One of the most important of the early Scottish pictures was an Irish co-production; *The Magdalene Sisters* (2003, directed by Peter Mullan) was so controversial a study of Catholic institutions for supposedly wayward Irish women that it had to be produced primarily outside the country.

The most developed of these new cinemas is that of the Republic of Ireland. In the late 1980s and the 1990s, its two best-known directors were the Irish novelist Neil Jordan, most of whose films were produced in England but who often drew on Irish materials, and the Irish playwright Jim Sheridan, who put the industry on the map with *My Left Foot*, in which Daniel Day–Lewis played Christy Brown, who became a writer and painter in spite of the cerebal palsy that left him able to move only one foot. Based on Brown's autobiography, the film was full of rough and nasty humor that kept it from being merely inspirational.

Sheridan's next picture, *The Field* (1990), starred Richard Harris as an Irish farmer, best described as an "angry old man," who becomes crazy and destructive when a field he has rented and improved for years is sold to an outsider. At times, the film seems as patriarchally driven as the old man. Sheridan took a deeper look at the Irish family—and at the politics of Irish rebellion and British injustice—in the largely factual *In The Name Of The Father* (1993), a melodrama in which power, strength, and renewal come from getting the truth told rather than letting the liars win.

Neil Jordan applies his lush visual imagination and sneaky wit to genre materials that only at first appear to be familiar. His adult look at the world of the fairy tale, *The Company of Wolves* (1984), is a bedtime story with a vengeance—and far more effective, as a horror film, than his later *Interview with the Vampire* (1994). *The Butcher Boy* (1997) cast the then notoriously antipapal Sinéad O'Connor as the Virgin Mary; one of the most violent and stylistically assured of his films, it may be the funniest family tragedy ever made, the story of the making of a crazy, likable killer who is perfectly OK with himself. The characters in *Mona Lisa* (1986) surprise the audience as much as each other, and the film manages to be funny and tough, with a romantic undertow. Much the same can be said of *The Crying Game* (1992), in which Stephen Rea (Fergus), Jaye Davidson (Dil), Forest Whitaker (Jody), and Miranda Richardson (Jude) negotiate a wilderness of sexual and political twists, and what begins as a story about a gang of Irish terrorists turns into an adult examination of race and sex, a witty and elegant game with the nature of barriers and distinctions in general.

Russia and the Former Soviet Union

After the death of Stalin, Soviet culture and filmmaking "thawed" under Nikita Khrushchev, and a number of cinematically fresh and emotionally engaging movies won critical acclaim at home and abroad: Mikhail Kalatozov's *The Cranes Are Flying* (1957), Sergei Gerasimov's *The Quiet Don* (1957), Grigori Chukhrai's *Ballad of a Soldier* (1959), Alexei Batalov's *The Overcoat* (1959), and Josef Heifitz's *Lady with a Dog* (1960). Other important and powerful films appeared in the next decade—Kalatozov's *I Am Cuba* (1964), Andrei Konchalovsky's *The First Teacher* (1966), Sergei Bondarchuk's seven-hour *War and Peace* (1967), Grigori Kozintsev's *Hamlet* (1964) and *King Lear* (1971). But under Khrushchev's successors, especially Leonid Brezhnev, the late 1960s and 1970s became an increasingly difficult period in which to work. Filmmaking was subsidized, but many films were not approved for production; art films were entered in festivals but rarely shown in Moscow or other big cities. Some filmmakers

were persecuted under the Brezhnev regime, and some left the country. Even so, enough great films were made to justify world attention to a Soviet Renaissance, whose most important directors were Sergei Paradjanov (born Sarkis Paradjanian) and Andrei Tarkovsky.

Paradjanov, Tarkovsky, and Others
Sergei Paradjanov was born in Georgia, was tutored by Dovzhenko, made most of his films in Ukraine (some in Georgia and Armenia), and died in Armenia in 1990. A musician, painter, and connoisseur of folk tales, Paradjanov became world famous with the Ukrainian *Shadows of Forgotten Ancestors* (1964), a lyrical explosion disguised as a movie. Set in the Carpathian mountains among a tribe "forgotten by God and men," *Shadows* episodically relates a folk tale of undying love. Its combination of realism and mythology evokes what is at once a vivid natural world and a magical realm brimming with the power of characters who are both simple and bigger than life (as in the folk legend and myth) and with psychological and supernatural forces that erupt into the wild daylight. Like the people it examines, its "prosaic days are for work, holidays for magic." But this world that has been so carefully re-created, both in its look and in its worldview, is observed by an utterly up-to-date camera that rushes to frame the action or follows it fluidly, or circles within or around the action—or *creates* the action, as in the early shot when a man is killed by a falling tree, but no tree is seen; as the tree is heard, the camera tilts down from a great height, gets a view of the man standing in the snow, and plummets until it appears to crush the actor. (The cinematographer was Yuri Ilienko.) The natural colors may be replaced at any time by flagrantly artificial lighting, shots taken through color filters, and special color effects achieved on an optical printer. From its swish pans to its slow motion, from its constantly changing music to its abrupt shifts in narrative tone, from its rough realities to its brilliant dreams, *Shadows of Forgotten Ancestors* was the most important Soviet film since *Ivan the Terrible, Part II*. Though Paradjanov was hailed as a new Dovzhenko, he ran into trouble when the film was accused of formalism—the demon of the old Stalinist censors—and of promoting Ukrainian nationalism. (They may have had

something there, for it was Ukraine's decisive move for independence in 1991 that precipitated the downfall of the Soviet Union.) His next ten projects were rejected, and he worked as a scriptwriter for years. But in 1968 he made a controversial film—*Sayat Nova*, also known as *The Color of Pomegranates*—that evoked the poems and the inner life of an 18th-century Armenian monk through a series of stunning images; when he refused to revise the film to suit authorities, it was recut by someone else and shelved. While he was serving many years at hard labor in the Gulag—for publicly protesting Moscow's cultural policies, although what he was accused of was homosexuality and trading in art objects—an early, unfinished (1971) version of *Sayat Nova* was seen by filmmakers and shown at festivals outside the country; Paradjanov completed the

film in 1978, after he got out of prison. His last major works were *The Legend of Suram Fortress* (1984, co-directed by Dodo Abashidze) and *Ashik Kerib* (1988). In *Sayat Nova*, where the camera almost never moves (the case in most of his later films), and *Ashik Kerib*, Paradjanov concentrated intensely on the almost iconically rich frame and de-emphasized movement and dialogue.

Andrei Tarkovsky, who died in 1986, was an astounding creator of worlds: worlds that had been (*Ivan's Childhood* or *My Name is Ivan*, 1962; *Andrei Rublev*, also spelled *Roublyov*, 1966—Soviet release 1971) and worlds that could never be (*Solaris*, 1972; *Stalker*, 1979, released 1982). And these worlds are transformed by the imagination: in *Andrei Rublev*, the attempts of medieval Russians to transcend their limits,

Fig. 16-18
Shadows of Forgotten Ancestors: *doomed lovers in a folk legend.*

whether by flying in a balloon or by discovering the secret of casting a perfect bell, and the icons painted by Rublev; in *Solaris*, the memories and dreams of a crew in orbit around a remote planet, a virtual sea of thought, that can materialize what they imagine. The most surreal of his films are full of cool, clean shots of nature, often of leaves and stones seen through running water (*Stalker*); his most natural films are never far from subjective vision (*Mirror*, 1974). Although Tarkovsky was allowed to make these films, which brought Russia international prestige, he was frustrated that they were so rarely, if ever, shown in his homeland for their intended audience. *Andrei Rublev*, based on the life of a major icon painter, used its central character—a monk whose wanderings and painting take him across a brutal stretch of 15th-century Russia—to focus its study of the relations between the suffering and grime of the world and the transcendent, almost impossible achievements of art and obsession; though it was shown abroad after winning a prize at Cannes in 1969, it was shown only once in Russia—in 1966—before it was grudgingly released there in 1971. The most political of his films, *Stalker*, was held back for years. Upset at these exhibition practices, Tarkovsky defected to the West in 1984, where he continued to make his slow, intensely meditative, magically evocative

films: *Nostalghia* (or *Nostalgia*) in Italy in 1983, and *The Sacrifice* in Sweden in 1986.

Among the many other filmmakers who came to prominence in this period, three more stand out: Larissa Shepitko, Nikita Mikhalkov, and Tenghiz Abuladze. Larissa Shepitko, who studied under Dovzhenko and was married to Elem Klimov (*Come and See*, 1985), was recognized as Russia's major woman director before she died in a car accident in her early 40s. Her best known works are *Wings* (1966), *You and I* (1971), and a harrowing, black-and-white, personal, poetic film called *The Ascent* (1977). Based on a famous story by the popular Kirghiz author Chingiz Aitmatov, *The Ascent* implies, through a tale of Soviet prisoners held by the Nazis, the senselessness and waste of human potential brought by the Stalinist purges. When she died in 1979, she was working on a film called *Farewell*.

Nikita Mikhalkov made the warmest and most inventive art-house hit the Soviets had produced since the days of Sputnik: *A Slave of Love* (1976), a reflexive romantic comedy that was exuberant and moving. His *Oblomov* (1980) was a solid adaptation of the classic Russian novel by Ivan Goncharov, and *Dark Eyes* (1987, made in Italy) adapted Chekhov to the talents of Marcello Mastroianni. It is Mikhalkov who mastered the

Tarkovsky's **Andrei Rublev.**

Fig. 16-19

new way to succeed in Soviet filmmaking: to direct international co-productions that sell tickets abroad and win prizes at festivals. His *Urga* (*Close to Eden*, 1993), shot in Mongolia, displeased the Russians as much as it pleased international audiences with its positive vision of multicultural harmony—released at a time when ethnic, religious, and political clashes were fracturing what was left of the former Soviet Union. His first post-Soviet film to be made in Russia was *Burnt by the Sun* (1994), an anti-Stalinist drama about a day in the life of a hero of the Revolution.

Tenghiz Abuladze, who died in 1994, came from and worked in Georgia. He is best known for the great trilogy on which he labored for nearly 20 years: *Molba* (*Prayer*, 1967, released 1969), a black-and-white drama full of winter, raw violence, and poems (read voice-over); *The Wishing Tree* (1978), a color film that could pass for a Czech tragicomedy if it were not such a Russian fable; and *Repentance* (1984, released 1987), a surreal black comedy about an official who resembles Stalin and who will not stay buried after his death, because someone repeatedly digs him up.

Glasnost and After

Repentance was shown to acclaim abroad and huge lines of patrons at home when it finally was released, its uncompromising and darkly amusing anti-Stalinism proof that a new openness (*glasnost*) was indeed beginning to flourish as the Cold War (1945–90) drew to a close.

For there had been a change in command. Mikhail Gorbachev began in 1985 a policy of restructuring (*perestroika*) and openness. Restrictions on Soviet art were virtually eliminated, and studio productions were expected to help pay for themselves. Subsidized production dropped; co-production, especially with companies abroad, substantially increased. Shelved films were released. New ideas were welcomed. The shadows of Brezhnev and stagnation were gone. Filmmakers replaced bureaucrats in key industry positions. And out of this, in the short-lived *glasnost* era (roughly 1985–92), came some daring and remarkable films, among the most influential of which were *Is It Easy to be Young?* (1987, directed by Juris Podnieks), an interview–documentary that traces the fortunes of several teenagers across two years; the antibureaucratic

satire *A Forgotten Tune for the Flute* (1987, directed by Eldar Ryazanov); *Little Vera* (1988, directed by Vassili Pitchul), a sexually frank and sometimes depressing, almost Neorealist look at a young woman's options under the oppressive sexual, economic, and political systems that are as inescapable as her family; *Fountain* (1988, directed by Yuri Mamin), an extremely funny fable about modern incompetence that portrays the Soviets as having lost their bearings and ruined everything by organizing and improving it; and *Get Thee Out!* (1990, directed by Dmitri Astrakhan), the first Soviet film about the pogroms. The script of *Little Vera* (by the director's wife, Maria Khmelik) went unproduced for four years but was approved under *glasnost*; its production and *Repentance*'s 1987 release indicated that the old restrictions on content and treatment truly were gone. Other significant *glasnost* films include Sergei Bodrov's *Freedom Is Paradise* (1989), Rachid Noughmanov's *The Needle* (1989), *Taxi Blues* (1990) by Pavel Lungin (often credited as Pavel Lounguine), and Vitaly Kanevsky's *Freeze, Die, Come to Life* (1990).

Perestroika opened the door to free enterprise, but also to inflation and food shortages; Soviet society became more vital, but also more threatened. In December 1991, the Soviet Union was disbanded, and its republics became separate countries; Russia, or the Russian Federation, remained the largest and was headed by its first elected president, Boris Yeltsin. Yeltsin called for a completely free-market economy and even tried to ban the Communist Party. Subsidized filmmaking was at an end. Mosfilm, the industry's largest studio, suffered so drastically from the loss of government backing that by 1993 its output had dropped from 45 to 7 pictures a year. An impossible thing had happened: Soviet filmmakers, who were supposed to focus on ideology rather than the box office, suddenly became post-Soviet filmmakers who had to make movies that would make money.

The problem is that the post-Soviet Russian movie business is no place to make money. Tickets are cheap, but very few people go. According to a 1993 poll taken in Moscow, only four percent of the respondents had any interest in seeing movies about daily life in Russia. But those movies—and nutty symbolic ones completely removed from the everyday, like Rachid Noughmanov's *The Wild*

Fig. 16-20

Tenghiz Abuladze's **Repentance.**

East (1993), a version of *Seven Samurai* whose bandits are bikers and whose farmers are midget "solar children"—continue to be made, even if their theatrical future is dismal. As weird and offbeat as daily life may appear in many of these films, it has an unpretentious and formidably amusing quality not approached by the formal masterpieces, let alone the Stalinist lectures and spectacles, of the Soviet past. Life on the real streets is shown with brilliant authority and insight in Vitaly Kanevsky's 1994 documentary, *We, Children of the 20th Century.*

This is not to suggest that the Russians have given up on making masterpieces and reconsidering the past. Alexander Sokurov's *Mother and Son* (1997) ranks with the best of Tarkovsky and Paradjanov; its muted colors, distorted perspectives, and slow tempo give the death of a mother the time it demands and make possible the rigorous search for the right images, images that seem to come from another world but go to the heart of ours. In addition to *Russian Ark* (2002; see Chapter 19), Sokurov made a "dictator trilogy" that treated Hitler (*Moloch*, 1999), Lenin (*Taurus*, 2001), and Hirohito (*The Sun*, 2009). And Petr Lutsik's low-budget comic epic, *Outskirts* (1998), parodied *Chapayev* and other films of the 1930s while telling, in black and white, a story that in the context of the 1990s was genuinely revolutionary: The heroes discover their collective farm has been sold to the new capitalists, and they work their way violently up the economic food

chain, growing in skill and determination, until they reach the big city, kill the top businessman, blow the place up, and save their farm. It was the only picture he ever directed, though he had co-written others, usually with his co-author on *Outskirts*, Aleksei Samoryadov. Born Pyotr Lutsik in 1960, he died in 2000 of a heart attack.

As the studios in Russia sought to make it on their own, securing international co-production deals on action and genre movies, agreeing to abide by international copyright laws, setting up (in 2009) a board to promote Russian films internationally, and making distribution deals that were completely independent of the old, centralized, official distribution system, studios and independents in the former republics began to develop self-supporting national cinemas. It had always been important to know from which region of the USSR a Soviet filmmaker came (Dovzhenko was Ukrainian to his bones), but now it became appropriate to speak of Noughmanov's *Wild East* as a film from Kazakhstan, in fact part of the "Kazakh New Wave." From the breakup of the Soviet Union came more than a dozen emerging national cinemas, each of them starting from scratch.

Iran

The Islamic Republic of Iran has produced state-supported and independent films of extraordinary quality; it also has a conventional film industry that is, in the words of director Abbas Kiarostami, "across the street" from where the real filmmaking is going on. Before the 1979 revolution that overthrew the shah, Iran had produced a total of 1,300 films, including a brief New Wave in the early 1970s. One of the best of the New Wave pictures was Sohrab Shahid Sales's *Still Life* (1974), a slow, realistic look at the lives of a railway-line guard and his wife, set in 1960, that shows their going about their daily routines and the destruction of that life when he is forcibly retired. A quiet and powerful film that remains a superb example of Iranian Neorealism, *Still Life* had a profound influence on Kiarostami and others. In 1984, Iran set the goal of producing at least 50 "Superior Iranian Films" every year, partly by making low-budget grants available for films that would teach worthwhile lessons and whose artistry would bring international prizes and bookings.

There were, of course, restrictions. Because a woman had to be covered when she left her house, even to go to a movie set and play an indoor scene, she still had to be covered in that indoor scene (as the wife was throughout *Still Life*); one result was that the majority of new Iranian films with adult characters were shot outdoors, even in cars like so many of Kiarostami's, to avoid shooting unrealistic indoor scenes in which, for example, a fully clothed couple talk things over in bed.

One of the most remarkable things about the Iranian cinema of the mid-1980s and later is that without portraying violence or sexual activity, let alone a woman's uncovered head, these pictures have revived Neorealism, the fable, and the children's film all at once. Many of these movies are about children and take them more seriously than adults, though they pretend to treat adults as equals. Most of them are about an ordinary person with a single big problem—a legacy of the most influential of all imports, *The Bicycle Thief*—and many are shot outdoors with nonprofessionals. The best have a solid sincerity and an apparent simplicity that sneaks the overwhelming into the frame, whether they are as matter-of-fact as Kiarostami's or as ugly and beautiful as those of Makhmalbaf (a radical sent to prison in the days of the shah), little tales with good advice or focused celebrations of human decency. Occasionally a rebellious film like Jafar Panahi's

The Circle (2000)—which circulates from one beset woman to another as they deal with the *chador* or overscarf, with the difficulty of going anywhere without a man or an ID card, with prostitution and jail, and with the possibility of solidarity—will challenge the system and find release overseas.

Abbas Kiarostami, an accomplished director of commercials, was asked to start the filmmaking branch of the Institute for the Intellectual Development of Children and Young Adults. Kiarostami began to write and direct short films in 1970, features in 1974 (*The Traveler*). He also wrote screenplays—treatments, really, with room for the actors to improvise the dialogue—that were directed by others but often edited by him; the most widely available of these are *The Key* (1986, directed by Ebrahim Forouzesh) and *The White Balloon* (1995, directed by Jafar Panahi). *The Key* is about a four-year-old boy who manages, when he figures out what the neighbors are yelling about, to save his baby sister and himself from a gas explosion in their locked apartment. *The White Balloon* is about a little girl who wants to buy a special goldfish for the New Year, the people who scare her, and the people who help her, especially her brother and a refugee who gives up the chance to sell his last balloon—the white one—to help her get her money from under a street grate. In 1987, Kiarostami directed *Where is the Friend's Home?* (or *Where is My Friend's House?*, as the French release title translates), a completely involving movie about a boy, Ahmad, who has accidentally picked up the school notebook of his friend, Mohammad Reza, and *has* to return it, in spite of the fact that he doesn't know where his friend lives, except that it's in another village, and the adults around him won't listen. Their rigid teacher has made it clear that he will expel Mohammad Reza if he doesn't bring his homework in tomorrow, in his notebook. Ahmad looks all over, for most of the movie, but doesn't find him. His solution—to do the homework in both notebooks and slip Mohammad Reza's to him just in time—cuts through the frustrations of the film and shows something important about friendship, right under the noses of the self-involved adults.

Where is the Friend's Home? is the first film in a trilogy. In 1991 the region where it was shot was hit by a terrible earthquake. In *Life, and*

Nothing More. . . (1992, also called *And Life Goes On*) a man like Kiarostami tries to drive with his son to that remote region, on roads that are mostly blocked, to find out whether the children he filmed are all right. He shows people a poster for the film and eventually hears good news that is likely to be reliable. He leaves his insistent son to watch a soccer game on a communal makeshift TV, and he almost reaches the village, but the film ends. The sequel is not, however, about getting to the village: *Through the Olive Trees* (1994) is a fictional film about the shooting of *Life, and Nothing More. . . .* This series of films is consistently realistic and increasingly reflexive. *Close-Up* (1990) is a semi-documentary treatment of the actual trial of a man who impersonated Makhmalbaf and said he was casting a movie. *Taste of Cherry* (1997), also called *The Taste of Cherries*, suspends its reflexivity until the final scene, a video take of the actors' setting up a shot.

Taste of Cherry is about a man who drives around looking for a stranger who will help him commit suicide—either by burying him or, if he's changed his mind and is alive, by pulling him out of the pit where he will or will not have killed himself by the next morning. As mentioned before, these films are often about people with a problem—how to drive to a quake-devastated village when the roads are practically gone, how to buy the fish in time—and Kiarostami's later ones often show the protagonist in a car, a subject he manages to make cinematically interesting, and entirely revealing of the culture and the land, for hours. (A woman took the wheel in *Ten*, 2002.) Although his earlier films and scripts snapped shut at the end as their structures were neatly fulfilled—the teacher's "Good" on the friend's homework marks the end of *Where is the Friend's Home?*—his later films have had strikingly open endings. Most of his films are Neorealist in spirit, structure, and method, but they are never violent, hysterical, or sentimental; they are as flat as Godard's but do not lecture. While dealing with the problems of everyday life, they address and leave open the questions of life itself.

Mohsen Makhmalbaf has worked in a variety of styles, from Neorealism to Expressionism, from raging satire to poetic mystery. He has even changed style in midpicture: *The Peddler* (1986) has three parts and three cinematographers. *The*

Cyclist (1989) moves from De Sica to Kafka, from a *Bicycle Thief* problem to a "Hunger Artist" problem. To get the money to pay his wife's hospital bills, a poor Afghan agrees to ride his bicycle in a small circle for a week, day and night; he once did this for three days. His son runs beside him with a bottle of water, nurses run along with beakers to test his urine for stimulants, men sell tickets, everyone makes bets. If anyone sees him fall asleep or collapse, his wife will die. But when he heroically, impossibly, and perhaps insanely finishes the week, he refuses to stop riding, even to collect the money.

Makhmalbaf's formal masterpiece, *Gabbeh* (1996), is a film of rich color and interwoven narrative lines; as a structure, it is woven. A *gabbeh* is a rug that shows a story; it is made of wool grown and sheared, dyed and woven, by a nomadic tribe in southeastern Iran. The Handicraft Industries Organization asked Makhmalbaf to make a movie about these weavers, expecting a documentary. Instead he made the story of a rug in the form of a rug. An old couple washes their prized blue wedding carpet in a stream; the *gabbeh* shows a distant horseman and a woman living with a tribe. The old man asks the *gabbeh* to tell its story, and a young woman in blue (Shaghayegh Djodat) materializes out of the rug; her name is Gabbeh, and her father is Weave of the Wool. She tells the old woman, who is dressed in the same blue, how she is waiting for her father to allow her to marry the man who waits for her, on his horse, in the distance. We see this romance played out, and the story of Gabbeh's uncle's search for a wife, while the old couple washes the rug. The old man wants Gabbeh to love him, but she of course is not interested; she prefers her lover, who howls like a wolf. At one point the uncle teaches a class, essentially to us, about color. He reaches out of the shot into another shot of a yellow, flowering field and pulls back a bunch of yellow flowers; he reaches out of the shot into the sky, and his hand comes back painted blue. "Love is color," says Gabbeh. At last the lovers run away, the father only pretends to kill them— and the old man howls his romantic longing like a wolf. The old couple may *be* the lovers in the story—the movie has just that kind of interreferential structure—or the story may come to life when they clean the rug.

The Apple (1998) was written and edited by Makhmalbaf but directed by his 18-year-old daughter, Samira Makhmalbaf. Her second film, Blackboards (2000), was a story about the will to teach, and beyond that a stark and vividly staged look at the clash between old and new cultures in Iran. She wrote and directed her next feature, At Five in the Afternoon (2003), based on a novel by her father; in it she confirmed her mastery of understated realism. Makhmalbaf is said to be preparing films for his other children to direct. The Apple is the true story, re-enacted by the actual family, of an overprotective man who refuses to let his blind wife and their two daughters leave their small, high-walled dwelling, and what happens when a social worker lets the kids out. But it ends with a sense of perfect, formal closure when the mother herself, left alone for the first time, finally walks outside and touches an apple, a piece of the richness of life, dangled by a playful neighbor.

The New Internationalism

The most striking change in film commerce since the mid-1960s has not been the introduction of individual national traditions but a leveling of national boundaries that has created a truly global market. The extent of international distribution, the number of international co-productions, the number of international film festivals, and the number of directors working outside their native industries have become more significant than any particularly national statistics.

To take only one example, Crouching Tiger, Hidden Dragon, which won Taiwan the Oscar for Best Foreign Language Film of 2000, was produced by companies in Mainland China, Hong Kong (where much of it was shot), the United States, and Taiwan. The director himself, Ang Lee, has worked across the world while maintaining a base in New York—the site of his first pictures, Pushing Hands and The Wedding Banquet—making films like Eat Drink Man Woman in his native Taiwan, Sense and Sensibility (a U.S.–U.K. co-production) in England, and Brokeback Mountain in the United States. He is an international director, and each country in his co-productions has added a significant presence, not just backing, as can plainly be seen in the contributions England made to Sense and Sensibility, from the Jane Austen novel and the Emma Thompson screenplay to the cast and the landscape. And if Brokeback Mountain is strictly American drama, Crouching Tiger is a film immersed in all of China, leaping from one region to another as gracefully as its characters bound across rooftops and basing itself in literature and in fable as well as in the history of Chinese cinema.

Directors had, of course, changed residence before: both Billy Wilder and Fred Zinnemann left Germany for Hollywood, as Hitchcock left England, and stayed, while Lang and Renoir worked in Hollywood for a while and then left. But in the 1970s and later it became more common to find directors working in several

Shaghayegh Djodat in Mohsen Makhmalbaf's Gabbeh.

Fig. 16-21

countries—like Louis Malle, who continued to make films in France after he began directing in America, or Wim Wenders, who made *Paris, Texas* in America, then hit the road for Tokyo (to make the documentary *Tokyo-Ga*, 1985) and Berlin. International crews and casts flourished as filmmakers satisfied the desire to work with the right people in the right place (Tarkovsky wanted his Swedish film, *The Sacrifice*, to be shot by Sven Nykvist) and learned from one another: Pavel Lungin's Soviet–French *Taxi Blues* was one of the first Soviet films to be shot with live sound—because it had a French sound crew.

It also became far more common to find films financed by groups or industries in several countries: international co-productions such as the French–German *Wings of Desire;* Sylvain Chomet's masterful French–Belgian–Canadian animated feature, *The Triplets of Belleville* (*Belleville Rendez-vous*, 2003); the Scottish–Irish *The Magdalene Sisters;* or the Italian–British–Chinese *The Last Emperor* (1987), which was directed by Bertolucci and shot by Vittorio Storaro (both Italian) on location in China—notably in the Forbidden City, where no Westerners had previously been allowed to film—and which starred John Lone (from Hong Kong), Joan Chen (from Shanghai), and Peter O'Toole (from Connemara, Ireland). Just as *The Last Emperor*'s location shooting was itself an event in the history of international cooperation, three years later *The Russia House* spread Moscow and Leningrad across the wide screen as no non-Soviet film had been allowed to show them before; it also had an Australian director and co-producer (Fred Schepisi), a British literary source and screenwriter (playwright Tom Stoppard's adaptation of John le Carré's *glasnost*-era spy novel), European co-financing and an American releasing company (MGM-Pathe), a distinguished supporting cast from America (Roy Scheider) and England (James Fox, director Ken Russell), and in the leading roles a Scot (Sean Connery), an American (Michelle Pfeiffer), and a German (Klaus Maria Brandauer).

A film may be co-produced because the filmmakers are living and working in different countries (Kieślowski's Swiss–French–Polish *Three Colors*), because economic opportunities arise (the 1987 co-production treaty signed by Canada and Hungary), because another country or

industry has the facilities—or politics—without which the project could not be realized (the controversial Chinese films co-produced in Taiwan and Hong Kong; *The Scent of Green Papaya*, shot in France because it posed production problems insurmountable in Vietnam), and because some projects require a great deal of funding from industries unable to support them single-handedly (*The Last Emperor*). Although it left tariffs and quotas against American films in place in the European Community (a demand pushed primarily by the French), the 1994 revision of the General Agreement on Tariffs and Trade (GATT, replaced in 1995 by the World Trade Organization) lowered international trade barriers and set up mechanisms to enforce copyright laws, making international production and exhibition deals simpler and more reliable.

It should be remembered that most films—made by studios or by independents, made in Hollywood or co-produced by people and industries in different countries—earn significant profits (or break even) only when they are exhibited worldwide. Alfonso Arau's *Like Water for Chocolate* (1991, released 1992, script and novel by Laura Esquivel) was a hit in Mexico, but abroad it sold more tickets than any Mexican film yet made, and in the United States it was the most successful foreign-language film yet released.

Although the Mexican cinema has long been known for films of romantic escapism—like the western musical *Allá en el Rancho Grande* (1936 and 1949, directed by Fernando de Fuentes) and horror films from the cheap *The Brainiac* (or *The Baron of Terror*, 1962, directed by Chano Urueta) to the polished *Cronos* (1993, directed by Guillermo del Toro)—and although *Like Water for Chocolate* was a work of Magical Realism, Mexico has also produced films that are realistic with an ironic edge, the best known of which are Buñuel's *Los olvidados* (1950) and Alejandro González Iñárritu's *Amores Perros* (*Love of Dogs* or *Love's a Bitch*, 2000, a long, fast, hard-hitting trio of interconnected tales about people who love their dogs even if some of them train dogs to fight and even if love can sometimes give you the short end of the stick, a film that reflects the international influence of Quentin Tarantino). Mexico's Alfonso Cuarón, the director of *Y Tu Mamá También* (2001), is also well known for his

Fig. 16-22
The Pearl: *a Mexican classic written by John Steinbeck, directed by Emilio Fernandez, and shot by Gabriel Figueroa.*

U.S. pictures, which include *A Little Princess* (1995) and *Harry Potter and the Prisoner of Azkaban* (2004). Guillermo del Toro followed *Cronos* with other brilliantly designed pictures made in the United States (*Mimic*, 1997; *Blade II*, 2002; *Hellboy*, 2004; *Hellboy II: The Golden Army*, 2008) and in Spain (*The Devil's Backbone*, 2001, a Spanish–Mexican co-production). In *Pan's Labyrinth* (2006, another Spanish–Mexican co-production), del Toro interwove the realistic and the fantastic with consummate skill, creating a narrative labyrinth at whose center is a choice between reading the story realistically and reading it as a fairy tale; the film gives full evidence for both positions. It was in 2006, when González Iñárritu's *Babel*, Cuarón's *Children of Men*, and *Pan's Labyrinth* were all on the world's screens at once, that critics noticed there was a vital new movement centered in Mexico, led by three friends who shot most of their films outside their native country and who went on to found a production company, Cha Cha Cha, that released its first picture in 2008 and that specialized in both Mexican and international productions; in 2009, it co-produced González Iñárritu's American picture, *Biutiful*.

International filmmaking has cross-fertilized the cinema. When John Ford decided to film *The Fugitive* (released in 1947) in Mexico, he hired a Mexican cinematographer, Gabriel Figueroa. Figueroa had been trained in Hollywood and had been particularly impressed by the style and example of Gregg Toland—not just in *Citizen Kane* but also in the films Toland shot for Ford and Wyler. One result was that *The Fugitive* looks almost as if Toland had shot it for Ford, but it also reveals Figueroa's own rich, developing style. Figueroa brought his international eye to many of the films he shot in Mexico, from Buñuel's *Los olvidados* and *The Exterminating Angel* (1962) to John Huston's *Under the Volcano* (1984). He also worked regularly with the greatest Mexican director of the 1940s, Emilio Fernandez, shooting—among others—his *María Candelaria* (1943) and the dramatically and visually powerful *The Pearl* (1946). *The Pearl* was itself the product of an international collaboration, for John Steinbeck wrote its script for Fernandez before rewriting it as a short novel. And Fernandez passed some of his tricks along to Peckinpah, for whom he played the role of General Mapache in *The Wild Bunch*.

Fig. 16-23
Emilio Echevarría in **Amores Perros.**

There have always been three reasons for film production to cross national boundaries— political, economic, and thematic. The first exodus of filmmakers from their homeland for political reasons was of Germans and other Europeans (Renoir and Clair, for example) from Hitler's Europe. Blacklisted American directors left the United States in the 1950s for England (Joseph Losey) or Greece (Jules Dassin), while the young Costa-Gavras left Greece to study and make films in a more politically receptive France (*Z*) and the United States (*Missing*, 1982). After the mid-1960s, the major political exodus was from Eastern Europe: Milŏs Forman, Roman Polanski, Agnieszka Holland, Krzysztof Kieślowski, Ryszard Bugajski, and Ivan Passer are among the many Eastern Europeans who deserted native production—temporarily or permanently—for the West. Related to the history of exodus is that of return. Renoir returned to Europe after the war, and Hitchcock went back to England long enough to shoot *Frenzy*. But there are also filmmakers who go back home to risk shooting controversial material under native conditions. Barbet Schroeder was born in Iran, spent part of his childhood in Colombia, and

established himself as a filmmaker in France, first working with Rohmer and then shooting his own features (*The Valley Obscured by Clouds*, 1972; *Reversal of Fortune*, 1990) and documentaries (*Idi Amin Dada*, 1974) wherever his camera took him. But in 1999 he returned to the streets and apartments of Medellín to make a violent, tender, realistic movie about love (and drugs, and fame, and—as is usual for him—the meaning of life and death) in contemporary urban Colombia: *Our Lady of the Assassins* (2000), a Colombian–French coproduction that was shot with small video cameras to minimize the security risks.

International co-productions also solve economic problems. Through this internationalism flows American investment capital for a Kurosawa to make a film deemed too extravagant and unpopular for the Japanese studios to support (*Kagemusha*); capital also flows the other way, allowing American filmmakers to raise money wherever they can find it (as Paul Schrader did for his Italian–American *The Comfort of Strangers*, 1990). The same applies, of course, in countries besides the United States. International co-productions often imply international casts—such as Robert De Niro, Burt Lancaster, Donald Sutherland, Dominique Sanda, Stefania Sandrelli, Sterling Hayden, and Gérard Depardieu in Bertolucci's *1900*—which may give the picture box-office appeal in more than a single country. The global marketplace of the early 21st century has created many new opportunities for international financing and distribution. For example, it was relatively easy to find the money for and arrange for the distribution of the Mexican–U.S. co-production *Sin nombre* (2009, directed by Cary Fukunaga).

Finally, some filmmakers shoot outside native boundaries because thematic commitments require the alternative visual or social environment. Peter Weir inspects American culture, while Werner Herzog requires savage and alien landscapes. *The Last Emperor* was a much better film for having been shot on location in China; conversely, the only place Terrence Malick could find the look of 1916–17 Texas for *Days of Heaven* was on the plains of Canada. To take a more recent example, *Slumdog Millionaire* (2008), a British picture with a British director and an Indian co-director, was shot in India with an Indian cast, Indian music, authentic locations, and nearly half of its dialogue in Hindi.

To the extent that international cinema depends on the interrelation of clearly defined national cinemas (like those of Sweden in the 1920s or Italy in the 1940s), it has had to be conceptually redefined in an era of globalization. An international co-production deal is made between two or more companies, not nations. A national cinema may be multicultural and may be borderless, open to influences from around the world. A nation itself, and the cultures within it, may be subject to shifting internal and external boundaries—spatial, temporal, ethnic, linguistic, economic, and so on. *Transnational cinema*, as a term, deals with this borderless condition, this openness to world culture, to world cinema, to living beyond boundaries, to multiculturalism, and to postcolonial hybridity. A film like *Chungking Express*, with its *femme fatale* and its multinational agenda, can be transnational without being the product of two nations. A film like *Café Lumière*, directed by a Taiwanese director in Japan, can be considered both transnational and international. A film like *The Suspended Step of the Stork* can be read as a study of borders in a transnational context. The concept of transnationalism has enriched our ways of thinking about local and global identity, and it has prompted a rethinking of the concept of national cinema (which can seem limited and old-fashioned in a global era), making it possible to imagine a cinema that transcends national boundaries according to a new model.

Luis Buñuel and Spain

One of the first models of the global career is that of the vagabond director Luis Buñuel, for 50 years a man without a cinematic country—making films in France, working as an editor and translator in America, then making films in Mexico, returning again to France, and only occasionally making a film in his native Spain. Made in spite of borders that were political, cultural, and logical, his films would be called transnational if he were working today.

Although the Spanish have a rich tradition of painting, poetry, theatre, and fiction, decades of political repression constrained the country's filmmakers until the death of Franco in 1975 and the emergence of three great directors: Víctor Erice (*The Spirit of the Beehive*, 1973; *The South*, 1983; *El sol del membrillo*, 1992), Carlos Saura (*The Hunt*, 1965; *Cría cuervos*, 1975; *Blood Wedding*, 1981; *Carmen*, 1983; *El amor brujo*, 1986—the last three choreographed by Antonio Gades), and Pedro Almodóvar (*Labyrinth of Passion*, 1982; *What Have I Done to Deserve This!!*, 1984; *Matador*, 1986; *Women on the Verge of a Nervous Breakdown*, 1988; *Kika*, 1993; *The Flower of My Secret*, 1995; *Live Flesh*, 1997; *All About My Mother*, 1999; *Talk to Her*, 2002; *Bad Education*, 2004; *Volver*, 2006; *Broken Embraces*, 2009). Almodóvar is most interested in melodrama, approached from a variety of angles, some of them skewed; he can be outrageous (*Women on the Verge*), symbolic (*Matador*), relatively realistic (*What Have I Done*), novelistic (*Live Flesh*), or subtly ironic (*The Flower of My Secret*), but he always gets top performances from his actors, who manage to be at home in—and sometimes, while performing, to comment on—a vast spectrum of roles. *Bad Education*, for example, is a daring treatment of pedophilia, but it is more about role-playing and what some people will do to make it in the film business; like *Live Flesh* and

Stirrings of a new Spanish cinema: two internationally popular examples. Fig 16-24: Antonio Gades and Laura Del Sol in Carlos Saura's Carmen; *Fig. 16-25: Carmen Maura (right) in Pedro Almodóvar's* Women on the Verge of a Nervous Breakdown.

Fig. 16-24

Fig. 16-25

others, it shows how he links comedy, tragedy, and history in melodrama. Saura is most interested in theatre, particularly the dance, and has made color and camera movement part of an all-embracing choreography. And Erice is most interested in light—like the indescribable color of a fruit a man works for months to paint (*El sol del membrillo*) or the light of a movie reflected on children's faces (*Spirit of the Beehive*); his films are evocative and careful, intimate and shrouded, symbolic and direct, reminiscent of the works of Werner Herzog and Zhang Yimou at their most romantic, but also of the intense and meditative pictures of Carl Dreyer. Other Spanish directors working today include Bigas Luna (*Jamón jamón*, 1992; *The Chambermaid on the Titanic*, 1998), whose films might be said to explore masculinity or just to take its extremes for granted, and Alejandro Amenábar (*Thesis*, 1995; *Open Your Eyes*, 1999; the American co-production *The Others*, 2001; *Agora*, 2009), who excels at cerebral horror but has gone on to other subjects. No work like this was going on in Spain in Buñuel's time.

Buñuel, a descendant of the Surrealism of Paris in the 1920s where he learned his craft from Jean Epstein, made films in a variety of styles: symbolic–Surrealist (*Un Chien andalou*, 1929; *L'Age d'or*, 1930), documentary (*Las Hurdes* or *Land Without Bread*, 1932), sociological case study *(Los olvidados)*, psychological case study (*El*, 1952), religious allegory (*Nazarin*, 1958; *Viridiana*, 1961), psychological–Surrealist allegory (*Belle de jour*, 1967), religious–Surrealist allegory (*The Milky Way*, 1969), political–Surrealist erotic drama (*That Obscure Object of Desire*, 1977), and social–Surrealist allegorical comedy (*The Discreet Charm of the Bourgeoisie*, 1972; *The Phantom of Liberty*, 1974). Through these differing styles over an amazingly long career shine the consistent Buñuel traits: the Surrealist's perception of the insubstantiality of reality coupled with the Surrealist's savage humor; the psychologist's interest in sexual fantasies and personal visions of experience that violate all the norms of the realists, the professional psychologists, and the Church; and, finally, his satiric, hostile preoccupation with the Church itself.

The first event in Buñuel's first film was a close-up of a razor slicing an apparently human (actually a dead animal's) eyeball. The brutality, the nausea, the visceral attack of this first action dominate the Buñuel canon. One of the most unflinchingly sadistic and brutal scenes in his work is the assault of the juvenile delinquents in *Los olvidados* (*The Forgotten Ones*; U.S. title, *The Young and the Damned*) on a legless beggar (cripples, dwarfs, blind men, hunchbacks, and freaks are as common in the Buñuel world as priests). The delinquents pull the cripple out of his cart, kick him, then gleefully send the empty cart careening down the street. The young hero ends up dead on a pile of garbage. As realistic as this depressing, nasty movie is, it still contains Surrealistic dream sequences—and a certain perverse tone—that make it utterly unlike any of the other children of Neorealism.

Viridiana, one of Buñuel's richest works as well as one of his most blasphemous, was filmed in Spain; apparently Franco and the Church misunderstood what it was going to be about and approved the production. (When it was finished, they tried to suppress it.) It begins in a monastery with the music of Handel's *Messiah*; it ends in the bedroom of a young lecher with rock music. The music and the settings mirror the film's journey. The young woman, Viridiana (Silvia Pinal), is a novitiate in a convent on the threshold of taking her final vows. Before taking those vows she makes the customary trip back to the secular world to be sure that she wants to leave it. She visits her rich uncle's estate. He falls under the spell of her beauty. Carried away by his passion, he drugs his niece with the intention of raping her insensate body. But instead of actually committing the rape, he merely tells her that she has been violated, daubing the sheets of her bed with blood to convince her of the physical fact of her sin. She decides not to return to the convent; her uncle kills himself in his shame.

Rejecting the formal teachings of the Church as a means of saving her soul, Viridiana takes the next step on the film's symbolic path. She turns to natural religion—good works, charity—as a means of helping humankind. Viridiana uses the money and the grounds of her deceased uncle's estate to establish a utopian community for the poor. Viridiana feels her soul strengthened by this Christian–Communist colony in which

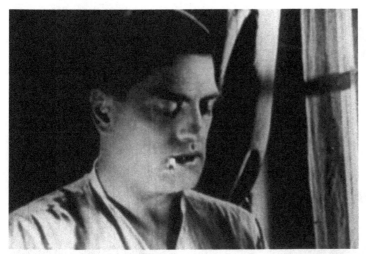

Fig. 16-26

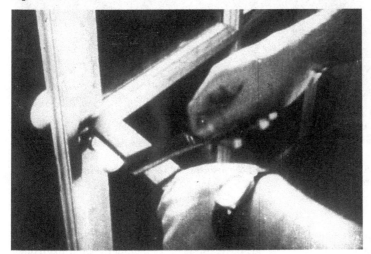

Fig. 16-27

The beginning of Buñuel's film career and of Un Chien andalou—*the filmmaker (Buñuel himself, Fig. 16-26) sharpens his razor to assault and alter human vision.*

everyone works together and no one goes hungry. But one day when Viridiana and the other masters leave on an excursion, the peasants break into the house, set out the fancy linen and china, and begin to devour a banquet of their own. They raucously break furniture and dishes; they drunkenly bloody the white linen with wine. One of the beggars takes a "picture" of the loathsome group; they pose in the positions of the disciples in da Vinci's "The Last Supper"; the beggar woman "snaps the picture" of the gathering by raising her skirt and exposing her naked groin. This lewd burlesque of the sacred scene deflates any hope that this human scum can be converted or helped by any means whatever. Viridiana has failed at both faith and charity. Seeing no hope at all, Viridiana wanders into the bedroom of her sensual cousin where he "plays cards," as he euphemistically puts it. As Viridiana sits down at the card table, her cousin tells her that he has always known she would one day play cards with him. Buñuel's allegory of the spirit and flesh is complete.

After *Viridiana*, Buñuel returned to Mexico (*The Exterminating Angel*, 1962, the disturbing tale of a group of people who find they are

Fig. 16-28
Alfonso Mejía as Pedro in Buñuel's **Los olvidados,** *one of the greatest of his Mexican features;*
cinematographer, Gabriel Figueroa.

unable to leave a party—for many weeks—for reasons they don't understand) and finally to France. *The Discreet Charm of the Bourgeoisie* develops the gap between the simple, concrete reality that bourgeois expectations assume (the banality of property, success, money, social intercourse, and, especially, eating dinner) and the complex levels of superrealities (wishes, dreams, imaginings, fancies) that actually exist. Expectations are memorably reversed in *The Phantom of Liberty*, where friends chat and defecate at a "dinner table" but excuse themselves to eat in a little room in private. One of the cleverest and most challenging of the late Buñuel films is *The Milky Way*, named after the route of pilgrimage from Paris to San Sebastian in Spain, where Christian pilgrims of the Middle Ages traveled to view the tomb of St. James.

Buñuel's film is more a pilgrimage in time than in space, for as his two modern "pilgrims" (one old, one young; both of them tramps) make the same journey, their "stopping places" are a series of religious heresies that have been debated and banned over the centuries. Buñuel's editing, audacity, and philosophical logic—the demands of the argument, realized as scenes—make it completely natural for the two 20th-century pilgrims to walk back and forth between centuries.

Even if filmmakers have always been able to make the fictitious appear real, Buñuel pushes this freedom into the realm of absurdity and contradiction. For example, the single female object of desire in *Obscure Object* cannot possibly be embodied by two different women, but there the two women concretely are, both of

Fig. 16-29
Viridiana: *Buñuel's beggars and cripples at his parody of "The Last Supper."*

them the single beloved the man would like to possess. The fact that she is two—and played by two actresses who do not resemble each other—underscores the impossibility of ever fulfilling the desire to possess, let alone define, another human being. For Buñuel the cinema has always been the realm of the impossible actual: Phenomena that in the reality of time and space cannot possibly occur can happen before the viewer's eyes because the cinema is free of reality's time and space. But for Buñuel this feature makes the cinema *more* like life and experience, not less, for reality is composed of thoughts, dreams, ideas, and desires as much as of tangible objects. The old heresy staged in a farmhouse *is there* on that Milky Way just as clearly as that farmhouse is there. The alternating objects of abstract desire are there, just as clearly as each of those actresses is there. In Buñuel's view, only when people realize the insubstantiality of our supposedly "objective reality" and of our opinions based on it will we be able to avoid doing violence both to reality and to one another. It was a view Buñuel maintained

ferociously for five decades, in country after country, until his death in 1983.

For Further Viewing

FILMS

THE NEW GERMAN CINEMA

RAINER WERNER FASSBINDER (1946–82)
Why Does Herr R. Run Amok? (1969)
Beware of a Holy Whore (1970)
The Merchant of the Four Seasons (1971)
The Bitter Tears of Petra von Kant (1972)
Ali: Fear Eats the Soul or *Fear Devour the Soul* (1973)
Effi Briest (1974)
Fox and His Friends (1974)
Mother Küster's Trip to Heaven (1975)
Chinese Roulette (1976)
Satan's Brew (1976)
Despair (1977)
The Marriage of Maria Braun (1979)
Berlin Alexanderplatz (1980)
Lola (1981)

Veronika Voss (1981)
Querelle (1982)

WERNER HERZOG (1942–)
Signs of Life (1968)
Even Dwarfs Started Small (1970)
Fata Morgana (1970)
Land of Silence and Darkness (1971)
Aguirre, the Wrath of God (1972)
Everyone for Himself and God Against All or
    The Mystery of Kaspar Hauser or The
    Enigma of Kaspar Hauser (1974)
The Great Ecstasy of the Sculptor Steiner (1974)
La Soufrière (1976)
Heart of Glass (1976)
Stroszek (1977)
Nosferatu: Phantom of the Night (1979)
Woyzeck (1979)
Fitzcarraldo (1982)
Cobra Verde (1987)
The Transformation of the World Into Music
    (1994). Made for TV
Little Dieter Needs to Fly (1997)
My Best Fiend (1999)
Grizzly Man (2005)
Encounters at the End of the World (2007).
    Wide release 2008
The Bad Lieutenant: Port of Call: New
    Orleans (2009)
La Bohème (2009)

VOLKER SCHLÖNDORFF (1939–)
Young Törless (1966)
The Lost Honor of Katharina Blum (1975).
    Co-director, Margarethe von Trotta
The Tin Drum (1979)
Circle of Deceit (1981)
The Legends of Rita (2000)
The Ninth Day (2004)

MARGARETHE VON TROTTA (1942–)
The Lost Honor of Katharina Blum (1975).
    Co-director, Volker Schlöndorff
The Second Awakening of Christa
    Klages (1977)
Sisters, or The Balance of Happiness (1979)
Marianne and Juliane or The German Sisters
    or The Leaden Time (1981)
Sheer Madness or Friends and Husbands
    (1982)
Rosa Luxemburg (1985)

Rosenstrasse (2003)
I Am the Other Woman (2006)
Vision (2009)

WIM WENDERS (1945–)
The Goalie's Anxiety at the Penalty
    Kick (1971)
Alice in the Cities (1974)
Kings of the Road or In the Course of Time
    (1976)
The American Friend (1977)
Lightning Over Water or Nick's Film (1980).
    Co-director, Nicholas Ray
The State of Things (1982)
Paris, Texas (1984)
Wings of Desire or The Heavens over
    Berlin (1987)
Far Away, So Close! (1993)
The End of Violence (1997)
Buena Vista Social Club (1999)
Don't Come Knocking (2005)

GERMAN MISCELLANY
The Captain from Koepenick (1956, Helmut
    Kautner)
Aren't We Wonderful? (1958, Kurt Hoffmann)
Not Reconciled (1965, Jean-Marie Straub and
    Danièle Huillet)
Yesterday Girl (1966, Alexander Kluge)
Chronicle of Anna Magdalena Bach (1967,
    Straub/Huillet)
Moses and Aaron (1974, Straub/Huillet)
Strongman Ferdinand (1975, Alexander Kluge)
Our Hitler (1977, Hans Jürgen Syberberg)
Knife in the Head (1978, Reinhard Hauff)
Germany Pale Mother (1979, Helma Sanders-
    Brahms)
Das Boot (1981, Wolfgang Petersen)
Parsifal (1982, Hans Jürgen Syberberg)
Class Relations (1983, Straub/Huillet)
Inside the Whale (1984, Doris Dörrie)
Benny's Video (1992, Michael Haneke; Austria)
71 Fragments of a Chronology of Chance (1994,
    Michael Haneke; Austria)
Lea (1996, Ivan Fila)
Funny Games (1997, Michael Haneke; Austria)
Lola Runs or Run Lola Run (1998, Tom Tykwer)
Enlightenment Guaranteed (1999, Doris Dörrie)
Heaven (2002, Tom Tykwer)
Caché or Hidden (2005, Michael Haneke;
    Austria/France)

The Lives of Others (2006, Florian Henckel von
   Donnersmarck)
The White Ribbon (2009, Michael Haneke;
   Austria)

THIRD WORLD CINEMA

CUBA

Lucía (1968, Humberto Solás)
Memories of Underdevelopment (1968, Tomás
   Gutiérrez Alea)
The Other Francisco (1975, Sergio Giral)
Alicia (1976, Victor Casaus)
The Last Supper (1977, Tomás Gutiérrez Alea)
Strawberry and Chocolate (1993, Tomás
   Gutiérrez Alea and Juan Carlos Tabío)
Guantanamera (1994, Tomás Gutiérrez Alea and
   Juan Carlos Tabío)
Who the Hell is Juliette? (1997, Carlos
   Marcovich)

LATIN AMERICA

The Pearl (1946, Emilio Fernandez; Mexico)
Yanco (1961, Servando Gonzalez; Mexico)
Vidas secas (1963, Nelson Pereira dos Santos;
   Brazil)
The Hour of the Furnaces: Notes and
   Testimonies on Neo-Colonialism, Violence
   and Liberation (1968, Fernando Solanas and
   Octavio Getino; Argentina)
Antonio das Mortes (1969, Glauber Rocha;
   Brazil)
Blood of the Condor (1969, Jorge Sanjinés;
   Bolivia)
El Topo (1969, Alexandro Jodorowsky;
   Mexico)
How Tasty Was My Little Frenchman (1972,
   Nelson Pereira dos Santos; Brazil)
The Harder They Come (1973, Perry Henzell;
   Jamaica)
The Promised Land (1973, Miguel
   Littin; Chile)
Xica (1976, Carlos Diegues; Brazil)
The Battle of Chile (1973–79). Part I released
   1975, Parts I and II released together in
   1977, Part III released 1979 (Patricio
   Guzmán; Chile)
Pixote (1981, Hector Babenco; Brazil)
Sugar Cane Alley (1983, Euzhan Palcy;
   Martinique/France)

Rodrigo D. No Future (1990, Victor Gaviria;
   Colombia). Completed 1989
Like Water for Chocolate (1992, Alfonso Arau;
   Mexico). Completed 1991
Central Station (1998, Walter Salles; Brazil)
No One Writes to the Colonel (1999, Arturo
   Ripstein; Mexico)
Our Lady of the Assassins (2000, Barbet
   Schroeder; Colombia/France). Completed
   1999
Amores Perros (2000, Alejandro González
   Iñárritu; Mexico)
The Devil's Backbone (2001, Guillermo del Toro;
   Spain/Mexico)
La Ciénaga (2001, Lucrecia Martel; Argentina)
Nine Queens (2001, Fabián Bielinsky; Argentina)
Y Tu Mamá También or And Your Mother Too
   (2001, Alfonso Cuarón; Mexico)
City of God (2002, Fernando Meirelles; Brazil)
The Dignity of the Nobodies (2005, Fernando
   Solanas; Argentina)
Pan's Labyrinth (2006, Guillermo del Toro;
   Spain/Mexico)
Sin nombre (2009, Cary Fukunaga;
   Mexico/U.S.)

AFRICA AND THE MIDDLE EAST

ABBAS KIAROSTAMI (1940–   )
The Traveler (1974)
The Report (1977)
Case No. 1, Case No. 2 (1979)
First Graders (1985)
Where is the Friend's Home? or Where is My
   Friend's House? (1987)
Homework (1989)
Close-Up (1990)
Life, and Nothing More . . . or And Life
   Goes On (1992)
Through the Olive Trees (1994)
Taste of Cherry or The Taste of Cherries (1997)
The Wind Will Carry Us (1999)
Ten (2002)
Five Dedicated to Ozu or Five (2003)
Shirin (2008)

MOHSEN MAKHMALBAF (1957–   )
Nassouh's Repentance (1982)
Two Sightless Eyes (1983)
Boycott (1985)
The Peddler (1986)

The Cyclist (1989)
Once Upon a Time, Cinema (1992)
Gabbeh (1996)
The Silence (1998)
Kandahar (2001)
Sex & Philosophy (2005)

OUSMANE SEMBENE (1923–2007)
Black Girl (1966)
Mandabi or *The Money Order* (1968)
Emitai (1971)
Xala or *The Curse* or *Impotence* (1974)
Ceddo (1978)
Camp de Thiaroye (1988). Co-director, Therno Faty Sow
Guelwaar (1992)
Faat Kiné (2000)
Moolaadé (2004)

AFRICAN AND MIDDLE EASTERN MISCELLANY
The Iron Gate or *Cairo Station* (1958), Youssef Chahine; Egypt)
The Night of Counting the Years (1969, Shadi Abdes-Salam; Egypt)
Still Life (1974, Sohrab Shahid Sales; Iran)
Work (1978, Souleymane Cissé; Mali)
The Exile (1980, Oumarou Ganda; Niger)
The Gods Must Be Crazy (1981, Jamie Uys; Botswana)
The Wind (1982, Souleymane Cissé; Mali)
Yol (1982, Şerif Gören and Yilmaz Güney; Turkey)
The Key (1986, Ebrahim Forouzesh; Iran)
Wedding in Galilee (1987, Michel Khleifi; Israel/Palestine/Belgium/France)
Yeelen or *Brightness* (1987, Souleymane Cissé; Mali)
Finzan or *A Dance for the Heroes* (1989, Cheick Oumar Sissoko; Mali)
The Need (1991, Alireza Davoudnejad; Iran)
Silences of the Palace (1994, Moufida Tlatli; Tunisia)
Guimba, un tyrant une époque or *Guimba the Tyrant* (1995, Cheick Oumar Sissoko; Mali)
The White Balloon (1995, Jafar Panahi; Iran)
Al-massir or *Destiny* (1997, Youssef Chahine; Egypt)
The Apple (1998, Samira Makhmalbaf; Iran)
Genesis (1999, Cheick Oumar Sissoko; Mali)
Blackboards (2000, Samira Makhmalbaf; Iran)
The Circle (2000, Jafar Panahi; Iran)

11'09"01—September 11 (2002, Youssef Chahine, Samira Makhmalbaf, and nine others; global)
Osama (2003, Siddiq Barmak; Afghanistan)
Paradise Now (2005, Hany Abu-Assad; Israel/Palestine)
Waltz with Bashir (2008, Ari Folman, Israel)

AUSTRALIA, CANADA, IRELAND, AND NEW ZEALAND

BRUCE BERESFORD (1940–   )
The Adventures of Barry McKenzie (1972)
Don's Party (1976)
'Breaker' Morant (1980)
Tender Mercies (1983)
Driving Miss Daisy (1989)
Black Robe (1991)

JANE CAMPION (1955–   )
Sweetie (1989)
An Angel at My Table (1990)
The Piano (1993). Completed 1992
The Portrait of a Lady (1996)
Bright Star (2009)

DAVID CRONENBERG (1943–   )
Stereo (1969)
Crimes of the Future (1970)
Shivers (1975). U.S. version, *They Came From Within*
Rabid (1977)
The Brood (1979)
Scanners (1981). Completed 1980
Videodrome (1983). Completed 1982
The Dead Zone (1983)
The Fly (1986)
Dead Ringers (1988)
Crash (1996)
eXistenZ (1999)
Spider (2002)
A History of Violence (2005)
Eastern Promises (2007)

ATOM EGOYAN (1960–   )
Next of Kin (1984)
Family Viewing (1987)
Speaking Parts (1989)
The Adjuster (1991)
Calendar (1993)
Exotica (1994)
The Sweet Hereafter (1997)

Felicia's Journey (1999)
Ararat (2002)
Adoration (2008)

PETER JACKSON (1961–   )
Bad Taste (1987)
Meet the Feebles (1989)
Heavenly Creatures (1994)
The Frighteners (1996)
Forgotten Silver (1996). Co-director, Costa Botes
*The Lord of the Rings: The Fellowship of the
   Ring* (2001)
The Lord of the Rings: The Two Towers (2002)
The Lord of the Rings: The Return of the King
   (2003)
King Kong (2005)

FRED SCHEPISI (1939–   )
The Devil's Playground (1976)
The Chant of Jimmie Blacksmith (1978)
A Cry in the Dark (1988)
The Russia House (1990)
Six Degrees of Separation (1993)

PETER WEIR (1944–   )
Picnic at Hanging Rock (1975)
The Last Wave (1977)
Gallipoli (1981)
The Year of Living Dangerously (1982)
The Mosquito Coast (1986)
Fearless (1993)
The Truman Show (1998)
*Master and Commander: The Far Side of the
   World* (2003)

AUSTRALIA, CANADA, IRELAND, NEW ZEALAND
MISCELLANY
The Story of the Kelly Gang (1906, Charles Tait;
   Australia)
Back to God's Country (1919, David M. Hartford;
   Canada)
The Viking (1931, Varick Frissell and George
   Melford; Canada)
The Luck of Ginger Coffey (1964, Irvin Kershner;
   Canada)
Nobody Waved Goodbye (1964, Don Owen;
   Canada)
Act of the Heart (1970, Paul Almond; Canada)
Mon oncle Antoine (1971, Claude Jutra; Canada)
Outback or *Wake in Fright* (1971, Ted Kotcheff;
   Australia/U.S.)

The Apprenticeship of Duddy Kravitz (1974,
   Ted Kotcheff; Canada)
The Picture Show Man (1977, John Power;
   Australia)
Murder By Decree (1978, Bob Clark; Canada)
Newsfront (1978, Phillip Noyce; Australia)
Mad Max (1979, George Miller; Australia)
My Brilliant Career (1979, Gillian Armstrong;
   Australia)
The Road Warrior or *Mad Max 2* (1981, George
   Miller; Australia)
Smash Palace (1981, Roger Donaldson; New
   Zealand)
Ticket to Heaven (1981, Ralph L. Thomas;
   Canada)
The Grey Fox (1983, Philip Borsos; Canada)
Man of Flowers (1983, Paul Cox; Australia)
The Company of Wolves (1984, Neil Jordan;
   Ireland)
My First Wife (1984, Paul Cox; Australia)
Crocodile Dundee (1986, Peter Faiman;
   Australia)
The Decline of the American Empire (1986,
   Denys Arcand; Canada)
My Left Foot (1989, Jim Sheridan; Ireland)
The Field (1990, Jim Sheridan; Ireland)
The Crying Game (1992, Neil Jordan; Ireland)
The Adventures of Priscilla, Queen of the Desert
   (1994, Stephan Elliott; Australia)
The Ugly (1996, Scott Reynolds; New Zealand)
The Butcher Boy (1997, Neil Jordan; Ireland)
The Castle (1997, Rob Sitch; Australia)
August 32nd on Earth (1998, Denis Villeneuve;
   Canada)
Heaven (1998, Scott Reynolds; New Zealand)
Innocence (2000, Paul Cox; Australia)
Atanarjuat the Fast Runner or *The Fast
   Runner* (2001, Zacharias Kunuk; Canada)
Moulin Rouge! (2001, Baz Luhrmann;
   Australia)
Rabbit-Proof Fence (2002, Phillip Noyce;
   Australia)
The Barbarian Invasions (2003, Denys Arcand;
   Canada)
Whale Rider (2003, Niki Caro; New Zealand)
Ten Canoes (2006, Rolf de Heer; Australia)
Hunger (2008, Steve McQueen; Ireland/U.K.)
District 9 (2009, Neill Blomkamp; U.S./New
   Zealand)
Samson & Delilah (2009, Warwick Thornton;
   Australia)

THE FORMER SOVIET UNION

TENGHIZ ABULADZE (1924–94)
Molba (*Prayer*, 1969). Completed 1967
The Wishing Tree (1978). Completed 1977
Repentance (1987). Completed 1984

SERGEI PARADJANOV (1924–90)
Shadows of Forgotten Ancestors (1964)
Sayat Nova or *The Color of Pomegranates*
    (1968–78). Shot 1968; early version released
    1971; completed 1978
The Legend of Suram Fortress (1984).
    Co-director, Dodo Abashidze
Ashik Kerib (1988)

ANDREI TARKOVSKY (1932–86)
Ivan's Childhood or *My Name is*
    Ivan (1962)
Andrei Rublev or *Andrei Roublyov* (1966).
    Shown abroad since 1969; Soviet release, 1971
Solaris (1972)
Mirror (1974)
Stalker (1982). Completed 1979
Nostalgia or *Nostalghia* (1983)
The Sacrifice (1986)

POST-STALINIST AND POST-SOVIET MISCELLANY
Boris Godunov (1955, Vera Stroyeva)
The Cranes Are Flying (1957, Mikhail Kalatozov)
The Quiet Don (three parts, 1957, Sergei
    Gerasimov)
Ballad of a Soldier (1959, Grigori Chukhrai)
The Overcoat (1959, Alexei Batalov)
Lady with a Dog (1960, Josef Heifitz)
Hamlet (1964, Grigori Kozintsev)
I Am Cuba (1964, Mikhail Kalatozov)
The First Teacher (1966, Andrei Konchalovsky)
The Wish (1966, Larissa Shepitko)
War and Peace (1967, Sergei Bondarchuk)
King Lear (1971, Grigori Kozintsev)
A Slave of Love (1976, Nikita Mikhalkov)
The Ascent (1977, Larissa Shepitko)
Oblomov (1980, Nikita Mikhalkov)
Come and See (1985, Elem Klimov)
A Forgotten Tune for the Flute (1987, Eldar
    Ryazanov)
Is It Easy to be Young? (1987, Juris Podnieks)
Fountain (1988, Yuri Mamin)
Little Vera (1988, Vassili Pitchul)
Freedom Is Paradise (1989, Sergei Bodrov)

The Needle (1989, Rachid Noughmanov)
Freeze, Die, Come to Life (1990, Vitaly
    Kanevsky)
Get Thee Out! (1990, Dmitri Astrakhan)
Taxi Blues (1990, Pavel Lungin *a.k.a.* Pavel
    Lounguine)
The Wild East (1993, Rachid Noughmanov)
Burnt by the Sun (1994, Nikita Mikhalkov)
We, Children of the 20th Century (1994, Vitaly
    Kanevsky)
Window to Paris (1994, Yuri Mamin)
Mother and Son (1997, Alexander Sokurov)
Outskirts (1998, Petr Lutsik)
Russian Ark (2002, Alexander Sokurov)
Room and a Half (2009, Andrey Khrzhanovsky)

SPAIN

PEDRO ALMODÓVAR (1951–   )
Labyrinth of Passion (1982)
What Have I Done to Deserve This!! (1984)
Matador (1986)
Women on the Verge of a Nervous Breakdown
    (1988)
Live Flesh (1997)
All About My Mother (1999)
Talk to Her (2002)
Bad Education (2004)
Volver (2006)
Broken Embraces (2009)

LUIS BUÑUEL (1900–83)
Un Chien andalou (1929). Co-director, Salvador
    Dalí
L'Age d'or (1930). Co-director, Salvador Dalí
Las Hurdes or *Land Without Bread* (1932)
Los olvidados or *The Young and the Damned*
    (1950)
The Adventures of Robinson Crusoe (1952)
Nazarin (1958)
Viridiana (1961)
The Exterminating Angel (1962)
Simon of the Desert (1965)
Belle de jour (1967)
The Milky Way (1969)
The Discreet Charm of the Bourgeoisie (1972)
The Phantom of Liberty (1974)
That Obscure Object of Desire (1977)

VÍCTOR ERICE (1940–   )
The Spirit of the Beehive (1973)
El sur or *The South* (1983)

El sol del membrillo or *The Sun of the Quince* or *Dream of Light* (1992)

DVDs

The Tin Drum (1979, **Volker Schlöndorff**). Criterion Collection. **Digitally remastered;** commentary by Schlöndorff. Includes deleted scenes; author **Günter Grass** reading from the novel in 1987; interviews with Schlöndorff, Grass, co-writer **Jean-Claude Carrière,** and others; the original ending of the script; and a documentary on the lawsuit.

AFRICA, CUBA, LATIN AMERICA, THE MIDDLE EAST, AND THIRD WORLD CINEMA

Amores Perros (2000, **Alejandro González Iñárritu**). Studio Home Entertainment. Includes a production commentary, music videos, and behind-the-scenes footage.

Central Station (1998, **Walter Salles**). Columbia TriStar. Commentary by Salles and others.

Close-Up (1990, **Abbas Kiarostami**). Facets Video. Includes an interview with Kiarostami and filmographies for him and **Mohsen Makhmalbaf.**

The Cyclist (1989, **Mohsen Makhmalbaf**). Image Entertainment.

The Devil's Backbone (2001, **Guillermo del Toro**). Columbia TriStar. Commentary by del Toro.

Genesis (1999, **Cheick Oumar Sissoko**). Kino International.

Osama (2003, **Siddiq Barmak**). MGM. Includes a documentary, *Sharing Hope and Freedom,* featuring Barmak.

Our Lady of the Assassins (2000, **Barbet Schroeder**). Paramount Home Video.

Pan's Labyrinth (2006, **Guillermo del Toro**). New Line Home Video. Platinum Series. Includes several short documentaries.

Pixote (1981, **Hector Babenco**). New Yorker Films.

Rodrigo D. No Future (1990, **Victor Gaviria**). Facets Video.

Strawberry and Chocolate (1993, **Tomás Gutiérrez Alea** and **Juan Carlos Tabío**). Buena Vista Home Video.

Sugar Cane Alley (1983, **Euzhan Palcy**). New Yorker Films.

Taste of Cherry (1997, **Abbas Kiarostami**). Criterion Collection. Includes an interview with Kiarostami.

Wedding in Galilee (1987, **Michel Khleifi**). Kino International.

Who the Hell is Juliette? (1997, **Carlos Marcovich**). Facets Video.

Xala (1974, **Ousmane Sembene**). New Yorker Films.

Yeelen (1987, **Souleymane Cissé**). Kino International.

Y Tu Mamá También (2001, **Alfonso Cuarón**). MGM/UA. Unrated edition; includes a commentary by the cast members in Spanish, a short (*Me la Debes*), a making-of documentary, and deleted scenes.

AUSTRALIA, CANADA, IRELAND, AND NEW ZEALAND

An Angel at My Table (1990, **Jane Campion**). Criterion Collection. Includes a commentary by Campion and others, an audio interview with Janet Frame, and more.

The Company of Wolves (1984, **Neil Jordan**). Hen's Tooth Video.

Dead Ringers (1988, **David Cronenberg**). Criterion Collection. Includes information on the medical instruments; a demonstration of the twinning/motion-control effects; the electronic press kit; and commentary by Cronenberg, star **Jeremy Irons,** and others.

Family Viewing/Next of Kin (1987 and 1984, **Atom Egoyan**). Zeitgeist Video. Contains both movies, with commentaries by Egoyan.

The Fast Runner (see Chap. 18 list).

Innocence (2000, **Paul Cox**). Columbia TriStar.

The Lord of the Rings: The Fellowship of the Ring, The Two Towers, and *The Return of the King* (2001–03, **Peter Jackson**). New Line Home Entertainment. Platinum Series. Special Extended DVD Editions. One four-disc set for each film in the trilogy, containing the extended version of the movie, commentaries by all concerned, and hours of documentaries and features about the background and production of the film, with especially good coverage of **digital effects, production design,** and the use of New Zealand **locations.** Even those who prefer the theatrical release versions will find the extras offered in these sets to be comprehensive, entertaining, and extremely informative.

Mad Max (1979, **George Miller**). MGM/UA. Special Edition. Includes the original Australian-language track, shorts on star **Mel Gibson** and the series, and more.

The Magdalene Sisters (2003, **Peter Mullan**). Miramax Home Entertainment. Includes a 1997 Channel Four documentary about the Magdalene Asylums, *Sex in a Cold Climate*.

Moulin Rouge! (2001, **Baz Luhrmann**). 20th Century Fox. Commentary by Luhrmann and others.

Picnic at Hanging Rock (1975, **Peter Weir**). Criterion Collection. Director's cut (three minutes shorter than the release version). Unlike the director's cut of *The Last Wave* (Criterion), which changes the ending, this one is an improvement.

Rabbit-Proof Fence (2002, **Phillip Noyce**). Miramax Home Entertainment. Includes a making-of documentary and a commentary by Noyce, author **Pilkington Garimara,** and others.

The Sweet Hereafter (1997, **Atom Egoyan**). New Line Home Entertainment. Commentary by Egoyan and writer **Russell Banks.**

Ten Canoes (2006, **Rolf de Heer**). Palm Pictures. Includes a making-of documentary, interviews, and a study guide.

Videodrome (1983, **David Cronenberg**). Criterion Collection. Includes *Fear on Film*, a 1982 discussion of horror by Cronenberg, **John Carpenter,** and others; the unrated cut of the film; a documentary and an interview about the effects; a 2000 Cronenberg short, *Camera*; the uncut Videodrome footage with Cronenberg's remarks; and commentaries on the feature by Cronenberg and by stars **James Woods** and **Deborah Harry.**

THE FORMER SOVIET UNION

Andrei Rublev (1966, **Andrei Tarkovsky**). Criterion Collection. The complete director's cut (205 minutes), new subtitles, a commentary and an essay by film scholar Vlada Petrić, and a timeline of Russian history and Rublev's life.

Come and See (1985, **Elem Klimov**). Kino Video. Includes interviews with the cast and crew, filmographies, and archival materials on Nazi brutalities and Belarus partisans.

The Films of Sergei Paradjanov (1964–88, **Sergei Paradjanov**). Kino Video. Contains *Shadows of Forgotten Ancestors, The Color of Pomegranates, The Legend of Suram Fortress*, and *Ashik Kerib*.

Little Vera (1988, **Vassili Pitchul**). Water Bearer Films.

Mother and Son (1997, **Alexander Sokurov**). Fox Lorber.

Outskirts (1998, **Petr Lutsik**). Facets Video.

Russian Ark (2002, **Alexander Sokurov**). Wellspring. Includes an excellent making-of documentary, interviews with Sokurov and others, filmographies, and more.

Sergei Eisenstein: The Sound Years (1935–46, **Sergei Eisenstein**). Criterion Collection. Contains *Alexander Nevsky* and *Ivan the Terrible, Parts I and II* (with deleted scenes); a stills-based reconstruction of *Bezhin Meadow*; an essay by film historian David Bordwell; and multimedia essays on Eisenstein's visual vocabulary, his collaboration with composer **Sergei Prokofiev,** and more.

Solaris (1972, **Andrei Tarkovsky**). Criterion Collection. Includes nine deleted and alternate scenes, many interviews, an essay by Tarkovsky scholars Vida Johnson and Graham Petrie, and an excerpt from a documentary featuring author **Stanislaw Lem.**

Stalker (1979, **Andrei Tarkovsky**). Image Entertainment. Includes an excerpt from Tarkovsky's diploma film, *The Steamroller and the Violin*; a documentary about Tarkovsky's home; and interviews with the cinematographer and the production designer.

SPAIN

L'Age d'or and *Un Chien andalou* (see Chap. 10 list).

Cría (1976, **Carlos Saura**). Miracle Pictures.

The Discreet Charm of the Bourgeoisie (1972, **Luis Buñuel**). Criterion Collection. Includes two documentaries on Buñuel.

The Exterminating Angel (1962, **Luis Buñuel**). Criterion Collection. **Digitally restored.** Includes a documentary, interviews, and a booklet that features an interview with Buñuel.

Live Flesh (1997, **Pedro Almodóvar**). MGM/UA.

The Spirit of the Beehive (1973, **Víctor Erice**). Criterion Collection. **Restored.** Includes an interview with the director and a documentary on the film.

Talk to Her (2002, **Pedro Almodóvar**). Columbia TriStar. Commentary by Almodóvar and star **Geraldine Chaplin.**

Tango (1998, **Carlos Saura**). Columbia TriStar. Includes a making-of documentary and a commentary by producer **Juan Carlos Codazzi** and star **Mia Maestro.**

That Obscure Object of Desire (1977, **Luis Buñuel**). Criterion Collection. Includes an interview with writer **Jean-Claude Carrière,** the text of an interview with Buñuel, and excerpts from a 1929 silent adaptation of the same source novel.

Viridiana (1961, **Luis Buñuel**). Criterion Collection. **Digitally restored.** Includes excerpts from a documentary on Buñuel's career.

What Have I Done to Deserve This!! (1984, **Pedro Almodóvar**). Wellspring.

17

The Return
of the Myths: 1977–

At some point in the late 1970s, the American cinema abandoned its attack on the genres of American movies and the myths of American life to embrace them both again. Though some critics sneeringly compared the new films to computerized video games, American movies were born as close cousins to the electrical and mechanical novelties in amusement arcades. The new films self-consciously defined movies as both the repository for cultural myths and the contemporary medium for their dissemination. They saw the movies as myth machines. The new films viewed these myths and mysteries not with the jaded eye of adulthood but with the hope and wonder of childhood; they set out to recapture or invent a kind of innocence.

In this period, muscular heroes in T-shirts, robots with hearts of gold, tough cops, resourceful teens, and benevolent masters rose up to vanquish purely evil villains. Instead of the intellectual and emotional complexity of such previous big films as *Lawrence of Arabia* and *The Godfather*, the typical blockbuster became a wide-screen, color, stereophonic *ride*, full of action and special effects, constructed for speed and thrills rather than contemplation, and with a simple, forceful, unthreatening message (for example, cheaters never prosper); examples range from Steven Spielberg's *Indiana Jones and the Temple of Doom* (1984) to Jan De Bont's *Speed* (1994) and J.J. Abrams's *Ştar Trek* (2009). Many audiences and most producers preferred what were called "feelgood" movies to "downers" and "bummers"; by far the majority of films had heroes to root for, villains to hate, and happy

endings. Movies fit once more into recognizable genres and embraced their conventions, even while harmlessly making fun of them.

Films that tackled difficult political or psychological material (or were considered too negative, like Ridley Scott's *Blade Runner*, 1982) sometimes had their endings changed by executives—although a few subversive, questioning films did sneak by. It was the period of the blockbuster, the sequel, the Dolby soundtrack, the videocassette and laserdisc and DVD and Blu-ray, the direct-to-video release, the camcorder, the computer, and the all-powerful talent agent—a time that began with the science fiction spectacles of George Lucas and Steven Spielberg and grew to include the creepy ironies of David Lynch and the political fables of Spike Lee. This period of American film history has continued into the 2000s, so its end remains unknown, but its aesthetic, technical, and economic elements are already clear enough. It is not an extension of the Hollywood Renaissance but an entirely new period: technically advanced and politically in retreat, devoted utterly to entertainment, with films that are innovative but rarely new (although many independents have made movies that leaned the other way). For a capsule version of the difference, compare the spiritual scenes in *Mean Streets* and in *Field of Dreams* (1989, directed by Phil Alden Robinson).

The late 1970s saw major changes in the film industry, film technology, and film content. The film business adopted a "blockbuster mentality," preferring to finance and distribute a few big films with the potential for enormous profits rather than a larger slate of modest films with modest profits. One "monster hit" or "tentpole picture" a year could keep a studio in business and help to pay for the flops and the less expensive movies it also produced. *The Godfather, Jaws, Star Wars, Close Encounters of the Third Kind, Grease,* and *Superman,* all from the 1970s, were among the top-grossing films of all time—as were their 1980s cousins *The Empire Strikes Back, E.T., Raiders of the Lost Ark, Return of the Jedi,* and *Batman.* The 1990s added *Titanic* and others to that list. *The Birth of a Nation, Snow White,* and *Gone With the Wind* may still be considered more commercially successful than most of these blockbusters—they made more profit in relation to their cost, and in more valuable dollars; in fact, when the figures are adjusted for inflation and the picture's many re-releases are added in, *Gone With the Wind* is ahead of *Titanic* (1997, directed by James Cameron). Inflation aside, *Titanic* is ahead of them all, with *The Dark Knight* (2008, directed by Christopher Nolan) right behind it in worldwide ticket sales. In the hope of repeating the kind of success introduced by *Jaws* in 1975, the studio attitude became to spend a lot of money to make a lot of money. *Titanic* cost and made so much that it confirmed this attitude all over again. At $200 million, it was the most expensive movie yet made, and it was the first to earn over $1 billion at the worldwide box office ($600 million domestic). A *blockbuster* is a picture that takes in over $100 million at the U.S. box office. "Small" films with relatively low budgets—many of which were "picked up" from independent producers and simply released by the studio—were given smaller openings and often had to make their profits overseas or on video. (Video itself made a difference, to be discussed later.) Given the cost of these spectacles—as high as $100 million or more, when to produce the average studio feature cost $11 million in 1981, $34 million in 1994, $55 million in 1997, $66 million in 2003, and $71 million in 2007—the films required tremendous advertising campaigns, which cost even more, and the theatre owner had to send a higher percentage of ticket earnings back to the distributor. Blockbuster or not, a movie that cost $90 million to make and $100 million or more to distribute but that grossed only $120 million would be in the red until the foreign box office and video raised its earnings. Theatres learned to make their profits at the concession stand, not at the box office. Theatres also were remodeled, or built, to house 2 or 4—or 16—screens; the multiplex cinema marked the era's biggest change in the practice of theatrical exhibition.

While the cost of the studio film rose, independent producers proved that even if they could not tie their new pictures into the total media complex available to the studios and to the huge communications companies by which most studios were owned (unless they released their completed films through studios, which often happened), they could still make profits with good low-budget pictures. Rebellious and creative directors found maverick producers and made their own films without "help" from the bottom-line studio bureaucrats. In 2001, Todd Field's *In The Bedroom* was produced for $2 million. In 1984, Lillian Vallish Foote and several other individuals produced *1918*, a quietly paced, intimate family drama that was written by her husband, Horton Foote, starred—along with a small group of excellent actors—their daughter Hallie, and was directed by Ken Harrison. *1918*'s central events—sickness and death at home in a time of war—might have appealed to Griffith but had no chance with a major studio, even if Horton Foote's track record included *Tender Mercies,* for which he'd just won an Oscar, as well as *To Kill a Mockingbird* and successful off-Broadway runs of the intense, personal plays (the *Orphans' Home* cycle, which includes *1918*) that he wanted to turn into movies. It was crucial that the writer be in creative control of the project, and that in itself ruled out working with a studio. With three co-producers and with help from friends (including Robert Duvall—whose contribution was to sing with Willie Nelson over the credits, who had made his mark in *Mockingbird* before *The Godfather,* and who had also starred in *Tender Mercies* as well as in Joseph Anthony's great 1972 independent feature, *Tomorrow,* adapted by Foote from a story by Faulkner), the family made the picture for $800,000. Robert Rodriguez became a medical test subject and maxed out his credit cards to raise the $7,000 it cost him to make *El Mariachi* (1992, released 1993), doing the writing, directing, shooting, and editing himself. By 2000, shooting on digital video, editing on a computer, and distributing on disc and over the Internet had brought ministudios to individual desktops, yielding projects that could be transferred to film in a lab or might lead to a job making a feature for a studio or an independent producer.

Independent production companies came in big and small sizes, but what defined them as independent is that they were not affilated with the MPAA, as the big studios were. The history of independent filmmaking in America goes back before Morris Engel, Ruth Orkin, and Ray Ashley made *Little Fugitive* (1953) and John Cassavetes directed *Shadows* (1959). In the 1980s, releases by independent production companies began to increase in number and popularity. Soon the independents were releasing two or three times as many features per year as the MPAA studios (in 2008, 462 as compared to the studios' 148). Much of the truly independent work, done by small groups and individuals rather than companies, was fostered by festivals and organizations such as the Sundance Institute, founded in 1981 by Robert Redford.

The major technical advances of the late 1970s were the introduction of the Dolby noise-reduction process, which drastically improved sound quality whether the final soundtrack was optical or magnetic; the Dolby Stereo Variable Area (SVA) soundtrack, which allowed 35mm prints to have four-track stereophonic *optical* soundtracks that had a subtlety, clarity, depth, and range previously possible only with magnetic sound; and the Steadicam, which combined the mobility of the hand-held camera with the smoothness of the old Mitchell studio camera mounted on a dolly. Just as it became normal, in the course of the 1960s, for features to be shot in color, stereo (usually with one or in some cases two surround channels that came from the sides and back of the auditorium) became the norm by 1980. In *Days of Heaven*, *Apocalypse Now*, *The Right Stuff*, and *GoodFellas*, the quality and aesthetics of the sound are as significant as those of the picture.

Finally, a new cultural attitude—a conservatism associated with but not limited to the presidency of Ronald Reagan—seems to have produced a shift in film content. The antiestablishment types who dominated American films from *Bonnie and Clyde* and *Midnight Cowboy* to *MASH* were replaced by more conventional, often beset citizens—like Donald Sutherland and

Mary Tyler Moore in Robert Redford's *Ordinary People* (1980)—who sought to find a meaningful place within conventional society. With the final singing of "God Bless America," the working-class, small-town protagonists of Michael Cimino's *The Deer Hunter* (1978) reintegrate themselves, both as individuals and as a group, into the fabric of American moral and social life, despite the agony their country has forced them to endure. The working-class hero of John Badham's *Saturday Night Fever* (1977) also seeks some meaningful place in American social life, beyond the escapist dream-dance world of the disco and the narrow moral and political provinciality of Bay Ridge. In the mythic sequel, *Staying Alive* (1983, directed by Sylvester Stallone), all the hero's fantasies—not of social, moral, and political growth but of dancing his own way in a big show—are fulfilled in an unbelievable manner, and the substance of his victory is simply that the Disco Kid keeps his personal style. The Dustin Hoffman of *Kramer vs. Kramer* (1979, directed by Robert Benton), who just wants to live lovingly with his son, would not give a dime on a cold day to the Dustin Hoffman of *Midnight Cowboy*.

The young welder of *Flashdance* (1983, directed by Adrian Lyne), who is not a feminist, wants to exchange her blue-collar job for the opportunity to express herself in ballet. The majority of 1980s studio pictures reflected a movement away from social rebellion and toward something else: something not to be angry about but to believe in. What might have been hissed or laughed off the screen in the politicized late 1960s and early 1970s became the stuff of dreams in the 1980s. As the song in *Flashdance*—and President Reagan—repeatedly asserted, anyone with determination and talent could "have it all," and that sweet hope fit well into a culture in which people tried to fulfill all the roles they thought they should (wife–mother–executive); in which they were encouraged to want more and buy more, even on credit; and in which poverty, disappointment, and suffering (the homeless could not "have it all") went unacknowledged. Long after Reagan, the movies were still concentrating on figures and dreams to believe in: 2005 alone saw *Batman Begins* (directed by Christopher Nolan), a new film about wizard-in-training Harry Potter, and a new *Star Wars* movie.

Star Wars and the New Mythology

These developments took place throughout the industry and across the country, but if any single film can be credited with opening the era—as *The Jazz Singer* cleared the way for the talkies—that film is George Lucas's *Star Wars* (1977), whose unprecedented use of Dolby Noise Reduction from the beginning to the end of production and whose Dolby SVA soundtrack led to what has been called the "second coming of sound," a complete revolution in the technology and aesthetics of film sound; whose use of a computer to control the camera was equally unprecedented; whose special effects changed the look not only of science fiction but of the fiction film in general—not to mention what they and the film's sound effects did to video games (in a way bringing the cinema back to the arcades where it began); whose phenomenal earnings led the industry to concentrate on big films designed for young audiences; whose creative interest in sequels was clear from the start, when *Star Wars* declared itself an episode of an otherwise unproduced series or serial; and whose successful integration of Zen philosophy, of Joseph Campbell's research into mythology and heroism, of serials and their heroes, of fantasy, of science fiction, and of fast-paced action and adventure announced the Return of the Myths.

Set "a long time ago" and as rooted in old movies as it was in the far older traditions of the saga and romance, this futuristic fantasy made the past new, a goal aspired to by the next three decades of American film, from the significantly named *Raiders of the Lost Ark* (1981) and *Back to the Future* (1984) to *Pulp Fiction* (1994)—not to mention an avalanche of sequels to hits, remakes of classics, and big-budget B pictures in familiar genres.

Superheroes, Slashers, and Cops

In addition to the *Star Wars* series and Spielberg's *Close Encounters* and *E.T.*, whose mythic figures come from outer space—and Lucas and Spielberg's Indiana Jones series, whose myths come from ancient and biblical mythology or from the movies—two other films helped to form the mythic consciousness of this period: Richard Donner's *Superman* (1978) and John G.

Avildsen's *Rocky* (1976). The comics have a presold audience of readers and their own mythology, and the perfect, moral, likable, mighty Superman (Christopher Reeve)—an Achilles whose "heel" is his vulnerability to Kryptonite—was a refreshing figure in whom the audience wanted to entertain belief. *Rocky*, a small film that became an unexpected hit, created its own life-sized but mythic hero in Rocky (Sylvester Stallone), the underdog who won't quit, the boxer who wins in spirit whether or not he wins a fight, the working-class Italian American who believes utterly in America. A hero created by the movies and its formulas, Rocky became the prototype for working-class overachievers like the heroine of *Flashdance* and, from Stallone's own Rambo to Sigourney Weaver's Ripley (the *Alien* series), at least 30 years of winners. There were very few films about losers.

In 2008, variations on these films were still being made; Darren Aronofsky's *The Wrestler* showed a wrestler's uplifting comeback, and *The Dark Knight* offered a mature view of Batman (Christian Bale), unable to solve one problem with which the Joker (Heath Ledger) confronts him, that of saving his beloved from a fatal explosion. Unlike Superman, Batman had long been a brooding figure, particularly in the graphic novels, and *The Dark Knight* reaffirmed his myth while probing more deeply into his situation. While it provided a guardian who did his best to deal with the emergencies of the 21st century, *The Dark Knight* also showed a bold cinematic style in its nighttime urban landscapes, the makeup of the Joker, and the computer effects that created the fallen crime-fighter, Two-Face (Aaron Eckhart), who could have come right out of a graphic novel.

The mythic, often escapist films generally had high production values, impressive stunts and special effects, and attractive heroes—many of whom, particularly in the era's conservative period, were police. Both *48 HRS.* (1982, directed by Walter Hill), starring Eddie Murphy and Nick Nolte, and *Lethal Weapon* (1987, directed by Richard Donner), starring Mel Gibson and Danny Glover, pit a team of crime busters—one black and one white, whose temperaments are comically mismatched but who come to like and depend on each other, and most of whose lines are jokes (they spar like the mates in screwball

Star Wars: *left to right, Peter Mayhew, Mark Hamill, Alec Guinness, Harrison Ford.*

Fig. 17-1

comedies)—against extremely violent and not at all funny villains. The hero of *RoboCop* (1987, directed by Paul Verhoeven) is both a man and a machine, and both are good cops. The hero of *Blue Thunder* (1983, directed by John Badham) is a good cop and the skillful pilot of an armed surveillance helicopter. The hero of *Top Gun* (1986, directed by Tony Scott) is a hotshot jet pilot who wins tests of skill and gets the girl. The hero of *True Lies* (1994, directed by James Cameron) is a virtually invulnerable secret agent who blows terrorists away with high-tech weapons and saves his marriage; one of its themes is that the workaday world is a boring fiction, but the movie-ish world is the real thing. There were also heroes who did not work for the police force—that is, who were not sheriffs and gunslingers in what were essentially the period's westerns. There were real-life heroes (Steven Soderbergh's *Erin Brockovich*, 2000), metaphysical heroes (Andy and Larry Wachowski's *The Matrix*, 1999), ordinary people forced to rise to extraordinary demands (Andrew Davis's *The Fugitive*, 1993), and people who had heroic fantasies (Alan Parker's *Fame*, 1980). The kids in *Fame* want to develop their skills, survive their personal trials, and become famous, and at the end it looks as if some of them may even have a chance; compared with the slew of 1980s films

about dancers and singers and groups who desperately want to succeed and, of course, do, *Fame* was almost realistic. So was Robert Townsend's *Hollywood Shuffle* (1987), which pointed out that if the hero couldn't make it as a Hollywood director, he could always find honest work at the post office.

Not every myth was of a hero; mythic villains were part of the same system. (After all, the Force has a Dark Side, and there are good and bad Terminators.) The young stockbroker in *Wall Street* (1987, directed by Oliver Stone), who wins morally even if he suffers, must defeat a tremendously powerful antagonist, a takeover artist who incarnates every evil known to capitalism. The "other woman" in *Fatal Attraction* (1987, directed by Adrian Lyne) has to be rejected, drowned, and shot at close range before the threat she represents can be destroyed. Although many of these films simply had nasty but mortal bad guys, others presented villains who might look human but were almost impossible to defeat or kill (James Cameron's *The Terminator*, 1984). The most common unstoppable villain of the era was the slasher, the compulsive madman (occasionally a woman) who kills one person after another—with a knife, with his bare hands, or with whatever happens to be around. If the prototype of the slasher was Cesare in *Caligari*, and if there have been others in such films as *M*, *Peeping Tom*, and the crucial *Psycho*, the sub-genre of the slasher film was defined and codified by John Carpenter's *Halloween* (1978), which brought together the essential elements of obsession, madness, one-by-one teenage victims, hints of the mythic and supernatural (the killer, who is compared to the boogeyman, is fueled, at least in part, by the energy and folklore of Halloween, when the dead are said to come home), the butcher knife, the mask, the unspeaking killer, the resourceful female survivor, and sex (that is, sex scenes that are associated with bloody death). *Halloween* was cloned by its own sequels as well as by countless low-budget independent productions, but its most famous imitator was the *Friday the 13th* series. In *Friday the 13th* itself (1980, directed by Sean S. Cunningham), as in the opening of *Halloween*, the camera shows not the killer but what the killer sees (not so the audience will identify with the slasher but so it won't discover her identity), and the villain turns out to be a woman who blames all sexually active teenagers for the death of her son, Jason. In the sequels (the best of which, *Friday the 13th Part 2*, 1981, and *Part III*, 1982, were directed by Steve Miner), the larger-than-life slasher is Jason. The next major slasher series, one of the most creative, began with Wes Craven's *A Nightmare on Elm Street* (1984), whose slasher attacks his victims in their dreams.

Most of the pro-myth films had little interest in politics—in *Footloose* (1984, directed by Herbert Ross), a bad government is one that forbids people to dance—but some of them were aggressively opposed to the politics, and particularly the feminism, of the 1960s and 1970s. One example of the backlash against feminism was *Die Hard* (1988, directed by John McTiernan), a film that was equally popular with male and female audiences. The hero, a New York City policeman (John McClane, played by Bruce Willis), copes with a dangerous situation to save his wife (Holly Gennaro McClane, played by Bonnie Bedelia). John is strong, smart, witty, nonracist, professional, and a regular guy. Holly is also strong and smart and good at her job. As the story begins, the policeman visits his estranged wife in Los Angeles on Christmas Eve; he goes to meet her at work, where he is irritated to find

that she is listed only under her maiden name. He also finds that she has just been awarded a Rolex watch for being especially good at her job. Then the high-rise office building is taken over by criminals pretending to be terrorists. After a lot of action, during which most of the criminals and some of the hostages are killed, we find the last and of course worst villain dangling from a 30th-floor window—holding on to Holly, who is being held and braced by her husband. John notices that the villain's grip is actually on the Rolex, not on Holly's forearm (the villain has his gun-hand free), and so he unlatches the watch—the explicit symbol of her independent professionalism—and the criminal falls to his death. When Holly and John finally leave the building, she identifies herself by her married name.

Myth and Antimyth

Two baseball pictures, Phil Alden Robinson's *Field of Dreams* (1989) and John Sayles's *Eight Men Out* (1988), clearly demonstrate that in this period, the escape from politics was a step into fantasy and mythmaking, and to confront political and economic corruption was to dismantle a myth. In *Field of Dreams*, an Iowa farmer (Ray, played by Kevin Costner) obeys a voice that tells him, more or less, that if he builds a baseball field on his property, the great "Shoeless" Joe Jackson will come there to play. Jackson had been one of the "Black Sox," members of the Chicago White Sox who conspired to throw the 1919 World Series and were barred forever from professional baseball; he represents a scandal this film would like to heal. In fact, the movie sets out to forgive and heal all of the failings of the 20th century, both personal and political. The key is to believe in one's dreams, to follow them with the innocent part of one's heart. And in this definitively mythic film, every dream comes true. When Ray builds the baseball diamond, the ghosts of Shoeless Joe and his teammates do appear; their suspension from the game has, in this magical time and place, been lifted, their sins forgiven. Given this second chance, the Sox think the Iowa field must be heaven, because heaven is where dreams come true. Another deceased ballplayer, whose dream of playing in the majors had almost but not quite been fulfilled, finally gets to go to bat against a major-league pitcher here. Even Ray gets a second chance and a wish

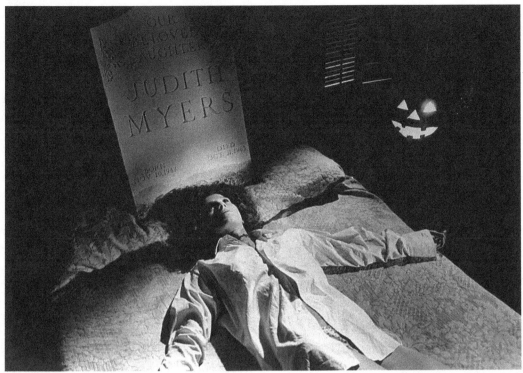

Fig. 17-2
Halloween: *The mythic ritual of formally arranged bodies and symbolic objects creates an atmosphere of eerie significance (Nancy Loomis as Annie).*

fulfilled: to reconcile with his dead father. Most significantly, the dreams of a black leftist writer (played by James Earl Jones) come true. He had been a major novelist and a concerned activist in the 1960s but finally lost faith in causes and in the improvability of American society; bitter and disillusioned, he had stopped writing. The writer's dream, which the hero helps to fulfill, is not to see social justice but to watch a great ballgame with the innocent eyes of his youth. In this film, to believe in the dream is to undo the failures of the past (the fixed World Series, Watergate) and set aside everything that has divided us (the hero's unfortunate fight with his father, the aroused political consciousness of the 1960s). And in a decade that saw thousands of farmers lose everything, the urgent financial problems of Ray and his family are solved when vast audiences drive to their farm to watch the games. The myth of America—the genuine America, as unspoiled as the ideal of baseball,

which can be a "heaven" where dreams come true—is renewed, and whatever was bad about the bad old times, including all those disruptive political struggles, is forgiven and forgotten; the past has been given back its innocence, and the present looks better too.

Eight Men Out tells the story of the Black Sox scandal in a firm, realistic style. If the myth of baseball is taken down a peg—the players are workers, the boss is cheap, and even the gamblers treat the players unfairly—the spirit of the game still comes across. Because of the depth with which it treats betrayed idealism, *Eight Men Out* manages to deal authentically with idealism. America, like baseball, is presented in a less-than-mythical light—a place that can be so hypocritical and economically corrupt that it is almost a fixed World Series in itself, full of betrayed, believing fans. The moral conflicts this film explores are intense, and the film argues that they need to be understood, not set aside—as history needs to be remembered and learned from. Erasing history is no way to defend or recapture the essence of an ideal. *Field of Dreams*, which did much better at the box office, is a "feelgood movie"; *Eight Men Out* is a "bummer." Studio executives used those words at the time. Distrustful of official institutions, refusing to offer simplistic solutions, and taking legendary figures with a grain of salt, *Eight Men Out* is an example of the period's "antimyth" movies. Although it was made in New Zealand, Niki Caro's *Whale Rider* (2003) is a good example of a mythic movie whose political content is feminist and that deals with traditional mythology.

Some of the antimyth films were low-budget independent productions; a few were studio extravaganzas. Tim Hunter's *River's Edge* (1986), which presented the American family as a dying institution and contemporary teenagers as unable to love or to feel anything deeply, and Gus Van Sant's *Drugstore Cowboy* (1989), which rejected the images of the 1980s' antidrug campaigns, were among the most forceful and negative of the small films. Kubrick's *Full Metal Jacket*, a war film; Ridley Scott's *Alien* (1979), a horror film set in outer space; and Michael Cimino's *Heaven's Gate* (1980), a western, spent their big budgets on unflattering portraits of militarism and big capitalism. While Barry Levinson's *Good Morning, Vietnam* (1987) implied that all the Americans and Vietnamese needed was to play a good baseball game together, *Full Metal Jacket*—released the same year—fired a metaphoric bullet at the myths of the Vietnam War and closed with an image of marching soldiers singing the "*Mickey Mouse Club* Song," whose "C: See you real soon" is reminiscent of *Dr. Strangelove*'s "We'll meet again." *Alien* has a strong, intelligent, fast-acting hero (Ripley, played by Sigourney Weaver), a metamorphosing monster as indestructible and rapacious as Ripley is heroic, and a bad-guy robot, all of which would seem to make this a mythic film. But the real villain—undefeated at the end—is the company that owns the spaceship and wants it to bring back the Alien, even at the cost of the crew, as a specimen from which to develop new weapons and troops.

Heaven's Gate told the story of the Johnson County Wars in 1890s Wyoming, increasing the body count and drawing explicit political connections between the federal government and the rich cattlemen who, in the course of the film, exterminate the peasant immigrants whose desire to work the land stands in the way of the cattlemen's plans. Read as "cattlemen vs. farmers," this is a standard western conflict, waiting for its Shane. But the marshal (Kris Kristofferson as Jim Averill) is not very effective. The head of the Cattlemen's Association (Sam Waterston as Frank Canton) is far better organized than the marshal, as well as cruel and cold, prejudiced and patrician. Canton's government connections are part of the upper-class world in which he moves—for *Heaven's Gate* makes the Old West the site of a class war. The members of the lower class gather in their community center, "Heaven's Gate," to dance in good times and debate in bad. They are not fancy folks, not all of them speak English, and some of them have stolen cattle (a capital offense) to feed their families, but they have the right to live and work in America despite what the Cantons think. When the peasants, at the cost of most of their number, are on the verge of winning the final battle, the cavalry, guided by Canton, rides to the rescue—of the bad guys. This cynical development, which causes a woman fighter to blow her brains out, climaxes the antimythic, disillusioned vision of *Heaven's Gate* and marks how far the narrative and thematic device of the last-minute rescue had developed since Griffith.

Heaven's Gate was the biggest box-office disaster in Hollywood history. Later films have lost more money, but this one brought down a studio. United Artists, which produced the film and was virtually destroyed by it, had to write off its $44 million cost and was acquired by MGM within a year (forming MGM/UA in 1981). *Heaven's Gate* opened for a week at its original length, 219 minutes, but was savaged by a New York critic. UA pulled the film, cut it to 147 much less interesting minutes, and forced Cimino to apologize publicly for his extravagance and poor artistic judgment. The original version, which has not played in a U.S. theatre since that first engagement, did good business in Europe throughout the 1980s. The common domestic judgment was that *Heaven's Gate* had no story, was depressing, and indicated the folly of letting an obsessive *auteur* get too far out of (studio) control. The complete version—available on video—does in fact have a story.

Fig. 17-3
Heaven's Gate: *In the community center where they go to enjoy themselves and to debate political matters, the immigrants are entertained by the violinist of the Heaven's Gate Band (David Mansfield).*

Painfully re-evaluating the myths of the western, of fair government, and of the hero, *Heaven's Gate* pushed the antimyth position farther than Hollywood was willing to go in this period. Its clearly articulated leftist message, which just as clearly referred to the social, economic, and political problems of the present, may have offended studio executives (as Cimino's arrogant behavior on the set certainly did) or may have been too out of step with current attitudes. That same year, Lucas's *The Empire Strikes Back* (1980, directed by Irvin Kershner) took creative mythology even beyond the achievements of *Star Wars* and took the box office along for good measure.

Popular Heroes and Postmodern Irony
But the debate over mythic values continued for decades, well after *Heaven's Gate* had closed. At a climactic point in *Lethal Weapon*, a villain smugly says there are "no heroes left"—and Mel Gibson rushes in to save the day. Incarnated by

Harrison Ford, Arnold Schwarzenegger, Sylvester Stallone, and others, the heroes of action–adventure films affirmed the power of the myths. The most cinematically impressive of these were Steven Spielberg's *Raiders of the Lost Ark* (1981), which started the Indiana Jones series; Ted Kotcheff's *First Blood* (1982), which started the Rambo series; and James Cameron's *The Terminator* and *Terminator 2: Judgment Day* (1991). Three personal and ambitious pictures, Spike Lee's *Malcolm X* (1992), Spielberg's *Schindler's List* (1993), and Gus Van Sant's *Milk* (2008), showed how real people, gifted and determined but not superhuman, could grow into heroes. On the other hand, a film like Eastwood's *Unforgiven* (1992) suggested that there may never have been any heroes, at least the way we like to think of them and the media (in *Unforgiven*, a writer who chronicles the exploits of gunfighters) like to construct them. Robert Redford's *Quiz Show* (1994) traced the fall of a phony hero. The way the media create heroes was analyzed in Oliver Stone's *Natural Born Killers* (1994), whose latter-day Bonnie and Clyde are killers with style. If that film was to be the period's *Bonnie and Clyde*, its *Graduate* was Robert Zemeckis's *Forrest Gump* (1994), in which Tom Hanks plays a character who is sometimes as passive and clueless as Dustin Hoffman in the earlier picture, but also less intellectual—a character elevated to mythic status without developing mythic consciousness, a blank that audiences filled with their own nostalgia for innocence, creating in the process a mythic vehicle, something apparently apolitical and innocent to believe in.

Popular culture continued to provide images and figures to renew. In *Superman*'s comic-book wake came such pictures as Tim Burton's *Batman* (1989) and Sam Raimi's *Spider-Man* (2002) and the many horror films whose gore effects and humor were inspired by EC Comics. At the same time, the comic books and graphic novels (in the United Kingdom and Japan as well

as the United States) became more aggressively cinematic and narratively complex: Frank Miller's *The Dark Knight Returns* (1986), Alan Moore's *V for Vendetta* (1988–89), Neil Gaiman's *Sandman* (1989–95). One adaptation that did its best to live up to the graphic novel that inspired it, from its narrative complexity to its bold use of color and effects, was Zack Snyder's *Watchmen* (2009); the original was written by Alan Moore, illustrated by Dave Gibbons, and colored by John Higgins, and Snyder respected what they had achieved in their at once mythic and antimythic tale of heroes and superheroes who try to manipulate a troubled world. Many films were made from TV series (*Star Trek*), remade from old movies, or set in the world of old movies. The recycling of imagery and genres was both a business decision (in favor of material the audience already knew and liked) and a tendency within Postmodern art. Reflexivity in these films was often a matter of dense or superficial references to other movies; sometimes, as in Tim Burton's *Ed Wood* (1994), the tone was inseparably homage and put-on.

Fig. 17-4
Raiders of the Lost Ark: *Indiana Jones (Harrison Ford) in a mythic world of old serials, ancient artifacts and forces, state-of-the-art effects, and up-to-date irony.*

As early as *Superman, Grease* (Randal Kleiser), and *Piranha* (Joe Dante)—all 1978—a reflexive, ironic distance had characterized many of the films that drew on received images and treated them from a contemporary perspective. Later, such films were recognized as Postmodern, but they were not the only variety. Wayne Wang's *Chan is Missing* (1982) offers an example of another kind of Postmodern film, a low-budget, independent picture that is in every respect the opposite of *Grease*. Chan does not appear in the film. A Chinese taxi driver who has, with a younger friend, been trying to locate Chan may be playing detective, but he is, as people often tell him, "no Charlie Chan." At the end, when the mystery film ends without solving the mystery and Chan remains unfound, the man who is not a Charlie Chan (and thus is the second Chan missing from this picture) sums up all the contradictory descriptions of Chan, leaving him a figure who cannot be defined simply or even defined at all. This absent figure who resists definition is the beginning of Postmodernism's inquiry, its ideal quest object.

As an intellectual movement, Postmodernism analyzes a world without a definitive center and dates from the 1970s. As a period in the history of culture, it appears to have begun after World War II and may be related to the widespread adoption of television. Appropriately resisting definition, the term has come to refer to the movement in the arts that came after Modernism. For some Postmodern artists, all the stories have already been told, and it is in style that the route to the new may be found. Much Postmodern art is reflexive, much of it builds on references to popular culture, and much of it sets out to be free of any ultimate truth or final synthesis. Some of it is purely commercial, reflecting cultural conditions rather than reflecting upon them. It was a Postmodern cycle when *Superman* went from a comic book to a TV show to a series of movies to a series of graphic novels (and eventually to another movie: Bryan Singer's *Superman Returns*, 2006). It was Postmodern for *Chan is Missing* to end without finding Chan, for *Eclipse* to show the absence of action when the characters don't show up for their meeting, and for Jim Jarmusch's *Coffee and Cigarettes* (2003) to be constructed out of an arbitrary but fixed set of terms (conversation, coffee, cigarettes, a table, and so forth).

While some filmmakers, like David Lynch, pursued irony and reflexivity into a truly Postmodern world of ungrounded textual play, others, like James Cameron, set out to create, without irony, state-of-the-art spectacles in which their heroes could do their stuff.

Leading Directors

Lucas and Spielberg

The master mythmakers of the era are George Lucas and Steven Spielberg. They are also the most powerful creative figures in the contemporary American film industry. Like P. T. Barnum, they are producers, showmen, masters of the revels; like Hitchcock, they are known by those who might not recognize the names of any other directors. As much captains and architects as personal stylists, they have worked with large teams of creative collaborators: the composer John Williams; special-effects artists like Douglas Trumbull (whose work includes *2001* and *Blade Runner* as well as *Close Encounters*), Dennis Muren, John Dykstra, and Richard Edlund; sound designers and editors like Ben Burtt and Walter Murch; and others: cinematographers, production designers, highly skilled technicians. Dolby Noise Reduction and Dolby Stereo owe much of their success to the impact of the *Star Wars* soundtrack. The special-effects house Industrial Light & Magic (ILM) is part of the Lucasfilm Ltd. empire, as is Skywalker Sound. Lucas also pioneered—and, as THX Sound, implemented—a system of standards for the quality and balance of theatrical sound. He has been a major force in the development of new editing technologies (beginning with SoundDroid, a digital sound-editing system, and the EditDroid, a computerized editing station that allowed movies to be edited on video) as well as in the marketing of movie-related merchandise and the creation of live amusements. In 1993, he announced that he would not begin work on the next three episodes of *Star Wars* until he and ILM had perfected the technology for seamlessly integrating simulated, digitized environments and live action; ILM's work on *Forrest Gump* and *Jurassic Park* was just a start. As a producer who controls a vast, multifaceted creative enterprise and whose cinematic fantasies have had an immense influence on more than a generation of children, Lucas has become the next Disney. As the director of the world's most popular spectacles, Spielberg has been called the next DeMille, but he also combines elements of Thomas Ince and Victor Fleming.

Lucas's first feature was *THX-1138* (1971), a stylized science fiction drama about a passionless, mechanized, regimented dystopia. *American Graffiti* (1973), a comedy about teenagers cruising the streets of a small town, was a major hit. (As previously mentioned, the soundtracks of *Easy Rider, Mean Streets*, and *American Graffiti* all achieved influential breakthroughs in the use of rock music.) His next film combined the adolescent coming-of-age drama with science fiction: *Star Wars*. Giving up directing to concentrate on producing, Lucas followed *Star Wars* with *The Empire Strikes Back* (1980, directed by Irvin Kershner) and *Return of the Jedi* (1983, directed by Richard Marquand); they are the fourth, fifth, and sixth episodes, or central trilogy, of a nine-part epic conceived as three trilogies. (By 2004, plans for the third trilogy had been abandoned.) Late in 1998, Lucas announced that he would direct the next episode himself (*Star Wars: Episode I—The Phantom Menace*, released 1999) and that it would introduce a new surround-sound format (Dolby Digital–Surround EX) with an additional rear-center channel that would allow sounds to be placed more precisely. In 2001, he announced that the shooting of the next picture (*Star Wars: Episode II—Attack of the Clones*, 2002) had been completed without exposing a foot of film, using a high-definition digital video camera: the new 24p (24 fps progressive-scan) camera, developed in 1997 by Sony with help from Panavision, that gave nearly filmlike results. (This technology is discussed in the next two chapters.) Shooting with a 24p allowed Lucas to avoid any loss of information when transferring a film original to digital for effects and editing; he simply started with a 24 fps digital original. The effects shots in *The Phantom Menace* had looked so much better on the computer than they did when transferred to film, and there were so many more computer-generated and -composited shots planned for *Clones*, that Lucas decided to go digital from pre-production to post, with a final product that would be projected digitally in some theatres and transferred to film for others (which is also how *The*

Phantom Menace was released). This was comparable to his much earlier decision to use Dolby Noise Reduction throughout the first *Star Wars*.

With *Star Wars: Episode III—Revenge of the Sith* (2005, also shot without film), Lucas linked the two trilogies into a coherent six-part saga, the story of the tragic fall and redemption of Anakin Skywalker, later Darth Vader, and the parallel adventures of his son, Luke. That "there is another" is a structuring principle: There are Luke and Leia, Anakin and Luke, the tale of the fall of the Republic (the first trilogy—that is, the one produced second, consisting of Episodes I–III) and the tale of the fall of the Empire (the second trilogy, consisting of Episodes IV–VI), two artificial hands, and so on. *Sith* forced audiences to rethink scenes they knew well: to see, for example, that when Darth Vader kills the Emperor in *Return of the Jedi*, he is not only saving his son, but also fulfilling his destiny as the Chosen One who will bring balance to the Force and destroy the Sith. When Anakin's forearm is cut off in *Clones* (the second film in its trilogy), it is not just to echo the scene in *The Empire Strikes Back* (also the second film in its trilogy) where Luke's forearm is cut off, but also to anticipate, revise, and strengthen that scene, to set it up that when Vader has wounded his son as he was wounded, he will declare their kinship. The interweaving and mirroring of elements from the episodes are intricate; thus both the first and fourth episodes contain the discovery of a young hero and both the third and sixth episodes contain ultimate confrontations with evil, but the conclusions of the third and sixth episodes are opposite in tone. The original *Star Wars* now took its proper place in the sequence; since the 1997 digitally augmented reissue, its official title had been *Star Wars: Episode IV—A New Hope*, and after *Sith* one understood that hope more clearly.

Raiders of the Lost Ark and its sequels were co-produced by Lucas and directed by Spielberg. With their cliff-hangers and nonstop action, the mythic Indiana Jones films owe even more to the 1930s and 1940s serials and pulp fiction than *Star Wars* does. One of the most entertaining and imaginative action pictures of the 1980s, *Raiders* deserves to be ranked with the greatest films ever made in the genre of action–adventure. *Indiana Jones and the Temple of Doom* took an "anything goes" attitude that encouraged more reflexive jokes and nonstop action. *Indiana Jones and the Last Crusade* (1989) set archaeologist Jones (Harrison Ford) on the trail of the Holy Grail, in the company of his father—played by Sean Connery, who as James Bond was the definitive hero of the action–adventure spectacle that leapt from one big action scene and exotic location to another, and thus *was* the cinematic father of Indiana Jones. *Indiana Jones and the Kingdom of the Crystal Skull* (2008) let Indy grow older, resolve some issues in his personal life, find a son (who may be intended to star in new Indiana Jones films, much as the 2009 *Star Trek* tried to win over new viewers with a younger cast), tackle Nazis and alien artifacts, and try to keep the picture exciting; highly computerized, it cost more than all the previous films combined, but it did not live up to them.

From *Duel* (1971) to *Temple of Doom*, it is Spielberg who established the movie as ride. *Jurassic Park* (1993), about dinosaurs and chaos theory and a theme park that gets out of control, is itself a theme park that offers the thrills of chaos but never slips out of control. His control of tension and pace is both tight and expansive; he may be better at grand, sweeping effects than any director since David Lean; and he has a firm, efficient sense of narrative structure. Spielberg's one flaw—which in some of his films works as a strength—is his apparent belief that scenes have to be "big" to work. Certainly the D-Day sequence in *Saving Private Ryan* (1998) is big and works. But overstatement and sentimentality derail the climax of *Schindler's List*. *Always* (1989, a remake of a movie he loved, Victor Fleming's 1943 *A Guy Named Joe*) paints the subtleties of emotion with such a broad brush that the result is emotionally unaffecting; *1941* (1979) has so much action that it's boring. But the majority of his films are rich experiences, both emotionally involving and kinetically charged, whose full, direct manner is appropriate and successful. *A.I. Artificial Intelligence* (2001; onscreen title, *Artificial Intelligence AI*), the project he inherited from Kubrick, has big scenes that are emotionally relentless, like the one in which the mother abandons her adopted robot child in a forest as threatening as that in any fairy tale; it has other fairy-tale moments that are involving without turning sentimental, like the ironic twist on *Pinocchio* or the dark use of W. B. Yeats's poem "The Stolen

Child" (uncredited); and it has an uncharacteristically subtle, quiet ending. Not only in theme (a robot who wants to be a real boy so the mother will love him, who ends up surviving the human race and is given an ironically limited and timeless reward by the robots who look back to him for their origin), but also in execution, it demonstrated the seamless integration of the worlds of live action and effects, and even if the film borrowed a little of its chill from Kubrick, it was still up to Spielberg to achieve the tone that made *A.I.* an emotionally rich and ironic *Pinocchio* for adults. His earlier science fiction pictures—which were, unlike *A.I.*, definitively mythic and more into the wishing-on-a-star aspect of Pinocchio— were big entertainments that kept in touch with individuals and their feelings: *Close Encounters of the Third Kind* (1977, revised 1980) and *E.T.— The Extra-Terrestrial* (1982) are engrossing spectacles whose visions are awesome and whose domestic, terrestrial scenes are usually well observed. *Duel* (about a motorist pursued by a crazy truck driver; his last TV movie) and *The Sugarland Express* (1974, about a couple fleeing the police to keep their baby; his first theatrical movie) have effective, linear trajectories—they know where they're going and keep moving. In the best of his early films, *Jaws* (1975), and in sequences like the silent drowning of the slaves in *Amistad* (1997), his style has the authority and economy of a master.

Like Lucas, Spielberg is also a producer; his first company was Amblin Entertainment. Though he rarely interfered with their directors, his creative stamp is evident on the films he produced, the best of which were *Poltergeist* (1982), directed by Tobe Hooper; *Gremlins* (1984), directed by Joe Dante; and *Back to the Future* (1985), directed by Robert Zemeckis. In 1994, when studio executive Jeffrey Katzenberg left Disney, he and Spielberg and record mogul David Geffen created a new studio: DreamWorks SKG. (In 2006, DreamWorks was acquired by Paramount, but in 2008, it moved to Universal, while DreamWorks Animation remained at Paramount.)

Close Encounters depicts a battle between earthly authority, which attempts to limit our knowledge of extraterrestrial life, and the higher power of the imagination—of people who *know*, without knowing how they know, that the beings exist. Those who know are bound by their common visions, induced by the aliens, and by earthly imagination and myth. The scientist who passionately seeks contact with the unknown is played by François Truffaut. As filmmaker–scientist he *produces* the climactic encounter between earthly and extraterrestrial beings and shares it with his audience in a display of sound and light, music and color—the resources of movies themselves.

E.T.—The Extra-Terrestrial begins where *Close Encounters* ends. Instead of an Earthling who departs with the extraterrestrials, an extraterrestrial creature is abandoned on Earth by his own people. E.T. is a kid's best possible magical friend. Spielberg clearly cares for children. The primary message of *Jurassic Park* is that children are good, and it is important to grow up and have them. *A.I.*, whose boy is real and artificial, complicates that message with the reminder that having or even designing children is not enough—one must love them and learn how to raise them. This reminder is consistent with the films in which Spielberg makes significant contact with his own parents' generation, as he did in *Saving Private Ryan*—telling their tales and not those of his own childhood. If Lucas has found a way to excite the child in moviegoers of all ages, Spielberg has offered a generation lessons on what it is to be a child and, all the way back to *Sugarland* and *Jaws*—and as recently as *War of the Worlds* (2005)—what it is to be a parent.

David Lynch

Nobody ever got lost trying to follow a Spielberg or Lucas film, but the films of David Lynch are something else. A unique stylist with a unique vision, Lynch has a fearlessly bizarre approach to the aesthetic challenges of narrative tone and structure. The world he presents is—as his characters often remark—a strange place. Of all the major directors whose first features appeared during or after 1977, Lynch is by far the most experimental.

An abstract painter and something of a cartoonist (in his long-running strip about the angriest dog in the world, the picture never changed), Lynch learned a great deal from the avant-garde. If the mechanical robin at the end of *Blue Velvet* (1986) can be traced directly to George Kuchar's *Hold Me While I'm Naked*, Lynch's emphasis on

intriguing, unexplained images whose presence not only *is* a mystery but also points obliquely to related mysteries can be traced back to the poetic devices of avant-garde cinema in general. The sound for Lynch's first four films—*Eraserhead* (1977), *The Elephant Man* (1980), *Dune* (1984), and *Blue Velvet*—was designed by Alan Splet, whose complex, ominous sound composites perfectly complement Lynch's haunting images.

Lynch's films—along with *Twin Peaks* (pilot, 1989; series broadcast 1990–91), the enigmatic TV series he created with Mark Frost, which was followed by the feature *Twin Peaks: Fire Walk With Me* (1992)—present and re-work a number of recurring themes and images. Life has a mystery. What lurks below the surfaces of ordinary reality may be horrible, unbearable (*Eraserhead*, *Blue Velvet*). Or there may be a secret knowledge, to uncover which is to solve a problem, grow in spiritual power, and fulfill one's destiny (*Dune, Twin Peaks*). The human body, though it may be kept squeaky clean (*Twin Peaks*), can be seen as fundamentally repulsive (*Eraserhead, The Elephant Man, Dune*). Sex is dangerous, unpredictable, and uncontrollable (*Eraserhead; Blue Velvet; Wild At Heart*, 1990). Children want love and suffer horribly (*Eraserhead, The Elephant Man*). The squirmy white things in *Eraserhead*—particularly a small one that opens its mouth, into which the camera plunges—resemble the sand worms of *Dune*, and both raise the question of creation from the body. As the camera moves into the severed ear in *Blue Velvet*, part of the ear is briefly seen as a sphere shaped by shadow, and a windlike but unnatural sound is heard; it is the sound heard in *Eraserhead* when the mysterious sphere, "the planet," is seen or entered. Jeffrey Beaumont (Kyle MacLachlan) explains the lure of the mystery in *Blue Velvet* this way: "I'm seeing something that was always hidden. . . . I'm in the middle of a mystery, and it's all secret." Following a mystery to its end can lead one into a dark and paradoxical space where personal identity is at risk—characters can even switch roles—while the official mystery remains unsolved (*Lost Highway*, 1996; *Mulholland Drive*, 2001). Even if he is capable of telling a perfectly moving, simple, true story about a man who drives a lawnmower hundreds of miles to visit his estranged brother

Fig. 17-5

Fig. 17-6

Close Encounters of the Third Kind: *the wondrous sight of the Mother Ship's landing (Fig. 17-5) and the wonder of childhood vision (Fig. 17-6, Cary Guffey).*

(*The Straight Story*, 1999), that control of the look of the world, in this case its wonderfully realized beauty and ordinariness, is essential to his creating surfaces that one might not like to look beneath, boxes and houses and ears that are rabbit holes. What one discovers in a Lynch film about people's private lives is usually awful. The innocent look of too-ordinary reality is clearly hiding something. The secret—the vision of the way life really is—may be the stuff of soap operas (*Twin Peaks*), of cosmic poetry (*The Elephant Man*), of *noirs* (*Blue Velvet*), or of sexual labyrinths (*Eraserhead*), and the ironic tone may be clean-scrubbed or gross, metaphysical or

Fig. 17-7
Blue Velvet: *Jeffrey (Kyle MacLachlan) hides in Dorothy's closet and peeks at the mystery.*

melodramatic. In most of his pictures, characters find out who they really or paradoxically are.

Eraserhead makes love and marriage, intercourse and reproduction, food and life all a bit horrible. Henry Spencer (Jack "John" Nance), who is "on vacation," marries Mary X (Charlotte Stewart) after they have a baby—although the hospital staff isn't sure that it is a baby: a skinless, screaming, goatlike head, linked by its skinny neck to a torso held together with swaddling. Mary is pitifully unhappy, makes weird sounds in her sleep when she can sleep, can't stand the baby's constant painful crying, and finally goes home to her nutcase parents. Henry, who has a dream in which his brain is made into erasers, eventually kills the baby (after it frightens away a beautiful woman Henry has had sex with, then *cackles*—the only time it's done anything but cry or eat) and perhaps ends up with the girl of his dreams, a tiny imaginary lady with huge cheeks whom he has watched perform on a stage inside the radiator. This is not the stuff of Hollywood romance. Its outdoors is geometric and muddy and bleak, its indoors claustrophobic and depressing, its characters maddening and unattractive and hurting badly. Dreams of creativity are squished in this wildly creative black-and-white black comedy, which became a major cult hit, often shown by itself at midnight on Fridays and Saturdays.

The Elephant Man, also in black and white (shot by Freddie Francis), is the essentially true story of John Merrick (John Hurt), a hideously deformed young Englishman, and Dr. Frederick Treaves (Anthony Hopkins), the anatomist who discovers him in a Victorian freak show and arranges for him to live in London Hospital and to meet members of London society—but, as an object of study, still to be on view. In the company of Mrs. Kendal (Anne Bancroft), an actress who believes that the theatre is "romance," Merrick even attends a play, where for the first time he can be in the audience rather than on stage (although at the end of the scene, Mrs. Kendal calls attention to him, and the audience gazes and applauds, this time without cruelty). Mrs. Kendal and Merrick's long-dead mother are the two beautiful women who almost magically accept him; he keeps their portraits together on his night table. When he dies, it is as if he projects his soul into starry space and toward the face of the mother. As she softly declares, "The heart beats—nothing will die," the screen fills with light.

Blue Velvet was Lynch's most popular film and the ancestor of another complicated mystery set in a strange small town, *Twin Peaks* (it is in *Blue Velvet*'s Lumberton, but could just as well be in Twin Peaks, that radio station WOOD announces, "At the sound of the falling tree, it's 1:30!"). At the beginning of the film, everything is bright and clean and in peaceful slow motion—until a man who has been watering his lawn suddenly falls, stricken with an ailment that is never identified. His son, Jeffrey (MacLachlan), comes home from school to work in the family store; he falls for a sweet girl, Sandy (Laura Dern), and everything is apple-pie normal—or, more precisely, heightened apple-pie normal—until Jeffrey finds a man's ear on the ground and sets out, with Sandy's help, to solve the mystery it poses. The key figures in that mystery are a violent psychopath named Frank (Dennis Hopper) and a sexual masochist named Dorothy (Isabella Rossellini). Dorothy does whatever Frank wants—sings "Blue Velvet," for example—because Frank and his cohorts have kidnapped her husband (whose ear Jeffrey found) and child. Sandy and Jeffrey have a love theme, played on a church organ; it is heard under their first kiss and under the scene in which Sandy expresses her hope that everything will be all right again, which will happen magically when the robins come back. The countertheme, "Blue Velvet," is the song of irresistible sexuality and dark, violent, obsessive perversity: Frank's

At the climax of Eraserhead, Henry (John Nance) watches as the mysterious "planet" cracks open.

Fig. 17-8

terrifying abuse (and the evidence that he was sexually traumatized when young, making him kin to the suffering children in *Eraserhead* and *The Elephant Man*), Dorothy's desperate performing onstage and off, the whole criminal and deviant world hidden beneath the clean, bright, artificial surface of Lumberton. When sung by Rossellini, it is a siren song that leads, so to speak, through a severed ear into the darkness that everyone hides. Like their leitmotifs, the innocent and corrupt worlds of *Blue Velvet* are as distinct as day and night. They are also equally stylized, extreme, and distant from reality. In the Happy Ending, when Jeffrey's dad has recovered and the flowers are again too bright against fences that are too white, Sandy and Jeffrey see a robin, an artificial one, with an artificial beetle in its beak.

If Anne Bancroft plays the Good Witch of the Theatre in *The Elephant Man*, Diane Ladd plays the Wicked Witch of Motherhood in *Wild At Heart*, a road movie filled with off-the-wall references to *The Wizard of Oz*; for example, two butchered men try to gather their blood and body parts together, losing a hand to a hungry dog, in an allusion to the scarecrow whose straw has been scattered by the flying monkeys but is stuffed back in by his friends. In this film, sex is hot and dangerous, like a struck wooden match;

weirdness and corruption are everywhere in a world that is menacing, crazy, rough, and passionate ("wild at heart and weird on top"). Dreams come true here ("If you're truly wild at heart, you'll fight for your dreams"), but through painful and fantastic means. The innocence of the young lovers (Laura Dern and Nicolas Cage) is relentlessly tested, destroyed, and celebrated. *Wild At Heart* is both a parody of 1980s mythic romance and the real thing, as *Twin Peaks* is and is not a soap. (When asked the relationship between *Wild At Heart* and *Twin Peaks*, Lynch replied that they both had a lot of wood in them.) *Wild At Heart* is an ironic artifice in the Postmodern mode of *Blue Velvet*, but it also has scenes of violence and of sexual self-knowledge that are acutely realistic. Like Lynch's previous films—and the next one, *Fire Walk With Me*—it deals with innocence, pain, and transformation in a stylized, mysterious world; unlike them, it was censored for U.S. release. *Lost Highway* wasn't censored, but its release was held up for a year while baffled and frightened people tried to figure out how to rate it, how to market it, how to *explain* it. Lynch distributed the long and difficult *Inland Empire* (2006) himself. After shooting *Inland Empire* on digital video, he announced that he was never going back to film.

Acknowledging that "film is beautiful, there's no two ways about that," he considered it "big and heavy and slow" to work with in comparison with digital, which "has its own look"—one he also found beautiful.

Mulholland Drive started as a pilot for a Disney series. When the studio rejected it, Lynch shot new footage to make what had been an anemone of stinging loose ends into a finished feature—in some cases, splicing the loose ends into Postmodern loops, so that one road led to another, one self to another, one clue to another, and so that the only answer to the mystery would be, as is often the case with Lynch, the whole film—a structure that is an answer to itself, a complete work of art that may have but does not require any external reference, that sets its own balance and its own definitions of identity in spite of the normal world, that reveals the beauty of the labyrinth.

Jim Jarmusch

Jim Jarmusch is a minimalist who constructs his films according to strict formal principles. *Stranger Than Paradise* (1984) was conceived as a black-and-white film consisting of nothing but sequence shots (each scene is presented in a single long take) linked by blackouts. While the scenes in *Stranger Than Paradise* follow one another in chronological order, those in *Mystery Train* (1989) are presented in an artificial order—simultaneous events are presented one after the other—that reflects a formalized approach to time. *Night on Earth* (1991) consists of five cab rides in five cities. In *Broken Flowers* (2005), a man goes to visit five of his former lovers. As simple as it sounds, he also plays with the number three: two men and a woman on the road in *Stranger Than Paradise*, three prisoners in *Down By Law* (1986), three interrelated but separated sequences in *Mystery Train*. Each of his films is a self-conscious response to a formal problem, almost in the manner of Godard; each patiently observes the so-called minor, aimless, and boring stretches of everyday life, almost like a Czech comedy; and each has a deadpan wit, an uncrowded *mise-en-scène*, and a love of rock-'n'roll that are reminiscent of Malick's cool, weird, ironic *Badlands*. He is as likely to allude to Elvis (*Mystery Train*) as to Ozu (the horse "Tokyo Story" in *Stranger Than Paradise*). His first film, *Permanent Vacation* (1980), was shot

Fig. 17-9

Fig. 17-10

Realistic mise-en-scène *and carefully balanced composition: Jim Jarmusch's* Stranger Than Paradise *(Fig. 17-9: foreground, Richard Edson; background, Eszter Balint and John Lurie) and* Down By Law *(Fig. 17-10: from left, John Lurie, Tom Waits, and Roberto Benigni).*

for $12,000 in 10 days and took its title from the lyrics of "My Boyfriend's Back." Tom Waits is in *Down By Law*. Eva (Eszter Balint), the immigrant heroine of *Stranger Than Paradise* (and the "Stranger In Paradise") calls Screamin' Jay Hawkins her "main man" and repeatedly plays her favorite song, "I Put A Spell On You." In *Mystery Train*, Screamin' Jay Hawkins himself plays the role of a desk clerk at the Memphis hotel where the main action takes place.

Jarmusch is a minimalist in another sense as well; to quote him: "My aesthetic is minimal. I make films about little things that happen between human beings." He avoids putting in too much, refusing to burden the film with extra props and dialogue and events that would get in the way of the subtleties that interest him—the peculiar, fortuitous way things happen. Very little takes place in his mundane scenes, but as they grow on you, they become very funny. Steering away from what Hollywood calls "action," he spends narrative time with matters Hollywood would skip over. As he told interviewer Brock DeShane McDaniel, "In most films, if a guy gets a phone call from his girlfriend, who says 'Come over,' the editor will cut to him at her door. I'm more interested in the guy on the way to his girlfriend's house than I am in the other two scenes. What did he see on the train? What did he eat? I'm more interested in those things in between." Jarmusch rejects Griffith's aesthetic of cutting out the inessential (and of calling attention to what is important in a scene through editing and camerawork) to dramatize what is, in another way, essential. He avoids cutting within scenes in order to present them in real time while reminding the audience—which gets restless when denied continuity editing—that it is watching a movie. If his films have, via their rock idols and their revisiting of genres (as in *Dead Man*, 1995), a touch of the mythic, no one could mistake them for "return of the myths" material; the lavish, conservative fantasies turned out by Hollywood are Jarmusch's polar opposite. In *Broken Flowers*, for example, the hero does not get his life together even if he does go on his romantic quest.

John Waters

John Waters is an ironist, like Lynch and Jarmusch, a writer–director of satirical comedies that at first were cult films in bad taste, then crossed into the mainstream when Waters restrained himself to what he calls "good bad taste." Shot and set in Baltimore, his home town, many of his films starred his childhood friend, the transvestite actor Divine (Harris Glenn Milstead), who died shortly after starring in *Hairspray* (1988). Among their first films together were *Multiple Maniacs* (1971), *Pink Flamingos* (1972), and *Female Trouble* (1975), milestones in the history of trash art. Waters established the outer limits of cinematic taste in *Pink Flamingos* (which ends with an unfaked shot of Divine's eating dog excrement), then moved on to the sense of smell in *Polyester* (1981), which was released in "Odorama."

There had been olfactory films before (Jack Cardiff's *Scent of Mystery*, 1960, in "Smell-O-Vision," identified a central character not with visual or sound cues but with her perfume), but they either circulated and dispelled odors through the theatre's air conditioners (AromaRama; *The Great Wall of China*, 1959) or shot perfumy mists into the audience's faces from tubing attached to the backs of the seats (Smell-O-Vision). Waters's system—reflecting his lifelong love of schlock movies, the gimmicks of William Castle, and the outrageous in general—was scratch and sniff. Each viewer of *Polyester* was given a card. In one of the cleverest gags in the history of film/viewer interaction, Divine reaches for some flowers, and a number flashes on the screen instructing the audience which area on the Odorama card to scratch off; the audience scratches, expecting flowers and dropping its guard (some of the earlier odors were vile), then smells instead the disgusting thing that is suddenly thrust in Divine's face. The viewer literally shares the character's sense of surprise as well as her unpleasant experience—a real step toward Bazin's "myth of total cinema." Waters's eleventh film, *Hairspray*, was his first hit with those who go to the movies before midnight. It was followed by *Cry-Baby* (1990), a high-energy teen romance with, as usual, arresting casting (from Patty Hearst, Polly Bergen, Troy Donahue, Traci Lords, and Dave Nelson to Johnny Depp as the hero and Kim McGuire as Hatchet Face); *Serial Mom* (1994), which starred Kathleen Turner as a cheery housewife who would kill to protect her vision of the clean bourgeois life, good manners, and family values; and his tale of independent film rebels, *Cecil B. Demented* (2000).

Hairspray, set in Baltimore in the spring and early summer of 1963, takes a nostalgic *and* parodistic look at the clichés of the period—but if that were all it did, it might have been nothing more than another *Grease*. However, into this apolitical world of dancing, romancing, feuding teenagers come the social and political struggles of the early 1960s. It is as if we were seeing a 1963 teen picture that dealt with the turbulent real world of 1963, something no such film ever did. The result is a humanistic political fable that is also a Postmodern satire.

Joel and Ethan Coen

Each of the Coen brothers' features concentrates on a separate genre—*Blood Simple* (1983), the *film noir*; *Raising Arizona* (1987), the romantic comedy; *Miller's Crossing* (1990), the gangster picture; *Barton Fink* (1991), the Hollywood-insider black comedy (imagine *Sunset Blvd.* directed by Polanski); *The Hudsucker Proxy* (1994), the rags-to-riches story; *Fargo* (1996), the cop picture; *The Big Lebowski* (1998), the buddy picture; *O Brother, Where Art Thou?* (2000), the Homeric epic; *No Country For Old Men* (2007, based on the novel by Cormac McCarthy), the rural crime thriller; *Burn After Reading* (2008), the spy melodrama. Each of the genres they parody and enrich becomes a jumping-off place for their twisted comic imaginations, offering not formulas for action and dialogue, but opportunities—as the formula that the police officer's romantic life must figure in the cop picture let the Coens make up, for *Fargo*, the policewoman's husband and their sweet, offbeat marriage. But nothing ever compels them to stick to one genre at a time—*Lebowski* is also a sports picture, a cowboy legend, and a parody of *noir*—and no genre dictates or constrains the eruptions of cockeyed Expressionism in their work.

In most cases Joel Coen directed, Ethan Coen produced, and they both wrote the scripts. With *No Country For Old Men*, they began to direct together. Although their tight, witty films are primarily concerned with style, calling attention to their clever camerawork, rich detail, and self-conscious distance from their subjects, each movie is also a genuine, effective genre work with strongly defined characters: *Blood Simple* is a superb neo-*noir*, as wickedly dark as *Raising Arizona* is wickedly funny. The result is that one admires the Coens' recreation of particular cinematic modes as well as their breezy modernity. They also write terrific voice-over narration: "Down here you're on your own" launches *Blood Simple* as brilliantly as "Maybe it was Utah" wraps up *Raising Arizona*.

The plot of *Blood Simple* is so complex, so full of betrayals and misunderstandings, that none of the characters ever completely figures it out. To the audience, however, it makes perfect sense. As when watching a Hitchcock film, one is rewarded for paying attention to details—in this case, for keeping track of a cigarette lighter and a pearl-handled .38, which are narrative elements as central as the main characters: an unnamed detective who narrates the film (M. Emmet Walsh); bar owner Julian Marty (Dan Hedaya); Marty's wife, Abby (Frances McDormand); and Abby's lover, Ray (John Getz). The violence, passion, pessimism, and look of *noir* are all here, and the tone is set at the start, as the detective observes voice-over that "nothing comes with a guarantee"—anybody can have something just go all wrong. When things go wrong in *Burn After Reading*, the story turns tragicomic before it settles into exasperated comedy, and in *No Country For Old Men*, where things turn out as badly as possible for many of the characters, the ironic tone moves between the intimate and the detached.

Jonathan Demme

Jonathan Demme has also worked in a number of genres, sometimes with an ironic edge and sometimes with scrupulous neutrality. In his concert films, *Stop Making Sense* (1984) and *Swimming to Cambodia* (1987), the camera observes the performers—the Talking Heads and Spalding Gray, respectively—and lets their own styles come through directly. This is not something that can be achieved simply by turning the camera on and recording the show; it requires discipline and clarity as well as a perfect understanding of the performer's aesthetics. Demme's restraint in *Stop Making Sense* is refreshingly different from the authorial intrusiveness of most concert films. (He returned to the genre in 2006 with *Neil Young: Heart of Gold*.) Demme's stylistic integrity is clear from his films but not foregrounded by them. His gangster comedy, *Married to the Mob* (1988), has none of *The Godfather*'s rich romanticism or *GoodFellas*'s muscular precision, but a sharply ironic touch and a zippy pace of its own. His thriller, *The Silence of the Lambs* (1991, from the novel by Thomas Harris), is full of ferocious, gruesome characters and events, portrays them without compromising their horrific nature, and becomes troubling without being troubled. The best of Demme's earlier narrative films—*Citizens Band* (1977), *Melvin and Howard* (1980), and *Something Wild* (1986)—are more offbeat, friendly, even affectionate in tone than *The Silence of the Lambs*, but in all his works

Fig. 17-11

Demme appears to like and care about his central characters as well as to understand them. That understanding, authorial transparency, and restrained balance had a great deal to do with the impact of *Philadelphia* (1993), one of the first mainstream features to deal with AIDS, and with the richness of characterization in *Rachel Getting Married* (2008), a comedy with hard emotional edges that concerns a disturbed young woman's relations with her family.

Terry Gilliam

Terry Gilliam, the American member of England's Monty Python group, first became well known as the creator of the animated sequences in their TV series, *Monty Python's Flying Circus*, and as the co-director (with Terry Jones) of *Monty Python and The Holy Grail*. After directing another two British pictures (*Jabberwocky*, 1977; *Time Bandits*, 1981), Gilliam shot two American-backed pictures in Europe—*Brazil* (1985) and *The Adventures of Baron Munchausen* (1989)—then returned to the United States for *The Fisher King* (1991) and *Twelve Monkeys* (1995, based on Chris Marker's *La Jetée*). *Brazil*, shot in 1984, is a dark social satire based loosely on George Orwell's novel *Nineteen Eighty-Four*. *Brazil*'s dystopia is an oppressive "free society" that spies on its citizens—a huge, inefficient, ruthless bureaucracy

devoted to red tape. The government has been under terrorist attack for 13 years but dismisses that as "beginner's luck." Crude instruments and cheap furniture dominate the cramped, ugly work environment; ducts are everywhere, and it is a crime to have anything fixed without going through Central Services (Robert De Niro plays an outlaw repairman). The hero (Sam Lowry, played by Jonathan Pryce) begins by tracking down a bureaucratic error—a fatal typo—and ends by falling in love with a terrorist (Jill Layton, played by Kim Greist). Sam meets his fate in Gilliam's version of Orwell's "Room 101," where a friend tortures him; Sam's escape is to retreat mentally—forever—to an idyllic fantasy inspired by the song "Brazil." In the American version of the film, what happens to Jill is not made explicit; in the English version, she definitely is murdered. For the director's cut, see The Criterion Collection's DVD. For the happy ending the studio wanted—in which the lovers get away before they are captured and actually move to Brazil—see the shortest of all the versions, released to TV. Taking a prodigiously creative look at stupidity, incompetence, vanity, and short-sightedness, the drab and dull and confused—with an undercurrent of passion and rebellion—*Brazil* is the best representative yet of Gilliam's satiric side, as *Time Bandits* remains the best of his fantasy–adventures. The battles

Fig. 17-12
Brazil: *Dr. Jaffe (Jim Broadbent) tries a new kind of plastic surgery on the hero's mother, Mrs. Lowry (Katherine Helmond).*

over releasing *Brazil* were a dreadful window on the film industry, which needs its rebels but often is comfortable destroying their work.

Carl Reiner and Others

Some of the period's comedies broke away from standard sex-role constructs, satirized contemporary society, or knowingly portrayed the traumas of growing up. Many bold talents took up the genre of the anxieties and worldviews of adolescents and young adults. There were John Hughes's *The Breakfast Club* (1985), Michael Lehman's *Heathers* (1989), Whit Stillman's *Metropolitan* (1990), Hal Hartley's *Trust* (1990), Richard Linklater's *Dazed and Confused* (1993), Kevin Smith's *Clerks* (1994), Terry Zwigoff's *Ghost World* (2001), Todd Solondz's *Palindromes* (2004, released 2005), and Jason Reitman's *Juno* (2007).

Paul Brickman's *Risky Business* (1983) was a commercially successful satire of capitalism, in which the perfect model for individualism and enterprise turns out to be converting an upper-middle-class home into a house of prostitution. The entrepreneur of *Risky Business* is no rebellious outsider, but a fresh, attractive,

all-American lad (played by Tom Cruise) who comes of age, both financially and erotically, thanks to a fresh, attractive, all-American prostitute (played by Rebecca De Mornay). As a result of this risky enterprise, the hero's American Dream comes true—fame, fortune (though temporary), and admission to Princeton. It is significant, and typical of the period, that preview audiences preferred this ending to the one originally planned and shot, in which the hero does not get into Princeton. As said before, it was a time for winners. Only a filmmaker with the clout of a Woody Allen could insist on keeping the sad ending of *The Purple Rose of Cairo* (1985).

Although most of the comedies were strictly boy-meets-girl, a few explored the complexities of sexual identity. Reversals of sexual roles and clothes are common motifs of films such as Blake Edwards's *Victor/Victoria* (1982), Sydney Pollack's *Tootsie* (1982), and Carl Reiner's *All of Me* (1984), which consciously descend from screwball comedy. *Victor/Victoria*, set in the Paris of Lubitsch (a Hollywood soundstage calling itself Paris), refers explicitly to the Lubitsch "touch" of suppressing visual information from the frame. The year of the film's action, 1934, is the very one in which Hollywood enforced its Production Code. *Victor/Victoria* seems a conscious return to the explicit sexual matters that the pre-Code Lubitsch had treated so deftly.

All of Me forces Lily Tomlin (Edwina) and Steve Martin (Roger) to share Martin's body. Martin acts the roles of both Edwina and Roger—not androgynously, but as separate male and female personalities in a male body. The audience sees Edwina when Roger does: when he looks in a mirror. They fight, learn from each other, and of course come to love each other. Eventually the soul of a conventionally attractive *femme fatale* (Terry, played by Victoria Tennant) ends up in the body of a horse, allowing Edwina's spirit to inhabit Terry's body and to explore another kind of intimacy with Roger—the kind that uses two bodies rather than one. But we and Roger have come to prefer Edwina to the "more attractive" woman, so when Roger and Edwina-in-Terry's-body begin to dance in the final scene, director Reiner rewards us by panning from Roger and Terry to a mirror that shows Roger and Edwina, so that we can celebrate the genuine romantic couple.

Carl Reiner, who was Sid Caesar's straight man on 1950s television and a cohort of Mel Brooks, also directed *The Comic* (1969) and *Oh, God!* (1977, in which George Burns is convincing as God, a role never previously filmed with any success). His son, Rob Reiner, began as an actor on the TV show *All in the Family*, then went into directing with *This Is Spinal Tap* (1984), a parody of a rock documentary that may be his finest comedy. It shares with his drama *Stand By Me* (1986) and his great tale of romantic adventure, *The Princess Bride* (1987), an unfailing ability to strike the right note at the right time, be it sad or uproarious, frightening or wistful. In both the Reiners' films, from *All of Me* to *Stand By Me*, interpersonal relationships are deeply explored, and what results is a moving understanding of the ways people bond together, the comedy and the drama of acceptance.

While most comedies entertained their audiences with funny lines and situations (for example, Bobby and Peter Farrelly's *There's Something About Mary*, 1998), two comedies stood out for their original uses of basic cinematic elements: *Being John Malkovich* (1999, directed by Adam Spiegel under the name Spike Jonze and written by Charlie Kaufman) let subjective camera and sound give the impression that characters—and the audience—could temporarily be, or at least share the experience of, the famous actor; *Groundhog Day* (1993, directed by Harold Ramis) used straight cuts and an alarm clock to start the same day over and over until the jerk of a hero (Bill Murray) learns how to use the day in the best possible way—the most effective and creative use of repetition in editing since Resnais's *Je t'aime, je t'aime* in 1968.

Robert Zemeckis

While Roger Corman can be credited with discovering and apprenticing Bogdanovich, Coppola, Dante, Demme, Sayles, and Scorsese—to name just a few—Spielberg's top discoveries to date are Frank Marshall (*Arachnophobia*, 1990; *Alive*, 1993; *Eight Below*, 2006) and Robert Zemeckis (*Romancing the Stone*, 1984; *Back to the Future*, 1985; *Who Framed Roger Rabbit*, 1988; *Back to the Future Part II*, 1989, and *Part III*, 1990; *Forrest Gump*, 1994; *The Polar Express*, 2004; *Beowulf*, 2007). Zemeckis's comedies are intricately plotted, full of zingy jokes and impressive special effects. *Romancing the Stone* pits fantasy against reality as deftly as *Back to the Future Part II* juxtaposes versions of the same character from different temporal continua. And just as *Forrest Gump*, a bit like Woody Allen's *Zelig*, puts its hero in the same frame as a president, *Who Framed Roger Rabbit* puts live actors and cartoon figures ("toons") in the same shots, as Disney often did. Co-produced by Spielberg's Amblin Entertainment and Disney's Touchstone Pictures, shot in London at Cannon Elstree Studios, with special visual effects by Lucas's Industrial Light & Magic, and putting together on screen for the first time the stars of both Disney and Warner Bros. cartoons—not to mention MGM and Fleischer cartoons—*Roger Rabbit* called on an extraordinary spectrum of major talents to create the most technically advanced and visually seamless cartoon-with-people ever made. *Roger Rabbit*'s reflexive conceits range from the wild notion that cartoons are *acted* in real time (so that when a refrigerator falls on Roger's head and he sees tweeting birds instead of stars, he is accused of blowing his lines) to an ending that is inseparably Warner Bros. and Disney (after Porky says "That's all, folks," Tinker Bell closes the film as if it were an episode of *Disneyland*). This is a world in which Daffy Duck and Donald Duck perform together on stage, with Daffy accusing Donald of having a speech impediment; in which Betty Boop *is* in black and white, as her films were, and has had trouble getting work in color cartoons; and whose detective story looks like and uses plot elements from both *The Maltese Falcon* and *Chinatown*. The 1940s Los Angeles of this film still has its streetcars, a reliable system of public transportation ("Who needs a car in L.A.?"). The villain—like the villain of *Chinatown*, who wants to control the city's expansion and the region's water—has a vision of shopping centers and gas stations, freeways and pollution, and wants to begin creating that Los Angeles on the site of Toontown. The villain is destroyed, the mystery is solved, Toontown and the streetcars are saved—but anyone familiar with today's Los Angeles must find this happy ending dark and sly, since the streetcars are gone, freeways and smog are everywhere, and no Toontown can be found on the maps. Alternate realities are indeed central to the comedies of Robert Zemeckis.

Tim Burton

The boldly designed films of Tim Burton, who once worked as an animator at Disney, turn to bright and dark subjects with equal zest. His lightest were *Pee-wee's Big Adventure* (1985), in which the childlike Pee-wee Herman (Paul Reubens) sets off in search of his stolen bicycle, and the science fiction comedy *Mars Attacks!* (1996); one of his darkest was the blockbuster *Batman* (1989), whose look and mood were inspired not by the early Batman comics but by the later, more pessimistic Batman graphic novels. Three of Burton's best films—*Beetle Juice* (1988), *Edward Scissorhands* (1990), and *Corpse Bride* (2005)—are horror fantasies revived as divine comedy. Like the animated *Corpse Bride*, which is at once whimsical and dark, *Beetle Juice* takes an original look at the exasperations and rules of the afterlife. *Edward Scissorhands*, a fable about why it snows, stars Johnny Depp in a brilliant re-imagining of *Frankenstein*. A film with heart and wit, *Edward Scissorhands* is set in a bland modern suburb that happens to adjoin a gothic castle inhabited by an old inventor (Vincent Price) and his creation, Edward (Depp). The inventor, as much a lonely, loving Gepetto as a Dr. Frankenstein, dies before he can give Edward normal hands; instead Edward's fingers are shears and blades—the tools of his art (sculpting) and the fate that separates him from others, whom he cannot readily embrace without cutting. In the end, when this sensitive artist has been exiled to the castle by a Tupperware torch party, Edward uses the scissors—the sign of his origin—to express his love in art, shaving ice sculptures to make the snow that falls on his beloved.

Like Burton's earlier films, *The Nightmare Before Christmas* (1993, directed by Henry Selick from Burton's story and produced by Burton) and *Ed Wood* are about eccentric characters who function within imaginary worlds, often as artists or, as in *Sleepy Hollow* (1999), investigators. If the worlds they invent and control are off-limits from the worlds of the living (*Beetle Juice*), nicer holidays (*Nightmare*), duller behavior (*Pee-wee*), and better movies (*Wood*), they are charged with the conviction of vision; the heroes reign in Hell rather than serve in ordinary comic Heaven.

Oliver Stone

The years since 1977 have also produced some filmmakers interested more in political and social problems than in the irrational, ironic, reflexive, comic, and fantastic.

Oliver Stone began as a screenwriter, receiving an Oscar for Alan Parker's *Midnight Express* (1978), then writing De Palma's remake of *Scarface* (1983) and Cimino's *Year of the Dragon* (1985). All this time he was trying to sell *Platoon*, a script based on his experiences in Vietnam. After directing *Salvador* (1986), a buddy film whose view of the politics of El Salvador was left

Deceptive surfaces in Victor/Victoria: *four "guys" out on the town (from left, Robert Preston, Julie Andrews, James Garner, and Alex Karras).*

Fig. 17-13

Fig. 17-14
Who Framed Roger Rabbit: *Detective Eddie Valiant (Bob Hoskins) finds himself in the same frame—and desk—as Roger.* © *Touchstone Pictures & Amblin Entertainment, Inc. All rights reserved.*

of center, he was given the chance to direct *Platoon* himself; released in the last days of 1986, it quickly attracted large audiences who proclaimed it the first film to portray accurately the experience of the American foot soldier in Vietnam. (The next film about which that was said was Patrick Duncan's excellent *84 Charlie Mopic*, 1989.) Although there are many characters in *Platoon*, the most important is first-timer Chris (Charlie Sheen). Like many of Stone's heroes, Chris is torn between two fathers, a good one (Sgt. Elias, played by Willem Dafoe) and a bad one (Sgt. Barnes, played by Tom Berenger). The good one opposes the massacre of civilians, takes care of his men, and even smokes dope with them. The bad one takes care of his men too, but he is contemptuous and ruthless; "There's the way it ought to be, and there's the way it is," he says to Chris, arguing against idealism and incarnating "the way it is." After Barnes kills Elias, Chris kills Barnes; his conclusion about the war is that Americans were really just

fighting each other on foreign soil—a conclusion dimwitted enough to rival that of *Metropolis*. Politics aside, *Platoon* does convey the experience of protracted jungle warfare, putting the audience through a long, rough tour of duty.

The opposed fathers in Stone's next film, *Wall Street* (1987), are an honest, hardworking businessman (Martin Sheen as Fox) and an unscrupulous corporate raider (Michael Douglas as Gekko). The hero is Fox's son, Bud (Charlie Sheen, Martin's real son), a stockbroker who learns from Gekko how to use confidential information and get rich in the inflated market of the mid-1980s, making money without creating anything, sometimes even by destroying. *Wall Street* drew on some earlier scandals and remarkably anticipated several that broke years later.

With his Vietnam movies (*Platoon; Born on the Fourth of July*, 1989, which starred Tom Cruise as a paralyzed veteran who becomes an activist; and *Heaven & Earth*, 1993, based on the autobiographies of a Vietnamese woman) and his

Fig. 17-15
Tim Burton's *Edward Scissorhands.*

powerfully edited *JFK* (1991), Oliver Stone has positioned himself as a vigorous rhetorician, whether he is acting as a trippy culture critic or as a political moralist. Near the end of *Wall Street*, an old broker (Hal Holbrook as Lou) gives Bud this advice, part Nietzsche and part Hemingway: "Man looks in the abyss. There's nothin' staring back at him. At that moment, man finds his character. And that is what keeps him out of the abyss." That confrontation and salvation occur in *Midnight Express, Salvador, Platoon, Wall Street, Born on the Fourth of July,* and *World Trade Center* (2006). The hero of *The Doors* (1991) embraces the abyss, and the hero of *Talk Radio* (1988) dances around it until somebody pushes him in. For Oliver Stone, Hell is where you find it.

If the camera circles its prey in *Talk Radio*, it pounces in *Natural Born Killers* (1994), Stone's richest satire and boldest cinematic experiment. *Natural Born Killers* is the story of Mickey and Mallory Knox (Woody Harrelson and Juliette

Lewis), lovers on a killing spree who become celebrities. Mickey and Mallory express what is chaotic, destructive, amoral, and crazy about America, and the film mirrors the chaos of its subject with a controlled, apparent chaos of constantly shifting images that is a filmlong montage. The camera, often tilted and hand-held, is sharp and restless; the rapidly edited images jump cut from color to black and white, from fine grain to grainy (some shots were taken on Super8 film and blown up), from film to video or animation or tinted stock; and the background readily becomes a rear-projection screen that allows the lovers to drive through the clouds or may flash their violent memories and thoughts. The world that is shown here is falling apart, but it is capable of being healed by love and by cultivating a harmony with the good spirits in nature; unfortunately, there is great power in nature's evil spirits (Mickey's rabbit) and in the demons that possess not only Mickey, but also the incarnation of the media, Wayne Gale (Robert

Downey, Jr.), who is most responsible for nurturing the tabloid and reality-TV cult that surrounds the killers and to whom they give a fatal lesson in reality. The film reaches its highest pitch of irony when it follows a romanticized shot of Mallory urinating outdoors and remembering how she and her lover met with a TV sitcom version of their meeting, shot on video and called *I Love Mallory*. While the father (Rodney Dangerfield) abuses the family, there are laugh tracks and happy music—even when he makes it clear that he has been having sex with his daughter. The first draft of the script was written by Tarantino.

Quentin Tarantino

Quentin Tarantino got most of his film education as a clerk in a video store. After he sold two scripts (later rewritten by others, a norm in the industry) to Oliver Stone (*Natural Born Killers*) and Tony Scott (*True Romance*, 1993)—both of which are about lovers on the run, creating their own mythology as they slide deeper into the world of violent crime, and both of which reflect the influence of *Badlands*—Tarantino became famous as the director of two stylish, violent, smart genre pictures: *Reservoir Dogs* (1992) and *Pulp Fiction* (1994). Unlike the films of Cimino and Stone, Tarantino's are unfettered by big messages; like them, they are cinematically intense, self-consciously *auteurist*, and at times charged with an almost physical energy. Although *Reservoir Dogs* is dominated by its sources (especially a Hong Kong police drama called *City on Fire*), it also has a rich, violent power that is convincing on its own. And *Pulp Fiction* is an original: bright, audacious, enigmatic, witty, violent, and surprising, with an unchronological narrative line that cleverly interrelates the events and characters in a triumph of style. Too hip to be *noir* and too slick to be pulp, *Pulp Fiction* is not an homage to the 1930s or 1940s but a 1990s Postmodern film in which words and images play in a self-referential field that has no definable underlying absolutes or moral center. *Pulp Fiction* became one of the most influential films of the decade, a model of formal complexity and stylized tone.

His next picture, *Jackie Brown* (1997), took a woman, played by Pam Grier, for its hero and let the camera take a long look at her. Slower and more intimate than the pictures that had made Tarantino the standard-bearer for a new American cinema of slam-bang style and knowing reference, *Jackie Brown* showed that Tarantino had looked deeply and well at thousands of movies and knew how to use them, to make them new and leave them old at once. For *Jackie Brown* is like a *noir* by some impossible collaboration of Kurosawa and Ozu, Fuller and Godard, opening with a parody of the opening of *The Graduate* and climaxing with a series of events that are, as in Porter's *Life of an*

Fig. 17-16

Pam Grier takes charge in Quentin Tarantino's Jackie Brown *(with Samuel L. Jackson, left).*

American Fireman, repeated whole from different points of view.

Tarantino has encouraged new directors and arranged for theatrical revivals of films most of today's viewers have seen only on video, such as Lucio Fulci's triumph of schlock style, *The Beyond* (1981), an Italian horror film that had been released in the United States for about a week under the title *7 Doors to Death* and that brought its new audiences, gagging, to their knees. He also brought Zhang Yimou's *Hero* (2002) to the United States in 2004, a film people strongly wanted to see but that had not yet found a Western distributor. His great enthusiasm for martial-arts pictures led to his fourth film, which was released in two parts: *Kill Bill Vol. 1* (2003) and *Kill Bill Vol. 2* (2004). Tarantino's powerful sense of rhythm in action, music, and editing made *Kill Bill* a nonstop experience charged with strength and cunning, pain and beauty, though its superb pacing could slow down at any time for an impressive silence or for a long, tense scene. It starred Uma Thurman as a mythic hero who overcomes incredible obstacles with immense energy, skill, and determination in her quest for revenge. As pure an action film as one could want, *Kill Bill* also created a meeting-ground for Eastern and Western action pictures. *Inglourious Basterds* (2009), which featured several of his characteristically long conversation sequences, took a spirited, humorous, but still violent look at World War II. Amid a slew of film references, two forces composed primarily of Jews manage to kill Hitler and his top associates during the premiere of a Nazi propaganda movie; the climactic explosion is fueled by nitrate film.

Robert Rodriguez

Robert Rodriguez got started with *Bedhead* (1990), a short about a girl who uses her special powers to get even with her gross brother; Rodriguez would return to the subject of gifted, imaginative children in *Spy Kids* (2001). *El Mariachi*, which as previously mentioned was made for $7,000, was released by Columbia in 1993 after another $1 million of post-production polishing. Its drama of mistaken identity, its command of action and romantic scenes, and its tight pacing established Rodriguez as an entertaining maverick and led to a sequel, *Desperado* (1995).

He and Tarantino were two of the four directors of *Four Rooms* (1995), and Tarantino co-wrote Rodriguez's vampire action movie, *From Dusk Till Dawn* (1996). Tarantino also directed a scene in *Frank Miller's Sin City* (2005), which was co-directed by Rodriguez and the author of the *Sin City* graphic novels, Frank Miller, who had become famous with his Batman graphic novel, *The Dark Knight Returns*. To credit Miller (and Tarantino), Rodriguez had to resign from the Directors Guild of America; the DGA allowed co-directors to be credited only when they always worked as a team, and it did not allow directors to team up on pictures when they happened to want to work together. The *Sin City* books had a white-on-black style with occasional patches of color, a look that Miller and Rodriguez matched. The tough-guy *noir* tone of the dialogue and the rough, violent stories worked with the stylized images to create an alternate world that was graphic on every level. No photographic adaptation of a graphic novel or of a comic book has ever succeeded in looking so "drawn," and few adaptations of any kind have been so faithful. In 2007, Rodriguez and Tarantino co-directed *Grindhouse*, a loving homage to the big, old, often decrepit movie-houses that kept themselves going in the 1960s and 1970s by grinding out double and triple features, most of them low-budget exploitation films. *Grindhouse* is a double feature—*Planet Terror* by Rodriguez and *Death Proof* by Tarantino—complete with trailers (three of them by Eli Roth, Edgar Wright, and Rob Zombie), scratches, and missing reels. The features are set in the early 2000s—the characters have cell phones—but capture the no-holds-barred, action-oriented style of the older genre films that so vitally engaged Tarantino, Rodriguez, and many others when they were learning about film in the crucible of the grindhouse.

John Sayles

John Sayles is an insightful writer with a good ear for dialogue and a director whose style is understated, meticulous, economical, and evocatively realistic. Sayles's understanding of character and his leftist politics are central to all his works, from his novel *Union Dues* and his first feature, *Return of the Secaucus Seven* (1979, released 1980), a comedy about a reunion of 1960s radicals, to *Men With Guns* (1997),

Fig. 17-17
Frank Miller's Sin City.

about a doctor who finds out how brutal the
police state in his Latin American country really
is. Sayles puts his characters in situations
where they have to figure themselves out (*Baby
It's You*, 1982, released 1983; *Lianna*, 1983;
Passion Fish, 1992), which they cannot really
do without figuring out the social, economic,
and political systems in which they live
(*Matewan*, 1987; *City of Hope*, 1991; *Lone Star*,
1996). *Eight Men Out*—Sayles's first script idea,
long put off because studios and producers
considered the idea box-office poison—
demonstrates that one way to gauge the health
or corruption of a society is to examine the conditions under which people work and the decisions they feel they have to make. Sayles also
has a talent for comic horror with a sociopolitical twist—evident in his scripts for Joe Dante's
Piranha (1978) and *The Howling* (1980, released 1981, co-written by Terence Winkless).
His science fiction fable, *The Brother from
Another Planet* (1984), performs a twist on *E.T.*
for good reason: Sayles was one of *E.T.*'s
uncredited writers, dropped from the project
because he disagreed about the direction it
should take. So he made his own *E.T.*, in which
the visitor from outer space is black.

Charles Burnett

In the late 1980s and early 1990s, so much attention was paid to the work of Spike Lee, John
Singleton (*Boyz N the Hood*, 1991), and the
Hughes brothers (*Menace II Society*, 1993) that
one of the greatest African-American directors,
Charles Burnett, was overlooked in the rush. Part
of the reason for this may be that Burnett's films
do not focus on the problems of crime and violence; instead, he makes poetically charged, dramatically resonant movies that are often about
black families dealing with some destructive
force that has to be identified and purged. His
first film, *Killer of Sheep* (1977), examined the
stress a man brings home from his job in a
slaughterhouse. It was added to the National
Film Registry in 1990, the year he released *To
Sleep With Anger*, a moral, convincingly acted
film about a black family that lives in South
Central Los Angeles but keeps in touch with its
biblical and Southern rural roots and what happens to them when Harry (Danny Glover), an old
friend of the father, Gideon (Paul Butler), comes
to visit. Harry is a superstitious con artist full of
the wild, bad ways of the old life, and like the
serpent in Eden, he seductively tests the weak
spots in the family until violence and illness and

Gideon (Paul Butler) and Harry (Danny Glover, right) in Charles Burnett's mysterious and affecting family drama, To Sleep With Anger.

Fig. 17-18

buried resentments erupt; the wife, Suzie (Mary Alice), finally throws him out, but Harry dies— killed, apparently, by supernatural forces—and is left for days in the kitchen, thanks to the efficiency of the city's services, while the family spontaneously heals and at last goes out for a picnic, so that the film ends with Harry still in the kitchen. But how it opens is even more poetically authoritative: Gideon sits in a room, dressed well and thinking; as he thinks, presumably about his experience with Harry—the story introduced by this opening frame—his shoes catch fire and the flames rise to his face, an image of purifying anger that is metaphoric without being arty and forceful without being pushy. His other films include *My Brother's Wedding* (1983), a tragicomedy set in another carefully observed family, and the problem-picture police drama *The Glass Shield* (1994).

Spike Lee

Spike Lee, son of jazz musician Bill Lee, was born in Atlanta; as a graduate student in NYU's film program, he made a thesis film—*Joe's Bed–Stuy Barbershop: We Cut Heads* (1983)— that won a Student Academy Award. Now an independent filmmaker based in New York— writing, producing, directing, and sometimes acting in his "40 Acres and a Mule" productions, many of which have been backed and distributed by major studios—Lee is the most prominent black filmmaker of his generation. His frank,

caustic, committed, reflexive style can best be described as "in your face."

Like *Bed–Stuy Barbershop*, a realistic drama about a barber who is more interested in cutting hair than in letting his shop be a front for the numbers racket, many of Lee's films are set and shot in the Bedford–Stuyvesant section of Brooklyn. His films tackle the clichés about black character and experience that pervade American culture, investigating and radicalizing them until the clichés are dismantled and—in the best of his works, but not all—the personal and social realities step forward. His first two features, *She's Gotta Have It* (1986) and *School Daze* (1988), addressed the images blacks have of each other, while the next, *Do The Right Thing* (1989), looked at interracial constructs. *She's Gotta Have It*—a film as important as *Stranger Than Paradise* and *Chan is Missing* in stimulating the 1980s' independent production movement referred to earlier in this chapter, since all three won festival prizes and attracted enthusiastic audiences without any help from Hollywood—is the story of a free spirit (Nola Darling, played by Tracy Camilla Johns) whose lovers want to change and control her. Each wants her for himself alone. Nola is passionate about Brooklyn, sex, honesty, and black consciousness. It is she who has to tell Spike Lee (who plays Mars Blackmon, one of the lovers) when Malcolm X's birthday is. The "It" in *She's Gotta Have It* at first appears to be promiscuous

Fig. 17-19
Do The Right Thing: *Radio Raheem (Bill Nunn, left) and Buggin Out (Giancarlo Esposito).*

sex, but it turns out to be personal autonomy, the freedom to explore and define and be herself. Nola is a new kind of "It" girl. Opening with a quote from a black woman writer, Zora Neale Hurston, *She's Gotta Have It* is about a woman who repudiates the clichés that surround her and refuses to be controlled by blacks or whites.

Do The Right Thing is set on a single block in Bedford–Stuyvesant on the hottest day of the year. Although it is a black neighborhood, there are no black-owned businesses, only a market owned by Koreans and a pizzeria owned by Italians (Sal, played by Danny Aiello, and his two sons). The Koreans are newcomers, but Sal has been in business for 25 years; although it is not his neighborhood, Sal is proud that its residents have grown up on his pizza. When Sal confides his pride and his dreams to his sons, sappy family-melodrama music can be heard beneath the dialogue; when Da Mayor (Ossie Davis) and Mother Sister (Ruby Dee), two of the neighborhood's older residents, remark how hot it is, the music plays variations on "Summertime"; this is

one way that the movie identifies artistic and social stereotypes reflexively, urging the audience to recognize the clichés and think. A stammering man, Smiley (Roger Guenveur Smith)—the film's "innocent"—begins the film by holding up a photo of Martin Luther King, Jr., and Malcolm X standing together and smiling; although the sociopolitical goals and tactics Malcolm proposed were more radical and revolutionary than those of King, who argued for nonviolent civil disobedience, the two assassinated leaders and their programs are linked in this photo. As the film's many characters go about their business, three men sit at a street corner in front of a bright red wall and comment on the action; these "Cornermen" are much like the chorus in a Greek tragedy, and their judgments are those of the attentive community.

The heat provokes confrontations and brings out latent racial antagonisms. Buggin Out (Giancarlo Esposito) demands that Sal add pictures of African Americans to the pizzeria's Wall of Fame, which has pictures only of famous Italian Americans; Sal refuses, and Buggin Out tries to organize a boycott. Mookie (Spike Lee), who delivers Sal's pizzas and has no developed political consciousness, unsuccessfully tries to defuse the suddenly growing antagonism between Buggin Out and Sal. At one point Da Mayor gives Mookie the simple, venerable advice, "Always do the right thing." "That's it?" says Mookie, who will find, along with the audience, that it is not always simple to know what the right thing is. Mookie's best friend, Radio Raheem (Bill Nunn), carries his prized portable stereo (a boom box) wherever he goes, loudly playing Public Enemy's "Fight the Power," a call to "fight the powers that be."

As tensions increase, Sal and the police are clearly revealed as the powers that be. As the pizzeria is closing for the night, Buggin Out and Radio Raheem repeat the demand that Sal acknowledge his black customers by putting up new photos; Raheem refuses to turn down the volume on his box, and Sal loses his self-control, allowing his latent racism to surface. Swinging a baseball bat, Sal smashes the radio to "kill" the music and all it stands for. Raheem attacks Sal in a rage, and they end up fighting in the street. The police break up the fight, arrest Buggin Out, and kill Radio Raheem with a chokehold. The Cornermen denounce the killing. When the police leave, Sal and his sons face the outraged community; Da Mayor urges everyone to think before doing something irrevocable. Politicized by the death of his friend—caused indirectly by

Sal, directly by the police, and generally by institutionalized white power—it is Mookie who starts the riot, picking up a garbage can and tossing it through one of the pizzeria's large windows. He does this dispassionately, not in a rage; his decision to do what he now considers right is a rational judgment. The pizzeria burns down; Smiley pins his photo of King and Malcolm on the burning wall. The next morning Sal and Mookie come to some kind of mutual understanding, but the political barriers between them remain clear.

Both Mookie and the neighborhood have taken a stand against racist oppression; the question is whether they were right to meet violence (Sal's destroying the boom box; the killing of Radio Raheem) with violence (destroying the pizzeria). This question is implicit in the two equally long, dialectically opposed quotations that end the film, one from King and one from Malcolm X. King argues against violence as a way of achieving racial justice: "The old law of an eye for an eye leaves everybody blind. [Violence] is immoral because it seeks to humiliate the opponent rather than win his understanding; it seeks to annihilate rather than convert.... It destroys community and makes brotherhood impossible.... Violence ends by defeating itself. It creates bitterness in the survivors and brutality in the destroyers." Malcolm argues that however many good people there are in America, "there are also plenty of bad

Do The Right Thing: *Da Mayor (Ossie Davis, left) offers Mookie (Spike Lee) some advice that will prove problematic: "Always do the right thing."*

Fig. 17-20

people...who seem to have all the power and be in these positions to block things that you and I need. Because this is the situation, you and I have to preserve the right to do what is necessary to bring an end to that situation." Malcolm advocates violence in the cause of self-defense, calling it "intelligence." These positions are absolutely opposed, since the community cannot decide to be violent and nonviolent. Yet there is something on which King and Malcolm agree: the need to recognize oppression and take an unalterable stand against it. The synthesis possible between them—as heroic, murdered champions of black power—may be implied by the photo of the two together, which fades in just before the quotations have finished scrolling up the screen and is the movie's final image. The synthesis that may emerge from their irreconcilable positions may have to be achieved over time and in history, as Hegel argued dialectical oppositions do collide and mutate. In the present historical moment, these different visions of the correct means to social, economic, and political change force a choice, and Mookie chooses the position articulated by Malcolm X.

But Mookie and Lee are not the same here, any more than they were in *She's Gotta Have It.* Lee chooses to dramatize the dialectic; like Brecht, he wants the audience to judge what it sees—decide for itself what "the right thing" is—rather than be spoon-fed a resolution. He does not vacillate between action and inaction; he knows that active resistance is necessary and that the choice is between ways of resisting. His project in *Do The Right Thing* is to expose the structure of racism. And as in all his films, his rude, upfront, catalytic technique is to come right out with what many people leave unsaid, or live with in silence—in this case, the injustice and racism that underlie the politics of contemporary America and determine many of its social conflicts. He also explores these conflicts in the moving documentary *4 Little Girls* (1997), about the children killed when the Sixteenth Street Baptist Church was bombed by anti–civil-rights terrorists in Birmingham, Alabama, in 1963; in the epic biography *Malcolm X* (1992); in the romantic melodrama *Jungle Fever* (1991), which also addresses the crack epidemic; and in the satire *Bamboozled* (2000), which plays like a cross between *The Producers* and *Putney Swope*

while suggesting that both satire and sincerity are doomed in the image-controlling world of contemporary media. (Other Lee pictures include *Summer of Sam*, 1999, a drama about a serial killer's impact on a community; the documentaries *The Original Kings of Comedy*, 2000, and *A Huey P. Newton Story*, made for cable in 2001, and *When the Levees Broke: A Requiem in Four Acts*, about Hurricane Katrina and its effect on the black community in New Orleans, made for cable in 2006; *She Hate Me*, 2004, in which a whistleblower does the right thing and finds his career derailed; *Inside Man*, 2006, the clever tale of a clever robbery; and *Miracle at St. Anna*, 2008, a story of black soldiers in World War II, a topic the movies had practically never handled.) Once those conflicts have surfaced and been articulated, there is no turning back for the community or the movie. Given what Malcolm X called "the situation," the one right thing is to fight the powers that be—"by any means necessary" (to quote the tail credits), including Mookie's violent decision and Lee's nonviolent one: to make a movie that explodes racial stereotypes and poses essential questions. The day may be hot, in fact inflammatory, but it is not any "Summertime" imagined by Gershwin.

Luis Valdez

Luis Valdez, the founder of El Teatro Campesino, began as a playwright and stage director. Working with his brother, Daniel Valdez, who composed the music and played one of the two leads (Henry Reyna), Luis Valdez wrote and directed *Zoot Suit*, a Brechtian musical about Chicano consciousness, which was produced in Los Angeles by the Center Theatre Group. Like the film adapted from it, *Zoot Suit* starred Edward James Olmos in the role of El Pachuco, the spirit of *machismo* and political awareness, who is part of Reyna's being, a figure of destiny, and the narrator of the work. *Zoot Suit* (1981), rewritten for the screen and directed by Luis Valdez, was set and shot in a theatre; sometimes it shows the audience watching the play, sometimes it is a movie with stage sets, and sometimes it is a movie shot as if the event were happening on location. It employs theatrical transitions, devices, and conventions as well as cinematic ones, all of which work together in a reflexive and blazingly cinematic style. El Pachuco calls for a cut to a new scene with a snap of his

Fig. 17-21
Zoot Suit: *Alice (Tyne Daly, left) offers her help to Henry Reyna (Daniel Valdez, center) and his co-defendants (in the background: Mike Gomez, left, and Kelly Ward). At the far right, in a skeptical mood, is El Pachuco (Edward James Olmos).*

fingers, or snaps to stop the action for commentary; he gestures for a swish pan or walks from one set to another as the stage revolves; he inhabits the stage as a solid presence only Henry can see—or through cutting momentarily becomes one of the characters; he interrupts the happy ending for the sober ending and then cues the dance ending. If the crucial film of the 1940s with which to study the relations between theatre and cinema is *Henry V*, the film of the 1980s is *Zoot Suit*. It is also one of the most colorfully designed, strikingly choreographed, and rhythmically edited films of the decade, with an extremely sophisticated narrative structure and a direct, engaging tone. Politically intense in its portrayal and analysis of the 1942 Sleepy Lagoon murder case, which was exploited in a racist anti-"Mexican" campaign that unjustly sent many *pachucos* (who today would call themselves Chicanos) to prison, the film is also irresistibly energetic and sardonically, boldly

funny. What it projects and is about is Style, inseparable from political awareness and incarnated in the zoot suit (a perfect example of the "objective correlative"). "Our *pachuco* realities will only make sense if you grasp their stylization," El Pachuco tells the audience. "To put on the zoot suit," he says, was "to play the myth" and to find "a style of urban survival." Tough, proud, and cool in the advice he gives Henry Reyna, one of the Sleepy Lagoon zoot-suiters sentenced to life (but freed on appeal two years later), El Pachuco becomes Henry's worst enemy and best friend, for the *macho* attitudes he represents and the advice he gives are both imprisoning and inspiring, keeping him back and thrusting him forward. One of the few significant musicals of the period (only Bob Fosse's *Cabaret* and *All That Jazz* approach it), and the most important Chicano film of the 1980s, *Zout Suit* was given a very limited theatrical release. Valdez's next movie, *La Bamba* (1987), was a more conventional approach to the mythic theme of Chicano heroism, a biography of rock star Ritchie Valens that was made in simultaneously released Spanish and English versions.

Gus Van Sant

Gus Van Sant began with eccentric, independent films (*Drugstore Cowboy; My Own Private Idaho*, 1991), then directed the less interesting but very successful *Good Will Hunting* (1997) and an ill-advised remake of *Psycho* (1998). He explored the moods and problems of the young in a series of low-budget, almost minimalist, tightly structured works, including *Elephant* (2003) and *Paranoid Park* (2007), before directing his next hit, *Milk* (2008). *Elephant* deals with a high-school massacre but spends much of its time following characters, often from behind, as they walk through the school's corridors; it is a low-key film that handles what could have been big emotional scenes in an understated light, making the horror more convincing. It is matter-of-fact, for instance, when it shows one of the shooters killing people in a computer game and then switching to a Web site where he can buy guns while the other shooter plays the piano for a long time. *Milk*, on the other hand, is a big film that builds both emotionally and logically to the heartfelt, engaged statements it makes about gay activism and the large-scale scenes in which Milk (played by Sean Penn) addresses crowds, which are balanced by more intimate views of the hero when he is alone or with friends. It deals with the political career and assassination of San Francisco Supervisor Harvey Milk, who was the first openly gay person to be elected to office in California, and it shows his becoming more powerful, both personally and politically, the more honest and forthright he is about his sexual preference and the more he wants to change society. He becomes another hero to believe in, but one based in reality.

Julie Taymor and Others

Feminist politics significantly affected American film theory as well as the makers of avant-garde and short narrative films in this period, but the feature-length narrative films, including those made by women, rarely were programmatically feminist. Mainstream cinema responded to the feminist movement of the 1960s and 1970s by creating more roles for strong women (or superficially revising the old roles) and putting sexism in the same "sensitive" category as racism—not to be treated in an offensive manner. But that was a far cry from exploring a gynocentric cinema, as women directors in Germany and France—and in the American avant-garde—were doing. Feminism was a subtext and a secondary concern in the American features directed by women, the majority of whom were fighting their way into the studio system with films that would entertain mainstream audiences—which is certainly one route to power in Hollywood, and often the only way to get a chance to direct *again*. But there were also brilliant directors, like Mary Harron (*American Psycho*, 2000) and Julie Taymor (*Titus*, 1999; *Frida*, 2002; *Across the Universe*, 2007), who made their mark by being stylistically daring and occasionally subversive. Among the unprecedented number of women directors to have come to prominence since the mid-1970s are Allison Anders (*Gas, Food Lodging*, 1992; *Mi vida loca*, 1994; *Things Behind the Sun*, 2001), Kathryn Bigelow (*Near Dark*, 1987; *Blue Steel*, 1990), Lizzie Borden (*Born In Flames*, 1983; *Working Girls*, 1986, wide release 1987), Martha Coolidge (*Not a Pretty Picture*, 1975; *Valley Girl*, 1983), Sofia Coppola (*Lost In Translation*, 2003, for which she won the Oscar for best original screenplay and was nominated for best director), Julie Dash (*Daughters of the Dust*, 1991), Nora Ephron (*Sleepless in Seattle*, 1993), Lisa Gottlieb (*Just One of the Guys*, 1985), Amy Heckerling (*Fast Times at Ridgemont High*, 1982; *Clueless*, 1995), Courtney Hunt (*Frozen River*, 2008, which went from an audience award at Sundance to an Oscar nomination), Patty Jenkins (*Monster*, 2003), Barbara Kopple (*Harlan County, U.S.A.*, 1976; *Keeping On*, 1981; *Wild Man Blues*, 1997), Mary Lambert (*Siesta*, 1987; *Pet Sematary*, 1989), Kasi Lemmons (*Eve's Bayou*, 1997), Penny Marshall (*Big*, 1988), Yvonne Rainer (*Film about a woman who ...*, 1974; *Kristina Talking Pictures*, 1976; *The Man Who Envied Women*, 1985), Susan Seidelman (*Smithereens*, 1982; *Desperately Seeking Susan*, 1985), Joan Micklin Silver (*Hester Street*, 1975; *Between the Lines*, 1977; *On the Yard*, 1978), Barbra Streisand (*Yentl*, 1983; *The Prince of Tides*, 1991; *The Mirror Has*

Two Faces, 1996), Betty Thomas (*The Brady Bunch Movie*, 1995), and Claudia Weill (*Girlfriends*, 1978; *It's My Turn*, 1980).

Julie Taymor came to wide attention with her Broadway adaptation of Disney's *The Lion King*, which showed a rich and varied theatrical imagination. Her first film, *Titus*, is a terrifically creative but ultimately faithful adaptation of one of Shakespeare's early tragedies, *Titus Andronicus*, and parts of it accordingly have great theatrical power and show a vivid command of blocking and choreography. In other parts the power is cinematic, notably in the authoritative camerawork, the montages that stylize what is going on, and the striking effects, all of which also show up in her later films. The settings, props, and costumes of *Titus* mix Ancient Rome with different parts of the 20th century, while the language is from the Renaissance, and Taymor makes all of it work together. Like *Frida*, a biography of Mexican painter Frida Kahlo (played by Salma Hayek), *Titus* is a visually exuberant treatment of a powerful figure (played by Anthony Hopkins), and Taymor makes each protagonist's obsessive preoccupation part of the look of the movie's world, from the way the design of *Frida* works with the colors and some other elements of Kahlo's paintings to the armor, honor, and muddy blood of *Titus*.

Mary Harron, born in Canada, demonstrated her skills at realism and tragicomedy in *I Shot Andy Warhol* (1996), but it was her scrubbed-white, violent satire *American Psycho*, based on the novel by Bret Easton Ellis, that scored a new high for black comedy as a vehicle of cultural analysis. She followed it with *The Notorious Bettie Page* (2005), a biography of the famous pin-up model that allowed Harron to analyze a range of images of women in film.

Ridley Scott and Others

Many directors, including Ridley Scott, followed the international marketplace to jobs in Hollywood. After the success of *Amores Perros* (2000), Alejandro González Iñárritu and writer Guillermo Arriaga produced its sequels, *21 Grams* (2003) and *Babel* (2006), in America. (Despite the backstage transition, it remains a tight trilogy; each film is constructed so that a single violent event integrates three apparently separate stories or sets of characters.) From

Hong Kong came John Woo (*Face/Off*, 1997); from Taiwan, Ang Lee (*The Ice Storm*, 1997); from the Netherlands, Paul Verhoeven (*RoboCop*; *Total Recall*, 1990; *Starship Troopers*, 1997); from Germany, Wolfgang Petersen (*In The Line of Fire*, 1993; *The Perfect Storm*, 2000); from Sweden, Lasse Hallström (*What's Eating Gilbert Grape*, 1993); from New Zealand, Martin Campbell (*The Mask of Zorro*, 1998); and from England, Mike Figgis (*Leaving Las Vegas*, 1995; *Timecode*, 2000) and Christopher Nolan (*Memento*, 2000; *The Dark Knight*).

Four British directors had joined the American industry in the 1980s, making pictures that were, for the most part, either hotly debated (Ridley Scott, Alan Parker) or uncritically enjoyed (Tony Scott, Adrian Lyne). The courses of their careers were determined by what their respective audiences demanded, and so they become interesting as a guide to the era itself. When Tony Scott and Adrian Lyne uncharacteristically made intricate, resonant, risk-taking films that departed from conservative mythic formulas and included unpleasant material, audiences stayed away; such was the fate of Tony Scott's *The Hunger* (1983, starring David Bowie and Catherine Deneuve as vampires). Even though Ridley and Tony Scott are brothers, the audiences for Tony's *Top Gun* (1986) and Ridley's *Blade Runner* (1982) were distinct camps: the former, much larger, looking to be blatantly entertained and subtly reassured; the latter preferring artistically ambitious films that were complex and revealing as well as entertaining.

All four directors had made commercials in Britain before turning to features; Tony Scott's fast-moving, seamlessly edited commercials were extremely influential in America, as were those of Adrian Lyne. Lyne's first major hit, *Flashdance* (1983), was the standard-bearer for the Reagan era, a movie that seductively preached that anyone who worked and dreamed hard enough could have everything she wanted. With its music-video colors and rhythms, likable heroine (Jennifer Beals), and denial of political and socioeconomic realities, *Flashdance* encouraged its audience to be uncritical. *Fatal Attraction* was as popular with adults as *Flashdance* was with teenage girls; it argued that committing adultery was the same as allowing a killer into the family (perhaps a reaction to the spread of AIDS) and that a single woman who looked autonomous and professional could secretly be crazy and demanding. Tony Scott's big films (*Top Gun; Days of Thunder*, 1990) also had a feelgood reliance on formula, but they were not as programmatically antifeminist as Lyne's; nevertheless, they reinforced conventional sex roles and demonstrated by their good box office that the mainstream audiences of the period could be happy with clichés.

Alan Parker's often violent and menacing films showed the dark side of dreams: a vacation that lands its drug-smuggling hero in a Turkish prison (*Midnight Express*), an "audition" that ends in sexual humiliation (*Fame*), the madness that engulfs a successful rock star (*Pink*

Floyd—The Wall, 1982, a British production; script and music by Roger Waters), a murder case whose successful solution destroys the detective (*Angel Heart*, 1987).

Ridley Scott's first picture, *The Duellists* (1977, British), was based on a story by Joseph Conrad; like most of his films, it was superbly designed and shot in Panavision and color. The ore-laden ship in his next film, *Alien*, was named the "Nostromo" in reference to Conrad's novel *Nostromo* (part of whose plot concerns the corrupting effect of a hoard of silver), an allusion that identified the greedy, colonialist owners of the ship as the primary villains. A nonsexist, nonracist, worker's perspective made itself felt in that film, and the ruthless gulf between masters and slaves—and between cops and "little people"—dominated the society portrayed in his

Fig. 17-22
Alien: *A search party from the "Nostromo" finds the remains of a nonhuman pilot, the "space jockey" who radioed a warning. Production Design, Michael Seymour; Director of Photography, Derek Vanlint; Costume Design, John Mollo; "Alien" Design, H. R. Giger; Art Directors, Les Dilley, Roger Christian; Set Decorator, Ian Whittaker; Concept Artists, Ron Cobb, Jean Giraud, Chris Foss; Visual Design Consultant, Dan O'Bannon.*

next picture, *Blade Runner*, which was based loosely on a dystopic novel by Philip K. Dick. Most of his later films (*Legend*, 1985; *Someone to Watch Over Me*, 1987; *Black Rain*, 1989; *Gladiator*, 2000; *Hannibal*, 2001; and *Black Hawk Down*, 2001) set leftist politics and ethically complex literature aside, but they were as tightly composed and often as moodily lit as their predecessors. *Thelma & Louise* (1991) struck that perfect balance of genre (the road movie), politics (sexual), and look (engrossing) that characterizes his best films, whatever the politics or the genre. A master of *mise-en-scène*, Ridley Scott has worked with some of the best cinematographers, production designers, concept artists, and special-effects wizards in the business. The look of *Blade Runner*—a neo-*noir* set in Los Angeles in 2019, some of whose scenes were shot in The Bradbury, a downtown building featured in many of the original *noirs*—with its towering buildings, endless rain, inescapable ads, richly dark color scheme, low-key lighting, and convincing special effects, survives in the release version. Unfortunately, the producers found the director's cut of *Blade Runner* too negative and confusing for their taste, so they added a voice-over narration that simplistically explained the story, then gave the film an astoundingly bad ending: a sequence that shows the lovers driving in a clean, sunny landscape (up to this point, a blue sky has been seen in only one shot—when the soul-like bird of a dead Replicant flies heavenward), accompanied by a voice-over that, like the sunny pictures, takes off all the pressure by announcing that the heroine (a robot, or Replicant, with a built-in four-year life span) just happens to have been constructed without a termination date. This self-destruct feature is what motivates most of the *Frankenstein*-like plot, in which the virtually human beings, artificially created and born full grown, seek out their creator to demand that he use his skills to extend their lives. The rest of the plot concerns the efforts of Deckard (Harrison Ford), a "blade runner"—an assassin who works for the police—who may be a Replicant himself, to locate and kill the rebellious Replicants. Fortunately, the director's cut of *Blade Runner* survived and was released in 1992.

Christopher Nolan and Others

Born in England, Christopher Nolan has made important films in the United States, both as an independent (*Memento*) and as a director of big studio pictures (*Batman Begins* and *The Dark Knight*). In *Memento*, a brain injury keeps a man from forming new memories. Although he can remember his name and his distant past, he cannot remember what just happened, and so he begins each new day or sequence with no memory of the days or even the hours that have come before. The film is in black and white and color by turns. The color sequences, which are dominant, unfold in reverse chronological order, so the audience does not know what happened in the "previous" (next to be shown) scene or sequence and shares the character's predicament. Intercut with the color sequences are black-and-white sequences that move forward in time; the end of the movie marks the midpoint of the story, and the last black-and-white scene changes to color to show the beginning of the actions we have watched in reverse. At the end of *Memento*, we know the reasons for the actions we saw at the beginning, which gives the picture a satisfying conclusion. Its black-and-white sequences set it apart from *Betrayal* and *Irreversible*, which move only backward in time. In his Batman films, Nolan puts his hero through trials of self-definition that are related to the problems of eruptive criminality and of maintaining order in a city that moves ever further out of control; as in *Memento*, what is at issue is the set of decisions an embattled, determined character makes about who he is and what he will do.

Both racial and sexual politics are explored in the understated, elliptical films of Wayne Wang and the sensitive dramas of Robert M. Young, both of whom are important independent filmmakers. Wang's most significant films include *Chan is Missing*, *Dim Sum: a little bit of heart* (1984), *Eat a Bowl of Tea* (1989), *Smoke* (1994, released 1995), *Blue in the Face* (1995, co-directed by Paul Auster), and *Chinese Box* (1998). Young's include *Alambrista!* (1977, released 1978), *Short Eyes* (1977), *The Ballad of Gregorio Cortez* (1982), *Dominick and Eugene* (1988), and *Caught* (1996); he was also the cinematographer and co-director of Michael Roemer's *Nothing But a Man* (1964).

The definitive late-1980s comedy of manners was independent Steven Soderbergh's first feature, *sex, lies, and videotape* (1989); it did for the video generation what *Carnal Knowledge* and *Trouble in Paradise* had done for their generations—addressed the present terms of intimacy—and in this movie, as in some of the films of Atom Egoyan, a video camera is the mediator of intimacy. Soderbergh's later works include *King of the Hill* (1993), *Out of Sight* (1998), *Erin Brockovich* (2000), and the two-part *Che* (2008).

Darren Aronofsky made a strong cautionary tale about the abuse of legal and illegal drugs, the sharply edited *Requiem for a Dream* (2000), but he is better known for his first feature, π (or *Pi*, 1998), a dark comedy about the search for the meaning of the universe at the intersection of mathematics and Jewish mysticism. Aronofsky moved to big science fiction with the lyrical *The Fountain* (2006), then back to the small film with the crowd-pleasing *The Wrestler*.

Joe Dante directed his first pictures for Roger Corman. *Piranha* was a parody of *Jaws* and many other movies as well as an attack on the Vietnam War and capitalist priorities. The first film Dante made without Corman, *The Howling*, was a tragicomic and satiric tale of werewolves, the media, and psychological fads. All of Dante's films are crammed with references to other films; for instance, after the tail credits of *The Howling*, Dante sends the audience on its way by cutting in part of a scene from *The Wolf Man*, in which the old gypsy (Maria Ouspenskaya) tells Lon Chaney, Jr., "Go now, and heaven help you!" Horror, reflexivity, and comedy are the mainstays of his movies, and they reinforce each other well in *Gremlins* (1984), which was produced by Spielberg, and in *Matinee* (1993), his salute to atomic mutant giant bug movies that is set in a world of bomb shelters, drop drills, protests, and the Cuban missile crisis.

Horror and reflexivity are also central to the work of Wes Craven, who got his start with the ruthlessly violent *The Last House on the Left* (1972), a remake of Ingmar Bergman's *The Virgin Spring*, then became famous when the Museum of Modern Art bought and showed a print of *The Hills Have Eyes* (1977), convinced that it was a work of art. When the slasher film was in decline, Craven renewed it with *A Nightmare on Elm Street* (1984) but sliced the

formula to fit his own purposes, making the slasher (Freddy Krueger, played by Robert Englund) talkative rather than silent and, following up Craven's career-long interest in dreams, having him attack the victims in their dreams, something Craven approached as a *cinematic* problem: how to interweave reality and dream in such a way that the audience, like the dreamer, believes a dream to be real until the moment of waking. Craven had little to do with the sequels, except for some input on Part 3, until he directed the reflexive *Wes Craven's New Nightmare* (1994), where Freddy enters the world of the moviemakers. Just as reflexive were *Scream* (1996) and its two sequels, in which the characters know all the rules of slasher films (and sequels) and use them to try to stay alive when real slashers go after them.

David Mamet perfected his cold, tense style with *House of Games* (1987); his interest in labyrinths and in confidence games overlap in that picture and in *The Spanish Prisoner* (1998). A playwright (*Glengarry Glen Ross*), Mamet is highly praised for his dialogue.

James Cameron established himself as one of the top action directors with horror and science fiction films—*The Terminator*, *Aliens* (1986), *The Abyss* (1989), *Terminator 2: Judgment Day* (1991)—in all of which he concentrated on the special effects to the point of mastery. He then put his knowledge of effects to work in the romantic drama *Titanic* (1997), a movie with no dramatic surprises but with a grand command of *mise-en-scène*. In contrast, Daniel Myrick and Eduardo Sánchez's *The Blair Witch Project* (1999) proved influential and effective because of its terrifyingly simple props and terms, its mix of video and 16mm, and its low-budget, improvised style.

David Fincher used special processing techniques to bring the silver back to the silver screen in *SE7EN* (1995, also called *Se7en*), a film whose dark, shimmering look makes its grisly tale of an insane murderer, his meticulously dispatched victims, and his effect on two policemen even more compelling. Like *Se7en*, Fincher's *Fight Club* (1999) is the story of an education in another way of being, but the lesson is empowering rather than horrific. It is also a skillfully executed tale of a man and his double. Fincher went on to direct *Zodiac* (2007), the story of the pursuit of a serial killer, and *The Curious Case Of Benjamin Button* (2008), the story of a man (played by Brad Pitt) who ages backward, growing from an old man to a baby; he shot *Zodiac* and most of *Benjamin Button* on high-definition digital video.

Paul Thomas Anderson, whose films often deal with conflicts between fathers or father figures and sons, directed two bold ensemble pieces influenced by the work of Robert Altman—*Boogie Nights* (1997), about the porn industry, and *Magnolia* (1999), about miracles and coincidences—before making *There Will Be Blood* (2007), the relentless, unsentimental story of a hardy and ruthless prospector (Daniel Plainview, played by Daniel Day–Lewis), a man who dislikes people in general and who becomes a successful oilman—in the process, raising and rejecting a boy who believes he is Plainview's son—until he finally destroys himself and his nemesis. Like the major films that preceded it, *There Will Be Blood* is long, involving, and perfectly paced.

Charlie Kaufman, whose principal interests seem to be the nature of the mind and of the creative process, as seen in his scripts for *Being John Malkovich* and *Adaptation.* (2002, Spike Jonze), became a director with *Synecdoche, New York* (2008), the story of a director (played by Philip Seymour Hoffman) who is awarded a large grant and decides to produce a theatrical model of life, mainly his life and the lives of the people he touches. At one point, he casts someone to play himself and direct the play, then someone else when that person commits suicide. The production, which is in rehearsal for decades and never opens, becomes a tragicomic mirror of the world, a part that stands in for the whole.

John Carpenter proved himself as a widescreen action director with the tightly paced *Assault on Precinct 13* (1976), then became famous with *Halloween*. His wide and cold, visually compelling *The Thing* (1982) is not a remake of *The Thing From Another World* (1951) but a return to the original story (John W. Campbell, Jr.'s "Who Goes There?"), in which there is not a single, easily identified adversary but a shapeshifter that can take on the form of any living being; thus, anyone might be the enemy—an idea utterly foreign to Hawks, who preferred to show a group of isolated humans fighting a known

enemy and growing closer as each person's character and the bonds between people are tested. Carpenter lets the group disintegrate until only a black man and a white man are left, and they establish a tentative truce on the verge of death. Interracial cooperation is an important theme in many of Carpenter's films, notably in *Prince of Darkness* (1987) and *They Live* (1988). In *They Live*, which remains one of the most politically critical films of the period, a white man (Nada—Spanish for "nothing"—played by wrestler Roddy Piper) and a black man (Frank, played by Keith David), workers who have lost their jobs in the Reagan era and have relocated to Los Angeles, discover that aliens—"they"—have recruited human collaborators and taken over the world. While "they live, we sleep," because humans cannot see the aliens in their true form without special glasses, thanks to a conditioning signal that is being sent across the world by satellite and played through TVs. The alien leaders echo the mythic rhetoric of some 1980s politicians: "It's a new morning in America—fresh, vital. The old cynicism is gone. . . . We must look to the strength of our nation, our ideals, a *vision*. We don't want to just survive; we want to succeed." When Frank and Nada destroy the conditioning transmitter at the cost of their lives, people can see the aliens for what they are. As the veil is lifted, one alien is saying on TV, "All the sex and violence on the screen has gone too far for me. I'm fed up with it. Filmmakers like George Romero and John Carpenter have to show some restraint." The ending that follows is, of course, unrestrained.

They Live is no *Close Encounters*; the aliens are evil. Times had changed between the making of those two pictures, and they continued to change. The period's intermittent conservatism yielded to an optimistic liberalism when the first African-American president was elected in 2008; nevertheless, terrorism remained a worldwide concern, and an economic recession had begun in 2007. In 2009, one result of that recession was that a lot of people went to the movies, many of them seeking escape and relatively inexpensive entertainment as they had during the Depression. Some of the big films continued to provide that escape (even if many of them had gone into production before the recession sank in, they were fortunate enough to be released when there was a strong market for them, and they remained popular on video), putting the happy ending back into romantic comedy or emphasizing exciting action that often led to personal fulfillment (Paul Greengrass's *The Bourne Ultimatum*, 2007; *Star Trek*, 2009), while some of the smaller films offered a less escapist view of the family than had been seen in years (*Before the Devil Knows You're Dead*, 2009; *Rachel Getting Married; Synecdoche, New York*) or tackled difficult economic and social topics (*Frozen River*, 2008). *The Dark Knight*, as of this writing the most popular film made in the 21st century, addressed the problems of the time in mythic terms that remained relevant, for it still mattered that a mythic figure could try to fix or protect the world, even if that was no longer a simple task and the hero had to discover his limits in the process. Confronting a villain who had become more formidable and confounding than any in his experience, a Postmodern version of the Joker, may have looked like a job for Superman, but it wasn't; what was required was a renewed Batman, a darker hero.

For Further Viewing

FILMS

CHARLES BURNETT (1944–   )
Killer of Sheep (1977). Completed 1973
My Brother's Wedding (1983)
To Sleep With Anger (1990)
The Glass Shield (1994)
Relative Stranger (2009). Made for TV

JAMES CAMERON (1954–   )
The Terminator (1984)
Aliens (1986)
The Abyss (1989)
Terminator 2: Judgment Day (1991)
Titanic (1997)
Avatar (2009). 3-D

JOHN CARPENTER (1948–   )
Assault on Precinct 13 (1976)
Halloween (1978)
The Thing (1982)
Prince of Darkness (1987)
They Live (1988)
In The Mouth of Madness (1995)

JOEL (1954–   ) AND ETHAN (1957–   ) COEN
Blood Simple (1983)
Raising Arizona (1987)
Miller's Crossing (1990)
Barton Fink (1991)
Fargo (1996)
The Big Lebowski (1998)
O Brother, Where Art Thou? (2000)
No Country For Old Men (2007)
Burn After Reading (2008)
A Serious Man (2009)

WES CRAVEN (1939–   )
The Last House on the Left (1972)
The Hills Have Eyes (1977)
A Nightmare on Elm Street (1984)
Scream (1996)

JONATHAN DEMME (1944–   )
Citizens Band or *Handle With Care* (1977)
Melvin and Howard (1980)
Stop Making Sense (1984)
Something Wild (1986)
Swimming to Cambodia (1987)
Married to the Mob (1988)
The Silence of the Lambs (1991)
Philadelphia (1993)
Beloved (1998)
Rachel Getting Married (2008)

BLAKE EDWARDS (1922–   )
Breakfast at Tiffany's (1961)
Days of Wine and Roses (1962)
The Pink Panther (1964)
The Pink Panther Strikes Again (1976)
10 (1979)
S.O.B. (1981)
Victor/Victoria (1982)

BOB FOSSE (1927–87   )
Sweet Charity (1968)
Cabaret (1972)
Lenny (1974)
All That Jazz (1979)
Star 80 (1983)

JIM JARMUSCH (1953–   )
Stranger Than Paradise (1984)
Down By Law (1986)
Mystery Train (1989)
Night on Earth (1991)

Dead Man (1995)
Coffee and Cigarettes (1986–2003). Released as
  feature 2003
Broken Flowers (2005)
The Limits of Control (2009)

SPIKE LEE (1957–   )
She's Gotta Have It (1986)
Do The Right Thing (1989)
Jungle Fever (1991)
Malcolm X (1992)
4 Little Girls (1997)
The Original Kings of Comedy (2000)
Inside Man (2006)
*When the Levees Broke: A Requiem in Four
  Acts* (2006). Made for TV
Miracle at St. Anna (2008)

GEORGE LUCAS (1944–   )
THX-1138 (1971)
American Graffiti (1973)
Star Wars or *Star Wars: Episode IV—A New
  Hope* (1977)
The Empire Strikes Back or *Star Wars: Episode
  V—The Empire Strikes Back* (1980, directed
  by Irvin Kershner)
Raiders of the Lost Ark (1981, directed by
  Steven Spielberg)
Return of the Jedi or *Star Wars: Episode VI—
  Return of the Jedi* (1983, directed by Richard
  Marquand)
Star Wars: Episode I—The Phantom Menace
  (1999)
Star Wars: Episode II—Attack of the Clones
  (2002)
Star Wars: Episode III—Revenge of the Sith
  (2005)

DAVID LYNCH (1946–   )
Eraserhead (1977). Completed 1976
The Elephant Man (1980)
Dune (1984)
Blue Velvet (1986)
Wild At Heart (1990)
Twin Peaks: Fire Walk With Me (1992).
  Completed 1991
Lost Highway (1997). Completed 1996
The Straight Story (1999)
Mulholland Drive or *Mulholland Dr.* (2001)
Inland Empire (2006)

TV series: *Twin Peaks* (pilot, 1989; broadcast
  1990–91). Co-producer, Mark Frost

JOHN SAYLES (1950–   )
Return of the Secaucus Seven (1980).
  Completed 1979
Baby It's You (1983). Completed 1982
The Brother from Another Planet (1984)
Matewan (1987)
Eight Men Out (1988)
The Secret of Roan Inish (1994)
Men With Guns (1997)

RIDLEY SCOTT (1937–   )
The Duellists (1977)
Alien (1979)
Blade Runner (1982)
Legend (1985)
Thelma & Louise (1991)
Gladiator (2000)
Hannibal (2001)
Black Hawk Down (2001)
American Gangster (2007)

STEVEN SPIELBERG (1946–   )
Duel (1971). Made for TV
The Sugarland Express (1974)
Jaws (1975)
Close Encounters of the Third Kind (1977).
  Revised 1980
Raiders of the Lost Ark (1981)
E.T.—The Extra-Terrestrial (1982)
Indiana Jones and the Temple of Doom (1984)
The Color Purple (1985)
Jurassic Park (1993)
Schindler's List (1993)
Amistad (1997)
Saving Private Ryan (1998)
A.I. Artificial Intelligence or *Artificial
  Intelligence AI* (2001)
Minority Report (2002)
War of the Worlds (2005)
Munich (2005)

OLIVER STONE (1946–   )
Platoon (1986)
Talk Radio (1988)
Born on the Fourth of July (1989)
JFK (1991)
Natural Born Killers (1994)

Quentin Tarantino (1963–)
Reservoir Dogs (1992)
Pulp Fiction (1994)
Jackie Brown (1997)
Kill Bill Vol. 1 (2003)
Kill Bill Vol. 2 (2004)
Grindhouse (2007). Co-director, Robert
  Rodriguez
Death Proof (2007). Expanded from *Grindhouse*
Inglourious Basterds (2009)

Julie Taymor (1952–)
Titus (1999)
Frida (2002)
Across the Universe (2007)

Gus Van Sant (1952–)
Drugstore Cowboy (1989)
My Own Private Idaho (1991)
Good Will Hunting (1997)
Elephant (2003)
Paranoid Park (2007)
Milk (2008)

John Waters (1946–)
Multiple Maniacs (1971)
Pink Flamingos (1972)
Female Trouble (1975)
Desperate Living (1977)
Polyester (1981)
Hairspray (1988)
Serial Mom (1994)

Robert Zemeckis (1951–)
Romancing the Stone (1984)
Back to the Future (1985)
Who Framed Roger Rabbit (1988)
Back to the Future Part II (1989), *Part III* (1990)
Forrest Gump (1994)
The Polar Express (2004). 3-D
Beowulf (2007). 3-D
Disney's A Christmas Carol (2009). 3-D

Recent American Miscellany
Between the Lines (1977, Joan Micklin Silver)
Saturday Night Fever (1977, John Badham)
Short Eyes (1977, Robert M. Young)
The Deer Hunter (1978, Michael Cimino)
Go Tell the Spartans (1978, Ted Post)
Grease (1978, Randal Kleiser)

National Lampoon's Animal House (1978, John
  Landis)
Superman (1978, Richard Donner)
The Stunt Man (1980, Richard Rush).
  Completed 1978
Heaven's Gate (1980, Michael Cimino)
Ordinary People (1980, Robert Redford)
Resurrection (1980, Daniel Petrie)
The Howling (1981, Joe Dante). Completed 1980
Body Heat (1981, Lawrence Kasdan)
Pennies From Heaven (1981, Herbert Ross)
Zoot Suit (1981, Luis Valdez)
The Ballad of Gregorio Cortez (1982,
  Robert M. Young)
Chan is Missing (1982, Wayne Wang)
Diner (1982, Barry Levinson)
Fast Times at Ridgemont High (1982,
  Amy Heckerling)
First Blood (1982, Ted Kotcheff)
Poltergeist (1982, Tobe Hooper)
Star Trek II: The Wrath of Khan (1982, Nicholas
  Meyer)
Brainstorm (1983, Douglas Trumbull)
Flashdance (1983, Adrian Lyne)
The Right Stuff (1983, Philip Kaufman)
Risky Business (1983, Paul Brickman)
All of Me (1984, Carl Reiner)
1918 (1984, Ken Harrison)
Brazil (1985, Terry Gilliam)
Rambo: First Blood Part II (1985, George P.
  Cosmatos)
The Return of the Living Dead (1985, Dan
  O'Bannon)
Henry: Portrait of a Serial Killer (1986, John
  McNaughton). Wide release 1990
River's Edge (1986, Tim Hunter)
House of Games (1987, David Mamet)
Lethal Weapon (1987, Richard Donner)
RoboCop (1987, Paul Verhoeven)
84 Charlie Mopic (1989, Patrick Duncan)
Field of Dreams (1989, Phil Alden Robinson)
sex, lies, and videotape (1989, Steven
  Soderbergh)
Edward Scissorhands (1990, Tim Burton)
The Grifters (1990, Stephen Frears)
Boyz N the Hood (1991, John Singleton)
Daughters of the Dust (1991, Julie Dash)
New Jack City (1991, Mario Van Peebles)
The Rapture (1991, Michael Tolkin)
Unforgiven (1992, Clint Eastwood)

El Mariachi (1993, Robert Rodriguez). Completed 1992

Addams Family Values (1993, Barry Sonnenfeld)

Clean, Shaven (1993, Lodge Kerrigan)

Groundhog Day (1993, Harold Ramis)

Menace II Society (1993, Allen and Albert Hughes)

Clerks (1994, Kevin Smith)

Hoop Dreams (1994, Steve James, Fred Marx, and Peter Gilbert)

The Shawshank Redemption (1994, Frank Darabont)

Smoke (1995, Wayne Wang). Completed 1994

SE7EN or *Se7en* or *Seven* (1995, David Fincher)

Caught (1996, Robert M. Young)

Eve's Bayou (1997, Kasi Lemmons)

L.A. Confidential (1997, Curtis Hanson)

Chinese Box (1998, Wayne Wang)

La Ciudad or *The City* (1998, David Riker)

π or *Pi* (1998, Darren Aronofsky)

The Blair Witch Project (1999, Daniel Myrick and Eduardo Sánchez)

Fight Club (1999, David Fincher)

The Matrix (1999, Andy and Larry Wachowski)

American Psycho (2000, Mary Harron)

Memento (2000, Christopher Nolan)

Timecode or *Time Code* (2000, Mike Figgis)

Frailty (2001, Bill Paxton). Wide release 2002

Ghost World (2001, Terry Zwigoff)

Harry Potter and the Philosopher's Stone or *Harry Potter and the Sorcerer's Stone* (2001, Chris Columbus). U.S./U.K.

Monster (2003, Patty Jenkins)

Spider-Man 2 (2004, Sam Raimi)

Palindromes (2005, Todd Solondz). Completed 2004

Frank Miller's Sin City or *Sin City* (2005, Robert Rodriguez and Frank Miller)

Good Night, And Good Luck. (2005, George Clooney)

Tim Burton's Corpse Bride or *Corpse Bride* (2005, Tim Burton)

Children of Men (2006, Alfonso Cuarón)

The Good Shepherd (2006, Robert De Niro)

Stranger Than Fiction (2006, Marc Forster)

The Diving Bell and the Butterfly (2007, Julian Schnabel). U.S./France

Enchanted (2007, Kevin Lima)

I'm Not There (2007, Todd Haynes)

There Will Be Blood (2007, Paul Thomas Anderson)

300 (2007, Zack Snyder)

Cloverfield (2008, Matt Reeves)

The Curious Case Of Benjamin Button (2008, David Fincher)

The Dark Knight (2008, Christopher Nolan)

Synecdoche, New York (2008, Charlie Kaufman)

Coraline (2009, Henry Selick). 3-D

Watchmen (2009, Zack Snyder)

DVDs

The Adventures of Indiana Jones (1981–89, **Steven Spielberg;** co-produced by **George Lucas**). Paramount Home Video. **Digitally restored** prints of *Raiders of the Lost Ark*, *Indiana Jones and the Temple of Doom*, and *Indiana Jones and the Last Crusade*. Includes a making-of documentary and shorts on the films' stunts, sound, music, and effects.

A.I. Artificial Intelligence (2001, **Steven Spielberg**). DreamWorks Home Entertainment. Special Edition. Includes two making-of documentaries; storyboards; interviews with Spielberg, the ILM effects group, and others; and more.

Alien Quadrilogy (1979–97, **Ridley Scott, James Cameron, David Fincher,** and **Jean-Pierre Jeunet**). 20th Century Fox. Includes release versions and special editions (in the case of *Alien*, the director's cut) of *Alien*, *Aliens*, *Alien³*, and *Alien: Resurrection*, with commentaries and many extras.

Blade Runner (1982, **Ridley Scott**). Warner Home Video. Four-Disc Collector's Edition. Contains the final 2007 cut, **digitally restored;** the 1982 U.S. and international versions; and the 1992 director's cut. Includes many documentaries.

Brazil (1985, **Terry Gilliam**). Criterion Collection. Includes the director's cut of the film (142 minutes) as well as the "Love Conquers All" edited-for-TV version (the U.S. theatrical release version is not included); a making-of documentary emphasizing the battles over releasing the picture; a commentary by Gilliam; storyboards; and interviews with the writers, designers, and composer.

The Curious Case Of Benjamin Button (see Chap. 19 list).

The Dark Knight (2008, **Christopher Nolan**). Warner Home Video. Two-Disc Special Edition. The entire film is presented in an aspect ratio of 2.4:1; the IMAX sequences may be viewed separately.

Daughters of the Dust (1991, **Julie Dash**). Kino Video. Deluxe Edition.

David Lynch: The Lime Green Set (1977–2008, **David Lynch**). Absurda. Includes *Eraserhead* (remastered, with separate soundtrack), Lynch's short films, *The Elephant Man* (with extras), *Blue Velvet* (remixed), *Wild At Heart* (with deleted scenes), *Industrial Symphony No. 1*, *Dumbland*, and a mystery disc.

Do the Right Thing (1989, **Spike Lee**). Criterion Collection. Includes a commentary by Lee, cinematographer **Ernest Dickerson,** and others; a making-of documentary; a visit to the locations; Lee's music video of **Public Enemy's** "Fight the Power"; storyboards; and the 1989 Cannes press conference with Lee and stars **Ossie Davis, Ruby Dee,** and **Joie Lee.**

Down By Law (1986, **Jim Jarmusch**). Criterion Collection. Includes interviews with Jarmusch, cinematographer **Robby Müller,** and others; the 1986 Cannes press conference with Jarmusch and stars **Roberto Benigni, Nicoletta Braschi,** and **John Lurie;** outtakes; unusually good production and location stills; and Jarmusch's phone calls with singer **Tom Waits,** Benigni, and Lurie.

Eraserhead (1977, **David Lynch**). Available only from the davidlynch.com store. Includes a terrific print of the film and a long interview with Lynch. The same Web site offers a selection of his shorts.

Fargo (1996, **Joel and Ethan Coen**). MGM/UA. Special Edition. Includes a documentary, an interview with the Coens and star **Frances McDormand,** and more.

Fight Club (1999, **David Fincher**). 20th Century Fox. Two-Disc Collector's Edition.

Frank Miller's Sin City (2005, **Frank Miller** and **Robert Rodriguez;** special guest director, **Quentin Tarantino**). Dimension Home Video. Recut and Extended Edition. Contains a *Sin City* paperback, the release version of the film, and an extended version, with commentaries by Rodriguez, Miller, and Tarantino.

Also includes a 15-minute version of Rodriguez's film school, numerous making-of shorts, and the complete greenscreen version of the movie.

Halloween (1978, **John Carpenter**). Anchor Bay. Divimax 25th Anniversary Edition. Includes a commentary by Carpenter, writer–producer **Debra Hill,** and star **Jamie Lee Curtis;** a documentary with many interviews; and a visit to the original location.

Heaven's Gate (1980, **Michael Cimino**). MGM Home Entertainment. The uncut version.

Jaws (1975, **Steven Spielberg**). Universal. 25th Anniversary Widescreen Collector's Edition. Includes a making-of documentary, storyboards, and deleted scenes.

The John Waters Collection (1972–98, **John Waters**). New Line Home Entertainment. Contains *Pink Flamingos, Female Trouble, Desperate Living, Polyester, Hairspray,* and *Pecker,* with commentaries by Waters.

Memento (2000, **Christopher Nolan**). Columbia TriStar. Includes the original story and puzzles that unlock information.

Men With Guns (1997, **John Sayles**). Columbia TriStar. With a commentary by Sayles.

Milk (2008, **Gus Van Sant**). Universal. Compare with *The Times of Harvey Milk.*

O Brother, Where Art Thou? (see Chap. 19 list).

Pulp Fiction (1994, **Quentin Tarantino**). Miramax Entertainment. Two-Disc Collector's Edition. Includes a documentary on the film, deleted scenes, critical analyses, and more.

SE7EN (1995, **David Fincher**). New Line Home Entertainment. Platinum Series. Includes commentaries by all concerned, an exploration of the opening title sequence, storyboards, alternate endings, and more.

Star Wars: Episode I—The Phantom Menace (1999, **George Lucas**). 20th Century Fox. Widescreen Edition. Episodes II and III are available in the same series of two-disc sets. Each thorough, informative set includes the feature with a commentary by Lucas and others, several short documentaries on the making and meaning of the film, deleted scenes, and a full-length documentary on, for example, everything that went into making a one-minute fight scene in *Sith* or how Yoda became a CG figure in *Clones.*

Star Wars: Episode IV—A New Hope (1977, **George Lucas**). 20th Century Fox. Limited Edition. Episodes V and VI are available in the same series of two-disc sets. One disc contains the film as originally released; the other disc has the digitally augmented version.

The Times of Harvey Milk (1984, **Rob Epstein**). New Yorker Video. **Restored** and with many extras. Compare this documentary with *Milk*.

Titus (1999, **Julie Taymor**). 20th Century Fox. Includes a making-of documentary, information about the costumes, articles on the film from *American Cinematographer*, a short about creating the nightmare sequences, and a Q&A between Taymor and students at Columbia.

18

Conglomerates and Video: 1975–

While filmmakers from Spielberg and Lucas to Scorsese and Lynch were pushing the American cinema to new levels of expression, many important developments took place in the business and technology of film. These changes were so extreme that by the beginning of the 21st century, almost every major studio had become part of a gigantic media corporation, the average studio picture cost more than $70 million to produce, an unprecedented number of films were sequels rather than risk-taking originals, and video—first analog, then digital—had become a viable medium for watching and even shooting motion pictures.

It's A Wonderful Deal

The Hollywood Renaissance ended shortly after the film industry became more interested in making deals than in making movies. Ironically, this change was motivated by the success of several key Renaissance films, notably the great sequel *The Godfather Part II* and the blockbuster *Jaws*. (Because it was the year of *Jaws* and the Betamax, 1975 has been chosen for the start date of this chapter.) Movies began to earn such high profits that more expensive films were made, designed specifically to make even more money. With higher costs came higher risks, so the movies became more formulaic and exciting, driven by increasingly sophisticated effects and calculated to be pleasing rather than disturbing. Movies were built around marketable elements—especially the stars, the book or picture the film would be based on, and the director—linked in a

deal, often before there was a final script and sometimes when there was only a vague notion of what the movie would be about. It was the package of stars and the genre, producers believed, that people went to see.

The reins of production passed into the hands of several kinds of executives: young business majors fresh out of school, former talent agents, corporate bigwigs, and producers of recent hits. Most of these new decision makers thought they were skilled at identifying projects that could turn into hits, but almost none of them had any visual training, on-the-set filmmaking experience, or grasp of film history (Chaplin, *Casablanca*, and *2001* about covered it). They rarely thought about what would make a good *film*, not just a good story or a good business opportunity. And they were desperate for appealing, entertaining, sure-fire projects.

Sequels and Blockbusters

Most film ideas were approved for production on the basis of market research and guesswork rather than experience and confident instinct. New ideas were rare, and when they succeeded, they were repeated in sequels. No period in film history (and this period has continued to the present) ever saw so many sequels, nor so many remakes—attempts to discover the old magic in old ideas, updating what had worked before. *The Big Clock* (as *No Way Out*), *The Blob*, *D.O.A.*, *The Last House on the Left*, *Out of the Past* (as *Against All Odds*), *Planet of the Apes*, and *Stella Dallas* (as *Stella*) were just a few that were remade, rarely with success. Screenwriter and novelist William Goldman summed up the studio mentality of the period with the motto, "NOBODY KNOWS ANYTHING."

Studio executives listened as writers pitched stories, producers outlined projects, and agents presented packages; put 100 projects into development when they knew they would make only 12; and ordered changes in completed films in response to the reactions of preview audiences and other executives. The great goal was to reach the desired (*target* or targeted) audience and earn its repeat business, then to reach other age and population groups—ideally, to see a picture with *legs* (the ability to grow in popularity on its own, without needing extra advertising, and to move from a few theatres to many) do so well that it became a blockbuster that could be kept in release a long time, be profitably distributed overseas and profitably licensed for TV and DVD, be the basis of a sequel, and perhaps even be rereleased. As discussed in the previous chapter, a blockbuster was a movie that took in at least $100 million at the U.S. box office during its first release. The *blockbuster mentality* of studio executives in this period consisted of (1) spending a lot of money on a few big pictures; (2) with rare exceptions, making only those pictures likely to appeal immediately to large audiences; (3) deciding a movie's fate on the basis of its opening-week box office; and (4) planning to subsidize the studio's less expensive pictures with the income from one or two immense hits each year, which allowed them to take a chance on a few pictures that might have an inherently limited appeal—but kept the hits officially in the red, unable to earn "net profits" until the studio itself was in the black, thanks to accounting practices that favored only the executives and the studio's owners.

For Hollywood executives, the new world began in 1975, when *Jaws* made money faster than any movie since *Gone With the Wind*, catalyzing the blockbuster mentality and identifying teenagers and young adults as the audience to please. Decades of teenpix came from this conception of the primary audience, but so did an unprecedented interest in and development of new sound technologies and special effects. *Star Wars* confirmed and expanded these priorities: special effects, young audiences, open endings leading to sequels, and impressive soundtracks.

And *Rocky*, released between *Jaws* and *Star Wars*, showed that the right medium-budget movie could make big money and that the public was looking for heroes. *Rambo: First Blood Part II* (1985, directed by George P. Cosmatos) provided what for many executives was the final revelation: that a sequel could earn more than the film on which it was based ($79 million, compared with *First Blood*'s $23 million).

Conglomerates

But not every studio executive was in Hollywood, or even in a studio. Beginning in the 1960s, many studios were taken over by bigger corporations whose executives saw filmmaking as part of their company's business rather than all of it, and strictly as a profit-making venture. (Imagine the difference it would have made if Mayer and Thalberg had had to answer to General Motors.) Universal-International was taken over by MCA (1962), Paramount by Gulf + Western (1966), United Artists by Transamerica (1967), Warner Bros. by Kinney (1969), and Columbia by Coca-Cola (1982)—and all of them went on to change hands. Even before *Titanic*, vast amounts of money rushed into the industry, which began to take in billions. Studios were valuable producers of salable entertainment, and when the dust had settled, most of them had been absorbed by media *conglomerates:* huge corporations made up of many diverse companies.

In 1994, the media conglomerate Viacom bought Paramount Communications, which included Paramount Pictures, Paramount Television, Simon & Schuster, and Madison Square Garden. Viacom owned the cable channels MTV, Nickelodeon, Showtime, and The Movie Channel, and by 2000, it had acquired CBS. That meant that in 2000, a Paramount movie could play in a Viacom theatre (Famous Players and United Cinema International; divestiture laws had long kept the studios from owning theatres, but many media conglomerates included theatre chains anyway; significantly, no one objected in 1997 when Sony Corp. and Cineplex Odeon merged their theatre businesses to form Loews Cineplex Entertainment) and then go to cable on a Viacom cable outlet (Showtime), to stores worldwide and in Viacom's video outlet (Blockbuster), and to network TV on a Viacom TV network (CBS), while the underlying novel was reissued by a Viacom publisher (Pocket Books), with ads for all these showings and products going out on Viacom's TV and radio stations. Publishing a movie on DVD could earn a studio more money than the film had made in theatres, and that was only one element of a conglomerate's exhibition and sales network.

The conglomerates were not monopolies but slices through the culture, communications structures that included some of the country's books, some of its newspapers, some of its channels, some of its cables and phone lines, some of its movies, some of its toys. Edison could have run one in a heartbeat. By cutting out the middleman and controlling virtually all aspects of production, distribution, and exhibition (even if the majority of theatre chains remained independent), the studios brought back vertical integration, only it was not the studio in charge but the conglomerate, which owned all the companies including the studio.

For Sale: Studio

Some studios were bought and sold repeatedly, even by the same people. Consider the fate of MGM. Investor Kirk Kerkorian gained control of MGM in 1969 and United Artists in 1981, forming the MGM/UA Entertainment Company. In 1985, Ted Turner, the owner of several major cable-TV stations, bought MGM and UA, but in 1986, he sold them back to Kerkorian, keeping the films. In 1986, Turner also sold the MGM lot and laboratory to Lorimar. Kerkorian sold MGM again in 1990 to Giancarlo Parretti of Pathe Communications (no relation to the legendary Pathé Frères). Parretti rang down the curtain on UA and formed MGM-Pathe, but he ran the studio for less than six months. (Like Turner's, Parretti's was a highly leveraged buyout. Little of the $1.3 billion Parretti paid Kerkorian for his 80 percent interest in MGM/UA was cash—the rest a transfer of paper assets, borrowed money, and anticipated revenues pledged by other companies for rights to the not-yet-owned films—and when it came to running the studio, the Italian financier had trouble paying the bills. In comparison, MCA's purchase of Universal for $11.25 million in 1959 was a simple transaction, as was Matsushita's acquisition of MCA in 1990 for $6.59 billion.) In 1992, MGM-Pathe was acquired by Crédit Lyonnais, a French bank, which stabilized and renamed the company—and revived UA in the process. By May 1992, Metro-Goldwyn-Mayer Inc., wholly owned by Crédit Lyonnais, included two filmmaking entities—MGM and UA—as well as such active units as MGM/UA Home Video. Incredibly, Kerkorian bought back the studio in 1996.

Although the studios survived, they no longer had permanent staffs of skilled artists and artisans—no Script Department with its group of experienced writers, no pool of directors, no costumers who worked for the studio on film after film and both understood and helped to create the studio's style, and not even the costumes themselves. Studios emptied their warehouses of props and costumes, from "Rosebud" to the dresses worn in *Gone With the Wind*, which saved them storage costs but made them no longer the rich producing entities they once had been, cornucopias of props, costumes, sets, and equipment. Just one result of this housecleaning was that far fewer period pictures were made; most films were set in the present, using costumes and props that could be bought in ordinary stores or rented from a supply house. A more significant result was that filmmakers became freelancers: Everyone was hired to work on a specific project—and without a project one was out of work, hoping for a call.

There was no studio staffed like the old MGM, which had actors like Judy Garland, Mickey Rooney, Clark Gable, and Spencer Tracy on the payroll, available to work on anything, as it had writers like Jules Furthman and Frances Marion, designers and choreographers who knew how to make an MGM musical, acres of outdoor sets, and its own film laboratory. The MGM lab, Metrocolor, was closed in the late 1980s. The old MGM back lot was sold long ago (by Kerkorian) to real estate developers, and the rest of the lot, with its soundstages and office buildings, passed from the control of MGM/UA to Lorimar-Telepictures to Warner Bros. to Columbia, which itself was finally bought by Sony. Even a highly successful studio like Disney, which has never changed ownership, began to hire "talent" on a film-by-film basis, only in rare cases going so far as to offer a contract to an actor or director for a set number of pictures.

In the Studio Era, a Paramount picture was approved, made, and released by Paramount, whether or not it was shot on the Paramount lot.

Today a Paramount picture is just as likely to have been made by an independent production company and "picked up" (as *Friday the 13th* was) by Paramount for release as "A Paramount Picture." In a *negative pick-up* deal, an independent producer sells the completed negative—the finished film—to a studio, thus recouping the costs of production and in most cases securing the rights to a portion of the film's earnings. But the deal may be made earlier, even before the film is shot, with the studio paying some or most of the cost of production; in this case, the filmmakers get more of their money at the "front end" of the deal—that is, right away—and are entitled to less of the film's profits. Generally, those who spend their own money or defer their compensation, whether they are producers, studios, directors, or actors, receive more money at the "back end" of the deal, after the film has been released. All the studios make pick-up deals—and there's no secret about it; it's made plain in credits like "MGM presents a GMT Production . . ." or when a studio logo (such as MGM's shot of the roaring lion) is followed by "An Acme Film." The important thing to realize here is that the studios themselves are not producing as many films as it appears; they have been working in partnership with independents for decades.

Throughout this period, a number of studio heads and major producers were former talent agents who brought their clients along with them. But the talent agencies themselves soon became as powerful as the studios. The sales of Columbia and Universal—whole studios—were arranged by talent agents. Michael Ovitz, until 1995 the head of Creative Artists Agency, not only acted as middleman between Matsushita and MCA in 1990, but in 1995 became (for a short time) the president of The Walt Disney Co. and its recent acquisition, Capital Cities/ABC Inc. With virtually everyone working on a contract basis—contracted to work on *a* film, with a profession but not a regular job—agents assembled prominent "elements" into a *package*, which in business terms was a package deal and the talent it bound: the basic idea and the key people who would make the film and attract the audience. This constituted putting a picture together, constructing the picture-as-deal and deciding, as studio producers alone once did, which movies would be made by whom. Indeed, the major

agent's list of clients, from whom the package of writer, director, and stars typically was selected, was the period's version of the studio's "stable" of talent. If Mickey Rooney and Judy Garland appeared together in a 1990s picture, it would be because they had the same agent, not because they worked for the same studio.

The Budget Explosion

The cost of making films went up throughout the period; it was not simply a matter of inflation when the average *negative cost* of a studio feature (the expenses involved in producing the negative—in other words, the cost of making the movie before any copies are struck) jumped from $11 million to over $20 million in the 1980s, then hit $50 million in the 1990s. In 2003, it cost Hollywood $64 million to make the average film and $103 million to distribute it; included in the latter figure was $39 million for prints and ads. By 2007, the cost of producing the average MPAA-affiliated-studio film had risen to $70.8 million, with prints and ads costing an average of $35.9 million.

The blockbuster mentality fed on itself. If a star's last picture had cost $10 million and earned $50 million, his or her fee on the next picture would be at least $1 million, possibly $20 million. If a picture was expected to do well—perhaps because it was the sequel to a hit—it appeared a safe investment, and more money was spent on it; thus, *Die Hard 2* (1990) cost much more than *Die Hard*. Studios spent more in the hope of making more. But if one spends $70 million on a *Die Hard 2*, and if conventional practices dictate that a film must take in three times its negative cost to break even (to cover the full costs of production, distribution, and interest), that overburdened sequel would have to sell $210 million in tickets before earning a penny. *Total Recall* cost $65 million, made almost twice that at the box office, and was a financial disappointment—but *Batman* cost $53.5 million and grossed over $253 million, and that was just from domestic ticket sales.

Studios hedged these enormous bets by selling *subsidiary rights* even before a picture was shot: licenses to distribute the film theatrically in other countries, to show it on cable and satellite, to broadcast it on network TV, to reproduce and sell it on videocassettes and laserdiscs (and later,

DVDs and Blu-ray Discs), to distribute it nontheatrically in 16mm, to sell a novel based on its plot, to consider it for a TV series, and to make toys and clothes inspired by its characters as well as many other trademarked items, from party napkins to computer games. These secondary revenues, especially the ones from video, could equal or surpass those taken in at the box office, and they had an effect on the way the film was shot: to play well in a theatre and acceptably on a TV set (in color, with more close-ups than long shots, and with crucial action often confined to the *TV safe area*, an inner rectangle the shape of a conventional TV screen).

Another commercial practice that had a marked effect on film content was *product placement*, which amounted to selling advertising space within the movie. Sometimes the product would show up subtly—everyone in the movie just happened to drink Budweiser or drive a Ford—but it could also make its presence felt blatantly. When a father and son go shopping in *Manhunter* (1986, directed by Michael Mann), the boy asks his dad what kind of coffee he likes, then says "You like that Folgers stuff, don't you? Mom likes it too." In older films, products were anonymous (studio-made boxes marked "Corn

Flakes") or bore invented names ("Wham" ham in *Mr. Blandings Builds His Dream House*, 1948), but in 1990, the Teenage Mutant Ninja Turtles ordered Domino's Pizza.

The studios were no longer the only game in town, though they remained extremely powerful. Many independent producers, directors "shopping projects" (trying to interest studios in them), agents, and writers with finished scripts "written on spec" (*on speculation*—that is, on one's own, with no guarantee that anyone would buy the work) visited the studios in the hope of selling an idea or a script, obtaining co-financing to produce a film, or convincing the studio to make a film. But many independents made films with no guidance or interference from any studio—films that usually cost under $10 million to produce and could turn out to be more profitable than any studio product. *The Blair Witch Project* (1999, directed by Daniel Myrick and Eduardo Sánchez) cost the original filmmakers, who used both film and video, $60,000. For $1.1 million, it was acquired by Artisan, which put another $300,000 into post-production polishing, so that its final cost was under $1.5 million— and it made $140 million at the U.S. box office, over 95 times its cost (or 2,333 times the cost of

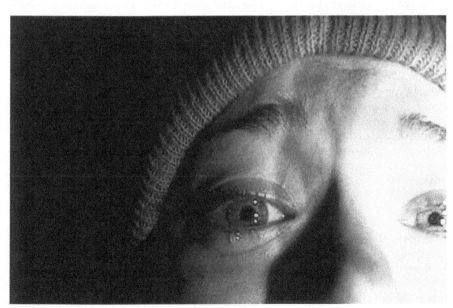

Fig. 18-1
***Heather Donahue in* The Blair Witch Project.**

the original version). Then it made even more on video and internationally. Artisan had expenses acquiring the film as well as polishing, printing, and advertising it, so Artisan may have made only about 20 to 50 times its investment, but any profit that starts at 2,000 percent is welcome. If *Blair Witch* stands out as one of the most profitable films of all time in relation to its cost, it is also remarkable for making its cheapest aspects—video, handmade props, and one-take rough framing—the most compelling.

Independent filmmakers who felt strongly about what they made could make pick-up deals with studios when the film was completed, on a take-it-or-leave-it basis, refusing to make cuts, but it was more common for them simply to deal with smaller releasing companies or independent distributors. Many other independent filmmakers struck co-financing deals with studios, instantly raising much of the production money they needed, gaining prestige, validating the payroll, and getting rid of the worry of finding a distributor in one fell swoop. Or they let the studio finance the project completely and more or less take over. The biggest problem independent artists found in working with studios on a creative level was that once they had sold their scripts or seen their productions become studio productions—subtly or grossly, the studio made its own version of the film, not theirs. It was often said that the only way to keep a good script from being rewritten was not to sell it.

Executive Decisions

The most frustrating pre-production experience any writer, producer, or director underwent at the hands of post-1970 studios was called "development hell," a good description of the years one might spend waiting for a studio to make up its mind to produce a project, ordering rewrites and other substantial but tentative revisions in the meantime—until one found that the project had been put in *turnaround*, offered to any other studio that might want it in exchange for reimbursement of the project's cost so far . . . where the cycle of indecision could begin again.

Yet the studios needed these outsiders—the writers, who gave them ideas, and the independents, who gave them films. If Hollywood demonstrated anything at the end of the 20th century, it was a hunger for ideas; it didn't

seem to know what to make. It wanted the lucid and the unexpected, material with a twist, a hook, a spin—in short, the simple–complex and the bold–subtle. Most consistently, Hollywood wanted the new–old. It wanted sequels to documented hits (*The Godfather Part III*); it wanted updated remakes of classics (*Cape Fear*) and Americanized remakes of overseas hits (*3 Men and a Baby*); it wanted revitalized genres (*Body Heat* and the "new *noir*"). The art of the sequel is one of *repetition with variation* (the *Godfather* films are quite different from one another, but each of them has near its start a ceremony that is both familial and religious, and each climaxes with a montage of murders), and the same can be said of the remake, the genre revival, and—according to conservative Hollywood—the aesthetics of the sure-fire investment. "Do it again, but differently," executives demanded, looking for a film idea that would "grab them" and thus, they assumed, would interest an audience.

The art most anxiously but consistently pursued by producers and agents in this period, whether or not they were also executives, was that of putting creative people together to work on viable projects. In many respects, the package was the movie. Entertainment lawyers made fortunes. Cinematography, sound, editing, and other cinematic matters were rarely considered; to hire a director was to indicate a preference for a certain style and pace. Since the agents and executives saw movies simply as stories acted out by stars in a repeatable medium, it was enough for them to determine the story, the stars, and the director, which were not only the key elements of the film as they saw it, but also the basis of its marketing campaign. And if overseas and video markets were willing to commit to this film, and if Chrysler wanted to donate all the cars for the chase scenes, so much the better. Even if the executives couldn't quite envision the movie they were approving, they could see the deal and knew precisely how to evaluate it.

Theatres

The conditions of film exhibition changed drastically in the course of the 1980s. Thanks to Dolby Stereo, theatres with optical sound projectors could present movies in four-channel stereo (before, stereo required a magnetic sound projector). The theatrical sound experience became more important, and sound editing and mixing became far more sophisticated than ever before, both technically and aesthetically.

The battle of the aspect ratios, which began with the wide-screen revolution of the 1950s, was settled in favor of two formats: American widescreen, a flat (nonanamorphic) format with an aspect ratio of 1.85 to 1 (written 1.85:1, it means that the screen is 1.85 times as wide as it is high), and Panavision, a scope (anamorphic) format with an aspect ratio of 2.35:1, later 2.4:1. (Early in the 1970s, Panavision widened its anamorphic aspect ratio to 2.4:1, while other scope films continued to be shot at 2.35:1. See "Aspect ratio" in the glossary. Also note that in Europe, flat widescreen is 1.66:1.) In the 1990s and 2000s, with the rise of high-definition television (HDTV), 16:9 or 1.78:1, also written 16×9, emerged as a film as well as a TV format.

The first 18-screen theatre was built in Toronto in 1979; it was conceived by veteran exhibitor Nathan A. Taylor, who together with Garth Drabinsky founded Canada's Cineplex Odeon Group. The *cineplex* (or *multiplex cinema*), now found in most cities, standing alone or in shopping malls, houses at least four—usually six or more—small theatres, each an auditorium with a big sound system and a relatively small screen. In the 1980s, virtually no new theatres were built except multiplexes, and that trend has continued into the 2000s. Many drive-ins and revival houses closed; by the early 2000s, very few were left. Some older theatres were upgraded to show the new spectacles, but many were partitioned, making way for two or three additional screens. The new exhibition spaces were smaller, but they were easier to fill than the cavernous single-screen theatres that had been built in times when far more people went to the movies.

A 1990 study found that only 25 percent of Americans went to more than five films a year. Between 1980 and 1994, the number of professional movie projectionists in America dropped 26 percent. The price of admission crept ever higher. By 1990, most theatres were not allowed to sell tickets for less than $5 except at bargain matinees. In 2009, the usual price of a big-city ticket was $10 or more. To take a family to the movies became an expensive proposition. The big films with big soundtracks were, audiences judged, worth seeing and hearing in big

theatres—or in a multiplex, even with the sound turned down so it wouldn't be heard in the other theatres, because even if the screen was small, what one saw on it was a *movie*, not a video.

In the 1980s and 1990s, audiences saw motion pictures in big theatres with state-of-the-art projection and sound equipment, in multiple-screen theatres with their many selections, in the older single-screen theatres that kept alive the "ordinary" moviegoing experience, or at home. Trading quality for convenience and economy, a family could rent a video of a recent movie, watch it on TV, and save $20 or $30. At that rate, a videocassette recorder–player (VCR) could pay for itself with a few skipped movies. By the early 2000s, when there were more DVD players than VCRs and a movie could be *bought* for the price of two or three tickets (let alone rented for far less than any single admission—and conveniently received through the mail from a company like Netflix or downloaded from the Internet), people chose to watch a movie at home far more often than in a theatre.

The growing cost of moviegoing made audiences more choosy. Since the 1960s they had been going to "a movie" rather than "the movies," but now they were going to a movie only when they felt confident they would enjoy it. In particular, audiences proved willing to pay to see sequels, new versions of movies they had already seen and knew they liked.

Studio Shakeups

The drama of buying, selling, merging, and taking over studios reached a historic climax in the late 1980s when Columbia and Universal were bought by Japanese companies and Warner Bros. merged with Time Inc. Movie companies had long been corporately linked with the publishing and recording companies that had, like them, been absorbed by conglomerates. Now the conglomerates renamed themselves "communications" enterprises and flung their nets of information and entertainment across the globe. Time, which owned several publishing and recording companies as well as Home Box Office (HBO, which showed new movies on cable), merged with Warner Bros. Communications in 1989 to form Time Warner, the world's largest communications conglomerate; in 1996, they acquired Turner Broadcasting in a merger. Time

Warner also founded a TV network and went on to acquire and develop the country's second-largest system of cable lines (after AT&T). In 2000, Time Warner and the Internet service provider America Online (AOL) announced a merger—really a takeover in which AOL acquired Time Warner; the deal creating AOL Time Warner was approved in 2001. Now the Internet was part of the conglomerate's package. With the improvement of broadband technology, it became possible to download or stream a digital copy of a movie (versions suitable for saving onto a DVD could be sent across the Internet by 2001). AOL Time Warner had a mammoth base of subscribers (from AOL to *Sports Illustrated*) and the cables to deliver, with the high-speed technologies of the future, digitized content not just from the Turner stations but from Warner Bros., New Line, and the other studios that had become part of Time Warner. Beyond being the largest company, it was the one that appeared most prepared for a digital future; however, AOL was dial-up and remained so for too long. Another media colossus had been created in 1994, when Viacom Inc., as previously mentioned, completed its acquisition of Paramount, making it possible to send *Star Trek* to audiences in almost any conceivable form. The Walt Disney Company stayed Disney—and eventually bought ABC.

But the other four majors were acquired by foreign companies. In 1985, 20th Century–Fox was bought by Rupert Murdoch's News Corporation, which was based in Australia; in the process Fox dropped its dash. Within a few years, the television arm of Fox had launched its own broadcasting network. In 1990, Fox sold its DeLuxe Laboratories to Britain's Rank Organisation, leaving no Hollywood studio with its own film processing and printing facilities, as hard as that is to believe; it's as if a professional 35mm photographer had no darkroom. As previously discussed, MGM was bought and sold all around the world, ending up in 1996 where it started, in California, as part of MGM/UA, and not owned or controlled by any other company. (A decade later, however, it was purchased by Sony and Comcast.) Columbia, which had merged with TriStar early in 1989, signed a merger agreement with Sony late in the year, and Columbia Pictures Entertainment became a Sony company—as did CBS Records soon after; now Columbia and

TriStar were listed under Sony. Finally, in 1990, Matsushita Electric Industrial Co. Ltd. bought MCA Inc., the parent company of Universal as well as of many recording companies, a TV division, and a publisher. Matsushita also owned Panasonic, Quasar, and Technics, which manufactured stereo and video equipment. When Columbia and Universal passed into Japanese hands, the new owners made it clear that they did not want to influence or supervise the studios' filmmaking activities. Their primary interest was the *software* for their hardware: the music for their CDs and CD players, the movies for their videocassettes and VCRs, laserdiscs and laser players (and after them the DVDs and DVD players, followed by the BDs—Blu-ray Discs—and BD players), monitors and TV sets—much as Time and HBO needed movies for their video and cable operations. (As if to confirm this, Columbia Pictures Entertainment, Sony Music Entertainment, and Sony Electronic Publishing became the Sony Software Corporation in 1991.) Magazines, books, records, tapes, data, movies—all had become information to be partially or entirely generated, stored, manipulated, formatted, sent, and retrieved electronically, on machines the majority of which were made in Japan or depended on Asian components. Sony, the inventor of Betamax (the first popular VCR and its half-inch video format), and Matsushita, its archrival and one of the chief developers of VHS (the competing format that took over the half-inch video market), now had studios to supply them with new films and old, grist for the mills of video.

But in 1995 Matsushita got out of the film and music business and sold MCA to the Seagram Company; it did not, however, get out of the video business. In 2000, Seagram merged with Vivendi (a French company with extensive holdings in publishing, advertising, and waste management) and Canal Plus (or Canal+, which has a film production entity—Studio Canal—and the largest pay-TV channel in France); the core of the deal was the sale of MCA, with all its music holdings as well as Universal Studios, to Vivendi. In 2001, Seagram bowed out, and the resulting company was named Vivendi Universal. So at the turn of the millennium, this is how it stood: the huge Disney, the new DreamWorks, the new Pixar, and the small MGM were self-owned; Columbia and TriStar were part of Sony; Fox was part of News Corp.;

Paramount was part of Viacom; RKO was long gone; Universal was part of Vivendi Universal; and Warner Bros. was part of AOL Time Warner.

In 2003, when America Online had become less powerful and was no longer seen as the key to the integrated digital future, AOL Time Warner changed its name back to Time Warner. As the MPAA listed them early in 2004, the seven *majors*—the major producers and distributors of movies in the U.S. at the time—were Buena Vista Pictures Distribution (The Walt Disney Company), Metro–Goldwyn–Mayer Studios, Paramount Pictures Corporation, Sony Pictures Entertainment (its status as a major continuing Columbia's), 20th Century Fox Film Corporation, Universal City Studios, and Warner Bros. Entertainment. But by the end of 2004, even if the studios still had those names, things had changed: Universal was no longer controlled by Vivendi, and a group of investors led by Sony and Comcast had put in a bid, accepted in September, to buy MGM and UA; that purchase was completed in 2005. In 2006, Disney bought Pixar. Also in 2006, Paramount completed its acquisition of DreamWorks, but that didn't work out, and in 2009, DreamWorks became relatively independent again and began to distribute its films through Universal, with DreamWorks Animation continuing to release through Paramount. In 2008, some of the studios closed or drastically reduced the size of the arms of their companies that had reached out to independents and had pursued relatively unusual ("specialty") projects, such as Picturehouse and WIP (Warner Independent Pictures) at Warner Bros., both of which were closed; that same year, New Line Cinema, once an important independent production company and then an active part of Warner Bros., became no more than a brand name at that studio. Finally, in 2009, Time Warner—which had spun off Time Warner Cable earlier in the year—went through the equivalent of a corporate divorce from AOL; they became separate companies, leaving Time Warner free to concentrate on creating media content.

NBC Universal was formed in May 2004. According to the deal, announced in 2003, Vivendi owned 20 percent of the new company, and General Electric—the parent company of NBC—owned 80 percent. Once again, a movie studio and a TV network had come together as parts of a gigantic business entity. It is ironic and significant that one of the two companies that had gone into the forming of General Electric in 1892 had been Edison General Electric. Thus GE's buying Universal might be thought of as the return of the Wizard in the age of the media conglomerate. A company descended from Edison now controlled Universal, one of the original Independents. Edison's spirit would be glad, no doubt, to be at the head of a media revolution based on the electronic storage and transmission of data, running a company with a global reach. But late in 2009, GE announced plans to acquire Vivendi's share in the conglomerate and then sell a controlling interest in NBC Universal to Comcast.

Movies in the Age of Video

From the late 1970s to the present, video has played important roles in the production and consumption of feature films.

In the 1950s and 1960s, television was at first the chief competitor and then the partner of the film industry. First demonstrated in the 1920s and improved throughout the 1930s, TV became a consumer item in the 1940s. As a broadcasting medium, it began as an inexpensive alternative to the cinema and a revolutionary upgrading of radio. By the 1950s, when TV's visual quality had improved enough to represent a threat, the movies were deliberately doing things TV couldn't do—be in color, in 3-D, in CinemaScope, in stereo—and TV was doing what movies couldn't do: present events as they unfolded, live rather than canned, with no admission charge. However, the TV industry soon found that it needed old movies and newly filmed programs to keep its schedules full and to attract more viewers. Movie companies found that they could make money from licensing the broadcasting rights to old films and could keep their facilities busy filming TV shows and, eventually, TV movies. Some studios even established TV divisions. From then on, the relationship between the film and TV companies became close and mutually beneficial, even if they remained official rivals.

In the late 1960s and 1970s, when a great many homes were first wired to receive cable TV and when color TV replaced black and white, the studios found themselves with two actively competitive and lucrative markets for their classics and their new color features—network TV (which is broadcast) and cable TV (which is a restricted-access system that can also transmit data and phone calls), soon to be followed by satellite TV. At the same time, public TV stations became the chief subsidizers of independent documentary filmmaking. Typically, studios and independents licensed their new features to be shown first on cable and then on network TV, obtaining some of the production money they needed by pledging these exhibition rights. Breaking new ground, Soderbergh financed *sex, lies, and videotape* almost entirely by selling the video rights to the as-yet-unshot film to RCA/Columbia Home Video.

Video (closed-circuit television) entered the consumer market in the mid-1970s and became a fact of life in the 1980s. The term includes both analog and digital video, and it refers most often to an electronic audiovisual work—or an electronic copy of an audiovisual work created in another medium, such as film—that can be stored on a tape, a disc, a hard drive, or another magnetic or optical device; in its original definition, "video" indicated that the work was designed to be seen on a television, but high-definition digital video (HDDV) is an important part of the digital cinema, which can be shown on a movie screen, and so the key to the definition remains that the storage and retrieval of the audiovisual material are electronic. By 1994, more than 85 percent of the American homes that had TVs also had VCRs. By then it was typical for a new film to be released first to domestic theatres, then to foreign theatres, then to video manufacturers and outlets, then to cable, then to 16mm distributors (a step often skipped), and then to network TV. In some cases, video distribution became as important to the studio as theatrical exhibition (in the U.S. and abroad, because every country that had TVs had VCRs and now has DVD players). If a film was not expected to do well, it might be released "direct to video" without appearing in theatres at all. In addition to using video as a dumping ground for films that died in theatres or were considered too expensive—in relation to expected revenue—to advertise for theatrical

exhibition (like *Slumdog Millionaire*, which was almost released direct to video because it wasn't expected to find a big audience), the film companies found that the sale of video copies of hit films could realize tremendous amounts of money. Disney's *Lady and the Tramp* (1955) made $50 million in theatres—counting its first release and all revivals—but it made $90 million on video. (Film companies made their money not when video copies were rented but when they were sold to rental outlets and to individuals—and, of course, when the duplication rights were first sold to the video companies.) Even movies with smaller followings were profitable to re-release on video; 50,000 devotees would not be enough to pay for a nationwide theatrical run, since 50,000 is not many tickets to sell, but it is a lot of cassettes and discs.

There used to be very few ways to see an old movie—not just a 1930s or 1940s movie, but any movie that was no longer playing in theatres. Films were released, played for a few weeks or months, then faded into memory. With luck, an old film might show up in 35mm at a revival house or in 16mm on a college campus. If for some reason one needed to see a particular film and couldn't wait for it to happen to show up in a theatre, on late-night TV, or in a film series, one would have to rent it in 16mm (if the film was in nontheatrical distribution and could be found in catalogs), buy it, find it in a collection, watch it at the Library of Congress, or ask a studio to get a copy out of its archive for a very expensive private screening. Then, in August 1976, the first prerecorded videocassettes were offered for sale.

Tape and Videotape

Videotape recording was conceived by a Russian scientist, Boris Rtcheouloff, in 1922; he was awarded a Soviet patent in 1927 but never built any instrument, let alone the tape to run through it. Videotape was invented in America in the early 1950s, and the video recorder with it.

In 1950, engineer Jack Mullin suggested to singer Bing Crosby, who was tired of broadcasting one show for the Eastern time zone and then, three hours later, another for the Pacific, that he could invent a "magnetic TV recorder." The technology would allow Crosby to time-shift on TV (to *time-shift* is to air a program at a different time than it was first broadcast, usually on the same day), doing the first show live, then playing a recording of the live show as the second show, just as Mullin's earlier use of *magnetic tape recording*—also called *audiotape recording*—had allowed Crosby to time-shift on radio.

The magnetic recording of sound (*audio*) on tape, from which videotape recording grew, had been invented in Germany and, as the Magnetophone, was first demonstrated in 1935. The wire recorder, which magnetized a silvery wire rather than a flat plastic tape, was invented in 1939 by an American named Marvin Camras. The Nazis began using the Magnetophone to delay or repeat radio programs in 1941, and Mullin—who brought a Magnetophone and some tapes home from the war—was one of the Americans who, like others around the world, replicated and perfected magnetic tape recording after World War II. The Ampex Corporation produced the first U.S.-made tape recorder in 1948. It was an analog recorder, like all the first audio and video recorders. In a development that would have huge implications, tape was first used to store data in 1951. Out of that came digital computer tape and the hard drive as well as *digital videotape* (DV; introduced by both Sony and Matsushita in 1995), which stores pictures and sounds as electronic zeros and ones. These terms require a digression.

Analog and Digital Information

Analog information is continuous, like a sound wave, with differences signaled by having more or less of something. *Digital* information is discrete, usually in the form of binary numbers, intermittent electronic pulses, or linguistic units that signify in "yes" or "no" terms rather than in "more" or "less" terms. To take a linguistic example of digital information, the presence or absence of the phoneme *b* distinguishes *block* from *lock*; it is either in the word or not. The digital world is binary, offering a choice between polar alternatives: on or off, yes or no, present or absent. An electronic switch can be open or closed. In the electronic and mathematical language of computers, a *one* (the equivalent of "yes" or "on") opens a switch, letting current flow through it as if through a sluice, and a *zero* ("no" or "off") closes it, stopping the flow. A character—say, "T"—can be stored as a *byte* of information, a unit consisting of 8 adjacent bits

that are processed together. Each *bit* (a contraction of "binary digit") is a minimal unit of information—or the memory needed to store it—in the form of a zero or a one. A binary number such as 10101101 could be an 8-bit byte recognized by a computer as a particular letter—or as the amount of red in a colored dot in a picture. A kilobyte (KB) is 2^{10} or 1,024 bytes; a megabyte (MB) is 2^{20} or 1,048,576 bytes; and a gigabyte (GB) is 2^{30} or 1,073,741,824 bytes, which is 1,024 MB or about a billion bytes. A megabit (abbreviated Mb) is 2^{20} bits.

Sampling and Conversion

What in analog might be a gradual curve would, if it was converted to digital information, be a staircase. The more steps there are, and the tinier and closer together they are, the more the staircase in this example will resemble a single curved line—that is, the more closely the digital version will sound or look like the analog original. The size and closeness of the steps depends on how often and at what level of detail the source—in this case, the curve—is checked. The curve's continuously changing shape is expressed in terms of its height or amplitude now, and now, and now, on the equivalent of a graph. (A curved line that goes up and down as time advances can be called a *wave* and plotted on a graph whose horizontal axis is time and whose vertical axis is the wave's amplitude, perhaps the volume of a sound.) This process of regularly dipping into an analog flow—or anything that can be represented as a waveform—to measure its position or value at the moment is called *sampling*. Sampling has to be done at absolutely regular intervals, thousands of times per second.

The difference between the highest and lowest frequencies of a signal is its *bandwidth*. A sound signal with greater bandwidth can reproduce more pitches with more clarity than can a narrow-bandwidth signal because it sends a greater range of data in the same amount of time and doesn't have to chop off the highest and lowest frequencies or levels. A video signal's bandwidth is invariable for a given system, such as conventional American TV broadcasting, and determines many of its properties.

Sampling is the first stage in *analog-to-digital conversion*. The changes that happen between samplings are not recorded. Assuming that samples of a curve can represent the whole curve is an application of theories of probability and statistics, and it depends on the further assumption that the curve or waveform will vary only within a predictable range. Each discrete sample is expressed in digital form at a specified level of complexity (*digitized*) and then is stored as a step in the digital staircase that is the encoded curve (that is, put into the digital *code* of zeros and ones). In the case of a frame, what is sampled is a picture whose light values have been translated into voltage. A device called a *telecine* converts a film image into a video signal and then digitizes it; it also synchronizes frame rates between film and video, using a process called *3:2 pulldown* to turn 24 film frames into 30 video frames (60 fields, with some film frames shown in two fields and some in three). Other devices may be used to digitize film or video, and still others are used to digitize sound. Sampling resembles a movie camera's regularly shooting discrete frames that show unmoving parts of a continuous motion.

The number of samples gathered per second is the *sampling rate* or *sampling frequency*. The number of bits in a sample is its *bit depth* or *sampling resolution*, which determines its complexity—that is, how many levels of detail the sample has. Sampling at an 8-bit depth gathers 8 bits per sample. The more bits are in each sample, the more information about the image can be sent per second. The speed—in megabits per second—at which the bits in the digitized samples can be sent over a connection (for example, from a telecine to a computer's memory—or from a DVD to a DVD player) is the *bit rate*. A good DVD has an average bit rate of about 7 Mb/sec and a good BD about 5 times that.

One bit can store 2 levels of information (0 or 1), and then the number goes up by powers of 2, so that 3 bits can store 8 levels (2^3), 4 bits can store 16 levels (2^4), 8 bits can store 256 levels (2^8); and 12 bits can store 4,096 levels (2^{12}); it takes n bits to store 2^n levels. If all color were reduced to 2 levels, one could choose between black and white. In 8 bits, one can specify a number from 0 to 255, one black-and-white shade on a 256-level gray scale (with the lowest level 0 and the highest 255), and so on. With 256 levels for each of the red, green, and blue component colors—abbreviated R, G, and B—that create the brightness and color of a

dot (actually a pixel, defined later) in a positive electronic image, a good video can show 16.8 million colors, the same number displayed by the monitor of a computer set to 24-bit color (in the terms above, 8-bit color, which has three 8-bit samples—for R, G, and B). Film, however, can display over 800 million colors. Where 8-bit sampling might capture the color "dark blue," 10- or 12-bit sampling might more accurately recognize and capture "lapis." If the bit rate is too low or the bandwidth too narrow, so that there is not enough information to produce a properly resolved image (with not enough data gathered in the first place or not enough received per second), a sharp image goes soft, and a diagonal line or a curve develops *jaggies* (little step-shapes) and truly looks like a staircase or a pile of boxes; similarly, a color becomes approximate and a sound tinny. If one listens to a CD very slowly, one can hear the steps: little abrupt changes and bumps instead of the perfectly flowing sound a full-speed CD imitates. Analog information is not just continuous, but made of infinitesimal changes; the steps or samples could never be too detailed or too numerous. All of these computer terms have become part of the lexicon of video and of digital cinema, even if audio and video recording began as analog systems.

Videotape Recorders

Thanks to Mullin's work, Bing Crosby Enterprises demonstrated the first *videotape recorder* (VTR) in 1951, the same year that Charles P. Ginsburg, leading a team at Ampex that included Ray Dolby—later the founder of Dolby Stereo—began work on a system that would be more reliable, produce a better image, and run more slowly instead of using an impractical amount of tape. In competition with Ampex, RCA Labs demonstrated Vladimir Zworykin's huge VTR in 1953.

In 1955, Ampex developed a videotape informally referred to as "rust scrapings on Scotch tape," and in 1956, Ampex marketed Ginsburg's fully realized video recorder, the first practical VTR, the Ampex VR-1000. Its heads spun while its 2-inch tape moved relatively slowly, solving the speed, frequency, and quality problems that had plagued other systems. It was meant to be used in a studio and, like the RCA machine, was too big to use anywhere else. The Ampex machines were put into use by TV stations as early as 1956, which is when CBS first time-shifted a news program. The rapid acceptance of this particular machine by stations and producers marked the start of the Video Era and changed TV forever. Along with live shows, movies, and filmed shows, TV now offered taped shows. TV, the live medium, became something that could be edited, and soon less live material was aired.

The first practical color VTR was developed after Ampex and RCA pooled their patents for that purpose in 1957. When portable VTRs were invented in the 1960s, more and more news events were shot on video, not on 16mm. "Canned"—as opposed to live—TV shows continued to be shot on video or on film for decades, though by the early 21st century most were shot on digital video. In the late 1960s and 1970s, portable VTRs that used reel-to-reel tape were widely used not only by TV news crews, but also by traveling activists who brought material the official media ignored ("the video underground") and by video artists.

Ampex developed a mobile VTR in 1959, but the future of the portable VTR belonged to Sony. Founded in Tokyo in 1946 by Masaru Ibuka and Akio Morita, the Sony Corporation specialized in applying advanced technology to consumer electronics, an emphasis evident in the home tape recorder it marketed in 1950, the transistor radio it invented in 1955, and the later products—including the CD player, CD-ROM, and DVD—that Sony invented in collaboration with Philips and other companies. After seeing the Toshiba Corporation's 1959 prototype of a *helical-scan* VTR—whose tape path, widely imitated, wound the tape tightly around a magnetic head in a helix, from a low feed reel to a higher take-up reel, for greater quality and efficiency—Sony began working on its own helical-scan machines, and so did JVC (the Victor Company of Japan, bought by Matsushita in 1953; the latter had been founded in 1918). In 1961, JVC demonstrated the first helical-scan color VTR. Also in 1961, Sony demonstrated a VTR that was the world's small-est yet. It used reel-to-reel tape and was designed for use in industry, education, the arts, and sports; the next year it was transistorized. In 1965, Sony marketed the world's first VTR for home use, and a color version followed in 1966.

Sony offered the world's first truly portable VTR in 1967.

Cassettes and Discs

But it was not until Sony invented the *video-cassette*—which kept videotape prethreaded in a plastic case, as audiocassettes did, rather than on open reels—that it revolutionized video recording and playback, not only in the home, but also for film and TV professionals. Sony's U-Matic cartridge, invented in 1971, used ¾-inch tape that recorded for one hour. Sony introduced the consumer *videocassette recorder* (VCR) in 1975; it used ½-inch tape and was called the Betamax. The Beta format proved to be convenient and of high quality. A year later, JVC introduced the VHS (Video Home System) format, which also housed ½-inch tape in a cassette but could record for a longer time and produced a relatively inferior image. Both VHS and Beta were color systems. RCA joined Matsushita, whose brand names included Panasonic and JVC, in the development of VHS tapes and VCRs.

The VHS format proved more popular than Beta and eventually replaced it in the home market (following the "format wars" of the 1980s). It first became widely available in the United States in 1977—the same year that 20th Century–Fox, sensing a trend, licensed Magnetic Video to sell its films on videocassette.

From 1976 to 1984, Sony was in court, accused—primarily by Disney—of encouraging copyright infringement on a massive scale by facilitating the home recording of TV programs and particularly of movies. The Supreme Court finally ruled that home taping was a legal technology as long as the copies were only for personal use. That 1984 decision made it legal for people to build their own collections of video copies of films, taping them off the air for purposes of entertainment and reference. (Buying legally prerecorded cassettes never posed copyright problems.) It was also in 1984 that Woody Allen's *Manhattan* was released on video, at his insistence, in what became known as the *letterbox* format: the complete, original wide-screen image, with black bars above and below, as if one were looking through the rectangular door of a mailbox. As VCRs were improved, so that later models could scan and locate images rapidly, record and play back in stereo, and display a single frame for several minutes, they became very useful tools for the study of motion pictures.

Even more versatile and useful was the *laserdisc* player, developed throughout the 1970s by Philips (in the Netherlands) and MCA—with both companies apparently building on the "optical disc" technology first patented in 1967 by American inventor David Gregg—and finally put on the market in 1978. Its single-frame display (on the standard-play or CAV discs) was perfectly steady, and the visual quality of the laserdisc image far surpassed anything possible with tape, as did the theatrical quality of its sound (the laserdisc is the ancestor of the compact disc or *CD*, introduced in 1982). Even an extended-play or CLV laserdisc could display single frames, though not as well as a CAV disc. A competing product, the grooved videodisc, came and went in the early 1980s. The laserdisc's fatal competition in the late 1990s was the *DVD* (which doesn't stand for anything, because its creators couldn't decide between *digital video disc* and *digital versatile disc*). The first laserdisc of a movie, marketed in December 1978, was MCA DiscoVision's *Jaws*, a three-disc boxed set. Two of the very last were *The Matrix* and *Enemy of the State* in 1999. Blu-ray, introduced in 2006, won its own format war (with HD DVD) and took over the high-definition disc market in 2007, without making the DVD obsolete. As optical discs, the laserdisc, CD, DVD, and BD were not magnetic media; they could be stamped out like phonograph records, whereas videotapes had to be recorded in real time—which cost more. (Floppy disks, computer tape, and hard drives or hard disks are magnetic. Magnetic disks are spelled with a *k*, optical discs with a *c*.)

DVDs

The DVD went on sale in Japan in 1996 and in the United States in 1997. By 2000, it had made the laserdisc obsolete, and DVD players were outselling VCRs. In the United States, the discs began to outsell prerecorded videos in 2002; the next year, more DVDs than tapes were rented. In the first six months of 2004, Americans spent 84 percent of their video budgets renting and buying DVDs—a record $10.7 billion, more than the film industry had collected at the U.S. box

office in all of 2003. In 2006, Americans and Canadians spent $9.13 billion at the box office, $7.39 billion to rent DVDs, and $15.65 billion to buy DVDs; VHS sales were negligible, and that same year the major studios announced that they would no longer release movies on VHS. Because of their high storage capacity, which began at 4.38 GB per side, soon nearly doubled, and would increase to 25 GB per side on a BD, DVDs could offer movies in an interactive format with a choice of versions and a full complement of background material.

Consumers enjoyed the DVD's visual quality and digital sound, which were much better than the picture and sound on a VHS tape; the DVD's instantaneous random access, which was inspired by the laserdisc and impossible with film or tape; and the supplemental materials with which DVDs were crammed, which built on the practice of the laserdisc but included more material. DVDs could include trailers, deleted scenes, interviews, detailed "making-of" documentaries and interactive demonstrations, other relevant films such as shorts by the filmmakers or newsreels, and more. DVDs also had subtitles that could be in different languages or could be turned off (film and all earlier video formats had had either one set of subtitles or none) as well as dubbed and original soundtracks. Some DVDs included both full-screen and wide-screen versions. Some offered a "director's cut" made before or after the film was released, a version that might differ significantly from the one shown in theatres. Some had running scene-by-scene and shot-by-shot commentaries by film scholars, and the majority had at least one running commentary track made by the filmmakers or constructed from interviews with them. A commentary could be turned off as easily as a particular sound format could be selected. Some older films were accompanied by the original soundtrack on one channel and a new digital stereo mix on another. Many DVDs also had programs, games, and links that were accessible when the disc was played on a computer; for example, the screenplay or score might be displayed along with the movie.

Because DVDs were digital, their data could be compressed, and because they were the size of a CD, the data had to be compressed, usually by a factor of 30 or more. (It was also possible to start with less data to compress in the first place—by gathering less information about each frame when it was digitized—but the image always suffered.) In the most common method of compression used for DVDs (the MPEG-2 compression scheme; the compression schemes used for Blu-ray Discs were different, but they worked according to the same basic principles), parts of the image that, in the computer software's view, did not change from frame to frame—perhaps the sky, a wall, or a range of mountains—could become image fragments repeated for each affected frame. This method saved storage space but usually left only one of every 12 frames in the form of a complete picture with full image data (an *intra frame*, also called an *I-frame* or *key frame*). The other frames were approximated by a computer when the image was compressed, with the average frame represented only in terms of its differences from the previous frame (a *predicted frame* or *difference frame*, called a *P-frame*). The changes from the last I-frame accumulated until they became too drastic and a new I-frame was required. A frame might also be a calculated approximation based on information in the frames before and after it (a *bidirectional frame* or *B-frame*); the assumption underlying a B-frame was that changes between frames followed a regular pattern. So most DVDs could not—unlike standard-play laserdiscs—precisely access and completely display, with full detail and resolution, any frame one desired; instead, they would show that frame or a nearby one as fully as possible. But there were exceptions. When The Criterion Collection made a DVD set of Stan Brakhage's films, *by Brakhage* (2003), they made every effort to ensure that the integrity of every one of Brakhage's frames was maintained in single-frame and extreme-slow-motion viewing. This required minimal compression and more I-frames than usual—as well as a respect for Brakhage's aesthetics of editing and color that determined the best possible compression scheme—because in many of his films, each frame is completely different from the others. True frame-by-frame viewing of a movie was possible on DVD, but few DVD publishers were willing to commit the extra time, care, bits, and money required.

In addition to compressing data, computer programs were used to clean up images after the frames had been digitized—removing dirt, filling in scratches, and so on. They were also used to get pops out of soundtracks. Sometimes, however, they automatically removed parts of the image they misread as imperfections—notoriously, a good number of the raindrops outside Susan's nightclub in the first DVD of *Citizen Kane*. To say the least, some DVDs gave more accurate frame information than others. But most of the makers and watchers of DVDs accepted the visual compromises involved in compression, because they made the small format and the extras possible.

Out of the Vaults

As a home-video format, DVD was strikingly different from tape in one respect: When introduced, it was only for playback. Although as rental items both tapes and DVDs were prerecorded and designed only to be played back, the first DVD players did not record, and every VCR did. One of the first appeals of the VCR had been that it allowed people to time-shift for themselves. They could record what they wanted and watch it when they wanted. They could erase it or keep it. They could skip commercials. Thus the VCR gave viewers control over the schedules and priorities of broadcast, cable, and satellite TV. So did its 21st-century offspring, the digital video recorder (DVR), though a DVR did not allow one to save a recording permanently.

In much the same way, renting or buying a video gave viewers control over both TV and theatrical movie programming—not just scheduling. No longer dependent on what the theatres happened to book or the stations happened to show, audiences could choose from a multitude of recent releases, nostalgia items, cult films, classics, favorites of all kinds that would never again play in theatres and might not even be shown on TV, subtitled movies, and even pornographic movies (video's first big hit). The picture was smaller than in a theatre, but there were advantages to being at home, including not having to hire a sitter, stand in line for a snack, or get to a theatre on time. Around the world, renting a movie to watch at home became one of the most common private and social pastimes, and seeing new movies on video became normal in cities—or countries—that could maintain only one or two 35mm theatres, if any.

In the video revolution, which by the end of the 20th century had completely changed people's access to movies, it was the rental outlet that first made available that great number and variety of pictures, movies that could be seen at will. People were able to see more old movies and more movies from around the world. In the rental and sales outlets taken as one big electronic *cinémathèque*, a great deal of film history—perhaps 10 percent of the world's surviving films—was in the video equivalent of "release" all at once. A brilliant video clerk like Tarantino could march into filmmaking with a staggering background, his years of watching films augmented by thousands of tapes and discs. Even though a movie's date of publication has almost always been its release date, it could be said that movies were *published on video* instead of being kept only on film, in archives and studio vaults, the way that paintings had been kept in museums and castles—until inexpensive, inferior copies had finally become widely available in the form of printed pictures. The cheap technology of video let ordinary people rent and buy movies. If one wanted to watch a particular film, getting a video copy of it became as simple as getting a book off the shelf of a personal or public library.

Home video also changed how people studied films. It became easy to examine a scene shot by shot, to capture a frame for printing, to check a detail, or to compare different versions of a picture (for example, the English- and Spanish-language versions of the 1931 *Dracula*, which had different casts and directors, or the original German and U.S. cuts of *The Blue Angel*). In many cases, descriptions and citations of films became more accurate, less dependent on memory. Of course, memories of films are interesting in themselves, but it was good to be able to be exact even when one didn't have access to a 16mm or 35mm print—when quoting dialogue, for instance, or analyzing a composition. The movies were out of the vaults.

Pixels and Lines

They were not exactly the movies, however. They were electronic copies. No video can truly reproduce a film image. The film frame contains far more information than all but the most advanced video frame. Film grain is finer than TV's dots and is not arranged in lines. Film colors are dyes.

To explain the fundamental ways in which film and video differ, one needs words like "pixel" and "scan."

A *pixel*, or picture element, is a single unit of an electronic image, one colored box or dot. Each pixel has red, green, and blue values that are sampled when the image is digitized, with at least 256 levels for each of the three component colors. (The component colors of a negative are yellow, cyan, and magenta.) Usually a pixel is a tiny square whose R, G, and B values (colors) have been mixed. By rough equivalence, the term can be applied to film, as if the frame were composed of—or could be broken down into—regular, minimal areas.

Pixels are lined up in rows that run horizontally across the frame. These rows are called *scan lines* because they were first drawn by an electron beam as it went back and forth across the screen of a cathode-ray tube (a conventional TV picture tube; in a CRT, both the electron gun and the phosphorescent screen, which glows briefly where the beam passes through a mask and hits it, are part of the same tube). The CRT is still in use, and though many displays employ other technologies, they still organize the image in lines. The lines can also be scanned onto other surfaces—for example, the raw stock in a *film recorder*, which uses a laser beam to scan onto film, one line at a time, a frame generated or modified by a computer. In a CRT and most scanning devices, the beam moves from left to right to left . . . and gradually downward, drawing horizontal lines until it reaches the bottom of the screen, when it is briefly shut off for a fast return trip to the top, where it begins to draw the next frame or set of lines.

A video camera or display has two kinds of *lines of resolution*: the stack of horizontal lines (the scan lines or *lines of vertical resolution*, sometimes simply called "lines") and, running perpendicular to them, the *pixel lines*, or *lines of horizontal resolution*, which are virtual vertical lines created by the pixels that are directly above and below one another. The number of pixel lines in a frame is the same as the number of pixels in a scan line. Each pixel in a line can also be called a *horizontal sample* of the image, because a pixel is *not* a one-for-one equivalent of the same area on the film, but a representation of an electronic sampling of that area. Pixel lines are responsible for a picture's horizontal resolution, scan lines for its vertical resolution. The number of piled-up scan lines gives the frame's height, while the number of pixels in each scan line gives its width. Multiplying the number of scan lines by the number of pixels in each line gives the frame's resolution and its area as the number of pixels in it, a figure that is usually expressed in megapixels (Mp; a *megapixel* is 1 million pixels) and that gives a general indication of image quality at a particular size. The information is tentative because the number of Mp does not indicate how much information has been supplied for each pixel (which depends on sampling and other matters), and it is related to the size of the display because a blown-up image does not have more pixels than the original; one needs more pixels for a larger image at the same level of detail. Enlarged too much, a video image becomes *pixelated*, clearly showing each pixel as a separate unit.

At the turn of the 21st century, worldwide, there were at least six primary TV systems, of which the most significant were NTSC, PAL, SECAM, and HDTV. The most common conventional systems were NTSC, used in the United States, Japan, etc.; PAL, used in China, most of Europe, etc.; and SECAM, used in France, Russia, etc. NTSC has 525 lines, each of which is 720 pixels wide, and it runs at approximately 30 fps (actually 29.97). The PAL and SECAM systems have 625 scan lines and run at 25 fps, differing only in their color technologies. The line numbers are complicated by the fact that not every line is displayed as part of the image. NTSC shows 480 *active lines* (lines with visual information) out of its 525, and PAL shows 576 of its 625. Some of the "inactive" lines are used for closed captioning, synchronization data, and *field blanking:* creating a blank interval between fields or frames that helps one to perceive apparent motion, as we saw in the discussion of visual masking in Chapter 2. Nor is every pixel in a line displayed; NTSC shows 640 of its 720.

Both PAL and NTSC have an *interlaced* image, which means that each frame is displayed in two successive fields. In an *interlace system*, which uses *interlaced scanning*, the even lines (one field) and the odd lines (the other) are drawn in separate batches as the tube is scanned by the electron beam. The brain combines the fields into a single frame. NTSC shows 60 fields per second; PAL shows 50. Computer monitors, most high-definition TVs, and many other devices use *progressive scanning*, in which the image is scanned onto the TV tube or display as a complete picture in a single pass. Where interlaced scanning would draw 50 or 60 fields per second, each consisting of every other line in a frame, progressive scanning would draw the same number of fields per second, but each field would contain all the lines in the frame. To the extent that it is seen whole, all at once, the progressive frame is comparable to a film frame. Because it shows each frame twice, the progressive system creates an effect similar to that of a two-bladed shutter, the kind used on many sound projectors to defeat flicker.

The types of scan are abbreviated i and p. With its 525 interlaced horizontal scan lines, NTSC can be described as 525i. The rest of this widely used means of describing a format is the number of fields per second, which makes NTSC 525i/60 and PAL 625i/50, but the i or p is not always included. In terms of the number of active scan lines, NTSC is 480i, and because only 640 pixels are visible in each NTSC scan line, the resolution of an NTSC image is 640×480 pixels.

High-definition television (HDTV, an advanced set of standards—incorporating Dolby Digital stereo—for digital television, or DTV), debuted in the late 1990s. In the early 2000s, HDTV offered several high-definition formats, including 720p, 1080p, and 1080i. The transitional standard-definition (SD) formats, which HDTV sets could also play, included 480p and 480i. HDTV was widescreen, with an aspect ratio usually referred to as 16×9 or 16:9 (1.78:1) as opposed to conventional TV's 4×3 (1.33:1). HDTV could letterbox some wide images to preserve their original shapes, or it could show them in its own 16×9, in which its programs and a growing number of movies were shot. On very large screens, interlaced scanning produced flicker, so most HDTV formats, such as 1080p, were progressive. The 1080p format called for 1,080 lines of 1,920 pixels (written 1920×1080—that is, 1,920 pixel lines by 1,080 scan lines), giving 2 Mp of information per frame. With HDTV, television became widescreen to come closer to the aspect ratios of most new movies. As film had led TV to be in color, it now led TV to be wide.

Film and Video Frames

The most advanced digital movie camera at the turn of the century, the *24p* or HDW-F900 invented by Sony in collaboration with Panavision, could shoot 2-Mp frames. As its name indicates, the 24p ran at 24 fps—to match film and to avoid the awkward conversion from 29.97 fps—and used progressive scanning to produce a more filmlike frame. (A later model is discussed in the next chapter.) But a newly printed frame of 35mm movie film, at the standard Academy-aperture size, has over *12.5 Mp* per frame—because it has the equivalent of *3,072 lines and 4,096 pixels*. (Since 1931, when it was adopted to make room for the soundtrack, *Academy aperture* has specified the dimensions of a full-sized frame on a 35mm print—0.868 × 0.631 inches, which is 25 percent smaller than the full frame that can be shot by a movie camera. Academy aperture actually has an aspect ratio of 1.375:1, but most filmmakers consider the difference negligible and refer to the Academy aperture aspect ratio—or the *Academy ratio*—as 1.33:1, the same as the aspect ratio of a true full frame. For more information, please look up these terms in the glossary.)

A frame whose horizontal lines have roughly 4,000 pixels is a "4K" image, where K is 1,000 pixel lines of resolution. The HDTV 1080p standard—with its 1,080 lines, each 1,920 pixels wide—gave a 2K image (1.92K is close enough; true 2K, the resolution shot by the first 24p camera, has 2,048 pixel lines), and so did Blu-ray. *High-definition digital video* (HDDV), shot on a high-resolution camera such as the 24p—or something less expensive—and with as few lines as 720, is informally called "high-def."

When watching a movie or a video, one deals not just with hard specifications but with *perceived resolution*, a focused image created by the brain from frames that, because the subjects were moving when photographed, are often blurred, much as the brain supplies motion to a series of stills. Most film prints have a literal resolution of 4K, in pixel terms, and a perceived resolution of 6K. The most advanced digital projection system contemplated in 2006 was 4K, with full sampling of R, G, and B values. 4K would be a big step up from the established (and still current) 1K and 2K systems; in tests it delivered a perceived resolution comparable to film.

Nevertheless, there is a big difference between a pixel and a grain of silver. Film is exposed at the molecular level, and there are millions of particles on a square inch of film, far more "dots" than there are in any video frame. Nor do molecules line up the way pixels do. The grain pattern—the shadows of the silver particles—is different in every frame, giving texture and a living quality to the movie-film image. (Of course, a compression program has to ignore these differences, or there would be no unchanging parts of any frame. "Grain" is added to many digital prints later.) A little galaxy of grain can define and color an area of film summarized as a pixel.

There is no fixed correlation between how many Ks an image is and how many megabytes are needed to store a digital version of it, because the information can be sampled in greater or lesser detail and because the sampled data can be compressed. An Academy-aperture film frame requires over 56 MB to store, uncompressed, and an NTSC frame takes just over 1 MB. Ideally, the film frame would be stored without compression to avoid any chance of software-introduced distortion, but the file or files containing an entire uncompressed movie would be immense; it makes one realize how much information film can store in the half a square inch of an Academy-aperture frame. To be perceived as "filmlike," an image requires a perceived resolution of 4K pixel lines or higher. To look good on a TV, even an HDTV, it needs much less.

Beyond the question of resolution and the fact that film can show many more colors than video are the issues of range and cropping. Video and film have different sensitivities; they differ markedly in their treatment of bright and dark areas, and some things that can be shot on film, like an extremely bright, unmoving light, could burn out a video camera or at least yield a poor image. (For a DV example, see the oil fire in *The Fast Runner*.) On the other hand, the only way Michael Mann felt he could capture the dark look of a city at night for his 2004 movie, *Collateral*, was to shoot most of the picture with a variant of the 24p on HDDV. Film can show more levels of brightness and contrast than can video, both in color and in black and white, and it can be exposed over a greater range; this usually gives the film image greater richness and detail.

Although video can show many colors, they are not film colors. Film colors are created chemically, TV colors electronically. Film colors are thrown on a screen as the projector's white light shines through the dyes on the film; TV colors emanate from the screen as glowing dots, which gives them an inevitable and uncinematic phosphorescence. (Actually it is inevitable only on a CRT. The best digital-projection systems avoid phosphorescence and electronic color by using microscopic mirrors to reflect the RGB values from a true white light onto the screen.)

When blown up to the size of a movie screen, the video image is relatively murky and subject to pixelation. Most people watch video on screens that are much smaller than those in theatres, so that a close-up does not have the impact—the sudden bigness—it would have in a theatre, and an extreme long shot may lose so much detail that it becomes unreadable. Keeping this in mind, many filmmakers have been shooting more close-ups than long shots, the way TV is shot.

Another way the video image is smaller is in terms of how much of the original is displayed. To stabilize the image electronically and to remove the possibility of an irregular outline, a TV tube usually "eats" the perimeter of any image. A viewer loses the whole rim of a 1.33:1 image and the left and right edges of a letterboxed image. This cropping can be overcome in advance by *windowboxing* the entire image—giving it a black perimeter on all four sides—or letterboxing at a width less than that of the display, but this is rarely done, perhaps because consumers prefer their screens to be as full as possible. The inner part of the cropped 1.33:1 image, the 95 percent or so of the frame that is displayed by a standard CRT and many other display systems, is called the *TV safe area*, and that rectangle is drawn or etched on the viewfinders of most studio cameras so that when the movies are shot in the first place, crucial actions can be kept within the purview of the tube.

When wide-screen films are copied for full-frame network broadcasting—or, scandalously, for release in 16mm—most of them are *panned and scanned* with an optical printer or its digital equivalent. In other words, only a 1.33:1 area of the image is recorded, and this image area is moved around to keep the "essential" action within the frame, sometimes by panning and sometimes by introducing cuts so that the action area can leap from one part of the frame to another. A Panavision film that is not letterboxed and also suffers the usual loss of perimeter is cropped so drastically that half the image is lost.

Fortunately, because most videos carry a film's original soundtrack, a movie *can* sound the same at home as it did in the theatre, if one has the right equipment.

While some of the differences between movies on film and movies on video depend on commercial practices and some on technical compromises, both of which are subject to change, the essential differences are significant. Whether one approaches the differences in terms of chemical and electronic colors, or how much data is in each frame, or how sampling and compression can affect a frame, or one's own responses, the fact is that movies on film and movies on video just don't look the same, and ultimately they provide different experiences.

Nevertheless, by the end of the 20th century, consumers had accepted videos as movies—or, to put it another way, they considered video close enough to film to serve as an adequate substitute. Most of the people who missed a movie in the theatre and then saw it on video felt they had seen the movie.

Theatres responded to the boom in home video by raising their prices, converting to surround sound and then digital sound, building multiplexes with larger auditoriums and screens, installing stadium seats, and hoping for pictures people would want to see right away and on a big screen. When a movie left the theatres, it stayed out of circulation as in earlier times and was hard to find on film. And that was when the video became available.

Changes on the Set

Film producers and studios responded to the Video Era in many ways. In the first place, they defined the "TV safe area." They set up optical printers to pan-and-scan movies for TV. They made money from licensing old and new movies for video—especially the old ones, which had stopped making money.

Very early on, the factories and labs noticed that consumers were buying and processing much less small-gauge movie film. Home movies were being shot on video. Portable VHS and Betamax cameras became available in 1982, and smaller units such as Kodak's integrated camera and recorder (*camcorder*) in 1984. When their prices went down—and with the introduction of DV in 1995 and the extremely convenient mini-DV shortly afterward—the home-movie business dropped film in favor of video, which didn't need to be processed and offered effortlessly synchronized sound. As the small-gauge market shrank, a number of film labs closed down, and the manufacturers made fewer kinds of film; 8mm black-and-white filmstock was the first to go.

The arts of film and TV had affected each other in the 1950s, making possible movies and teleplays that were well-written, efficiently directed, and powerfully acted. In the 1980s the greatest indication of their mutual influence was the *music video*, which built on the montage aesthetic as well as the tradition of the *Soundies* and other music shorts (films of singers, played in special jukeboxes and in theatres) while lending its own style—which, it was feared, decreased one's attention span—to filmmakers like Oliver Stone, whose *Natural Born Killers* intercut different film stocks and video at top speed.

Film producers and distributors began to pay more attention to the question of electronic rights, and soon a film's showings on cable (and satellite, the Internet, and phones and other mobile devices) and its video release were as important as its showings in theatres. Video director's cuts flourished.

On the set, one of the most important new devices was the *video tap* in a 35mm movie camera, which allowed what was filmed to be displayed on a monitor. The director often watched the video display—called *video assist*—instead of the set, to see how the action worked within the frame. The greatest boon to rehearsal was the video camera, which allowed actors and directors to work with a scene and evaluate it before shooting.

With the rise of DV and HDDV, many movies were shot on video and transferred to film for theatrical exhibition. Shooting film was expensive. Video was cheap and erasable, and a video camera could easily shoot for 45 straight minutes—a great aid to documentary filmmakers who were waiting for the right moment to happen—while film cameras almost never shot more than 20 minutes. For these reasons, most early-21st-century documentaries were shot on digital video.

The analog video in *The Blair Witch Project* looked like video, which was part of the movie's aesthetic: to mix 16mm and video footage, keeping track of which character was behind each camera. One of the first DV movies that looked as though it truly had been shot on film was a Dogme95 production, *The King is Alive* (2000, directed by Kristian Levring). Agnès Varda made her first use of mini-DV part of the subject of *The Gleaners and I* (2000); as in her work shot on film, the image was as sharp as the technology allowed. In 1999, four DV cameras shot four simultaneous feature-length takes for Mike Figgis's *Timecode* (2000), all of which were shown at once on the split screen, with characters moving from one screen to another as they walked, for example, from a car to an office. That movie could not have been made without video.

Together with the computer, video opened the doors to a new generation of independent filmmakers, because shooting on digital video reduced costs and often looked all right when the results were "filmed out" or put on film. That was the case with the first widely circulated Inuit movie, the legend of *Atanarjuat the Fast Runner* (or *The Fast Runner*, 2001, directed by Zacharias Kunuk), and with an American independent thriller, *Open Water* (2003, directed by Chris Kentis). *Zodiac* (2007), shot with a variant of the 24p, looked terrific on film. On the other hand, Ingmar Bergman held up the theatrical release of his last movie, *Saraband* (2003), for over a year because he had shot it on DV as a TV movie and was dissatisfied with the visual quality of the attempts made to transfer it to film.

Nonlinear Editing

In the 1980s, some editors began to edit movies by working with video copies of shots instead of bits of film. By the late 1990s, those shots were not video clips but digital video files, and nearly all movies were edited on a computer, even though some continued to boast in their tail credits that they were "Edited on Film." In 1995, about half of Hollywood's movies were edited on film; after a 1996 movie edited on computer won the Oscar for Best Film Editing—Anthony

Minghella's *The English Patient*, edited by Walter Murch—the number of computer-edited movies increased. In *nonlinear editing*, which was to a film splicer what the first word processor was to a typewriter, shots that had been transferred to video could be pulled in any order and assembled and rearranged easily, rather than be committed to the spliced, linear sequence of a workprint. Many of the first nonlinear editing machines worked with video files that had been transferred to laserdiscs or hard drives. In *digital nonlinear editing*, each shot was digitized—unless it was shot on digital video in the first place—and stored on a hard drive or archived until the editor was ready to work with it. The *online* (or *on-line*) editor called up the shots in the desired order to see how they played, and by punching in a few frame numbers or moving a mouse (instructing the computer which part of the shot to display) could trim a shot to the desired length. The editor could also make the shot end with a fade, move it to a

different scene, and so on. Then the negative was cut to match the *Edit Decision List* (EDL), a computer printout of all the shots and cuts, where previously the negative would have been cut to match the workprint. It was not long before a movie could be edited on a laptop.

Copies and Originals

From the point of view of the film production and distribution companies, the worst thing about video was the ease with which movies could be pirated—and the worst thing about digital video was that it allowed copies to be made that were indistinguishable from the digital original. It was not unusual for a pirate to sneak a video camera into a theatre and copy a first-run movie. To discourage piracy, distributors put copyguards on videos and other encryption schemes on discs and digital prints. Some studios even put flashing dots in the image area of 35mm prints (so that a copy would reveal from which print it had been made), a practice first widely objected to by the audiences of Peter

Fig. 18-2
Atanarjuat the Fast Runner *was shot on DV. Some video distortion can be seen in the face in the background.*

Weir's *Master and Commander: The Far Side of the World* (2003).

From the point of view of 16mm film distributors, the worst thing about video was that many people were renting video copies rather than movies. This was true even of film professors, whose tight budgets sometimes mandated the showing of videos instead of films in film classes. The fewer prints were rented, the more distributors had to charge for them; the less a particular print was rented, the less incentive the distributor had to strike a new copy of that movie when the old print deteriorated. Thus many films began to go out of 16mm distribution, as distributors began to go out of business. With the closing of most revival houses, the distribution of old films in 35mm suffered equal casualties. As much as professors enjoy the ability to stop a video on a frame, it is literally essential that students also be exposed to the actual movie—what might these days be called the film version of the film—uncut, uncropped, and projected at the correct speed. After that, it is valuable, convenient, and cost-effective to use a video for further study, particularly since that protects the celluloid print from excessive handling. Home video has wonderfully improved our access to copies of films, but the films themselves are becoming ever harder to locate.

Finally, from the point of view of film purists, who were delighted at all the uncut and restored prints released on video, there were two problems with the new technology. First, it threatened to replace film. Second, it could be abused to create censored or revised versions that would circulate along with—or in some markets, instead of—the originals. The first matter has not been settled, but even if the digital cinema realizes all its goals, individuals and schools will still be able to collect and project 16mm and 35mm films. Of the second problem there was evidence right away, as classic films began to be colorized for release on video and showings on TV.

Colorization

Colorization was the practice of electronically adding color to videos of black-and-white movies. Later, the technology was used to help make movies rather than change old ones.

The first films to be colorized, in 1984, were shown in 35mm as well as released on video: two

Laurel and Hardy shorts and the features *Topper* (1937) and *Of Mice and Men* (1939). The colors were electronic, assigned by computer to specific areas of each frame (blue to Cary Grant's jacket, brown to his hat). Nor did the colors have any necessary relationship to the original colors of whatever was photographed: In the computer-colored version of *Suddenly* (1954), Frank Sinatra's famous blue eyes were brown.

Movies were colorized to make them better TV programs, in line with the assumptions that a color TV was wasted if it wasn't showing a program in color, and that black-and-white films *lacked color* rather than *had* their own unique scale of tones. Many colorizers argued that black-and-white films would have been made in color if the money or technology had been available. But as Eisenstein and many others recognized, color film and black-and-white film raise extremely different aesthetic problems and opportunities. John Huston could have made *The Maltese Falcon* in color, but he chose not to. When Ted Turner (whose purchase of the MGM/UA film library also netted him the pre-1950 Warner Bros. films controlled by UA, among them *The Maltese Falcon* and *Casablanca*) had the film colorized over his objections, Huston said the result was like a roast that had been covered with teaspoon after teaspoon of sweet syrup.

Electronic Cinema

One of the most creative applications of video was the "electronic cinema" championed by Francis Ford Coppola and used extensively in *One from the heart* (1982). Inspired by the ease with which TV studios could create and revise complex effects electronically, Coppola decided to use the video camera, a computer, and a video-effects generator as a painter might use a sketchbook and as a writer might assemble a first draft.

On a single screen he combined a background (a sketch or photo rather than a fully constructed set), the actors, and any materials to be superimposed or matted in. The soundtrack could be tentatively assembled just as the picture was, adding music and effects to the dialogue to see how the whole thing played. Or he could string together photos and sketches of the backgrounds he intended to use, from first scene to last. A cross between a rough draft of the film and an

Fig. 18-3
On the set of One from the heart.

extensively illustrated script, the video composite let Coppola see just how much of the set would actually show up on camera and have to be constructed, how the actors and dialogue worked in this visual context, how the scene looked with and without camera movements or lab effects, and which visual elements yielded the most effective composites. It also let him present to co-workers and possible backers an electronic sketch of his vision of the film.

Coppola has further ambitions for electronic cinema, including the possible satellite transmission of high-definition images for playback in theatres. Whether this leads to a cinema without film (once considered a contradiction in terms) remains to be seen. Coppola's influence in this period may turn out to have been as strong as Lucas's, because electronic cinema—transcending its roots in TV effects and using more computers, building on its ability to try out compositions by combining visual and musical elements on the fly, perfecting video assist, experimenting with high-definition video, letting the director work on different parts of the project at once, considering satellites and

the Internet as distribution portals, and fitting in naturally with the concept of nonlinear editing—has become a model for the digital cinema. Just as Lucas's desire for a better editing system led to the first nonlinear editing machine (part of his push for computerized work in every aspect of production), Coppola's demand for an all-embracing system that would allow him to be more creative and productive provided part of the impetus that brought the programmers, the hardware designers, the sound editors and cinematographers, the distributors and communications experts—in short, the film people, the TV people, the computer people, and the phone people—together to invent a newly integrated way of filmmaking.

For Further Viewing

FILMS

MISCELLANY: THE AGE OF VIDEO
Point of Order (1964, Emile de Antonio)
Numéro deux (1975, Jean-Luc Godard and Anne-Marie Miéville)

One from the heart or *One From The Heart*
(1982, Francis Ford Coppola)
Family Viewing (1987, Atom Egoyan)
Julia & Julia (1987, Peter Del Monte)
The Celebration (1998, Thomas Vinterberg)
The Idiots (1998, Lars von Trier)
The Blair Witch Project (1999, Daniel Myrick
and Eduardo Sánchez)
The Gleaners and I (2000, Agnès Varda)
Our Lady of the Assassins (2000, Barbet
Schroeder)
Timecode or *Time Code* (2000, Mike Figgis)
Atanarjuat the Fast Runner or *The Fast
Runner* (2001, Zacharias Kunuk)
Russian Ark (2002, Alexander Sokurov)
Open Water (2003, Chris Kentis)
Inland Empire (2006, David Lynch)
[Rec] (2007, Jaume Balagueró and Paco Plaza)
Zodiac (2007, David Fincher)
Diary of the Dead (2008, George A. Romero).
Completed 2007
Cloverfield (2008, Matt Reeves)
Paranormal Activity (2009, Oren Peli). First
version 2007

DVDs

The Blair Witch Project (1999, **Daniel Myrick**
and **Eduardo Sánchez**). Artisan
Entertainment. Includes a commentary by the
directors; the TV documentary, *Curse of the
Blair Witch;* a map and dossier in the DVD-
ROM section; and deleted scenes ("newly
discovered footage").
Brazil (see Chap. 17 list).
The Celebration (see Chap. 14 list).
Cloverfield (2008, **Matt Reeves**). Paramount.
A good example of the handheld-video look
(actually shot with a larger HDDV camera),
with a making-of documentary.

Diary of the Dead (2007, released 2008,
George A. Romero). Dimension Extreme.
Includes a making-of documentary and
other extras.
Family Viewing (see Chap. 16 list).
The Fast Runner (2001, **Zacharias Kunuk**).
Columbia TriStar. A good example of the shot-
on-video look; the film transfer shown in
theatres looked much the same.
The Gleaners and I (see Chap. 13 list).
One from the heart (1982, **Francis Ford
Coppola**). Fantoma/American Zoetrope.
Special Edition. Includes a remastered, high-
definition transfer of the film, with a
commentary by Coppola; a documentary on
electronic cinema; a making-of documentary; videotaped rehearsals; a documentary on
composer **Tom Waits;** deleted and alternate
scenes; a look at Zoetrope Studios; and
Coppola on the digital future.
Open Water (2003, **Chris Kentis**). Lion's Gate.
A good example of the low-budget, independent, mainstream feature shot on digital video
and released on film.
[Rec] (2007, **Jaume Balagueró** and **Paco Plaza**).
Sony Pictures. Includes a making-of
documentary and an interview with the
directors. Excellent use of the long take and
the motivated video camera.
Russian Ark (see Chap. 16 list).
Timecode (2000, **Mike Figgis**). Columbia
TriStar. This excellent disc includes the
complete first version as well as the release
version of the movie—takes 1 and 15—with
commentaries by Figgis; the ability to hear
the sound from *any* quarter of the split-
screen image; Figgis's video production diary;
and, in the DVD-ROM section, the "shooting
score."

19

Digital Cinema: 1999–

The digital cinema is a comprehensive approach to producing and distributing movies without using film. Movies may be shot on digital video or generated entirely on a computer. (In a more limited sense of the term, digital cinema is the mastering, distribution, and exhibition of a digital print, also called a *digital cinema package* or DCP, regardless of whether the movie originated on film or digitally.) What is altered and edited is a digital copy of the footage, and the filmmakers can work on different parts of the movie in whatever creative order suits them. The final product of the digital mastering process is a file that can be packaged for digital projection or transferred to film. This is not a far-fetched vision; most of it is already in place. Though there are still relatively few digital theatres, prints are being made for them, and though most pictures are still shot on film, the number of movies shot on high-definition digital video (HDDV) continues to increase. Most films are converted to an electronic format for digital processing. Effects work consisting partly or entirely of computer-generated imagery (CGI) and digitally modified frames has made most optical special-effects technology obsolete; digital effects (DFX) dominate post-production. Digital mixing and the digital soundtrack have become standard. Film prints carry both analog and digital soundtracks, but the analog track is there only in case of a breakdown. If the digital cinema is ever completely realized, film prints and analog tracks will become as rare as silent movies did, and the projection of movies stored as huge digital files will become the norm.

Although the first feature film generated entirely on a computer was Pixar's *Toy Story* (1995, directed by John A. Lasseter), it is that movie's sequel, *Toy Story 2* (1999, Lasseter, with co-directors Lee Unkrich and Ash Brannon), that marks the beginning of the digital cinema, because *Toy Story 2* was the first film to be entirely generated, edited, mastered, *and exhibited* in digital form, even though it was also released in 35mm. It was also in 1999 that the long-take DV breakthrough *Timecode* (2000, directed by Mike Figgis) was shot; that the digital intermediate process was perfected for *O Brother, Where Art Thou?* (2000, directed by the Coens); that *The Blair Witch Project* (1999) exploited the Internet as a publicity vehicle; and that Lucas's *Star Wars: Episode I— The Phantom Menace* (1999)—which was not a completely digital project like *Toy Story* or Lucas's *Star Wars: Episode II—Attack of the Clones* (2002)—was projected both digitally and in 35mm. For these reasons and more (discussed later), but especially because *Toy Story 2* was the first movie to fit the entire package and because digital projection had just been introduced, it appears correct to give 1999 as the year that the digital cinema arrived. This is not a simple or final decision, however. After all, *The Jazz Singer* was not a fully realized talkie, but it was the film that gave the most momentum to the transition to sound, and the picture comparable to that is the first *Toy Story*, because it made so many people aware that a feature could be made entirely on a computer. That would make 1995 the key year, as it may in fact be. If one prefers to date the period from the first *live-action* mainstream feature produced

Fig. 19-1
Toy Story 2: *Woody shows Buzz Lightyear (left) an episode of his old TV show, "Woody's Roundup," and is entranced by his video image.*

without shooting a foot of film and still exhibited both digitally and in 35mm, that would be 2002 and *Clones*—but the computer film began with animation, most CGI is a variant of animation, and that the *Toy Story* movies were created entirely on a computer gives them an apt separation from the world of photography from which the analog cinema grew.

Doing without Film

Film is heavy. Tapes and discs are light. Film costs a lot to ship in those big boxes and cans, but a hard drive or a set of discs containing a digital print of a movie is extremely portable, and streaming a movie to a theatre via satellite or a broadband connection is weightless and practically free. On a Hollywood set, 35mm film costs about 100 times more than digital videotape; the makers of *Clones* spent $16,000 on the

220 hours of high-def digital tape they used to shoot the picture, rather than the $1.8 million they would have spent on buying and developing 220 hours of film. A great advantage that digital video, or any video, has over film is that it is instantly available for playback, requiring no trip to the lab.

A copy of a film has more contrast and less detail than the original, and copying is an essential part of working with film—but a digital copy is the same as the original. With each *generation* of copying (the negative is the first generation, a copy of it is the second, a copy of that copy is the third, and so on), the analog image becomes more "dupey" and the optical soundtrack more harsh. The same thing happens with tapes, which build up surface noise with each generation until there is more noise than signal, or at least a conspicuous loss of fidelity. More than three generations can easily separate the camera negative from the release print even if no effects

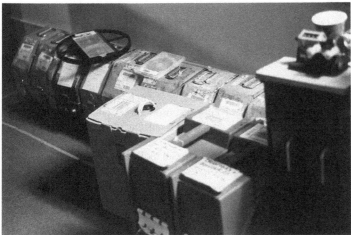

Heavy 35mm films in their sturdy shipping cans and cases. Usually there are two cans, each with two or three 2,000-foot reels, per feature. The envelope near the left contains a digital soundtrack on a CD-ROM, which is being shipped with one of the prints. Photo by Victor Jendras.

Fig. 19-2

work is involved. If effects work is involved, what might have been scores of generations of copying appear to be no generations at all; every part of the digital image remains as rich and sharp as it started out, with none of the unfortunate effects of copying. Furthermore, the act of copying film, for example when making a positive release print from an intermediate negative (IN, also called an internegative), can damage the film slightly—or grievously if it is scratched or picks up dust while being handled or run through a printer. Showing a film in a projector almost always damages it, and a new print needs to be made after a few hundred showings—but making that print slightly wears down the IN, so that eventually a new printing negative has to be struck from the interpositive (IP), the positive copy of the edited camera negative. Digital prints, however, do not suffer a loss of quality when they are copied, and they are not damaged by being projected. Every showing is as clean, stable, and clear as the first.

If a film is scratched, many frames can be ruined, but the film will still run through a projector; if an optical disc is scratched or a hard drive is dropped, a new copy will have to be made, because a damaged disc or drive will not play reliably, if at all. Still, making that new digital copy costs less than making a new film print, and the former will look more like its original than the latter will. On the other hand, the film print will have a film image. In other

words, a digital copy is famous for being identical to the original, but a digital original is not the same as a film original. Digital video has sharper edges, no grain, greater depth of field, and so on. The digital print has the disadvantage of needing to be played back on the software and equipment that created it, at least long enough to be transferred to some future medium, and both software and computers have a history of vanishing—or becoming useless or impossible to fix—once they go off the market.

Film isn't easy or cheap to copy, modify, or send, but a digital file certainly is. The convenience of digital work comes from a change of medium, which cannot help but bring a change in quality. A change in quality is not necessarily good or bad; the point is to be aware of the change. For example, electronic color is not worse than photochemical color, but it doesn't look the same. Analog does not have the characteristics of digital, which makes analog both inconvenient and irreplaceable. What "replaces" it will be standing in its place but will be quite different.

A classical recording on a CD has no surface noise and a cleaner, more distinct sound than the same recording on an LP, but the analog recording has a smoother, fuller sound and a quality of "presence" like that in a concert hall—except for all the scratches, pops, and hiss. The subtle shades of analog recording were traded for the noise free and nondegradable aspects of digital recording in the 1980s, and most people considered it a good trade—but it wouldn't have happened if CDs hadn't sounded so good that consumers were willing to switch media. Accordingly, the technical goal the digital cinema has set for itself in the early 21st century is to shoot and project an image that looks as much like film as possible. This is comparable to the problem of making a CD sound like a perfect LP or a great tape recording; it can't be done, but one can get close. If the theatrical digital experience proves close enough to the analog experience, with extra advantages provided by the digital format (such as digital 3-D), mass acceptance will follow.

Digital has already become absolutely central to post-production work, its role in pre-production is constantly growing, and enthusiasts see no reason that the entire moviemaking process should not become digital from first to last. Indeed, one of the primary arguments in favor of the total digital cinema is that the image is already being transferred from film to digital media for editing, effects work, and so on, then transferred back to film; all this costs money, and there is no loss of information in digital-to-digital copying, so why not skip the converting and transferring and just work the whole time with digital files? The argument is strong if taking film out of the cameras and projectors does not impoverish the image.

A major argument in favor of computerized filmmaking is that a digital image can be manipulated completely and seamlessly. This makes possible extraordinary special effects that look as real as anything else in the picture, subtle color corrections that can be applied to an entire movie, and changes in what was originally photographed, even to the extent of changing a camera angle or the lighting. It also makes possible *convincingly* combined images whose subjects were never in physical or temporal proximity, so that a living actor can touch a dead president (*Forrest Gump*, 1994)—a variation on Kuleshov's artificial landscape or creative geography, where shots taken at different places could be cut together to create the impression of a single event happening in a single place. But Kuleshov's shots *were* taken at certain times and places, and they have a physical and even metaphysical relationship with the photographed world—whose light touched and affected the filmstock—that critic André Bazin considered essential to the narrative and

documentary cinema: a "fingerprint" linking the shot to the physical subject that reflected light into the lens and onto the film, where the light was recorded without the need for human intervention. A digital image can be generated without any exposure to the world, like an animated film, or it can be modified so completely that it appears autonomous, entirely unconnected from any act of recording physical reality—presenting, in fact, an imitation of photography. Digital effects can look as if they were *photographed live*. In comparison, all earlier effects showed their seams. Painting, digital animation, digital composites, and CGI are found throughout the 21st-century "live" feature. Thus digital cinema has allowed a basic link between photography and physical reality to change: It is no longer self-evident that a live-action shot presents any live action.

This is not a question of fiction and acting; it is a matter of the presumed connection between image and reality. Even if special effects have long made it possible to show the impossible, those effects shots and other opticals were spread throughout films that were, primarily, photographed live action—and the effects weren't always as visually convincing as normally photographed scenes in the rest of the movie. Now that the effects are a seamless part of the image and everything appears equally real, in some movies the whole frame has begun to resemble an effect and to be accepted, paradoxically, as *un*real or, at best, not necessarily real. Watching Fred Astaire dance or Jackie Chan slide down a building, one applauds what the actor did in the presence of the camera; when Spider-Man swings through the city (*Spider-Man 2*, 2004, directed by Sam Raimi), one applauds the effects. For the willing suspension of disbelief to take hold, one has to believe the effects shots and the rest of the movie's world are equally real—to believe, for example, that in *Spider-Man* (2002, Raimi) and its sequels both the actor and the graphic are the character—but many people are pulled out of that suspension when they notice how well an effect has been achieved, how cool and accomplished it is. The widely known fact that any image in a contemporary movie may have been digitally modified has led to a change in the ways some people respond to movies: as anything-goes, purely artificial structures. This is a step in the direction of painting and music and away from photography—a medium that implies the subject was present to be photographed, and thus that what one is watching somehow did happen or is happening, no matter how outrageous or made up the action is. In the presence of an impressive image that may never have been photographed or an event that may have happened only in part, the contemporary viewer feels both awe and distrust. This new attitude is one of the most important effects of the digital revolution, along with the conviction that any kind of story, no matter how fantastic, can now be told.

It is possible that Hitchcock would have made *Rope* (1948) in one take if his camera hadn't been limited to ten-minute reels. One problem with film is that it keeps running out. Using DV, as in *Timecode*, or a hard drive, as in *Russian Ark* (2002, directed by Alexander Sokurov), or more recent technology, a digital moviemaker can shoot a feature in a single take, in real time, as Hitchcock could not. In this sense, the digital cinema is a step toward the long take of stage drama—or of the surveillance camera—opening up new possibilities in filmmaking. Working in real time, after all, enhances the possibilities of realism, and reality itself is comparable to an infinite long take, even if many aspects of consciousness and our lived experience correspond to the instantaneous changes of editing. While Bazin would regret any severance between the photographic image and physical reality, he would enjoy the renewed emphasis on the long take, which has never been able to be so deeply explored as it is in the digital cinema. The Lumières would find nothing wrong with a single-shot movie, and Méliès would be on the computer all day, designing transformations. It seems that the digital cinema can continue to work with the aesthetic and practical matters that have concerned filmmakers all the way back to the beginning—a computer could have helped Griffith experiment with the tints, tones, and lights for *Broken Blossoms*—while it also poses a monumental change in the medium.

The digital cinema was made practical by advances in computer technology. Just as computer monitors made TV viewers want higher video resolution, creating the push to DV and HDTV, the computer revolution made workers in many fields want to share in the speed and convenience of the digital world, to which many of them were introduced by the Internet. When personal computers offered more memory, faster microprocessors, and greater storage capacity, and when correspondents began to use e-mail more than the postal service and researchers to use the Web more than the library—all of which happened in the mid-1990s—consumers and programmers found more uses for computers. By the end of the 20th century, people were able to load, play at full speed, alter, and save huge digital video files on home and office computers, instead of watching tiny computer videos and their boxy pixels jerk along. They could store their work on recordable DVDs and portable hard drives. They could transfer their old home movies to video, make new DV movies, and digitally edit both picture and sound. Later, they could do all that in HD. Filmmakers found that they could send each other digital files over the Internet and work on them together, modifying them with no loss of information; they found that workers spread across the globe could watch and evaluate a clip together in real time; they became interested in the way a project could evolve in digital space; and they saw the advantages of digital editing. They realized that digital was clearly the technology of the future and, in fact, the present, and they took up Coppola's dream of an electronic cinema—now seen entirely in the digital terms advanced most prominently by Lucas—hoping someday to be able to sit down at a computer and compose a whole movie.

But there is still more to the digital cinema than integrating production and distribution with an electronic network, more even than digitizing images so they can be manipulated on a computer, or getting rid of film. Digital cinema is a new paradigm, a *nonlinear* system that allows the movie to be produced in practically any order and that allows all the filmmakers to work on the digital files—the shots, the sound rolls, the composites, the music—at the same time. This model has already begun to replace the linear system of moviemaking, in which—to take just one representative example—the film has to be shot and then edited one reel at a time before the sound-effects editor can start to build a sound reel. This nonlinearity is possible only if the filmmakers use computers.

Beginnings

The first computer film artist was John Whitney. He started by designing and using mechanical drawing machines that created abstract patterns on cels that could then be conventionally photographed with an animation camera. Saul Bass shot the graphics for the opening credits of *Vertigo* on Whitney's "animation machine" in 1957, and Whitney shot *Catalog* on it in 1961; he considered *Catalog* a "sample reel" of computer-graphic effects, not a film. Whitney then invented coordinated mechanical systems that would draw on film with moving light and then advance to the next frame, eliminating the need to photo-graph the drawings; these abstract images were then systematically varied and combined by an analog computer according to principles Whitney was investigating that opened up a visual harmony, a mathematics and music of form moving in time. The computer varied and processed the images, then displayed them one frame at a time on a cathode-ray tube. A 35mm camera photographed the displayed images, which were in black and white; then Whitney used filters and an optical printer to color and combine the images onto a conventionally reproducible color negative. His experiments, funded by IBM from 1966 until his death in 1995 and executed on their huge digital mainframe computers, opened the door to the slit-scan techniques used in *2001* and to his own abstract shorts and demonstration films, including *Permutations* (1968), *Experiments in Motion Graphics* (1968), *Matrix* (1971), and *Arabesque* (1975), as well as his brother James's *Lapis* (1966).

Once Douglas Engelbart had invented the computer mouse and hypertext in 1968, computers were on the verge of new ways to navigate the world of data and instructions. The invention of the *graphical user interface* (GUI), which replaced typing a command with clicking on a picture linked to a command, is important to mention here because it made it possible for computers to display and manipulate visual files. The GUI was developed at Xerox's Palo Alto Research Center (Xerox PARC) and demon-strated in 1974 on the Xerox Alto, a computer that was not put on the market. The GUI made its definitive public appearance in 1984 as part of Apple Computer's Macintosh. Apple had been founded by Steve Wozniak and Steve Jobs in 1976, and in 1977, they had invented and marketed the Apple II, the most successful and versatile of the early personal computers. IBM countered with its own personal computer in 1981 (appropriating the name; an IBM-compatible machine was a "PC"). As part of that project, in 1980 IBM asked Bill Gates and Paul Allen to provide an operating system for the PC, allowing the two to keep the rights to that system, which was DOS. (They based part of their work on an earlier system written by Gary Kildall.) Gates and Allen, who had founded Micro-Soft in 1975, changed its name to Microsoft; the company became a software giant that specialized in operating systems. After Steve Jobs saw the Xerox Alto, Apple developed its own GUI for the Lisa computer, a problematic machine soon replaced by the Macintosh, and the IBM systems had to scramble to compete. In 1990, Microsoft marketed Windows 3.0, which brought a workable GUI to IBM-compatible machines. Soon Windows was improved and took over in most offices, while the Mac became the professional standard for graphics work and the emerging field of computer-based editing. By the mid-1990s, nearly every computer had a graphical interface. Beyond any issue of convenience—vital because it allowed untrained people to use computers—the GUI made visual data as important as text to the next generation of filmmakers and filmgoers, who learned to use computers in childhood.

The Internet grew out of a U.S. defense project designed to keep data flowing in case power lines and equipment failed in a national emergency. The Advanced Research Projects Agency (ARPA) gave its name to the ARPAnet, first tested in 1969. In 1972, Ray Tomlinson wrote a program for the ARPAnet that allowed him to send the first e-mail. As a tool with broader uses than those required by the Defense Department, the Internet was conceived by a team headed by Vinton Cerf. In 1983, Cerf and Robert Kahn wrote the Internet Protocol, the gigantic network's means of sending packets of data between computers. Now subsidized by the National Science Foundation rather than the Pentagon, the Internet went into operation in 1983. In 1989, Tim Berners-Lee wrote the "http" protocol that allowed his dream of globally accessible information to become a reality when the World Wide Web, a subset of the Internet, was officially launched in 1991. (In the course of inventing the Web, Berners-Lee had set up his first server in 1990.) Berners-Lee had written a program called "Enquire Within About Everything" in 1980, and now that was possible—especially with the aid of the Web browser (Mosaic in 1993, Netscape in 1994). In 1993, Berners-Lee put his Web technology in the public domain, making it permanently free. In 1984, there were about a thousand *hosts* (computers that make their data and programs available) on the Internet; in 1992, a million; in 2001, a hundred million; in 2009, 625 million. Online services expanded in the late 1990s; they and local networks made it easy to link workers—as well as their files and virtual desks—to explore new ways of creating, modifying, and approving projects, especially large collaborative ones.

In the 1990s, people realized they had entered a digital age. Virtually every aspect of public and private life had been touched by computers. All one's preferences were in a database somewhere, and anything from a cellular phone to a fuel injector was being run by a chip. Everyone—not just everyone on a project—was connected to everybody else and to vast resources of information. Not all that information was true or complete, but it was certainly easy to find. E-mail had become a primary means of communication. Beginning in the mid-1980s, the film industry had shifted many operations to networked desktop computers, as did so many companies between then and the turn of the century. Every "business" aspect of the film business was computerized, from the executive's calendar to the accountant's spreadsheet, the Legal Department's contracts, the distributor's booking schedule, the theatre's receipts, and the statistician's demographic analysis of box-office performance. These and other changes, like the storyboard's being animated, were not evident on the screen. If audiences noticed that computers had come to filmmaking, it was thanks to decades of increasingly sophisticated special effects.

The first feature film to use a motion-control camera was *Star Wars* (1977). As its name suggests, the motion of the camera was controlled by a computer so that the camera could move exactly the same way—usually in relation to models and miniature sets—over and over again. With each *pass* (of film through the camera; the same term is used when film runs through a printer) the same footage was re-exposed, but some element or aspect of the visual field changed. In a *Star Wars* battle, for instance, each ship was shot separately, and so was the field of stars. If the camera appeared to swoop around an asteroid and after a ship, it had to move precisely the same way when the model ship was being shot as when the model asteroid was being shot—and in the other passes when the star background was being shot, or the ship was not illuminated but silhouetted against a bluescreen (also "blue screen"), or a foreground object exploded. This precise repetition, ensured by the computer, allowed perfect composite images to be created in the camera; it also made it much easier to create the elements for such conventional composites as traveling mattes, which were put together on an optical printer. By 2000, the technology was obsolete. The motion-control camera was used most effectively in Cronenberg's *Dead Ringers* (1988), where it followed Jeremy Irons as he played one brother, then his twin, in the same frame, while panning between them or tracking with them through an apartment.

The 20-second "Genesis" sequence in Nicholas Meyer's *Star Trek II: The Wrath of Khan* (1982), in which a lifeless planet undergoes a sweeping, fiery transformation into a lush, green, brand-new world, was CGI from start to finish, the first of its kind. (Steven Lisberger's Disney film *TRON*, which also used CGI, came out a month later. 1982 was also the year of *One from the heart* and electronic cinema.) Created entirely within the computer, this historically crucial sequence pointed the way to the purely digital cinema. It was the work of a team headed by Ed Catmull at the computer-graphics division of Lucasfilm. In 1986, Catmull approached Steve Jobs with an idea for generating whole movies on computers. Jobs bought the CG division from Lucas in 1986; then he and Catmull co-founded Pixar Animation Studios. The most important animation company since Disney, Pixar released its first features through Disney and was eventually bought by Disney.

Another founding member of Pixar, John A. Lasseter, directed the company's first film, a short called *Luxo Jr.* (1986), which introduced their hopping lamp and was nominated for an Oscar. As previously mentioned, Lasseter directed *Toy Story* in 1995, the first feature generated entirely on computers, and *Toy Story 2* in 1999, the first digitally generated and mastered film to be digitally projected. These "3-D animations" looked like a cross between drawings and photographed puppets or models; their rich shadows and textures were the result of Pixar's ever-more-sophisticated software. The next Pixar features—*a bug's life* (1998, directed by Lasseter and Andrew Stanton), *Monsters, Inc.* (2001, directed by Pete Docter), *Finding Nemo* (2003, directed by Stanton), *The Incredibles* (2004, directed by Brad Bird), and *Cars* (2006, directed by Lasseter and Joe Ranft)—were so intricately planned that some frames took hours for even a computer to generate. One frame from *Finding Nemo* that showed complex underwater light on a coral reef took a 2,000-processor network 10 hours on Pixar's "RenderMan" software. Using a competing process, DreamWorks entered the field of digital animation with *Antz* (1998, directed by Eric Darnell and Tim Johnson) and had great success with *Shrek* (2001, directed by Andrew Adamson and Vicky Jenson) and its sequels. The first completely CG character was a probing water-thing in *The Abyss* (1989, directed by James Cameron).

The first computerized editing machine was Lucas's EditDroid, developed between 1984 and 1986; it worked with shots that had been transferred to laserdisc and was a nonlinear editor. The first feature cut on it was *The Patriot* (1986, directed by Frank Harris) in 1985; another was *The Doors* (1991, directed by Oliver Stone), which was also one of the first films with a digital soundtrack (CDS, discussed below). The Avid Film Composer, which became the industry standard for editing film as well as for creating certain effects formerly made only on an optical printer, was invented in the early 1990s. Film that had been transferred to video was fed into the Avid, which was a dedicated Macintosh computer (later, a program that could run on other computers) with two monitors and an array of hard drives. A digital nonlinear editor, the Avid digitized the video and kept the shots—that is,

the picture and sound files—directly accessible in any order and ready to be modified. While it was mostly used for editing films, the Avid naturally could also edit projects that originated on analog or digital video. In the early 2000s, Avid introduced the Nitris, an editor that digitized images at a 10-bit depth, creating high-quality HD video files with resolutions as high as 2K and 4K. *The English Patient* (1996) was not the first movie whose picture and sound were edited on Avid, but it was the first to win an Oscar for film editing—and another, equally influential, for sound. By the end of the century, most films were edited on Avid or one of its rivals. By 2007—when the equivalent of an effects house could be run on a laptop—the most successful of Avid's rivals was Final Cut Pro. Walter Murch, who had edited *The English Patient*, edited *Cold Mountain* (2003) on Final Cut Pro and went on to use it for such projects as Coppola's *Youth Without Youth* (2007).

The digital soundtrack was introduced by IMAX in 1988. The first mainstream digital soundtrack was developed by CDS (Cinema Digital Sound) and premiered on 70mm prints of *Dick Tracy* (1990, directed by Warren Beatty). The CDS track was not widely adopted because the industry was waiting for Dolby Labs to come up with a digital track that had an analog safety net.

Dolby Laboratories Inc., founded in 1965 by engineer Ray Dolby, first became known for its system of reducing system noise when re-recording tape: *Dolby Noise Reduction* (NR) selectively compressed and expanded the signal to suppress the frequencies where tape hiss and surface noise were recorded, increasing the signal-to-noise ratio and making possible several generations of clean copying and a better audio master. Dolby decoders soon became part of most home stereo systems—at first because recording and playing back with Dolby NR increased the fidelity of audiocassettes, whose thin tape was only ⅛-inch wide and ran four times slower than the 7½ inches per second (ips) at which reel-to-reel tape begins to record music well; cassettes needed all the help they could get.

Dolby Labs introduced the revolutionary *Stereo Variable Area* (SVA) soundtrack in 1975, which allowed optical 35mm prints to carry four channels of stereo surround sound on two tracks (decoded in the projection booth into left, center, right, and surround channels). Previously, except for the very first multiple-optical-track experiments, stereo had been confined to magnetically striped—or mag—prints. All Dolby's analog optical sound-tracks are variable-area tracks, which admit more or less light as they widen and narrow (as opposed to variable-density tracks, which are of a fixed size but grow brighter and darker). *Star Wars* used Dolby NR throughout production, from the first recording to the final mix, and it had a Dolby SVA soundtrack; from then on, Dolby was the recognized leader in film sound. Dolby technology was also used to improve the mag tracks on 70mm prints.

In 1986, Dolby improved the four-channel analog track with "spectral recording," increasing its ability to record and play back very soft and very loud sounds accurately, and *Dolby SR* became the standard optical surround soundtrack. The six-channel *Dolby Digital* optical track was invented in 1991 and first used on Tim Burton's *Batman Returns* (1992). At that time it was called Dolby SR•D, and the six channels were left, center, right, left surround, right surround, and bass effects; prints also carried a Dolby SR soundtrack in case the digital system broke down or the theatre had conventional projection.

Soon there were two more digital systems, the six-channel *Digital Theater Systems* (DTS) and the eight-channel *Sony Dynamic Digital Sound* (SDDS). Most film prints now carry at least one of the three leading digital soundtracks and one analog track. A *tri-format print*, common at the turn of the century and shown in Figure 19-3, was compatible with Dolby Digital, DTS, and SDDS. Dolby Digital and SDDS sound-tracks were on the print. IMAX put its sound on a hard drive, DTS on a CD-ROM, and what was on the print was a synchronizing code. DTS was *double system* sound, with two machines linked as the old Warner Bros. projector and record player were, but by more reliable means. Magnetic striping, used from the 1950s to the 1990s, especially on 70mm prints, was costly. Like any optical track, a digital soundtrack was far less expensive than a mag track and did not have to be recorded in real time; it was also of better quality than any earlier optical format, and it could be printed wherever it would fit. Dolby Digital was printed between the sprocket holes

on one side of the print. The analog track ran alongside the DTS track, which was a code that controlled the CD, and both of them fit between the sprocket holes and the image area (the "frame" itself). SDDS was printed as a stream of microscopic dots on the left and right sides of the film, between the outside edges and the rows of sprocket holes. The first DTS film was Spielberg's *Jurassic Park* in 1993. SDDS premiered with John McTiernan's *Last Action Hero*, also in 1993.

From the late 1980s through the 1990s, digital special effects rapidly became more common. Still, audiences were surprised to find that hundreds of the people shown in long shot in *Titanic* (1997, directed by James Cameron) were made in a computer. The DFX in *Titanic* were state of the art but not unique; neverthe-less, they were the ones that made many view-ers recognize that the new effects in movies were specifically digital. Others realized that fact when Lucas publicized the digital aspects of his revision of the *Star Wars* trilogy in the same year, 1997, but it had been clear as early as 1991, when Cameron's *Terminator 2: Judgment Day* foregrounded its extreme digital effects, or in the aptly named "Genesis" sequence of 1982. The rise of CGI and digital-image processing stretched from *Star Trek II* to *Toy Story 2*—and beyond to such milestones as *The Lord of the Rings: The Return of the King* (2003, directed by Peter Jackson), whose film footage was mixed with CGI and digitally modified in un-precedented ways—or the previous year's *The Lord of the Rings: The Two Towers*, whose Gollum was the most expressive and technically advanced of digital characters, created by a computer and a digitally replaced live actor, Andy Serkis.

The first feature shot on HD video and trans-ferred to film was an Italian–British co-production, *Julia & Julia* (1987, directed by Peter Del Monte). Starting in the late 1990s, many films were shot on DV and transferred to film. In Denmark, for example, Lars von Trier's Dogme95 picture, *The Idiots*, was shot on DV and edited on Avid in 1998. *Timecode* was shot on DV, late in 1999, because the longest that Figgis could shoot film continuously was just over 20 minutes, and he wanted to shoot a feature in one take. The four takes in *Timecode* lasted between 85 and 94½ minutes. The takes

A tri-format 35mm anamorphic print of Steve Miner's **Lake Placid** *(1999) in projection position, shown here at almost twice its actual size. The squeezed image will be widened and inverted by the projection lens. Note the three digital soundtracks and the analog track.*

Fig. 19-3

started and ended at different times, but the cameras were perfectly synchronized with each other (by a time code, or timecode) so that 85 minutes of the film showed four simultaneous views of a sequence of events as it unfolded in real time, in locations that were adjacent to or far from each other but that always were reached in a continuous manner, by following a driving or walking character.

The four soundtracks varied in volume so that one scene could be concentrated on at a time.

Late in 2001, Alexander Sokurov shot *Russian Ark in* one 90-minute take in St. Petersburg's Hermitage Museum (the other six minutes of the movie are credits). Sokurov wanted a better image than DV could provide, and HD tape was limited to 52 minutes. At that

Fig. 19-4

A detail of part of the soundtrack area of one frame from the same print. The distance from the left side of the film to the image area is 5/16 of an inch. Starting near the outer edge of the film and looking from left to right: The field of dots running vertically to the left of the sprocket holes is half of the SDDS track, which is light purple. The square patterns between the sprocket holes are the Dolby Digital track, which is in black and white; there is a tiny Dolby logo, resembling two Ds facing away from each other, in the center of each block. The two wavy lines—white against a black background—are the stereo analog track, Dolby SR. The line of blips is the DTS control code, also white against black. Then the image area begins. In Fig. 19-3, the rest of the frame is visible: There is no soundtrack between the right sprocket holes, and the rest of the SDDS track runs along the right edge.

Gollum, from The Lord of the Rings: The Two Towers.

Fig. 19-5

time, shooting in HD at feature length required that the camera feed its data not to tape but to a hard drive, which was carried along by the camera crew; they were limited to four tries before they ran out of the experimental, unerasable drives, and they got it on the fourth take. The perfectly choreographed *plan-séquence* that constitutes the movie, a shot as continuous as one's presence in the world and in some dreams, shows what an unnamed character (whose thoughts and speech were recorded by Sokurov) is given to see—a bit like Dante, but there is a strong sense that he is dreaming, along with a hint that he may be seeing all this after death. The modern-day narrator is never on camera because the entire movie is a POV shot (subjective camera) showing what he sees; it is also a mindscreen because what he is looking at is the world of his own dream or vision and

because he is telling about it. We look through the narrator's eyes as he walks, often accompanied by a diplomat sometimes called the Stranger (the Marquis de Custine, who visited Russia in 1839), through a museum whose rooms are filled with people who once danced or gathered there or in rooms like these—Russian history comes alive, one artistic period at a time. History, art, society, and the observer are linked in an unbroken flow of perception, moving as the narrator does from one time to another without any cutting. They are also linked by the museum, an ark loaded with what needs to be saved and that seems at the end to be moving through a mist. The lighting (candles and daylight, since there was no time to set up, hide, and break down lights) was as carefully planned as the movement within the building of hundreds of actors. When the image and sound had been

Fig. 19-6
The four simultaneous long takes of **Timecode.** *Moviestore collection Ltd/Alamy.*

Fig. 19-7
Russian Ark: *The Stranger, Custine (Sergei Dreiden), admires the palatial museum of art and time.*

slightly polished, *Russian Ark* was transferred to film and exhibited in 2002.

In 1998, computer technology was put to a new use, previously explored only in commercials: the digitizing of an entire film after it had been edited. The makers of *Pleasantville* (1998, directed by Gary Ross) transferred all their color-film footage to an electronic format, selectively removed the color from it, and then transferred the results to film: a black-and-white image that sprouts color here and there as the characters, who live in the world of an old TV show, begin to discover the more passionate and unpredictable aspects of life. In 1999, Lucas digitized all of *The Phantom Menace* to mix live-action and CG footage seamlessly. But it was also in 1999 that the Coens' *O Brother, Where Art Thou?* (2000) was completely digitized to make it look more realistic.

O Brother was shot in the lush South but was supposed to have been set in the Dust Bowl, which meant that many greens would have to be changed to browns. These changes, among others, were made in 1999 on a *digital intermediate* (DI). The fact that the changes were made without distorting the skin tones of the actors was the most impressive aspect of the *electronic*

intermediate process, as it was also called, and because the changes were made not in the service of effects but as a way of fixing and polishing a normal movie, the DI caught on and was used on most studio pictures after 2000.

Once *O Brother* had been edited, the negative—including the completed effects shots—was scanned by a laser beam and fed into a computer as a digital data file; this file was the electronic intermediate (EI) or the DI. Once the color changes had been made, the DI was recorded by laser onto intermediate stock (the three major kinds of film stock are camera, intermediate, and print) as the *digital intermediate negative* or DIN. The DIN was copied to an IP, and INs were made from the IP for striking release prints. Both the EI, the creative space, and the DIN, the final product, were part of the DI process. As the process became more versatile and complex, it became common to cut in effects shots during the DI stage and to revise the film in numerous ways, from changing the lighting to formatting the film in its final aspect ratio.

The frames in the DI could be altered to fill a miniature set with full-sized actors, polish skin

Fig. 19-8
A digital intermediate was used to change the colors of the vegetation without altering the colors of the faces in O Brother, Where Art Thou?

texture with a fairy glow, make composites, and more. Any changes in exposure or color could be applied throughout the film; this resembled—and in some labs replaced—timing. (*Timing* a print, or adjusting its brightness and color levels in a printer, had been invented shortly after the beginning of contact printing in the Silent Era; the digital version, which offered more possibilities, was called *digital grading* or *digital timing*.) At this point, color, brightness, effects, framing, and even locations were all equally capable of being changed. And all these changes, no matter how many and no matter how significant, were merely changes in the zeros and ones into which the image had been digitized, revisions in a numerical file. When the revised digital image was scanned back onto film by a laser in a film recorder, the rearranged zeroes and ones were just as digitally fresh as they ever were, and the revised DI was identical in quality to the original DI, still only one generation away from the negative.

The image went from the edited camera negative to the digital intermediate, then back to negative film with no discernible loss of image quality. The result of the DI process was a new 35mm negative with perfectly integrated live

action and effects as well as corrected exposure, almost as though the final picture had been captured by the original camera. This was the most important change in post-production since digital nonlinear editing.

The year 1999 saw the shooting of *Timecode*, the DI work on *O Brother*, and the *dual release* (that is, in both 35mm and digital prints) of the first feature made and projected without film, *Toy Story 2*, and it also saw the dual release of *The Phantom Menace*, the first live-action feature to be digitally projected—and, crucially, digital projection itself. In the history of digital cinema it was, as previously argued, the defining year.

Two competing digital projectors were invented in 1999, by Texas Instruments (Digital Light Processing—DLP—a *micromirror* projector) and by Hughes–JVC (a liquid-crystal display, or LCD projector). The DLP projector reflected light onto the screen with incredibly tiny mirrors on three chips (optical semiconductors called *digital micromirror devices*, with each DMD chip dedicated to R, G, or B). DLP started with a pure white source and used a prism to direct the light to the three DMDs, which reflected R, G, and B light—one mirror per color per pixel—back into a prism that mixed the red image, the green image, and the blue image into a single frame and directed it toward the screen. The millions of mirrors on each chip tilted to reflect or block the light thousands of times per second, creating a deeper blue, for example, by flashing the blue mirrors for the pixels with that color more often per frame; sky blue, by flashing them less often. LCD projectors shone white light through an electronic LCD panel. By the time that *Clones*, shot entirely on 2K HDDV, was digitally projected in 2002—after Lucas had spent a long time on the DI, tweaking the actors' performances by manipulating their faces and reconstructing frames—the highest-resolution projectors were also 2K. Micromirror projection was used for *Phantom Menace* and *Clones*, as well as *Toy Story 2* and *Finding Nemo*. By 2004, DLP dominated the market.

In 2003, the studio group charged with adopting standards for digital projection (Digital Cinema Initiatives, or the DCI) endorsed 2K but called for systems that could be upgraded when higher-resolution technology was perfected. A year later, Sony privately demonstrated a 4K projector with *full-bandwidth*, or 4:4:4, RGB data. (Some video formats and equipment provided full data for red but less for the other two. Ordinary DV was 4:1:1 for NTSC and 4:2:0 for PAL.) Sony's 4K projector was offered to the public in 2005.

In a digital theatre, the CG elements in *Clones* were brilliantly vivid and sharp. However, the 24p-photographed images of the actors were a bit dim and fuzzy in comparison; they suffered from the lower resolution. When *Clones* was transferred to film, the actors looked the same as they had, but the CG elements were less impressive. The effects had looked best on a computer monitor, and they had looked nearly the same when digitally projected, but they had not transferred well to film. By the time *Revenge of the Sith* (shot on a more advanced 2K camera, a CineAlta with 4:4:4 color) came out in 2005, the bugs had been worked out, and both the 35mm prints and the digital prints were excellent.

The light-sensing area in the 24p cameras used on *Clones* and *Sith*—the "target area" behind the lens where light used to hit film but now encountered a chip—was small. Measured diagonally, it was only ⅔ as long as a 35mm frame. The chip, called a *sensor*, was a *charge-coupled device* (CCD) covered with photocells. Each photocell registered, as an electronic signal, the amount of red, green, or blue light falling on it; an analog-to-digital converter, usually built into the chip, digitized the information and sent it to a video recorder that was part of the camera or attached to it. There was one photocell on the CCD per primary color per pixel. In some other cameras, a beam splitter directed the light to three separate R, G, and B chips. After Sony introduced the 24p in 1997 as the HDW-F900, several companies introduced their own 2K cameras. David Fincher used the Viper camera on *Zodiac* and *The Curious Case Of Benjamin Button*. *Clones* used a Sony camera whose body had been adapted by Panavision, which had worked with Sony on the 24p from the start.

In 2004, Panavision released its own 24p, a second generation of the camera that had a target area the size of a frame of Super 35 film, which is slightly larger than a standard 35mm frame. In the early 2000s, Super 35 was the large format of choice, because it was no longer necessary to use 70mm and mag to get an excellent soundtrack, and the Super 35 image, on 35mm film that cost much less than the 65mm stock used for 70mm prints, was considered detailed enough to be blown up to 70mm if one desired. Panavision's new 24p could use the same lenses as 35mm movie cameras (those for the first 24p had been smaller) and match film's depth of field. It captured far more information on the larger frame. It could run at 24 fps or any speed from 1 to 50 fps. It was completely portable, requiring no cable to connect it to the dockable video recorder, and it was the right size and weight to be hand-held, used in a Steadicam, or set on a tripod. It shot 12.6 Mp frames at 4K—equivalent to the resolution of 35mm film. (The first film shot at 4K was *Superman Returns* in 2006.) It recorded full-bandwidth color. Its format was designed to work with the DI process, creating a digital original perfect for a 4K electronic intermediate. In an unintended but wonderful historical irony, Panavision called its "Super 35 Digital Cinematography Camera System" the Genesis. That invention brought digital camerawork into its maturity, and soon other 4K camera systems were put on the market.

Production and Distribution

Even in a digitized industry, making a movie begins when someone gets an idea. After that, the usual step is writing a script, but in the digital cinema one might also begin with a computer sketch, a set of picture and sound files that expands and develops. As a digital file, whether it is written with an ordinary word processor or with special software, a script can be (but rarely is, yet) illustrated with digital pictures, sounds, and clips that clarify how the writer envisions the movie.

The first stage of production is called development, and the usual key collaborators are the producer and the writer. When the story and approach have been agreed upon, the producer hires the writer to do a full-length script—or buys the script if the writer approached the producer with a finished one. Finding a producer is an important part of development: getting the money. Lawyers get out their digital templates and prepare contracts. When a screenplay has been judged satisfactory, the producer keeps the writer (or new writers) around for revisions and hires a director, usually trying to interest her or him by showing the script. Sometimes, of course, a director can bring his or her own idea or script to a producer.

Working with DV is so inexpensive, however, that an independent filmmaker can write, direct, shoot, edit, and mix a digital video before having to find a company to pay for the transfer to film, make the prints, and distribute them. The filmmaker might even be able to produce the movie (pay for it) if the *mise-en-scène* isn't lavish and the actors either are unknowns or agree to be paid after the movie has been released. Independent filmmakers used to have this kind of freedom when working with 16mm, but 16mm expenses have soared far above those of DV. At present, many independents are making features on high-def or standard DV and breaking into the business with pictures that are of sufficiently high visual quality to be shown in 35mm theatres but that cost as little as $500 or as much as $2 million to produce, while the average Hollywood feature costs over $70 million.

A digital filmmaker can take a project from the first idea to the final *digital video master* (which can be scanned onto film or used to make videos and digital prints), playing all the key creative roles or working with others, without waiting years for a conventional producer to get behind a $70 million idea. Using the digital master, the filmmaker can bypass a film release altogether and output his or her work in PAL, NTSC, SECAM, or HDTV and sell it to TV worldwide; or make a DVD and enter that market; or post it on the Internet for paid or free downloading; or show it in digital theatres. But in whatever order the nonlinear artist approaches filmmaking, the tasks conventionally done in development, and then in pre-production, production, and post-production (all four of which constitute the production phase, which ends with the approval of a sync-sound print), and finally in distribution do all have to be done eventually.

One of the biggest changes the computerization of the industry has brought to development is screenwriting software, both because it has affected how movies are written and because it presents the script in a format that can be read and analyzed by other programs. These other programs can "break down" the script to determine the production requirements for each scene, decide which scenes can be shot with the same actors and sets, and construct a budget—not a budget inflated by actors' and directors' salaries but a practical estimate of what it will cost to shoot the movie. Most of this happens in pre-production, well after the script has been approved.

The major stars may be signed during development, which is when agents do most of their work, but the majority of casting is done in pre-production, along with many other tasks. Casting agencies use computers to match actors with roles, location scouts use them to find places to shoot, and agents use them to keep track of their clients' accomplishments. Production software breaks down the script into blocks to be shot on certain days. Accounting software keeps track of expenses. Programmers examine the script and drawings to design computer games based on the film.

Drawings can be scanned into a computer or generated on one, then lined up in the order of the script, creating a story outline that resembles a comic strip and is called a *storyboard*. The physical drawings used to be pinned on walls or big boards. Making a storyboard has been a basic practice ever since Eisenstein sketched his shots. Using arrows and several drawings per shot, a storyboard can indicate every camera, prop, and character movement. In a computer, the comic strip can turn into a cartoon or *animatic* (a computer-animated storyboard, usually with 3-D models), with the intermediate actions between the drawings filled in. The sound—or trial sounds—can be synchronized with the animatic. The characters, props, and sets can be moved in relation to each other—a creative, experimental process that can help one discover the best action, camera angle, lighting, blocking, or choreography; determine whether certain props are needed or which costume designs look best; and make it possible to begin designing sets, models, miniatures, and effects to scale. Only what will be photographed needs to be built, occupied, driven, hung, or worn; the rest still needs to be designed but can be added electronically. A growing set of files lets a digital rough draft of the film develop as each of its elements is tried out or completed. A pre-production animatic can serve as the visual spine of a movie, much as a screenplay is its dramatic spine.

The majority of design work is still done in pre-production, most of it with the aid of computer graphics. Research is carried out during development and pre-production: to get period details correct, for example, or to make sure no real person with a character's name lives in the city where the story is set. Much design and background research is now done on the Internet.

In the digital cinema, production is the period in which live action is photographed. In conventional terms, it is "principal photography," the period when the principal performers and major scenes are shot. A high-def digital camera, now called a *camera system*, or a 35mm film camera is used on the set. The camera system produces an electronic image, digitizes it, and records the digital negative. The 35mm film is run through a telecine or another device that digitizes the image, as previously explained.

The video tap built into the camera, which sends a picture that is watched while the scene is being shot (video assist), is recorded for reference—in sync with the digital sound that is recorded on the set, such as dialogue. The shots, kept in sync with their sounds, are digitally logged using the edge numbers on the film negative, which are put there by the manufacturer and are unique, or a time code on the digital video. The script supervisor, who keeps track of the details of each take as it is shot, now works on a laptop, and her or his notes are included in a database linked to the shots. Mechanical special effects, such as explosions and car crashes, and special-effects makeup, such as zombie wounds, are shot on the set. However, it is less dangerous and sometimes gives acceptable results to create the explosions or stunts on a computer and mix them with live-action footage during post-production. It is during production that the director gets the performances he or she wants from the actors and consults with the cinematographer about lighting and composition. (The director's official job is simply to make the best use of the resources the producer has provided.) In post-production, the director normally works with the film editor, the composer, the sound supervisor, and the digital-effects companies.

Digitizing a feature intended to be released on film or digitally is usually done at the highest possible resolution—from 2K to 4K with 10- or 12-bit color—to create the materials for a good master or print. Compressed and lower-resolution files can be made from the full-resolution version. Effects work and grading can be done at 2K, but 1K is sufficient for editing and is fine for standard DV and for *rushes* or *dailies* (digital copies of each day's shooting, which unlike the film prints formerly used are ready to be shown without any lab work; rushes got their name from having to be rushed through the lab).

Even if effects work can be done at 2K, many effects are created at full resolution on a digitized frame to achieve top quality. As previously mentioned, a standard Academy 35mm frame, uncompressed, consumes 56 MB. (The format using the smallest amount of the frame takes up 44 MB.) This does not pose a problem in an effects house, partly because most effects shots are short and are worked on frame by frame, but it's too much for a desktop computer to display in real time and too big to edit. If a 1.33:1 color movie is digitized at theatrical resolution, it runs at 1.34 GB per second, uncompressed. No one is yet working on a feature on an 8,000-GB drive. A conventional dual-layer DVD could hold almost seven seconds of uncompressed footage per

The T-1000 (Robert Patrick) prepares to pull a pole out of its side—sideways—in Terminator 2: Judgment Day.

Fig. 19-9

side. Thus a DVD release is heavily compressed, as discussed earlier, and DVDs meant to be loaded onto the drive of a digital projector are also compressed, sometimes to 10 or 15 discs per feature.

In post-production (though parts of this may now be begun earlier), the film is edited, the effects are generated, the DI is adjusted, the music is composed, and the sound effects are recorded. The *D–M–E* (dialogue, music, and effects) soundtrack is mixed on computerized equipment while the mixer watches the edited print, which consists of the image and dialogue; all these tracks are digitally encoded, logged, and if necessary, fixed. Sound mixing is entirely digital; the final result is at least one digital soundtrack, along with an analog track that may have fewer channels and may have been con- verted from the digital sound master. The final stage of post-production is making a series of trial prints until a final version—the answer print, which must receive the approval of the cinematographer and the producer—is agreed on. Making multiple prints is part of distribution.

Dialogue is often replaced in post-production, with the actors delivering their lines right into a mike and trying to sync with their performances on screen; as dubbing, it goes back to the first sound films. The difference now is that the

recordings may be sped up or slowed down by a computer to achieve sync or alter the delivery of a line; beyond that, any recording may be changed in any number of ways thanks to a host of digital filters, equalizers, and so on. The music may be written earlier in a nonlinear production, so that a film could be edited to match the music instead of the usual practice, in which the composer watches the edited film and writes the music to it.

It is the essence of digital special effects that any image from anywhere can be seamlessly added to the original photograph (if there is one) or computer graphic, just as any area of the original can be electronically removed; there are no bluescreen lines (where the elements of a traveling matte might have joined imperfectly) leaking out at the seams. A frame or shape can be constructed in the computer and then have a photographed image superimposed on or "stuck" to it—which is how, in Charles Russell's *The Mask* (1994), a character is smashed flat as a pancake by a fall, then peels himself off the sidewalk and pumps himself back to his original volume, because the image of the actor (Jim Carrey) has been deformed to the shape of the computer-modeled "pancake" and rides it through all its changes; this is also one way that the evil Terminator, the T-1000 (Robert Patrick),

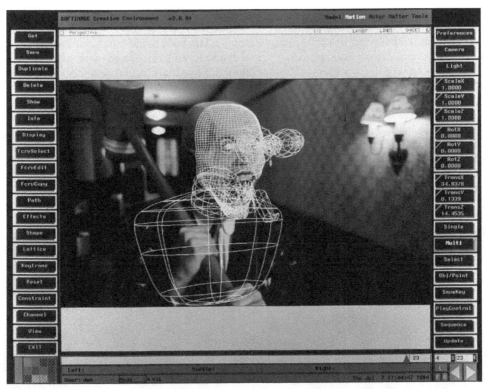

Fig. 19-10

Fig. 19-11
The Mask: *the wire frame superimposed on the photographic plate, as seen on the computer monitor (Fig 19-10), and the completed image as it appears in the movie (Fig 19-11).*

in *Terminator 2* bears the guise of a policeman–robot over its computer-modeled body (supposedly of liquid metal, so that it can be sliced and heal, or change into any shape). Another technique perfected in *Terminator 2*, called *morphing* (from "metamorphosis"), allows one image to change into another—not with a dissolve, for example from the T-1000 as a cop to the T-1000 as a housewife, but with a series of intermediate steps created by the computer, each one a complete and focused image, that begin 100 percent cop/0 percent housewife, then go to 99 percent cop/1 percent housewife, through 50/50 (which in a dissolve would be the most unreadable, double-exposed part of the transition, whereas in morphing this stage is

clear and credible) all the way to 100 percent housewife/0 percent cop. Computers allowed the T-1000's body to close its gaping mercury wounds, to walk through the steel bars of a door in a hospital corridor, and to shine with the right metallic quality.

If Industrial Light & Magic (ILM) could send a herd of dinosaurs romping over a huge landscape and then through and around a group of running actors (not merely behind or in front of them, as with rear projection, but interacting with them in their space), thus giving *Jurassic Park* the credibility that makes it work so well as a fantasy, they could also use computers to allow cartoons and actors to interact in *Who Framed Roger Rabbit* and to allow Jim Carrey to behave

Fig. 19-12

Mighty Joe Young *(1998): To create the illusion that a 13½-foot gorilla is destroying a car because its alarm irritates him, first a car was imploded on a full-sized set, crumpling the middle and blowing its back end upward; this was photographed and became the film plate. Then the actor who played Joe (John Alexander in a suit designed by Rick Baker) pulled up the back of a 40-percent-scale lightweight dummy car (scaled down because the suited actor was 40 percent the size Joe was supposed to be) on a bluescreen set. Computer animators generated, with the aid of much new software—for example, to create and light the thousands of hairs that made up its fur—a CG Joe that matched Alexander's actions and digitally inserted it into the film plate, along with its CG shadow. This shot had to match other shots taken of Alexander against a bluescreen on a 40-percent-scale set.*

like a cartoon in *The Mask*, in each case making the incredible vivid and the suspension of disbelief easier. There are many points in *The Mask* when Carrey behaves like a character in a Tex Avery cartoon—usually Wolfie. To create the shot (Fig. 19-11) in which his eyes bug out of his head and he wags his suddenly long tongue, a regular production shot was made of Carrey, in his green mask makeup, walking down a hallway with a mallet, then opening his mouth and imitating the cartoonish action. Then a CG model of the bugged-out face—a *wire frame* of polygons—was superimposed on the plate of Carrey (the original photographed image). The wire frame changed with every frame of the shot and could be played with until it assumed the desired shape and comic movement. Then a CG image of the mask, eyes, and tongue was *rendered* (created as a picture from all the numerical data, based on the lighting of the scene, the desired colors and textures, and the digital properties of the model), and that animation was wrapped around—or became a high-resolution version of—the wire frame. Where untransformed parts of Carrey could be seen around the animated computer imagery, they were erased (like his real tongue) or allowed to remain (like his hands, holding the mallet). Then the computer put the graphic through its changes, frame after frame, until the electronic-effects shot was complete. Finally, that shot was transferred to film, ready to be cut into the rest of the movie and looking as if it had been photographed along with everything else.

The most common optical effect is the composite (a *digital composite* is one created on a computer instead of an optical printer), which combines into one frame elements that were photographed or generated at different times— like the actors, the alien landscape, and the 3-D animated giant bugs in Verhoeven's *Starship Troopers* (1997) or the many elements combined in the digital composites shown in this chapter from *Mighty Joe Young* (1998, directed by Ron Underwood; a remake of Ernest B. Schoedsack's 1949 original, which had been stop-motion animated by Willis O'Brien and optically printed by Linwood Dunn, using the techniques he and the others had used on *King Kong* in 1933) and from *The Phantom Menace*. In the shot from *Mighty Joe Young*, the final image of the huge gorilla

(Joe) was CGI, digitally inserted frame by frame into a live-action scene. The CG Joe replicated and replaced a man who played Joe through most of the film and who had been photographed in front of a bluescreen in an animatronic gorilla suit (*animatronics* use electronics, cables, and valves to control movement, say on a gorilla's facial apparatus, remotely), crumpling a 40-percent-scale model car on a 40-percent-scale set of Hollywood Boulevard—so he'd look over 13 feet tall. A real car had been imploded on a full-sized set, watched by full-sized actors, and that became the film plate into which the CG Joe was placed, along with his CG shadow and parts of the small-scale set. In the course of making this picture, Kodak discovered flaws in their finest-grain film, artifacts that could be found only with a computer, and they created a new filmstock that would improve all future bluescreen and greenscreen work. (A greenscreen is used if a character is wearing blue, which would create a hole in the picture—that is, in the character's image—and for most video composites.) The pod race in *The Phantom Menace* (Fig. 19-14) was built from an animatic storyboard, and every element in this composite is CGI; there was no film original. In the climactic battle scene (Fig. 19-15) there were no extras, and the cost of outfitting an army was eliminated by creating multiple groups of warriors that were all based on one CG character and that were moving, by groups, in repeated patterns that were difficult to trace. Live warriors were digitally modified. Figure 19-13 is a perfect digital composite; from the 1930s to the 1980s it would have been an optical composite made with traveling mattes on an optical printer. See the color insert for a digital composite from *Revenge of the Sith*.

In 2008, the state of the art was represented by Fincher's *The Curious Case Of Benjamin Button;* based loosely on a short story by F. Scott Fitzgerald, it told the tale of a man who ages backward, born as an old man and dying as a baby, and it offered Brad Pitt (Benjamin) the opportunity to play a character's whole life instead of being one of several actors who would play Benjamin, the normal means of dealing with such a story. Several actors did play Benjamin as an old man and as a boy, but their faces and, in fact, their heads were replaced with Pitt's. For his middle years, Pitt played Benjamin in his own body and using conventional makeup. When he went on to look younger than that, the makeup for Pitt was digital; the computer stripped away the signs of age and built him a younger face. The digital composite that put Pitt's head seamlessly on what looked like an old man's body (see the color insert for an example) was not as remarkable as the technology that went into making the image of that head, which was generated in a computer. The CG image of Pitt at a particular age was made to conform with a *motion-capture* performance (in which all his movements were recorded on a computer) executed by Pitt and confined to his head. The eyes, which establish contact with a character and a sense of his or her inner being, were especially difficult and important to render, for it was necessary—for the emotional structure and strategy of the picture to work—that the audience feel that Benjamin is a single, living character, and as an old man he is played largely by a graphic. The love of Benjamin's life, Daisy (Cate Blanchett), was played as a child by a child; the adult Daisy was played by Blanchett, who was made to look younger through digital processing and older through digitally augmented conventional makeup. For the dancing scenes, Blanchett's head was joined to the body of a younger woman. Both Pitt and Blanchett dubbed the voices for their characters at all ages, in some cases with the aid of a digital equalizer to modify the pitch and shape of the sound to achieve the proper impression of youth or age. The evidence of the computer was seen throughout *Benjamin Button*, from the aerial view of Paris in the 1950s (a computer simulation, looking three-dimensional, precise in every detail, and subtly moving, where earlier effects technicians would have used a matte painting—a painting on glass that shows a background or a location) to the ocean scenes where the tugboat was on a dry soundstage and the water was a program that simulated the behavior of an ocean. Some of the environments and props (the clock that runs backward) were digitally created, and some of the characters were digitally modified, but the viewer still seemed to have been to all these places and times and to have watched and related to all these people, as a story that could never happen was made to look real.

Distribution is the phase in which prints are struck, trailers and ads appear, the movie is released, and prints are sent to theatres. The DIN can be used to make film prints or to generate printing materials. The preparation of a digital print is more complicated. When mastering the digital print, further changes may be made to the DI (for example, to repair a scratch), the final picture is synced with the audio tracks, subtitles are added (in multiple languages), any needed restoration is performed, the image is letter-boxed or squeezed to conform to the desired screen format, closed captioning is added, watermarks are included to enhance security and to control such theatrical events as the opening and closing of curtains, display control data are incorporated, and all these actions and more are referenced to the print that was approved at the end of post-production. The final master may be used to make video masters, film printing materials, and digital prints. Once the master has been encrypted and compressed, the resulting digital print is called a digital cinema package; about 100 GB, it is usually on a portable hard drive or a set of DVDs or BDs. Once it reaches the theatre, the DCP is loaded on the hard drive of a digital projector; decrypted and uncompressed, it can be projected. The DCP offers the exhibitor many choices—for example, to show a film with or without subtitles, which are generated by the digital projector, or in a dubbed version.

After a movie has played theatrically, it is distributed to such nontheatrical markets as airlines, sold on video, rented to cable and satellite companies, and eventually rented for broadcast. It could, of course, skip the theatrical run and be released directly to video or be posted for downloading to desktops and laptops, to portable players, and to cellular phones. (A movie was sent to phones in India in 2004. Shortly thereafter, full-length movies could be played on the video iPod, and by 2009, on the iPhone.) The Internet has opened new avenues of film distribution as well as new opportunities for marketing with more direct and immediate feedback (for example, how many people watch which version of a trailer). By 2006, a filmmaker could post a digital video on a Web site such as YouTube, making it available as a free download, and reach a huge audience; this bypassed the problem of finding a distributor, and the posted sample of his or her

Fig. 19-13

Fig. 19-14

Fig. 19-15
Three digital composites from Star Wars: Episode I—The Phantom Menace. *In Fig. 19-13 the city is a model, the sky is a separately filmed shot, the landscape is a composite of several shots of hilly countryside that were digitally joined and then anamorphically squeezed for a look that was both otherworldly and Earthlike, and the activity on the ground and in the skies is computer generated. No element of Fig. 19-14 was photographed; the landscape (artifically blurred because fast-moving objects blur when shot with a movie camera), the racing pod, and the rest were all created in the computer. The landscape in Fig. 19-15 was created the same way as that in Fig. 19-13, but the shot has no models; thousands of CG warrior–extras (modified from the Jar Jar CG character) were digitally generated and composited frame by frame into a digitally modified landscape.*

DIGITAL CINEMA: 1999–   677

work might make it easier for the filmmaker to find an agent or a distributor for future work. In 2008, Wayne Wang posted his feature *The Princess of Nebraska* (2007) on YouTube so that it could reach a larger audience than it had in theatres. In 2009, YouTube struck a deal with Sony and other companies to provide full-length movies on the site, protected by copyright and supported by ads, and Netflix began streaming many of its titles.

In what might be thought of as the final stage of distribution, the film negative is stored under ideal conditions—in a salt mine, for instance—ready for a re-release or the striking of an archival print. A film negative will outlast a digital print or master by a factor of ten or more. As mentioned earlier, storing a digital print, whether magnetically or on optical discs, means that the file has to be readable in the future. It will have to be copied onto fresh media before the tape or drive or discs containing the file—which never deteriorates and is always the same as it was—degrades, and it will require working equivalents of the equipment and software that created it. Every transfer will cost money, and it is unlikely that enough funds will always be available to save every movie; thus many will be lost. Even if a movie has been a digital project from the start, it is best to transfer it to 35mm film for archiving and storage—preferably on three black-and-white negatives, one for each primary color.

When a film is distributed in 35mm, hundreds of prints are made, and many of them have no business use after a few months of playing in theatres—because they have been scratched or because there is no more demand for them. Making prints and hauling them around the country account for at least half of a distributor's expenses, so most distributors would prefer to release movies in a digital format.

A digital print can be sent to the theatre on a set of discs, on a portable hard drive, by satellite, or over a broadband Internet connection. It weighs from a couple of ounces to nothing. A copy of a digital print costs very little to make, and there is no problem if one wants to release a picture in a few theatres and then make more prints if there is a demand for them; in a film lab, it is more economical to make all the prints at once.

Most theatre owners and projectionists do not see digital distribution and exhibition in such a positive light. A movie still arrives at the theatre, by whatever means, and still has to be loaded onto the projector. With film, the only inconvenience is splicing the shipped reels together into the single big reel that is loaded on the platter of a contemporary projector, then unsplicing them to return the movie to its shipping cans. That is simpler than dealing with an entirely new technology.

Conversion to digital projection would cost a theatre at least $150,000 in the early 2000s, and it was really for the distributor's convenience. Theatres already had digital sound. What could they significantly gain by presenting a digital rather than a film image? Converting theatres would prove economical only if audiences demanded to see digital prints as they once demanded sound . . . and digital sound. By 2009, the desire to see the new digital 3-D pictures appeared to have created a demand for digital projection, and many more projectors were installed worldwide.

The Look of the Future

In 1993, a company announced that it was perfecting the technology that would allow the image of Buster Keaton to star in a new comedy. In 2004, the image of Laurence Olivier was digitally made to perform a new role in Kerry Conran's *Sky Captain and the World of Tomorrow*. And in 2008, Brad Pitt's CG image co-performed the role of the aged Benjamin Button in a fully realized landscape and while interacting with other players.

Now that anything can be constructed as a digital image, the narrative film and the animated film have come closer together. The cinema is at an interesting crossroads, where it can explore the realism of the long take as readily as it can cut itself off from photographic reality. Acknowledging the importance of video and animation, as well as the fact that many movies are not shot on and may no longer be printed on celluloid, some Film Studies programs have renamed themselves Moving-Image Studies.

With 4K shooting and projection, the digital cinema is finally a complete system. It stands ready to replace 35mm film. What will happen depends on whether cinematographers and audiences embrace the new technology. Doubtless, many movies will still be shot and released on film, but many will avoid film entirely. Dual distribution will continue until one medium wins out, which could take a decade. The question is not how great a role video and computers will play in the cinema of the future, but how great a role *film* will play.

For it is clear that digital video and the other technologies described here have transformed the film industry and its product. At this point a cellphone can shoot a movie that can be distributed on YouTube. It is equally clear, looking back, that cinema was the crucial art of the 20th century. But if the age of digital information is taken as license to store films on computer media and if film, which gave the silver screen its silver glow, becomes an obsolete medium for the presentation of movies, then the cinema as an art of projected films may end shortly after its first century. The dialectical conflict of film and TV, or the photochemical and the electronic, will have ended with a synthesis.

It may come down to an issue of what people get used to seeing. The brightness, sharpness, contrast, range, and dyes of the film image used to be recognized, respected, and considered among the essential and definitive characteristics of a unique medium. The film frame is an analog storage system. If it turns out that film is "warm" and the digital image "cold" in the same way that analog sound is said to have a fuller, richer quality than digital sound, then the digital image may lose something that is essential to film—some incalculable part of its visual range—no matter how "filmlike" a frame or a color can be.

Digital cinema may be adopted simply because of its convenience. Reel-to-reel tape has better quality, is transported more evenly, has more surface area, and can run at a faster speed than a tape cassette, but the cassette made it obsolete as a consumer item.

Films still look better in 35mm theatres than they do on the best TVs, although the combination of a BD and a large HDTV can offer a very good 2K experience. One prediction that can be made with assurance is that full-sized theatres will continue to be patronized because of their big screens and auditorium-scale sound. It is equally clear that the home video market will become an ever more significant source of revenue for the film industry, continuing to take in more than the box office every year, and that people will continue to consider the home, or the home theatre, a convenient and satisfactory substitute for the public theatre. Pay-per-view (video on demand) and Internet sales will become more significant distribution channels, as will phones, and one can expect to see more DVDs and BDs making their way to consumers through the mail and more movies being downloaded from the Web. It will become more common to download a movie to a portable player via wireless technology. The future includes a nearly infinite library for download and display.

One can also predict that independent production will increase and that more new pictures will be shot on digital video and edited (as well as being put through the rest of post-production) on portable computers. HD will open the market to many new filmmakers, as DV already has, but at a higher level of quality and with theatre-ready product. Comprehensive standards will be agreed upon for digital color and projection, and that will facilitate the transition to the complete digital cinema. Common video and DV standards and user expectations will expand to high-def as HDTV replaces standard TV, but 2K will begin to look shabby compared with 4K.

The adoption of digital filmmaking is an expanding worldwide movement. Zhang Yimou fell in love with computer effects in *Hero* (2002), where he made, for example, a fighter run crashing through the rain—not a rainstorm, but the individual drops. In his next film, *House of Flying Daggers* (2004), whose digital effects are masterful, there is a wonderful moment when snow covers a fall landscape, as gorgeous as the most painterly digital effect—but what actually happened was that it started to snow, and they decided to keep shooting because they were out of time. There will always be a place for the natural cinema.

International co-production will continue to increase and to inspire the growth of new industries and companies, but it may well be interpreted in a transnational context. The world's sense of borders is changing, thanks in great part to the universe of converging media that has made us virtual citizens of all countries and cultures. We can hope that this will be accompanied by a worldwide expansion of distribution, taking advantage of the culturally more open networks so that more films can be seen outside their countries of origin. More ways will be found to distribute movies and other audiovisual content over the Internet, not just to individuals and theatres, but also to portable digital projectors. The evolving, interconnected digital world will take the movies along with it into a globalized future.

The next stage of digital development will leave video technology behind. Some of the camera chip's information is sacrificed when recording on tape. Recorded directly on a hard drive or flash-memory device, a frame taken by a camera can be purely digital. The tapeless digital workflow—the completely digital procedure of acquiring and modifying data (frames as files), which runs from pre-production to post-production—now in its infancy, will become predominant.

In the United States, it is likely that independent producers will continue to make more films than the major studios, and less expensive ones. A new generation of independent as well as studio filmmakers, raised on computers, will be impatient with the old networks and imperatives and will establish new priorities and procedures.

It can, of course, be foolhardy to make predictions. Disney said it was through with 2-D animation as of 2004, and the trendy nature of some digital advances might have made it seem likely that all new animation, not just at Disney, would soon be 3-D. But any look at a masterpiece like *Spirited Away* or *The Triplets of Belleville* makes it clear that 2-D animation is by no means finished.

One trend that shows strong signs of continuing is the interest in restoring classic movies. In this respect, the look of the future includes the look of the past.

Film preservation and restoration are urgent matters. As of 2006, 50 percent of the films made before 1950—and more than 80 percent of the films made before 1920—had been lost.

Restoration is the art of taking an old, perhaps damaged film, many of whose shots may be missing or out of order, and undoing the damage, finding and assembling the best surviving prints and fragments—and doing a staggering amount of research—in order to strike a new print that is as close as possible to the film as originally released. Ever since the enthusiastic reception of Kevin Brownlow's painstaking restoration of Abel Gance's *Napoleon* (produced and presented in 1981 by Robert A. Harris and Francis Ford Coppola), the commercial value of the pictures gathering dust and turning to nitrate soup in their vaults has impressed itself on film companies both in America and abroad. Harris's own restoration of *Lawrence of Arabia*, which took three years and resulted in the best possible 70mm print of the film as David Lean had intended it to appear—a good 20 minutes longer than the abridged version that had been in circulation, including every shot that had been cut at the producer's orders shortly after the picture first opened—was one of the most significant film events of 1989. Indeed, Columbia's re-release of *Lawrence* received as much public attention as its purchase that same year by Sony, the former as important in the history of the art as the latter is in the history of the business. Spectacularly visual, elegantly paced, sweepingly historic, intellectually and emotionally profound, and with a perfectly clean soundtrack, the restored *Lawrence* hit a generation of film students right in the eyes—students who had seen films projected in 70mm (like *Alien*, blown up from 35mm) but nothing *shot* in 70mm—that is, nothing with the perfect detail of the 65mm camera negative. In a time of action–adventure teenpix and little adult pictures with two characters who come to appreciate each other, *Lawrence* appeared like the conscience of narrative film.

In 1987, Paramount began to inventory and preserve its film and television archives—200,000 cans of material. In 1990, it opened a building for the archive and announced a program of re-releases. By June 1990, both Warner Bros. and Columbia had announced their own film preservation campaigns, and eight filmmakers—Woody Allen, Francis Ford Coppola, Stanley Kubrick, George Lucas, Sydney Pollack, Robert Redford, Steven Spielberg, and the president of the board, Martin Scorsese—had formed The Film Foundation to raise at least $30 million for restorations to be carried out jointly by studios and archives. That same year, Disney completed a restoration of *Fantasia* for the film's 50th anniversary, the first time in decades that it had been seen full-frame. Also in 1990, at France's Gaumont, Pierre Philippe and

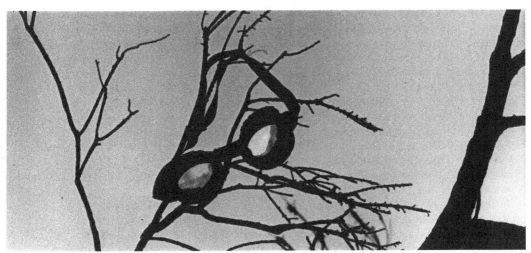

Fig. 19-16
Lawrence's goggles, snagged on a branch: the last shot in the sequence of Lawrence's fatal motorcycle accident and the first shot restored to **Lawrence of Arabia.**

Jean-Louis Bompoint restored Jean Vigo's *L'Atalante*, which had been released in 1934 in a version recut by the producers, who found the director's cut gloomy and uncommercial—the only version available from 1934 to 1990 (when Vigo's cut was found in the archives of the British Film Institute), the one that earned classic status and has been analyzed shot by shot for years. The restored director's cut of *L'Atalante* is a real historical surprise, 10 minutes longer and with a more flowing, less jumpy rhythm, revealing a complex, mature break with the style of *Zero for Conduct*. It is also as stunningly beautiful, as clean and fresh and strange, as it was in 1934. The 1998 restoration of *Touch of Evil* did not clean up or lengthen the release version, but tossed it. Editor and sound designer Walter Murch and producer Rick Schmidlin went back to the original reels of sound and picture, then edited and mixed them according to the instructions Welles had left in a 58-page memo, written immediately after he had seen the studio's cut. It was like seeing the film for the first time.

Many restorations are now done on computer, not on film. In a *digital restoration*, the best available film elements are fed into a computer, which can use all the resources of a DI and more to clean up and otherwise restore the image and sound. From 1998 to 2002, *Metropolis* was restored at 2K; it was released

on both film and DVD, and the film version looked as good as an average 35mm print— except that it was longer, more coherent, more carefully motivated, and less silly. DI technology is becoming more important in digital restoration, and the result can be a new negative—whether or not new prints are struck and shown—as well as a video release that pays for the restoration.

Computers can alter films in many ways, good and bad. Colorization, which evolved into a creative tool for a picture like *Pleasantville*, still is practiced and remains the opposite of restoration. In Joe Dante's *Gremlins 2—The New Batch* (1990), a cable station, modeled on one of Ted Turner's, announces a showing of *Casablanca*, "Now in color, with a happier ending." In 1990, Turner owned 2,200 MGM films, 750 RKO films, and 750 pre-1950 Warner Bros. films—not just their TV rights but the movies themselves as well as their domestic theatrical distribution rights. He showed them on his stations, exposing millions of people to films that had not been out of the archives for decades. But Turner had some popular black-and-white films colorized, convinced that he was improving them, and he upset many people with his widely announced plans to colorize *Citizen Kane*. As it turned out, a clause in Welles's original RKO contract, which remained binding on any owner of the film, specified that no changes could be made in *Citizen Kane* without Welles's approval—or that of his heirs, who were not about to give it. Welles had the right of final cut on *Kane*, and even from the grave the final word: No. Denied the right to colorize *Kane*, Turner had it restored. A new 35mm negative was prepared under the supervision of the film's original editor, Robert Wise, and Turner arranged for the new prints to be distributed theatrically by Paramount. *Citizen Kane* opened in ten cities on May 1, 1991, exactly 50 years after its opening at the RKO Palace in New York.

In 1993, in the largest digital film-processing project yet attempted, all 120,000 frames of *Snow White* were cleaned in a computer, the dust removed and the scratches stitched together with excellent results. In the early 2000s, Charles Burnett's *Killer of Sheep* was restored by UCLA. The film had been shot on 16mm, and Burnett had never cleared the music rights; thus its 1977 "release" was underground. Cleaned despite considerable damage, blown up to 35mm, and with the rights finally cleared (a process that took years), *Killer of Sheep* opened in 2007, perhaps the first film to have been restored before it was officially released.

The more films are restored to their original look and length, and the more new movies appear, the more the art and history of motion pictures will live and grow. We can only hope that many of those movies will be shot and printed on celluloid, because we want all the information every one of those frames can give us.

For Further Viewing

FILMS

PIXAR ANIMATION STUDIOS
Luxo Jr. (1986, John A. Lasseter)
Toy Story (1995, John A. Lasseter)
   a bug's life (1998, John A. Lasseter and Andrew Stanton)
Toy Story 2 (1999, John A. Lasseter, Lee Unkrich, and Ash Brannon)
For the Birds (2001, Ralph Eggleston)
Monsters, Inc. (2001, Pete Docter)
Finding Nemo (2003, Andrew Stanton)
The Incredibles (2004, Brad Bird)
Cars (2006, John A. Lasseter and Joe Ranft)
Ratatouille (2007, Brad Bird and Jan Pinkava)
Wall-E (2008, Andrew Stanton)
Up (2009, Pete Docter and Bob Peterson). 3-D

MISCELLANY: DIGITAL CINEMA
Catalog (1961, John Whitney)
Permutations and *Experiments in Motion Graphics* (1968, John Whitney)
One from the heart or *One From The Heart* (1982, Francis Ford Coppola)
Star Trek II: The Wrath of Khan (1982, Nicholas Meyer)
TRON (1982, Steven Lisberger)
The Abyss (1989, James Cameron)
Dick Tracy (1990, Warren Beatty)
Prospero's Books (1991, Peter Greenaway)
Terminator 2: Judgment Day (1991, James Cameron)
Batman Returns (1992, Tim Burton)
Jurassic Park (1993, Steven Spielberg)
Last Action Hero (1993, John McTiernan)
Forrest Gump (1994, Robert Zemeckis)
The Mask (1994, Charles Russell)
The English Patient (1996, Anthony Minghella)
The Nutty Professor (1996, Tom Shadyac)
Titanic (1997, James Cameron)
Star Wars: Episode I—The Phantom Menace (1999, George Lucas)
O Brother, Where Art Thou? (2000, Joel and Ethan Coen)
The Lord of the Rings: The Fellowship of the Ring (2001, Peter Jackson)
Shrek (2001, Andrew Adamson and Vicky Jenson)
Waking Life (2001, Richard Linklater)
Hero (2002, Zhang Yimou)
The Lord of the Rings: The Two Towers (2002, Peter Jackson)
Russian Ark (2002, Alexander Sokurov)
Star Wars: Episode II—Attack of the Clones (2002, George Lucas)
Cold Mountain (2003, Anthony Minghella)
The Lord of the Rings: The Return of the King (2003, Peter Jackson)
House of Flying Daggers (2004, Zhang Yimou)
The Polar Express (2004, Robert Zemeckis). 3-D
Ryan (2004, Chris Landreth). Canadian short
Sky Captain and the World of Tomorrow (2004, Kerry Conran)

Spider-Man 2 (2004, Sam Raimi)
Star Wars: Episode III—Revenge of the Sith
(2005, George Lucas)
A Scanner Darkly (2006, Richard Linklater)
Superman Returns (2006, Bryan Singer)
Harry Potter and the Order of the Phoenix
(2007, David Yates)
300 (2007, Zack Snyder)
Bolt (2008, Byron Howard and Chris Williams).
3-D
The Curious Case Of Benjamin Button (2008,
David Fincher)
Avatar (2009, James Cameron). 3-D
Disney's A Christmas Carol (2009, Robert
Zemeckis). 3-D

DVDs

Bit rates: See *The Mummy* (Chap. 11 list) and
Lawrence of Arabia (Chap. 14 list).
The Curious Case Of Benjamin Button (2008,
David Fincher). Criterion Collection.
Includes a very long and comprehensive
making-of documentary that may also be
viewed as a set of featurettes, augmented by
storyboards, costume sketches, and more.
Hero (see Chap. 14 list).
The Lord of the Rings (see Chap. 16 list).
*Master and Commander: The Far Side of the
World* (2003, **Peter Weir**). 20th Century Fox.
Widescreen Collector's Edition. Includes a
making-of documentary emphasizing Weir's
involvement from pre- to post-production, an
interview with Weir, edited sequences that can
be broken down into takes, a demonstration
of microphone placement, a short on sound
design, and clear demonstrations of **digital
effects.**
Monsters, Inc. (2001, **Pete Docter**). Buena Vista
Home Entertainment. Collector's Edition.
Includes a **Pixar** short, *For the Birds;*
information about the making of the film, laid
out in a production-timeline menu; and more.
O Brother, Where Art Thou? (2000, **Joel and
Ethan Coen**). Touchstone Video. Includes a
documentary about the **digital intermediate**
process, a music video, and a script-to-
storyboard-to-scene comparison.
One from the heart (see Chap. 18 list).
Restored versions are **boldfaced** in all the lists:
See *Metropolis* (Chap. 7), *The Passion of Joan
of Arc* (Chap. 10), *Touch of Evil* (Chap. 11),
Lawrence of Arabia (Chap. 14), *The
Godfather* (Chap. 15), etc.
Russian Ark (see Chap. 16 list).
Star Wars (see Chap. 17 list).
Terminator 2: Judgment Day (1991, **James
Cameron**). Artisan Entertainment. Ultimate
Edition. Includes the release cut and the
extended cut, storyboards, the script, and
hours of making-of documentaries and shorts.
Timecode (see Chap. 18 list).
Toy Story: The Ultimate Toy Box (1995–99,
John A. Lasseter). Disney/Pixar. Collector's
Edition. Contains both of the movies and a
third disc with excellent making-of
documentaries and demonstrations.

For Further Reading

NOTE: Within an authorial entry, books are listed in the order in which they were first published but are given in their most recent editions; earlier versions may be available in the library.

CHAPTER 1: INTRODUCTORY ASSUMPTIONS

GENERAL HISTORIES OF FILM AND REFERENCE WORKS

Acker, Ally. *Reel Women: Pioneers of the Cinema 1896 to the Present.* New York: Continuum, 1991.

Allen, Robert C., and Douglas Gomery. *Film History: Theory and Practice.* New York: McGraw-Hill, 1993.

Alvarez, Max Joseph. *Index to Motion Pictures Reviewed by VARIETY, 1907–1980.* Lanham, Md.: Scarecrow Press, 1982.

Altman, Rick. *Silent Film Sound.* New York: Columbia University Press, 2004.

The American Film Institute Catalog. Feature Films, 1911–1920. 2 vols. Berkeley and Los Angeles: University of California Press, 1988.

———. *Feature Films, 1921–1930.* 2 vols. New York: Bowker, 1971.

———. *Feature Films, 1931–1940.* 3 vols. Berkeley and Los Angeles: University of California Press, 1992.

———. *Feature Films, 1941–1950.* 3 vols. Berkeley and Los Angeles: University of California Press, 1999.

———. *Feature Films, 1961–1970.* 2 vols. Berkeley and Los Angeles: University of California Press, 1997.

———. *Within Our Gates: Ethnicity in American Feature Films, 1911–1960.* Berkeley and Los Angeles: University of California Press, 1997.

Armes, Roy. *Third World Film Making and the West.* Berkeley and Los Angeles: University of California Press, 1987.

ASC Manual. See Burum.

Barnouw, Erik. *Documentary: A History of the Non-Fiction Film.* 2nd rev. ed. New York: Oxford University Press, 1993.

Barsacq, Léon. *Caligari's Cabinet and Other Grand Illusions: A History of Film Design.* New York: New American Library, 1978.

Barsam, Richard. *Nonfiction Film: A Critical History.* Rev. ed. Bloomington: Indiana University Press, 1992.

Bogle, Donald. *Toms, Coons, Mulattoes, Mammies, and Bucks: An Interpretive History of Blacks in American Films.* 4th ed. New York: Continuum, 2001.

Bordwell, David, Janet Staiger, and Kristin Thompson. *The Classical Hollywood Cinema: Film Style and Mode of Production to 1960.* New York: Columbia University Press, 1985.

Bowser, Eileen, ed. *Film Notes.* New York: Museum of Modern Art, 1969.

Brakhage, Stan. *Film Biographies.* Berkeley: Turtle Island, 1977.

Brownlow, Kevin. *The Parade's Gone By. . . .* Berkeley and Los Angeles: University of California Press, 1976.

Burum, Stephen, ed. *American Cinematographer Manual.* 9th ed. Hollywood: ASC Press, 2004.

Carr, Robert E., and R. M. Hayes. *Wide Screen Movies: A History and Filmography of Wide Gauge Filmmaking.* Jefferson, N.C.: McFarland, 1988.

Cherchi Usai, Paolo. *Silent Cinema: An Introduction.* 2nd. ed. (Formerly *Burning Passions.*) London: BFI, 2008.

Conant, Michael. *Anti-trust in the Motion Picture Industry.* Berkeley and Los Angeles: University of California Press, 1960.

Cook, David A. *A History of Narrative Film.* 4th ed. New York: Norton, 2004.

Cripps, Thomas. *Slow Fade to Black: The Negro in American Film, 1900–1942.* New York: Oxford University Press, 1993.

Dunn, Linwood, and George E. Turner, eds. *The ASC Treasury of Visual Effects.* Hollywood: American Society of Cinematographers, 1983.

Everson, William K. *American Silent Film*. New York: Oxford University Press, 1978.

Fell, John L. *A History of Films*. New York: Holt, Rinehart, 1978.

Ferreux, Huguette Marquand, ed. *Musée du Cinéma Henri Langlois*. 3 vols. Paris: Maeght Éditeur, 1991.

Fielding, Raymond. *A Technological History of Motion Pictures and Television*. Berkeley and Los Angeles: University of California Press, 1967.

————. *The Technique of Special Effects Cinematography*. 4th ed. Burlington, Mass.: Focal Press, 1985.

Finler, Joel W. *The Hollywood Story*. 3rd ed. London: Wallflower Press, 2003.

Focal Encyclopedia of Film and Television Techniques. See Spottiswoode.

Halliwell, Leslie. *See* Walker.

Harpole, Charles, general editor. *History of the American Cinema*. 10 vols. New York: Scribner's, 1990–2003; Berkeley and Los Angeles: University of California Press (reprints), 1994–2006.

Haskell, Molly. *From Reverence to Rape: The Treatment of Women in the Movies*. 2nd ed. Chicago: University of Chicago Press, 1987.

Hayes, R. M. *3-D Movies: A History and Filmography of Stereoscopic Cinema*. Jefferson, N.C.: McFarland, 1989.

Hines, William E. *Job Descriptions for Film, Video & CGI*. 5th ed. Los Angeles: Ed-Venture, 1999.

James, David E., and Rick Berg, eds. *The Hidden Foundation: Cinema and the Question of Class*. Minneapolis: University of Minnesota Press, 1996.

Jowett, Garth. *Film, The Democratic Art: A Social History of American Film*. Burlington, Mass.: Focal Press, 1985.

Kattelle, Alan. *Home Movies: A History of the American Industry, 1897–1979*. Nashua, N.H.: Transition, 2000.

Katz, Ephraim. *The Film Encyclopedia*. 6th ed. Revised by Ronald Dean Nolen. New York: HarperCollins, 2008.

Kawin, Bruce F. *How Movies Work*. Berkeley and Los Angeles: University of California Press, 1992.

Kisch, John, and Edward Mapp. *A Separate Cinema: Fifty Years of Black-Cast Posters*. New York: Farrar, Straus & Giroux, 1992.

Kuhn, Annette, and Susannah Radstone, eds. *The Women's Companion to International Film*. Berkeley and Los Angeles: University of California Press, 1994.

Luhr, William, ed. *World Cinema Since 1945*. New York: Ungar, 1987.

Macgowan, Kenneth. *Behind the Screen*. New York: Delacorte, 1965.

Maltin, Leonard, ed. *Leonard Maltin's Movie Guide*. Annual vols. New York: Signet.

Mannoni, Laurent. *The Great Art of Light and Shadow: Archaeology of the Cinema*. Translated and edited by Richard Crangle. Exeter, UK: University of Exeter Press, 2000.

Manvell, Roger. *The International Encyclopedia of Film*. New York: Crown, 1972.

Mast, Gerald, ed. *The Movies in Our Midst: Documents in the Cultural History of Film in America*. Chicago: University of Chicago Press, 1982.

McGee, Marty. *Encyclopedia of Motion Picture Sound*. Jefferson, N.C.: McFarland, 2001.

Monaco, James. *How to Read a Film: Movies, Media, and Beyond*. 4th ed. New York: Oxford University Press, 2009.

New York Times Film Reviews, 1913–1998. 18 vols. plus annual vols. Hamden, Conn.: Garland, 2001. Later vols. from Routledge (New York).

Pratt, George C. *Spellbound in Darkness: A History of the Silent Film*. Rev. ed. Greenwich, Conn.: New York Graphic Society, 1973.

Randall, Richard S. *Censorship of the Movies*. Madison: University of Wisconsin Press, 1968.

Reisz, Karel, and Gavin Millar. *The Technique of Film Editing*. 2nd ed. Burlington, Mass.: Focal Press, 1968.

Rhode, Eric. *A History of the Cinema from its Origins to 1970*. New York: Hill and Wang, 1976.

Rotha, Paul, and Richard Griffith. *The Film Till Now*. Rev. ed. Boston: Twayne, 1960.

Russo, Vito. *The Celluloid Closet: Homosexuality in the Movies*. Rev. ed. New York: Harper & Row, 1987.

Ryan, Rod. *A History of Motion Picture Color Technology*. Burlington, Mass.: Focal Press, 1978.

Sadoul, Georges. *Histoire Générale du Cinéma*. 5 vols. Paris: Editions Denoël, 1946–54.

————. *Dictionary of Film Makers*. Translated and updated by Peter Morris. Berkeley and Los Angeles: University of California Press, 1972.

————. *Dictionary of Films*. Translated and updated by Peter Morris. Berkeley and Los Angeles: University of California Press, 1972.

Salt, Barry. *Film Style and Technology: History and Analysis*. 2nd ed. London: Starword, 1992.

Sarris, Andrew. *The American Cinema: Directors and Directions, 1929–1968*. New York: Da Capo Press, 1996.

Segrave, Kerry. *Drive-in Theaters: A History from Their Inception in 1933*. Jefferson, N.C.: McFarland, 2006.

Singleton, Ralph S., and James A. Conrad. *Filmmaker's Dictionary*. 2nd ed. Edited by Janna Wong Healy. Hollywood: Lone Eagle Publishing, 2000.

Sitney, P. Adams, ed. Film Culture *Reader.* New York: Cooper Square Press, 2000.

Sklar, Robert. *Movie-Made America: A Cultural History of American Movies.* Rev. ed. New York: Random House, 1994.

———. *Film: An International History of the Medium.* 2nd ed. Upper Saddle River, N.J.: Prentice Hall, 2001.

Slide, Anthony. *The New Historical Dictionary of the American Film Industry.* Lanham, Md.: Scarecrow Press, 2001.

Spottiswoode, Raymond, et al. *The Focal Encyclopedia of Film and Television Techniques.* Burlington, Mass.: Focal Press, 1969.

Thompson, Kristin, and David Bordwell. *Film History: An Introduction.* 3rd ed. New York: McGraw-Hill, 2009.

Thomson, David. *The New Biographical Dictionary of Film.* Expanded and updated ed. New York: Knopf, 2004.

Variety International Film Guide. Annual vols., changing editors. Los Angeles: Silman-James Press.

Variety Obituaries, 1905–1992. 14 vols. Hamden, Conn.: Garland, 1993.

Wagenknecht, Edward. *The Movies in the Age of Innocence.* New York: Limelight, 1997.

Walker, John, ed. *Halliwell's Who's Who in the Movies.* 4th rev. ed. (Formerly *The Filmgoer's Companion.*) New York: HarperCollins, 2006.

Weis, Elisabeth, and John Belton, eds. *Film Sound: Theory and Practice.* New York: Columbia University Press, 1985.

Willis, Donald C. *Horror and Science Fiction Films: A Checklist.* 4 vols. Lanham, Md.: Scarecrow Press, 1972–97.

Willis, John. *Screen World.* Annual vols. New York and London: Applause.

CHAPTER 2: BIRTH

Abel, Richard, ed. *Encyclopedia of Early Cinema.* New York and Milton Park, UK: Routledge, 2005.

Anderson, Joseph, and Barbara Anderson. "The Myth of Persistence of Vision Revisited." *Journal of Film and Video,* Vol. 45, No. 1 (Spring 1993).

Aumont, Jacques. *The Image.* Translated by Claire Pajackowska. London: BFI, 1997.

———. *L'Image.* 2nd ed. Paris: Nathan, 2000.

Barnes, John. *The Beginnings of the Cinema in England: 1894–1901, Vol. 1: 1894–1896.* Rev. ed. Exeter, UK: University of Exeter Press, 1998.

Ceram, C. W., *pseud. See* Marek.

de Lauretis, Teresa, and Stephen Heath, eds. *The Cinematic Apparatus.* New York: Palgrave–Macmillan, 1985.

Dickson, W. K–L. *The Biograph in Battle: Its Story in the South African War Related with Personal Experiences.* Trowbridge, U.K.: Flicks Books, 1995.

Dickson, W. K–L., and Antonia Dickson. *A History of the Kinetograph, Kinetoscope, and Kineto-phonograph.* New York: Arno, 1970.

Elsaesser, Thomas, with Adam Barker, eds. *Early Cinema: Space—Frame—Narrative.* London: BFI, 1990.

Gunning, Tom. "The Cinema of Attractions: Early Film, Its Spectator and the Avant-Garde." *Wide Angle* Vol. 8, No. 3–4 (Autumn–Winter 1986). Reprinted in Elsaesser and Barker, *Early Cinema,* above.

Hendricks, Gordon. *The Edison Motion Picture Myth.* Berkeley and Los Angeles: University of California Press, 1961.

———. *Eadweard Muybridge: The Father of the Motion Picture.* New York: Grossman, 1965.

Jenkins, C. Francis. *Animated Pictures.* Washington, D.C.: McQueen, 1898.

Mannoni, Laurent. *The Great Art of Light and Shadow: Archaeology of the Cinema.* Translated and edited by Richard Crangle. Exeter, UK: University of Exeter Press, 2000.

Mannoni, Laurent, Donata Pesenti Campagnoni, and David Robinson. *Light and Movement: Incunabula of the Motion Picture.* Gemona: Le Giornate del Cinema Muto, 1995. Distributed by BFI.

Marek, K. W. (Ceram, C. W.) *Archaeology of the Cinema.* New York: Harcourt, Brace, 1965.

Münsterberg, Hugo. *The Photoplay: A Psychological Study.* New York: Appleton, 1916. (Reprinted as *The Film: A Psychological Study: The Silent Photoplay in 1916.* New York: Dover, 2004.)

Musser, Charles. *The Emergence of Cinema: The American Screen to 1907.* Vol. 1 of Charles Harpole, ed., *History of the American Cinema.* New York: Scribner's, 1990; Berkeley and Los Angeles: University of California Press, 1994.

———. *Edison Motion Pictures, 1890–1900: An Annotated Filmography.* Washington, D.C.: Smithsonian Institution Press; Gemona: Le Giornate del Cinema Muto, 1997.

Muybridge, Eadweard. *Human and Animal Locomotion.* 3 vols. New York: Dover, 1979.

Newhall, Beaumont. *The History of Photography: From 1839 to the Present Day.* rev. ed. New York: Museum of Modern Art, 1964.

———. *Latent Image: The Discovery of Photography.* Garden City, N.Y.: Doubleday, 1967.

Sadoul, Georges. *Louis Lumière.* Paris: Seghers, 1964.

Watson, Robert Irving. *The Great Psychologists.* 5th ed. Upper Saddle River, N.J.: Prentice Hall, 1991.

CHAPTER 3: FILM NARRATIVE, COMMERCIAL EXPANSION

Abel, Richard. *The Ciné Goes to Town: French Cinema, 1896–1914*. Updated ed. Berkeley and Los Angeles: University of California Press, 1998.

———, ed. *Encyclopedia of Early Cinema*. New York and Milton Park, UK: Routledge, 2005.

Addams, Jane. *The Spirit of Youth and the City Streets*. New York: Macmillan, 1909.

Arvidson, Linda. *When the Movies Were Young*. New York: Benjamin Blom, 1968.

Balshofer, Fred J., and Arthur C. Miller. *One Reel a Week*. Berkeley and Los Angeles: University of California Press, 1968.

Barnes, John. *The Beginnings of the Cinema in England: 1894–1901*. 6 vols. Exeter, UK: University of Exeter Press, 1997– . Volume 1 rev. 1998. Volume 5 covers 1900.

Blaché, Alice Guy. *See* Slide.

Bowen, Louise de Koven. *Five and Ten Cent Theatres*. Chicago: Juvenile Protective Assn., 1911.

Bruno, Giuliana. *Streetwalking on a Ruined Map: Cultural Theory and the City Films of Elvira Notari*. Princeton: Princeton University Press, 1993.

Crafton, Donald. *Before Mickey: The Animated Film 1898–1928*. Cambridge, Mass.: MIT Press, 1982.

———. *Emile Cohl, Caricature, and Film*. Princeton: Princeton University Press, 1990.

Elsaesser, Thomas, with Adam Barker, eds. *Early Cinema: Space—Frame—Narrative*. London: BFI, 1990.

Fell, John L. *Film and the Narrative Tradition*. Berkeley and Los Angeles: University of California Press, 1986.

———, ed. *Film Before Griffith*. Berkeley and Los Angeles: University of California Press, 1983.

Frazer, John. *Artificially Arranged Scenes: The Films of Georges Méliès*. Boston: Twayne, 1980.

Grau, Robert. *The Theater of Science*. New York: Broadway Publishing, 1914.

Guy, Alice. *See* Slide.

Low, Rachel, and Roger Manvell. *History of the British Film (1896–1918)*. 3 vols. London: Allen & Unwin, 1948–50.

McMahan, Alison. *Alice Guy Blaché: Lost Visionary of the Cinema*. New York: Continuum, 2002.

Musser, Charles. *The Emergence of Cinema: The American Screen to 1907*. Vol. 1 of Harpole, Charles, ed., *History of the American Cinema*. New York: Scribner's, 1990; Berkeley and Los Angeles: University of California Press, 1994.

———. *Before the Nickelodeon: Edwin S. Porter and the Edison Manufacturing Company*. Berkeley and Los Angeles: University of California Press, 1991.

Niver, Kemp R. *Motion Pictures from the Library of Congress Paper Print Collection 1894–1912*. Berkeley and Los Angeles: University of California Press, 1967.

———. *Biograph Bulletins 1896–1908*. Los Angeles: Artisan Press, 1971.

Slide, Anthony. *The Big V: A History of the Vitagraph Company*. Lanham, Md.: Scarecrow Press, 1987.

———. *Early Women Directors*. New York: Barnes, 1977.

———. *Early American Cinema*. Rev. ed. Lanham, Md.: Scarecrow Press, 1994.

———. *The Memoirs of Alice Guy Blaché*. Rev. ed. Lanham, Md.: Scarecrow Press, 1996.

———. *The New Historical Dictionary of the American Film Industry*. Lanham, Md.: Scarecrow Press, 2001.

Smith, Albert E., and P. A. Koury. *Two Reels and a Crank*. New York: Garland, 1984.

CHAPTER 4: GRIFFITH

Affron, Charles. *Lillian Gish: Her Legend, Her Life*. New York: Scribner's, 2001.

Barry, Iris, and Eileen Bowser. *D. W. Griffith: American Film Master*. New York: Museum of Modern Art, 1965.

Bernardi, Daniel, ed. *The Birth of Whiteness: Race and the Emergence of U.S. Cinema*. New Brunswick, N.J.: Rutgers University Press, 1996.

Bitzer, G. W. *Billy Bitzer: His Story*. New York: Farrar, Straus & Giroux, 1974.

Bowser, Eileen. *The Transformation of Cinema: 1907–1915*. Vol. 2 of Harpole, Charles, ed., *History of the American Cinema*. New York: Scribner's, 1990; Berkeley and Los Angeles: University of California Press, 1994.

Cherchi Usai, Paolo, ed. *The Griffith Project*. Annual vols. London: BFI.

Dixon, Thomas. *The Leopard's Spots: A Romance of the White Man's Burden—1865–1900*. New York: Doubleday, Page & Co., 1903.

———. *The Clansman: An Historical Romance of the Ku Klux Klan*. New York: Grosset & Dunlap, 1905.

———. *The Traitor*. New York: Doubleday, Page & Co., 1907.

———. *The Reconstruction Trilogy*. (Includes *The Leopard's Spots*, *The Clansman*, and *The Traitor*.) Newport Beach, Calif.: Noontide Press, 1994.

Gish, Lillian, with Ann Pinchot. *The Movies, Mr. Griffith, and Me*. Englewood Cliffs, N.J.: Prentice-Hall, 1969.

Griffith, D. W. *The Man Who Invented Hollywood: The Autobiography of D. W. Griffith*. Edited by James Hart. Louisville, Ky.: Touchstone, 1972.

Gunning, Tom. *D.W. Griffith and the Origins of American Narrative Film: The Early Years at Biograph.* Urbana and Chicago: University of Illinois Press, 1991.

Henderson, Robert M. *D.W. Griffith: The Years at Biograph.* New York: Farrar, Straus & Giroux, 1970.

———. *D. W. Griffith: His Life and Work.* New York: Oxford University Press, 1972.

Huff, Theodore. *Intolerance: Shot-by-Shot Analysis.* New York: Museum of Modern Art, 1966.

Jesionowski, Joyce E. *Thinking in Pictures: Dramatic Structure in D. W. Griffith's Biograph Films.* Berkeley and Los Angeles: University of California Press, 1987.

Niver, Kemp R. *D.W. Griffith: His Biograph Films in Perspective.* Los Angeles: John D. Roche, 1974.

Stern, Seymour. *Griffith: I—"The Birth of a Nation."* Film Culture #36 (Spring–Summer 1965). New York: Film Culture, 1965.

CHAPTER 5: MACK SENNETT AND THE CHAPLIN SHORTS

Agee, James. "Comedy's Greatest Era." In *Agee on Film.* 2 vols. New York: McDowell, Obolensky, 1960.

Arnheim, Rudolf. *Film as Art.* Berkeley and Los Angeles: University of California Press, 1957.

Asplund, Una. *Chaplin's Films.* Translated by Paul Britten Austin. London: David & Charles, 1971.

Bergson, Henri. *Laughter: An Essay on the Meaning of the Comic.* Translated by Cloudesley Brereton and Fred Rothwell. New York: Dover, 2005.

Chaplin, Charles. *My Autobiography.* New York: Simon and Schuster, 1964.

Huff, Theodore. *Charlie Chaplin.* New York: Henry Schuman, 1951.

Lahue, Kalton C., and Terry Brewer. *Kops and Custard.* Norman: University of Oklahoma Press, 1968.

McCabe, John. *Charlie Chaplin.* Garden City, N.Y.: Doubleday, 1978.

Payne, Robert. *The Great God Pan.* Garden City, N.Y.: Hermitage House, 1952.

Robinson, David. *Chaplin: His Life and Art.* New York: Da Capo, 1994.

Sennett, Mack. *King of Comedy.* New York: Doubleday, 1954.

Sullivan, Ed. *Chaplin vs. Chaplin.* Hollywood: Marvin Miller Enterprises, 1965.

Tyler, Parker. *Chaplin: Last of the Clowns.* New York: Horizon, 1972.

CHAPTER 6: MOVIE CZARS AND MOVIE STARS

Abel, Richard, and Rick Altman, eds. *The Sounds of Early Cinema.* Bloomington: Indiana University Press, 2001.

Acker, Ally. *Reel Women: Pioneers of the Cinema 1896 to the Present.* New York: Continuum, 1991.

Anger, Kenneth. *Hollywood Babylon.* New York: Dell, 1981.

Barnouw, Erik. *Documentary: A History of the Non-Fiction Film.* 2nd rev. ed. New York: Oxford University Press, 1993.

Barr, Charles. *Laurel and Hardy.* Berkeley and Los Angeles: University of California Press, 1968.

Barsam, Richard. *The Vision of Robert Flaherty: The Artist as Myth and Filmmaker.* Bloomington: Indiana University Press, 1988.

Berg, A. Scott. *Goldwyn: A Biography.* New York: Penguin Putnam/Riverhead Books, 1998.

Blesh, Rudi. *Keaton.* New York: Macmillan, 1966.

Bowser, Pearl, Jane Gaines, and Charles Musser, eds. *Oscar Micheaux and His Circle: African-American Filmmaking and Race Cinema of the Silent Era.* Bloomington: Indiana University Press, 2001.

Brooks, Louise. *Lulu in Hollywood.* New York: Knopf, 1982.

Brownlow, Kevin. *The Parade's Gone By....* Berkeley and Los Angeles: University of California Press, 1976.

———. *Behind the Mask of Innocence: Sex, Violence, Prejudice, Crime: Films of Social Conscience in the Silent Era.* New York: Knopf, 1990.

———. *Mary Pickford Rediscovered: Rare Pictures of a Hollywood Legend.* New York: Abrams, 1999.

Brownlow, Kevin, and John Kobal. *Hollywood: The Pioneers.* New York: Knopf, 1979.

Cooke, Alistair. *Douglas Fairbanks: The Making of a Screen Character.* New York: Macmillan, 1940.

Croy, Homer W. *How Motion Pictures Are Made.* New York: Harper, 1918.

DeMille, Cecil B. *Autobiography.* Englewood Cliffs, N.J.: Prentice-Hall, 1959.

Durgnat, Raymond, and Scott Simmon. *King Vidor, American.* Berkeley and Los Angeles: University of California Press, 1988.

Endres, Stacey, and Robert Cushman. *Hollywood's Chinese Theatre: The Hand and Footprints of the Stars from the Silents to "Star Trek."* Los Angeles and London: Pomegranate Press, 1992.

Everson, William K. *The Films of Laurel and Hardy.* New York: Citadel, 1967.

Finler, Joel. *Stroheim.* Berkeley and Los Angeles: University of California Press, 1968.

———, ed. Greed: *A film by Erich von Stroheim.* (Includes the script.) New York: Simon & Schuster, 1972.

Green, J. Ronald. *Straight Lick: The Cinema of Oscar Micheaux.* Bloomington: Indiana University Press, 2000.

———. *With a Crooked Stick: The Films of Oscar Micheaux.* Bloomington: Indiana University Press, 2004.

Grierson, John. *Grierson on Documentary.* Edited by Forsyth Hardy. Rev. ed. London: Faber, 1966.

Irwin, Will. *The House that Shadows Built.* New York: Doubleday, 1928.

Keaton, Buster, with Charles Samuels. *My Wonderful World of Slapstick.* Garden City, N.Y.: Doubleday, 1960.

Kerr, Walter. *The Silent Clowns.* New York: Da Capo, 1990.

Kisch, John, and Edward Mapp. *A Separate Cinema: Fifty Years of Black-Cast Posters.* New York: Farrar, Straus & Giroux, 1992.

Koszarski, Richard. *An Evening's Entertainment: The Age of the Silent Feature Picture, 1915–1928.* Vol. 3 of Harpole, Charles, ed., *History of the American Cinema.* New York: Scribner's, 1990; Berkeley and Los Angeles: University of California Press, 1994.

Lindsay, Vachel. *The Art of the Moving Picture.* New York: Macmillan, 1915.

Lloyd, Harold. *An American Comedy.* New York: Dover, 1971.

MacCann, Richard Dyer. *The First Tycoons.* Lanham, Md.: Scarecrow Press, 1987.

Marsh, Mae. *Screen Acting.* Los Angeles: Photostar Publishing, 1922.

May, Lary. *Screening Out the Past: The Birth of Mass Culture and the Motion Picture Industry.* Rev. ed. Chicago: University of Chicago Press, 1983.

McCabe, John. *Mr. Laurel and Mr. Hardy.* New York: Dutton, 1975.

Micheaux, Oscar. *The Conquest: The Story of a Negro Pioneer.* Lincoln: University of Nebraska Press, 1994.

Moews, Daniel. *Keaton: The Silent Films Close Up.* Berkeley and Los Angeles: University of California Press, 1977.

Norris, Frank. *McTeague, A Story of San Francisco.* New York: Doubleday & McClure, 1899.

Oberholtzer, Ellis Paxson. *The Morals of the Movie.* Philadelphia: Penn Publishing, 1922.

Reilly, Adam. *Harold Lloyd: The King of Daredevil Comedy.* New York: Macmillan, 1977.

Robinson, David. *Hollywood in the Twenties.* Cranbury, N.J.: Barnes, 1968.

———. *Buster Keaton.* Bloomington: Indiana University Press, 1969.

Scarborough, Dorothy. *The Wind.* Austin: University of Texas Press, 1979.

Slide, Anthony. *Lois Weber.* Westport, Conn.: Greenwood Publishing Group, 1996.

Taves, Brian. *The Romance of Adventure: The Genre of Historical Adventure in the Movies.* Jackson: University Press of Mississippi, 1992.

Vidor, King. *King Vidor on Film Making.* New York: McKay, 1972.

———. *A Tree Is a Tree.* New York: Monarch, 1976.

———. *King Vidor: A Directors Guild of America Oral History.* Interviewed by Nancy Dowd and David Shepard. Lanham, Md.: Scarecrow Press and the Directors Guild of America, 1988.

Weinberg, Herman G. *The Complete* Greed *of Erich von Stroheim.* New York: Dutton, 1973.

———. *The Complete* Wedding March *of Erich von Stroheim.* Boston: Little, Brown, 1974.

———. *Stroheim: A Pictorial Record of His Nine Films.* New York: Dover, 1975.

Chapter 7: The German Golden Age

Brooks, Louise. *Lulu in Hollywood.* New York: Knopf, 1982.

Cherchi Usai, Paolo, and Lorenzo Codelli, eds. *Before Caligari: German Cinema, 1895–1920.* Madison: University of Wisconsin Press, 1990.

Eisner, Lotte H. *The Haunted Screen: Expressionism in the German Cinema and the Influence of Max Reinhardt.* Berkeley and Los Angeles: University of California Press, 1969.

———. *Murnau.* Berkeley and Los Angeles: University of California Press, 1973.

———. *Fritz Lang.* New York: Da Capo, 1988.

Elsaesser, Thomas. *Weimar Cinema and After: Germany's Historical Imaginary.* New York and Milton Park, UK: Routledge, 2000.

Elsaesser, Thomas, with Michael Wedel, eds. *The BFI Companion to German Cinema.* London: BFI, 1999.

Gunning, Tom. *The Films of Fritz Lang: Modernity, Crime and Desire.* London: BFI, 2000.

Hinton, David. *The Films of Leni Riefenstahl.* 3rd ed. Lanham, Md.: Scarecrow Press, 2000.

Hull, David Stewart. *Film in the Third Reich.* Berkeley and Los Angeles: University of California Press, 1969.

Kaes, Anton, Martin Jay, and Edward Dimendberg, eds. *The Weimar Republic Sourcebook.* Berkeley and Los Angeles: University of California Press, 1994.

Kobal, John, ed. *Great Film Stills of the German Silent Era.* New York: Dover, 1981.

Kracauer, Siegfried. *From Caligari to Hitler: A Psychological History of the German Film.* Princeton: Princeton University Press, 1966.

Kreimeier, Klaus. *The Ufa Story.* Translated by Robert and Rita Kimber. New York: Hill and Wang, 1996.

Leiser, Erwin. *Nazi Cinema.* New York: Macmillan, 1974.

Petley, Julian. *Capital and Culture: German Cinema, 1933–45*. London: BFI, 1979.

Petro, Patrice. *Joyless Streets: Women and Melodramatic Representation in Weimar Germany*. Princeton: Princeton University Press, 1989.

Riefenstahl, Leni. *Leni Riefenstahl: A Memoir*. New York: St. Martin's, 1993.

Robinson, David. *Das Cabinet Des Dr. Caligari*. London: BFI, 1997.

Saunders, Thomas J. *Hollywood in Berlin: American Cinema and Weimar Germany*. Berkeley and Los Angeles: University of California Press, 1994.

CHAPTER 8: SOVIET MONTAGE

Babitsky, Paul. *The Soviet Film Industry*. New York: Praeger, 1955.

Barna, Yon. *Eisenstein*. Bloomington: Indiana University Press, 1974.

Bordwell, David. *The Cinema of Eisenstein*. Cambridge, Mass.: Harvard University Press, 1993.

Constantine, Mildred, and Alan Fern. *Revolutionary Soviet Film Posters*. Baltimore: Johns Hopkins University Press, 1974.

Dickinson, Thorold, and Catherine de la Roche, eds. *Soviet Cinema*. London: Falcon Press, 1948.

Dovzhenko, Alexander. *Alexander Dovzhenko: The Poet as Filmmaker*. Translated by Marco Carynnyk. Cambridge, Mass.: MIT Press, 1973.

Eisenstein, Sergei M. *The Film Sense*. Rev. ed. Edited and translated by Jay Leyda. New York: Harcourt Brace Jovanovich, 1969.

———. *Film Form: Essays in Film Theory*. Edited and translated by Jay Leyda. New York: Harcourt Brace Jovanovich, 1969.

———. *Notes of a Film Director*. Rev. ed. Translated by X. Danko. New York: Dover, 1970.

———. *Immoral Memories: An Autobiography*. Translated by Herbert Marshall. Boston: Houghton Mifflin, 1983.

———. *Non-Indifferent Nature: Film and the Structure of Things*. Translated by Herbert Marshall. Cambridge and New York: Cambridge University Press, 1987.

———. *Selected Writings, 1922–34*. Edited and translated by Richard Taylor. Bloomington: Indiana University Press, 1987.

———. *Towards a Theory of Montage*. Edited by Richard Taylor and Michael Glenny; translated by Michael Glenny. Bloomington: Indiana University Press, 1994.

———. *Selected Writings, 1934–47*. Edited by Richard Taylor. Bloomington: Indiana University Press, 1996.

———. *Beyond the Stars—The Memoirs of Sergei Eisenstein*. Edited by Richard Taylor. Bloomington: Indiana University Press, 1996.

Geduld, Harry, and Ronald Gottesman. *Sergei Eisenstein and Upton Sinclair: The Making and Unmaking of* Que Viva Mexico! Bloomington: Indiana University Press, 1970.

Horton, Andrew, and Michael Brashinsky. *The Zero Hour: Glasnost and Soviet Cinema in Transition*. Princeton: Princeton University Press, 1992.

Kenez, Peter. *Cinema and Soviet Society: From the Revolution to the Death of Stalin*. London: I. B. Tauris, 2000.

Kuleshov, Lev. *Kuleshov on Film*. Translated by Ronald Levaco. Berkeley and Los Angeles: University of California Press, 1974.

Lawton, Anna. *The Red Screen: Politics, Society, Art in Soviet Cinema*. London: Routledge & Kegan Paul, 1992.

Leyda, Jay. *Kino: A History of the Russian and Soviet Film*. 3rd ed. Princeton: Princeton University Press, 1983.

———, ed. *Eisenstein: Three Films*—Battleship Potemkin, October, Alexander Nevsky. Scripts translated by Diana Matias. New York: Harper and Row, 1974.

Leyda, Jay, and Zina Voynow. *Eisenstein at Work*. New York: Pantheon, 1982.

Marshall, Herbert. *Soviet Cinema*. London: Russia Today, 1945.

———. *Masters of Soviet Cinema: Crippled Creative Biographies*. London: Routledge & Kegan Paul, 1983.

Mayer, David. *Eisenstein's* Potemkin: *A Shot-by-Shot Presentation*. New York: Grossman, 1972.

Montagu, Ivor. *With Eisenstein in Hollywood*. New York: International, 1969.

Nilsen, Vladimir. *The Cinema as a Graphic Art*. Translated by Stephen Garry. New York: Hill and Wang, 1959.

Pudovkin, V. I. *Film Technique and Film Acting*. London: Vision Press, 1959.

Roberts, Graham. *Forward Soviet! History and Non-fiction Film in the USSR*. London: I. B. Tauris, 1999.

———. *The Man with the Movie Camera: The Film Companion*. London: I. B. Tauris, 2001.

Seton, Marie. *Sergei M. Eisenstein*. New York: Grove Press, 1960.

Sitney, P. Adams, ed. Film Culture *Reader*. New York: Cooper Square Press, 2000. Includes a brilliant translation of Vertov's manifestos.

Taylor, Richard. *The Politics of the Soviet Cinema: 1917–1929*. Cambridge: Cambridge University Press, 1979.

———, ed. *The Eisenstein Reader*. Translated by Richard Taylor and William Powell. London: BFI, 1998.

Taylor, Richard, and Ian Christie, eds. *The Film Factory: Russian and Soviet Cinema in Documents 1896–1939*. Cambridge, Mass.: Harvard University Press, 1988.

Taylor, Richard, Nancy Wood, Julian Graffy, and Dina Iordanova, eds. *The BFI Companion to Eastern European and Russian Cinema*. London: BFI, 2000.

Thompson, Kristin. *Eisenstein's Ivan the Terrible: A Neoformalist Analysis*. Princeton: Princeton University Press, 1981.

Tsivian, Yuri, with Paolo Cherchi Usai, Lorenzo Codelli, Carlo Montanaro, and David Robinson, eds. *Silent Witness: Russian Films 1908–1919*. London: BFI, 1990.

Vertov, Dziga. *Kino-Eye: The Writings of Dziga Vertov*. Edited by Annette Michelson; translated by Kevin O'Brien. Berkeley and Los Angeles: University of California Press, 1984. *Also see* Sitney.

CHAPTER 9: SOUND

Abel, Richard, and Rick Altman, eds. *The Sounds of Early Cinema*. Bloomington: Indiana University Press, 2001.

Altman, Rick. *Silent Film Sound*. New York: Columbia University Press, 2004.

Brown, Bernard. *Talking Pictures*. London: Pitman, 1931.

Crafton, Donald C. *The Talkies: Hollywood's Transition to Sound, 1926–1931*. Vol. 4 of Harpole, Charles, ed., *History of the American Cinema*. New York: Scribner's, 1997; Berkeley and Los Angeles: University of California Press, 1999.

Eliot, Marc. *Walt Disney: Hollywood's Dark Prince*. New York: HarperCollins, 1994.

Eyman, Scott. *The Speed of Sound: Hollywood and the Talkie Revolution, 1926–1930*. Baltimore: Johns Hopkins University Press, 1999.

Franklin, Harold B. *Sound Motion Pictures*. Garden City, N.Y.: Doubleday, 1930.

Green, Fitzhugh. *The Film Finds Its Tongue*. New York: Putnam, 1929.

Hijiya, James A. *Lee de Forest and the Fatherhood of Radio*. Cranbury, N.J.: Lehigh University Press, 1993.

Merritt, Russell, and J. B. Kaufman. *Walt in Wonderland: The Silent Films of Walt Disney*. Baltimore: Johns Hopkins University Press, 2000.

Milne, Tom. *Rouben Mamoulian*. London: Thames & Hudson, 1969.

O'Brien, Charles. *Cinema's Conversion To Sound: Technology and Film Style in France and the U.S.* Bloomington: Indiana University Press, 2005.

Paul, William. *Ernst Lubitsch's American Comedy*. Cambridge, Mass.: MIT Press, 1983.

Schickel, Richard. *The Disney Version: The Life, Times, Art, and Commerce of Walt Disney*. New York: Simon and Schuster, 1968.

Thomas, Frank, and Ollie Johnston. *Disney Animation: The Illusion of Life*. New York: Abbeville, 1982.

Thrasher, Fredric. *Okay for Sound*. New York: Duell, Sloan, & Pierce, 1964.

Walker, Alexander. *The Shattered Silents: How the Talkies Came to Stay*. London: Elm Tree, 1978.

Weinberg, Herman G. *The Lubitsch Touch*. 3rd ed. New York: Dutton, 1977.

Weis, Elisabeth, and John Belton, eds. *Film Sound: Theory and Practice*. New York: Columbia University Press, 1985.

CHAPTER 10: FRANCE BETWEEN THE WARS

Abel, Richard. *French Cinema: The First Wave, 1915–1929*. Princeton: Princeton University Press, 1984.

———. *French Film Theory and Criticism: A History/Anthology, 1907–1939*. 2 vols. Princeton: Princeton University Press, 1988.

Bazin, André. *Jean Renoir*. Edited by François Truffaut. New York: Simon and Schuster, 1973.

Braudy, Leo. *Jean Renoir: The World of His Films*. Garden City, N.Y.: Doubleday, 1972.

Brownlow, Kevin. *Napoléon: Abel Gance's Classic Film*. New York: Knopf, 1983.

Clair, René. *Reflections on the Cinema*. London: Kimber, 1953.

———. *Cinema Yesterday and Today*. New York: Dover, 1972.

Crisp, Colin. *The Classic French Cinema, 1930–1960*. Bloomington: Indiana University Press, 1994.

Durgnat, Raymond. *Renoir*. Berkeley and Los Angeles: University of California Press, 1973.

Ehrlich, Evelyn. *Cinema of Paradox: French Filmmaking Under the German Occupation*. New York: Columbia University Press, 1985.

Flitterman-Lewis, Sandy. *To Desire Differently: Feminism and the French Cinema*. Urbana and Chicago: University of Illinois Press, 1990.

Fraigneau, André. *Cocteau on the Film*. New York: Dover, 1972.

Gilliatt, Penelope. *Jean Renoir: Essays, Conversations, Reviews*. New York: McGraw-Hill, 1975.

Leprohon, Pierre. *Jean Renoir*. New York: Crown, 1971.

Lourié, Eugène. *My Work in Films*. New York: Harcourt Brace Jovanovich, 1985.

Mitry, Jean. *René Clair*. Paris: Éditions Universitaires, 1960.

O'Shaughnessy, Martin. *Jean Renoir*. Manchester: Manchester University Press, 2000.

Ray, Man. *Self Portrait*. Boston: Little, Brown, 1963.

Renoir, Jean. *My Life and My Films.* New York: Atheneum, 1974.

Sadoul, Georges. *French Film.* London: Falcon Press, 1953.

Salles Gomes, P. E. *Jean Vigo.* Berkeley and Los Angeles: University of California Press, 1971.

Sitney, P. Adams. *Modernist Montage: The Obscurity of Vision in Cinema and Literature.* New York: Columbia University Press, 1990.

Slavin, David Henry. *Colonial Cinema and Imperial France, 1919–1939: White Blind Spots, Male Fantasies, Settler Myths.* Baltimore: Johns Hopkins University Press, 2001.

Vigo, Jean. *The Complete Jean Vigo.* Surrey: Lorrimer, 1983.

Williams, Alan. *Republic of Images: A History of French Filmmaking.* Cambridge, Mass.: Harvard University Press, 1992.

Williams, Linda. *Figures of Desire: A Theory and Analysis of Surrealist Film.* Berkeley and Los Angeles: University of California Press, 1992.

Chapter 11: The American Studio Years: 1930–45

Acker, Ally. *Reel Women: Pioneers of the Cinema 1896 to the Present.* New York: Continuum, 1991.

Adamson, Joe. *Groucho, Harpo, Chico, and Sometimes Zeppo.* New York: Simon and Schuster, 1973.

Adler, Mortimer J. *Art and Prudence.* New York: Longman's, 1937.

Affron, Charles. *Cinema and Sentiment.* Chicago: University of Chicago Press, 1982.

Altman, Rick. *The American Film Musical.* Bloomington: Indiana University Press, 1999.

Auiler, Dan. *Hitchcock's Notebooks: An Authorized and Illustrated Look Inside the Creative Mind of Alfred Hitchcock.* New York: Avon/Spike, 1999.

Balio, Tino. *United Artists: The Company That Changed the Film Industry.* Madison: University of Wisconsin Press, 1987.

———. *Grand Design: Hollywood as a Modern Business Enterprise, 1930–1939.* Vol. 5 of Harpole, Charles, ed., *History of the American Cinema.* New York: Scribner's, 1993; Berkeley and Los Angeles: University of California Press, 1996.

Basten, Fred E. *Glorious Technicolor: The Movies' Magic Rainbow.* Cranbury, N.J.: Barnes, 1980.

Bazin, André. *Orson Welles: A Critical View.* Translated by Jonathan Rosenbaum. New York: Harper, 1978.

Beauchamp, Cari. *Without Lying Down: Frances Marion and the Powerful Women of Early Hollywood.* Berkeley and Los Angeles: University of California Press, 1998.

Behlmer, Rudi, ed. *Memo from: David O. Selznick.* New York: Random House, 2000.

Berg, A. Scott. *Goldwyn: A Biography.* New York: Penguin Putnam/Riverhead Books, 1998.

Bergman, Andrew. *We're in the Money: Depression America and its Films.* New York: New York University Press, 1971.

Bernstein, Matthew. *Walter Wanger, Hollywood Independent.* Berkeley and Los Angeles: University of California Press, 1994.

Blumer, Herbert. *Movies and Conduct.* New York: Macmillan, 1933.

Bogdanovich, Peter. *John Ford.* Rev. ed. Berkeley and Los Angeles: University of California Press, 1978.

Bordwell, David, Kristin Thompson, and Janet Staiger. *The Classical Hollywood Cinema: Film Style and Mode of Production to 1960.* New York: Columbia University Press, 1985.

Callow, Simon. *Orson Welles: The Road to Xanadu.* New York: Penguin, 1997.

———. *Orson Welles Volume 2: Hello Americans.* New York: Penguin, 2007.

Capra, Frank. *The Name Above the Title.* New York: Da Capo, 1997.

Carney, Ray. *American Vision: The Films of Frank Capra.* New York: Cambridge University Press, 1986.

Carringer, Robert L. *The Making of* Citizen Kane. Berkeley and Los Angeles: University of California Press, 1985.

———. The Magnificent Ambersons: *A Reconstruction.* Berkeley and Los Angeles: University of California Press, 1993.

Cavell, Stanley. *Pursuits of Happiness: The Hollywood Comedy of Remarriage.* Cambridge, Mass.: Harvard University Press, 1980.

Charters, W. W. *Motion Pictures and Youth.* New York: Macmillan, 1933.

Corliss, Richard. *Talking Pictures.* Woodstock, N.Y.: Overlook, 1974.

Cowie, Peter. *The Cinema of Orson Welles.* New York: Barnes, 1965.

Curtis, James. *Between Flops: A Biography of Preston Sturges.* New York: Limelight, 1984.

Dale, Edgar. *The Content of Motion Pictures.* New York: Macmillan, 1933.

Doane, Mary Ann. *The Desire to Desire: The Woman's Film of the 1940s.* Bloomington: Indiana University Press, 1987.

Durgnat, Raymond. *The Strange Case of Alfred Hitchcock.* Cambridge: MIT Press, 1975.

Eames, John D. *The MGM Story.* New York: Crown, 1985.

Eyman, Scott. *Ernst Lubitsch: Laughter in Paradise.* Baltimore: Johns Hopkins University Press, 2001.

———. *Print the Legend: The Life and Times of John Ford.* Baltimore: Johns Hopkins University Press, 2001.

Facey, Paul W. *The Legion of Decency: A Sociological Analysis of the Emergence and Development of a Pressure Group.* New York: Arno, 1974.

Fielding, Raymond. *The March of Time.* New York: Oxford University Press, 1978.

Finler, Joel W. *The Hollywood Story.* 3rd ed. London: Wallflower Press, 2003.

Forman, Henry James. *Our Movie-Made Children.* New York: Macmillan, 1933.

Francke, Lizzie. *Script Girls: Women Screenwriters in Hollywood.* London: BFI, 1994.

Gallagher, Tag. *John Ford.* Berkeley and Los Angeles: University of California Press, 1985.

Goldner, Orville, and George E. Turner. *The Making of King Kong: The Story Behind a Film Classic.* New York: Ballantine, 1976.

Gomery, Douglas. *The Hollywood Studio System: A History.* London: BFI, 2005.

Gottesman, Ronald, ed. *Perspectives on* Citizen Kane. New York: G. K. Hall, 1996.

Gottlieb, Sidney, ed. *Hitchcock on Hitchcock: Selected Writings and Interviews.* Berkeley and Los Angeles: University of California Press, 1997.

Halliwell, Leslie. *Mountain of Dreams: The Golden Years of Paramount Pictures.* London: Hart-Davis, MacGibbon, 1978.

Harley, John Eugene. *World-Wide Influence of the Cinema.* Los Angeles: University of Southern California Press, 1940.

Harris, Robert A. *The Films of Alfred Hitchcock.* Secaucus, N.J.: Citadel, 1976.

Hay, Peter. *MGM: When the Lion Roars.* Atlanta: Turner Publishing, 1991.

Hays, Will H. *The Memoirs of Will H. Hays.* Garden City, N.Y.: Doubleday, 1955.

Hecht, Ben. *A Child of the Century.* New York: Simon and Schuster, 1954.

Henderson, Brian, ed. *Five Screenplays by Preston Sturges.* Berkeley and Los Angeles: University of California Press, 1985.

Higham, Charles. *The Films of Orson Welles.* Berkeley and Los Angeles: University of California Press, 1970.

———. *Hollywood Cameramen.* Bloomington: Indiana University Press, 1970.

Hillier, Jim, and Peter Wollen, eds. *Howard Hawks: American Artist.* Bloomington: Indiana University Press, 1997.

Hirschhorn, Clive. *The Warner Bros. Story.* New York: Crown, 1979.

Hochman, Stanley, ed. *From Quasimodo to Scarlett O'Hara: A National Board of Review Anthology, 1920–1940.* New York: Ungar, 1982.

Horton, Andrew, ed. *Three More Screenplays by Preston Sturges.* Berkeley and Los Angeles: University of California Press, 1998.

Huettig, Mae D. *Economic Control of the Motion Picture Industry.* Philadelphia: University of Pennsylvania Press, 1944.

Hurst, Richard M. *Republic Studios: Between Poverty Row and the Majors.* Lanham, Md.: Scarecrow Press, 1979.

Inglis, Ruth A. *Freedom of the Movies.* Chicago: University of Chicago Press, 1947.

Jacobs, Diane. *Christmas in July: The Life and Art of Preston Sturges.* Berkeley and Los Angeles: University of California Press, 1992.

Jewell, Richard B. *The RKO Story.* New Rochelle, N.Y.: Arlington, 1982.

———. *The Golden Age of Cinema: Hollywood 1929–1945.* Malden, Mass. and Oxford: Blackwell, 2007.

Kael, Pauline. *The* Citizen Kane *Book.* (Includes the script and the final shot-by-shot cutting continuity.) New York: Limelight, 1984.

Kawin, Bruce F., ed. *Faulkner's MGM Screenplays.* Knoxville: University of Tennessee Press, 1982.

Klingender, F. D., and Stuart Legg. *Money Behind the Screen.* London: Lawrence & Wishart, 1937.

Kobal, John, ed. *Hollywood Glamor Portraits: 145 Photos of Stars 1926–1949.* New York: Dover, 1976.

Koppes, Clayton R., and Gregory D. Black. *Hollywood Goes to War: How Politics, Profits, and Propaganda Shaped World War II Movies.* Berkeley and Los Angeles: University of California Press, 1990.

Leff, Leonard J., and Jerold L. Simmons. *The Dame in the Kimono: Hollywood, Censorship, and the Production Code from the 1920s to the 1960s.* New York: Grove Weidenfeld, 1990.

Lewis, Howard T. *The Motion Picture Industry.* New York: Van Nostrand, 1933.

Loos, Anita. *Kiss Hollywood Goodbye.* New York: Viking, 1974.

Manvell, Roger. *Films and the Second World War.* New York: Dell, 1976.

Martin, Olga. *Hollywood's Movie Commandments.* New York: Wilson, 1937.

Marx, Groucho, with Richard J. Anobile. *The Marx Brothers Scrapbook.* New York: Norton, 1973.

Marx, Samuel. *Mayer and Thalberg: The Make-Believe Saints.* New York: Random House, 1975.

———. *A Gaudy Spree: The Literary Life of Hollywood in the 1930s When the West Was Fun.* New York and Toronto: Franklin Watts, 1987.

Mast, Gerald. *Howard Hawks, Storyteller.* New York: Oxford University Press, 1982.

———. *Can't Help Singin': The American Musical on Stage and Screen.* Woodstock, N.Y.: Overlook, 1987.

Mayne, Judith. *Directed by Dorothy Arzner.* Bloomington: Indiana University Press, 1994.

McBride, Joseph. *Orson Welles.* New York: Viking, 1977.

———. *Hawks on Hawks.* Berkeley and Los Angeles: University of California Press, 1981.

McCarthy, Todd, and Charles Flynn. *Kings of the B's.* New York: Dutton, 1975.

McGilligan, Pat, ed. *Backstory: Interviews with Screenwriters of Hollywood's Golden Age.* Berkeley and Los Angeles: University of California Press, 1986.

Moley, Raymond. *Are We Movie Made?* New York: Macy-Masius, 1938.

———. *The Hays Office.* Indianapolis: Bobbs-Merrill, 1945.

"The Motion Picture Production Code of 1930." In Mast, Gerald, ed., *The Movies in Our Midst.* Chicago: University of Chicago Press, 1982.

Mueller, John. *Astaire Dancing.* New York: Knopf, 1985.

Nielsen, Mike, and Gene Mailes. *Hollywood's Other Blacklist: Union Struggles in the Studio System.* London: BFI, 1996.

Nizer, Louis. *New Courts of Industry.* New York: Longacre, 1935.

Parish, James R. *The Golden Era: The MGM Stock Company.* New Rochelle, N.Y.: Arlington, 1974.

Perlman, William, ed. *The Movies on Trial.* New York: Macmillan, 1936.

Peters, Charles C. *Motion Pictures and Standards of Morality.* New York: Macmillan, 1933.

Place, J. A. *The Non-Western Films of John Ford.* Secaucus, N.J.: Citadel, 1979.

Powdermaker, Hortense. *Hollywood the Dream Factory: An Anthropologist Looks at the Movie Makers.* North Stratford, N.H.: Ayer, 1979.

Production Code. *See* Motion.

Quigley, Martin. *Decency in Motion Pictures.* New York: Macmillan, 1937.

Rohmer, Eric, and Claude Chabrol. *Hitchcock: The First 44 Films.* Translated by Stanley Hochman. New York: Ungar, 1979.

Rosenbaum, Jonathan. *See* Welles.

Rothman, William. *Hitchcock: The Murderous Gaze.* Cambridge, Mass.: Harvard University Press, 1982.

Rushdie, Salman. *The Wizard of Oz.* London: BFI, 1992.

Sarris, Andrew. *The Films of Josef von Sternberg.* New York: Museum of Modern Art, 1966.

Schatz, Thomas. *Boom and Bust: The American Cinema in the 1940s.* Vol. 6 of Harpole, Charles, ed., *History of the American Cinema.* New York: Scribner's, 1997; Berkeley and Los Angeles: University of California Press, 1999.

Schulberg, Budd. *What Makes Sammy Run?* New York: Random House/Vintage, 1993.

Seldes, Gilbert. *The Movies Come from America.* New York: Scribner's, 1937.

Siegel, Joel E. *Val Lewton: The Reality of Terror.* New York: Viking, 1973.

Sinclair, Upton. *Upton Sinclair Presents William Fox.* Los Angeles: the author, 1933.

Sloan, Jane E. *Alfred Hitchcock: A Filmography and Bibliography.* Berkeley and Los Angeles: University of California Press, 1995.

Smith, Steven C. *A Heart at Fire's Center: The Life and Music of Bernard Herrmann.* Berkeley and Los Angeles: University of California Press, 1991.

Staiger, Janet, ed. *The Studio System.* New Brunswick, N.J.: Rutgers University Press, 1995.

Stott, William. *Documentary Expression and Thirties America.* New York: Oxford University Press, 1973.

Sturges, Preston. *Four More Screenplays.* Berkeley and Los Angeles: University of California Press, 1995. *Also see* Henderson *and* Horton.

Telotte, J. P. *Dreams of Darkness: Fantasy and the Films of Val Lewton.* Urbana and Chicago: University of Illinois Press, 1985.

Thomas, Bob. *King Cohn: The Life and Times of Harry Cohn.* New York: Putnam, 1967.

Thomas, Tony. *The Busby Berkeley Book.* Greenwich, Conn.: New York Graphic Society, 1969.

Truffaut, François, and Helen G. Scott. *Hitchcock.* Rev. ed. New York: Simon and Schuster, 1985.

Tuska, Jon, ed. *Close Up: The Contract Director.* Lanham, Md.: Scarecrow Press, 1976.

Tyler, Parker. *Magic and Myth of the Movies.* New York: Simon and Schuster, 1970.

———. *The Hollywood Hallucination.* New York: Simon and Schuster, 1970.

Von Sternberg, Josef. *Fun in a Chinese Laundry.* New York: Macmillan, 1965.

Walsh, Raoul. *Each Man in His Time: The Life Story of a Director.* New York: Farrar, Straus & Giroux, 1974.

Weaver, Tom, Michael Brunas, and John Brunas. *Universal Horrors: The Studio's Classic Films, 1931–1946.* 2nd ed. Jefferson, N. C.: McFarland, 2007.

Weinberg, Herman G. *Josef von Sternberg.* New York: Dutton, 1967.

Welles, Orson, and Peter Bogdanovich. *This Is Orson Welles.* Edited by Jonathan Rosenbaum. New York: HarperCollins, 1992. (Four hours of the original interviews are available on audiocassette as *This Is Orson Welles*, Caedmon/HarperCollins, 1992.)

Wellman, William. *A Short Time for Insanity: An Autobiography.* New York: Hawthorn, 1974.

West, Mae. *Goodness Had Nothing to Do with It.* Englewood Cliffs, N.J.: Prentice-Hall, 1959.

Wood, Robin. *Howard Hawks.* Rev. ed. London: Secker and Warburg, 1979.

———. *Hitchcock's Films Revisited.* New York: Columbia University Press, 1989.

Zukor, Adolf. *The Public Is Never Wrong.* New York: Putnam, 1953.

CHAPTER 12: HOLLYWOOD IN TRANSITION: 1946–65

Agee, James. *Agee on Film.* 2 vols. (Vol. 1 contains his reviews and essays; vol. 2, his scripts, including *The African Queen* and *The Night of the Hunter.*) New York: McDowell, Obolensky, 1960.

Altman, Rick. *The American Film Musical.* Bloomington: Indiana University Press, 1987.

Battcock, Gregory, ed. *The New American Cinema.* New York: Dutton, 1967.

Beck, Jerry, and Will Friedwald. *Looney Tunes and Merrie Melodies: A Complete Illustrated Guide to the Warner Bros. Cartoons.* New York: Henry Holt, 1989.

Belton, John. *Widescreen Cinema.* Cambridge, Mass.: Harvard University Press, 1992.

Bentley, Eric, ed. *Thirty Years of Treason.* New York: Viking, 1971.

Bessie, Alvah. *Inquisition in Eden.* Berlin: Seven Seas, 1967.

Brodsky, Jack, and Nathan Weiss. *The* Cleopatra *Papers: A Private Correspondence.* New York: Simon and Schuster, 1963.

Carr, Robert E., and R. M. Hayes. *Wide Screen Movies: A History and Filmography of Wide Gauge Filmmaking.* Jefferson, N. C.: McFarland, 1988.

Casper, Drew. *Postwar Hollywood: 1946–1962.* Malden, Mass. and Oxford: Blackwell, 2007.

Casty, Alan. *The Films of Robert Rossen.* New York: Museum of Modern Art, 1969.

Ceplair, Larry, and Steven Englund. *The Inquisition in Hollywood: Politics in the Film Community, 1930–1960.* Champaign: University of Illinois Press, 2003.

Ciment, Michel. *Kazan on Kazan.* New York: Viking, 1972.

Cogley, John. *Report on Blacklisting. I. The Movies.* New York: Fund for the Republic, 1956.

Dick, Bernard F. *Billy Wilder.* Rev. ed. New York: Da Capo, 1996.

Dowdy, Andrew. *The Films of the Fifties: The American State of Mind.* New York: William Morrow, 1975.

Feuer, Jane. *The Hollywood Musical.* 2nd ed. Bloomington: Indiana University Press, 1993.

Fordin, Hugh. *The Movies' Greatest Musicals: Produced in Hollywood USA by the Freed Unit.* New York: Ungar, 1975.

Geist, Kenneth L. *Pictures with Talk: The Life and Films of Joseph L. Mankiewicz.* New York: Scribner's, 1978.

Goodman, Ezra. *The Fifty Year Decline and Fall of Hollywood.* New York: Simon and Schuster, 1961.

Goodman, Walter. *The Committee.* New York: Farrar, Straus & Giroux, 1968.

Halliday, Jon, ed. *Sirk on Sirk.* New York: Viking, 1969.

Handel, Leo A. *Hollywood Looks at Its Audience.* Champaign: University of Illinois Press, 1950.

Hardy, Phil. *Samuel Fuller.* New York: Praeger, 1970.

Hayes, R. M. *3-D Movies: A History and Filmography of Stereoscopic Cinema.* Jefferson, N. C.: McFarland, 1989.

Horne, Gerald. *Class Struggle in Hollywood, 1930–1950: Moguls, Mobsters, Stars, Reds, and Trade Unionists.* Austin: University of Texas Press, 2001.

HUAC Hearings, 1947 and 1951–52. Lengthy excerpts in Mast, Gerald, ed., *The Movies in Our Midst.* Chicago: University of Chicago Press, 1982.

Jones, Chuck. *Chuck Amuck.* New York: Farrar, Straus & Giroux, 1989.

Kahn, Gordon. *Hollywood on Trial.* New York: Boni & Gaer, 1948.

Kanfer, Stephan. *A Journal of the Plague Years.* New York: Atheneum, 1973.

Kitses, James. *Horizons West: Mann, Boetticher, Peckinpah.* Bloomington: Indiana University Press, 1969.

Knox, Donald. *The Magic Factory: How MGM Made* An American in Paris. New York: Praeger, 1973.

Kozloff, Sarah. *Invisible Storytellers: Voice-Over Narration in American Fiction Film.* Berkeley and Los Angeles: University of California Press, 1988.

Lardner, Ring, Jr. *I'd Hate Myself in the Morning: A Memoir.* New York: Thunder's Mouth Press/Nation Books, 2000.

Lev, Peter. *The Fifties: Transforming the Screen.* Vol. 7 of Harpole, Charles, ed., *History of the American Cinema.* New York: Scribner's, 2003; Berkeley and Los Angeles: University of California Press, 2006.

Lumet, Sidney. *Making Movies.* New York: Knopf, 1995.

McGilligan, Pat, ed. *Backstory 2: Interviews with Screenwriters of the 1940s and 1950s.* Berkeley and Los Angeles: University of California Press, 1991.

Miller, Merle. *The Judges and the Judged.* Garden City, N.Y.: Doubleday, 1952.

Minnelli, Vincente, with Victor Arce. *I Remember It Well.* Garden City, N.Y.: Doubleday, 1974.

Monaco, Paul. *The Sixties: 1960–1969*. Vol. 8 of Harpole, Charles, ed., *History of the American Cinema*. New York: Scribner's, 2000; Berkeley and Los Angeles: University of California Press, 2003.

Morgan, Hal, and Dan Symmes. *Amazing 3-D*. Boston: Little, Brown, 1982.

Navasky, Victor S. *Naming Names*. New York: Penguin, 1991.

Nevins, Francis M. *Joseph H. Lewis: Overview, Interview, and Filmography*. Lanham, Md.: Scarecrow Press, 1998.

Ottoson, Robert. *American International Pictures: A Filmography*. New York: Garland, 1985.

Powdermaker, Hortense. *Hollywood the Dream Factory: An Anthropologist Looks at the Movie Makers*. North Stratford, N.H.: Ayer, 1979.

Pratley, Gerald, and John Frankenheimer. *The Films of Frankenheimer: Forty Years in Film*. Bethlehem, Penn.: Lehigh University Press, 1998.

Preminger, Otto. *Preminger: An Autobiography*. Garden City, N.Y.: Doubleday, 1977.

Quart, Leonard, and Albert Auster. *American Film and Society Since 1945*. New York: Praeger, 1985.

Ray, Nicholas. *I Was Interrupted: Nicholas Ray on Making Movies*. Edited by Susan Ray. Berkeley and Los Angeles: University of California Press, 1993.

Reemes, Dana M. *Directed by Jack Arnold*. Jefferson, N.C.: McFarland, 1988.

Richie, Donald. *George Stevens: An American Romantic*. New York: Museum of Modern Art, 1970.

Ross, Lillian. *Picture*. New York: Doubleday, 1993.

Schatz, Thomas. *Boom and Bust: The American Cinema in the 1940s*. Vol. 6 of Harpole, Charles, ed., *History of the American Cinema*. New York: Scribner's, 1997; Berkeley and Los Angeles: University of California Press, 1999.

Schechter, Harold. *Deviant: The Shocking True Story of Ed Gein, the Original "Psycho."* New York: Pocket Books, 1989.

Schrader, Paul. "Notes on *Film Noir*." In *Schrader on Schrader & Other Writings*, edited by Kevin Jackson. London: Faber and Faber, 1992.

Schumach, Murray. *The Face on the Cutting-Room Floor*. New York: Morrow, 1964.

Segrave, Kerry. *Drive-in Theatres: A History from Their Inception in 1933*. Jefferson, N.C.: McFarland, 2006.

Shindler, Colin. *Hollywood Goes to War: Films and American Society, 1939–52*. London: Routledge & Kegan Paul, 1979.

Sikov, Ed. *On Sunset Boulevard: The Life and Times of Billy Wilder*. New York: Hyperion, 1998.

Silver, Alain, and Elizabeth Ward, eds. *Film Noir: An Encyclopedic Reference to the American Style*. 3rd ed. Woodstock, N.Y.: Overlook Press, 1993.

Telotte, J. P. *Voices in the Dark: The Narrative Patterns of* Film Noir. Urbana and Chicago: University of Illinois Press, 1989.

Truffaut, François, and Helen G. Scott. *Hitchcock*. Rev. ed. New York: Simon and Schuster, 1985.

Trumbo, Dalton. *Additional Dialogue: The Letters of Dalton Trumbo, 1942–1962*. Edited by Helen Manfull. New York: M. Evans, 1970.

Vaughn, Robert. *Only Victims*. New York: Putnam, 1972.

Warren, Bill. *Keep Watching the Skies! American Science Fiction Movies of the Fifties*. 2 vols. Jefferson, N.C.: McFarland, 1982, 1986; 1 vol. ed., 1997.

Warshow, Robert. *The Immediate Experience: Movies, Comics, Theatre, and other Aspects of Popular Culture*. Enl. ed. Cambridge, Mass.: Harvard University Press, 2002.

Wood, Robin. *Hitchcock's Films Revisited*. New York: Columbia University Press, 1989.

CHAPTER 13: NEOREALISM, THE NEW WAVE, AND WHAT FOLLOWED

Almendros, Nestor. *A Man with a Camera*. Translated by Rachel Phillips Belash. New York: Farrar, Straus & Giroux, 1984.

Andrew, J. Dudley. *André Bazin*. New York: Oxford University Press, 1978.

Armes, Roy. *French Cinema Since 1946*. 2 vols. New York: Barnes, 1966.

———. *The Cinema of Alain Resnais*. New York: Barnes, 1968.

———. *French Cinema*. New York: Oxford University Press, 1985.

Bacon, Henry. *Visconti: His Life, His Films*. Cambridge and New York: Cambridge University Press, 1998.

Bazin, André. *What is Cinema?* 2 vols. Edited and translated by Hugh Gray. Berkeley and Los Angeles: University of California Press, 2005.

———. *Bazin at Work: Major Essays and Reviews from the Forties and Fifties*. Edited by Bert Cardullo. London: Routledge, 1997.

Bondanella, Peter, ed. *Italian Cinema: From Neorealism to the Present*. 3rd ed. New York: Continuum, 2001.

———. *The Cinema of Federico Fellini*. Princeton: Princeton University Press, 1992.

Bresson, Robert. *Notes on Cinematography*. Translated by Jonathan Griffin. New York: Urizen, 1977.

Brown, Royal S., ed. *Focus on Godard*. Englewood Cliffs, N.J.: Prentice-Hall, 1972.

Browne, Nick, ed. *Cahiers du cinéma 1969–1972: The Politics of Representation*. Cambridge, Mass.: Harvard University Press, 1989.

Brunette, Peter. *Roberto Rossellini*. Berkeley and Los Angeles: University of California Press, 1996.

———. *The Films of Michelangelo Antonioni*. Cambridge and New York: Cambridge University Press, 1998.

Bruno, Giuliana, and Maria Nadotti, eds. *Off Screen: Women and Film in Italy*. New York: Routledge, 1988.

Cahiers du cinéma. See Browne, Hillier, *and* Wilson.

Cameron, Ian, ed. *The Films of Robert Bresson*. New York: Praeger, 1970.

Cocteau, Jean. *Cocteau on the Film*. New York: Roy Publishers, 1954.

Cowie, Peter. *Antonioni, Bergman, Resnais*. New York: Yoseloff, 1964.

Crisp, C. G. *Eric Rohmer: Realist and Moralist*. Bloomington: Indiana University Press, 1988.

Dixon, Wheeler Winston, ed. *The Early Film Criticism of François Truffaut*. Bloomington: Indiana University Press, 1993.

Duras, Marguerite. *Hiroshima Mon Amour*. Translated by Richard Seaver. New York: Grove, 1961.

———. *India Song*. Translated by Barbara Bray. New York: Grove, 1976.

Durgnat, Raymond. *Nouvelle Vague: The First Decade*. Essex: Loughton, 1963.

———. *Franju*. London: Studio/Vista, 1967.

Fellini, Federico. *Fellini on Fellini*. New York: Da Capo Press, 1996.

Forbes, Jill. *The Cinema in France: After the New Wave*. Bloomington: Indiana University Press, 1994.

Godard, Jean-Luc. *Godard on Godard*. Translated by Tom Milne. New York: Da Capo Press, 1986.

Godard, Jean-Luc, and Youssef Ishaghpour. *Cinema: The Archaeology of Film and the Memory of a Century*. Translated by John Howe. Oxford and New York: Berg, 2005.

Greene, Naomi. *Pier Paolo Pasolini: Cinema as Heresy*. Princeton: Princeton University Press, 1990.

Guzzetti, Alfred. *Two or Three Things I Know about Her: Analysis of a Film by Godard*. Cambridge, Mass.: Harvard University Press, 1981.

Harvey, Sylvia. *May '68 and Film Culture*. Rev. ed. London: BFI, 1980.

Henderson, Brian. *A Critique of Film Theory*. New York: Dutton, 1980.

Hillier, Jim, ed. *Cahiers du cinéma: The 1950s: Neo-Realism, Hollywood, New Wave*. Cambridge, Mass.: Harvard University Press, 1985.

———. *Cahiers du cinéma: The 1960s: New Wave, New Cinema, Reevaluating Hollywood*. Cambridge, Mass.: Harvard University Press, 1986.

Insdorf, Annette. *François Truffaut*. Rev. ed. Cambridge and New York: Cambridge University Press, 1995.

Kael, Pauline. "The Come-Dressed-as-the-Sick-Soul-of-Europe Parties." In *I Lost It at the Movies*. New York: Boyars, 1993.

Kawin, Bruce F. *Mindscreen: Bergman, Godard, and First-Person Film*. McLean and London: Dalkey Archive Press, 2006.

Landy, Marcia. *Fascism in Film: The Italian Commercial Cinema, 1931–1943*. Princeton: Princeton University Press, 1987.

Leprohon, Pierre. *The Italian Cinema*. New York: Praeger, 1972.

Liehm, Mira. *Passion and Defiance: Film in Italy from 1942 to the Present*. Berkeley and Los Angeles: University of California Press, 1984.

Lucas, Tim. *Mario Bava: All the Colors of the Dark*. Cincinnati, Oh.: Video Watchdog, 2007.

MacBean, James Roy. *Film and Revolution*. Bloomington: Indiana University Press, 1975.

MacCabe, Colin. *Godard: Images, Sounds, Politics*. Bloomington: Indiana University Press, 1980.

———. *Godard: A Portrait of the Artist at Seventy*. New York: Farrar, Straus & Giroux, 2004.

Margulies, Ivone. *Nothing Happens: Chantal Akerman's Hyperrealist Everyday*. Durham, N.C.: Duke University Press, 1996.

Monaco, James. *The New Wave*. New York: Oxford University Press, 1976.

———. *Alain Resnais*. New York: Oxford University Press, 1978.

Pasolini, Pier Paolo. *Heretical Empiricism*. Edited by Louise K. Barnett and translated by Ben Lawton and Louise K. Barnett. Bloomington: Indiana University Press, 1988.

———. *Poems*. Selected and translated by Norman MacAfee with Luciano Martinengo. New York: Farrar, Straus & Giroux, 1996.

Petrie, Graham. *The Cinema of François Truffaut*. New York: Barnes, 1970.

Robbe-Grillet, Alain. *Last Year at Marienbad*. Translated by Richard Howard. New York: Grove, 1962.

———. *For a New Novel: Essays on Fiction*. Translated by Richard Howard. New York: Grove, 1965.

Rosenbaum, Jonathan. *Rivette: Texts and Interviews*. London: BFI, 1977.

Roud, Richard. *Jean-Luc Godard*. Rev. ed. Bloomington: Indiana University Press, 1970.

Stack, Oswald, ed. *Pasolini on Pasolini*. Bloomington: Indiana University Press, 1969.

Tonetti, Claretta Micheletti. *Bernardo Bertolucci: The Cinema of Ambiguity*. New York: Twayne, 1995.

Truffaut, François. "A Certain Tendency of the French Cinema." Reprinted in Nichols, Bill, ed., *Movies and Methods*, vol. I. Berkeley and Los Angeles: University of California Press, 1976.

Truffaut, François, and Helen G. Scott. *Hitchcock.* Rev. ed. New York: Simon & Schuster, 1985.

Van Wert, William F. *The Film Career of Alain Robbe-Grillet.* Pleasantville, N.Y.: Redgrave, 1977.

Ward, John. *Alain Resnais, or The Theme of Time.* New York: Doubleday, 1968.

Williams, Alan. *Max Ophüls and the Cinema of Desire: Style and Spectacle in Four Films.* New York: Arno, 1980.

———. *Republic of Images: A History of French Filmmaking.* Cambridge, Mass.: Harvard University Press, 1992.

Wilson, David, ed. *Cahiers du cinéma 1973–1978: History, Ideology, Cultural Struggle.* New York and Milton Park, UK: Routledge, 2000.

Wollen, Peter. *Signs and Meaning in the Cinema.* 3rd ed. Bloomington: Indiana University Press, 1972.

Wood, Robin, and Michael Walker. *Claude Chabrol.* New York: Praeger, 1970.

Zavattini, Cesare. *Sequences from a Cinematic Life.* Translated by William Weaver. Englewood Cliffs, N.J.: Prentice-Hall, 1970.

Chapter 14: National Cinemas 1: 1945–

Andrew, Dudley, and Carole Cavanaugh. *Sanshô Dayû/Sansho the Bailiff.* London: BFI, 2000.

Balcon, Michael. *Twenty Years of British Film.* London: Falcon, 1947.

Barnouw, Erik, and Subramanyam Krishnaswamy. *The Indian Film.* 2nd ed. New York: Oxford University Press, 1980.

Barr, Charles. *Ealing Studios.* London: Cameron & Taylor, 1977.

———, ed. *All Our Yesterdays: 90 Years of British Cinema.* London: BFI, 1986.

Bergman, Ingmar. *Four Screenplays of Ingmar Bergman:* Smiles of a Summer Night, The Seventh Seal, Wild Strawberries, The Magician. Translated by Lars Malmstrom and David Kushner. New York: Simon and Schuster, 1960.

———. *Three Films by Ingmar Bergman:* Through a Glass Darkly, Winter Light, The Silence. Translated by Paul Britten Austin. New York: Grove, 1970.

———. Persona *and* Shame. Translated by Keith Bradfield. New York: Boyars, 1994.

———. *Images: My Life in Film.* Translated by Marianne Ruuth. New York: Arcade, 1994. *See also* Duncan.

Berry, Chris. *Postsocialist Cinema in Post-Mao China: The Cultural Revolution after the Cultural Revolution.* New York and Milton Park, UK: Routledge, 2008. ed.

———. *Perspectives on Chinese Cinema.* 2nd ed. London: BFI, 1991.

Betts, Ernest. *The Film Business: A History of British Cinema, 1896–1972.* London: Allen & Unwin, 1973.

Björkman, Stig, Torsten Manns, and Jonas Sima. *Bergman on Bergman.* Translated by Paul Britten Austin. New York: Da Capo, 1993.

Blackwell, Marilyn Johns. Persona: *The Transcendent Image.* Urbana and Chicago: University of Illinois Press, 1986.

Bock, Audie. *Japanese Film Directors.* New York: Kodansha, 1985.

Bordwell, David. *The Films of Carl-Theodor Dreyer.* Berkeley and Los Angeles: University of California Press, 1981.

———. *Ozu and the Poetics of Cinema.* Princeton: Princeton University Press, 1988.

———. *Planet Hong Kong: Popular Cinema and the Art of Entertainment.* Cambridge, Mass.: Harvard University Press, 2000.

Bose, Mihir. *Bollywood: A History.* UK: Tempus, 2007.

Browne, Nick, Paul G. Pickowicz, Vivian Sobchack, and Esther Yau, eds. *New Chinese Cinemas: Forms, Identities, Politics.* Cambridge and New York: Cambridge University Press, 1994.

Brunette, Peter. *Wong Kar-Wai.* Champaign: University of Illinois Press, 2005.

Burch, Noël. *To the Distant Observer: Form and Meaning in Japanese Cinema.* Revised and edited by Annette Michelson. Berkeley and Los Angeles: University of California Press, 1979.

Butler, Ivan. *The Cinema of Roman Polanski.* Cranbury, N.J.: Barnes, 1970.

Callow, Simon. *Charles Laughton: A Difficult Actor.* New York: Fromm International Publishing, 1997.

Chakravarty, Sumita S. *National Identity in Indian Popular Cinema, 1947–1987.* Austin: University of Texas Press, 1994.

Cheng, Jihua, Li Xiaobai, and Xing Zuwen. *History of the Development of Chinese Cinema.* 2 vols. Beijing: China Film Press, 1963.

Christie, Ian, ed. *Powell, Pressburger, and Others.* London: BFI, 1978.

Coates, Paul, ed. *Lucid Dreams: The Films of Krzysztof Kieślowski.* Trowbridge, UK: Flicks Books, 1998.

Cowie, Peter. *Swedish Cinema.* Cranbury, N.J.: Barnes, 1969.

———. *Ingmar Bergman: A Critical Biography.* New York: Scribner's, 1982.

Das Gupta, Chidananda. *The Cinema of Satyajit Ray.* Rev. ed. New Delhi: National Book Trust, 1994.

Desser, David. *Eros plus Massacre: An Introduction to the Japanese New Wave Cinema.* Bloomington: Indiana University Press, 1988.

Dick, Eddie, ed. *From Limelight to Satellite: A Scottish Film Book.* Bloomington: Indiana University Press, 1991.

Dissanayake, Wimal, ed. *Colonialism and Nationalism in Asian Cinema*. Bloomington and London: Indiana University Press, 1994.

Dreyer, Carl Theodor. *Four Screenplays:* The Passion of Joan of Arc, Vampyr, Day of Wrath, Ordet. Translated by Oliver Stallybrass. Bloomington and London: Indiana University Press, 1970. *See also* Skoller.

Duncan, Paul, and Bengt Wanselius, eds. *The Ingmar Bergman Archives*. Los Angeles: Taschen America, 2008.

Ehrlich, Linda C., and David Desser. *Cinematic Landscapes: Observations on the Visual Arts and Cinema of China and Japan*. Austin: University of Texas Press, 1994.

Fullerton, John, and Jan Olsson, eds. *Nordic Explorations: Film Before 1930*. Bloomington: Indiana University Press/Stockholm Studies in Cinema, 2000.

Ganti, Tejaswini. *Bollywood: A Guide to Popular Hindi Cinema*. New York and Milton Park, UK: Routledge, 2004.

Gomez, Joseph A. *Peter Watkins*. Boston: Twayne, 1979.

Goulding, Daniel J., ed. *Five Filmmakers: Tarkovsky, Forman, Polanski, Szabó, Makavejev*. Bloomington: Indiana University Press, 1993.

Graham, Allison. *Lindsay Anderson*. Boston: Twayne, 1981.

Grierson, John. *Grierson on Documentary*. Edited by Forsyth Hardy. Rev. ed. London: Faber and Faber, 1966.

Holloway, Ronald. *Z Is for Zagreb*. Cranbury, N.J.: Barnes, 1972.

Horton, Andrew. *The Films of Theo Angelopoulos: A Cinema of Contemplation*. Princeton: Princeton University Press, 1997.

———, ed. *The Last Modernist: The Films of Theo Angelopoulos*. Westport, Conn.: Praeger, 1997.

Iordanova, Dina. *Cinema of Flames: Balkan Film, Culture, and the Media*. London: BFI, 2001.

James, David, and Kyung Hyun Kim, eds. *Im Kwon-Taek: The Making of a Korean National Cinema*. Detroit: Wayne State University Press, 2001.

Kawin, Bruce F. *Mindscreen: Bergman, Godard, and First-Person Film*. McLean and London: Dalkey Archive Press, 2006.

Kelly, Richard. *The Name of this Book is Dogme95*. London and New York: Faber and Faber, 2001.

Kurosawa, Akira. *Something Like an Autobiography*. Translated by Audie E. Bock. New York: Knopf, 1982.

Kurzewski, Stanislaw. *Contemporary Polish Cinema*. London: Wischhusen, 1980.

Last, Antonia. *Blackout: Reinventing Women for Wartime British Cinema*. Princeton: Princeton University Press, 1991.

Lau, Jenny Kwok Wah, ed. *Multiple Modernities: Cinemas and Popular Media in Transcultural East Asia*. Philadelphia: Temple University Press, 2003.

Lawrence, Amy. *The Films of Peter Greenaway*. Cambridge and New York: Cambridge University Press, 1997.

Leyda, Jay. *Dianying: Electric Shadows: An Account of Films and the Film Audience in China*. Rev. ed. Cambridge, Mass.: MIT Press, 1979.

Liehm, Antonín J. *Closely Watched Films: The Czechoslovak Experience*. White Plains, N.Y.: International Arts, 1974.

———. *The Miloš Forman Stories*. White Plains, N.Y.: International Arts, 1975.

Liehm, Mira, and Antonín J. Liehm. *The Most Important Art: East European Film After 1945*. Berkeley and Los Angeles: University of California Press, 1977.

Low, Rachel. *The History of the British Film: 1896–1939*. 6 vols. London: Allen & Unwin, 1948–79.

Luhr, William, ed. *World Cinema Since 1945*. New York: Ungar, 1987.

Marks, Leo. *Peeping Tom*. (Includes the script.) London: Faber and Faber, 1998.

MacCabe, Colin. *Performance*. London: BFI, 1998.

Michalek, Boleslaw. *The Cinema of Andrzej Wajda*. Translated by Edward Rothert. Cranbury, N.J.: Barnes, 1973.

Milne, Tom. *The Cinema of Carl Dreyer*. Cranbury, N.J.: Barnes, 1971.

———, ed. *Losey on Losey*. Garden City, N.Y.: Doubleday, 1968.

Minh-ha, Trinh T. *Cinema—Interval*. New York: Routledge, 1999.

Morris, Meaghan, Siu-Leung Li, and Stephen Chan Ching-kiu, eds. *Hong Kong Connections: Transnational Imagination in Action Cinema*. Durham, N. C.: Duke University Press, 2006.

Napier, Susan J. *Anime From* Akira *to* Princess Mononoke: *Experiencing Contemporary Japanese Animation*. New York: Palgrave, 2001.

Orr, John, and Elzbieta Ostrowska, eds. *The Cinema of Andrzej Wajda: The Art of Irony and Defiance*. London: Wallflower Press, 2004.

Palmer, James, and Michael Riley. *The Films of Joseph Losey*. Cambridge and New York: Cambridge University Press, 1993.

Pensel, Hans. *Seastrom and Stiller in Hollywood*. New York: Vintage, 1969.

Portuges, Catherine. *Screen Memories: The Hungarian Cinema of Márta Mészáros*. Bloomington: Indiana University Press, 1993.

Powell, Michael. *A Life in Movies: An Autobiography*. New York: Knopf, 1987.

————. *Million Dollar Movie*. New York: Random House, 1995.

Quant, James, ed. *Shohei Imamura*. Bloomington: Indiana University Press/Cinémathèque Ontario Monographs, 1999.

Quinlan, David. *British Sound Films: The Studio Years, 1928–1959*. Totowa, N.J.: Barnes and Noble, 1984.

Rai, Amit S. *Untimely Bollywood: Globalization and India's New Media Assemblage*. Durham, N.C.: Duke University Press, 2009.

Rajadhyaksha, Ashish, and Paul Willemen. *Encyclopedia of Indian Cinema*. Rev. ed. London: BFI, 2008.

Ray, Satyajit. *Our Films, Their Films*. Bombay: Orient Longman's, 1977.

Rayns, Tony, ed. *Wong Kar-wai on Wong Kar-wai*. London and New York: Faber and Faber, 2006.

Rayns, Tony, and Scott Meek, eds. *Electric Shadows: 45 Years of Chinese Cinema*. London: BFI, 1980.

Richie, Donald. *The Japanese Cinema: Film Style and National Character*. Garden City, N.Y.: Doubleday, 1971.

————. *Ozu: His Life and Films*. Berkeley and Los Angeles: University of California Press, 1974.

————. *The Japanese Movie*. Rev. ed. Tokyo: Kodansha, 1982.

————. *A Hundred Years of Japanese Film*. Tokyo: Kodansha, 2001.

Richie, Donald. Additional material by Joan Mellen. *The Films of Akira Kurosawa*. 3rd exp. ed. Berkeley and Los Angeles: University of California Press, 1999.

Richie, Donald, and Joseph Anderson. *Japanese Film: Art and Industry*. New York: Grove Press, 1960.

Rotha, Paul. *Documentary Diary: An Informal History of the British Documentary Film 1926–1939*. London: Secker & Warburg, 1973.

Sato, Tadao. *Currents in Japanese Cinema*. Translated by Gregory Barrett. Tokyo: Kodansha, 1982.

Schrader, Paul. *Transcendental Style in Film: Ozu, Bresson, Dreyer*. Berkeley and Los Angeles: University of California Press, 1972.

Sen, Mrinal. *Views on Cinema*. Calcutta: Ishan, 1977.

Shin, Chi-Yun, and Julian Stringer, eds. *New Korean Cinema*. New York: New York University Press, 2005.

Simon, John. *Ingmar Bergman Directs*. New York: Harcourt, Brace, 1972.

Skoller, Donald, ed. *Dreyer in Double Reflection: Translation of Carl Th. Dreyer's Writings About the Film (Om Filmen)*. New York: Dutton, 1973.

Skvorecký, Josef. *All the Bright Young Men and Women: A Personal History of the Czech Cinema*. Toronto: Martin, 1971.

Soderbergh, Steven, with Richard Lester. *Getting Away With It*. London and New York: Faber and Faber, 1999.

Stok, Danusia, ed. *Kieślowski on Kieślowski*. London and New York: Faber and Faber, 1995.

Sussex, Elizabeth. *The Rise and Fall of British Documentary*. Berkeley and Los Angeles: University of California Press, 1975.

Taylor, Richard, Nancy Wood, Julian Graffy, and Dina Iordanova, eds. *The BFI Companion to Eastern European and Russian Cinema*. London: BFI, 2000.

Teo, Stephen. *Hong Kong Cinema: The Extra Dimensions*. London: BFI, 1998.

Törnqvist, Egil. *Between Stage and Screen: Ingmar Bergman Directs*. Ann Arbor: University of Michigan Press, 1995.

Varia, Kush. *Bollywood: Gods, Glamour, and Gossip*. London: Wallflower Press, 2009.

Widmer, Ellen, and David Der-wei Wang, eds. *From May Fourth to June Fourth: Fiction and Film in Twentieth-Century China*. Cambridge, Mass.: Harvard University Press, 1993.

Wood, Robin. *Ingmar Bergman*. New York: Praeger, 1969.

————. *The Apu Trilogy*. New York: Praeger, 1971.

Zhang, Zhen, ed. *The Urban Generation: Chinese Cinema and Society at the Turn of the Twenty-first Century*. Durham, N.C.: Duke University Press, 2007.

Zsuffa, Joseph. *Béla Balázs, The Man and the Artist*. Berkeley and Los Angeles: University of California Press, 1987.

CHAPTER 15: HOLLYWOOD RENAISSANCE: 1964–76

Anger, Kenneth. *Hollywood Babylon*. New York: Dell, 1981.

Brakhage, Stan. *Brakhage Scrapbook: Collected Writings 1964–1980*. Edited by Robert A. Haller. New Paltz, N.Y.: Documentext, 1982.

————. *Film at Wit's End: Eight Avant-Garde Filmmakers*. New Paltz, N.Y.: McPherson & Co., 1989.

————. *Essential Brakhage: Selected Writings on Filmmaking by Stan Brakhage*. Edited with a foreword by Bruce R. McPherson. Kingston, N.Y.: Documentext, 2001.

Brunette, Peter, ed. *Martin Scorsese: Interviews*. Jackson: University Press of Mississippi, 1999.

Carney, Raymond. *American Dreaming: The Films of John Cassavetes and the American Experience*. Berkeley and Los Angeles: University of California Press, 1985.

————. *The Films of John Cassavetes: Pragmatism, Modernism, and the Movies*. Cambridge and New York: Cambridge University Press, 1994.

FOR FURTHER READING   701

————, ed. *Cassavetes on Cassavetes*. London and New York: Faber and Faber, 2001.

Ciment, Michel. *Kubrick: The Definitive Edition*. Translated by Robert Bononno and Gilbert Adair. London and New York: Faber and Faber, 2001.

Cook, David. *Lost Illusions: American Cinema in the Shadow of Watergate and Vietnam, 1970–1979*. Vol. 9 of Harpole, Charles, ed., *History of the American Cinema*. New York: Scribner's, 1999; Berkeley and Los Angeles: University of California Press, 2000.

Coppola, Eleanor. *Notes / on the Making of* Apocalypse Now. New York: Limelight, 1991.

Cowie, Peter. *The* Apocalypse Now *Book*. New York: Da Capo, 2001.

Curtis, David. *Experimental Cinema*. New York: Universe Books, 1971.

Elder, R. Bruce. *The Films of Stan Brakhage in the American Tradition of Ezra Pound, Gertrude Stein & Charles Olson*. Waterloo, Ont.: Wilfrid Laurier University Press, 1998.

Falsetto, Mario. *Stanley Kubrick: A Narrative and Stylistic Analysis*. 2nd ed. New York: Praeger, 2001.

Farber, Stephen. *The Movie Rating Game*. Washington, D.C.: Public Affairs Press, 1972.

Houston, Penelope. *The Contemporary Cinema*. Rev. ed. Baltimore: Penguin, 1971.

Jacobs, Diane. *Hollywood Renaissance*. Cranbury, N.J.: Barnes, 1977.

————. *. . . But We Need the Eggs: The Magic of Woody Allen*. London: Robson, 1982.

James, David E. *Allegories of Cinema: American Film in the Sixties*. Princeton: Princeton University Press, 1989.

Kael, Pauline. *For Keeps*. New York: Dutton, 1994.

Kelly, Mary. *Martin Scorsese: The First Decade*. Pleasantville, N.Y.: Redgrave, 1980.

————. *Martin Scorsese: A Journey*. New York: Thunder's Mouth, 1992.

Kolker, Robert Philip. *A Cinema of Loneliness: Penn, Stone, Kubrick, Scorsese, Spielberg, Altman*. 3rd. ed. New York: Oxford University Press, 2000.

Le Grice, Malcolm. *Abstract Film and Beyond*. Cambridge, Mass.: MIT Press, 1977.

Lewis, Jon. *Whom God Wishes to Destroy: Francis Coppola and the New Hollywood*. Durham, N.C.: Duke University Press, 1995.

Lovelace, Linda (Linda Boreman), with Mike McGrady. *Ordeal: An Autobiography*. New York: Bell, 1983.

Lumet, Sidney. *Making Movies*. New York: Knopf, 1995.

Monaco, Paul. *The Sixties: 1960–1969*. Vol. 8 of Harpole, Charles, ed., *History of the American Cinema*. New York: Scribner's, 2000; Berkeley and Los Angeles: University of California Press, 2003.

Nichols, Bill, ed. *Maya Deren and the American Avant-Garde*. Berkeley and Los Angeles: University of California Press, 2001.

Quart, Leonard, and Albert Auster. *American Film and Society Since 1945*. 2nd ed. New York: Praeger, 2001.

Rees, A. L. *A History of Experimental Film and Video*. London: BFI, 2008.

Renan, Sheldon. *An Introduction to the American Underground Film*. New York: Dutton, 1967.

Rosenthal, Alan. *The New Documentary in Action: A Casebook in Film Making*. Berkeley and Los Angeles: University of California Press, 1971.

————, ed. *New Challenges to Documentary*. Berkeley and Los Angeles: University of California Press, 1987.

Schrader, Paul. *Transcendental Style in Film: Ozu, Bresson, Dreyer*. Berkeley and Los Angeles: University of California Press, 1972.

Sitney, P. Adams. *Visionary Film: The American Avant-Garde 1943–1978*. 2nd ed. New York: Oxford University Press, 1979.

————. *Modernist Montage: The Obscurity of Vision in Cinema and Literature*. New York: Columbia University Press, 1990.

————, ed. Film Culture *Reader*. New York: Cooper Square Press, 2000.

————, ed. *The Avant-Garde Film: A Reader of Theory and Criticism*. New York: Anthology Film Archives, 1987.

Stuart, Frederic. *The Effects of Television on the Motion Picture and Radio Industries*. New York: Arno, 1975.

Thompson, David, ed. *Altman on Altman*. London: Faber and Faber, 2006.

Thompson, David, and Ian Christie, eds. *Scorsese on Scorsese*. London: Faber and Faber, 1996.

Tyler, Parker. *Underground Film: A Critical History*. New York: Grove, 1969.

Weddle, David. *"If They Move . . . Kill 'Em!": The Life and Times of Sam Peckinpah*. New York: Grove, 1994.

Wees, William C. *Light Moving in Time: Studies in the Visual Aesthetics of Avant-Garde Film*. Berkeley and Los Angeles: University of California Press, 1992.

Whitney, John. *Digital Harmony: On the Complementarity of Music and Visual Art*. New York: McGraw-Hill, 1980.

Williams, Linda. *Hard Core: Power, Pleasure, and the "Frenzy of the Visible."* Berkeley and Los Angeles: University of California Press, 1989.

Wood, Robin. *Arthur Penn*. New York: Praeger, 1969.

Youngblood, Gene. *Expanded Cinema*. New York: Dutton, 1970.

CHAPTER 16: NATIONAL CINEMAS 2: 1968–

Acevedo-Muñoz, Ernesto. *Buñuel and Mexico: The Crisis of National Cinema.* Berkeley and Los Angeles: University of California Press, 2003.

——. *Pedro Almodóvar.* Hants, UK: Palgrave Macmillan, 2008.

Armes, Roy. *Third World Film Making and the West.* Berkeley and Los Angeles: University of California Press, 1987.

Berg, Charles Ramirez. *Cinema of Solitude: A Critical Study of Mexican Film, 1967–1983.* Austin: University of Texas Press, 1992.

Besas, Peter. *Behind the Spanish Lens: Spanish Cinema under Fascism and Democracy.* Denver: Arden, 1985.

Bhabha, Homi K. *The Location of Culture.* New York and Milton Park, UK: Routledge, 2004.

Buñuel, Luis. *My Last Sigh.* Translated by Abigail Israel. New York: Knopf, 1983.

——. *An Unspeakable Betrayal: Selected Writings of Luis Buñuel.* Translated by Garrett White. Berkeley and Los Angeles: University of California Press, 2000.

Burton, Julianne. *The New Latin American Cinema: An Annotated Bibliography.* New York: Smyrna, 1983.

——, ed. *Cinema and Social Change in Latin America: Conversations with Filmmakers.* Austin: University of Texas Press, 1986.

——, ed. *The Social Documentary in Latin America.* Pittsburgh: University of Pittsburgh Press, 1990.

Busch, Annett, and Max Annas, eds. *Ousmane Sembène: Interviews.* Jackson: University Press of Mississippi, 2008.

Byg, Barton. *Landscapes of Resistance: The German Films of Danièle Huillet and Jean-Marie Straub.* Berkeley and Los Angeles: University of California Press, 1995.

Chanan, Michael. *The Cuban Image: Cinema and Cultural Politics in Cuba.* London: BFI, 1985.

——. *Cuban Cinema.* Minneapolis: University of Minnesota Press, 2004.

——, ed. *Twenty-Five Years of the New Latin American Cinema.* London: BFI, 1983.

Corrigan, Tim. *New German Film: The Displaced Image.* Rev. ed. Bloomington: Indiana University Press, 1994.

——, ed. *The Films of Werner Herzog: Between Mirage and History.* New York: Methuen, 1987.

Cyr, Helen W. *A Filmography of the Third World.* Lanham, Md.: Scarecrow Press, 1985.

——. *The Third World in Film and Video, 1984–1990.* Lanham, Md.: Scarecrow Press, 1991.

Diawara, Manthia. *African Cinema: Politics and Culture.* Bloomington: Indiana University Press, 1992.

D'Lugo, Marvin. *The Films of Carlos Saura: The Practice of Seeing.* Princeton: Princeton University Press, 1991.

Durgnat, Raymond. *Luis Buñuel.* Berkeley and Los Angeles: University of California Press, 1968.

Edwards, Gwynne. *Indecent Exposures: Buñuel, Saura, Erice, and Almodóvar.* New York: Boyars, 1995.

Ehrlich, Linda C., ed. *An Open Window: The Cinema of Victor Erice.* Lanham, Md.: Scarecrow Press, 2000.

Eickelman, Dale F., and Jon W. Anderson, eds. *New Media in the Muslim World: The Emerging Public Sphere.* 2nd ed. Bloomington: Indiana University Press, 2003.

Elsaesser, Thomas. *New German Cinema: A History.* New Brunswick, N.J.: Rutgers University Press, 1989.

——. *Fassbinder's Germany: History Identity Subject.* Ann Arbor: University of Michigan Press, 1996.

Elsaesser, Thomas, and Michael Wedel, eds. *The BFI Companion to German Cinema.* Bloomington: Indiana University Press, 2000.

Fawal, Ibrahim. *Youssef Chahine.* London: BFI, 2001.

Gabriel, Teshome. *Third Cinema in the Third World: The Aesthetics of Liberation.* Ann Arbor: UMI Research Press, 1982.

Gittings, Christopher E. *Canadian National Cinema.* New York and Milton Park, UK: Routledge, 2002.

Gorbachev, Mikhail. *Perestroika: New Thinking for Our Country and the World.* New York: Harper & Row, 1987.

Goulding, Daniel J., ed. *Post New Wave Cinema in the Soviet Union and Eastern Europe.* Bloomington: Indiana University Press, 1989.

Grant, Michael, ed. *The Modern Fantastic: The Films of David Cronenberg.* Trowbridge, UK: Flicks Books, 2000.

Greenberg, Alan. *Heart of Glass.* Munich: Skellig, 1976.

Gugler, Josef. *African Cinema: Re-imagining a Continent.* Bloomington: Indiana University Press, 2003.

Gutiérrez Alea, Tomás. *Memories of Underdevelopment.* (Includes the script and the source novel.) New Brunswick, N.J.: Rutgers University Press, 1990.

Handling, Piers, ed. *The Shape of Rage: The Films of David Cronenberg.* Toronto: General Publishing, 1983.

Harrow, Kenneth. *Postcolonial African Cinema: From Political Engagement to Postmodernism.* Bloomington: Indiana University Press, 2007.

Hershfield, Joanne, and David R. Maciel, eds. *Mexico's Cinema: A Century of Film and Filmmakers.* Wilmington, Del.: Scholarly Resources Books, 2000.

Hopewell, John. *Out of the Past: Spanish Cinema after Franco*. London: BFI, 1986.

Horton, Andrew, and Michael Brashinsky. *The Zero Hour: Glasnost and Soviet Cinema in Transition*. Princeton: Princeton University Press, 1992.

Hutton, Anne, ed. *The First Australian History and Film Conference Papers, 1982*. North Ryde, NSW: Australian Film and Television School, National Library, 1982.

James, C. Rodney. *Film as a National Art: NFB of Canada and the Film Board Idea*. New York: Arno, 1977.

Johnson, Randal. *Cinema Novo x 5: Masters of Contemporary Brazilian Film*. Austin: University of Texas Press, 1984.

Johnson, Randal, and Robert Stam, eds. *Brazilian Cinema*. Rev. ed. New York: Columbia University Press, 1995.

Kaes, Anton. *From Hitler to Heimat: The Return of History as Film*. Cambridge, Mass.: Harvard University Press, 1989.

Kinder, Marsha. *Blood Cinema: The Reconstruction of National Identity in Spain*. Berkeley and Los Angeles: University of California Press, 1993.

King, John. *Magical Reels: A History of Cinema in Latin America*. New ed. London and New York: Verso, 2000.

Kolker, Robert P., and Peter Beicken. *The Films of Wim Wenders*. Cambridge and New York: Cambridge University Press, 1993.

Koos, Leonard R., ed. "Transnational Cinema." Special issue, *Post Script* Vol. XXV, No. 2 (Winter/Spring 2006).

Kovács, Katherine S., ed. "The New Spanish Cinema." Special issue, *Quarterly Review of Film Studies* Vol. VIII, No. 2 (Spring 1983).

Khan, Mohamed. *An Introduction to Egyptian Cinema*. London: Infomatics, 1969.

Kraidy, Marwan M. *Hybridity, or the Cultural Logic of Globalization*. Philadelphia: Temple University Press, 2005.

Kronish, Amy, and Costel Safirman. *Israeli Film: A Reference Guide*. Westport, Conn.: Greenwood/Praeger, 2003.

Lawton, Anna. *The Red Screen: Politics, Society, Art in Soviet Cinema*. London: Routledge & Kegan Paul, 1992.

Luhr, William, ed. *World Cinema Since 1945*. New York: Ungar, 1987.

MacBean, James Roy. *Film and Revolution*. Bloomington: Indiana University Press, 1975.

McFarlane, Brian. *Australian Cinema*. New York: Columbia University Press, 1988.

Malkmus, Lizbeth, and Roy Armes. *Arab and African Film Making*. London: Zed Books, 1991.

Martin, Michael, ed. *New Latin American Cinema*. 2 vols. Detroit: Wayne State University Press, 1997.

Mora, Carl J. *Mexican Cinema: Reflections of a Society 1896–1988*. Rev. ed. Berkeley and Los Angeles: University of California Press, 1990.

Morris, Peter. *Embattled Shadows: A History of the Canadian Film, 1895–1939*. Montreal: McGill–Queens University Press, 1979.

Noriega, Chon A., ed. *Visible Nations: Latin American Cinema and Video*. Minneapolis: University of Minnesota Press, 2000.

Oshana, Maryann. *Women of Color: A Filmography of Minority and Third World Women*. New York: Garland, 1984.

Paranaguá, Paulo Antonio, ed. *Mexican Cinema*. Translated by Ana López. London: BFI, 1996.

Pfaff, Françoise. *The Cinema of Ousmane Sembene: A Pioneer of African Film*. Westport, Conn.: Greenwood, 1984.

———. *Twenty-Five Black African Filmmakers: A Critical Study, with Filmography and Bio-Bibliography*. Oxford: Greenwood Press, 1988.

———, ed. *Focus on African Films*. Bloomington: Indiana University Press, 2004.

Pick, Zuzana M. *The New Latin American Cinema: A Continental Project*. Austin: University of Texas Press, 1993.

Pines, Jim, and Paul Willemen. *Questions of Third Cinema*. Bloomington: Indiana University Press, 1989.

Rayner, Jonathan. *Contemporary Australian Cinema*. Manchester: Manchester University Press, 2001.

Reade, Eric. *History and Heartburn: The Saga of Australian Film, 1896–1978*. East Brunswick, N.J.: Fairleigh Dickinson University Press, 1981.

Rentschler, Eric. *West German Film in the Course of Time: Reflections on the Twenty Years since Oberhausen*. Bedford Hills, N.Y.: Redgrave, 1984.

Rodley, Chris, ed. *Cronenberg on Cronenberg*. London and New York: Faber and Faber, 1997.

Saeed-Vafa, Mehrnaz, and Jonathan Rosenbaum. *Abbas Kiarostami*. Champaign: University of Illinois Press, 2003.

Salmane, Hala. *Algerian Cinema*. London: BFI, 1977.

Sánchez-H., José. *The Art and Politics of Bolivian Cinema*. Lanham, Md.: Scarecrow Press, 1999.

Schmidt, Nancy. *Sub-Saharan African Films and Filmmakers: An Annotated Bibliography*. London: Hans Zell, 1994.

Shafik, Viola. *Arab Cinema: History and Cultural Identity*. Rev. ed. New York: The American University in Cairo Press, 2007.

Shohat, Ella. *Israeli Cinema: East/West and the Politics of Representation*. Austin: University of Texas Press, 1989.

Stevens, Donald F., ed. *Based on a True Story: Latin American History at the Movies.* Wilmington, Del.: Scholarly Resources Books, 1998.

Strauss, Frédéric, ed. *Almodóvar on Almodóvar.* Translated by Yves Baignères. London and New York: Faber and Faber, 1998.

Tarkovsky, Andrey. *Sculpting in Time: Reflections on the Cinema.* Translated by Kitty Hunter-Blair. Austin: University of Texas Press, 1989.

Taylor, Richard, Nancy Wood, Julian Graffy, and Dina Iordanova, eds. *The BFI Companion to Eastern European and Russian Cinema.* London: BFI, 2000.

Triana-Toribio, Núria. *Spanish National Cinema.* New York and Milton Park, UK: Routledge, 2003.

Ukadike, Nwachukwu Frank. *Black African Cinema.* Berkeley and Los Angeles: University of California Press, 1994.

———. *Questioning African Cinema: Conversations with Filmmakers.* Minneapolis: University of Minnesota Press, 2002.

Veroneau, Pierre, ed. *The Canadian Cinemas.* Ottawa: Canadian Film Institute, 1979.

Wenders, Wim. *On Film: Essays and Conversations.* London and New York: Faber and Faber, 2001.

Xavier, Ismail. *Allegories of Underdevelopment: Aesthetics and Politics in Modern Brazilian Cinema.* Minneapolis: University of Minnesota Press, 1997.

Young, Robert J. C. and Raji Sunder Rajan, eds. *Postcolonial Studies Companion and Reader.* New York and Milton Park, UK: Routledge, 2010.

CHAPTER 17: THE RETURN OF THE MYTHS: 1977—

Allen, William Rodney, ed. *The Coen Brothers: Interviews.* Jackson: University Press of Mississippi, 2006.

Bach, Steven. *Final Cut: Dreams and Disaster in the Making of* Heaven's Gate. New York: William Morrow, 1985. (For other industry-related books, see Chap. 18 list.)

Falsetto, Mario. *Personal Visions: Conversations with Contemporary Film Directors.* Los Angeles: Silman–James Press, 2000.

Friedberg, Anne. *Window Shopping: Cinema and the Postmodern.* Berkeley and Los Angeles: University of California Press, 1993.

Fuchs, Cynthia. *Spike Lee: Interviews.* Jackson: University Press of Mississippi, 2002.

James, David E. *Power Misses: Essays Across (Un)Popular Culture.* London and New York: Verso, 1996.

Klotman, Phyllis Rauch, ed. *Screenplays of the African American Experience.* Bloomington: Indiana University Press, 1991.

Levy, Emanuel. *Cinema of Outsiders: The Rise of American Independent Film.* New York: New York University Press, 1999.

McConnell, Frank. *The Spoken Seen: Film and the Romantic Imagination.* Baltimore: Johns Hopkins University Press, 1975.

———. *Storytelling and Mythmaking: Images from Film and Literature.* New York: Oxford University Press, 1979.

Peary, Gerald, ed. *Quentin Tarantino: Interviews.* Jackson: University Press of Mississippi, 1998.

Phillips, Julia. *You'll Never Eat Lunch in This Town Again.* London and New York: Faber and Faber, 2002.

Prince, Stephen. *A New Pot of Gold: Hollywood Under the Electronic Rainbow, 1980–1989.* Vol. 10 of Harpole, Charles, ed., *History of the American Cinema.* New York: Scribner's, 2000; Berkeley and Los Angeles: University of California Press, 2002.

Pye, Michael, and Linda Myles. *The Movie Brats: How the Film Generation Took Over Hollywood.* New York: Holt, Rinehart, 1979.

Quart, Leonard, and Albert Auster. *American Film and Society Since 1945.* 2nd ed. New York: Praeger, 2001.

Reid, Mark A. *Redefining Black Film.* Berkeley and Los Angeles: University of California Press, 1992.

Rodley, Chris, ed. *Lynch on Lynch.* London and New York: Faber and Faber, 1999.

Rosenbaum, Jonathan. *Film: The Front Line—1983.* Denver: Arden Press, 1983.

Russell, Carolyn R. *The Films of Joel and Ethan Coen.* Jefferson, N.C.: McFarland, 2001.

Schaefer, Dennis, and Larry Salvato. *Masters of Light: Conversations with Contemporary Cinematographers.* Berkeley and Los Angeles: University of California Press, 1984.

Schechter, Harold. *The Bosom Serpent: Folklore and Popular Art.* 2nd ed. New York: Peter Lang, 2001.

Smith, Thomas G. *Industrial Light & Magic: The Art of Special Effects.* New York: Del Rey, 1991.

Vale, V., Andrea Juno, and Jim Morton, eds. *Re/Search #10: Incredibly Strange Films.* San Francisco: Re/Search Publications, 1986.

Vaz, Mark Cotta, and Patricia Rose Duignan. *Industrial Light & Magic: Into the Digital Realm.* New York: Del Rey, 1996.

Williams, Linda. *Screening Sex.* Durham, N.C.: Duke University Press, 2008.

Wood, Robin. *Hollywood from Vietnam to Reagan . . . and Beyond.* New York: Columbia University Press, 2003.

Wyatt, Justin. *High Concept: Movies and Marketing in Hollywood.* Austin: University of Texas Press, 1994.

CHAPTER 18: CONGLOMERATES AND VIDEO: 1975—

Bach, Steven. *Final Cut: Dreams and Disaster in the Making of* Heaven's Gate. New York: William Morrow, 1985.

Bart, Peter. *Fade Out: The Calamitous Final Days of MGM.* New York: William Morrow, 1990.

Billups, Scott. *Digital Moviemaking 3.0.* 3rd ed. Studio City, Calif.: Michael Wiese Productions, 2008.

Blake, Larry. *Film Sound Today.* Hollywood: Reveille Press, 1984.

Dunne, John Gregory. *The Studio.* New York: Random House/Vintage, 1998.

Goldman, William. *Adventures in the Screen Trade: A Personal View of Hollywood and Screenwriting.* New York: Warner, 1983.

Jenkins, Henry. *Convergence Culture: Where Old and New Media Collide.* New York: New York University Press, 2006.

Kauffmann, Sam. *Avid Editing: A Guide for Beginning and Intermediate Users.* 4th ed. (Includes DVD.) Burlington, Mass.: Focal Press, 2009.

Kawin, Bruce. *How Movies Work.* Berkeley and Los Angeles: University of California Press, 1992.

Kent, Nicolas. *Naked Hollywood: Money and Power in the Movies Today.* New York: St. Martin's, 1991.

Kinder, Marsha. *Playing with Power in Movies, Television, and Video Games: From Muppet Babies to Teenage Mutant Ninja Turtles.* Berkeley and Los Angeles: University of California Press, 1991.

Lees, David, and Stan Berkowitz. *The Movie Business.* New York: Vintage, 1981.

Litwak, Mark. *Reel Power: The Struggle for Influence and Success in the New Hollywood.* New York: William Morrow, 1986.

Marc, David, and Horace Newcomb. *Demographic Vistas: Television in American Culture.* Rev. ed. Philadelphia: University of Pennsylvania Press, 1996.

McClintick, David. *Indecent Exposure: A True Story of Hollywood and Wall Street.* Rev. ed. New York: Dell, 1983.

McNeil, Alex. *Total Television: A Comprehensive Guide to Programming from 1948 to the Present.* 4th ed. New York: Penguin, 1996.

Monaco, James. *How to Read a Film: Movies, Media, and Beyond.* 4th ed. New York: Oxford University Press, 2009.

Murch, Walter. *In the Blink of an Eye: A Perspective on Film Editing.* 2nd ed. Los Angeles: Silman–James Press, 2001.

Obst, Lynda. *Hello, He Lied—and Other Truths from the Hollywood Trenches.* Boston: Little, Brown, 1996.

Ohanian, Thomas A., and Hans C. Ohanian. *Digital Nonlinear Editing: Editing Film and Video on the Desktop.* 2nd ed. Burlington, Mass.: Focal Press, 1998.

Prince, Stephen. *A New Pot of Gold: Hollywood Under the Electronic Rainbow, 1980–1989.* Vol. 10 of

Harpole, Charles, ed., *History of the American Cinema.* New York: Scribner's, 2000; Berkeley and Los Angeles: University of California Press, 2002.

Spottiswoode, Raymond, et al. *The Focal Encyclopedia of Film and Television Techniques.* Burlington, Mass.: Focal Press, 1969.

Squire, Jason E., ed. *The Movie Business Book.* 3rd ed. Berkshire, UK: Open University Press, 2006.

Staten, Greg, and Steve Bayes. *The Avid Handbook: Advanced Techniques, Strategies, and Survival Information for Avid Editing Systems.* 5th ed. Burlington, Mass.: Focal Press, 2008.

Wasko, Janet. *Hollywood in the Information Age.* Austin: University of Texas Press, 1995.

Wyatt, Justin. *High Concept: Movies and Marketing in Hollywood.* Austin: University of Texas Press, 1994.

CHAPTER 19: DIGITAL CINEMA: 1999–

WEB SITES

Note: Some of this information is not yet in books but is available on the Web sites of the studios and certain other major companies.

Avid: http://www.avid.com

Buena Vista (Disney): http://www.disney.com

Dolby Laboratories: http://www.dolby.com

Metro–Goldwyn–Mayer: http://www.mgm.com

The Motion Picture Association of America (MPAA): http://www.mpaa.org

Panavision: http://www.panavision.com

Paramount: http://www.paramount.com

Pixar: http://www.pixar.com

Sony: http://www.sonypictures.net

Twentieth Century Fox: http://www.foxstudios.com

United Artists: http://www.unitedartists.com

Universal: http://www.nbcuni.com

Warner Bros.: http://www.warnerbros.com

The Internet Movie Database (IMDb) is the best place to start when looking up a person or a movie online, and it is usually accurate: http://www.imdb.com

MAGAZINES AND TRADE PAPERS

Many more could have been listed, but these offer the most up-to-date, accurate, comprehensive information about the film industry, cinematography, and digital effects.

American Cinematographer. Published by the American Society of Cinematographers. Professional articles on film and digital production techniques—with an emphasis on the practice and aesthetics of conventional, special-effects, and digital cinematography— along with well-researched articles on historic movies and great cinematographers.

Cinefex. A state-of-the-art journal of special effects, usually covering 1–3 new movies per issue. Old issues are collectible and hard to find.

Daily Variety. Can be mailed outside the Los Angeles area; subscribers may search http://www.variety.com and receive electronic daily bulletins. The weekly version of *Variety* does not cover the film business as thoroughly as the daily one. Authoritative data on films, especially in the reviews; all showbiz obituaries; worldwide industry news—and the occasional nonstory, printed to see whether it arouses interest in a project. Special issues on Women in Film, the Oscars, etc.

The Hollywood Reporter. An alternative to *Daily Variety*, preferred by many readers. Unless you're a studio, you don't need to get both every weekday.

BOOKS AND ARTICLES

Belton, John. "Digital Cinema: A False Revolution." *October*, No. 100 (Spring 2002).

Billups, Scott. *Digital Moviemaking 3.0.* 3rd ed. Studio City, Calif.: Michael Wiese Productions, 2008.

Cherchi Usai, Paolo. *The Death of Cinema: History, Cultural Memory, and the Digital Dark Age.* London: BFI, 2008.

Gauntlett, David, and Ross Horsley, eds. *Web.Studies.* 2nd ed. London: Hodder Arnold, 2004.

Jenkins, Henry. *Convergence Culture: Where Old and New Media Collide.* New York: New York University Press, 2006.

Kauffmann, Sam. *Avid Editing: A Guide for Beginning and Intermediate Users.* 4th ed. (Includes DVD.) Burlington, Mass.: Focal Press, 2009.

Koppelman, Charles. *Behind the Seen: How Walter Murch Edited* Cold Mountain *Using Apple's Final Cut Pro and What This Means for Cinema.* Berkeley: New Riders, 2005.

Murch, Walter. *In the Blink of an Eye: A Perspective on Film Editing.* 2nd ed. Los Angeles: Silman–James Press, 2001.

Ohanian, Thomas A., and Hans C. Ohanian. *Digital Nonlinear Editing: Editing Film and Video on the Desktop.* 2nd ed. Burlington, Mass.: Focal Press, 1998.

Ohanian, Thomas A., and Michael E. Phillips. *Digital Filmmaking: The Changing Art and Craft of Making Motion Pictures.* 2nd ed. Burlington, Mass.: Focal Press, 2000.

Poole, Curtis, and Janette Bradley. *Developer's Digital Media Reference: New Tools, New Methods.* Burlington, Mass.: Focal Press, 2002.

Poole, Curtis, and Ellen Feldman. *The Digital Producer: Getting It Done With Computer-Based Tools.* (Includes CD-ROM.) Burlington, Mass.: Focal Press, 1999.

Prince, Stephen. "True Lies: Perceptual Realism, Digital Images, and Film Theory." *Film Quarterly*, Vol. 49, No. 3 (Spring 1996).

Slide, Anthony. *Nitrate Won't Wait: A History of Film Preservation in the United States.* Jefferson, N.C.: McFarland, 2000.

Smith, Thomas G. *Industrial Light & Magic: The Art of Special Effects.* New York: Del Rey, 1991.

Staten, Greg, and Steve Bayes. *The Avid Handbook: Advanced Techniques, Strategies, and Survival Information for Avid Editing Systems.* 5th ed. Burlington, Mass.: Focal Press, 2008.

Svanberg, Lasse, ed. *The EDCF Guide to Digital Cinema Production.* Burlington, Mass.: Focal Press, 2004.

Swartz, Charles S., ed. *Understanding Digital Cinema: A Professional Handbook.* Burlington, Mass.: Focal Press, 2004.

Vaz, Mark Cotta, and Patricia Rose Duignan. *Industrial Light & Magic: Into the Digital Realm.* New York: Del Rey, 1996.

Whitney, John. *Digital Harmony: On the Complementarity of Music and Visual Art.* New York: McGraw–Hill, 1980.

Young, Rick. *Focal Easy Guide to Final Cut Pro 6.* Burlington, Mass.: Focal Press, 2007.

Distributors

The following is a list of major 16mm distributors that were active as of 2009. Asterisks identify distributors whose large and diverse holdings make them particularly useful when setting up a survey course in film history, but every company listed here is an important resource.

California Newsreel
http://www.newsreel.org

Cambridge Documentary Films
http://www.cambridgedocumentaryfilms.com

Canadian Filmmakers' Distribution Center
http://www.cfmdc.org

Canyon Cinema*
http://www.canyoncinema.com

Chicago Filmmakers
http://www.chicagofilmmakers.org

The Cinema Guild
http://www.cinemaguild.com

Criterion Pictures*
http://www.criterionpicusa.com

EmGee Film Library*
(818) 881-8110 Fax: (818) 981-5506

Film-Makers' Cooperative*
(212) 267-5665

First Run Features
http://www.firstrunfeatures.com

Flower Films
http://www.lesblank.com

Frameline
http://www.frameline.org

Icarus Films
http://icarusfilms.com

Janus Films*
(212) 756-8822, ext. 335

Kino International*
http://www.kino.com

Milestone Film & Video
http://www.milestonefilms.com

The Museum of Modern Art Circulating Film Library*
http://www.moma.org

Penn State Media and Technology Support Services
http://www.libraries.psu.edu/mtss

Pyramid Media
http://www.pyramidmedia.com

The Rohauer Collection (The Douris Corp.)
(614) 469-0720

Swank Motion Pictures, Inc.*
http://www.swank.com

Third World Newsreel
http://www.twn.org

Wellspring Media
http://www.geniusproducts.com

Women Make Movies
http://www.wmm.com

Zeitgeist Films
http://www.zeitgeistfilms.com

Zipporah Films
http://www.zipporah.com

Glossary

Academy aperture. Also **sound aperture.** The exact dimensions of the Sound-Era image area (also called the picture area or the frame) on 35mm movie film: .868 × .631 inch, with an aspect ratio of roughly 1.33:1. Also, the rectangular opening in the camera that admits light only to an area of that size on the film. In the Silent Era, a true **full frame** was 1.33:1 and measured .980 × .735 inch; that full frame, the whole 4 × 3 area bounded by the sprocket holes and the frame lines, is also called the **camera aperture, full aperture,** or **silent aperture,** and some lenses and formats still use that entire area when shooting. In 1931, the size of the picture area was reduced and slightly reshaped to make room for the soundtrack, creating the Academy aperture or sound aperture. A 1.33:1 flat image that uses the entire Academy frame can be called a full-frame image or a **full frame,** even though it is only ¾ the size of a true full frame or **full-aperture frame.** Note that through all these changes, the film remained 35mm wide with four sprocket holes on the left and right sides of each frame. *See* Academy ratio.

Academy ratio. The standard proportions of a 35mm image: four units wide by three units high (4 × 3), expressed as an aspect ratio of 1.33:1. In the Sound Era, when the Academy aperture was adopted, the actual aspect ratio of the frame became 1.375:1. However, the difference between 1.333:1 and 1.375:1 is widely ignored because it has a negligible effect on composition, and the Academy ratio is still referred to as 1.33:1. *See* Academy aperture *and* Aspect ratio.

Actualité. A nonfiction film that records a real event in an unbiased manner.

Additive color. *See* RGB.

Alienation effect. *See* Brechtian cinema.

Analog. Information that is continuous, like a wave, and that indicates difference by having more or less of something, as the amplitude of a sound wave rises with an increase in volume; in an analog recording, the electrical waveform is analogous to the acoustic waveform, changing as it changes and continuing as it continues. *See* Digital.

Anamorphic. Any wide-screen process, lens, or format in which a wide field of view is **squeezed** (horizontally compressed) during shooting and **unsqueezed** (restoring normal width-to-height relationships) during projection. *See* Flat *and* Wide screen.

Anamorphic lens. A lens that compresses or widens the horizontal dimension of an image without affecting the vertical dimension. The camera lens squeezes a wide image to fit onto standard-sized film, then the projection lens spreads out the skinny image to fill a wide screen.

Animatics. Computer-animated storyboards; moving rough drafts of scenes—often 3-D graphics developed from photos, drawings, and models.

Animation. The process of making inanimate drawings or objects appear to come to life and move—usually by shooting sequential drawings, or an object in sequential positions, one frame at a time.

Animatronics. Moving puppets, robots, masks, etc. by electronically activating remotely controlled pumps and other implanted electromagnetic devices.

Anime. Japanese feature-length animated films.

Answer print. The final trial composite print; the first approved copy of the movie in its final form.

Aperture. An opening through which light passes, especially in a lens or camera.

Aperture plate. A flat piece of metal with an opening that is the dimensions of the desired frame; it can be slid into most cameras, printers, and projectors just in front of the film.

Art director. The person who designs a movie's sets and decor. *See* Production designer.

ASA. A measure of the photosensitivity of an emulsion, following specifications established by the American Standards Association; the higher the ASA, the faster the "speed" and the greater the sensitivity of the film.

Aspect ratio. The ratio of the width of the image (written first) to its height (a constant). A full 35mm frame is 1⅓ times as wide as it is high; its aspect ratio (1⅓ to 1, or 4×3) is written 1.33:1. The electronic equivalent is usually written 4:3 or 4×3. Other common aspect ratios are 1.44:1 (IMAX, a flat format), 1.66:1 (35mm European widescreen, a flat format), 1.78:1 or 16:9 or 16×9 (HDDV and HDTV, the high-definition digital video and television aspect ratio also used for flat theatrical prints), 1.85:1 (35mm American widescreen, a flat format; called Super 1.85 when shot on Super 35mm film), 2.2:1 (70mm flat), 2.35:1 (late CinemaScope, early Panavision, and generic "scope"—35mm anamorphic; also the aspect ratio of wide-screen Super 35mm, which is shot flat but squeezed during printing and projected anamorphically), 2.4:1 (Panavision's 35mm anamorphic aspect ratio since the early 1970s, a shape that makes it easier to hide splices), 2.55:1 (CinemaScope's original aspect ratio), and 2.75:1 (70mm anamorphic). Today, most movies are 1.66:1 (European flat), 1.78:1 (HDDV flat), 1.85:1 (American flat), or 2.4:1 (scope), though some are still 1.33:1 (full-frame flat). Aspect ratios of video formats are sometimes expressed as the number of horizontal pixels, written first, by the number of vertical pixels (i.e., the number of pixels in a horizontal line by the number of horizontal lines). It is also common for electronic aspect ratios to use a colon or to close up the space around the "×" and not to express the height as a constant; thus, 16×9 (or 16:9) and 1920×1080. *See* Academy aperture, Academy ratio, Anamorphic, Flat, Pixel, Wide screen, *and* Widescreen.

Auteur. A filmmaker—usually a director, but sometimes a producer or writer—with a distinctive style and thematic vision that are developed throughout a body of work. French for "author"; thus, the primary creator of a movie, who guides the collaborative filmmaking project so that it expresses his or her creative intentions. Strictly, a director with a distinctive style and vision who also writes and edits the films.

Barney. A padded bag placed over the camera to soundproof it. *See* Blimp.

Base. The flexible component or vehicle of film stock, made of a cellulose compound and coated with a photographic emulsion.

BD. A Blu-ray Disc. A type of high-definition DVD.

Beat. In theatre, the pulse created by actions, dialogue, and pauses; also the length of a unit of this pulse. An effective pause may last a beat or a double-take occur on a beat, etc.

Benshi. In Japan, the live narrator of a film.

Beta movement. *See* Phi phenomenon.

Bildungsroman. (1) A novel about the formative experiences of a central character; e.g., Joyce's *A Portrait of the Artist as a Young Man.* (2) A movie with the structure of such a novel.

Bi-pack. Also **bipack.** A double load of film. *See* Printer.

Bit. A minimal unit of digital information, or the memory needed to store it, in the form of a zero or a one. *See* Byte.

Bit rate. The speed, usually given in megabits/second, at which the bits in digitized samples can be sent over a connection; the amount of information available per second to define a frame, reproduce a sound, etc.

Blacklist. A list that prohibits the hiring of specific individuals and/or a particular class of people, such as left-wing screenwriters. Also the agreement to enforce such a list.

Blade. The part of a shutter that blocks the light; a shutter may have several blades.

Blimp. A rigid cover placed over the camera to soundproof it; a **blimped camera** is one with internal soundproofing. *See* Barney.

Block booking. The practice of forcing an exhibitor to rent a group of films rather than to bid on individual titles.

Blockbuster. A major box-office hit, conventionally defined as one that grosses $100 million or more during its first domestic release.

Blocking. Planning and rehearsing the positions and movements of the actors and of the camera within a shot or scene.

Bluescreen. Also **blue screen.** A bright blue background against which action or models may be shot; when filtered and printed, the blue area may be rendered opaque or transparent, permitting the generation of traveling mattes and composites. If the foreground subject is blue or wearing blue, this **color difference process** won't produce usable results, so a contrasting **greenscreen** or **redscreen** is used instead. TV effects use greenscreen.

Blu-ray. *See* BD.

Bollywood. The commercial cinema of Mumbai (formerly Bombay).

Boom. (1) The arm of a crane, which supports the camera platform and moves it through the air. (2) The lightweight pole from which a microphone is suspended above the actors (whose movements it accompanies) and outside the frame.

Boom shot. Also **crane shot.** A shot taken from a crane.

Bourgeois. Middle-class.

Bourgeois cinema. Films, and the industry behind them, that encourage audiences to identify with fictional characters and situations, to forget their troubles, and to feel satisfied with fictional resolutions. Escapist fictions that make political analysis appear irrelevant and unnecessary. *See* Brechtian cinema.

Box-office grosses. *See* Gross.

B picture. (1) A film meant to appear at the bottom of a double bill. (2) A relatively inexpensive film, usually a genre picture without big stars.

Brechtian cinema. Films, and certain devices within them, that encourage audiences to remain critically distant from the fiction, to analyze the dramatized situation in political terms, and to keep in mind the theatrical or cinematic nature of the spectacle; the opposite of bourgeois cinema. Inspired by the "epic theatre" of German playwright Bertolt Brecht (1898–1956) in which a variety of reflexive and stylized devices engage the audience's critical awareness. Brecht's *Verfremdungseffekt* or "estrangement effect," often called the **alienation effect,** removes or estranges the spectator from the illusion of reality in the spectacle and from the temptation to empathize with its characters and get lost in the illusion; from this distance, the spectator can study and judge the characters as well as the political and ethical implications of their problems and of the measures taken to solve them.

Breen Code. *See* Production Code.

Byte. Eight adjacent bits that are processed as a unit.

Camera aperture. *See* Academy aperture.

Cameraman. Also **cameraperson.** (1) The person in charge of lighting and shooting a movie. Also known as **cinematographer, DP, director of photography.** (2) Loosely, the camera operator.

Camera platform. A small metal platform that can support the camera, which is usually on a tripod, and two or three people. Often equipped with wheels. *See* Crane *and* Dolly.

CARA. The Motion Picture Association of America's Classification and Rating Administration, the board that awards a film its **MPAA rating** (G, PG, R, etc.), determining how old one must be—implicitly, how mature one ought to be—to see it.

Celluloid. Transparent material chemically derived from cellulose; cut into strips to be used as film base or into sheets (**cels**) on which to paint individual elements of composite drawings.

CCD. Charge-coupled device. A chip that registers the amounts of red, green, and blue light falling on it as voltage levels, capturing the frame as an electronic signal and converting that analog signal to digital information. The photocells on a CCD— sometimes called **photosites**—are usually square, are arranged in adjacent horizontal lines, and may be covered with microlenses and/or filters. Each site records R, G, or B information for a particular pixel.

Some cameras have one CCD; others have three (one each for R, G, and B); still others use **CMOS** (complementary metal oxide semiconductor) chips. A photosensitive chip is often called a **sensor.**

CFF. *See* Critical flicker frequency.

CG. (1) Computer-generated. (2) Computer graphics.

CGI. Computer-generated imagery.

Changeover. The instantaneous switch from one projector to another, as the reel on the first projector ends and the next reel begins.
Changeover marks, usually little circles in the upper right corner of the frame, appear near and at the end of the reel (before the tail leader) to cue the projectionist in a two-projector system.

Channel. The sound meant to be played through a particular speaker; e.g., the left, center, right, and surround channels of a Dolby Stereo analog soundtrack.

Chiaroscuro. The artistic arrangement of light and dark elements in a shot or in any pictorial composition.

Chip. (1) A wafer of silicon or another semiconductor material. (2) An integrated circuit on such a wafer, together with its connecting pins or wires. (3) A microprocessor. *See* CCD.

Cinéaste. (1) A knowledgeable film enthusiast. (2) Literally, a film producer, writer, or camerman.

Cinema. (1) The art of motion pictures; "the movies" in general. (2) A movie theatre. (3) The films of a country or group.

CinemaScope. The 35mm anamorphic process introduced by 20th Century–Fox in 1953. *See* Aspect ratio.

Cinématographe. The Lumière brothers' 35mm camera, which could also be used as a projector and a printer.

Cinematographer. Also **director of photography** and **DP;** sometimes **cameraman.** A motion picture photographer; the head of the camera crew.

Cinéma vérité. French for "film truth"; *kinó-pravda* in Russian. An unscripted documentary in which the catalyzing presence of the camera, with which the subjects interact, is acknowledged. In most cases the crew is small, sometimes only one person to run the camera and one to record the sound, and the equipment is lightweight. *See* Direct cinema.

Cineplex. Trade name of the first multiplex cinema.

Cinerama. Triptych format (three cameras, three projectors) employing a high, wide, deeply curved screen, yielding a panorama or a three-panel image that extended nearly to the limits of peripheral vision; a fourth projector played the stereo sound. Original aspect ratio about 2.75:1 but 2.1:1 when viewed from the center. Introduced 1952; changed from a multi-film system to a large-negative anamorphic system in the early 1960s.

Close shot. Also **CS**. (1) Unlike the far shot, a shot in which the camera is near the subject—or, thanks to a long lens, appears to be near the subject. (2) A shot whose field of view is slightly broader than that of the close-up; in terms of the human figure, the head and upper chest might fill the frame.

Close-up. Also **closeup, CU**. A shot whose field of view is very narrow; in terms of the human figure, a face or hand might fill the frame.

Color difference process. *See* Bluescreen.

Completion date. (1) The year a film is finished and ready to be released; usually the year it is copyrighted. (2) The day the final trial print is approved. *See* Answer print *and* Release date.

Composite. *See* Digital composite, Optical composite, *and* Sound composite.

Composition. The arrangement of the elements of an image in relation to the boundaries of the frame and to each other.

Composition in depth. The composition of a visual field in relation to the axis that runs from the camera to infinity; in most cases, significant elements are distributed from the foreground to the background of the image. *See* Deep focus.

Conglomerate. A huge corporation made up of many diverse companies. A **media conglomerate** might include a film studio, a TV network, a cable or satellite system, a video chain, a games company, a music company, and a publishing house.

Constructive editing. Also **linkage editing.** A variety of montage in which many brief, distinctly individual shots (which are considered complementary and related rather than in polar conflict) accumulate into a dynamic whole; formulated by Vsevolod Pudovkin.

Contact printer. *See* Optical printer *and* Printer.

Continuity. (1) The narrative structure of a film, laid out in sequence; the plot as a string of scenes. (2) A list and description (including dialogue) of all the shots in the final version of a film, prepared by the editor; the film as a series of shots. Also known as **cutting continuity.** (3) The matching of details that allows shots taken at different times to appear to be recording a single, continuous event; the impression that conditions established in one shot continue to exist in later or related shots. (4) A list of the details—such as the length of a cigarette, the condition of a tablecloth, or the number of buttons left unbuttoned on a shirt—that have to be matched from shot to shot, either within a scene or from one scene to another. (Once the boot has been eaten in *The Gold Rush*, continuity demands that from then on, scene after scene, the tramp must have only one boot, and the correct foot must be wrapped the same way.)

Continuity editing. Also *découpage*. Editing to create the impression that events flow seamlessly from shot to shot; the opposite of montage (in which cuts are called to the audience's attention and discontinuity is heightened).

Continuous signal. (1) A signal that is perceived as uninterrupted; e.g., a flickering light that appears to be shining continuously or a rapid series of beats that is heard as a single sound. (2) A signal that actually is uninterrupted. *See* Critical flicker frequency.

Contrapuntal sound. Sound that is synchronized to clash with what is shown; a soundtrack that works against the image track or in counterpoint with it. Audio-visual montage.

Contrast ratio. *See* High-key lighting *and* Low-key lighting.

Co-production. A film produced by two or more business entities (studios, partnerships, producers, companies, etc.) that may be in different countries.

Core. A plastic hub on which film is wound.

Crane. (1) A vehicle equipped with an arm (or boom); at the end of the arm is a camera platform that can be lifted and moved through the air. (2) A lightweight boom that supports a remote-controlled camera. *See* Boom shot.

Cranking back. Rewinding the film a short distance in the camera, usually so it can be re-exposed. Invented by R. W. Paul.

Creative geography. Also the **artificial landscape.** Creating through montage an impression of spatial contiguity that does not otherwise exist. Formulated by Lev Kuleshov.

Credits. Also **titles.** A list including the name of the film, its distributor, copyright and other notices, and the names and contributions of those who worked on it, found at or near the film's start (**head credits** or **opening titles**) and/or at its end (**tail credits** or **end titles**). *See* Intertitle *and* Title.

Critical flicker frequency. Also **CFF.** The slowest rate (48 alternations of light and dark per second) at which the human eye perceives a flickering light as an uninterrupted light—i.e., as a continuous signal. The point at and above which **flicker fusion** (perceiving "on-and-off" light as if it were always "on") occurs. *See* Continuous signal *and* Flicker.

Cross-cutting. Also **parallel montage.** Cutting back and forth between ongoing actions—usually between scenes that are presented as occurring in different locations at the same time and that are dramatically or thematically related. *See* Intercutting.

CRT. Cathode-ray tube. An ordinary TV picture tube.

Cult film. A movie, usually but not necessarily weird, with an insatiably devoted following.

Cut. (1) An instantaneous transition from one shot to another; also called a **straight cut**. (2) To splice one shot to another; also the splice itself. (3) The way a particular version of a film has been edited, as in the *director's cut*. (4) The instruction to stop shooting or to end a shot. (5) Abridged.

Cutaway. A cut away from a shot—or setup, figure, or action—to which the editor will soon return; the return is a **cutback.** A cut to a shot whose function is to provide a break from, offer information about, or evade a flawed portion of the primary shot, or to intervene between two similar shots so that their joining will not create a jump cut.

Cycle. A group of similar films made at a particular time, usually fueled by audience and industry support for movies with a certain tone, approach, or subject matter; a flurry of films in a particular genre, released continuously until audience interest dries up and the cycle ends.

Dailies. Also **rushes.** Film or digital copies of each day's shooting.

Day-for-night. Shooting in the daytime while using filters or underexposing to create the impression of night.

DCP. *See* Digital print.

Deconstruction. The critical process of dismantling the logical, ideological, or fictional structures that support and are reflected in a text; analyzing the ways a work comprises contradictions and defers rather than delivers meaning. Formulated by Jacques Derrida.

Découpage. *See* Continuity editing.

Deep focus. A visual field that is in sharp focus from foreground to background (extreme depth of field) and whose foreground and background planes appear to be widely separated (impression of a deep visual field, usually created by a wide-angle lens); often used to accentuate composition in depth.

Density. Degree of opacity of processed film.

Depth of field. A measure of the range of focus in an image; specifically, the range before and behind the plane of focus within which objects remain acceptably sharp. (A lens might be focused at an object 8 feet away but still keep objects that are from 5 to 11 feet away in focus; at a setting yielding a greater depth of field, that same lens might be focused at 8 feet and keep objects in focus from 4 feet to infinity.) Thus, the distance between the nearest and farthest objects that are in focus, measured along the axis from the camera to infinity.

DFX. Digital special effects. Effects achieved on a computer.

Dialectical montage. Also **intellectual montage.** A variety of editing in which shots "collide" or significantly conflict with each other, ideally generating a synthesis (which may be a metaphor or a concept) in the mind of the viewer. Formulated by Sergei Eisenstein.

Dialectics. The theory and practice of systems that develop through conflict between opposites. The **thesis,** or first term, gives rise to its opposite or opponent, the **antithesis,** and out of their conflict emerges a **synthesis** that becomes the first term in a new dialectical cycle.

Diegesis. The world of the story and what is real in and for it.

Diffusion. The dispersion, unfocusing, or scattering of light, creating "soft" rather than "hard" effects.

Digital. Information that is discrete, like a flipped switch, and that signifies in yes/no, on/off, present/absent terms rather than varying an uninterrupted signal; usually in the form of electronically stored data, binary numbers, intermittent electronic pulses, or linguistic units. *See* Analog.

Digital cinema. (1) Nonlinear production, using digital video and computers, of motion pictures that are shot, edited, and distributed without using film. (2) The mastering, packaging, distribution, and exhibition of movies in a digital format. (3) A theatre equipped with a digital projector.

Digital composite. Any image created by combining two or more digital images or image elements on a computer.

Digital editing. *See* Nonlinear editing.

Digital-image processing. Modifying a frame in a computer.

Digital intermediate. Also **DI; an electronic intermediate** or **EI.** A digital copy of the edited film negative, which may be digitally modified in any way. After all the changes have been made—without adding any photographic generations—the revised DI is scanned onto celluloid in a film recorder, creating a digital intermediate negative or **DIN.**

Digital print. Also **digital cinema package** or **DCP.** A digital master that has been encrypted and compressed so that it is ready to be loaded on a digital projector.

Digital restoration. Using a computer to improve the images and sounds taken from the best surviving film elements, returning the movie to the look and sound it had when it was new—e.g., by removing scratches and fixing colors. *See* Restoration.

Digital soundtrack. *See* Dolby Digital, DTS, *and* SDDS.

Digital video. *See* DV *and* HDDV.

Direct cinema. The Canadian, British, and American version of *cinéma vérité*; in general, the camera is less intrusive, with the filmmaker more like an invisible observer and all the sound indigenous. The films of Frederick Wiseman are good examples of direct cinema.

Director. The person who guides the actors in performance, determines the staging of the action, supervises all aspects of shooting, and works with the producer, writer, and designer before production and with the film and sound editors after production to ensure the consistency and excellence of the movie as well as the best possible use of the personnel, materials, and resources provided by the producer.

Director's cut.   The film as the director would like to see it released; the final version presented to the producer or studio, usually with the contractual understanding that it may be altered without the director's approval.

Dissolve.   Also **lap dissolve.** A superimposed fade-out and fade-in; a transitional device in which one image vanishes evenly and gradually while another gradually appears.

Documentary.   A nonfiction film that organizes and presents factual materials to make a point.

Dolby Digital.   (1) A digital surround soundtrack from Dolby Laboratories (six channels in a 5.1 configuration: left, center, right, left surround, right surround, and bass effects); the optical soundtrack is printed block by block in the spaces between one line of sprockets of the 35mm film print. (2) An electronic version of that format, found in HDTV and on some discs and digital prints.

Dolby noise reduction.   Also **Dolby NR.** A process for reducing system noise, particularly tape hiss, by compressing the signal during recording and expanding or decoding it during playback.

Dolby Stereo.   (1) Also **Dolby SVA** (Stereo Variable Area), replaced in 1986 by **Dolby SR** (Spectral Recording). A Dolby NR-encoded, optical, variable area analog soundtrack that carries four channels (left, center, right, and surround) on two tracks; found on most 35mm prints; first major use, *Star Wars* (1977). (2) A magnetic soundtrack, each of whose six or more channels has been Dolby NR—encoded and is carried on its own track; most often found on 70mm prints; now rare. *See* Dolby Digital.

Dolly.   A camera platform with rubber wheels that allow it to move (be pushed) freely over a floor, unlike the earlier steel wheels that had to run on steel rails (tracks). *See* Track shot.

Double system.   Two machines that are interlocked—e.g., to present the separate picture and sound of a movie.

DP.   Director of Photography. *See* Cinematographer.

DTS.   Digital Theater Systems and its six-channel, double-system (the sound is on a CD-ROM controlled by a synchronizing code on the print) digital surround sound format.

Dubbing.   (1) Replacing one performer's voice with that of another (as in *Singin' In The Rain*). (2) Replacing all the performers' dialogue with dialogue spoken in another language, usually by other performers. (3) Re-recording with the same performer, especially when an actor replaces his or her dialogue as recorded during shooting with a new performance, under ideal sound conditions, of the same dialogue. Also known as **looping.** *See* Loop. (4) Copying or transferring a recording.

Dupe.   A print copied from another print.

Dutch tilt shot.   *See* Tilt.

DV.   Digital video. (1) Digital videotape. (2) A program, movie, or audiovisual signal recorded on digital videotape, a hard drive, or another digital medium. (3) Standard digital video as opposed to a high-definition format. *See* HDDV.

DVD.   A Digital Versatile Disc or Digital Video Disc. There is no standard name, so a DVD is a DVD.

Editing.   The art of selecting, trimming, and assembling in order the shots (film editing) and/or the tracks (sound editing) that make up the finished motion picture.

Electronic cinema.   The use of video and computers to storyboard, sketch, render, combine, and alter images from, for, or as a film. Invented by Francis Coppola.

Electronic intermediate process.   *See* Digital intermediate.

Emulsion.   The light-sensitive component of film stock. *See* Base.

Establishing shot.   (1) A long shot, early in a movie or scene, that shows where the action takes place. (2) Any shot that introduces a location.

Exposure.   (1) The amount of light that is allowed to reach the film. Overexposure indicates too much light, underexposure too little. (2) The act of allowing light to reach film; the instant in which this happens.

Expressionism.   (1) The artistic movement that held that the look and style of the visible, external universe could take its shape, color, and texture from the artist's intuition of its essential inner being or from human emotions and sensations. (2) The art of rendering inner states as aspects of the outer world. (3) Emotionally intense creative distortion.

Exterior.   (1) An outdoor shooting location. (2) A scene that is set outdoors. *See* Interior.

Extreme close-up.   Also **ECU, tight close-up.** A shot with a very narrow field of view; the camera appears to be extremely close to the subject. In terms of the human figure, an eye or mouth might fill the frame.

Extreme long shot.   Also **ELS.** A shot with a very broad field of view; the camera appears to be extremely far from the subject. An adult might be less than one tenth the height of the frame.

Fade.   (1) A transitional effect in which the image gradually and evenly disappears into darkness (a **fade-out** or **fade to black**) or appears from darkness (a **fade-in**). (2) A dissolve to any monochromatic field (**fade to red, fade to white,** etc.). (3) To effect a fade; to fade out (rarely used alone to mean "to fade in").

Far shot.   Unlike the close shot, a shot in which the camera is or appears to be distant from the subject.

Fast film.   Film whose emulsion has a high "speed," making it extremely reactive to light and useful in low-light conditions.

Fast motion.   Also **undercranking.** The effect of speeded-up movement, achieved by exposing fewer than the normal number of frames per second (i.e., shooting at a rate lower than the projection rate).

Faux raccord.   A jump cut with a false impression of continuity; often a match of action over a change of scene. Perfected by Maya Deren.

Feature.   (1) A movie whose running time is an hour or more. (2) A theatrical, narrative film that usually lasts over 85 minutes.

Film.   (1) The flexible medium, consisting of a perforated base coated with an emulsion, on which images are photographically imprinted. (2) Perforated film base coated with magnetic oxide; **magnetic film** is the same gauge as the film run through the camera and can easily be kept in frame-by-frame sync with the picture and with other tracks. Also known as **fullcoat, mag film, mag, mag stock.** (3) A movie. (4) Like **cinema,** a general term for the art of motion pictures. (5) To shoot a motion picture.

Film d'Art.   Early silent French "art" films consisting of filmed stage productions.

Film noir.   (1) An American genre of the 1940s and 1950s (named by French critics who noticed the resemblance between these "black" or "dark" films and the series of dark mystery novels—many of them by American pulp writers—published as the *Série noire*) characterized by sudden violence, tough romantic intensity, deceptive surfaces and emblematic reflections, unsentimental melodrama, narrative complexity, low-key lighting, and themes of entrapment and corruption, honor and duplicity, desire and revenge, compulsion and madness, betrayal and disenchantment, irony and doom. (2) A latter-day film with the characteristics of a *film noir*; also called neo-*noir.*

Film out.   To transfer from a digital medium to film.

Film plane.   In the camera, the line formed by the upright frame that is held in the gate, ready to be exposed. The location of the film and its distance from the back of the lens, indicated by a line etched on the camera body.

Film recorder.   A device that uses a laser to scan onto film, one line at a time, an image that has been digitally generated or modified.

Film stock.   Also **filmstock, raw stock, stock.** Unexposed film.

Final cut.   (1) The right given to some directors to have the director's cut released without any changes. (2) The final version of a film, after which it will not be re-edited.

Flashback.   A cut to an earlier event, usually followed by a return to the present.

Flat.   (1) Not anamorphic; a spherical-lens format. (2) Not 3-D; a two-dimensional format. (3) Not glossy; a dull, matte, or nonreflective surface.

Flicker.   The rapid alternation of light and dark caused by the opening and closing of the projector's shutter. Noticeable below 48 fps. Dealt with by using a two- or three-bladed shutter to show each frame several times. *See* Critical flicker frequency.

Flicker fusion.   *See* Critical flicker frequency.

Flip book.   A book with a drawing on every page. By bending the pages against one's thumb and flipping through the pages, one could see the drawing move. Invented by John Barnes Linnett.

Focal length.   The distance in millimeters from the film plane to the optical center of the lens when the lens is focused at infinity. In 35mm Academy-ratio cinematography, a "normal" lens has a focal length of 50mm, a short or wide-angle lens has a focal length shorter than that (e.g., 28mm), and a long or telephoto lens has a long focal length (e.g., 200mm). *See* Zoom lens.

Formalism.   Whether practiced by an artist or a critic, the emphasis on the form, structure, and strategies of a work of art, rather than on its subject or the circumstances under which it came to be created.

Format.   The physical and optical characteristics of a negative or print, such as whether it is flat or anamorphic, the gauge of the film, the aspect ratio of the image, and the number of perforations per frame; also the placement and other characteristics of the soundtrack (single or double system, analog or digital).

Fps.   Frames per second; the rate of exposing and/or projecting frames. Most sound films run at 24 fps; silent films ran at speeds that varied from 16 fps to 24 fps, with 16 fps common for most films before 1920. On today's projectors, "silent speed" is 18 fps, since most films in the mid-1920s ran at 18–22 fps. To simplify matters, the convention is to define silent speed as 16 fps. *See* Sound speed.

Frame.   (1) An individual photograph or picture area on a strip of film. *See* Academy aperture. (2) The perimeter or boundary line of the picture area. (3) In the narrative film, a story or narrative situation within which another story or sequence is bracketed or presented. (4) A one-frame length of film.

Frame enlargement.   A printed enlargement of an individual frame from a movie.

Freeze frame.   Also **freeze-frame.** A sudden cessation of movement created by the continual reprinting of the same frame.

Full aperture.   Also **camera aperture** and **silent aperture.** A format in which the camera exposes the entire picture area, including the area usually reserved for the soundtrack. *See* Academy aperture.

Full frame. *See* Academy aperture.

Full shot. Also **FS.** A medium long shot that offers a relatively complete view of the set and shows the human figure from head to foot.

FX. Effects. *See* DFX *and* Special effects.

Gate. In a camera, printer, or projector, the apparatus through which film passes as it is exposed to light.

Gauge. The width of a strip of film in millimeters.

GB. A gigabyte, consisting of 2^{30} or 1,073,741,824 bytes, which is 1,024 MB.

Gendai-geki. In Japan, a film set in the present or recent past; the film of modern life.

Generation. A stage separating a copy from a source. A copy of an original is a first-generation copy; a copy of that is a second-generation copy.

Genre. (1) A subcategory of the narrative film, defined by the choice and treatment of subject—mystery, musical, western, and so forth. A group of films, or a narrative approach, that deals with a specific avenue of human experience in a character-istic manner (or a variation of it), structuring the story and its presentation in relation to a recurring set of terms, themes, values, figures, and images. (2) A particular variety or type of motion picture. Within the nonfiction film, for example, *cinéma vérité* and the newsreel are distinct genres.

Grading. *See* Timing.

Greenscreen. *See* Bluescreen.

Gross. The amount of money earned by a film before any expenses are deducted. The **domestic box-office gross** is the amount spent on tickets to a particular movie in the country where it was produced. After deductions by the exhibitor and distributor, the amount returned to the filmmaker or production company is the **producer's gross.** *See* Net.

GUI. Graphical user interface.

Hays Office. Colloquial name for Hollywood's bureau of self-censorship, the Motion Picture Producers and Distributors of America, as adminis-tered by its first president (1922–45), Will Hays. *See* MPAA *and* Production Code.

HD. High definition.

HDDV. High-definition digital video, abbreviated **high-def.** Current standards range from approxi-mately 1–4K resolution and up to 12.6 Mp per frame.

HDTV. High-definition digital television. Common formats are 720p (1280 × 720, progressive), 1080i (1920 × 1080, interlaced), and 1080p (1920 × 1080, progressive). The sound is Dolby Digital, and the screen has an aspect ratio of 16:9.

Head. The beginning of a reel of film or tape. *See* Tail.

High-angle shot. A shot in which the camera looks downward toward the subject. *See* Low-angle shot.

High-key lighting. A lighting plan in which the set is brightly lit and there is a low contrast ratio (in other words, the dark areas of the image are not much darker than the bright areas). *See* Low-key lighting.

Hollywood montage. *See* Montage.

Hommage. A shot, a scene, or an element within either that is reminiscent of and pays tribute to the work of an earlier filmmaker.

Horizontal lines of resolution. *See* Line.

House. A theatre.

I. *See* Interlaced scanning.

Ideology. A set of interlocking assumptions, values, and expectations held by a person, group, or culture.

Imbibition printing. *See* Technicolor.

IN. Intermediate negative; also **interneg.** A printing element, made from an IP, that is used instead of the camera negative, to protect it. Used to make positive prints and positive intermediates (interpositives). *See* Digital intermediate *and* IP.

Independent. (1) Also **Indie.** Always capitalized; other senses of the word are lower case. A film production company not affiliated with the Motion Picture Patents Company. (2) A filmmaker who works without studio support or interference and who may distribute the film personally or license it to a company that specializes in alternative, nonstudio products. (3) A producer or small company that makes a film autonomously but that may have a distribution deal with a studio.

Insert. A shot, usually of an unmoving object, that is cut into a scene or a sequence; the principal actors, if they or any part of them should appear, are represented by doubles.

Intercutting. (1) Inserting one or more shots into another series of shots or into a master shot. (2) Interweaving shots from separate scenes, not necessarily in a cross-cutting pattern but usually to imply relatedness. *See* Cross-cutting.

Interior. (1) An indoor set. (2) A scene that takes place indoors. *See* Exterior.

Interlaced scanning, abbreviated **i** or **I.** Drawing a video image as two successive fields, one containing the even-numbered scan lines and one the odd lines. The brain combines or interweaves the lines of the two fields into one picture. *See* Progressive scanning.

Intermittent. Any movement, signal, etc. that starts and stops, starts and stops . . . usually at regular intervals.

Intertitle. Any title or title card, whether or not it is superimposed on another image, that appears anywhere between the head credits (or opening titles) and the tail credits (end titles) of a movie. Most subtitles are excluded. *See* Credits, Subtitle, *and* Title.

IP. Interpositive; a positive intermediate. Made from the camera negative or from an IN, and used to make a final negative or another IN. *See* Digital intermediate *and* IN.

Iris. (1) A circular mask. *See* Mask. (2) A transitional device in which the image appears as an expanding circle (an **iris in**) or disappears as a contracting circle (an **iris out**).

Iris shot. A shot whose picture area appears within a circle, whether or not the circle changes size.

Jaggies. *See* Pixelation.

Jidai-geki. In Japan, a costume drama or period piece set in the feudal past.

Jump cut. (1) A cut between two shots that are so similar that the subject appears to jump from one position to another. (2) A disjunctive, disorienting cut; a sudden transition that may be illogical, mismatched, or impatient with normal continuity and that—unlike the match cut—calls attention to itself. *See Faux raccord.*

K. 1,000 pixel lines of resolution, also called lines of horizontal resolution; the lines run vertically. A frame each of whose horizontal or scan lines has roughly 4,000 pixels is a **4K** image, regardless of how many horizontal lines it has (i.e., regardless of the height of the frame). *See* Line.

Kammerspielfilm. In German silent cinema, an intimate "chamber drama," relatively free of intertitles and usually concerned with the close psychological observation of a small number of characters who must deal with the problems of everyday life in realistic but evocatively lit settings; inspired by the *Kammerspiele* of Max Reinhardt (a theatre so small that the audience could see the actors' subtle gestures; also, the plays performed there). Formulated by Lupu Pick in reaction against Expressionism.

KB. A kilobyte. *See* MB.

Kinetograph. Edison's first motion picture camera.

Kinetoscope. Edison's electronically operated peephole viewer.

Leader. (1) Opaque film spliced to the beginning (**head leader**) and end (**tail leader**) of a reel; used to thread film in a projector and protect it when stored on a reel. (2) Also **Academy leader.** The **countdown** head leader that permits the projectionist to adjust focus and framing as well as to load the projector for a proper changeover (by stopping right after the last number displayed, usually a "3"). (3) Film base cut into a workprint or printing element, the same length as the missing or complementary footage it replaces.

Leitmotif. (1) A recurring musical theme that is associated with a recurring narrative element or theme; perfected by Richard Wagner. (2) A thematically significant narrative element that recurs and develops in the course of a movie.

Level. Degree of volume, intensity, contrast, brightness, pitch, color, etc.; amount of power.

Line. (1) A **scan line,** also called a **line of vertical resolution** or simply a **line;** a horizontal row of pixels. (2) A **pixel line,** also called a **line of horizontal resolution** and a **pixel line of resolution;** a vertical column created by pixels whose positions on their scan lines place them directly above and below each other. (3) The dividing line of a budget; **above-the-line** personnel include the director and stars; **below-the-line** personnel include the crew. (4) An imaginary line running across a set. The camera and action stay to one side of this line in order to maintain screen direction; **crossing the line** reverses screen direction.

Linkage editing. *See* Constructive editing.

Lip sync. Perfect synchronization between picture and sound, so tight that an actor's lip movements and recorded dialogue absolutely match.

Live sound. Tracks recorded during shooting.

Location. A shooting site that is not on a studio lot; often a place where the film's fictional events are set or actual events occurred.

Long lens. A lens with a long focal length and a narrow field of view, which flattens depth relationships and appears to bring the subject closer; a very long lens is called a **telephoto lens.** *See* Focal length.

Long shot. Also **LS, far shot.** A shot that gives a wide, expansive view of the visual field; the camera appears to be far from the subject. In terms of the human figure, a person might be less than half the height of the frame.

Long take. A shot that lasts longer than a minute.

Loop. (1) In the threading path of a camera, printer, or projector, a short length of film that is left slack; originally called the **Latham loop.** (2) A strip of film, tape, or magnetic film whose beginning is joined to its end. (3) To postsynchronize dialogue, specifically by **looping** (listening repeatedly to the live sound, and recording the new reading, on a loop of magnetic film loaded in a dubber that is synchronized with a projector). *See* Dubbing.

Low-angle shot. A shot in which the camera looks upward toward the subject. *See* High-angle shot.

Low-key lighting. A lighting plan in which the set is dimly lit, with rich shadows and occasional highlights, and there is a high contrast ratio (in other words, the dark areas of the image are much darker than the bright areas). *See* High-key lighting.

Mag. Short for **magnetic.** Magnetic tape or film.

Magnetic film. *See* Film.

Magnetic soundtrack. One or more stripes of magnetized iron-oxide particles bearing the final soundtrack, either on magnetic film that is played by a machine synchronized with the projector or bonded onto the release print (running alongside the frames) and played by the projector.

Majors. Hollywood's biggest studios, especially during the Studio Era, when they were Columbia, Fox, MGM, Paramount, RKO, Universal, and Warner Bros.

Mask. A sheet of metal (a **matte plate**) or cardboard (a **matte card**), painted flat (**matte**) black—or a strip of exposed film (a **fixed matte**) that is transparent in some areas and opaque everywhere else—that admits light only to specific areas of the frame. Used to re-shape the frame or in connection with the making of optical composites. *See* Matte.

Master. (1) An electronic original from which copies can be made. (2) To produce a final electronic version from which copies can be made.

Master shot. A long take, usually a full or long shot, that covers all the major action of a scene and into which closer or more specific views are intercut.

Match cut. A cut over which an action appears to continue seamlessly. *See* Jump cut.

Matrix. *See* Technicolor.

Matte. (1) Any surface or coating that is "flat" (nonreflective) rather than shiny; most photographic and lighting equipment and accessories are matte black. (2) A mask that admits light freely to certain areas of the frame and completely blocks it from reaching other areas. In most cases, a **mask** is a rigid physical object or camera accessory, and a **matte** is a selectively opaque shot or shot element. *See* Mask *and* Traveling matte.

Matte box. A black, accordion-like device mounted in front of the camera lens (and often fitted with a sunshade or **lens hood**), capable of holding matte cards and filters.

Mb. A megabit, consisting of 2^{20} bits.

MB. A megabyte, consisting of 2^{20} or 1,048,576 bytes. 1,024 KB (a **kilobyte** is 2^{10} or 1,024 bytes).

Mechanical special effects. *See* Special effects.

Medium long shot. Also **MLS.** A shot whose field of view is narrower than that of a long shot but broader than that of a medium shot. *See* Full shot.

Medium shot. Also **midshot, MS.** (1) A shot whose field of view is midway between those of the close shot and the far shot. (2) More precisely, a shot whose field of view is midway between those of the close-up and the full shot. In terms of the human figure, a view from head to waist or thigh might fill the frame.

Melodrama. A popular narrative form that is characterized by intense emotions and romantic, sensational incidents and that draws strong, vivid distinctions between good and evil.

Mindscreen. The field of the mind's eye.

Miniature. A small, model set.

Mise-en-scène. The atmosphere, setting, decor, and texture of a shot. The way a scene has been designed and staged for the camera.

Mix. (1) To balance, combine, and re-record separate tracks, creating an intermediate or final composite soundtrack. (2) A mixing session. (3) The composite soundtrack. (4) A dissolve.

Monopack. Also **integral tripack.** A compound emulsion used in color photography; the three layers of the negative are sensitive to red, green, and blue and record them as cyan, magenta, and yellow.

Montage. (1) The dynamic editing of picture and/or sound. (2) The intensive, significant, and often abrupt juxtaposition of shots. *See* Constructive editing, Continuity editing, *and* Dialectical montage. (3) Rapid cutting; pioneered by Abel Gance. (4) A series of overlapping images; in the sound film, usually accompanied by music and used as a transitional device; also known as **Hollywood montage.**

MOS. Minus optical sound; i.e., shot silent. Said to have originated with silent-trained German directors in Hollywood, who preferred to shoot "mit-out sound."

Motion capture. Recording the movements, usually of a person, on a computer.

Motion Picture Patents Company. Edison's patent-sharing trust, comprising the nine leading film companies of 1908 (Edison, Biograph, Vitagraph, Essanay, Lubin, Selig, Kalem, Méliès, and Pathé) as well as inventor Thomas Armat and distributor George Kleine. The combine was incorporated and activated in 1908; Méliès was included in 1909, the same year that Eastman agreed to sell perforated raw stock only to members of the MPPC. Disbanded 1917.

Motion Picture Production Code. *See* Production Code.

Movie. (1) A motion picture. (2) A feature-length narrative film.

Movietone. The sound-on-film (**optical sound**) process introduced by Fox; very similar to Phonofilm. *See* Phonofilm, Photophone, *and* Vitaphone.

Mp. A megapixel; 1 million pixels.

MPAA. The Motion Picture Association of America, formerly the **MPPDA** (Motion Picture Producers and Distributors of America). The major studios' trade association.

MPAA rating. *See* CARA.

MPPDA. *See* Hays Office *and* MPAA.

Multiplex cinema. A theatre with many separate auditoriums. *See* Cineplex.

Mutoscope. Biograph's peephole viewer; each frame was printed on paper and mounted on a card, and the cards flipped by as the viewer turned a crank.

Narration. (1) The act of telling or relating, whether or not the account is fictive, the presenter (**narrator**) is personalized, the act is deliberate, or words are employed. (2) Also **narrative.** A text or discourse; the words and/or images delivered by a narrator—who may be a character (*Citizen Kane*), the writer (*The Last Laugh*), a persona (*Annie Hall*), the filmmaker (*2 or 3 Things I Know About*

Her), an impersonal voice (*Jules and Jim*), or the system of filmmaking itself, functioning as a third-person narrator (*The 400 Blows*). (3) In sound film, a voice-over commentary; in silent film, the intertitles attributed to a narrator (usually impersonal; sometimes a character).

Narrative. (1) The adjective for **narration.** (2) That which is narrated, whether true or false; the story (or series of events and perceptions) and the discourse in which it is presented. *See* Plot.

Narrative film. (1) A movie whose story is primarily or entirely fictitious. (2) Any movie that tells a developing story; this general sense includes many nonfiction, avant-garde, and animated films.

Naturalism. A deterministic realism that accounts for behavior through the close observation of hereditary, instinctive, psychological, social, economic, and political forces, rejecting theistic explanations along with sentimentality.

Negative. (1) Film stock that turns black where it has been exposed to light. Also color negative stock, which reverses the color values in the original; *see* Monopack. (2) The camera original; the negative film run through the camera. (3) The completed movie; the edited and perfected final negative, from which release prints may be struck directly or from which a printing element can be made. (So that the negative isn't worn out making prints, it is copied to an IP, which is copied to an IN, from which the prints are struck until it wears out and another IN is made from the IP.)

Negative cost. The cost of producing a movie, exclusive of making and distributing multiple prints. All the expenses, from optioning the first script to paying the last bill from the lab, incurred in making one copy of the film—i.e., the final negative, from which the first approved print was struck. *See* Answer print.

Negative pick-up. Also **pickup.** A deal whereby a studio buys (or belatedly co-produces) and distributes an independently produced film.

Neorealism. Particularly in Italy after World War II, a "new realism" characterized by location shooting, scripted dialogue that sounds improvised, the use of nonprofessional actors in the majority of roles, an emphasis on the everyday struggles of common people and the unvarnished look of nonstudio reality, the rejection of bourgeois fantasy as well as of Expressionism, and the determination to present the characters in relation to their real social environments and political and economic conditions.

Net. The amount of money earned by a film after all expenses are deducted. *See* Gross.

New Wave. (1) In France in 1959–60, the sudden appearance, on many fronts, of a host of brilliant films by directors who had not previously made features or whose earlier work had gone unnoticed. Also

la nouvelle vague. (2) Any sudden appearance of many exciting new filmmakers in a country whose films have been unremarkable for a long time.

Nickelodeon. The first permanent movie theatre in America, which was converted from a store, opened in 1905; it was called a nickelodeon because admission to the theatre (*odeon* in Greek) cost a nickel.

Nitrate film. Film whose base is made of cellulose nitrate; explosive, and obsolete since 1951, but often visually superior to safety-base film.

Nonlinear editing. Assembling randomly accessible electronic copies of shots into temporary or final sequence, whether they are stored as video clips or—in the case of **digital nonlinear editing**—as digital files.

Normal lens. A lens whose focal length is neither long nor short and that reproduces perspective much as it is seen by the human eye. *See* Focal length.

NTSC. The conventional TV system used in the U.S., Japan, and many other countries. It shows 30 fps as 60 interlaced fields. The standard calls for 525 lines, of which 480 are displayed.

Off-angle shot. *See* Tilt.

Offscreen. Also **OS.** Outside of camera range.

Optical composite. Any image created by combining elements from two or more separately photographed images, or combining two or more complete images, usually on an optical printer. The term can also apply to a digital visual composite made on a computer.

Optical printer. A film copier in which the original and the printing stock are not in physical contact during the instant of exposure (in a contact printer, they are); instead, one or more optical systems intervene, allowing part or all of the original image to be rephotographed with or without modifications. An image might be cropped, flipped, repeated, superimposed on another, distorted, filtered, used in a special-effects composite, and so forth. The optical printer itself might be thought of as a camera facing a projector. *See* Printer *and* Special effects.

Optical soundtrack. A continuous black-and-white, **sound-on-film** image area running down one edge of the film (adjacent to the frames), containing the movie's final soundtrack and designed to allow varying amounts of light to pass through it to a photocell.

Orthochromatic film. Early black-and-white film stock, sensitive to blue and green (and, much less so, to yellow) but not to red or orange; replaced **monochromatic film,** which was sensitive only to blue. *See* Panchromatic film.

Overcranking. *See* Slow motion.

P. *See* Progressive scanning.

PAL. The conventional TV system used in China, most of Europe, and many other countries. It shows

25 fps as 50 interlaced fields. The standard calls for 625 lines, of which 576 are displayed.

Pan. (1) To pivot the camera horizontally, turning it from side to side. (2) Also **panning shot** and **panoramic shot.** A shot within which the camera pivots on a vertical axis, turning in a horizontal plane.

Pan-and-scan. To copy a wide image to 1.33:1—usually for TV broadcasting, flat film prints, or full-screen video—by using an optical printer to move around a 4 × 3 frame (whose contents will be copied to the print, while the rest will be discarded) within the image, sometimes by panning and sometimes by cutting.

Panavision. The 35mm anamorphic format that replaced CinemaScope; also the company that developed a new line of cameras and lenses. The aspect ratio was 2.35:1 until the early 1970s, when it was changed to 2.4:1.

Panchromatic film. Black-and-white film stock, in use since 1926, that is sensitive to the entire spectrum. Because its speed, or photosensitivity, was less than that of the orthochromatic film it replaced, it required wider lens-aperture settings and yielded inferior depth of field.

Paper print. A positive copy of a film, made on sheets of paper and sent to the Library of Congress (until 1907, when copyright law was revised to allow the registration and protection of materials not printed on paper) to establish copyright on each of the photographs that constituted the movie.

Parallel montage. Cross-cutting between two or more separate actions (different enough to "collide" when juxtaposed) to imply that they are dramatically or thematically related.

Patents Company. *See* Motion Picture Patents Company.

PCA. *See* Production Code.

Perf. Perforation. Informal term for a sprocket hole.

Perforated stock. Film or mag stock that has sprocket holes along one or both edges.

Persistence of vision. Retinal retention of a bright image that is followed by darkness.

Phantom. A transparent image. *See* Superimposition *and* Traveling matte.

Phi phenomenon. Also **phi effect.** The process of combining perceived fragments into a mental whole, as when preconsciously deducing and hallucinating movement from a series of stills, believing that one sees a continuous action rather than a series of consecutive but frozen phases of motion. In the first experiments, the subjects saw a light move from position A to position B when, in fact, the unmoving light at A had flashed, followed by the unmoving light at B. What they saw is called **beta movement** if the light appears to traverse the whole distance

from A to B (as a figure in a movie might appear to move from position A in frame 1 to position B in frame 2); seeing beta movement, or any apparent movement of "the" light, depends on the distance between the lights and the interval between the flashes. Discovered by Max Wertheimer.

Phonofilm. The sound-on-film process invented by Lee de Forest. *See* Movietone.

Photocell. Also **photoelectric cell.** A device that converts light into electrical impulses—e.g., when responding to light that has passed through an optical soundtrack.

Photophone. The sound-on-film process developed by RCA; it used a variable area optical soundtrack (as most contemporary systems do) rather than a variable density track. *See* Movietone, Phonofilm, *and* Vitaphone.

Photosensitivity. The degree to which an emulsion reacts to light.

Pickup. *See* Negative pick-up.

Picture. (1) A movie. (2) The image track of a movie, as distinct from the soundtrack. (3) The image area of a frame.

Pixel. Picture element. (1) The basic unit of an electronic image; the smallest block in a video display or frame. Usually square and displaying a single mixed color. The term is used whether the video frame is analog or digital. Pixels are laid out in tightly adjacent rows, creating a rectangle composed of tiny squares. The area, aspect ratio, and resolution of a frame can be calculated using the number of pixels in each scan line or horizontal row (the horizontal dimension) and the number of such rows (the vertical dimension, equal to the number of pixels from the top to the bottom of the image). (2) Loosely, the smallest discernible component of a film image. In pixels, a 35mm Academy frame is 4096 × 3072 (4K; 12.6 Mp; 1.33:1). *See* Aspect ratio, K, *and* Line.

Pixelation. Enlarging a video image or reducing its resolution so much that the individual pixels can be seen as little blocks; e.g., a diagonal line develops **jaggies** (jagged lines of blocky pixels where a line or curve should be smooth) and looks like a staircase or the blade of a hand saw.

Pixel lines of resolution. *See* K *and* Line.

Pixillation. The art of animating a person or an object that is capable of moving under its own power—and may well move between exposures. *See* Stop-motion animation.

Plan-séquence. *See* Sequence shot.

Plastic material. Visually expressive objects and images. Formulated by Vsevolod Pudovkin.

Plot. The order in which the events that make up a story are presented. (In the story itself, all the events are in chronological order.)

Positive. An image or print whose color or black-and-white values correspond to those in the subject; created either by shooting **reversal** film (which yields a direct positive image) or by making a negative of a negative.

Post-production. The phase of filmmaking during which picture and sound are augmented and edited into final form, after the conclusion of principal photography.

Post-synchronization. (1) The process of recording, after the picture has been shot, a track that is to accompany a particular MOS (silent) shot—or to be substituted for a track recorded during production—and of synchronizing this and other wild tracks with the picture. *See* Dubbing *and* Wild track. (2) The process of creating and synchronizing a soundtrack for a film shot silent or in a foreign language.

POV shot. Point-of-view shot, also known as **subjective camera.** A shot in which the camera adopts the vantage point of a character's physical eye or literal gaze, showing what the character sees.

Pre-production. The practical planning phase of filmmaking, including all the work (location scouting, set construction, costume design, etc.) that must be done before shooting can begin.

Primary color. *See* RGB.

Principal photography. The process of shooting the principal performers and every dialogued scene in the script; the core activity of the production phase of filmmaking.

Print. (1) A positive, projectable copy of a film. (2) Any printed copy of a film, whether positive or negative, intermediate or final. (3) To duplicate a frame, a shot, a reel, or a complete movie, with or without making alterations.

Printer. A film-copying machine that directs light through processed film (the original) onto raw stock (which, when processed, becomes the print). A **contact printer** is used for relatively simple duplication, such as making a release print from a final negative, a workprint from a camera negative, or a brighter copy of a shot that is too dark. A **bi-pack printer,** or a contact printer adapted for the purpose, exposes two or more sandwiched filmstrips at once to the blank film. An **optical printer** is used to create optical special effects. A **film recorder** "prints" a digital image on film.

Problem picture. An issue-oriented feature film, particularly one that calls attention to a contemporary, real-world topic of concern.

Processor. *See* Chip.

Producer. (1) The person who selects and hires the creative team to write and shoot a film, pays all the costs of filmmaking, owns the finished product, and arranges for the film's distribution. (2) The business entity that collectively performs the functions of an individual producer. (3) The studio or production-company executive who authorizes and directly or indirectly supervises the making of a film.

Production. (1) A filmmaking project. (2) The activity of making a film. (3) The shooting phase of filmmaking, particularly that involving the principal actors (which is called **principal photography**).

Production Code. Also **The Motion Picture Production Code of 1930.** A moralistic list of what could and could not be shown or endorsed in a Hollywood film. A producer's self-censorship guide, considered preferable to censorship by groups outside the film industry, the Code was drawn up in 1930, approved by the Hays Office, and officially adopted by producers and distributors that same year. It was first enforced in 1934, when Joseph Breen was appointed to run the Production Code Administration.

Production designer. An art director responsible for designing the complete look of a film, coordinating and integrating its sets, dressings, props, costumes, and color schemes.

Production effects. *See* Special effects.

Production still. (1) A photograph, shot with a still camera, that is taken on the set, often approximating a scene in the film or illustrating some aspect of the making of the film. (2) The photographs included in a film's press kit, including production and publicity stills.

Program picture. A run-of-the-mill feature; a film made to fill basic programming needs, because theatres had to show *something*.

Progressive scanning, abbreviated **p** or **P.** Drawing a complete video image as a single field in a single pass. In most systems, each frame is shown twice to avoid flicker. *See* Interlaced scanning.

Prop. Also **property.** A physical object handled by an actor or displayed as part of a set; the term excludes set dressings and costumes.

Property. (1) An owned work. (2) A concept, script, or pre-existing work (a **literary property**) that is being considered for production. (3) A film currently in production. (4) A prop.

Rating. *See* CARA.

Raw. Unexposed and unprocessed.

Reaction shot. A cutaway or reverse shot that shows how one or more characters react to an offscreen action, usually one that has been shown in the preceding shot.

Realism. A representational style that attempts to present a state of affairs without distortion.

Rear projection. Also **back projection.** The projection of stills or footage onto a translucent screen, from behind that screen, to provide a background for the live action that is performed between the screen and the camera.

Reel. (1) 1,000 feet of 35mm film—in practice, between 900 and 990 feet—wound on a reel or core; in 16mm, a full reel is 400 feet of film. At silent speed, a full reel is approximately 13–17 minutes long; at sound speed, approximately 11 minutes long. (2) Up to 2,000 feet of 35mm film, wound on the metal reels in use today. In practice, 15–20 minutes at sound speed. Also **double reel.** (3) A metal or plastic spool on which film or tape is wound; unlike a core, a reel has outside rims or flanges.

Reflexivity. (1) Self-referentiality, displayed by a work or by its creator. (2) Also **self-consciousness.** The implication that a work of art is aware of itself as a work of art, either as an artifice in a particular creative tradition or as an autonomous and self-directing structure.

Release date. The date—loosely, the year—a film is first shown to a public audience, not on a sneak-preview basis but as an official opening. *See* Completion date.

Release negative. The final negative of the release version, from which IPs and release prints are struck.

Release print. An original positive print (not a dupe of such a print) that is officially put into distribution and designed to be projected.

Release version. The approved, final cut; the text or version of a movie that is approved for release and distribution.

Rendering. Using a computer (or a network of them) to generate the lighting, textures, and colors of a digital environment.

Resolution. The degree of fine detail within an image; the extent to which a fuzzy circle, glob, or polygon can be seen as the sharp circle it's supposed to be; the extent to which the smallest components of a picture cohere into an image. Related to the number of dots per inch in a photograph and to the number of pixels in an electronic image at a certain display size. Resolution increases as the size of the smallest picture elements decreases and their number increases.

Restoration. Ideally, returning a film to the condition it was in when it was new and complete. The work is done with the best surviving film and sound elements. *See* Digital restoration.

Reversal. *See* Positive.

Reverse-angle shot. Also **reverse shot.** (1) A shot that reverses the field of view over a cut, as if the camera had turned 180° to the rear. (2) One in a series of alternating, complementary views (a **shot/ reverse-shot** pattern) whose angles are usually separated by 120–160°; often used for conversations.

Reverse motion. Action that runs backward, achieved by printing or projecting a shot from last frame to first.

RGB. Red, green, and blue. (1) The **additive** or **light primaries,** as distinct from the subtractive, pigment, or dye primaries. Full-strength red, green, and blue lights add to white light. **Subtractive** or **colorant primaries** (yellow, cyan, and magenta, or **YCM,** used in color negative film), equally mixed, subtract all their color values from white and produce black, as do RGB dyes. Film is a subtractive color system, removing its colors from the projector's white light; TV is an additive color system. (2) The level, shade, brightness, etc. of the red component of a color image is its **R** or **red value;** RGB is shorthand for those three values, which mix to produce the color of a pixel.

Rushes. *See* Dailies.

Safety-base film. Camera or printing stock that has a slow-burning base made primarily of cellulose tri-acetate (originally, cellulose acetate), in contrast to the explosive base of nitrate film, which it replaced.

Sampling. The process of regularly dipping into an analog flow, or anything that can be represented as a waveform, to measure its position, voltage, shade, or other value at that instant; done thousands of times per second. Each discrete sample is converted to digital form at a specified level of complexity (**digitized**); the number of bits per sample (and per second) directly affects the color accuracy and resolution of a digitized frame—or, in music, the richness and complexity of a digitized sound.

Scan. (1) To draw an image by moving a laser or other tight beam (originally, the beam in a cathode-ray tube) across a surface in a series of horizontal lines. *See* Film recorder *and* Line. (2) To capture an image, including a frame, with a laser-beam scanner.

Scan lines. *See* Line.

Scenario. A film script or screenplay.

Scene. (1) A dramatic action or interaction that takes place in a single location. (2) A complete unit of action that is capable of being covered in a single shot, regardless of how many shots are actually used to cover it. (3) The shot(s) in which a scene is presented.

Schüfftan process. A production special effect that allows actors, artwork, partial full-scale sets, and miniature sets to be photographed together; developed by Eugen Schüfftan.

Scope. Anamorphic; derived from "CinemaScope."

Score. (1) The original music composed for a film. (2) The music arranged for a film.

Screen direction. (1) In the interests of spatial continuity and logic, the practice of keeping track of the directions in which people or objects are facing or moving. (2) The trajectory of movement (or direction of a gaze, orientation of an object, etc.) within, across, and in relation to the borders of the frame (e.g., toward screen right); its orientation to real or hypothetical three-dimensional space (e.g., toward the east window); and the continuity of that space as it is created by the continuity of trajectory from shot to shot (e.g., to indicate in a cross-cut sequence that X and Y, who are never seen in the same shot, are running in the same direction up opposite sides of the street, X runs up the west side of the street and toward screen right, and Y runs up the east side of the street and toward screen left). *See* Line.

Screen left. The left half or side of the screen, as seen by the audience.

Screen right. The right half or side of the screen, as seen by the audience. *See* Stage left.

Screenwriter. The author or co-author of a screenplay; the artist who first determines the structure, characters, themes, events, and dialogue of a film as well as many of its crucial images.

SDDS. Sony Dynamic Digital Sound, an eight-channel digital surround soundtrack that is printed, as a stream of microscopic dots, on the outer edges of the 35mm filmstrip.

Segue. A sound dissolve; pronounced *seg-way*.

Self-consciousness. *See* Reflexivity.

Semiotics. Also **semiology.** The study of signs and signifying systems.

Sensor. *See* CCD.

Sequel. A film whose action follows or predates (as a **prequel**) that of a previously released film, whose essential narrative and thematic elements it sets out to vary, extend, and repeat. Unlike the films in a series, the original and its sequels are meant to be shown in numerical order (or release order, if the films aren't numbered).

Sequence. (1) Any group of consecutive shots and/or scenes. (2) A series of interrelated shots that is not restricted to covering an action in a single location and that has its own beginning, middle, and end (subtly limited structure) and distinct project (function, style, or concern) within the whole of the film; e.g., the dream sequence that opens *Wild Strawberries* or the Odessa Steps sequence in *Battleship Potemkin*. (3) A series of interrelated scenes with a consistent dramatic project, constituting a significant unit of the structured narrative; e.g., the Bernstein sequence in *Citizen Kane* or the chain-gang sequence in *Sullivan's Travels*.

Sequence shot. Also *plan-séquence*. A scene that is covered in a single long take whose camera movements are, in most cases, intricately blocked.

Serial. A film made of chapters that are shown at regular intervals—in most cases, weekly.

Series. (1) A set of films that feature the same main characters and generally may be shown in any order. (2) Loosely, a set of sequels.

Set. (1) A decorated sound stage. (2) An artificially constructed setting, whether interior or exterior. (3) Any site where a movie is shot.

Set dressing. (1) Furniture, fixtures, and objects attached to the walls or floor of an interior set. (2) Integral parts of an exterior set. *See* Prop.

Setup. The position (location and angle) of the camera, fitted with a particular lens, at the start of a take; any number of shots may be taken from the same setup.

70mm. Film that is 70 millimeters wide; most often used for release prints of films that have been shot on 65mm negative stock; also used for 35mm anamorphic films that have been blown up.

SFX. Sound effects.

Shomin-geki. In Japan, the drama or comedy about ordinary, modern-day people, usually from the lower-middle class; a subgenre of the *gendai-geki*.

Short lens. A lens with a short focal length and a broad field of view, which exaggerates depth relationships in the visual field; a very short lens is called a **wide-angle lens.** *See* Focal length.

Shot. (1) A continuously exposed series of frames, beginning and ending with a cut or other transitional device. (2) A take. (3) In animation and special effects, a series of individual or composite frames that gives the impression of having been continuously exposed.

Shot/reverse-shot. *See* Reverse-angle shot.

Shutter. A device that, when open, allows light to reach and expose the film in a camera or printer—or shine through the film and the lens in a projector—and that, when shut, keeps out light and allows the next frame to be advanced into position.

Silent speed. Approximately 16–20 fps, but conventionally defined as 16 fps. *See* Fps.

16mm. Film that is 16 millimeters wide; the smallest professional gauge and a low-budget format.

Slow film. Film whose emulsion has a low "speed," requiring bright lighting.

Slow motion. Also **overcranking.** The effect of slowed-down movement, achieved by exposing more than the normal number of frames per second (i.e., shooting at a rate greater than the projection rate).

Socialist Realism. The Stalinist insistence that art serve the interests of the state and be clear to anyone; to be arty was to be elitist and confusing, and to deviate from the Party line was to fail to communicate plain reality.

Sound composite. Any recording created by mixing other recordings, whether analog or digital.

Sound on disc. *See* DTS *and* Vitaphone.

Sound on film. *See* Movietone, Optical soundtrack, Phonofilm, *and* Photophone.

Sound speed.   24 fps, although some formats have been designed for higher rates (multi-film Cinerama ran at 26 fps, early Todd-AO at 30 fps). *See* Fps.

Sound stage.   Also **soundstage.** A large, windowless, soundproof building in which sound films are shot on artificially lit sets.

Soundtrack.   Also **sound track.** (1) The final sound composite; all the sounds heard in a film. (2) The optical, digital, or magnetic track(s) in which that composite is stored; usually an integral part of the release print. *See* Channel.

Special effects.   (1) Physical effects that can be staged for the camera and shot in real time (e.g., a tree crashing through a window). Also known as **production effects.** (2) Production effects that entail the use of machines (e.g., an electronically detonated explosion). Also **mechanicals, mechanical special effects, special mechanical effects.** (3) Photographic illusions created through nonroutine shooting or printing techniques, usually during post-production (e.g., a traveling matte in which a bicyclist crosses the face of the moon). Also **opticals, optical special effects, special optical effects, special effects cinematography, SPFX.** (4) Visual effects achieved on a computer; also **digital effects, DFX.**

Speed.   (1) The rate at which frames are exposed or projected. *See* Fps. (2) The degree to which an emulsion reacts to light and the rapidity with which it does so; the "faster"—more photosensitive—an emulsion is, the less light is required for adequate exposure and the grainier an image is likely to be. (3) A measure of the light-gathering ability of a lens.

SPFX.   Special effects, especially those achieved on an optical printer. *See* Special effects.

Spherical lens.   A lens that preserves the normal horizontal and vertical relationships found in the subject. *See* Anamorphic lens *and* Flat.

Splice.   (1) The physical bond that joins one piece of film to another. (2) To make such a bond, usually with glue or tape.

Split reel.   (1) A film that is half a reel or less in length (where a full reel is 1,000 feet of 35mm film). (2) A reel, one of whose sides may be unscrewed to allow the insertion or removal of film that has been tightly wound on a core.

Split screen.   Also **split-screen.** Any frame containing two or more separate and distinct frames or images.

Sprocket.   Also **sprocket wheel.** The toothed wheel that engages and advances film in a camera, printer, or projector.

Sprocket holes.   Also **perforations, perfs.** The regularly spaced, usually rectangular perforations—into which the pins of claw mechanisms and the teeth of sprocket wheels precisely fit—that run along one or both edges of motion picture film and one edge of mag film.

Squeeze.   (1) The degree to which an image is horizontally compressed. (2) To make an image less wide, especially when photographing a wide field on normal film. *See* Anamorphic.

Stage left.   The left half of the stage, as seen by a performer who is facing the audience. *See* Screen right.

Steadicam.   A camera mount, worn by the operator, that allows the camera to remain level even when the operator moves, ensuring extremely smooth hand-held traveling shots.

Still.   A single photograph, taken by a conventional still camera rather than a movie camera.

Stock.   *See* Film stock.

Stock footage.   Miscellaneous shots and scenes kept in a studio's film archive for repeated use; sufficiently famous (major news events) or anonymous (planes in flight) to be cut into a movie without the expense of new shooting.

Stop-action photography.   Also **stop-motion photography.** Stopping the camera, making a change take place in the action area, and then restarting the camera, creating what appears to be a continuous shot within which everything suddenly shifts position or something is instantly changed into something else.

Stop-motion animation.   Frame-by-frame shooting of a model (e.g., King Kong), a cutout, or any object incapable of moving under its own power. *See* Pixillation.

Storyboard.   A series of drawings that shows how a film or a sequence unfolds, often with several pictures per shot and with indications of character, prop, and camera movement. *See* Animatics.

Straight cut.   *See* Cut.

Studio.   A large production company with its own lot; ideally, equipped with everything necessary to plan, shoot, edit, mix, and release motion pictures.

Studio system.   The control of virtually all aspects of film production, distribution, and (when legal) exhibition by a small number of big studios. (Their only competitors were the smaller studios and the independents.) Also the division of labor within the studio, with one department for writing, another for costumes, etc., and the practice of keeping all employees—including directors and stars—answerable to the studio executives' plans for their careers, decisions about which films should be made, and concepts of the studio's "house" style and entertainment mission.

Subjective camera.   (1) A shot or setup that shows what a character sees; a **POV** (point-of-view) shot. (2) Loosely, a shot, scene, or sequence that shows what a character remembers, relates, dreams, hallucinates, or imagines; a mindscreen.

Subjective sound.   A track that presents what a character hears, does not hear (e.g., if deaf), or imagines hearing.

Subtitle. A line of words printed near the bottom of the screen; in most cases a condensed translation of foreign-language dialogue. Considered intertitles only when part of the original movie.

Subtractive color. *See* RGB.

Superimposition. Multiple exposure; printing or shooting one image over another.

Super 35mm. Film that is 35mm wide and that is shot full aperture—using the entire available picture area, including the area normally reserved for the soundtrack. *See* Academy aperture *and* Aspect ratio.

Surrealism. An avant-garde movement that sought to pursue within artistic structures the juxtapositions, transitions, and bizarre logic characteristic of dreams and the unconscious.

Surround. In theatrical stereo, a channel played through speakers on the side and rear walls of the auditorium. In **split-surround** (used in *Apocalypse Now* and later in Dolby Digital), there are two distinct surround channels, permitting sounds to be placed in the left rear or right rear of the sound field, or a sound source to appear to move diagonally above the audience.

SVA. *See* Dolby Stereo.

Swish pan. A panning movement so rapid that the image is reduced to streaks.

Sync. Synchronization, especially between picture and sound. *See* Lip sync.

Tail. The end of a reel of film or tape. *See* Head.

Take. (1) An unedited shot, beginning when the camera starts exposing film and ending when the camera stops. (2) An attempt to photograph a usable shot; the attempts that prove satisfactory are printed.

Technicolor. **Imbibition printing,** also called the **dye transfer process,** and the company that perfected it. The process of applying dyes directly onto the print (rather than putting the dyes through the film developing process) by means of a **matrix,** which is a celluloid strip bearing various thicknesses of hardened gelatin that is capable of absorbing and shedding dyes. In three-strip Technicolor, each of the three matrices is a black-and-white record of the red, green, or blue in the image (in negative, the cyan, magenta, or yellow, respectively).

Telecine. An apparatus that converts a film image to a video signal and then digitizes it; it can also synchronize frame rates between film and video.

Telephoto lens. (1) A lens with a very long focal length and a very narrow field of view; it has a high factor of magnification (as if telescopic) and flattens depth relationships. (2) Loosely, any long lens. *See* Focal length *and* Wide-angle lens.

35mm. Film that is 35 millimeters wide; the standard professional film gauge.

Tilt. (1) To pivot the camera upward or downward. (2) A shot within which the camera pivots on a horizontal axis, moving in a vertical plane; a tilting movement. Also known as **tilt shot, tilting shot.** (3) A shot in which the camera is tilted to the side, so that the top and bottom of the frame are not parallel to the lateral horizontal axis of the set. Also known as **Dutch angle, Dutch tilt shot, off-angle shot.**

Time code. Also **timecode.** Time information, recorded on film or tape; used for synchronization and for locating particular scenes or frames. Originally developed for synchronizing videotape and film, it can also synchronize multiple devices. (1) A windowed display of the elapsed time the picture has been running, in hours, minutes, seconds, and frames. (2) A crystal-generated pulse that is invariable and for which a start time, shared by two or more devices, can be established; from then on, all the devices run on the same time and in perfect sync, driven by or referenced to the time code. Any irregular film and tape they might produce can be sped up or slowed down in reference to the time code.

Timing. Also **color grading, color timing.** Correcting overexposure, underexposure, and color values when making a print. When digital instruments are used, the term is **digital grading.**

Tinting. The process of evenly and monochromatically coloring an originally black-and-white shot, either by dyeing the film or by printing on colored stock. In a tinted shot of a face, the whites of the eyes are colored. *See* Toning.

Title. (1) A shot consisting primarily or entirely of words; it may appear on its own, as did most of the narrative and dialogue intertitles in silent film, or be superimposed over another shot. The term includes head and tail credits, intertitles, title cards, scrolling titles (titles that "crawl" up the screen), and subtitles. (2) The name of a work.

Title card. A stable, full-frame title; also the card (which may or may not be decorated) on which the words are drawn or printed, and the shot of the card. Includes virtually all head and tail credits, all narrative and dialogue titles in silent film, and the majority of superimposed or stand-alone titles today, but excludes crawls and subtitles.

Titles. (1) The sequence of title cards that includes the name of the film. (2) The opening or closing credits. (3) The intertitles, considered as a group.

Toning. The process of chemically converting a black-and-white image to a monochromatic color image; the darker the image (i.e., the greater the concentration of exposed silver crystals), the deeper the color. In a toned shot of a face, the whites of the eyes are white. *See* Tinting.

Track. (1) An individual recording. *See* Channel, Dolby Stereo, Mix, *and* Soundtrack. (2) One of the steel rails on which the steel wheels of a camera platform could smoothly ride; also one of the boards, laid over uneven terrain, on which the rubber wheels of a dolly may ride. (3) To move the camera forward, backward, to the side, diagonally, or along a curve, usually with perfect smoothness. The term excludes pivoting (pans and tilts), crane, and aerial movements as well as apparent camera movements (zooms in the camera or an optical printer). *See* Dolly, Track shot, *and* Traveling shot.

Track shot. Also **tracking shot, trucking shot.** (1) A shot taken from a camera platform whose steel wheels ride on steel rails (**tracks**); characterized by smooth movement along straight lines and relatively gentle curves. (2) Any shot in which the camera moves (**tracks**) forward, backward, to the side, diagonally, along a curve, or across the ground; the term excludes shots taken from a crane or plane—as well as pans, tilts, and zooms. *See* Traveling shot. (3) A track shot taken from a dolly; also known as a **dolly shot.**

Transnational. That which extends beyond, transcends, or redefines the concept of national boundaries.

Traveling matte. Also **travelling matte.** (1) A matte that can vary the contours of its opaque area(s) from frame to frame; a film of a moving silhouette. (2) An optical composite that seamlessly, and without see-through ("phantom") effects, integrates elements from different shots into one image; isolated through special photographic and printing techniques, the elements are combined in an optical printer. (3) A video or digital composite, created by electronic matting techniques, of moving elements from separate sources.

Traveling shot. Any track shot, dolly shot, crane shot, following shot, hand-held shot, or aerial shot in which the camera moves from one place to another. The term excludes pans and tilts (in which the camera only pivots) and zoom shots (in which the lens is adjusted and the camera stays put).

Tri-format prints. Also **triformat prints.** Release prints that include Dolby Digital, DTS, and SDDS digital soundtracks.

Trust. A group of companies in the same field, formed to reduce competition and control prices. Illegal.

TV safe area. The part of a film image that is sure to be displayed on a properly working conventional television. Vital actions often are kept inside it.

24p. A digital video camera that can expose 24 progressive frames per second at 2K or 4K. The first model was Sony's HDW-F900.

Two-shot. A shot of two people.

Uncut. Unabridged.

Undercranking. *See* Fast motion.

Underscoring. Music that accompanies a shot, scene, or sequence but is not being played by any character or object (radio, record, etc.) in the movie; nondiegetic music.

Variable area track. An optical soundtrack whose amplitude or contour varies but whose density (a measure of opacity) remains constant.

Variable density track. An optical soundtrack whose dimensions remain constant but whose degree of opacity (**density**) varies.

VCR. *See* Videocassette recorder.

Vertical integration. An economic structure in which every aspect of production and distribution is controlled from the top.

Vertical lines of resolution. *See* Line.

Video. (1) Closed-circuit television. (2) The art and technology of television. (3) A work made to be televised or shown on a monitor. (4) A videotape, laserdisc, DVD, or BD copy of a movie or of a video work. (5) An electronic image or work that can be electronically displayed or transferred to film. (6) Digital video.

Videocassette recorder. Also **VCR.** A videotape deck that electronically records and plays back audiovisual information that may be displayed on a television; the videotape is wound on cores in a case, so that the tape itself need not be handled.

Visual masking. The phenomenon whereby the brain stops processing a frame that is followed by an instant of visual noise, clearing the mental slate for the next frame and defeating any image-confusing effects that might be caused by persistence of vision.

Vitaphone. The **sound-on-disc** process first used by Warner Bros.; eventually made obsolete by the sound-on-film process. *See* Movietone, Optical soundtrack, Phonofilm, *and* Photophone.

Vitascope. Edison's first projector, invented by Thomas Armat and C. Francis Jenkins and incorporating the Latham loop. *See* Loop.

Voice-over. Also **voice-over narration, V-O.** A commentative dialogue track (sometimes presented as an interior monologue) that is not being delivered aloud by any onscreen or offscreen indigenous source; instead it is laid "over" the indigenous sounds of the scene.

Wide-angle lens. (1) A lens with a very short focal length and a very broad field of view; it deepens or exaggerates depth relationships in the visual field and produces distorted, bowed images of objects that are very near the camera. (2) Loosely, any short lens. *See* Focal length *and* Telephoto lens.

Wide screen. Any film format, whether flat or anamorphic, that has an aspect ratio greater than 1.4:1. The adjective is **wide-screen.**

Widescreen. A 35mm flat format whose aspect ratio is 1.85:1 in America, 1.78:1 in HDDV, and 1.66:1 in Europe. The adjective is **widescreen.**

Wild track. Also **wild recording, wild sound.** A recording made without camera synchronization.

Wipe. A transitional effect in which one image appears to push another off the screen (the moving boundary between the images is the **wipe line**) or in which parts of one shot are removed while parts of the next shot appear in their place.

Workprint. Also **work print.** A working copy of the film, edited on film into rough final form; also the positive print of the camera footage, which is cut and recut by the editor. The final, approved workprint is used as a guide when mixing the sound and cutting the negative. Made obsolete by computerized editing.

Writer. *See* Screenwriter.

Zoom. To adjust the focal length of a zoom lens while the camera is running; also a shot taken while the zoom is being adjusted. As the focal length is shortened (a **zoom out** or **backward zoom**), the lens behaves more like a wide-angle lens, exaggerating depth relationships, decreasing magnification, and widening the field of view so that the camera appears to move away from the subject; as the focal length is increased (a **zoom in** or **forward zoom**), the lens behaves more like a telephoto lens, flattening depth relationships, increasing magnification, and narrowing the field of view so that the camera appears to move closer to the subject.

Zoom lens. A lens with a variable (rather than a fixed) focal length, which allows the camera operator or assistant to widen or narrow the field of view without moving the camera or stopping to change lenses.

Acknowledgments

Film Stills

The author and publisher wish to thank the following for making available photographic stills:

from *Scorpio Rising;* courtesy of Kenneth Anger.

from *Wavelength;* courtesy of Anthology Film Archives.

A Kinetoscope Parlor and *Fred Ott's Sneeze;* reprinted courtesy of Arno Press, Inc., 1970.

from the films *Diary of a Country Priest, 8½, Closely Watched Trains, Viridiana, Pather Panchali, Throne of Blood,* and *The Bicycle Thief;* courtesy of Audio-Brandon Films.

from *La strada;* courtesy of Avco-Embassy Films.

from the films *Mothlight* and *existence is song;* courtesy of Stan Brakhage.

from *Faces;* courtesy of Ray Carney and the Estate of John Cassavetes. Frame enlargement from *Faces* reproduced by permission; copyright © Faces International Films. Photography by Al Ruban.

from *Terminator 2: Judgment Day;* courtesy of Carolco Films.

from *The White Balloon* by Jafar Panahi, 1995, Iran. Reproduced by permission of Celluloid Dreams, Agent for Jafar Panahi.

from *Women on the Verge of a Nervous Breakdown;* courtesy of Cinevista, Inc.

from *Blood Simple* and *The Killer;* courtesy of Circle Releasing Corporation.

from the films *Lawrence of Arabia,* copyright © 1962, and *On the Waterfront;* both courtesy of Columbia Pictures Industries, Inc. All rights reserved.

from *Halloween;* courtesy of Compass International Pictures.

from the films *Breathless, Vivre sa vie, The Children of Paradise,* and *A nous la liberté;* courtesy of Contemporary Films/McGraw-Hill.

from *La Cienaga;* Courtesy Cowboy Pictures.

from *Blue Velvet;* courtesy of DEG Communications.

from *New York Stories;* courtesy of The Walt Disney Company. Used by permission, copyright © The Walt Disney Company.

from the films *Mighty Joe Young, Steamboat Willie,* and *The Skeleton Dance;* © Disney Enterprises, Inc.

from *The Fall of the House of Usher;* courtesy of the George Eastman House.

from *The Book of All the Dead,* Canada. Reproduced by permission of Bruce Elder.

from *Once Upon a Time in America;* copyright © 1984 Embassy International Pictures.

from *A Trip to the Moon, The General, The Pawn Shop, One A.M., The Last Laugh,* and *Easy Street;* courtesy of Em Gee Film Library.

from *Hiroshima Mon Amour,* 1959, France, Argos Films S. A. R. L. Reproduced by permission of Gades Films International Ltd.

from *France/Tour/Détour/Deux/Enfants;* courtesy of Jean-Luc Godard.

from *Stranger Than Paradise;* courtesy of the Samuel Goldwyn Company. © 1984 Cinesthesia Productions Inc.

from *Chunhyang,* Courtesy Korean Film Commissioner Hong-Joon Kim.

from *Iphigenia;* courtesy of Andrew Horton.

from *Down By Law;* courtesy of Island Pictures Inc. © 1986, Black Snake, Inc. All rights reserved.

from the films *The 39 Steps, The Rules of the Game, Jules and Jim, The 400 Blows, L'avventura, Citizen Kane, Ugetsu, Wild Strawberries, The Seventh Seal, The Blue Angel,* and *Grand Illusion;* courtesy of Janus Films.

from *Grass;* "Protest by the Hollywood Ten," courtesy of Paul Jarrico.

from *Salt of the Earth;* courtesy of Paul Jarrico.

from *The Jazz Singer* © 1927 Turner Entertainment Co. An AOL/Time Warner Company. All rights reserved. Everett Collection.

from *Interrogation,* 1982. Courtesy of Circle Releasing. Reproduced by permission of Kino International.

from *Ménilmontant,* 1925, France. Courtesy of Circle Releasing. Reproduced by permission of Kino International.

from *Sop'yonje,* 1993, Korea. Reproduced with permission of the Korean Cultural Center, Los Angeles.

from *The Passion of Joan of Arc;* courtesy of La Societé Nouvelle des Establishment Gaumont.

from *Lola Montès;* courtesy of Les Films de la Pléiade.

from *Speedy;* courtesy of The Harold Lloyd Trust.

from *Raiders of the Lost Ark;* courtesy of Lucasfilm Ltd. TM & Lucasfilm Ltd. (LFL) 1981. All rights reserved.

from the films *Star Wars; Star Wars: Episode I–The Phantom Menace;* Courtesy of Lucasfilm Ltd.

from *Eraserhead;* courtesy of David Lynch.

from the films *Black Narcissus, Blonde Venus, Brazil, The Breakfast Club, Do The Right Thing, Foolish Wives, Frankenstein (1931), The Last Temptation of Christ, The Mummy (1932), The Scarlet Empress, They Live, Trouble in Paradise, Videodrome,* and *Zoot Suit;*

from *2001: A Space Odyssey* © 1968 Turner Entertainment Co. An AOL/Time Warner Company. All rights reserved.

from *The Maltese Falcon* © 1941 Turner Entertainment Co. An AOL/Time Warner Company. All rights reserved.

from *The Treasure of the Sierra Madre* © 1948 Turner Entertainment Co. An AOL/Time Warner Company. All rights reserved.

from the Warner Bros. releases: *Bonnie and Clyde* © 1967 Warner Bros.-Seven Arts and Tatira-Hillar Productions; *Day for Night* © 1973 les Films du Carrosse S.A.; *Full Metal Jacket*, copyright © 1987 Warner Bros., Inc.; *McCabe and Mrs. Miller* © 1971 Warner Bros., Inc.; *Mean Streets*, copyright © 1973 Warner Bros., Inc.; *A Star is Born* © 1954 Warner Bros., Inc.; *The Wild Bunch* © Warner Bros.-Seven Arts, Inc.

from *New York Stories: Life Lessons*; courtesy of Touchstone Pictures and Martin Scorsese. © Touchstone Pictures.

from *Nosferatu* and *Destiny*; courtesy of Transit Films.

from *The Last Wave*; copyright © 1977 Turner/United Artists.

from *Stagecoach*; courtesy of TV Cinema Sales Corporation.

from *Alien*, © 1979; courtesy of 20th Century–Fox Film Corporation. All rights reserved.

from *Edward Scissorhands*, *Lacombe Lucien*, and *Walkabout*; courtesy of 20th Century–Fox.

from *Kiss of Death* © 1948 20th Century–Fox Film Corporation. All rights reserved. Reproduced by permission.

from the films *Lucía*, *Xala*, *Memories of Underdevelopment*, and *The Last Supper*; courtesy of Unifilm.

from the films *Annie Hall*; *Carrie*, © 1976; *Gold Diggers of 1935*; *Heaven's Gate*, © 1980; *The Jazz Singer*; *The Manchurian Candidate*, © 1962 M. C. Productions; *Persona*; *Red River*; and *Raging Bull*, courtesy of Martin Scorsese, © 1980. All courtesy of United Artists Corporation. All rights reserved.

from *The Mummy's Ghost*; copyright © 1944 by Universal City Studios, Inc. Reproduced by permission of and courtesy of Universal Studios Publishing Rights, A Division of Universal Studios Licensing, Inc. All rights reserved.

from the films *The Kiss*, *The Magic Lantern*, *Life of an American Fireman*, *The Great Train Robbery*, *The Adventures of Dollie*, *A Corner in Wheat*, *The Musketeers of Pig Alley*, *Barney Oldfield's Race for a Life*, *Making A Living*, *Kid Auto Races*, *Fatima*, *Sherlock Jr.*, *Berlin: Symphony of a Great City*, *M*, *Strike*, *The Man with a Movie Camera*, *Storm Over Asia*, *Return to Reason*, *Un Chien andalou*, *Zéro de conduite*, *Blackmail*, *Pickup on South Street*, *Viaggio in Italia*, *The Battle of Algiers*, *H₂0*, and *Open City*; courtesy of the University of Chicago Film Archive & Study Center.

from the films *Once Upon a Time in America*, © 1984 Embassy International Pictures; *Rebel Without a Cause*, copyright © 1955; *The Road Warrior*, © 1982 Kennedy Miller Entertainment Pty. Ltd. All courtesy of Warner Bros., Inc. All rights reserved.

from *Gun Crazy* © 1949 Pioneer Pictures Corporation. Reproduced by permission of Warner Bros.

from *Finding Nemo*; © Disney Enterprises, Inc./Pixar.

from the films *The Lord of the Rings* (Gollum), *The Lord of the Rings: The Two Towers*, and *Sin City*; courtesy of Photofest.

from *Way Down East*, *The Greatest Question*; courtesy the Museum of Modern Art/Film Stills Archive.

from *Whale Rider*; Newmarket Films/Photofest.

from *Duck Soup*; Paramount Pictures/Photofest.

from *Russian Ark*, *Amélie*, *Stan Laurel and Oliver Hardy*, *Body and Soul*; Photofest.

from *Time Code*; Red Mullet Productions/The Kobal Collection/Marks, Elliot.

from *Lake Placid*; © 1999 20th Century–Fox. All rights reserved.

from *Sop'yonje*; reproduced with permission of the Korean Cultural Center, Los Angeles.

from *Monkeyshines no. 1 and no. 2*; courtesy Library of Congress.

from the films *The Love Light*; *Run Lola Run*; *Amores Perros*; *The Blair Witch Project*; *Atanarjuat the Fast Runner*; *One from the heart*; *O Brother, Where Art Thou?*; courtesy Academy of Motion Picture Arts and Sciences.

from *Who Framed Roger Rabbit*; courtesy Touchstone Pictures & Amblin Entertainment, Inc. All rights reserved.

from *Toy Story*; © 1999 Disney Enterprises, Inc. Pixar. Original *Toy Story* elements © Disney Enterprises, Inc.

from *Slumdog Millionaire*, *Ashes of Time Redux*, *The Curious Case Of Benjamin Button*, *Star Wars: Episode III—Revenge of the Sith*, *Watchmen*, *The Dark Knight*; Photofest.

Nonfilm Stills

The Capitol Theatre ("Bank Nite"), opening of *The Tigress*, Grauman's Chinese Theatre, Haggar's Royal Electric Bioscope, Interior of the Roxy, from the ceiling to the orchestra, The Carthay Circle Theatre, The Carthay Circle Theatre: one of the many snack bars, The Carthay Circle Theatre: the mezzanine, The Carthay Circle Theatre: the painted asbestos curtain at the front of the circular auditorium; courtesy of the Academy of Motion Picture Arts and Sciences.

Cans of film; Photo by Victor Jendras © Used by permission.

Lobby card for the Lone Defender; courtesy of Robert Harris.

Douglas Fairbanks's name and prints in cement; Roy Rogers's imprints of his gun and horse along with his hands and boots; Mary Pickford's name and prints in cement; Courtesy of Bruce F. Kawin.

Mary Pickford and Douglas Fairbanks; The Mary Pickford Foundation.

Lobby card for *The Blot*; courtesy of the Museum of Modern Art/Film Stills Archive.

Stage Show; Katherine Hepburn; Dorothy Arzner; courtesy of the Academy of Motion Picture Arts and Sciences.

Index

Cagney, James, 260, 264, 335
Cahiers du cinéma, 384, 397, 398, 402
Cain, James M., 334, 364
Caine, Michael, 423
The Caine Mutiny, 327
Calcutta '71, 462
Calcutta Film Society, 459
California Split, 495
Caligari, 2, 175, 182, 447, 514, 529, 589
Callas, Maria, 411
Call Northside 777, 316
Calloway, Cab, 231
Calmettes, André, 66
Calvalcanti, Alberto, 236
camcorder, 585, 650
Camera, 583
Camera Buff, 442
The Cameraman, 156
camera obscura, 18
Cameron, James, 586, 589, 593, 595, 623, 625, 628, 662, 663, 682, 683
Camille, 270, 280
Le Camion, 404
Cammell, Donald, 434, 475
Camouflage, 441
Campbell, Eric, 109, 110, 116
Campbell, John W., Jr., 624
Campbell, Martin, 620
Campion, Jane, 465, 553–554, 578, 582
Camras, Marvin, 641
Camus, Albert, 358
Camus, Marcel, 350, 410
Canada, 567, 570, 637
Canadian cinema, 146, 508, 516, 520–521, 525, 526, 548, 554–558, 567, 578–579, 582, 682
Canadian Film Development Corporation, 554–555
Canal Plus (Canal+), 638
Canet, Guillaume, 410
Cannon Elstree Studios, 607
Cantata, 443
The Canterbury Tales, 372
The Canterville Ghost, 506
Cantet, Laurent, 410
Cantor, Eddie, 67, 220
Canudo, Ricciotto, 234
Cape Fear, 636
Capital Cities/ABC Inc., 634
Capra, Frank, 3, 124, 153, 154, 231, 266, 277–278, 288, 292, 293, 296, 308, 316, 338, 449, 490, 492
The Captain's Paradise, 423, 482
CARA (Classification and Rating Administration), 490–491
Les Carabiniers, 32, 390, 391, 412
Carbutt, John, 22
Cardiff, Jack, 424, 476, 603
Carefree, 262
Carey, Harry, 74, 79, 148, 288, 289
Cargol, Jean-Pierre, 388
Carmen, 103, 570, 571
Carmen Jones, 141
Carnal Knowledge, 505, 623
Carne, 404
Carné, Marcel, 186, 253–256, 257, 376, 377, 378
Carnival in Flanders, 253
Carnival of Souls, 509
Caro, Marc, 405, 410

Caro, Niki, 553, 579, 592
Carol, Martine, 379, 380
Carousel, 140
Carpenter, John, 508, 583, 590, 624, 625, 629
Carradine, Keith, 495
Carré, Ben, 148
Carrey, Jim, 672, 675
Carrie, 504, 508
Carrière, Jean-Claude, 582, 584
Carroll, Madeleine, 298
Cars, 662
Carson, Jack, 324
Carstensen, Margit, 530
Casablanca, 189, 261, 268, 486, 631, 652, 681
Casanova, 366
Casarès, Maria, 254
Casaus, Victor, 577
Case, Theodore, 222
Casler, Herman, 42, 43
Cassavetes, John, 9, 341, 415, 435, 492, 499, 505, 506, 522, 526, 587
Cassel, Seymour, 492
Castellani, Renato, 476
Castle, William, 603
Castle-Hughes, Keisha, 553
The Castle, 551
Castro, Fidel, 540, 547
Castro Street, 520
Catalog, 516, 660
Catch-22, 505
Catmull, Ed, 661
Cat People, 148
Cattaneo, Peter, 432
Caught, 378, 622
Caught in a Cabaret, 106
Caught in the Rain, 106
Cavalcanti, Alberto, 185, 257, 423, 475, 514
Cayrol, Jean, 395, 396
CDS (Cinema Digital Sound), 662
Cecil B. Demented, 603
Ceddo, 541
Ceiling, 437, 438
The Celebration, 415, 481, 654
Celebrity Pictures, 140
Céline and Julie Go Boating, 398
celluloid, 10, 11, 21, 22, 24
censorship, 63, 130–131, 182, 203, 251, 436, 438, 458, 464, 465, 518, 601
Central Station, 582
Centro Sperimentale (film school), 358
Cerf, Vinton, 660
Cervantes, Miguel de, 159
César, 250
C'est la vie, 403
CG, 674, 675, 676, 678
Chabrol, Claude, 384, 397, 407–408
Cha Cha Cha, 568
Chacon, Juan, 318
Chadha, Gurinder, 463
Chahine, Youssef, 578
Chakravarty, Utpalendu, 462–463
Chamberlain, Richard, 550, 552
The Chambermaid on the Titanic, 572
Chambers, Jack, 516
Chan, Jackie, 470, 658
Chandler, Raymond, 334, 490
The Big Sleep, 294

Chaney, Lon, 120, 148, 164, 165, 167, 168, 429
Chaney, Lon, Jr., 623
Chang: A Drama of the Wilderness, 150
Chang Cheh, 470, 480
Chan is Missing, 595, 614, 622
Le Chant du styrène, 412
The Chant of Jimmy Blacksmith, 550
Chaos, 375
Chapayev, 217, 437, 563
Chaplin, Charles, 30, 50, 64, 92, 101, 102, 103, 106–115, 116, 117, 118, 120, 123, 124, 151, 152, 153, 154, 155, 156, 157–159, 161, 164, 168, 175, 198, 205, 225, 229, 231, 232, 243, 250, 251, 272–275, 338, 382, 423, 490, 492, 493, 495, 545, 631
Chaplin, Geraldine, 584
Chaplin, Sydney, 115
Chapman, Graham, 430, 431
The Charge of the Light Brigade, 268, 428
Charles and Lucie, 403
Charles Urban Trading Company, 42
Charley Varrick, 508
Charlie Wilson's War, 505
Charulata, 460
Chase, Charley, 152, 167
Chasney, Jasmine, 396
Chávarri, Jaime, 581
Chayefsky, Paddy, 330
Che, 623
The Cheat, 118, 135, 167
Chekhov, Antonin, 561
The Chelsea Girls, 518
Chen, Joan, 567
Chen Kaige, 464–465, 467, 478, 483
Cherrill, Virginia, 272, 273
A Chess Dispute, 60
Chess Fever, 207
The Chess Players, 461
Cheung, Leslie, 465
Cheung, Maggie, 405
Chevalier, Maurice, 227, 228, 262, 376
Cheyenne Autumn, 289
The Chicago, 127
Chicanos, 617
Chico Marx, 226
Un Chien andalou, 235–236, 257, 515, 572, 573, 583
La Chienne, 245, 250
Childhood of Gorky, 217
A Child of the Big City, 193
The Children Are Watching Us, 361–362
Children of Men, 568
The Children of Paradise, 254–256, 257, 377
Chilean cinema, 405, 539, 540, 541, 577
Chimes at Midnight, 308
China Is Near, 374
Chinatown, 335, 441, 490, 526, 607
Chinese Box, 622
Chinese cinema, 463–468, 464, 478, 480, 481, 483, 566, 567
The Chinese Connection, 470
A Chinese Ghost Story, 470
Chinese Roulette, 529, 530
Ching Siu-tung, 470, 480
La Chinoise, 390, 393
Chloe in the Afternoon, 397

Kanevsky, Vitaly, 562, 563, 580
Kang Je-Gyu, 471, 472
Kang Woo-Suk, 471
Kanin, Garson, 280
KAOS, 375
Kaplan, Nelly, 403, 410
Karina, Anna, 391, 392, 412, 529
Karloff, Boris, 187, 423, 505
Karnad, Girish, 462
Karno, Fred, 151
Karras, Alex, 608
Kasaravalli, Girish, 462
Kasdan, Lawrence, 627
Kaspar Hauser, 534
Katyń, 441
Katz, Sam, 127
Katzenberg, Jeffrey, 597
Kaufman, Boris, 214, 251, 329, 330
Kaufman, Charlie, 607, 624, 628
Kaufman, Mikhail, 185, 214, 215, 218
Kaufman, Philip, 517, 627
Kaul, Mani, 462, 480
Kautner, Helmut, 576
Kaye, Danny, 338
Kazakh New Wave, 563
Kazan, Elia, 329, 330, 331, 344, 346, 353, 356, 378
Kazantzakis, Nikos, 444, 500, 501
Keaton, Buster, 8, 50, 101, 117, 120, 151, 153, 154–157, 158, 164, 165, 167, 168, 226, 274, 275, 281, 338, 358, 382, 492, 678
Keaton, Diane, 494
Keats, John, 553
Keeler, Ruby, 264, 339
Keeping On, 619
Keighley, William, 268, 309, 312, 325
Keitel, Harvey, 500, 554
Keller, Marjorie, 516
Kellerman, Annette, 120
Kelly, Gene, 3, 9, 323, 339, 340, 352, 356
Kelly, Grace, 298, 343
Kelly, Ned, 81
Kemp, Will, 260
Kennedy, Jeremiah J., 64
Kentis, Chris, 650, 654
Kenton, Erle C., 312
A Kentucky Feud, 58
Kerkorian, Kirk, 633
Kern, Jerome, 262
Kerr, Deborah, 423, 424, 427
Kerr, Richard, 516
Kerrigan, Lodge, 628
Kershner, Irvin, 330, 579, 596
Kessel, Adam, 64, 106
Keystone Company, 101, 106, 115, 152
Keystone Kops, 103, 109
The Key, 564
Khan, Mehboob, 480
Khanjian, Arsinée, 558
Khleifi, Michel, 539, 578, 582
Khmelik, Maria, 562
Khrushchev, Nikita, 559
Khrzhanovsky, Andrey, 580
Kiarostami, Abbas, 564–565, 577, 582
Kid Auto Races at Venice, 106, 107
The Kid, 113
Kieślowski, Krzysztof, 403, 410, 442–443, 477, 482, 483, 537, 567, 569
Kika, 570

Kildall, Gary, 660
Kiley, Richard, 341
Kill Bill Vol. 1, 612
Kill Bill Vol. 2, 612
The Killer, 470, 470, 471
Killer Bait, 356
Killer of Sheep, 613, 682
Killer's Kiss, 510
The Killers, 508
The Killing, 510
The Killing of a Chinese Bookie, 9, 492
Kim Il-Sung, 471
Kim Jee-Woon, 472, 481
Kim Kyu-Chul, 472
Kimmins, Anthony, 423, 475
Kim Myung-Gon, 472, 473
Kind Hearts and Coronets, 423, 482
Kinemacolor, 42, 325
Kinetograph, 24, 26, 31, 33
Kinetophone, 219
Kineto-phonograph, 28, 219
Kinetoscope, 24, 26–27, 28, 31, 33, 34, 37, 42, 43, 44, 122
King, Henry, 129, 140, 167, 207, 266, 353
King, Stephen, 504, 556
The King and I, 127
The King and the Clown, 472
King & Country, 506
King David, 549
The Kingdom, 414, 415
A King in New York, 274–275
The King is Alive, 415, 650
King Kong (1933), 151, 177, 266, 322, 553, 675
King Kong (2005), 553
King Lear, 559
The King of Comedy, 500
King of Kings, 327, 518
King of the Hill, 623
Kingsley, Ben, 423
Kings of the Road, 398, 529, 534, 535
King Solomon's Mines, 141
Kinney, 632
Kinó-Eye, 215, 218
Kinó-Nedelia, 194
Kinó-Pravda, 148, 215, 392
Kinski, Klaus, 533, 534, 535
Kinski, Nastassia, 535
Kinugasa, Teinosuke, 446, 447, 456, 480
Kircher, Athanasius, 29
Kirsanov, Dimitri, 8, 236, 257, 376, 447, 514
Kismet, 340
The Kiss, 39
The Kiss in the Tunnel, 55, 56, 59
Kiss Me Kate, 320, 340
Kiss of Death, 316, 334, Color Plate 30
Kitano, Takeshi, 3, 457, 458, 480, 481, 483
Kleine, George, 44, 62
Klein-Rogge, Rudolph, 175
Kleiser, Randal, 595, 627
Kleist, Heinrich von, 397
The Kleptomaniac, 58, 60
Klimov, Elem, 561, 580, 583
Kline, Kevin, 527
Klondike Annie, 283
Klos, Elmar, 3, 437, 439, 476–477
Kluge, Alexander, 528, 536, 576
K.M.C.D., 42, 43
Knife in the Water, 441, 482

Knock on Any Door, 344
The Knockout, 106
Kobayashi, Masaki, 206, 446, 456, 480, 483
Kodak, 22, 675
Kohner, Susan, 349
Konchalovsky, Andrei, 559, 580
Kontroll, 443
Koopman, Elias, 42
Kopple, Barbara, 619
Korda, Alexander, 256, 423, 443
Korean cinema, 470–473, 478, 481, 483
Korean Wave, 471
Kore-eda, Hirokazu, 457–458, 480, 481
Körtner, Fritz, 171
Korty, John, 524
Koster, Henry, 322, 355, 356
Koster & Bial's Music Hall, 34
Kotcheff, Ted, 549, 555, 579, 593, 627
The Koumiko Mystery, 399
Kovacs, Laszlo, 488
Koyaanisqatsi, 515
Kozintsev, Grigori, 217, 218, 559, 580
Kracauer, Siegfried, 48, 173
Kragh-Jacobsen, Søren, 415, 474
Kramer, Stanley, 328, 329–330, 353
Kramer vs. Kramer, 587
Krauss, Werner, 171, 172, 174, 182, 183, 189
Krazy Kat cartoons, 145
Kren, Kurt, 516
Kristina Talking Pictures, 619
Kubelka, Peter, 516
Kubrick, Stanley, 322, 355, 510–513, 523, 526, 527, 592, 597, 680
Kuchar, George, 516, 518
Kuchar, Mike, 516, 518, 525
Kuleshov, Lev, 51, 194–195, 207, 213, 216, 217, 218, 658
Kunuk, Zacharias, 555, 579, 650, 654
Kureishi, Hanif, 434
Kurosawa, Akira, 3, 9, 206, 324, 370, 375, 446, 447, 448–452, 453, 454, 456, 479, 483, 484, 485, 491, 496, 569, 611
Kurys, Diane, 403, 404
Kurz, Emilie, 181
Kusturica, Emir, 444, 478
Kwaidan, 206, 456
Kwak Jae-Yong, 472
Kwak Kyung-Taek, 471
Kyo, Machiko, 449, 451, 454

Labyrinth of Passion, 570
Lacan, Jacques, 6
LaCava, Gregory, 268, 284, 312
The Lacemaker, 402
Lach, Robert, 183
Lacombe Lucien, 402
Ladd, Diane, 601
Ladies and Gentlemen, 373
Ladri di biciclette, 350, 361, 362, 375, 411, 459, 564, 565
Lady and the Tramp, 640
Ladybird Ladybird, 432, 433
The Lady Eve, 279, 313
The Lady from Shanghai, 307, 308
The Ladykillers, 423, 482
Lady of the Pavements, 92
The Lady Vanishes, 297
Lady Windermere's Fan, 67, 147